D0805737

477

The Younger Pitt

By the same author

The Younger Pitt : The Years of Acclaim

THE
YOUNGER PITT

THE RELUCTANT TRANSITION

JOHN EHRMAN

CONSTABLE LONDON

First published in Great Britain 1983
by Constable and Company Limited
10 Orange Street London WC2H 7EG
Copyright © 1983 by John Ehrman
All rights reserved
ISBN 09 464930 8
Set in Monophoto Baskerville 11 pt.
by Servis Filmsetting Ltd, Manchester
Printed in Great Britain by
St Edmundsbury Press
Bury St Edmunds, Suffolk

DA
522
.P6
E35
1969
v.2

137666

Contents

Illustrations

vii

Illustrations

Introduction

The central volume of a biography, it has been said, should be the keystone of an arch. A man's life, however, does not necessarily resemble an arch; and Pitt's career in mid-term does not seem to me to follow a sustained curve. Such divisions of time of course are retrospective, and mainly a matter of chance. They depend on an unforeseeable length of life, and conditions beyond a man's own control. Pitt's life in point of fact did show a pattern in the end. But that was marked most clearly in its first and last stages: the intervening years, particularly the early years of the French Revolutionary War, lacked on the one hand the acclaim of his peacetime achievements, and on the other the stubborn grimness of an ever more testing struggle which, amid all the weaknesses and failures, turned him into a symbol and a legend. This last was the period above all that would be enshrined in 'the immortal memory', as the 1780s were that of 'the wonderful youth'. The years which fill the greater and notably the latter part of this volume, by contrast, have less visible form and unity, and contributed little to his fame. They do not witness an apex or fruition. But they were significant for his development. For by the time that the First wartime Coalition drew to its close, in 1796–7, they were subjecting his outlook and his methods to an irreversible change.

The process should not be etched too sharply. Even in Pitt's lifetime it was becoming customary to divide his career in two, contrasting the forward-looking early successes with later repression and failure in war. Of course a division was ultimately true: Pitt himself drew attention to it when he once told the Commons that he of all men must long for a return of peace to pursue his reforms. But the transition took time: his assumptions, and fortunes, were not changed at once. Some attitudes, taken as typical of wartime, were displayed while peace was still assured, and a frame of mind inherited from peacetime could be observed in the early stages of war. Pitt surprised some of his supporters with what they saw as evidence of illiberality before the French Revolution ever began. He was also thought weak or complacent by a range of political opinion for not moving sooner, and then more fiercely, against unrest when unrest arose. Such facts suggest an adherence to concepts – to an interpretation of constitutional values – straddling what came to be accepted as the divide. Pitt in fact was rather slow in this respect to adapt to pressures. He took some initial cautionary steps, and when he struck he struck increasingly hard. But the timetable shows an approach carrying traditional overtones which spanned a period longer than is often portrayed.

A similar process may be seen over a wider front. In matters of government Pitt remained a reformer; he looked for improved effectiveness, where possible through improved institutions. But he had always done so with – through – a keen sense of familiar strengths and limits. His adaptation to circumstances was accordingly uneven; and in the management of the war itself this was accentuated by the war's own character. The years of the First Coalition are as unsatisfactory to follow as they were to live through. Notable moments, for good and ill, occurred in the endless chain of advances and failures: at sea with the Glorious First of June, in the flow and ebb of West Indian operations, on the French coasts at Toulon and Quiberon, even in the Low Countries as York's 'ten thousand men', after marching to and fro for two campaigns, retreated in a bitter winter to their expulsion from the continent. There was drama; but dramatic tension is lessened by an absence of theme, for all too often the British effort – like those of the other Allies – was a series of reactions to events it did not control. This very incoherence however – this continual disappointment of a vision of victory within the grasp – determined, against the political and administrative assumptions available, the pace and scope of adjustments which proved to be important. It was the middle nineties, particularly one might argue the years 1795–6, with their deepening military frustration, economic and financial pressures, and sometimes frightening surges of unrest, that forced responses which would take time to mature and harden, but, incomplete as they remained, were shaped in outline then. These were formative years, for the nation and for Pitt himself. For they showed – and in the end too starkly for him to evade it any longer – that the end of the struggle might be indefinitely prolonged.

Pitt's recognition of this fact was certainly unwilling. Once fully accepted, his first reaction – an urgent move for peace – disturbed some of his colleagues. The growing strain began also to show in his health and sometimes his spirits. The public image remained what it had always been; and the impression

Of an accosting profile, an erect carriage

would not have been diminished by events calling increasingly for a 'balancing subterfuge'. But the image was not forced: it was natural enough; and so was his behaviour in private. Pitt's intimates continued to marvel at the way in which he usually bore his burdens: cheerful, full of fun, sardonic, and buoyed up by hope. The sudden spells of depression were the more noticeable when they came; and the friends themselves perhaps the more necessary as the isolation increased. For Pitt's private life, particularly after the first year of the war, was becoming more private than ever; the days were now bounded almost wholly by Downing Street, the House of Commons, his retreat at Holwood and the little castle of Walmer bestowed on him the year before war began. We know less about them than we do about his final decade, on which a rising generation and survivors' memories largely dwelled. But little changed in essence from the earlier years. Pitt's relationships remained simple and affectionate, and he depended greatly on them – as was revealed when the needs of Government led to a long breach with his brother Chatham. Late in 1796, when this volume closes, a possible new prospect was dawning, as he embarked on, or drifted into, his one serious approach to romance. But if serious it was scarcely ardent; it would end in anti-climax within a few months; his life continued on an older pattern, amid the now relentless calls of office.

I have been very fortunate, once more, in the help received while writing this volume. I wish to record my acknowledgment and gratitude for permission to consult papers in the possession of the Duke of Buccleugh and Queensberry, the Marquess Camden, the Marquis of Normanby, Earl Amherst, Earl Bathurst, the Trustees of the Fitzwilliam (Wentworth) Estates, the Earl of Harewood, the Administrative Trustees of the Chevening Estate, Lord Cottesloe, Lord Redesdale, Lady Anne Cavendish-Bentinck, Sir Hector Monro, the late Mr George Fortescue, Mr Richard Head, Mrs Camilla Pretyman, and Mr W.H. Saumarez Smith. Unfortunately Countess Spencer felt unable to allow me to see the papers of the second Earl Spencer at Althorp. I wish further to make grateful acknowledgment to the authorities of the Bodleian Library, the British Library (particularly Dr Daniel Waley and Dr Robert Smith), Cambridge University Library, Edinburgh University Library, the Guildhall Library of the City of London, the History of Parliament Trust (particularly Dr Roland Thorne, who generously allowed me to read material in advance of publication), the John Rylands Library of Manchester University (particularly Dr Frank Taylor), Lambeth Palace Library (particularly Mr Geoffrey Bill), the Leeds City Archives Department, the National Library of Scotland (particularly Dr Denis Roberts), the National Maritime Museum Greenwich (particularly Dr Roger Knight and Dr R.A. Morriss), Nottingham University Library, Pembroke College, Cambridge, the Public Record Office (particularly Dr Nicholas Rodger), St Andrews University Library, the Scottish Record Office (particularly Miss Myrtle Baird), Sheffield City Libraries, the County Archives or Record Offices of Buckinghamshire, Devon, Hampshire, Kent, Northamptonshire, Suffolk (Ipswich), and West Sussex, the William L. Clements Library of Michigan University, Duke University Library, North Carolina, and the Huntington Library and Art Gallery, California.

Mrs Rosemary Bigwood, Dr Paul Kelly, and Dr R.F. Mullen examined certain groups of documents for me. I am very grateful. I am also greatly indebted to those who have answered my questions, read parts of the book, or eased my path in other ways, as some of them kindly did for the earlier volume: to Dr R.C. Alston, Professor M.S. Anderson, Miss Sonia Anderson, Professor D.A. Baugh, Professor J.S. Bromley, Mr Handasyde Buchanan, the late Sir Herbert Butterfield, Professor Ian Christie, Dr Michael Duffy, Mr Clive Emsley, Dr Howard V. Evans, Dr Walter Ehret, Dr David Geggus, Professor A. Goodwin, Dr Paul Kelly, the late Dr G.S.R. Kitson Clark, Miss Sheila Lambert, Professor Jerzy Lojek, Dr Piers Mackesy, Dr F. O'Gorman, Dr J.C. Sainty, the late Dame Lucy Sutherland, Mr S.P.G. Ward, Professor William Willcox, Professor Gwyn A. Williams. I must record my thanks for permission to read unpublished theses, as detailed in the Notes on Sources to Chapters, by I.S. Asquith, P.J. Brunsdon, R.A. Cooper, S.R. Cope, Michael Duffy, Clive Emsley, Alan G. Jamieson, Agnes King, Austin Vernon Mitchell, J.T. Murley, P.K. O'Brien, Christopher Oprey, Norman Frank Richards, M.W.B. Sanderson, W.A.L. Seaman, James Walvin, and the late J.R. Western. The Syndics of the Cambridge University Press have given me leave to make use of material in my book *The British Government and Commercial Negotiations with Europe 1783–1793*, and the Editors of *History Today* have done likewise for an article, 'Pitt the Younger and the Ochakov Affair', which appeared in that journal.

Her Majesty The Queen has given me gracious permission to reproduce Reynolds's portrait of the 2nd Earl of Moira (fig. 11a). Other illustrations have been reproduced by kind permission of the Trustees of the National Portrait Gallery (frontispiece, figs 4, 5, 8, 9a, 10b, 15, 19a), Sir Hector Monro (fig. 1a; photo. Scottish National Portrait Gallery), the Baltimore Museum of Fine Art (fig. 1b), the Trustees of the British Museum (figs 2, 3, 14, 16), the Trustees of the National Gallery (fig. 6; photo. National Portrait Gallery), the Governing Body of Christ Church, Oxford (fig. 7), the Royal Marines, Plymouth (fig. 9b; photo. National Portrait Gallery), the Trustees of the National Maritime Museum (fig. 10a), the National Trust (fig. 11b), the Controller of H.M. Stationery Office, for a Crown copyright document in the Public Record Office (fig. 12), Lady Teresa Agnew (fig. 13; photo. National Portrait Gallery), the British Library Board (fig. 17), Messrs Spink & Son (fig. 18), the Provost and Fellows of Eton College (fig. 19b; photo. Courtauld Institute of Art), the Earl of Malmesbury (fig. 20; photo. Courtauld Institute of Art). Miss Sarah Wimbush, Mrs Alison Opyrchal and Miss Judith Prendergast of the National Portrait Gallery gave welcome aid in my inquiries.

Finally I must record my very real gratitude to my two excellent typists: Miss Winifred Millard, who patiently dealt with large batches of manuscript over a long period, and her equally impeccable successor Mrs Jennifer Martin.

April 1982   J.E.

Abbreviations

I	John Ehrman, *The Younger Pitt, the Years of Acclaim* (1969).
A.C.	*The Journal and Correspondence of William, Lord Auckland*, ed. The Bishop of Bath and Wells (4 vols, 1861–2).
B.L.	British Library.
Buckingham	The Duke of Buckingham and Chandos, *Memoirs of the Courts and Cabinets of George the Third* (2 vols, 1853).
C.A.O.	County Archives Office.
C.R.O.	County Record Office.
Ec.H.R.	*The Economic History Review.*
E.H.R.	*The English Historical Review.*
H.C.J.	*Journals of the House of Commons.*
H.L.J.	*Journals of the House of Lords.*
H.M.C.	Publications of the Historical Manuscripts Commission.
Holland Rose, II	J. Holland Rose, *William Pitt and the Great War* (1911).
L.C.G. III	*The Later Correspondence of George III*, ed. A. Aspinall (5 vols, 1962–70).
N.L.S.	National Library of Scotland.
P.H.	*Cobbett's Parliamentary History of England . . . 1066 to 1803*, ed. William Cobbett (36 vols, 1806–20).
P.R.	*The Parliamentary Register: or, History of the Proceedings and Debates of the House of Commons [House of Lords]*, ed. John Debrett (45 vols, 1780–96, and *3rd series*, 1796–).
P.R.O.	Public Record Office.
R.O.	Record Office.
S.R.O.	Scottish Record Office.
Stanhope	Earl Stanhope, *Life of the Right Honourable William Pitt* (4 vols, 1861–2).
Stockdale	*Debates and proceedings of the House of Commons*, ed. John Stockdale (4 vols and unnumbered, 1784–90).

Tomline   George Tomline, *Memoirs of the Life of the Right Honorable William Pitt* (2nd edn, 3 vols, 1821).

Trans. R. Hist. S.   *Transactions of the Royal Historical Society.*

Part One

CHAPTER I

The Ochakov Affair

I

In the summer of 1789 the political climate in England was calm. Party warfare was at a low ebb after the recent Regency crisis, and Pitt's standing was higher than it had ever been. There was no obvious domestic issue, as it seemed, which he could not handle. The country by and large was prosperous, after a recession in the north the year before. And while the harvest looked uncertain in places – always a possible cause of trouble – there was little fear of a general failure to shake the general peace.

So matters stood in England at one of the great symbolic turning-points for Europe, in the year which came to be taken as marking the end of an age. In Pitt's own career, too, the next three years are something of a watershed, as events on the continent first led him in a new direction, and then helped shape a new role for him at home. The process, however, was not a sudden one. The historic confrontation was delayed. And indeed for much of the fateful period between 1789 and 1793 European diplomacy was agitated by a quite different set of problems.

The early stages of the upheaval in France of course made a great sensation, and never more so than in the first half of that summer. On 14 July the Bastille fell. Coming on top of the other developments of a dramatic two months – the meeting of the Estates General, riots and troop movements, the dismissal of the popular Minister Necker – it raised to a fresh intensity the fascinated gaze of Europe. The monument of the most imposing of monarchies had fallen to a mob in the centre of the capital, and the fact seemed scarcely credible, even in a decade of growing continental unrest. There was applause and doubt, revulsion and amazement, wherever politically conscious men were gathered together. But within the Governments themselves, aware though some might be of deeper implications, the most immediate concern was the likely effect on the standing of France as a Great Power. There was talk from the start of contagion and example; but the statesmen in their cabinets sat down to their familiar task of adjusting the diplomatic odds.

The same applied across the Channel, though with lesser weight. The British Government had other things to think about, in various parts of the world, particularly where the Regency crisis had held up business for several months. There is a marked absence of comment on events in Paris in Ministers' letters at this time. But those most concerned with foreign affairs were on the whole rather pleased. 'I defy the ablest Heads in England', wrote the Foreign Secretary, 'to have planned, or its whole Wealth to have purchased, a Situation so fatal to its Rival, as that to which France is now reduced by her own intestine Commotions'. And Pitt himself, on 14 July, before he had heard the latest astonishment, could remark complacently that 'Our neighbours in France seem coming to actual extremes', a scene which made 'that country an object of compassion, even to a rival'.[1]

Given recent circumstances, the tone of these remarks was hardly surprising. In September 1787 the two countries had almost gone to war over Holland, and Pitt's Ministry, and he himself, had scored a notable triumph. In the summer of 1788 a Triple Alliance had been formed by England, Holland and Prussia, primarily against France.[2] And in this very summer of 1789 the British Government was becoming involved in central and eastern Europe, where an active and traditionally hostile France could add grave complications. Her virtual removal, however temporary, from the international scene therefore seemed an uncovenanted mercy at an interesting point.

This assessment held good very largely over the next two years.[3] For diplomatic concern throughout that period focused increasingly on the east of Europe, and while there was a distraction in London in 1790, in the shape of a sharp quarrel with Spain, that too underlined the British relief at France's embarrassments.[4] By the autumn of 1790, when the Spaniards suffered a diplomatic defeat, it could be argued that England was once more 'in possession of the balance of Europe'.[5]

This was gratifying, after the end of the American War only seven years earlier. National prestige had risen again, and without much expense. Nor did the immediate future look particularly discouraging; certainly less so, in the likeliest trouble spot, than it had recently been. From June 1789 to June 1790 Pitt was watching a scene in central Europe which seemed to be getting out of hand. By the autumn it was quieter, and much of the credit for this was ascribed to England.

The verdict was reasonable in part. In the later eighties, as France

1. Duke of Leeds to Duke of Dorset [British Ambassador in France], Private, 31 July 1789 (B.L. Add. Ms 28064); Pitt to Hester Countess of Chatham, 14 July 1789 (Stanhope, II, 38).

2. See I, 520–42.

3. There were spasmodic fears in the summer of 1789 that France might take risks abroad in order to divert attention from her troubles at home. But such apprehensions had largely disappeared by the winter.

4 See I, 554–68.

5. Op. cit., 551 – a claim made, by the British Ambassador in Madrid, at the beginning of the year, which the events of later months served to strengthen.

declined in the reckoning, the two main focal points of continental unrest were the rivalries of Russia and Turkey, and of Austria and Prussia. Within that uneasy quadrilateral, formed of two old vulnerable empires and two newly thrusting states, most of the other now endemic disturbances – in Poland and the Baltic, and the Austrian dominions – were heightened or distorted in greater or lesser degree. So far as England was concerned, the first point of interest was Prussia's intentions, for by the recent alliance we could be involved if she was at war. And this seemed not unlikely at times, for Prussia was proving an uncomfortable partner; her restless ambitions were being pushed as far as unstable conditions would bear. In the past three years, while Russia and then Austria were at war with Turkey, she had been pursuing a 'complex, cynical and impracticable scheme'.[1] Its proportions changed with the pace of Court intrigues – rising since the death of Frederick the Great – and as short-term advantage appeared to dictate. But in the first half of 1790 it settled into an extreme form. The central object remained the same throughout: to gain the port of Danzig and its fortress of Thorn, which would strengthen Prussia's coastline and through which her trade passed within Polish territory. The Poles therefore should cede this area, receiving the province of Galicia in return, which Austria had taken from them in the First Partition of 1772. The Austrians however would be comforted by securing some Balkan gains from the Turks, who themselves would be assuaged by offers of support (or even perhaps armed assistance) if Austria did not comply with a general guarantee of their other Balkan territories, and possibly by a Prussian attack on Austria if Galicia was not given to the Poles. Finally the Russians, Prussia's rivals in Poland and suspicious of her wooing of the Turks, were to be mollified by an easing of her friendship with a Sweden which was hostile to themselves, and above all by pressure in favour of their great object in the Turkish war, the retention of the captured Black Sea port of Ochakov and part of Bessarabia to the west. Everyone – except the unfortunate Swedes – would thus be satisfied in part, although everyone except Prussia would have to forgo something.

But if she was to realise so ambitious a plan Prussia could hardly advance on her own, and she needed a stronger connexion than the Poles or the Turks could provide. This could come only from the other partners of the Triple Alliance of 1788, and above all from England, for the Dutch in this instance counted for less. But why should England let herself be involved, in areas hitherto of marginal concern, and under a Ministry which by and large had shown itself reluctant to intervene in Europe?[2] The answer lay partly in the terms of the alliance, if the case could be shown to meet them; but also, as the Prussians saw it, in the

1. See I, 539.
2. Op. cit., 467–77, 516.

change of atmosphere which had brought about that treaty, and more particularly as time went by in signs of a growing British interest in Poland.

With this the wheel came full circle, back to Danzig and the Prussian trade. But it raised severe complications, for the aims of England were not the same as her ally's. Indeed, while they overlapped, in the last resort they were contradictory, for the object of British policy came to be the maintenance of the territorial *status quo*. The main target, moreover, was different in either case; in that of Prussia it was generally Austria, in that of England, Russia throughout. British involvement had in fact first arisen as a consequence of a trade negotiation with Russia which, since 1786, had failed to yield a result.[1] Sparked off by the need to replace an earlier treaty which had just expired, its lack of progress gradually turned the Ministry's attention, and above all Pitt's, to an alternative scheme. Trade with Russia, though it showed an adverse balance, was accepted as a hopeful element in that rapid commercial expansion which marked his first decade. The market was growing, its raw materials were useful to British industry, and Russia remained a prime source of supply for essential naval stores. But if the old advantageous terms were not to be repeated – and it seemed that they might not – a possible replacement arose elsewhere. The plains and forests of Poland and Prussia could provide hemp and timber for the fleet; their ports and rivers could take British goods for sale in central and eastern Europe. Two minor markets might thus be enlarged, and Russia too might still be exploited, for if entry to St Petersburg was legally restricted the Polish rivers gave access to the east. A thriving trade in this central area could thus have commercial and strategic advantages; and all the more so – for this was an aspect which came increasingly to dominate the plan – if Russia's approach to the Mediterranean was effectively blocked. It was true that she was now established in the Crimea, and had freedom of navigation in the Black Sea; but the Crimea was badly served for an outlet to the south. The Allies should therefore seek the return of the port of Ochakov, and its neighbouring territory across the mouths of the Bug and the Dniester, to the Turks.

But if this object was to be achieved, it could best be done by insisting on the principle of the *status quo ante bellum* – a return to the territorial position before the Russo-Turkish War. And in that case the Austrian province of Galicia should not be cast as a necessary bargain in an arrangement over Danzig between Prussia and Poland. The British in any case did not want to alienate Austria any further; on the contrary, they were hoping to wean her from her connexions with Russia and France.[2] If the 'Imperial Powers' were to be divided, and the European

1. Op. cit., 502–6.
2. See op. cit., 467–75.

balance correspondingly tilted, Prussian ambitions must be firmly restrained.

In the autumn of 1790 it looked as if this might be so, for a few months earlier there had been a dramatic change of policy in Vienna. The Austrian Empire was suffering from the strains imposed by the Turkish war, and the accession of a new Emperor early in the year paved the way for a reconciliation with Prussia. Encouraged by the British, this took place in the summer at the village of Reichenbach, and the Reichenbach Convention was signed at the end of July. Austria thereby agreed to an armistice with Turkey, pending the meeting of a wider Congress for peace. She and Prussia recognised the principle of the *status quo ante bellum*, subject to the possibility of minor amendments. And both countries welcomed the efforts of the Triple Alliance to achieve peace between Russia and Turkey, and to settle the problems of the Austrian Netherlands, which were in revolt against Vienna and already the subject of British intercession.[1] The danger of war in central Europe seemed thus to have receded; and England, and Pitt himself, were largely identified with the result.

II

It was from this starting point that ideas in London began to harden in the winter of 1790. The elements of a plan had been present for over a year, but it now began to take shape. Foreign policies by this time awaited Pitt's detailed decision,[2] and Pitt had not considered the detail carefully before. The summer and autumn had been occupied chiefly by the quarrel with Spain, and it was early in November before this was resolved. He was then free to turn his eyes elsewhere, and he did so at once. By the middle of that month he was hard at work on the affairs of Poland and eastern Europe.

There was reason enough for this. The promise of the late summer had not been fulfilled, and indeed seemed to be in some danger of fading. Russia, which had made further gains against Turkey, had also made a sudden peace with Sweden, and was the less disposed to accept a call for a strict *status quo*. Her relations with England showed no sign of improving, and the Alliance itself was running into trouble, for Prusso-Polish relations had taken a turn for the worse. The Poles, who had never liked the thought of ceding Thorn, were now divided on the cession of Danzig, and were negotiating with the Turks for a river access to the south which might give 'an entire new direction to [their] trade'.[3]

1. Op. cit., 547–51.
2. See op. cit., 570–1.
3. Daniel Hailes [Minister in Warsaw] to Leeds, 1 December 1790 (P.R.O., F.O. 62/3).

This naturally alarmed the Prussians, who did their best to obstruct the talks, and meanwhile they had failed in their efforts to persuade Austria to part with Galicia. The Allied initiative was thus receding. Prussia was once more casting around. The Turks remained in a bad way; and the unfinished business could scarcely be dropped. The approach of winter would afford a breathing space before the next campaigning season. It was clearly time for Pitt to think of taking a hand.

Nevertheless he might not have acted so promptly, or precisely on the lines he did, if a particular influence had not emerged at that point. The British Minister in Berlin, Joseph Ewart, had been heard of increasingly in recent years – in the Dutch crisis and, more prominently, during the Northern War.[1] Of the same age as Pitt, he had risen fast once he got started, and was now a leading member of that group of Scottish diplomats who largely filled the Legations of northern and central Europe.[2] Married to a Prussian lady of noble family, and making the most of his contacts with the Court, he was ambitious, ingenious, persuasive, a young man very much in a hurry. His febrile restlessness was not diminished by an illness which brought him to England early in November, and he waited on Pitt at once. Always a keen advocate of the Anglo-Prussian connexion, he saw it as the cornerstone of something larger – an edifice in which the name of Ewart would be enshrined. The Government in London had wished at the start of the alliance for a wider federation of Powers:[3] he had now been arguing for several months that this was not only desirable, but essential. The great object was to curb Russian expansion in south-east Europe, which threatened the whole balance of the centre and the north. If this could be achieved, everything else would fall into place, and the effects would be felt from the Baltic to the Mediterranean. But if it were not, the same effects would benefit Russia, for this was not a situation which was likely to yield a middle result.

> I beg leave [he wrote to Pitt after their first series of meetings] to recall Your attention to the effects which a cordial cooperation with Prussia . . . could not fail to produce not only at Berlin, but likewise at Warsaw and at Constantinople, by establishing the influence of England on the most permanent footing, and it would likewise make one of the inferior Baltic Powers immediately put itself under the

1. See I, 522, and also 544n1.
2. It is a somewhat remarkable fact that of the nine British envoys affected most directly by the Ochakov affair six were Scots: Ewart from Berlin, Daniel Hailes in Warsaw, Robert Liston in Stockholm, Sir Robert Keith in Vienna, the young Lord Elgin on a special mission to the Emperor, and Sir Robert Ainslie in Constantinople. The exceptions were Sir Charles Whitworth in St Petersburg, Lord Auckland in The Hague, and Francis Drake in Copenhagen. The Scot Hugh Elliot had left Copenhagen in 1789.
3. I, 540–2.

protection of the Allies . . . But should Russia be extricated from her present difficulties . . . without restoring everything to the Porte [Turkey], she would probably very soon recover her influence at Warsaw, at Copenhagen, at Stockholm, & even at Constantinople . . . while the influence of the Allies would sink at all those places, in the same proportion; and the unbounded confidence in the Naval power of Great Britain, by which Prussia has been & may continue to be directed, would be destroyed.[1]

But could such a policy succeed without a war? Ewart was confident that it could. Russia was extended, militarily and financially. She had gained successes against the Turks, but the current campaign seemed to be slowing down, and in November 1790 her armies were held up before the fortress of Ismail. Trade was disturbed, credit was short (thanks partly to the reluctance of resident British merchants to provide it), and as a result the rouble was depressed. The consequences might be inferred; but the Empress's stubborness might soon make them plain, for if England took a stand she was open to the threat of a British Baltic squadron and a Prussian army. It was true that her recent peace with Sweden had relieved that particular flank. But the King of Sweden was greedy, he would extract a high price for keeping quiet, and the appearance of British ships might swing him to the Allies. Even if it did not, and he opted for Russia, this would have a good effect on Denmark, since the two Baltic Powers, recently at war, thoroughly distrusted one another. There was therefore little to fear, and as long as England was resolute 'I should think she [Russia] must certainly knock under'.[2]

Ewart could clothe his case in an array of local knowledge, and he found the Prime Minister in sympathetic mood. Surprisingly so, one might think, considering Pitt's marked reluctance to combine too closely with Prussia over the past two years. But a variety of arguments was now leading him on, and they were precisely of the sort to arouse his interest. He was always attracted, in the first instance, to a 'grand design' – he had shown this in the cases of Ireland and finance, and now there was an opportunity in foreign affairs.[3] The design moreover on this occasion had one particularly congenial aspect; for the problem was one of trade as well as power – of the interaction of trade and power – exactly the kind with which he felt most at home. As with Nootka Sound, so with Ochakov in a more complex diplomatic setting, it was the commercial prospects that sparked off his concern. Ewart was soon made aware of this, he turned it to advantage, and by the third week in November 'Things were so much advanced' that Pitt authorised him to 'open the

1. Ewart to Pitt, 13 December 1790 (P.R.O. 30/8/133). He repeated his reasoning in almost the same words to Auckland at The Hague on the 18th (B.L. Add. Ms 34434).
2. Ewart to Auckland, 28 November 1790 (loc. cit.). And cf. Ewart to Pitt, 13 December 1790 (P.R.O. 30/8/133).
3. See I, 195; and possibly, one might add, op. cit., 202n3.

business' of trade with the Polish envoy in London.[1] Matters however then took a different turn. For Ewart, unimpressed by the latter's capacity, urged the Poles to send as an emissary their new Minister at The Hague, the young Count Michel Ogínski; the idea was seconded by Auckland; and Ogínski soon arrived. None of the British authorities knew that he came in fact on his own authority, possibly before his superiors were informed and even perhaps with Russian approval.[2] Ewart saw to it that he was officially received, and in an interview with Pitt Ogínski discovered that the Minister was thinking in terms of a positive plan.

It is hard to be sure exactly how this was proportioned, or indeed how far it stretched, for Ogínski left two accounts at different dates which do not agree. There seems no real reason to doubt that Pitt moved from the starting point of a commercial agreement, by which Poland would increase her exports to the west and Britain its markets in central Europe. But he now sketched, as an immediate prospect, a farther design. He wished to see a treaty of trade and alliance between the two countries; and – according to Ogínski's contemporary report – was prepared for the British to take the initiative. Whether the connexion was to be purely bilateral or, as Ogínski stated much later, part of a treaty between Britain, Holland and Prussia on the one hand and Poland on the other, it is unfortunately impossible to say from the discrepancies of his accounts. But the latter, as indeed was soon to be made clear, must have been the final object, whether or not it could be reached in one step; for this was not only Ewart's thinking but also a potential sequel to the settlement of the old Danzig/Thorn dispute, itself necessary for an increased British transit trade.

Pitt's overture in fact fitted into an evolving diplomatic scheme, whose features, if still imprecise, were emerging fast enough for Ewart to be hopeful that things would go his way. 'In regard to Russia', he wrote after talking to Pitt, 'on va lui mettre de nouveau le couteau sur la gorge';[3] and if he was premature in judging the decision he was probably right about the intent. Pitt had never had any luck with Russia: the Empress was a stumbling block from the start. In 1785 she had taken

---

1. Ewart to Auckland, 18 December 1790 (B.L. Add. Ms 34434), referring to his 'stay in London', which had ended at some time between 24 and 28 November. On the latter date he had written that the 'commercial advantages' were thought 'of the greatest consequence' (same to same, loc. cit.); and see also his letters of 14 November to Auckland (loc. cit.), and to F.J. Jackson, the chargé d'affaires in Berlin (Ewart Mss, Kirtlebridge, Dumfriesshire).

For recent thoughts of a commercial treaty with the Turks as well, see John Ehrman, *The British Government and Commercial Negotiations with Europe 1783–1793* (1962), 143.

2. He had in fact just taken Russian citizenship in addition, to claim some rights of property. For his mission and the background see Jerzy Łojek, 'The International Crisis of 1791 – Poland between the Triple Alliance and Russia' (*East Central Europe*, II, no. 1; Pittsburgh, 1975), which corrects my account in op. cit. (n2 above), 131–2.

3. To Auckland, 28 November 1790 (B.L. Add. Ms 34434).

umbrage at the German *Fürstenbund*, in which George III was involved; the sole result of the trade talks in 1786 had been a Franco-Russian treaty in 1787; in 1788 she had been angry at the Ministry's refusal to allow her to hire transport vessels for her fleet – a decision taken to underline British neutrality in the Russo-Turkish war; she had been angrier still at the Triple Alliance; was known to favour Fox in the Regency crisis; and more recently, after a temporary thaw, was suspected of encouraging Spain over Nootka Sound.[1] Russia in fact was now seen as an unfriendly Power which would exploit any British reverse, and whose attitude hampered our need for trade and peace in the Baltic. Only firmness, it seemed, would bring her to a reasonable frame of mind, and in so doing help settle the peace of Europe east of the Rhine. The very confusion which was so prevalent made an extended Allied 'system' the more desirable, and the need for our influence was growing, as senior British diplomats pointed out.[2] With the ending of the Russo-Turkish war on Allied terms there would be a widespread reduction of tension; and those terms must be the restoration of the *status quo*, allowing for minor amendments, for there was no going back on the Reichenbach Convention. Having guaranteed the Austrian armistice, England must now insist that comparable conditions applied to Russia in a general peace.

This was the approach, and the point at issue was Ochakov, with its neighbouring territory commanding the mouths of the Dniester and the Bug. Elsewhere Russia had at times seemed prepared to revert to a *status quo ante*; but the Black Sea port with its river access had not been negotiable so far. It had been captured in 1788, and there was no hint of its being returned in a peace treaty under Allied mediation. The Empress indeed may well have thought that Ochakov could hardly cause a war with England, and it is doubtful in fact how important the town appeared in London at the start. It was true that a Russian presence in the Black Sea was now seen as a danger, giving France and Spain access to the naval stores and the prospect of greater Mediterranean trade, hampering Polish commercial expansion, and posing a more direct strategic problem for the Turks. The shape of the threat was fast becoming clearer, Russia's success increasingly disturbing, in the uncertainty for the future of the traditional Baltic supplies. But there is no evidence to suggest that the significance of Ochakov itself was closely assessed. As the Russians pointed out, there had been no Allied reaction to its capture at the time, and Ewart, after his conversations with Ministers, was explicit. The 'necessity', he reminded Pitt after a second round of talks, 'of Russia's being made to restore all its conquests to the Porte' was 'not so much on account of Oczakow and its district, which

1. See I, 473–4, 502–6, 545–6, 508; David Bayne Horn, *Great Britain and Europe in the Eighteenth Century* (1967), 223.
2. Cf. Malmesbury at The Hague in 1788 (I, 552) with Auckland now, when the resolution of the Russo-Turkish troubles remained the 'only embarrassment' (to Pitt, 22 December 1790; P.R.O. 30/8/110).

however important to the Turks, are only secondary considerations when compared with the decisive influence which the issue of the present discussion between the Allies & Russia must have on the strength & permanency of the actual system of politicks of this country'.[1] He was weighting the case unduly, for he was neglecting the Polish aspect: the restoration of the area had figured in the first British argument for a trade agreement,[2] and an access to the south by arrangement with Turkey was now a cherished object of the Poles themselves. But no regional survey was available in London, no study of alternatives was called for, and if Ewart underrated an important factor Ochakov remained the occasion, not the cause, of the affair. As such it was to prove embarrassing. But that had to be accepted; for this was one of the times when a far-reaching policy turns on an apparently minor demand.

Such then were the arguments to which Pitt responded, under Ewart's impetus. He may have done so the more readily in the light of his fortunes over the past few years. There was a feeling of great confidence in the Foreign Office, and among many British envoys abroad, after a run of diplomatic victories. 'We seem to have got into a very good way', wrote one of the Under Secretaries, Bland Burges, 'of persuading people to do what they do not like'.[3] Pitt himself did not talk like this; but he may well have felt much the same, and, drawn step by step into a tangled situation, he was now resolved to cut the knot. 'Mr Pitt is no timid man', the experienced Malmesbury had noted a year before.[4] He was quite ready to confront the Empress, if conditions allowed and the need arose.

Nevertheless there was much to be done before such a step was taken. If he was to have his way without a war, the ground should be prepared. This would take time, for some of the Courts concerned were three to four weeks distant; but time was available, though not plentiful, since a squadron could not operate in the Baltic until the spring. He would also have to carry the Cabinet; for while Pitt was the man who mattered, and the Foreign Secretary as almost always was responding to an active policy, their colleagues had not been collectively consulted and must now be brought up to date. Relations with Prussia were still officially restricted to 'general Assurances' of support, and the language to the

1. 15 January 1791 (P.R.O. 30/8/133). He had written ten days earlier in the same strain to Auckland (5 January 1791; B.L. Add. Ms 34435). By 'politicks' Ewart meant, as was common usage, foreign policy.

2. See I, 507–8 for consul Durno's proposals in 1789.

3. To Sir Robert Keith, 15 August 1790 (B.L. Add. Ms 35543). See likewise his letter to Auckland of 6 August, in B.L. Add. Ms 34432, and Hailes's to Keith of 11 September, in B.L. Add. Ms 35543. Jeremy Bentham, who had been alarmed for some time by Pitt's attitude to Baltic affairs, had earlier described him as 'stalking over Europe. . . , spitting in the face of one sovereign and giving a kick to another' (quoted in Mary P. Mack, *Jeremy Bentham, An Odyssey of Ideas 1748–1792* (1962), 398).

4. To Ewart, 29 August 1789 (Ewart Mss).

Russians was still temperate, if cool.[1] In October and again in November we had repeated our offers to help towards peace, and much would now depend on the Empress's reply. But this had not arrived by the end of December, Pitt was anxious to start his inquiries, and in the New Year he began to move.

On 8 January 1791 a crop of despatches was completed, for Stockholm, Copenhagen, Warsaw, Berlin, The Hague, Vienna, and Madrid. Between them they amounted to a grand design. The despatch for Vienna was purely informative, repeating the object of British policy and stating that a naval force was being maintained while the issue remained in doubt. The instructions to Madrid were based on signs of an improvement in relations after Nootka Sound,[2] and the traditional Spanish dislike of a possible Russian access to the Mediterranean. They sought diplomatic backing for the British demand in St Petersburg, which might carry some weight in view of Russia's recent sympathy with Spain. Auckland in The Hague was told – as was often the case with the Ambassador in that focal point – to read the other despatches under 'flying seal',[3] and inform the Dutch as our allies. The plan itself was contained in the messages for the two Northern capitals, and for Warsaw and Berlin. The Poles were offered their commercial treaty on the terms disclosed to Ogínski, coupled with an invitation to join the Triple Alliance.[4] The approaches to Denmark and Sweden were more 'delicate',[5] particularly to Sweden, reflecting the uncertain and anxious position in either case. The Danes were to be told that the time had come for them to go beyond their normally friendly protestations. If they showed signs of listening, they should be handed a Note proposing a connexion with the Allies, in the event (which seemed not unlikely) of a Russo-Swedish alliance. But if that looked impossible, they were to be asked to use their good offices with Russia, and in the background was the implication that they might open their ports to a British force. The object of course was to play on the Danes' habitual fear of Swedish aggression, which had been notably increased by the sudden end of the Russo-Swedish war. But Sweden was still undecided: her policy would

1. Leeds to F.J. Jackson, 14 November 1790 (B.L. Add. Ms 28066); same to Count Simon Woronzow [Vorontsov, the Russian Minister in London], 9 October 1790 (B.L. Add. Ms 34433); same to Sir Charles Whitworth [Minister in St Petersburg], no. 10, 19 October 1790, no. 13, 14 November 1790 (P.R.O., F.O. 65/19).

2. See I, 500. The Spaniards had recently appeared quite friendly over various questions.

3. I.e. left open for him to seal for onward transmission. He could not however always read the enciphered passages, about which he was apt to show 'insatiable' curiosity (eg George Aust to Keith, 20 July 1790; Holland Rose, II, 480n1).

4. See p. 10 above.

5. Leeds to Auckland, no. 1, 8 January 1791 (P.R.O., F.O. 37/33).

yield to the highest bidder, and the British Minister in Stockholm was urging the Allies to act. He was accordingly sent 'most secret & confidential' orders to offer an Allied subsidy of £100,000, on the understanding that Sweden remained quiet and 'assisted' us if required.[1] This must be done adroitly, for details must not leak out. But if a British squadron was to operate freely, an effort should clearly be made to avoid antagonising the Swedes while we were wooing the Danes.

These tactics dictated the message to the Prussians, who were now pressing for a clear-cut response, and some of whom indeed were calling on the British to come to a point. It was rather curious at first sight that this should have been so, when less than a year before they had thought of supporting the Russian claim to Ochakov.[2] But in the maze of the efforts for territorial gain – so singleminded and so unstable – and the shifting struggles for power around an inert and capricious King, Prussian policy was easily addicted to extremes, searching endlessly for the partner who would offer the best return. Careful handling was therefore necessary, for tension was rising again in Berlin, and if the anglophiles were disappointed there was always the danger of a sudden reaction. The British despatch was friendly and hopeful; but a decision was avoided, for 'before any distinct Declaration is made . . . it is necessary to ascertain precisely what are the Means for inforcing' it.[3] A long account followed of our approaches elsewhere; and while the picture admittedly was still confused, there was reason to think it would soon start to lighten, and then the Allies could act.

Pitt and the Foreign Office were optimistic. They could scarcely believe that 'all our engines will fail', and 'If any of them succeed, our point must be carried'.[4] A comprehensive plan of this kind was indeed perhaps the best hope, for as the news spread among the capitals so should the cumulative effect. There were moreover some grounds for confidence, particularly in Denmark, where the British party was strong and had earlier seemed inclined to help.[5] The Poles too might well be influenced, the King of Sweden was now in the market, and Austria was thought to be anxious for a general peace. Even the Empress, it was argued, could hardly defy such odds; and in the last resort there was always the British fleet.

But not everyone was convinced. The Cabinet was unsure. There was apparently a general wish to postpone a decision until Parliament had

1. Same to Liston, no. 1, sd (F.O. 73/12).
2. See p. 5 above.
3. Leeds to Jackson, no. 1, 8 January 1791 (F.O. 64/20).
4. Burges to Auckland, Private, sd (B.L. Add. Ms 34435). For Pitt, see Ewart to Auckland, 5 January 1791 (loc. cit.).
5. The Foreign Office indeed went so far as to call one of its former statements an 'unequivocal assurance' (Leeds to Fráncis Drake [Minister in Copenhagen], 8 January 1791; P.R.O., F.O. 22/13. And see Drake to Leeds, no. 8, 11 December 1790, loc. cit.).

risen, which it was hoped would be in the middle of April.[1] Ministers seem to have reserved judgment, while content to let the approaches go ahead. But if there were doubts – and there probably were – they may soon have been strengthened by Auckland at The Hague. For Auckland was becoming worried, and was making his views heard. He had a keen nose for trouble, and he smelt it at this point. In the first place he did not trust Ewart – his judgment or his information. He suspected that things were not nearly as certain as that young man chose to believe. There were strong, if temporarily muted, forces in Prussia which dreaded a Russian war; he was sure that Russia would not climb down; and what could the Allies do then? Prussian operations, and a British squadron, would not affect the Empress materially. They could strike only at the fringes of her empire, and as long as she avoided an encounter a naval force in the Baltic would suffer severely from wear and tear. The war would probably be indecisive, expensive and highly unpopular. It might not be supported in Holland; and there was another great fact to be faced. For, sitting in the cockpit of Europe, Auckland was gloomy about France. Far more than most people in London, he feared the effects of the Revolution. 'If that Russian business could happily be settled we might sit still & look at the French Story like Spectators in a Theatre'.[2] But if we risked and lost our prestige, or forced a general distraction and conflict, we would weaken the hope of containing a disturbance which might easily spread.

Auckland was never the man to shrink from airing his opinions. He wrote to his colleagues in other countries, to Ewart and Burges, to Grenville, Leeds and Pitt.[3] He was not in a particularly strong position to reverse the tide. Despite his situation in an Allied capital and his professional and political claims, he was generally unpopular, and particularly – for what that was worth – with Leeds.[4] He had been wrong before, and been reprimanded;[5] and he was competing with a man who had now gained Pitt's ear. For Ewart, who had gone to Bath for his health late in November, was recalled to London a month later, and by his own account had been 'almost constantly in Downing Street or at Whitehall since'.[6] He had not got all that he wanted: he would have preferred immediate action. But his policy held the field, and his

1. Ewart stressed this point to Auckland on 5 January, adding that the King of Prussia would be told in confidence (B.L. Add. Ms 34435), as apparently he was (Ewart to Pitt, 11 February 1791; P.R.O. 30/8/133).

2. Auckland to Morton Eden, 11 January 1791 (B.L. Add. MS 34435).

3. Ewart apparently assumed throughout January that Auckland agreed with him. It came as a shock in February to find that he did not.

4. See I, 484–5, 499–500, 429–34.

5. Op cit., 489–90, 492, and particularly 533–4.

6. To Auckland, 5 January 1791 (B.L. Add. Ms 34435). According to Leeds a month earlier, 'Every body who has had any Conversation with him, is full of his commendation' (to Jackson, Private, 29 November 1791; B.L. Add. Ms 28066).

reputation was high. The significance of Auckland's objections lay in the future rather than at the time. But judging by later events they may well have had an effect on Grenville, and, perhaps through him, given other Ministers cause to reflect.

To receive a reply from northern Europe generally took about a month, and some of the answers in this case were not likely to be hurried. As the messengers made their way back across the wintry northern plains – and almost every messenger in the Foreign Office books was now on the move – they carried the normal run of diplomatic reports, while the British proposals were still being scrutinised.

The reports were rather disquieting. No one expected good news from Russia; but, probably in the first half of February, the answer to the earlier messages arrived.[1] It was as uncompromising as had been feared – an absolute refusal – and the British Minister in St Petersburg saw no solution other than to 'proceed to extremes'.[2] Spain meanwhile made a démarche, but this too had little effect; and it was followed by the news that the Russians had captured the Turkish strongpoint of Ismail.[3] Despite friendly remarks from Vienna, the Austrians made no real move to help, and their talks for peace with Turkey were badly bogged down. Matters in Poland looked rather more hopeful, and the British Minister was hard at work – 'he negotiated, conferred, promised, apostrophized, and threatened; he resorted to pamphlets and broadsides; in short, he left no stone unturned'.[4] But the result was still in the balance, the Polish politicians were excited and corrupt, and perhaps their only point of agreement was an intense distrust of Prussia which not even the prospect of British protection might overcome. The Alliance itself was in an uneasy state. The Dutch were openly reluctant to repeat their effort of the year before against Spain, and provide ships to act with a British squadron.[5] They were being treated sternly at just this time in their lengthy talks with London over Far Eastern trade,[6] and they saw little point in making Ochakov a pretext to 'pluck a feather from the cap of the Empress'.[7] They seemed apathetic and cautious; and the Prussians were thought to be intriguing once more. The chargé d'affaires in Berlin could not decide what was going on, but Ewart, who had his own sources, feared that overtures were being made elsewhere. This indeed

1. See pp. 12–13 above.

2. Whitworth to Leeds, no. 2, 10 January 1791 (P.R.O., F.O. 65/20). There is no endorsement of the date of receipt.

3. Same to same, nos, 5, 7, 25 January, 7 February 1791, (received 21 and 26 February), no. 8, 18 February 1791 (loc. cit.). See p. 9 above for Ismail.

4. Robert Howard Lord, *The Second Partition of Poland* . . . (1915), 171.

5. I, 563.

6. Op cit., 432.

7. As Ewart put it to Pitt, 11 February 1791 (P.R.O. 30/8/133).

was true. A Prussian envoy had set out on a secret mission to Vienna, to revive the old ideas of a territorial exchange and propose an arrangement at Poland's expense. Any such plan, if successful, would of course split the Imperial Powers. But it would also destroy Pitt's Polish design, and furthermore – though this was in the background – a Prusso-Austrian understanding might have implications for British policy towards France. The Foreign Office was in the dark; but it was uneasily aware that something was stirring which might affect 'the very existence of Prussia, as a powerful or useful Ally'.[1]

So matters stood – or rather eddied – while Ministers waited for news from the North. As it began to come in, it could be taken either way. The King of Sweden was happily making the most of his situation: he did not sign an agreement with Russia, and he capped the Allies' proposal at once. In response to the figure of £100,000 he asked for £1½ million for 'each campaign', the command of a combined naval force, and a peacetime subsidy to follow.[2] The Danes, or rather the anglophile party, remained as helpful as they could. They agreed to approach the Empress, they listened to the offer of an alliance, some of them stated that there would be no obstruction and that Copenhagen would provide supplies. But even the best disposed made it clear that Denmark would remain neutral, and in a 'remarkable answer' pleaded 'for God's sake leave us in peace'.[3] Silence then descended. The Danes got in touch with the Russians. But as the time for decision drew closer nothing concrete was heard.

It had long been assumed in London that the probable deadline would be the middle of April,[4] for if a Baltic squadron was to be effective it should sail by the end of that month. After a partial reduction of the fleet at the end of the Nootka Sound crisis, a virtual standstill had been ordered in December, so as to retain a force of 35 to 40 ships of the line. In January Lord Hood was ordered to hoist his flag in the *Victory*, cruisers were sent to their stations in February, and in March the squadron assembled at Spithead. By the end of that month there was a force of 36 of the line and 29 smaller vessels – a fleet larger than Nelson commanded at Trafalgar. Meanwhile the supply departments were turning their attention to a Baltic campaign, for 'the Service was entirely new, at least to any One now living'.[5] Two storeships were hired, and a full complement of stores was ordered in case local replenishments could

---

1. Ibid. And see also his letter to Pitt of 23 January (loc. cit.).

2. Liston to Leeds, no. 8, Secret, 17 February 1791 (P.R.O., F.O. 73/12). And see also his no. 9, 19 February 1791, Most Secret & Confidential.

3. Francis Drake to Leeds, no. 16, 4 February 1791 (F.O. 22/13). See also same to same, no. 13, 15 January 1791.

4. See Ewart to Auckland, 5 January 1791 (B.L. Add. Ms 34435).

5. P.R.O. Adm. 106/3037; the Surveyor of the Navy's retrospective 'Observations' on the Armaments of 1790 and 1791.

not be obtained. It was unfortunate that the only British sailor with local experience was not available, for Captain Sidney Smith, of future Mediterranean fame, who had been serving with the Swedish fleet, was abroad. But he was in any case suspect in London – his activities had caused diplomatic trouble – and there is no evidence that his information was sought. The Admiralty indeed had little to go on, and the only advice that the Government received came from the Prussian General in prospective charge of the land campaign, who suggested that a British officer should be sent to inspect the area, and forwarded some ideas for naval operations.[1] The Department confined itself to fitting out the force on the best rough estimate it could make, and the ships were victualled and stored by the time that the Ministry wished.

In the middle of March little more had therefore emerged to influence a decision, and the Foreign Office, and Pitt himself, were now disposed to act.[2] They might have waited longer, although they were growing impatient;[3] but in the third week of the month matters came to a head. For the King of Prussia by then had heard the results of the secret talks in Vienna, and while Austria, it seemed, was not going to risk a war, she would also not engage in a territorial exchange.[4] The British alliance therefore was best; his flank appeared to be safe; and on the 11th he sent brief instructions in his own hand to his Minister in London, calling on the British Government to join in an immediate attack on the Empress. He demanded a 'definite declaration', in default of which 'the cession of Ochakov would be [the] natural outcome'.[5] The message was received on the 19th or 20th, and the Cabinet met: possibly on the 21st, certainly on the 22nd, and almost certainly again on the 27th. At the end of the session on the 22nd a Minute was drawn up, resolving that a force of 39 sail of the line, with frigates, should be prepared for despatch to the Baltic towards the end of April; that measures should be taken for further reinforcements, and for sending 10 or 12 sail of the line to the Black Sea; that a secret treaty should be offered to the King of Sweden, promising an Allied subsidy of £200,000 or 'even' £300,000, in return

1. Jackson to Leeds, nos. 8 and 13, 23 January, 6 February 1791 (P.R.O., F.O. 64/20), transmitting General Möllendorff's views. From the later remarks of a British consul, it looks as if information on the Danish ports and coast was not sought very urgently by the Legation (John Mitchell to Drake, 20 May [1791]; F.O. 97/116), and certainly nothing was passed on to London. Recent reports on the Baltic passages were lying in the Admiralty, from a reconnaissance mission sent, in connexion with the Nootka Sound crisis, in the summer of 1790; but little notice seems to have been taken of them.

2. For the Foreign Office see Leeds to Auckland, 11 March 1791 (B.L. Add. Ms 34436). Pitt's attitude may be inferred from Ewart to Auckland, 8 March 1791 (loc. cit.), and Ewart to Jackson, 11 March 1791 (Ewart Mss).

3. See Burges to Auckland, 21 March 1791 (B.L. Add. Ms 34436).

4. See p. 17 above.

5. J. Holland Rose, *William Pitt and National Revival* (1911), 608. A copy, untranslated, is enclosed in Jackson to Leeds, no. 23, 11 March 1791 (P.R.O., F.O. 64/20). Cf. p. 14 above.

for his neutrality and the use of his ports; and that an ultimatum should be sent at once to Russia for joint delivery with the Prussians. Ewart and the Prussian Minister waited on Pitt after the meeting, and Pitt, Leeds and Chatham (First Lord of the Admiralty) saw the King the next day. On the night of the 27th the despatches left London for the capitals concerned; the King's Message for the necessary supplies was read to Parliament on the 28th; and on the 31st a naval press was put into effect.[1]

So the die was apparently cast. There were several strange features about the decision. The Cabinet Minute was specifically based on 'the supposition that the Danes will adhere to their assurances of not obstructing the Sound, as well as of observing a strict neutrality, & of giving the use of their ports to your Majesty's ships';[2] but no firm assurance of this nature had been received. The idea of sending a small force to the Black Sea had been mentioned vaguely before; but no preparations or inquiries had been made as to its functions or maintenance. The *casus belli* was Ochakov; but no detailed study had been made of its importance, and indeed none was available until March. Even then it came not from a British but from a Dutch source, and the information was volunteered by Auckland, who had been talking to an Admiral with local experience. The report as it happened proved awkward, for it discounted the value of the port to the Turks, and although Pitt then took up the question it was late in the day and he did not pursue it long.[3] His approach in fact was altogether in contrast to his usual form. A distinguishing mark of his Administration had been the care with which he sought the facts, and his insistence on detail before he formed a plan. Even in 1784, on his first essay into foreign affairs, one can see him probing a scheme for Baltic alliances with some precise

1. According to Leeds, writing later (*The Political Memoranda of Francis Fifth Duke of Leeds. . .* , ed. Oscar Browning (1884), 150), the Cabinet met on the 21st as well as on the 22nd, but it was the latter meeting, which was a long one, that attracted the attention of various newspapers. For the Minute, and the attendance, see *L.C.G.III*, I, no. 663; alterations to the draft by Leeds and by Pitt, in each case substituting 'preparations' and 'measures' for immediate action, and in Pitt's case also tightening up the demands on Sweden, are to be found in P.R.O., F.O. 64/20. According to one newspaper (*The Gazetteer*, 23 March 1791), Hawkesbury from the Committee of Trade, who was not yet a member of the Cabinet (see I, 433n1), was also present on the 22nd; and Ewart, too, claimed to have attended the same meeting, and to have 'waited on' the Cabinet again on the 27th before the despatches were sent off (to Jackson, 22 March 1791, and Note of 27 March 1791; Ewart Mss). By the wording of Pitt to Marquess of Stafford [Lord Privy Seal], 28 March 1791 (P.R.O. 30/29/384), there seems to have been a Cabinet meeting on this latter date. The various interviews and audiences were reported in several newspapers. The ultimatum to Russia was in the form of a 'Representation' drawn up by Pitt (draft in his hand, and Leeds to Whitworth, no. 1, 27 March 1791; P.R.O., F.O. 65/20).

2. *L.C.G. III*, I, no. 663.

3. See *A.C.*, II, 382–3, and for a good account of the episode Holland Rose, op. cit., 603–5.

queries about the port of Gothenburg.[1] Now he was risking a war with Russia ostensibly for a cause about which he made no inquiries, and to which he had earlier seemed largely indifferent.[2] No proper information was available on the Baltic, where our ships were to act. There was no real basis for assessing the future trade with Poland, which underlay the policy. And the very existence of the 'grand System', which was the object and means of the exercise, remained, at the point of decision, entirely in doubt.

All this is curious; and it is perhaps true that if the Prussians had not forced the pace some of the omissions might have been made good. But despite the earlier British arguments, they were not in fact central to Pitt's thinking. He had been growing impatient before the Prussians' message, and his behaviour really reflected his belief, under Ewart's prompting, that success would follow on a firm stand. If England was shown to mean business, everything else would fall into place. The very indecision in the Baltic and Poland was an argument for boldness, and his information from the Legation in Russia was that the Empress would yield to force. Given this reasoning the unanswered soundings of January could become a basis for action in March, impelled by the approaching campaigning season and the Prussian demand. The point was now reached which Ewart had foretold: the 'existence of Prussia, as a powerful or useful Ally' seemed to be 'at stake',[3] and in these circumstances the challenge to Russia appeared to be well worth while. For one gains the impression that very few people in London really believed that the worst would happen. At the Navy Office, amid the preparations, 'it was generally thought there would be no war with Russia'; the Foreign Office remained sanguine; and most Ministers agreed that 'an additional armament would produce the best effect'.[4] They did not all do so with equal enthusiasm, or even with the same expectations. Grenville was lukewarm, but seems to have approved because the force might form a counter in a negotiation, Thurlow hid his doubts as far as possible in a familiar sullen silence, and Richmond and Stafford ended by having serious fears. But even the self-confident Richmond shrank from opposing what he took to be 'the Majority' of his colleagues,[5] or the general feeling that the matter had best be left to Pitt. For there was undoubtedly a widespread 'confidence', as one envoy

1. I, 471.
2. See pp. 5, 7, 12, 19 above.
3. Ewart to Pitt, 11 February 1791 (P.R.O. 30/8/133). See p. 17 above.
4. Surveyor of the Navy's 'Observations', referring to early April (P.R.O. Adm. 106/3037); Leeds to Auckland, 11 March 1791 (B.L. Add. Ms 34436); Burges to Auckland, 21 March 1791 (loc. cit.); *Political Memoranda of Leeds*, 150, quoting Grenville's opinion.
5. Richmond to Pitt, 27 March 1791 (Alison Gilbert Olson, *The Radical Duke . . .* (1961), 220–1). Stafford's apprehensions by that date are revealed in Pitt to Stafford, 28 March 1791 (P.R.O. 30/29/384). Thurlow's attitude remained until early in April as it had been since January (17 January to Ewart; Ewart Mss).

called it later, 'in Pitt's star';[1] and it was a sentiment that Pitt himself shared. If he envisaged a campaign it was a short one, and his policy in essence was an exercise in brinkmanship. He had been in that situation before, and emerged victorious; and he had brought himself to the conviction that he could do so again.

III

Perhaps he might. But the matter was never put to the test. Instead the naval mobilisation raised a storm of protest at home.

Outside the small circle of Ministers and officials, the news came as a shock. Ever since the reduction of the fleet had been halted after Nootka Sound, Government newspapers had been mentioning the possibility of such a step. But the public did not pay much attention or expect a war, the Funds by and large remained steady, and when the Cabinet's decision was known its supporters were acutely embarrassed. The reactions of the Ministerialist newspapers reflect their dismay. Most of them kept as quiet as they could while they waited to see what would happen, and even *The Times*, which was perhaps the best informed at this point and felt the greatest obligations, was frankly taken aback. On 23 March it had 'the best reasons to believe that no future circumstances . . . will induce Mr Pitt to involve the country'. On the 26th it believed that we were going to support Prussia in 'forcing' peace on the Empress. On the 28th it looked forward to 'a speedy war', and reminded its readers that Pitt had always proved right so far. On 1 April it concluded that the campaign would not be an 'active one'. On the 4th it announced, in capital letters, 'there will be NO WAR'.[2]

This confusion was not surprising. The City and Parliament were also confused. The Funds by now had fallen steeply, although there was a slight rally at the turn of the month, due perhaps to Dutch buying after earlier sales; and both the Lords and the Commons were thoroughly upset. Not the least of Pitt's misfortunes indeed was that Parliament was still sitting – a consummation which Ministers had devoutly hoped to avoid.[3] In the crises of 1787 and 1790 they had been able largely to do so, and the outcome on this occasion amply justified their fears. As soon as the King's Message was read there were discussions in both Houses, and it became apparent that the Ministry was in trouble. Government backbenchers seem to have been uncertain and generally silent at the outset; but it was disturbing that one steady supporter and one hitherto friendly, if prickly, independent were quick to oppose the motion for

---

1. W.W. Fawkener [special envoy to Russia] to Ewart, 28 June 1791 (Ewart Mss).
2. It is fairly clear that the paper's best information came from the Admiralty or the Navy Board, where the same opinion may finally have prevailed (see p. 20 above).
3. See pp. 14–15 above.

granting supplies.[1] It passed by what the King thought 'very handsome' majorities in both Houses.[2] But Ministers knew that the figures did not reflect the mood. Over the next fortnight the doubts came to the surface, and by mid-April the message was clear. In two further debates in the Commons, on the 12th and 15th, Government held its majorities by 253 to 173 and 254 to 162.[3] But as George Rose of the Treasury remarked, 'There are Circumstances attending this Business which render it a mortifying as well as a distressing One',[4] and the mortification was almost complete by the time he wrote. For, majority or no majority, the Ministry had by then been reduced to 'a line of concession, which what has happened . . . compels us to adopt'.[5]

Pitt was in a delicate position for a debate. Very few people could see the point of his acting as he did. Very few had thought about Ochakov, many hardly knew where it was, and this was indeed 'a quarrel in a far-away country between people of whom we know nothing'. It seemed quite absurd to risk a war for the place, or go to the expense of fitting out a fleet. And it was very difficult for the Minister to make his wider case convincing. To invoke the Allies' 'defensive system' as a safeguard of the balance of power invited the response – which was not slow in coming – that his proposal was aggressive, and had little effect when that balance was traditionally thought of in terms of France. It was indeed hard for him to enter into his reasoning in any depth, for this would focus unwelcome attention on the plans for Poland and the role of Prussia, and might even – a point of importance – prejudice the Allies' secret talks in the North. He had moreover to contend with the fact that there was a good deal of sympathy for Russia – rather mild and residual perhaps, but again the legacy of a long tradition, stretching back through the 1760s when Chatham had talked of 'a natural alliance', to the later days of Walpole and even to the age of Peter the Great. It had been battered by recent events, since the Armed Neutrality of 1780.[6] But it was not dead yet, there were still old antipathies towards the Turk, and it was not entirely fanciful to fear, as some in official circles now did, the emergence of a 'Russian party' under Opposition, and particularly Fox.[7]

For this was a golden opportunity for Fox, and one moreover that suited him well. He had always been a champion of Russia – it was one of

---

1. John Somers Cocks and James Martin, on 29 March (*P.R.*, XXIX (1791), 39–40).

2. *L.C.G. III*, I, no. 666; and see also *H.M.C., Dropmore*, II, 42–3. The figures were 97 to 34 in the Lords, and 228 to 135 in the Commons.

3. *L.C.G. III*, I, no, 670, which is to be preferred for the first set of figures to *P.R.*, XXIX, 153.

4. To Auckland, Most private & confidential, 19 April 1791 (B.L. Add. Ms 34436). He had already confided his doubts to his own memoranda on 28 March (N.L.S. Ms 3795; I owe this reference to Dr Paul Kelly).

5. Grenville to Auckland, 16 April 1791 (B.L. Add. Ms 34436).

6. See I, 49–50.

7. Auckland and Burges were both aware of this possibility.

the planks of an old-fashioned foreign policy[1] – and these particular circumstances were tailored to his use. One might fear Russia's attitude in the Baltic, with its implications for our naval supplies. One might resist her arguments over neutral rights, which could threaten our maritime power. But the quarrel here concerned eastern Europe, and what had we to do with eastern Europe, and the rigid preservation of the Turkish northern frontiers? Fox developed a powerful attack[2] enthusiastically swelled by his colleagues, exploiting their first real Parliamentary chance since the disastrous Regency crisis. They found a surprisingly easy target, for, caught in the net of his undertakings, Pitt put up an uncharacteristically weak performance. He had even to fall back on that last refuge, the need for official discretion: 'Confidence must be given to those in whose hands the Administration was entrusted'.[3] Government spokesmen, as Thurlow complained, were thereby '*gagged* in the debates',[4] although the appeal, as so often, had a certain effect. Several backbenchers gave their support, on the ground that one must trust the Ministry. But most of them did so reluctantly, and the sense of bewilderment remained. By the time that the Commons' debate was resumed in the middle of April, the House and the country were no wiser than they were at the start.[5]

By then, however, the Government was on the run. The Cabinet was thoroughly alarmed, and when it met on the evening of 30 March Stafford added his doubts to Grenville's and to Richmond's growing opposition. The next day Camden showed signs of wavering – he 'seemed much agitated, and lamented the difficulties' – and by that evening, when there was to be a further meeting, the Foreign Secretary expected 'a direct and abrupt change' of course.[6] He hinted at his resignation if this were to happen, and at first it seemed that it would, for Pitt, Leeds and Chatham found themselves at odds with Richmond, Stafford and Grenville, while Camden said very little and Thurlow pretended to be asleep. In the end, however, something of an escape was found. In the past few days a message had arrived from Denmark, containing further friendly remarks about assistance, and some proposed modifications of the British demand which, the Danes thought, the Empress might accept. These related to the boundaries of the Ochakov area, so as to leave the lower reach of the Dniester to the Turks

1. For another see I, 493, 613n2.
2. Speech of 29 March, of which there is a somewhat fuller account in *The Senator; Or Clarendon's Parliamentary Chronicle. . . ,* II (nd, but 1791) than in *P.R.,* XXIX.
3. Speech of 29 March; *P.R.,* XXIX, 48–9. The same sentiment had been heard, but not in that case defensively, in the early stages of the Nootka Sound crisis.
4. *Political Memoranda of Leeds,* 159.
5. There had been a further debate in the Lords on 1 April, after a first one on 29 March. Both were damaging to Government, and the first was indeed reported more amply in most London newspapers than the debate of the same day in the Commons (cf. I, 53).
6. *Political Memoranda of Leeds,* 152–4.

(and thus, by implication, available to the Poles); and while neither the British Minister in Copenhagen nor the Foreign Secretary was much impressed, the Cabinet as a whole grasped eagerly at the straw. They resolved to return 'a civil answer' to the Danes, taking note of the prospect of assistance, but seeking a 'written and official Answer' on 'a Point of so much Importance'. Meanwhile they would send a message to the Prussians, seeking a brief postponement of the ultimatum on ground which might appear less likely to be taken as an earnest of retreat in Berlin. Leeds remained unhappy; but he finally agreed. The meeting closed at one in the morning, and the messenger left within two hours.[1]

This was all pretty shaky, and Pitt himself was now shaken – more so perhaps than at any time since the Irish business almost six years before. As on that occasion, a complicated scheme was showing signs of going badly wrong, and it was hard to see how many of the balls could be kept in the air. Faced with a divided Cabinet, he must demonstrate a public strength which, as things stood, was beyond his grasp. His only hope was to 'lay open' his case, and this he refused to contemplate – 'there was great difficulty in doing that in Parlt',[2] as indeed there was. His friends and advisers were increasingly alarmed and for the most part un-convinced, and while he showed a brave face at first to Ewart[3] he was in fact losing heart. 'He felt an inclination' by 4 April 'to throw up in finding a measure he was convinced was right liable to such difficulties as might render it futile if not impracticable';[4] and some ten days later he revealed his feelings in a rare – a very rare – show of emotion. In a talk of 'several hours' with Ewart he stressed that his view had not changed; 'he was convinced there never had existed a discussion in which the interests, both political & commercial of this country, were more committed'.

> 'But . . . all my efforts to make a majority of the House of Commons understand the subject have been fruitless; and I know for certain that, tho' they may support me at present, I should not be able to carry the Vote of Credit. In short, Sir, You have seen that they can be embarked in a War from motives of passion, but they cannot be made to comprehend a case in which the most valuable interests of the Country are at stake.' . . . After stating several facts in confirmation, and repeating, even with tears in his eyes, that it was the greatest mortification he had ever experienced, he said he was determined not to knock under but to keep up a good countenance.

The fleet would be kept ready to sail, and he hoped some compromise

1. Op. cit., 156–8; Drake to Leeds, no. 25, 12 March 1791; Leeds to Drake, no. 3, 31 March 1791 (P.R.O., F.O. 22/13); Leeds to Jackson, no. 7, 31 March 1791 (F.O. 64/20).
2. *Political Memoranda of Leeds*, 160, for 4 April.
3. Pitt to Ewart, 6 April (Ewart Mss).
4. *Political Memoranda of Leeds*, 160.

might be found; but 'he was well aware that the difference . . . would always be very great and extremely mortifying'. He was, so Ewart reported, 'much embarrassed' throughout, and 'extremely affected by the violence' of the most recent debate.[1]

The interview indeed took place at a singularly bad moment, for Pitt had just experienced one of the worst days he had ever had in the House. It was true, as he observed, that no financial vote of credit – the great test – was involved;[2] but Opposition's language had been fierce and confident, his majority fell to 80 on a vote of 326, and he himself was restricted to a few brief remarks after the division.[3] 'His efforts' to make them 'understand the subject' had in fact really been abandoned – he had landed himself in a straitjacket from which he could see no escape. Three days later he emerged rather better, with a majority of 92 on a vote of 316 – thanks possibly to a fear that Fox might actually topple the Ministry and to the fact that he chose the occasion to air his views once more about France.[4] But the recovery was limited, the damage had gone too deep, and while the debates were under way Pitt was in process of dismantling his plans.

The retreat was hastened by a growing surge of public hostility. For the Parliamentary tempest reflected a feeling which quickly took root. Government newspapers remained embarrassed, and some showed ominous signs of ratting; Opposition journals breathed a new confidence, and there was a spate of pamphlets and caricatures.[5] Not all of this, as usual, was quite what it seemed. The Russia Company recruited its resources, and the Russian envoy Simon Vorontsov – normally an admirer of Pitt's and a convinced anglophile – set out to mobilise opinion in a cause that was going his way. Starting with pieces in the London newspapers, and the supply of information to useful quarters – from Fox himself and leading peers and MPs to merchants and coffee house politicians – he was soon organising pamphlets and articles farther afield. He had his paid agents of course, and Opposition helped; there is

1. Ewart to Jackson, 14 April 1791 (Ewart Mss). The reference to 'a War from motives of passion' obviously refers to Nootka Sound. Holland Rose, who quotes from this letter (op. cit., 617), ascribes the meeting to 'on or about 10th April'. But the mention of the debate in the Commons must date it after the 12th. Pitt however had talked to Leeds and written to Rose in the same strain on the 10th (*Political Memoranda of Leeds*, 162; *The Diaries and Correspondence of the Right Hon. George Rose*, ed. L.V. Harcourt, I (1860), 110–11).

2. The motion, brought by Grey, had been 'to state . . . propositions' on the preparations for a war with Russia (*P.R.*, XXIX, 103, 111).

3. Op. cit., 153. According to the Opposition newspaper *The Morning Chronicle* on 13 April there were another 25 MPs who would have voted against Pitt had they been present.

4. *The Senator*, II, 530–45, gives the clearest report of Fox's speech although *P.H.*, XXIX alone elaborates on the French part of it.

5. See M.S. Anderson, *Britain's Discovery of Russia 1553–1815* (1958), ch. VI, to which this paragraph is much indebted.

a hint that the first of the pamphlets was composed by Fox.[1] But he did not have to count on such sources alone, for there were others in plenty: spontaneous meetings and unsolicited treatises – one of the first was from 'a rich gentleman in Devonshire' – with which the Ministry's efforts, distinctly half-hearted, could not compete. By his own account, indeed, Vorontsov spent only £250 of his Government's money, and the attack drew its strength undoubtedly from 'une affaire . . . absolutement impopulaire'.[2] The groundswell of opposition was not confined to London; it was equally apparent in the provinces and Scotland. 'The country throughout' in fact '. . . told Mr Pitt they will not go to war'.[3] Nor was there much enthusiasm in the Service which would have to carry out the policy. Hood himself disliked the prospect; and a potentially greater voice was heard. 'How', wrote Nelson of the Empress Catherine, 'we are to get at her fleet I don't see'. 'Narrow seas', he wrote prophetically, 'and no friendly ports are bad things'.[4]

On 15 April Pitt therefore went into reverse, as it had been predictable for some days that he would. He set to work to draft despatches, particularly one for Prussia which he completed the next day.[5] Parliamentary opposition and 'the public impression' had made it 'very difficult' to go to war. The former policy must accordingly be dropped, and we must hope that the Danes' suggestion would offer 'some middle term'.[6] This was 'a line of concession' with a vengeance, and it sparked off one immediate result. For the Foreign Secretary had already decided that he would not sign the despatch. By the 15th in fact he was ready to resign. He now attended his last Cabinet meeting, and after a pause for the necessary arrangements delivered up his Seals on the 21st.

Leeds's departure was not entirely unwelcome, although it increased the impression of defeat. He had long been a lightweight, and resented the fact, and his going eased the way for an obvious successor. For though gossip made free with the choice, it could not be seriously in doubt. At a Cabinet on 16 April Grenville read out the offending despatch; he acted for Leeds in the next few days; and he now took over the post.[7]

With his arrival the new policy was put into effect. Since a 'middle

1. 'Composé' actually by Fox's young follower Robert Adair, of whom more anon, but 'sous la dicte de monsieur Fox' (*Archiv Knyazya Mikhaila Illarionovicha Vorontsova*, ed. P.I. Bartenev, IX (1876), 196).
2. Op. cit., VIII (1876), 23; IX, 190, 192.
3. Anthony Storer to Auckland, 6 May 1791 (*A.C.*, II, 388).
4. To William Cornwallis, 4 April 1791 (*H.M.C., Various Collections*, 369).
5. See *Political Memoranda of Leeds*, 160–2, and for a fuller text of Leeds's objections as early as 9 April, P.R.O. 30/8/151.
6. Grenville to Ewart, no. 1, 20 April 1791 (P.R.O., F.O. 64/21). For the dating of the final draft see *Political Memoranda of Leeds*, 162–4.
7. Op. cit., 166–7; *H.M.C., Dropmore*, II, 54–5. There had been rumours in March that Leeds would be superseded (*Political Memoranda of Leeds*, 148–9). For Grenville's growing part in foreign affairs in recent years see I, 570.

term' must be found, three possibilities were advanced. The region of Ochakov, as originally defined, might be depopulated and declared neutral; or it might be ceded to Russia on condition that it was then left waste; or the frontier might be drawn east of the Dniester, as the Danes had suggested, no fortresses being built in the Russian area. These terms were not specified in detail in Grenville's first round of despatches, for the Ministry had decided to send a special envoy to negotiate in St Petersburg. The idea seems to have been taking shape for some days, and the choice fell on William Fawkener, the senior clerk in the Privy Council Office, who had earlier been employed on a mission to Portugal.[1] He left early in May via Berlin, and meanwhile Ewart had been sent ahead to break the news to the Prussians and enlist their co-operation. It was a bitter moment for him, and his nerves were on edge. As he passed through Holland, he left a note for Auckland asking him not to interfere any more.[2]

The epilogue was protracted, but the result was much as might have been foreseen. Fawkener and the British Minister did their best, but the proposals were brushed aside, and on 26 July the Allies agreed to Russia's retention of Ochakov and all the area to the eastern bank of the Dniester, subject only to an assurance of free navigation down the river. This face-saving formula, for what it was worth, reflected a rising worry over France which was leading the Courts of Europe to avoid quarrelling too much with each other. But it scarcely affected the issue, for the prospective beneficiary was Poland, and the Empress was already making plans for Poland's future. Meanwhile the terms contrasted sadly with Pitt's language at the start. No one really expected otherwise, whatever faint hopes there might be in London, least of all the new Foreign Secretary, who wished to wind up the affair. 'An appearance of firmness', he allowed, remained 'necessary' while the talks were under way,[3] and the naval force was not in fact demobilised until August.[4] But the idea of a Black Sea squadron had been dropped before Fawkener left England, and the fate of the Baltic fleet was finally decided when the Danes, after all that had passed, replied that they could not promise the use of their ports.[5] It was an ironical end to a policy which was supposed to have rested on their 'assurances'.[6]

1. I, 495.
2. 23 April 1791 (B.L. Add. Ms 34436). On the 14th he had described the events leading to the change of policy as 'a pretty strong *symptom of bitching*' (Ewart to Jackson; Ewart Mss).
3. To Auckland, 16 April 1791 (*H.M.C., Dropmore*, II, 50–1). And see his assertions to Ewart, qualified though they were, as late as 6 July (loc. cit., 123–4).
4. It became a holiday sight. Pitt himself was rowed round the ships with Dundas late in July, and entertained to a meal of turtle and wine aboard the *Victory*.
5. Grenville to Fawkener, 6 May 1791 (P.R.O., F.O. 65/21); Drake to Leeds, no. 35, 21 April 1791 (F.O. 22/13).
6. P. 14n5, 19 above.

So far as Ochakov itself was concerned, then, the whole business proved pointless. Nor did the result, on the face of it, greatly affect Anglo-Russian relations. Trade did not suffer, there was talk of a new commercial treaty again within a few months, and the next year, as the French scene darkened, an alliance was in the air. By then indeed the affair had begun to look as transient as it has done ever since, 'probably . . . of small importance in the eyes of posterity, and . . . already almost forgotten' at home.[1] Nevertheless, Ochakov made its contribution to events which cast their shadow ahead. For the aftermath of the crisis produced a major reassessment in a setting from which the British influence was removed. The Prussians, relieved – whether openly or tacitly – that a fluctuating venture had been decided for them, and increasingly worried, like the other continental monarchies, by developments in France, turned again to Austria, and a preliminary Convention in July was followed by an alliance in August. The Swedes allied themselves with Russia in October; Russia, Austria and Turkey made peace the next January; and the way was then open for the predatory Powers to settle the fate of Poland. This indeed had been foreshadowed even while the British policy was collapsing, for in May 1791 the Poles produced a new Constitution inspired – it was alleged – by French ideas. The Empress made it plain that she would not accept it, in the summer of 1792 her troops marched in, to be followed early the next year by the Prussians. Pitt's 'grand system' was a vanished memory, Russia stood on the ruins, and the reviving jealousies in central Europe, and the mutual disenchantment of Prussia and England, bedevilled the first stage of the struggle with France. The crisis which began in 1789 raised echoes in 1793–5, in the background to the animosities of the First wartime Coalition.[2] Meanwhile Pitt was forced, and his countrymen were satisfied, to 'watch events and keep ourselves quiet',[3] passive spectators of the upheavals whose effects were soon to engage them again.

In this sense, Ochakov may be taken as the start of the Eastern Question for England. In other respects the overture barely resembled the subsequent theme. There was little emphasis, in particular, on that concern for the Turkish Empire as our passage to India which governed later strategic thought. Dundas showed interest from the India Board, and Pitt himself took note; but not as a pivotal factor in his calculations.[4]

---

1. *The Annual Register . . . for the Year 1792* (1793), 33.
2. See I. 553.
3. Pitt to Ewart, 2. September 1791 (Holland Rose, op. cit., 629). And cf. Ewart to Pitt, 9 September 1791 (P.R.O. 30/8/133).
4. For Dundas, see N.L.S. Ms 3944; for Pitt, P.R.O. 30/8/195, undated notes on the case for intervention. The argument was not used publicly by Government. It is interesting, however, that a Ministerial publicist, W.A. Miles, already employed by Pitt (see I, 531n2, 541n3, 566–7, 606), and soon to be semi-officially involved in the preliminaries to the French Revolutionary War, published in 1791 a warning pamphlet on this theme, which advocated the building of a Suez canal as an artery for British trade (*An Enquiry into the Justice and Expediency of Prescribing Bounds to the Russian Empire*).

It is true that if things had gone differently for England in 1791, there might have been a basis for rather greater activity in the eastern Mediterranean. Trade with the Black Sea might have expanded, agents have been established in the Levant and Egypt.[1] But the interest was still peripheral, and the issue of Ochakov was seen primarily in other terms: in the interlocking prospects for the Baltic and Poland and the Prussian alliance. The arguments took place in fact 'in the age of Chatham rather than in that of Palmerston'.[2] Nevertheless, within that context they suggested a significant change. For, seen as a European problem, the Ochakov crisis challenged old assumptions: British friendship for Russia, the dismissal of Turkey as a factor in continental affairs, the exclusion of the eastern regions from the balance of power. Pitt's reasoning had little effect. His demands seemed out of character, and they were too unfamiliar and badly presented. The adjustment was much too quick; it needed far better preparation, and the pretext itself was particularly weak. His case stood little chance at home unless it proved effective abroad; and he had miscalculated there at almost every point. Ochakov came as a bolt from the blue, and was disastrously mishandled. It was one of those curious episodes which are real to those involved in it, and unreal to almost everyone else. Pitt was led into the preliminaries reluctantly, and then suddenly saw great dangers and a great design. But it contained elements which persisted through the upheavals of the next fifteen years; and he had cause increasingly to remain persuaded that the fiasco, so largely his fault, proved in point of fact that his vision had been correct.

The affair had some immediate repercussions on both Ministers and diplomats. It brought Grenville to the Foreign Office – an important event – and paved the way for his succession by Dundas at the Home Office,[3] thereby completing the inner Cabinet circle which was to conduct the war with France. It strengthened Auckland's hand within the diplomatic service; for his warnings had proved right, and Ewart, already in Grenville's disfavour, and soon to be further embarrassed when he mishandled the legal arrangements for the marriage of the Duke of York to a Prussian princess, retired through ill health in the autumn and was replaced by Auckland's brother. It left an unhappy taste among some of the British envoys involved, whose mutual relations had suffered from the confusion of the past few months. Not all of them were pleased that the Foreign Secretary had resigned; they felt the humiliation, and were doubtful of the future: 'The palinoidal concerto', as one of them put it, 'in which I have been obliged to perform is certainly not the musick which is the most agreeable to my taste'.[4] But

1. See I, 438–40.
2. Anderson, op. cit., 178.
3. See I, 634, 458n1.
4. Robert Liston, from Sweden, to George Aust [an Under Secretary at the Foreign Office], 29 May 1791 (P.R.O., F.O. 97/39). He told Jackson in Berlin that he was 'disgusted' with his instructions (17 May 1791; F.O. 353/64).

above all, of course, Ochakov was a crisis for Pitt: his first major setback in Europe, a nasty threat to his Ministry, and the only occasion in the peacetime decade on which he wondered if he should resign.

It has sometimes been held that he should, and the fact that he did not has been taken, then and since, as evidence of his love of office. He was in no danger of a defeat in the Commons once he decided to change his policy. His lowest majority was 80 (which *was* low for him on a major issue), and the figure quickly improved – a very different position from that, for instance, of North in 1782.[1] This may well have been due partly to the knowledge that in fact he was going to retreat, for the sense of the Cabinet must have been known and Fawkener's mission may even have been rumoured.[2] But it was also due precisely to the fear that the Ministry might have to resign, in which case presumably it might be replaced by Fox. Indeed it was this, according to Rose, that dissuaded Fox from a further attack, for he knew that 'our best Friends . . . had a greater Dread of his coming into Power than even of a Russian War'. The assessment may well have been right, and it was not necessarily confined to best friends alone. Had Fox been a 'fresh man', reported a former Coalition MP, he would have had 'little difficulty in getting into office'; but as it was, he and 'his party' stood little chance. 'Il est vrai', Vorontsov concluded in a review of the whole affair, 'que quoique monsieur Pitt aya perdu de sa popularité, la nation l'aime encore et veut le conserver en place'.[3] The House and the country in general wanted him to stay, and his resignation would undoubtedly have been deplored.

It may still be argued that he should have gone, and left others to drop his policy. He seems early on in fact to have had some thought of doing so: on 4 April he talked of 'an inclination to throw up'. But he gave various reasons for staying, the first on that same day.

> One consideration [he then told Leeds] strongly impressed his mind. The country he had no doubt (supposing a change of Govt to happen) would soon right itself, but what would become of the King?[4]

He repeated the argument soon afterwards, with a different emphasis.

1. Pp. 20–3, 25 above (though n3 on p. 25 must be taken into account), and I, 78. On 8 May 1940, Neville Chamberlain saw his majority fall to 81 at the end of the debate which led him to resign.

2. It was at any rate confidently forecast on 19 April by the well informed Professor of Modern History at Cambridge, John Symonds (to Arthur Young; *The Autobiography of Arthur Young. . .* , ed. M. Bentham-Edwards (1898), 205). The newspapers seem to have been slower off the mark; *The Times* mentioned Fawkener only on the 24th.

3. Rose to Auckland, 19 April 1791 (B.L. Add. Ms 34436); Anthony Storer to Auckland, 6 May 1791 (*A.C.*, II, 389); Simon Vorontsov to Alexander Vorontsov, 13 July 1791 N.S. (*Archiv Vorontsova*, IX, 202). Fox himself admitted that he was unlikely ever to run Pitt closer than he had done on 12 April (F. O'Gorman, *The Whig Party and the French Revolution* (1967), 62).

4. *Political Memoranda of Leeds*, 160.

What, then, remains to be done? Certainly, to risk my own situation, which my feelings and inclination would induce me to do without any hesitation; but there are unfortunately circumstances in the present state of this country which make it certain that confusion and the worst kind of consequences might be expected, and it would be abandoning the King.[1]

Later, in a message designed for the Prussians, he added the effect on foreign affairs.

To speak plainly: the obvious effect of our persisting would have been to risque the existence of the present Government, and with it, the whole of our system both at home and abroad. The personal part of this consideration it would have been our duty to overlook, and I trust we should all have been ready to do so. . . : but the overthrow of our system here, at the same time that it hazarded driving the Government at home into a state of absolute confusion, must have shaken the whole of our system abroad. It is not difficult to foresee what might have been the consequence to Prussia . . .[2]

And Prussia had become the linchpin of our policy in northern and central Europe.

There was a significant inconsistency between the first and the later of these statements. In one Pitt 'had no doubt the country . . . would soon right itself': in the others, there would be 'confusion and the worst kind of consequences'. Here, one might say, are clear signs of a politician finding an excuse, on reflection, to stay. One could well be right. Pitt's initial remarks about wanting to resign should probably not be dismissed too lightly. His temperament must be remembered, and the picture that he held of himself. This was just the personal kind of issue on which he would have liked to take a Roman stand.[3] But equally he was fond of power, and it is not surprising if he was affected by that sense of indispensability which few Prime Ministers avoid. Probably all these elements were present; but the choice was not seriously in doubt. There were reasons enough to be found for staying, and he was soon giving them full weight.

Should one, however, go farther? Was the King's name itself an excuse? Pitt was not on the best of terms with George III at the time. The

1. Conversation of? 12–14 April with Ewart (Ewart Mss; see Holland Rose, op. cit., 617).

2. To Ewart, 24 May 1791 (Tomline, III, 262). The draft is in P.R.O. 30/8/102. It may be noted that there is no mention of the state of France as an argument.

In his extensive notes on the whole subject (see p. 28, n4 above) which were probably made later, Pitt used the further argument '? danger of the War if entered upon being stopped. Change of Government.'

3. And see also the account of his remarks to Burges on 19 April as given in Rosebery, *Pitt* (1891), 110–11.

King was unenthusiastic about the Canada bill, which was passing through Parliament during these months, and he was opposed to the abolition of the slave trade, which Wilberforce was bringing up again with Pitt's support.[1] More to the point, he disliked Catherine II, and can hardly have relished this reverse, including as it did the loss of his Foreign Secretary. He had sometimes been treated without much consideration over appointments and honours, always matters of delicacy; and the Regency crisis itself had indeed left sore feelings – however unreasonably – when George III read of the Ministry's decisions as to his medical treatment and saw that he had been regarded effectually as a lunatic under the Regency bill.[2] He was also unlikely to have been happy about Pitt's relations with his Chancellor Thurlow, which, seldom cordial, were suffering currently from a dispute over the course of Hastings's long trial.[3] For Thurlow was still a force, 'the Keeper of the King's Conscience' in the Cabinet and, despite his behaviour in the Regency crisis, still personally acceptable to George III. Such facts were not to be dismissed, and Opposition drew comfort from them. Their leaders indeed were persuaded that the Minister was now 'tottering in the Closet', and Fox even thought that there was 'no objection on the part of the K. to take F. into his service'.[4]

This last may well have been wishful thinking, the likely response of any Opposition encouraged by a sudden turn of events.[5] There was no sign that George III had forgotten the events of 1783, and the fact that Fox was now moving, uneasily but publicly, towards a firm commitment to the French Revolution can scarcely have endeared him to a monarch who was congratulating Burke on the *Reflections*.[6] Nor was the King likely to have wished to call on the more conservative Whigs, for there was no reason to suppose that they would come in without Fox. Any such transaction might upset him after his illness two years before. If Pitt meant by 'the worst kind of consequences' his replacement by Opposition, he was therefore probably sincere in thinking that he would be 'abandoning the King'.

1. See I, 367–9, 398–9.

2. For the latter see John Brooke, *King George III* (1972), 342–3; for the former, eg I, 642, which was soon followed by other controversies, affecting Buckingham and Dundas.

3. For Thurlow's attitude to the trial in January 1791, see *The Correspondence of Edmund Burke*, VI, ed. Alfred Cobban and Robert A. Smith (1967), 197–9; for his relations with Pitt in recent years, I, 368, 398, 628, 655.

4. Duke of Portland to Earl Fitzwilliam, 21 April 1791 (quoted in L.G. Mitchell, *Charles James Fox and the Disintegration of the Whig Party 1782–1794* (1971), 161–2).

5. Though a confidential note from William Grenville to his brother Thomas (the latter in Opposition) mentioning Fox's name, together with those of Lord John Cavendish and Portland, as possibilities for office in a reshuffled Cabinet, may help show why their hopes were raised (nd, but endorsed 1791; Grenville Correspondence, Ms D/56/1/1, Buckinghamshire C.R.O.).

6. As he first did in February 1791 (*Correspondence of Edmund Burke*, VI, 219).

It might be held, however, that he had a different possibility in mind: the formation of a less hostile Ministry which might have included some of his own colleagues.[1] Such an outcome in point of fact need not have been inconceivable; for it did not really follow that if Pitt went the rest of the Cabinet must do the same. Collective resignation on a matter of policy would have been highly unusual, and several Ministers, despite their final Minute,[2] had felt growing doubts in this case. What was there to stop George III from calling on one of them to take over, or on a fresh figure, with whom some might serve, who was not connected with Fox? Was there not indeed a possibility, if Pitt suggested resigning, of the King abandoning him rather than of his abandoning the King? Of course Pitt dominated his colleagues, his disappearance would greatly have weakened them, and it would have been a major political event. But the political world is adaptable, things as strange had happened before – and would happen later – and however great the disturbance there was no real need to turn to Fox at once. Opposition's strength by all the evidence was confined to this one point. The politicians might well have rallied to prevent the risk of another royal malady. And Pitt himself, for the same reason, would probably have had to bless the arrangement. There might have been an alternative to him; and there was one colleague who would gladly have sought it. A Ministry on such a basis would have been grist to Thurlow's mill.

Pitt would certainly have disliked such an outcome, and he must have been alive to the King's reservations. All the same, it seems doubtful if this was what he feared. Unless he was indulging in his well-known sarcasm he could scarcely have expected it to produce 'the worst kind of consequences', whatever the immediate 'confusion' or risk to 'the existence of our system both at home and abroad'.[3] The system presumably would have endured, while Opposition remained in opposition. But as far as one can see, the alternative did not seriously cross his mind. He appears genuinely to have assumed that if he went the Government would fall. He never talked in any other sense, and while one could argue that this was disingenuous, designed in fact to force the issue, the remarks seem to ring true. Indeed they show all the signs of a natural, unpremeditated approach; when Pitt spoke of 'our duty', and trusted 'we should all have been ready', he was really seeing the issue in personal terms throughout.[4] He was sure that he *was* the Ministry, and

1. There was a further choice, which Grenville at least had considered or heard of. In a paper of 28 March there is the suggestion of a Cabinet in which Opposition would be included, Fox being possibly one Secretary of State and Pitt himself the other (see E.A. Smith, *Whig Principles and party politics . . .* (1975), 124, 141). The idea does not seem to have gone any farther.

2. P. 18 above.

3. P. 31 above. For his sarcasm see I, 611.

4. Loc. cit. And this is further supported by the conversation with Ewart on ? 12–14 April (p. 25 above). See also his notes in P.R.O. 30/8/195.

he judged the consequence in that light. The decision to stay was doubtless fortified by a liking for power: it may be held also to have reflected the strength of George III in his weakness, and Pitt's instinctive attitude towards his colleagues and himself.

IV

This lofty conception of his role and his conduct – of the part he was born to play – is again suggested by a singular incident which took place while the affair was dying down. It excited some interest at the time; but it was not cleared up, for the facts remained hidden while Pitt was alive, and indeed for long after his death.

Opposition were naturally eager to keep the Ministry on the hook, and they pegged away at the Russian question until the summer recess.[1] The subject had staled by the winter, but they made a final effort soon after the new session began in January 1792. The first attack came on 20 February, the second was launched on the 29th, and on the 24th Burges of the Foreign Office was 'closetted' with Pitt about it. He expected a dramatic climax, for there was information to be revealed, and 'if I mistake not, . . . the fate of the Opposite Parties . . . will finally be settled, and Mr. Fox and his Adherents for ever ruined and undone'.[2] But the revelation was not forthcoming, Pitt in the end kept silent, and Burges never forgave him for missing what he thought could have been his greatest coup.

The secret at which Burges was hinting lay in his and Pitt's own papers. It concerned a mission by Fox's supporter, Robert Adair, to St Petersburg in the summer of 1791. Fox indeed seemed to many at this time to be acting like an alternative Foreign Secretary: he wrote to a member of the French Constituent Assembly suggesting the despatch of an Opposition observer, and Adair was widely assumed to be his 'Envoy . . . to the Empress'.[3] Such behaviour aroused the Ministry's wrath, and equally its surprise. 'Is not the idea', wrote Grenville, 'of Ministers from Opposition to the different Courts of Europe a new one in this Country? I never heard of it before, & should think that if it could be proved, I mean legally proved, it would go very near an impeachable misdemeanour.'[4] Soon afterwards he and Pitt had cause to suspect that in one case it did.

---

1. In May and June in both the Commons and the Lords (*P.R.*, XXIX, 516–55, 597–617; XXX (1791), 158–73, 305–16).

2. To Anne Burges, 24 February 1792, referring to meetings held that morning (Burges Ms 47, Bodleian Library). He referred to a debate 'on Monday', which was the 27th; in the event it started on the 29th.

3. Grenville to Auckland, Private, 1 August 1791 (B.L. Add. Ms 34439). The intention of the letter to Paris was in fact probably less heinous than was supposed; for the background see L.G. Mitchell, *Fox and the Disintegration of the Whig Party*, 174–5.

4. To Auckland, Private, 29 July 1791 (B.L. Add. Ms 34438).

The notion of the Russian journey seems to have come from Adair himself. It arose in part from a plan to do some stockjobbing on the prospects of peace or war. The Funds were still depressed when he left in May, there was money to be made from timely information, and Adair had made his arrangements with his bankers in advance.[1] He told Fox of his intention, and Fox did not gainsay him. 'Well: if you are determined to go', he is supposed to have said, 'send us all the news', and he gave Adair a 'cypher' (actually a code) used by Burgoyne in the American War.[2] Armed with this and, by what followed, detailed guidance and instructions, the young man (he was twenty-eight) set off for Vienna, where he stayed a few days. He then went on to St Petersburg, which he reached in mid-June, soon after Fawkener arrived. He carried introductions from Vorontsov, and one from the Duchess of Devonshire to the British Minister, Sir Charles Whitworth, which induced the latter to present him reluctantly at Court. Adair indeed went further, calling frequently on the Legation, and making use of its facilities to send some of his letters home. These seem all to have been written in the last ten days of July (he had fallen ill meanwhile): two or possibly three to Fox, two to the Opposition MP Samuel Whitbread – some under cover to forwarding addresses, of whom one, Stephen Rolleston, was a Clerk in the Foreign Office – and the rest to his bankers and the main intermediary, his mistress. They were well informed, and they contained interesting news.[3]

Exactly how interesting in every instance it is impossible, alas, to say, for the coded passages seem not to have been broken at the time, and they have not been broken since.[4] But quite enough remains in the lengthy passages *en clair* (much the largest part of the correspondence) to justify the authorities' concern. For these show that the Russians

1. They were Ransome, Moreland & Hammersley, of Pall Mall.

2. *Memorials and Correspondence of Charles James Fox*, ed. Lord John Russell, II (1853), 384.

3. Copies are to be found in P.R.O. 30/8/337 and in Burges Mss 62, 95. Neither set is complete, and they complement each other.

4. The difficulty lies in identifying the book to which the code, known to be a book code, was applied, and in the comparatively small amount of coded material in the letters. For although the book was one of those used by Fox and General Burgoyne in their correspondence during the American War (see above), no clue has emerged as to its title; and the works known to have been used at that time by Burgoyne himself (see Howard Peckham, 'British Secret Writing in the Revolution'; *The Michigan Alumnus Quarterly Review*, 43, no. 11) do not appear to fit this material, since the former are dictionaries in more than one volume, with more than one column to the page, while the latter suggests a single volume of about 300 pages, arranged in continuous lines. It is perhaps more likely that a well-known work would have been chosen, in a handy edition; for Adair might not have wished to load his baggage with a bulky and thus potentially suspicious volume, particularly if by rights it should have formed part of a multi-volumed set. Inquiry in London and Cheltenham, however, has failed to produce an answer on such lines.

I am grateful to Professor William Willcox and Mr Handasyde Buchanan in particular for help on this conundrum.

informed Adair of the main exchanges with the British representatives, and quote verbatim from the papers on both sides. They reveal in detail his advice to the Russians on Fawkener's proposals for navigation down the Dniester. They contain what Adair supposed to be the valuable news that, if the Turks refused the final terms, the Allies at the end of four months would 'abandon them to the events of war'.[1] And they discuss the effects of those terms on the Austrian claims, as yet unsettled. On this last question, Adair reported that he had talked to the Austrian Ambassador, to whom he bore a letter from Vorontsov; and 'You [Fox] may guess of course the Conversations which have passed'. They appear to have turned on the chances of Austria retaining Belgrade, an object which the Triple Alliance had consistently opposed; and the Ambassador had made '*very particular mention* of them, in his Dispatches to Vienna'.

Adair sent his last batch of letters by the hand of the Secretary of the Legation, William Lindsay, who was returning to London. Despite some momentary qualms, he could not resist the chance of a speedy conveyance, and had decided it was safe. He proved to be wrong. Lindsay, like Whitworth and Fawkener, had been unhappy about Adair from the start, although none of them at first could credit the rumours that he had come to hamper the negotiation – 'a transaction' which 'appeared to them so extraordinary and so infamous that they could not readily believe Englishmen capable of so far forgetting their duty to themselves, and to their Country'[2] By the time that Lindsay left, however, they had changed their minds. For the Secretary had opened Adair's first letter to Fox, and shown it to his superiors, and he felt no hesitation in accepting the latest packet and handing it to Burges on arrival. The Foreign Office in any case was already on the alert; it was watching the mails through the European capitals, and intercepted most (if not all) of Adair's other letters. By the end of August it had an interesting file. But it failed to find the code book, despite the efforts of the Post Office decipherers and those of the Customs officers when Adair came home.[3]

The evidence was very damaging. Adair's reports (due no doubt to inexperience) were not in point of fact always correct. Fawkener did rather better than he represented, and he misunderstood some of the finer points. But the limitations of the agent did not affect the purpose.

---

1. This passage, underlined by Adair, was included in a transcript of one of Fawkener's and Whitworth's papers to the Russians.

2. Lindsay, 'Some particulars concerning Mr. Adair's Mission to St. Petersburg' (P.R.O. 30/8/337). The paper was written on his return, at Burges's request.

3. 'The Examining Officer . . . might, *without seeming to do so*, bestow the necessary attention on this point, in tumbling over that Gentleman's baggage' (Burges to Mr Cox [Chief Customs Officer at Harwich], 20 August 1791; copy in Burges Ms 47). For similar efforts in Paris, see John Ehrman, 'Pitt the Younger and the Ochakov Affair', *History Today*, IX, no. 7.

Adair could be proved to have connived with the Russians in opposing his own Government's efforts, and to have sent news of his activities to prominent members of Opposition. His conduct was not in fact so very far removed from the 'impeachable misdemeanour' of which Grenville had written; and if it was made public, how would Fox appear? Whether or not he had written to Adair – and there is no surviving proof that he had[1] – he was deeply implicated by the correspondence, by its contents and its tone;[2] and the revelation must have dealt a heavy blow to so controversial a character. It is hardly surprising that Burges was sure that 'Mr. Fox and his Adherents' would be 'for ever ruined and undone'. When Pitt did not use the material, the Under Secretary was aghast.

Why in fact did Pitt decide at the last moment to keep quiet? The answer must be considered in the light of two later events. The momentary speculation about Adair's mission, such as it was, soon died away; it had done so very largely, indeed, before the final debates. No one thought any more about it until in February 1797 a letter from Burke to the Duke of Portland, written in September 1793, was published as a pamphlet. It contained a passage about Ochakov, in which Burke accused Adair of having aided the Russians and kept in touch with Fox; and while Fox's own behaviour did not perhaps amount to 'absolute high treason' – since Russia had not been at war with England – it was 'in law, . . . undoubtedly a most unconstitutional act, and a high treasonable misdemeanour'.[3]

The charge had no public effect. Burke's wilder moods by then were seldom taken seriously, and this, it seems to have been thought, might be one of their products. The pamphlet moreover was first published without the author's sanction, from a copy in the possession of a clerk, and Burke's friends at once successfully brought an injunction to stop it. Adair accordingly did not feel obliged to do more than issue a denial, and the matter was again laid to rest. But there was one significant consequence. For when the pamphlet appeared, Grenville, who was still Foreign Secretary, decided to refresh his memory. He asked Burges's successor, George Hammond, to look out the correspondence in the Foreign Office; but Hammond could not find it, he applied to Burges, and Burges wrote to Grenville to explain.

---

1. According to Burges on 7 July, 'I know he [Adair] has received Letters from Mr. Fox since his arrival' at St Petersburg (to Ewart; copy in Burges Ms 84). But I have found no evidence of them.

2. As Adair himself stated many years later, he 'expressed much exultation' to Fox at the end of the negotiation (*Two letters from Mr. Adair to the Bishop of Winchester. In Answer to the Charge of a High Treasonable Misdemeanour . . .* (1821), 9). It had not been confined to that moment.

3. *A Letter from the Rt. Honourable Edmund Burke to His Grace the Duke of Portland. On the Conduct of the Minority in Parliament . . .* (1797), 7.

Mr Hammond has this morning communicated to me your Lordship's desire, that I would give you such information as is in my power respecting the business of Mr Adair. It was not from want of respect to Mr Hammond that I avoided to acquaint him with what I know . . .; but, as I held myself to be bound by a promise to Mr Pitt, as well as by the nature of the business itself, not to mention anything relating to it to any one except himself and your Lordship, I thought it on every account better to adopt this mode of communicating what I knew of it.

Your Lordship is already well apprized of the circumstances which led to this discovery. [Burges then repeats the details] . . . As soon as [Adair's letters] arrived here, they were, in the customary way, sent to the Post Office, where copies of them were taken. These copies continued for some time in the Office. After the meeting of Parliament [in 1792], Mr Pitt desired me to give them to him. I accordingly did so, and he locked them up in one of his own boxes; since which time I have not seen them.

He was, however, able to enclose Lindsay's account of the affair, which, being his own document, he had kept.[1]

Nothing more happened after this for twenty-four years. And then in 1821 Bishop Pretyman Tomline published the first instalment of his Life of Pitt.[2] He repeated Burke's accusations, and added for good measure that he found their accuracy 'attested by authentic documents among Mr. Pitt's papers'.[3] Such a statement from such a source could hardly be ignored, and Adair wrote to the Bishop demanding its withdrawal. He was by then a respected veteran diplomat, a few years later to be a Privy Councillor, and he may have thought with the passage of time that the evidence was slight. Challenging Tomline to produce the letters, he asked why, if the statement was true, the Government of the day had not done more about it. Pitt had hinted briefly in the debates at the possibility of a future inquiry; but Fox had declared himself ready to meet it, and nothing more was heard.

Tomline would not withdraw. He acknowledged that it might be difficult to prove the charges so long after the event; 'and yet

---

1. 18 February 1797 (P.R.O. 30/8/337), and see p. 36, n2 above. Grenville showed this letter and its enclosures to Hammond, and asked him to continue looking for the papers, although 'the hope of recovering [them] . . . is not very great' (loc. cit; no address and unsigned, but in Grenville's hand, and endorsed later, in Tomline's hand, as referring to Lindsay's account).

Pitt could not know that Burges had in fact retained his own copies of part of Adair's correspondence (p. 35, n3 above) – a matter on which the former Under Secretary seems to have kept quiet for the rest of his life.

2. See I, xi.

3. Tomline, II, 445.

circumstances might leave no doubt' of their truth, and Fox had never openly denied the rumours. Ignoring Adair's challenge to produce the evidence, he stated that he was not going to alter the passage, and Adair thereupon published the correspondence, taking a stronger line than before. If Fox had not replied to the rumours 'it was Mr. Pitt himself who made it impossible'. For he had said nothing specific, and in fact his 'threatened investigation seemed to be the signal for dropping the subject everywhere' until Burke had revived it.[1] This reply was generally accepted, and Adair was thought to have had much the best of the exchange. He himself certainly believed so, and his last reference to the subject reflects his satisfaction with the result. Indeed, he then felt himself free to join with his detractors in condemning the conduct of which he had been accused. 'I subscribe', he wrote in 1824, '. . . to everything he [Burke] says of its indecorum, of its criminality, and of its danger. Such a conduct would be faction in its very essence, which *party*, in the true Whig sense of the word, holds in utter abhorrence'.[2] Such was Sir Robert Adair's final verdict on the episode of his youth.

Against this background we may try to assess Pitt's motives. One may dismiss the possibility that he found the evidence inconclusive. He certainly seems to have accepted it before the debate, and his later action in locking it away does not suggest that he changed his mind. Nor does he seem seriously to have doubted that Fox was involved, whether or not he could be proved to have written to Adair. There is indeed a piece of interesting evidence as to Pitt's view on this point. In March 1792 Gillray produced a caricature based on the news, which received great publicity, that the Empress Catherine had placed a bust of Fox in her cabinet between those of Demosthenes and Cicero. Beneath the picture were some verses, which included these lines:

> Who now, in this presumptuous hour,
> Aspires to share the Athenian's praise?
> The advocate of foreign power,
> The Aeschines of later days.

They were reprinted in 1798 in Canning's paper *The Anti-Jacobin*, and James Boswell the younger wrote in the margin of his copy, early in the

1. *Two letters from Mr. Adair to the Bishop of Winchester.* . . , 49, 53–4.
2. To John Allen (*Memorials and Correspondence of Fox*, II, 386). Lord Stanhope investigated the matter in his turn for his biography of Pitt, published in the 1860s, and dismissed it after searching in vain for Tomline's evidence. But Tomline's biographer in *D.N.B.* found the copies of the letters, and upheld the passage, and Holland Rose briefly did the same, though without much interest, in 1911 (*William Pitt and National Revival*, 622).

next century, that Pitt's nephew had then told him that the verses were by Pitt himself.[1]

It is likely, therefore, that Pitt believed that the charges would stick. Various reasons can be put forward for his keeping quiet. It might first be argued, from what was to follow, that he acted as he did because there was a prospect of a junction with some of his opponents, brought about by symptoms of possible domestic unrest. It is true that soundings took place in the course of 1792, and that Pitt then said that he had no personal objection to Fox. But there was no serious thought of an arrangement before May, Fox's name did not figure until June, and, on the lowest view, Pitt's supremacy within any form of coalition might have been secured more easily if Fox had earlier been discredited rather than preserved, albeit hypothetically, for office.

There is a second argument, however, which may carry greater weight. Pitt may well have wanted to let the whole Ochakov affair be forgotten. He had emerged from it shaken but not unseated; the excitement had largely died down; and he was certainly not anxious to revive it, as his disclosure would be bound to do. If there was political advantage to be gained there was also some to be lost by concentrating attention on this episode of the past.

This was doubtless true. But it fails to account in itself for Pitt's action later and for Tomline's behaviour. Political advantage, in Burges's terms, *could* have been served in 1797 by letting it be known that Burke was not talking nonsense. It was a time of real anxiety and distress, Fox was widely held to be a dangerous man, and the state of the war could be represented as justifying his suppression. Instead Pitt kept the papers as closely as before;[2] and Tomline's stubborn silence long afterwards, preserved at some cost to his reputation, can best be explained on the premises that he was respecting his old master's views. Taking the story in its entirety, it is hard to resist the conclusion that Pitt was not prepared to discredit Fox in this way.

Again there may be more than one reason. Two earlier episodes should be borne in mind: the Westminster scrutiny of 1785, and Mortlock's case in 1786. In the first Pitt had learned the dangers of

1. *Poetry of the Anti-Jacobin*, ed. C. Edmonds (1890), xxxi. The whole verse, of five stanzas, is indeed suggestive.

The 'nephew' may have been one of Pitt's step-nephews, the young Stanhopes, for in fact he had no nephew. But he treated the children of his former brother-in-law Stanhope's second marriage as his own family, and one of them would therefore seem to have been a likely source.

Aeschines, the lifelong rival of Demosthenes, escaped impeachment in Athens for his part in negotiations with Philip of Macedon. Sent earlier to aid resistance to Philip in the Peloponnese, he (with his fellow emissary) had abandoned the policy and advocated peace.

2. And the fact that Grenville's note, with Burges's letter to him, are preserved in Pitt's files (p. 38, n2 above) suggests that the Foreign Secretary was asked to hand them over, to be kept with the rest.

appearing personally vindictive; when he persisted in trying to keep Fox out of Parliament he was surprised by the result. And the lesson had borne fruit a year later, when he was moving against Mortlock and a deputation told him that 'his supporters . . . took it ill his taking such a part against an individual'.[1] The same charge might be made again, and perhaps he recoiled from the prospect, after his earlier inclination to go ahead. It could have been politically damaging; it may also, on reflection, have offended his sense of what was due to himself. It may furthermore, by a natural extension, have offended his sense of what was due to Fox: this was not the way in which to strike at a great opponent. Adair had in fact hit on the answer, though not in the sense he claimed, when he noted that 'it was Mr. Pitt himself who made it impossible' for Fox to answer the rumours. And the outcome was an example, though far from ordinary in its application, of that blend of rectitude and political good sense which had become associated with Pitt's name.

In the autumn of 1788 Fox visited Gibbon in his retreat at Lausanne. 'We had few politicks', the historian recorded, but 'he gave me in a few words such a character of Pitt as one great man should give of another his rival'.[2] The magnanimity is familiar. It was not suspected during their lifetimes that, less than four years later, Pitt had been generous to Fox.

---

1. See I, 220–3, 232–3. In an earlier discussion of the matter (*History Today*, IX, no. 7) I did not specify these two occasions, which I had not then examined closely and now seem to me to have been significant.
2. *The Letters of Edward Gibbon*, ed. J.E. Norton, III (1956), 132.

CHAPTER II

France on the Horizon

I

In August 1791, a few weeks after the Ochakov question was settled, Auckland declared that 'All political speculation will now turn to France'.[1] Looking out from his window at The Hague across the frontiers of Europe, it was a fairly obvious forecast to make. The summer of 1791 saw the first indications, however cautious and confused, that the continental monarchies might intervene in French affairs; and the indications seemed to many to be more prominent than the caution. The process, begun without undue zeal by Marie Antoinette's brother the Emperor of Austria, had been gathering way since the failure of the flight to Varennes in June. Shortly before that event he was thought to have agreed to a defensive alliance with Prussia. He then issued his Padua Circular calling for combined action; hastened the completion of a general peace with Turkey at the Congress of Sistovo;[2] and, even as Auckland wrote, was conferring in person with the King of Prussia. On 27 August the two monarchs issued the Declaration of Pillnitz, announcing that the fate of Louis XVI was a matter of concern to all European sovereigns, and the émigré French princes, indulging in their usual unhelpful zeal, called on their unfortunate head to reject a new French Constitution. Speculation was certainly turning to France, and affecting the relations between the continental Powers. But, relieved of its recent embarrassments, the British Government kept clear. 'The conclusion of the Sistovo business,' wrote Grenville from the Foreign Office, 'has removed every difficulty which there was in the way of our speaking out, and avowing our determination of the most scrupulous neutrality in the French business.'[3]

The determination was not new, however muted the speaking out had been. Ever since the summer of 1789 the Ministry had scrupulously stood aside. No one had been more careful to follow this line than Pitt. He learned caution in 1787, when the Dutch crisis killed his hopes of an improvement with France,[4] and as the troubles grew across the Channel

1. To Morton Eden, 12 August 1791 (quoted in *The Cambridge History of British Foreign Policy*, I (1922), 208).
2. See p. 28 above.
3. To Auckland, 23 August 1791 (*H.M.C., Dropmore*, II, 171).
4. For which see I, 313, 441–2, 486–94.

he remained watchful but aloof. The advent of the much heralded Necker in 1788 left him notably unmoved, and when Grenville – not yet in the Cabinet – suggested a personal letter of welcome, he appears deliberately to have ignored the advice.[1] He was going to behave correctly, but not going to be involved, and this determination was reflected on the eve of the first great Revolutionary crisis. The results are of some interest, not only as indicating his approach, but also because they helped foster a legend which was soon to cling to his name.

The year of 'the Death-Birth of a World'[2] was ushered in appropriately by wet weather; for the most familiar cause of trouble throughout the old Europe was dearth or a rise in the price of bread. The corn harvest of 1788 had been widely affected by drought; its successor seemed to be in greater danger from rain. There was no great margin of European (including British) grain crops in the eighties as a whole: human and animal populations were rising, distribution and prices were vulnerable, and shortages made up increasingly from the American continent. Despite a reasonable harvest in some of the French provinces there was widespread hardship in the winter and spring, and by the summer of 1789 'la Grande Peur' was deepening throughout the country. In Paris above all the situation was becoming explosive: the hated contractors fixed their prices, official efforts were failing to halt them, and in May and June the food riots grew. On 25 June the French Government sought the British Government's help, and Necker enclosed in the Ambassador's instructions a personal letter for Pitt. The Ambassador accordingly requested an interview, Pitt consulted some of the corn merchants, and he then forwarded the case to the Committee of Trade, which met in two sessions attended by himself.[3]

The French wanted consignments of flour, and this meant lifting the British corn laws; for as they stood, export of wheat or flour was forbidden when the price of wheat reached 44 shillings a quarter.[4] It had been higher than that early in the year, and was a good deal higher now – between 48 and 56 shillings in London at the beginning of July. Such a

---

1. Pitt to Grenville, 29 August 1788 (*H.M.C.*, *Dropmore*, I, 353), alluding almost certainly to a despatch of 26 August from Paris (see *Despatches from Paris 1784–1790*, II, ed. Oscar Browning (1910), 93–5); Grenville to Pitt, 1 September 1788 (P.R.O. 30/8/140); Pitt to Grenville, 5 and 10 September 1788 (*H.M.C.*, *Dropmore*, II, 354–5). Pitt in fact, like many in official positions, was soon disenchanted with Necker – in contrast to Necker's continued respect for the son-in-law that might have been (see I, 112).

2. To quote, inevitably, Carlyle.

3. Marquis de la Luzerne to Pitt, 28 June 1789, enclosing Necker to Pitt, 25 June 1789 (P.R.O. 30/8/143); P.R.O., B.T. 5/5, for meetings of 2 and 3 July; p. 92 below. Necker's letter is printed in Tomline, III, 83n. The members of the Committee present on the two days were Hawkesbury, the Earl of Effingham, and Pitt. Pitt's attendances, which had been irregular in recent months, were frequent throughout July.

4. 13 Geo. III, c. 43; 14 Geo. III, c. 64; 21 Geo. III, c. 50, the last applying to London, Essex and Kent alone.

level had not in practice stopped cargoes from finding their way abroad, under cover of the usual frauds and devices to square the regulations. But the demand was now for legal export, if necessary with Parliamentary sanction, and it was the feasibility and scale of this that Pitt and his colleagues had accordingly to weigh.

They did so against an uncertain and somewhat unpromising background. In contrast to earlier decades, England had become a net importer of wheat over the past twenty years, and the export restrictions moreover were proving notoriously unsuccessful.[1] In the past twelve months there had been heavy shipments to Europe, as well as to British garrisons overseas, and after the patchy harvest of 1788 stocks of wheat in London were low.[2] Reserves of flour however were adequate, and the price was not unduly high, thanks perhaps to recent technical improvements in milling. And since it was flour for which Necker had asked, the Committee concentrated on the question whether an export of 10,000 sacks might be allowed – roughly a week's consumption for the capital. The evidence varied: one merchant, Robert Wilson,[3] thought that it might, but others were more pessimistic, and all were agreed that unless the shipments went 'unobserved' the price would rise at once. The real obstacle however would be the effect on wheat prices, and the consequent danger of a general panic. Much of course turned on the prospects for the harvest, on which no one cared to pronounce. There were regional variations; all might yet be well if the weather improved; but transatlantic supplies were doubtful, owing to competing European demands and, it was alleged, a shortage of United States shipping,[4] and with stocks already low at home there was a real risk of shortage.

Governments were always sensitive to that ominous word, leading all too easily to 'Distress and sometimes popular Commotions'.[5] The Committee's fears were further heightened on learning that there were rumours of a much larger export, and that prices were already rising again in London and the south-east. Fresh warnings followed in the next few days, from merchants and MPs. But by then in fact Pitt had made up

1. So much so, in fact, that a further law was passed in July 1789 (29 Geo. III, c. 58). But that too was inadequate, and the whole position had to be reviewed in 1791.

2. P.R.O., B.T. 5/5. But according to official figures produced later, 'foreign exports' of wheat (i.e., other than smuggled shipments) were substantially lower than in the three preceding years (B.R. Mitchell and Phyllis Deane, *Abstract of British Historical Statistics* (1962), ch. III, table 9). This of course would not include garrisons overseas, some of which were supposed to have received large amounts after a failure of the Canadian harvest in 1788.

3. For whom see p. 45 below.

4. The latter aggravated, so one witness told Pitt and Hawkesbury, by 'the Measures of this Country' since the end of the American War (B.T. 5/5, 2 July). Shades of the Navigation Act of 1786, and the complementary Orders in Council (see I, 332–41).

5. Committee of Trade to Pitt, report of 8 March 1790 (B.T. 6/182).

his mind. On 3 July he wrote to the French Ambassador.[1]

> Mr Pitt . . . has felt the strongest desire to be able to recommend sending the supply of flour dèsir'd by Monsr Necker, and had hopes from the information at first given him by Mr Wilson that it would be practicable; but, having afterwards received some contrary information, he thought it necessary that the subject should be examined by the Council for the Affairs of Trade . . . Mr Pitt has now the mortification to find that, according to the accounts of the persons most conversant with the corn trade, the present supply in this country compar'd with the demand, and the precarious prospect of the harvest render it impossible to propose to Parliament to authorize any exportation.

He reported accordingly to the Commons, in answer to a question, on the 6th.[2]

The decision was perfectly explicable, given the weight of advice. Pitt would have been told that charity began at home, and he was in no position to disagree. The harvest indeed turned out to be as poor as had been feared in some areas; some local rioting and trouble ensued, and this might have been worse if prices had risen earlier, sparked off by permission to export. He had taken the case sympathetically – the conservative Hawkesbury was clearly alarmed – and he was not just seeking excuses, as the French very naturally felt.[3] Nor need one endorse the historical verdict that 'the gift of 20,000 sacks of flour outright would have been the best bargain of Pitt's career'.[4] The sacks in fact would have been sold, not given; and while his recent popularity in France[5] certainly suffered, there was no real reason to suppose that a different response would have transformed Anglo-French relations for long. The difficulties were genuine. One may note at the same time that this was not an occasion on which Pitt persisted against them. He accepted the

1. Holland Rose, *William Pitt and National Revival*, 543. According to Wilberforce, he had come to a decision on the 2nd (Robert Isaac Wilberforce and Samuel Wilberforce, *The Life of William Wilberforce*, I (1839), 227).

2. *P.R.*, XXVI (1789), 356–60. William Windham, who asked the question, noted that it attracted little attention from Members (*The Diary of the Right Hon. William Windham 1784 to 1810*, ed. Mrs Henry Baring (1866), 182).

3. There is perhaps a further sign of an initial desire to help the French. In mid-May, before Necker wrote, the British Ambassador in Paris was told to send details of the scarcity of grain, 'which is likely . . . to be very severely felt by the lower Classes of People' and was 'an Object of too serious a Nature not to attract His Majesty's particular Attention' (Leeds to Dorset, 15 May 1789; P.R.O., F.O. 27/32). Pitt's hand is surely evident in this.

4. Holland Rose, op. cit., 544.

5. See I, 666, and also Montmorin [Foreign Secretary] to Luzerne, 10 May 1789 (intercept in F.O. 95/2).

objections, and held out no hopes; and his reply to the French did not ease the effect. It was commendably prompt, strictly correct, addressed to the Ambassador, and left at that. As he had not made contact with Necker the year before, so he did not do so now, for Necker had written to him through the Embassy. Perhaps a direct answer in friendly terms would have softened the blow;[1] certainly there was no sign of straying from the official channel, or enlarging on the matter in hand. It was a stance which the Government was to favour amid the pitfalls that lay ahead. In this first instance it gave rise to suspicions in France which were soon to deepen and then take root.

II

The Ministry's policy over the next four years followed a simple pattern. It maintained a strict neutrality, which looked increasingly like a quarantine.

The element of quarantine took shape slowly: as a weapon of state it was muted at the start. For the two features of the Revolution that could pose a real threat to England – a challenge to British obligations in Europe, and an open appeal to sedition abroad – were absent in the early stages, and the first was implicitly renounced. In external affairs, as in other departments, reason was to be the guide: a modern, rational order at home would preclude old-fashioned adventures. All was benevolence and aspiration among the spokesmen of 1789, and they roused in various ways much foreign sympathy or satisfaction. It would probably be going too far to say that 'the French Revolution was approved at first by the common judgment of mankind'. In England at least the response 'varied between enthusiasm and indifference'.[2] Some fine spirits, particularly the young, were fired almost to madness by this wonderful union of the Age of Reason with the promise of romantic hope:

> When Reason seemed the most to assert her rights
> When most intent on making of herself
> A prime enchantress. . . .[3]

In wider circles there was lively pleasure, or measured commendation. 'Don't I remember,' one Victorian matron recalled of those early days, 'your glorious grandmother dancing round the Tree of Liberty at

1. As indeed Auckland told Pitt after talking to Necker himself (27 August 1789; P.R.O. 30/8/110).
2. Acton's *Lectures on the French Revolution*, opening to ch. IX; *The Debate on the French Revolution 1789–1800*, ed. Alfred Cobban (1950), 4.
3 Wordsworth, *The Prelude*, Book XI.

Norwich with Dr Parr!'; and the Vice-Chancellor of Cambridge in 1790 awarded his Latin prize to an essay endorsing the Revolution as 'likely to prove advantageous to this country'.[1] More widely still perhaps there was a feeling, not unkindly but rather dismissive, that, with good cause and reasonable motive, 'They had been playing the fool in France'.[2] But few could seriously condemn a programme which, so frequently and flatteringly, proclaimed a debt to the Glorious Revolution of a century before. When the first surprise died down there was a wave of, often vague, condescending goodwill. And set against this background, Ministers were content to see French pretensions reduced. 'The main point,' wrote Grenville in the late summer, 'appears quite secure, that they will not for many years be in a situation to molest the invaluable peace which we now enjoy'.[3]

Pitt himself said little – nothing publicly for several months – and when he first spoke, in February 1790, it was in a cool, uncommitted tone. He did so in a debate on the Army estimates, which he wished slightly to increase, at a time when the first news of Nootka Sound had just been received.[4] Much of his contribution therefore was made with that background in mind, and with reference to the level of overseas establishments. But turning to events in France, he struck a balance between hope and caution. He decried 'the unqualified nominal liberty of the French at present, which was, in fact, the most absolute, direct, and intolerable slavery'. But this referred to the present, not necessarily to the future, and viewing the prospects his initial reaction was not to despair.

> The present convulsions in France must, sooner or later, terminate in harmony and regular order; and notwithstanding that the fortunate arrangements of such a situation might make her more formidable, it might also render her less obnoxious as a neighbour . . . [For then] she would enjoy that just kind of liberty which he venerated . . ., nor could he . . . regard with envious eyes, an approximation in neighbouring States of those sentiments which were the characteristic feature of every British subject.

However,

easier, he would admit with the right honourable gentleman was it to

---

1. Janet Ross, *Three Generations of Englishwomen*, I (1888), 8 (for Dr Parr see I, 609 and p. 000 below); Samuel Romilly to Madame G -, 20 August 1790, *The Memoirs of Sir Samuel Romilly* . . ., I (1840), 404.
2. A reaction voiced, typically, by Addington; quoted in Philip Zeigler, *Addington* (1965), 65.
3. To the Marquess of Buckingham, 14 September 1789 (Buckingham, II, 165). Cf. p. 4 above.
4. See I, 554.

destroy than rebuild; and therefore, he trusted that this universally acknowledged position would convince gentlemen that they ought, on the present question, not to relax their exertions for the strength of the country . . .[1]

Unexceptionable sentiments, reflecting the climate of opinion. They had already been acted upon, and the confidence was not lessened in the next two years. From the start the Government was anxious to preserve normal relations with France. It was quick to rebut the charges, already spreading, of 'English gold' to foment the troubles. It allowed the British Ambassador to come home, at his request, when he was found to have written indiscreetly to one of the émigré princes. It told the Embassy to keep British subjects out of trouble as far as it could. It passed on a proposal from a Frenchman to burn men of war at Brest.[2] As the 'invaluable peace' became disturbed elsewhere, the attitude was preserved. When Pitt made use of private envoys in Paris at the height of the Nootka Sound crisis, they were able to say that England accepted the Revolution. At the same time, when they urged on London the advantages of an Anglo-French alliance, they were met with an uncompromising silence.[3] The policy was made more explicit after Ochakov, as Grenville forecast. The Ministry temporised over the Padua Circular of May 1791,[4] when peace in eastern Europe had still to be signed and Austria kept in play. But its views were common knowledge, they were not altered by the flight to Varennes – 'we are all anxious *spectators*,' wrote Pitt of that event – and a few months later the Government 'spoke out'.[5] When the British were invited to support the Declaration of Pillnitz, the authors were sent a firm reply. 'The King has determined not to take any part in supporting or opposing' action on behalf of Louis XVI.[6] This did not in fact cause much surprise, or for that matter much regret in Vienna, where there was still a strong

1. 9 February 1790 (*P.R.*, XXVII (1790), 79–80, 103). The right honourable gentleman was Fox, which gave Pitt a nice opening. He went on to ask his audience 'to improve, for our security, happiness, and aggrandisement, the precious moments of peace and leisure which were before us'. But this again must have referred to Spain's action at Nootka Sound.

2. See *Despatches from Paris 1784–1790*, II; P.R.O., F.O. 27/32, 33A; B.L. Add. Ms 28064, *passim*.

3. See I, 547–8, and Howard V. Evans, 'William Pitt, William Miles and the French Revolution' (*Bulletin of the Institute of Historical Research*, XLIII, no. 108, 196–8); W.A. Miles to Pitt, 30 December 1795 (*The Correspondence of William Augustus Miles on the French Revolution, 1789–1817*, ed. the Rev. Charles Popham Miles, II (1890), 281); Pitt to Hugh Elliott, – October 1790 (copy in P.R.O. 30/8/102).

4. P. 42 above.

5. Pitt to Hester, Countess of Chatham, 2 July 1791 (Stanhope, II, 126); p. 42 above.

6. Grenville to Keith [in Vienna], no. 9, 19 September 1791 (P.R.O., F.O. 7/28). And cf. Grenville to Ewart, no. 26, 26 August 1791 (F.O. 64/22), Grenville to Whitworth, no. 6, 27 September 1791 (F.O. 65/22). The same series contain earlier warnings.

reluctance to divert too much attention from central Europe. It may have been a greater blow to the émigré princes, who had been held at arm's length hitherto, and whose envoy was now given equally short shrift.[1] As Burke, who was in touch with him, found, 'there was no moving [Ministers] from their neutrality', and when the new French Constitution was announced in September 1791 they hastened to repeat their desire to 'maintain, and improve, the good understanding which so happily persists'.[2]

There was one limit, indirect but significant, to this scrupulous abstention.[3] In 1789 and 1790 England undertook a new commitment in the Low Countries. The revolt of the Austrian Netherlands – the Belgic provinces – in 'the year of revolution' had quickly elicited a firm British response. Their grievances had been supported in the name of the Triple Alliance, but hopes of independence had been discouraged, to the Prussians' disgust.[4] This was partly because the British Government did not want to offend Austria, and was trying to restrain its restless partner, who as usual was fishing in troubled waters. But even more important was the fear of French influence over what would be a new, divided state, in an area traditionally of British concern. The prevention of a union between the provinces and France, Pitt stated, was 'worth the risk, or even the certainty' of war; but while he was worried about 'the enthusiasm of the present spirit', the policy was not aimed at the Revolution as such. It was 'the rashness of [French] councils', which was far from new, and the familiar threat to the Channel, that evoked a familiar and predictable reaction.[5] He had his way in January 1790, when he gained acceptance of the principle that the Allies should be associated with the rights of what remained a semi-independent Austrian possession. Their role was reaffirmed by the Reichenbach Convention in July;[6] but the dispute was far from over, and in the winter a crisis arose. For the Austrian representative then refused to extend the period for local discussions, and in November the Allies were warned that their mediation no longer held good. Austrian troops moved towards Brussels; the British mediator, Auckland, protested fiercely; and

---

1. For the visit of the Chevalier de la Bintinnaye in September see *Correspondence of Edmund Burke*, VI, 385–446; for the Government's reply F.O. 90/17, ff. 102–3, and Grenville to George Aust [at the Foreign Office], 20 September 1791 (F.O. 27/37). Pitt's relations with the émigrés from 1789 to 1791 are followed best through his dealings with the princes' adviser, the former Minister Calonne, for which see Note on Sources to this chapter, p. 653 below).

2. *Correspondence of Burke*, VI, 409–15; Grenville to Lord Gower [Ambassador in Paris], no. 6, 5 October 1791 (F.O. 27/37).

3. For a possible but qualified second exception see I, 550n3.

4. I, 547–8.

5. Loc. cit.; *The Cambridge History of British Foreign Policy*, I, 189.

6. I, 551.

the Government, at first reluctantly, decided to back him up. The fleet was still partly mobilised after the end of the Nootka Sound crisis, and Pitt prepared to send it if the Austrians broke the agreement.[1] The Emperor's forces reached Brussels quickly, and the long-simmering revolt was quashed. But a Convention was signed in December restoring the provinces' ancient privileges, and the Triple Alliance was recognised as the guarantor. The threat of the fleet had been made against Austria. But it was a warning to the whole of Europe that the Belgic coast was a region of high importance to British security.

At the beginning of the winter of 1791 the official position was therefore clear. England would do nothing to intervene in France, or help others to do so. The attitude was not shaken by the growing confusion of the next few months: if anything, indeed, it was strengthened and confirmed. France had been a counter, easily played, in the Spanish crisis of 1790, and she had been entirely discounted in London in the Ochakov crisis of 1791.[2] She remained of curiously marginal interest now that the picture was changing, and she was herself becoming a focus of continental debate. As the scene darkened in the new year, as the Allied sovereigns and the French factions were alike propelled, in a mutual reaction, towards the attractions of a sudden attack, and despatches from the British Embassy spoke of anarchy and 'impending war',[3] the Government stood firmly on its declared policy, to an extent indeed that raised hopes in Paris itself. French suspicions of England were as lively as ever, and the official statements from London were viewed in a context of reported divergencies and doubts. Every rumour – and there were plenty – was seized on, magnified and distorted, as fears and expectations swept the Revolutionary Committees from day to day. But at least the official statements were there, to give some substance to the hopes, and in the mounting uncertainty it seemed worth while to test them out. A French mission was sent to London in January 1792, to discuss the possibility of a 'mutual guaranty'. The chief emissary was Talleyrand, and his watchful eye soon saw that Ministers really wanted to mean what they said. For while they would not negotiate officially – since the mission bore no official credentials – they were quite prepared to listen, and to repeat their desire not to 'foment or prolong the disturbances . . . with a view to any profit . . . to this country'. Talleyrand even thought that if hostilities started England might accept

1. For the evidence of Pitt's leading part in the decision see Holland Rose, op. cit., 534. There was some unhappiness at the start about Auckland's handling of the dispute, and the Foreign Secretary, seldom an admirer, remained convinced that it had been inept.

2. See p. 4, n3 above.

3. See *The Despatches of Earl Gower from June 1790 to August 1792* . . ., ed. Oscar Browning (1885), 137, 145, 154, 159.

Robert Adair, *by Gainsborough*

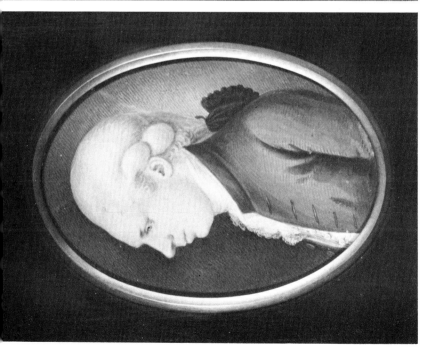

Joseph Ewart. *Unknown*

'Design for the new Gallery of Busts and Pictures', by Gillray, March 1792

a 'defensive' French deployment into a part of the Austrian Netherlands. He was certain at any rate, when he left in March, that she would
not join in a continental war.[1]

This indeed was now the general impression, in the most varied
quarters. The British Government, came a complaint from the exiled
princes' headquarters, 'aujourdhui plane tranquilement Sur la poli-
tique de l'Europe'. 'England,' wrote Auckland disgustedly on a visit
from The Hague, 'has little concern now in what is going forward on the
Continent'.[2] It was an attitude compounded of both mood and reasoned
argument, the latter drawing strength very largely from the former. For
Ochakov had done its work; the Government had drawn in its horns,
and the country followed events from a return to isolation. And Pitt
himself, reacting from his setback, was also reacting from his recent bout
of interest. He was indeed, as he was told, now 'gliding' over foreign
affairs,[3] and quite ready, with that facility which so often preserved his
balance, 'to expect' from a change of circumstance 'that doubtful
contingencies would have a . . . favourable issue'.[4] Given this temperament, better prospects could be argued for either side of the Rhine. To
the east, the danger had lessened: the Russo-Turkish War was over,
Prussia and Austria had survived their quarrels, the cause of our
involvement no longer obtained. Poland, it was true, was still of moral
concern; but we were not bound by treaty, and no one now expected us
to act. Those regions would not engage us further. And we need not be
too apprehensive about the west, for while it was hard to tell what would
happen, the result either way could be accepted so long as our interests
and obligations in the Low Countries were observed. The European
sovereigns – Austria and Prussia, encouraged by Russia and Sweden –
might still prove unwilling to declare war on France: there was some
reason to suppose so, from their continuing mutual distrust. But if they
did, they would soon win, for what could France do in her present state?
And if the French themselves attacked Austria (which alone would have
territories at risk) who again could expect a different result? A campaign
should settle the matter, and then the future might be more assured.
Alternatively, if nothing happened, France would painfully settle
herself; 'the present convulsions . . . must, sooner or later, terminate in
harmony and regular order'.[5] After all, this was not the first, though it
was much the greatest, of recent disturbances; there had been troubles in

1. Grenville to Gower, no. 6, 9 March 1792 (F.O. 27/38); Talleyrand to A. de V.
Delessart [Foreign Minister], 2 March 1792 (*Correspondance de Talleyrand: La Mission de
Talleyrand à Londres, en 1792* . . ., ed. G. Pallain (1889), 137–8).

2. Calonne (see p. 49, n1 above) to Pitt, 28 January 1792 (copy in P.R.O., P.C. 125,
no. 366); Auckland to Lord Henry Spencer, 20 March 1792 (*A.C.*, II, 397–8).

3. See above.

4. Wilberforce's 'Sketch of Mr. Pitt' (*Private Papers of William Wilberforce* . . ., ed. A.M.
Wilberforce (1897), 62).

5. P. 47 above.

the past decade in Hungary, Sweden, Holland and Liège, in Geneva, Poland and the Austrian Netherlands, and except perhaps in Poland none now threatened European peace. France would emerge chastened, probably exhausted, and almost certainly pacific: there, as elsewhere, tumult would be followed by suppression or consolidation. Western Europe could therefore be left to work out its future – provided, again, that our commitments to the Low Countries were recognised.

Such would seem to have been the background to Pitt's celebrated forecast early in 1792 – one of the most ill-fated predictions that a British Prime Minister has ever made. It was produced, ironically, at a moment of triumph, in the greatest of his budget speeches, reviewing the achievements of almost a decade of peace.[1] In contrast to the past two years he was proposing a net reduction of the armed forces, and the first widespread cut in taxes since he came to office. This was gratifying, at a time when the country could do with some reassurance. But Pitt's greatest pride was the further prospect of feeding his cherished Sinking Fund, to reduce uninterruptedly the volume of the National Debt. Seeking to illustrate the process, he took a period of fifteen years – probably in fact because this produced a round figure at the current rate. But he went on to justify it, and his Estimates, in a fatal passage.

I am not, indeed, presumptuous enough to suppose that when I name fifteen years, I am not naming a period in which events may arise, which human foresight cannot reach, and which may baffle all our conjectures. We must not count with certainty on a continuance of our present prosperity during such an interval; but unquestionably there never was a time in the history of this country, when, from the situation of Europe, we might more reasonably expect fifteen years of peace, than we may at the present moment.[2]

He spoke on 17 February. On 20 April the European war began.

---

1. See I, 273–5.

2. *P.H.*, XXIX (1817), 826. This is the best text, for reasons given in I, 274n1. The contemporary collections *P.R.* (XXXI, 1792) and *The Senator* (IV, nd but 1793) greatly curtail and generalise the passage; so for that matter does Tomline (II, 285), who publishes much of the rest of the speech in *oratio directa* and is a good source in this instance. But the wording appears in *The Speech of the Right Hon. William Pitt, Chancellor of the Exchequer, on Friday, the 17th day of February 1792* . . . which was printed for Robinson and Stockdale at the time; and since we know that Pitt, in a rare instance, passed that for publication, it may be taken as authentic. Several of the London newspapers, too, gave the gist of the passage more or less closely on 18 February, including the specific figure of fifteen years.

The King's Speech at the end of January had itself referred to the good prospects for peace (Pitt's draft or copy is in P.R.O. 30/8/234).

CHAPTER III

'Until the Day of Judgment'

I

In pursuing a quiet foreign policy Pitt knew that he had general support, in Parliament and, to all appearances, the country at large. Whatever their sympathies, few people early in 1792, and certainly very few Members – one is tempted to say no Member except Burke – were prepared to become involved in a war over France. There was less agreement on how to treat 'French ideas' in England; but the issue was still open, and moreover throughout this period it was one that embarrassed Opposition rather more than the Minister himself.

The relative strengths of the Parliamentary parties were still much what they had been some two years before, on the eve of the general election which was held in the summer of 1790. Indeed, in so far as one can judge from the evidence, they had not changed significantly since the general election of 1784. It would be rash to claim too much for any calculations – those that have been made raise queries reflecting the uncertainties hedging the problem. But Opposition may have made a modest gain between 1784 and 1790, mainly from by-elections; suffered a small loss at the general election; and recouped that loss over the next two years. By one estimate, it could be said to have increased its definable numbers in the Commons by a net ten to twelve in the course of some eight years.[1]

The qualifications to such figures are obvious. Contemporaries would not have agreed on a precise answer any more than historians can do.[2] The degrees of attachment, the sources of attachment, the extent of discipline in different cases – the degree of identity and its effect – may be assessed in various ways. The short period from the Regency crisis to the troubles of 1792 has its place in the history of party, for it was the link – the corridor, as it were – between diverging sets of conditions. Viewed from within Parliament, it showed certain signs of a further sharpening

1. The calculation is that of F. O'Gorman, *The Whig Party and the French Revolution*, Appendix I. But it must be stressed that this is open to some detailed objections.

2. Cf. op. cit. with two calculations of 1788, themselves differing from each other (I, 618), and with that of Donald Ginter, using division lists as a guide to 'voting potential', in *Whig Organization in the General Election of 1790* (1967), xiii. This last includes Members, not necessarily regarded as firm party men, who supported Opposition on particular issues.

of focus, under the impact of two political crises and the preparations for the election. The events of 1788–9, renewing the conflict of five years before, and the sudden upset of Ochakov in 1791, stiffened and enlarged the loyalties – almost desperate by this time – which were shared by the survivors of 1784. And drawing strength from the familiar issues, the Whig machinery was improved to cover more directly some of the outlying ground. Publications were subsidised, contacts with newspapers extended, Parliamentary candidates controlled more closely, a Whig Club – founded earlier – revivified.[1] The core perhaps hardened, the fringes seemed to be more definitely fringes of a core, at least when office beckoned or old constitutional cries were invoked. It is noticeable that in 1788–9 and again in 1791 Government newspapers referred disparagingly to 'The Party' – a fact suggesting both its existence and its limits.

The latter merit attention as well as the former. The renewal of battle had its effect on political attitudes at large, after the quieter period of the middle eighties. 'I am certainly a Partyman', Dundas confessed in the autumn of 1791, 'and more so now than I ever thought of being';[2] and his reaction had earlier counterparts beyond Westminster itself. In the fleet assembled for Nootka Sound in the summer of 1790 'Party runs very high and they are sadly disunited';[3] Gibbon, watching events from Switzerland, could not repress his indignation 'at the use of those foolish obsolete, odious, words Whig and Tory'; and on the eve of the general election an able pamphleteer declared that 'the spirit of party is become the vivifying principle of public conduct'.[4] This last view had been heard before – for as long indeed as men could remember. It was less familiar to conclude that 'a neutral conduct' had become 'useless and ridiculous'. The novel analysis, however, produced a more traditional response: the remedy was to transform parties by persuading the independent Members to support them, since 'An independent man, and a party man, are very different and opposite characters'.[5] It was not a definition that owed much to Burke,[6] and a distinction in fact was widely drawn

---

1. See I, 616–18.

2. Dundas to Edmund Burke, 6 October 1791 (*Correspondence of Burke*), VI, 429.

3. Duke of Clarence to Prince of Wales, 12 July [1790] (*The Correspondence of George Prince of Wales 1770–1812*, ed. A. Aspinall, II (1964), no. 513). From other naval correspondence of the time it seems likely that the situation can be explained in political as well as in professional and personal terms.

4. Gibbon to Lord Sheffield, 7 August 1790 (*Letters of Edward Gibbon*, 3, no. 762); [William Combe], *Reflections on the Approaching Dissolution of Parliament . . .* (1790), 9. Combe, one of the more interesting minor writers of the day – he was later to be the author of *Dr. Syntax* – may have been on the Ministry's payroll by this time.

5. Combe, op. cit., 9. The implications were not worked out. But the process might be said to have been inherent already in the practice of the Commons as a whole. As Combe continued, 'Independence is a relative term' (op. cit., 12), and it was not to be measured in the last quarter of the century by the conduct of the strictly independent MPs alone.

6. Cf. I, 35.

between organised Opposition, now admitted more openly as a legitimate activity, and party in the old factious sense of the term. 'The Opposition', ran a passage in a pamphlet almost certainly reflecting Pitt's own views, 'is a sort of public body, which, in the practice at least of our Government, is perfectly known and established'.[1] But to be acceptable and effective, precisely because it could perform a proper function, it must act within recognised limits and behave responsibly as an 'ex-official body'. All depended, in short, on 'the manner in which its faculties are exercised'[2] – and the Regency crisis had shown what that manner should not be. A statement which may seem to posterity to point towards a development of party appeared to many contemporaries very largely to condemn it.

It was therefore easy to portray 'the Party', now firmly associated with the name of Fox,[3] as something exceptional, which right-minded men abhorred. It is not so easy, given the reasons for its impact in the later eighties, to say if, on that basis, the body would have grown or endured. For while loyalties could be polarised on controversial occasions, Opposition was still working for the most part within what was often a 'very loose' House.[4] It throve, as Oppositions do, on excitement; could its progress have survived a further period of quiet? It certainly might not have seemed so in the summer of 1789, when, as indeed again in 1790, there were bickerings and signs of disillusionment. Fox himself wrote of the 'habitual spirit of despondency and fear that characterises the Whig party',[5] and while this was at a bad moment such symptoms of a perennial Opposition endured. If the organisation was improving, and pressures for unity were clear, there appeared also to be a real danger that the inner ranks themselves might suffer increasingly from the state in which their cohesion had developed. Years in the wilderness are bad for the nerves. What might have happened if the question had faded on which, as it seemed, 'the Party' lived; if the role of the Crown, so prominent in the eighties, had receded in the nineties, without its replacement by the fresh storms that unexpectedly swept the scene, and Pitt had quietly pursued his reforms, in areas largely distant

---

1. [Henry Mackenzie], *A Review of the Principal Proceedings of the Parliament of 1784* (nd, but 1792), 174. He had used much the same language, calling Opposition 'a kind of public department', in 1791 (*Additional Letters of Brutus* (nd, but 1793), Letters X and XI, 18 May and 21 November 1791); and Camden, one of Pitt's colleagues, expressed a somewhat similar view in 1788 (see A.S. Foord, *His Majesty's Opposition 1714–1830* (1964), 412). For Mackenzie's connexion with Pitt see I, 39n2, and Mackenzie to Pitt, 13 May 1792 (P.R.O. 30/8/154).

2. *A Review*, 174–7.

3. Sometimes indeed with a differentiation from respectable Whigs such as the Duke of Portland (see *The Letters of Brutus to Certain Celebrated Political Characters* (1791), Letter IX, 21 March 1791).

4. I, 519; 210–11, 230–1.

5. To Richard Fitzpatrick, 17 February 1789 (*Memorials and Correspondence of Fox*, II, 302).

from the old disputes?[1] One cannot tell, and the ifs of history serve only to make historians careful of their terms. One can but say, on the brink of events which were to introduce a new dimension, that a 'formed Opposition' was in being, grouped around an issue which might have been shrinking, in a way that allowed continuity in the very process of change.

The picture was reflected in the general election itself. 'The Party's' preparations were more concentrated and perhaps more far-reaching than before, and some at least of the candidates talked directly in terms of Fox and Pitt. Pitt himself indeed accepted a broad polarisation; towards the end he thought that 'the whole force for Government' would approach 340, Opposition would be about 190, 'and the remainder neutral or doubtful'.[2] This left only 28 under the last heading: a marked drop from the analyses only two years before.[3] The best retrospective survey bears out his figures: 340 Ministerialists, 183 Opposition, 29 independents, 6 doubtful.[4] At the same time the grounds for such a calculation remained complex, and the yields variable. Forecasts followed familiar lines – 'Remain for', 'Remain against', 'Remain doubtful', 'May gain', 'May lose', 'Sure to gain', 'Sure to lose', 'Uncertain' – and they related to categories producing differing degrees of commitment.[5] Ministerial estimates, reasonably accurate in the aggregate, were far from being so in the particular. There were more contests than had been expected – 92, compared with 87 in 1784 – and the Treasury, as in 1784, was often proved wrong on specific cases.[6] It could claim 19 accurate and 9 fairly accurate predictions in the 40 English counties, 15 accurate in the 32 large boroughs, 16 accurate and 4 fairly accurate in the 32 medium-sized boroughs, with higher proportions in the 139 small boroughs, over half of which depended on the patron's decision.[7] These results came from an organisation which had not changed greatly in the past six years. For the sharpening and extension of Opposition's surveillance seems not to have been matched on the Government's side. The Ministry was prepared for an election which, not legally required until 1791, had been rumoured at intervals

1. See I, 619, 636.

2. To Edward Eliot, 9 July 1790 (quoted in the Introductory Survey to the forthcoming volume for 1790–1818 in *The House of Commons* series of *The History of Parliament*. I am very greatly indebted to Dr Roland Thorne for permitting me to read and cite this source before its publication).

3. Cf. I, 618–20.

4. *History of Parliament* as in n2 above.

5. Op. cit. One forecast with such headings, emanating possibly from Grenville and subsequently kept up to date, relates probably to a period running quite closely to the election. Others, dating from 1788 and perhaps '89, followed earlier examples – eg I, 124 – with 'Pro', 'Con', 'Hopeful', 'Doubtful'.

6. Cf. I, 147, 149 (where the figure of contests should be altered from 83).

7. *History of Parliament*, op. cit. The final estimate of those mentioned in n5 above produced 351 pros and hopefuls against 207 cons and doubtfuls.

as political conditions see-sawed over the previous twenty months. By January 1790 Pitt claimed indeed that 'the ground laid . . . was very firm and solid';[1] and so it was, in the customary terms. There was no more likelihood of an Administration losing than there had been throughout the century, and in the event it held, or even improved on, the success of 1784.[2] Rose at the Treasury had nothing in particular to fear. The fact was reflected in Government's approach; in its limits and its strength.

Growth and spread in party feeling thus took place within a structure that could both accommodate and define it. In a general election, local and personal factors with their own distinct significance were brought to weigh on the national scales.[3] This of course did not change in 1790. But neither did it prevent a keener sense of identity informing Opposition and rubbing off on other parts of the House. The consequences were not regularly evident over the next few years in the conduct of many of the Members, whose habits, in business and debates, did not greatly change. They turned up or not much as they were used to do; their voting patterns – constant or occasional – were not radically altered by the existence of a rather more predictable allegiance on notable occasions.[4] At the same time, many Parliamentarians – certainly the more professional – felt themselves 'Partymen . . . more so now' than before.[5] Life went on in recognisable ways in an assembly conscious of fewer poles of reference, but not always of a corresponding discipline. And if a stimulus to party extended unevenly through the regions, it was in turn contained and penetrated by their indigenous concerns.

II

These could operate in more than one direction. In 1790 in point of fact there was one subject of concern in the country, as well as at Westminster, which may have enlarged a feeling of party even if it did not materially affect the election results. Many Dissenters on that occasion seem to have swung away from Pitt. Precisely where and how far they did so it is hard to say, for as so often the evidence is not firm enough. Election addresses, in constituencies where the Dissenting interest mattered, seldom stressed its aims or its attitude to Government. Few candidates, it would seem, committed themselves in the hope of

---

1. To Sir Archibald Macdonald [Attorney General], 3 January 1790 (quoted op. cit.). The rumours had been intermittent since the start of the Regency crisis (I, Ch. XX) and through Pitt's subsequent popularity.
2. Cf. I, 42, 146–7.
3. Op. cit., Ch. II, section II.
4. This is examined for the years 1790–4 in the Introductory Survey to the forthcoming volumes of *The History of Parliament*.
5. See p. 54 above.

securing Dissenting votes. In some places at least Pittite Members were returned once more with Dissenting support. Nevertheless there seems little doubt that earlier sentiment had often changed. Some elements of Opposition certainly had high hopes; in November 1789 Fox saw 'a *chance* of [the Whigs] getting very important support' from Non-conformity, and Burke, in full agreement, was already urging him to make sure.[1] Circumstances changed to some extent for politicians in the next few months; but not greatly, in all likelihood, for many of the Nonconformists themselves. The historian William Belsham, himself a Dissenter, remarked a few years later that 'they had the gross indiscretion, in many of their public votes, to recommend a marked preference' for Fox.[2]

The reason lay, above all, in Pitt's rejection of the movement to repeal the Corporation and Test Acts, those seventeenth-century enactments whereby Dissenters were barred from public office unless they agreed to subscribe to a sacramental test. He had opposed it on three occasions, in 1787, 1789 and 1790 itself; and in 1790 had spoken harshly, against a background of rising alarm. From this last date in particular, indeed, it has often been assumed that he was simply reacting to the French Revolution. But in fact his attitude stemmed from a time when that prospect did not exist, and it was formed initially on purely domestic grounds.

At first sight this is very surprising, and the Dissenters themselves were completely surprised. There were many good reasons in 1787 for them to expect Pitt's support. They could recall the legacy of a past when Chatham had shown them favour, and maintained close if fluctuating ties through much of his career. Thomas Hollis, David Erskine, Richard Baron offered different glimpses of a varied relationship. The Dissenters were ready to approve of his son, and Pitt in his turn had some early links, though these were more general or held at one remove. His friend Dudley Ryder[3] was an example of that not uncommon phenomenon, the Anglican of Dissenting stock who remained sympathetic. Shelburne's circle had its share of Dissenters – he appointed one to be tutor to his son – including Richard Price, whom Pitt liked and respected. Wyvill, Wilberforce, William Mason were closely in touch with that Yorkshire connexion which, in its marriages and friendships, crossing the boundaries of denomination, was laying one of the bases of the nineteenth-century intellectual aristocracy. More pervasive and important perhaps there was the influence of Cambridge, Lockeian, latitudinarian, and now touched with a rising earnestness inspired both

1. Fox to Earl Fitzwilliam, 13 November 1789 (Wentworth Woodhouse Muniments, Sheffield, F115a); Burke to Fox, 9 September 1789 (*Correspondence of Burke*, VI, 15). Both were referring to the general election which had to come by March 1791.

2. *Memoirs of the Reign of George III. To the Session of Parliament Ending A.D. 1793*, IV (1795), 278.

3. See I, 108, 310.

by Anglican Evangelicalism and by Dissent. For in Cambridge the two streams met which carried divergent Anglican currents towards an avowed, if latterly uneasy, respect for the disestablished sects. 'The prevalent Heterodoxy in the Establishment', it was stated in 1786, 'takes its Rise in *Cambridge*';[1] and of that broadening, rational movement Watson, Tyrwhitt, Hey were still active examples. The Feathers' Petition of the early seventies, for the removal of the Thirty Nine Articles as a test within the Church, had been largely a University effort. In the next decade the new generation of Simeon, Atkinson, Jowett, John Venn was building on the Evangelical precept of Berridge of Everton. In their very different, indeed contrasting, ways both schools admitted an obligation, the first intellectual, the second primarily moral, to Dissent. Pitt had little personal contact, particularly with the earnest Evangelicals. Pembroke was not a College that was much affected. But some of the other influences impinged. He had attended Dr Hey's lectures;[2] his friend Euston's father the Duke of Grafton – the Chancellor of the University – became virtually a Unitarian; above all his favourite author Paley,[3] the epitome of the Cambridge tradition, had recently restated the arguments for toleration in Church and State. It was a background from which the Dissenters might look for practical results. And there was a more specific cause for hope; for in the election of 1784 they had plunged enthusiastically into Pitt's support. 'They ranked among his most zealous adherents', seeming to 'act', as one MP recalled, 'in Corps';[4] and while the effect may be hard to isolate within the pattern as a whole, there were places, particularly in the eastern counties, where it was clearly marked. In Cambridgeshire itself their role was crucial in the county poll, and hopes of repeal of the Acts had been one of the rallying cries. To the possibly more tenuous links of family sympathy and educational influence the sects could therefore add a direct political debt.

The time might also have seemed ripe for the Acts to be repealed. Religious toleration was not in question: it was civil disability that was at stake, and here there were clear signs of a more propitious climate. For it was not only Dissenters who felt that legal exclusion from public office was now 'one of those Gothic absurdities, which are suited only to the ages of ignorance and barbarism'.[5] A more widespread attack and sense of doubt were ready to be mobilised, after a lull following the earlier varied efforts for religious reform. To rationalist thought the Acts were ridiculous, and to rationalist morality wicked; and the feeling affected

1. See Charles Smyth, *Simeon and Church Order* . . . (1940), 102.
2. I, 16.
3. See I, 396n1.
4. W. Belsham, *Essays Philosophical and Moral, Historical and Literary*, II (1799), 109; Edmund Burke to Richard Bright, 8–9 May 1789 (*Correspondence of Burke*, V, 471).
5. Joseph Towers, *Thoughts on the Commencement of a New Parliament* . . . (1790), 52–3. Towers was a Dissenting minister.

many who remained conventionally within the Church. There was a good deal of, rather superficial, anticlericalism in that still unconstrained society, extending indeed beyond questions of privilege to property itself. Wilberforce recalled that in his early life, when he 'mixed with very various circles', he 'could hardly go into any company where there was not a clergyman present without hearing some such measure [for seizing Church property] proposed'.[1] Lay disposal of ecclesiastical places could be happily accepted: lay appointments by confessional allegiance offended modern sense. 'Not even a bug can be destroyed within the purlieus of the royal household but by the hallowed fingers of a communicant'.[2] This remark in a Dissenting pamphlet could have come equally well from a London drawing room or club.

The position seemed the more illogical in view of its evasions, extensions and exceptions. It was not very difficult, given goodwill, to escape the Corporation Act – unless a charge was preferred within eighteen months the offender need not take the sacrament. It was harder but not impossible to escape the Test Act; on the other hand, this covered by custom certain important if non-'public' places.[3] The system was full of anomalies: a man could sit in Parliament, for instance, to represent a borough in which he was prevented from holding or voting for a post. It encouraged dishonesty: you could satisfy the demands, as many did over several generations, by performing a ceremony in which you did not believe once a year under the Indemnity Acts.[4] It had been made worse, paradoxically, by a recent enlargement of the original Toleration Act, whereby the whole body of Dissenting ministers was admitted to the sanctions of the other sects.[5] For, now exempt from religious, they qualified for civil restriction on exactly the same terms as those already in 'the half-way house'. The sense of grievance was finally heightened by the feeling that the offending Acts were bearing hardest on those against whom they had not been primarily designed. For when they were passed, under Charles II, the enemy was Roman Catholicism, and the Dissenters had submitted in order to protect the true liberties of the realm. Now conscientious Protestants, long the supporters of the Hanoverian Succession, were suffering from an embargo intended

1. Robert Isaac Wilberforce and Samuel Wilberforce, *The Life of William Wilberforce*, I, 261. In France, however, a clergyman might have been present, and theoretically in agreement.

2. [Samuel Heywood], *The Right of Protestant Dissenters to a Complete Toleration Asserted* (1787), quoted in Anthony Lincoln, *Some Political & Social Ideas of English Dissent 1763–1800* (1938), 240n2.

3. To positions in the Bank of England, and the Russia, South Sea, and East India Companies; and perhaps (it was uncertain) to Censors of the College of Physicians.

4. Which were passed annually from 1727. The Corporation of Nottingham, to take one instance, was said as late as the 1830s to have existed for years almost entirely on Occasional Conformity and the Indemnity Acts.

5. 10 Geo. III, c. 44, extending 1 W. & M., c. 18.

chiefly for a different creed. They formed an important part of the nation in its economic and intellectual life. Their connexions and friendships were extensive. They included highly respectable men. Yet they had been granted no direct easing of their disabilities, in a period during which the Roman Catholics themselves had enjoyed some relief.[1]

The case looked, and was, a strong one. But it had another side. The Hanoverian Church of England has had many hard things said of it, and certainly in very many ways it was supine, unenthusiastic and corrupt. Seen from the heights of Victorian worship the view was depressingly flat. But 'those plains of rational piety'[2] yield their rewards on closer inspection, and, as in other parts of society, the picture held light and shade. Parish life was often moribund, and the clergy sometimes a disgrace. But by no means always – current research is restoring a more varied impression – and in a century of clerical hymn-writing not all of it was Methodist. Old abuses flourished and some, such as pluralism, were even being extended. But they did not extinguish a scattered awareness of rising dangers and rising needs. The Sunday and primary school movements, the growing missionary movement, the attempts to start hospitals for 'sick poor', the foundation of the Proclamation Society and the revival of the Society for the Reformation of Manners, the forwarding of Acts for sabbath observance and for aid to oppressed curates, even for Poor Law reform and Church reform itself: all these efforts of the seventies and eighties, the headwaters of a later flood, announced a stirring of conscience and a striving for 'benevolence'.[3] The impulse – whatever the later claims – did not come only from Evangelicals and Methodists, still held, the latter uneasily, within the body of the Church: indeed it was shared, sometimes in partnership, by men who disliked the rest of their works. The Establishment was largely dormant. It was rich, and growing richer. It called for renewal. But it had not lost faith in itself, or become entirely ossified.

It also still commanded a perhaps surprisingly deep attachment. Against the scepticism in London society, the almost total lack of contact with the urban poor, the earnest disapproval on the part of Dissent, must be set much quiet Anglican observance. Gibbon was amazed, when *The Decline and Fall* appeared, to find that 'the majority of English readers were so fondly attached even to the name and shadow of Christianity';[4] and the strongest attacks – notable tributes to conviction rather than to scholarship – were launched by orthodox Anglicans, not Methodists or Dissenters. The Age of Reason in its narrow sense was in fact already

1. By the Act of 1778 (18 Geo. III, c. 60) protecting priests, after taking an oath of allegiance, against some of the earlier penalties levied on their calling, and allowing all Roman Catholics, on the same oath, to inherit and purchase landed property.

2. G.F.A. Best, *Temporal Pillars* . . . (1964), viii.

3. A word often to be found in the Anglican literature of the period.

4. *Memoirs of My Life*, ed. Georges A. Bonnard (1966), 159. The first instalment of the great work was published in 1776.

declining in England, even while it was bearing its most spectacular fruits abroad. The structure stood; but it had been shaken intellectually and emotionally – Hume and Wesley in their very different ways had beaten on the walls – and in any case the design had always incorporated older features. There were strong traditional, insular strains running through English thought in the century in which it had been at its most universal. Its very impact on the European pattern masked yet in a sense stemmed from the contrasts, and these were nowhere imbedded more firmly than in the fabric of public life. The Church of England was part of that fabric; it was an integral part of the Constitution. And the Constitution commanded the loyalties of reason and tradition alike.

And now it was under debate. The relations of Church and State were in question. A weight of genuine doubt was added to the more predictable fears. It was to be expected that Anglican Corporations would seek to protect their own, and use elevated arguments for highly practical ends. The same reasoning, held more honourably, would feature in orthodox apologetics. But there were reservations in more surprising quarters. William Mason, the disciple of Chatham and friend and associate of Dissenters; William Wilberforce, politically indebted and embarking as a colleague on a great cause; Samuel Parr, that stalwart Foxite and the Whigs' answer to Dr Johnson, make a curious trio to find opposed to repeal in 1787. But, like many others, they still felt that 'a toleration and a test should always go together',[1] and that whatever the faults of the Establishment its role must be preserved. Without an appropriately privileged Church the State as it was known would change its nature: without appropriate support from the State the Church as it was known could disappear. To many it was very shocking that the connexion should be weakened, and even latitudinarians, questioning its essence, could rally in defence against too headlong a threat. The influential Paley himself had just done so, in terms which struck a responsive chord. There was no reason in principle why 'men of different religious persuasions, may not sit upon the same bench, deliberate in the same council, or fight in the same ranks'. It was wrong, and useless, to try 'making of the church an engine, or even *an ally*, of the state; . . . or regarding it as a support of regal in opposition to popular forms of government'. But – a famous and far-reaching phrase – 'the authority of a church establishment is founded in its utility', and 'the general tendency' of 'the public happiness' must be taken into account. There should be a union, and balance, of 'the right of private judgment, with the care of public safety'; and this meant a '*complete* toleration of all dissenters from the established church, without any other limitation or

---

1. A pronouncement of Bishop Warburton's in his celebrated discourse, *The Alliance between Church and State*, which, produced in the 1730s, held its influence for half a century.

exception, than what arises from the conjunction of dangerous political dispositions with certain religious tenets'.[1]

This last was a significant statement in the middle eighties, for it was just then that doubts were being voiced about the 'dispositions' of Dissent. They had nothing to do as yet with the French Revolution; but a good deal to do with the American, and the general questioning of assumptions of which it had become a focus. For one of the most noticeable features of that generation was a 'dramatic change' in the expression of the Dissenters' political thought.[2] No longer could they all be taken as faithful followers of the reigning house, or of the *status quo* as that had been generally accepted. Of course many could, and the Dissenting Interest was no more a political than a theological unit. On the contrary it was fissiparous by nature, as indeed was evident in these very decades in a drift away from some of the older bodies towards offshoots or breakaway movements. Nonconformity was stirring and shifting, and the process was confused. But one of the catalysts was precisely a new intellectual conviction that secular problems should be tackled in secular terms. This 'croisade laïque', as it has been called,[3] naturally yielded different answers: 'As Dissenters', it was rightly observed, 'we have no peculiar principles of civil government at all'.[4] But it was equally true – indeed a logical sequel – that 'Modern nonconformity naturally leads us to study government',[5] and the spirit of rational inquiry altered relations with the outside world. Some of the results damaged the campaign against the Corporation and Test Acts itself. For, in contrast to the previous generation, Dissenters had been prominently connected with most of the agitations of the past twenty years: with Wilkes and Liberty, the American upheaval, the various movements for reform; and while they were not peculiar in this – while in fact it widened and strengthened their contacts – their efforts, high-minded and zealous, carried a particular flavour. It was paradoxical, indeed, that the claim to be judged by purely secular standards ended rather in a new label being pinned to the old sectarian coat. For the Dissenters were notable publicists – notable pamphleteers and preachers – and the fact underlined the impression of denominational discontent. It had not taken firm hold in the middle eighties; but the speed with which it was soon to do so owed a good deal to the growing antipathy of

1. *The Principles of Moral and Political Philosophy* (1785), bk. VI, ch. X, and particularly 555–6, 573–4, 582, 586. The earlier part of the passage was quoted by a supporter of repeal in one of the Parliamentary debates a few years later (William Smith, in 1789; *P.R.*, XXVI, 113).
2. Gerald R. Cragg, *Reason and Authority in the Eighteenth Century* (1964), 261.
3. Lincoln, op. cit., 18.
4. Joseph Priestley, *A View of the Principles and Conduct of the Protestant Dissenters, with respect to the Civil and Ecclesiastical Constitution of England* (1769), 37.
5. R. Robinson, *A Plan of Lectures on the Principles of Nonconformity* . . . (1778), 49.

those years. Rational Dissent was far from popular: in the hands of men like Priestley and Robinson of Cambridge it could indeed frighten and offend the more conservative brethren themselves. Often Unitarian in theology, and undeferential in politics, some of its most influential spokesmen were calling for more than society would give. In their arguments against the Acts they went on to question the Establishment.[1] It was hardly surprising if many felt that repeal could be the thin end of a wedge.

In one respect, moreover, it would be the wedge itself. For what would happen to the boroughs if Dissenters were openly admitted? One of the Acts, after all, was the Corporation Act: it was local as well as central offices that were involved. To admit Nonconformists officially to those bodies would be to lay open the way to a change in the nature of control of some very important institutions. Corporations could affect the choice of Parliamentary candidates. They could bring pressure, sometimes weighty, to bear on MPs. The incidence of private Parliamentary bills, the whole pattern of national and local connexions, made the character of borough government a matter of intimate concern. Repeal touched entrenched private interests in a highly sensitive point, and this was accordingly a factor, not necessarily decisive but of real substance, which Pitt – which any Minister – could not afford to ignore.

The background was therefore less simple than the Dissenters appeared to think. They may also have underrated one advantage so far as Pitt himself was concerned. Their electoral support in 1784 and their subsequent goodwill rested largely on his efforts for Parliamentary reform. This was not at all unreasonable, for Pitt had fought hard for the cause, and a great deal harder than Fox, whose actions had always been ambivalent.[2] Nevertheless the alliance, like all such connexions between leading Parliamentarians and campaigners outside, contained divergent views as to what the objects should be. Pitt's strategy had been conservative, centred on what he thought was possible, and he was soon expressing distrust of 'schemes, founded in visionary and impracticable ideas'. He was correspondingly wary of the external pressures on which he relied – 'I wish Mr. Wyvill had been a little more sparing of my name', and Wyvill at the time was his close associate in the cause. As early as 1783 there were signs of mutual disillusionment between the young Parliamentary champion and the more radical figures in the country. They did not lessen in the next few years, and some of the more outspoken doubts came from the ranks of the more vocal Dissenters. Capell Lofft, a leading campaigner in Suffolk – where the sects had rallied conspicuously in 1784[3] – specifically rejected Pitt's proposals

1. Eg. Priestley's *A Letter to the Right Honourable William Pitt . . . on the Subjects of Toleration and Church Establishments . . .* (1787).
2. See I, Chs. III, particularly 60–76, and V, 223–8, on which the following part of this paragraph is based.
3. P. 59 above.

while giving them tactical support. But by 1787 in any case Pitt had decided that the issue was dead: the country was prosperous and satisfied, and the agitation had faded away. As Wyvill himself agreed, any further immediate effort was hopeless,[1] and radical cries and pressures were not – to say the least – required. If the Dissenters accordingly reckoned to improve their fortunes in this way, they were blurring an earlier distinction and in danger of misreading current signs.

The motion for the repeal of the Acts was entrusted to the respected MP Henry Beaufoy, an Anglican of Dissenting connexions who was active in many fields of 'improvement'.[2] It had its first reading on 28 March 1787, and Pitt had by then sounded out the ground. He talked to a Dissenters' deputation in mid-January,[3] and soon afterwards he asked the Archbishop of Canterbury to collect the Bishops' views. The Archbishop was John Moore, 'of a disposition naturally mild and generous', whose reputation was 'neither to adopt any steps to inflame the minds of the Dissenters on the one hand, nor to alarm the friends of Orthodoxy on the other'.[4] A report from such a source was unlikely to stem from archiepiscopal pressure: it might safely be taken as reflecting opinions received. These were of limited statistical value, for only 16 of the 27 prelates met; but they included both the Archbishops, and of those present only two – Watson and Shipley, both noted reformers – voted for repeal.[5] The Bench might thus be said to have spoken clearly, and the fact could not but influence Pitt. Indeed it was probably decisive in determining his course.[6] If the Dissenters' memories are to be trusted, he had received them sympathetically; 'the expressions used by him in the . . . conferences . . ., though far from amounting to a promise of support,

1. I, 228; Christopher Wyvill to Pitt, 29 July 1787 (*Political Papers, chiefly respecting the Attempt . . . to effect a Reformation of the Parliament: Collected by the Reverend Christopher Wyvill*, IV (1802), 31–40).
2. See I, 266, 291, 351–2, 389. The statement in *D.N.B.* that he was a Dissenter is incorrect; see Sir Lewis Namier and John Brooke, *The History of Parliament: The House of Commons 1754–1790.*, II (1964), 72–3.
3. On the 19th (Guildhall Library Ms 3084/1, f.2v). He received a deputation again early in February, to accept the printed 'Case' (loc. cit., ff. 4–5).
4. Belsham, *Memoirs of the Reign of George III*, IV, 219; John Nichols, *Literary Anecdotes of the Eighteenth Century . . .*, VIII (1814), 95.
5. Both Watson and Shipley moreover hailed from Welsh sees, which were not generally thought of much account. Copies of the Minutes of the meeting, which was held at the Bounty Office in Westminster on 10 February, and of Moore's reply to Pitt on the 12th, are in Archbishop Moore's Mss at Lambeth Palace Library, no. 17.
6. He may also have been affected by Bishop Sherlock's *Arguments against a Repeal of the Corporation and Test Acts*, which is said to have been shown to him and his friends by Pretyman (*Letters of Theophilus Lindsey*, ed. Herbert McLachlan (1920), 64). This celebrated pamphlet, originally entitled a *Vindication* of the Acts some seventy years before, was reissued in 1787 with an unsolicited dedication to Pitt – as indeed was an answering *Refutation* of the same earlier period.

. . . were considered as certain indications of a favourable disposition'.[1] But when the debate followed he opposed the motion, and he left no doubt that he spoke Ministerially, with a view to influencing the vote.

Pitt based his case on the argument that there should be no 'deprivation' of civil right 'unless there is reason to see substantial inconvenience in the participation'.[2] He submitted however that there was, and that Parliament in its turn could not be deprived of its 'discretionary power' of decision. An Established Church was necessary; many of its members were alarmed; and it was from the statements of some of the Dissenters that the alarm arose. These were therefore questions of 'expediency': 'If I were arguing upon principles of right, I should not talk of alarm; but I am acting upon principles of expediency'. For what was the position? Many of the Dissenters were moderate men. But there were others who were more extreme, and who questioned the existence of the Establishment itself. Nor would they be backward, if repeal was granted, in using their new influence in the local Corporations; for it was 'towns and corporations' that would be 'their object', the benefit would not be 'so immediate' in the counties, and 'an exclusive corporation brought into the hands of the Dissenters was a very different thing from a dissenting member sitting in the House'. Repeal of the Acts was quite another matter from granting the customary annual indemnity:[3] the latter simply showed that Parliament did not wish to enforce the restrictions farther than it need. He had a high opinion of Dissenters in general; but in current circumstances there could be a threat to the union of Church and State, which might not be 'probable' but was not 'chimerical'. Such a view was widely held, and therefore 'I cannot vote for the repeal without alarming a great body of the Legislature'. Nor indeed were the present arrangements intolerable in practice. A 'spirit of moderation' prevailed, and Government would continue to afford every 'mental privilege, of perfect toleration' to the Dissenters' religious beliefs.

Pitt had thus come down unambiguously against the motion. He had not, as perhaps he might have done, given the House its head.[4] It was an important, quite possibly a decisive intervention, for in fact there had been doubts beforehand how the vote would go. The Dissenters and the Archbishop of Canterbury were agreed that repeal might perhaps have been gained if the Ministry had not shown that it meant to give a lead.[5]

---

1. Belsham, op. cit., IV, 127. This is a rather stronger impression than that recorded in the minutes of the meeting (p. 65, n3 above), and it was given retrospectively. But Belsham is generally trustworthy, and his statement rested on information from one of those present.

2. *P.R.*, XXI (1787), 562–5.

3. See p. 60, n4 above.

4. 'He could not with decency give a silent vote on such an occasion' (*P.R.*, XXI, 562).

5. Belsham, *Memoirs of the Reign of George III*, IV, 128–9; Moore to Auckland, 6 April 1787 (B.L. Add. Ms 34424). Some of the newspapers, however, had predicted that the motion would fail.

It is hard to tell; there was probably a fairly hard core of some 150 MPs from whom a variable combination of votes for repeal – as it turned out, some two-thirds of this total – could be expected in most circumstances. Reformers of various brands, attaching to sections of Opposition, were likely to be actual or potential supporters of the small number of Dissenting MPs themselves.[1] All therefore would turn on how, and how strongly, a body of the less committed Members felt. In 1787 the feelings of 'alarm' were balanced against a reluctance to appear intolerant, and to uphold restrictions which went against the intellectual grain. 'Many of the independent Members', it was held, were for the motion;[2] Fox came out in support;[3] a substantial part of the House may have waited to see what Pitt would say. Had he then misjudged the atmosphere, and been unnecessarily cautious? If so, some of his backbenchers might have felt it was not for the first time.[4] As it was, the motion was lost by 178 to 100, a comfortable majority in a rather thin House.[5]

The attendance does not suggest that the questions aroused intense excitement. Nor does Pitt's behaviour suggest that he himself held strong views. He was quite capable of striving hard for a cause that he had at heart, as the example of the slave trade was to show the next year.[6] But this was not the case here; he took objections as he found them, from a certain groundswell of apprehension, the uneasiness of borough Corporations and local magistrates – where Anglican ministers were well represented – and more specifically from the Bishops' vote. 'The Bishops all together lead Mr. Pitt', it was later remarked;[7] and while the verdict came from an uninformed quarter, it was in fact true of a subject about which he felt no intimate concern. He was never stirred by theological disputes; he was a thoroughgoing Erastian, and as an Erastian took his advice from the appropriate department. He may have done so the more readily because the Bishops sat in the Lords, who would thereby have been the more encouraged to throw out the measure if it passed the Commons; and also because their opinion would have been echoed by the King, who was thinking – *absit omen* – of his coronation oath and

---

1. See G.M. Ditchfield, 'The parliamentary struggle over the repeal of the Test and Corporation Acts, 1787–1790' (*E.H.R.*, LXXXIX, no. 352), 551–69.

2. *The Public Advertiser*, 27 March 1787.

3. For an interesting tale, which may be baseless, of how he made up his mind, see Herbert S. Skeats, *A History of the Free Churches of England, from A.D. 1688–A.D. 1851* (1868), 488 n.

4. Eg Daniel Pulteney to the Duke of Rutland, 15 March, 11 April 1785 (*H.M.C., Fourteenth Report, Appendix, Pt. I*, 190, 198).

5. Some accounts give 176 to 98.

6. It must of course be said here that a decision on the slave trade was not a Ministerial matter involving Government. But at least at the start this was not by Pitt's wish (see I, 392–5).

7. William Cowper to Lady Hesketh, 23 June 1789 (*The Works of William Cowper, Esq. . . .*, ed. Robert Southey, VI (1836), 248). And there is little doubt – though there is no reason to suppose this was conclusive – that Pretyman, living in Downing Street and soon to become a Bishop himself, was against repeal (see p. 65, n6 above).

would have been prepared, so he said, to make his views publicly known.[1] Pitt moreover may well have thought that by taking the Bishops' advice in an instance affecting the Constitution so closely, he was unlikely to arouse a fierce or prolonged debate. For in declaring his position as the King's Minister he was not only accepting responsibility; he was also seeking to forestall controversy and keep the temperature low. The political situation was relaxed, after the disturbance of earlier years, and he was reaping growing benefits from a period of quiet. It was a welcome change, remembering the setbacks of the first year or so in office,[2] to experience a session which had 'proceeded triumphantly' hitherto.[3] There was other business – not all Parliamentary – to occupy his mind: the last stage of the Anglo-French commercial treaty, the talks with France over India, the rising trouble in Holland, above all the Consolidations Act.[4] In all these circumstances, and gives his rather marginal personal interest, he would need strong inducements to make him risk trouble on the Dissenters' behalf.

The decision did him little immediate harm. There was no further immediate debate, Opposition reaped little advantage, and the country in general dismissed the matter. Pitt's reputation was consolidated over the next two years, by his financial and diplomatic successes and his handling of the Regency crisis. By the spring of 1789 he was at the height of his popularity, and many of the Dissenters approved his policies at large. But the episode was significant, and it was to have significant effects. For the sects, whatever their other differences, 'were in the last degree astonished and chagrined at the part taken by Mr. Pitt in this debate'.[5] If he was not prepared to support them, they thought that at least he might have abstained from so prominently stating a decisive opposition. They noted that he had found himself for once on the same side as Lord North, and in fact warmly referred to that old un-touchable;[6] and they drew the natural conclusion that 'it was not possible for [him], on this grand question, to stand well at once with the Court and the Dissenters'.[7] The first parting of the ways was in prospect

1. This was a statement made after the motion had been defeated (George III to Pitt, 29 March 1787; *English Historical Documents 1783–1832*, ed. A. Aspinall and E. Anthony Smith (1959), no. 452). I know of no evidence that Pitt consulted the King in advance. But he must have known his mind.

2. See I, 610 & n2.

3. Henry Dundas to Sir Archibald Campbell, 23 March 1787 (Holden Furber, *Henry Dundas, First Viscount Melville, 1742–1811* (1931), 68).

4. I, 492, 441–2, 525–6, 271. There was also the fourth charge against Warren Hastings (op. cit., 450).

5. Belsham, op. cit., IV, 127.

6. See I, 103, 129 n2, 140. The MP Nathaniel Wraxall indeed believed that this was the first time that Pitt ever gave 'spontaneous recognition' of North's 'talents and principles' (*The Historical and the Posthumous Memoirs of Sir Nathaniel William Wraxall 1772–1784*, ed. Henry B. Wheatley, IV (1884), 438).

7. Belsham, loc. cit., 128.

between the combined forces which hitherto had given the Minister his unique appeal. For by the argument of expediency Pitt had adopted a position which he may have expected events to change for him, but which on the contrary they were to reinforce.

The Dissenters were far from finished. They were determined to try again, and, like the slave trade abolitionists, they expected to succeed.[1] Their confidence was not without grounds. The defeat had scarcely been overwhelming; support could perhaps have been organized better; and 'the Court' itself, though adverse in the votes, had not appeared violently so. An opportunity to reintroduce the motion came in May 1789, and when Beaufoy rose to speak on the 8th the Dissenters were full of hope.

They were narrowly disappointed. The House was even smaller than in 1787, and the fact may have been partly due to a widespread uncertainty and wish to abstain.[2] The vote was quite close – the nearest to victory that the Dissenters in fact came for 39 years – the numbers being 122 to 102.[3] The arguments remained the same; for although two speakers (one being Fox) mentioned continental examples, the shadow of France had not been cast as yet. Pitt contented himself with repeating his earlier objections, and perhaps the most important new element was Fox's declared growing concern.[4] It was therefore almost certain that another attempt would be made. The Dissenters felt that only one more push was needed now. '. . . The present times are highly favourable to liberality of every kind'; another 'calm and reasonable presentation of our case' would surely carry the day.[5] The motion was revived within a year, and this time by Fox. He gave notice of his intention in February 1790, and the debate took place on 2 March.[6] But the result was very different from the campaigners' hopes. A new spirit was abroad, fear and hostility had been roused, Pitt himself came down heavily, and the motion was lost by 294 to 105.

The reasons were not far to seek. In the narrower party sphere

1. Cf. I, 396.
2. Thus Wilberforce, who had voted against repeal two years before, now absented himself, 'my mind not being made up' (*Life*, I, 217).
3. *P.R.*, XXVI, 128. The likely attitude of the Lords, however, can be inferred from their rejection two months later of a bill by Earl Stanhope to repeal a number of obsolete laws affecting Anglican observance.
4. Op. cit., 93, 128. Pitt certainly does not seem to have resented Beaufoy's trying again: in some notes in his hand for a list of possible appointments, undated but clearly made in May or early June 1789, there is one 'Secy. India Board – Mr Beaufoy' (P.R.O., 30/8/197) – a post which he in fact obtained in 1791.
5. *The Conduct to be observed by Dissenters in order to procure the Repeal of the Corporation and Test Acts, Recommended in a Sermon Preached . . . at Birmingham, November 5, 1789 . . . By Joseph Priestley* (nd), 10–11.
6. *P.R.*, XXVII, 108, 139–96.

leadership of the campaign had now passed increasingly to the Foxites, and there was perhaps a corresponding tendency to harden on the Ministerial side. But wider influences were more cogently at work, which stemmed very largely from the actions of the Dissenters themselves. For, exasperated by obstruction and, as they thought, with victory in sight, their more passionate advocates had flung themselves into the fray. A spate of pamphlets and sermons poured forth which could hardly be called 'calm and reasonable', and, more disturbing to the sober-minded, meetings were held throughout the country. In London and Yorkshire, in Lincoln and Worcester, above all in the Midlands the Dissenters gathered. There were even plans for a National Convention on the eve of the debate, which judging by some of the provincial resolutions would have been a stern affair. 'Framed in terms for the most part harsh and revolting', as one of the more moderate brethren put it,[1] they went far beyond the specific case for repeal. Disestablishment, Natural Justice, 'citizens'' rights, the Rights of Man themselves – such cries had not been heard in such a tone from such quarters before. The more conservative Dissenters, whatever their misgivings, could not entirely stand aside, for the fight united the sects as they had not been united for years. The reaction was not slow in coming. Both Church and State took fright. The signs were growing throughout the winter, in a counter-flood of meetings and publications. By February 1790, it was said, 'the consideration of the repeal of the Test and Corporation Acts engrosses . . . the serious thoughts of almost every denomination of people throughout the Kingdom'.[2] It was probably true. 'No proposal', it has been stated, 'had stirred such national interest since 1784'; it 'roused a storm', to take a longer perspective, '. . . which recalls the days of Hoadly and Sacheverell'.[3] The Dissenters' resolutions were met by an equal host from the parsons and gentry: from the clergy of London and York and Chester, and the Society for Promoting Christian Knowledge, from county and borough assemblies in almost every part of the country. The cry of 'the Church is in danger' was heard again in the land. The uneasy indifference of 1787, the uncertainty of 1789, had suddenly been replaced by a wave of intense alarm.

Such a change was largely due to events in France – or rather to the way in which the more vocal Dissenters applied them. The distinction is important, for there was still no widespread fear of what was happening across the Channel: rather the reverse. Let the French continue with

---

1. Belsham, op. cit., IV, 278.

2. Quoted, from a debate of the Common Council of London in Guildhall on 25 February, in *The Gentleman's Magazine* (1790), I, 267. And cf. Fox in the Commons on 2 March (*P.R.*, XXVII, 139).

3. Eugene Charlton Black, *The Association, British Extra-Parliamentary Organization 1769–1793* (1963), 213; M. Dorothy George, *English Political Caricature to 1792 . . .* (1959), I, 206.

their efforts to advance on an English model; in many ways it was time they did, and it should keep them out of mischief. Burke had not yet published his great philippic, the Revolution still seemed primarily a domestic affair, and the violence of its early days appeared in part to be dying down. But it was another matter to point to France as an example to this country, as some of the leading sectaries had been doing from the start. It proved to be their greatest error – understandable, but highly unpopular – and it did much to heighten resistance to what had been a purely native demand. When Price moved an Address to the French National Assembly at the end of 1789 he sparked off the first of all counter-Revolutionary prints, and repeal of the Acts lay at its centre.[1] A new note indeed was now to be heard, and it was echoed in the Commons' debate. Fox and Beaufoy, and Pitt less directly, acknowledged the impact of the Revolution, and Burke stepped into the arena, for the first time on this subject, with the second of his major declarations on France.[2]

Such then were the circumstances of the Dissenters' third attempt. Pitt widened the scope of his objections in the course of his speech.[3] He repeated those of 'policy and expedience'; but, as he had not done before, he now added with 'force and confidence' arguments 'on the ground of right'. 'Toleration could, by no means, be considered an equality'. The restrictive laws protected an Establishment which was part of the Constitution, and the fact that tenure of civil office was made dependent on a religious test was paralleled by the religious test ('the oath of abjuration') imposed on members of the Commons and the Lords. There was no inherent claim to any post; posts were granted by authority, and he 'had no idea of such Levelling principles as those which warranted to all citizens an equality of rights'. The Dissenters' behaviour had confirmed his caution, and his wish to preserve the prerogative. 'He must, therefore, give his negative to the motion';[4] and, as he knew it would, the House did the same.

So the matter ended, to the Dissenters' disgust and distress:

1. The Address was moved on 4 November, and published at the end of December. The print appeared on 16 February 1790 – the day after Fox gave notice of his intention to introduce his motion for repeal.
2. See *P.R.*, XXVII, 147–8, 162, 174, 178–87. Burke's first speech on France had been made three weeks before, on the same occasion as Pitt's (see p. 47 above).
3. *P.R.*, XXVII, 155–63.
4. *P.H.* has 'decided negative'. It is worth noting, however, that Pitt had been careful to define the prerogative. Repeal indeed could extend it dangerously, by enabling sovereigns to favour minority creeds at the expense of the Established Church, as James II had tried to do in another direction.

A blot that will be still a blot, in spite
Of all that grave apologists may write.[1]

In the general election that followed, despite their efforts and Fox's hopes,[2] they failed to make a significant impact on events. There had been speculation how far they might do so, and opponents of repeal had even been praised after the Parliamentary debate for defying trouble by voting as they did.[3] But at the polls – where they occurred – the resentment which certainly existed was not embodied to great effect in the lists of Members returned. In some relevant constituencies, indeed, there was little discernible consequence, and in some the threatened concentration of effort did not emerge. Norwich for instance, that old centre of Dissent, was quiet. In Bristol there was a compromise. In Great Yarmouth and Bridport contingent factors held some Dissenters in the Ministry's camp. At St Davids there was no contested poll in the end. In Liverpool and Coventry and Maldon Opposition candidates may well have benefited, but it is hard to tell exactly how far, and in Suffolk and Ipswich they probably did not. Similarly, a supporter of repeal defeated at the poll did not necessarily owe his defeat to repeal. Of the fifteen cases in question, very few if any can be confidently thus described.[4] Despite switches in votes there was not a completely uniform sectarian response. More telling perhaps, many vulnerable constituencies were in fact so constructed that the enfranchised Dissenters by themselves could not produce a change.

Nevertheless, the results of the three years' campaign cannot be so summarily dismissed. If there was no great electoral consequence, there were less tangible long-term effects. The unusual alliance of 1784, which had given Pitt his distinctive strength, was under some pressure after 1787 and splintered in 1790. Dissent was cooler where it was not alienated, and Dissent was a significant element in that body of 'improving' effort which he was generally thought to represent. He had hitherto reconciled in his person traditional and radical support; the combination was weakened now, and it would not be seen in the same way again. For whatever Pitt's, rather vague, hopes at the start that opinion would slowly settle in favour of a measure which he could then

1. Cowper's 'Expostulation'. The poem (a protest against the recent relief to the Roman Catholics; see p. 61, n1 above) was written in 1781, and published in 1782. Cowper referred to it now as showing what he thought of the result of the debate (to Lady Hesketh, 8 March 1790; *Works of William Cowper*, VI, 287). It was a rare example at this moment of surviving Evangelical sympathy.
In May 1791 a motion was defeated for the repeal of the penal laws in Scotland, where however the issues were different.
2. P. 58 above.
3. Eg *Life of Wilberforce*, I, 258–9.
4. I am indebted to Dr Thorne for information here. See also Ditchfield, loc. cit., 572–6.

adopt, and whatever regrets he may have felt later, when the consequences were plain,[1] he had committed himself at a time when familiar conditions would soon be changing, fresh forces making ground and old calculations largely destroyed. The fact that the efforts for repeal reached their climax in the first, open phase of the French Revolution did much to hasten a reaction against it which then pressed farther on the Dissenters themselves. It was no accident that the first anti-revolutionary riots were staged in the name of 'Church and King':[2] the agitation for repeal had clinched the tendency – welling up on the one side from a recumbent Anglicanism, and markedly advanced on the other by Rational Dissent itself – to associate religious with secular questions and views. In many respects, indeed, the whole affair heralded the forthcoming troubles. It identified Dissent in the public mind with whatever was coming from France – a development that was soon to lead to much heart-searching among the sects. It pushed many Dissenters – not all of them readily – into partnership with the reforming Whigs, and revived old cries of Court influence before these were heard in a wider context. On the eve of urban troubles, it hardened the existing division between Corporations and Nonconformists in the rising centres of industrial growth. It may have carried a stage farther the advances in popular organisation, particularly in the form of associations, which harked back to the American War. It ranged against Pitt with a personal sharpness some of the most formidable men in the country, from within those intelligent earnest communities of solidly Puritan stock which by teaching and social condition were suited to share and spread the new Word. In a different setting, it was a curtain-raiser to the great conflict of ideas which was so profoundly to shape his later career.

III

In one respect the connexion was direct. The conflict was articulated by pamphlets, and the most influential succession was launched by a leading Dissenter at the height of the campaign for repeal of the Acts. Price–Burke–Paine: so the sequence runs, for Price's *A Discourse on the Love of Our Country* sparked off the *Reflections on the Revolution in France*, which in turn precipitated the First Part of the *Rights of Man*. These last two achievements, of course, were the peaks in a crowded landscape of lesser but notable heights, Sir James Mackintosh and Mary Woollstone-craft for example. They gave to the immediate debate a transcendent

1. According to Lord John Russell, referring long afterwards to the debate of 1790, 'Mr. Pitt, as is now well known, did in a few years . . . completely change his mind on the subject, and express a wish that the Test and Corporation Acts should be repealed' (in the successful debate on repeal in 1828; Hansard's *Parliamentary Debates*, *N.S.*, XVIII (1828), 678). I know of no conclusive evidence that this in fact was so.
2. See p. 103 below.

value and enduring fame. They also did much to shape public attitudes in what proved to be a period of transition.

That period might be said to have lasted to the closing months of 1791. For 1792 was the decisive year, witnessing the 'second revolution' in France, the worsening of the European situation, the flare-up of trouble at home and its expression in new, suspect forms. The propertied orders – perhaps society at large – then felt themselves progressively threatened. But this was not so in the earlier years, when the renewal of dispute was indeed a renewal, along largely familiar lines through familiar patterns of organisation. If a slope was forming towards a watershed, it was at an angle which concealed the fact. There were reasons in 1790, and even in 1791, to view the prospects as more hopeful than those of ten years before.

This was certainly the impression of the reviving exponents of reform themselves. They now saw their efforts as an aspect of progress, not an antidote to collapse.[1] 'The present times are highly favourable to liberality of every kind',[2] and, viewed domestically, the fact was due precisely to the calm of recent years. The fresh stirring of interest began with the centenary of the Glorious Revolution, not least as a timely means of heartening a flagging Parliamentary Opposition. The meetings and dinners throughout the country bolstered the party's self-respect, and helped augment the preparations for a general election. It was appropriate that Price's sermon on the love of country[3] should have been preached to the London Revolution Society, and the anniversary, in November 1789, was transformed by the events in France. For the most vivid stimulus within the movement came from the French Revolution, that offspring, as many saw it, which was now outstripping its English parent. The force of the impact varied at first in different quarters among the reformers: the leading organ of a decade before, the Society for Promoting Constitutional Information, remained largely aloof for about a year from what it regarded as its foreign pupils. But the leaven was at work, most obviously in the London Revolution Society itself, the other, lesser survivor from the last great campaign. In the autumn of 1789 it plunged into correspondence with its French counterparts, sending Addresses and advice in return for tributes to 'the instructors and examples of the . . . World'.[4] The Jacobin Club – then a most respectable body – may even have been founded in emulation: there was a wave of sentiment 'as if the Strait between Calais and Dover were no more'.[5] Within two years of the Bastille falling, the Society was

1. Cf. I, 59–60, 160–1.
2. P. 69 above.
3. P. 73 above.
4. The Patriotic Union of the Town and Castleward of Lille to the London Revolution Society, 26 November 1789 (quoted in George Stead Veitch, The *Genesis of Parliamentary Reform* (2nd edn., 1965), 129).
5. London Revolution Society to the Patriotic Club at Marseilles, 27 March 1791 (op. cit., 154).

in contact with over forty institutions in France. And while it was unique in this respect in London, and new provincial bodies were slow to emerge – the first of any substance was founded in Manchester in the autumn of 1790[1] – the established Whig Clubs and Constitutional Societies, and the flourishing societies of inquiry and debate,[2] were busily sowing the seed which was to produce a bumper crop. It was a time of confidence and expectation, of solemn resolutions and fraternal greetings. In the light of what followed it was touching, sometimes rather absurd, and sad.

Many of the hopes were bound to be channelled into a fresh demand for Parliamentary reform. They found some popular expression in the veteran Horne Tooke's candidature for Westminster in June 1790,[3] and within the Commons themselves in a motion three months before. The sponsor perhaps was rather unfortunate: he was the great Irish orator Henry Flood, who since 1783 had sat, interruptedly, for English seats. It was natural enough for him to try, as the current chairman of the Society for Constitutional Information. But despite his fame in Dublin he cut little ice at Westminster, where his rare interventions had failed to impress a very different audience. He was in fact a rather isolated figure, who had first supported and then criticised Pitt without achieving acceptance as a respected independent. He certainly had no close ties with Opposition – he voted with Government in the Regency crisis – and they were not involved in the initiative in any way. Flood seems indeed to have acted without much hope for immediate success; his motive was rather to ventilate the question in the light of the Societies' enthusiasm, and extract statements of goodwill from Parliamentary leaders facing an election. The proposals themselves were distinctly cautious, more so in some ways than Pitt's in 1785: 100 extra Members for the counties, to be elected by all 'resident householders' paying tax of at least 50 shillings a year, the addition in seats being met, if required, by removing one of the two Members for certain agreed (obviously close) boroughs.[4] This was modest enough in all conscience, solidly based, as Flood said, on property, and eschewing those features of Pitt's earlier plans which had helped defeat them. It scarcely mentioned the more populous boroughs, though there was a hint of the need for new constituencies. The plan was essentially traditional. But it failed even to come to a vote.

It was killed in effect by Pitt himself, resting on the mood of the House. The Minister asked for an adjournment, but declared that if pressed he

---

1. And that was established primarily to counter the local Church and King Club which had arisen in the battle over the Corporation and Test Acts.

2. See I, 168.

3. An inconvenient invasion of the cosy agreement reached between Government and Opposition after earlier financial experiences, which in effect gave the constituency to the Foxites (see I, 617n1).

4. *P.R.*, XXVII, 196–297. Cf. I, 226–7 for Pitt's scheme in 1785, and op. cit., 75–6 for 1783.

would vote against the motion. The reason given was its untimeliness – though Pitt was also dubious of some of the details. His own efforts had been frustrated by 'the charge of innovation', and while he still thought that mistaken it had been enough to carry the day. It was this memory that deterred him from supporting a cause of which 'he continued to be as firm and zealous a friend as ever'. He would 'most certainly' try again at 'some more favourable' time; but there was no 'utility' in arguing 'certain practical principles of reform, consistent with the genius of the Constitution, to remedy peculiar abuses, which . . . they did not feel at that moment'.[1] Other speakers agreed, the avowed opponents of reform with relief, and several of its earlier supporters with a well tempered reluctance. Even Wilberforce and Duncombe, from the old stronghold of Yorkshire,[2] echoed the case for postponement, and Fox, while seeking a division, called it 'a sleeping question, for the present'.[3] So the House agreed, predictably enough; the motion for adjournment was carried, and the issue shelved until sterner times.

The discussion took place in the shadow – or the glare – of the debate on the Corporation and Test Acts. It followed in fact immediately, two days later, on 4 March.[4] The tumult of recent months discouraged any form of 'innovation'. But one of the strongest elements in the reaction had been the Dissenters' use of the French example, and the same influence loomed over this separate case. Burke was in full cry in the second debate, impelled precisely by such a combination; and the feeling was beginning – just beginning – to infect some others·within Opposition. A significant intervention came from William Windham, a regular party member since 1784. 'What, would the right honourable gentleman [Flood] advise them to repair their house in the hurricane season!'[5] Windham, it was true, was an opponent of Parliamentary reform. But he was no extreme enemy to the Revolution as a French domestic affair – he favoured the export of corn in June 1789,[6] and visited Paris later that summer, and again in 1791, without visible distaste. He had no connexion with Burke on the subject, and was indeed rather impatient of him while at the same time he nursed a general suspicion of Pitt. He had supported repeal of the Corporation and Test Acts in 1789. The speech was therefore widely noticed; and while it marked no break with his associates, and indeed served to show that the whole question was still quite open, it was·a possible pointer to

1. *P.R.*, XXVII, 209–10. A slightly different version of the speech is given in John Gifford's *A History of the Political Life of the Right Honourable William Pitt*, I (1809), 553.

2. See I, 67–76, 223–8.

3. *P.R.*, XXVII, 211. Fox of course had earlier been an ambivalent friend to Parliamentary reform.

4. P. 69 above.

5. *P.R.*, XXVII, 208. *P.H.*, (XXVIII, 467) follows the wording in *Speeches in Parliament of the Right Honourable William Windham . . .*, I (1812), 192.

6. See p. 45, n2 above.

future embarrassments which would gradually become more prominent, and would play their part in Pitt's own developing plans.

That process was visible in 1791. Throughout most of the preceding year Opposition was not greatly troubled by France. The debates of February and March 1790, in which Burke first showed his fears, were followed by a period of conscious forbearance. After all, this could be an election year, in which they were trying to act as a party. It was no time for breaking ranks, and in any case the subject was not yet central to their thinking. Nothing had happened in France itself to crystallise opinion further, and the main topics for the rest of the session were the Tobacco Excise bill and Nootka Sound.[1] Burke of course was increasingly alarmed, and going his own way, and Sheridan at the other extreme was flirting increasingly with reform. Their relations, strained since the Regency crisis, were now undeniably worse, and the great Whig lords were becoming rather uneasy. But at the end of the summer of 1790 Opposition was in quite good heart – in better heart, indeed, than it had been a year before – and the awkward question had been held successfully in the wings.

It could not be kept there much longer while Burke felt as he did. The publication of the *Reflections*, in time to greet the new session in November, was followed by his break with Fox in May 1791 in the debate on the Canada bill,[2] and three months later there appeared the *Appeal from the New to the Old Whigs*. Party zealots later ascribed their misfortunes to one or other of these events, and perhaps the first was the most serious, though the least direct in its Parliamentary effects. For the appearance of the *Reflections* put squarely before the public an issue which was soon developed in the First Part of the *Rights of Man* and the host of lesser pamphlets that followed.[3] The controversy was not yet polarised: many of the authors held intermediate positions, and Burke

1. See I, 246, 291–2, 553–9. The Excise bill provoked a good deal of activity from Opposition in its later stages – greater than I have suggested in my earlier volume.

2. I, 370.

3. It has been calculated that Burke's pamphlet, published on 1 November 1790, sold over 13,000 copies in the first five weeks, and some 19,000 in England, Scotland and Wales by the end of May 1791. Paine's, published in March 1791, is thought to have sold 14,000 in two months, and 16,000 in Britain (and some 40,000 in Ireland) by November. Burke cost five shillings, and Paine three: sums beyond the reach of poorer readers. But Paine was subsidised or reprinted in part by the reform Societies.

At least 25 other pamphlets can be listed in 1790–1 – there were more later – in response to Burke, and at least 24 in response to Paine. In some cases they too went through several editions. One must remember, however, that it had not been unusual for publications of current interest to attract a ready sale over the past decade: witness Sheffield's pamphlet on the prospects for trade at the end of the American War, and Wraxall's on the state of politics in 1787 (see I, 160 n1, 604). The size of the editions of course (on which evidence is scarce) is relevant.

and Paine themselves did not concentrate entirely on the French Revolution. Their arguments were directed to basic attitudes in the light of domestic circumstances which as yet were very largely independent of that event. But if the interaction was still in the shaping it had certainly been carried a stage farther, and the fact was underlined by a fresh wave of activity among the London Societies. After something of a pause towards the end of 1790, following the Parliamentary setbacks – the Society for Constitutional Information recorded 'no particular business' in the last quarter of the year –[1] a new impetus could be seen from the spring of 1791. Contact was established with provincial Societies, more use was made of the newspapers, arrangements were put in hand to circulate the *Rights of Man*. The anniversary of Bastille day was turned into a great occasion, leading, in an organised counterblast, to a serious 'Church and King' riot.[2] Mob violence was nothing new, and the excesses in this instance were confined almost entirely to Birmingham and its neighbourhood. The reformers' purpose and hopes remained bright, if no longer undimmed. But public caution was growing – the flight to Varennes had now taken place – and if many were still dismissive rather than hostile that fact itself could not be dismissed.

The Parliamentary Opposition had accordingly to be the more careful. The pressures were greatest of course on Fox himself. Thrust now somewhat on the defensive, his attitude would be crucial if a position had to be defined in due course. That time had not come yet, and throughout 1791 he succeeded largely in postponing it. He manoeuvred indeed with some skill in awkward though not wholly adverse conditions, relegating Burke to the sidelines and refusing to commit himself too far. It might be argued that he had forfeited some useful freedom already; that his language on the Revolution had already been too explicit. But if he had mounted a tightrope Fox was now able to keep his balance, and stay on his feet for another year. Although damaged by some further injudicious remarks – most notably in the Ochakov debate of 15 April[3] – and the subsequent split with Burke, he managed nevertheless to keep his options open. If he had earlier alarmed the Whig nobles he now made some conciliatory moves; if he had given some comfort to the Societies he now held aloof;[4] and the foundation of a Fox Club the year before, if it might seem to overlap with existing Whig bodies, gave him a more specific base from which to make his influence felt. In all this he was greatly helped by the general desire of Opposition not to be split or distracted at an otherwise hopeful time. For the great issue in 1791 was Ochakov, at least until the autumn, and as the Whigs moved to the assault other questions could be held in suspense. This was

1. P.R.O., T.S. 11/961, f. 219.
2. For which see pp. 131–2 below.
3. P. 25 above.
4. And even, though rather tactlessly, tried to counsel moderation to the French themselves (see p. 34, n3 above).

their best opportunity since the winter of 1788; there were correspondingly strong incentives to paper over the cracks.

The same considerations helped shape Pitt's reaction. If Fox was
concerned to blur the differences he was prepared to exploit them. He
had welcomed Windham's intervention early in 1790;[1] he was now
happy to accept Burke's, and drive the advantage home. There was
certainly good reason to do so in the spring and early summer, when the
Minister's position was shaken – some thought threatened – by the
Ochakov crisis. But despite Opposition's alarm the contacts seem still to
have been slight: while Ministers made polite noises to Burke over the
Canada bill, and also Warren Hastings's continuing impeachment, and
Pitt himself talked of 'co-operation' to defend the Constitution, the
overtures yielded no specific result.[2] The process, however, was greatly
advanced in the late summer and early autumn, after the publication in
August of *An Appeal from the New to the Old Whigs*. For Burke's attack then
moved from generalities to his own associates, and Government was
quick to accept the gift. Brought into closer conversation by the French
émigrés' affairs,[3] Ministers started to woo their old antagonist in earnest.
Camden and Dundas praised the pamphlet soon after it appeared,
Burke dined with Hawkesbury and then with Dundas,[4] and before the
end of September with Pitt. 'The reconciliation . . . of Mr. Burke with
the Ministry'[5] was now perceptibly under way, to its own satisfaction
and Opposition's grief.

These were good political tactics. But tactics after all relate to attitudes,
and one must try to define Pitt's at this time with some care. He certainly
did not share much of Burke's thinking on the Revolution: he remained
firmly neutral in foreign policy,[6] and he did not much fear 'French ideas'
at home. So far as one can judge, he was not unsympathetic to the earlier
hopes in France, and if Varennes was rather disturbing it was followed

1. *P.R.*, XXVII, 209.

2. See I, 369–70, 450–1, and *P.R.*, XXIX, 352 for Pitt's speech on 6 May. For doubts
as to the extent of his wish to exploit Opposition's embarrassment, which I cannot fully
share, see Herbert Butterfield, 'Sincerity and Insincerity in Charles James Fox',
Proceedings of the British Academy, LVII, 245n.

3. See p. 49 above.

4. This was perhaps the more indicative of straight political advantage since, while
Dundas had been helpful over Hastings's impeachment, he remained unwilling to be
involved too deeply in Burke's efforts for the émigré Princes; to Grenville, 15 September
1791 (*H.M.C., Dropmore*, II, 193).

5. *The Anecdotes and Egotisms of Henry MacKenzie*, ed. H.W. Thompson (1927), 144,
referring to the dinner with Dundas, at which he himself and Pitt had been present. Pitt
then 'pressed' Burke to stay the night in Downing Street, which he did, though politics
were not discussed (see I, 588, where the date in n3 should be 1 September). At
Grenville's prompting they dined in Downing Street in September, and in October Pitt
began to talk to Burke's son Richard about Irish affairs.

6. Pp. 42–3, 47–52 above.

by a lull.[1] The evidence is sketchy, but suggestive. In November 1790 Wilberforce recorded, after dining with Dundas, 'Much talk about Burke's book. Lord Chatham, Pitt and I seemed to agree, contra Grenville and Ryder'. Almost a year later he noted again, after dining at Downing Street, 'They talk much of Burke, particularly Grenville – and against La Fayette, who rather defended by Pitt'.[2] In general Pitt seems to have viewed 'the battle of the books' from something of a distance. 'Rhapsodies', he observed of Burke's 'French' writings later, '. . . in which there is much to admire, and nothing to agree with',[3] and while circumstances governed his response in practice there is a story – not a very firm one – that he may even have had some private sympathy with Paine.[4] If so, it might have been prompted by a matter of tone; for Paine's approach, whatever his object, was that of a true eighteenth-century man, the heir to a tradition of critical, hopeful 'common sense', whereas Burke's passionate thank-offering, in its more complex emotional dimensions, was a defence that yet, in feeling, held the seeds of a 'revolt against the century'.[5] Pitt would have known where he was with Paine – and he might have liked the prose style.[6] He was not drawn, by contrast, to apocalyptic fears.

But neither he nor Fox was in fact much swayed by this kind of warfare: Fox did not read the *Reflections* until the later part of 1791. Their judgments of events were made from their own positions and interests, and on occasions they could still find themselves not so very far apart. Party warfare seemed real enough to the actors in 1791, and when Pitt pleaded a 'risque' to 'our system both at home and abroad', and Dundas

1. P. 48 above.

2. *Life of Wilberforce*, I, 284, 315. Holland Rose, in his *William Pitt and National Revival*, 599, concluded that it was Grenville, not Pitt, who was unimpressed by Burke in 1790 (perhaps taking 'contra' in that sense, rather than as being 'contra' Chatham, Pitt and Wilberforce). But surely this would not have been the attitude of a man whom some months later was expressing '*utter* dislike' of the Revolution (see Lord St. Helens to Grenville, 15 June 1791; *H.M.C., Dropmore*, II, 99). Wilberforce himself, it should be noted, tried to prevent the quarrel between Burke and Fox in May 1791 (*Life*, I, 300).

3. To Auckland, 8 November [1795]; *A.C.*, III, 320.

4. 'Mr. Pitt used to say that Tom Paine was quite in the right; but then he would add, "What am I to do? . . . It would be very well, to be sure, if every body had sense enough to act as they ought; but as things are, if I were to encourage Tom Paine's opinions, we should have a bloody revolution; and, after all, matters would return pretty much as they were" . . .' (*Memoirs of the Lady Hester Stanhope, as related by herself in Conversations with her Physician . . .*, II (1845), 22). This, it must be remembered, would have applied to the later Part II as well as Part I of the work. Dr Meryon, who recorded the conversation, is probably reliable enough; but Lady Hester is certainly not – though her recollection, dating from a period when 'bloody revolution' had seemed a real possibility, may appear to be so surprising that it could not have been entirely wrong. Pitt may in fact have said something of the kind – it would not be out of character – which was then subjected to her habitual extreme exaggeration. It would be uncharacteristic of him, for instance, to have found any political theorist 'quite in the right'.

5. *Common Sense*, the title of an earlier famous pamphlet by Paine; cf. Alfred Cobban, *Edmund Burke and the Revolt against the Eighteenth Century . . .* (1929).

6. See I, 15, 396 n1.

confessed some months later to being 'certainly a Partyman',[1] the attitudes to France and reform were part of the spectrum. Ministerial suspicions of Fox were real, and at times acute, on these matters. But from different points of departure some of the leaders on either side were moving at a tangent here rather than in systematic conflict, and both Fox and Pitt themselves promoted measures which the other could support. They remained at one, of course, on the separate issue of the slave trade, and there was other non-party business, as usual, on which they were broadly agreed.[2] There were also two more striking and relevant proposals which, in a period of adjustment, disclosed patches of common ground.

One was Fox's libel bill, brought forward in the midst of the attacks on Ochakov.[3] Its aim was to transfer the decision in such cases from the judge to the jury. As things stood, the latter were confined to pronouncing on the facts of publication; subject to a discretional direction in law, they should now be responsible for the general verdict. Pitt agreed, and the motion passed through the Commons without a division. After a delay caused by the Parliamentary timetable, and despite fierce protests from Thurlow and Chief Justice Kenyon, it passed the Lords early in the summer of 1792.[4] There were cogent reasons in this instance for Pitt to have acted as he did. The law had not been working well, particularly in the past decade: it was widely held to be no longer suitable, and juries were reluctant to convict. As the Minister said, the change was unlikely to favour the obvious libeller, and convictions in fact increased after the Act came into force. The cause moreover had a history dating back to the days of Chatham; it had been argued by his favourite lawyer Camden against his bête noire Mansfield, and it was part of the tradition in which his son had been brought up. It was a palladium of whig liberties. Nevertheless the bill came at a time when Pitt was counselling caution on reforms which he might have been expected to support. The effect was of fundamental importance. 'Freedom of discussion is . . ., in England, little else than the right to write or say anything which a jury, consisting of twelve shopkeepers, think it expedient should be said or written'.[5] A palladium of liberty most certainly, and one that was soon to give Pitt himself some bad moments. But it was secured while he could still concur with Fox.

In the same period, the two men agreed on another question. In the spring of 1791 they supported a bill for the relief of the English Roman

1. Pp. 31, 54 above.
2. See I, 398–9 for the slave trade at this time. Other questions on which they did not oppose each other included Grey's motion for a committee to consider the effects of imprisonment for debt, Dundas's bill for the encouragement of seamen, and the Sierra Leone settlement bill. There was also agreement over Horne Tooke's petition on the Westminster election (p. 75 above).
3. On 20 May 1791. He had given notice of his intention in February.
4. On 21 May 1792. The Act was 32 Geo. III, c. 60.
5. A.V. Dicey, *Introduction to the Study of the Law of the Constitution* (10th edn., 1959), 246.

Catholics. Coming shortly before the Ministry's final refusal to aid any section of the Protestant Dissenters,[1] this pointed a contrast which yet derived from a similar context of feeling and argument. As with the Nonconformists, the business dated from the later eighties: in this instance from 1788. In February of that year an English Catholic committee had approached Pitt for help in removing restrictions which it claimed were now irrelevant as well as unjust. Relief, it was agreed, must be conditional on an oath of allegiance first being taken, as in the earlier Relief Act of 1778 and one of 1774 for Ireland,[2] and Pitt advised that authoritative views should therefore be collected on the extent of the Papal dispensing power. This was done, from the domestic clergy and some of the Catholic universities of Europe, and the answer emerged that the Church of Rome had no civil authority in England. With the help of Lord Stanhope, that unwearying reformer, a 'protestation' was then drawn up, and a petition prepared for Parliament.[3] Trouble followed, for the Catholic bishops (or rather Vicars Apostolic, for they had no sees) objected to the wording of the oath of allegiance, and were soon at odds with a large section of their flock. But although the dispute led to delay the motion for relief went ahead, and was introduced by the backbencher John Mitford, the future Law Officer and Speaker, who was an acquaintance and supporter of Pitt. It passed through the Commons without a division in April 1791; the wording of the oath was settled in the Lords; and the measure became law in June.[4]

The Act allowed Roman Catholics, on taking the oath, to occupy some local offices themselves or by deputy, and to practise at the Bar. It admitted Catholic peers, likewise after oath, into the King's presence like their Protestant fellows.[5] It regulated the practise of free worship indoors, and of free attendance at registered schools. It suspended many old, largely obsolete, penalties, and removed the old summary power to order Catholics (after taking the oath) to leave the cities of London or Westminster. Many restrictions still prevailed; the Act did not apply to Scotland,[6] and the test of an oath, and a large variety of specific

1. See p. 72, n1 above.

2. P. 61, n1 above for the former, and, for the wording of the latter, see the Irish statute 13 and 14, Geo. III, c. 35. The English Act of 1778 itself had an equivalent in Ireland, 17 & 18 Geo. III, c. 49.

3. Hence the description of the bill as initially announced, somewhat curiously at first sight, 'for the relief of Protestant Roman Catholic Dissenters' (*P.R.*, XXIX, 2). The title was later widened to include all English Roman Catholics, not only those 'protesting'.

4. 31 Geo. III, c. 32. It was perhaps fortunate that Thurlow was absent at the time through illness.

5. See I, 44.

6. Hardly surprisingly, perhaps, since the Act of 1778 had been successfully kept out of the northern kingdom. Scotland was however brought into line in 1793 (33 Geo. III, c. 44). Ireland of course was a separate matter, subject to its own Parliamentary proceedings (see n2 above). Catholic Relief Acts followed there in 1792 and again in 1793 (33 Geo. III, c. 21).

'The Repeal of the Test Act A Vision', *by Sayers, February 1790*

Edmund Burke. *Sculp. Thomas Poole*

Thomas Paine,
by Auguste Milliere after G. Romney

Major John Cartwright.

Engraved by G. S. Facius after Hoppner

Charles Grey. *Unknown*

exclusions and limitations, meant that the Roman community remained in a special class. Catholic Emancipation had to be won in the following century. But a very real step had been taken, and subject to its continuing provisos 'the position of Catholics who took the . . . oath', if not equal, 'was now . . . secure'.[1]

The bill was supported in the Commons by Fox and Windham and Burke and Pitt. All shades of leading opinion in fact were for once agreed. Pitt himself took a prominent part, as he had done from the beginning. Although he counselled delay on one occasion, to settle disputed points,[2] it was he who originally suggested the idea of obtaining opinions from the European universities. He intervened in the protracted quarrels over the wording of the oath; tried, unsuccessfully, to have the old penal statutes repealed and not merely suspended;[3] and lent the weight of his influence to seeing the measure through. 'He watched over the bill during its passage through the House, with the greatest assiduity . . ., removed the obstacles which opposed it, and . . . participated in the joy of the Catholics, at its ultimate success'. 'For this', wrote the secretary of their committee, who was a firm friend and supporter of Fox, 'they were indebted to none more than him'.[4]

It may seem remarkable that the Act should have passed with so little obstruction; still more that it led to no popular unrest. After all, the smaller measure of 1778 had been followed at no great interval by the Gordon riots. Old fears of Popery died hard; but, like Fox's libel bill if for other reasons, the Catholic Relief bill was fortunate in its time. It might have run into trouble earlier, and although its counterparts for Scotland and Ireland were passed later[5] an initial attempt for England might well have been opposed by then. In the mounting suspicion of change which gathered pace from 1792 even so widely acclaimed a reform could have raised serious doubts. But as it was, the consensus embraced both reforming zeal and conservative reactions, the result of an unusual conjunction of timing and cause. For in 1791 the Catholics were the beneficiaries of a distrust of the French Revolution which could yet live, at this stage, with an effort for 'liberal improvement'. The case appealed in almost equal degree to forces normally contrasted with each other, and if the supporters' arguments varied they were combined in their effect. The French clergy had suffered; the impression rubbed off on the English community; and there was no question here of the high-flown radicalism which had helped ruin the Dissenters' campaign. Nonconformists were busy, sometimes noisy, and their views were often contentious: the English Catholics were quiet, and few showed much liking for

1. Lecky's *History of England in the Eighteenth Century*, V (1887), 187.
2. Bernard Ward, *The Dawn of the Catholic Revival in England 1781–1803*, I (1909), 158.
3. See p. 82 above.
4. *Reminiscences of Charles Butler, Esq. of Lincoln's Inn*, II (1827), 68.
5. P. 82, n6 above.

events in France.[1] It was safe enough for Pitt at this point to further a reform which, in its direction and its limits, could also be taken as a defensive move.[2]

There was a somewhat similar background to another project, which in this case was dropped. Towards the end of 1791 Pitt formed a plan for the partial commutation of tithes. Based on some recent individual enclosure bills it sought, as national policy, to substitute cash payments for the surrender of corn in kind. The object, Pitt wrote to the Archbishop of Canterbury, was to 'obviate . . . complaints' – tithes of course were always apt to be a ready source of grumbling – which 'at the present moment' might be particularly important. For 'there are appearances which but too strongly indicate that [the subject] is likely to be agitated in different parts of the country', and any remedy would come best from 'those who wish well to the Establishment'. It was a clear warning to forestall trouble from radicals or Dissenters – the easier since two good harvests gave no cause to fear serious dearth – and the proposal seems to have come 'from the Minister himself'. So at least it was said a year later by a Bishop who claimed to know, and Pitt indeed stressed at the time that the scheme was drawn up at his own desire.[3] He had certainly been supplied with papers, and he expected action, for the subject figured among those 'likely to afford employment in the Christmas recess'.[4] In the event, however, it did not; the Bishops procrastinated, and the matter lapsed. It was revived towards the end of the decade, in a different setting and again unsuccessfully: tithes in fact

1. Thus Bishop Horsley, who did as much as anyone to see the Catholic bill through the Lords, organised an address from his clergy at just this time thanking Pitt for his 'steady opposition . . . to the repeated attempts of the Dissenters to sap the foundations of the Constitution by the abolition of the Test' (to Pitt, 9 April 1791; P.R.O. 30/8/146).

Pitt himself had feared at one point that 'the application of the Catholics . . . certainly can never be agitated without a possibility of its being improperly confounded with the question of the Dissenters' (to Grenville, 11 January 1791; *H.M.C., Dropmore*, II, 13). He proved to be wrong. The Dissenters themselves, to their credit and in contrast to their behaviour in 1778–80, supported the Catholic claim.

2. It might be argued that his attitude could also have owed something to Ministers' suspicion that Fox had (illegally) mobilised Roman Catholic votes in the famous Westminster election of 1784 (see Paul Kelly, 'Pitt versus Fox: The Westminster Scrutiny, 1784–5', in *Studies in Burke and His Time*, XIV, No. 2, 156–7). 1788, the year in which the Catholics approached the Minister (p. 82 above), saw a further by-election there. But the approach had been in February, five months before the need for the election arose with one of the sitting Members, Lord Hood, being appointed to the Admiralty Board.

3. Bishop of Bangor [John Warren] to Archbishop of Canterbury, enclosing papers, 23 January 1793 (Archbishop Moore Ms no. 8, Lambeth Palace Library); Pitt to Archbishop of Canterbury, 16 December 1791 (loc. cit., no.17).

The Minister's initiative might have been prompted, or at least stimulated, by a group of MPs in Devon who were involved in talks with the local Dissenters and others over a protest against the tithes, and were worried by a threat of pressure on Parliament from an association based on Devon and Sussex (John Rolle to Pitt, 17 November 1791, P.R.O. 30/8/173; and see also same to same, 19 January 1792, loc. cit.).

4. Pitt to Edward Eliot, 8 December 1791 (Pretyman Ms 435/39, West Suffolk R.O., Ipswich). His own papers on the subject are in P.R.O. 30/8/161.

were not commuted nationally until 1836. But the incident suggests an attitude towards which Pitt now appeared to be moving: a readiness to plug likely gaps in the defences by timely limited reforms, when the chance was presented and his fellow defenders could be brought to agree.

This, it might be held, was nothing much, and the question arises whether Pitt could and should not have done more from 1789 to 1791. It was the last period, one can argue, in which he had a freedom of manoeuvre of the same kind and, broadly speaking, as substantial as that which he had enjoyed so far. Thereafter the skies began to darken as fears and scares developed and, in the early wartime years, demands for reform could be shouted down. But in 1789 and 1790 Pitt was in a strong position, widely accepted in the country and with no rival clearly in sight. And again in 1791, particularly when the Ochakov crisis had passed, he could hope to influence a Parliament and a public that might still respond. Did he not throw away the chance of a broader unity among men of moderate views, in a way that might at least have lessened the extent of later divisions? These proved to be important years; they were seen as such by some at the time. Did he not allow them to become 'The Years of Lost Opportunity'?[1]

Perhaps the best opportunity, ironically, had already been lost. Pitt's greatest default in the pre-war period – as he himself may have come to recognise[2] – was probably his treatment of the Dissenters, which was decided in 1787. His arguments then, which may have tipped the scales, made it virtually impossible to disengage when the verdict might have been reversed in 1789, and by 1790 it was too late in the light, or heat, of the ensuing controversy. As the issues began to change – or as the French example began to impinge – he was already partly identified with a certain attitude. Looking back a few years later, a Dissenting historian concluded that it was here that political intolerance had first revived. 'That most important of political truths remained to be discovered – that mankind are with infinitely more ease and efficacy to be governed by mildness than severity'.[3]

Pitt's reaction to other pressures, whether applauded or condemned, should therefore be seen with this example in mind. His refusal to aid the Dissenters, or at least to remain on the sidelines, sharpened a wider attack which in turn provoked a sharper defence. But his posture on other issues was likely in any case to have been defensive, given his style and his reading of events. An atmosphere had been created on the

1. Donald Grove Barnes, *George III and William Pitt, 1783 to 1806* (1939), title to Chapter VI, where the dates however are 1789 to 1793.
2. P. 73, n1 above.
3. Belsham, *Memoirs of the Reign of George III*, IV, 286. And a postscript was added in May 1792, when Pitt opposed an unsuccessful motion by Fox to repeal certain statutes affecting specifically the Unitarians.

Corporation and Test Acts which was very important; which affected the line-up of forces; but hardly the subsequent decisions themselves. One may indeed wonder if these would have differed significantly in other hands, for they reflected a conception of government that was widely accepted and hard to oppose. But in any case it was one to which Pitt himself subscribed, and which, in the light of his conditions and forecasts, his temperament underlined.

The central charge of course, particularly in retrospect, was his attitude to Parliamentary reform. This in fact was the one specific instance that could be taken as springing from this time. In some others, as has been suggested, he moved cautiously forward; but the impression was naturally outweighed by his inaction here. The case for the defence was obvious. Whether he proposed a scheme of this kind or supported another, Pitt would be committed to facing the results. But the Commons were certain to reject a motion unaccompanied by a weight of petitions; feeling in the country had indeed been roused against 'innovation'; no Parliamentary group or leader was active: the time simply was not ripe. In the background moreover stood the King, who of course would be strongly opposed, and whose peace of mind had now to be taken into account. If Pitt had failed twice before, in the aftermath of a real agitation, how could he succeed now? There was no proper chance at all. However his strength might be gauged in general – and its limits must always be carefully assessed – he was in a weak position on this subject, and had no right to cause unnecessary friction for no return. Furthermore, it might be wrong. He was generally ready to respect opinion, and the circumstances had changed since his earlier attempts. The public then had been anxious and divided: it was now prosperous and broadly content, and events in France, which more than any others lay behind the demand, could be taken as a caution rather than an incentive. Why then countenance this question, for the sake of appearing consistent, when it was neither practical politics nor indeed to be desired?

Such reasoning was convincing to most men at the time: the critical reforming Societies stood for a small minority. But it does not really answer the retrospective charge. For conditions can easily change; they were to do so again very soon; and Pitt's own earlier arguments then proved apposite, and in tune with a stronger approach. Speaking on the subject in 1784, for the first time as the Minister, he was reported as saying that 'if once again a war should arise, the sense of the people could not surely be accurately obtained by the present mode of representation'.[1] Did this not turn out to be relevant in the early and middle

1. 16 June 1784; *Stockdale*, II (1785), 53. The speech is much less fully reported, and this passage does not appear, in *P.R.* and *P.H.* Pitt also then said that 'it was a cause that he would at any time take a pride to espouse' (loc. cit., 51). It was perhaps ironical that these remarks occurred in a speech against the introduction of a scheme in that session which he thought premature (see I, 223); and that when he spoke in 1790 in the opposite sense, it was in the first stage of the Nootka Sound crisis, which itself could have led to war.

nineties, and an argument for a wider franchise which was yet defined on his own terms?[1] One might object that it would have been cynical to support a cause which he knew would fail; but apparent cynicism at one level can mean wisdom and honour at another. It was not enough to speak mildly for a principle which you then promptly put aside. You then reached the position that reform was undesirable when the immediate future looked doubtful, and pointless or otiose when it did not. When precisely, it might be asked, would Pitt's conditions be fulfilled? His function was not simply to reflect opinion: there were occasions when a Minister should lead and persevere. If Pitt, it would be argued, had shown at that moment a readiness to act on his old beliefs, he could have reaped a reward in the course of the next few years. For when he embarked on repressive measures, which many accepted reluctantly, he would have achieved a more willing consensus if he had first tried for a moderate reform.

One may debate if such a result was likely, or how much difference it would have made. But in any event Pitt's perspective was not like this. He did *not* expect a war, or a sudden surge of unrest: on the contrary, as so often, he was hopeful of the future. France would settle down, or alternatively lose the first continental campaign; and he was confident of the prospects at home. The economy was booming in 1790 and 1791. The doubtful harvest of 1789 was followed by two years of plenty, the mild depression of 1788 had lifted, domestic industry was forging ahead. In almost every sector, as Wedgwood wrote of his own, manufacture 'darts forward at . . . an amazing rate',[2] and foreign trade was if anything moving even more dramatically. From 1789 to 1792 inclusive English exports rose by almost 50 per cent, and the figures had their effect on a Minister always alert to economic trends. When he came to draft the King's speech at the start of 1792, Pitt gave more space to the financial prospects than he had done in recent years. 'The continued and progressive improvement', he ended, 'in the internal situation of the country . . . must . . . operate as the strongest encouragement to a spirit of useful industry among all classes . . ., and above all, must confirm and increase their steady and zealous attachment to [the] constitution'.[3] The connexion, as so stated, expressed his firm and instinctive belief.

It also held a warning. Pursue political speculation too far, and the connexion might fail of its effect. Pitt acknowledged the possibility, he now felt it necessary to say so, it had entered into some of his speeches over the past two years. But he had not been seriously worried by the extent of reforming activity, for the prime example seemed likely to fail of its effect.

As to the publications . . . stated to have been disseminating

1. See p. 75 above for the similarity of Flood's proposals in 1790 to his own in 1785.
2. To Auckland in January 1792; quoted in T.S. Ashton, *Economic Fluctuations in England 1700–1800* (1959), 167.
3. *P.R.*, XXXI, 4. A draft or copy of the speech is in Pitt's papers, in P.R.O. 30/8/234.

throughout this country, with a view to extol the French revolution . . ., and to induce the people to look into the principles of their own constitution, he did not venture to think that there might be no danger arising from them; but . . . he saw no cause for immediate alarm . . . since he could not think the French revolution, or any of the new constitutions, could be deemed an object fit for imitation in this country, by any set of men . . .'[1]

The answer therefore was to be careful, to discourage immediate innovation, and above all for Government to pursue its steady well-tried course. For the point is that these questions now appeared of marginal importance to Pitt, both for the true situation of the country and for the policies of immediate concern. It was Nootka Sound and Ochakov abroad, and the familiar efforts for improvement at home, that occupied the Ministry throughout the greater part of these years. As for France, and the balance of the Constitution – well, time would be the best guide; meanwhile, as the like minded Grenville put it, 'peace and economy are our best resources; and with them I flatter myself *we* have not . . . much to fear'.[2] Of course the estimate was wrong. 'Patience' did not prove a good guide here, and Pitt could be accused once more of reading the signs in 'a counting-house spirit'.[3] He certainly showed his usual optimism and his inherent inclination, where he was not deeply engaged, to work with the grain.[4] He was relying on the methods and policies which by and large had served him well, there was no great change of attitude, his strengths and weaknesses remained the same. So far from suffering a sudden reaction he continued as before, content for the moment with smaller advances and otherwise to wait and see. He was not looking beyond the pattern with which he was familiar, and within which his energies and vision had been expressed. The less familiar forces were foreign to his instinct, and he found it hard to envisage their growth: viewing events abroad and at home he felt no premonition. 'Never fear', he told Burke towards the end of September 1791, '. . . depend on it we shall go on as we are, until the day of judgment'.[5]

1. Speech in the Commons on 6 May 1791; *P.R.*, XXIX, 351–2.
2. To Auckland, 23 August 1791 (*H.M.C.*, *Dropmore*, II, 172).
3. I, 88, 493 (where the charge was made by Burke); and see also op. cit., 280.
4. See I, 325.
5. This was at dinner in Downing Street (see p. 79, n5 above), and the source is Addington, who was there (the Hon. George Pellew, *The Life and Correspondence of the Right Honble. Henry Addington, First Viscount Sidmouth*, I (1847), 72). 'Very likely, Sir', Burke is said to have replied, 'it is the day of *no* judgment that I am afraid of'.

Part Two

CHAPTER IV

1792: The Dimensions of Unrest

I

On 21 May 1792, eight months after those words were spoken, a Royal Proclamation was issued for the preventing of seditious meetings and writings. Seven months later, in December, another was issued to call out part of the militia, the sea and land forces were increased, and an Aliens' bill was introduced. The confidence of a year before had been rudely shaken, and Government faced the possibility of war with France and the spectre of domestic unrest.

The two developments were linked, and reacted on each other. The apparent spread of 'the French infection' here in turn encouraged the French. It was indeed this double danger that raised such intense alarm: the position appeared quite different from that on the eve of a normal war. Nevertheless, internal unrest had its own causes and its own momentum, distinct in many aspects from the influence of 'French ideas'. Many of the troubles of that year, spasmodic at first and spreading later, owed little directly to any intellectual ferment. At the same time, without that pressure they would not have been viewed as they were, so that familiar symptoms were subsumed in a strange new threat. One must try to weigh the factors – some coincidental, some others contrasting – which accounted from the very start for the course and fate of discontent.

At this point, therefore, we must stand back from the course of the narrative. We need not, and cannot, examine in detail the ferment of political and social ideas which in varying forms carried their influence across the Channel. Nor can we follow the precise variations and relationships among the British movements. Nor, again, assess in detail the constituent domestic factors, some of which, in thought and attitude, have already been glimpsed. We can seek only to suggest categories in the pressures on Government; and above all to hold in mind the great persistent question why in fact there was not a British revolution as there was a French, when so many people thought it might come and when indeed certain factors in this country – exposed as it was in unique degree to economic change, familiar with popular organisation, at once a home of liberal thought and notorious for mob violence – might have seemed propitious. In proposing explanations we move some distance from Pitt himself and his immediate problems. But only in order to try the better to measure their real extent, and gauge the nature of the threat which henceforward was so greatly to colour his actions and, at first unevenly and then irresistibly, the attitudes of a generation.

The full impact of the French example fell towards the end of 1792. The first Proclamation, in May, was published at a time of little violence. In terms of actual disturbance, in fact, the first third of the year was quiet, and where there were undertones of apprehension – mostly in the midlands and parts of Lancashire and Yorkshire – they were largely the legacy of the Birmingham riots of the year before.[1] These had been sudden and highly unpleasant; but they were suppressed when action was taken, and the threat of contagion soon died away. They caused a more than local alarm, and ruffled the general impression of peace; but not unduly, and not for very long. Such other troubles as had been reported in the period since 1789 were of familiar kinds, in their nature and extent. Eighteenth-century England was well acquainted with riots: they were something that the system both digested and feared. But in these scattered incidents, average in number and mostly short-lived, there was nothing to suggest that experience could not cope.

The long age of seminal disturbance was indeed ushered in by a series of reports of the most familiar kind of all. In July and August 1789 there were bread riots in North Wales.[2] For throughout the century the most frequent single source of unrest had been the shortage or price of food, and particularly of wheat. Every decade had witnessed the effects, and they could be really serious – some of them worse, except perhaps for Birmingham, than anything happening in England between 1789 and 1794. There was nothing then to equal in scope the food riots of 1766, which had swept through almost every county south of the Trent; no incident so dramatic as that of two years later, when a mob protesting at prices invaded the courtyard of St James's Palace.[3] Bad harvests could frighten the magistrates of the towns as well as the farmers, and some trouble was not unlikely in 1789.[4] It was limited in the event, and there was no more from that cause in the next two years, when the wheat crops – particularly in 1791 – were very good.[5] But one of the depressing features of 1792 was a rainy summer, and the results swelled the grievances of the winter months.

1. See p. 78 above. There had also been a crop of disturbances, starting with an enclosure riot, in Sheffield late in July 1791 (possibly influenced by the excitement in Birmingham), and a seamen's strike in Liverpool (not a violent one) in the late summer. But they did not attract the same attention or bequeath the same fears as the Birmingham outrage.

2. P.R.O., H.O. 42/14, 50/381; taking the fall of the Bastille as a useful starting point. No unrest had been reported to the Home Office in the first half of the year.

3. All the more so in the latter instance because food riots were much scarcer in London than in the provinces throughout the century.

4. See p. 3 above.

5. 1791 was in fact the last year in English history in which the nation did not have to depend for part of its bread on imported supplies.

The decisive importance of food in the poor man's budget could be reflected in protests aimed specifically at other objects. It was one element – not always a major one – in the enclosure riots, in riots over lack of work, and demands for higher wages. Simple forms of industrial action had been known throughout the century, and indeed had led to counteractive legislation. A series of Acts since the 1720s (some forty by the middle nineties) forbade 'combinations' in particular trades, reinforcing the old common law against conspiracy. They were not markedly effective. Small-scale organisation persisted in the charitable friendly and benefit societies, which in fact proliferated so fast – and so typically of the age[1] – that an Act was passed in 1793 to regulate and protect them.[2] And, partly under such cover, collective bargaining and strikes went on: it was as a member of the Breeches Makers Benefit Society in 1793 that the young Francis Place found himself involved in a wages' strike. Not all trades moreover were covered fully by the various Acts, and some of the most important were not covered at all. But the protests of course in practice paid little heed to the exact state of the law. There were some notable instances in the second half of the century, with weavers and wool-combers, miners – particularly colliers – and seamen well to the fore. The results could be impressive. A seamen's strike for higher wages at Liverpool in 1775 produced prolonged and ugly riots, and the seamen of the Tyne made their power felt, more quietly, in 1792. It was on this type of labour unrest that food prices made the clearest impact, and could be angrily invoked as an urgent cause for redress.

But matters of livelihood in general could easily cause trouble. There were riots against taxes and turnpikes, imports and machinery, the introduction of new methods, competition over jobs. The authorities tended to lump them together as a single problem; and in some ways they were right. For whatever the contingent differences the causes were all directly economic, and sometimes they can be linked to broad economic trends. This is a truism; but it may bear stressing when one is following the events, so largely political, of the 1790s. Depression on a national scale was an obvious – though not invariable – cause of disturbance. It had been noticeably so, for instance, in the recessions of 1765–9, of 1772–3 and 1778–81, and the unrest had sometimes included political troubles – the 'Wilkes and Liberty' movement in the first case, the Association movement in the last. The same correlation can be observed in the nineties, and perhaps the most striking example was the year 1792 itself. For 1792 marked the turning point, of crucial importance in Pitt's career, between a cycle of broadly based prosperity and one of sharp economic fluctuations. More immediately, it saw the

---

1. See I, 168.
2. 33 Geo. III, c. 54. It was introduced by the joint Secretary of the Treasury, George Rose.

peak of a major three years' boom ending in a sudden if transient crisis in the winter of 1792–3. The setback was the more painful because it had scarcely been expected, and the boom had been on an unprecedented scale. In the early months of 1792 all seemed to be well. Manufactures and trade were flourishing even beyond the experts' hopes,[1] recent harvests had been abundant, money appeared plentiful, investment well spread. The economy seemed to be advancing to the highest level in the country's experience. But restraints in fact were present, in a classic form. For credit was over-extended, the money supply coming under great demand, and a sizeable proportion moreover had gone into overseas trade. There had indeed been some drain of bullion late in 1791, and the continuing process could be seen in retrospect as a '*hazardous Expansion of the Capital of the Kingdom*'.[2] When the skies began to darken abroad and the harvest failed at home confidence was shaken and there was also some shortage of coin. For wages had been rising in places in response to shortages of labour in the boom, and there was an added export of bullion to pay for imported wheat. The pressures began to combine: bread prices moved upwards, market rates of interest were already doing so, private securities came under strain, and the country banks – many recently established – found themselves hard pressed. The signs multiplied from the autumn; there was something of a panic in December; and the onset of war soon afterwards deepened a crisis already under way. By the standards of a few years later it was not of the first magnitude, and recovery followed in the spring of 1793, helped by action from Pitt. But peacetime conditions had gone for good, and his great budget of February 1792, so assured and so optimistic, served instead as their epitaph.

A reading of the national indices therefore supplies a broad economic background to the surge of dissatisfaction late in 1792. A similar correlation, with the factors in different balance, can again be suggested a few years later, for 1795–7. It is possible indeed to construct a chart of 'social tension' for the whole decade in which busines cycles and average wheat prices are the leading components.[3] The exercise has its value in a period of diverse agitation, for its reminder that disturbance rises most readily from causes with simple effects. It also offers a frame of reference, crude though it may be from the nature of the sources, against which to set the incidence of the disturbances themselves. At the same time one must be careful, for apart from the shortcomings of some of the figures, national trends and average levels are defined perforce in general terms. The impact on the other hand has to be measured by local conditions,

1. Cf. I, 163 (in 1790), 276n4 (February 1792).

2. Sir Grey Cooper [a former joint Secretary of the Treasury] to Henry Addington, enclosed in Addington to Pitt, 2 July 1793 (Stanhope Ms S5 01/1, Kent C.A.O.).

3. W.W. Rostow, 'Business Cycles, Harvests and Politics' (*The Journal of Economic History*, I, no. 2).

time lags are often uncertain,[1] and in a largely unindustrialised society irregularities are the more marked. A rather closer look at the labour unrest of 1792 discloses, within the overall pattern, a distinctly varied scene.

In the first place one is struck by the great differences in time scale, and particularly by the speed with which trouble could start and, often, die down. This last in fact was true of the whole range of unrest. The Home Office papers are filled with letters from authorities taken unawares, and relieved a little later by the disappearance of the immediate threat. 'The last riot having happened . . . quite suddenly and unexpectedly'; 'I have just heard that the sailors have refused to go to sea'; 'everything here is now in a State of Perfect Tranquillity' again[2] – such remarks recur, though of course by no means universally, very much as they had done over past decades. Labour disturbances are apt by nature to produce sudden shifts of mood, and in this period they were often stopped by sending in the troops. But not always, and such a measure could itself have varying effects, for much turned on the precise source of trouble and on local relationships. One may cite two contrasting examples from this particular year. In May 1792 there was a riot in Leicester over the cost of meat, entirely unforeseen and soon successfully dispersed. The prices in point of fact were not unduly high compared with those in neighbouring areas, and indeed they were said to have been lower than a short while before. But the cost of food of course was a sensitive subject, easily affected by rumour, and Leicester was a market town with a well-earned reputation for riot. The respectable inhabitants, however, rallied under an energetic Mayor, and the affray was virtually over when a troop of horse arrived. Five months later a wages' strike began among the seamen on the Tyne. The men in this instance were more highly disciplined, their case was effectively put, and many of the shipowners felt uneasy about the merits of their own arguments in a region over which the magistrates in any case had slender control. The local authorities were therefore cautious and not unsympathetic, there was little violence, and when soldiers – and in this case sailors – were sent they in turn behaved with restraint. As a result the strike was prolonged,

1. One has also to choose the time unit. In the chart for the nineties mentioned above it was taken as the calendar year, which can give a curious impression. Thus 1792, the peak of a business cycle, is shown as registering the lowest social tension of the period 1790–1806 – which would have surprised the Government – and the tension in 1797 is given as less than that of 1795–6 (loc. cit., 220). Furthermore there is the importance of timing within the cycle. Food riots, the most direct product of adverse conditions, did not necessarily occur at the worst moment of a trough, but often in response to sudden sharp temporary movements of supplies and prices.
2. Copy of Mayor of Leicester to Secretary at War, 15 October 1792; Marquess Townshend to Dundas, referring to King's Lynn, 31 October 1792; Charles Stisted to Home Office, referring to Ipswich, 18 November 1792 (all in P.R.O., H.O. 42/22).

but it was settled by negotiation, through the efforts of a respected local MP.[1] To the Government, called on for troops, the two episodes were items in a series. But their courses responded to the different conditions in either case.

The range of such conditions turned very largely on the site of the trouble. Locality is crucial in any assessment of unrest. The point was brought out clearly in the summer of 1792, when the Deputy Adjutant General of the Forces set out to inspect the midlands and southern Lancashire and Yorkshire. In Manchester at that moment he found more cause for uneasiness in some of the 'higher description' than in 'the lower class of the inhabitants'. Liverpool, recently the scene of wage protests, appeared now to be 'firmly' and loyally 'united'. Sheffield on the other hand provided 'a picture of a very different complexion': it was a 'centre of . . . seditious machinations', filled with 'violent language, and . . . extreme views'. Chesterfield, twelve miles distant, was contentedly the 'opposite'. Nottingham showed a mixture of prosperity and tendency to riot; Loughborough, not far away, was quiet, though perhaps uneasily so. Leicester as ever was 'extremely prone to Riot'; Birmingham more peaceful, but subject to 'frequent little affrays'.[2] One of the authorities' worst fears, indeed, was always the danger of imported disturbance, from restless spirits, or roving bands of workers, or simply men seeking jobs from outside. In the aftermath of the Birmingham riots in 1791 the Lord Lieutenant of Warwickshire and the High Sheriff of Oxfordshire were on the watch for 'stragglers' who might carry the virus farther afield. In Manchester at the same time it was 'the very numerous and *foreign* population' (meaning mostly from other areas, though the Irish were also included) that posed the main threat. When wage riots seemed possible in Liverpool in the spring of 1792, 'many colliers . . . from distant parts' arrived in the hope of fomenting trouble. Colliers again tried to raise the countryside in the summer following protests over wages at Bristol, and a few months later bands of English miners were roaming discontentedly through North Wales. Coventry looked doubtfully at Birmingham, Leeds at Sheffield, Derby at Nottingham; Truro feared the 'tin men' of Bodmin.[3] The shadows of contiguity stretched across a patchwork scene.

Such apprehensions often centred on certain industries and trades.

1. See Town Clerk of Leicester to Home Office, 23 May 1792 (loc. cit.) for the first case. Norman McCord and David E. Brewster, 'Some Labour Troubles of the 1790's in North East England' (*International Review of Social History*, XIII, Part 3), and Austin Vernon Mitchell, 'Radicalism and Repression in the North of England, 1791–1797' (M.A. thesis, Victoria University of Manchester, 1958), offer balanced accounts of the second.

2. Lieut. Colonel Oliver de Lancey to Dundas, 13 June 1792 (H.O. 42/20). This sums up a series of reports.

3. H.O. 42/19–22 *passim*.

This had been so since medieval times. Miners and sailors were obvious examples of the effect of structures or traditions which lent themselves to cohesive and often self-contained organisation. Some groups of textile workers, too, had histories of protest – the Wiltshire wool-combers and weavers and the Spitalfields silk workers were well known. Their continued prominence suggests that the problem still had little to do with the rising feature of the newer factory system: in the troubles of 1792, indeed, the emphasis often fell the other way. For while the face of industry and the balance with agriculture were beginning to change, small-scale patterns were still predominant, and in fact often encouraged by the early stages of the industrial revolution. It was precisely this kind of organisation that was said to be the trouble in Sheffield. 'The Manufactures of this Town are of a nature to require so little capital . . ., that a Man with a very small sum of Money can employ two, three, or four Men, and this being generally the case, there are not in this, as in other great Towns, any number of persons of sufficient weight who could by their influence, or the number of their dependants, act with any effect in case of a disturbance'.[1] It would indeed be rash to try to proportion unrest in this period between any one scale of industry or trade and another: the occupations most prone to disturbance, such as those already cited, themselves comprised units of varying types and size. And beyond their ranks in turn, the crowds of the early nineties seem to have had their fair share of unattached masters and their men. Often in fact, as in France, these provided the driving force. And this is not surprising, for they were both vulnerable to economic pressures and, placed in their own diversity at a sensitive point in the social order, could be highly conscious of its threats, opportunities and constraints.

For protest, whatever the pattern of work, was not the product of hardship alone. Distress – direct distress – was of course a major cause of trouble, and with ample occasion; but it was not the only one. In Manchester in 1791 there was held to be a mixture of reasons for 'the very general Spirit of Combination among all Sorts of Labourers and Artizans'. There was 'the Introduction of Machinery to abridge Labour in Weaving'; there was also the fact that trade on the whole was 'wonderfully prosperous', which unfortunately produced its own 'attendant Evils'. Men 'estranged, unconnected, and in general . . . in a species of Exile' – a penetrating description of change and mobility in the countryside as in the towns – were flocking to take up work and disturbing the local balance. 'High' wages offered greater leisure, and

---

1. De Lancey to Dundas, 13 June 1792 (H.O. 42/20). Another paper reaching Dundas at this time stressed the same contrast between the structure of the cutlery industry of Sheffield and the patterns in the Yorkshire 'clothing' towns (from Lord Loughborough, 24 April [1792]; S.R.O. Melville Castle Ms GD 51/1/17/2).

thus – a familiar cry – 'filled with Liquor' they 'engaged in very *desperate* Affrays'.[1] In Nottingham a year later it was 'the facility of getting money in the manufactures, and the dissipation which accompanies it' that was said to 'dispose' people to riot.[2] It was not indeed always the worst paid who rioted or struck. The miners of Cornwall were more obstreperous than those of Anglesey, where wages were lower; some wage rates were higher on the troubled Tyne than at Hull, which was still a quiet port. The real wages of cotton weavers, of London artisans and of agricultural labourers may possibly have reached their peaks precisely in 1792. But to the authorities' dismay this did not always mean social peace: sometimes in fact it seemed to produce the opposite. '. . . As the wages given to Journeymen' in Sheffield 'are very high, it is pretty generally the practice for them to work for three days, in which they earn sufficient to enable them to drink and Riot for the rest of the Week'.[3]

Such accusations, once more, were thoroughly familiar. Improvidence and idleness had long been charges levied at 'the lower sort'. And if some, like Adam Smith, suggested an answer in higher payments, more were disposed to turn to stricter discipline or education. A whole literature existed on the subject. But the cause was hard to remedy, for it lay largely within the structure and practices of labour itself. If one looks at many trades, including agriculture, in this phase of industrialisation, the endemic feature was still *under*employment rather than *un*employment. Mines and factories and larger workshops could doubtless have done with greater discipline, and employers throughout the century tried in various ways to secure it. But they were by no means always successful – particularly perhaps in the mines – and old habits were widespread and stubbornly persistent. This indeed was bound to be so, for if many men worked no harder than they had to, the working week itself was different for many from its nineteenth-century successor. Many forms of labour were still part-time, leaving opportunity for others: for farm-work above all, or for cultivating a patch of land. Some might pay well enough for a man, given the traditional background, to lay off for a few days or even (as with sailors) weeks. They might (as with builders or tailors) vary in intensity at different times. And they were apt to be highly uncertain, open to the winds of chance. When one talks of economic disturbance one must recall what the economy was: one in which, in a decade of rising prices and intermittent trade depressions, it was the casual nature of so much employment – as with building labourers or dockers in this century; the incidence in varied, often static, conditions of shifts of occupation, particularly among younger men – the

1. Thos. Bayley and Henry Norris to ?, 19 July 1791 (H.O. 42/19).
2. De Lancey to Dundas, 13 June 1792 (H.O. 42/20).
3. Loc. cit. Similar complaints were made at the same time from Leicester, where wages in the dominant hosiery trade had been rising in the past few years. And cf. *The Torrington Diaries . . .*, ed. Cyril Bruyn Andrews, III (1936), 33.

journeyman, by definition mobile, was still, as earlier, a focus of protest;[1] the impact on local structures of growing urban, but not necessarily factory, populations; and the vulnerability of local markets for the smaller master and his pool of labour, that went far, at this quite early stage in a long process of increasing change, to define the immediate connexions between economic pressures and social unrest.

II

There were also connexions that were not so immediate, or leave a fainter trace. By no means every riot could be put down, simply or at a remove, to wages or jobs or the price of food. There were 'collateral difficulties', to recall a phrase of Pitt's on a former occasion of serious disquiet,[2] and even when economic and social tensions were obviously combined they could contain overlapping areas, and sometimes inner contradictions. In the enclosure riots, for instance – fewer in the eighties and early nineties, in a lull between the earlier and later spates of enclosure bills – direct economic grievance was only part of the story. The developments in farming methods, without which food production could not have risen, undoubtedly caused real hardship and injustice. The enclosures themselves played some part – how large it is hard to say – in the uneven drift from the land to the towns. They also brought benefits to other farming households, and if its national proportion may have been shrinking the size of the agricultural labour force is thought to have increased. So possibly did the numbers of small farmers and cultivators (full or part-time), compensated for their shares in the old open fields. The effects on living standards are disputable, and there were factors other than enclosure at work: the rapid growth of population, and the unequal pace of local developments. As so often in an economic process, much was blamed on what could readily be seen. But that was the more likely because the impact here fell on a way of life. And this was very important, in the kind of reaction provoked.

> Those fenceless fields the sons of wealth divide,
> And even the bare-worn common is denied.

> The poor in these parishes may say, and with
> truth, 'Parliament may be tender of property:

1. Cf. Peter Laslett, *The World we have Lost* (2nd edn., 1971), 13–14.
   One must be careful all the same not to overemphasise the static nature of many communities: recent research has suggested degrees of mobility in some areas at least, at different points in a long period, greater than had been assumed. The point is rather that the normal condition of a community was held to be one of stability, and its administration was designed on that premise.
2. I, 59.

All I know is that I had a cow and an Act of
Parliament has taken it from me'.[1]

Such feelings ran deep, sometimes with justice and always understandably, and they were not to be dispelled by the latest arguments
from above. For that matter, reasoned argument was not always very
conspicuous, when it came it all too easily bade self-love and social be the
same, and in any case men do not always take kindly to being improved.
They did so quite often in point of fact where they could affect the issue,
and successful resistance, too, might lead to something worse. Un-
enclosed lands, often but not always among the poorest by nature,
supported in wartime conditions some of the worst villages in the
country; and the problem impinged on the towns as well. If the common
lands of Nottingham and, still more, Coventry for instance had been
enclosed, building could have spread, probably with happier social
results. As it was, gross overcrowding was the cost of preserving ancient
rights. Familiar aids to subsistence, perhaps above all familiar custom –
the tried and well-worn ways – could exact a high price.

In both these urban cases the commons were the property of the
Corporation: private landlords were the main agents of change. The
history of the enclosures again points the need to look closely at local
relationships in judging movements of national scope. England was a
country both highly integrated and minutely differentiated, and the
interaction of central policies with regional patterns and interests is a
basic, and for long was a prominent, theme of English history. This
certainly remained true of the movements of the 1790s; and 'Sacrifice
the Parts, What becomes of the Whole?'[2] We do not know enough: we
need a modern Domesday Book of local studies before we can properly
reassemble the evidence. But the more precise the investigations, and the
deeper they go, the clearer it is that general categories were sharply
refracted in particular forms. The presence or absence of a great
landlord, or of a well established squirearchy – for the country was not
simply a series of manorial estates; the impact of county families, whose
own mutual relationships varied, on the varied patterns of the local
towns; the presence or absence of an urban Corporation – for some of the
fastest growing centres were not incorporated, with significant effects on
their identities and strength; the nature and extent of the Parliamentary
franchise, and the vigour or otherwise of the electors – much could turn
on the qualifications for the Freedom, deriving largely from local trades;
the strength and complexity of denominational loyalties, in the country

1. Oliver Goldsmith, *The Deserted Village* (1770), lines 307–8; Arthur Young, quoted
in J.L. and Barbara Hammond, *The Village Labourer 1760–1832* (1911), 83–4.
Goldsmith's target, unlike Young's qualification, was really 'luxury' rather than
efficiency.
2. William Blake, annotations (c. 1808) to Sir Joshua Reynolds's *Discourses* (1788),
Discourse IV, 83.

as in the towns – the relations between Church and Chapel, and the fortunes of the different branches of Dissent: such factors must always be considered in assessing the sum of local responses to questions and policies of wider concern. There was a crowded historical palimpsest, subject to continual accretions and erasions. Social networks contained and reflected particular blends of convention and law.

Unrest in such a context could be aimed at local or at national issues, the former sometimes expressed in the latter's terms, the latter sometimes embodied rather oddly in the former. There were examples to be found in any decade, from almost any county or town. A dispute over paving or a right of way could be invested with the weight of national divisions; equally the line-up of national forces could be revealed in a parish dispute. The currents ran in either direction, and with very real strength. For the pattern of regional identities did not mean a lack of definition at the centre: local responses varied within a unified whole. One common denominator indeed was the fact and the role of the riot itself, on lines and within limits that were nationally accepted. Popular tumults of course had long been a common occurrence throughout Europe: they were very far from being English property alone. But open individual violence *was* a well known English characteristic, a byword abroad and in some ways a source of self-satisfaction at home. Though now declining in some of its forms it was constantly erupting, and at different social levels: in the street and the market, the camp and the theatre, the entertainment garden and the public school. Pleasures and spectacles were still often brutal – the cockfight, the prizefight, the pillory – and grievance or, equally, enthusiasm was readily vented on the spot. Foreigners were always noting the fact, and deploring or occasionally half admiring it. They put it down to native animalism, and sometimes also to native independence.

This last was true enough in its way, for such behaviour had a moral aspect. It contained, often confusedly, assertions of right. Jostling in the streets, stones thrown at windows which had not been lighted for a popular occasion, cheering, hissing and mobbing powerful persons – such things were the reverse of the coin, the underside of a society built on deference. When the Crown Prince of Denmark visited London he found that 'no one, not even a common sailor, gave the wall to him'.[1] When George III recovered from his illness in 1789, the Prince of Wales was forced to give three cheers outside the doors of Brooks's. Anything strange above all was unpopular, as the unfortunate foreigners found: they were still apt to be insulted, and their belongings pilfered, as a

---

1. M. D'Archenholz, *A Picture of England . . . translated from the French* (Dublin, 1791), 4. London of course was the great object of foreign comparison, and not by foreigners alone:

The fairest capital of all the world,
By riot and incontinence the worst (William Cowper, 1785).

matter of habit.[1] Novelty was generally suspect, and old sanctions were jealously protested, even if – often because – they could not be preserved. There was a strong, and articulate, feeling for 'the rights of the freeborn Englishman', and these could be held to apply to the action of the crowd, or mob. The food riot perhaps in particular had its 'moral economy', its sense of justice, and when this was felt strongly enough collective behaviour could reflect the fact. The crowd could sometimes show its own discipline, and confine itself to chosen offenders.[2] Violence, if endemic, was not always indiscriminate. It claimed a place within an order of which it was a part.

The sense of inclusion was indeed very strong. It both directed and limited much of the unrest. The 'moral economy' of the food riots had a basis in the decline of the Elizabethan statutes of price regulation, themselves deriving from medieval concepts. It was a demonstration against the impact of freer market forces on a hierarchical paternalistic structure. Wage strikes and riots, too, had something of the same element: it was the survival of the regulating system in the ribbon trade of Coventry, for instance, that largely saved the town from the disorders of the 'freer' hosiery trades in Leicester and Nottingham. In so far as the protests over livelihood had an explicit political content it was in fact very largely an appeal to a better past. And this could very often lead to a distinction being made between the politicians in power and the more enduring elements of the state. The Ministry of the day might be hissed and hooted, but the system itself was disassociated from the complaints. 'However the people [of Liverpool] might differ in relation to their opinions of the present Administration, yet in support of the general government and constitution of the country they were, with few exceptions, firmly united'. The seamen of the Tyne, in their wages' strike, greeted a man-of-war which ran aground on arrival, 'We know well enough, by God Captain, what you've come about, but, damn it, we'll save His Majesty's ship for all that'.[3] These are examples from 1792, which could be paralleled in earlier years. They could also be contrasted with cries of an opposite kind. The King might be cursed, gentility damned, old rights of equality cheered; there is evidence both ways, and it can be cited according to choice. Such remarks in fact do not in themselves throw a very clear light on the balance of sentiment: on degrees of disaffection and acceptance and support. That is not to say

1. When the French refugees arrived in large numbers in 1792, one of the first cares of those trying to look after them was to protect their baggage, known to be foreign, on the roads to London.

2. For the argument, and examples, see E.P. Thompson, 'The Moral Economy of the English Crowd in the Eighteenth Century' (*Past and Present*, no. 50); R.B. Rose 'Eighteenth Century Price Riots and Public Policy in England' (*International Review of Social History*, VI, no. 2).

3. De Lancey to Dundas, 13 June 1792 (H.O. 42/20); McCord and Brewster, loc. cit., 375.

there were not forces at work which would change the tone of articulate protest. It does suggest that, as things stood, protest had not been systematic, and that at the level of professed motive it included a highly conservative strain.

This was shown – perhaps at first sight curiously – in those riots, fewer in number, which were or were supposed to be directly political or religious. For more often than not these were mounted ostensibly to defend the Constitution. From the days of Sacheverell, the Ormonde riots, and Walpole's excise tax to the militia riots of the sixties and seventies[1] and the Gordon and Birmingham disturbances, the mob or its instigators were not out to challenge the system, but on the contrary to save it from an alleged threat. It was similarly not very hard to start a demonstration in favour of war – however fierce the resistance when pressing for the forces began. The first specifically political riot in England in the age of the French Revolution was a Church and King demonstration at Manchester in 1790. Like the anti-Catholic troubles of ten years before and those against Dissenters a year later, it reflected the force of an appeal to the legacy of the past.[2]

This did not mean that all those taking part necessarily did so for the same reasons, or that the demonstrations were always exactly what they seemed. Some were countenanced, and may have been incited, by respectable men – squires or parsons or merchants – for their particular ends. 'Raising a mob' was an old device, though it might sometimes take strong nerves. The crowd was a facile instrument, easily moved and often very frightening, which could be used to underline one's power, or press a case, or defeat one's opponents. Wilkes was the archetype of this exploitation on a major issue; Parliamentary politicians – including Fox – were usually more cautious,[3] and it was the minor provincial figures who generally played that kind of, more restricted, game. But the crowd itself too, at least on occasions, seems to have followed its own purposes, which could give a rather different look to the ostensible cause. In the Gordon and the Birmingham riots, for example, there is evidence to show that destruction of property was limited largely to the most prosperous offenders. The poorer Catholic and Nonconformist dwellings, and even places of worship, were left more or less alone: it was the homes of the powerful and well-to-do, and the more fashionable chapels and meeting houses, that on both occasions suffered the heaviest damage. This may suggest, as has been argued, that things were not

1. One of which, at Hexham in 1761, produced the worst casualties inflicted by troops in any provincial riot of the century: said to be over 100 killed and wounded.

2. Of course there were political disturbances which were not related to such general themes, for instance the Keppel riots of 1780 (see I, 21–2). For the role of the election riot see pp. 169–70 below.

3. As a radical of an earlier generation put it, 'they who raise mobs raise the Devil'; William Beckford in 1768, quoted in John Cannon, *Parliamentary Reform 1640–1832* (1973), 69.

quite as they might appear: that a respectable rallying cry could be a pretext for dangerous sentiments. The banner of Church and State may have covered a '"levelling" instinct'; even perhaps have allowed 'an explosion of latent class hatred'.[1]

One must not forget that later in the nineties, when the levelling instinct had been well aired, riots still took place against Jacobins and democrats. None the less it would be unwise to dismiss the first of these findings, even if the second raises terminological – and thus deeper – doubts. Nor in fact need one be surprised that social resentments should have found an outlet in a constitutional cause. The basic feeling of poor against rich was by no means incompatible with stubbornly conservative protest in society as it stood. Folk memories were immensely strong. They penetrated radical thought itself. And in any case these non-radical cries had always had their radical element. Fear of Popery, in so far as it was not simply xenophobic, was remembered by the London mob as a weapon against the Court, the synonym for power;[2] leading Dissenters, who combined so effectively a Protestant ethic with worldly success, were a natural target, particularly in the midland towns. Such subversive emotions might well find a home in the body of respectable tradition, when the old seventeenth-century revolutionary theories had sunk into hidden streams. For popular unrest, even when it was overtly political, lacked a visible intellectual framework other than that of the established order itself. The outbreaks had long been specific and largely unconnected, clothed very often in the terms of the system within which they were contained. This still held good in the 1780s, and if the position was now to change – if the familiar types of disturbance were to be fused into something different – one ingredient therefore must be a fresh impact of ideas.

III

In the winter of 1791–2 the reforming movement underwent some changes of far-reaching importance. It contracted in some respects and expanded in others, with profound effects both for the short and for the longer term. The existing London Societies were busy, although the balance between them was shifting. The Whig Club[3] remained officially sympathetic, though increasingly divided by doubts. But it was concerned with the Parliamentary struggle rather than with reform as such, and it was not designed to promote the cause in the country. That

1. George Rudé, *The Crowd in History . . . 1780–1848*, 224; R.B. Rose, 'The Priestley Riots of 1791' (*Past and Present*, no. 18), 84.

2. So it had been used a century before by Shaftesbury, the greatest manipulator of the mob before Wilkes.

3. P. 54 above. The contribution, if any, of the more recent Fox Club (p. 78 above) is obscure.

there were not forces at work which would change the tone of articulate protest. It does suggest that, as things stood, protest had not been systematic, and that at the level of professed motive it included a highly conservative strain.

This was shown – perhaps at first sight curiously – in those riots, fewer in number, which were or were supposed to be directly political or religious. For more often than not these were mounted ostensibly to defend the Constitution. From the days of Sacheverell, the Ormonde riots, and Walpole's excise tax to the militia riots of the sixties and seventies[1] and the Gordon and Birmingham disturbances, the mob or its instigators were not out to challenge the system, but on the contrary to save it from an alleged threat. It was similarly not very hard to start a demonstration in favour of war – however fierce the resistance when pressing for the forces began. The first specifically political riot in England in the age of the French Revolution was a Church and King demonstration at Manchester in 1790. Like the anti-Catholic troubles of ten years before and those against Dissenters a year later, it reflected the force of an appeal to the legacy of the past.[2]

This did not mean that all those taking part necessarily did so for the same reasons, or that the demonstrations were always exactly what they seemed. Some were countenanced, and may have been incited, by respectable men – squires or parsons or merchants – for their particular ends. 'Raising a mob' was an old device, though it might sometimes take strong nerves. The crowd was a facile instrument, easily moved and often very frightening, which could be used to underline one's power, or press a case, or defeat one's opponents. Wilkes was the archetype of this exploitation on a major issue; Parliamentary politicians – including Fox – were usually more cautious,[3] and it was the minor provincial figures who generally played that kind of, more restricted, game. But the crowd itself too, at least on occasions, seems to have followed its own purposes, which could give a rather different look to the ostensible cause. In the Gordon and the Birmingham riots, for example, there is evidence to show that destruction of property was limited largely to the most prosperous offenders. The poorer Catholic and Nonconformist dwellings, and even places of worship, were left more or less alone: it was the homes of the powerful and well-to-do, and the more fashionable chapels and meeting houses, that on both occasions suffered the heaviest damage. This may suggest, as has been argued, that things were not

1. One of which, at Hexham in 1761, produced the worst casualties inflicted by troops in any provincial riot of the century: said to be over 100 killed and wounded.

2. Of course there were political disturbances which were not related to such general themes, for instance the Keppel riots of 1780 (see I, 21–2). For the role of the election riot see pp. 169–70 below.

3. As a radical of an earlier generation put it, 'they who raise mobs raise the Devil'; William Beckford in 1768, quoted in John Cannon, *Parliamentary Reform 1640–1832* (1973), 69.

quite as they might appear: that a respectable rallying cry could be a pretext for dangerous sentiments. The banner of Church and State may have covered a ' "levelling" instinct'; even perhaps have allowed 'an explosion of latent class hatred'.[1]

One must not forget that later in the nineties, when the levelling instinct had been well aired, riots still took place against Jacobins and democrats. None the less it would be unwise to dismiss the first of these findings, even if the second raises terminological – and thus deeper – doubts. Nor in fact need one be surprised that social resentments should have found an outlet in a constitutional cause. The basic feeling of poor against rich was by no means incompatible with stubbornly conservative protest in society as it stood. Folk memories were immensely strong. They penetrated radical thought itself. And in any case these non-radical cries had always had their radical element. Fear of Popery, in so far as it was not simply xenophobic, was remembered by the London mob as a weapon against the Court, the synonym for power;[2] leading Dissenters, who combined so effectively a Protestant ethic with worldly success, were a natural target, particularly in the midland towns. Such subversive emotions might well find a home in the body of respectable tradition, when the old seventeenth-century revolutionary theories had sunk into hidden streams. For popular unrest, even when it was overtly political, lacked a visible intellectual framework other than that of the established order itself. The outbreaks had long been specific and largely unconnected, clothed very often in the terms of the system within which they were contained. This still held good in the 1780s, and if the position was now to change – if the familiar types of disturbance were to be fused into something different – one ingredient therefore must be a fresh impact of ideas.

III

In the winter of 1791–2 the reforming movement underwent some changes of far-reaching importance. It contracted in some respects and expanded in others, with profound effects both for the short and for the longer term. The existing London Societies were busy, although the balance between them was shifting. The Whig Club[3] remained officially sympathetic, though increasingly divided by doubts. But it was concerned with the Parliamentary struggle rather than with reform as such, and it was not designed to promote the cause in the country. That

1. George Rudé, *The Crowd in History . . . 1780–1848*, 224; R.B. Rose, 'The Priestley Riots of 1791' (*Past and Present*, no. 18), 84.
2. So it had been used a century before by Shaftesbury, the greatest manipulator of the mob before Wilkes.
3. P. 54 above. The contribution, if any, of the more recent Fox Club (p. 78 above) is obscure.

The composition of both these bodies followed the founders' intentions. At the start both recruited some members from higher social levels. A few professional men – even one small country gentleman – belonged at first to the Sheffield society,[1] and Horne Tooke, John Frost and Maurice Margarot, Joseph Gerrald and John Thelwall, all early members of the London body, were broadly from 'the middling sort'. There may have been a similar sprinkling at Leicester, and rumours were heard in various places of financial support from 'respectable persons'. But it seems to have been only a sprinkling, and the contributions were limited: the vast bulk of the members and the stimulus came, for the first time, from the lower orders. 'Tradesmen, mechanicks, and shopkeepers' and 'journeymen of all denominations' was Hardy's own description of the LCS in 1792, and an account for Government at the end of the year talked of 'clerks and shopmen to haberdashers etc:'.[2] A more detailed list, again made for Government, in the winter of 1792–3 showed an ample spread over the smaller scale London trades: hatters and tailors, weavers and dyers, frameworkers, cabinet makers and watchmakers, stationers, shoemakers, hosiers, hairdressers, butchers and bakers, bricklayers, warehousemen. Shoemakers and cordwainers, by another account, were particularly prominent; but precise analysis is impossible, and there are things we shall never know. 'Mechanics', 'artisans' and 'labourers' are mentioned quite often; but what were their exact definitions, and what were the relations between different kinds of masters, self-employed tradesmen, and their journeymen and apprentices? The lower and lower middling orders had their gradations like others, jealously regarded, as the fortunes of their Societies in harder times were to show. But the Societies were primarily theirs, and one thing is clear. This was a popular movement, and the members were almost wholly 'men hitherto regarded as being beyond the political pale'.[3]

So indeed they thought of themselves at first, with a mixture of apology and pride. 'Have we, who are Tradesmen, Shopkeepers and Mechanics' – so ran the title of an early LCS debate – 'any right to obtain a Parliamentary reform?' The Sheffield Society, perhaps the most radical, hoped in 1792 that 'men of more respectable characters and greater abilities would step forward'.[4] But it did so in order to reprove its betters, and as time went by the note of apology declined. This was partly because the lines were drawn more sharply as conditions hardened, and the popular Societies were thrust on the defensive. But it

1. See Mitchell, loc. cit., 21–3, contrary to the general impression.
2. Quoted in Seaman, 'British Democratic Societies', 29.
3. Loc. cit., 30–3; and see also Walvin, 'English Democratic Societies and Popular Radicalism', 101–6. E.P. Thompson, *The Making of the English Working Class* (1963), 155–6, gives an account of occupations in the LCS a few years later; Rudé, *The Crowd in History*, ch. Thirteen, provides a comparison with France.
4. Quoted in Thompson, op. cit., 18; *The Annual Register for . . . 1792*, 94.

was also due to the fact that their confidence had risen by then as their organisation – a largely novel one – evolved. For those small shop-keepers, artisans and craftsmen built an impressively effective structure, which had to cope both with rapid expansion and with subsequent repression and decline. Following a model adopted in Sheffield it was based on the 'division', a cellular group sending a delegate to a larger meeting which in turn sent up its delegates, and so on ending in a central committee. This was not only aimed directly at a democratic ideal; it also produced a flexible working pattern, which – like later cells – proved resistant when circumstances changed. Pitt himself paid reluct-ant tribute to 'the peculiar construction'.[1] Despite many mishaps and reverses it was a notable feat, and its initial success did much to bolster morale in the early, hopeful phase.

This new growth may be measured against developments in the older Societies. For in the course of 1792 a contrast emerged. The climate which favoured the former held its threats for the latter, as men of property began to be frightened by events abroad and at home. The appearance of popular bodies began to pose problems for the SCI; the rising correspondence, which at first seemed to promise a wider influence, was soon raising awkward questions and internal disputes. Members now had to consider how far they would go, and – in a sense paradoxically – their uncertainties were increased by a complication from quite another quarter. For in the spring of 1792 a further new Society appeared, but of a type very different from the rest and the last of its kind for a very long time.

The Friends of the People began their life in April.[2] They did not spring from the people themselves. Nor indeed were they strictly comparable even with the SCI: their membership was more aristocratic and more predominantly Parliamentary, and in fact they had a directly Parliamentary origin. While there may have been earlier rumours that something of the sort was brewing, the stimulus came from a law case

---

1. In the Commons, 17 November 1795 (*The Senator*, XIII (nd), 331).

2. There are two other Societies of this period which were possibly of the same type; but both doubtfully so. A Grand Lodge, or perhaps Society, of Constitutional Whigs seems to have existed or been founded late in 1791 – which later confusingly added to itself the name Friends of the People. It has been tentatively classed with the SCI as a Society of the older kind (Seaman, loc. cit., 16). But if it was the body of which a little more was heard a year later, it may well have been a popular Society, meeting (possibly) in Soho under the presidency of a leather-cutter (Veitch, op. cit., 213, n8). There was also the Association for Preserving the Freedom of the Press, which was founded in December 1792. This certainly included men of social standing; but it seems to have been a heterogeneous, indeed shapeless, body of mixed membership and views (see Black, *The Association*, 254).

arising out of an election.[1] According to a well known if simplified story it was then transformed into action in a way typical of the participants and the age. Charles Grey, the young Opposition MP, is said to have dined with a company of like spirits, and 'after having drunk a considerable quantity of wine, they pledged themselves to bring forward the reform of Parliament'.[2] A statement was issued over 147 signatures, 24 of which were MPs', and the Association of the Friends of the People entered on its controversial career.

The title, perhaps unconsciously, had its own significance. For in its flavour and composition the new Society reminds one of the committee of the Westminster Association twelve years before.[3] Both had their origins in the same constituency; both were organs of an Opposition group;[4] both, from the same social background, flirted uneasily with radical reform. The young MPs who led the Friends of the People indeed resumed exactly where their predecessors stopped. As they themselves said, they were 'not aiming at Reforms unthought of by wise and virtuous men; . . . our opinions neither possess the advantage, nor are liable to the objection of novelty'.[5] They had no truck with the *Rights of Man*. They sent no Addresses to France, and specifically disclaimed the French example. From the outset they were on strained terms with the SCI – which was sympathetic to Paine, in touch with France, and increasingly sceptical of Parliamentarians – and when its founder Cartwright was elected to the new Society a few of the Friends of the People resigned. At the same time their Parliamentary prominence attracted the interest of the popular bodies: Sheffield approached them early on – with little success – and they corresponded with the LCS. Their name was even adopted in some surprising quarters – the Holborn Friends of the People, for instance, were among the most radical of popular groups. Such contacts proved to be of little importance: the differences were too great for any real meeting of minds. Nevertheless

1. The Westminster election of 1790. George Rose, as a Secretary of the Treasury, had been ordered by the Court to pay a sum found to be owing to a publican for the usual kind of services. A meeting of electors, called by Opposition interests, debated if Rose should be impeached, and a proposal was made on the spot to form a Society to promote Parliamentary reform. It failed, but was soon followed up as appears below.

2. This is Lady Holland's account (*Journal of Elizabeth, Lady Holland*, ed. the Earl of Ilchester, I (1908), 101). She described the party as being at Lord Lauderdale's. Lord Holland wrote that it was at Lord Porchester's, but agreed that Lauderdale had 'wrought upon Grey' (*Memoirs of the Whig Party during My Time*, I (1852), 13–14). The Holland House version depended mainly on Fox, and so became part of the Whig tradition. More recent treatment has placed the episode against an ampler background.

3. See I, 64–8.

4. Of the twelve initial members of the Committee of the Friends of the People eight were MPs, and 23 of the 24 MPs who signed the opening manifesto stayed with Fox after the split in Opposition two years later.

5. Address to the People of Great Britain, 26 April 1792 (*Political Papers . . . Collected by the Rev. Christopher Wyvill*, III, Appendix, 137). A second address, in May (loc. cit., 165–73), was even more concerned to disclaim innovation.

the Friends of the People made their impact on the movement at large. Emerging as a recognisable factor in the Parliamentary events of 1792, they probably played their part in turning Government's mind towards the preventive Proclamation of May,[1] and acted to some extent as a forcing ground for the attitudes of Fox and of Pitt. They thereby publicised developments outside, and helped harden the reactions to them: the attention – the notoriety – they gained had significant results. They also affected the pattern of the movement itself, briefly suggesting fresh alignments and soon revealing the obstacles. In these various ways they served to highlight the growing difficulties of 'reform from above', and further to complicate its prospects in the country.

No one, however, could have foretold throughout most of 1792 how the balance would tilt between the reformers' opportunities and their problems. It took a long time in fact for the legacy to be fully judged. For 1792 saw a radical alliance, however uneasy and incomplete, which made a unique impress on the next few years before it vanished for a generation. Whatever their differences – and as in all such movements these were seldom far below the surface – reformers then did share certain traditions and aspirations, which splintered and were engulfed as the pressures grew. The divisions deepened thereafter, in the bitter decades; Whigs in the end were talking of 'irreconcilable war' with Radicals,[2] while Hardy's craftsmen and artisans sullenly went their ways. It was not until the 1820s and '30s, when the cause revived, that men of different backgrounds could hope to recall the joint efforts of an earlier day.[3]

They did so at that time from an emerging new pattern of assumptions. The alliance of the nineties rested on assumptions and doctrines that had long been held. It was indeed their persistence that made it possible and decided its character; their inner divergencies, and fresh influences, that determined its limits. The influence of the doctrines was strong: as has been well said of the popular Societies, 'Intellectually, the democratic demands of 1792 were not original'.[4] The new pro-

1. P. 91 above. According to the Whig grandee Fitzwilliam, this was certainly so (see Goodwin, op. cit., 207, n181). But the extent and accuracy of his knowledge are uncertain: he and his friends were apt to leap to conclusions.

2. As James Mackintosh, the author of the celebrated early reply to Burke (see p. 73 above) and once the Secretary of the Friends of the People, did to Lord John Russell in 1819, reflecting on – of all things – Peterloo.

3. It was not surprising that a middle-class survivor of the LCS, such as John Gale Jones, should have reminded an audience in 1830 of the 1790s. But memories of the long-buried alliance were already stirring: 'Weel, sir!', said a northern shopkeeper to the veteran Whig lawyer John Clerk at a political meeting in 1820, 'ou're at the auld wark again' (Henry Lord Cockburn, *Memorials of His Time* (1856), 376).

4. Walvin, loc. cit., 76. For the complicating attitude to property, which one commentator (Cannon, *Parliamentary Reform 1640–1832*, 138–9) has argued was a new element, see p. 167 below.

gramme broke no new ground at first. All the immediate objects had been stated before. Some indeed were common to the whole of the reforming movement; shorter Parliaments and a redistribution of seats were familiar enough. And if the LCS and its kindred bodies, unlike the Friends of the People and most of the SCI, called for universal suffrage, so had John Jebb and the Duke of Richmond over ten years before.[1] The popular bodies set to work in fact within a framework already erected, not least by the labours of the SCI itself. Certain precedents were accepted, certain axioms taken for granted, and the prime object had long been the same. The strength of Parliamentary institutions was reflected once more in the unanimity with which the critics fastened on Parliamentary reform.[2]

Parliament stood as the guardian of the Constitution. The popular Societies, like their opponents, professed their reverence for that 'beautiful frame'.[3] 'To allay . . . the heat of party, to prepare the *public mind* for deliberate investigation, and to prove that our *Liberties* may be renovated without destruction of the Constitution or personal sacrifice, is the immediate purpose, endeavour and intent of this Society'. So spoke the earliest of these bodies, in Sheffield. Each of its members had to declare himself 'an enemy of all conspiracies, tumults and riotous proceedings', and the LCS similarly expressed its '*abhorrence* of tumult and violence'. 'Reform, not anarchy' was its watchword,[4] and the new Societies' leaders at first were certainly anxious to proceed within the law. The qualification of time is necessary, for the mood was less certain by the outbreak of war, and even towards the end of 1792 the LCS was voicing fiercer sentiments. But these could be contrasted strongly with others; constitutionalism for long remained a potent force, and the early resolutions of the Societies were, sometimes naïvely, well-meaning. '. . . Men need only to be made acquainted with the abuses of government and they will readily join in every lawfull means to obtain redress' – this was from the United Constitutional Societies at Norwich in March 1792. And when the LCS published a statement of its principles in April, it sent a copy to the Home Secretary claiming his protection.[5]

The Constitution was invoked. But what exactly did the Constitution mean? Its general acceptance had long been fortified by its flexibility. Politicians sought its support in contradictory situations, and glosses abounded on a doctrine of few basic texts. According to approved political thought it now centred on the settlement of 1689, which earlier events had prepared and against which they were to be measured. The results might be ambiguous, and interpreted according to taste; but if

1. See I, 64, 70.
2. Cf. I, 59. Thus the LCS could write in October 1792 to the reforming Society in Stockport, 'We expect everything from an honest and annual Parliament' (quoted in Walvin, loc. cit., 217).
3. Cf. I. 45.
4. *Wyvill Papers*, III, 576–8; B.L. Add. Ms 27811, ff. 2–3.
5. P.R.O., H.O. 42/20; Veitch, op, cit., 205–7.

the content was disputable there was broad agreement on what to exclude. At the same time, however, there existed another tradition, which had been at once a contributory influence and a failing rival to this dominant theme. Providing a section of the foundations for the eighteenth-century structure, it was very largely concealed as that design took final shape. But it was still visible to those who looked for it, and they could do so legitimately because, however much out of fashion, it remained a part of the fabric itself.

This was the historical – if also pseudo-historical – element in the old 'Commonwealthman' tradition.[1] Like so much reforming doctrine it looked back to supposedly better times. For it was an article of faith with reformers that it was not they who were the innovators, but rather it was the servants and managers of a corrupt executive.[2] The model could sometimes be traced back very far indeed. One of the most persistent strands in reforming literature was the appeal to Anglo-Saxon purity – that happy state of equality and freedom which was destroyed by 'the Norman Yoke'. Its origins were ancient – possibly as old as the Conquest itself – and it gained fresh vigour in the upheavals of the seventeenth century. Discredited by that experience, above all by its use in the Commonwealth, the tradition disappeared for a time, but had recently been revived. A crop of publications from the 1770s, centring on King Alfred as lawgiver, helped reinstate the men of Wessex as the rude forefathers of the Constitution. Like the Constitution itself, indeed, their appeal was varied and wide.[3] But it was strongest with the radicals recalling a lost popular representation.[4] At times it clearly struck a vivid, intimate note. When the popular Society at Sheffield first set up its divisions,[5] it named them, in groups of ten, after the Anglo-Saxon tythings.

Here then was a reconstruction essentially historical in its nature, reflecting the strength of the instinct to seek support from the past. But that was not the whole story, for such an evocation of a distant age merged with an essentially different approach. 'This Saxon model of

1. As treated in Caroline Robbins, *The Eighteenth Century Commonwealth Man* (1950).

2. Cf. I, 59, 71.

3. Cf. for instance the anti-Ministerialist pamphlet *Three Letters to the People of Great Britain, by 'Alfred'*, of 1785, with the Ministerialist *Alfred's Letters* (anon., but by James Bland Burges of the Foreign Office) of 1793. Erskine, the future defence counsel for Paine and Hardy and Horne Tooke, won a prize at Cambridge in the '70s with a declamation on 'Anglo-Saxon liberty' and 'Norman feudalism' (though partly adverse to the first); and Pitt himself on one occasion praised the Anglo-Saxon example, and described the Norman system as a 'temporary interruption' to progress (26 November 1795; *P.R.*, XLIII (1796), 417).

4. For the apogee and slow decline of the revival see Christopher Hill, 'The Norman Yoke', in *Democracy and the Labour Movement. . .*, ed. John Saville (1954), 13. There was a similar movement in France in the early days of the Revolution: 'Back to the Gauls', and above all to Vercingetorix.

5. See p. 108 above.

government, when reduced to its first principles, has a strong resemblance to the natural order of things'.[1] If in some important ways it contrasted with, in others it complemented, the kind of thought that was now most alarming: the appeal to 'metaphysic rights'.[2]

For the great new element in 1792, in its extent and intensity, was the influence on popular thinking of an assertion of natural claims. In a sense of course this was older than any reliance on a constitution, and it had its own history, mostly underground and often inarticulate.

> When Adam delved and Eve span,
> Who was then the gentleman?

This basic human cry recurred in different ages, seldom emerging hopefully for very long. The two strands had been linked before in that memorable period when Levellers and Diggers and their kindred had ended with statements of inherent right. The combination now reappeared, with fresh force and remarkable impact. For if 1792 marks a watershed, it was not only as the founding year of the popular Societies, but also for some of the doctrines which they eagerly discussed.

What led them along such paths? 'The answer, in two words,' it has been said, 'is Tom Paine'.[3] So bald a statement needs some definition to underline its point. Paine, in the form particularly of the Second Part of the *Rights of Man*, which appeared in 1792, was not solely responsible for the kind of arguments that distinguished these Societies' debates from those heard earlier in bodies like the SCI. The popular Societies themselves were not uniform, though they all had much in common, and in any case several of the elements are traceable to a combination of sources. Nor did Paine in fact represent as sharp a break with the past as he assumed. Although he claimed that the new Part of the *Rights of Man* was 'a work, written in a style of thinking and expression different to what has been customary in England',[4] this was by no means wholly true of the thinking. Paine's approach was moulded by the Age of Reason;[5] his great examples of America and France – and America perhaps was the central influence – were rooted in sophisticated intellectual origins and societies initially with limited aims; and he had direct precursors in some respects in England itself.[6] The argument was not entirely novel: if it were, it might not have been so readily grasped. But the expression was

1. Hill, loc. cit.
2. *Reflections on the Revolution in France*, 90; and see op. cit., 88–92.
3. Thompson, *The Making of the English Working Class*, 84.
4. Preface to *Rights of Man. Part the Second . . .* (1792), vii.
5. See p. 80 above.
6. Eg James Burgh in his *Political Disquisitions* (c. 1774–75), in which the historical arguments are sometimes balanced with those of natural rights. Paine himself, in *Common Sense* (1776), had made use of the Anglo-Saxon ideal, and he referred to it again, if rather briefly, now (eg *Rights of Man. Part the Second*, chs. II, IV).

another matter; there was, for England, a real difference of tone.[1] The message came over like a clarion call. It looked to the future, not the past. Though not written directly for the common people, it was in language that all could understand. 'All the great laws of society are laws of nature'. 'Man has no authority over posterity in matters of personal right'. 'All hereditary government is tyranny', a system 'as absurd as it is unjust'. The idea of the Constitution itself – a thing that 'has got into circulation . . . by being chalked up in the speeches of parliament' – was 'a sepulchre of precedents', a 'Political Popery'. 'Government on the old system, is an assumption of power, for the aggrandisement of itself'. But 'When a nation changes its opinion and ways of thinking, it is no longer to be governed as before'. The age of revolution had begun, and the 'spark' would catch. 'I do not believe that monarchy and aristocracy will continue seven years longer'. It might not even be so long, if Paine's final passage was not purely figurative. 'It is now towards the middle of February. Were I to take a turn into the country, the trees would present a leafless winterly appearance'. But 'I might observe that a *single bud* had begun to swell', and 'I should reason very unnaturally . . . to suppose *this* was the *only* bud in England which had this appearance . . . though the vegetable sleep will continue longer on some trees and plants than on others, and though some may not *blossom* for two or three years, all will be in leaf in the summer, except those which are *rotten*'. The forecast was qualified in one important respect: in a revolution directed, as this would be, to 'some great and positive good', reason, not violence, would be the natural guide. 'The heart, rather animated than agitated, enters serenely upon the subject'. But the assertion was hardly calculated to bring serenity to his opponents; taken in context, they were more likely to dismiss it out of hand. For the Second Part of the *Rights of Man* was no tract for the study alone. It called men to action: the language was immediate. It breathed a purely secular spirit, absent in the previous century, and the confidence of the rhetoric introduced a new dismissive note.[2] In the last analysis Paine was right: his work was 'different to what has been customary'. It opened new vistas in an exciting – or ominous – way.

Above all, it reached the people. The First Part of the *Rights of Man* had caused a notable stir: some 50-60,000 copies may have been in circulation by the end of 1791.[3] Its circulation was greatly exceeded by

1. I am indebted to Professor Gwyn A. Williams for a suggestion that the emphasis of the style was really American, itself perhaps derived in part from the precept of current Scottish rhetoric.

2. Not least in the references to the King, eg op. cit., 22, 26–7, 38. The note was well caught by Hazlitt: 'Paine affected to reduce things to first principles, to announce self-evident truths'; Character of Cobbett', in *Table Talk* (1821). It was not the smallest part of his legacy to nineteenth-century radicalism.

3. See p. 77, n3 above.

that of the Second Part in February 1792, and the impact mounted as time went by. One cannot say exactly how many copies of either or both Parts were sent out in the next few years, but the numbers were certainly prodigious by existing standards, even if one excludes Ireland where the book sold like hot cakes. Perhaps, on this last basis, some 200,000 copies were printed by 1794; and very many of those would have been read by more than one person. They were said to be 'in almost every hand'; to be 'dropped, not only in cottages, and in highways, but into mines and coal-pits'; 'every cutler' in Sheffield was supposed to have one; 'even children's sweetmeats' were 'wrapped up with parts'.[1] In 1790 Burke had written of the SCI's distribution of literature, 'whether the books so charitably circulated, were ever as charitably read, is more than I know'.[2] The answer in one instance was not long delayed.

Of course not all Paine's readers were admirers of his work. Many went to it out of curiosity, or to learn the worst. But it could not fail to make an impression; Government took it seriously from the start, and in humble quarters its influence was as notable as its circulation. The *Rights of Man* became at once 'as much a standard book . . . as Robinson Crusoe and the Pilgrim's Progress'.[3] And the effect endured. '. . . The writings of Paine', a Scottish cabinet maker prophesied in the summer of 1792, would prove 'as famous in future generations as the Laws of Solon were'.[4] He was not far wrong, for two generations at least. Paine's books, and this one in particular, were on the shelf or hidden in the drawer of every active working-class radical for much of the nineteenth century. The *Rights of Man* became almost a bible, and Paine himself an object of veneration: 'God Save Great Thomas Paine' was still being sung in Sheffield in the 1840s. The initial impact was caused by the fact that the Second Part was issued very cheaply: the SCI distributed it at sixpence, compared with three shillings for the First.[5] It was thus brought within the popular reach, and the contents did the rest. Methods, message and occasion were singularly well met.

The achievement throws some light on – if it raises more questions about – the capacity and vigour of the reading public. Paine was not subtle or profound: his strengths lay elsewhere. But he required more intelligent study than most of the current cheap literary warfare, the simple radical tracts and the equally simple rejoinders. *Hog's Wash* and *The Reign of George the Last* on the one hand, Job Nott and Will Chip on the other, were less demanding than the *Rights of Man*, but they were not necessarily more effective. One must also note how easily a printing

---

1. First three quotations from Thompson, op. cit., 108; the last from a speech by the Attorney General at the prosecution of Paine in his absence in 1792 (*A Complete Collection of State Trials*, ed. Thomas B. Howell, XXII (1817), 381).
2. *Reflections on the Revolution in France*, 3. Cf. p. 78 above.
3. Benjamin Vaughan to Evan Nepean, 30 November 1792 (P.R.O., H.O. 42/22).
4. Walter Miller to John Horne Tooke, 4 July 1792, quoted in Walvin, loc. cit., 207.
5. P. 77, n3 above.

demand of any kind could be met; there was little expense in bringing out an edition of a popular work, and large numbers could be envisaged and seem on occasion to have been put in hand. When a young breeches-maker could make himself responsible for a run of 2,000 copies of a pamphlet, and the SCI could talk, however hypothetically, of issues of 100,000,[1] there was clearly a wide and variegated audience, ready to respond to more than one level of thought.

Such bridges were very important, even if many of them later collapsed. They enabled men on one side of a financial gulf to cross to some of the pastures on the other. The circulation of political literature among the popular Societies and beyond was novel in its nature within living memory, and probably entirely novel in extent.[2] It was a precursor, however limited its capacity for immediate survival, of the growth of working-class readership in the following century. The process was two-way. If some publications were subsidised, some at least of the Societies reserved funds with which to buy books.[3] One would like to know how far they also bought the newspapers which promoted radical views. For the developments in the early nineties had their effects on journalism, particularly in those regions where the Societies were strong at first. In London, the old Foxite interest ensured a good hearing for the cause, and the excitements of 1792 were amply reflected in the press. It was nonsense to say, as one Ministerialist did, that 'almost all' the papers 'were in the pay of the Jacobins';[4] Government by then was paying allowances to no fewer than nine London journals. But Ministers were certainly dissatisfied with the results and alarmed by the general mood, and in the autumn they founded a new evening daily.[5] Over the

1. See Place's *Autobiography*, 159–60 for the first (he recovered his costs); R.K. Webb, *The British Working-Class Reader 1790–1848* (1955), 39 for the second. Single editions of 100,000 were a pipe dream for the SCI, and it suffered financially from the variety of its publications. But these do seem on occasions to have been produced successfully in large numbers, and the celebrated *Cheap Repository Tracts*, with better backing, are said to have sold altogether no fewer than two million copies in their first year, 1795 (information from Dr R.C. Alston).

2. One does not know at all precisely how far the Puritan prints of the 1640s and '50s, and those of the Levellers, Diggers, Anabaptists and Fifth Monarchy Men in particular, reached the populace at large; or for that matter the voluminous political literature in the early part of the eighteenth century. One can only guess that improved facilities favoured a proportionately wider circulation among the increased population of the early 1790s.

3. This was one of the first resolutions of the Revolution Society in Norwich, and a stated object of the Constitutional Society of Sheffield.

4. Bland Burges to Auckland, 2 February 1793, referring to the previous year (*A.C.*, II, 494–5).

5. *The Sun*, 'established', according to Burges much later, 'under the sanction of Mr. Pitt' in October (quoted in A. Aspinall, *Politics and the Press c. 1780–1850* (1949), 78). A morning paper, *The True Briton*, sometimes said to have been started at the same time, came into existence in fact in January 1793. One advantage in an evening daily was that such papers seem to have circulated much more freely in the provinces than did the London morning dailies.

next few years the London newspapers were closely embroiled, and their circulation almost certainly increased.[1] But a more novel, if parallel, development took place in the provinces. For although Opposition had made some use of provincial journals in the eighties,[2] only a small proportion of the total could then be said to have political views. Of the fifty or so (all weeklies) the great majority was produced simply to record local doings and display advertisements. They were in fact broadly in the state in which most London papers had been earlier, and when they included national news it was generally in a brief stereotype from London agents. There were exceptions – the *Cambridge Journal* for instance, some of the Norwich newspapers, the *Sheffield Register* – most of which were owned and run by Dissenters. But at the turn of the decade a new spirit could be seen. Prompted partly by the controversy over the Corporation and Test Acts, and partly by the desire to report events in France, many of the existing journals, particularly in the midlands and the north, awoke – often sluggishly – to the rising political concern. More important, new journals were founded between 1790 and 1793 most of which held political opinions from the start. By no means all were radical, and, combined with the older newspapers, the anti-radical press in fact managed to hold its own. If one takes the northern counties alone, it has been calculated that there were 28 journals at one time or another between 1791 and 1797, of which ten (later eleven) might be classed as favouring reform, ten (later nine) as the opposite, while eight had no discernible views.[3] But the reforming papers were active, some had links with the popular Societies, and they, as well as some of their opponents, enlisted readers on a new scale. Where the provincial sheets had earlier been numbered in their hundreds, the *Manchester Chronicle* (opposed to reform) was printing over 2,000 copies in 1789 and well over 4,000 in 1793, and the radical *Sheffield Register* over 1,500 in the latter year. Such figures, as far as can be seen, were not grossly untypical, and the distribution was sometimes quite wide. The *Sheffield Register* for example was read in parts of Derbyshire and Nottinghamshire, the Newcastle papers in the neighbouring counties, the Cheshire papers in north Wales.[4] Both sides put forward their efforts. Government turned

---

1. The scale may be judged by a statement from the Post Office, which Pitt retained, that from 15 to 20 June 1789 77,573 newspapers passed through its hands (P.R.O. 30/8/196).

2. See I, 606n3.

3. See Mitchell, 'Radicalism and Repression in the North of England', 310–27. The north, as there defined, covers Cumberland, Westmorland, Northumberland, County Durham, Yorkshire, Lancashire, and Cheshire.

The annual sale of newspaper stamps in Britain rose in round numbers from 14,100,000 in 1780 to 17,000,000 in 1793. The appearance of new journals may have accounted for much of the increase.

4. How many provincial readers there were on average to a copy it is very hard to say. A generation later, in 1829, there were said to be seven or eight (Aspinall, op. cit., 25 n1). In London on the other hand there was an estimate of 20–30 in 1789 (see I 605, n4).

its attention to the provinces, sending news and providing money, while the Societies inserted advertisements and some numbered the editors in their ranks. It can hardly be doubted – though one would like to know more – that, at a probable average cost of $3\frac{1}{2}$d a week,[1] they and many of their members were among the subscribers in 1792.

In the main, one is still talking here of a particular section of the people. Paine's appeal was exceptional, which was why he caused exceptional alarm. But the working public which was in the habit of studying pamphlets and reading newspapers, though a reasonably wide one and keenly interested, obviously had its limits. Broadly speaking – for throughout this subject one is generalising, and on uneven evidence – it consisted of an intellectual, and perhaps a largely occupational, 'aristocracy of workers'. 'The class of tradesmen and artisans' – the backbone of the LCS – 'formed the dividing line, in this period, between the reading and non-reading public'.[2] Above them, in the 'middling sort', itself an increasingly elaborate hierarchy, facilities and habits were fostering a steady interest in public affairs. The varied movement of 'benevolence'[3] was laying extensive foundations for a more earnest and regular concern. This process was reflected in a rising stream of publications, didactic, investigative or descriptive, and also – partially, often uncertainly – in less direct and weighty forms. In the novel for example, reviving from the decline of a generation, a greater realism and a social conscience co-existed with the stirrings of Romance.[4] Nor was it unimportant that some of the most popular authors of this school were women; for an audience which contained wives and daughters had its own effect. For every reader of the social preaching of Mary Woollstonecraft in the early nineties there may have been ten of Clara Reeve and Charlotte Smith, whose tales had their own political tone.[5] Other purveyors of fiction were more direct in the first half of the decade. The group of 'revolutionary' novelists – Holcroft, Godwin, Robert Bage – had something new to say and said it with effect. Their example was followed within the decade by kindred spirits and opponents alike, and the battle spread to the essayists and the poets. It was both a development and a break, like the political strife itself, and its influence was guaranteed by material developments long under way. The

1. Donald Read, *Press and People 1790–1850* . . . (1961), 67. The cost was very soon to rise. Almost all provincial papers remained weeklies until well into the nineteenth century.

2. Richard D. Altick, *The English Common Reader* . . . (1957), 72, 65.

3. P. 61 above.

4. The stage on the other hand, was retreating from reality.

5. For Mary Woollstonecraft see p. 73 above. But it is of interest that she herself, who in 1792 had made the familiar attack on the 'flimsy' novel as a corrupter of feminine taste and intelligence (see her *Vindication of the Rights of Woman*, ch. XIII, sect. II), had already written a novel on the newer lines in 1788. When she died in the later nineties she was well on the way to completing another. Hannah More, in the opposite camp, was to follow a similar course.

circulating library, the subscription library, the bookselling shop, the magazine, the cheap reprint: all sprang from and served the needs of spreading prosperity and leisure. The physical and moral conditions existed, and the politics themselves were pressing. The circulation of Burke and the First Part of Paine underlined and developed the point.

But what of the mass of people who lay at the other end of the scale, beyond the reading, often self-improving, tradesman and artisan? The extent and degree of national literacy are hard to define. They may have been greater and more variously served than many contemporaries assumed. '. . . All ranks now READ', proclaimed James Lackington, the successful bookseller, in the early nineties, and a decade earlier a German visitor in London 'conversed with several people of the lower class, who all knew their national authors, and who all have read many, if not all of them'.[1] Such remarks do not take one as far as one would wish; perhaps not much farther than the kind of men and women we have already mentioned. But many of those had learned at the start in a rude but not unlettered world. Basic literacy had probably been increasing since at least the middle of the century, promoted above all by religious instruction whether Anglican or Nonconformist. The Charity and Sunday School movements were becoming well established, and Dame Schools too were now spreading fast, devoted largely to the same purpose. Such developments were beginning to produce their own kind of reading matter, complementary to the Bible and to the catechism in the parish schools. The popular example of Mrs Sarah Trimmer, who catered mainly for children but also 'for the instruction and amusement of cottagers and servants',[2] argues a familiarity with some basic texts and simple tales. Certain kinds of literature undoubtedly did very well. The almanac, the ballad and the chapbook (the last perhaps beginning to fade), sold by hawkers and on the stalls, purveyed rhymes and prognostications and accounts of executions.[3] Nor should one ignore the broadsides and handbills, and even words chalked on the walls, which 'made the streets a sort of poor man's library'.[4] Sometimes they carried

---

1. *Memoirs of the Forty-Five First Years of the Life of James Lackington* (edn. of 1810), 257 (first published in 1791); Carl Philip Moritz, *Travels . . . through Several Parts of England in 1782*, ed. Percy Ewing Matheson (1924), 43 (first published in 1783, translated in 1795). Such observations are receiving confirmation from current bibliographical work, centred on the British Library, on the *Eighteenth Century Short Title Catalogue*, which has disclosed the existence of over a thousand bookshops throughout Great Britain – of one kind or another – by 1800.

2. *D.N.B.* She flourished from the early eighties.

3. The last were still being sold well into the nineteenth century. The English public has always greatly enjoyed the drama of death.

According to the bookseller Lackington again, in the northern towns the sales were conspicuously not of 'established authors' but of 'common trifling books' – 'nothing but trash' (and see B.L. Add. Ms 27828 *passim*).

4. R.K. Webb, op. cit., 24. For a vivid example in Whitehall, see *Autobiography of Francis Place*, 229.

their own political warfare. In the winter of 1788, in the Regency crisis, handbills praising Pitt were stuck on the Foxite Devonshire House. Four years later there was a regular battle on the London walls, as loyalists and dissidents tore down or covered up each other's prints.[1] And beyond all this lay what may best be described as the hearing public, listening to a reading in a cottage or tenement or inn. It might be the Bible, or Pilgrim's Progress, or a newspaper, or Tom Paine. It all supplied what Hazlitt later called 'food for our stomachs'.[2]

Materials therefore existed, hitherto inert but potentially volatile, which in certain circumstances could conceivably explode. The Royal Proclamation of May 1792 recognised the possibility. Coming suddenly after the complacency of the autumn and early winter, it specified publications as an immediate threat. They did not stand alone in Ministers' minds; within the offices of Whitehall, Government was embarking on other inquiries and precautions. But at a moment when neither domestic unrest nor French interference was as yet a serious fact, seditious writings, and one above all, lay at the centre of the problem. The completed *Rights of Man* was pervading the country: a focus, a target, and something like a creed. When one recalls Pitt's confident words of exactly a year before,[3] the Proclamation, while not occasioned solely by it, was a remarkable tribute to a single book.

1. I, 659n2; S.M. to John Reeves, 10 December 1792 (B.L. Add. MS 16921).
2. 'What Is the People?' in *Political Essays, with Sketches of Public Characters* (1819).
3. Pp.87–8 above.

CHAPTER V

1792: The Dimensions of Unrest

I

The Government's action of May was seen in some quarters as premature. Six months later, at a graver moment, it was held by some to have been unwise. In 1791, when Paine was left alone, his First Part had had limited influence; but after the publicity of attempted suppression 'it appears, that the book . . . is now made a standard book'.[1] The argument has its force; but there is some evidence to the contrary, and one must look more closely at the Ministry's area of choice. The Second Part of the *Rights of Man* placed it under pressure, and the nature of its possible weapons has to be understood.

At the beginning of 1792 the means of ensuring law and order were very largely those with which the Hanoverian Succession faced its early threats. Indeed in some respects they were less, for the measures introduced against Jacobitism were partly dismantled in the decades following the failure of the '45. The executive's legal powers were circumscribed; and its practical resources remained as slight as, by accepted tradition, they long had been. In the last resort the Government had to call in the troops; and the last resort was often uncomfortably close. The machinery of civil enforcement was slender, unreliable and largely chaotic. At the same time it was too venerable to be summarily disturbed. Contained for the most part within the old units of local government, it was mainly controlled, at their different levels, by the county and the parish. The men on the ground were attached above all to the parish vestries, which partly appointed and generally paid the constables and watchmen and marshals and beadles. The duties were then regulated – and appointments also made – by the county magistrates, the omnipresent, usually part-time unpaid justices of the peace. For the JPs remained the linchpin of the system of order: the Court of first instance in most cases, the issuers of licences and warrants, the readers of the Riot Act, the most immediate bastions of the law. Their jurisdictions covered the towns as well as the country

1. Benjamin Vaughan to ?Evan Nepean, 30 November 1792 (P.R.O., H.O. 42/22); and cf. Dundas's public acknowledgment in December of the existence of such a view (*P.R.*, XXXIV (1793), 56). The Archbishop of Canterbury reported a 'prevailing opinion' of scepticism as to the need for the Proclamation at the time (to Auckland, 22 May 1792; *A.C.*, II, 408).

districts; where Corporations and boroughs had their own powers it was because the mayors and aldermen were sworn of the Commission. The county had great authority, which extended under direction into a central area of national concern. For it was the Lord Lieutenant, acting on a quota set by the Privy Council and an order issued through a Secretary of State, who embodied the county militia in an emergency. The protection of life and property in varied situations was thus held in local – often very local – hands, bringing with it the complexities and anomalies of an ancient pattern.

The system rested on historic views of direct responsibility. Parishes, wards and precincts elected or appointed their officers from their inhabitants: pay was for part time – the post of constable was often correspondingly unpopular – and powers were limited to the immediate district. The principle, and in the last resort the practice, were carried farther afield. The Posse Comitatus – the force of the county – could be invoked in a riot, and any subject sworn by the justices to act as a special constable; and the militia in turn derived from the common law obligation to take up arms in defence of the realm. The theory, medieval – or Anglo-Saxon – in origin, was of course often honoured in the breach, or more strictly speaking by well-tried extension or circumvention. Some payments were swelled by fees, some offices performed by deputy; others were being placed on a rather more professional basis. But if there were loopholes in the observance the principles were held in respect, and they would not be easily overturned.

For the attitudes to enforcement derived from assumptions affecting government itself. The central administration of Britain in the late eighteenth century was highly developed for certain purposes. It had enabled the country to become a Great Power, and to bring its growing wealth to bear. In the collection of revenue, the waging of war (for which revenue was mainly needed), the pursuit and maintenance of overseas trade and consequentially of empire, effective instruments lay to hand even when they were not effectively used. But while such purposes were willingly acknowledged they were well defined and narrowly watched; it was indeed this blend of strong and of limited government that gave the system its flavour. Certain areas of overlapping interest were particularly sensitive, where the recognised claims of the state met those of private or corporate rights. The standing army was the classic instance; there was another in the Excise, whose processes served the revenue at a possible cost to personal freedom.[1] But any extension in the existing resources of the Crown was apt to cause resentment, and anything new was likely to rouse vociferous concern. The twin gods of individual liberty and low taxation would be affronted: better accept the paradox of a readier recourse to the troops. The few additions to the weapons of order, and the failure of one recent proposal, suggest the

1. See I, 291–2.

strength, despite recognised dangers, of this point of view.

It is noticeable that the innovations, such as they were, took local forms, even where the body concerned was in part centrally controlled. Local Acts for cleansing, paving or lighting sometimes led Corporations and parishes to consider means of regulation which could have a wider effect. When special Commissioners for instance were set up with such duties and powers, they sometimes formed their own staffs which took on some of the work of policing.[1] Even so it was very unusual for older arrangements to be superseded: if something new was devised it was more often simply added to what was there. The point is underlined by the one experiment that had been concerned with policing the capital itself. The famous Bow Street runners made their appearance in the 1750s. In some ways they showed signs of an attempt at central control. For one brief year in the sixties they drew in part on Governmental funds, and Government was soon occasionally using them beyond the bounds of the Bow Street Court. They could even be sent – though not very often – into the provinces on special cases, and by the 1780s their name had passed into the language. The complementary horse patrol moreover, also under the local magistrate, had a certain authority over the capital's highways at large. But these powers were jealously watched, with growing effect. The force was recruited, in very small numbers – by the eighties it had shrunk to four runners and two horsemen – from the existing parish officers; the experiment of Government pay was very soon withdrawn; and if the horse patrol, and a foot patrol which was added in 1790, could operate beyond the Bow Street district, both were restricted in the wider area to the designated 'highways' and 'streets'. Changes were to come in the nineties; but at the start of that decade the only specific police force in Westminster and London, or indeed in Britain, was largely beholden to older bodies, and its powers were closely defined.

The results were correspondingly limited, and the problems of crime and disorder grew. The Gordon riots of 1780 added to a growing concern, and in the next few years efforts were made to meet it. Shelburne's reforming Ministry tried its hand in 1782–3; but it was not in office long, and the attempt was confined to two bills affecting penalties and the definition of vagrancy, intended 'for the improvement of the police of the metropolis and its environs'.[2] Two years later there was a more comprehensive and direct attack. In June 1785 Pitt's

1. Eg the 'Manchester and Salford Police Act' – as it became known – of 1792 (32 Geo. III, c. 69), for which the way had been partly prepared by a local Cleansing and Lighting Act of 1765 and an Improvement Act of 1776. The word 'police' did not figure in the title of this 1792 Act, which was 'for cleansing, lighting, watching, and regulating the Streets'.

2. *P.R.*, IX (1783), 207. The first bill, introducing the death penalty for receivers of stolen goods, failed; the second, amending the Vagrancy Act of 1744, passed. Shelburne himself later claimed, rather typically, that he had wider measures in store.

Solicitor General introduced a 'London and Westminster Police bill'.[1] Drafted for the Home Office by John Reeves, an energetic barrister of whom more was to be heard, it aimed, in its author's words, at 'a strong executive'.[2] Westminster and London were taken as a single area, for which three Commissioners would be responsible, to be nominated and paid by the Crown. From an office provided by Government they would supervise the work of nine stipendiary magistrates, who would be assisted by non-resident colleagues, in nine Public Offices. The Commissioners would have powers of search and arrest – slightly extended again under the Vagrancy Act[3] – issuing warrants on their sole authority except in the City, where endorsement was required by the Lord Mayor or an alderman. Enforcement would be in the hands of a High Constable responsible to the Commissioners, who himself would be in charge of nine Chief Constables, one for each district. Their duties would not entirely supersede those of the officers of the parishes and wards; there would be co-ordination, with the Commissioners exercising partial control.

The bill went about as far as it could. As has been claimed, it was 'far-reaching in its consequences',[4] and it certainly overlaid existing arrangements. The old authorities did not disappear, but they lost their unfettered jurisdiction. The Commissioners were given large powers, on the understanding that they were deemed to be JPs. It was a major reform, on the model of the Bow Street Court. Within its limits, it struck at interests which were very strongly entrenched.

Objections therefore could be expected. Nevertheless the prospects seemed quite good, for, as Pitt himself said, the proposals arose from 'the necessity of something being done to prevent the enormous grievance that every body complained of'. It was, he asserted, something that 'had long been an object in his mind'.[5] Unfortunately he allowed the Ministry to mishandle the case. The new system would fall under the Home Office, and the Home Secretary Sydney – seldom impressive[6] – did little if anything to prepare the ground. He should really have known better, for it was he, as Shelburne's Home Secretary, who had been concerned with the bills of 1783.[7] But he muddled the business,

1. This was its popular name. Its title was 'for the better prevention of crimes, and the more speedy punishment of them' in the areas specified (*P.R.*, XVIII (1785), 522, which is to be preferred to *Stockdale*, III (1785), 497). The bill appears in the list of contents for the volume as 'the Solicitor-General's Police Bill'.

2. To Lord Sydney [Home Secretary], 29 June 1785 (P.R.O., H.O. 42/7). See also Reeves to Pitt, 18 July 1785 (P.R.O. 30/8/170).

3. See p. 123, n2 above.

4. Leon Radzinowicz, *A History of English Criminal Law and its Administration from 1750*, III (1956), 108–9.

5. *P.H.*, XXV (1815), col. 907. This debate, on 29 June, is not reported in *P.R.*, XVIII or *Stockdale*, III. *Stockdale*, however, reports debates on the earlier stages of the bill (op. cit., 497–509, 511–12).

6. See I, 130, 184–5.

7. P. 123 above.

contriving in particular to ignore the City – the copy of the bill for the Lord Mayor's comments was sent a fortnight late, so that there was no time for proper consideration. Pitt in turn, whatever his sentiments, seems not to have studied the scheme; he confessed that he was not 'perfectly master of the subject', and to being 'incapable of forming a competent judgment'.[1] He was very busy throughout those months, above all with the Irish Propositions, and this was not the only sign of miscalculation in a rather disappointing year.[2] The bill thus got off to a poor start, and the procedure moreover was faulty, for since it contained financial provisions the measure should have gone first to a Committee of Supply. Resistance soon mounted. The City protested at losing full control of its officers, who indeed were generally admitted to be more effective than those elsewhere; and the sitting part-time magistrates – who, unlike their provincial brethren, were notoriously venal – naturally did not look forward to being summarily removed. Despite the desire for improvement, fears of the executive carried the day. The House was uneasy, and the bill was dropped.[3]

So ended, as it seemed, the only attempt at a real reform. At the turn of the decade the system continued as before. Whatever the signs of a change in attitude it had proved ineffectual, and in point of fact the change had not gone very far. Men on the whole still thought along older lines. The word police itself had recently entered general usage; but it had not yet gained official sanction,[4] and was employed very often as a term of dislike. As Sheridan had said earlier, 'it was not an expression of our law, or of our language', although it might now be 'perfectly understood'.[5] Stress was often laid on its French origin, which was hardly a recommendation – it was typical of Shelburne's tactlessness that he should have cited the French example in recommending an English reform.[6] Other authorities, including reformers themselves, were more generally cautious or hostile: from Blackstone and Adam Smith to Martin Madan and (at first) Romilly himself. A police force under Government could be an instrument of tyranny. It would certainly extend the patronage of the Crown. It would confuse or weaken ancient jurisdictions and the self-reliance of communities. One influential pamphlet had even argued only a few years earlier that the old Posse Comitatus should rather be strengthened as a 'people's police'.[7]

---

1. *P.H.*, XXV, col. 907.
2. See I, 209–12, 610 and n2.
3. *P.H.*, XXV, cols. 900–13.
4. Eg pp. 123 n1, 124 n1 above.
5. In the Commons, 5 March 1781 (*P.R.*, II (1781), 98).
6. Speech in the Lords of 3 June, 1780; *P.H.*, XXI (1814), col. 680. For an attempt to elucidate his baffling personality, see I, 86–7.
7. *An Inquiry into the Legal Mode of Suppressing Riots* (1781). It was by William Jones, the lawyer and great orientalist who was soon to be knighted as an East Indian judge.

Government therefore was left, in the capital and beyond, to depend on the army if a riot looked like getting out of hand. But the army was of limited use if there were too many riots at once: it was thinly spread and sometimes badly placed for quick intervention, and its presence was undesirable for too long at any one time. The duties were not greatly welcomed by the civil authorities or the military themselves. Commanders, and sometimes the War Office, had their reservations, and the quartering of soldiers on a district, with the likely possibility of incidents, was apt to be a fruitful source of local complaint. In May 1792, when the Royal Proclamation was issued, the troops were quite well distributed on paper. The 'effective' strength in England was some 41,000 men – almost 6,000 below establishment – the two main concentrations being in the London area, and in the midlands and southern Lancashire and Yorkshire.[1] The latter moreover consisted mainly of cavalry, which with its relative speed of movement and more formidable appearance was generally favoured for quelling a riot. The deployment of both horse and foot, however, suffered from certain constraints. There were not many barracks, in the shape of old 'garrisons' and 'fortresses', outside the London district, and where they existed they were usually small and sometimes remote. Forces of any description were accordingly 'parcelled up in small packets',[2] regiments of horse being often split into tented 'troops' over a wide area, and infantry often lodged in taverns, from which it was slow to assemble and hard to check. No military force could be summoned, moreover, except on request from the magistrates, who were often reluctant to act until serious damage was done.[3] While it usually proved effective once it reached the spot, the army could therefore be placed under pressure if disturbance was widespread.

II

Riot of course was a crime – the Riot Act had extended the circumstances – and its suppression in general could not be divorced from that of crime itself. The two problems were closely linked in the minds of the authorities; it was the Gordon riots in particular that stimulated the 'police' bills of the 1780s, the political troubles of the '90s that aided new thought on the policing system at large.[4] The same connexion lay behind many of the voluntary associations formed,

1. P.R.O. 30/8/340, papers of 5 May 1792. 'Effective' forces excluded Companies of 'Invalids' borne on the strength, who garrisoned castles and forts.
2. As Dundas put it to Pitt, 22 November 1792 (P.R.O. 30/8/157).
3. It was George III's insistence that the troops should act 'without waiting for directions from the Civil Magistrates' that brought the Gordon riots of 1780 under belated control.
4. For the connexion within the Middlesex magistracy, in the person of Patrick Colquhoun, see Radcinowicz, op. cit., III, ch. 9.

notably in the eighties, to protect private property. The Gordon riots again gave an impetus to a process already under way as a result of the general spread of crime. A crop of Voluntary Associations for Defence sprang up in and around the capital, some of which seem to have continued when the immediate danger died down. Some older, rather different bodies, both official and unofficial – the London Military Foot Association and the Honourable Artillery Company are notable examples – began also from this time to act occasionally as a kind of police; and groups for guarding property were to be found in some of the suburbs and surrounding villages. Their existence, the product of lawlessness, should not be ignored as part of the background to the loyalist associations which political trouble was soon to produce.

In its alarm at the rise in crime, which was generally acknowledged but could not be met by a stronger police, society at large looked to the Courts. Parliament had certainly done so for the greater part of the century, enacting severer sentences and above all widening the scope of the death penalty. The process had been hastened over the past thirty years. But the response from the Courts themselves was patchy and often ambivalent, for the very multiplicity of capital offences was tending to defeat the object. Reliable figures are hard to come by for the country as a whole: the legal statistics of the age are quite as confused as many others. Judges and juries were certainly as savage on occasions as the law decreed; but they were becoming, rather more frequently, as evasive as it allowed. Perhaps about a third of those so convicted were hanged in the event;[1] remissions were not uncommon, and in the more serious cases the penalty was now quite often changed to transportation. But there were still plenty of executions, transportation itself could be a dreadful fate, and the effect of the sentences was not the less brutal for their unpredictability. The arguments for extreme measures were fortified by the state of the prisons, put under extreme pressure as the work of the assizes grew. For the gaols, most of them old and many of them decrepit, were grossly overcrowded and largely insecure. Crammed with a miscellany of offenders and unfortunates, very often in shocking conditions, and manned by corrupt or brutalised jailers, lax or savage as the case might be, they were a notorious scandal and frequently a menace. Official papers are filled with complaints and urgent demands for new buildings, and by the later eighties some were projected or even under way. Meanwhile the hulks took the overflow, which in turn they failed to hold completely, and New South Wales, to replace America, was no answer in itself.[2] In the last decade of the century transportation, as the alternative to hanging, was equally in danger of failing to meet the case.

1. Radzinowicz, op. cit., I, 147–51, 157–9, on figures for London and Middlesex and the Home Circuit.
2. See I, 407–8.

It was thus not so much of a paradox as it might appear that this age of extended punishment saw the birth of the efforts for criminal reform. While men and women were being hanged or transported for stealing a sheep or a few shillings' worth of goods, the great tide of rational inquiry was beginning to gather pace. A few of the fruits reached the statute book; more were defeated on the way; most were still confined to literary debate, though John Howard's revelations on the gaols had some practical effect. The contrasting reactions largely stemmed from the same rising pressures, producing fresh calls for repression on the one hand, a questioning of methods and principles on the other. But the contrast was not always complete; the responses could overlap, and reform itself was not invariably aimed at mitigation. If much of it sprang from humane sentiment and the movement for 'benevolence', much was directed chiefly to tidying up the muddled state of the law. And the object here was not necessarily – though it was often – lesser punishment: some of the first plans for reform in fact called for heavier selective sentences.[1] Meanwhile the more conscientious Ministers coped as best they could, often uncertainly and sometimes inconsistently. Shelburne, the most open of all to the trends of reforming thought, headed a Government which tried to introduce the death penalty for receiving stolen goods; and Pitt, who according to a knowledgeable source 'was convinced of the improper severity of our laws', and even 'had it in contemplation to submit the whole . . . penal code to . . . revision', opposed in 1787 a motion for such an inquiry.[2]

The treatment of crime in the eighties, and the methods retained for keeping order, suggest current notions of what could be taken as acceptable. On the one hand the ancient mixture of haphazard licence and stern repression was coming under attack from ideas of more equable and sure control. But this process was in its infancy, and older attitudes drew their strength from the fact that lawlessness could still be seen as an ugly but not an insupportable threat. This is not to say that there were not sometimes serious misgivings. 'Justices – the few there are – are afraid of the felons; constables are not to be found; the poor must plunder because not provided for; ladies dare not live in the country . . .'.[3] But things were not usually taken as being as bad as that, at least in the countryside which was here, unusually, singled out. Despite the

1. For a general discussion see Radzinowicz, op. cit., I, Part III.
2. See p. 123, n1 above for Shelburne; Cobbett's *Parliamentary Debates*, XIX (1812), Appendix, cols. lxxvi–lxvii for Wilberforce's retrospective statement on Pitt's views; *P.R.*, XXII (1787), 213 for Pitt's attitude in 1787, when he pleaded the need for time to consider and for lawyers to agree on 'proper data and principles'. The Solicitor General's scepticism of the effects of 'extreme severity', in the first debate on the Police bill of 1785 (*Stockdale*, III, 499; see pp. 123–4 above), may have reflected his leader's views at the time.
3. *The Torrington Diaries*, II, 87; entry for 25 June 1789. Colonel John Byng, who became Torrington, was a professed contemner of the present times.

incessant sporadic disturbance, life in the middle and higher ranks was tolerably peaceful for most of the time, and the structure of society itself had so far absorbed the level of violence. If in some ways things were worse with a fast-rising population, in others they were ordered rather better than before. Streets were better lit, highways rather safer, new prosperous suburbs brought physical separation; the 'reformation of manners' was beginning to bite. The parish constable might be hard to find, and not much use in practice; but there seemed to be no absolute need to replace him over most of the country with new methods of control. The general opinion at the start of the nineties was still that England could be lightly governed: the extent of disorder, worrying as it could be, did not undermine stability and freedom. Such terms indeed are always relative, and men at the time know broadly what they mean. At this point, as always, they have to be interpreted in the idiom of the day.

Given such premises, the balance of order could be seen as both delicate and firm. It could take a good deal of pressure, but the pressures themselves could raise real alarm. The outbreaks of the mob, that dreaded word, were at once evanescent and frightening; and none the less frightening because they were not the work of criminals alone. For while there was often – perhaps particularly in London – a criminal or floating fringe, the 'faces in the crowd'[1] seem to have been largely those of men from a range of working trades. Evidence from the Gordon riots of 1780 suggests that it was the small shopkeepers, craftsmen and artisans (particularly the younger men) who comprised the bulk of convicted rioters; and in Birmingham in 1791 (though the detail is less adequate) it seems again to have been artisans and, in this case, industrial labourers. Scattered accounts of other urban troubles tend to reinforce the impression, with the addition of peddlars and domestic servants – the latter a fruitful source of crime; in the country there is also mention of miners and small-scale textile workers, farm labourers and small cultivators, whether freeholders or tenants. Again, while perhaps one should not lay too much stress on the geographical origins of riot in the capital – for most areas, including the poorer ones, contained mixed levels of population – it was not necessarily the worst districts that saw the start of trouble, though their inhabitants might then happily join in. Riots now began less often in St Giles's or Holborn or the neighbour-hood of Fleet Street – the ancient rookeries and thieves' kitchens – than in the working quarters: the City and Southwark, Shoreditch, Spital-fields, the Strand. Quite respectable citizens could sometimes be involved. The fact had been noted in the Wilkite troubles, and when Pitt was attacked in 1784 as he returned from receiving the Freedom of the

---

1. Rudé, *The Crowd in History*, title to ch. Thirteen.

City, 'he was attended by a great concourse of people, many of the better sort, all the way down the Strand, as well as by a considerable Mob' which ended by fighting in St James's Street.[1]

But this was the point. It is not surprising that contemporaries should have picked on the thieves and drunken harridans who roamed the streets in the wake of any major outburst; nor perhaps that this impression dominated later accounts. The sight, in all conscience, was arresting enough. But really it was not so much that the mob might include the dregs of society as that working men and tradesmen of fixed address could very largely make up a mob. 'John Bull in a crowd is always John Bull in a mob': this was a statement with which Pitt himself, remembering the shopkeepers and apprentices in 1785, would no doubt have readily agreed.[2] The fact that a man was described as following a given occupation, while socially significant, did not sanction his behaviour. Football hooligans today have their trades, and seldom show a regular criminal record, but they can smash and riot none the less. The authorities' practical concern was the ease with which accepted rowdiness[3] could turn into mass action, whatever the source.

The mob had certain features which the word itself describes. 'Mobile (short for the Latin *mobile vulgarus* the excitable crowd)' – this seventeenth-century definition of the noun is given as slightly predating that of 'Mob' itself.[4] Mobility, of various kinds, was the characteristic danger. It contained in the first instance the prime ingredient of the physical threat.

> The gath'ring number, as it moves along,
> Involves a vast involuntary throng.[5]

It was movement – the movement from one quarter into others, attracting fresh elements and unpredictable action – that in London posed the challenge which was so hard to meet at the start. And in the provinces, in both town and country, it was movement again that the authorities feared: the progress of the crowd, but also the vagrant, the dispossessed countryman, the roving band of workmen, the incitement or involuntary pressure from outside. There were other less direct connotations: not physical but social. For if riots often sprang from certain well defined industries[6] they also had a seed-bed in that area of

1. See I, 140–1. The incident had the further familiar feature of direction from above (ibid).
2. Op. cit., 145, 254 and n4.
3. See pp. 101–2 above.
4. *O.E.D.*
5. Pope, *The Dunciad*, Bk. IV, lines 81–2. It has been suggested that the 'horrifying picture' of this whole passage anticipates prophetically the nightmare of the Gordon riots (Pat Rogers, *Grub Street, Studies in a Subculture* (1972), 106).
6. See pp. 96–7 above.

society which was peculiarly prone to sudden change. The small master, the small farmer, the shopkeeper, the aspiring journeyman and mechanic, might hope to profit and prosper, but he might also fall. The abyss was always there, and it could be a terrifying sight. Social mobility was a gratifying feature of English life by European standards. There were few legal barriers to prevent a rise in the scale. To some it seemed, as the century wore on, that 'each of the different ranks of men are perpetually pressing upon that above them', and that the process applied 'even' to 'the lower class'.[1] The rider needs strong qualification: the lower class was not in the same position as the rest.[2] But the very possibility of movement in any case meant that the ladder was fairly narrow. An active crowd, particularly urban, was jostling at the foot. And if opportunities for betterment existed, which themselves had their unsettling aspect, so equally did the dangers of a crash, bringing fear and resentment and the threat of unrest.

The behaviour of the crowd was assumed to be unpredictable. It might prove 'reasonable, or good-natured' if boldly faced;[3] it might have its inner discipline and limited targets. But no one could be sure, and in any case the limits were not much consolation to the sufferers. The degree of violence need not depend upon the ostensible aim: the worst political or religious riots since 1780 had in fact been those on behalf of 'Church and King'. Their excesses stiffened Government's attitude to disturbance from any quarter, and in 1792 it could point to a recent ugly case. The Birmingham or Priestley riots (so called from the most famous victim) showed many features from the past projected into a time of change. While the trouble was sparked off by a celebration in honour of the French Revolution – by a Bastille dinner on 14 July 1791 – it was linked at least as closely with the reaction to the campaign for the repeal of the Corporation and Test Acts. The two local leaders in that effort had been Unitarians; Priestley himself had become a bogyman;[4] and there was a long history, stretching back for at least three-quarters of a century, of riots against Dissenters from 'the bustling, booby-faced Birmingham mob'.[5] The dinner in 1791, for that reason, had carefully been chaired by an Anglican; it was held expeditiously, and Priestley himself stayed away. But a crowd gathered – its clarity of mind was shown by some shouts of 'No Popery' – and after the diners had dispersed the tavern was wrecked. Threats and destruction followed for

1. *The London Chronicle* in 1773, quoted in Harold Perkin, *The Origins of Modern English Society 1780–1880* (1969), 93.
2. See pp. 151–3 below.
3. Lord Eldon's – of all people – comment, recalling his success in arguing a mob out of dragging him from his carriage when he was Attorney General during the treason trials of 1794 (*Lord Eldon's Anecdote Book*, ed. Anthony L.J. Lincoln and Robert Lindley McEwen (1960), 101).
4. See p. 64 above.
5. See R.B. Rose, loc. cit., 70–1.

the inside of a week. Priestley's library and laboratory were destroyed, and his house and chapel burned down. So were the houses, shops and chapels of some other prominent Dissenters. The crowd then moved out into the countryside, burning, looting, seizing food and drink. On the 18th the Dragoons arrived, and Birmingham itself was brought to order. It took a few more days for the riots as a whole to be suppressed.

The damage was calculated at £100,000, of which about a quarter was paid in compensation. Seventeen people were tried, four found guilty, and two hanged. These facts, and the length of time which elapsed before the troops' appearance, deepened suspicions already raised by the behaviour of the local magistrates. The strong Anglican and conservative traditions of the Birmingham authorities had for some years been growing more specific under pressure from Dissenting wealth and the complementary spread of a lively intellectual activity. The divisions were becoming sharper as prosperity increased and the city emerged as 'the Great Toy Shop of Europe'.[1] When the Priestley riot began the justices seemed curiously slow to act. They appear to have countenanced the burning of chapels and done little to disperse the mob, and while special constables were enrolled the two magistrates present at the start were even said to have been heard cheering on the violence. It is hard to tell how far in fact there was active connivance or worse at first: the justices may have been hoping by such tactics to limit an outburst they could hardly control. But certainly they were dilatory and at best indecisive, content to keep their heads down until the troops arrived. In this indeed they were not untypical of many magistrates elsewhere: rough parallels may be drawn with Manchester and other northern and midland towns. But all in all it was not surprising, and it may have been justifiable, that the local authorities should have been accused of initially favouring the crowd.

Similar accusations were levied against Government. The slow movement of the troops, the small number of prosecutions and their relative failure, led to charges that the victims had been deliberately ignored. On a closer look this contention cannot be sustained. The Ministry was not deeply frightened by the events at Birmingham: it viewed them, rightly, as of limited importance.[2] But it was not disposed to gloss them over or evade its authority, and in fact it acted with all the force it could. The magistrates' letter calling for troops was sent to London on 15 July; others from private persons followed over the next two days. The Home Office and the Secretary at War moved at once. The first order went out on the 16th, and others the next day. The former reached Nottingham on the morning of the 17th, and the

1. Burke's phrase. See in general J. Money, 'Birmingham and the West Midlands, 1760–1793 . . .' (*Midland History*, I, no. 1). The famous Lunar Society of Birmingham, which included Priestley himself, was at the apex of a pyramid that contained the less exclusive Amicable and Robin Hood debating societies.
2. Cf. p. 78 above.

Dragoons were under way within the hour. But they were heavy cavalry, they had almost sixty miles to go, and it was evening before they reached the outskirts of the town. They entered the next morning, and remained in the area for three or four days, while other forces were held in reserve, largely against the danger of riots elsewhere.[1] By the end of the week they could be withdrawn, but foot troops replaced them. On the 19th Samuel Garbett wrote that Birmingham was under a 'great obligation' for the Home Secretary's speedy response.[2]

Throughout the rest of July troops reinforced the midlands, particularly in Warwickshire and as far afield as Oxford. The Government meanwhile tried to bring the offenders to book. 'It being His Majesty's earnest desire that every measure should be taken for bringing to punishment the Persons concerned in the violent Outrages', the Treasury Solicitor, accompanied by a barrister and one of the Bow Street magistrates – 'In order to give a greater appearance of solemnity . . ., and the more strongly to mark the attention of Government to this object' – were sent to investigate and if necessary 'order a special Commission for . . . more speedy Trial'.[3] They moved as fast as they could. But the juries would seldom convict. 'The prejudices are . . . strong in favour of the Rioters', and on the first acquittal 'Exultation began to take place in the Court' – this was from Worcester, where several offenders had been picked up. '. . . The same Spirit ran through the whole town, and the Rioters wanted not for Friends' – this was from Oxford;[4] and in general the picture held good. In Birmingham itself it proved impossible to count on informers, despite the rewards. The Treasury Solicitor and his team found it hard going.

Not unnaturally some authorities took some comfort from 'the Spirit'. The 'Zeal' of the juries, 'however Mistaken arose', it could be said, 'from Loyalty',[5] and the King himself was not dismayed by the thought that 'Priestley is the sufferer for the doctrines he and his party have instilled'.[6] The Lord Lieutenant in Ireland voiced a similar satisfaction: 'I am not sorry even for the *excess, excessive as it has been*'.[7] It seems highly doubtful, however, if more sophisticated Ministers felt the same. Dundas at the Home Office certainly did not, and as a Home Secretary of less than three months' standing he was unlikely to have written as he did to a

1. Eg in Coventry, Wolverhampton, Manchester, Leicester, and Bristol. Troops of Dragoons as far afield as Bradford and Trowbridge were held ready to move.

2. To Nepean (P.R.O., H.O. 42/19, on which with H.O. 43/4 and *L.C.G. III*, I, nos. 691–2, this paragraph is mainly based).

3. Copy of Dundas to William Chamberlayne, 21 July 1791 (H.O. 42/19).

4. Chamberlayne to Nepean, 10 August, 26 August 1791 (loc. cit.).

5. Same to same, 26 August 1791 (loc. cit.).

6. To Dundas, 16 July 1791 (*L.C.G. III*, I, no. 691). He continued, 'yet cannot approve of their ['the people'] having employed atrocious means of shewing their discontent'.

7. Marquess of Buckingham to W.W. Grenville, 19 July 1791 (*H.M.C., Dropmore*, II, 133). For his temperamental shortcomings see I, 130–1.

county authority unless his sentiments were shared by Pitt. It was not only that violence on this scale was intolerable, whatever its cause. The cause itself was not served by such means, and indeed it was not clear-cut. No doubt a riot for Church and King could 'create a prepossession in its favor. But it must not be forgot that dangerous precedents generally originate in commendable motives', and how commendable indeed were the motives when it came to the point? The concentration of violence against prosperous citizens suggested that in point of fact it might have arisen very largely from a 'levelling principle'.[1] This was a shrewd judgment, in face of the prevailing view. It may have been influenced by a report from the senior officer on the spot, who was surprised that 'the standard' raised had not been that of 'sedition'.[2] 'The people' was a dangerous entity. Its emotions were fickle. William Grenville, a recent Home Secretary, may have spoken for the inner ring of his colleagues when he declared 'I do not admire riots in favour of Government much more than riots against it'.[3]

A year later the danger came from the latter rather than the former. The Ministry's view of the reforming, and above all the popular, Societies was coloured by the fact. It was sad – one might say tragic – that this should have been so: that the latter's early genuine desire for legality could not have been given greater weight. It may seem clear to us that their intentions, so far from relying on the pressure of violence, were directed on the contrary to peaceful means at the start. In many respects they could have been contrasted, not linked, with the mob. But aware of its limited resources as revealed once more by recent experience, Government was unlikely to draw distinctions of this sort. The men who formed the popular bodies came precisely from those social levels which so often gave momentum to unrest; the more articulate they became, and the more they corresponded with the older Societies, the greater the danger of support from more powerful quarters. If political debate seemed to the participants an alternative to violence, it seemed to the authorities in this case a potential incitement. Associations on the old lines were one thing, working men's gatherings quite another; and the possible combination could have unknown effects. The literature for discussion now added to the dangers: new ideas were working on old forces, sedition itself now had its text. As events in France grew worse, the novel gave point to the familiar. Continuity and discontinuity were about to meet.

1. Draft of Dundas to the Earl of Orford, September 1791 (H.O. 42/19). Cf. p. 104 above.

2. De Lancey to Sir William Fawcett, 21 July 1791 (*L.C.G. III*, I, no. 692).

3. To Auckland, 22 July 1791 (*H.M.C., Dropmore*, II, 136). Auckland, from across the Channel, was not so sure. 'I heartily adopt your . . . abhorrence of popular riots', he answered, 'whatever may be their pretext or object; but under the present circumstances . . . in Europe, I cannot lament the late scandalous scenes at Birmingham, though I am sorry for the distresses and losses to which many individuals have been exposed' (26 July 1791; loc. cit., 140).

III

When the Ministry decided on preventive action in May 1792, it knew that success could not follow from itself alone. Government did not command effective means of enforcing censorship, any more than it commanded an effective police. However one approaches the problem, one is impressed by the extent to which containment of disorder relied on the co-operation of the propertied ranks. This of course is generally so in a pluralistic society; in England in the late eighteenth century it was the case in exceptional degree. The boundaries within which Ministers moved – the extent of other interests' immediate control – demanded a wide measure of mutual agreement based on a broad common approach. This is how oligarchies work when they are in their heyday, whatever the degree of centralisation or of dispersal of functions. Their capacity for survival under pressure can further turn on the extent to which they appeal to the less powerful elements within the limits of the oligarchic pattern.[1]

The first and greatest line of defence was of course the gentry. Indeed if the gentry was hostile or split the edifice would crack. The nobility, for all its weight, did not form a separate interest: neither its privileges nor influence were generically distinct. It was the gentry, culminating in the peerage, that ran local affairs and supplied the Parliamentary class, and whose attitudes and way of life were accepted (not always applauded) and widely (not always) copied as a governing norm. Its support had long been of vital concern to the Crown, and as the clouds began to gather a familiar appeal was heard, one that for over three centuries had lain at the root of English government. When Henry VIII's new ecclesiastical order had to be enforced, the sheriffs and justices of the counties were the men 'especially elected and chosen . . . for this purpose, . . . such men as unto whose wisdom, discretion, truth and fidelity we might commit . . . a matter of such great weight'. When trouble spread in 1792 Ministers turned to 'the magistrates and gentlemen of the country', for 'In truth, without [their] assistance . . . it is very vain for Government' to try to act.[2] The gentlemen of the shire were the leaders and guides of their 'countries'. As justices they had the legal authority to act and to judge. They were the central link in the chain of that 'Constitutional Doctrine of reciprocity' which was one of mutual protection and support.[3] Given 'a Government such as the

1. I am disregarding here the arguments of some social scientists that power in all forms of society, however defined, is in practice oligarchic. The term is used in its valid historical sense.

2. Quoted from the royal letter of 1535, in G.R. Elton, *Policy and Police, The Enforcement of the Reformation in the Age of Thomas Cromwell* (1972), 239–40; Grenville to Buckingham, 14 November 1792 (Buckingham, II, 226). The Home Office had said something similar after the Birmingham riots in 1791 (draft to Orford, September 1791; P.R.O., H.O. 42/19).

3. Marquess Townshend to [?Dundas], 7 September 1791 (H.O. 42/19).

Constitution has made ours', the maintenance of order fell squarely on them.[1]

So too, as in the past, did the best hope of proper information.[2] Throughout the peacetime decade following 1783 the Ministry seems to have employed few paid agents of its own. This applies, perhaps unequally, to both foreign and domestic intelligence, but particularly to the latter, including the years 1789–93. One cannot be entirely certain of the facts from correspondence or the financial accounts, for in such matters neither are necessarily complete. But within its limits the evidence is fairly convincing. Home Secret Service was met from the Civil List, with an annual ceiling of £10,000 which had been set by Burke's Economical Reform Act of 1782. There were some other possible sources in the Crown's reserved revenues, which were allocated by the King and to some extent by Ministers unhampered by Parliamentary control; and while some of these funds had vanished with the loss of the American colonies, others, such as the income from the Duchy of Lancaster, remained.[3] But the Home Secret Service allowance itself varied little over this period: after an immediate post-war drop to £3,000 in 1784 it was £7,000 in 1785, £10,600 in 1786, £10,000 in 1787 and 1788, £8,000 in 1789, and £10,000 for each of the next three years.[4] There may possibly have been some further disbursements out of the Home Secretary's Foreign Secret Service funds, which for administrative convenience may also have covered certain items at home.[5] But the

1. Grenville to Buckingham, 14 November 1792 (Buckingham, II, 227).

2. Cf. the address of Thomas Wriothesley [Cromwell's Secretary] to the Hampshire Quarter Sessions in April 1539 (Elton, op. cit., 370).

3. See J.E.D. Binney, *British Finance and Administration 1774–92* (1958), 120–1; John Norris, *Shelburne and Reform* (1963), 187–8.

4. The sources are various, and broadly those used by Alfred Cobban to compute payments for Foreign Secret Service (also borne on the Civil List) in his article 'British Secret Service in France, 1784–92' (*E.H.R.*, reprinted in his *Aspects of the French Revolution* (1968), ch. 10). Discounting possible small payments by the Home Secretary himself (see below), Home Secret Service was met, out of Class VIII in the Civil List, by the Treasury. The retrospective 'Account of. . . Secret Service Money, for the last Twenty-five Years', of 1798–9 (*Parliamentary Papers . . ., 106, Accounts and Papers*, XLVIII), when checked against P.R.O., T.38/168–70, 53/56–60, 60/26–8, A.O. 1/2121, is generally reliable; where there are differences, I have relied primarily on T.38/168–9, 60/26–8. The 'Report from the [Commons'] Committee on the Civil List Accounts' of 15 March 1802 (*Parliamentary Papers, Miscellaneous, 1801–2*), which also gives figures, is rather less satisfactory. There is a volume of Secret Service payments, 1782–1789, kept by Evan Nepean of the Home Office, in the Sydney Mss at the William L. Clements Library in the University of Michigan; but this covers foreign as well as home payments, and the two categories cannot always be distinguished. The same applies to Dundas's Secret Service accounts from 1792 (not extensive) in the Melville Mss at Duke University, North Carolina; and to the requests for money from the Home Office to the Treasury in P.R.O., H.O. 36/4–7. For these sources see R.R. Nelson, *The Home Office, 1782–1801* (1969), Ch. Five.

5. See 22 Geo. III, c. 82, art. xxvii. The Home Secretary's Secret Service payments, unlike the Treasury's which were generally listed as being for 'Home' or 'Domestic' Secret Service, were listed exclusively as being for 'Foreign Secret Service'. Any sums applied to the domestic purposes prescribed by the Act should therefore have been included with the 'foreign' disbursements.

totals from this source were not large, and since the higher payments from the middle eighties corresponded with crises abroad the allocations to genuinely domestic purposes were probably quite small.[1] One other form of payment, under the same Class in the Civil List, seems at this stage to have had nothing to do with Home Secret Service: this was the variety of disbursements for Special Services, which covered quite other favours, functions and dues.[2] Issues to the Post Office for secret service, discontinued under that name by Burke's Act, were now made from the Foreign Secret Service funds – probably in part at least by the Home Secretary – and before 1792 at any rate were confined largely to intercepting foreign mails.[3]

When it is remembered that some of the funds went on newspaper subsidies for political services,[4] the scale of paid domestic intelligence (even allowing for the Crown's reserved revenues) would thus appear to have been quite modest. The same impression arises from the scattered references to agents in Ministerial papers and the Home Office files. Few of those employed at the start appear to have been spies pure and simple: more often, in this small circle, they were or had been associated with the law. There were some 'watchers', used irregularly, several of whom seem to have begun by volunteering their services. One such followed the newspaper editor Sampson Perry and a suspect associate in 1789; another, Thomas Parker, who had kept (or failed to keep) an eye on the Latin American Miranda in 1790,[5] 'perambulated the Town' in 1792; a few professionals were used in the late eighties to watch such assorted figures as the Chevalier D'Eon, Calonne, and the French and Spanish and Russian envoys; a certain de Cruchant or de Cruchent, patronised by the royal Duke of Gloucester, reported sometimes on French visitors and refugees. Barely distinguishable from such men were some of the informers who (where they were not anonymous) wrote in hope of a reward. But here again a proportion came from the lower reaches of the law. The most effective agents were often of this type – William Metcalfe and John Groves, who penetrated the London Corresponding Society, were or had been practising attorneys.[6] They did not form an organised network, and few of them were as yet highly regarded: the Home Office was obliged to use or to listen to them, but it did so cautiously and often

---

1. Not allowing for fees, the totals (to the nearest £) dropped from £5,965 in 1784 to £1,000 in 1785, £1,500 in 1786, £4,000 in 1787 (the Dutch crisis), £1,000 in both 1788 and 1789, £3,460 in 1790 (the Nootka Sound crisis), £1,580 in 1791, and £3,434 in 1792 (sources as in p. 136, n4 above).

2. See P.R.O., T.38/741–2, 744.

3. Kenneth Ellis, *The Post Office in the Eighteenth Century* (1958), 67–9, Appendix 3.

4. I, 143–4, 605–6. Election expenses on the other hand – though these were now a declining item – were removed from Secret Service funds by the Act of 1782.

5. For whom see I, 385–6.

6. See in general P.R.O., H.O. 42/14 *et seq*; Secret Service payments, Sydney Mss, Clements Library, Michigan; Clive Emsley, 'Public Order in England 1790–1801' (M. Litt. thesis, Cambridge University, 1970), 224–53. Nelson, op. cit., 87–94, is useful for names and activities in the earlier and middle eighties.

at arm's length.[1] This was sometimes easier, as well as less expensive, because in the early nineties groups of magistrates were beginning to employ their own agents direct. But Government had employed a regular 'spymaster', William Clarke, since the early eighties at least, and when the system was enlarged on the outbreak of war he was either reinforced or succeeded by another – Hugh Cleghorn, recently Professor of Civil History at St Andrew's – to act as a screen between the Office and its paid informants.

More weight was usually placed on intelligence from the Post Office – mostly from intercepted mail, sometimes from postmasters' news. Officials of all kinds indeed, above all in the ports and the coastal regions, supplied reports and rumours in a growing stream. They were paralleled by others from private 'respectable' voluntary sources, particularly from the clergy and gentry headed by the magistrates themselves. The volume and often the quality of such news was again highly uneven: Grenville lamented over one incident that 'of all the King's good subjects, who are exclaiming against its not being noticed, not one thought it worth his while to apprise the Secretary of State'. He added that on inquiry the story had no real foundation; but 'It is not unnatural, nor is it an unfavourable symptom, that people who are thoroughly frightened, as the body of landed gentlemen in this country are, should exaggerate these stories as they pass from one mouth to another'.[2] The Ministry indeed was in a dilemma familiar to Governments in time of unrest, heightened by the ethos and resources of the age. Unable and unwilling in those early years to build an effective system of its own, it must rely as widely as possible on voluntary information. But the more it could do so – the more it could draw on public support – the harder to weigh the results, and attitudes largely but not always shared. In the event the balance was often held in specific cases – a good deal better in fact than one might sometimes expect. Ministers received, and knew they received, plenty of false or prejudiced tales, and within the framework of their own apprehensions tried to keep their heads. They certainly did not always succeed, and some of them stopped trying. But while they could be swayed and sometimes panicked by informers' and spies' reports, they remained more sympathetic to those from the gentry and the regular officials, who might be nervous or stupid or self-interested but did not live by selling their wares. In this indeed they were probably right, for so far as can be seen news and impressions from 'respectable' persons formed the most reliable source, taken as a single category, in this initial phase.

1. Eg its treatment of Parker.
2. To Buckingham, 14 November 1792 (Buckingham, II, 227–8). Grenville was then acting as Home Secretary for Dundas, who was on a visit to Scotland.

'The body of landed gentlemen' 'are thoroughly frightened'.[1] It was possible to write in this way not only from the nature of the threat but also because the gentry was now at heart a homogeneous force. It had hardly been so a century, and certainly not a century and a half, before, and very real divisions had persisted into the reigns of the early Hanoverians. Whig and Tory gentry then could often be distinguished by financial as well as political fortune. But while the former discrepancies had if anything increased between the larger and smaller landowners, the latter's definition had become progressively blurred. The criss-cross of political connexions, which reflected intricate relationships, also argued by its very existence the limits within which they moved; and if in a crisis such as the American War a genuine conflict could re-emerge, it was not entirely on earlier lines and could as quickly decline. The dynastic question had long been settled; religious issues were less obtrusive; and with a broader consolidation and variety – though not a levelling – of its wealth, with legal refinements of inheritance, and a temporary drop in purchase from outside, the landed order in a period of general agricultural prosperity could really be taken as something very like a whole. So at least its reactions to the older forms of unrest might suggest. There was less occasion for dissatisfied squires to support or countenance popular protest out of hostility to mercantile interests or the larger landowners or the Court. They still sometimes showed paternal protection, particularly perhaps in the case of a bread riot or when the unpopular Excise was involved.[2] But the instances seem to have been rarer than in the first half of the century, when political loyalties partly reflected and partly intensified social interests. The two were not yet fused together as tightly as they were soon to become, and local allegiance to Opposition could still make itself felt. There were places where magistrates were reluctant to act as vigorously as Government wished: in Sheffield and Nottingham, in parts of the west country, occasionally in the north-east. Sometimes they hung back out of caution, sometimes from Foxite sympathies in a period in which these were not yet automatically suspect. But as the pressures grew, above all after a year of war, the essential solidarity of the gentry was revealed.

The propertied orders as a whole, however, embraced a wider range; downwards to the yeomen and freeholders, elsewhere to other forms of wealth which were penetrated by the landed order, but not always friendly to it or so readily accustomed to a natural role in public affairs. 'The Safety of the Country', Dundas told Pitt – and while he was writing from Scotland his remarks applied to England as well – 'must I am

---

1. P. 138 above.
2. For opinion on the Excise in general see I, 253, 291–2; for one clear and typical instance at this time, which found its way to Pitt, Lord Grimston and William Plumer (from Ware) to ?, 9 January 1789 (P.R.O. 30/8/242).

persuaded depend on the Body of the well effected [*sic*] to the Constitution . . . taking an open, an active and declared part'.[1] He was not thinking here of the nobility and gentry alone; and he was posing a serious problem in seeking to engage other 'well-informed and weighty' elements[2] in positive support.

For there was less opportunity and incentive for such men to 'take an active part'. Merchants and manufacturers, the larger shipbuilders, a wide range among the lawyers, dons and sections of the parish clergy and the Dissenting ministers, a variety of persons with an 'independence' derived at a remove from land or from trade – such categories, listed in the tables at the turn of the century,[3] were at once more diffuse and often less immediately involved. Many of their members, thanks to the irregularities of the Parliamentary franchise, the weighted choice of Parliamentary candidates, and the religious limitations of local government, were at best on the fringe of that regular contact with the springs of authority which was still so largely vested in the landed order itself. In theory, and to some extent in practice, it was a proud English boast that 'the great mass of property, both landed, monied and commercial, finds itself represented'. But it remained a fact of government, local as well as central, that 'Landed property is the basis on which every other species of material property rests'.[4] The landed peers and squires and their families were the main dispensers and receivers of patronage. However unpolitical some of them might be, they were linked with the system and familiar with its terms. And while their ranks were being constantly extended by marriage or achievement, this was a limited process which left the bulk of the 'middling ranks' untouched. 'Trade', it had earlier been declared, 'is . . . far here from being inconsistent with a gentleman'.[5] But the dynamic by its nature was selective, and industry as yet was scarcely involved. It was not by adoption that the mass of property was to be enrolled in the protection of social order so much as by mutual agreement that diverse interests were equally at stake.

Such agreement could not always be taken for granted; and where it could it might have to be changed from passive acquiescence into active support. Neither the mercantile nor the manufacturing interest, to take the main entities, was cohesive; both contained variety as did the landed interest, but the internal links were far less strong. Certain great trading bodies – the Chartered Companies, the West India merchants – were used to dealing with Government or speaking in Parliament as groups. More recently, the manufacturers had coalesced briefly in a General

1. 22 November 1792 (P.R.O. 30/8/157).
2. See I, 145.
3. See George Chalmers's edition (1804) of Gregory King's seventeenth-century lists, and Patrick Colquhoun's publications of the same decade.
4. Arthur Young, *The Example of France* . . . (1794), 106; William Marshall, *On the Landed Property of England* (1804), 1.
5. Daniel Defoe, *The Complete English Tradesman* (1726), 376.

Chamber, and even voiced resentment at their exclusion from 'the great council of the nation'.[1] But the General Chamber did not last long: it was split by quarrels and suspect to Ministers – including Pitt, who far less than most was 'unacquainted with their real interests'.[2] And the very solidarity and exclusiveness of the great mercantile bodies underlined their mutual divisions and weakened a collective voice.[3] In such circumstances, sectional influences were strong in shaping answers to national themes. The textile oligarchy of Leeds differed greatly in outlook from those of Derby or Nottingham; the maritime merchant community of Liverpool from those of Hull or the Port of London itself. The social and political resemblances were often less immediate than the distinctions. Neither the industrial nor even the mercantile interest was a coherent national force.

One of the important differentiations could be religious allegiance. There was only one continuing family of Dissenting peers, and the squirearchy was mainly Anglican. Merchants, manufacturers, attorneys, members of the 'useful professions' – not to mention shopkeepers and opulent tradesmen – were affected more often by denomination. Creed, whatever the degree of tolerance or of alliance in a given cause,[4] was a separating element in the old society, and the developments of the 1790s both pointed and complicated the effects. Some of the lines were blurred, others were sharpened or altered as parts of the social structure began unmistakably to change. This is not to say – it is far from saying – that men, directly or indirectly, accepted that their religion was primarily a social or an economic function. Neither ministers nor the practising laity, of whatever complexion, would have admitted to holding their faith by reference to secular ends. But precisely because religious practice was imbedded in the national life it was bound to affect and be affected by the national experience.

The results, diversified and complex, penetrated the people at large. They did much to define the attitudes of sections of the 'middling sort'. Beyond its division into Anglican or Nonconformist, with Wesleyan Anglicans moving from the Church, the relative strengths of the sects were shifting, as they had been for some time. The English Presbyterians and the Quakers – the latter often rich and highly respectable – were approaching a crisis following a decline; the General Baptists were losing ground to the Particular Baptists and the Unitarians; almost all the older connexions were subject to schism and fresh dissent. So again was

1. See their declaration in 1784, quoted in Perkin, op. cit., 29.

2. Ibid. See I, 208–9, 486, 491–2.

3. Perhaps the closest that varied trading interests came to achieving an association was in the General Meeting of Merchants in London, which seems to have been a semi-permanent body consulted – together with merchants in the outports – by Government on several occasions between 1786 and 1788 (see I, 289n3). But it does not appear to have attained a lasting formal identity.

4. See pp. 58–60, 62 above.

Methodism once John Wesley died; his overshadowing authority had held the burgeoning movement together. And on the remoter fringes old and new smaller congregations were active – Sandemanians, Shakers, Swedenborgians, Anabaptists, Moravians, Muggletonians. The pattern, in so far as there was one, was partly personal and often regional; set by leading preachers or administrators, and old areas of concentration. But it was widely spread, the shifting movements testified to its vitality, and they both contributed and responded to those of political events.

For the old strengths of Nonconformity were again displayed in contrasting ways, as was always liable to happen in unsettled times. Respectability and protest were equal manifestations of Dissent, representing different strands and each able to claim biblical support. Men of property – often small property – in the Nonconformist, and now the Wesleyan, chapels were apt to find themselves in an anomalous position. The internal disputes and attacks – from rival, openly radical sects, or from radicals in solidly established congregations, or activists in quietist communities – drove many of them, not always willingly, towards support for a political order which yet, and indeed now all the more firmly, continued to limit their secular rights. They faced both ways, mostly (for as always there was a trickle of prosperous Dissenters to the Church itself) unwilling to identify too closely with the landed Anglican interest, but also gravely perturbed by the challenges from within. In the short run, their dilemma was to save Pitt from some of the consequences of his recent behaviour over the Corporation and Test Acts.[1] In the longer term, and despite the great gains made by Nonconformity throughout the country, it was to weaken the social ties which had marked the old Dissent. But neither process, particularly the latter, could be clearly foreseen in 1792. These were early days; the religious scene was confused. And if the middling and the upper orders were to be drawn into developing relations, the results could not always be taken for granted when Government first looked round for support.

The influence of sectarian and social development was felt beyond the sects themselves. 'Dissent, old and new, helped to carry over and transform the latent vertical antagonism of the old society into the overt class hostility of the new'.[2] We are indeed standing here, as throughout, uneasily on the verge of class. The exact significance of the term at this time is open to discussion.

Contemporary usage itself was imprecise, and can seem ambiguous. 'Class' could be taken – as in school and at the Wesleyan meeting – in the simple sense of classification while the categories were still described by

1. See pp. 72–3 above.
2. Perkin, op. cit., 281.

other names. Thus Adam Smith had written of 'classes of people' in listing the 'orders of society',[1] and such broad terminology went back to Defoe at least. In general indeed, when the word had been used it was a convenient variant on other expressions deemed to be of a similar kind. 'Ranks' or 'orders' or even 'degrees', 'interests' when the theme was more directly economic – these terms, which to us can imply distinctive connotations, were often taken as interchangeable with 'classes' themselves. The Scottish professor John Millar, one of the 'fathers of sociology',[2] wrote in this sense in 1771, on the rare occasions that he mentioned classes in his account of *The Origin of the Distinction of Ranks*. And the same approach can be seen in the eighties and nineties: the evangelical Thomas Gisborne published in 1795 an *Enquiry into the Duties of Men in the Higher Ranks and Middle Classes of Society in Great Britain*, and when Hannah More in the following year addressed tracts to 'Persons of the Middle Ranks' she noted that they were widely bought by 'the gentry and middling classes'. Evangelicals indeed seem to have been rather in the habit of talking, loosely, of classes; but there were examples from very different quarters. 'The phrase "higher classes"', it has been said, 'was used for the first time by Burke in his *Thoughts on French Affairs* in 1791'.[3]

The same variation applied farther down the scale. Jonas Hanway in 1772 published his *Observations on the Causes of the Dissoluteness which reigns among the Lower Classes of the People*; half a century later, Francis Place and the new Quarterly reviews alike were talking quite as often of 'people' and 'sorts'. This was the last generation to do so, as the social consequences of industrialisation reached a stage at which terminology hardened into new forms. It was a change which was accompanied by the equally gradual transformation in the accepted meaning of the phrase 'the public'.[4]

The inexactitudes of terminology, in an age when social structures were receiving fresh study – when new foundations for such studies were indeed being laid – may reasonably be held to reflect the conditions of its employment. Classes as we think of them spring from industrial society; ranks, orders and degrees suggest older social forms. In the prolonged early phases of capitalism the two could, jaggedly, interlock; conceptions of status and incentives to class could conflict and co-exist. But even where economic pressures might foster the latter, they were neither wide

1. See *The Wealth of Nations*, Bk. I, ch. 11.
2. See eg Ronald L. Meek, 'The Scottish Contribution to Marxist Sociology', in *Democracy and the Labour Movement*, ed. John Saville (1954).
3. Asa Briggs, 'The Language of "Class" in Early Nineteenth Century England', in *Essays in Labour History . . .*, ed. Asa Briggs and John Saville (1960), 51. He also notes an interesting use of 'middle classes' by the General Chamber of Manufacturers in 1785.
    The interchangeability of these terms in this period, however, did not perhaps entirely remove an older distinction between 'orders' and 'estates' as defined by law on the one hand, and 'interests' and 'classes' as purely economic or social categories on the other.
4. See I, 144.

nor deep enough seriously to upset the former's strength. 'Class' has been defined, among many definitions, as not only 'a group of people', but equally 'a force or mechanism that operates to produce social attitudes'. For this it has first to develop into 'a force that unites into groups people who differ from one another, by overriding the differences between them'.[1] In the late eighteenth century social groupings had scarcely begun to alter; and attitudes and organisation generally follow at a remove. Contemporaries were more conscious of the pace of mobility within an older system than of the first signs of a prospective basic change. For two centuries at least economic development had embraced 'vertical' and 'horizontal' structures; but with an emphasis on the former that preserved appropriate social ideas. Who would now envisage a fundamental shift, rather than a further stage in a known if hastening process? Social arrangements could still be conceived as a broad-based pyramid, the unbroken lines of which were angled to a peak.[2] It would indeed have been far-seeing at this point to postulate at all precisely a class structure of society in place of more familiar norms.

The fact had political implications – perhaps one might say a political equivalent. The concept of class at the least implies, and more often postulates, struggle. Very few men in the late eighteenth century – no major British political theorist – had a developed vision of normal political conflict. Such a 'point of departure', it has been argued, 'is [now] so familiar that we take it for granted': whatever names are applied '– progress and reaction, liberalism and conservatism, movement and order, left and Right – . . . that is what politics are about'.[3] It is so powerful an interpretation that it can be imposed retrospectively on periods and situations which did not consciously respond. When the latter did so, in whatever degree, the interest is naturally intense: in the Great Rebellion in England for example, above all in the French Revolution. Political disturbance on such a scale, against a background of economic pressures, can certainly be a forcing ground for the development of social concepts; in the terms in which we have been talking, 'class is more important when times are bad, status when they are good'.[4] But the intellectual framework of the late eighteenth century had still to be refashioned; 'thesis', 'antithesis' and 'synthesis' lay in the,

1. T.H. Marshall, 'The Nature of Class Conflict', in *Sociology at the Crossroads* . . . (1963), 171.

2. Perhaps one might again illustrate here, if parenthetically, by the use of terms. In the closing phases of a long age, in the early nineteenth century, the words 'chain' and 'bond', soon to be synonymous with exploitation, retained their old sense of approval. 'Bond of attachment', 'chain of connection' – such phrases appear, if by then defensively, not only in writers such as Southey and Cobbett but in a range of Nonconformist literature.

3. J.M. Roberts, 'The French Origins of the Right', in *Trans. R. Hist. S., Fifth Series*, 23 (1973), 27.

4. W.G. Runciman, *Social Science and Political Theory*, (2nd edn., 1969), 142.

not very remote, future. If in the narrower Parliamentary terms party warfare in England was still widely suspect,[1] the concept of inherent social conflict, imposing a pattern of continuous movement, was similarly alien to the main stream of political thought.

That is not to say that political balance was held to exclude its own kind of movement. In England of all places this was certainly not the case. As industrial society did not spring out of a static traditional economy, but rather from a long period of developing forms, so likewise political concepts had evolved in that period which introduced elements of dissolution into an earlier order. England indeed, it could be (and was) said, was the native home of the process, the model for its adoption in America and France. The Protestant ethic was strong, with its implications for individual freedom. The emphasis on political liberty, enshrined in the settlement of 1689, could be a counter-weight to prescriptive hierarchy as well as to doctrines of equality. The entrepreneurial ideal, and the conditions for differing interests, 'took off', like the economy itself, from the new technical advance. Locke and the spinning jenny, prerequisites and symbols of 'improvement', might stand in large measure for the English contribution to the Age of Reason. That age culminated on the continent in the French Revolution; how was it that these potent forces, essentially of movement, were not politically more disruptive in Britain itself?

In one sense perhaps the question may be wrongly put. It might suggest that revolutions are an easy result of movement, or even unrest. In point of fact of course they are not: it takes a great deal to spark off a revolution, a mixture of pressures and circumstances which does not readily occur. One need not postulate as a norm the extremes of stability and its overthrow: 'Political stability is a comparatively rare phenomenon in the history of human society'.[2] Taking a conventional measure, people subsist far more often in some instability; and even when the degree is marked it is likely to turn into revolution (in the immediate sense of a sudden change in the form or content of existing institutions) only when it pervades vital political areas. In the late eighteenth century, as was shown in France, this meant sections of the governing orders themselves. Although it might be theoretically possible, it was historically unknown for the lower orders to act effectively without a prior impulse from above. And that impulse, as it proved, was lacking in Britain. One has only to compare the situations in the early 1790s and the early 1830s to appreciate the fact.

It has even been suggested, indeed, that the real thwarted revolution in this country came not in the early 1790s but in the early eighties, when the county Association movement emerged and faltered and failed.[3] One need not accept the argument to recognise its starting point: the

1. Cf. I, 30–1, 47–8, 614–21.
2. J.H. Plumb, *The Growth of Political Stability in England 1675–1725* (1967), xvi.
3. H. Butterfield, *George III, Lord North, and the People, 1779–1780* (1949). And see I, 59, 67–73.

crucial importance of the attitudes of the gentry and mercantile interests. When allied, however uneasily, with Parliamentary spokesmen, these were the quarters from which a serious threat could come. For as with a Ministry, so with a propertied society itself, 'it was ; . . very difficult to bring [it] down from outside, unless it was already ripening for a fall from within'.[1] In 1792, and even some years later, there were few signs of such internal decay: on the contrary, external dangers strengthened defences that were full of vigour. Initial complacency and subsequent alarm produced the same broad effects. The established order first expected and then resolved to contain the threat.

The complacency had been strengthened by the successes of recent years. This indeed was Pitt's contribution to the atmosphere at the start. The confidence of 1791 was not overturned but tempered by the precautionary movements of the following summer. In point of fact, in many ways the first half of 1792 was a very confident time. The economic boom seemed to be reaching fresh levels, 'a load of taxes' was 'repealed',[2] and while party activity in Parliament had risen following the stimulus of Ochakov, political feeling in the country soon quietened down again. France was not yet giving cause for serious alarm; but in so far as comparisons were drawn, events across the Channel strengthened many Englishmen's self-esteem. The country was prosperous, the King more popular than he had been for many years. As they measured the extent of recovery since the end of the American War, men of property felt good reason to reaffirm their faith in the Constitution.

Much indeed could be made of the contrast with France over the past decade, following a struggle in which she seemed to have redressed the earlier balance. For on the contrary, as could now be seen, her misfortunes in the later eighties had been largely caused or compounded by the effects of that war. The critical strain on her central finances threw into glaring relief the impact on a wide range of particular interests. It proved to be the catalyst of disaster which had been feared, but avoided, in Britain, forcing into combination a series of not necessarily complementary pressures.[3] No single great trade in this country had recently suffered a major crisis, as the wine trade for instance suffered in France. There had been no industrial contraction, as followed in France – or could be held to follow – from the commercial treaty with Britain of 1786.[4] The fruits of prosperity themselves, such as the French peasant proprietors glimpsed for a spell, had not vanished largely in taxes and seigneurial dues. The Government here had not declared itself bankrupt, leading to changes of Ministers and measures. There had not been a period of mounting doubt and savagely critical

1. I, 236.
2. Op. cit., 274.
3. See op. cit., 157–61.
4. Op. cit., 190–1. The setback to the British cotton industry in 1787–8 was limited and short-lived (see op. cit., 276–7).

self-analysis, in a climate, widely accepted, of intellectual attack.

Nor had there been, arising from such problems, the particular element of a growing struggle for power and recognition within the superior orders themselves. In one important sense indeed there could not be a close parallel here, for many Governmental places in France were tied in theory to descent by inheritance. Financial reward, political power and – not least – social advancement could all depend on the possession of posts which often conferred hereditary privileges. For over a century the French Crown had oiled the administrative and social wheels with the ameliorating device of purchase of offices. But as the returns grew increasingly attractive in a period of rising financial pressures, and the Crown embarked in half-hearted desperation on new administrative reforms, the 'haves' – the existing privileged groups – drew closer together against the 'have nots', a process greatly facilitated by legal codification. The result was a diversified mass of social and political resentment which the advent of revolutionary conditions brought to a point, particularly among the unaccommodated in the high and middle bourgeoisie. Merchants and manufacturers in England too (though hardly lawyers, unlike in France)[1] might resent their exclusion from direct political power; social weight, local and national, might be too narrowly defined. But there had been no concerted successful effort to reverse familiar practices, and there was no code of office by birth or purchase to be exploited in defence.[2] However influence was acquired in England, it was not governed by such regulation; this was largely what was meant by a free society, to those who could rise in the scale. There might well be obstacles in practice, but they did not arise from legal inducements to a 'feudal reaction' such as was witnessed across the Channel. The *machinery* of power and influence in Britain, with the notable exception of the Parliamentary franchise, did not seem by contrast to demand fundamental review. There was no call here, as there was in France, to construct a constitution from first principles – or to engage in the resulting theoretical 'endless disputes'.[3] If improvement was desired, it could be specific and pragmatic. 'The question now is not general: it is not for or against all innovation; but what the nature of the innovation shall be?'[4]

1. The role of the lawyers was important. Could figures such as Thurlow, it has been asked (Alfred Cobban, 'The Myth of the French Revolution', in *Aspects of the French Revolution*, 103), or more strikingly the Scott brothers Lords Eldon and Stowell – the sons of a Tyneside coal factor – have attained high office in the eighties in France? Almost certainly not, and the frustrations of their counterparts across the Channel led a large and able group of men eventually into the Revolutionary process.

2. The nearest exception to this statement lay in the manner in which certain offices granted for life by the British Crown had come to be regarded as the property of their occupants (see I, 177). But while the practice had not been tested in the Courts, it remained – and logically for that reason – a matter of convention and not of law.

3. Grenville to Buckingham, 14 September 1789 (Buckingham, II, 165).

4. Arthur Young, *The Example of France, A Warning to Britain* (1793), 97–8.

Such an attitude in England drew its strength largely from the feeling that there was a reasonable balance between individual rights, the organs of the state, and the rights of sectional interests. Much turned on the feeling for personal rights as embodied above all in the Common Law, that unique expression of ordered liberty, a binding force in the national consciousness, an instrument whose processes were closely followed and, it might be said, instinctively assessed. Much turned, too, on the interpretation and treatment of corporate liberties – of those sectional relationships which in various forms distinguished European civilisation as a whole. For throughout most of the continent, as in Britain, there was a pattern of established institutions: in trade and industry, finance and agriculture, learning, religion and the law itself. Often drawing directly on the central power as the guarantor of their privileges, they could also be balanced with it in arrangements which had certain broad features in common. 'Constituted bodies', as they have been called[1] – assemblies in which interests were represented, and certain rights and functions constitutionally, if sometimes marginally, enjoyed – existed in most regions west of Russia and the Ottoman Empire to aid and check the governing power, where the assemblies were not also (as in some republics) the governing power themselves.[2] The central Diets of Sweden and Poland, the provincial Diets in Prussia, the Diets of Bohemia and Hungary, the City Councils in the Holy Roman Empire, the Council of the Venetian Republic, the cantonal Councils in Switzerland, the Estates of the Dutch and the Austrian Netherlands, the provincial Estates and Parlements of France, the Parliaments of Great Britain and Ireland, and formerly the colonial American Assemblies – such bodies could all, on their various bases, air grievances and discuss taxation, and within widely differing limits protect the subject's or the citizen's rights. But the differences of course were quite as prominent as the similarities, and in France and Britain – in some ways closely comparable – the former were very real indeed. In France, the regional Parlements were critically important in embodying the resistance of privileged groups to the reforming interests of the Crown. But in Britain the forces of property and privilege were not assembled in this way; the central system sought consent obtained by other means. For the authority of the British system was held to derive from its *penetration* by interests which accordingly did not require autonomous powers. They had their identities and legal rights; England was adept at evolving such forms.[3] But their representation and their liberties were lodged in a single Parliament, which unlike most continental assemblies was legally in continuous session and, far more than any such assembly, checked and forwarded the work of Govern-

1. R.R. Palmer, *The Age of the Democratic Revolution*, I (1959), ch. II.
2. There were exceptions in Denmark, Bavaria, parts of northern and southern Italy, Portugal, and a part of Spain, where old rights had fallen into disuse.
3. Cf. I, 168.

ment. So too in the final judgment were the defences of personal freedom; it was the High Court of Parliament, and no other, that made statute law. And in this capacity it embodied a limitation on privilege, for 'all private rights, which encroached on the legal authority of the Crown, tended to erect petty tyrants at the expense of the people's liberty'.[1] The equilibrium in fact in Britain lay within the central authority itself: 'every branch of our civil policy supports and is supported . . . by the rest'.[2] The theory extended to – was based on – the national polity as a whole, to reconcile freedom with authority, effective government with personal rights.

The concept of individual freedom was thus not viewed in isolation. The social philosophy was not atomistic; the Philosophical Radicals were still around the corner. Civil liberties, enshrined in law, could be expressed in corporate arrangements which were not divorced from but related to the will of the King in Parliament. This interpretation of an open society shaped the reaction of the propertied orders to the sudden combination of domestic and foreign threats. On the one hand it posited a habit of open debate and reliance on the law which it would take a very bad fright indeed to undermine. At the end of 1792, when that fright was first widespread, there was not in fact a concerted move to oppression. The Ministry was certainly alarmed, and opinion in the country certainly hardened. Many radically minded men themselves felt serious doubts. 'The *revolutionary*-party', as one of them put it, had 'revolted' reformers.[3] Nevertheless Ministers should not count on easy support for anything they might choose to do. There was now undoubtedly a 'dread of novelties', which would produce 'a great *shew* of unanimity in the higher ranks'; but deeply rooted English principles, and the trend of opinion over a generation, had not been suddenly or drastically transformed. 'Corruption or tyranny' would still provoke protest, expensive wars would be unpopular, Parliamentary reform remained a defensible ideal. These views came from a respectable Nonconformist MP with friends in responsible places. They were those of a minority now out of favour, but still in the stream of public life. And many of the sentiments, if not the deductions, were shared by a wider public, and in fact were not unknown to officials and Ministers themselves. The alarm of 1792–3 evoked a broad response from the ranks of property; but not, in every instance, in similar degree. While there was very little open dissent from the Government's precautions, and a flow of assurances of

1. Charles Yorke, the son of Lord Chancellor Hardwicke, in conversation with Montesquieu, who had favoured the dispersal of legal powers (P.C. Yorke, *The Life and Correspondence of Philip Yorke, Earl of Hardwicke*, II (1913), 173).

2. Blackstone's *Commentaries on the Laws of England*, quoted in I, 46.

3. Benjamin Vaughan to ? Nepean, 30 November 1792 (P.R.O., H.O. 42/22). And cf. Wilberforce later – 'I well remember that in 1792 or '93 . . . numbers who formerly had been sworn friends of reform were afraid of strengthening the Enemies of the Constitution' (notes on Pitt, nd, in Wilberforce Ms C34, f. 31; Bodleian Library).

active support, there were also tacit reservations in places from which it would have liked more positive help. Political diversity did not disappear; Pitt's doubters and opponents were not suddenly converted. And the Ministry for its part, through the Home Office, recognised limits beyond which it should not go. The belief in an open society did not vanish overnight; nor did the reliance on a Constitution which the established order was resolved to defend.

But the open society was collective, and the resolve was very strong. If there was an ingrained respect for freedom there was an equal determination that the structure which embodied that freedom should survive. The double threat from below and abroad was precisely of a kind to raise such a response; particularly since the foreign danger came from the hereditary enemy, France. Reasoned argument and fear, old principles and interests, national and sectional, a dread of new forces all the keener for the example on which they seemed to draw, combined in that exceptional winter of 1792 to foster a common instinct of self-preservation. If the Ministry could not count on a moratorium from its Parliamentary opponents, or the same intensity of support from every quarter of the political public, it soon found that it need not reckon with serious active opposition or significant divisions in the ranks of property faced with popular unrest.

Political principle and economic interest in fact pointed in the same direction over a wide enough social range to produce a formidable defence. There was not a comparable fusion of conditions for the active forces of discontent; the articulate groups were still highly uncertain of the extent of their demands, and the mass of people was unlikely to be, or stay, roused except by severe hardship. Emerging on a scene in which their superiors had not already moved appreciably – in which there had been no prior revolt or decay within the more powerful orders themselves – they faced immense obstacles, which were not likely to be quickly removed. The popular Societies at the outset were anxious to work with other interests; but respectable reformers were shutting the doors. A mass appeal could be sustained only if there was persistent economic distress; and no one could tell at the time if the recession would last. There was thus little immediate prospect of penetrating the existing system, and a completely unknown prospect of raising the pressure from below. For as matters stood these exponents of grievance – in contrast with France – must work from outside; and the more they had to do so the more they were confined to that role. In a diversity of local situations they must develop a national momentum which would not be aided, on current showing, by a loss of will elsewhere. The conclusion was implicit, though not all of them drew it, or indeed would have liked it. Their hopes of success must really rest on a tide of national misfortune, to attract the active sympathy of better placed elements, and to keep the people at large engaged.

But how far were the people at large involved, or sympathetic? They were by no means an undifferentiated mass. On the contrary, the gradations and differences within the lower-middling and lower orders were in some ways as elaborate as those higher up the scale. 'The people', 'the subordinate classes', lacking easy means of intercommunication, were perhaps circumscribed by local influences more directly than their superiors. The conditions of the countryside on the one hand and of many of the towns on the other, though there were areas of overlapping,[1] suggested some broad divisions of response. And in both urban and rural populations, and increasingly in the former, the lower levels had their own strata, even though the lines were often imprecise. It was indeed inherently difficult to tell exactly where those levels began; the upper edges were blurred where they merged into the 'middle ranks', as was shown by contemporary diversities of definition.[2] So too were some of the gradations among the skilled and semi-skilled men: the hierarchies of craftsmen and small tradesmen, small farmers and the more substantial smallholders, artisans, mechanics, higher estate and domestic servants. But there were hierarchies none the less, as could be seen at the lower end, where such men, enjoying their own status and self-respect and sometimes ambitions, were distinguished from the floating mass of mainly unskilled labour, and again from the vagrants and paupers – the real urban and rural poor. Such categories, well understood within the lower ranks themselves, could produce their differences of attitude when tested by unsettled times.

The distinctions however, particularly in the towns, were seldom recognised clearly from above; and there were countervailing reasons why this should have been so. The lower orders had been generally inarticulate, and organised at best on a local scale. They sent no spokesmen from their ranks to Parliament; they formed no recognised interest, and their pressures were spasmodic and generally short-lived. They were simply material to be governed, which did not enter the process of governing. They had always been regarded as being 'beyond the political pale'.[3] This attitude naturally sprang from a hierarchical social structure, in which crafts and occupations descended often in families, and men and women knew their places – quite literally in the countryside, where the generations succeeded in the cottage and the farmhouse as well as the Hall. But it was reinforced, at this particular stage and in a sense paradoxically, by the impact of the least static elements among the lower sort. For in important, indeed in the most

1. See pp. 96–9 above.
2. Eg the different lines drawn at this point by Patrick Colquhoun and Francis Place.
3. P. 107 above.

vocal and forceful, sectors of the working orders there was a frequent – at least potential – contrast between the continuity of their categories and the personal fluctuations of the men who composed them. Compared with the broad situation higher up the scale, individuals could not count so firmly on maintaining their standing throughout their lives. Of course personal fortunes could change in the upper and the higher middle ranks: there were declining noblemen and gentry, poor relations of established families, needy placemen, failed merchants and manufacturers, and the opposite movements from below. But generally speaking a man in those reaches was born to a given status with which he could identify, and expect to be identified. Continuity lower down, even where apparently assured, was far more vulnerable: the rural pattern was changing under agricultural development, and in the towns, above the large irreducible numbers who never rose above the lowest levels, working men were surrounded by the hazards and chances of change. A man might rise; he might suddenly fall; he might move from job to job. But he scarcely commanded his fate,[1] and the very growth of differentiation tended in this period to underline the fact. As trades and industries enlarged, as wealth spread and made more complex demands, so did the distinctions in function and attitude among those engaged. In due course it could be claimed, with perhaps only moderate exaggeration, that 'the difference between skilled workmen and common labourers is as strongly marked as [a generation earlier] was the difference between the workman and his employer'.[2] But such developments were still in an early stage towards the end of the eighteenth century, and if degrees of status were becoming clearer certainty of status very often was not. Insecurity – at the lowest levels meaning a roof or the next meal, at higher levels the standard of employment or of opportunity – was a great binding force on the lower sort as a whole, a common factor which made it an entity and distinguished it from its betters. And the gap, if not always wide, was deep. Some men could cross it; but until they did so they lay, and knew that they lay, below the hierarchy of articulate interests, among their 'subordinate' fellows who dwelt beneath the line.

This broad sense of identity, refracted though it was within a social order which did not accept or indeed yet rest on a developed conception of class, existed when poverty itself might not be the immediate problem. Compared with many European countries, indeed, the necessaries and even some luxuries of life were spread, as was frequently noted, surprisingly far down the scale.[3] There was dire hardship and squalor in the warrens of the increasingly crowded towns, in mouldering rural

1. See pp. 97, 131 above, with its implications for the character of the mob.
2. Francis Place's *Improvement of the Working People* . . . (1834, written in 1829), 5–6. It must be remembered that his personal experience was confined to London.
3. See the quotations in Perkin, op. cit., 93–4.

cottages, in the large community of the floating poor.[1] There was also a fair degree of comfort in many households of the lower sort, and – a fact sometimes praised, sometimes deplored – a lively spirit of emulation.[2] It was a feature for example of this peculiarly English state of affairs that the cycle of fashion in dress – a product of attitude as well as of means – was widely and quickly followed among the lower orders. The idea of an open society did not vanish at the point at which they began, and it permeated many who accepted the system as well as those who did not. It could in fact co-exist, as elsewhere, with the idea of ordered degree. But while the propertied orders viewed the connexion in terms of opportunity and balance – of the opportunities of the open society, and its necessary balance with a stable structure – it was the uncertainties and risks of the former, and the boundaries of the latter, that gave men in the lower ranks, whether well or ill disposed or simply passive, a common starting-point from which to reckon, and the context in which they moved.

The developments of 1792 increased the authorities' inclination to take the lower orders as a whole – scarcely surprisingly given the tone of the new 'seditious' texts. The unprivileged as a body were being urged to press their claims, and the growing 'appetite for reading' among 'the common people' was producing 'dangers and temptations . . . beyond any former period'.[3] The Ministry counterattacked in kind, at first by attempted suppression, soon reinforced by the encouragement of loyalist pamphlets and tracts. But such measures postulated an audience swayed but not governed by the temptations, and this judgment in turn was based on an older view of the people's needs. In Government's experience, disaffection was usually linked with economic distress; in the new puzzling conditions, which Ministers could not hope to gauge exactly, their immediate instinct was to place their faith mainly in the persistence or return of prosperity. It was the familiar panacea: the maintenance of normal food supplies and wages, the avoidance of higher prices – above all food prices – and taxes.[4] 'Continued and progressive improvement' was the key to the harmony of 'all classes', the most likely way to 'confirm and increase their . . . attachment to [the] constitution'. So Pitt thought at the start of 1792, as Grenville had thought earlier: 'peace and economy are our best resources; and with them I flatter myself *we* have not . . . much to fear'.[5] The hopes died hard under the

1. The last – paupers and cottagers, and vagrants – was estimated by Colquhoun in his *Treatise on Indigence* of 1803 as comprising some 334,000 families out of a national total of over 1,346,000. The proportion by then may have been rather greater than ten years earlier, as a result of wartime distress.

2. Cf. p. 131 above.

3. Advertisement to Hannah More's *Tales for the Common People* (originally the series of *Cheap Repository Tracts*) in her collected *Works* (1801), V.

4. For the theoretical role of taxation in this context see I, 248.

5. Pp. 87–8 above.

impact of recession and war. 'The very circumstances of the present stagnation [of credit] was a proof of the power and energy of the country'. The 'facility of markets', while to some extent affected by the general European war, was 'impeded very little' by the fact that the enemy was France, and 'that effect did not reach the internal state of the cash and commerce of this country'. Thus Dundas and Pitt argued in the spring of 1793, as they awaited a recovery from the crisis of recent months.[1]

This was taking a view of the national economy as a whole. The remedies in practice were applied to particular occasions and places. There had been typical examples in the past few years. The export of grain was stopped in East Anglia in the bad harvest of 1789, and Pitt himself responded to a plan for forwarding ordnance works at Plymouth to help relieve local distress.[2] Similar specific responses were visible in 1792: Government again acted, if belatedly, over the export of grain from the eastern counties.[3] But the effect was – as it was meant to be – limited; treatment was given for exceptional cases; it did not seek to raise normal standards on a national scale. And indeed the treatment itself in this period was not always helped by the rising doctrine of what was best conducive to the national interest. Pitt above all, who liked where possible to hold his pragmatism in a framework of theory,[4] was by no means always willing to subordinate the latter to the former. 'I imagine', Dundas wrote ruefully from Scotland late in 1792, 'you must have some good reason for not having stopped the export of grain . . . and of course no consideration will ever prompt you to encroach on sixpence on the regular sinking Fund you have established'. But if further trouble was to be avoided in the lowland towns the Ministry must make a greater short-term allowance for 'the exigencies of the Times', and above all 'a plentiful supply of Food to the People'.[5] The dilemma was real enough, as many Governments have found since, within and beyond the period of classical economic thought. It obtruded at a moment when that thought was not in tune with the traditional immediate means of assuaging local distress.

For paradoxically, if Governments viewed social peace most directly in economic terms, they were placing their faith in processes which they acknowledged would respond only slightly to their prompting. '. . . Trade, industry and barter would always find their own level, and be

1. In the debate on the revival of public credit, on 30 April (*P.R.*, XXXV (1793), 335, 339). See p. 94 above.

2. For the latter see Duke of Richmond to Pitt, 27 August 1789; P.R.O. 30/8/171.

3. There was also some disposition to approve the raising of wages (by private persons) in various parts of the country as 'of a hundred times more importance' than any form of official repression (Grenville to Buckingham, 7 November 1792; Buckingham, II, 224).

4. See I, 277–80, 512.

5. To Pitt, 12 November 1792 (P.R.O. 30/8/157). For the Sinking Fund see I, 260–9.

impeded by regulations which violated their natural operation, and deranged their proper effect'.[1] The social implication of this statement of Pitt's might not have pleased earlier generations; but they could hardly have denied the strength of the limits to economic management. For whatever their intentions, Governments disposed of clumsy weapons, and liberal doctrine rationalised a situation which it may have accentuated but did not create. A legislative framework could certainly be built to accommodate 'natural' progress: a century of advance bore witness to the fact. But there was little that a Ministry could do directly to affect short-term fluctuations, or indeed to anticipate movement whose significance time alone would reveal. The crisis of 1792–3 confirmed the first truism; and beyond it two major long-term factors were at work in the 1790s, both fundamentally adverse and the first at least not yet fully grasped. In the important matter of food supplies, and most immediately of bread, the country had entered on an age in which it could no longer be self-sufficient.[2] The improvements of the long agricultural revolution had in fact yielded most of their increase, England had become a net importer of wheat, and the population was rising fast. There was an inherent and lasting difficulty now in meeting the needs of the people. And this was the more serious because it was beginning to bite at a time when the fastest rate of growth had settled in the industrial towns, with the prospective emergence of a new urban identity. These pressures, falling on the accepted limits of control, were inescapable; they would have operated whether there had been a French Revolution and a war or not. But they were underlined, and the effects perhaps hastened, by the long hard war, adding to the problems of providing cheap food and distorting the patterns of urban trades. There was to be neither the peace nor the even prosperity to which Ministers had looked forward. The people must support or acquiesce in the system when those blessings did not exist.

How far, again, would they do so? It was hard indeed to tell. In the first year of gathering tension evidence could be cited either way. On the one hand there were the alarming reception of Paine's inflammatory pamphlet, the mounting reports of disaffection, the rise of the popular Societies; on the other, comforting signs of popular loyalty, particularly rural, and of popular reactions against the French, confirmed at the outset of war. The contrasts indeed continued throughout the decade, when the war had become unpopular and distress was really frightening. When urban discontent had been largely contained, unrest spread in the countryside. While subversive tracts grew more violent, the

1. Pitt in the Commons, 12 February 1796 (*P.R.*, XLIV (1796), 23). He was speaking in a debate on wages.
2. See p. 92, n5 above.

counter-propaganda found its own wide audience. If desertion, and trouble in individual units, were endemic in the armed services, and there were large-scale mutinies in the fleet in the dark year of 1797, there was no comparable rising in the army at home or overseas, and many of the naval mutineers made it clear they would fight the enemy if he appeared. While Government could usually count on support from provincial juries, it was roundly defeated by London juries at an early stage. If the King was stoned or shot at in his carriage on one notable occasion, the organised meetings of protest in the capital, which grew larger as the years went by, were almost always well behaved and troops did not have to be used. The picture was far from simple; it varied from place to place and time to time. It was hardly surprising that Ministers at moments should have feared the prospect of revolution, and proclaimed at others, equally warmly, that the heart of the country was sound.

It can be argued however that all this evidence must be viewed in a particular context, which was entirely different from that of recent times; that the 1790s were a decade of repression which opened a new period, and that the symptoms of popular support may have been due very largely to fear. Government most certainly took all the steps it could to strengthen and extend its measures. New Acts and regulations were imposed, important freedoms curtailed, new police courts set up in the capital, barracks built, the home forces increased and the county militias embodied. These official efforts were sustained by the growing cohesion of the propertied orders, commanding informal as well as formal means of support. The armed forces, on whom so much turned, continued to be held in an iron discipline, which was never weakened by strainings of loyalty from above. For unlike the case of France in the later eighties there were no doubts among the officers,[1] and when less draconian means failed the King's Regulations held their ancient terrors. It took a bold man to face the punishments which disobedience would bring. And there were heavy risks, less certain but threatening, in the country at large. They were not confined to action by the Courts. If a suspected agitator or his sympathisers could not be brought to trial, they were often open to other deterrents. Innkeepers might be warned of a danger to their licences, tradesmen of a loss to their custom, labourers could lose their cottages, dependants or workmen their benefits or jobs. More substantial dissidents – a threat by example – could feel the same weight of discouragement, in the Universities, the professions, the network of places and honours. A formidable social reaction underpinned the measures themselves, creating an unmistakable climate with far-ranging effects.

All this was very real, and must be given great weight. The question follows why it should have been as effective as it was. For the

1. A few army officers were suspect – three in fact were cashiered – in 1792. But their example was an exception that served to prove a rule.

transformation was not complete, even by the later nineties. The lower orders had been subject to plenty of risks and punishments before, as a reading of the statute book or a visit to the gaols and hulks would reveal; and familiar restraints for their part did not vanish overnight. The social pressures, while very strong, were still patchy: they did not govern every area; and official repression itself had its limits. Laws were changed, and Ministerial powers increased against the private subject. But the concept of law did not disappear – sometimes inconveniently for Ministers – and the Courts, and less visibly the Home Office, could still protect as well as condemn. The physical weapons of order themselves remained rudimentary. England was not an armed camp, and there was still no system of police. Yet the defences held; the deterrents, in retrospect, worked. Why were they not challenged more effectively by those on whom they fell?

The same point may be reached by another route. Were the dangers as real as was claimed; or were they magnified unnecessarily? Did the propertied orders overrate, or Ministers distort, the extent of the threat? Pitt and his colleagues have often been accused – they were accused at the time – of over-reacting, possibly deliberately, possibly out of panic. In either case, if this was so why had the challenge not been greater? Why did the people, for whatever reasons, accept that the system would prevail?

Government itself looked, if uncertainly, to some reassuring symptoms. One – much proclaimed – was held to be the impression made by the fresh events in France, followed by the wave of sentiment when the war began. The former may have been overplayed. It is open to doubt how greatly the flow of French refugees in 1792, the arrest of King Louis, the September massacres, shocked the English lower classes. One leading popular Society at least seems to have suffered a fall in recruitment; but this was temporary, and the numbers were rising again by the end of the year.[1] The feelings may often have been very faint, unlike those of the middle and upper orders, and the hardships of the winter of more immediate concern. But the outbreak of war in 1793 was a more familiar rallying point, enlisting instinctive loyalties for an old and intimate cause. For patriotism was a strong force – one of the strongest forces of all – and love of country ran as deeply through the lower as through the higher ranks. In some ways indeed perhaps it ran more deeply, for lack of privilege meant a lack of choice: the less power and property a man has the less scope for making reservations. Persons of substance nourished their allegiance by their sense of possessing 'a stake in the country'; where the stake was small or non-existent, the country itself remained. National occasions have often shown the strength of such feelings among the poor; the flags fly thickly in the smaller streets. And in the Old Order in Europe, including England, the point bears

1. P. 106 above.

particular emphasis, for the reservations of men of position could be very real. The state – the King – could claim only so much; there were independent rights to be asserted; a gentleman could withdraw his services if the limits were transgressed. A whole body of political thought had been built on such premises, and on the social processes from which they derived. It was the pride of Englishmen in the eighteenth century that the tensions had been largely resolved; that a satisfactory balance had been achieved and maintained. But the fact that the lower orders were largely excluded from its active enjoyment did not prevent more primitive loyalties from being lodged in an ancient home. This did not mean that labourers and workmen expected or wanted to enlist; on the contrary, the press was loathed and the army despised, as always, as the last resort of the misfit or the adventurer or the man in trouble. Nor, underlying these attitudes, was war itself a fact of daily life: it was something that happened elsewhere, in other countries or at sea. When the effects of this particular struggle, indeed, fell with unprecedented impact, there was an unprecedented degree of resentment and discontent. But old attitudes died hard, if indeed they died at all. Love of country remained a formidable binding force.

The fact moreover that the enemy was France made it easier to identify patriotism with the preservation of the existing structure. For the national feeling among the poor was not necessarily wedded to the defence of oligarchy; on the contrary, it could be invoked in attack. But violent revolution was a new ingredient to add to the ancient hatred of the French: it could indeed partly replace Popery as the ideological foe. The war was not begun on ideological grounds; Ministers were driven by traditional reasons of strategic interest. But once it had begun, the 'French infection' could be readily invoked as a threat to 'the poorest he' in England as well as 'the greatest he'.

This was a cause embracing religion, in the face of a levelling atheism; and religion was again a force on which the authorities might draw. Ironically, they gained a significant response from quarters they did not much like: from large sections of the Methodists and of the Dissenting sects. Its springs and its quality varied, and the latter can be misunderstood. The great historian Elie Halévy maintained in a famous judgment that 'Methodism was the antidote to Jacobinism', and that its influence saved England from revolution.[1] Later opinion has chipped parts of the argument away. Methodism was not, as had been suggested, the sole basis of the evangelicalism – largely conservative in

---

1. *A History of the English People in the Nineteenth Century*, I (English transln., 2nd edn., 1949), 590–1, 387. And see op. cit., Part III, ch. 1 *passim*. The argument was not new, though it had never been developed so forcefully. It had been suggested, for example, by Lecky.

secular matters – which was the period's great religious force.[1] The movement, though unified in structure, had never been a coherent whole; it contained serious divisions in the early nineties, and soon started to hive off connexions some at least of which held men with radical political views. The social doctrines included different, even contrasting, strands – they had shown strong sympathies for the state of the poor, and in the early days indeed Wesleyans were sometimes accused of levelling tendencies. And even the most respectable congregations were not consistently active supporters of Government's interpretation of loyalty in all its forms. After all, these were precisely the years in which they broke finally from the Anglican Church, a decision which scarcely favoured whole-hearted acceptance of the system as a whole. But when all this has been said a potent truth remains. The main stream of Methodist teaching did not countenance secular rebellion; more important, its emphasis lay in a different direction, at a deeper level. For the quality of the Methodist response was formed not so much by political engagement as, conversely, by a concentration on less transitory concerns.

This was to be seen among the more discontented Methodist sects themselves. Their crises and renewals were theological, secular action was deemed to be secondary, and if their members often came to be linked with the growth of working-class organisations that was a result of local conditions rather than a necessary consequence of their faith. The peripheral importance of politics was more clearly visible in the central teaching. For the very heightening of spiritual conscience which lay at the root of the Methodist ethos allowed a wide latitude to the secular power. The Christian's concern was with his soul, his enjoyment of Grace, his hopes of redemption; for the rest, he moved in a world whose order his Maker had ordained. So long as his spiritual life was respected he in turn owed respect; there was indeed a strain – often repellent – in the mainstream of Methodist preaching which demanded a welcome of temporal suffering as a test of eternal salvation. Rebellion was justified by false doctrine, not by social injustice; the rewards of the saved lay beyond the grave. Methodists could most certainly be socially active: their influence on society was becoming distinct. Many of them were prospering by the Protestant ethic of steady work and steady behaviour – it was noted in the 1780s that they made excellent factory managers. But this was a private ethic, resting on a given public order, and the ethic in itself was not central to the creed. 'Methodism was much more than a school for citizens; it was a school for saints'.[2] In essence it was scarcely a vehicle of political philosophy at all.

The effects of the movement's influence reflected the fact. They can

---

1. P. 61 above.

2. John Walsh, in *A History of the Methodist Church in Great Britain*, I, ed. Rupert Davies and Gordon Rupp (1965), ch. IX, 313.

perhaps be over-estimated in the early and middle nineties. Forceful and spreading though it was, Methodism was still restricted in geography and numbers; in 1791 there were under 80,000 declared members, with possibly as many undeclared attendants, compared with something under half a million Dissenters of various kinds. But it was a working leaven, and it reached down into quarters where radical Dissent was likewise at work. For Dissent harboured sharper contrasts in social and political doctrine; not all its branches were content with so passive a secular role. Like the Methodists, the sects insisted on the primacy of personal redemption; but the duties and claims of the godly could be read in more than one way. Christian was at spiritual war with Apollyon, but Apollyon dwelt in the seats of power, and the wrestlings of the righteous had often taken worldly forms. The effects could be confusing, not least at the extremes, where 'enthusiasm', that old bogy which was now raising its head once more, could fire contrasting attitudes depending on the preaching imbibed. The quietism of the Quakers was met by the chiliasm of the Shakers; faith by works, that great Nonconformist doctrine, by apocalyptic claims. For in the excitements of the 1790s millenarianism revived: the end of the world was at hand, the Second Coming awaited. And as in the seventeenth century, such essentially unworldly expectations cast their own shadows over current political events. Some of the wilder religious movements rejected the relevance of worldly affairs; others carried their radicalism into political causes. But all brought their peculiar flavour to the secular scene. Whatever its direction, 'enthusiasm' by nature was an emotionally disruptive force.

Such extreme manifestations were seen most frequently among the very poor. The bulk of the Dissenting congregations was hard-headed, but again divided. The old strains of militant Puritanism, never dead, now emerged more clearly under the stimulus of a new political debate. Dissent harboured and to some extent nurtured the infant developments of popular struggle, and the growth of 'Paineite' doctrines took place, as elsewhere, below a broad social line. The process was of high importance: the Chapel became a Trade Union form. At the same time a weight of teaching fell the other way. For in many of the Dissenting congregations, particularly in the largest and the best established, the doubts and problems of the more prosperous were repeated lower down the scale. The fear of ungodly revolutionary excess was not confined to the wealthiest brethren; there was still a strong strain of Reformed doctrine that prescribed respect for established authority. Many humble sectarians continued to be governed throughout the period by the belief that secular order in itself was divinely ordained. Many too showed distaste for mass action on the part of a mob to which they felt superior, and whose ways were not their ways. The old self-confidence – self-righteousness – was strong. It could set its face against Courts and Bishops. It could also turn its back on riot when the cause was not its own.

But if Methodism largely, and Dissent partially, could produce acquiescence or support, Government itself did not greatly appreciate the fact. Sectarianism had been linked too recently with grievance and aggressive political views.[1] If many Dissenters were well-affected, many more were not. They were the heirs of those stiff-necked men who had once destroyed a King; and who could say now that the old hostility was dead? It was easy to believe in worsening conditions that 'all the Dissenters . . . are republicans'.[2] And if the Methodists preached subordination, they too were leaving the Established fold. The combined activity was disturbing; the licensed disestablished places of worship, some 1,300 in the seventies, some 1,600 in the eighties, rose to almost 4,000 in the next decade. This was not the kind of religion that the authorities wanted. They preferred to look to the Anglican Church. The Established Church was the natural partner of the established state; and serious loss to the one could not be ignored by the other. 'The Church of England', Pitt said later, 'as by law established, [was] so essential a part of the constitution that whatever endangered it would necessarily affect the security of the whole'.[3] However sincerely rival congregations wished to maintain the fabric of order, their very existence could be viewed as a threat to one of its acknowledged supports.

The authorities did not look in vain. Anglicanism rallied in defence. The early effects on itself, indeed, were more immediate than those on the state. For while the French Revolution made little difference to the short-term prospects of political reform, which for several years had subsided into quiescence, it made an immediate impact on the Anglican spirit. There was both loss and gain, and the loss was soon obvious. Already stiffening in the struggle over the Corporation and Test Acts, the ecclesiastical hierarchy now froze in a 'granite conservatism'.[4] Any prospect of internal reform, or of working contacts with Dissent, vanished;[5] in defending the state the Church came to claim something more like exclusive than superior rights. Latitudinarianism faded in the face of this new rigidity. So did the appeal of orthodox Anglicanism to large elements in the rising population. When the Methodists left they tore the web which, however tenuous, had held growing numbers of the lower orders within the parent church. Contact with the urban poor, the main area of growth, declined further almost to vanishing point, and Anglicanism suffered also in parts of the countryside. Vital religion was now associated even more widely with Nonconformity, and when England next entered on an era of reform the Establishment looked out

1. Pp. 63–4, 69–71 above.
2. John Newton, the Anglican Evangelical pastor who helped to convert Wilberforce, in 1795; quoted in Walsh, loc. cit., 303.
3. *P.H.*, XXIII (1814), col. 557.
4. Sykes, *Church and State in England in the XVIII Century*, 2.
5. See pp. 58–60, 70 above.

from 'a besieged city'.[1] Its identification with the secular power had been achieved all too well. It was unmistakably an arm of government. Any hope of comprehensiveness had gone.

Such loss was quickly apparent, even if its full extent could not be foreseen. It was not so easy to measure the gain which emerged from the same conditions. This perhaps was partly because the contrast was not distinct; where there was gain it often took shapes which themselves were associated with the hardening attitude. For the hopeful developments in Anglicanism centred on the heightening of personal example, shown above all by the Anglican Evangelicals who were also among the strongest supporters of Government. The need, already implicit in the growing movement of 'benevolence', was emphasised dramatically by events in France. Anglicans as a body pointed to the effects of French rationalism. 'Religion, that held the materials of the fabrick together, was first systematically loosened', and the process opened, or at least cleared, the way for attacks on a secular authority which 'could not stand on authority alone'. The remedy lay in a fresh spirit. 'Situations formerly supported persons. It now became necessary that personal qualities should support situations'.[2] The Evangelicals, already active, were well placed to utter such warnings, and to focus a feeling which now spread in a specifically Anglican form. If social differences should be accepted, social duties were reciprocal. If men were called to different stations, each station had its obligations. The traditional teachings had a new urgency, and they found a ready and deepening response. The survival of Anglicanism as a factor in nineteenth-century England owed much to this discipline of 'personal qualities', which the age of unrest underlined.

The impact fell most directly on those with a situation to support – even though the Evangelicals themselves were sometimes keenly disliked.[3] But the message was aimed equally at the lower orders, and the effects there are more problematical. It certainly failed to restore to the Church a mass of alienated urban poor, and it had limits of its own making in the rural parishes. For many of the audiences were captive, and some at least must have been resentful; to men and women enduring hardship it must have seemed a mockery to be told to count their blessings. They heard the same perhaps from the Methodists – though often they were urged to count their sufferings – but compared with the Methodists, Anglican preaching came so very obviously from above.[4]

1. Sykes, op. cit., 2.
2. Edmund Burke, *Letter to William Elliott, Esq.* . . . (1795), in *The Works of the Right Honourable Edmund Burke*, VII (1826), 363–4. This of course was written a few years later, by one who was no Evangelical. It expressed the more cogently an attitude which by then had become an accepted part of the wider Anglican ethos.
3. Cf. p. 61 above.
4. The more so as the rising value of glebe land made clerical life increasingly attractive to the gentry, removing the country parson a stage farther from the daily life of his flock.

Nevertheless, given the volume of effort – the tracts, the sermons, the day schools, the visits – it would be rash to dismiss the results. They may well have played a part in securing a measure of popular acquiescence in a structure for which they provided a moral defence. For whatever the movement's shortcomings the Evangelicals did not lack confidence; and they added a fresh dimension of earnest, high-minded missionary zeal to a system that in past decades had come to depend largely on habit.

Habit in a wider sense, however, was not necessarily a disadvantage. If no longer always self-sufficient, it remained a pillar of the system as a whole. It was something indeed, under various names, in which the governing class still placed great faith. The concept was hierarchical, from the family to the state,[1] and it centred on – was founded in – a rural society. 'A nobleman, a gentleman, a yeoman – that is a good interest'; the old saying of Cromwell's in his later days summed up an enduring sentiment. In some ways one might well argue that the approach was becoming inappropriate, for society after all was embarked, if patchily, on change. There was the great new feature of the rising towns, where the populations – though not always the areas – were growing, and the capital itself expanding at an ever increasing pace. London and its environs now formed the largest city in Europe, and when the first census was taken at the turn of the century they accounted for over ten per cent of the nation. Such a proportion was not unfamiliar, but given the absolute increase in size the aggregation posed problems that were becoming new in kind. So did the manufacturing centres, and urban concentrations in general; and the challenge was not only one of scale but of balance with the countryside itself. For urban growth, while now self-generating, was also swelled materially by rural drift, and agricultural labour was in proportional, if not necessarily absolute, decline.[2] Traditional theories of social relationships were thus, as so often, being given fresh emphasis at a time when the social pattern was in some state of flux.

The legacy was to haunt succeeding generations. The rural social ideal was so strong, the habit of mind went so deep, that 'for long it obstructed . . . the formation of a true philosophy of urban life'.[3] But if this was so in the nineteenth century there was little to upset it at the end of the eighteenth, when two out of three English men and women still lived outside a town of any size, and only one in six in a town of over

---

1. For the basic importance of degree in the family and the household see, as typical examples, the influential William Paley's *Reasons for Contentment; addressed to the labouring Part of the British Public* (1792), and his sermon on *The Duties of Servants* (*Sermons on Various Subjects by William Paley*, ed. the Rev. Edmund Paley, I (1825)).

2. For the qualification see p. 99 above.

3. G.M. Young, *Victorian England, Portrait of an Age* (1936), 21–2.

20,000. Whatever the future implications, society remained predominantly agricultural; and the size of many of the towns themselves imposed close contacts with their immediate areas. For many centres still existed mainly to serve the neighbouring countryside, and their patterns of life as well as of government were affected by rural influences. The very pace of the influx moreover, from displaced agricultural labour and domestic outworkers, brought into the larger centres men used to thinking in village terms. It would take some decades of massive growth before even such places as Manchester and Birmingham lost the last traces of their country character and achieved a self-contained civic pride. Meanwhile, at a time when few towns outside London were remote from the fields and commons, the ethos of the land still pervaded the greatest commercial nation in the world.

But Manchester, Birmingham and others *were* growing, and manufactures spreading in the countryside itself. Landed values were becoming a conditioning rather than a frequently integral element, a confusion rather than a standard of reference, for much industrial and mercantile life. Commerce and industry themselves, however, had their own hierarchical features, and in many instances – old and new – the paternalistic strain was strong. Indeed it was perhaps sometimes stronger in certain towns than in certain villages – textile villages in the south-west for instance, or mining villages in the midlands and north. Place and scale were very important, but they did not impose rigid patterns: the importance of the former indeed was precisely that it did not.[1] Towns differed in character according to their trades, and industrial size alone did not dictate results. Some of the largest new factories themselves (still semi-rural rather than urban) were highly paternalistic: Cromford, Belper, Etruria illustrate the point. The factory system in fact, the classic stimulant of a developed class consciousness, was not its most prolific seed-bed at this formative stage. It might be true, as one radical noted, that 'whatever presses men together . . . is favourable to knowledge', so that 'every large workshop and manufactory is a sort of political society' by nature.[2] But like most of his articulate colleagues he was not himself a factory worker, and such places were not yet the foci for politically inquiring men. The factories were generally subject to a discipline the continuity of which was exceptional, and in a society geared to underemployment unrest sprang more easily from earlier forms. It was still in fact experienced more often in certain industries of older structure, and from men involved – often interruptedly – in small-scale trades and crafts. The example of Sheffield, that nest of sedition, could not be universally applied; but

1. See pp. 96, 100–1 above.
2. John Thelwall in 1794, quoted in H. Collins, 'The London Corresponding Society' (*Democracy and the Labour Movement*, ed. John Saville), 126.

precisely because it could not, its significance was underlined. If the finance required for an undertaking was 'little', and the number of 'dependants' few, there was a corresponding lack of 'persons of sufficient weight . . . to act with . . . effect'.[1]

But while the strength of hierarchical connexions naturally varied with the type of work, it was also subject in some degree to a more pervasive inner threat. For paternalistic attitudes – the guidelines accepted, whatever the practice – were being increasingly invaded by the doctrine of economic laissez-faire. The old regulations for prices and employment had been weakened, often abandoned,[2] and the rural order itself was developing in new ways. The yeomen were under pressure, the tenantry's situation was altering; enclosure, whatever its benefits, meant economic and social change. Such facts were reflected to some extent in the assumptions of masters and landlords: a shift of attitude, it has indeed been held, came first from above. In Carlyle's telling retrospective phrase, it involved an 'abdication on the part of the governors'[3] quite as radical in its effects as pressures from below. The twin developments of manufactures and agricultural increase were remodelling an order whose expansion they had so far maintained. And this, it can be argued, was a further severe limitation on an appeal to the virtues of that order by the guardians themselves.

The process as yet, however, was partial, and the implications were obscure. The liberal economists had now revealed the insecurity of doctrines which in practice had long been under pressure. But they did not seek to replace them in every aspect, the message could bear varying interpretations,[4] and the economic movements themselves were outstripping social instincts that were still widespread. Much of the discontent from below was phrased in cries for a return to the past; and if the upper orders looked hopefully to the future their own values were not consciously changed. One might say that in point of fact they expected to have their cake and eat it; to sustain economic progress on the society they knew. Hitherto at least they had assumed that the framework would endure, that advance was possible within – was made possible by – the balance already achieved. Contradictions might now be emerging; they might be apparent in some legislation. But events so far had moved slowly, and the serious tests had still to come.

Paternalism stems from a prevalence of face to face relationships. The rural ideal remained strong because it could still be taken as the archetype. Whatever the emerging social consequences of agricultural change the vital features of social authority were as yet undisturbed. The squire, the parson, the farmer, the cottager, in all the variety of local

1. See p. 97 above.
2. Cf. p. 102 above.
3. In *Chartism* (1839).
4. See I, 512n4.

circumstances, were still thought of as embodying the pattern of connexion in community life. The units of parish and manorial government regulated duties and responsibilities, determined by magistrates and rectors, church wardens and overseers. Vagrancy and poor laws, the granting of licences, the punishment of minor illegalities, much local education, the fixing of some wages, lay within their hands. And beyond these formal powers, so did voluntary charitable relief: the landlord above all was looked on for help – often the only help – above legal limits. Given the incursion of the landed interest into local 'improvement' and industry, the same values penetrated those areas as well. The fact was largely accepted – often for want of an alternative – by the recipients, the more desperately when times were bad and the dispenser of charity himself might be retrenching at their expense.

> . . . To Bright Earl Ashburnham be honour and praise
> His Lordship deserves it for his virtuous ways
> For his kind attention to the Poor at Pembrey,
> With Alms he assist them, their cause he'll survey
> He suffer not one in a destitute state
> If he'll be aware he'll render his fate
> Success and good fame to Ashburnham's name
> Sweet joy to his family for ever the same.[1]

This was written during the French wars by a colliery blacksmith at a pit belonging to the Earl which was on short working. It was a response that was still widespread, and made its sometimes unconscious demands, even when the same men might be driven to protest and riot.

One may like or dislike this situation. It was a fact of life. Landlords as usual might be good or bad, or 'like most of us . . . a little bit of both'. The better ones could not complain of a lack of freedom of manoeuvre. The English landowner was fortunate that (unlike his counterpart in France) he was not associated with direct taxation; not marked off – however irrelevantly in practice – by feudal privileges and dues. Agricultural prosperity allowed him very often to indulge his benevolence without undue strain, as it also provided much of his capital for the profitable stimulation of other interests. The shock of the French Revolution pointed the need for an activity which in any event was no new experience or idea. His personal responsibility continued; he could be identified, for good or ill; he remained an immediate target for praise or abuse. Many of the urban troubles indeed were held to be due to the fact that such relationships were inadequately reflected in the growing towns. It was the more serious when unrest later spread over the countryside.

---

1. Quoted in G.E. Mingay, *English Landed Society in the Eighteenth Century* (1963), 274.

Demands of this type on a superior were part of 'the freeborn Englishman's rights'. How far did they affect attitudes to property, including political property? The last in fact may have seemed to the higher orders the most immediate threat, for while there were attacks throughout the 1790s on inequalities as such they were usually expressed most specifically in the cry for a universal franchise. The calls for more equal wealth were scattered, and seldom strictly formulated. The more sophisticated were generally tentative and reached a limited public – Pitt is said not to have been worried by Godwin's *Political Justice*, because it sold at three guineas – and detailed proposals at the other extreme were very rare indeed. The saintly crank Thomas Spence, advocating the nationalisation of land from his Holborn barrow, had his followers in the Corresponding Societies, but they were seldom explicit or effective as yet. Perhaps John Thelwall of the LCS was the most influential of the popularists who carried a stage farther the generalised assaults of Paine himself. He was indeed a potentially seminal figure, taking 'Jacobinism to the borders of Socialism'[1] more precisely and logically than the mass of cheap seditious tracts. For if the propertied orders feared the 'wild work'[2] which Paine's teachings might bring, it was because they foresaw social revolution coming first in terms of political change.

This in fact, one might say, was the link between the claims of the popular Societies that their aims were constitutional and their opponents' conviction that they were nothing of the kind.[3] Given such a background – very different from that of John Jebb and the Duke of Richmond[4] – universal suffrage, the initial target which persisted through all the later programmes, certainly ran clean against the defence of existing rights. For that defence rested firmly on property, however the case might be deployed: usually on the doctrine of 'indirect representation', one of the bulwarks of the old system, but also now increasingly on the argument, preached and disseminated in the pamphlets, that many of the lower sort were in fact already involved. Freehold, copyright, scot and lot, burgage tenure: such rights were extensive, if erratically distributed. The very anomalies of the pattern brought 'the people' within its scope. And if it was abandoned for universal suffrage, what would the consequences be? Not a rectification of the franchise to admit more of the worthier sort, but the denial of the very basis on which the structure stood. The political balance would be destroyed, and with it part of the fabric of law which had been built in its wisdom to cover all sections of the community. Such a consequence, it was held, would damage the people themselves. 'Of the two' indeed,

1. E.P. Thompson, op. cit., 160.
2. The reformer Christopher Wyvill's phrase (*Political Papers* . . ., V, 237.
3. See pp. 111–14, 134 above.
4. P. 111 above.

poor and rich, 'it is rather more the concern of the poor to stand up for the laws . . .; for it is the law which defends the weak against the strong, the humble against the powerful, the little against the great'.[1] It was the familiar argument of the thin end of the wedge. If the principle of the franchise was overturned, there was no reason why social principles should not follow suit.

This was a comprehensive case. In point of historical justification it might have been stronger if a reverse process had not already taken place. For it seems highly probable in fact that the franchise had been narrowed earlier in the century, and its manipulation by powerful elements effectively increased. We need to know more for the period as a whole; but from the figures of population, and evidence extracted from polls stretching back into the seventeenth century, it is likely – to put it at its lowest – that the numbers of the unenfranchised rose. So probably did the influence exerted on the enfranchised themselves: by the buying of votes and placing of voters, control of Parliamentary petitions, not least the increasing avoidance of a contested poll.[2] Many of the calls for a return to the past may here have been rooted in some reality, even if the newer processes were grafted on the old. The change was not complete: we need to know more about earlier habits and the extent of abstention; it may have been gradual, almost insensible; but there was almost certainly a change. The argument that the lower orders were pro-portionately included would sound better if their numbers had not grown, and their votes, where held, had been rather more free.

At the same time the argument may have had, or been felt to have, some force. One should probably be wary of underrating the pressures that lower-middling or lower class voters, in certain cases at least, could bring to bear on their MPs. Regional studies are uncovering processes and patterns which suggest that representatives, however elected, had sometimes to pay heed to quite inferior interests. But argument in any case may often have been weaker than sentiment or habit. This indeed was a possibility which the teachers themselves seemed often to sense. 'The old English ways', 'our old secure bulwarks', 'our King and Nation mixed' – such phrases reappear to exhaustion in the counterattacks.[3] That famous English predilection for ascribing antiquity to quite recent developments – for absorbing change, if decently disguised, into a tenacious myth of the past – may have had its effect here when confronted by direct assault. The experience of the last decade had shown how quickly reforming aspirations could subside among the higher orders, given a return of prosperity and peace. How far they were endemic in the lower orders it is difficult to say. There was no doubt a reality in what Dr Johnson had called 'a reciprocal pleasure in

1. Paley, *Reasons for Contentment*, 3. And cf. p. 149 above.
2. Cf. I, 33, 149.
3. Eg the collection of pamphlets in *Association Papers . . . Addressed to All the Loyal Associations*, of 1793.

governing and being governed',[1] and in some country districts this may have been particularly marked.[2] At the same time the familiar fact that discontent, whatever its origins, could so often be translated into campaigns for Parliamentary reform suggests that, confusedly perhaps or partially, and generally directed from above, the call held an instinctive popular appeal. The sentiments are hard to proportion. Meanwhile however there was one occasion on which the lower orders as a body might hope to come into their own. For if one can hardly weigh exactly political sentiments and instincts in general, one must take account of the peculiar impact of the Parliamentary election itself.

The conditions, again, were set by the practice – the developments – of past decades, to which attitudes and habits had insensibly been attached. They were far from elevating. 'The Englishman's rights' in an election had become largely a synonym for bribery and tumult, and while any such occasion might be promising – an election for a Corporation or even for a vestry[3] – the climax of course was a Parliamentary contest. Even where there was no actual contest, so that 'the peace of the County (or borough) might not be disturbed' – a practice which occurred increasingly from the 1740s – there was apt to be some raising of favours, some largesse and celebration, some pretext for familiarity, some sense of excitement. And these were increased immensely when there was a choice and the stakes were raised – sometimes to levels which could ruin a candidate. The circuses as well as the bread were then liberally provided: an hypocrisy born of, but also imposed on, power out of residual rights. The election riot was an occasion of its own, something rather like the old court of misrule, limited in time and purpose, when troops if possible were never used.[4] The chief beneficiaries of course were the electors, and there was doubtless force in the statement that those 'common people' who received the inducements were jealous of their status, and rejoiced in the fact.[5] But the unenfranchised too had their day, booing, cheering,

---

1. *Boswell's Life of Johnson* . . ., ed. George Birkbeck Hill, I (1934), 408.

2. The importance of the *urban* penetration of counties as a factor in the voting patterns of the early eighteenth century is stressed by, eg, Geoffrey Holmes, *The Electorate and the National Will in the First Age of Party* (1976). The limits to its extent, as assessed by poll books a century later, in the generation leading to the first Reform Act of 1832, are suggested by the table (admittedly incomplete) in Cannon, *Parliamentary Reform*, Appendix 5. This last naturally does not take into account the further limitation suggested by the varying natures of the towns themselves (eg p. 100 above). On the other hand there were rather more contested polls for the counties in the early nineteenth than in the middle and later eighteenth century.

3. Occasionally to such an extent that it reached the ears of the Home Office (see P.R.O. series 42 *passim* for the early nineties).

4. When they were summoned in one instance in the general election of 1790, this was said to be quite exceptional (Sir George Yonge [Secretary at War] to Grenville [Home Secretary], 3 July 1790; P.R.O., H.O. 50/382).

5. See eg Soame Jenyns in *Thoughts on a Parliamentary Reform* (1784), republished in *The Works of Soame Jenyns, Esq.*, II (1790).

parading, drinking, lifting their exuberant disrespect to its highest constitutional pitch. It was true, as the defenders claimed, that there was nothing quite like it elsewhere in Europe. So far as it went, it was unique to the English scene. The corrupt open-handed election had its own savour and its own attractions for those who were indulged in the doles and the licence as well as those who reaped the real rewards.

Looking back on the popular movement as it emerged in the 1790s, its significance lies in what it represented rather than what it achieved. Something really different was coming to the surface, allied to older attitudes and often clothed in older forms. I have tried to suggest causes that promoted, and also some factors that may have limited the effects, social and political, on the populace itself. The existence of such factors may help to account for the practical failure of an appeal which, in troubled times, might have been expected to yield greater results. For there was – there must have been – a combination, economic, physical and moral, which enabled the authorities in England to hold their repression at the levels they did. One may look indeed at what happened in Scotland, and much more in Ireland, to see that the English conditions were different in degree or (compared with Ireland) in kind.[1] If elements are taken in isolation it is sometimes hard to explain their effect. Some after all were not entirely different from their counterparts in France, where there was a revolution. One may doubt if the English lower orders were more conservative, or patriotic, than the French, or regional differences greater in England than across the Channel. French trades and industries nourished relationships as close as those in this country; and the smaller French landowners, though not the greater, remained close to the soil. It was the combination in England that can be offered in contrast: of an enlargement of wealth with a broad correspondence between political and administrative attitudes,[2] important reserves of Protestant doctrine, the ethos and structure of the laws. The unifying forces in the early nineties seem to have been stronger than those making for conflict, far enough down the social order to allow a resolute defence at the top. For that defence had two aspects. On the one hand it was born of fear; on the other it was exercised through weapons, all of them limited and some of them weak, which were not radically remodelled and whose effect rested in the end on deterrence. The lower orders could not hope to succeed if they encountered their superiors' resistance. They could hardly move to any purpose without a prospect of support. But some such signs might have materialised, cracks might have opened and resistance weakened, if the measure of agreement had stopped decisively too high up the social scale.

1. See Ch. VII below.
2. For the, still limited, growth of strain here, and the response, see I, 167–8.

This however is far from saying that the discontent was not deeply felt. Of course it was; otherwise the 1790s would not have been what they were. It is rather to suggest that in such a situation, falling on a people with an instinct for their rights, but one that was attuned and still largely confined to specific causes and occasions, there were strong internal as well as external constraints on unity of purpose, which did not disappear even at times of particular hardship. It is also far from saying that the propertied orders were not really alarmed and, at least at moments, felt they had good cause. Revolutions as serious as that which they dreaded may need unusual combinations of causes;[1] but for that very reason suspicions are easily roused. The comfortable classes found it hard to gauge degrees of support, or consent, or indifference; and even if the result seemed favourable that was not necessarily enough in itself. For complacency could be dangerous: conspiracy must not be ignored: small groups of men can cause great upheavals, sometimes from trivial events. The fear of the mob was always present, and it was coming closer to the surface again. England may have been broadly, nationally, peaceful for a couple of generations, but it had a reputation for violence, and crime was growing apace.[2] One can look with hindsight, and judge probabilities; that is no consolation at the time. And this was particularly true of the winter of 1792–3, when the familiar kinds of unrest were being overlaid by something new. The reports of riots, of fresh Societies, of seditious pamphlets, and now of French intrigues, fell on a bad harvest and rising food prices, on a failure of credit, on a possible war. Events across the Channel as well as at home were taking an ominous turn. The Ministers in London were under strong incentives to act.

1. Cf. p. 145 above.
2. Pp. 101–2, 126–9 above.

CHAPTER VI

Party Talks and French Events

I

The Royal Proclamation in May was not only an event of some national importance. It also reflected movement within the closer Parliamentary sphere. For the draft had been shown to some Opposition leaders, they had objected to certain passages, and the results were seen in the final text. This was a notable development, after the sharpening of party in the last two years.[1] But it was not wholly divorced from that process. It showed the Whigs' growing uneasiness in the face of current pressures. It also showed Pitt in a mood which took account of the recent past.

The uncertainties of Opposition were dramatically heightened by the Friends of the People. Hitherto it had held together well enough to absorb Burke's attacks.[2] But Grey and his companions provided a fresh embarrassment, particularly since action followed at once in the Commons. The Association was formed on 11 April; on the 30th Grey gave notice that he intended to introduce a motion in the coming session for Parliamentary reform. Other sections of 'the party' had already been meeting, at the Duke of Portland's Burlington House,[3] and finally decided not to give concerted support. The debate went accordingly. The tone for the most part was cautious, in an attempt to avoid dissension and remain on amicable terms. But there was a marked sense of strain; the cracks were barely papered over; and it was as well that the occasion did not call for a vote.[4]

The Whigs' greatest anxiety centred on Fox's intentions, for it was his attitude to the Friends of the People that in fact made them of such concern. In themselves they were of minor importance, on ambivalent terms with other reformers and significant in the country mainly as a symbol for attack. But they posed a real party problem because Fox would not condemn them, and they could – and frequently did – claim him for their own. The pressure was predictable and shrewd: the Society knew it could play on his sympathies, and it was eager to force his hand

1. See pp. 53–6 above.
2. Pp. 77–9 above.
3. See I, 616, 620–1.
4. *P.R.*, XXXII (1792), 449–98.

when he was anxious not to be forced. Its members appealed to so much that he valued – to some of the deepest springs in his nature – to the inheritance and the instincts that made him the man and the figure he was. They epitomised indeed the kind of Whiggery in which he felt most at home: aristocratic, self-confident, active, looking to the public as the natural ally, under its traditional guides and guardians, in restraining the executive power. And – though in this they were not exceptional – they were young, the coming generation:[1] a fact which was always apt to carry weight with Fox. As he himself said, 'he did not like to discourage the young ones'.[2] It was hard to deny the demands of so congenial a band.

At the same time, however, Fox was annoyed and apprehensive. He felt grave misgivings about what the young ones had done. This was not the moment to raise the old issue, about which in any case he had mixed feelings;[3] he had almost certainly not been consulted, and would have liked to see the matter dropped. As the debate approached he became increasingly alarmed – not without personal cause, for he had been excluded from Portland's last meeting.[4] But there was more to it than that, and the stakes were high. For Fox's supreme object was to keep the Whigs in being, and with them so far as possible Opposition as a whole. If they were badly weakened Pitt and the King would be the beneficiaries – the one thing that must be prevented at virtually any cost. In the debate itself he spoke accordingly in temperate and temporising terms. He could not oppose Grey's intention; he himself had been a friend to reform; but as to timing, 'he should have hesitated' to raise the subject now.[5] The prevarication was not disingenuous. Fox thought it wrong to define the choices. Opposition's duty was to stay together, to avoid being outmanoeuvred, and to go on pressing Ministers where it could unite.

These priorities, and old connexions with which they were bound up, held Fox within the main body of the great Whig interests; and indeed it would still have seemed almost unnatural to contemplate a break. There was the less inclination to do so since he and some of his colleagues thought they could see signs of weakness within the Ministry's ranks. This was not because they scented the prospect of a great Parliamentary triumph; the last debate on Ochakov fizzled out in February, and as Fox himself had already admitted, Government was 'too . . . superior in

---

1. It has been calculated that in 1792 almost half the reliable Foxites, among whom they were numbered, were under forty years old (Mitchell, *Fox and the Disintegration of the Whig Party*, 254). But so were over a third altogether of the members of the House of Commons.

2. Charles Grey, *Some Account of The Life and Opinions of Charles, Second Earl Grey* . . . (1861), 11.

3. Cf. p. 76 above.

4. See p. 172 above.

5. *P.R.*, XXXII, 470.

numbers' in general to permit 'a struggle for power'.[1] But recalling its own experience, Opposition placed its hopes elsewhere. It still clung to the earlier impression that George III was not happy with Pitt. The arguments remained the same: the Minister had failed in the eyes of Europe and been publicly weakened at home, the King disliked some of his other policies, and there had been some trouble over appointments.[2] These hopes were latent in April, when the issue of the slave trade emerged once more. They rose sharply in May: 'The King is supposed to want to get rid of Pitt, but dares not in these times'; even so there was 'a very strong and general idea' of 'some change or other' from within.[3]

Such expectations might well seem excessive. But they were set against a shifting background. Foreign affairs in the first place were taking a shape which perhaps could be turned to good account. New problems of neutrality or alliance might yield a party advantage – though this in fact could be an issue which would recoil on its promoters' heads. More immediately, however, there were developments to assess at home. Pitt's approach in advance of the Proclamation was clearly something to be weighed. And its significance appeared to be heightened by an intriguing event which, rumoured for some weeks, suddenly occurred in May.

For in April there was talk of a personal quarrel inside the Cabinet. Such a prospect was indeed exciting: just the kind of thing to hearten the troops. And the rumours moreover were true; an old antipathy was coming to a head. Pitt and Thurlow had never liked each other, and relations had long been uneasy. Since 1788 they had been growing worse. The Regency crisis left a sour taste,[4] which was preserved by a series of incidents, over pensions and posts and legal processes, that suggested a deeper state of strain.[5] The episodes were not unduly important, for Thurlow did not dare go too far. But as memories of the Regency crisis faded – and perhaps after Pitt was shaken by Ochakov – his surly resentment became increasingly plain. In May 1792 it suddenly burst forth. On the 8th he spoke in the Lords against the Commons' recent resolutions on the slave trade, which had been moved, though not

1. On 17 February, in the debate on the budget (*P.R.*, XXXI, 232). For the Ochakov debates of the 20th and 29th see p. 34 above.

2. See p. 32 above.

3. Sir Gilbert Elliot to Lady Elliot, 19 May 1792 (*Life and Letters of Sir Gilbert Elliot. . .*, ed. the Countess of Minto, II (1878), 29). He was closely in touch with Portland at the time.

4. See I, 652, 655–6; and for earlier relations op. cit., 185, 368, 394–5.

5. Most prominently over a pension for Auckland proposed by Pitt in 1789; a Scottish appointment proposed by Dundas in 1790; the legalities attending the Duke of York's marriage in 1791, which led to a quarrel between Thurlow and Grenville; and a running objection on Thurlow's part, which reached its climax in 1791, to the appointment of George Rose (his former protégé) as Clerk of the Parliaments. His opposition to repeal of the penal laws against the Scottish Episcopalians may perhaps also be cited.

Ministerially, by Pitt. And six days later he turned sarcastically on a direct Ministerial measure, Pitt's bill to attach arrangements for a sinking fund to all future loans.[1] This second attack was so unexpected that Government was 'nearly beat' in the upper House.[2] It proved to be the breaking point, and the end for Thurlow himself.

For Pitt's patience had already been severely tried. The King had had to intervene more than once, as had several Ministers, who now felt however that there was no more they could do. Grenville, earlier 'a Cement of Connexion', had come to dislike the Chancellor; Stafford, while still friendly to him, had spoken and failed; Camden had given up; Hawkesbury, an ally from an older period, was not close enough to Pitt.[3] Nor could George III himself keep the peace any longer. Thurlow had banked throughout on the Lord Chancellor's position as the monarch's particular representative in Cabinet, on the King's continued personal friendship, and Pitt's reluctance to excite the King.[4] It was not enough in the face of this open provocation, and the King knew very well what the result, if pressed, must be. He could not even postpone a decision, for on 16 May Pitt 'stated the impossibility of his sitting any longer in Council' with Thurlow. The only question therefore was 'which of the two shall retire', and the Chancellor was told he must go, though the time was left open and for convenience was delayed until June, when both Parliament and the Court of Chancery rose.[5] The King was upset – 'a decision', he wrote to Thurlow, 'so revolting to my feelings'; and Thurlow was surprised – 'I did not think that the King would have parted with me so easily'.[6] The Great Seal was placed in commission.

1. See I, 402, 268.

2. Grenville to Buckingham, 15 May 1792 (Buckingham, II, 207). The voting was 28 to 22.

3. For the King at different times in 1789 and 1790 see Stanhope, II, Appendix, ix, xi, *L.C.G. III*, I, no. 562, Pitt to Stafford, 21 November [1790], P.R.O. 30/29/384; for Grenville, Stafford to Grenville, 27 September 1789 (*H.M.C., Dropmore*, I, 524), Dundas to Stafford, 22 October 1791 (P.R.O. 30/29/1/15); for Thurlow' relations with Stafford, the former's correspondence in P.R.O. 30/29/1, and Tomline, III, 402; for Camden, his letter to Lady Frances Stewart, 21 May 1792, in Camden Ms C3/24, Kent C.A.O.; for Hawkesbury, Thurlow's two notes of 17 May 1792 in B.I. Add. Ms 38192.

4. See I, 104, 185, 368 for the Chancellor's position, and Stanhope, II, Appendix, ix for an occasion on which the King pleaded his 'late . . . illness' as a reason for reconciliation.

5. The course of events may be followed in Stanhope, II, 149–50 and Appendix, xv; and *L.C.G. III*, I, no. 754. Pitt's draft notification to Thurlow of 16 May is in P.R.O. 30/8/102.

6. George III to Thurlow, 17 May 1792 (*L.C.G. III*, I, no. 755); Horace Twiss, *The Public and Private Life of Lord Chancellor Eldon . . .*, I (1844), 213, containing a supposedly verbatim account of Thurlow's reaction. He was said to have added, 'As to that other man, he has done to me just what I should have done to him if I could'. On 5 June, while still nominally Lord Chancellor, he fired his last broadside by speaking in the Lords against a bill, moved in the Commons by Pitt, for encouraging the growth of timber in the New Forest.

The search for a successor was to be involved in the party manoeuvres which by then were under way.

For Pitt had been making tentative approaches before Thurlow was dismissed. He was able to move at the start against a hinge in Opposition. There were still traces within its ranks of the separate bodies which had joined in the ill-fated Coalition of 1783.[1] The followers of North and the Rockinghams' successors had not entirely lost their identities, at least, and perhaps most visibly, in their social ties. One of the ablest Northites was Alexander Wedderburn, Lord Loughborough, a former Law Officer and now Chief Justice of the Common Pleas. Intensely ambitious, alert and adroit, and long an envious rival of Thurlow, he had kept in touch, if intermittently, with his old colleagues Eden (Lord Auckland) and – since schooldays – his fellow Scot Dundas. He seems at this point to have been moving into closer contact with them both, possibly going so far as to pass on news of Opposition's meetings;[2] and Pitt in return used him as an intermediary, certainly through Auckland and perhaps Dundas as well.[3] The latter indeed appears to have suggested the form of the approach which the Minister adopted as soon as the debate on Grey's notice of a motion was out of the way.[4] On the following day, 1 May, Pitt proposed a meeting of the Privy Council which Portland, Lord Fitzwilliam (his close associate and Rockingham's heir), Lord Guilford (the former Lord North), Loughborough 'and other Leading Persons' might attend, to consider such measures against disaffection 'as the present circumstances may require'.[5] The reaction was favourable enough for the Minister then to get in touch with Portland direct, and the two men met in Downing Street

1. I, 101.
2. This is suggested in Pitt to Auckland, 1 May 1792 (B.L. Add. Ms 46519). Auckland had been in England for several months on leave from his post at The Hague. For earlier signs of contact, mostly on legal matters, see Pitt to Auckland, 27 March 1792 (B.L. Add. Ms 34441); Dundas to Loughborough, 22 October 1791, and Loughborough to Dundas, 24 April 1792 (S.R.O., Melville Castle Ms G.D. 51/1/17/1–2; and see p. 97, n1 above).
3. Pitt to Auckland, 1 May 1792 (B.L. Add. Ms 46519). There is a letter from Dundas, endorsed to Loughborough 1792, which if correctly ascribed to 5 May of that year shows the two men closely in touch by that time (Melville Castle Ms G.D. 51/1/17/3). Auckland also took soundings of Opposition sentiment through his brother-in-law Gilbert Elliot, like himself and Loughborough originally a Northite but in close touch with all shades of opinion; see Loughborough to Auckland, 4 May 1792 (P.R.O. 30/8/153), and *Life and Letters of Elliot*, II, 18.
4. See Dundas to Pitt, and Pitt to Dundas, nd but clearly before 1 May 1792, in Melville Castle Ms G.D. 51/1/17/4.
5. Pitt to Auckland, 1 May 1792 (B.L. Add. Ms 46519). Fitzwilliam would in fact, as Pitt recollected while he wrote, have first to be made a Privy Councillor.

There may have been a parallel here, at least in the experienced Dundas's mind, with the Gordon riots of 1780, in the aftermath of which the Rockinghams had attended a Privy Council – and then received an offer of a Coalition from North. I owe this suggestion to Dr Paul Kelly.

on 10 May.[1] Pitt put his proposition, and told the Whig leader of 'the only measure . . . thought of maturely' – the Proclamation against seditious meetings and writings. He seems in fact to have given him a draft on the spot; Portland showed it to some of his colleagues, including Fox; and the paper was returned with a few amendments. The idea of attending a Privy Council was turned down, for Portland feared that such a gesture might be 'misrepresented and misunderstood'. At the same time, however, he was prepared to say that in this matter 'We may act in concert though not in conjunction'.[2]

That was on 13 May. Three days later Thurlow was dismissed. The political world was highly stimulated, not least the inner ranks of Opposition. There was much for them to discuss, possibly to hope for, perhaps to fear, and some of them at least now saw Pitt's invitation in a different light. Was the Proclamation really being issued for the reasons proclaimed? Might not 'Paine's book' and the threat of unrest be of lesser importance than the wish to exploit the Friends of the People and to counteract Thurlow's dismissal? There could be a trap, into which their 'Dissention' might lead them.[3] And yet there was an opportunity, if they could avoid the risks. For George III might be feeling resentful at having had to act under dictation, and Government would be weakened and embarrassed in the Lords. It could therefore be the case that 'the Duke of Portland and his friends would be by no means unacceptable for these separate reasons to the King and perhaps not to Pitt'.[4]

Meanwhile the approaches continued, and some offers were now mentioned. As soon as Thurlow received his dismissal, Pitt and Dundas turned again to Loughborough. The prospect of the Seals was dangled before him, possibly at first without other changes but very soon as part of a wider arrangement.[5] Three other Cabinet places, some Privy

1. Pitt to Portland, 9 May 1792 (draft in P.R.O. 30/8/102); Portland to Pitt, sd (P.R.O. 30/8/168). Loughborough apparently said later, in June, that he 'took *no* notice' of Auckland's letter (*Diaries and Correspondence of James Harris, First Earl of Malmesbury* . . ., ed. by his Grandson . . ., II (1844), 458). This is not the impression given in his own letter to Auckland of 4 May, in P.R.O. 30/8/153. Auckland later claimed in his turn that he had 'never written' to Loughborough 'since I knew of the intended dismission of Ld. Thurlow', i.e. after 14 May (to Lord Sheffield, 24 July 1792; B.L. Add. Ms 45728).

2. Portland to Pitt, 13 May 1792 (P.R.O. 30/8/168); *Life and Letters of Elliot*, II, 23–4, 26; *Diaries and Correspondence of Malmesbury*, II, 458.

3. Thomas Pelham to Lady Webster [later Lady Holland], 28 May 1792 (B.L. Add. Ms 51705). Pelham was seeing a certain amount of both Portland and Fox at this time.

4. Gilbert Elliot to Lady Elliot, 22 May 1792 (*Elliot*, II, 30).

5. The sequence of events is not completely clear. Loughborough knew by 18 May that he might become Chancellor (see H. Butterfield, 'Charles James Fox and the Whig Opposition in 1792', in *The Cambridge Historical Journal*, IX, no. 3, 330 Postscript), and he may even have been sounded on the day on which Thurlow made his fatal attack in the Lords (p. 175 above). A letter from Dundas of 'Thursday 14th' refers to 'the Vacancy in the Seals which will immediately be open' and for which a Commission would have to be issued immediately (S.R.O., Melville Castle Ms G.D. 51/1/20/7). Wider offers are first mentioned specifically, as having been recently received, on the 25th (see p. 178, n2 below).

Councillorships, the Lord Lieutenancy of Ireland were in the air.[1] The bait was not taken, though it was not ignored; Portland 'bestowed much more thought upon it than I should have thought necessary'. But the posts were said to be too few, the accompanying patronage too 'insignificant', and 'nothing like a situation of equality . . . in either House' was held out.[2] The Whigs in fact were not prepared to give hostages to a fortune controlled by the Minister. They must not endanger their uneasy equilibrium, or allow a section to be absorbed. The Proclamation was about to be published, and discussed in Parliament. Fox made an eloquent appeal for party unity, and when the Commons' debate was over Portland rejected the Ministry's suggestions as 'utterly inadmissible'.[3]

No doubt. But the seed had been sown, and Loughborough was hungry for office. Since he dared not come in by himself – he had an earlier notorious change of sides to live down, and he could not now quite face being a second Eden[4] – he did his best to bring the two sides closer together. At first he appeared to be having some success. The pressures on the Whig Lords were growing. Burke was lobbying Loughborough and Portland, and, more important, the diplomat Lord Malmesbury, whose advice on Europe was greatly respected, was being increasingly consulted and showed himself in favour of further talks.[5] So too were others 'of weight and influence',[6] some even prepared to welcome coalition – a word that was now beginning to be used. Above all, Ministers themselves seemed anxious to explore farther. Loughborough saw Pitt and Dundas on 14 June.

> Pitt . . . wore every appearance of sincerity and frankness; . . . he stated no difficulties or objections, but assured him [Loughborough]

1. *Diaries and Correspondence of Malmesbury*, II, 458–9. Loughborough was careful to remind Portland a few days later that this had not been a formal offer: 'It was rather a rapid sketch of situations that were or might be open' (nd, but late May 1792; Portland Ms PWF 9220, University of Nottingham). The Governor Generalship of India seems also to have been in contemplation (*Malmesbury*, II, 468–9).

2. Portland to Loughborough, 25 May 1792 (Portland Ms PWF 9220).

3. Loc. cit. He had already warned Pitt on the eve of the debate not to be disappointed by the limits to Opposition's support (24 May 1792; P.R.O. 30/8/168).

4. I, 484–5. The analogy with Eden is not exact, for the Lord Chancellor's position was unique in its personal relationship to the King. But the precedent was uncomfortably close. The earlier occasion was in 1771, when Loughborough (then still Wedderburn) had become Solicitor General.

5. For Malmesbury (Sir James Harris) see I, 521–22. He had the further advantage of a certain influence over the Prince of Wales. On the other hand Pitt now disliked him intensely, following his reversion to his old Foxite connexion in the Regency crisis (op. cit., 521, 622n1); see Gilbert Elliot to Malmesbury, 8 April 1793 (N.L.S., Minto Ms 11111).

6. A list given later by Malmesbury is in *Political Memoranda of Leeds*, 181. William Windham may be added to it.

Lord Loughborough, *by William Owen*

Charles James Fox, *by Thomas Day*

it was his wish to unite cordially and heartily – not in the way of bargain, but to form a strong and united Ministry. His only doubts were about Fox, and these, he said, *might* be got over. He was a little apprehensive of Fox's opinions relative to the French Revolution, and hinted that he was afraid he had gone *too far*. – That this was an objection to his coming *at once into the Foreign Department*, because it would look like a change of system.[1]

The Minister confessed that he was talking without the King's express command. But he was confident that this could be obtained, and Loughborough's own view was that he would return to the subject after speaking to Grenville and to George III.[2]

The programme however did not go like that. Pitt saw Loughborough again eleven days later; but only to put a damper on the hopes. The difficulty, he said, was to persuade his friends 'to the measure of coalescing with Fox at present'; and while he himself still felt no objection he had therefore not talked to the King. From the way in which he spoke it seemed to Loughborough that the negotiation was 'only suspended, not *broken off*'.[3] But meanwhile, if Pitt was in earnest, he still had his two hurdles before him: one known (or stated) in the shape of his associates, the other unknown in George III.

But was Pitt in earnest? Portland and his associates were far from sure. Were the alleged feelings within the Ministry just a tactical excuse? Had Pitt and Dundas not simply tried to split Opposition, and as soon as they met complications found a pretext to think again? The former Rockingham Whigs in particular could not really believe that Pitt himself would accept a balanced coalition. Hence Portland's reaction, influenced by Fox, to the offer of posts outlined in May;[4] and hence the far more vivid suspicions of Fox himself. From diverging points of

1. Malmesbury's account in his diary for 17 June (*Malmesbury*, II, 463). And cf. Portland to Malmesbury on the 15th (loc. cit., 460). Some variations of wording appear in *Elliot*, II, 42–4, and *Correspondence of Burke*, VII, 194. Pitt is also said in one account (*Elliot*, II, 43, citing Malmesbury) to have remarked that, whatever the difficulties raised by Fox's current attitude, 'his conduct in the year '83 and during the time of the discussion about the Regency' was now 'entirely obliterated from the *Royal memory*'.

A great deal of course turns on the accuracy, indeed the honesty, of Loughborough's reporting. It is hard to pronounce on this, since there is no independent check. Some of the Whigs later suspected him of exaggerating Pitt's expressions in his eagerness for office. But there seems to have been no complaint from Pitt himself or from Dundas – perhaps, however, because they remained anxious to keep Loughborough in play – and there is an emphasis in the Minister's wording which can hardly be explained away even supposing the shading to have been heightened.

2. Pitt was in fact quoted as saying that 'he would be responsible that it would please the King *and the Queen*' (*Malmesbury*, II, 460).

3. Loc. cit., 467–9; *Elliot*, II, 53–4; Portland to Fitzwilliam, 27 June 1792 (Wentworth Woodhouse Muniments, F31a; Sheffield City Libraries).

4. Pp. 177–8 above.

vantage both men in fact were tempted. Portland and his like-minded peers – Fitzwilliam, Carlisle, the Duke of Devonshire – were genuinely anxious to support Government in the face of possible unrest. They were frightened by the popular Societies,[1] and by the Friends of the People, and at moments at least were driven to believe that 'circumstances . . . made a Coalition with Pitt a very necessary measure'.[2] The fruits of office also beckoned, if they were substantial enough. And Fox for his part could not wholly dismiss the prospect. Office held very real attractions to one of his views and situation: the exercise of his talents as well as a relief to his finances, and equally the chance of attaining a share of power as a group. 'As a Party man, he thought it a good thing for his party to come into office, were it only for a month', and he was not deterred by the thought of coalition – '*he loved coalitions*'. The 'circumstances of the country' moreover made 'a strong Administration' desirable; a junction indeed sometimes seemed '"*so d – d right, to be sure, that I cannot help thinking it must be*"'.[3] But when all this had been said, it went very hard to enter into coalition with Pitt – the faithless victor of '84, the promoter of the Westminster Scrutiny, the prime target of party resentment, the heir to hereditary rivalries.[4] If an agreement were to be reached it must be on well secured conditions; and their guarantee should be that Fox himself was shown not to be subordinate. He could rationalise the case, and the arguments were well deployed. Personal equality of status with Pitt was necessary to prove that Pitt meant business, that Opposition would be given proper weight, and true Whig principles thereby preserved. It would not be to 'the honour *and pride* of the Party' that he should enter on any other terms. But the wound may have gone much deeper than the reasoning, and the pride at stake was not the party's alone. Fox had seemed '*a little hurt*' at the outset that Pitt had not approached him instead of lesser figures, and he could not believe that in the end his rival 'would admit him to an equal share of power'. His tone when he spoke of Pitt was unusually 'impractical' and 'acrimonious'. Even when he admitted, as he did on one occasion, that he might have to join an arrangement, he talked of leaving the Commons for the Lords if he was given an office lower than Pitt's. The strength of his feelings made him bad tempered, and his opinion swung to and fro. He was 'peevish' and 'not inclined to speak' – an unusual

---

1. The specific effect of Sheffield (see p. 105 above) was very important here. Fitzwilliam had his palace of Wentworth Woodhouse nearby, and had been receiving worrying reports of the town for some time. Chatsworth and Castle Howard and Welbeck – though the Duke of Portland lived at his older seat Bulstrode in Buckinghamshire – were also not so very far away.

2. *Malmesbury*, II, 464, 454. Cf. *Correspondence of Burke*, VII, 149.

3. *Malmesbury*, 462, 466, and *Elliot*, II, 45, quoting Fox at first and at second hand – in the latter case from Portland – respectively.

4. See I, 134, 217–22, 137.

symptom; then 'more accommodating and less taciturn'; then 'harsh
. . . and opiniative' again.[1]

Fox's advice carried great weight. It reaffirmed the definition of party
as proclaimed in the American War and developed as a lifeline in the
past decade. And his moods were anxiously watched, for he still held the
key. While the other leaders deplored his refusal to condemn the Friends
of the People – while indeed they acknowledged that on several great
issues they and he held contrasting views[2] – they, and Portland perhaps
most keenly, were still reluctant to risk a break, bringing the loss of their
friend and inspiration and perhaps his lurch towards a more extreme
position.[3] It was hard to know how to act, for 'there was no doing
without Fox or with him', and so, as Burke observed, his 'coach *stops the
way*'.[4] But with varying degrees of enthusiasm, they decided they must
'insist' that he should be 'not only a member of the Cabinet' but 'in as
respectable and efficient a situation' as in 1782–3.[5]

The decision led to a curious episode which put paid for a time to any
further talks. For, by this argument, Pitt's real intentions could be
gauged by an acid test. He said that he wished to form 'a strong and
united Ministry'; that meant Fox on proper terms; that in turn could
best be achieved if Pitt left the Treasury for another post. Portland and
Fitzwilliam had in fact been playing with this idea since the middle of
June, and of some 'neutral man' being placed at the head of the new
Ministry. One name had even risen to the surface – that of the Duke of
Leeds, Pitt's own former Foreign Secretary, a friend of Malmesbury's,
and endowed with the rather misty virtue of having once opposed the
American War.[6] The news not unnaturally reached Leeds, and in mid-
July he visited Portland. He then decided, with Portland's consent, to

1. For his remarks and changes of mood throughout these weeks see above all
Malmesbury, II, 459–69; for a hardening of attitude in July, loc. cit., 472 and B.L. Add.
Ms 47561. The sensitive point of precedence in the Commons is brought out in *Elliot*, II,
46.

According to Fox's nephew Lord Holland, writing many years later, Fox had 'a very
secret interview' with Pitt, in which 'the latter proposed a coalition', at about this time.
Fox refused, because no post was to be given to Sheridan. I have not found any other
evidence for this; it seems inherently unlikely, even if allowance is made for inaccurate
detail; and Holland himself was 'not confident' about the date (*Memoirs of the Whig Party*,
I, 30–1; II, 46).

2. Others being '*The Abolition of the Slave Trade, The Repeal of the Test Act*, and the
system to be observed *relative to French politics*' (*Malmesbury*, II, 460–1, recording a
conversation with Portland). Cf. *Elliot*, II, 44.

3. For this last consideration see O'Gorman, op. cit., 98n2.

4. *Malmesbury*, II, 466.

5. When he had been Foreign Secretary. Portland to Fitzwilliam, 27 June 1792
(Wentworth Woodhouse Muniments, F31a). The Duke actually wrote '–92 & –93', but
clearly meant '82–'83.

6. *Malmesbury*, II, 459, 465. And see I, 185, 522.

place the proposition before the King.[1]

Leeds felt little diffidence in putting himself forward. After all, he had been a Secretary of State, and he was a Duke, qualified by station – like Portland earlier – to grace a junction of abler men. In any case he had never been disposed to underrate his qualities, and he was doubtless gratified by the thought of so splendid a return, and at Pitt's expense. He entered on the process with due solemnity and a lively sense of filling a need; and Portland and Fox were content to watch, without much hope but – the latter particularly – ready and willing to see how far their reading of Pitt was confirmed.[2] They were also greatly interested in the King's attitude; to discover how far he was prepared to sanction the kind of proposals his Minister had raised. They had a vivid sense of the royal power after their experience of nine years before; Fox indeed considered, or affected to consider, that 'the success of the whole' depended upon it.[3]

The result was farcical. Leeds was always apt to mishandle a negotiation: he had done so more than once in his time, as George III and Pitt had had to point out.[4] He was now plunging into a delicate situation, inadequately briefed and ill equipped. When he had his audience, on 14 August, it was to find to his consternation that the King was not, as he had assumed, 'informed of everything that had passed'. Pitt had not spoken to him on the subject 'for a long time', in fact for 'some months', and then only to mention 'something like an opening on the part of the Duke of Portland and his friends'. George III's own comment moreover had been, '*Anything Complimentary to them, but no Power*' – a statement to which poor Leeds put three exclamation marks in his account. Worse followed, for when the King asked the Duke who was supposed to take over the Treasury, and the latter said – one imagines uneasily – 'some one upon terms of Friendship and Confidence with both Parties', 'H.M. replied . . . that whoever was the First Lord must either be a Cypher or Mr. Pitt appear as a *commis*'.[5]

It took the King about half an hour to dispose of Leeds. Soon afterwards the Duke learned – possibly through Loughborough – that Pitt would like to hear from him.[6] The two men met on 22 August, and

1. *Malmesbury*, II, 470; *Political Memoranda of Leeds*, 175, 179, 183; Portland Mss PWF 9223–4. It is not entirely clear on whose initiative the meeting, or the approach to the King, was proposed.

2. For Leeds's experiences of Pitt see I, Chs. XVI, XVII, and Ch. I above; for the attitudes of Portland and Fox, *Malmesbury*, II, 470–2, and Butterfield, loc. cit., 314.

3. Malmesbury to Leeds, retailing Fox's views, 31 July 1792 (*Malmesbury*, II, 473).

4. See I, 474–6, 554–5.

5. *Political Memoranda of Leeds*, 187–90; and see also Pitt to George III, 18 August 1792 (*L.C.G. III*, I, no. 774) and George III to Pitt, 20 August 1792 (Holland Rose, II, 38). Cf. also the King's silence in June when the subject had been brought up at Court (*Malmesbury*, II, 465–6) – a reaction, however, which had then been thought to indicate his 'full acquaintance' with what was said to be going on.

6. See Holland Rose, II, 38. According to Burke (to William Burke, 3 September 1792; *Correspondence of Burke*, VII, 193–4), Loughborough had known in advance of the plan for Leeds, but had not dared mention it to Pitt.

the atmosphere was chilly. Pitt, who 'did not appear quite at his ease', listened to the account, and then said 'that *there had been no thoughts of any alteration in the Government, that circumstances did not call for it, nor did the people wish it, and that no new arrangement, either by a change or coalition, had ever been in contemplation!!!*'[1] Leeds, staggered by this reply, admitted that Fox posed a problem. Pitt agreed. He also agreed that he had talked to the King 'on a former occasion', as the King had stated. He wished that the Duke had come to him first, before doing anything else. He thought there was 'no purpose whatever' in a further meeting of himself and Portland.

So Leeds 'withdrew'.[2] He was followed by everyone else. The talks had failed, and when next they arose it was in graver circumstances. Pitt, however, made it clear to Portland that he remained on friendly terms. If he was not going to share power he was prepared to be 'complimentary'.[3] In July – before the fiasco – he had obtained the King's permission to offer Portland the Garter, and although the Duke refused the Ministry continued to make itself agreeable by promoting and supporting his candidature for the Chancellorship of Oxford University.[4] He was elected, which greatly pleased him. It was a sign that Pitt had not closed the door, even if 'all Idea of *New Arrangements*' was now 'excluded' in the form proposed.[5]

In the week that ended the prospect of an accession to Pitt's Ministry there was an accession of great future significance to himself. On 26 July the young George Canning, something of a protégé of Sheridan's and Fox's after his precocious triumphs at Eton and Oxford, sat down in his rooms in the Temple to write a letter to Pitt. He may have been encouraged by a word from Thomas Orde, an old acquaintance of the Minister and Chief Secretary of Ireland at the time of the Propositions;

Bland Burges of the Foreign Office later maintained that George III told the Minister of Leeds's proposal, in front of the Duke, on the terrace at Windsor immediately after the meeting (to Anne Burges, 14 October 1794; Bland Burges Ms 10, Bodleian Library). It seems unlikely.

1. *Political Memoranda of Leeds*, 194. The Duke was driven to exclamation marks on several occasions during this affair.

2. Op. cit., 194–6. For Dundas's reaction to Leeds's 'preposterous' behaviour see Melville Castle Mss G.D. 51/1/17/11–13.

3. P. 182 above.

4. The first steps had in fact again been taken just before Leeds saw George III. But support continued to be given thereafter. For other suggestions of honours and posts to Opposition in July, see O'Gorman, op. cit., 103.

5. Dundas to Loughborough, 29 August 1792 (Melville Castle Ms G.D. 51/1/17/13). Auckland, the first avenue of approach, may be allowed the last word. Although he doubted if Pitt would be 'permanently strengthen'd' by a coalition, 'I have no doubt, that it is becoming & wise in you to leave the door open, at least till the commencement of the session' (to Pitt, 4 September 1792; P.R.O. 30/8/110).

his decision was taken, by his own account, out of disgust with the Friends of the People, which made it impossible, despite his connexions, to give his loyalty to Opposition.[1] Instead it was now 'personally with Yourself that I am ambitious of being connected', and in return he was invited to call at Downing Street.[2] He did so on 15 August. Pitt at first seemed 'awkward', but after a time expressed his readiness to help find a seat when the chance arose. Canning, who was also feeling awkward, said he did not want one from a borough owner, 'such a man, for instance, as my Lord Lonsdale' – who had given Pitt his first chance.[3] But the Minister pointed out that his Departmental patronage was 'very small', and that even when a Treasury borough came up it normally meant personal expense. He could therefore almost certainly help best by using his influence with a proprietor, with whom however Canning need not have dealings thereafter, although he should be prepared to resign his seat if he differed too firmly from the patron's views. As for himself, he was willing to say that he would not 'fetter' opinion on issues which did not directly involve the Ministry's position. He accepted as an example the repeal of the Test Act, which Canning had raised; 'A general good disposition towards Government was what he hoped to find'.[4] The two men parted well pleased with each other. It was a notable coup for Canning; and Pitt for his part must have welcomed the prospect of an addition to his personal following[5] in the shape of a young Whig hopeful at this particular time. A seat was found ten months later, and the connexion began which was to forge a personal attachment and help shape a political tradition.

Pitt's motives in approaching Opposition have often been discussed, on the more recent occasions mainly from Opposition's point of view. They are of interest, for the talks took place in what might be called the final period in which current conditions gave him a reasonable freedom of choice. Events were soon to narrow the area, more swiftly perhaps than he saw. But in the spring and summer of 1792 he was still moving in familiar territory, shadowed by a cloud which might be threatening but, he might hope, would pass away. His conduct moreover raises questions which were not answered at the time. When Leeds retired from the scene

1. The letter of 26 July is in Stanhope Ms S 501 series, Kent C.A.O.; Pitt's reply, of the 28th, in Canning Mss, bundle 30, Harewood deposit, Leeds Archives Department. The 'Mr. O–' mentioned in Canning's later account (see *Miscellanies Collected and Edited by Earl Stanhope, Second Series* (1872), 57–64) appears in his letter as Orde; further possible contacts with Pitt are discussed in Dorothy Marshall, *The Rise of George Canning* (1938), 32–3. For Orde himself see I, 198–215.

2. Letters of 26 and 28 July.

3. See I, 25–6.

4. Stanhope, *Miscellanies, Second Series*, 59–60.

5. Whose numbers within the Ministry's normal voting power were small; see I, 619, for an estimate in 1788.

it was in a state of complete bewilderment. How could Pitt admit to having talked to the King if no new arrangement had ever been thought of? How could his statements be reconciled with Portland's; whose information or memory was wrong? There must have been 'some *strange* mistake'.[1] He could not find the clue, and there have been differing explanations ever since.

In the first place, was Pitt himself really responsible for the initiative? Opposition leaders after a time were not entirely sure. They were soon struck, and rather surprised, by Dundas's role; for Dundas was not yet generally looked on as a figure of the first rank. He had been made a Secretary of State the year before with some hesitation as a stopgap, and there was still an impression that he remained on a temporary basis.[2] Yet here he was, making the running in these important conversations, the third attendant at Pitt's meetings with Loughborough, the Minister's confidant in the affair. Portland indeed came to the conclusion that 'D. hurried P. into the negotiation';[3] and certainly it was he who suggested inviting the Opposition notables to a Privy Council, who did most of the talking about appointments, and looked forward to remaining in touch at the end.[4] He was, or became, sure of his ground: 'Mr. Pitt felt exactly as I do'; 'Mr. Pitt . . . feels exactly on the Subject as I do'; 'We' can be reached at Wimbledon on a certain day, or in London on another.[5] He had clearly risen in Pitt's trust and friendship over the past few years.[6] Despite the outcome, this negotiation may have further hastened the ascent of his fortunes.

Dundas moved against the background of the Home Office, which explained his involvement at the start. He was departmentally responsible for enforcing the Proclamation, and his anxiety to widen political support met with Pitt's ready response. The Minister in point of fact seems himself to have been thinking on similar lines, and he at once suggested following up a meeting of the Privy Council with one of all peers and MPs, at which attendance would be understood to mean that those present 'act in Concert in their several Counties during the Summer'. He expected a response from 'all the Peers and *four* fifths of the House of Commons';[7] but the idea was dropped when the invitation to the Council was declined. One need not doubt that this first offer was made on the ostensible grounds. The Proclamation by its nature would carry more weight the wider its Parliamentary support, Dundas at least

1. *Political Memoranda of Leeds*, 194–5, 197–8.
2. See I, 458, and *Leeds*, 198.
3. To Fitzwilliam, 27 June 1792 (Wentworth Woodhouse Muniments, F31a). And cf. *Elliot*, II, 54.
4. P. 176 above; *Malmesbury*, II, 458, 460, 464, 468; *Elliot*, II, 35; Melville Castle Mss G.D. 51/1/17/3, 5–9, G.D. 51/1/20/1 and possibly 7–9.
5. Melville Castle Mss G.D. 51/1/17/7, 13, 5.
6. See I, 456–8, 584.
7. To Dundas, nd (S.R.O., Melville Castle Ms G.D. 51/1/17/4). And cf. Pitt to Auckland, 1 May 1792 (B.L. Add. Ms 46519).

was impressed by the growing anxieties of the Opposition grandees,[1] and he and Pitt were in earnest in seeking a public demonstration that these last were prepared to commit themselves.

But what about the subsequent offer to join the Ministry? If agreement could be reached it would clearly strengthen Government's hand. There would be a proof of substantial unity, encouragement to the forces of order, a promise of greater freedom of action without much Parliamentary risk. The French would be shown how matters stood. Agreement would bring obvious public advantages. But these were scarcely so compelling as to force an offer in themselves. Pitt had been thinking of accompanying the Proclamation with other precautionary measures – possibly embodying part of the militia and taking powers to expel foreigners.[2] But he had not 'maturely considered' them,[3] and on reflection they were laid aside, for in fact Ministers were not deeply disturbed. They certainly felt that a warning was needed, that it was 'high time for the Executive Government to interfere': as Dundas hinted, they were coming under pressure from the counties, and the Whig peers' 'concert' carried pressure too.[4] But they were content then to see how the warning worked, to make some precautionary dispositions, and otherwise remain vigilant but restrained. Their language was moderate; they did not want to rush to extremes. The mood was probably expressed by Auckland, after he had been in touch with Pitt: 'My alarm is not great, because I think that the good part of the country predominates, and is awake to the danger, but it may be essential to the whole that so good a disposition should be kept in activity and well directed'.[5]

Pitt's approach could therefore have rested on more than this precautionary concern; and as so often in such cases the motives in fact may well have been mixed. One must ask if Opposition may not have been right: if the main object was not simply to split them, as Fox and Portland came to believe. The Whigs' suspicions where Pitt was concerned were of course endemic by now: it was almost an article of faith to presume that he was unprincipled.[6] This kind of assumption – which was applied equally in reverse to Fox – usually misleads those who

1. See Dundas to Thurlow, 9 May 1792 (N.L.S., Melville Ms 6).
2. This was Thomas Pelham's account, at a time when he was in touch with Portland (to Lady Webster, 28 May 1792; B.L. Add. Ms 51705). See also *Elliot*, II, 24 or 14 May. Pitt himself wrote on the 1st of 'other Measures' (to Auckland; B.L. Add. Ms 46519).
3. *Elliot*, II, 24.
4. Pitt in the debate on the Proclamation on 25 May (*The Senator . . .*, V (nd), 935); and see Dundas's interesting remarks on the same occasion (*P.R.*, XXXIII (1792), 178). Cf. pp. 133–8 above.
5. To Loughborough, 1 May 1792 (*A.C.*, II, 403). His continental experience, however, made him add that 'the peace and serenity of these Kingdoms' might yet be involved.
6. Eg Portland to Burke, 12 September 1792; quoted in Butterfield, loc. cit., 315n71.

make it. Issues are simplified by preconceptions which more often than not are ill informed. But in this case an argument could certainly be built on the premise, in a sequence which seemed to explain the series of statements and manoeuvres. First, it could be held, Pitt tried to separate Portland and his 'respectable' colleagues from the Friends of the People, and inferentially from Fox, who was not invited by name to the Council. Secondly, he tried to entice Loughborough on his own, the more urgently when Thurlow was suddenly dismissed. Thirdly, having failed to do so – and still under pressure from Thurlow's going – he tried to enlist a few of the others, on unattractive terms. Fourthly, on finding that Fox must be included, and in a major post, he pretended to have no personal objection, knowing that – fifthly – his colleagues and supporters would provide a suitable excuse. By the same token he did not bother to keep the King informed, reckoning correctly that he could extract himself if his initial tactics failed. Leeds's unwelcome proposal merely clarified an earlier decision, taken before Pitt was faced with the proposal of stepping down to an 'equality' with his rival. The motive throughout was to weaken his opponents at what seemed to be an opportune moment, taken from a position – as they continued to think[1] – which was weaker than before.

No hard evidence exists to refute directly such a reading of Pitt's intentions. He had certainly shown himself ready earlier, within recognised limits, to exploit Opposition's embarrassments, and he is said to have remarked now that its proceedings in April had led him to over-estimate its divisions.[2] He would obviously have been glad to discomfit 'the party', as well as to gain wider positive support. The question really is if the first of these motives filled the whole space of his political thinking. Can it account entirely for the way in which he and Dundas behaved? Or might the sequence be better suited by another reading, not necessarily excluding this explanation but embracing a wider choice?

For in some ways Pitt might appear to have been taking unnecessary risks, if his sole intention was as Opposition thought. One may argue whether or not he was wise to neglect the King so seriously, leaving him to pick up such news as reached him – which of course it did.[3] One might think it risky to name appointments after the King's initial response.[4] These hazards perhaps were not unduly serious: Opposition had to know the size of the proposals, and a Minister had always to judge how to handle the monarch. It was more open to suspicion to hold out appointments, some affecting the Cabinet, without confiding – so far as

1. See p. 174 above.
2. P. 173 above; *Elliot*, II 43.
3. *Malmesbury*, II, 465–6; *Elliot*, II, 45, 54. Cf. *Political Memoranda of Leeds*, 185.
4. For which see p. 182 above.

is known – in any of his colleagues except Dundas.[1] It could hardly have pleased Grenville, as Opposition noted, to learn that his post had been mentioned; and others might have been worried by the naming of non-Cabinet places in which Dundas continued to indulge at least into July.[2] Prospective rearrangements of such importance of course demanded confidential talks; but this was an unusually strict initial exclusion of those currently in office. Above all – for here was the crux – one might think that Pitt was clumsy to risk their resentment by stating so firmly that he had no personal objection to Fox. He could well have been less categorical, and not committed himself so far – or indeed hinted so explicitly (and perhaps disingenuously) at an easing of the King's historic attitude.[3] It might be argued that such inducements were needed to lure Opposition into the trap; to make Portland and his friends and Fox himself face a possibly destructive choice. But what was the point if the lure was then to be so swiftly withdrawn, by the statement a week later that any arrangements must be postponed? For someone held to be so machiavellian Pitt's tactics on this reading seem maladroit, calculated to raise suspicion in every quarter at once. He may have used his colleagues to redefine a prospect which was showing signs of becoming awkward; but if he had never meant what he said about Fox, why say it precisely in this way?

Perhaps because there was rather more to it than a fairly obvious ruse, suggested and adopted under Dundas's influence. One may indeed cite some evidence to support a broader explanation. Pitt, it might be argued, had reasonable cause to open his options at this moment. It was he after all who took the initiative, with the problems which that entailed; he could have left Opposition to its own embarrassments with perhaps equal success. But in fact he could have seen incentives for a form of action which might combine an advantage to the public with a useful realignment of his own position. In the first place, despite its regular majorities the Ministry was short of talent, and notably weak in several important respects. Pitt's personal performance had earlier been seen against an otherwise 'vast vacuity',[4] and despite the improvements of the past two years, as Grenville and Dundas were given more power, Government still had little debating strength, particularly in the Lords, and remained hard pressed to find able men for a variety of posts. It had

1. The two other Cabinet Ministers mentioned at times are Grenville and Richmond; but neither of them as having been consulted by Pitt or Dundas until the third week in June. Grenville would seem to have known the position by the 21st (see Buckingham, II, 212). For the state of informed – or uninformed – knowledge outside the Cabinet as late as mid-July, see George Rose to Auckland, 13 July 1792 (*A.C.*, II, 417–18); for the effect of rumour, Gower to Pitt, 3 August 1792 (P.R.O. 30/8/139).

2. Eg O'Gorman, op. cit., 103.

3. For which see p. 179, n1 above. And he went out of his way, by one report, to repeat his personal lack of objection to Fox in his second interview with Loughborough, when the arrangements were postponed (*Elliot*, II, 54).

4. I, 604; and see op. cit., 621–2, 634.

the numbers but not the quality, and this was galling at times to a Minister who set a premium on competence. Eden had once rescued him from a dilemma over the trade talks with France; Cornwallis had reluctantly done the same over India.[1] But Cornwallis was now retiring – or so it seemed – and a successor was not in sight; Thurlow had gone, and indeed might need skilled and resolute handling in the Lords; and as the situation looked more uncertain, abroad and possibly at home, there was much to be said for strengthening Government as well as its Parliamentary support. In mid-July Portland heard that Pitt still wished to appoint one of three Opposition members to India, 'as three of the properest men to be chosen from'.[2] It was a problem that was genuinely worrying him and Dundas alike, and if the post was a bait to Opposition, Opposition had the candidates to fill the post.

More important and pressing was the Lord Chancellorship itself. The approach to Loughborough opened the way to a chain of possibilities. If he accepted on his own it would serve the limited purpose of replacing Thurlow and detaching an experienced opponent in the Lords. If he insisted on some of his colleagues, there might be other advantages: the Ministry would rise as on a seesaw to the extent that Opposition sank, the King's Government would benefit in quality and support. Such possible results could be generally gauged. And Pitt himself may have thought of another; not bearing so directly on the King's Government as on his own relationship to the King.

One must not exaggerate here. The Minister's position was strong. He had just triumphed over Thurlow, he had earlier had his way over Cabinet changes,[3] and shortly before the talks collapsed he received a personal mark of favour. On 5 August the former Lord North (for the past two years Lord Guilford) died. He had held the office of Lord Warden of the Cinque Ports, carrying with it Walmer Castle and some £3,000 a year, and the next day the King offered it to Pitt. Indeed he did more: in a note to Dundas, he stated that he would 'not admit of this favour being declined'.[4] Pitt of course was famous for declining favours, and he had rejected one from George III already: in the winter of 1790, after Nootka Sound and the general election, he refused the glittering honour of the Garter and asked that it should be bestowed on his brother Chatham instead.[5] He was now being offered financial aid in an acceptable form, and he had little option but to bow to the King's

1. Op. cit., 485, 453.
2. *Malmesbury*, II, 469. The men in question were Lord North (son of the former Minister), William Windham, and Thomas Grenville. On the Ministerial side, Pitt was thinking – though perhaps rather doubtfully – of bringing Eden back from The Hague to a Cabinet post.
3. See I, 634–5.
4. Stanhope, II, 160; cf. op. cit., Appendix, xv–xvi.
5. Which it was in December. This also resembled the action of his father in 1761 in declining the offer of a peerage, one being granted instead to his wife (see I, 6n4).

declared wish.[1] Nevertheless, if the gift related very largely to a private situation, it also had a political advantage which Dundas at least saw a need to grasp. The King, he wrote, still seemed prepared to show signs of favour to Thurlow. It would therefore be 'politically wrong to refuse . . ., and lead to constructions in the View of the Publick not favourable to the Strength of your Government'.[2]

A similar note was struck again in Dundas's comments on the talks themselves. Both he and Pitt were at pains to point out that the Ministry 'was not so pressed to form an arrangement' that it was obliged to do so on disadvantageous terms.[3] This was true enough, and when Opposition revealed the scale of its demands Pitt in turn made it clear that he did not intend to be swamped. But there was sometimes a suggestively defensive air; when the talks ended, for example, Dundas asserted that they had not been begun from any lack of internal 'vigour', or from a dissatisfaction on the part of the King which would have countenanced '*New Arrangements*'.[4] Strictly true again – and in accord with Pitt's careful statement to Leeds that 'there had been no thoughts of any alteration in the Government'.[5] But the wording reflected some sensitivity, and perhaps enough caution about the monarch to give colour to the rumours in Opposition, even if these led to wishful thinking. Pitt himself admitted that the King did not like his recent conduct over the slave trade,[6] only a fortnight before he insisted on Thurlow's dismissal. He may have been conscious of some weakness on that flank, not critical but unwelcome; and in such a case have been attracted to the idea of an enhanced independence. An accession from Opposition would be useful in that respect, provided it could be kept under suitable control. When Pitt talked of 'a strong and united Ministry', 'not in the way of bargain', this was one consideration which he could have had in mind.[7]

1. Even so, Wilberforce later recalled George III's anxiety to enlist Dundas's aid, 'knowing Mr. Pitt's Indifference to his own pecuniary interests' (endorsement, of 1817, on Pitt to Wilberforce, 8 August 1792; Pembroke College, Cambridge, Mss). Dundas was glad to oblige (*L.C.G. III*, I, no. 771 and notes). See also Tomline, III, 408, for the King's thought in May 1790 of granting Pitt a financially advantageous sinecure.
2. 5 August 1792, on the eve of Guilford's death (P.R.O. 30/8/157). The mark of favour must have been the conferment in June of a remainder of Thurlow's barony on his nephews' male heirs, he himself being unmarried.
3. Portland to Fitzwilliam, 27 June 1792, noting Loughborough's report of Pitt's conversation (Wentworth Woodhouse Muniments, F31a).
4. To Loughborough, 29 August 1792 (S.R.O., Melville Castle Ms G.D. 51/1/17/13).
5. See p. 183 above. The words 'change' and 'coalition' (ibid) could be strictly, if scrupulously, interpreted in the same sense. Cf Barnes, *George III and William Pitt*, 252.
6. *Malmesbury*, II, 464. See I, 400–1.
7. P. 174 above. This argument is perhaps reinforced by a memorandum on a change of Ministry written by Lansdowne (Shelburne), which is said to have followed a summons by the King, while the negotiation was under way, 'to obtain his views on the situation' (see Lord Edmond Fitzmaurice, *Life of William, Earl of Shelburne . . .*, III (1876), 500–4). Gillray even depicted him driving to St James's to kiss hands. No more was heard of the episode, but it must have given Pitt to think.

Portland and some colleagues would have suited well enough for the purpose. They would also have added desirable 'acres' to the 'abilities' of Pitt's Cabinet.[1] In both respects indeed they would have played their part in a familiar process; not only in the balancing of property and talent, but in the system as a whole. For of course, viewed purely as a process, Pitt was following a well-worn course, by which eighteenth-century Governments continually 'sought to absorb . . . opposition', potential or actual, 'within the existing ministerial arrangement'.[2] However wicked some of 'the party' might find it, such a move was normally aimed at a section; but it could be directed at the centre itself. For if the great Whig lords would not accept without Fox, serious arguments could be suggested, for a politician not committed to those party principles, to consider taking him in. Such a step certainly raised obvious problems, at Court, in the Ministry, and perhaps in the country: 'the people are the avowed enemies of coalitions',[3] and this would be one to cause plenty of talk. On the other hand, Fox's accession – unlike, it could be held, the junction with North – could bring some public advantages; it would disassociate him from the Friends of the People, and could have a good effect at home and abroad. Nor need a reconciliation in fact have seemed impossible to Pitt in person if the terms were right. A Ministry containing himself and Fox would be seen to be more free of Court influence; it would represent a balance of moderation and safety with the mainstream of 'improving' ideas. It would be a return in a sense to the point from which Pitt had started, before the parting of the ways that had begun ten years before. Perhaps he would not have been entirely sorry to emphasise the fact: he disliked being branded as a tool of the Court, he cherished the tradition of '*an Independent Whig*'.[4] At the same time he was no subscriber to party in the Burkeian sense, and was not unduly constrained by its demands.[5] In some ways indeed he was closer to Fox than he was to Portland. On several great questions, as the Duke himself noted, the two of them differed from him and his friends, and a few months later he even suspected Pitt of re-hatching a plan for Parliamentary reform.[6] There had been moments in the past two years when the rivals moved along parallel lines.[7] Given certain conditions, their collaboration was not unthinkable.

But those conditions were paramount as far as Pitt was concerned. In

1. See I, 635 for Lord Chesterfield's remark at this time, 'We cannot go on well unless we have some acres added to our abilities'.
2. Paul Kelly, 'British Parliamentary Politics, 1784–1786' (*The Historical Journal*, XVII, no. 4), 734. And cf. p. 33, n1 above for the tentative consideration in March 1791.
3. William Elliot to Sir Gilbert Elliot, 29 June 1792 (*Elliot*, II, 51).
4. I, 58.
5. 'They [Dundas and Pitt] know not what party is' (Portland to Burke, 12 September 1792; quoted in Butterfield, loc. cit., 315n71). And see I, 65–6, 136.
6. *Malmesbury*, II, 460–1; Portland to Loughborough, 11 and 16 November 1792 (Portland Mss PWF 9228–9).
7. Pp. 80–4 above.

the first place, as every one knew, Fox could be taken into Government only if he changed his attitude to the Friends of the People and above all to 'French politics'. And secondly, if Pitt was indeed thinking along the lines suggested, it was because he was determined to stay unequivocally at the head of affairs. This was a cardinal difference, for instance, between his remarks about Fox now and his wish to save the King from a change the year before.[1] In the earlier instance the question had been whether or not he should resign; in 1792 it was how best to fortify his position. Any notion that Pitt should leave the Treasury and accept another post equal with Fox was doomed to immediate failure, as Fox himself predicted and Malmesbury and Loughborough and others pointed out. Any notion, too, of giving Fox a share of the lead in the House of Commons was bound to raise a resistance that could not be overcome.[2] Leeds's intervention was fatal because it brought these ideas to a point. As soon as he learned what was brewing, Pitt put an end to the affair.

Such a reading of Pitt's intentions could explain his treatment of the King, his remarks about Fox, his statements to Leeds, and the sequence of events. It would show him working, as he liked to work, to a pattern in which the lines converged, exploiting a series of prospects, themselves related to varying needs, from which – an important point – he could withdraw at any stage. If nothing happened, he might hope to have deepened his opponents' embarrassments. If some of them joined him and others did not, he would gain either way. If they insisted on bringing in Fox he assuredly faced problems, but also a new prospect which in some ways might add to his strength. The invitation was his, and as long as he stayed at the head of the Ministry – on which he was determined – he trusted himself to remain in control. And beyond the political adjustments, providing their impulse and justification, lay the promise of a broader, more fully committed national support. Pitt's position was multi-faceted. It looked out over several fronts. His manoeuvres, it may be argued, had more than one object in view.

The outcome pointed to the future: to the clash of principle within Opposition, leading in the end to a split and the broad wartime Government. Whether the talks encouraged such a process, as Pitt himself seems to have thought,[3] or rather delayed it by inducing his opponents to try to close ranks once more, they faced in a direction from which there proved to be no return, and which became much clearer at the end of the year. At the same time, their course was affected

1. Pp. 179, 30–1 above. And cf. p. 33, n1 above for the fate of a suggestion then that Pitt might step down to an equality with Fox in some kind of Coalition.

2. Loughborough to Portland, nd but probably late May 1792 (Portland Ms PWF 9220); *Malmesbury*, II, 459, 465, 472; *Elliot*, II, 46, 55.

3. He saw 'very strong indications that even without any regular treaty, all serious hostilities from any but the violent set are at an end' (to Pretyman, 22 July 1792; quoted in O'Gorman, op. cit., 93).

throughout by the legacy of the past: the new pressures were imposed on old struggles and the resulting attitudes and balance of forces. Memories of 1783–4 above all coloured a scene in which national conditions had not yet altered enough to force a major political change. For if a watershed was now in sight the summit had still not been reached, and it was as natural to move by familiar landmarks as to peer uncertainly ahead.

II

Once it had begun, the course of this negotiation was not affected by public events. Their rapid movement began to be felt only as the talks ended. The summer months at least into August were a period of waiting: to see what would happen abroad, and how the Proclamation worked at home. The other ideas which Pitt had mentioned were not followed up. No more was heard of embodying the militia, and while the Law Officers seem to have been consulted an Aliens' bill was likewise dropped.[1] This may perhaps have been because there was little time left in the Parliamentary session; but such measures in any case would have been irrelevant to the position as the Ministry itself saw it – and might well have been widely greeted as unnecessarily extreme.[2] For in fact there was no hard information of deliberate conspiracy or threats in England, either from native or from foreign quarters. Although the Attorney General's 'disposition' in May was 'extremely *Dictatorial* with respect to Aliens',[3] few émigrés were actively suspect, and except in the Channel Islands the numbers were not such as to cause great alarm. The correspondence of some was opened, reports were sometimes made, and a few Englishmen were subject to the same attentions. But officially at least only twelve names attracted this treatment from the Home Office, and few serious suspects emerge from the reports of the summer – still quite sparse, and generally trivial – supplied by the Department's usual sources of information.[4]

It could therefore have been hard to prove conditions in which part of the militia should have been called out, or foreign subjects made liable to unaccustomed powers. The greatest single inducement to action lay in

1. See p. 186 above.
2. And cf. pp. 146, 149 above.
3. Sir Archibald Macdonald to ? Dundas, 10 May 1792 (P.R.O., H.O. 119/1).
4. For which see pp. 136–8 above. A copy of the Secretary of State's Warrant for opening and copying mail, dated 28 April 1792, is in P.R.O., H.O. 42/208. The list includes Paine, Horne Tooke, and Talleyrand. Interceptions however could also have been practised less officially (see Ellis, *The Post Office in the Eighteenth Century*, ch. 6); one of the fruits may be seen in a copy of a despatch from the French Embassy of 28 April in Pitt's papers (P.R.O. 30/8/333). Other notes on suspects for this period are in H.O. 42/20 (undated) and 42/21 (28 July 1792). For the Channel Islands see H.O. 98/2.

the effect of a specific book,[1] and the Proclamation sufficed for steps to be taken over that at once. Paine himself had come under various pressures over the past year: he had been burnt in effigy, attacked in newspapers and in a biography written pseudonymously by a Government official, and there were semi-official complaints to American authorities who appeared to lend sanction to his work. In January 1792 the printer of the Second Part of the *Rights of Man* suddenly withdrew – an event which may have sprung at least in part from Governmental prompting. The decision to issue the Proclamation now paved the way for direct measures. Paine's new printer was summonsed on 14 May, and Paine on the 21st. He appeared in Court on 8 June, to hear – to his disappointment – that his trial was postponed until the winter. Nothing daunted, he had already published an open letter to Dundas; he followed it up with another, *on the Late Proclamation*; and in September he left England for Paris as a delegate to the National Assembly, nominated under the French citizenship to which he had been elected the month before.

Meanwhile efforts were mounted to stifle the spread of the offending work, with other pamphlets and the like deemed to be seditious. Entrusted mostly to local hands, they were thought to be having some success. For while it may have been true, as was said, that the publicity confirmed Paine as a national figure,[2] the attentions of magistrates and hostile neighbours seem to have had a cautionary effect. Many of Paine's readers became more secretive; many others may have been frightened off. This last was soon the authorities' impression, and in those months they were probably right.[3] Magistrates in some counties at least kept a sharp eye open for seditious meetings; the first prosecutions for selling pamphlets appeared; so did the first legal warnings to publicans not to harbour Societies – a division of the London Corresponding Society may have been the first to experience the result. Above all, local Addresses were organised in favour of the Proclamation, and if there was hesitation in some areas, opposition in others and occasional failures, a steady stream of support flowed in from June until the end of August.[4] The climate affected the older Societies – the SCI to some extent, the Friends of the People more seriously. There were some defections, a growing uneasiness in the membership at large, and a consequential lull in activity which was also noticeable elsewhere. At the end of July Burges at the Foreign Office found it 'astonishing how completely Mr. Paine

1. P. 120 above.
2. See p. 121 above. In November one of the toasts of the British Revolutionary Society in Paris was 'Paine and the new way of making good books known by a royal proclamation and a King's Bench prosecution' (John G. Alger, *Englishmen in the French Revolution* (1889), 98).
3. The later radical tradition itself shared their view (see Richard Carlile's opinion, quoted in Moncure Daniel Conway, *The Life of Thomas Paine*, I (1892), 346).
4. Over 340 loyal Addresses by 1 September (*The Annual Register for 1792*, Chronicle, 36). And see Black, *The Association*, 232n47.

and his adherents are extinguished', and Grenville had already written of an 'entire . . . deadness'.[1]

Their satisfaction was to prove short-lived. But even while it lasted it had certain limits. If the Proclamation at first seemed to need no complementary legislation, the Ministry did not entirely neglect other precautions. It had been a sign of Pitt's optimism early in the year that the military establishment was marginally lowered.[2] In May the dispositions were overhauled, and in June there was a meeting in Dundas's house at Wimbledon, attended by Pitt himself, which agreed on an immediate and significant step. Orders were given to build new barracks for cavalry at or near Sheffield, Manchester, Nottingham, Birmingham, Coventry and Norwich. The work was well under way in August, and finished in October. At the same time a new Barrackmaster General's department was formed for administration – a scheme worked out in consultation with Pitt, which was to have expensive results.[3]

The provision of barracks for these manufacturing towns lessened the drawbacks of dispersal, and reflected experience at Birmingham only a year before.[4] The importance of the military was underlined by the shape of a separate development aimed at a failure of the previous decade. After the Government's defeat on its 'police' bill for the capital in 1785, it showed no sign of being prepared to try again.[5] But in the spring of 1792 a private Member, Francis Burton, returned to the charge, and his efforts received Ministerial support. The new bill was based to some extent on the earlier attempt.[6] It proposed eight, in place of nine, Public Offices, each containing three stipendiary magistrates and financed from a consolidated fund.[7] The magistrates, appointed by the King on the advice of the Lord Chancellor, were to be debarred from taking fees, and from standing for Parliament or voting in the Parliamentary elections of the wider metropolitan area. There was to be a Receiver in charge of finance, appointed by the King on the advice of the Privy Council. Each office was to have not more than six constables,

---

1. Burges to Auckland, 31 July 1792 (*A.C.*, II, 423); Grenville to same, Private, 19 July 1792 (B.L. Add. Ms 46519), and sd to Gower (*H.M.C., Dropmore*, II, 294). See also *L.C.G. III*, I, no. 767. Cf. p. 186 above.

2. See p. 52 above. The reduction specified – from an increase in 1790 for Nootka Sound – was from 17,448 to 17,013 men.

3. Colonel de Lancey, who had recently visited the midlands (see p. 96 above), was put in charge of the work, and made 'Superintendent-General' of the barracks. See his report of 12 October 1792 (P.R.O., H.O. 42/22), his account of the June meeting quoted in Charles M. Clode, *The Military Forces of the Crown . . .*, I (1869), 245, and George III's note on progress of 29 August 1792 (H.O. 42/20).

4. Pp. 126, 131–3 above.

5. See pp. 123–5 above. The provisions, virtually unaltered, were however introduced into the Irish Parliament in 1786, and passed without much difficulty as the 'Dublin Police Act' (26 Geo. III, c. 24).

6. Cf. p. 124 above.

7. Cf. I, 90–1.

acting under the justices, whose powers would include the preventive arrest of suspicious persons as defined by the Vagrancy Act.

The measure, not surprisingly, ran into opposition. There were the familiar suspicions of paid magistrates appointed by the Crown, and a concession was extracted that the King should act on the advice of the Privy Council, as was already proposed for the Receiver's appointment. The clause for preventive arrest was also attacked; concessions again were made, to narrow the categories of persons liable and permissible places of apprehension. The bill indeed came under close scrutiny. But feeling in the Commons now favoured action of some kind, for the main target, the existing justices, no longer commanded much sympathy. Of low social standing, inefficient and notoriously corrupt, most of them outside Bow Street itself and the City were known to be 'very unequal to the Office'. 'A Tallow Chandler and transacts often his business as a Justice across his Counter'. 'Underwent a Commission of Bankruptcy. Was afterwards in the King's Bench prison – then turned trading Justice'. 'A feeble minded old man'. '4 or 5 years ago escaped from the Fleet Prison' – such descriptions fill most of a list made for the Home Office in the summer of 1792.[1] The passing of the Act in June[2] soon led to fresh appointments of a higher calibre, and the experiment was hailed, at least in some quarters, as a success. But it remained on trial. The Act was limited initially to three years, and although it was renewed thereafter the stipendiary magistrates were still often viewed with suspicion. Nor did their introduction lead – it was not meant to lead – to that of a police force. Unlike the bill of 1785, the Act of 1792 made no provision for High and Chief Constables responsible to central Commissioners and impinging on older authorities. The few constables allowed to the justices continued to be maintained by the parishes and wards.[3] As Patrick Colquhoun, the most distinguished of the new magistrates, remarked a generation later, 'the Act of 1792 . . . did no more than establish a purer Magistracy' and confer limited powers of preventive arrest.[4] The administration of justice was improved in the capital, and some of the arrangements began to be copied in a few other towns. To that extent there was a new weapon in the armoury of order. But the means of civil regulation were virtually unchanged, and Government's strengthening of the facilities was accordingly directed to the army alone.

Meanwhile the continental Powers were on the move. On 20 April

1. 'List of the Present Acting Justices', endorsed August 1792 (H.O. 42/21). Only three out of thirteen men were said to be 'of better reputation'. 'Acting' here has the meaning of 'existing'.
2. 32 George III, c. 53.
3. Cf. p. 121 above.
4. Statement in 1816; quoted in Radcinowicz, op. cit., III, 134–5.

France had declared war on Austria.[1] A period of mounting tension and the death of the Emperor Leopold II had left the war parties of both countries in charge, and in the end it became a question of who would act first. The new French Foreign Minister, Dumouriez – a veteran of the old royal secret diplomacy – at once revived a favourite policy of the *ançien régime*. Austria was to be isolated by securing the neutrality of Britain and Prussia, an object which, it was held, would be encouraged by the conquest of the Austrian Netherlands and the creation of a neutral Belgic state.[2] Things however did not go as expected. The offensive campaign in the Netherlands misfired. Continuing economic troubles led to conspiracies and riots in south-east France. There was another change of Ministry in June, and Dumouriez left for a command in the field. And Paris saw the arrival in July of detachments of provincial National Guards, which, allied with the radical sections or ward assemblies in the capital, brought a standing militant presence to bear on confused events. In all these circumstances it was not surprising that the French diplomacy failed. So far in fact from responding to the overtures, the Prussians moved the other way. Early in June they dismissed the French envoys from Berlin, and on 24 July they joined Austria in the war.

The reasons were not far to seek. Frederick William of Prussia had been more bellicose than Leopold of Austria for at least a year, and following the Emperor's death he could see events going his way. Early French reverses at the front and signs of growing internal confusion now suggested the need for quick action if a great chance was not to be missed. For Prussia was not driven exclusively by moral zeal. It would be sad indeed if Austria was in a position to dictate the peace. Agreement had already been reached that joint action would bring joint 'indemnities', and while details had not been specified the Prussians had their list. Such gains would arise in the west, at their ally's as well as their enemy's expense. But, perhaps more significant, there was a prospect of others in the east which again might accrue from the same crusade.

For Prussia, like Austria and Russia, sought her sphere of interest in central Europe, and her policy in the west was largely dictated by the fact. The end of the Russo-Turkish war and the ensuing realignment allowed the rapid revival of a persistent dream. Possession of the Polish port of Danzig and adjoining territory, with rights up the lower Vistula, remained a prime strategic and commercial object. Since the summer of 1791 the prospect could be envisaged in altered terms: no longer in concert with Britain and Holland, but in some form with Austria and Russia.[3] The steps in the process were hard to predict, for the interests of the three Powers differed, the Austrians' and Russians' in fact essen-

1. See p. 52 above.
2. Which however was a radical misunderstanding of the British position (see I, 547–8).
3. See pp. 5–6, 28 above.

tially, in the Polish sphere. But the Prussians were not dismayed; they were always prepared to adjust, and there were important developments to exploit. The Empress Catherine was determined to annul the 'jacobinical' Polish constitution of 1791. She also wished to see the French Revolution suppressed. She was therefore doubly anxious that Austria and Prussia should attack in the west, leaving her the more free to act in Poland and removing the focus of European discontent. Austria for her part was set on achieving her own persistent aim of the Bavarian Exchange – gaining the German Electorate in exchange for ceding the Netherlands –[1] for which she might have to make some concessions elsewhere. In these stimulating circumstances the Prussians might extract a return from each Imperial Power for entering the war against France. They began to set the ground early in the year, when the future was still clouded. In February they signed an alliance with Austria, in which the article on Poland was left ambiguous. In the same month they learned, with Austria, that Russia meant to see the offending constitution removed. In April they discreetly revised their reading of an earlier guarantee of Polish territory.[2] In May the Empress gave the order to march, and they and the Austrians stood aside. In July, when they moved against France, the position in the east remained doubtful; the Russians had driven as far as Warsaw, and the other two Powers were becoming disturbed. But the Prussians were still not unhopeful: although they were far from being sure of Austria, events might yet induce her finally to support their claim, and Russia was now in their debt for committing troops to a different front. The seeds of discord were being sown once again, but the spectre of revolution might serve for a time. The Polish Patriots had compounded their crimes by embracing French ideas in central Europe; the French themselves must be brought to heel for the sake of universal order. An immediate consensus overlay the 'vice' of separate 'public interests'.[3] It was judged vital in Berlin to take advantage of the fact.

In assessing their Polish designs none of the central Powers had to reckon with Britain. This indeed was in striking contrast with eighteen months before. In January 1791 the British Government had tried to add Poland to the Triple Alliance:[4] in the summer of 1792 it rejected Polish appeals for help. There was no longer any enthusiasm for a central European policy; Pitt and Grenville in fact, after Ochakov, were determined not to burn their fingers again. In the summer of 1791 they declined to join any guarantee of the new Polish constitution, and while they told the Prussians early the next year that they feared a revived Russian influence in Poland, they confined themselves to expressions of regret when the crisis came. Such inaction aroused concern among admirers of the Polish reforms, and efforts were made to mobilise

1. See I, 473.
2. By their alliance with Poland of 1790, for which see I, 547.
3. See op cit., 553.
4. P. 13 above.

pressure, led by some Opposition MPs. Pamphlets were written, subcriptions raised, public meetings organised. Government however remained entirely unmoved. The situation indeed was one which is fairly familiar to ourselves: a Ministry remains passive over an issue on which it has suffered an earlier failure, and is then attacked on grounds of principle by those who had helped cause the reverse.[1] The decision was unambiguous: 'no Intervention . . . could be serviceable to Poland', at least without greater effort than could be justified.[2] The Foreign Secretary himself had no doubts: 'We have . . . no other concern', he wrote in July, 'in the miseries and misfortunes of other countries than what humanity calls for'.[3]

This remark was made to the Ambassador in Paris, and it applied to France as well. The expressions of British neutrality, repeated in the summer, were interpreted as strictly as before.[4] Such assurances did not reflect sympathy: rather the reverse. The Foreign Office was increasingly exasperated by the succession of transient figures in Paris, and the chill was felt by their representatives in London. The new Ambassador, the young Marquis de Chauvelin – scarcely the sinister figure of *The Scarlet Pimpernel* – provoked contempt by his Government's weakness and his own ineptitude. When he protested against some of the wording in the Royal Proclamation of May, he was answered – perhaps unwisely – in a public rebuke, and his growing contacts with a well-marked francophile circle of Opposition did little to sustain an inherently difficult role. The 'ignorance and absurdity of the French Mission' aroused Grenville's disdain;[5] a complementary temporary embassy was treated carefully, but at arm's length. For when Chauvelin had been sent to London, in April, he was followed at once by Talleyrand, returning on a second visit to try to build on his recent talks.[6] The effort succeeded to the extent that on 24 May the French Government was given a declaration amounting to neutrality in the war with Austria, subject to respect for Britain's treaty obligations and rights.[7] But while Pitt had already spoken in the same sense to a deputation of London merchants, and a Proclamation was published forbidding British subjects to serve with any enemy of France, he refused to make public the text of this communication to Paris, and Talleyrand's attempts to revive the earlier suggestion of an alliance were firmly rebuffed. Dumouriez had hoped to tempt the Ministry with some concessions,

1. See Ch. I, section III above.
2. Grenville to Colonel William Gardiner [Minister in Warsaw], no. 2, 4 August 1792; quoted in Holland Rose, II, 54.
3. Grenville to Gower, 19 July 1792 (*H.M.C., Dropmore*, II, 294).
4. See p. 50 above.
5. To Auckland, 19 June 1792 (*H.M.C., Dropmore*, II, 281). For the exchanges with Chauvelin see P.R.O., F.O. 27/39.
6. See pp. 50–1 above.
7. Grenville to Chauvelin, 24 May 1792 (*La Mission de Talleyrand à Londres, en 1792*, ed. G. Pallain, 305–6). See also op. cit., 332.

including an offer of the West Indian island of Tobago, in return for a compact and a British loan. The proposals fell on deaf ears; so did an appeal in June, through Chauvelin, for British mediation with Prussia and other neutrals to refrain from attacking France and, in the case of Prussia, Poland as well.[1] When Talleyrand left London early in July he could therefore reaffirm British neutrality, but without hope that it would be interpreted in any but a purely passive spirit.

Pitt has sometimes been attacked for failing to respond to the French appeal of June. The point is academic, for the Prussians by then were not going to be deterred by British opinion. Something concrete would have had to be offered to counteract the rewards of entry, and Pitt and his colleagues did not intend to tread that maze again. They were not now going to mobilise the fleet, or urge the Baltic Powers to co-operate against Russia, or launch a diplomatic offensive to settle central European affairs. That issue was dead beyond immediate recall, and representations alone would have been pointless. Prussia's course was set. Despite their hopes of isolation, the British were not to be immune from the results.

For the Prussians' declaration of war set events in motion which probably tipped the immediate balance in France. On 25 July their commander, the veteran Duke of Brunswick, issued the celebrated manifesto to which he reluctantly gave his name. His refusal to apply the rules of war to the French National Guards, the threats of reprisals for defending French territory, the promise of retribution to Paris if the King or Queen was harmed, heightened tensions in the capital which were already almost at breaking point. On 3 August the sections[2] united with only one dissenting voice to demand the deposition of Louis XVI. On the 10th the Tuileries were invaded for the second time, and the notorious 'massacre' took place. The King, fleeing to the Assembly, was suspended from his powers and imprisoned with his family. The fortress of Longwy was surrendered and Verdun fell to the Prussians, and Lafayette went over to the Austrians in the north. The road to Paris seemed open. Tales of treachery swept the city. Bands of toughs and criminals invaded the prisons, and news of the September massacres sped abroad.

The repercussions began to be felt in England at once. Official channels of communication suffered from the suspension of the royal

1. Pitt's replies to Talleyrand's approach are allegedly recorded in an undated note, 'Proposition de M. d'Autun [i.e. Talleyrand as Bishop of Autun]. Réponse de M. Pitt', in Calonne's papers, P.R.O., F.O. 95/630, no. 339. There is a copy of the appeal of June in Pitt's papers, P.R.O. 30/8/333. The cession of Tobago in return for British aid was not a new idea: Calonne and the exiled Princes had considered it as early as 1789 (see Norman Frank Richards, 'British Policy and the Problem of Monarchy in France, 1789–1802' (Ph.D. thesis, University of London, 1954), 13).

2. See p. 197 above.

powers. For there was now no authority in France to which foreign Missions were accredited, and the neutral Ambassadors were hurriedly withdrawn. Gower was recalled on 17 August and left ten days later, and Ministers decided on reflection not to leave a chargé d'affaires behind.[1] A greater responsibility accordingly fell on the French Embassy in London; unfortunately there were new developments which further weakened its reputation. Dumouriez's successor as Foreign Minister, the former journalist Lebrun, was perhaps a less inadequate figure than has often been suggested. But he was committed to the revolutionary theory of a network of agents abroad, and Chauvelin dated from an earlier dispensation. The unfortunate Ambassador, who was now beginning to adjust rather better to his surroundings, found himself 'assisted' by personalities and missions often more powerful than himself. Talleyrand was back yet again; more important – for he was now simply sheltering from Paris, with no specific instructions and no wish to draw attention to his presence[2] – there was a variety of unofficial emissaries, without valid credentials but directly in touch with Lebrun. Mostly young and inexperienced, they were a singularly unimpressive lot, who indeed were to do a good deal of damage through their misleading reports. Meanwhile their activities and the quarrels with Chauvelin, of which the British Government was kept posted, brought the Embassy finally into disrepute.

The 'secret missions', as Paris called them, were not only confusing; they were also suspect. For even the agents who bore a semi-official character were despatched in an atmosphere of hostile suspicion. The instructions to the head of the first such group have been described as resembling those of a Jesuit sent into England in the sixteenth century.[3] Other agents came simply as observers or spies, and Government began to be worried by the growing number of reports. Its uneasiness was greatly increased by the stream of refugees now crossing the Channel, in the wake of the new tumults and in particular of a decree against nonjuring clergy. For where the entrants had been numbered in their tens and hundreds they were now suddenly in their thousands, and who could be sure that these did not include 'many Emissaries . . . under the denomination of Emigrants'?[4] The new arrivals had a mixed reception,

---

1. *The Despatches of Earl Gower*, 209–11; *H.M.C., Dropmore*, II, 302–3, 310.

2. He was however seen by Pitt on 17 August, and shown the despatch for Gower's recall (*H.M.C., Dropmore*, II, 302). Pitt also saw Chauvelin separately (loc. cit., 303), but only to agree to return a note, at the Ambassador's 'agitated' insistence on its recall, which the latter had written earlier in the day calling once more for British intervention with the Allies and deploring the events, 'criminels et désastreux', in Paris in the past week.

3. J.T. Murley, 'The Origin and Outbreak of the Anglo-French War of 1793' (D.Phil. thesis, University of Oxford, 1959), 37–8. The man, François Noël, happened in fact to be an unfrocked priest.

4. Lord Hood [from Portsmouth] to Pitt, 20 September 1792 (P.R.O., H.O. 42/21). See also Burges to Grenville, 14 September 1792 (*H.M.C., Dropmore*, II, 315).

but it included many acts of kindness; organisations sprang up in the coastal towns, funds were raised in London, lodgings acquired. The Ministry gave some limited support – not very graciously or substantially. It also kept as close a watch as possible on signs of incitement and intrigue.

After the relaxation of the summer, the atmosphere in the early autumn in fact became not unlike that in France in relation to England over the past few years. Among the upper and middling orders there was now the same suspicion, the same rumours of foreign gold, heightened in this case by sudden shock. The reaction of the respectable public may well have been greater than that of Government; it is hard to say how deeply Ministers were alarmed. They and their officials foresaw growing danger from the scale of the influx; they suspected French contacts with some London newspapers, and were worried at the thought of subversion in Ireland.[1] At the same time they seem to have taken some of the reports with a pinch of salt, and they were certainly not prepared to change the normal life of a summer recess. The Cabinet dispersed as usual to its and its friends' country houses, including, as usual, the small 'effective' nucleus.[2] Grenville, who married Pitt's cousin Anne Pitt in mid-July and started his honeymoon at Pitt's house Holwood,[3] was out of London with one short break until mid-September. Dundas, who had been minding shop for him, left early in October for his annual visit to Scotland. And Pitt spent some five weeks based on Downing Street out of some three months. He went down to Burton Pynsent to see his mother[4] at the beginning of August, returning about a fortnight later for a Cabinet meeting to consider Gower's recall, and leaving again for his new residence at Walmer in the third week of September. He clearly liked what he found there, for he changed his plans and stayed until 10 October.[5] This does not suggest undue perturbation, and neither does the Ministry's behaviour in general. It took no exceptional steps to deal with such suspects as it could identify among the émigrés; and although its new journal *The Sun* adopted an alarmist tone in October, there is no

1. H.O. 42/21 *passim*.
2. See I, 321. 'We get every day deeper and deeper into inaction', wrote one of the officials left behind, as late as mid-September (Burges to Auckland, 14 September 1792; *A.C.*, II, 442).
3. I, 591.
4. I, 8,590.
5. The movements are traceable in correspondence and notes in *L.C.G. III*, I, *H.M.C.*, *Dropmore* II, Buckingham II, Stanhope II, P.R.O., H.O. 42/21–2, P.R.O., P.C. 1/128, Pretyman Ms 435/39 (Suffolk R.O., Ipswich). The King, as was now his custom, was at Weymouth from the middle of August to the end of September.
It was towards the end of these holidays that Sir Robert Keith, returned from Austria, failed to find 'a single soul' at the Foreign Office (see I, 514n3). Pitt's and Dundas's absence from London attracted some attention (LM [Lady Louisa Macdonald, wife of the Attorney General] to Lady Stafford, nd but 1792; P.R.O. 30/29/4/6).

evidence of a coherent effort to whip up public excitement.[1] In weighing the merits of 'directing' a 'good disposition'[2] and maintaining a low-keyed approach, the Ministry seems to have been content to rest on the earlier Proclamation, more perhaps because of the natural limits of a period of balance than from any deliberate concerted decision.

The rising uncertainty and disgust affected the context of foreign policy. It did not however change the policy itself. The earlier neutrality was strictly maintained, and the fact repeated to all concerned. It continued to apply to the Revolution as well as to the war; when Gower was recalled, he was told to make it clear that Britain proposed 'strictly to adhere to the principles of neutrality in respect to the internal government of France'.[3] The attitude was tested late in September, for the French monarchy was then abolished. The Ministry confined itself to a decision, recently taken, to join the courts of Austria and Naples (at their instance) in warning that if harm befell Louis XVI those responsible could not seek asylum. 'Humanity' went that far,[4] but its extent was clearly defined. 'Undoubtedly', wrote George III, 'there is no step that I should not willingly take for the personal safety of the French King and his family that does not draw this country into meddling with the internal disturbances of that ill-fated Kingdom'.[5] Ministers had no such intention. They had made it clear for the past month that nothing effective could be done for the French royal family.[6] Pitt's response now to the abolition of the monarchy, according to

1. See p. 116, n5 above for *The Sun*. This newspaper may have been founded partly because some of the Ministerial experts – George Rose and Charles Long (successor to Tom Steele: see I, 131) at the Treasury, Dundas and Nepean at the Home Office, Burges at the Foreign Office, Hawkesbury at the Committee for Trade – were dissatisfied with the other journals receiving official funds. One of them, *The Oracle*, had even been recently involved in an official prosecution for libel. It was doubtless against such a background that John Walter of *The Times* saw Pitt in October and passed on information about sedition; but his tone suggests that Government was certainly not taking a marked initiative (to ? [probably Nepean], 29 October 1792; H.O. 42/22).

Official libel actions in July – arising of course from earlier transactions – against Sampson Perry of *The Argus*, Richard Tattersall and William Williams of *The Morning Post* (both anti-Ministerial papers), and John Bell of *The Oracle* (in receipt of Ministerial funds), were no more frequent than in earlier years.

2. P. 186 above.

3. Dundas [acting for Grenville] to Gower, 17 August 1792 (*Despatches of Lord Gower*, 200–1).

4. See p. 199 above.

5. To Grenville, 22 September 1792 (*H.M.C., Dropmore*, II, 317). The King would not then have heard of the decision to abolish the French monarchy, which was taken on the 21st. Gower had been instructed to convey on his departure 'earnest and anxious hopes' that the royal family would 'at least be secure from any acts of violence' (*Despatches of Gower*, 210).

6. When a royalist emissary, the Bishop of Pamier, was sent to London later in August to plead energetic support for this cause, he received no encouragement (Richards, loc. cit., 55).

Calonne who saw him at Walmer, was 'enveloppé dans beaucoup de Circumspection ministérielle'; and when Grenville was asked what would happen if recognition of a Republic was sought, he replied after an interval that he doubted if it should be granted at once, but that it might follow if the Republic survived.[1]

When this opinion was given, the war itself had changed. The 'promenade to Paris' which Europe awaited when Prussia joined Austria in July was dramatically halted and then reversed as summer drew to a close. After his early successes in August Brunswick moved ponderously forward, awaiting a popular aid which he expected but could not find, contemplating his supplies and his sick lists, conforming to the manoeuvres of a long career. On 20 September his main forces faced a cannonade at Valmy, east of Rheims; it was enough to make him withdraw, and soon enter into talks which allowed him to retreat without interference. By the end of October he was back beyond the frontier; the French were spread along the Rhine between Frankfurt and Speyer; and after declaring war on the Kingdom of Sardinia, had overrun its territory in Nice and Savoy. Early in November the northern front, now reinforced and stabilised, was set alight. On the 6th Dumouriez[2] beat the Austrians near the village of Jemappes by Mons, the prelude to what proved to be a swift advance through the Austrian Netherlands.

The events of September and October if anything heightened the British Government's belief in the wisdom of its choice. The more uncertain things became the more leading Ministers trusted not to become involved. Brunswick himself was left in no doubt that the policy of neutrality meant what it said, and while his procrastination and then his failure were greeted with disappointment at first, Ministers soon accepted the results philosophically.[3] The Foreign Office and Pitt gave some thought in October, under pressure from an appeal for financial support from Sardinia, to possible consequences in the event of '*un nouvel ordre de choses*'. Pitt suggested that 'the French retaining Savoy, or any

1. Note in Calonne's papers of 30 September 1792 (P.R.O., P.C. 1/128, no. 260); Grenville to Auckland, 6 November 1792 (*A.C.*, II, 466). See also same to same, no. 14, 21 August 1792 (F.O. 37/39). For Calonne see p. 49, n1 above.

2. See p. 197 above.

3. For Ministers' disappointment with the campaign see Grenville to Chatham, 11 October 1792 (B.L. Add. Ms 58937) – where the retreat was seen as an encouragement to unrest in England and Ireland – Buckingham, II, 217, 219, and *A.C.*, II, 454; for the communication to Brunswick – which was in reply to 'strong' and 'repeated' questions from him (Sir James Murray to Grenville, 25 August 1792; F.O. 26/18) – see Dundas (for Grenville) to Murray [sent as military observer to Allied headquarters], 12 September 1792 (F.O. 26/19). There is some slight mystery here. Grenville was still out of London (see p. 202 above). A draft to Murray in his hand, nd but probably early in September, gives the latter an opening – carefully qualified – to receive Austrian and Prussian 'ideas' through Brunswick. No such suggestion however is included in the letter as sent from the Foreign Office.

other acquisition great or small, might be argued to come within' such a 'description'.[1] But this was all hypothetical, and the Prussians' misfortunes did not arouse great sorrow in London after the history of recent years. They and the Austrians would have to 'begin again in the spring'; meanwhile the Foreign Secretary was thankful that 'we had the wit to keep ourselves out of the glorious enterprize . . ., and that we were not tempted by the hope of sharing the spoils in the division of France, nor by the prospect of crushing all democratical principles all over the world'. Hostilities would continue next year, 'twice as difficult' for the Allies as before. But the other Powers, at least north of the Alps, were unlikely to be involved, and as for Britain, 'We shall do nothing'.[2] The affirmation was unambiguous, and so were the hopes. As long as our nearest interests were respected we could hold aloof. There was no diplomatic basis for dealings with France, and we had no desire to venture; but we were not party to a crusade, or to the ambitions of the crusading states. We had our own affairs to see to, our own health to guard. We wished to pursue a splendid isolation, resting on our wealth and minding our peace.

1. To Grenville, 16 October 1792 (*H.M.C., Dropmore*, II, 322). For the appeal and the negative reply see John Trevor [Minister in Turin] to Grenville, no. 79, Secret, 8 October 1792; Grenville to Trevor, 18 October 1792; Trevor to Grenville, no. 91, 7 November 1792 (F.O. 67/10).
2. Grenville to Buckingham, 7 November 1792 (Buckingham, II, 221–5).

CHAPTER VII

The End of Peace

I

1792 was a year with its share of irony. Grenville sketched his 'tableau of Europe' on 7 November,[1] at the very opening of the events which were to lead England into war within three months. Following Jemappes on the 6th,[2] Mons fell the next day. On the 14th the tricoleur flew in Brussels, and Louvain, Liège (which witnessed a second rising)[3] and Antwerp were taken in the next two weeks. Fired by these triumphs, by the conquest of Savoy and signs of disarray in the Rhineland, the French uttered their defiance, as it seemed, in a series of decrees. On the 16th they ordered the pursuit of the Austrians wherever they might retreat – a threat to the German states and equally to the Dutch. On the same day they proclaimed freedom of navigation through the estuary of the Scheldt. On the 19th they promised brotherhood and aid to all peoples wishing to 'recover their liberty'. On the 27th they incorporated Savoy in France. On 3 December, while these headlong pronouncements were still being digested, the National Convention determined on the trial of Louis XVI.

The British policy of neutrality was thus faced by a new situation. At the very least there was the need to decide what the decrees might mean. They did not of course all bear equally on the British position. The possible annexation of Savoy had already suggested itself as the first awkward development of the war,[4] and the event marked it out from the personal proceedings of some of the generals, or the semi-official pressures from Paris, which were being witnessed elsewhere as the armies advanced. It overturned the earlier assurances that the Revolution was not interested in foreign territory. But it did not directly challenge a British obligation or interest.[5] The decision to try Louis XVI for treason was again revolting to the feelings. It raised more acutely the unhappy problem of the royal family's fate. It made the prospect of peace less likely at a moment when the Allies' failure was leading to

1. Buckingham, II, 224.
2. P. 205 above.
3. See p. 52 above.
4. Pp. 204–5 above.
5. As indeed was obvious from the tone of Grenville to Trevor, no. 10, 18 October 1792 (P.R.O., F.O. 67/101).

doubts and recrimination in Vienna and Berlin. But it was not in itself a cause for British action, let alone armed intervention, perhaps whatever the outcome and certainly not at this stage. For no one could tell what would happen, what the verdict or the sentence might be; and this indeed applied to the other decrees, apart perhaps from that on Savoy. How far would they be carried out? Did they represent policy or propaganda? Who were really in charge now in Paris, and what did they really want? These were to be crucial questions in the weeks ahead. It was to prove peculiarly difficult to find proper answers.

In considering the military scene itself, two of the decrees were of immediate concern. The threat to Dutch territory posed by the Austrians' retreat, and the proclamation on the Scheldt, thrust to the fore the demands of treaty engagements. An invasion of Holland – whatever was said about limiting the object to pursuit of the enemy – or a proven effort to change its constitution, could bring into force the Anglo-Dutch alliance of 1788.[1] The opening of the Scheldt – however strongly old arguments of Natural Law were invoked – would defy the terms of the Treaty of Munster of 1648, which had been repeated in a sequence of Anglo-French agreements over the past eight decades and again in the Dutch Alliance of 1788.[2] The exact force of those terms for the estuary might be viewed with some scepticism; in 1784–5 Pitt had seemed prepared to see them changed, at a time when the Dutch were quite as disturbed by that prospect as they were now. But he had then been at the start of his career, and anxious to avoid continental entanglements; Holland had not been our ally – on the contrary, she had recently been our enemy; and above all it was the Austrians, not the French, who were seeking the change, and a distant Austria with remote suzerainty was a different matter from a neighbouring France. By 1790 Pitt's anxieties had hardened; in 1792 they were acute.[3] The dangers to the Low Countries began to take shape in November even before the first of the decrees. The risk of a French movement through Holland indeed seemed 'to press so much in point of time' that Pitt and Grenville acted at once, without consulting the Cabinet or perhaps the King.[4] It was, Pitt wrote, 'absolutely impossible to hesitate as to supporting our ally in case of necessity', and on 13 November Auckland at The Hague was instructed to say that there would be 'no hesitation as to the

1. See I, 538.

2. For the status of the Treaty of Munster as a corner-stone of the European system see op. cit., 532.

3. I, 50, 468–9, 472–3, 547; pp. 49–50 above. And even in 1785 Pitt had stressed the danger of French influence in the area; see Paul Bernard, *Joseph II and Bavaria* (1965), 213.

4. Pitt to Grenville, 11 November 1792 (not 5–12 November as in *H.M.C., Dropmore*, II, 328; see Murley, loc. cit., 1911). Other members of the Cabinet were informed after the event, Stafford for instance on the same day, Hawkesbury only fifteen days later (Pitt to Stafford, 13 November 1792, Stanhope II, 173–4; same to Hawkesbury, nd but 28 November 1792, B.L. Add. Ms 38192). I have not found any evidence for the King.

propriety of . . . assisting the Dutch Republic, as circumstances might require against any attempt to invade its dominions or to disturb its Government'.[1]

As the despatch went on to state, the object of the *démarche* was to warn the French as well as to reassure the Dutch themselves.[2] It was an indication of what was to follow that this important part of the exercise misfired. One has always to remember the pace of communications in any piece of eighteenth-century business. Depending on the wind, it took two days or more for a despatch to reach The Hague, and in the confusion of those weeks it was taking some eight days for despatches from The Hague to reach Paris. Auckland received the instructions of 13 November either late on the 15th or on the 16th. Their contents had not reached Paris by the 20th, when the National Convention ratified the Executive Council's decrees of the 16th. The British Ministry, or rather Pitt and Grenville, had decided to publish the pledge to the Dutch in the newspapers.[3] It appeared on the 22nd, after allowing a proper interval for the despatch to have reached its destination. Within the same forty-eight hours, therefore, England and France had publicly committed themselves to the prospect of opposite courses of action over Dutch territory and rights. Burges, the Under Secretary at the Foreign Office, had wanted the warning sent direct to Paris 'by some proper person (without character)' at the same time that it was sent to The Hague.[4] The suggestion was not approved, for what he himself accepted were 'strong reasons' of procedure. Whether or not it would have made any difference in this particular instance, the pattern of events was symptomatic of the difficulties ahead.

The situation was made worse while the statements were appearing. For on 21 November French gunboats entered the Scheldt. Their destination was Antwerp, to aid the developing attack, and their presence seemed to show that French pronouncements meant what they said. The news aroused the deepest misgivings in London, where it was received on the 26th. 'Quiet' preparations were put in hand for a 'rapid increase of naval force', though – partly to preserve its confidentiality – no ships were to be despatched at once. A Cabinet was quickly called, and held on the 29th. And the Dutch were then told, in answer to an

---

1. Pitt to Stafford, 13 November 1792 (*Diaries and Correspondence of George Rose*, II, 114–16); Grenville to Auckland, no. 20, Most Secret, 13 November 1792 (P.R.O., F.O. 37/41).

2. The fact was underlined also in Pitt to Grenville, 11 November 1792 (p. 208, n4 above) and Burges to Auckland, 13 November 1792 (*A.C.*, II, 468).

3. Grenville to Auckland, Private and most Secret, 13 November 1792 (*H.M.C., Dropmore*, II, 332).

4. Burges to Auckland, 13 November 1792 (*A.C.*, II, 468). 'Without character' of course means without official character. On the pace of communications cf. I, 513–14.

appeal, that a squadron would be sent if needed to uphold British treaty commitments.[1]

That much was clear. There was much else that was not. A fortnight earlier, on the same day that the initial assurance was given to Holland, Pitt and Grenville had decided to act on a suggestion from Auckland, and seek an 'explanation of. . . views' from Austria and Prussia as to the chances of a general peace.[2] Nothing more specific was proposed; 'a Confidential Communication' was desirable, but that must depend on the Allies' response.[3] The Government would obviously benefit from some up-to-date knowledge, particularly with respect to the Austrian Netherlands where the legal position was obscure. For while the British and the Prussians and the Dutch – the partners of the Triple Alliance – looked on themselves as guarantors of the provinces' rights, the Austrians had never ratified the Convention of 1790 to this effect, and in the 'unforeseen events' in Flanders some clarification would be useful.[4] Eight days later an earlier Spanish overture for an exchange of views was cautiously accepted, if the British envoy in Madrid thought it worthwhile.[5] These approaches and responses marked a departure from the isolation of recent months. But at the end of November no replies had been received.[6]

More immediately to the point, there was contact with the French themselves. One line of communication had opened in Holland. The French envoy there, Emmanuel de Maulde, a friend and client of Dumouriez, was hoping to retain a shaky tenure of his post by encouraging a peace negotiation. In mid-November he approached the Dutch Grand Pensionary, who thought the matter well worth pursuing

1. Grenville to Auckland, no. 24, 26 November 1792 (F.O. 37/41); Pitt to Hawkesbury, nd but 28 November 1792 (B.L. Add. Ms 38192); Grenville to same, 27 November 1792 (B.L. Add. Ms 38228); Minute of Conversation between Grenville and Baron Nagel [Dutch Ambassador], 29 November 1792 (F.O. 37/41). No Minutes of the Cabinet meeting seem to have survived; cf. I, 629. For the Dutch appeal see Holland Rose, II, 77.

2. Auckland to Grenville, 9 November 1792; Grenville to Auckland, 13 November 1792 (*H.M.C., Dropmore*, II, 330, 332). They did not however accept the Ambassador's accompanying, and typical, proposal that both operations should be entrusted to his brother Morton Eden, the envoy in Berlin.

3. Grenville to Morton Eden, no. 19 (F.O. 64/26); same to Alexander Straton [chargé d'affaires in Vienna], no. 2 (F.O. 7/31), both of 13 November 1792.

4. See p. 50 above. Grenville had raised the point again with Auckland earlier in the summer (no. 2, 11 May 1792; F.O. 37/38).

5. F.J. Jackson [Minister *ad interim* to Spain] to Grenville, no. 25, 4 October 1792; Grenville to Jackson, no. 7, 21 November 1792 (F.O. 72/25). The continuing shifts of attitude in Spain may be followed in Jackson's despatches *passim*, loc. cit.

6. Or were likely to be in that time. Communications with Spain were always, and with Austria and Prussia often, slow. In the event the despatches to Madrid and to Berlin reached their destinations in the third week of December; that to Vienna by the end of November (F.O. 72/25, 64/26, 7/31).

and secured Auckland's agreement to a trial of Dumouriez's views. They authorised de Maulde, on their own initiative – though Auckland seems to have kept in the background – to raise the possibility of their Governments' mediation in return for the safety of the French royal family. In reporting this to London Auckland suggested a financial sweetener, a prospect of which de Maulde was aware; and Pitt and Grenville, with the King's consent, were prepared to send £10,000 in case of success. Shades of Harris a few years earlier, and reflections of Pitt's gold.[1] But the sum was agreed without great expectations, and the scepticism was justified, for de Maulde in his anxiety mishandled the affair. He thought it advantageous to report to Paris as well as to Dumouriez; and while the General proved less pacific than had been reported – not surprisingly after his recent advance – the Executive Council was misled into thinking that a formal intercession was proposed. The episode may have contributed to the rising tide of misunderstanding which was to be so evident in the next two months. It had no other effect, for Paris was not keenly interested, and de Maulde himself was recalled after all. Although the talks continued, neither the Dutch nor the British took them seriously after a time. But at the end of November Pitt and Grenville had at least the impression that Dumouriez, once more a central figure, might not be out of reach.[2]

Conversations also opened in London, through more than one channel. As in Holland, they were not unconnected with personal ambitions and fears. The one thing on which the leading French agents, official and unofficial, agreed was the likely importance of the Dutch alliance to British policy. They took for granted, as all Frenchmen did, the financial importance of Holland to England, and as Dumouriez's operations raised the possibility of a further advance they competed in efforts to impress the point on their patrons in Paris. Chauvelin himself was active, seeking an interview with Grenville for 19 November. He was rebuffed, since the Ministry was determined to avoid official recognition of an unconstitutional régime. But the Foreign Office had recognised since August that 'It is not easy to determine beforehand the precise steps to be adopted in Consequence of these Principles'; the news of the Scheldt decree, when received on the 26th, had its effect; Chauvelin had already renewed his request, easing the way this time by asking for a 'Conversation particulière'; and on the 28th he was asked to call at the Foreign Office the next day.[3] The result was inconclusive, and

1. See I, 522–8, and p. 48 above.

2. For the affair see the correspondence between Auckland and Grenville in F.O. 37/41–2, 97/247, and B.L. Add. Ms 34445; and between Grenville and George III in *H.M.C., Dropmore*, II, 339. Murley follows it in detail, loc. cit., 220–43. Auckland, referring to de Maulde, had earlier noted 'the dangerous Character of the Man' (to Grenville, Most Secret, 3 August 1792; F.O. 37/39).

3. The correspondence of the 19th to the 28th is in F.O. 27/40; the remarks about 'precise steps', on the occasion of Gower's recall from Paris (p. 201 above), in Grenville

The Duke of Portland, *by Romney*

William Windham, *by Reynolds*

gave rise to accusations later – not surprisingly perhaps, given the uncertainties which both men felt. Grenville, trying to sound out the ground, may have been too imprecise in his language; Chauvelin, anxious to restore his credit with Paris, was too emphatic in reporting a continued desire for neutrality and a possible British recognition of the Republic. Shades of meaning seem to have been lost in a tangential discussion.[1] But the Ambassador in any case was not to have the chance immediately of testing his impressions. For his competitors were more effectively at work. The principal 'secret agent' Noël[2] talked to the MP William Smith, a reforming but Pittite Dissenter who had access to Pitt himself, and then crossed the Channel to see Dumouriez and report to Paris. And at the end of the month one of his lesser colleagues, or rivals, brought about – in a sense by chance – the first real exchange of views.

The manner in which this happened was typical of the prevailing conditions. Among the 'secret agents' in London was a young man called Scipion Mourgue, as eager as any of the others to make his mark with his patrons, and even by their standards unusually headstrong and foolish. But he had one claim, as it proved, to attention, for he was known to William Miles, that indefatigable fringe figure who had a way of cropping up briefly in the face of troubled events.[3] Miles in fact had certain qualifications to act as a go-between in this instance. He knew Paris well, was a friend of Lebrun, the former journalist who was now Foreign Minister, and as one of Pitt's confidential emissaries to France at the time of the Nootka Sound crisis would have appeared to be an obvious channel of approach.[4] Mourgue for his part had persuaded himself – wrongly – that Lebrun had authorised him to negotiate, and he got in touch with Miles in mid-November. The word was passed on, it would seem to Charles Long, the joint Secretary of the Treasury, and after some hesitation Long announced that he would hear what Mourgue had to say. It was a significant response, for Long was an intimate of Pitt's – a friend since Cambridge days, one of the select band who could address the Minister solely by his surname,[5] brought into Parliament in 1789 and made successor to Tom Steele[6] two years later

---

to Auckland, no. 14, 21 August 1792 (F.O. 37/39). Chauvelin's proposal of a 'Conversation particulière' was useful. As he himself stressed when he met Grenville, it was designed to avoid the difficulties arising from 'any Point of Form' (copy of Grenville's note of conversation, 29 December 1792; F.O. 27/40).

1. Both sides subsequently published their versions. Chauvelin's in the form of his despatch to the Foreign Minister Lebrun of 29 December, Grenville's in that of his note of the same day (see above).

2. See p. 201, n3 above.

3. He will be familiar to readers of I (see its Index); and see also pp. 28n4, 48n3 above.

4. He might also have been thought a good contact with Grenville, through a long-standing connexion with the Foreign Secretary's elder brother Buckingham. An old friendship with Lafayette was by now of more doubtful use so far as Paris was concerned.

5. Which even Dundas for instance did not do; and see I, 132.

6. See op. cit., 107, 109n1, 131.

when Steele was appointed joint Paymaster General. He saw Mourgue on the 30th. The meeting was a fiasco, the agent haranguing his disgusted listener on the claims and successes of the Revolution. But at the end, whether by premeditation or invaded for once by a gleam of doubt, he suggested that Ministers should talk to a more senior emissary. One happened to be at hand, staying with Mourgue himself: a senior official in the French Foreign Ministry, Hugues Bernard Maret, who was in London on private business over which he had been delayed, and had agreed to stand in for Noël[1] while he remained. Long went at once to Pitt, and Pitt agreed to a meeting. With this decision matters entered on a new stage.[2]

This was on 1 December. Considering the point from which they started, Pitt and Grenville had moved some way in the past three weeks. They had given a public assurance to Holland, agreed to seek the views of Austria and Prussia, and were ready to listen if Spain wanted to talk. Their own expectations remained fluid in the sudden turn of events. Until very recently they had been hopeful that Holland would not be attacked,[3] and in taking precautions they were not inclined to act precipitately over the Scheldt. They had also tried, and been disposed, to keep foreign policy distinct from domestic concerns.[4] But the latest news had shaken Grenville at least in both respects. He now saw a 'concerted plan' on the part of the French 'to drive us to extremes'; and he linked this specifically with 'a view to producing an impression in the interior of the country'.[5] Pitt as yet may possibly not have wished to go so far: it may have not been fortuitous that his summons to the Cabinet which was held on 29 November was 'in consequence of Accounts from Abroad and the dispatches from the Hague', and nothing else.[6] Within

---

1. P. 210 above.

2. The sequence of events from Miles's and Long's point of view is fairly clear, from the former's papers as used in Howard V. Evans's article cited p. 48, n3 above, and the selection in *Correspondence of . . . Miles*, I, 347–63. It is not so precise from Pitt's, for he may already have heard of Maret from William Smith (see above). It seems he was acting temporarily in Noël's place.

3. See Grenville to Auckland, 23 November 1792 (F.O. 37/41).

4. Cf. the tone of Stafford to Pitt, 16 November 1792 (P.R.O. 30/8/180) with that of Grenville to Buckingham, 14 November 1792 (Buckingham, II, 226–8).

5. Grenville to Auckland, 27 November 1792 (*H.M.C., Dropmore*, II, 344).

6. To Hawkesbury, nd but 28 November 1792 (B.L. Add. Ms 38192). Grenville on the other hand wrote on the same occasion that the intention to open the Scheldt 'with many particulars of our internal situation seems to call for some immediate and decisive resolution' (to same, 27 November 1792; B.L. Add. Ms 38228).

There is one mystery at this point. In *D.N.B.*, the article on Burges states that Pitt asked him to write a pamphlet to prepare the public mind for war with France; and while no date is given, material in Burges's papers in the Bodleian Library is both suggestive and inconclusive. A note to that effect in his 'Concise Diary of Events . . . 1752–1806' (Burges Ms 73) is placed under 1792. It states, 'I write, jointly with Pitt, a Pamphlet on the Proceedings of the French Convention, which is published'. There is

the next few days he opened a line to Paris. Nevertheless, as he was to make clear, the subsequent talks were bound to be affected by the connexion which Grenville had made. For the 'unforeseen events' abroad were now not the only danger; they had been accompanied by a wave of unrest at home. Riots and rumours of sedition were spreading in the very weeks of the French advances, and they mounted to a fresh peak as the decrees were flourished in the face of Europe. One of these in particular struck home to an insular people. The fraternal decree of 19 November might increase Ministerial fears for Holland, where there were constant reports of the raising of an insurrectionary 'Batavian legion'. Its application to Britain aroused a wider public as well, at a time when Frenchmen in England were already suspect and the 'secret agents' were being watched. However he might choose to treat it, and however anxious he might be for peace, no Minister therefore could ignore the conjunction of these simultaneous threats.

II

It may have been the harder by this stage to disentangle native and external pressures because in point of time the second, however loosely, had preceded the first. While the Cabinet was still dispersed, and the machinery of Government in general 'inactive',[1] the small band of officials at the Home Office had had to take some precautions. The sudden descent of large numbers of émigrés on the Channel ports excited a public wariness which the authorities shared.[2] If committees of aid sprang up, so did widespread feelings of a different kind, particularly in the coastal counties which saw the landings at first hand. There was much 'prejudice and uneasiness' in Sussex, the people disliked French papists in Devon.[3] Dundas and Nepean and their clerks tried to step up the surveillance. Requests for information were sent to mayors and Customs officers, there were inquiries into dockyard security, attempts to scrutinise passages to Ireland. The methods remained rudimentary, for nothing on this scale had arisen hitherto. Meanwhile Dundas thought it wise to pursue an earlier thought. In mid-September he

---

also a note, in Burges Ms 29, of a letter from John Heriot editor of *The Sun*) of 28 December 1792, referring to a pamphlet written jointly by Burges and Pitt and apparently entitled 'Observations on some late proceedings of the French Convention'. I owe this information initially to Dr Howard V. Evans, who has searched for the pamphlet without success. If Pitt was thinking along these lines in November (rather than December) he was presumably not very far removed from Grenville's scepticism of peace, however anxious he may have been to postpone, and thereby possibly prevent, the issue. But much of course turns on the dating.

1. P. 202, n2 above.
2. See p. 202 above.
3. Lord Sheffield to ?, 25 September 1792; JR [John Rolle] to ? [both at Home Office], 29 September 1792 (H.O. 42/21).

sought legal opinion – and now more seriously than before – on permissible means of controlling foreigners' entry and movements. His main anxiety in point of fact was still related to a hypothetical prospect: the arrival of Brunswick's armies in Paris, followed by a flood of revolutionary refugees. Even so, this would merely compound problems that were already growing, which (Dundas forecast wrongly) were about to be discussed in Cabinet.[1]

In these same weeks more familiar trouble was brewing. The wheat crop was failing, and commercial credit was coming under strain.[2] The summer had been generally bad, and soaking rains in August and September fell on an unpromising harvest in almost every part of the country. By late September the western home counties were in 'a vortex of mud, clay and water'. A month later, the eastern counties were calling for an embargo on the export of grain. By then prices of provisions were 'extraordinarily high' in the midlands, and in the next few weeks the same was true of the north.[3] Nor were provisions the only articles to suffer a rise; coal was reported to be 'unusually dear' at least in the midlands, and raw wool and cotton seem to have shown a sharp increase. The levels, with the exception perhaps of wool, were not unprecedentedly high: all had probably been reached and most surpassed on earlier occasions in the past twelve years.[4] But the index of domestic commodities rose noticeably from August,[5] and it did so at a time when trade was beginning to fall and confidence to be shaken. Higher wages in selective cases[6] were not an adequate counter to the pressures which, led by foodstuffs, came at an uncertain point. If foreign troubles had their effects, material and psychological, on the economy,

1. Dundas to Lords Chief Justices of the King's Bench and the Common Pleas, Chief Baron of the Exchequer, Attorney and Solicitor General, 12 September 1792 (H.O. 48/2); same to Duke of Buccleugh, 19 September 1792 (S.R.O., Buccleugh Ms 30/9/9). For the inquiry in May see pp. 186, 193; for Brunswick's advance, pp. 197, 200 above.

2. See pp. 92, 94, 154 above.

3. Eg Buckingham to Grenville, 23 September 1792 (*H.M.C., Dropmore*, II, 318); Charles Townshend to Pitt, 10 October 1792; Mayor of Leicester to Secretary at War, 15 October 1792; Mayor of Norwich to Dundas, 25 October 1792; Mayor of Yarmouth (Norfolk) to Secretary at War, 28 October 1792, and to Dundas, 1 November 1792; the Rev. Sproule to ?, 24 November (H.O. 42/22).

4. As so often the picture is by no means clear. Thus whatever was said about coal in the midlands, the price in London for the *year* is shown in one account as lower – while in another as higher – than that for 1791. Wheat and corn prices too can yield different results from different sources (cf. B.R. Mitchell and Phyllis Deane, *Abstract of British Historical Statistics*, ch. XVI, with T.S. Ashton, *Economic Fluctuations in England 1700–1800*, Appendix, Tables 1, 2, 15, 16; and see also the latter, 25, 167).

5. According to one calculation from 78.3 in July to 80.4 in August, and monthly thereafter to 80.9, 86.9, 85.2, 83.5 (Arthur Gayer, W.W. Rostow and Anna Jacobson Schwartz, *Growth and Fluctuation of the British Economy*, II (1953), 468–70, which modifies the impression given by the annual mean as reproduced in Mitchell and Deane, op. cit., 470).

6. See pp. 97–8 above.

there were factors independent of them which were classic ingredients of unrest.

It is not always easy to proportion causes when the unrest came. Some of it may have been adventitious, like the seamen's riots for wages on the Tyne and at Ipswich, which were doubtless encouraged but not necessarily impelled by these immediate strains.[1] As a colliers' agitation in Somerset indeed had shown in the quiet month of August, trouble could arise in conditions of a boom, and reflect subtler relationships.[2] Some other disturbances were ascribed directly to food prices, or prices in general. In others again the authorities were not entirely sure. For a note of doubt sometimes creeps in: a riot on market day at Great Yarmouth was said to be 'under the pretence of the high price of provisions'; food prices, it was forecast from Pitt's old constituency of Appleby in Westmorland, 'will be an Excuse . . . for popular tumult'.[3] Such doubts did not refer to the symptomatic element which this form of protest could contain: to the sense of helplessness and dislocation in the face of unregulated market forces.[4] On this occasion the meaning was specific. There was 'suddenly' a 'mutinous disposition of the lower order of People',[5] which was being fanned under the turn of events in France.

The connexion of course was easy to make. It was sometimes almost certainly wrong, sometimes dubious, and very often impossible to prove. Part of the winter's unrest would probably have arisen anyway, and some of the rioters would not have taken kindly to hearing that they responded to a foreign stimulus. The interaction of political ideas and economic pressures is seldom clear-cut. But that very fact gave rise to alarm now. For if there were riots over prices there was simultaneous political disturbance, and a fresh surge of organisation to give a contemporary expression to both.

This last came, in greater volume, from the popular Societies, suddenly expanding again after the summer lull. For while there was some activity higher up the scale, among the Friends of the People,[6] it was from the institutions of the lower orders that the danger was most keenly felt. Many of the existing Societies probably grew larger – the LCS more than doubled its membership in a month[7] – and throughout October and November new ones were being founded almost weekly. In

1. Pp. 93, 102 above.
2. This was in fact a rather interesting episode, in which a well organised 'combination' for higher wages was said to have succeeded partly because 'Shoemakers and other tradesmen' had recently shown the way, and partly because of tacit support from the owners 'in order to have a pretence to raise the price of Coals' (Captain George Monro to ?, 9 August 1792; H.O. 42/21).
3. Mayor of Yarmouth to Secretary at War, 28 October 1792; the Rev. Sproule to ?, 24 November 1792 (H.O. 42/22). For Pitt and Appleby see I, 25–6.
4. See p. 102 above.
5. Mayor of Leicester to Secretary at War, 15 October 1792 (H.O. 42/22).
6. See pp. 108–110 above.
7. P. 106 above.

England alone, the Home Office learned, 'seditious' associations were formed or forming in some thirteen towns, and there was one report of 'Country Clubs' as well.[1] The list swelled in the next two months, perhaps most markedly in East Anglia, and it was not only in numbers that the movement grew. For within the limits of local variety it could now more definitely be called a movement, and there was some evidence of tentative moves towards centralisation. Some at least of the Societies were in regular touch, the LCS was emerging as a focus, by mid-November there was even talk of a national Convention. Such a possibility, as one radical journal observed, 'which is music to the honest patriotic ear, is a dreadful sound to that of placemen, pimps, and parasites'.[2] The apparition of both a spread and a concentration of disaffection was bound to arouse both a spate of rumour and a more considered alarm.

The evidence of organisation seemed to be supported by the series of Addresses which now flowed from the Societies to France. The LCS in combination with some other London groups and Manchester and Norwich; Newington, Aldgate, Sheffield, Rochester, Derby; the Revolution Society and the SCI,[3] were the more prominent among the bodies which congratulated the National Convention on the repulse of Brunswick and, sometimes, the deposition of the King. The wording was fervent; it was given full attention in the official *Moniteur*, which reported the Convention's equally fervent replies. In a few instances representatives were sent to Paris – Redhead Yorke and William Brooks Johnson for Derby, Joel Barlow and John Frost for the SCI. In others they called on the French Embassy in London. Their doings were blazoned in the daily press.

By mid-November such contacts were often being looked on as the tip of an iceberg; for warnings of all kinds were now pouring in. One has only to stand the volumes of Home Office correspondence side by side to see how quickly fears were mounting in the last quarter of the year. They covered the whole spectrum, from the trivial to the general, but with a broad consistency that was increasingly hard to ignore. Handbills and verses, scrawlings on doors, remarks in inns, preaching by Dissenters; tales of 'conversations' among Guardsmen at Hounslow or troopers of the Greys at Manchester; strikes in the north-west – at Wigan and Liverpool –, in Yorkshire and the midlands – Wakefield, Sheffield and Coventry –, on the east coast from Suffolk to the Tyne: the reports piled up, conveying an impression of impending strife. 'The people in the North' were in a 'firment'; two-thirds of the inhabitants of Newcastle-under-Lyme were 'ripe for revolt'. As such impressions spread it was small wonder that men of different backgrounds could see an 'encreasing

1. Anon. lists, endorsed October, in H.O. 42/22.
2. *The Argus of the People*, 13 November 1792; quoted in Seaman, 'British Democratic Societies in the Period of the French Revolution', 153. See also loc. cit., 151–2.
3. For this Society and the SCI see p. 74 above.

appearance of Republican Principles among the People of this Country', and suspect that 'the lower orders' were 'forming the basis of future deep events'.[1]

Most alarming of all were the tales of weapons being made and hidden. The authorities spent a great deal of time on one mysterious case. Dr Maxwell of York, an open admirer of the Revolution, was said to have ordered thousands of pikes and daggers from Birmingham, and the affair – which shrank on investigation – became famous when Burke dramatically threw a dagger on the floor of the House of Commons.[2] But there were other reports, mostly starting in November – of orders for muskets in the London area, of threats to the Tower and the Excise Office, of cargoes of arms landing from France. Taken with the rest of the evidence, given the sketchy means of testing, it might suddenly have seemed that nothing like this had been seen in England before.

And not only in England. Scotland and Ireland were as bad if not worse. By the end of November 'matters' there, it was said, were 'far less moderate'; 'the thief has entered in'.[3] Since the early summer there had been riots in some of the larger Scottish towns – in Aberdeen and Perth, Dundee and Edinburgh itself. Other outbreaks were reported from the villages of Berwickshire and Lanark, Easter Ross and the north; and in the late summer and early autumn Societies began to form. Expanding fast from October to December, they displayed some formidable features from the start, seeking a wide and cheap membership very much on the pattern of the LCS, and exhibiting a spirit of fiery radicalism and the Lowland capacity for organisation. The pace of development indeed was startling. In August there was a single Society, the Friends of the People in Edinburgh. In mid-December some 160 delegates, representing eighty bodies, met in the capital in a General - Convention.

This upsurge was the more remarkable because Scotland had been, or seemed, quiet for so long. Movements for reform which had burgeoned in the eighties did so against a background of widespread apathy. The decade had been marked by efforts on behalf of county and burgh reform and – fiercer and more strictly native – doctrinal battles for the soul of the Kirk. But the political campaigns lost much of their impetus,

1. These views were held respectively by John Walter of *The Times* – in receipt of a Ministerial subsidy (to ?, 29 November 1792), and Benjamin Vaughan – for whom see p. 149 above (to ? Nepean, 30 November 1792; H.O. 42/22). For the rest of the paragraph see loc. cit., *passim*, and the theses of Seaman, Walvin, Mitchell, and Murley (Notes on Sources, Chs. V, VI). Diaries, correspondence and newspapers convey a vivid impression of the atmosphere of that month.

2. In the debate of 28 December. He had obtained it from Bland Burges. See *Correspondence of Burke*, VII, 328, and for the Government's investigation, which had begun in September, H.O. 42/21–2.

3. Vaughan to ? Nepean, 30 November 1792 (H.O. 42/22).

the Moderates in the Kirk beat the 'Wild Brethren', the Episcopalians, moving for repeal of the old anti-Jacobite laws, did so gently; and in the early years of the French Revolution the mass of the country to all appearances followed 'the taciturn regularity of ancient affairs'.[1] In so far as there had been any political demonstrations from the lower orders, they had in fact – not dissimilarly from England – been on behalf of State and Kirk. Mobs had once rioted against Wilkes and Liberty (since Wilkes was no lover of Scotland), and the Gordon riots of 1780 in London, led by a Scot, followed a wave of anti-Catholic feeling that had started north of the border. Two episodes however ruffled the surface in 1791: the failure of a renewed campaign to abolish the Episcopalians' penalties, which had been under way for over a year; and, more seriously at a popular level, the passing in London of a further Corn Act, the bounties and import restrictions of which worked against the interests of the manufacturing towns.[2] This last indeed was to prove a major point of discontent in 1792, as the poor harvest which struck England fell with equal effects on the north.

Such manifestations of feeling suggest similarities as well as differences between the pressures making for unrest at this point on either side of the border. For there were important features in common. In Scotland as in England the popular Societies more often than not disapproved of, and sometimes tried to discourage, violence. In Scotland as in England, too, some of the riots themselves owed little or nothing to political incentives. Thus in Berwickshire the trouble came from turnpikes, in Lanark from enclosure, in Ross from well-founded suspicions that lairds were turning land over to sheep. The price of bread figured largely, as it did farther south. But the resentment in Scotland was fuelled in this instance by the recent Corn Law, passed by the Parliament at Westminster primarily on behalf of the English landowner. Tensions that were common in fact to both countries, and arose in degree from common causes, took much of their colour, here as elsewhere, from a particular context. For in Scotland there were latent forces which might give discontent a cutting edge: a transformation of the economy which affected the balance of social relationships the more noticeably from the smaller scale of the economy itself, and an old national pride, resentful of a dominant neighbour – perhaps the more so now in the light of the remarkable native Enlightenment. The Constitution lauded in England did not mean the same thing in Scotland; if there had been half a century of quiet, it had been imposed and its pattern partly shaped from outside.

A threat of disruption was therefore likely to meet with a hard, because nervous, response. The nervousness was the greater in the early winter because troops were rather thin on the ground. Their establish-

1. John Galt's phrase in *Annals of the Parish* (1821); quoted in Henry W. Meikle, *Scotland and the French Revolution* (1912), 41.
2. See pp. 72n1, 44n1 above.

ment was slightly below strength and, as in England, the regiments were 'parcelled up in packets' – the legacy of a quiet life. There were moreover peculiar difficulties in containing riots in the larger Scottish towns, for cavalry, always a favourite weapon, was hampered by 'the particular construction of the Streets'. 'Sailors and Marines' were the best answer where the populous centres lay on the coasts; but there seemed little recognition of this fact in Whitehall.[1] The alarm not unnaturally was stoked by the fierceness of the rioters' proceedings, more violent and often more openly political than in England at this stage. Trees of liberty were set up in the eastern towns and some of the villages; French successes were toasted – bells were rung and windows lit in Perth when Dumouriez entered Brussels; the Home Secretary, Dundas, became quite used to being burned in effigy. London for its part was made aware of the authorities' fears by Dundas himself, passing through Edinburgh in October on his annual visit home.[2] 'Unless something effectual can be done', he wrote on arrival, 'to check the indiscriminate practice of associations, they will spread the fermentation of the country to such a height it will be impossible to restrain the effects'. A month later, there were 'great attempts to do Mischief in . . . Edinburgh, Glasgow, Paisley, Perth, Dundee, Montrose and Aberdeen. In a word I might have said all the Towns whose Manufactures are flourishing'. In another ten days, 'If the Spirit of Liberty and Equality continues to spread with the same Rapidity it has done since the failure of the Duke of Brunswick's Army, it will be in vain for any Military that can possibly be spared . . . to quell that Spirit which ferments at such a rate that it must break out into open Sedition'. He was hard at work on counter-measures: addressing sheriffs and clergy, trying to cope with hostile newspapers, reviewing military dispositions, supervising the distribution of bread and fuel, urging an embargo on the export of grain.[3] As another of Pitt's Scottish correspondents later remarked of these months, there seemed to be 'such a Mine of Mischief charged' that 'any Accident' might have been 'sprung with the most calamitous Effects'.[4]

Ireland in some ways was a more serious case. There was not a spate of violence on the scale of Scotland. But there had been corn riots since the

1. See Dundas to Pitt, 12 and 22 November 1792 (P.R.O. 30/8/157). Cf. pp. 126, 132–3 above.

2. See p. 202 above.

3. To Nepean, 14 October 1792 (quoted in Meikle, op. cit., 94); to Pitt, 12 and 22 November 1792 (P.R.O. 30/8/157).

4. Henry Mackenzie [for whom see p. 55 above], 23 December 1793 (P.R.O. 30/8/154). Not every one however was so greatly impressed. David Scott (see I, 414) reported sceptically on the troubles in Perth and Glasgow in November (to ? Pitt, 13 November 1792; P.R.O. 30/8/176); and Sir Gilbert Elliot, fresh from the Borders, wrote of the fear of insurrection he found in London, 'This is certainly ridiculous to those who live in Scotland and know the truth' (to Lady Elliot, 13 December 1792; *Life and Letters of Elliot*, II, 81).

summer, there was swelling 'republican' agitation in the north, and a Convention of Roman Catholic delegates, intent on the removal of disabilities, was due to meet early in December. The passage of arms and French agents was suspected intermittently, in an atmosphere now of increasing alarm. Behind these events, indeed, there lay pressures that were to grow in the next few years, leading to one of the notable failures in the long Irish tragedy. They can be examined better at that point;[1] an outline here must serve to sketch the problems and conditions for the immediate British response.

This was concentrated on political objects – which in Ireland of course meant politico-religious. Unlike the last occasion of discontent, in the later stages of the American War, the Irish economy had not been giving cause for concern. On the contrary, like the English, it had flourished since the middle eighties,[2] and while – as in England – there was now a bad harvest and the boom was faltering, this was not the main reason for alarm. The authorities' fears arose rather from two separate developments, usually contrasting, which for some time had seemed to be moving on converging lines. In the north, centred on Belfast, the Protestant Dissenters had been raising fresh cries for Parliamentary reform. They were doing so, however, not in the old manner of the Irish Whigs – of Grattan, Charlemont and Flood – but with a militant flavour now heightened by French military success. The split in English radical Nonconformity had little counterpart here, against the background of a more circumscribed episcopalian Ascendancy, a more openly corrupt representation, and an ambivalent attitude to the British Crown. The agitation – and it was a fierce agitation, with its share of meetings, speeches and pamphlets – had been under way since 1790 and mounting since 1791. At the same time the Roman Catholics were likewise on the move. The old Catholic Committee, broadly resigned to a slow easement of existing disabilities, was taken over by a more thrusting leadership based on the Dublin trading interest. Its aims found an echo among the northern Dissenters, themselves campaigning against disabilities and feeling their strength against the landed establishment. The two movements, from opposite quarters, drew together in the autumn of 1791, when the young Dublin Protestant Wolfe Tone published his *Argument on Behalf of the Catholics of Ireland* under the pseudonym of A Northern Whig, and with Thomas Russell of Belfast founded the first Society of United Irishmen.[3] There was now a focus for combined

1. Ch. XI below.
2. See I, 50, 196, 213.
3. In September and October respectively. There has always been doubt – fed by himself – as to how far Tone's disaffection had been precipitated by an earlier failure to make a career in London, and in particular to interest the British Government in ideas which he put forward in 1788 for an expansion of empire in the Pacific (see his letters to Pitt in P.R.O. 30/8/183). Certainly Pitt's own characteristic lack of response or even of acknowledgment (cf. I, 323–4) did not help, and perhaps could have tipped the scale in what was to prove an important case.

action; in the second half of 1792 the Catholics – still mainly loyal, but calling for some admission to the Parliamentary franchise – improved their own mutual contacts with a view to a national Convention; and as the autumn turned to winter, and the news from the continent flooded in, the authorities in Dublin, at first complacent, became increasingly worried. In the last weeks of November their uneasiness was changing to alarm. The spectre of a revived Volunteer Movement in the spirit of '79–'82,[1] but one in which Catholics were full and active members (where they had been tacit on the earlier occasion) and the Protestants were inspired not (as before) by the gentry but by francophile Nonconformists, faced the Castle[2] and the Ministry in London at a generally anxious time.

The latter had already tried, ineffectually, to forestall the Catholic danger. In the winter of 1791–2 it had canvassed the prospect of a Relief bill which would have gone beyond the recent Act for Catholics in England[3] and included the right to the franchise on a propertied basis in Irish county – though not borough – elections. Pitt and more particularly Dundas, who as Home Secretary was departmentally responsible, had been anxious to separate Catholic resentment from that of Protestant Dissent; they had been impressed by the claims of the Catholic Committee;[4] and Pitt, if rather vaguely, would have liked once more to 'look to a permanent system'.[5] They soon came up against the Castle. The Lord Lieutenant, the Earl of Westmorland (one of Pitt's friends at Cambridge, a supporter and later a junior member of his Government, and installed in Dublin since 1789),[6] with his forceful Chief Secretary Robert Hobart, mustered the usual arguments against. The property qualifications, however closely based on the English model, would have quite different results owing to the Irish leasehold system which, unlike that in England, amounted virtually to tenure for life. The introduction of Catholics to the county suffrage would overturn the political balance, and in due course – perhaps quite soon – destroy the relations between Church and State. At the very least, consultation was needed with the Protestant community; and should the shift of

1. See I, 50. The organisation had in fact never died, and underlay that of the Belfast Dissenters.
2. As the Irish Government was commonly known.
3. For which see pp. 81–3 above.
4. Represented in London over the past year by Burke's son Richard, who was to be dismissed – partly at least as the victim of events – in the following summer.
5. Robert Hobart [Chief Secretary in Ireland] to Earl of Westmorland [Lord Lieutenant] 25 January 1792, reporting a conversation with Pitt (W.E.H. Lecky, *A History of Ireland in the Eighteenth Century*, III (1892), 53). Cf. I, Ch. VIII.

For the proposals see Lecky, loc, cit., ch. VI. They were almost certainly put to the Cabinet in December (see Pitt to Auckland, 14 December 1791; Pembroke College, Cambridge Mss.). For the distance that Pitt had moved since 1785, the year of his Irish Propositions, cf. I, 200.
6. See I, 17. He was appointed joint Postmaster General in July, and Lord Lieutenant of Ireland in October, 1789.

influence in the Catholic Committee be taken as reflecting Catholic opinion at large? Confronted by these vigorous objections, Pitt was quick to yield. If the Irish Government would countenance a measure broadly on 'the line of the recent English concession, . . . I believe that will keep everything quiet for a time'. A few weeks later Hobart could write, after talking to the two Ministers in London, that 'all idea of a Catholic game (if such ever was entertained) is at an end'.[1]

The lesser measure followed in the Dublin Parliament. Even so the Castle arranged for it to be moved – as in England – by a private Member, and confined itself to holding the ring. The bill passed later in February – 'a . . . miserable mockery', the Committee's London agent called it.[2] Disabilities were removed in four respects: from the qualifications required for practising law, for intermarriage by members of the legal profession, for permission to run an educational establishment (and also to be educated abroad), and employing apprentices in trade. It did not do the trick. The Catholic agitation continued and rose. The alarm of the coming winter underlined its seriousness. And a year after these limited concessions a very different bill was passed through the Irish Parliament on the motion of the Irish Government.

Meanwhile the Ministry in London had to decide how to act on the ground. There was no very clear guidance from Dublin, where the authorities were still not certain how grave the position really was. Throughout the greater part of November the Lord Lieutenant was reporting a scene in which potential dangers had not reached a point of explosion. London likewise was not sure – Pitt himself was inclined to think that the Catholics might try 'to carry their point by force'; but in view of the dangers in England, and still more in Scotland, he and his colleagues were prepared to accept the risk. The evidence indeed was disputable. Following investigations, both the Irish Administration and British Ministers were inclined to discount the scale of arms' shipments. The stories of French agents were worrying, and again occupied much attention; but the remedy in this case would come most easily from measures for the Kingdom as a whole. Pitt and Dundas, now pressed for resources on their side of the Irish Sea, were not willing to weaken them in the light of what they had heard. As the Castle began seriously to wonder if there might not be a rising after all, they decided that Ireland should not be immediately reinforced.[3]

1. Pitt to Westmorland, 6 January 1792; Hobart to Westmorland, 25 January 1792 (Lecky, loc. cit., 45, 54).

2. Richard Burke to Edmund Burke, referring to the terms when first learned, c. 29 January 1792 (*Correspondence of Burke*, VII, 47). See p. 82, n6 above. The Act was 32 Geo. III, c. 21 (with an indemnifying Act in c. 22). It was introduced by Sir Hercules Langrishe, the recipient of Edmund Burke's public *Letter to Sir Hercules Langrishe . . .* which was published in February.

3. P.R.O., H.O. 100/38 *passim*. And see George III to Grenville, 26 November 1792 (*H.M.C., Dropmore*, III, 341).

In the course of November, and particularly in the last two weeks, these combined developments drove the Ministry along a new path. Its response until then had seemed to many uncertain, and indeed puzzling; and even in the middle of the month Pitt's own attitude gave rise to speculation. 'I am not sure', wrote Buckingham to Grenville on the 8th, 'that your Government have been *doing* enough; . . . and be assured these are not my opinions only, but I have heard them from all ranks of people with great dissatisfaction'. A week later, partly soothed, he still felt a significant reserve: 'I knew that (as far as you were concerned)' the 'apparent inattention' 'could not proceed from neglect'.[1] At the same time Portland, watching anxiously from the troubled ranks of the Whig potentates, was prepared to listen to a rumour that Pitt was about 'to propose a plan of Parliamentary reform'.[2] Fantastic as this might seem, the story appears to have been quite widespread. Early in the month, Lord Sheffield wrote that 'Pitt is suspected of democracy, and it is said by some lately that he will himself move a Plan of reform next Session'; and a fortnight later Chauvelin told Paris that the Minister might resign and embrace reform, if he were not dissuaded (as was almost certain) by his love of power.[3] They were wrong; Pitt was in fact making notes of possible measures, several considered before and some of which were to be taken soon:

> Association of Persons to be called out in Case of Necessity as annexed to Corps of Militia . . .
> Law to define Sedition, and make it punishable by Banishment –
> To give Power to call out Militia in cases of Riot in particular Places . . .
> Suspension of Habeas Corpus
> Power to take Security at least as to Foreigners . . .
> No. of Householders to be ready to mount and arm their Servants (Private Signal)
> . . . Intelligence from France.[4]

Government's hesitation had been due to two causes. It had not been

1. Buckingham to Grenville, 8 and 15 November 1792 (*H.M.C., Dropmore*, II, 327, 333); and see the passage in Grenville to Buckingham, 7 November 1792 (Buckingham, II, 224). Cf. also Stafford to Pitt, 16 November 1792 (P.R.O. 30/8/180).
2. To Loughborough, 11 and 16 November 1792 (Portland Mss PWF 9228–9 University of Nottingham). While he was 'disposed to think it impossible . . . in the present circumstances', he had 'such authority for believing that a very contrary language has been held by persons very nearly connected and certainly very strongly attached to him' that he admitted to being shaken.
3. Sheffield to Gibbon, 5 November 1792 (see *The Letters of Edward Gibbon*, 3, 303n4); Chauvelin to Lebrun, 21 November 1792 (cited in Murley, loc. cit., 147). A background was suggested by Buckingham, writing to Grenville on the 24th of a public 'disposition to give way upon points of reform' (*H.M.C., Dropmore*, II, 338).
4. 'November 9th' [endorsed 1792]; P.R.O. 30/8/198. Cf. p. 193 above.

sure that in England at least the trouble was as bad as was widely thought. Grenville, by temperament the hardest of the inner group,[1] was not disposed as late as mid-November to give too much credence to the scares: 'It is not unnatural, nor is it an unfavourable symptom, that people who are thoroughly frightened, as the body of landed gentlemen in this country are, should exaggerate these stories as they pass from one mouth to another'.[2] Dundas, who by now was out of daily touch, seems to have felt rather the same – perhaps influenced by the keener air of danger, and what he conceived to be the needs, in Scotland.[3] Pitt's own attitude can be judged only by the evidence of omission and the apparent impression in the political world that he was not fully alert.[4] Secondly there was a feeling – apparently illogical in view of the public alarm, but resting on the gap between attitudes and action – that Government would do better not to move too far until it was sure of the response. There must be a promise of real support by those in whose hands any measures must lie, and 'I wish', wrote the acting Home Secretary, 'this was more felt and understood'.[5] How far such a process could be advanced officially was a tricky question; but whatever the answer, the timing should be very carefully judged.

From the middle of November this uncertainty shrank. In the following weeks indeed we can watch the transformation of an attitude, in circumstances that gave the process a lasting significance. The rising tide of unrest was now reaching a stage in which regular troops might be stretched too far, possibly in England and probably in Scotland.[6] It had also to be seen, for the first time seriously, against the possibility of a struggle with France. The impact of the Revolutionary victories had been noted for over a month: Pitt, Grenville and Dundas all agreed on the effect of Brunswick's failure.[7] To the enthusiasts in the Societies the Old Order was in retreat: the adverse impression of the September

1. I, 133.

2. To Buckingham, 14 November 1792; Buckingham, II, 228 (and see the whole tenor of the letter). See p. 138 above.

3. Eg Dundas to Nepean, 25 November 1792 (P.R.O., H.O. 103/6). And cf. to Pitt on the 22nd (P.R.O. 30/8/157), showing no particular anxiety about the date of his return south.

4. Which survived certainly in some quarters to the end of the month: 'the Ministerial Coterie I understand', wrote one Opposition MP, 'affect to *Query*' the 'Alarm' (Charles Yorke to Earl of Hardwicke, endorsed 27 November 1792; B.L. Add. Ms 35392). See also pp. 202–3 above.

5. Grenville to Buckingham, 14 November 1792 (Buckingham, II, 227). Cf. p. 138 above.

6. Eg Dundas to Pitt, 12 November 1792 (P.R.O. 30/8/157). Official communications had already made the point. Cf. pp. 126, 218–19 above.

7. Grenville to Buckingham, 14 November 1792 (no above) – 'the real fact is, that these people [seditious pamphleteers] were completely quelled, and their spirit destroyed, till the Duke to Brunswick's retreat'; for Dundas on 22 November see p. 219 above; for Pitt, in January 1793, *P.R.*, XXXIV, 301.

massacres[1] was overlaid by the new triumphs; there was an exciting feeling that men were 'seeing the future, and it works'. Ministers for their part had now to digest the portents for the Low Countries, and to recognise that disaffection at home might have to be dealt with in the context of war. It was in these circumstances that they contemplated their first new step, which was decided the more easily when news reached London of the recent French decrees and entry into the Scheldt.[2] They had already taken some action along the earlier lines: instructions went out in the middle of the month, under the Proclamation of May, to buy up copies of published 'libels' with a view to prosecution. But this was not enough in itself – and there was even a question if it could be repeated.[3] The army should now be reinforced, and well-affected forces brought into play. In the last ten days of November the Ministry decided to embody parts of the militia, a measure discussed probably before the 26th and decided by the end of the month.[4] By an Act of 1786 Parliament had then to be summoned within fourteen days, and it met on 13 December, about a month earlier than had been planned.[5] Six days later Government introduced a bill 'for establishing Regulations respecting Aliens arriving in this Kingdom, or resident therein in certain places'; and this passed into law on 8 January 1793.[6]

The embodiment of the militia at first affected certain counties only, in England and Scotland. Meanwhile regular troops were being quietly moved near London and the Tower was made secure. Surveillance of Englishmen and foreigners increased; radical newspapers were closely scrutinised; Paine, at last tried, was found guilty in his absence;[7] special constables were enrolled in the capital, meetings widely harried, prosecutions begun. The hand of Government fell suddenly, and in places heavily, in December. The effects were the greater from new signs of support in Parliament and outside.

It would have been surprising if Opposition had not been confused by the growing troubles, falling on a body already under strain from Fox's

1. See p. 200 above.

2. Which, it will be remembered, it did of the latter on 26 November (p. 208 above).

3. 'A thing that can be done but once'; Grenville to Buckingham, 14 November 1792 (Buckingham, II, 227). Why? This interesting doubt of magistrates and juries does not appear in Home Office correspondence; but see pp. 390–1 below.

A circular letter to the Lords Lieutenant of counties, to enforce the Proclamation of May strictly, went out on the 25th.

4. See Buckingham, II, 229–30. The necessary Royal Proclamation was issued on 1 December.

5. The Act was 26 George III, c. 107; a summons had been optional before that date. In the dog days of August Pitt and Dundas, in 'very jolly' mood, had even 'talk'd of no necessity of Parlts. meeting till the middle of February' (John Hatsell [Clerk of the House of Commons] to John Ley, 6 August 1792; Ley of Trehill Mss, Devon R.O.).

6. 33 Geo. III, c. 4. It provided for the registration of aliens, their deportation if necessary, and restrictions on their movements.

7. See p. 194 above. The trial opened on 18 December.

behaviour. He himself exposed the rift as soon as Parliament met. For Fox had now been brought – had brought himself – to the point of decision, after the long period of ambiguity which had been intensified in recent months. Impelled by a highly personal blend of temperament and principle, of pique and intellectual loyalties, old-fashioned ideas and an instinct for growth, he moved swiftly, almost desperately, to a choice whose origins were far from simple but which was to place him justifiably in his future symbolic role. His attitude to France, if not fully formed, was enthusiastic once more. Like so many others, he had been discouraged and shocked by events in August and September, but Brunswick's retreat restored his pleasure in the Revolution. 'The Kings and Princes' had been discomfited; it was like America all over again, and 'no public event, not excepting Saratoga and York Town, ever happened that gave me so much delight'.[1] He was not quite certain of the consequences when the French moved into the Low Countries. An independent Belgic state seemed acceptable, but he was said to be 'ready to defend Holland'.[2] This last must have been a reluctant, and was a qualified, admission: it did not include the preservation of Dutch rights in the mouth of the Scheldt, and while Fox was not prepared to swear that the French might not invade he thought the Ministry would be 'mad' to enter a war which he was sure could be avoided 'with honour'.[3] His remarks on the subject were brief and tangential. He did not really wish to face that particular point.

Domestic affairs, however, posed a more straightforward challenge, and one which struck a particularly sensitive nerve. Fox had spent the late summer and autumn largely at his house at St Anne's Hill near Dorking; as others noted, he was not closely in touch with the swing of sentiment. He came to London in mid-November impressed by the French successes, and vigilant to defend 'the Spirit of Liberty' against any 'growth of Tory principles'.[4] It was not clear for some days how he meant to act; but his attitude hardened in the last week of the month. The forecast of an aliens' bill struck him as 'abominable'. He was blind, Portland found, to 'the danger' of 'an inundation of Levelling Doctrines', and moving fast, it was said, into 'a violent . . . opposition' to Government. When Fitzwilliam saw him on 1 December, after an

1. Fox to Mrs Armistead, nd but October 1792 [endorsed wrongly 7 October] (B.L. Add. Ms 45780); same to Lord Holland, 12 October 1792 (*Memorials and Correspondence of Fox*, II, 372). And cf. Portland to Fitzwilliam, 23 November 1792 (Wentworth Woodhouse Muniments, F31a).

2. For his reported views on the Austrian Netherlands see Burke to Fitzwilliam, 29 November 1792 (*Correspondence of Burke*, VII, 316); for those on Holland, Fitzwilliam's report of 1 December (quoted in O'Gorman, op. cit., 112), and Malmesbury's note of one conversation on the 11th (*Diaries and Correspondence of Malmesbury*, II, 474).

3. On the Scheldt see *Malmesbury*, ibid; for the rest, Fox to Holland, 23 November 1792 (*Memorials and Correspondence of Fox*, II, 379–80).

4. Burke to Fitzwilliam, 29 November 1792, reporting a conversation between William Windham and Fox earlier in the month (*Correspondence of Burke*, VII, 315).

absence of some months, the impression was unfavourable – 'I by no means like him'.[1]

The embodiment of militia roused Fox to further fury. 'If they mention danger of *Insurrection*, or rather, . . . of *Rebellion*, . . . I shall grow savage, and not think a French *lanterne* too bad for them'.[2] On 4 December he took the plunge at a dinner of the Whig Club, declaring for 'The Rights of the People' in a manner which shocked many of the audience and led Portland to dissociate himself publicly from the occasion. On the eve of the new session, coming late to a meeting with the leading Opposition peers, he 'disapproved highly' of their intention not to oppose the Address in the Lords, and 'with an oath declared *that there was no address at this moment Pitt could frame, he would not propose an amendment to, and divide the House upon*'.[3] The debates that followed proclaimed his determination. In a brilliant opening speech he opposed the embodiment of the militia, calling for evidence of insurrection and attacking an abuse of executive power. He promised renewed efforts against religious disabilities, and for Parliamentary reform. And moving to foreign affairs, proposed the despatch of an envoy to Paris, and the desirability of acknowledging the French Republic. All this happened between 13 and 15 December. In those few days, in essence he crossed the great divide.

Fox's decision was shaped by the principles and emotions of the past decade. But it gained its particular force from what was happening at this point to the Whigs themselves. He was always roused by a threat to their cohesion – so long as it came from someone else – and in the past few weeks he had been alerted to a fresh danger. For during his stay at St Anne's Hill there had been new approaches to and by the Ministry, and when he came to London it was 'to counteract some of Lord L[oughborough]'s mischief'[4] and a disturbing move by William Windham and Burke. This trio indeed had been coming closely together since the middle of October, trying to persuade Portland to declare support for the measures that Government might need to take, and, led by Burke himself, to persuade Government to take them. A meeting between Burke and Pitt to this effect, probably on 9 November, produced no result, and the Minister remained cautious at a meeting on

1. Fox to Holland, 23 November 1792 (*Memorials and Correspondence of Fox*, II, 380); Portland to Fitzwilliam, 30 November 1792 (Wentworth Woodhouse Muniments, F31a), reporting a conversation of the 24th; J. Anstruther to Windham, 30 November 1792 (see Butterfield, loc. cit., 326); Fitzwilliam to Countess Fitzwilliam, nd (see O'Gorman, op. cit., 112). On Fox's initial hesitation in mid-November see O'Gorman, op. cit., 110.
2. To Portland, 1 December 1792 (*Memorials and Correspondence of Charles James Fox*, ed. by Lord John Russell, IV (1857), 291). He wrote on the same day in similar terms to the party manager William Adam [for whom see I, 616]; B.L. Add. Ms 47568.
3. *Diaries and Correspondence of Malmesbury*, II, 475. See also *Life and Letters of Sir Gilbert Elliot*, II, 79–82.
4. To Holland, 23 November 1792 (B.L. Add. Ms 47571).

the 13th of himself and Grenville with Burke and Windham. Heartened by apparent signs of Portland's acquiescence, the two members of Opposition then raised the prospect of support for 'a line of measures against the doctrinal arms of France', in return for information and without seeking 'a change of Ministry' or 'official arrangements'. The Ministers replied that such co-operation would require 'more certain and definite assurances' from (as Burke put it) 'the heads of the party',[1] and the next few days showed that the time was not ripe. Meanwhile however Pitt offered Loughborough the Seals.[2] Here Portland and his friends were on more certain ground; they disapproved, as before, of his accepting unaccompanied by others, and on the 24th he accordingly declined.[3] By then Fox was in town, and Portland unhappily in the toils. Ministers' 'hopes of anything really useful from Opposition' had again 'nearly vanished'.[4] But in a sense this was too pessimistic, for the conversations, if abortive, had brought their great rival to the verge of extremes.[5]

Opposition's embarrassments soon emerged in the Parliamentary debates. The Whig peers did not move an amendment to the Address – the only such step came from Lansdowne, who as Shelburne had been their old enemy, but was now bitterly hostile to Government[6] – and when Fox moved an amendment in the Commons it was beaten by 290 votes to 50, 37 of the latter, it has been reckoned, coming from committed members of 'the party'.[7] That was on 13 December; two days later, moving for a negotiation with France and recognition of the Republic, he did not dare press for a division. There was not a final split, for Portland was desperately anxious to avoid one, and subjected once

1. Burke to Fitzwilliam, 29 November 1792 (*Correspondence of Burke*, VII, 309–11). Cf. pp. 172, 180, 191n5 above.

2. On the 17th (see John Lord Campbell, *The Lives of the Lord Chancellors*, VI (1847), 360); Pitt to Grenville, 18 November 1792 (*H.M.C., Dropmore*, II, 335–6). The decision to do so was taken, 'without any other arrangement', and the King's approval obtained, by the 15th (Pitt to Dundas of that date, quoted in *L.C.G. III*, I, 630n1). Cf. pp. 177–8 above.

3. P.R.O. 30/8/153. Portland's advice was sent on the 23rd (Portland Ms PWF 9230). See also Loughborough to Burke on the 27th (*Correspondence of Burke*, VII, 303–4).

4. Grenville to Buckingham, 25 November 1792 (Buckingham, II, 228), which makes it sound as if the Ministry, not Opposition members, had made the running. See also Pitt to George III, sd (*L.C.G. III*, I, no. 807).

5. See the emphasis that Fox placed on them in letters at the end of November (to Robert Adair on the 26th and 29th; B.L. Add. Ms 47565).

6. He found a seconder, however, in the Whig Duke of Norfolk, who earlier had agreed to his colleagues' line. Portland (though apparently he alone) had been shown the draft of the King's Speech in advance (Auckland to Pitt, 9 December 1792; P.R.O. 30/8/110).

7. *P.R.*, XXXIV, 73; O'Gorman, op. cit., 114. There is an interesting, if fallible, list of Members supposedly attached to Portland in December in N.L.S., Minto Ms 11196.

more to Fox's mesmeric influence he shuffled through the month.[1] Indeed, despite a fiasco in which he allowed one supporter in the Commons to disavow Fox's views and his own son to follow with a violent attack on Pitt, Opposition was still formally united at the end of the year. Fox himself, taken aback by the hostility among those he still 'loved and esteemed',[2] made some half-hearted gestures of reconciliation. But the gaps widened under the pressure of events. On 16 January 1793 Malmesbury decided to support the Ministry, and on the 28th Loughborough accepted the Seals. Thirteen days later, when war had come, Windham and Burke formed a self-styled 'Third Party' – a loose grouping of members who soon offered Government their co-operation.

From the middle of December, therefore, Pitt could count on Parliamentary backing for his domestic measures and his policy towards France. There was also evidence by then of strong support outside. 'I am more and more convinced', Grenville had written early in November, that one of the best ways to avoid 'the evils' affecting the continent was by 'endeavouring to nurse up in the country a real determination to stand by the Constitution when it is attacked'[3] The spirit he sought found expression in the next few weeks.

It came in the shape of Loyal Associations, a counterblast to the Associations and Societies for reform. Numbers are impossible to assess, and many local meetings – some perhaps held only once – may have been dignified by a more imposing name. One friendly calculation claimed more than 2,000 such bodies throughout the country; another, hostile, conceded 150 in London alone.[4] The movement sprang up and made its mark within a period of two months. It began in the capital, at a meeting at the Crown and Anchor Tavern on 20 November, when 'The Association for Preserving Liberty and Property against Republicans and Levellers' came to life. The begetter and chairman was John Reeves, a barrister who had filled a variety of official posts. A product of Eton and Merton College, Oxford, and a Fellow of Queen's, he had been a Commissioner of Bankruptcy, Counsel to the Mint, Law Clerk to the Committee of Trade, and in 1791 was appointed to the new office of Chief Justice in Newfoundland. Returning to England the next summer, he became Receiver of the Public Offices under the new Justices' Act for Westminster, a task on which he entered with his usual

---

1. 'Fox is his vampire'; Malmesbury to Leeds, 29 December 1792 (quoted in Mitchell, *Charles James Fox and the Disintegration of the Whig Party*, 208). But a week earlier even Windham had not believed that an 'irreparable breach' was necessary (*Diaries and Correspondence of Malmesbury*, II, 481). The struggle for the Duke's soul at this time can be followed in *Malmesbury*, II and *Elliot*, II.
2. To Robert Adair, 26 November 1792 (B.L. Add. Ms 47565).
3. To Buckingham, 7 November 1792 (Buckingham, II, 224).
4. See Austin Mitchell, 'The Association Movement of 1792' (*The Historical Journal*, IV, no. 1), 62.

energy.[1] Capable as a lawyer, an interesting writer,[2] clearly a born organiser, he does not leave a particularly sympathetic impression. He seems to have been a forceful, rather hectoring man, with a hard unaccommodating intelligence – a minor Croker, if one may make a comparison in what would soon once more be Tory terms. The new Association was quickly at work, inserting its proceedings in the London newspapers, encouraging the creation of similar bodies, printing and circulating pamphlets and books. Some of these soon became well known – Dr Vincent's *Short Hints upon Levelling*, Paley's *Reasons for Contentment*, at a humbler level 'Thomas Bull's' *One Pennyworth of Truth, Poor Richard*, above all *Village Politics*.[3] As Reeves had intended, his committee was soon supervising a national campaign with himself in charge: advice went out, reports came in, there was a strong flavour of central guidance.[4] Amid the alarm which reached a peak in the last six weeks of the year, he was at a personal peak of vigour and, one feels, fulfilment.

How genuinely spontaneous, and how representative, was all this? There has been some debate whether or how far Government was involved. Reeves himself stated categorically that it was not. '. . . None of the King's Ministers knew or heard of this Association, till they saw the first advertisement in the public prints. It was planned without their knowledge, and has been conducted . . . without their aid'. This was a public announcement made within a matter of months. Three years later, when he was again organising a loyal Address at a bad moment, he told Pitt that he did so 'as on a former occasion, without any consultation or concert with anybody at Whitehall'.[5] It is hard to believe him if the claim is confined to prior knowledge; impossible if it is extended to subsequent aid. Reeves may not have approached any Minister in person, or supplied any one in Whitehall with a prospectus.[6] But Grenville, temporarily in charge of the Home Office, seems to have known that an Association was in the offing some days before it was

---

1. *D.N.B.*; Black, *The Association*, 235–6. He was also active in other spheres of London life: FSA in 1789, FRS in 1790. For the Westminster Justices' Act see pp. 195–6 above; Reeves had been interested in its unsuccessful predecessor in 1785 (pp. 123–5 above), and was soon hard at work on this occasion (to ? Nepean, endorsed as received 28 July 1792; same to Nepean, 1 August 1792, H.O. 42/21).

2. Eg I, 614n1.

3. Hannah More's pseudonymous success. *Association Papers* . . . (1793) contains the proceedings and publications of the Crown and Anchor Society: 22 of the latter, most of them including more than one piece. Pictorial weapons were also enlisted, and Rowlandson and Fores were both in touch.

4. The picture emerges in the papers retained by Reeves, B.L. Add. Mss 16919–31.

5. *Association Papers*, iv (and see also v), June 1793; Reeves to Pitt, 7 November 1795 (P.R.O. 30/8/170).

6. Austin Mitchell, loc. cit. (see p. 96, n1 above), 59n19, cites a draft declaration for an Association of 17 November, sent to the Home Office. But this was not from Reeves, and its origin is obscure (it was said to be from Lord Dalrymple (H.O. 42/22), but there was no one of that title at that time).

formed.[1] He might indeed have heard from his Under Secretary Nepean, who knew Reeves and was in touch with him over his magistrates' business; and Nepean, together with officials in some other departments – some of the latter possibly with Pitt's blessing– certainly helped the Association's work once it had begun.[2] Grenville himself knew about, and may have advised on, the formation of the committee – 'a few persons of rank cannot be kept out of it, but we mean it chiefly to consist of merchants and lawyers, as a London society, and that the example should then be followed by each county or district'.[3] There may have been a difference of emphasis as to Government's direct encouragement: Dundas in Scotland thought it 'a very delicate Point', Grenville had fewer misgivings, Pitt may have avoided – as on some other occasions – 'any commitment' of himself.[4] But there is no need to doubt that when they decided to embark on stronger measures, Ministers were well pleased with an outcome which strengthened their hands.

There was thus discreet approval and some quiet co-operation. They were scarcely needed to 'nurse up' an attitude,[5] or even perhaps to turn it into practical steps. Grenville in England and Dundas in Scotland were 'called upon on all sides for counter associations', 'pressed almost from every quarter', before news of Reeves's offspring had spread.[6] In so far as any initial political stimulus was given to that body, it may in fact

1. See Buckingham to Grenville, 18 November 1792 (*H.M.C., Dropmore*, II, 337), referring it would seem to an Association in London, and in answer to a letter from Grenville which I cannot trace.

2. For help from Nepean with at least one Ministerial newspaper see John Heriot, editor of *The Sun* (p. 116, n5 above), to Reeves, 29 November 1792 (B.L. Add. Ms 16919); for action by the Post Office and the naval Victualling Office, Black, op. cit., 240; *Association Papers*, iv, admits some aid from 'Officers of Government' (as distinct from Ministers), but only as individuals loyal to the Crown. Reeves himself indeed claimed that Pitt 'gave us the use of the Post Office' once the Association was formed (to William Windham, 2 August 1794; B.L. Add. Ms 37874).

3. To Buckingham, 25 November 1792 (Buckingham, II, 229). He also remarked that 'we are preparing an association in London, which is to be declared in the course of next week' (ibid). This was strictly correct, for the meeting of the 20th was followed by the first meeting of the committee on the 29th.

4. Dundas to Pitt, 22 November 1792 (P.R.O. 30/8/157); I, 607. I know of no primary evidence for Pitt other than Reeves himself, who stated later (to Windham, 2 August 1794; B.L. Add. Ms 37874) that 'Mr. Pitt had the curiosity to make enquiries after it', and talked to him twice or thrice (see also same to same, 1 August 1794; loc. cit.). But he insisted that the business 'began without any communication with any of them' [Ministers]. One subsequent account (J. Gifford, *A History of the Political Life of the Right Honourable William Pitt* . . ., III, 200–9) states that the Minister had doubted the expediency of Associations – because he wished to ban all political meetings – but that Reeves persuaded him otherwise. Another, better informed (Tomline, III, 463), claims however that he was not consulted upon the plan before it was proposed; 'he considered it far better, that the measure should appear as it really was, perfectly unconnected with government'. This sounds nearer the mark.

5. P. 229 above.

6. Grenville to Buckingham, 25 November 1792 (Buckingham, II, 229); Dundas to Pitt, 22 November 1792 (P.R.O. 30/8/157).

have come from the Windham group rather than from Ministers themselves.[1] But by mid-November there was an alarm and a desire for action which really needed little prompting and for which Reeves supplied a ready spark. His dictatorial control of his committee, the co-ordination of local efforts, the pressures of publicity at an exceptional time, seem more likely to have heightened than imposed a pattern. The Associations drew their leadership, depending on area, from the minor clergy and gentry and the 'middling orders' – an indication of the levels which consent could reach. Reeves's papers indeed hold remarkably little from 'persons of rank' or notable names:[2] the pages are filled rather by country rectors and squires (often the smaller squires); trading and financial organisations, a wide range of merchants and tradesmen. Not every region responded equally, and the quality of support itself was not uniform. There were the invariable local limits or restraints, and the views of adherents were not always the same. Scattered areas in the north, in East Anglia and the west country, defeated efforts to form Associations, sometimes for rather unexpected reasons.[3] Some Associations were fairly weak. Not every one who was invited accepted – some indeed of the most respectable in London did not. And others again who did so had their reservations, or started from positions much more moderate than that of the leading spirits. Public opinion can be an elusive entity even when one knows the local detail. But from Reeves's correspondence and also from the language of loyal resolutions, one may sense the existence of a middle ground which it would be foolish to underrate. It has been argued that many of the declarations do not take one very far; that they expressed anodyne sentiments 'capable of representing every type of . . . position short of revolutionary re-publicanism'.[4] And indeed it may be true that many men joined the Associations from a feeling for the Constitution which did not mean abandoning its constraints. There was a widespread desire to rally against sedition and unrest; it is less certain that every one agreed with everything put out in their name.

Reservations themselves, however, posited hopes for success. If the

1. It was Windham who drew up the declaration that emanated from the meeting at the Crown and Anchor of 20 November (Austin Mitchell, loc. cit., 58), and he and Loughborough were certainly in touch with the Association later (Windham to [Reeves], 16 January 1793; B.L. Add. Ms 16924).

2. P. 231 above.

3. 'The bulk of the people . . . are friends of the Constitution . . . I do not know of any person of property or consequence in this vicinity who would be willing to come forward, and in a public manner support you: and some of them are not your friends' (R.B. Nickolls, Dean of Middleham, Yorkshire, to [Reeves], 8 December 1792; B.L. Add. Ms 16919). See in general Black, op. cit., 252.

4. Donald E. Ginter, 'The Loyalist Association Movement of 1792–93 and British Public Opinion' (*The Historical Journal*, IX, no. 2), 187. This article concentrates on the meetings; B.L. Add. Mss 16919–28 contain examples of refusal to join, reservations, and differences of emphasis.

Associations were not always an exact gauge they were perforce the pledge of a support for Government's measures. The effect was not long in doubt. The solid bulk of the propertied interests began swiftly to assert itself; and at the lower end of the scale the wave of radical protest was met by a wave of counter-demonstrations – loyal toasts, processions, Paine burnt in effigy – which was not necessarily unreal for being favoured or doubtless sometimes primed. The authorities took heart. 'The spirit of the people is evidently rising', Grenville observed early in December. A fortnight later, 'the change . . . is little less than miraculous', and by January there were 'abundant' signs of 'increased loyalty and zeal'.[1] Feeling was such that Fox himself joined the Association in his parish of St George's, Hanover Square – even while he was being toasted by the rival short-lived Association for the Freedom of the Press.[2] Early in the New Year the danger was held generally to be receding, and many of the Associations themselves ceased to meet. In mid-January it was possible to collect the declarations of the past two months 'as a Memorial to the present Generation, an Example and Instruction to Posterity'.[3]

III

By that time England and France were very close to war. There had been some signs in December of a rather more hopeful kind. Pitt's decision to sound the ground himself was followed by an amicable meeting with Maret,[4] of which the participants' accounts, for once in this short period, convey much the same sense. The two men met on the 2nd. They seem to have agreed that there could usefully be talks 'by private agents, with no official character'. Pitt then fastened on the danger of a move which could start an uncontrollable sequence.

> I . . . mentioned to him distinctly that the resolution announced respecting the Scheldt was considered as proof of an intention to proceed to a rupture with Holland; that a rupture with Holland on this ground or any other injurious to their rights, must also lead to an immediate rupture with this country . . .

If such a train of events was to be avoided, the onus therefore lay on

1. Grenville to Buckingham, 5 December 1792 (Buckingham, II, 232); same to Auckland, 18 December 1792 (quoted in Austin Mitchell, loc. cit., 75); Archbishop of Canterbury to Auckland, 3 January 1793 (*A.C.*, II, 478).
2. Both in December. Fox's gesture was of course designed very largely to reassure the conservative Whigs, after the shock – mutual at this point – of the past few weeks.
3. Meeting at the Crown and Anchor Tavern, 11 January 1793; *Association Papers*, Number II, 2.
4. See p. 212 above.

France; and if the atmosphere was to be lightened there was one other thing to be done. The fraternal decree,[1] 'avowing a design of endeavouring to extend their principles of government by raising disturbances in other countries', could not but appear 'as an act of hostility to neutral nations'. Maret himself must have seen the impression it had produced, and 'till we had full security on this point, no explanation could answer its purpose'.[2]

Maret was conciliatory. Glossing over the implications of the use of the Scheldt, he 'believed there was no design' to attack Holland, and a real desire for good relations with England. Lebrun, Dumouriez, and the Executive Council all held this view, and while public opinion in France might try to demand an official negotiation he was inclined to think that private talks could be agreed. His despatch suggests that he was impressed by what he took to be the Minister's sincerity and readiness to be flexible within the permissible limits. He was also struck by Pitt's apparent suspicion of Chauvelin and Noël,[3] and stated – perhaps hopefully – that he would be preferred for the talks himself.[4]

Pitt and Maret were sensible men – Maret's qualities led him ultimately to become Napoleon's Foreign Minister as Duc de Bassano. His report was sent off at once, and there were straws to grasp at in the fitful wind. The French advance had halted, and some ground indeed was about to be lost; for the first time since Valmy the Allies were having a minor success. Dumouriez in particular was in some trouble; supplies were short, his citizen troops discontented, and there were sizeable desertions. He was at least temporarily at a standstill, and on 13 December was ordered to respect Dutch neutrality and establish himself in winter quarters. At the same time there were currents in Paris favouring continued peace with Britain, and intermittently at least a real anxiety to secure it. The effect of the November decrees had not been fully foreseen; the two most provocative, those on the Scheldt and on fraternal liberation, had been issued in a heady atmosphere, and the second in fact almost on the nod. There is no real sign that Lebrun had grasped the full significance for British opinion of the claim to 'natural rights' in the estuary; and indeed while this certainly contained an

1. Of 19 November; p. 206 above.

2. Pitt's Minute of the meeting; Holland Rose, II, 80–1. Apart from a preamble, this reproduces a text of which there are copies in the Pretyman Mss (Suffolk R.O., Ipswich), the Stanhope Mss (Kent C.A.O.), and B.L. Add. Ms 34446, ff. 28–30. There is a preceding memorandum by Pitt, from which the fuller version was probably written, in Stanhope Ms S5 09/14. For Maret's account in a despatch of December to Lebrun, its incomplete publication in Paris, and a reproduction with further inaccuracies in *The Annual Register* for 1792, see Murley, loc. cit., 267.

3. See pp. 199, 201 above.

4. Although he wrote that Pitt suggested this, Pitt does not mention it. Maret also implied that he had been firm about French claims in respect of the Scheldt; again Pitt's fuller account does not tally, and Dr Murley suspects that the impression was designed for Maret's masters at home (ibid).

element of challenge, it had been raised partly to attract support from commercial interests in Antwerp against plans said to be hatching for a monarchy under a Dutch or German prince.[1] The 'fraternal' proclamation for its part had slipped through in a moment of confusion. As Maret told Pitt, 'it went beyond what was intended',[2] and the Executive Council now found little difficulty in acknowledging the fact. When Maret's despatch had been digested, Chauvelin was instructed that the decree applied to hostile belligerents alone.

There were thus some signs in mid-December of a physical and emotional pause. But only some, and other developments were decidedly forbidding. Antwerp was said to be about to be fortified; there were continuing reports of French subversion in Holland; and missions of Belgic Patriots to Paris, seeking an independent state with French guarantees, revived a threat which Pitt a few years earlier had thought worth preventing at 'the risk, or even the certainty' of war.[3] The prospect of discreet Anglo-French conversations was also threatened as soon as it appeared by a growing demand in Paris for the recognition of Chauvelin's credentials. The Ambassador's own attempt to ease the difficulty,[4] and now the hint of an alternative channel, aroused a determination in the Executive Council – perhaps not surprisingly – to use him to force acceptance of the Republic. It came at a particularly bad moment, just as Louis XVI was about to stand trial. On 9 December Maret was told to see Pitt again; but only in order to refer him to Chauvelin, the accredited envoy through whom any talks must proceed. And if, on the credit side, the Executive Council limited its application of the fraternal decree, it declined simultaneously, for the first time, to recognise the guarantee of the Dutch constitution which the Triple Alliance had given in 1788.[5] Worse was very soon to follow. Belgian independence might not suit Britain; but on 15 December even that possibility was effectually removed, and with it indeed the last vestige of the French foreign policy of '89.[6] For a further decree was then issued levying revolutionary and confiscatory war: the wealth of occupied countries in future would be used towards the conqueror's expenses, 'feudal' structures would be abolished, the properties sequestrated and the political rights removed. Any state maintaining such a system would be looked on as an enemy of France. For good measure, action was ordered to uphold her natural rights in the Scheldt. It was a turning-point, the most far-reaching decision taken so far; curiously enough it was taken quietly, and once again with very little debate. Once again, however, the effect throughout Europe was profound, and

1. See *The New Cambridge Modern History*, VIII (1965), 710.
2. Holland Rose, II, 81.
3. In August 1789 (I, 547). And see pp. 49, 207 above.
4. Pp. 210–11 above.
5. See I, 538–42.
6. Cf. p. 46 above.

it was deepened in England a few days later by a speech from Lebrun in which he disclosed the existence of the talks in London, pretended they had been sought by Pitt and not by a French agent, and publicly derided the force of any British threat. On the 20th a despatch went to Chauvelin, ordering him to ask the Foreign Secretary in person if England regarded the opening of the Scheldt and the 'fraternal' decree as pretexts for war. He was further required to demand an official answer, and to insist on timely recognition of his credentials.[1]

'Menaces always do harm to a negotiation'.[2] Why did Lebrun act as he did, risking a prospect which he privately favoured at the very time that contact had been made with Pitt? One might argue that the risk was small, in view of the order to Dumouriez to respect Dutch neutrality – the key to the situation. Given that fact, popularity could be earned by abusing England in public, while further limited movements in the Scheldt would presumably provoke no stronger action than their predecessors had done. But this is too simple as a complete explanation. It assumes a degree of control over Dumouriez that was far from certain, an assured control of Dutch internal subversion – or alternatively a confidence that change within Holland would not bring an extreme British response[3] – and a domestic political authority on the part of the Executive Council which current conditions were known not to warrant. This last indeed was a part of the answer. Authority by now was splintered, as the power which had slipped from the Executive Council to its committees and thence to the Convention was contested by the great factions, themselves composed of shifting groups. Lebrun confessed at this time in private that he had virtually lost control. There was hardly the possibility of a careful approach.

But it was not only failing authority. The Executive Council was badly informed. The French agents in London, and the Ambassador himself, were ill equipped to judge events. Their accounts – as distinct from factual reports by spies on such matters as dockyard preparations – had been largely misleading for months: 'a . . . record of futility and incompetence'.[4] It was not so much that they were excited by the evidence of unrest – so was a large British public, and in the end the British Government. Or that some of them exaggerated the chances of Opposition when Parliament met – Pitt had some similar misgivings at the same point.[5] Their inadequacy lay in their failure even to try to strike a balance, their eagerness to believe what suited them – and their patrons – which sprang largely from the narrowness and the quality of their sources. For so far from inciting the popular Societies or the strikers

1. It overtook instructions sent on the 15th which were worded even more stiffly.
2. Translation from François de Callières, *De la manière de négociér avec les Souverains* (1716).
3. See pp. 210, 235 above.
4. Murley, loc. cit., 63.
5. See p. 238 below.

and rioters, as was feared, the agents were scarcely in contact with them and knew virtually nothing of their methods or thoughts. With very unimportant exceptions they kept themselves in London, and in London their knowledge was mainly at second hand. It seems curious for instance that no French emissary seems to have talked to Thelwall or Hardy, although Hardy lived a few hundred yards from their favourite base.[1] They mostly sat in the coffeehouses and taverns, reading the papers and listening to gossip, and nourishing their hopes on those ardent sympathisers who were still prepared to keep in touch. At a higher level, Chauvelin and the senior agents were confined to meeting increasingly unrepresentative politicians. They do not seem in this critical period to have spoken to Fox, either at St Anne's Hill or on his visits to London;[2] and figures such as Sheridan and Lansdowne were not well placed to give reliable advice. Perhaps the most useful informant, at least at moments, was the respectable William Smith;[3] but it is hard to tell how much he knew, or how far his knowledge was absorbed within a group of inexperienced and mutually jealous men. It was against this background that a stream of reports reached France in November confidently forecasting an English revolution. They found ready readers, including Lebrun. For the Foreign Minister was inherently suspicious of the British Government, and while genuinely anxious to keep its neutrality he now reckoned he spoke from strength. The news from London, the flow of Addresses from reforming and popular Societies, the expectations of a radical British colony in Paris swollen by recent refugees, all ministered to a feeling in the early part of December that 1789 was about to be repeated across the Channel. There were still some uncertainties: warnings over Holland – even from Sheridan – remained as strong as ever, and the embodiment of militia came as a shock. But, buffeted by domestic conflicts and varied pressures from the Low Countries, the nominal directors of policy listened expectantly to what they were told.

The reaction in England was swift. Maret saw Pitt again on 14 December, to convey the Executive Council's reply of the 9th.[4] The meeting was brief. Pitt listened in silence, remarked that Chauvelin could not be treated as an accredited envoy, and refused to say anything more.[5] When Parliament reassembled on the 13th it was hard to say how

1. See pp. 106–7 above. Hardy lived above his shoemaker's shop at 9 Piccadilly, the other end of the street from the great coaching White Bear Inn, where the agents circulated.
2. P. 227 above.
3. See p. 211 above.
4. P. 235 above.
5. Pitt's note of the conversation is in the Stanhope Mss, in a file of 'Notes by Mr. Pitt re Budget Speech December 1798, etc:'.

things would go; for if Opposition was obviously divided, the Ministry too had its problems. As Pitt knew, it was on debatable ground in embodying militia without explicit proof of an insurrection. This was required by law, and 'as we have looked more to the substance than to the form, I doubt whether we could, from our present materials, give as precise an answer as we should wish to cavils of this nature'.[1] Pitt may indeed have already been returning to his earlier doubts of the extent of the danger, after the pressures of recent weeks.[2] He may also have been troubled by the fact that he would miss the debates for some days, while he awaited re-election after accepting a place of profit under the Crown – the Cinque Ports.[3] His forecast was right; Fox attacked at once exactly in the way he had feared. But although the speech was acknowledged to be brilliant it had no effect on the voting; Fox lost credibility by his ensuing attacks; and the Minister returned on the 19th to the strong support of the House.[4] The Aliens' bill caused little difficulty, considering its scope. Meanwhile steps were being taken against a possible war. Export of arms and grain to France had already been forbidden – the latter the more easily as scarcity spread at home.[5] A naval armament was being urgently prepared, and bounties were now issued for men. 'Observers' were at sea watching movements in an area from Dunkirk to Brest. New lists were compiled of possible foreign 'incendiaries' in England. The Home and War Offices, the Admiralty and Navy Board, were all hard at work. The Foreign Office too was busy, as closer contacts began to be made.

For in the second half of December the Government modified its stance. Hitherto it had confined itself to assurances to Holland and requests for information from other Powers.[6] Successive developments now moved it from a passive to an active neutrality in which it circulated general proposals to Europe, for the first time for over eighteen months.[7] The Convention's decree of 15 December and Lebrun's subsequent speech[8] went far to convince Ministers that war had become much more

---

1. Pitt to Dundas, 4 December 1792 (Stanhope, II, 177).

2. See the same letter, loc. cit., 176.

3. P. 189 above. And see I, 128n1.

4. P. 227 above. Those days, so disastrous for Fox, were indeed fortunate for Pitt. The Ministerial speeches were distinctly weak, and there really might have been 'an opportunity', as the Duke of Leeds observed in a draft for a pseudonymous open Letter to the Right Honourable William Pitt, 'for your rival to have profited by yr. Absence' (B.L. Add. Ms 27916).

5. See p. 154 above. Grain was included with arms on the old British argument that certain foodstuffs were as much contraband in war as were munitions. Pitt, in the debate on the outbreak of war in February 1793 (p. 258, n1 below), defended the action on the ground that the French infraction of treaties had produced a situation so uncertain that it was only prudent to deny such supplies.

6. Pp. 207–9 above.

7. Cf. pp. 13, 19 above.

8. Pp. 235–6 above.

likely. But these were not the only events at this crowded moment, for on the 19th a contrasting approach was received from elsewhere. It came in the shape of a verbal statement from the Russian Minister in London, conveying a proposal from the Empress for a Coalition of which Britain should form a part.[1] Pitt and Grenville had thus to take stock of a situation which was forcing them beyond an attitude on one restricted front.

The results appeared at the end of the month. By then Chauvelin had transmitted the gist of his instructions of the 20th,[2] and it was decided that the time had come to reply in form. No interview was granted by Grenville or by Pitt; the response was stated in a Note of 31 December which was made public just over two weeks later, after Chauvelin had published his own.[3] It was an important document, the principles of which, never rescinded, were to be tested severely as circumstances changed. The immediate argument was formidable. The French avowal that the fraternal decree of 19 November did not apply to neutrals was placed in the context of the speeches and conduct of French authorities since that date, and particularly of the encouragement of disaffection in Holland. The statement that the Dutch would not be attacked so long as they observed 'an exact neutrality' echoed an assurance, heard in June,[4] which had since been followed by open infractions of Dutch rights in the Scheldt. France had broken a series of treaties by her actions, and declared that she was free to do so by natural rights. What then about the other engagements to which she had been party? 'England never will consent that France shall arrogate the power of annulling at her pleasure, and under the pretence of a . . . natural right, of which she makes herself the only judge, the political system of Europe, established by solemn treaties, and guaranteed by the consent of all the powers'. She must 'shew herself disposed to renounce her views of aggression, . . . and confine herself within her own territory'. Nor could the British Government watch 'with indifference' the establishment, 'directly or indirectly', of French sovereignty over the Low Countries. France must not enlarge herself at the expense of other states, or disturb their domestic peace, if she really wished for 'friendship and peace' with England.

The same theme was put to other Powers, with a consequential policy. On 29 December a despatch was sent to St Petersburg in response to the

1. The evidence as to the date and nature of the approach may be sought in Grenville to Vorontsov, 28 December 1792 (F.O. 65/23).

2. P. 236 above. The précis, which had caused him some agony, was received in the Foreign Office on the 27th.

3. On 16 January 1793, in the Ministerial newspapers *The True Briton* and *The Sun*; Chauvelin's Note of 27 December appeared in *The Morning Chronicle* of 7 January.

The documents were included in the series presented to Parliament on 28 January – a kind of White Paper for the British case. They appear in the collections of the debates under that date, as well as in publications such as *The Annual Register*.

4. See pp. 199–200 above.

Russians' proposal. which was repeated to The Hague, Berlin, Vienna and Madrid.[1] Pitt and Grenville did not embrace the Bear; on the contrary, they remained suspicious. Recent memories were vivid, Pitt had never had much luck with the Empress,[2] and he was not yet prepared to abandon neutrality however defined. There was not much trust of the Russians in official quarters.[3] If they were to work together, it should be on British terms. And the first of these were on the lines about to be stated to the French themselves.

> . . . The withdrawing of their Arms within the limits of The French territory; the abandoning their conquests; the rescinding any Acts injurious to the sovereignty or rights of any other Nations, and the giving, in some public, and unequivocal manner a pledge of their intention no longer to foment troubles, or to excite disturbances against other Governments.

The second, and distinctive, part followed. If these 'stipulations' were met, the other interested Powers should make a 'return'. They

> might engage to abandon all measures, or views of hostility against France, or interference in their [*sic*] internal affairs, and to maintain a correspondence, and intercourse of amity with the existing Powers in that Country with whom such a treaty may be concluded.

The proposals should be put to Austria and Prussia by 'those not hitherto engaged in the war'; if agreement was reached, the neutrals could then propose peace terms to France. But if the French refused the stipulations, the other interested Powers should take

> active measures for the purpose of obtaining the ends in view; And it may be considered whether, in such case, they might not reasonably look to some indemnity for the expenses, and hazards to which they would necessarily be exposed.[4]

In short, a French return to the foreign policy of 1789 would bring a general recognition of the Republic; a persistence in the opposite course might bring England into a hostile alliance, and seeking indemnities as the Austrians and Prussians had earlier agreed to do.

---

1. Grenville to Whitworth, no. 13, 29 December 1792 (F.O. 65/23), and see also same to Vorontsov, 28 December, loc. cit.; same to Auckland, no. 33, 29 December 1792 (F.O. 37/42); to Morton Eden, nos. 21, 22, sd (F.O. 97/324); to Straton, no. 4, sd (F.O. 97/59); to Jackson, no. 10, sd (F.O. 72/25).
2. See I, 505, 546; Ch. I above.
3. Eg in Grenville to Auckland, no. 33 (n1 above).
4. Grenville to Whitworth, no. 13 (loc. cit.).

All these exchanges, and those that followed in the last month of peace, took place in conditions which might reasonably be called un-precedented. Certainly British Ministers found them so, and one can see why. The Government's position was distinct from that of continental Powers, for its neutrality had still to be weighed seriously in Paris. But that very fact raised unusual problems in the agitated weeks spanning the turn of the year. As reports flowed in from France and the Low Countries, Pitt and Grenville faced a situation in which the confident and the uncertain, the calculating and the committed – the humdrum and the daemonic – continuously clashed and fused. One need not fail to recognise their errors or their limitations to appreciate the dilemma in which they were uneasily caught.

Its character was heightened by two factors, one familiar, one unfamiliar. As the volume of the messages grew, so did the constraints imposed by pace. No example perhaps shows more clearly in the late eighteenth century the effect of the state of communications than these critical months. Its significance was not the less real for probably not having been decisive – for one can hardly say that war would not have come in any case. But the time lags compounded the consequences of impressions which it needed every aid to control and often to correct.

Much of this of course was an old story. But the context was strange. Diplomacy perforce was geared to the pace of the sailing ship and the horse;[1] it had to reckon at this point with forces which the framework might not hold. The usual means of contact, now more vulnerable, had to carry the burden of talks with a revolutionary Government lacking foreign recognition and, very largely, domestic power. The dangers were obvious; and they were the more acute when there was added, partly from principle and partly under pressure, a rapidly growing French addiction to 'open diplomacy'. The frequent revelations of exchanges with London, which was fast becoming a habit in Paris, led the British Government to follow suit but without settled plan. At the same time it adhered to normal forms and practices with other Powers, and in some crucial respects with the French themselves. The combi-nation increased the risks, already high, of ill will and mischance. Negotiations, by nature delicate, were bound to be hard to handle when their processes were subjected to such novel strains.

The results were to be seen at their sharpest between mid-December and mid-January. The importance of timing was then soon exposed. For just as Lebrun was raising his tone, the French emissaries in London, whose reports had contributed to it, were lowering theirs. The embodiment of militia, the promise of an Aliens' bill, the success of the Loyal Associations, the run of the Parliamentary debates, dented the

1. Cf. I, 167.

confidence in an early revolution.[1] A crop of letters in mid and late December spelt out the message. The temper of the country had changed; the Foxite Opposition was unpopular; the best hope indeed now lay in Pitt's own anxiety for peace. Maret – worried by the Minister's attitude when they met again on the 14th –, Noël – returned from the continent[2] and shaken by what he found –, Chauvelin – veering from his predictions of the past few weeks – warned Lebrun in terms repeated more generally by their lesser associates. Miles too wrote in alarm, urging an understanding of Pitt's position.[3] But the turn was too sudden and too late to affect the prevailing mood. It could not dampen the 'elation' in Paris[4] or stop the Foreign Minister from expressing it in the very weeks in which the reports were being written.

The confusion grew worse if anything in the first half of January. There had been time by then for the news from England to make its mark in France. It did not remove the public belligerency, or the deep feelings in parts of the Convention: Grenville's Note of 31 December was rejected in a long uncompromising statement, there were fiery speeches from the floor, the prospect of war with England was proclaimed. Nevertheless uncertainty was spreading, in the Executive Council and, perhaps more importantly now, within the political groups. It was known that Dumouriez, among his bayonets, was not necessarily resigned to a passive role;[5] it was also borne in on men who had not fully grasped the implications of their statements that England really was prepared to make good her assurances to Holland. As a result, support was growing for a measure of restraint in foreign policy: an uneasiness reflected – though that was not the sole cause – in doubts as to the sentence to be passed on the King.[6] The problem in relation to England was how to keep her neutral without abandoning positions publicly staked and claimed.

It was not a simple task. And it was not going to be eased now in London. For the British Government had hardened in its turn. The surge of support at home encouraged it 'to talk to France in the tone which British Ministers ought to use' at such a time; the messages from Paris made it feel more strongly than ever 'the probability of things being brought speedily to a crisis'.[7] Early in December Pitt had thought that peace could be preserved by defensive preparations; a month later he seemed to one observer – admittedly a partial one – 'a convert to

1. See pp. 236–7 above.
2. Pp. 211–12, 237 above.
3. See Murley, loc. cit., 296–9; *Correspondence of Miles*, I, 389–90, 393–7, 400–4.
4. See Miles to M. Fabry, 9 December 1792 (*Correspondence*, I, 378).
5. P. 210 above.
6. See p. 235 above. The choice of treason as the charge necessarily carried the possibility of the death penalty.
7. Grenville to Auckland, 18 December 1792, 1 January 1793 (*H.M.C., Dropmore*, II, 360, 362).

war.[1] In the sense that he expected hostilities, this was doubtless true; and he was unlikely to budge from his own declared positions, particularly perhaps since he had now stated them in Parliament. For the debates, almost inevitably, were contributing to the war of words, and Pitt himself attacked the conduct of French agents in England (with the example of French support for the Patriots in Holland), the infraction of treaties, the November decrees, and the results in territories overrun. He justified the withdrawal of the British Ambassador, and the refusal to re-establish him with authorities who were not legitimate and had behaved 'with barbarity' to Louis XVI. The language indeed was very strong – 'a conduct [in the treatment of the King] which at once united the highest degree of cruelty and insanity', and would, if the death sentence was passed, be 'to France eternally disgraceful, and to the world detestable'; 'a code of laws [in France itself] . . . of anarchy and ambition', and 'principles [applied to other states] which were inconsistent, with . . . every regular government'; 'a war [as declared, and practised for instance in Flanders] of extirpation'.[2] Some of these remarks, the French Government could claim, interfered with its internal affairs; none showed any sign of accepting its explanations, or indeed of acknowledging its legitimate existence.

This last charge, it might be said, was disingenuous when the French envoy was to be made the test. Chauvelin's superiors had not paid much regard earlier to his status vis-à-vis their 'secret agents', and they continued to use him more for show than for serious talks. On 7 January Lebrun himself sent Miles a copy of an important paper with further information intended for Pitt which the Ambassador was not shown.[3] But whatever his masters' inconsistencies, the question of the envoy's position did relate to a wider issue which may be asked of Pitt himself. Granted that the Minister was not prepared to recognise Chauvelin's credentials, could he not have devised other means of approaching the French?

For the striking feature of the British Government's handling of relations directly with France was its confinement strictly to response. Pitt was prepared – as, less comfortably, was Grenville – to receive approaches on their own terms: neither took steps to initiate approaches themselves.[4] There was one moment when it seemed that they might do

---

1. Pitt to Dundas, 4 December 1792 (Stanhope, II, 176); Minute by Miles, 7 January 1793, after talking to Pitt (*Correspondence of Miles*, II, 3). Miles's accuracy and judgment are discussed on pp. 251–2 below.

2. Speeches of 20 December 1792 (*P.H.*, XXX (1817), cols. 143–5), 4 January 1793 (*P.R.*, XXXIV, 295, 299).

3. See Howard V. Evans, loc. cit., 204, discussing Miles's Minute of 12 January 1793 and his letter to Pitt of the 13th in *Correspondence of Miles*, II, 28, 39.

4. The suggestion of mediation conveyed to de Maulde (p. 210 above) was in response to his approaches.

so. Following Grenville's talk with Chauvelin on 29 November,[1] they seriously considered sending a representative secretly to Paris. They probably went so far indeed as to draft instructions, and the King was informed; a rumour even crept into the London press. The emissary was named there as William Lindsay, late of the Embassy in Paris; but in point of fact he would have been Pitt's friend Charles Long.[2] The talk with Maret, however, postponed the event while the Ministers waited to see if the French would 'open a communication',[3] and the worsening of relations thereafter seems to have put an end to the idea. When Fox about a fortnight later called in Parliament for the despatch of 'a Minister' (or accredited envoy) to Paris, it did him more harm than anything else. If he had been content to limit his argument to *de facto* dealings – as he began by doing – it might have appeared more attractive and, as later claimed, justifiable.[4]

A rather different problem emerged almost at once. For at the end of December the British did take an initiative. The proposals made to Russia, and repeated to Holland, Austria, Prussia and Spain,[5] offered perhaps the best hope of peace at that unpromising time. But, as happened in November when the Government made clear its position to the Dutch, the information was not sent to the French,[6] or on this occasion made public in England. It was a decision which, then and later, gave rise to dispute and blame. 'I never was so earnest with Mr. Pitt on any other occasion', recalled Wilberforce, in whom the Minister confided soon afterwards, 'as I was in my entreaties before the war broke out, that he would declare openly in the House of Commons, that he had been, and then was, negotiating this treaty'. And when Pitt at length disclosed the transaction in Parliament more than seven years later, Fox was reported to have replied that, having learned of it, he 'completely approved' of the contents; but 'it wanted but one essential thing . . . to be acted upon'. 'If this paper had been communicated to Paris', might it

1. Loc. cit.

2. Who was in touch at this time with Miles and Scipion Mourgue (p. 211 above). For his identification see Grenville to George III, 1 December 1792 (*L.C.G. III*, I, no. 812); for undated instructions, P.R.O., F.O. 27/40. Lindsay, who was named in *The Morning Chronicle* of 26 November, had been left briefly to clear up in Paris after Gower's recall (p. 201 above). He had earlier helped to uncover Adair's transactions in St Petersburg at the time of Ochakov (p. 36 above).

As might have been expected, Miles offered himself as an emissary at this interesting point (*Correspondence*, I, 360, 372).

3. *L.C.G. III*, I, no. 812. It must be remembered that the centre of a negotiation in eighteenth-century practice was accepted as falling by agreement in one of the capitals involved (cf. Ehrman, *The British Government and Commercial Negotiations with Europe*, 6, n6). That the assumption clearly survived here although the 'communication' would not be 'in form' reflects the mixture and confusion of attitudes and circumstance.

4. Debate of 15 December 1792 (*P.R.*, XXXIV, 98, 150–2). The effect of the speech, and retrospective apologia for it, are discussed in L.G. Mitchell, op. cit., 204–6.

5. Pp. 239–40 above.

6. See p. 208 above.

not have been 'productive of most seasonable benefits'? 'It was a fine theory, which Ministers did not think proper to have carried into practice'.[1] The regrets have often been repeated, and not by Whig historians alone. They lie indeed at the heart of the argument that Pitt could have tried harder to prevent the war, or alternatively that he actively welcomed the prospect.

The charges are not strictly refuted by an event unknown to the earlier critics, and very largely ignored by their successors. For in point of fact the British proposals did become known in Paris quite soon. It is indeed permissible to wonder if the Ministers in London did not suspect this might happen; for a circulation which included Spain, as well as Holland when there was still contact with de Maulde,[2] could not be considered unduly secure. It is even conceivable that there was a deliberate leak, since the information, taken from the despatches of 29 December, was sent on the 31st by an agent who may have been a double agent. The affair is mysterious, the evidence slight and obscure.[3] But whatever its truth, one cannot dismiss the possibility that Pitt and Grenville took into account a disclosure which would not involve themselves.

This however is not an answer. Rather, it would underline Pitt's decision not to engage in a direct approach. Differing reasons have been put forward to account for his argued rigidity or restriction of effort here or throughout. He has been accused of accepting war as a means of countering domestic unrest, or, more ominously, as the final step in a process of ruining the Foxites which he had begun by stimulating panic over unrest and its French connexion, Or again of a determination, typical and by now familiar, to cling on to office rather than resist pressures from others, above all from George III. Or of a desire to emulate his father and repeat his triumphs, avenging the loss of America and the recent memory of Ochakov. Or, finally, of allowing his temperament – his pride and his chilly reserve – to lead to an obstinate regard for form which was tragically inappropriate. Judgment must turn on the impressions derived from what has been said so far, of Pitt's response to unrest in the autumn and of earlier backgrounds. For there is not enough firm evidence at this juncture to assess directly the relative importance of political pressures and his own disposition.

There was undoubtedly one respect in which the former carried great weight, from the general sentiment but above all the King's. Recognition of the Republic, and thus of its envoy – unlikely so soon in any

1. Wilberforce to William Hey, 14 February 1801 (R.I. and S. Wilberforce, *Life of Wilberforce*, II, 13); Fox's speech of 3 February 1800 (*P.R., 3rd series*, X (1800), 352).
2. See pp. 209–10 above.
3. It is discussed by Murley, loc. cit., 420–2. The agent was a certain Martin, who was in touch with Paris (see Evans, loc. cit., 204n1) as well as with Chauvelin. The suggestion that he may also have worked for the British Government arises from a letter, cited by Murley, from an Under Secretary in the Home Office (John King; P.R.O., H.O. 1/1).

case[1] – was bound to be refused while Louis XVI was on trial. No public man, including Fox, could readily call for *de jure* acceptance before the sentence was known[2] and George III's own feelings were naturally profound. It was true that this attitude, which Pitt shared, did not preclude talks on another footing, as Chauvelin on one occasion successfully pointed out.[3] But unfortunately for himself the Ambassador had already largely queered his pitch, and as the crisis deepened his freedom of action was virtually lost. Personally unsympathetic,[4] usually maladroit, known to be on an uncertain footing in Paris, he was not the man to handle a mission which any diplomat would have found taxing. His inadequacies crowned a failure made probable by his instructions, themselves the victims of timing and ignorance as well as the products of fervour and defiance. One may speculate if Maret, for instance, might not have achieved a *modus vivendi* in the critical weeks of November which might have forestalled the subsequent deadlock. But he or any one else would have had to meet his own domestic pressures if he was to avoid making a demand which could not be met.

Beyond this significant issue it is harder to assess the impact of political constraints on Pitt's own preferences. As so often, George III was singled out at the time. Pacific like his Ministers until recently, and markedly pacific in the past decade, he was held now to be urging a tough line. He certainly made it clear that he disliked the idea of sending a spokesman to Paris, and had little hope of the outcome of any talks.[5] Pitt of course had to reckon with his views, and the knowledge that he felt deeply. There is not the evidence to go farther than that. The rumours of disagreement centred at the time on the treatment of domestic danger;[6] on foreign policy they grew firmer in retrospect,[7] and mostly on predictable lines. The King, sometimes with Hawkesbury, was set up against Pitt: the familiar picture of the Closet dictating to the Minister. But one report, from Maret, may have been nearer the truth. Stressing Pitt's desire for peace at the beginning of December, it distinguished him from Hawkesbury[8] and most of the Ministers, who were said to be for

1. See pp. 204, 210 above.
2. (*P.R.*, XXXIV, 80–1, 88, 98). Though Fox at one point went near to doing so; see his various remarks, of differing tendencies, on 14 and 15 December.
3. P. 210, n3 above.
4. Cf. Maret's impression of Pitt's feelings at their first meeting (Baron Ernouf, *Maret Duc de Bassano* (2nd edn., 1884), 97).
5. To Grenville, 3 December 1792 (*H.M.C., Dropmore*, II, 351). See also, for a month later, *L.C.G. III*, I, no. 821.
6. P. 223 above.
7. Among contemporaries, from the Foxites during the long years of isolation and from Miles after he had turned against Pitt in the middle nineties.
8. It is impossible in fact to tell how often Pitt and Hawkesbury saw each other in these months. They were certainly in touch over an approach that was made in December and January by representatives of the French West Indian islands of Guadeloupe and Martinique, for British protection and possibly sovereignty (see B.L. Add. Mss 38192, f. 93; 38228, 38351–2 *passim*). Otherwise there is very little evidence bearing on Hawkesbury's role and influence, whether directly or at a remove.

war, and equally from the Portland Whigs, who would accept it readily
enough. This may well have been a better appreciation than the stock
antitheses, even if for obvious reasons it may have stressed Pitt's hopes
too much. For in fact the distinctions were probably a matter of
emphasis, within parameters set by the political world at large. The
Court was one factor in a situation which contained Parliament and the
public as well; and Pitt's experience and priorities combined with the
circumstances to point him on a course, pursued individually, which was
broadly theirs. The starting point was his own. A faith in domestic
prosperity as the prime weapon against unrest, and a distrust of
European entanglements stemming from Ochakov, could serve as
powerful motives to preserve neutrality and peace; a record of firm,
sometimes tough, diplomacy which had failed only on that one occasion
– and in one other instance at least had been tougher than George III's[1]
– suggested a readiness to stand by his case. But the case here was both
strictly defined and such as to command widespread support –unlike
that of Ochakov – thus reducing the likelihood of a sudden reversal.[2] For
Pitt had made it clear that he subscribed to a cardinal axiom of British
policy: that the fate of the Low Countries and the Scheldt estuary was a
vital national interest. This had resulted in naval preparations twice
within the past six years; and Dutch rights and territorial integrity
moreover were now guaranteed by treaty engagement. So long as that
was acknowledged peace was perfectly possible; and the prospect would
improve if the French would renounce, more categorically than
hitherto, any fraternal support for an English revolution. This last point
was linked increasingly, after the decree of 15 December, with the need
to reassert the basis of international relations, which in turn could be
maintained only if France would 'shew herself disposed' to abandon 'her
views of aggression' and 'confine herself within her own territory'. As it
was, her activities seemed to be all of a piece. In the British context, they
would be judged by her treatment of British commitments, and if the
threats to these were not removed there would be war on the principles
invoked.[3] This was not a stance which allowed ample room for
manoeuvre, for conciliation must come from the same quarter as the
provocation. Nor would it be easy to reach an agreement which both
Governments could defend in public, particularly when one would not –
and scarcely could – recognise the other. If Pitt wished to remain neutral
– as perhaps he did more keenly than any of his colleagues – it was on

---

1. In the Dutch crisis of 1787; see I, 525–6, 528.

2. Cf. pp. 21–6 above.

3. A distinction should be observed here. The terms proposed for British *mediation* (pp.
239–40 above) were not necessarily those on which Britain would go to *war* if the terms
were not agreed in every case. A continued occupation of Savoy, for instance, would not
have been a basis for hostilities if British interests in the Low Countries were preserved.
Terms of *mediation* took account of existing belligerents' aims; they would become British
terms for *peace* only when Britain was at war as a result of their violation in one strategic
instance.

terms which the confrontations with Paris soon underlined. One may doubt if he surrendered unwillingly to political pressures, because the conditions for such a conflict did not materialise.

A role of strictly qualified response was beset by unusual difficulties in circumstances which, it has been suggested, raised unusual problems for negotiation.[1] None of those involved could claim to be a master of events; Pitt differed from the Executive Council in Paris in knowing where he finally had to stand. Most of the charges against him indeed have posited a far-sightedness which the available evidence does little to support. His shifts of mood, his very rigidities, convey a rather different impression, of a statesman interpreting his case amid scenes which he did not fully understand. He moved from a slow start, intending to feel his way into a situation that soon began to go wrong. The caution over contacts and direct information, the insistence on correct diplomatic forms, reflected in this setting not only inherent imaginative limits[2] but also perhaps a feeling that it was best to stick to the well known paths in surroundings from which the signposts were being suddenly removed. The early friendliness followed by chill which Maret so swiftly encountered was symptomatic of a natural, and typical, reaction to a rebuff, not necessarily of psychological warfare aiding a predetermined plan. If there were constants affecting Pitt's course, indeed, they would seem to have been formed less by foresight than by one immediate tactic and one underlying premise. The tactic was to delay: partly in the hope of a turn for the better – itself a sign of uncertainty – and partly for prudential reasons. It was possible that the French would climb down, or recognise restraints: the belated proposal for a mediation was directed to that end. And if they did not, time was useful to prepare and extract advantages: to fit out ships and warn overseas forces, to allow – or persuade – the Dutch to prepare, to learn other Powers' plans, and put the French publicly in the wrong. There were good arguments for postponement. But if hostilities were unavoidable, they could be faced on a premise which all the British Ministers shared. For while these months could be seen later as the prelude to the struggle of a generation – to the Great War, as it long was known, which ended only at Waterloo – Pitt and his colleagues had no such perspective. They assumed that the war, if it came, would be short. They thought it could be over within a year.

The last hope of peace virtually vanished in mid-January. Slight and ambiguous, such as it was it came from the French. Pitt's show of interest early in December had been nipped by what followed; there was now the

1. See p. 241 above.
2. Cf. pp. 43, 45–6, 245 above.

ghost, if insubstantial, of another chance. The immediate antecedents were not encouraging. A request by Chauvelin to see Pitt was turned down on 4 January, by Charles Long on his own initiative, but since the envoy had reverted to something like his earlier view, and was reporting that England might yet yield to pressure, a meeting might not have produced very good results. In the next few days in any case relations deteriorated further, for a fresh message, dated 31 December, was received from Lebrun. Chauvelin was told to make two new protests, one against the Aliens' bill and the other against the stoppage of shipments of grain to France.[1] He did so on the 7th, in two Notes. They were returned within the hour, as 'assuming a character' for the author 'which is not acknowledged'. On the 9th he tried again for a meeting. He was told that he could be received unofficially, but that the French 'resolutions' on the British complaints must be known before 'any new explanations' could be given. On the 11th he accordingly returned, rather reluctantly, to his instructions, which had ordered him to revoke the commercial treaty of 1786 – infringed, it was argued, by the denial of trade and now of free travel and residence – if he did not receive satisfaction within three days. His letter announcing this was sent back without comment on the 12th. At that point therefore it would have seemed highly likely that negotiations had finally failed.[2]

But on the 13th they were revived, and simultaneously from two quarters. For events were outpacing communications once again. While Chauvelin was making his protests, the Executive Council in Paris had decided to see if it could not keep the British still in play. Despite the public condemnation of Grenville's Note of 31 December,[3] Lebrun sent a reply on 8 January which refrained from closing the door. French rights in the Scheldt were reasserted, and stated to be 'a question . . . absolutely indifferent to England'. If the English persisted in their 'haughty language', and continued to make 'hostile preparations . . . in the . . . ports', the French would prepare and fight. But a saving clause was inserted – 'after having exhausted every means to preserve peace'; the language for the most part was more moderate than before; and the commercial treaty was not rescinded outright. To Chauvelin's embarrassment, this paper reached him a few hours after he had written to Grenville on the 11th. He at once sought an interview to explain how matters stood, and after further exchanges this was granted on an unofficial footing for the 13th. Nothing very much happened. Grenville, after listening in silence, remarked that 'the circumstances were too

1. See pp. 225, 238 above. Both were represented as contravening the commercial treaty of 1786.

2. The more important documents here, which were placed before Parliament on 28 January, are to be found as in p. 239, n3 above. A fuller account of these few days is given in Murley, loc. cit., 423–30. For the English text of the commercial treaty see *P.H.*, XXVI (1816), cols. 268–72.

3. Pp. 239, 242 above.

critical' for him to answer on the spot. He established that Chauvelin 'at present' was asking for talks '*sous la même forme* that he had now come'; and the two men then parted – not in the event to meet again.[1]

Chauvelin's anxiety to secure his interview was heightened by a separate approach which reached London at the same time, and of which he was partly aware. He may not have appreciated that his Foreign Minister had entrusted Miles with 'a statement' for Pitt in addition to a copy of the paper sent through the Embassy.[2] He must have known that Miles had also received a communication from Maret, now back in Paris as 'Premier Chef' in the Foreign Department.[3] The two letters would seem to have said much the same thing; and their tone was more benign than that of the official despatch. Miles himself believed that they represented a fresh departure, which cast an entirely new light on the paper that Chauvelin had received. Lebrun's letter

> authorised me to declare to Mr. Pitt that the Scheldt would be as good as given up; that the Convention would do away by a revision of its law all the offensive matter contained in the decree of the 19th November [the 'fraternal' decree], and that the Executive Council had rejected the offers of Liège and some of the Belgic provinces to incorporate themselves with France.

Maret's, he noted for Pitt, was to the same effect, suggesting also that 'all the offensive matter in the two decrees of November 19th and December 15th' (levying revolutionary war) was likely to be removed 'preliminary to the British Cabinet acknowledging the Republic'. He himself suspected that 'an agent will be sent over to treat with Mr. Pitt, confidentially, in the event of the Minister expressing such a wish'.[4] Excited by the possibilities, he asked to see the Minister on the 13th. He arrived during, or possibly just before, a Cabinet meeting, and his impression of what happened is best given in his own words.

> Pitt received Maret's letter with great good humour from me, with all

1. Transcripts of the letters arranging the meeting are in P.R.O., F.O. 95/99–100; Grenville's account of it (13 January 1793; F.O. 27/41) is printed in full in Holland Rose, II, 104–5. The translation of Lebrun's paper of the 8th is included in the collection of documents presented to Parliament (p. 249, n2 above). Pitt kept copies of most of the papers (P.R.O. 30/8/333).

2. P. 243 above. This personal letter was also sent to Miles, with the main document, through the Embassy; but its contents would not have been known. Chauvelin, who was certainly suspicious, asked Miles indeed not to communicate with *Grenville* until he had done so himself (M. Reinhard [for Chauvelin] to Miles, 13 January 1793; *Correspondence of Miles*, II, 41).

3. It arrived at the Embassy, like the other letter, on the 12th (Murley, loc. cit., 431).

4. Miles to Lord Fortescue, 15 January 1793 [on Lebrun's letter]; Minute, given as 13 January, on Maret's letter (*Correspondence*, II, 44, 42). Maret's letter is published loc. cit., 28–36.

the marginal notes[1] exactly as I had scribbled them, went into the Cabinet with it, and in half an hour came out furious, freighted with the whole of its bile, with the addition of Mr. Burke, who attended tho' not of the Cabinet; and returning me the paper, prohibited me from corresponding with the French Executive Council on the subject of Peace or War. I went away chagrined.[2]

The episode requires comment. Miles certainly saw it at that moment as disastrous. He had been deeply depressed by the 'inconsistency' and 'insolence' of the French a few weeks before;[3] Lebrun's letter now raised his expectations equally high. 'The Cabinet', he had told Pitt, 'if it is not resolved upon war, may have peace on terms honourable to the country';[4] and his chagrin after the meeting is easy to understand. The account itself raises some problems. Was it written at the time or some years later, at a date when Miles had turned bitterly against Pitt?[5] Why did he concentrate apparently on Maret's letter rather than on Lebrun's – surely the more important – and what exactly had Lebrun written; for that letter has disappeared?[6] Can all the detail be trusted? Miles stated the next day, for instance, that Grenville countermanded Pitt's embargo on further correspondence, but according to Grenville himself 'the mode of intercourse' was definitely stopped.[7] Pitt himself in any case had warned Miles in distinctly chilly terms, before the latter brought Maret's letter, that it would be 'impossible to have any Communication with You respecting its Contents'.[8] Such caveats may be minor; the real question turns on Miles's judgment. For if he was right – if the French were in fact prepared to meet the substance of the British case, and if Pitt was stopped by others against his inclination from following up the approach – the Cabinet's reaction on 13 January could indeed have been a decisive event.

One can only offer ones own opinion. I would agree with that given elsewhere, that Miles was disposed to grasp at a straw, and was too much

1. See directly above.
2. This text is given in Evans, loc. cit., 204, as taken from Miles's papers. Referring to 13 January 1793, it dates retrospectively from 1 March 1804. A similar but not identical text is published in *Correspondence*, 42 under the date 13 January; but Dr Evans has kindly sent me evidence to show that it is the less reliable of the two.
3. To Long, 15 December 1792 (P.R.O. 30/8/159).
4. 13 January 1793 (*Correspondence*, II, 40).
5. P. 246, n7 above.
6. Miles stated that he gave it to Pitt – who then gave it to Long (Joseph Smith [Pitt's secretary] to Miles, 14 January 1793; *Correspondence*, II, 44) – and that it was never returned.
7. Minute by Miles, 14 January (loc. cit., 43); Grenville to Auckland, 15 January 1793 (*H.M.C., Dropmore*, II, 366). The Minute itself, however, seems to have come from Miles's retrospective compilation of notes in March 1804 (information from Dr Evans).
8. 13 January 1793 (copy in P.R.O. 30/8/102).

impressed by Pitt's 'good humour'.[1] Like many intelligent ambitious men who attain and remain on the fringe of affairs,[2] he was easily led to magnify his contribution; like many who have lived in the twilight world of confidential commissions, where the private and the public, the official and the clandestine meet, he attached inordinate significance to 'secret history'. He had lived by his wits, and this time they had brought him closer to the centre than he had been before. Genuinely committed to hopes of peace, he was bound to view from a particular angle the result of his contacts with men who were anxious to keep in touch with Pitt. Miles saw a part of the game; but there was more that he could not see, and it was not surprising if some of the Cabinet may have suspected he was being used. For Ministers were faced by the discrepancies between one statement and another: whom were they to take most seriously, Lebrun in public, or Lebrun to Chauvelin, or Lebrun and/or Maret to Miles? And what precisely did these last letters mean – for shades of meaning were all-important? Was not Miles seeing in ambivalent phrases all that he wanted to see? To a sceptical eye, they could be taken rather as an exercise in procrastination; looked at closely, there was nothing specific on which to seize. It did not need Burke to cast doubts on Maret's carefully worded paragraphs. Against a highly confused background, the Cabinet could do that for itself.

Nor would it take long for Pitt to agree, if indeed he had been captured by Miles's enthusiasm. It is possible, to give Miles the benefit of the doubt, that he was. He had been on the brink of war before, with France, with Spain, with Russia, and on two of those three occasions the opponent had yielded at the last minute. Was there now a sign that this might happen again? If so, it would be a triumphant relief. But when the evidence was examined it seemed much too indistinct. It could even be taken in parts to point the other way: Grenville certainly thought so, though he acknowledged that the 'tone' was 'greatly lowered'; and a further letter to Miles from Paris written on the day of the meetings – from his friend Mourgue, who was in touch with Lebrun – could soon have reinforced that view.[3] Pitt's anger may have been sparked by appearing to have been led briefly up a garden path. The Ministry returned no immediate answer, and the outlook remained dark.

But still neither side was prepared to take a decisive step. In Paris, as in Dumouriez's headquarters, opinions and pressures swung to and fro, with a harassed and weakened Executive Council anxious on the whole to wait and see. Ministers in London for their part were also uncertain. They could see no real way out, and by 20 January Pitt was said to view

1. Cf. Evans, loc. cit., 205; Murley, loc. cit., 431–7.

2. See I, 531n2, 541n3, 566–7, 606.

3. Grenville to Auckland, no, 6, 13 January 1793 (F.O. 37/43); same to same, Private, sd (B.L. Add. Ms 34447). Mourgue's letter, which did not reject the British demands directly, but warned that the French would not 'consent to abandon Belgium, or any of our conquests', is cited in Evans, loc. cit., 208.

war as 'inevitable, and . . . the sooner it was begun the better'.[1] The
Government had decided by then on its answer to the French
statements. Disregarding the choice, or the ambiguities, offered by the
private letters, it fastened on the threat in the instructions to Chauvelin,
and rejected it out of hand. Brief and icily hostile, this Note of the 18th
held out no hope: indeed it was clearly intended to be taken or left as the
French might choose.[2] Pitt himself saw some advantage in bringing
matters now to a head; he was apparently impressed by the prospect,
currently raised, of an easy seizure of the French West Indies, and public
opinion 'was disposed for war, which might not be the case six weeks
hence'.[3] At the same time there were very real merits in waiting for
France to make the fatal move: our own case had been published, and
our ally Holland was not yet fully committed to a resolute response.
Dutch Patriots still looked to France, there were other voices favouring
concessions, and above all the physical defences were not yet complete.
The British Government had been urging Auckland for some time to
press for greater urgency; it now told him that a few more weeks' grace
would not come amiss.[4] Nor were our relations with other Powers clear
or satisfactory, for the proposal of a mediation had been singularly
unsuccessful. The Austrians and the Prussians avoided making a reply in
Vienna and Berlin; and when they did so in London, by a joint
statement through their envoys on 12 January, it stipulated a return of
the French monarchy and dwelt on the nature of 'indemnifications' –
the Bavarian Exchange for Austria, acquisitions for Prussia farther east.[5]
The answer in fact had less to do with France than with the imminent
partition of Poland; Prussian troops began to cross the border on the
14th. And the Russians for their part – whose approach had led to the
British proposal – were soon to underline the fact that they had
something quite different in mind. After some delay they let it be known
that they did not intend to negotiate with a régime they refused to
recognise. They wanted England to declare war – an object, it was
suspected in London, designed on familiar lines to give them a free hand
in central Europe. By mid-January only the Spaniards had answered

1. This was Loughborough's account, after seeing Pitt with a view to accepting the
Lord Chancellorship (*Malmesbury*, II, 501; and see p. 229 above). Murley has suggested
(loc. cit., 450n3) that the Minister may have talked as he did – and expressing confidence
in the outcome – as an extra inducement to Loughborough to join.
2. See *P.R.*, XXXIV, 366–8.
3. *Malmesbury*, loc. cit., 501–2. See p. 246, n8 above for the talks on Guadeloupe and
Martinique.
4. F.O. 37/42–3, B.L. Add. Mss 34446–7, *passim*. Even on 5 February Grenville was
writing that 'a week or two' might help the Dutch; 'But for God's sake let them avail
themselves of it to the utmost' (to Auckland, Private; B.L. Add. Ms. 34447).
5. See pp. 239–40 above. Grenville's Minute of 12 January 1793 (F.O. 64/27);
Morton Eden to Grenville, no. 2, 5 January 1793 (loc. cit.); Straton to same, nos, 2, 3, 7
of 5, 8, 20 January 1793 (F.O. 7/32).

amiably if vaguely.[1] If war came at once there was therefore the prospect of an alliance in which the other partners' aims would be far removed from our own.[2]

But a fresh development brought war even closer. On 23 January the reports reached London of the execution of Louis XVI. They were greeted with horror, but not with much surprise by the Government: George III and Pitt prepared the day before for a Privy Council 'whenever the news came'.[3] The meeting was held on the 24th, and Chauvelin was ordered to leave by 1 February. In the event he started without waiting on the 25th. 'The business', wrote Grenville, 'is now brought to its crisis, and I imagine that the next dispatch . . ., or the next but one, will announce the commencement of hostilities'. 'Probably' the French would start them. But 'a great force' was now ready here, and once 'all hope of satisfactory explanation' had died the British Government might cut the knot.[4] Either an assault on Holland or a rejection of the latest British Note[5] could settle the matter. But in the event there was one last unexpected twist.

For on 24 and 26 January two emissaries left Paris, one for The Hague and the other for London. The first was de Maulde, now restored to a wavering favour;[6] the second was Maret – accompanied by Mourgue – heading for Pitt once more. Maret carried alternative letters, to be used according to circumstance: one naming him as chargé d'affaires in place of Chauvelin, who on the 22nd – before his expulsion – was sent news of the mission and officially recalled; the other empowering him to dispose of the Embassy's records if the mission failed. For the second time, and now finally, the unfortunate man was out of step with events. He had not heard of Chauvelin's dismissal when he left Paris, he did not know that Chauvelin had in turn left London without hearing of his coming, and when he caught up with the situation, at Dover on the 29th, he wrote to Lebrun asking for fresh advice. Arriving in London on the 30th, he saw Miles – and, briefly, Lansdowne – at once. But Miles had been warned by Pitt not to 'make himself' a go-between; and Maret, uncertain of his own credentials and denied access through his old intermediary, remained at a loss over the next few days. He informed the Foreign Office that he was charged with responsibility for the Embassy's papers;

1. Whitworth to Grenville. nos. 4, 8 of 11, 27 January 1793 (F.O. 65/24); Jackson to Grenville, no. 1 and enclosure, 1 January 1793, endorsed as received 14th (F.O. 72/26).

2. The prospect of the alliance was recognised at the turn of the year, when Sir James Murray (see p. 204, n3 above) was again sent to the Prussian headquarters (Grenville to Eden, no. 1, 4 January 1793; F.O. 64/27).

3. Pitt to Grenville, 23 January 1793 (*H.M.C., Dropmore*, II, 372).

4. Grenville to Auckland, 24 January 1793 (loc. cit., 372–3). Cf. Mourgue's statement of the 13th (p. 252, n3 above).

5. See p. 253 above.

6. See p. 245 above.

having done that, he seems to have stayed in the Embassy, seeing Miles but no one else. On 4 February, by which time he had still not received instructions, he was ordered to leave England at once.[1]

The offer that was said to have been brought was retailed to Pitt by Miles on 6 February, when Maret had gone and 'the ban of the Empire'[2] no longer applied.

> He informed me that France would give up Nice, Mayence, Worms, & all its conquests on the Rhine. That it would renounce Liège, the Low Countries (provided Great Britain would guaranty their independence), the Scheldt, & contrive the means of detaching Savoy from France.

Every territorial surrender in fact that Britain could demand, and that Miles had counted on earlier in January. And, perhaps above all,

> . . . should you listen to this offer, he had instructions to propose M. Dumouriez to finally negotiate and arrange with you, & that on being assured of the protection of the laws, he would come over, and when you had settled matters he would be invested with authority to sign and exchange and that the National Convention would ratify whatever he agreed to.[3]

Not unnaturally, Miles lamented what he saw as lost opportunities: first in mid-January, and again now.[4] In point of fact, the Government had known of the prospect of talks with Dumouriez before Maret was sent home, if not before he arrived. George Rose had heard something as early as 22 January, and Talleyrand sent news – 'je sais positivement' – from his Surrey retreat on the 28th.[5] Confirmation from a firmer source arrived on 2 February, contained in despatches from Auckland which had been delayed for some days by Channel storms. The Foreign Office

1. For this mission, the significance of which has been disputed, see Murley, loc. cit., 469–79 and Evans, loc. cit., 205–7, which are to be preferred to Holland Rose, II, 109–12. Chauvelin did in fact receive Lebrun's despatch of the 22nd after he left London, on his way to the coast; but, rattled and resentful, he failed to send the news of Maret's coming to the British Government, and moreover passed Maret himself at night on the road from Calais without informing him of that fact. Pitt's warning was conveyed to Miles on 28 January by Charles Long (*Correspondence of Miles*, II, 52), probably after being informed about the mission (see n5 below).
2. Miles to Aust, 4 February 1793 (*Correspondence*, II, 57).
3. P.R.O. 30/8/159. Cf. the text in *Correspondence*, II, 62–3.
4. Minute of 4 February 1793; Miles to Aust, 5 February 1793 (loc. cit., 59–60).
5. Rose to Auckland, 22 January 1793 (B.L. Add. Ms 34447); Talleyrand to Grenville, 28 January 1793 (*H.M.C., Dropmore*, II, 374–5). He included news of Maret's forthcoming arrival for good measure. An acquaintance of Auckland's, Bartholomew Huber, reported similarly on the 29th (to Grenville; P.R.O., F.O. 27/41).

at first was sceptical.[1] But when further reports were received a day later the Cabinet met and instructions were sent. On 27 January de Maulde had handed the Ambassador a letter from Dumouriez proposing a meeting on the Netherlands' border. He had also – typically and confusingly[2] – opened a negotiation himself, telling Auckland that Dumouriez intended to seek 'a plan for restoring peace' at the head of his army, and wished to make contact personally with the British in advance. Auckland, though cautious, was stirred by this approach – his stream of despatches was voluminous even for him.[3] He thought that the General might be in earnest, he trusted himself not to be hoodwinked, and delay at the least could do no harm, particularly since the Dutch Government was now belatedly calling for time.[4] A little bribery might help – every one had the lowest opinion of de Maulde. All in all it would be well worth seeing what Dumouriez had to say.

The Cabinet agreed. Dumouriez was a bigger fish than Maret, and contact through a senior Ambassador distinctly preferable to reliance on 'other channels' such as Miles. Auckland was told on 4 February to listen to any proposals. He was to enter into no engagements, and to make it clear that there must be 'an express disavowal of the offensive decrees, and a sufficient security for a disposition to conclude peace with Austria, Prussia, and Sardinia on such terms as those Powers may reasonably expect'. These would clearly include 'The abandonment of all conquests made by France, and of all means tending to disturb the tranquillity of other Countries'. A general pacification indeed was necessary to remove the dangers raised by the separate issues. France must take no more provocative action; and this now included any intention of sending a naval force to the West Indies while there was still peace with ourselves.[5] The terms of mediation of December were revived and extended, and the Prussians informed.[6] But by the time the despatch left London it was in fact out of date. It must always remain doubtful how far either Maret or Dumouriez could have delivered the goods – assuming that Miles reported Maret correctly and that Dumouriez was ready to concede. Quite possibly he was, for he was now worried and dissatisfied: uncertain of military success, and shocked by the King's death.[7] He knew moreover that there were men in office and others in

---

1. Auckland to Grenville, nos. 17–20 and private letters, 28–29 January 1793, and endorsements (F.O. 37/43–4); Grenville to Auckland, 3 February 1793 (*H.M.C., Dropmore*, II, 377); Burges to same, 2 February 1793 (*A.C.*, II, 492–4).

2. See pp. 209–10 above.

3. F.O. 37/43–4, 28 January–5 February *passim*. For his epistolary habits see Ehrman, *The British Government and Commercial Negotiations with Europe*, 36–7.

4. P. 253 above.

5. Grenville to Auckland no. 17, 4 February 1793 (F.O. 37/44). The King of Sardinia was sovereign in Savoy (p. 204 above).

6. Grenville to Eden, no. 5, 5 February 1793 (F.O. 64/27); same to Murray, no. 3, 6 February 1793 (F.O. 29/1).

7. Cf. pp. 252, 254 above.

the Convention who were dismayed by the thought of war with England and anxious to extract themselves.[1] But whether they were strong enough to enforce instructions or – as Dumouriez claimed later – were reduced to passing them in secret, the question is irrelevant in the last resort. For there is no sign from other documents that the French Government would have backed such concessions, if Maret indeed had proper authority to speak as he was said to have done. Nor is it easy to suppose that the terms could have been carried through the various committees and the Convention itself. The evidence indeed suggests otherwise. The moderates, as they had become, were being elbowed off the stage. The King had been executed, the political scene was confused, excited and unforeseeable, the Mountain was advancing, Marat was in fully cry. And then on 29 January Chauvelin arrived in Paris, with the news of his expulsion by the British Government. It roused a public storm. The commercial treaty was rescinded at once, an embargo was laid on British and Dutch shipping, and it was provisionally agreed on the same day that Dumouriez should be ordered to invade Holland. These decisions were taken therefore before Maret reached London or Auckland's despatches were received.[2] On the 31st the Executive Council decreed that the Dutch Republic should be attacked, and the Dutch Patriots were ordered to stir up insurrection. On 1 February the Convention voted to declare war on Holland and Britain, and – as the fraternal decree then dictated – appealed to the British people to rise.

The news reached London on the morning of the 7th, and was accepted by the Foreign Office on the 8th. It was received almost quietly after the tension of recent weeks. The Government had already imposed an embargo on French shipping in return for the French measure. It now took 'the necessary steps' to enter on hostilities. The formalities were not hurried. The House of Commons was engaged that week on hearing election petitions – or rather it was meant to be, for quorums were proving hard to find. The King's Message announcing war was presented on 11 February, and on the 12th Pitt moved an Address in reply. According to tradition – and a newspaper story which caused some hilarity – he was the worse for wear after a drinking bout with Dundas. None the less he seems to have made a lengthy speech, bringing the Government's case up to date and examining the French claims. It was a methodical narrative, which in fact may have 'wearied the patience of the House', for so much of the story had been told before. But it summed up the British case, and it met the mood. The final sentence, before he sat down, looked to the future.

---

1. See for instance the evidence of the writer and lecturer David Williams, who visited Paris in December and was pressed to undertake a peace mission to London at the end of January (David Williams, 'The Missions of David Williams and James Tilly Matthews to England (1793)', in *E.H.R.*, LIII, no. CCXII).
2. Pp. 254, 256 above.

It now remains to be seen [Pitt concluded] whether, under Providence, the efforts of a free, brave, loyal, and happy people, aided by their allies, will not be successful in checking the progress of a system, the principles of which, if not opposed, threaten the most fatal consequences to the tranquility of this country, the security of its allies, the good order of every European Government, and the happiness of the whole of the human race![1]

1. *P.R.*, XXXIV, 459, which is followed by *P.H.*, XXX, cols. 345–61. *The Senator*, VI (nd), 304–17, gives a briefer account. The text of the King's message is given in all three publications under the proceedings of the 11th. For the question of Pitt's state on the 12th see I, 585.

The House had had to adjourn on every day from the 5th to the 9th because not enough Members were present to ballot on the petitions (see *H.C.J.*, 48, (1803) 136–7).

Part Three

CHAPTER VIII

The First Campaign

I

On 8 February 1793 Pitt received a 'Plan for Internal Defence' from the Duke of Richmond, the Cabinet's military member for the past nine years. He sat down to make a précis, and add some notes to his own.[1] As so often when enemy landings have had to be considered, the most likely region was taken to be Hampshire and, more strongly, Sussex and southern Kent. Naval squadrons were accordingly proposed for Weymouth, Dungeness and the Downs, with light vessels in the small harbours east of Selsey Bill. Regular troops should be concentrated to reinforce local resistance by 'Sudden Levies'; and provision was made for 'Driving the Country' – the removal of horses and transport from the danger areas. The paper formed the outline of a comprehensive scheme which was to be elaborated in the next few years. Appearing on the day after news of the French declaration reached London, it represented the first duty of a Government at war.

The shape of that war itself had almost certainly not been considered. Neither Pitt nor any one else appears to have given the matter close thought. In broad terms, this was not as surprising as it might seem to us, steeped in the concept of planning in an age of sophisticated conflict and threats. The series of eighteenth-century wars in which Britain had built European alliances bequeathed lines of strategic preference, but no tradition of preparatory detail. On the basis of a fleet in being – with all that implied for national attitudes, to administration as well as to strategy – resources were mustered as occasion arose. And on this occasion, even if Ministers had spared much thought from their immediate labours, almost every strategic factor was obscure. There had

---

1. P.R.O. 30/8/245; paper in Pitt's hand, endorsed by him 'D of R. Plan for Internal Defence Feb 8th 1793'. I have failed to find Richmond's original in any collection.

The Duke was Master General of the Ordnance, an office recognised as carrying military advice though not necessarily within the Cabinet. But he himself had been included in January 1784, as he had been in two earlier Ministries (I, 94, 139), and continued since in the absence of a Commander-in-Chief; and while the veteran Lord Amherst was appointed late in January to the post of Commander-in-Chief – vacant since the end of the American War – Richmond remained a colleague professionally involved in such arrangements, and the one with the greatest knowledge of them at this time.

been no real contact until very recently with any of the states at odds with France; only one of them, Prussia, was already an ally in potentially relevant circumstances; and we could not tell what to expect from other possible partners. We had no understandings with Austria or Sardinia, with Russia or with Spain. Nor did we know any details of the Prussian or Austrian military plans.[1]

The only reference to the European theatre, if war should come about, seems indeed to have been to the old favourite of coastal raids on France. In December 1792, when Grenville replied to the Russians' overture,[2] he mentioned such landings as a possibility. As was soon to be shown, this was a persistent theme, not least with Pitt himself, and it had a long and respectable history. But it was mentioned then merely in passing, and no study was made. Specific pre-war orders in fact were confined to another traditional sphere: to the equally favoured theatre of the West Indies.

Even so, these were an extension of earlier defensive measures, themselves dating back to the rising of negroes and mulattoes in French and Spanish Haiti – St Domingue and San Domingo – in 1791.[3] There had been concern ever since for the safety of the British islands: arms were supplied on request to the whites in St Domingue from nearby Jamaica, and that colony was itself later reinforced. So were the Windward Islands, as Ministers reversed the earlier policy of reducing the local forces which Pitt, as Chancellor, had pursued.[4] At the outbreak of war there were just under 6,000 British troops in the Caribbean, with a small replenishment promised; and it was on that basis that the Government accepted pleas for offensive operations. The largest would be against St Domingue, which seemed likely to welcome it; for in 1791 and again late in 1792 the French planters in the island had offered allegiance to the British Crown in return for military aid.[5] When war began to seem probable, they were given a friendly hearing. Grenville agreed that in such an event 'our attention would naturally . . . be turned to the West Indies'; St Domingue could not survive in independence, and he would then consider means to take it 'under the sovereignty and protection of England'. French supplicants from Martinique and Guadaloupe were meanwhile approaching Hawkes-bury;[6] and while the Ministry would not approve action unless or until war was declared, it instructed the command in Jamaica to prepare for

---

1. See pp. 253–4 above.

2. Pp. 239–40 above.

3. See I, 399–400.

4. Eg P.R.O. 30/58/8, 30/8/193 (letters from Sir George Yonge, at the War Office), 348, 352; Dundas to Pitt, 15 and 18 October 1792 (P.R.O. 30/8/157).

5. Pitt's copy of the Manifesto of 1791, from the island's Assembly, is in P.R.O. 30/8/149.

6. Grenville's Note on meeting with M. Malouet, 1 January 1793 (P.R.O., W.O. 1/58); for Hawkesbury see B.L. Add. Mss 38351–2, and Pitt to Hawkesbury, 17 December [1792], in B.L. Add. Ms 38192.

St Domingue, and in February sanctioned attacks on the French Windward Islands and Tobago.[1]

In so far as a pattern existed it was thus familiar. But the Caribbean offensive was limited to local resources, and after making due allowance for the general European uncertainties the lack of reference to the continent in pre-war months might still seem strange. For there was one clear British obligation: the protection of Holland, and that being so one might have expected discussions on possible military aid. As it was, talks were confined to the sending of a small naval squadron, and if anything else was considered in London it would appear to have been dismissed.[2] This was due in part to continued hopes that the worst would not happen. It also reflected, once more, a customary approach. For the commitment of troops to the mainland was never lightly sanctioned or, on past precedent, approved in advance of war. Historically, it meant prior agreement with allies on intentions and costs; but in January the Dutch were calling for an earnest of British support with no apparent sign that they meant to help themselves, and nothing was known of Prussia's plans as a member of the Triple Alliance.[3] It was not very hard, given recent experiences and the obvious pressures, to fit out the fleet; there was no difficulty in principle in reinforcing the colonies. Operations in Europe, whatever the limits, were another matter, normally the subject of negotiation and treated with care.

But in the event the Government's hand was forced. In fact it had to move within a fortnight of the outbreak of war. As late as 14 February there were still some hopes of Dumouriez: of some form of understanding with him, or at least that he would act with restraint.[4] At the same time, however, the position in Holland was slipping fast: the declaration of war caused a panic, and confusion grew at The Hague. Auckland asked urgently for a General from England, who would advise and rally the Dutch and be followed if possible by some British troops. He had scarcely written when Dumouriez suddenly attacked. Advancing from Antwerp on the 16th, his troops were soon moving through western Holland, received with rapture by the Dutch Patriots and meeting no real resistance. The extent of the crisis was not fully understood in London at once: on the 19th Ministers were still prepared only to lend financial assistance. But on the 20th they reluctantly decided to send a Guards' contingent of some 1,500 men.[5]

The reluctance was extreme. 'Although the determination had been

1. These approaches from the islands were clearly a factor in the insistence, in what proved to be the last British terms for continued peace, that no French naval force be sent to the West Indies (see p. 256 above).

2. Pp. 208–9 above.

3. For the Dutch see p. 253 above.

4. See pp. 255–7 above; Grenville to Auckland, no. 25, 13 February 1793 (P.R.O., F.O. 37/44); Auckland to Grenville, 12 and 14 February 1793 (*H.M.C., Dropmore*, II, 378–9).

5. Auckland to Grenville, 15 and 20 February (loc. cit., 379–80; no. 36, F.O. 37/44); Grenville to Auckland, no. 26, 19 February, no. 27, 20 February 1793 (F.O. 37/44).

taken to resist all applications for sending troops to Holland from this Country in the present moment, yet the circumstances . . . have appeared so urgent' that they had had to change their minds. But the support was to be temporary, confined to the crisis; and this must be explained in 'distinct and unequivocal terms'.[1] The orders to the commanders were explicit. They were to co-operate with the Dutch, but not to move without further instructions more than twenty four hours' march from Helvoetsluys, where the force had landed and from which it could be re-embarked.[2]

The Ministry may have felt both the more annoyed and the more obliged to send British troops because it was already helping to provide others in more familiar form. At the turn of the year arrangements had been made to finance a corps of Hanoverians which George III ordered into Holland as Elector and a member of the Germanic Diet.[3] But this force was not ready when the crisis arose, so that more immediate help was needed. On the other hand its commander was available to help the Dutch. He was in fact the Duke of York, George III's favourite son and a trained soldier, who was appointed to 'these foreign troops' before England was at war.[4] It was indeed for York that Auckland called in his plea for a General from England, and when the British troops were sent the Duke was placed in command of them as well. So the choice was made which was to have an unforeseen significance, in Ministers' relations with the King and the conduct of the war itself.

For with the despatch of its Guards battalions the Government became involved in operations from which it found it could not disengage. The crisis in Holland proved indeed to be temporary; the commitment to the Low Countries did not, and the fact was crucial for British policies over the next two years.

The immediate operations might seem in themselves to have opened the way to the force's return. In the course of March the Austrian army in Flanders won a series of battles – Aldenhoven, Neerwinden, Louvain – which cleared the province and left the invaders of Holland exposed. They retreated to Antwerp. By then Prussian troops were on Dutch soil,

1. Grenville to Auckland, no. 27, 20 February 1793 (loç. cit.). See also Pitt to Auckland, 2 March 1793 (B.L. Add. Ms 46519).

2. Grenville to Auckland, no. 27 (n1 above); instructions for Duke of York and for Major General Gerard Lake, 23 February 1793 (P.R.O., W.O. 6/10; fair copies of final drafts, W.O. 6/7, 6/9).

Pitt was also anxious to remove the naval force, sent before the war, as soon as possible for general services, possibly leaving some seamen to be drafted into Dutch ships (to Auckland, 2 March 1793; B.L. Add. Ms 46519).

3. The body representing the German states and nominally owing allegiance to the Holy Roman Emperor (the Emperor of Austria), which could raise forces to protect a threat to territorial integrity.

4. Duke of York to George III, 19 January 1793 (*L.C.G. III*, I, no. 826).

and the Hanoverians were approaching from the east. Holland therefore looked safe, and the Austrian Netherlands had been recovered. The British, on that basis, might leave the fight to their allies.

But on the contrary they were soon sending reinforcements, and planning their own operation within the main campaign. On 19 March the earlier restriction on movement was lifted, and leave given to advance in the Low Countries in co-operation with other forces. This was still a limited concession, designed to harass the French retreat;[1] but in the next few weeks it was followed by a fresh, and different, step. The reasons now lay beyond the battle front, in the area of the national interest itself. Their military expression arose from the fortuitous presence of British troops.

The first and perhaps most compelling cause stemmed from the revival of an old fear. In January, when the Austrians had replied with Prussia to the suggested British terms for a general peace, they had repeated their familiar wish to exchange the Austrian Netherlands for Bavaria. Such a development had never been favoured in London, and despite some brief wavering – for in order to effect the exchange, it was appreciated that the Netherlands must be recovered – it was not favoured now.[2] Austrian sovereignty over the area had long been a principle of British policy, and the question therefore was what inducements were needed to maintain the *status quo*. This indeed was to become a leading feature of British diplomacy and strategy. When combined with the circumstances of the moment, it suggested a particular response.

The idea took shape in April. At the beginning of that month Pitt was still looking to the return of the troops, if not immediately at least fairly soon.[3] But meanwhile he was prepared to increase them to carry out 'a particular service': an operation which in his view could be supported on several grounds. This was for the capture of Dunkirk, now coming within striking distance. The arguments were complementary, forming an attractive case. Dunkirk was a seaward element in the chain of fortresses which formed the barrier, on both sides of the frontier, between Flanders and France. If the Austrian Netherlands were to remain Austrian their defences should be strengthened, and an expansion of the province to include French strongpoints would be an inducement to drop the Exchange. The port moreover was an ideal base, as George III pointed out, for the passage of siege materials against the fortresses which the Austrians would need.[4] Its possession would

---

1. Dundas to Sir James Murray [see p. 254, n2 above], 19 March 1793 (P.R.O., W.O. 6/7). See also Pitt to ? Loughborough, 2 March 1793 (P.R.O. 30/8/153).

2. For past history see I, 473, p. 198 above; for Grenville's reactions from mid-January to early February, M. Duffy, 'British War Policy: the Austrian Alliance, 1793–1801' (Oxford D. Phil. thesis, 1971; hereafter referred to as Duffy, 'War Policy'), 17.

3. To Grenville, 30 March, 1 April 1793 (*H.M.C., Dropmore*, II, 388–9).

4. To Grenville, 29 March 1793 (loc. cit., 387).

strike a blow at the French privateers – a wartime preoccupation since the sixteenth century. And this last argument could be used, better perhaps than any alternative, to allay the public suspicion of mainland operations.

The exchanges that followed disclosed different Ministerial points of view. Indeed the plan for Dunkirk produced the first indications of how Pitt and some of his leading colleagues saw the shape of the war. Pitt himself was hopeful, as he usually was,[1] and the extent of his optimism was soon revealed. The decision was opposed from the start by Richmond, who sent him letters early in April[2] which led to a long conversation between the two men. It was one of considerable interest, for Pitt argued along lines that were to become familiar over the next few years; and the discussion epitomised, at this early point, many of the features and the basic problems of strategic thought. Pitt accepted (unlike Richmond) the immediate commitment to reinforce in Flanders, though he did not like the expense of taking up the necessary transports. But this should not interfere with other prospects.[3]

He then briefly run over the returns [from recruiting] & his Expectations which in general amounted to the raising this summer towards 20,000 Men Infantry and Cavalry, which with what we had before might enable us . . . within the year to sent [*sic*] 10,000 Men to the D. of York & to have 15,000 Men for Expeditions & other Services. These He seem'd to consider as possible in the following order. To have a Corps of about 10,000 British to act in June July or August upon the Coast of France, to send the same Force with some reinforcements it might get from Gibraltar to the Mediterranean in August or September, & to detach again from it in october a sufficient corps to the West Indies for great operations there.

For the first purpose it might be possible to help by drawing on Hanoverians and Hessians, and 'it was by no means unlikely' that the Russians – with whom we were in continuing communications[4] – would provide a force. If they did, a combined attack might be made by sea on Brest; otherwise Havre might be the best of several choices. The Mediterranean might be served if a combined army could be gained, of hired Swiss together with Austrian, Sardinian (i.e. northern Italian) and Spanish troops; this, with 'an English Force supported by an

---

1. Cf. I, 109, 322, 588–9.
2. On the 3rd and the 5th: see J. Holland Rose, 'The Duke of Richmond on the Conduct of the War in 1793', in *E.H.R.*, XXV, no. XCIX, 554–5. The originals are in Stanhope Ms S5 03/14 (Kent C.A.O.).
3. 'Minutes of Conversation with Mr Pitt Wednesday 10 April 1793' (P.R.O., W.O. 30/81). The long paper (of some 16 pages) would seem probably to have been written a few days later. It is not signed, but is in Richmond's hand throughout.
4. See p. 262 above.

English & Spanish Fleet . . . might attack Toulon or Marseilles', before the English detachment left for the Caribbean in October, 'which was the proper season for that Service.'[1] One might also, he speculated later, manage an attack on Mauritius, the French island in the Indian Ocean which could threaten our lines to the East.

Such ideas clearly depended on diplomatic action and the provision of enough British troops. Pitt kept himself informed of estimates as to ways and means. But there were two factors which he did not appreciate. Unlike the returns from a buoyant revenue or a strictly administrative reform, or even the preparation of a naval force from improved dockyards and a pool of men, the basic material in this instance – the size and quality of the land forces – was not inherently favourable, and could not be stretched too far. Even if the numbers could be met – and Pitt was not grossly unrealistic here – the questions had to be asked whether they could be maintained despite wastage and how good the troops might be. And equally it was essential to allow for administrative shortcomings in a series of distinct but administratively connected operations. Pitt has been regularly accused, as a wartime Minister, of a deep lack of strategic grasp. The contemporary arguments will emerge from the pattern of demands and events. But one thing can be said at the start: strategy relies on its materials, and in this first disclosure of his thinking he showed his ignorance of what that could involve.

So it struck Richmond, who had been a commander as well as head of a military Department. His comments might stand as a classic example of the professional response.[2]

> To all this I stated to Mr Pitt that I thought He was going on much too fast in His Calculations. That men just raised upon paper were not soldiers . . . that I thought it required at least six months . . . assembled in Corps either in Camp or in quarters to make them at all fit for Service & that even then they would be but very young & raw Soldiers.

Britain moreover was not like Austria or Russia, with a large reserve of men 'having little Else to do than to come forth for War when wanted'. We could not raise large land forces at the expense of agriculture and trade: 'We ought' therefore 'very much to aconomise [*sic*] our Men for we have no second army to produce if we waste the first'.

Richmond then turned to the timing of operations.

> I particularly represented to Mr Pitt that very proper [as] His schemes & Ideas were they were much too vast to be executed within

1. A postponement from the pre-war calculation (pp. 262–3 above).
2. W.O. 30/81. Richmond had taken part in some of the operations against the French coasts in the Seven Years War, as well as commanding troops successfully at Minden, and had emerged from that war as a Major General.

any Thing like the Time He talked of. that . . . by undertaking too much He would do nothing well. That great & long Preparations were necessary for all Military Services, and that He could not too soon fix upon the precise Plan He meant to pursue, determine His force . . . appoint His Commander & fix the time for His operations.

Admirable advice, if hard to act on, particularly in eighteenth-century conditions. It struck no spark: Pitt 'contended strongly that the Service in Flanders would not interfere with any of His other Plans & talked eagerly about them as what He really had in view'.[1] The exchange ended not untypically of colleagues when the matter does not press. 'I told him that He would find himself mistaken & He said I should find He was not, & so we parted in great good Humour'.

The good humour did not last, as Richmond himself was to make clear. His own strategy, unlike Pitt's, concentrated on one object; although it was one included in the Minister's plans. There were not enough troops to 'fritter away . . . aiming at Conquests in french Flanders and the West Indies, in the Mauritius and the Mediterranean and in Britanny [*sic*]'. They should be thrown into the area in which they could do most good; and that, by the early summer, was in north-west France.[2] It was in this region, which in 1793 was alive with discontent, that we 'might be able at once to terminate this War'; for Richmond was much impressed by information reaching London of a movement which might deliver the port of St Malo to a British force. If that could be achieved, and a garrison installed, we could ensure supplies and finance which would enable French royalist forces to combine. The alternative was an 'endless war against fortified Towns' in Flanders, which, indeterminate as it probably would be, would not serve our best interests.[3]

The concentration on western France, as the spearhead for support of the French royalists, was to develop into one of the strategic themes of the next few years. Its rejection now was explained by Dundas, to whom Richmond expressed these views and who as Secretary of State was responsible with him for directions on military affairs.[4] Objections could be raised both to the operation itself and to its implications. Was an expedition, in the first place, as simple and self-contained as the Duke

---

1. And cf. pp. 263–4 above.
2. By this term, as used henceforth, I mean the area lying broadly west of Paris and north of the Loire; between 47° and 50°N, and 5°W and 2°E.
3. To Dundas, 1 July 1793 (B.L. Loan Ms 57 (Bathurst), vol. 107). This was in some degree a retrospective argument. But from internal evidence it represented Richmond's earlier views, which had been urged in conversation, it would seem in Cabinet. The movement which impressed him was led by a certain Gaston, whose influence was to be overtaken by others.
4. To Richmond, 8 July 1793 (loc. cit.). For the Home Secretary's position in relation to the armed forces see I, 82, 309–10, 312, 570.

assumed? It would need a protective fleet, and depend on this group of royalists living up to its promise – a hazardous prospect, since so little was known. And then might not the British force become unavoidably involved in prolonged commitments, such as Richmond himself opposed when talking of the Flanders front? In any case, objects of war could not be reduced to 'one precise point'. They were 'intermixed together, and render the Question a complicated one'. To throw the available British forces into Brittany would be to accept the principle that our main aim was to restore 'good order' in France – and to rely on one source for that object. But this was not so, necessary as such an end might be for future peace. We had gone to war to preserve the safety of Holland – there had never been 'any difference' on that – and 'it has been assumed . . . as a Corollary . . . that We must, if possible, retain the Netherlands in the House of Austria, as the only secure Barrier to the United Provinces against the Power and Ambition of France'.[1] These 'have ever been held uncontrovertible Maxims of British Policy'. The operations in Flanders *were* therefore serving a major British interest, and moreover they pinned down a French force far greater than any garrison in St Malo could do. Nor was Flanders, though of prime significance, the sole interest for this country. There were objects in the West and East Indies as important as those on the French coast.

> Success in those quarters I consider of infinite Moment, both in the view of humbling the power of France, and . . . of enlarging our National Wealth and Security. If we were called upon to decide whether the operations now going forward on the Continent or those other objects . . . were to be totally abandoned, I should feel the Alternative a very disagreeable one. But I trust we have no such alternative before us.

There were resources enough, if 'properly applied'.

Dundas wrote when things seemed to be going well, if rather slowly, on the Flanders front. But he had given his views earlier on much the same lines, and with a further argument to support the use of troops against Dunkirk itself. For if the case held good for operations in Flanders, 'some cogent reason' was none the less needed 'to procure the approbation of the People of this Country to the application of its strength in any other direction' than 'the Operations of [the] Fleet'.[2] As every one knew, there were always 'strong prejudices against Continental Wars' and a 'strong prepossession' in favour of a strictly maritime strategy. The capture of Dunkirk, with its maritime importance, might therefore meet this attitude: a benefit on which Dundas laid

1. By the Netherlands, as the sentence makes clear, Dundas of course meant the Austrian Netherlands, as was normal usage.
2. To Sir James Murray, 16 April 1793 (W.O. 6/7).

some stress. But if he was aiming at traditional sentiments he had an added inducement to do so, and the argument came well, at that particular point. For in the spring of 1793, as events in the field began to shape policy, the old 'prejudices' were inflamed by recent diplomatic events.

II

Since the summer of 1792, when the Russians marched into Poland, feeling in England had been roused against all three of the original partitioning Powers. The Empress was up to her old games, Prussia and Austria had kept quiet, and their inaction in that suspect quarter looked uncommonly like collusion. When the Prussians in turn marched in January, there was a highly vocal storm, with Opposition once more prominently engaged.[1] The prospect of a second Partition was much more unpopular than the first, some twenty years earlier. There was greater sympathy for the Poles after their constitution of 1791, and greater dislike of the predatory states with their unrelenting ambitions. The Government was embarrassed. It made its feelings clear to Prussia,[2] but the invasion occurred at a time of potentially closer contact, and after their confinement to expressions of moral disapproval the year before Ministers were certainly not going to do anything now. While they perforce condemned the action in public as in private – Pitt did so in April – they were anxious to separate events in the east from those in the west.

> . . . Measures of ambition were as odious in a Crowned Head as in a Republican or any other Power. But . . . shall we, because a partition was made of Poland, abate that resistance without which we must fall a prey to the destruction levelled at all Europe . . .?[3]

As the prospect of military co-operation arose for the first time, the attractions of Dunkirk as a specifically British venture increased.

The arguments for the operation centred on Austria – on the need to keep her in the Low Countries – and Austria, it might have seemed, had earned less disapproval. After all, she had not invaded Poland as Prussia had done. Nevertheless she was included in the public attacks, and these were recognised in Vienna as a possible danger to better relations. For developments in the east in point of fact, and somewhat paradoxically,

1. See pp. 198–9, 253 above.
2. P.R.O., F.O. 64/27 *passim*; Grenville to Sir James Murray, 4 January 1793 (F.O. 29/1). See also Grenville to Morton Eden, no. 5, 5 February 1793 (F.O. 64/27), same to Murray, no. 3, 6 February 1793 (F.O. 29/1).
3. Pitt on 25 April (*The Senator*, VII (nd), 686–7; here to be preferred to *P.R.*, XXXV).

were soon driving the Austrians to seek a closer understanding with Britain. By April, when the detail of the Russo-Prussian agreement was known, they had learned the extent of their diplomatic loss. The two Powers had seized more of Poland than expected, and bound themselves to defend it; and the Emperor was offered merely the promise of aid towards a future Bavarian Exchange in return for immediate consent to the Partition. Austria had been isolated, and her main territorial hope in the west placed in doubt. But now that England was a co-belligerent, a new weight might be thrown in the scales.

At this formative stage, therefore, there was an inherent contradiction between the pressures on the British and on the Austrians to concert their plans. But both sides could list enough advantages to make the effort worth-while.[1] We have seen the immediate reason why this was so in England: Austrian policy for its part might benefit even if its immediate aims were not achieved. In the first place there was a real fear of the French Revolution's expansion, which certainly weighed with the new Chancellor, Baron Thugut, who had just replaced a discredited predecessor. The war with France must go on, to nullify her conquests; and this was necessary even in order to check the damage from the new Polish Partition. For if the Austrians abandoned the French war they would risk forfeiting the support of Britain, and be exposed on their own to a Russo-Prussian alliance. On the other hand, if they recognised the Partition they would risk the withdrawal of Prussia from the west, where she was engaged largely in order to secure acceptance of her eastern gains.[2] Thugut hated the Prussians, and he saw greater danger in leaving them free to pursue their ambitions than in keeping them involved in the war. And beyond this immediate object he could envisage a greater prize, an alliance with Britain which would pave the way, through contacts with Russia, to a triple alliance, by which Prussia would be isolated while France was subdued. The great object must be to enlist British sympathy against the Partition and for the Exchange. But if this proved impossible at once, co-operation still had much to offer.

The British too could see benefits beyond the immediate object; and these appeared to grow with the Austrians' success. Their victories in the spring aroused widespread admiration, and encouraged memories of the Old System – the old alliance with Austria, overturned in the 1750s – which doubtless looked the more attractive from experience of Prussia in the past few years. If the French were to be beaten quickly, the Austrians seemed to be the men to do it; and with the restoration of peace the ancient 'natural' partnership, glimpsed briefly in the eighties, might be revived.[3] It was perhaps not purely for tactical reasons that Grenville

1. The following two paragraphs draw largely on Duffy, 'War Policy', 30–8.
2. P. 197 above.
3. Cf. I, 467, 471–5.

now talked in this way.[1] There was much to be said for bringing Anglo-Austrian relations in from the cold.

Starting in April, the two Governments therefore began to talk seriously, through their commanders on the continent and more widely in London and Vienna.[2] At the same time, the British did not view the discussions in isolation; on the contrary, they saw them as part of a comprehensive scheme. At the start of the war, their stated intention was to 'bring down every power on earth to assist them';[3] and if this was so there would be consequences beyond the military sphere alone. An agreement with Austria that was not related at least to agreements with Holland and Prussia must indeed have led to problems in both the short and the longer term. But relations within the Triple Alliance were not yet themselves properly worked out. British efforts centred on this triangle over the next few months, against a background of changing military events.

The hope in London was to form a network of Conventions[4] limited to the conduct of war, whereby the contracting parties in each case would not make peace on their own, and their responsibilities towards operations, supply and wartime trade would be specified. This would leave the detail of post-war indemnities as far as possible to the peace table: the principle was admitted, but its application should be reserved.[5] Such a hope however, not surprisingly, proved to be chimerical; claims were soon being raised and pressed, and even when Conventions were secured they were far from meeting their limited objects as a result.

The Prussians gave the greatest cause for anxiety at the start. Deeply suspicious of the Austrians, as the Austrians were of them, and determined to secure recognition of their Polish gains, they were going slow on the western front, in their own sector on the middle Rhine and farther north on the Austrian flank. Nor were they ready – or perhaps able – to take the British into their confidence on strategy. Despite a professed willingness to do so in February, after Sir James Murray was attached to their headquarters,[6] subsequent reports conveyed an

1. Count Starhemberg [Austrian Minister in London] to Thugut, 24 May 1793 (*Quellen zur Geschichten der deutschen Kaiserspolitick Österreichs während der französischen Revolutionskrieg*, ed. A. von Vivenot and H.R. Zeissberg, III (1882), 79).

2. The British had earlier hoped for a conference of principals in London (see Duffy, loc. cit., 24). But nothing had come of this, and even a visit from Count Mercy, the veteran Austrian diplomat in Brussels, fell through.

3. Dundas in the Commons, 12 February 1793 (*P.R.*, XXXIV, 477).

4. Which in international usage had the force of treaties; though the full extent of associated obligations could be rather more easily disavowed (see p. 276, n2 below).

5. For the first see p. 240 above, and Pitt's statement of 25 April (*P.R.*, XXXV, 302); for the second Grenville to Murray, 15 February 1793 (F.O. 29/1), where the restoration of conquests by France without any details was said to be the only formula 'which affords a reasonable prospect of forwarding the objects of common interest'.

6. P. 254, n2 above.

atmosphere of distrust and reserve. Late in June it was therefore decided to send an emissary to open talks. By then there were difficulties with the Austrians and the Dutch.

The Dutch had not become more popular in London since the outbreak of war. They had been preserved, it was widely held, by Auckland and the Austrians, their own showing had been lamentable, and now they were sinking back into their old lethargy and disputes. The strong francophile party of course was hostile, mercantile interests were divided, and the House of Orange in the form of the Stadtholder commanded little respect.[1] The British connexion was under strain. It was partly for this reason that the Dutch Ministers who maintained it sought support for their wartime claims. First raised in April, these centred on the Austrian Netherlands: on a restoration of territories granted to the latter since 1715, particularly two strongpoints yielded in 1785 which overlooked the Scheldt, and a corridor (at the expense of Liège) giving better access to the fortress of Maastricht.[2] The pressure was stepped up by complaints about their role in the partnership – their subordination to a command and a policy resting on an Austrian campaign. The demands posed an unwelcome problem: not only for the obvious effect on Austria, but also, as one Dutch Minister put it, because the secrecy which that engendered must be made the closer by Prussian jealousies which could 'affect . . . the whole Conduct and Fate of the War'.[3]

It was not therefore surprising that the British in the early summer tried to stall the Austrians' own demands. Early in May it was made clear that the Government would not help over Poland, and remained opposed to the Bavarian Exchange. These responses naturally seemed to indicate 'not a very warm friendship';[4] but Thugut was prepared to make the concessions which he had foreseen might be required. He intimated that he might forgo support for the Exchange if offered a suitable acquisition in France,[5] and that he would not insist on a British stand against the Polish Partition. In return, however, he wished to know what the British might want for themselves; and here he received no precise answer. Grenville preferred to leave such matters to the peace table: a reply which appeared the less satisfactory when at the same time he raised the question of a Dutch indemnity at the Austrians' expense.

1. See I, 521.
2. Michael Duffy, '"A particular service": the British government and the Dunkirk expedition of 1793' (*E.H.R.*, XCI, no. 360), 534 and n2; hereafter cited as Duffy, Dunkirk. For the Dutch concessions in 1785 see I, 472–3. There was also a claim for gains in the West Indies.
3. Auckland to Grenville, 9 August 1793 (F.O. 37/48).
4. See Duffy, 'War Policy', 41, quoting Mercy.
5. It seems best to put it like this, because Thugut hoped to retain the option of the Exchange as a bargaining counter with Prussia, and was therefore anxious to suggest an alternative to the British alone.

How moreover, it occurred to Thugut, did Dunkirk figure in all this? Were the British going to claim it, while the Dutch were strengthened on the other side of the Austrian Netherlands? When Grenville went on to talk of signing an agreement as progress was made with the other co-belligerents, the Austrians in turn decided to slow the pace. They had hoped to conclude the negotiation in London. Now Thugut called for the draft proposals to be sent to Vienna before they could be agreed. This was done in mid-July. By then the British talks with Prussia had reached a point where a strictly bilateral Convention could be signed.

For the fading hopes of prior broad consent between the various partners finally disappeared in those conversations. When the emissary reached Prussian headquarters,[1] and spoke of the Dutch and the Austrians, he was told that any agreement must be confined to England alone. That being so however, the prospect, if limited, was quite simple, for both sides were content to avoid raising awkward points. The British did not want to discuss indemnities, and the Prussians wished to keep their hands free; the British were interested in opening the way to support for their military operation, the Prussians in creating conditions for some form of financial help. The talks thus went well enough, for there was little directly to hold them up; and an Anglo-Prussian Convention was signed on 14 July.

It provided for a framework, rather than the substance, of co-operation. The parties contracted to plan and act together; not to 'lay down their arms but by common consent' until the French returned conquests taken from themselves or their joint allies; not to export war stores or provisions to France from their ports, and to 'injure' her trade; and to prevent neutral states from allowing similar exports. Taking their cue, the Austrians in turn insisted on excluding the Dutch from a Convention which they agreed could follow the same lines. This was conceded, and the document was signed on 30 August.[2] It completed the structure of what became known as the First Coalition.

For the Conventions with Prussia and Austria were not the only ones of that year. There were others, four of which provided on similar lines for co-operation: with Russia, Sardinia, Spain, and The Two Sicilies. The first in point of time was the Russian, on 25 March; and it in fact suggested a formal model for the agreements with Prussia and Austria themselves.[3]

1. P. 273 above. He was Lord Beauchamp, who became Earl of Yarmouth a few weeks later, and Marquess of Hertford in June 1794 – the father of Thackeray's 'Marquess of Steyne' and Disraeli's 'Monmouth' who amassed the Wallace Collection.
2. French texts of both agreements are in *The Consolidated Treaty Series*, ed. Clive Parry, 52 (1969), 93–5, 109–11; English texts in (*inter alia*) *P.H.*, XXX, cols. 1052–5.
3. See Grenville to Beauchamp, Most Secret and Confidential, 27 June 1793 (F.O. 29/1).

The Earl of Chatham. *Studio of Hoppner*

The Duke of Richmond, *by Romney*

Lord Hood, *by Abbott*

Earl Howe, *by Copley*

Although the earlier exchanges had been abortive,[1] the entry of Britain into the war at once revived proposals in St Petersburg for a 'mutual connexion'.[2] The approach was received cautiously in London, for it might mean assent to the conquests in Poland; but there were certain prospective advantages for both sides. The Empress's hatred of the Revolution was real – strong enough indeed for her to swallow the renewal of a commercial treaty with England which she had been fighting for the past seven years.[3] She might also hope to win support for control of the Baltic against her neighbour Sweden, and at least a balance in the British attitude to her relations with Austria and Prussia. The enlistment of naval power, and perhaps of an influence on Vienna and Berlin, was undoubtedly tempting. And in London too the prospect had its attractions, one in particular of immediate substance. There might be the bonus of the commercial treaty, secured once more on favourable terms. More important, the obnoxious League of Armed Neutrality, formed by Russia in the American War and preserved in principle since,[4] would have to be suspended if not abolished. This was an object on which the British placed particular weight, underlying as it did the whole treatment of seaborne trade in war. The right to prevent the passage to an enemy from a neutral of warlike stores and certain foodstuffs had long been a fundamental claim, upheld at the cost of war itself. Its successful challenge in the most recent conflict had been a severe blow; but if Russia now became a co-belligerent 'the Principle' would be 'set aside'.[5] Russian influence moreover might work on Denmark to ensure favourable access to the Baltic naval stores. And something too might be gained for operations themselves. The Russians were prepared to send a squadron to act with the fleet in the Channel and North Sea. British Ministers – certainly Pitt himself – had hopes of a more telling contribution. When he talked to Richmond of his preference for the French coasts, he included Russian troops in the possibilities.[6] It was a prospect that would be pursued while the First Coalition lasted; and one that became reality – on French-controlled coasts – in the Second.

Meanwhile the talks went ahead on an immediate agreement. They were taken briskly, the Cabinet in London granting latitude over wording.[7] Two Conventions resulted, one for revived commercial

---

1. Pp. 239–40, 253 above
2. Whitworth to Grenville, no. 18, 5/14 March 1793 (F.O. 65/24).
3. Ehrman, *The British Government and Commercial Negotiations with Europe*, 134–5.
4. See I, 49–50, 503.
5. Whitworth to Grenville, no. 8, 27 January/7 February 1793 (F.O. 65/24).
6. P. 266 above; and see Grenville to Whitworth, no. 4, 26 March 1793 (F.O. 65/24).
7. Grenville's 'Note circulated to the Cabinet with the Drat. to Mr. Whitworth', 15 March 1793 (loc. cit.); Grenville to George III, 18 March 1793 (*L.C.G. III*, II, no. 858); George III to Grenville, 19 March 1793 (*H.M.C., Dropmore*, II, 385). Richmond had had some comments to make (loc. cit., 384–5).

arrangements, the other for co-operation in the war. At the latter's centre lay the terms (as copied with Prussia and Austria) for restrictions on belligerent and neutral trade. Otherwise it provided (again as in the later Conventions) for joint action and continued belligerency until French conquests were restored.[1] In pursuance of these principles the Russians proposed, as expected, to send a squadron to the Channel fleet.

George III's comment on the agreement was that it 'completely destroys the whole Russian system of an armed neutrality'. The official view, as received by Pitt later, concluded that the immediate effect 'went much further' than the Government had dared to hope.[2] For the Russians began at once to exert pressure on the neighbouring neutrals, fitting out a naval squadron and leaving Sweden and Denmark in no doubt as to their views. The sudden transformation of poacher into gamekeeper raised some diplomatic problems of its own. But the British welcomed it in their dealings with the other Baltic states.

These in turn were bound to be difficult, for the conflict between belligerent and neutral interests, sustained throughout the century, had been brought to a fresh point in the American War. Not only had the conflicting arguments been restated and elaborated: the League of Armed Neutrality, as its title showed, had provided for armed protection, and the Baltic Powers had then been joined, at least in theory, by others – Holland, Prussia, Austria, Portugal, The Two Sicilies. Hence the British emphasis now in all the Conventions on the denial of supplies to France. And hence the insistence to the neutrals themselves on two principles heightened by the American War: the legitimacy of Prize Court procedures, and a realistic definition of blockade.

Neither of course was new. But both gathered new importance from the increased experience and potential of naval strength. The first was to gain lustre in a few years' time from the judgments of Sir William Scott in the Admiralty Court, which gave a new dimension to this area of international law. The second – affected in due course by those judgments – was thrown into relief by an unprecedented freedom of manoeuvre for the British fleet. Like other aspects of neutrality, in fact, the formulation rested on realities of power, and their consequences in treaties embodying 'contracts . . . and certain mutual advantages'. For the treatment of neutrals developed from treaties, rather than from Natural Law, comprising as it did 'bonds of equity which have been found alone too weak to hold the nations of the world'. This was a

1. P. 240 above; French and Russian texts are in *Consolidated Treaty Series*, 51 (1969), 493–7, 52, 3–6; English texts in (*inter alia*) *P.H.*, XXX, cols. 1030–3.
2. *H.M.C., Dropmore*, II, 385; anon. paper 'Conduct of Russia respecting Neutrals since 1793'; from an official source by internal evidence, after 1799 (P.R.O. 30/8/196). One of the advantages to Russia of a Convention rather than a treaty was indeed said to be that she could ignore the provisions of the Armed Neutrality more easily (Hawkesbury's 'Observation' on a despatch of 28 January 1794, noted loc. cit.).

traditional British contention: as it had been proclaimed recently, treaties were 'to the statesman . . . of the same use, that a collection of statutes is to a lawyer'.[1] Reinforced now by the French Revolution's contrasting appeal to natural rights, the argument was applied unwaveringly to the Northern Powers.

In the course of 1793 a familiar pattern emerged. One of the facts of life in the Baltic was the mutual suspicion of Denmark and Sweden, and the British hoped at first to build on the fact in Copenhagen at least.[2] When the inevitable offer to join an alliance against France had predictably been declined, the Government still trusted to the Danish Ministry's known fears of the Revolution. As a member of the Imperial League, Denmark indeed had sent troops into Germany for defence. But this did not affect her determination to maintain the existing 'perfect Neutrality'.[3] While the Danes rejected a Swedish proposal for a joint squadron to protect their trade, they doubted if the British could blockade the French ports effectively, and were certainly not going to make concessions at the very start of a naval war. The Swedes for their part, more inclined to France, scarcely responded to messages from London. Meanwhile the merchants began to reap their rewards, and the British envoys in both capitals to urge 'compulsory Measures' for bringing them to heel.[4] One deterrent lay in the Russians' threats; but these, while helpful, caused some embarrassment when the Empress declared in the summer that she would stop all neutral vessels sailing for France. This was going far beyond the British claim to stop contraband stores: it struck at the basis of legitimate trade.[5] The Government proclaimed its own intentions in an Order in Council in June, specifying the rules governing search at sea, retention of goods, adjudication and payment. The Swedes received favourable treatment in the first of these matters, under a treaty of 1661.[6] But not surprisingly, relations with both countries suffered as the cases mounted, and by the winter reports were reaching London of a rising affection for France. By then, too, a Russian demonstration had suggested limits to its effectiveness: a naval squadron, putting to sea in late summer, soon put back in disrepair, having had no discernible impact on the neutral Baltic trade.

1. Charles Jenkinson, *A Collection of all the Treaties of Peace, Alliance, and Commerce, between Great Britain and other Powers, From . . . 1648 . . . up to 1783* (1785), I, xix, iv. While Hawkesbury (Jenkinson) first published the work in 1785, when he was a Minister, the introduction, from which the quotations are taken, had been written in 1757.
2. Cf. pp. 13, 275 above.
3. David Hailes [Minister in Copenhagen] to Grenville, no. 14, 5 March 1793 (F.O. 22/16).
4. Same to same, no. 35, 22 July 1793 (F.O. 22/17); and cf. Henry Wesley [chargé d'affaires in Stockholm] to Grenville, no. 12, 19 April 1793 (F.O. 73/14).
5. See the précis of communications in P.R.O. 30/8/196.
6. Grenville to Charles Keene [chargé d'affaires in Stockholm], no. 3, 4 July 1793 (F.O. 73/15, enclosing the recent Order in Council). The treaty of 21 October 1661 is in Jenkinson, op. cit., I, 166–9.

At the other end of Europe, there was soon evidence of the British intention to 'bring down every power on earth to assist them'.[1] Negotiations opened, in the Cabinet's phrasing, for 'some regular & fixed plan of Concert & co-operation' with 'Spain, Sardinia, Naples, &c.'[2] The results appeared on 25 April in a Convention with Sardinia, on 25 May in one with Spain, and on 12 July with The Two Sicilies (Naples). And on 10 September a treaty of defence was signed with Portugal implementing the terms of the ancient alliance.

If the efforts in the north were concerned mainly with commercial warfare, those in the south were more directly operational. Soundings had been taken of Sardinia and Portugal before England was at war; the talks with Spain and The Two Sicilies followed on the French declaration.[3] Sardinia figured first in the design, as she did in the event. For her mainland territory was strategically important. The older title of the King of Sardinia was King of Savoy, and in Piedmont (which he retained, after the loss of Nice and Savoy itself)[4] he held the key to northern Italy, and to an offensive against south-east France. His northern border rested on Switzerland, that reservoir of skilled mercenaries; to the south – though without direct access – was the sea, where British power might support a coastal advance. Early in January, Grenville asked if Sardinia would join in proposals for a general peace, or alternatively in an alliance if it came to war.[5] In the latter case operations might be launched to recover Savoy and Nice, for the first of which aid from Switzerland would be 'of the highest importance' while the second would benefit from a British naval force. There was a 'considerable probability' that a fleet would soon be sent to the Mediterranean, and with French forces spread as they were the attacks should succeed. The Sardinians were eager to listen. They thought they might well reach an agreement with some of the Swiss cantons. They naturally welcomed a British fleet, and were prepared to move against Nice. 'Money alone was wanting', and they suggested a subsidy (such as they had had in the past) or a loan on the London market.[6] The talks went ahead fast, and no great difficulties were encountered. Sardinia undertook to provide an army of 50,000 men; England to send 'a

1. P. 272 above.
2. Cabinet Minute, 17 April 1793 (B.L. Add. Ms 59306).
3. In the last case the initiative coming from Naples and being taken up at once (see Grenville to Sir William Hamilton [Minister in Naples], no. 6, 22 March 1793; F.O. 70/6).
4. P. 204 above.
5. To John Trevor, no. 1, 10 January 1793 (F.O. 67/11). He had already talked to the Sardinian Minister in London.
6. Trevor to Grenville, no. 8, 30 January 1793 (loc. cit.). See p. 204 above for an earlier request, before England was at war.

respectable fleet' into the Mediterranean, and to pay a subsidy of
£200,000 a year.[1]

The presence of a fleet in the Mediterranean was of course desirable
on several counts: to deny the large force in Toulon easy access to the
Atlantic, where commerce could be raided or the other French fleet in
Brest supported; to impress and support, or restrain, other Mediterranean Powers; to nourish local offensives; and protect a sensitive trade.
Naval freedom of action demanded a secure friendly port in the central
area, well to the east of Gibraltar, the only British base. Naples filled the
bill well, and in more than one way. For besides its strategic importance
the Kingdom of The Two Sicilies contained an army generally held to
be perhaps the best in Italy. Talks opened in March, and were soon
going well; agreement was reached in June, and a Convention signed in
July. The Two Sicilies agreed to 'unite' 6,000 troops, and four ships of
the line with four frigates and four small vessels, to the British forces in
the Mediterranean, and increase them later if possible. They would
close their ports to trade with France, and open them to British warships
for shelter and supply. In return the British would meet the costs of
transporting the Sicilian troops by sea and their subsistence outside the
Kingdom, and would afford protection to Sicilian vessels sailing in
British convoy. They would 'keep a respectable fleet of ships of the line in
the Mediterranean, as long as the danger of the Two Sicilies . . . shall
require'; and an undertaking was included not to make peace except by
common consent, as in other Conventions.[2]

One of the incentives for the Bourbons in Naples to secure a British
connexion was their ancient coolness with the Bourbons in Spain, who
now refused to guarantee aid if the Neapolitan territories were
attacked.[3] For the British themselves an agreement with Spain was a
prize to be valued, an object of substance in the naval war. Her hostility
would of course raise grave problems: a constant threat to a Mediterranean fleet, a pressure on Atlantic dispositions, a further commitment
in the West Indies; and neutrality itself would leave uncertainties in all
these respects, reflected no doubt in fluctuating favours to be conferred
on either side. An alliance, conversely, would not only remove such
pressures but might yield direct offensive advantages: added strength for
the watch on Toulon, and so for naval operations to the east, and
perhaps in certain circumstances the use of Spanish troops. But snags
could easily be foreseen. While the Spaniards hinted in January at a
'concert' with England if France appeared to threaten them, a

1. English text of the Convention in *Consolidated Treaty Series*, 52, 25–7, and *P.H.*,
XXX, cols. 1033–5.
2. French text in *Consolidated Treaty Series*, 52, 79–82; English in *P.H.*, XXX, cols.
1050–2.
3. Hamilton to Grenville, no. 11, 19 April 1793 (F.O. 70/6).

commitment was unlikely until they were sure of seeing a strong British fleet. They might try to use a wartime agreement to gain their objects in a new commercial treaty, over which the two parties remained far apart after talks lasting several years. British arrogance was resented in Madrid; Spanish gloom and lassitude sniffed at in London.[1] Nevertheless, on these unpromising foundations an alliance was imposed. The Spaniards dropped their efforts for a comprehensive trade agreement, the British announced the prospect of a fleet for Gibraltar; they would take Spanish seaborne trade into convoy, the Spaniards would shut their ports to the French. The treaty of May was not greeted by either partner with unrelieved enthusiasm: the fleet had not yet arrived, the Spaniards were proving awkward over plans and questions of command. The British Ambassador, about to leave for another post, looked back with some regret to the 'distant footing' on which he had earlier lived. 'They are infinitely more untractable and difficult to deal with', he wrote sourly, 'as friends, than as Enemies'.[2] But freedom of naval manoeuvre had been gained in two important areas; and within the next few months the connexion indeed was to offer an inviting prospect.

The cordon in the Atlantic was not complete without a friendly Portugal, and in their talks with Spain the British were anxious to keep the Portuguese in play. They encouraged co-operation between the Iberian Powers, and worked for an agreement with Lisbon themselves. The Portuguese however were not prepared to break with France until their summer convoy was in from Brazil and British naval dispositions had been seen to be effective. They sent a squadron designed to cruise in the Atlantic with the Channel fleet; but they did not like the terms on supplies for the enemy accepted by other Allies, and tried for some months to secure limitations to a full trade war. They were also suspicious of favours being granted to Spain at their expense. Agreement however was reached at length in September, broadly on the lines laid down elsewhere. The Portuguese did not declare war on France. But they declared themselves an 'auxiliary' ally in compliance with the existing treaties of mutual defence. Mutual convoy protection was promised; Portuguese ports were closed to the French; and trade with France was restricted as the British wished.[3] A Portuguese treaty of defence with Spain had been signed already. On paper at least, a system of alliances existed in the central Atlantic and the western Mediterranean.

1. F.O. 72/26, January to March 1793 *passim*. For the commercial negotiation see I, 497–501. There were also still some problems to be settled finally over the rights and relations at Nootka Sound.

2. Lord St Helens to Grenville, 29 May 1793 (F.O. 72/27). For the treaty see *Consolidated Treaty Series*, 52, 43–50 (Spanish and French texts), and *P.H.*, XXX, cols. 1048–50 (English text).

3. F.O. 63/16–17 *passim*; for the treaty see *Consolidated Treaty Series*, 52, 149–56 (Portuguese and English texts), and *P.H.*, XXX, cols. 1055–7 (English text).

So the Coalition was framed. Beyond its boundaries the diplomatic war was waged steadily in some places, languidly in others. In the south the British had to reckon with and where possible draw on Austrian interests, as they worked where possible with Russia in the north. The Ottoman Empire, the duchy of Tuscany, and the Genoese republic were the neutrals to be considered most immediately in Mediterranean affairs. Turkey, important for the Levant trade, was tired from its recent wars and – in spite of Ochakov – attracted by a possible influence in its dealings with the Imperial Powers. It seemed quite anxious therefore to establish closer contact, even to the extent – an unfamiliar prospect – of sending an Ambassador to London. Tuscany and Genoa, deriving their significance from ports which were a natural outlet for Piedmont – for supplies, and for transport of troops if required by sea – would probably respond as they sensed events might dictate. Both, despite the Tuscan rulers' Hapsburg connexion, were proving distinctly cautious: both contained a strong francophile faction, and were conscious of the French army in Savoy. The British representatives had their difficulties;[1] the Government in London counselled patience, pending the effects of a stronger fleet and perhaps a Sardinian advance.

It was also necessary to look in part beyond the Alliances for auxiliary troops which could be placed under direct British control. The traditional answer, for a country with a small standing army, lay in the German principalities, particularly Hesse Cassel and Hesse Darmstadt and of course Hanover. Arrangements with the first and last were soon put in hand. In March, Hanover undertook to supply some 13,000 men for continental service – and march them immediately into Holland – in return for pay, transport and maintenance; and in April a treaty was signed with Hesse Cassel for 8,000 men for three years, the same expenses being met and an annual payment made to the Landgrave's exchequer. The number was augmented to 12,000 by a further agreement in August, and in the next two months treaties were made with Baden for some 750 men and Hesse Darmstadt for some 3,000. Even before all the arrangements were concluded York had received 17,000 German mercenaries, at a time when he disposed of some 6,500 British troops.[2]

There was one important case, however, in which the British were

---

1. And they themselves were not in any case very suitable at the start. Matters in Genoa were in the hands of the Consul until a new Minister – the energetic Francis Drake, from Denmark – arrived in August. Lord Hervey in Florence, who exhibited some of his family's curious characteristics, had soon to be told not to be too 'warm' (Grenville to Hervey, no. 3, 5 July 1793; F.O. 79/8).

2. This was in August 1793. For the treaty with Hanover see *Consolidated Treaty Series*, 51, 481–8; for those with Hesse Cassel op. cit., 52, 9–18, and *P.H.*, XXX, cols. 1024–9; with Baden, loc. cit., 131–6; with Hesse Darmstadt, loc. cit., 159–64. There is a memorandum on the terms for Hesse Cassel among Pitt's papers in P.R.O. 30/6/338; their negotiation (of interest since they formed the basis of other such agreements) can be followed in F.O. 26/20, 31/5 *passim*.

involved, not unilaterally but in Allied efforts, with wider implications and without success. Switzerland was the home of some of the finest soldiers in Europe, veterans of other countries' battlefields, the guards of the French Kings and the Popes. It also occupied a place of great strategic significance. 'Like a bastion frowning over converging valleys, that Alpine tract dominates the basins of the Po, the Inn, the Upper Rhine, and the Upper Rhone. He who holds it . . . can determine the fortunes of North Italy, Eastern France, South Germany, and the West of the Habsburg domains'.[1] And, it can be added, he who employs its resources strengthens his own as he rests on its flanks. In the last weeks of peace cautious soundings had been taken in some of the Cantons judged hostile to France, which might be prepared in some way to commit their troops. There was no prospect of involving the country as a whole in an alliance: parts of it were under strong French influence, Geneva indeed had had its own revolution, and the Federation – the Helvetic Body – would certainly not engage as one. The first approaches were unsuccessful: the French armies were too close for any of the Cantons to wish to take a risk. But in the spring the Sardinians gained some ground in Savoy in a local offensive, the British Minister in Berne worked hard through the summer, and in September he was optimistic. In the autumn, however, he was forced to acknowledge disappointment.[2] The efforts then took a less direct, though not less ambitious, turn.

For the tasks demanded of the Swiss, at least in prospect, were ambitious. As well as reinforcing the Sardinians they were 'to act in conjunction with His Majesty's Naval Forces against the Southern Provinces of France'.[3] The troops in fact were required as part of a strategy adumbrated early in the war, which began to take shape as the year progressed. It was a broad conception based initially on the presence of a Mediterranean fleet, Sardinian operations, and, not least, developments in France itself. The opportunity – the test – was to come soon: sooner indeed than was entirely expected. Its outlines could be glimpsed, if imprecisely, in the pursuit of connexions stretching in an arc from the Atlantic through the Mediterranean to the Alps.

III

While the negotiations with the two main partners, Prussia and Austria, were under way, the battlefront itself called for co-ordination. The

1. Holland Rose, II, 374.
2. F.O. 74/3 *passim*; Grenville also received private reports throughout the year, which are in B.L. Add. Ms 59051. For Pitt's hope in April, see p. 266 above; for the Sardinians' role and views, Grenville to Trevor, no. 1, 10 January 1793, Trevor to Grenville, nos. 8, 15, 30 January, 20 February 1793 (F.O. 67/11), no. 33, 4 May 1793 (F.O. 67/12).
3. Grenville to Lord Robert Fitzgerald [Minister in Berne], no. 5, 15 March 1793 (F.O. 74/3).

expulsion of the French from Holland meant the end of a short-term crisis, and the presence of the Duke of York introduced a new commander in the north. At the end of March the Austrian commander, the Prince of Coburg, suggested a conference, and this was held in Antwerp on 7 April. The Powers' embarrassments were soon revealed. The shape of future operations could not be divorced from territorial aims – from the respective claims for indemnities which were being raised at just this time.[1] Nor were the Austrians themselves united on basic policy: while Thugut wished to continue the war and secure their indemnifications,[2] Coburg wanted peace and indeed had just issued a statement abjuring the retention of conquests all round. The Prussians for their part were hanging fire on the Rhine while they awaited events; and the British were developing their own plan to reconcile Allied and domestic pressures.[3]

The conference, and the exchanges that followed, succeeded in producing an interim strategy. Coburg was induced to withdraw his proclamation, and a plan was agreed which benefited immediately both the Austrians and the British. The main army, including some Prussians, would advance on the fortresses athwart the frontier: it would reduce Condé, which it was already investing, and Valenciennes inside France, thereafter moving northwards to mask the strongpoint of Lille. In order to complete these operations while maintaining a cordon along the length of the front, Coburg wanted troops from the British command, hitherto held near the coast.[4] This should enable him to take Valenciennes. The ensuing containment of Lille would support an attack on Dunkirk, which could otherwise be threatened from that fortress; and in return for their earlier help he would consent to the British operation and aid it as far as his resources allowed. York secured Dutch and Hanoverian participation – the Dutch remaining on the coastal flank – and the Government, after a visit from Murray, agreed to the plans.[5] In May, the Duke moved to Valenciennes, and took part in the clearing attacks. The investment then proceeded methodically; but sieges were usually deliberate affairs and this was no exception. The British became impatient: 'Our Ideas about the Duration of the Siege vary like the Price of Stocks', Dundas was told in June.[6] At length however – and before it

---

1. See pp. 265, 273–4 above.

2. P. 271 above.

3. For the Prussians see pp. 272–4 above.

4. Pp. 264–5 above. In the plan as it finally emerged on 1 May, Coburg put his combined forces in mid-May at 92,000, with 13,000 more early in June. The cordon, to cover strongpoints from Maubeuge to Ostend, would require 40,000 men.

5. The first instructions for the Dunkirk operation were sent on 16 April, and a revised version on 10 May (P.R.O., W.O. 6/7, drafts in 6/20). The steps towards agreement can be followed loc. cit. and in W.O. 1/166 and F.O. 37/47–8, 29/1. Murray had been appointed Adjutant General (effectively chief of staff) to York in March, and attended the Antwerp conference: a series of letters from him to Pitt, showing the hardening of views in June and July, are in P.R.O. 30/8/162.

6. By Murray, 14 June 1793 (W.O. 1/166).

was finally expected – the fortress surrendered on 28 July. The success followed closely on two others: Condé capitulated on the 10th, and on the 22nd the Prussians finally entered Mainz. At the end of that month the Allies had therefore secured some substantial gains, and the British could turn to their own distinctive task.

But not without a choice of options being presented at this last point; and while they were rejected, from York's headquarters without even the need to refer home, the response requires some explanation of a reasoning firmly shared. Coburg proposed two consecutive operations, which he now preferred to Dunkirk: first, to continue joint action, principally against Maubeuge, so as to extend the breach in the barrier fortresses; and then, in mid-August, for a farther joint strike into France, besieging Cambrai with the main army and marching towards Paris itself.[1] York and Murray were naturally not impressed by a farther reduction of strongpoints without immediate relevance to their particular aim. But an advance on Paris might have seemed to be another matter. Why was it not even considered, as against Dunkirk?

The proposal, it could have been thought, held the greater attraction in the light of developments inside France itself. Indeed, whatever its origin, it could hardly have been made seriously without them.[2] For at the end of July the Republic was at a very low ebb: it had been living with the possibility of failure and political disruption for the past three months. In April, after the defeat in Holland, Dumouriez had deserted to the Austrians. Throughout the early summer, reports flooded in from all fronts of indiscipline and low morale. In Paris, the struggle between Girondins and Jacobins ended in the latter's victory in June, bringing to a head growing revolts in the southern provinces centred on Lyons, and in Brittany and the Vendée in the north-west. In mid-June the royalist peasants of the Vendée captured Saumur; a month later – on the day that Condé fell – Lyons rose against the central Government. The Sardinians were threatening from Savoy, the British Mediterranean fleet reached Gibraltar, Corsica was in a state of revolt, and the Allies had crossed the frontier in the north-east. Even the Spaniards took some posts in the Pyrenees. A circumspect approach from Lebrun to London, shortly before he was dismissed, probing the chances of peace, had been dismissed in May.[3] Now the prospect of invasion and collapse stared his successors in the face.[4]

---

1. The plan of the first phase was put forward between 29 July and 3 August, the second on 13 August.

2. According to the British envoy in Brussels it in fact came from Mercy, desperately anxious to save the life of Marie Antoinette who was about to be tried for treason. He suggested taking Cambrai and threatening the capital: Coburg changed this – whether after deliberation or not – to marching on the capital (see Duffy, *Dunkirk*, 535n5).

3. Richards, 'British Policy and the Problem of Monarchy in France', 130.

4. Cf. Pitt in the Commons as early as 17 June: 'every circumstance concurs to favour the hope of our being able completely to accomplish every object of the war' (*P.R.*, XXXV, 675).

In some ways the peril looked even greater than a year before.[1] It was met with the same – or even fiercer – resolution. The Allies' opportunity, if it existed, proved in fact to be fleeting. In mid-August the great Carnot was appointed to the Committee of Public Safety, already reviving and imposing its ferocious will. The fighting in the provinces began to swing in the central Government's favour; the southern front, at one time a real prospect, faded in the autumn; there was no attack on Cambrai, the last major fortress east of Paris. Coburg had suggested one course, in theory at least, to achieve sudden victory. Others, invoking support inside France, could also be envisaged. All fell within the British frame of reference. In greater or lesser degree, most would have had to be weighed against Dunkirk.

Something has already been said about Ministers' thoughts on north-west France.[2] The process will be followed later, together with the action taken to support the risings in the south. This last did not bear on the men and supplies earmarked initially for Dunkirk; but the experience then encountered raises the question of how effectively British resources, in this first year of war, could have been redistributed in the north itself. For some redistribution would have had to take place, once involvement was accepted in the Low Countries,[3] and the reasons for that acceptance bore in turn on Coburg's proposal. This in fact was received less than three weeks after York had been sent fresh confirmation of his Government's aim to capture Dunkirk as soon as circumstances allowed.[4] It was generally agreed that the time was favourable now that Valenciennes had fallen, and the operation still held its place as a link in the structure of the First Coalition. Throughout the campaign Ministers had refused to 'give blind co-operation to measures not distinctly explained'.[5] They feared being drawn into an orbit not of their choosing or to their advantage; and the unresolved questions surrounding the connexions with the Prussians, the Dutch and the Austrians themselves placed Dunkirk at this time in the centre of their thinking. This indeed was underlined at the beginning of August, when the instructions were confirmed for the attack to go ahead. For, looking to success, the Government then laid down that 'the Surrender must be taken by the

---

1. P. 197 above.

2. Pp. 262, 266–9 above.

3. The last indication of the Ministry's belief in its freedom of action was on 16 April, when Dundas repeated (to Murray; W.O. 6/7) the hope of British troops being released for operations elsewhere. But he added the rider that they must be kept in Flanders if 'truly essential' to Coburg's immediate movements; and that effectively settled the matter.

4. Coburg's proposal being received on 19 August (cf. p. 284, n1 above), and instructions being sent from London on the 1st (Dundas to Murray, no. 26; loc. cit.). They repeated in the current context the object of despatches of 16 April and 10 and 30 May (loc. cit.; see p. 283, n5 above).

5. Dundas to Murray, Private, 16 April 1793 (copy in B.L. Add. Ms 34449). Cf. same to same, 10 May 1793 (P.R.O., W.O. 6/7).

Duke of York in the Name of His Britannic Majesty'.[1] Such a stipulation might seem rash, or stupid, given the main argument for the operation – the retention of the Austrian Netherlands by Austria, with the bait of an extension to the west. But it was made, as Ministers explained later, to satisfy the unhappy Dutch at a time when their suspicions had been rising over indemnification.[2]

> . . . it would be advantageous to have that place [Dunkirk] in our hands when the Peace should be negotiated; because meaning as we should to deliver it to Austria we might however obtain in return from the Emperor such concessions for the Dutch on their frontier and respecting Antwerp and the navigation of the Scheld[t].[3]

The manoeuvre might therefore lead to a solution of the Scheldt problem as experienced in the eighties. It might also persuade the Dutch to release their troops for a later Allied advance into France.[4]

The operation was thus related directly to the peace settlement which must come for a region always accepted as of prime importance to British interests. But was this not a case of sharing the lion's skin while neglecting to slay the lion first?[5] It was true that Dunkirk would be a useful port for British nourishment of a forward movement,[6] and an incentive to the Dutch to play their part. But did this compensate for failing to aid an immediate forward movement itself? It is possible that Ministers knew that Coburg might have some decisive object in mind, for they seem to have been aware that he hoped, once he took Valenciennes, to bring the French army to a general action.[7] But they were not required to take note of the specific proposal for Cambrai and Paris, for they had not been informed;[8] and if they had, one may wonder about the response. For opinion in London appears to have grasped that

1. Same to same, 1 August 1793 (loc. cit.). For an earlier rumour, and the Austrians' suspicion that this might be done, see *A.C.*, III, 68, 79.

2. See p. 273 above.

3. Sir Gilbert Elliot's journal, 8 September 1793, after talking to Dundas and Loughborough (Duffy, Dunkirk, 535). Elliot was then designated as Governor or Commissioner for Dunkirk.

4. For the Scheldt in the eighties see I, 470–3; for the release of a Dutch corps, Grenville to Morton Eden, no. 8, 7 September 1793 (Duffy, ibid.).

5. Cf. The Hon. J.W. Fortescue, *A History of the British Army*, IV – Part I (1915), 88; referring in that instance to the discussion in April.

6. Cf. p. 265 above.

7. At least to judge from Grenville to the Earl of Elgin [Minister in Brussels], no. 9, 13 September 1793 (F.O. 26/21). How much weight had ever been attached to this in London is not clear.

8. P. 284 above. See Duffy, Dunkirk, 535n6. Murray had privately discussed the capture of Paris only a week or so earlier (to Pitt, 23 July 1793; P.R.O. 30/8/162). But he did so as a possible operation for 1794, not 1793; and by the time that Coburg's proposal was received, York's headquarters reckoned in any case that the die had been cast firmly for Dunkirk.

a decisive action was impossible unless the French forces were conveniently massed – as they were not at that time. And there is no sign
that the British believed – any more than Coburg himself usually did –
that a major advance could succeed until such a battle had been won.[1]
Any average commander – and Coburg was very average – might have
hesitated to leave strong forces in his rear: to a disciple of the strict
eighteenth-century school, concerned for security by cordons and sieges,
the risk might well have proved unacceptable had it come to the point.
The idea looks tempting in retrospect, at least superficially. But given
the resilience of the French, the Allies' mutual distrust, Coburg's own
vacillations, the pace of his proceedings and the limited campaigning
time after Cambrai might have fallen, it is far from certain that such a
plan would have worked. Brunswick failed in 1792; Coburg could well
have done so in 1793. If his proposal was disregarded, it reflected the fact
that British hopes of a French collapse, which persisted over much of the
year, turned on expectations other than that of a march from Flanders to
Paris.[2]

York began to move north on 15 August. He reached the coast on the
21st, after beating off some French resistance on the way. The
preparations for the siege had been in train for just over a month at
home. They formed an instructive example of wartime administration
facing its first serious continental test for over thirty years. As might have
been expected, it did not emerge well. Pitt's own role is not entirely easy
to follow. At the start, as has been said, he was 'all energy and bustle'.[3]
This was to be the first fruit of British strategy, and the British command,
in the campaign; and perhaps the memory of Chatham's reputation
echoed in his son. There were sufficient reasons for his early stimulation.
It was not always well received, and the pace died down. This was due in
some measure to personalities, for most of the requirements fell on the
Ordnance Office, and the Master General of the Ordnance was
Richmond, already opposed to the strategy and moreover disgruntled
that York, with whom his family had quarrelled and who as a General
was junior to himself, should have been given the principal field

---

1. Grenville to Elgin (p. 286, n7 above), where these points are specifically made. Pitt
himself appears to have dismissed the possibility without much question, judging by a
conversation with Windham in August (Windham to Edmund Burke, 17 August 1793;
Correspondence of Burke, VII, 411).

2. It is also interesting that Murray, discussing possible operations some weeks later,
was convinced that the capture of Paris could be at best 'problematical' if only because of
'the general attachment of the Inhabitants to the cause they are fighting for' (to
Grenville, 27 September [1793]; F.O. 29/2).

3. Duffy, Dunkirk, 538. Unless otherwise stated, my account now follows this
admirable study. P.R.O. 30/8/338 contains lists of ordnance requirements received by
Pitt in July.

command.[1] He was not pleased to be hustled for information on behalf of a plan he disliked, and his co-operation was distinctly formal at first.[2] But the difficulties went deeper, and they were real enough. As the demands came in from York's headquarters the Ordnance soon appreciated, after initial confidence, that it lacked both material and men. The estimated needs in point of fact had been inflated: Dunkirk was not a fortress in the proper sense, for its defences, long dismantled, had been repaired only slightly in recent years. Poor intelligence, soon to be evident throughout, was producing its first consequence. But necessary stores were lacking in any case – artillery carriages, timber, mortars, ammunition – as were horses and both skilled and unskilled men. There were not enough trained gunners, or even soldiers to unload and pull the guns into position; and a proposal to take a thousand seamen for the purpose met with short shrift. A less daunting alternative seemed to lie in shipping the siege-train to the nearest harbour in British hands, at Nieuport, and thence by canal to the area of attack. But faulty intelligence again left every one – in the field and in London – unaware not only of the details of the canal but also that the enemy controlled the sluices.[3] The fall of Valenciennes, rather sooner than expected,[4] gave the programme fresh urgency. But the means to achieve it were problematical indeed.

The difficulties were heightened because of the need to preserve the security of the precious siege-train, on its journey from Woolwich Arsenal to Dunkirk. Secrecy was indeed jeopardised from early in August, when some of the London newspapers were openly speculating; it survived, however, until York's march north took the French by surprise. But it imposed a strict timetable for the army to receive the material; and in the event the junction was not achieved. The tides at Nieuport restricted access to a few days in every fortnight, and to convey a range of stores and men in the right order and at the right point, after a passage subject to the elements, was asking a good deal. Given the untried, circumscribed system, the odds were steeply against success.

1. Not only was Richmond a General with seniority 1782, while York was a Lieutenant General, seniority 1784; York's command had been restricted initially to the small British force sent for a specific service in Holland and extended since by stages to a wider Allied command. In 1789 Richmond's nephew, Charles Lennox (later his successor as Duke), had fought a duel with York of which the family approved.

2. For Richmond's opinion of Pitt's knowledge of war see pp. 267–8 above. He did not think highly of Dundas's either. His temper was also not improved at the start by being woken in the night when he was out of London to answer Pitt's first questions on ordnance, by a messenger sent through Nepean, an Under Secretary in the War (not even his own) Office.

3. Ministers knew that the storeships could enter Nieuport on the spring tides, which meant for the immediate purpose in a period ending 24 August. But the local agent sent to spy the canal was given the wrong canal to spy; and – possibly because of the insistence on secrecy – no proper information was received until later on the state of Dunkirk's facilities and defences.

4. See pp. 283–4 above.

The result was critical, for the force must be ready for the stores when they arrived, without having to wait too long if it was found necessary to mount a prepared attack.[1] Misled by the first confident response, York accordingly moved forward; only to find himself in position eight days before the train reached Nieuport, let alone himself.

There was indeed a catalogue of misfortunes at the English end. The Ordnance decided, reasonably enough, to ship the stores in two consignments; but the Admiralty muddled the escort arrangements, the first convoy was late and missed the spring tides at Nieuport, and much of its cargo had to be landed at Ostend, which meant changing from one canal to another for Dunkirk. Some of the vital material moreover had been packed in the wrong order, causing further delay on arrival, and York was still waiting to open his bombardment more than a fortnight after he had hoped.

The delay was fatal. There is general agreement that, given a bombardment, Dunkirk would probably have surrendered by the end of August. As it was, the French had time to flood the marshes to the south-east, forcing the British into a coastal belt which exposed them to fire from enemy gunboats, and above all leaving the western and southern approaches open to French reinforcements. York called for ships and more troops to counter the inconvenience. He was promised four regiments, destined for the West Indies, to be returned within three or four weeks; but no one had foreseen the possible need for a naval squadron, and when some ships were assembled – as they were quite quickly – the conditions for keeping station in the shoals were found to be unsuitable.[2] They were forced to make their base up the coast. Meanwhile the French, who late in July had decided to reinforce the Flanders front at the expense of the area between the Rhine and the Moselle, were hastening troops to the north. York applied to Coburg for help. But unfortunately for him, he had been overtaken by a fresh outburst of Allied jealousies at this very time. The enemy had been able initially to contemplate switching his strength thanks to Prussian dilatoriness on the central front; but early in August the Prussians were planning an advance west of Mainz,[3] which would have pinned down substantial forces and made such disengagement difficult. At this point however the Austrian Government, still seeking gains to offset failure in Poland, hit on a fresh idea, to invade Alsace.[4] A force moved from their Rhine army; but the march required Prussian cover, and the Prussians,

1. I put it like this, because Dundas claimed later, in conversation, that Murray at one point wrote him privately that Dunkirk would surrender without a siege (see Duffy, loc. cit., 544n1). If so, the scale of the demands from headquarters for siege stores was even more inadmissible.
2. Neither Ministers nor the Admiralty had consulted the charts. Shades of the preparations for Ochakov (see p. 18, n1 above) in even less excusable circumstances.
3. See p. 284 above.
4. Which, while not preventing an attack on Cambrai – for there were troops enough for both – was scarcely consonant with the idea of a march in strength on Paris.

resenting their ally's intentions, called off their planned advance. The French were left free to move a force of over 30,000 men, and they sent it in a body to relieve Dunkirk.

York was therefore in real trouble, though he did not appreciate its extent. As late as 3 September his headquarters were sanguine enough to invite Pitt and Dundas over to see the sport.[1] The Dutch to the westward were by then under pressure, and while this led Coburg to spare some troops it also weakened the British covering force. Poor intelligence played its part once more. The pace and scale of the French reinforcements took York by surprise until the eve of the massive attack which came on the 6th. He was in fact facing over 45,000 men with some 14,500, and not surprisingly was forced to retreat, abandoning much of the siege-train which had arrived just in time for its fate. The British suffered some 10,000 casualties. The Dutch were routed a few days later. And while the enemy was then halted with Austrian help, Dunkirk itself remained in his hands. No further attack on it could be envisaged, and on 13 September York was ordered to rejoin Coburg to the south.

The failure of the operation was followed naturally by a public row. The scapegoats were primarily Richmond and Pitt's brother Chatham at the Admiralty. As so often on such occasions, some of the attacks were inaccurate and should at least have been more widely aimed. In a sense indeed they were unfair, for the two Departments ended by meeting enough of the demands to have supplied what was required. By early September the first half of the siege-train – which would probably have sufficed – had reached its goal, and naval support was on its way, though the operations had had to be replanned. The War Office sent the extra requirements as asked. Defeat was due to the French reinforcements, the result of Austro-Prussian rivalry; if they had been held on the Rhine, Dunkirk might well have fallen in the course of the month. The British could point to their allies as the cause of their misfortune. But in another sense the attacks were justified. There had certainly been incompetence in the relevant offices: absurd early optimism at the Ordnance, and a lack of supervision in the packing of its stores; muddled orders from the Admiralty, and extraordinary ignorance of the North Sea coast. This however was not the whole story: such shortcomings were compounded by others at field headquarters and within the Cabinet itself. Allowing for all their bad luck, York and Murray made their mistakes: intelligence was poor, estimates of material were widely excessive, and the enemy's possible reactions consistently underplayed.[2] Although

1. Murray to Dundas, Private, 3 September 1793 (W.O. 1/167).
2. The muddle over the canals (p. 288 above) was the fault of a subordinate commander; but the lack of information at headquarters and of efforts to acquire it are obvious throughout. And while Dundas – so he claimed – had wondered about the desirability of naval support, and Pitt had thought of looking into it, it had escaped York's and Murray's serious attention (see Duffy, Dunkirk, 547 and ns2, 3). For their prolonged optimism see n1 above.

York was said later to have 'Condemned the whole measure of Dunkirk',[1] he gave no sign of doing so when he undertook it. Better appreciation might have reduced the losses, although it could scarcely have changed the outcome once the French were free to move in strength. But that was the point. Only greater forethought and swifter action at home could have produced a different result; and it is here that the gravamen of the charge must really lie. For the Ministers responsible for an arguably sound design were involved in an execution for which they were ill prepared. Speed proved to be of the essence, and they could not act fast enough for Dunkirk to be taken while the odds were on their side.

It was perhaps not surprising. The great enemy of contemporary administration – in Europe as well as England – was time: it was always difficult to do complicated things quickly. Even the French, now in apparent and unpredictable contrast, were imposing great bursts of energy on periods of exhausted disarray. In their own fashion, they were putting an inherited situation to the strain; elsewhere the limits were more traditionally defined. In England, the structure of government, its underlying assumptions, and the peculiar features of an island base, demanded ampler warning of allocations, transport and supply. Given time, it was possible to mount a well-found expedition, as the first colonial venture was indeed soon to show. But there were very real problems, and they were illuminated by the shifts of events and fortunes surrounding the change from peace to war. The limitations were reflected in the attitude, enhanced by his temperament, of Pitt himself. The spasmodic quality of his impetus was partly personal, partly enforced. Acting, with his closest colleague Dundas, in the context of diffused powers, his interventions were of limited value in themselves. For it was not by proddings alone that a Minister could hope for effective action: a framework was essential within which they could find their place. This had been Chatham's unusual achievement – for, contrary to legend, he too had had to work largely to accepted limits, the force of which however he reduced by personality, political adroitness and what perhaps might be called the illusionist's flair. But persistence was also important; and in the face of a sudden demand Pitt's personal efforts were not fully sustained. The initiatives in July were followed by short visits to friends and odd days at Holwood before he left to see his mother at Burton Pynsent in the second half of August. Accompanied by Dundas, he then went down to Walmer for as long as he could spare – though, as he pointed out, this was handy for news from Dunkirk.[2] One must not exaggerate. The Home Counties and Kent at least were in easy reach of London, and Richmond, who after his earlier coolness was co-

---

1. Malmesbury, *Diaries and Correspondence*, III (1844), 18; diary for 6 December 1793.
2. Duffy, *Dunkirk*, 553–4; Pitt to Hester, Countess of Chatham, 31 August 1793 (P.R.O. 30/8/12). For the customary dispersal of Ministers see Auckland to Lord Henry Spencer, 9 August 1793 (*A.C.*, III, 104).

operating fully, did so for a time from camp in Sussex, where he followed the local manoeuvres as Lord Lieutenant.[1] The lack of written evidence, moreover, for Pitt's role at least in the later stages may stem largely from the fact that Dundas was with him; for Dundas was the Secretary of State concerned, and it was doubtless for this reason that he was asked to Walmer. Nevertheless the impression remains that the Minister was breathing holiday air: he thought himself freer in August than he had done in June and the first half of July, when the operations in Flanders were among the business that kept him in town.[2] His ready optimism was supported by the feeling in York's headquarters, and the reverse came as a shock, particularly after the Allies' recent gains. Ministers by and large were not neglectful, and they thought they did quite well. But as Pitt and Dundas walked up the partridges,[3] and Richmond looked to affairs in Sussex, they were removed in spirit as in circumstance from the relentless, desperate men in Paris.

The affair had wider consequences than its scale might have suggested. The public criticism was not in itself necessarily a serious matter, but it came at a time of some reaction from the opening hopes. There was already some disappointment, particularly with events at sea. As so often in the first stages of a war, the navy was expected to sweep all before it; the more easily in view of the reported demoralisation of the French fleet. In point of fact the exercise of seapower was pursuing its unspectacular course: squadrons cruised in the focal areas, trade was sustained with acceptable loss. Provisions for convoy, quickly introduced, were proving broadly successful; but there were delays, and some damaging attacks on unprotected shipping in the Channel approaches, all of which provided ammunition for debate.[4] A deeper if less specific frustration stemmed from the motions of the main Channel fleet. For five months after the outbreak of war Lord Howe and his command were still at Spithead; and while this was due partly to valid impediments – to priorities accorded to foreign stations, to the difficulties of manning a substantial force while merchantmen were at sea with peacetime crews, to the immediate demands of operations in the Low Countries – there was justified impatience by the time he finally set sail. Nor did he then give greater satisfaction, for in the next few weeks – during which he

1. Chatham however was in London for much of the period.
2. Pitt to Hester Countess of Chatham, 7 June, 15 July, 31 August 1793 (P.R.O. 30/8/12). But see also p. 299 below. One may note, too, that Pitt's personal correspondence with the Commissary General in Flanders, (the official responsible for supply), sustained earlier and later, is missing for this period (see P.R.O. 30/8/187).
3. See Pitt to Auckland, 8 September 1793 (*A.C.*, III, 114).
4. As Dundas pointed out in the winter, there had been both coastal and deep-sea convoys (fifty of the latter), and no ship in convoy had been taken by the enemy (speech of 21 January 1794; *P.R.*, XXXVII (1794), 149). On the same occasion, however, Pitt was sufficiently disturbed to call for a defence from the Admiralty and make some detailed notes of his own (P.R.O. 30/8/196, ff. 213–16v).

sighted but could not catch a French squadron – he was forced back twice by gales. The fleet had done nothing by September to meet the country's hopes, and there were signs of 'an uneasy sensation' arising from the 'want of success at sea'.[1] The fiasco, as it seemed, of Dunkirk focused a rising irritation, superficial no doubt but unfortunate coming in the later part of a campaign which was to be followed at no great distance by the Parliamentary session.[2]

There was irritation too, naturally enough, among the commanders and Ministers concerned. By the autumn, Howe was said to be discontented:[3] Dunkirk raised sharper feelings, and not all the resentments died down. York, upset by the post mortem, was complaining in private by the end of the year, and the stigma of failure did not help when the Government later lost confidence in him. Chatham's reputation also suffered, although he made no immediate fuss; but Richmond, criticised and critical, was not one to remain quiet. He was still voicing his complaints of strategy on the morrow of the defeat, and his sense of neglect increased shortly afterwards when Dundas sent a list of fresh requirements for the West Indies. His answering tone led Pitt to threaten dismissal, which in turn drew a bitter rejoinder;[4] and while the differences were patched up they were bound to leave their mark. Richmond felt himself isolated; he withdrew into his shell, and the Cabinet virtually lost the advice of one of its ablest members. Its cohesion was weakened, and some mutual suspicions remained. The King was not best pleased by the misfortune to his favourite son. And although Pitt and Dundas themselves escaped fairly lightly, the Ministry's standing suffered its first setback of the war.

There were also material consequences for the Alliance. This indeed was soon evident. The Austrians had only recently signed their Convention with England: a full treaty of alliance had still to be agreed.[5] The question of indemnities lay at the heart of discussions on the conduct of war, and the British decision to take Dunkirk in the name of George III – implemented when York on arrival called for its surrender in that form – at once revived lively suspicions in Vienna.[6] Nor was the

1. William Eliot [chargé d'affaires at The Hague] to Auckland, 21 August 1793 (B.L. Add. Ms 34452), commenting on the latter's impressions on returning home.

2. It is seldom easy to gauge degrees of disappointment and their significance when they are not of critical importance. My impression derives from the tone of a range of correspondence and newspapers, not always to the same effect. For the significance of the summer recess cf. p. 202 above.

3. Lord Apsley to Pitt, nd but between August and November 1793 (P.R.O. 30/8/112).

4. Pitt to Richmond, draft, 17 September 1793; Richmond to Pitt, sd (B.L. Loan Ms 57, vol. 107); Dundas to Richmond, 21 September 1793 (P.R.O., H.O. 50/369); Richmond to Dundas, 22 September 1793, and correspondence of the 24th (B.L. Loan Ms 57, vol. 107).

5. See p. 274 above.

6. Pp. 285–6 above.

explanation well received when it came, for the Austrians were not comforted by the assurance that they would be given the port at the peace.[1] How, they continued to wonder, did all this relate to the Dutch demands? Agreement on that issue was going to be difficult in any case, and it is hard to say how far the limited inducement might have helped. But its absence – the failure to capture Dunkirk – certainly did not ease the task of intercession, and the question of the Dutch indemnity affected the war effort for the next two years. It proved to be an immediate obstacle to the conclusion of an Anglo-Austrian alliance, which in turn affected co-operation for the next campaign; it also limited the co-operation, and sometimes the support, of the Dutch themselves, to an extent that eventually helped lead to their own defeat. The military failures of 1794 and 1795 cannot be understood without reference to the diplomatic stalemate in the later part of 1793. The British were committed to the north-east front; but the main object of the commitment lacked the full participation of the forces required to bring it about.

Failure at Dunkirk thus underlined a problem which success was meant to mitigate. The diplomatic repercussions were compounded by a military effect. For there was now no distinct British initiative in Flanders; and the very limits on British resources for a continental campaign accordingly increased the dependence on future Austrian plans. But these in turn must take account of the Prussians. When York rejoined Coburg, there was thus a clear incentive to achieve a coherent Allied design.[2]

Subsequent developments in the autumn made this the more necessary, as commanders and Governments began to look to the following year. In the closing months of the campaign, before the armies – at least the Allied armies – took up winter quarters, the core of the Coalition seemed to be falling apart. The trouble came once more, and now acutely, from the Prussians. For as they looked at events in the west, they were wondering if the game was worth-while. Although they had signed their Convention with Britain in July, and moved more purposefully on the Rhine,[3] they were not prepared to do too much without proper reward. Their ideas on indemnity remained obscure, and were suspected of being excessive; and hints were soon heard of the need for financial support in any further campaign.[4] The British began to wonder if Prussia might not in fact withdraw,[5] and in the third week of September the suspicions seemed in danger of being confirmed. For Ministers then received a demand for a subsidy, as well as recognition of the gains in Poland, in return for further participation in the war. At the

1. See p. 286 above.
2. See in particular Grenville to Morton Eden, no. 9, 13 September 1793 (F.O. 7/34).
3. Pp. 274, 284 above. Pitt, characteristically, had hopes of their more vigorous action at that time (copy to Murray, Private and Confidential, 19 July 1793; P.R.O. 30/8/102).
4. Grenville to Yarmouth, no. 5, 26 July 1793 (F.O. 29/1), no. 15, 7 September 1793, Yarmouth to Grenville, 10, 29 September 1793 (F.O. 29/2).
5. Grenville to Yarmouth, no. 18, 26 September 1793 (F.O. 29/2).

same time, Frederick William, who was with his army on the Rhine, announced that he would be leaving for Poland, and he did so within the next two weeks.[1] The recent Austrian move into Alsace had had its effect; so too had the defeat at Dunkirk and the ineffectiveness of the British effort.[2]

> Les Promenades eternelles de l'Admiral Howe deviennent un enigme indechiffable . . . Vous me dites que le succès de l'Entreprise sur Dunkerque peut seul calmer le mécontentement du Public; mais le Siège est levé . . .

One conclusion could be drawn, particularly since Parliament would be meeting later. 'Dans des Conjonctures aussi embarraissantes il est neccessaire que vous redoublez d'attention pour observer la contenance du Ministère'. The misfortunes of the year could make a real Prussian contribution the more desirable. Pitt, it seemed, was in some difficulty. It might usefully be increased.

The British were not prepared to yield to this kind of pressure at once. Grenville's reaction was to accept that there seemed little hope of effective Prussian aid 'in the present War', and to see how far it could be replaced from elsewhere – perhaps from Bavaria and Brunswick, certainly if possible from Switzerland.[3] The Prussians themselves should be called on to meet their more limited engagement under the Alliance of 1788 – an idea apparently suggested by the Austrians which was at once taken up.[4] Pitt, while agreeing that no countenance could be given to gains in Poland, was at first disposed to temporise over money; to hear – indeed to ask – what the Prussians had to say, and perhaps discuss less direct measures if a subsidy was out of the question.[5] The matter was referred to the Cabinet, which took a middle line: 'on the whole, our idea was that our language in the first instance should, though firm and distinct, be in some degree conciliatory; but that if necessary it must be peremptory'.[6] An approach was worked out on this understanding; but it failed to gain much response, for while the Prussians did not – as was momentarily feared – withdraw their forces from the western front, they would not promise to meet their obligations under the earlier treaty. Pitt

1. Yarmouth to Grenville, no. 9, 24 September 1793, no. 14, 7 October 1793 (loc. cit.).
2. Frederick William of Prussia, letter signed 'expressly' by the Ministers Fincken-stein, Alvensleben and Haugwitz, to Baron Jacobi [Prussian Minister in London], 22 October 1793 (copy of the decypherment, in Pitt's papers P.R.O. 30/8/338). Jacobi was no anglophile, and consistently reported all the bad news he could find.
3. Grenville to Pitt, 8 October 1793 (P.R.O. 30/8/140); Grenville to Yarmouth, no. 22, 19 October 1793, no. 25, 30 October 1793 (F.O. 29/3). See also p. 282, n2 above.
4. See Duffy, 'War Policy', 64; Grenville to George Henry Rose [chargé d'affaires in Berlin], no. 3, 20 October 1793 (F.O. 64/28). For the treaty of 1788 see I, 538–9, 541–2.
5. See his letters to Grenville from 2 to 8 October in *H.M.C., Dropmore*, II, 433–40.
6. Pitt to Grenville, 10 October 1793 (loc. cit., 442). The Foreign Secretary had been unable to attend.

accordingly informed the Minister in London that there could be no financial support.[1] This produced a slight softening – admittedly very slight, but one that seemed enough to be worth a further effort,[2] and Pitt and Grenville decided to send a special envoy to Berlin. Clearly the best man was needed, and fortunately he was available; for Lord Malmesbury, generally accepted as the leader of his profession and the negotiator of the Triple Alliance of 1788,[3] was at leisure and known to be eager for employment. It was in fact an enforced leisure, since his opposition to Government in the Regency crisis, for which Pitt did not forgive him for several years. But relations had recently improved somewhat – the party talks of the previous year doubtless helped[4] – and in mid-November Malmesbury was offered and accepted the task. He left late in the month, carrying the burden of discussions potentially critical for a full Coalition in 1794.

The possible loss of the Prussians strengthened the leanings towards the Austrian alliance,[5] supported in any case by military facts. In August there were some 93,000 Austrians in the Low Countries and 38,000 on the Rhine, compared with 22,000 British and British-paid and 15,000 Dutch in the north, and 46,000 Prussians in the centre. The Austrians moreover were being reinforced on both fronts, unlike their partners; and they also disposed of a smaller but important force in Italy.[6] They were favoured furthermore by their quality, for while York's headquarters were not impressed by Coburg, the troops were accepted as the most professional in Europe and the command after all had the best Allied record so far. Serious efforts were therefore made to build on the recent Convention, and achieve a fuller alliance which would regulate the next campaign. A negotiation took place throughout the autumn on conditions for peace, the broad nature of indemnities, increased trade, and further military commitments. But while progress was made on some of the issues, construction of a package was held up by the continuing stalemate over indemnities for the Dutch.[7] The atmosphere moreover was soured by difficulties in the south, where the prospect of a fresh front was becoming more urgent;[8] and decisions on

1. The Prussians argued that the treaty of 1788 required the British to keep an army on the continent larger than was there now – presumably meaning one of British troops – and that the recent Convention, which had superseded it for the purpose of the present war, allowed for a co-operation dependent cn circumstances.

2. Grenville's 'Minute of Conference with Baron Jacobi, Nov. 7th & 8th'; F.O. 64/28.

3. See I, 538–42.

4. See p. 178 above. For the better relations in 1793, see Malmesbury to Pitt, 23 January 1793 (P.R.O. 30/8/155), and N.L.S., Minto Mss III 38–9, 11159–60.

5. Expressed clearly by Grenville on 17 September to Whitworth in Russia (*H.M.C., Dropmore*, II, 425), and reinforced thereafter.

6. See Duffy, 'War Policy', 60; and p. 307 below.

7. See p. 294 above. Duffy, loc. cit., 48–78 follows the negotiation in detail to the end of the year.

8. See Ch. IX below.

the various problems were further delayed by the expectation of a conference with the Emperor himself, who was supposed to visit his Netherlands in September or October. He had not left Vienna, however, when Malmesbury set out for Berlin; and as the time approached for consideration of military policy in 1794, its necessary context remained entirely uncertain.

Meanwhile operations continued on the Rhine and the Flanders front. Prussian activity virtually ceased with the King's departure, and the Austrian incursion in Alsace petered out after a spirited start.[1] Farther north, the enemy consolidated on the barrier fortresses from Maubeuge through Lille to Cassel. His morale was still uncertain, confusion always incipient, and enough of the season remained for an Allied strategy still to be worth-while. The British Government, caught unawares by Dunkirk, had no settled preference itself. A further attack there – intermittently considered – might mean holding the troops designed for the West Indies, and others now in demand.[2] A thrust towards Paris, briefly considered this time, did not survive review.[3] York's main force was therefore allowed to rejoin Coburg, who wished to besiege Maubeuge. It was a reasonable plan, for the fortress was a hinge in the French, and a threat to Austrian, lines of communication, and a magnet for a French concentration in its extensive entrenched camp.[4] But the Austrians were driven off before the Allied dispositions were complete, and then a series of attacks in the north forced the remaining British and Austrians back along the coast. In October in fact there seemed to be a danger that York would be cut off from his base, and a further reinforcement had hastily to be sent from England to Ostend. Acting with the troops left in the area, they managed to halt the French advance until the main British force arrived from the south and restored the situation. The Government had been on tenterhooks at the thought of a further defeat, and it was with relief that early in November orders could be sent to return the reinforcements.[5] By then the campaign was clearly at an end, and both York and Coburg were looking to winter quarters. Minor offensive operations were envisaged for the British, to keep so unpredictable an enemy from gaining an advantage.[6] But as the troops prepared to enter 'fixed Cantonments', thoughts in London were largely concentrated, as they had been indeed ever since Dunkirk, on opportunities elsewhere.

1. Pp. 295, 289 above.
2. See pp. 262–3, 266–7, 285n3 and n1 above. The possibility of a further attempt – at what particular time was not decided – seems finally to have been dropped in mid-October (W.O. 6/8, 14 September–13 October 1793).
3. And see p. 287, n2 above.
4. See p. 284 above.
5. W.O. 1/167, 174, 177, 6/8 *passim.*
6. Dundas to Murray, no. 63, 9 December 1794 (W.O. 6/8). See also *L.C.G. III*, II, no. 983.

CHAPTER IX

Victory in France?
The North-West and Toulon

I

At midnight on 13 September 1793, while Pitt and Chatham were sitting with Dundas in his house at Wimbledon, a messenger arrived with news that the Mediterranean fleet, with a Spanish squadron, had landed troops at Toulon on 27–8 August at the city's request. The excitement was great, at an otherwise embarrassing point, only five days after York had been driven off from Dunkirk. When his colleagues left, Dundas sat up completing a special Gazette, which he took to Windsor at first light and then to breakfast with Grenville at Dropmore. The two Secretaries of State carried on to town, to the drafting of despatches and a meeting of Ministers; and at the end of the day there was a lively dinner, with Dundas himself, Pitt, Chatham, Loughborough, Malmesbury and others 'in the highest spirits' over 'a great deal of Turtle' and plenty of claret.[1] The event was indeed worth celebrating, for it came not only as a timely relief, but also as a potential climax to opportunities, intermittently envisaged in London, for the Allies to achieve a presence and end the war inside France itself.

Such prospects centred at first on the north-west, where a fresh levy for the army in February had sparked off the active discontent of regions populated largely by peasants faithful to the Church and acutely hostile to the larger towns. A rising in Brittany in March was soon linked with others in Normandy and the Vendée, all grouped around the royalist cause. As so often on such occasions the rumours were enticing; names began to filter through, agents to get in touch. Reports were now received on matters quite different from the ship movements and dockyard activities which had hitherto comprised the bulk of hard intelligence. Tales of an overall commander, the mysterious Gaston on

1. Dundas to Duke of Buccleugh, 14 September [1793] (S.R.O., Buccleugh Ms GD 224/30/9/12); Amberst's diary, vol. II, sd (Kent C.A.O.); Gilbert Elliot's diary 11–14 September 1793 (N.L.S., Minto Mss 11159–60), in which the entry for the 13th must have been written on the 14th.

Some intimation of the event may have been received as early as the 7th (see Pitt to Grenville, attr. to that date, in *H.M.C., Dropmore*, II, 422). But if so the information seems to have been less precise, and in fact it probably referred to a report of the situation developing before the result. As late as the 13th itself Pitt was very uncertain what was going on (to Edward Eliot, 13 September; Stanhope Ms S5 07).

whom Richmond pinned his hopes,[1] led the exiled Princes, the Dutch and the British all to try to contact him in the early summer. But the obstacles to support, let alone co-operation, were severe. The scale and control of British means of information, at least beyond the strictly naval, were rudimentary. The sums spent on secret service in France had hitherto been modest, yielding corresponding results to which a possible exception in the London-based missions of 1790 proved the rule.[2] Political intelligence now remained confined to Paris, and its quality was not high; while warning and news of military movements were proving conspicuously thin. The obvious point of contact with the north-west was the Channel Islands; but the celebrated 'Correspondence' of later years was then in its infancy.[3] The attempt to reach Gaston – distinctly amateurish – was controlled direct from England,[4] and the lack of background knowledge, of co-ordination between the ,islands' authorities, and resources in trained men and vessels, produced more smoke than light. As was to be proved in the course of the war, and has been amply shown since, it takes hard-won experience to assess and aid resistance in any form. In March 1793 Evan Nepean, the able Under Secretary at the Home Office, observed that 'We have been out of luck with our Intelligence'.[5] Until that position could be improved, it was premature to count on anything more.

But improvement did not keep pace with events. It was not until June that reliable contact could be established with Brittany, and not until August that answers were received to specific British inquiries. These were pondered in the early autumn.[6] But by then the season was changing, the insurgents' first impetus had died away, and Toulon was engaging more immediate thought. The five months required to elicit proper intelligence had in fact been those of the rising's best hopes.

The tenor of the replies when they came, however, pointed other difficulties. The Bretons and Vendéans had been disappointed of their principal aim: after capturing Saumur, which could have threatened the western approaches to Paris itself, they had turned their main effort in the other direction against the port of Nantes, which they failed to take. But they were still planning to gain some coastal outlet, at which

1. P. 268, n3 above.
2. See Cobban, 'British Secret Service in France, 1784–92' (*E.H.R.*, LXIX, no. 271), and p. 136, ns 3–5 above. For Miles and Elliot in 1790 see I, 566–7 and p. 48, n3 above.
3. A. Cobban, 'The Beginning of the Channel Isles Correspondence, 1789–1794' (*E.H.R.*, LXXVII, no. 302), republished as ch. 11 in his *Aspects of the French Revolution* (1968).
4. It failed.
5. To Philippe Fall [Lieutenant Governor of Jersey], 13 March 1793 (Cobban, *E.H.R.*, loc. cit., 40).
6. For a summary of early contacts, followed by the more successful missions of the Chevalier de Tinténiac, see Cobban, loc. cit., 42–5, and N.F. Richards, loc. cit. (p. 200, n1 above), 90–4. A retrospective précis of communications from June 1793 is contained in P.R.O., W.O. 1/389.

they could receive aid, and they wanted this in the shape of an émigré force. The idea took London rather by surprise, for however different their views on the merits, British Ministers had been assuming that support of a rising would mean the provision of British troops. Richmond called for them to hold St Malo, Dundas's opposition turned on British commitments, and Pitt thought in terms of British resources for his favoured coastal assaults.[1] But by May, before Richmond's opinions became a matter for Cabinet discussion, the strategy for the Low Countries had been agreed, and there was nothing effective to spare for northern France. Nor for that matter was the Channel fleet ready to cover the Western Approaches.[2] Even if the needs had been known precisely, resources of the kind envisaged were short.

Similar considerations might have applied to émigré troops. At the least, it would have taken time to assemble such an expedition: when supplies and terms of service had been settled, transports and convoy had still to be found. But in any case the problems then would not have been military alone; indeed the latter's solution would have precipitated the rest. For to have despatched an émigré force would have meant facing at the very outset the question of British intervention in the future settlement of France.

Both these problems – the constraints on resources, and the definition of aims – of course had connotations for the Alliance as a whole. This became clear in one quarter even before the main framework of the Coalition was complete. The British predilection early in the war for assaults on the French coasts encouraged the search for European troops when the commitment in the Low Countries emerged. This was not solely for their use in Flanders. The early arrangements with Hanover and Hesse Cassel kept the options open;[3] and in one other instance the emphasis on coastal operations was direct. The Convention with Russia in March 1793 provided for a naval squadron to augment the British fleet.[4] But this had not in fact been urged from London: the Admiralty was lukewarm about the offer, which came from the Russians themselves. The British, as they made clear, would have preferred some troops; and they pressed the point as soon as the Convention was signed.[5] The objects moreover were specific. A Russian force was wanted either for joint operations in Flanders, or for 'attacking the vulnerable parts of the French Coasts in the Channel or on the Ocean so as to distract the

1. Pp. 266–9 above.
2. See pp. 263–4, 282–3, 292 above.
3. Pp. 264, 281 above. Those with Hesse Cassel were broadly in line with the arrangements in the War of American Independence.
4. P. 276 above.
5. For their emphasis before signature, see Grenville's note to Vorontsov, 15 March 1793, and immediately afterwards, Grenville to Whitworth, no. 4, 26 March 1793 (P.R.O., F.O. 65/24).

attention of the Enemy, and to encourage any favourable dispositions which may shew themselves in the Provinces'. It was impossible at that point to decide between the two; but in either case we would provide the sea transport and should be empowered to make the choice.[1]

This thinking was reflected in Pitt's remarks in April, when he speculated to Richmond on the prospect of using Russians against a French port; and Whitworth in St Petersburg was quite correct in stressing the coastal alternative when he presented his Government's views.[2] There was a further inducement to do so; for, as he observed, Russia had already refused troops as a form of assistance for the main operations whenever this had been broached by Austria and Prussia. His own efforts, however, failed. For if the Russians were anxious now to co-operate with Britain, this did not mean a change to military involvement in the war in the west. On the contrary, a maritime partnership could buttress the pursuit of independent interests; and it was not hard to see a way in which this aim could be linked with their own views on the future in France.

The Empress Catherine's hatred of republicanism, as a revolt against a lawful sovereign, was as real as her use of the ensuing events to serve her own concerns.[3] The execution of Louis XVI heightened her determination to see the legitimate dynasty restored to the throne. While not quite prepared to take the step of acknowledging the captive Dauphin as King, she welcomed a visit from the Comte d'Artois – the younger of his two uncles – and encouraged his proposal for the service of an émigré corps which Russia would support. The idea indeed had several attractions, and was raised at an apposite point. Its adoption would meet her genuine wish to preserve and help the royalists. It would balance Austrian and Prussian influence, and promote a claim to help shape the peace. And it could be used, as it was at once, in response to the British approach, to meet the request for troops in a less committed form. A reply was quickly prepared, advocating an émigré force under d'Artois, to be paid by Russia which in turn would receive – as under an earlier alliance – a British subsidy.[4] D'Artois himself was sent on to England, to further the project and consult on plans. It was all, wrote Whitworth, well 'suited to the whole system of this Country, being a Compound of Magnificence and Misery'.[5] It was certainly suited to the range of objects which the Empress had in view.

1. Grenville to Whitworth, no. 4, 26 March 1793 (loc. cit.).
2. P.R.O., W.O. 30/81 (see p. 266 above); Whitworth to Grenville, no. 24, 5/16 April 1793 (F.O. 65/24).
3. There was indeed a certain analogy with her attitude in the War of American Independence, when she refused to supply the British with troops as they asked, but also to recognise the United States.
4. By art. 6 of the Anglo-Russian subsidy treaty of 1755. The proposal was sent in April in the form of a Counter Project.
5. To Grenville, no. 27, 18/29 April 1793 (F.O. 65/24). By 'misery', as is clear from the context, he meant 'miserliness'.

The proposal was received angrily in London – so angrily in fact that Whitworth at the other end did his best to tone down the response. The demand for a subsidy aroused instant resentment: unless it was dropped, Grenville insisted, 'all possibility of a future concert is at an end'.[1] But Ministers were not only upset by the idea of paying for what they regarded as a moral obligation, or even by a call for payment without forfeiting direct control. They were also alarmed by the implications of financing one particular group of Frenchmen, and thereby seeming to give it political support.[2]

There was also some immediate embarrassment in that the leader was d'Artois; for the Prince had earlier run up debts in England which laid him open to arrest. The likelihood now indeed seemed to be such that the Government discouraged him from landing, and he was persuaded to sail on to Ostend. But this was a marginal nuisance, which could be overcome. The important point, as Grenville observed, was that we maintained we were not at war to impose an authority on France without referring to French wishes.[3]

That was clear, as far as it went. The war aims had been stated publicly on more than one occasion: they were 'indemnity for the past, and security for the future'.[4] Any French Government that would treat on such terms and carried effective authority could be accepted for the purpose of negotiation. As Pitt now confirmed, 'if sufficient security and reparation could be had for this country', he would not necessarily refuse to 'allow their Government to remain even upon its present footing'.[5] But of course this raised its own questions, given the nature of that Government and the emergence of a resistance which was calling for external support. When the British reply was sent to Russia it was not yet known that the insurgents wanted aid in the shape of an émigré force; but they were known to be royalists, and since they seemed to be gaining ground it might 'perhaps be desirable not to neglect' a chance of putting

1. To Whitworth, no. 9, 14 June 1793 (loc. cit.); and see his first reaction in no. 7 of 17 May. Whitworth's answer to no. 9 was made in his no. 41 of 24 June/5 July (F.O. 65/25).

The severity of the reaction showed that the Government had not expected to include Russia in the 'hiring' of foreign troops which it accepted at the start of the war, even though Pitt had stated in a debate on 11 March that foreign contingents might have to be secured on such terms 'in order to press on all sides of the common enemy', and was privately hoping for a Russian force to that end.

2. These feelings were intensified by a temporary misunderstanding, for Grenville at any rate interpreted the proposal initially as applying to a joint French and Russian force – which indeed he learned later had been suggested at one point by d'Artois himself ('Minute of Conference with Count Vorontsov, July 11th, 1793', in F.O. 97/342). This would strengthen the identification of a British connexion with Frenchmen who would actually be operating with a subsidised ally, and therefore be less likely to fall under any real British control.

3. To Whitworth, no. 9, 14 June 1793 (F.O. 65/24).
4. Pitt in the Commons, 25 April 1793 (*P.R.*, XXXV, 302).
5. Speech of 17 June 1793 in the Commons (loc. cit., 675).

a Bourbon at their head.[1] Ministers went no farther, and they drew no consequences. 'There was no intention,' Pitt stated, 'if the country had not been attacked, to interfere in the internal affairs of France. But having been attacked, I affirm, that there is nothing . . . which pledges us not to take advantage of any interference in the internal affairs of France that may be necessary'.[2] If aid was given, it was as an operation of war.[3] The implications for the future should, and could, not be specified.

The exiled Princes themselves indeed had so far been held at arm's length. The Government had declined to recognise a Regent, and helped persuade the Austrians to do likewise. When d'Artois in March suggested meeting Pitt the acceptance was distinctly cautious, and he opted for a warmer welcome in St Petersburg instead. He was now returned to the continent without setting foot in England.[4] Ministers were as chary as ever of underwriting the strict Bourbon cause,[5] while the discussions with Russia for a further alliance soon moved away from an émigré force. The insurgents' replies to the British question reached London on 7 September. When the news of Toulon followed six days later, no clear response had emerged.

II

Over the next few weeks reports flooded in on events in the south: from the Mediterranean fleet, from British envoys, and commanders and advisers quickly deployed. For there was a rapid application of effort to this new, exciting prospect: a pressure as concentrated in aim as its ramifications were widespread – in Madrid and Naples, Turin and Verona, Berne and Vienna and the Flanders camps.

Such extensive activity stemmed from the belief that the cession of Toulon was a blow, as Pitt put it, 'in every view the most important which could be struck towards the final success of the war'.[6] There was the promise of a combination more powerful than Brittany and the

1. Grenville to Whitworth, no. 9, 14 June 1793 (F.O. 65/24).
2. Speech of 17 June (*P.R.*, XXXV, 675).
3. Cf. Pitt in the Commons on 30 May 1794, in a retrospective review: 'I at the same time assert[ed], that if an opportunity should occur, in which we might interfere with advantage in the internal government of France, we certainly should avail ourselves of every such opportunity, as an operation of the war' (*P.R.*, XXXVIII (1794), 371–2).
4. Richards, loc. cit., 128–31; and see p. 301 above. On the other side, Talleyrand, sent over once more in May to discuss reparations – in the colonies – was given a chilly reception (see pp. 199–200 above).
5. Cf. pp. 203–4 above.
6. To Westmorland, 15 September 1793 (Cambridge University Library Add. Ms 6958/7). And cf. Grenville to Buckingham, sd – 'I am much mistaken, if the business at Toulon is not decisive of the war' (Buckingham, II, 241–2); Dundas to Murray, 14 September 1793 (P.R.O., W.O. 6/8).

Vendée yet offered: a base from which to support the risings of large urban – as against predominantly rural – populations, in an area now made accessible to Allied forces by sea as well as by land. Toulon was one of the two great naval ports, equalled only by Brest in the north; its possession – and presumably with its fleet intact – would secure control of the Mediterranean.[1] This in itself would have important effects on the bordering states, and on the force of the arguments for a southern strategy. But the hopes were higher than that, for they centred on a more immediate opening: the success, or at least continuance, of revolts which had been spreading in south-east France, and might yet, with Allied help, light a fuse which would end the war.

For Toulon was the third southern city to defy the Government in Paris. It followed Lyons and Marseilles in the struggle – at one time spread through sixty *départements* – that rose to a peak when the Jacobins in Paris crushed the Girondins. The decision owed as much perhaps to the British blockade, sustained since July, as to other factors, and it came moreover at a moment when the risings were suffering a partial reverse. Indeed the step was taken when Government troops had largely cut off landward supplies, and were advancing on Marseilles itself. But Lyons was still in friendly hands – as strongly, it seemed, as before – and the injection of Allied troops might well turn the tide. The whole position in France was confused. The Rhone valley and Provence were still up in arms. Here above all was an opportunity for a vigorous blow.

This state of affairs, since mid-summer, had underlined the British arguments for a greater co-ordinated pressure in the south. Their programme for Toulon in September could scarcely indeed have been formed so quickly had they not already been thinking about Mediterranean operations.[2] Toulon itself, and Marseilles, had figured in these earlier speculations, for the naval blockade led the city authorities in July to open a cautious line to Hood. But that was one possibility – and not then the most prominent[3] – in a fluid situation, for which provision should be made if resources could be found. In June, while the Government sought to reach closer contact with the Sardinians, it tried to persuade the Austrians to increase their forces in that quarter.[4] In July, Pitt thought of withdrawing some British and German troops from Flanders, to be sent to the Mediterranean for whatever might come about. The aim was to 'distress the enemy on more sides than one while their internal distraction continues'; and Dundas contemplated sending a force of 4–5,000 men to Gibraltar, to take advantage of any

1. Pp. 266–7 above.
2. See pp. 278–80 above.
3. As late as 27 August Pitt was earmarking a possible force for attacking Toulon, but in the summer of 1794 (P.R.O. 30/8/196). See also Dundas's conversation early in September, in Gilbert Elliot's diary, 8–9 September 1793; N.L.S., Minto Ms 11159.
4. Grenville to Morton Eden, no. 2, 11 June; and see further his no. 4, 12 July 1793 (F.O. 7/33).

opportunity.[1] This might be in Provence, or conceivably in Corsica where the inhabitants were in revolt. With the advantage of a fleet on station, it was desirable to be prepared.

The summer hopes had not been realised, and indeed they were far from firm. The Austrians were not impressed by the proposal to increase their strength in Italy, particularly when the prospects were brightening on the main front. They might consider doing so in return for some territorial advantage; but this was unlikely to commend itself to the Sardinians.[2] The detachment of men from the Low Countries was also not immediately possible; the plans for Dunkirk were about to be confirmed, as well as those for later operations, and even north-west France, a closer target, could not be allotted British troops. Pitt and Dundas were beginning to talk in terms of Hessians for the fronts outside Flanders.[3] But whatever the obstacles Ministers at least had considered a policy, and given the necessary requirements some thought.

It was thus possible now to embark on a train of action at once. There was indeed no delay in taking the first steps. By the time that Dundas and Pitt met at dinner on 14 September, orders had been drafted for 5,000 Hessians from Flanders and two British companies in each of the five battalions in Gibraltar, and for the preparation of two regiments in Ireland destined for the West Indies. The British Minister in Turin was instructed to ask for 5,000 Austrians from northern Italy at once; and Sir William Hamilton in Naples for 5,000 Neapolitans under the terms of the recent Convention.[4] The Hessians, it was hoped, would soon be replaced in Flanders by others from the same source, and since York had recently been sent eight British regiments which he knew he could keep until early October, he should not be too badly off in the aftermath of Dunkirk.[5] On 16 September Pitt was envisaging a force of 9,700 British and Germans for Toulon. His general pool was enlarged in the next fortnight, when half of York's reinforcements were ordered back to England; but these in theory could not be called on, for they were intended for the West Indies. Even so, by the end of the month a respectable body was earmarked on paper, to swell the 4,400 British and

---

1. Pitt to Murray, 19 July 1793 (J. Holland Rose, 'Pitt and the Campaign of 1793 in Flanders'; *E.H.R.*, XXIV, no. 4), 748; Dundas to Grenville, nd but July 1793 (*H.M.C., Dropmore*, II, 408). See also Dundas to Lord Mulgrave, Secret, no. 1, 8 July 1793 (H.O. 50/455). As early as April Pitt had envisaged sending a force to the Mediterranean in August or September, after an attack on the north-west coasts (see p. 266 above).

2. Duffy, 'War Policy', 53.

3. Correspondence with Murray in July, in P.R.O. 30/8/102 and 162, W.O. 1/166 and 6/7.

4. Despatches throughout the Toulon episode were listed and summarised for Grenville after the event, and the Abstract may be found in B.L. Add. Ms 59064. The documents themselves are scattered through the relevant F.O., W.O. and H.O. volumes in the P.R.O. (see Note on Sources to this Chapter). See p. 279 above for the Convention with The Two Sicilies.

5. See pp. 289, 297 above.

Spaniards already landed from the ships at Toulon.[1]

The main hope, however, lay in the other Allies: in a direct contribution, and also if possible in covering operations. This was not unreasonable, given the initial British thoughts on the war. Efforts in Europe, whether coastal assaults or on a main Allied front, were viewed in the context of a more extensive strategy. The West Indies in particular claimed resources, military as well as naval, and these were not seen in London as conflicting seriously with services nearer home. Dundas reflected the Government's mind when he wrote in the summer that it was not called on to make a 'disagreeable' choice: there was enough strength available 'if properly applied'.[2] The application could mean an Allied contribution, as it had meant a British force in Flanders; and Pitt indeed had already been thinking along those lines. In the spring he had speculated on a detachment of British troops for a Mediterranean attack, after which they would carry on to the Caribbean. But this was designed by its nature as a limited task, and when wider prospects beckoned he had postulated an Allied force.[3] He now saw this increasing quickly to some 23,000 men – 3,000 Spaniards, 6,000 Neapolitans, 5,000 Austrians, 9,000 Sardinians – with large additions in 1794. A further 11,000 Sardinians and 10,000 Austrians, with possibly 10 or 12,000 Swiss, and smaller bodies of Corsicans and Saxons (from Baden) might be gathered by the early spring; perhaps joined in the summer by 4 or 5,000 British returned from the West Indies if operations there had gone well. The final total 'allowing for deductions would be an Army in the south of France of near 60,000 Men', of whom some five-sixths would come, by agreement or hire, from the continent.[4]

Some of these immediate reinforcements were in fact acquired. Early in September the British envoys in Italy, who of course learned the news before it reached London, were urging their needs under treaty; and with partial success. Two thousand Neapolitans were in Toulon by the end of the month, 2,000 more early in October, and by then over 1,400 Sardinians had also arrived.[5] More of these last were asked for; but while

1. Pitt's paper is in P.R.O. 30/8/196. For the instructions on York's reinforcements see Dundas to Murray 14, 18, 23, 28 September 1793 (W.O. 6/8); the loss of four battalions was notional, since they had not in fact disembarked when ordered home. A return of 18 September gives 1,262 British (as compared with Pitt's 'Marines landed – 1500' in his paper of the 16th) and 3,161 Spaniards ashore ('Troops arrived at Toulon at the different periods . . .'; B.L. Add. Ms 59064).

2. See p. 269 above. And see also Dundas to Murray, 14 September 1793 (P.R.O., W.O. 6/8).

3. Pp. 266–7 above for his thoughts in April; Pitt to Murray, 19 July 1793 (P.R.O. 30/8/102); and see his paper of 27 August 1793 (p. 304, n3 above), in which he contemplated an Allied army totalling 50,000 men.

4. P.R.O. 30/8/196. There are some inconsistencies in the paper, for both figures and timing; but this seems to be the broad conclusion.

5. B.L. Add. Ms 59064; correspondence in F.O. 67/12, 70/6. The news of Toulon seems to have reached Italy first via Nelson in the *Agamemnon*. For the Convention with Sardinia see pp. 278–9 above. Trevor in Turin suggested hiring troops from Malta and the Papal States as well.

The Duke of York. *Attributed to Mather Brown*

The Earl of Moira, *by Reynolds*

Sep.r 18th

Force which it is supposed may be
collected at Toulon, by the End
of October or early in November

Brit[ish]   Rank & File.
Marines landed   1500.

Flank Companies
from Gibraltar }   6 00
Flank Companies
from Ireland   }   20 00
Two Battallions
from Flanders to be
replaced by detach.t } 12 00
from the Guards
                         5 3 00
Cavalry from Ireland }   9 00
                         6 2 00
Hessians from Flanders
to be replaced by the add.l
Corps ordered —   5 000

                                          11. 2 00
                    Spanish (approx)   8 000
                    Neapolitans   6 000
                    Sardinians   9 000
                    Austrians   5 000
                                          3 8. 2 00

This Force may be estimated (allowing
for some deduction) at 30 000 Men.
To this may properly be added
some time from Corsica, and
probably early in the Spring, an
additional Body of 11 000 Sardinians
brought here or of 10 000 Austrians
and some Troops of Baden from hence
51   Probably also a Body of Swiss; and
in the Course of the Summer (if
the Expedition to the West Indies is

successful) about 4 or 5 000 British
on their Return from the Islands.
If 10 or 12 000 Swiss can be secured
It seems not unreasonable to expect
that by the Beginning of next Year
there may be an Army in the
South of France of near 60 000 Men

Force to be employed in Flanders
or on the Coast of France in the
Channel and the Ocean

Force now in Flanders   110. 000
Regiments to be disposable
from hence early in
next Year.
Nine Reg.s drafted
to be compleated 4 800   7 000
Other Reg.s —   6 00
Guards   1 500
5 New Reg.s per unions   5 000
Cavalry —   2 000   21. 000 (52)
                            21.300

                                          13 0. 0 00
To this it is hoped may be
added an additional Force of
Austrians   2 0. 000
Bavarians (to be employed
on this side or substituted
in place of an additional
Corps of Austrians drawn
from Alsace & Lorraine)   2 5. 000
                                          1 75. 000

Toulon — Army —

52

Pitt's notes on troops for Toulon, September 1793 (P.R.O. 30/8/196)

Toulon itself was given priority, the British still hoped for continuing – indeed increased – pressure from the Sardinians elsewhere. For if the French were not to concentrate their efforts on recapturing the city, they must be put under greater threat farther afield. The proposed advance against Nice should be mounted, though not at the expense of Toulon itself,[1] and operations renewed in the Alps to recover Savoy. The former in fact was expected shortly, and ships from the fleet were ready to support. The Alpine front was in less good shape, for the French had recovered some of their summer losses, a counter-offensive was rumoured, and the Sardinians were known to be over-stretched. When Grenville sent off his first crop of despatches, they therefore included further proposals for aid to Sardinia, as one aspect now of the measures to exploit Toulon.[2]

There were two other sources from which troops might be gained, whether or not their supply would release Sardinians for Toulon. One was Switzerland. But the efforts there failed after rising hopes in August; the French influence was too strong and the prospects on the Rhine were too uncertain.[3] The other was Austria, which already had 8,000 men under treaty with the Sardinians, and a permanent force in its own territories of 'the Milanese' to the east. Negotiation was needed if any of the latter were to be secured, but the British efforts to this end had hitherto yielded no result.[4] Fresh exhortations were therefore sent to Turin and Vienna to compose their differences and seize the advantage which might be opening in the south.

But more was soon wanted directly for Toulon. The most recent demand on the Austrians had been for 12–15,000 men. While their co-operation with Sardinia was still required, to be gained by territorial agreements, they were now asked to send 5,000 to the port itself, with 15,000 to follow.[5] These forces should come from northern Italy, shipping at Genoa and/or Leghorn – a proposal which would need diplomatic handling in two distinctly francophile states.[6] At first it seemed likely that the immediate request would be met in Vienna; possibly as an inducement to the British to maintain their strength in Flanders.[7] On 25 September, an offer was made of 5,000 men. But no

1. Grenville to Trevor, no. 12, 14 September 1793 (F.O. 67/12). By mid-October the emphasis had shifted somewhat in favour of the more distant operations (see précis of despatches in B.L. Add. Ms 59064).

2. Cf. pp. 284, 306 above.

3. Pp. 282 above. Only a small body, raised 'clandestinely', was in prospect (Fitzgerald to Grenville, Confidential, 6 September 1793, F.O. 74/3); and even this did not materialise. For Grenville's anxiety to use Swiss resources to support operations in southern France see eg his letter to Fitzgerald of 26 September 1793, in *H.M.C.*, *Dropmore*, II, 427.

4. See pp. 296–7 above. Relations between Austria and Sardinia were also suffering from disagreements on the front itself.

5. Duffy, 'War Policy', 61n1; Grenville to Trevor no. 12, 14 September 1793 (F.O. 67/12). Cf. p. 305 above.

6. See pp. 296–7 above.

7. See Duffy, loc. cit., 68.

orders followed, and in the next few weeks it began to look as if they might not be sent.

For as September gave way to October the Toulon project was assessed, in Vienna as in London, in its strategic context. And seen from that quarter, the rating was not high. The Austrians had not favoured efforts in the south when the campaign in the north was going well; they were no more inclined to do so now that it was slowing down again. If a serious diversion was intended, Provence and the Rhone were too far away. If it was designed to sway matters in Paris, the same argument applied. North-west France met both these aims better, and might perhaps better merit support. On military grounds the Austrians could thus see little attraction in the British demand. Nor were they disposed on reflection to meet it at a time when military proposals turned so critically on the diplomatic effects. There was much business now in train, the different aspects of which were connected: the settlement of strengths and dispositions with that of future indemnities, the shape of European strategy with the rising question of finance. There were exchanges to be made, bargains to be struck, in a developing situation. To Austria, the south was something of a side-show in these central affairs.

No troops from the Milanese therefore reached Toulon in October. Other reinforcements were received there after the first week in the month. Just under 1,000 Spaniards, over 600 Sardinians, and some 1,250 British, brought the total landed from the start to some 12,900.[1] These additions, which would have been respectable in the early stages, were now falling short of both intentions and needs. Only Naples, it seemed, could be counted on for any further immediate strength: the Sardinians were coming under pressure in the Alps, and the movement against Nice was under way; no more was expected from Spain, and there was no sign of the Hessians and the British from the north. These last reinforcements were in fact not even on their way: of the 9,700 whom Pitt had listed, a Gibraltar contingent alone had arrived. The troops from Ireland, some approaching readiness, were held for lack of transports; and those in Flanders by the developments after Dunkirk.[2] It was early in November before any British could be spared, and later in that month before a Hessian force embarked. By then both were destined for another service.

---

1. Returns in B.L. Add. Ms 59064. There were also 450 Toulonese. Hood managed to hire some 1,500 Maltese to replace seamen landed from his fleet (see p. 306, n5 above).

Holland Rose, II, 151 gives a figure at this date of 16,912. The difference lies mainly in higher numbers for the Spaniards and the friendly French.

2. See pp. 305, 297 above, and Fortescue, op. cit., 141–50, 157–66, 174–5 for details and comments.

The prospect of troops from Ireland was still being coupled with those from Gibraltar in mid-October (Dundas to Commissioners in Toulon – see p. 310 below – 18 October 1793; précis in B.L. Add. Ms 59064).

The situation on the ground at Toulon began slowly to change as a result. This was due in part to the French Government's successes elsewhere. The revolt at Lyons was suppressed on 9 October, Marseilles was already virtually reduced, and more troops were available to concentrate against the Allies. As ominous, though no one could have guessed it, was the earlier posting of the young Captain Buonaparte to control the artillery on the heights beyond the port. For Toulon was dominated by hills, and as the weeks went by the odds lengthened against inadequate numbers stretched on a front of over three miles. The attackers were turned defenders, awaiting fresh strength to command the high ground. Nor were the British happy about the quality of their partners. The Spaniards were not pulling their weight, the Neapolitans were deteriorating. By the end of October Hood, hitherto confident, was beginning to lose heart.[1]

The silence from Vienna was expressive of the internal problems of the Coalition. From Toulon itself the need soon arose for a statement of policy towards France. It was indeed precipitated by one from the commander on the spot, which, designed to meet his own situation, raised – as so often in such cases – an immediate embarrassment for his Government at home.

Hood had acted in response to the prospect of an invitation to enter the city, for which a proclamation of his intentions was required. This he issued on 23 August, pledging assistance in return for a declaration in favour of the monarchy and the disarming of the ships and forts. The Toulonese replied by recognising Louis XVII as King, and 'A Monarchic Government' on the lines laid down by the National Assembly and formulated in 1791. On the 28th, having landed safely, Hood acknowledged their decision, and took possession in trust for Louis XVII.[2]

This was awkward. Ministers appreciated the ease with which the prize had been gained. But was it necessary to stipulate monarchy to secure the invitation; and should possession have been taken in trust (unlike Dunkirk when in prospect),[3] and for a named King? Hood was reminded that 'the true ground of the War' was 'to repel an . . . unprovoked Aggression'; the restoration of monarchy had not been declared as an object, and while circumstances justified an 'interference' to re-establish 'some regular Government', this was solely in order to

---

1. To Dundas, 27, 28 October 1793 (P.R.O., H.O. 28/14), where he still professes a guarded if diminished optimism; to Chatham, Private, 20, 27 October 1793 (P.R.O. 30/8/367), where he begins to talk of 'fatigue' and 'despair'.

2. Hood to Dundas, 25, 29 August 1793 (H.O. 28/14). The Toulonese declaration is in P.R.O., P.C. 1/125, and was published, together with Hood's two Proclamations, in *The Annual Register* for 1793, State Papers, 171–3.

The Toulonese referred to the constitution of '1789'; but in the context that meant the constitution of 1791, which the Assembly then adopted.

3. See pp. 285–6 above. There were of course other factors involved then.

hasten peace.[1] Familiar words. But they were beginning to need elaboration; with British – and Allied – troops now on French soil, and holding a city by request, something more would soon have to be said. Even if Hood's proclamations had accurately conveyed Government policy, they could scarcely have been allowed to stand on their own. As it was, an authoritative statement was undoubtedly needed, in a matter of such importance where every word had to be weighed.

It was not only in public that Government had to speak. It had to lay down guidelines for relations with the French and for conduct inside France. As soon as news was received of the landings, Ministers agreed that a 'ministerial' – or political – personage should be sent out. The choice fell on Gilbert Elliot, who had been earmarked for Commissioner at Dunkirk; and his appointment was combined with that of a commander already despatched for the forces ashore, Lieutenant General O'Hara, and of Hood himself as Commissioners for Toulon.[2] The task, as Elliot remarked with satisfaction, was 'infinitely important, and equally delicate', and he was soon closeted with Pitt, Dundas and the Lord Chancellor in drafting the Commission's instructions. The final version owed much to Pitt. It gave substance to the public statement which the Ministry issued on 29 October, and was supplemented by a proclamation to the Toulonese from the Commissioners on 20 November.[3]

In facing the consequences of apparent success, Ministers had to find a formula which would translate the sense of earlier statements into a working arrangement. The result demands some scrutiny, for it has provoked varying assessments. The public statement of 29 October followed on Pitt's remarks in June.[4]

1. Chatham to Hood, 25 September 1793 (H.O. 28/14). Cf. Dundas in July on the growing difficulty of separating the restoration of 'good order in France' from the 'professed' objects of the war, in circumstances in which future security was making the former 'certainly the most material object' (to Richmond, 8 July 1793; B.L. Loan Ms 57, vol. 107).

2. It was dated 29 October 1793, when Elliot left. He had learned as early as 14 September that he would probably be going, and was told definitely on the 17th (diary; N.L.S., Minto Ms 11160). For his proposed Commissionership at Dunkirk see p. 286, n3 above. On 25 October, in view of the importance of the mission, he was made a Privy Councillor.

3. Elliot's diary (loc. cit.) throws some light on the drafting of the Instructions; Pitt's contribution (which is stressed there, and see also Pitt to Grenville, 3, [5], 9, [11], 17 October; *H.M.C., Dropmore*, II, 435–47) appears in his annotations to the draft, in P.R.O. 30/8/334. The final version is in F.O. 95/4/6, and is printed almost in full in Paul Cottin, *Toulon et les Anglais en 1793* (1898), 419–25. P.R.O. 30/8/334 also contains a draft of the Declaration of 29 October with a few small corrections by Pitt. The final version was published in *The London Gazette*, and may be found, with the text of the Commissioners' Proclamation of 20 November 1793, in (*inter alia*) *P.H.*, XXX, cols. 1057–61. The French text is in P.R.O., P.C. 1/125. The contents of the Commissioners' Proclamation were discussed with Elliot before he left England in October.

On the evidence, I cannot agree with *The Cambridge History of Foreign Policy*, I, 243 (which perhaps took it from E.D. Adams, *The Influence of Grenville on Pitt's Foreign Policy*, 22–5) that Grenville's attitude here 'was more flexible than that of Pitt'.

4. P. 303 above.

His Majesty by no means disputes the Right of France to reform its Laws. It never would have been his wish to employ the Influence of external Force with respect to the particular Forms of Government to be established in an independent Country. Neither has He now that Wish, except in so far as such Interference is become essential to the Security and Repose of other Powers. Under these Circumstances, He demands from France, . . . the Termination of a System of Anarchy, which has no Force but for the Purpose of Mischief. . . . The King demands that some legitimate and stable Government should be established, founded on the acknowledged Principles of universal Justice, and capable of maintaining with other Powers the accustomed relations of Union and Peace. . . .

So far, so good. But how to bring that about?

His Majesty invites the Co-operation of the People of France. . . . He calls upon them to join the Standard of an hereditary Monarchy, not for the purpose of deciding, in this Moment of Disorder, Calamity, and Public Danger, on all the Modifications of which this Form of Government may hereafter be susceptible, but in order to unite themselves once more under the Empire of Law, of Morality, and of Religion. . . .

The combination was echoed in the Commissioners' statement of November. 'His Majesty . . . by no means desires to prescribe the form of [France's] Government'. But in drafting the French text, the words 'un gouvernement regulier' were changed to 'la monarchie héréditaire'.[1]

The object was thus defined by two circumstances; a fact which was to have repercussions as circumstances changed. 'Interference' in the form of French government was held to be justified because a peace giving future security could not be reached with the 'system' as it stood. And secondly, given the nature of the current resistance, the rallying point was taken to be an hereditary monarchy. For whatever the opinions of different men who opposed the Jacobins in different places, they were led in arms mostly by royalists under the Bourbon flag.[2] Against the background of Hood's commitment, it was on this ground that Pitt

---

1. Richards, loc. cit., 110–11. The English text (*P.H.*, XXX, col. 1060) has 'monarchy'.

2. Though not in Marseilles, which flew the tricolour throughout. But the young Buonaparte, not unlike Pitt, drew his conclusions from the effects.

'*The Marseillais*: Vendée wants a King, wants a counter-revolution. . . . Do we not fly the tricolour flag?

. . . *The Soldier*: It is no use bothering with words. It is necessary to analyse actions; and you must admit that in sizing up yours it is easy to prove you counter-revolutionaries' (*Le Souper à Beaucaire* (July 1793), transl: Somerset de Chair, 1945).

Some of those opposing the central Government did so as supporters of a southern federalist movement which had grown up in the past two to three years, and was not itself royalist.

argued, in the course of drafting, for 'a more pointed recommendation of monarchical government with proper limitations'. He could not see 'any way so likely to unite considerable numbers in one vigorous effort'.

> This by no means precludes us from treating with any other form of regular government, if, in the end, any other should be solidly established; but it holds out monarchy as the only force from which we expect any good, and in favour of which we are disposed to enter into concert.[1]

Hereditary monarchy then, at least as the immediate proposition. But what brand of hereditary monarchy? The Government was anxious not to be identified with any one party, and above all with immediate claims from members of the royal family itself. This was made abundantly clear – only one émigré was allowed to leave for Toulon, and he was stopped at Genoa at the last moment[2] – and by none more than Pitt. He commented emphatically in this sense on the instructions to the Commissioners: on the need for an amnesty in areas falling under their authority, except to those involved in Louis XVI's death, and on the nature of that authority – pending the establishment of 'a regular Government', or a change of events requiring fresh instructions, 'It will be impossible to admit the Exercise of any Authority in the Name of Any of the French Princes', particularly 'under the Character of a Regent'.[3] This last injunction was dramatically illustrated in the next few weeks. News reached London late in October that Louis XVI's eldest surviving brother, the Comte de Provence – the future Louis XVIII – might be proposing to head for Toulon. It caused considerable alarm. The British Minister in Genoa, where the Prince might embark, was told to try polite but 'forcible' dissuasion, and if necessary to say that the commanders in Toulon could not let him land without explicit instructions; and when, in November, it was thought that he was on his way, a strong message was sent to Turin, where his peripatetic Court was then based. Hood and his colleagues had already been ordered not to receive the Prince if he arrived; the Sardinians were now asked to help

---

1. To Grenville, [5 October 1793] (*H.M.C., Dropmore*, II, 438–9).

2. For this episode see *Correspondence of Edmund Burke*, VII, 428–9, 463 n4, 477 n11, 486 n1.

3. P.R.O. 30/8/334. Grenville had been discussing this last point, pointing out that if the Constitution of '91 was adopted there should be no pressing problem, since it seemed to provide for an elected Regent, but that there might be difficulty 'if hereditary Monarchy only is restored, & that in the person of a minor or captive King' (to Pitt, 4 October 1793; J. Holland Rose, *Pitt and Napoleon Essays and Letters* (1912), 257). No European Government had recognised any claim to the title of Regent since Louis XVI's death.

in case the British failed to intercept.[1] The project was abandoned. Its threat had revealed a nervous determination in London not to be caught out.

There was indeed every reason to avoid embarrassment. While Toulon was flying the Bourbon flag, it had not declared for a Regent, and many of its citizens – like those of Marseilles – were in fact non-Jacobin republicans.[2] The exiled Princes had always rejected the 'moderate' constitution of 1791;[3] and the British Government itself had links with the 'constitutional' royalist party. Malouet, Lally Tolendal, Mallet du Pan could generally command a hearing; and a closer connexion was being formed at this very time. For as the response from Switzerland remained disappointing, a prominent 'constitutionalist', Jean-Joseph Mounier, was sent under Government auspices to see what could be done. He was put in touch with the British Minister, financial support was authorised, and an intelligence network soon set up.[4] It was the start of a process that was to become a significant feature of policy, and bring the constitutionalists themselves into the centre of strategic thought. Even at this point, when nothing was decided, it did not augur well for the Princes' cause.[5]

But meanwhile there was more to the British approach than caution over royalist differences. For if the Government remained wary of the Princes and their advisers, it was equally 'by no means an advocate of the Constitution' of 1791. The Foreign Secretary had always been sceptical, and he was still convinced that the document as it stood would provide a 'precarious and insecure . . . footing'.[6] There was no commitment to its supporters, and the desire to avoid a Regent moreover did not refer to French domestic issues alone. It arose in fact quite as much from a British claim in a matter of immediate but wide-ranging concern.

This turned on the nature of Allied control at Toulon itself. There was

1. Grenville to Francis Drake, no. 3, 22 October 1793 (F.O. 28/6); same to Trevor, no. 21, 30 November 1793 (F.O. 67/13). The Prince informed George III of his intention to go to Toulon, and to assume the functions of Regent; but very belatedly (his letter was received only on 29 November), and without acknowledging the consequences of British possession of the port in trust.

2. P. 311, n2 above.

3. See p. 42 above.

4. Grenville to Lord Robert Fitzgerald, Private, 26 September 1793 (*H.M.C., Dropmore*, II, 427); Fitzgerald to Grenville, no. 28, 13 November 1793; Grenville to Fitzgerald, no, 9, 3 December 1793 (F.O. 74/3). See p. 282 above.

5. As Burke, their great champion, may have appreciated (see *Correspondence*, VII, 486 n5).

6. Grenville to St Helens [in Madrid], no. 28., 22 October 1793 (F.O. 72/28). Again (see p. 309, n2 above) the term used was 'the Constitution of 1789'. For his reaction initially see p. 147 above; for his strong distrust of the Princes' advisers, his no. 19 to St Helens of 9 August 1793 (F.O. 72/27) and his letter to Malmesbury of 9 December (*H.M.C., Dropmore*, II, 476).

no difficulty over the Sardinian and Neapolitan troops, for they were stipulated by treaty as falling under British command. Swiss mercenaries would pose no problem, any more than Hessians; and the Austrians had not yet appeared. But the Spaniards were another matter, with a sizeable naval squadron and a land force considerably larger than the British themselves.[1] Hood indeed had appointed the junior of the two Spanish Admirals, Gravina, commandant of the city and in overall land command. For a time this worked quite well, for Gravina was able and friendly, and co-operated with the subordinate British commander. But the local arrangement was overtaken by considerations of higher policy, aggravated by a misfortune on the spot. Towards the end of October Gravina was wounded, and his superior, Admiral Langara, claimed the right to nominate his successor. Hood resisted, on the ground that Toulon had accepted *British* support, that Spain therefore disposed of no right, and that though Spanish troops were currently predominant the British were in charge of growing Allied forces from elsewhere. He was in accord with his Government, for acting on the same basic argument that Toulon had invited British aid, Ministers were framing an appropriate form of control. The Commission of three was to be British, with Elliot responsible for 'all the points of a Civil Nature' and General O'Hara as military governor and commander of the land forces.[2] Not surprisingly, this exacerbated the rising feelings in Madrid, fully voiced by a francophile Ambassador in London.[3] But they received short shrift. The British repeated their rights. They also argued their inability to transfer command of other Allied troops, and the danger of divided military control. This last applied to Toulon itself; but it was the more important because Toulon was designed to become 'the centre of operations which may extend themselves . . . in the South of France'.[4]

This in turn pointed a further question. For the dispute over command – keenly felt, as such disputes usually are – was also symptomatic of a larger problem. It was one which was causing the Spaniards some uneasiness: what part, they wondered, did possession of Toulon play in British ambitions? The Court of Madrid was not best pleased by the strong reaction to the Comte de Provence; for while it had not recognised him as Regent, it had – as the British suspected – known and approved of his proposed entry into France.[5] What did his rejection

1. Pp. 298, 305–6, 308 above.

2. See p. 310 above. Hood to Dundas, 27 October 1793 (H.O. 28/14); Grenville to St Helens, no. 28, 22 October 1793 (F.O. 72/28). Pitt's firm line is apparent in the correspondence of 17–20 October in *H.M.C., Dropmore*, II, 447–8.

3. Del Campo, for whom see Ehrman, *Commercial Negotiations*, 19n2, 89n4. See Grenville to St Helens, no. 36, 1 December 1793 (F.O. 72/28).

4. Same to same, no. 32, 30 November 1793; no. 26, 4 October 1793 (loc. cit.), and see also Grenville to Pitt, sd (P.R.O. 30/8/140) for early ideas on the implications for civil control.

5. Same to same, no. 33, 30 November 1793 (loc. cit.). And see pp. 312–13 above.

imply, when coupled with the measures for unilateral control? Both seemed to impinge on the vital question of indemnities. And this was something about which the Spaniards had been worried from the start: they suspected designs on their West Indian islands under the cover of the Alliance, they wanted a share in the French fleet at Toulon, and they now feared a British claim to the port itself, under cover this time of holding it in trust for a captive King.

Much of this suspicion, the British assumed, was habitual – the reaction of a Power accustomed to being a lesser partner. Much, too, doubtless arose from the chequered history of trade negotiations, and something from the quarrel over Nootka Sound.[1] But the fears in fact were not groundless, for the British were soon suggesting that Spain should find her reward along the Pyrenean border – 'preferable to distant conquests, especially in the West Indies'[2] – while they themselves remained imprecise about their aims. They were prepared to say, in November, that they would seek their indemnities 'only' in 'places not on the Continent of Europe'.[3] But this statement – not calculated in itself to calm Spanish apprehensions – contained nothing about the French fleet, or for that matter Corsica, the home of an old independence movement and an island about whose future Spain was known to be concerned. Nor did it remove the assumption of immediate control over parts of France itself which would serve in due course as a pledge for more permanent claims elsewhere. Madrid remained worried about British policy and resentful of the Toulon Commission; and the disagreement did not ease relations between the commanders on the spot, as their operations came under growing strain.

For throughout November the situation deteriorated. A stalemate had supervened, and stalemate could be fatal to the Allies. The lie of the land was against them, so that reinforcements were vital; and the 3,800-odd that arrived from Italy scarcely matched losses in wounded and sick.[4] Nor were the troops used to the best advantage. It takes time and an exceptional commander to weld a mixed force together, and both were lacking at Toulon in 1793. Hood, at first in general command and later the senior Commissioner, was a fine seaman, well versed in affairs, in

---

1. On the first point see St Helens to Grenville, Private, 10 April 1793 (F.O. 72/27); on the other two, p. 280 above.

2. Grenville to St Helens, no. 19, 9 August 1793 (F.O. 72/27). And see Grenville to Pitt, 4 October 1793 (P.R.O. 30/8/140).

3. In the Toulon Commissioners' Declaration of 20 November. In Grenville to St Helens, no. 31, 30 November 1793 (F.O. 72/28) the words are 'only in French possessions outside Europe'.

4. The fresh troops totalled 3,786, mostly from Naples. In mid-November, over 3,000 men were out of action through sickness alone.

Nelson's view 'the first officer in our Service'.[1] But age – he was rising sixty-nine – and a certain acerbic self-sufficiency did nothing to reduce the inherent difficulties of his task. A seasoned survivor of professional rivalries from the bitter days of the American War, he was hard and wary in official relations as he remained assured in action. Masterful, proficient, but now rather worn, and keenly aware of the odium of failure, he was not backward in voicing his opinions of soldiers and allies. He had been fortunate at first in a military subordinate acquired by chance. Lord Mulgrave, a soldier by trade and a political friend of Pitt and Dundas, had been sent on one of the special missions which Government favoured in 1793 – Murray's, Yarmouth's, Malmesbury's on a higher level[2] – to learn the Sardinians' plans and assess their resources. As soon as he heard of the landings he left Turin for Toulon, where Hood was able to make use of his knowledge and gave him the British land command. Mulgrave was active and clear-headed, as his reports direct to Ministers showed.[3] He worked closely with Gravina,[4] and conducted operations well. But he was not prepared to take a lesser place when Lieutenant General O'Hara arrived, together with a second in command, Major General David Dundas.[5] Neither of these officers proved of much comfort. O'Hara, personally gallant, desponded from the start, and Dundas in due course openly lamented his fate. Neither was a negligible figure: Dundas indeed was to end as Commander-in-Chief of the Army. Nor could any one in all probability have gained the time required to persuade the Allies to send reinforcements for the coming year: Mulgrave himself had warned of the outcome if no support came. It was rather that the atmosphere was one of deepening gloom, not conducive to ingenuity or heartening to the troops. The Spaniards for their part nursed their resentment, and did as little as possible. There was little inducement for them to do anything else.

As November wore on, the French strength and efficiency increased. Successes in the Alps against the Sardinians freed further numbers, and performance improved from a change in command. On the 29th the Allies suffered a disaster. An attack on a battery failed with serious losses,

---

1. 8 June 1795 (see GEC, *The Complete Peerage*, VI (1926), 569 n(a)). Collingwood on the other hand thought that 'Lord H's ambition' was 'far exceeding his abilities' (2 March 1794; *The Private Correspondence of Admiral Lord Collingwood*, ed. Edward Hughes (1957), 43).

2. Pp. 254n2, 274n1, 296 above.

3. They may be found in H.O. 50/455, and see also J. Holland Rose, *Lord Hood and the Defence of Toulon* (1922), Appendix F. For the impression they made at home see *H.M.C., Dropmore*, II, 449. Mulgrave's elder brother had also shown capacity, as a member of the Board of Control for India (see I, 427, 439, 441, 456–7).

4. See p. 314 above.

5. It rather looks as if Richmond, baulked of the command in Flanders (pp. 287–8 above), had wanted to control the 'extensive operations' in prospect 'in the South'. But Pitt declined to fall in with his wishes (Pitt to Richmond, 17 September 1793; B.L., Bathurst Loan 57, vol. 107).

including the capture of O'Hara himself. Worse soon followed, for the enemy's build-up continued, to a total of over 30,000, while news came from England that only a modest cavalry detachment could be expected reasonably soon. General Dundas was in despair, and when Hood turned down his advice to withdraw, their relations, already cool, became badly strained. In the same period the atmosphere altered in London. Ministers hitherto had remained optimistic, on the basis of despatches up to three weeks old; they had not fully appreciated the problems of terrain, and they still hoped that the Austrians would move.[1] Now however the mood began to change, as less favourable reports were received, at a time moreover when decisions had to be taken for other areas as well. A spell of confusion followed in mid-November. On the one hand, the Cabinet did not wish to drop plans some of which had been hardening while the British reinforcements for Toulon had been delayed.[2] On the other, a holding operation there was still thought to be feasible until Allied aid, not yet ruled out, restored the original prospect. Some troops from home thus remained desirable, and were envisaged as arriving in the winter.[3] At this point Mulgrave reached London and was able to bring his experience to bear. His presence increased the sudden sense of urgency: Hood was told to prepare for withdrawal if necessary, but pressure was renewed on the Austrians, and a fresh effort made to speed the transports to Ireland.[4] Events however now took charge. On 17 December, after several days' bombardment, the French captured the key western defences, and drove the British – unsupported by the Spaniards – from their positions on the northern heights. On the 18th Hood agreed to evacuate; the main fleet moved to the outer roadstead, the troops were concentrated on the inner harbour, and a plan was drawn up to burn the arsenal and the enemy ships. It partly misfired – literally, for the Spaniards again failed to act. But in the event fourteen men of war were burnt (with eleven more put temporarily out of action), another nineteen carried off, and many stores – including masts – destroyed. Hood embarked some 8,000

---

1. On the latter, see Pitt to Grenville, [10 November 1793] (*H.M.C., Dropmore*, II, 464); Grenville to Trevor, 11 November 1793 (F.O. 67/12). See also in general Amherst's diary as late as the 16th (vol. II, Amherst Mss, Kent C.A.O.). Ministers also drew some wider comfort from a continued expectation that France would collapse during the winter (see Grenville to Auckland, 11 November 1793; *A.C.*, III, 143).

2. For causes of delay see p. 308 above. The other plans are discussed on pp. 321–5 below.

3. Some indication of the process can be gathered from correspondence on 16–17 November in *L.C.G. III*, II, nos. 969, 972; Holland Rose, *Pitt and Napoleon*, 225–6; B.L. Add. Ms 38310 (for Hawkesbury's views, which were adverse to Toulon).

4. For possible evacuation see Dundas to Hood, Private, 23 November 1793 (H.O. 28/14); for the Austrians Duffy, 'War Policy', 70: for Mulgrave's effect, Pitt to Grenville, nd but 23 November (*H.M.C., Dropmore*, II, 471). Mulgrave's report was the more telling because on his way home he had talked to the Austrian commander in the Milanese.

troops, and some Toulonese to put the latter beyond reach of reprisals.[1] On 20 December, the Mediterranean fleet was anchored along the coast in the Bay of Hyères.

The failure at Toulon, like that at Dunkirk, left its immediate scars. It did not promise well for amity in further southern operations: Hood had no confidence in General Dundas, Dundas had no love for Hood. It soured relations with Spain at the opening of the alliance, and depressed those with Austria at a formative time. It revealed fresh administrative shortcomings, and caused further Ministerial resentments. It left Government with another setback to explain and defend. All these aspects of the case emerged quickly enough. If the Admiral and the General felt sore, so too did the Admiralty, surveying the impact on resources increasingly stretched. Chatham later wrote an account, self-justifying but not unreasonable, concluding that either Toulon should have been given full priority over other commitments or abandoned 'the moment' that doubts arose if it could be held. His sense of grievance was clear: 'My opinion was treated with no great respect'.[2] It was an echo, if fainter, of Richmond's complaints and, in its own context, of his early warning against too tight a programme. As forces were shifted on paper between different tasks, and supplies and transports failed to keep pace, professional reservations, so far largely ignored, seemed indeed to be justified. George III, anxious for the future of his son's command, had made the same point earlier. 'The misfortune of our situation is that we have too many objects to attend to, and our force consequently must be too small at each place'.[3]

There was a persuasive case to be made in reply. Chances – invitations – should be grasped when the odds on success seemed open, and the strategic consequences might be so profound. What would have been said if the opportunity had been turned down? With hindsight, the greatest flaw perhaps lay once more in a neglect of intelligence – this time particularly at home:[4] a lack of appreciation of the lie of the ground

1. There is a great discrepancy in estimates of the latter. Elliot at the time put the number at some 4,000 (to Auckland, 24 December 1793; B.L. Add. Ms 34452), Hood later claimed almost 15,000, which has generally been repeated since.
2. P.R.O. 30/8/364. From the contents, this paper was written after the autumn of 1794 (possibly at the turn of 1794/5). His attitude closer to the time is suggested in the draft of a letter to Hood of 28 January, or possibly March, 1794 (loc. cit.).
3. To Pitt, 14 September 1793 (Holland Rose, *Pitt and Napoleon*, 225). For the connexion with Flanders see same to same, 17 November 1793 (loc. cit., 225–6), following same to Dundas, 16 November 1793 (*L.C.G. III*, II, no. 969).
It was a misfortune that this argument seems never to have been put – certainly not forcibly – by Amherst, the Commander-in-Chief. On the contrary, he appears generally to have thought there were enough troops, and furthermore to have confined himself to that aspect of a wider administrative case.
4. Cf. pp. 288, 290 above.

at Toulon which, with the usual administrative inadequacies, helped undermine the effort needed to speed support. The means once more proved unequal to ends arguably good in themselves; and in so far as this lay within the strictly British compass it embraced the system as a whole. It was the failure to produce transports on an adequate scale which bedevilled troop movements from October, so that the Cabinet's decision on Toulon in mid-November made little difference in any event.[1] But Ministers would not have accepted such an argument as conclusive. They had seen Toulon from the start as an opportunity for the Alliance as a whole; they had reason to think that a response was coming, and felt badly let down. Their defence in public was hampered by the need to refrain from blaming their partners;[2] but in private they made their views very clear. The Austrians above all were left in no doubt of the gravity of the issue. The British envoy in Vienna had been told at the start that 'non-compliance' with the request for troops 'would endanger the very foundation of all future cordiality and connection'.[3] The stream of pleas and reproaches continued over the next two months, dying down when the promised instructions showed signs of being sent and renewed when they were not. On 13 December the Government threatened to withhold undertakings for the next campaign in Europe.[4] It was ironical that the orders left Vienna the next day – in the week that Toulon fell.[5]

Might success there have proved, as Ministers hoped, 'decisive of the war'?[6] So it has often been held, and Pitt and Dundas (and by implication Grenville) have been accused of missing that point, as well as, less absurdly, of misjudging the resources required.[7] In point of fact it

1. That shortage, already affecting movements from Ireland and greatly aggravated by the need, as it was seen, to protect Ostend after Dunkirk, was the root cause of the subsequent confusion. Even if British reinforcements for Toulon had sailed in mid-November, they could not have got there in time. Fortescue's strictures, loc. cit., 175, should be read with that in mind.

2. It was in fact confined, in various debates early in the new session of Parliament, to the line taken in the King's Speech of 21 January 1794: the attack had 'greatly distressed' French operations (by holding down substantial forces), and 'an important and decisive blow has been given to their naval power'.

3. Grenville to Eden, no. 11, 27 September 1793 (F.O. 7/34).

4. Same to same, nos. 22–24, 13 December 1793 (F.O. 7/35). And see loc. cit. throughout October and November. Dundas's letters to the commanders in Toulon, in H.O. 50/455, convey the feelings.

5. The British message of the 13th had not of course arrived by then. It was also ironical that on 18 December Hood was told that at least 2,000 men, of whom he had received word from home on 30 November following the Cabinet's latest decisions (p. 317 above), were now coming from Ireland (H.O. 50/455).

6. P. 303, n6 above.

7. There is a certain historiographical interest in the development of the first charge, which of course can, but need not, be taken as the basis for the second. It was in fact often so taken at the time and in the early nineteenth century, and then largely abandoned when the papers came to be studied from the 1860s. More recently it seems to have revived.

could be argued conversely that they expected too much of an advance from Toulon: that an Allied command in which, at least initially, different nationalities were in close support, relying – at least initially – on seaborne supplies, and moving at a traditional pace, might well have got bogged down in a region open to extensive counter-attack. But who can tell? Resolute action *might* have rekindled a royalist resistance fading in October, dislodged the French from the coast and the Alps, and turned the scale in the south. The effects *might* have led to a political collapse, or to military victory the next year. One may take leave to doubt. Nevertheless, if such results are thought probable, failure at Toulon was failure indeed.

Certain diplomatic consequences were less hypothetical. For the public commitment to royalism engendered by Toulon had results for British policy that were of interest in the longer term. The Ministry, forced to decide, had tried to take a middle line; to acknowledge royalists as the visible organised opponents of a system inimical to peace, and accordingly as recipients of external support, without limiting that support to any particular group or recognising any as the heir to the future. By its nature, this was not an easy path to follow: once money or men were sent, approval was bound to be inferred. Nor was the careful definition of the commitment itself always borne in mind. The statements of October and November[1] were widely, indeed generally, taken as pledging more than in fact they meant. If they acknowledged a restored monarchy as legitimate sovereign of its former territory, they specifically refrained from endorsing its pre-Revolutionary form; and, contrary to later comment, they did not preclude negotiation with a Republican authority on the basis of aims announced at the start of the war.[2] The course of events was to show the relevance of this position to wartime strategy: it allowed the British the freedom to foster a resistance which was not dependent on the émigré 'ultras' and at one time seemed more likely to succeed. But the provisos and distinctions, important as they were in themselves and to Government's thinking, naturally made less impression on the public at large; and indeed they could not always be sustained by Government itself. It may have been unfortunate for the course of the war, but it was not entirely so for Ministers, that insurgence had no real point of focus inside France. There was never the need finally to choose between distinct or antagonistic movements separated in space and usually peaking at different times. All the same, it was the essence of the policy to give support where results might follow, and royalists of all shades were taken under the umbrella first unfurled at Toulon. Political opinion in England meanwhile welcomed or deplored the pronouncements as either a new expression or an extension of war

1. Pp. 310–12 above.
2. For this last see particularly the wording in the first of the paragraphs quoted ibid; also Pitt's letter to Grenville quoted on p. 312, n1 above.

aims. The Foxites were quick to condemn them as a predictable departure from the pretence that the Ministry did not wish to impose a government on France: the Portland Whigs were as promptly delighted. – Pitt's 'shyness' in avowing 'the object of the War' had now been removed, and the people of England, given 'a little time', would 'adopt the principle'.[1] Burke, from his own point of vantage, best understood the position. Government had put 'the War at length upon a proper footing'; but its wording showed 'too much art': we were still not prepared to acknowledge a crusade, and were relying too much on the theorists of 'what is called the constitution' – men, as he put it, 'who do not know whether they are Jacobins or not'.[2] To Pitt and Grenville, their moves at Toulon – their statement, the discouragement of the Comte de Provence, the retention of control strictly in British hands – were designed to relate policy to a developing weapon of war.[3] To the world at large, as to later opinion, 'Co-operation with the royalists . . . involved the British in the ideological conflict' as the 'one lasting effect' of the affair.[4]

III

The fall of Toulon ended any hopes of a presence in France for the time being. It virtually coincided with a disappointment in the north-west. For while the Allied troops were pinned down in the Mediterranean the British Government had resolved to send aid to the continuing resistance in the Vendée. This was one of the commitments which the Cabinet upheld in mid-November, the other being a West Indian expedition. I have suggested that the decision did not affect the outcome in the south, because the resources which might have been spared could not by then have arrived in time.[5] But this argument is no endorsement of the northern design. If the fate of Toulon cannot be laid at the door of the Vendée, that does not mean that the plan for the Vendée was well prepared or carried out.

1. For the Foxites see Fox to Lord Holland, 2 November [1793] (B.L. Add. Ms 47571), and Sheridan and Fox in the Commons on 21 January 1794; for the Portland Whigs, Fitzwilliam to Thomas Grenville, 7 November 1793 (B.L. Add. Ms 42058). There were equally doubts on the other side – eg John Hatsell to Auckland on the fears likely to be felt by 'some of the best Friends of Administration' (20 September 1793, on Hood's Declaration; B.L. Add. Ms 34452).
2. *Correspondence of Burke*, VII, 434–5, 480–1, 486. It was at about this time that he wrote the 'Remarks on the Policy of the Allies with respect to France', in which such views are embodied.
3. Cf. p. 303 above.
4. Steven Watson, *The Reign of George III 1760–1815* (1960), 367–8; a balanced expression of a verdict sometimes put in more extreme form – eg Holland Rose, II, 163: 'The Toulon episode, more than anything else, bound . . . Pitt, albeit unwillingly, to the irreconcilable Royalists'.
5. P. 319, n1 above.

It emerged early in November. The insurgents' message received early in September, on the most useful forms of aid, had been considered in the light of the news from the south and a flow of émigrés' proposals.[1] At last, in mid-October, the Ministry made up its mind. On the 17th it replied that it could shortly send some arms and ammunition, with clothing, tents, some cavalry equipment, and a sum of money. Shipping could also be provided for émigrés to join the resistance; but, contrary to earlier assumptions, British troops were not promised – they had not been asked for, and as Dundas put it privately, 'any handful' secured by 'starving' other services would be of little use.[2] This message was followed by another suggesting co-operation – on the same basis of an émigré contingent – in an attack on St Malo.[3] Over the next fortnight, however, a fresh plan was conceived. It was dictated by two concurrent developments: by news of a fresh royalist success in the Vendée, and by a favourable turn of events in Flanders. The former was in fact rather misleading. The insurgents had stemmed a long series of reverses by a victory late in October which set them marching once more towards the coast. But they were in worse condition than the reports of their movements suggested, and, 'half fugitives and half invaders',[4] their prospects were obscure. The impression spread nevertheless that there was a 'Critical State of things' which might be tipped decisively by rapid support.[5] At the same time the recovery in Flanders and the safe retention of Ostend freed the British regiments recently sent to that port.[6] On 8 November they were ordered to re-embark within a week if possible, and by the 18th Ministers decided to mount a descent on the French coast.[7] A commander was quickly appointed; and in some ways it was a surprising choice. For it fell on the Earl of Moira, until recently known as Lord Rawdon,[8] who had abandoned his support of Government in 1787, become an intimate of the Prince of Wales, and been prominent in the Regency crisis. He had moreover been on bad terms

1. See p. 303 above. The most substantial of the latter came from M. (later General) de Jarry, who was patronised by Auckland. There were also proposals from the exiles in the Channel Islands.

2. P.R.O., W.O. 1/389; Dundas to Burke, 13 November 1793 (*Correspondence of Burke*, VII, 450). For the earlier assumption on British troops see p. 300 above.

3. On 21 October (W.O. 1/389). For an enthusiastic response from the Channel Islands, see the copy in Pitt's papers of M. du Dresney to Dundas, 8 November 1793 (P.R.O. 30/8/334).

4. Stanhope, II, 208.

5. Pitt's wording, to the Earl of Moira (see below), – November 1793 but between the 10th and 12th (draft in P.R.O. 30/8/102). See also Grenville to Yarmouth, 30 October 1793 (*H.M.C., Dropmore*, II, 452).

6. See p. 297 above. Rumours of preparations for a French attack on Jersey, current in October, also died away – as it proved, only temporarily – at this time.

7. Dundas to Sir Charles Grey [commanding in Ostend], 8 November 1793 (W.O. 6/8); draft of Pitt to Moira as in n5 above; *L.C.G. III*, II, nos. 972, 974.

8. He had succeeded to the Earldom in June.

with Richmond, with whom he would now have to work – they had quarrelled publicly in the early eighties, and Moira furthermore had acted as the Duke of York's second in his duel with Richmond's nephew.[1] But to set against these disadvantages he had a high reputation as a soldier who had distinguished himself in the American War. His selection in fact was due largely to Cornwallis, under whom he had then served, and he was of suitable rank as a recently promoted Major General. For the descent was to be in some force: 10–12,000 men were proposed.[2] The object was to enable the mainland royalists, with such strengthening and stiffening, to 'assemble in an organized Body capable of undertaking [a] serious operation'. The first question therefore was to decide if there could be an immediate coastal junction or if the expedition must capture a base before contact could be made.

Moira based himself on the second assumption. Of two possible points of attack, the Isle de Noirmoutiers (near the mouth of the Loire) or St Malo, he favoured the former as a prelude to a combined assault on Nantes.[3] He would need 12,000 men for the landings and subsequent operations, 2,000 being cavalry, of which the royalists were known to be short. The chief bottleneck would be artillery, for that branch had been starved in peacetime and very little could be spared from either Flanders or home defence. Moira prepared to adjust, but he drew attention to the danger,[4] and the shortage in fact proved the first of the obstacles he had to meet.

These were soon in evidence. Moira found it hard to lay hands on even half the gunners he needed, and he was quickly in trouble over the guns themselves. The overall size of the force moreover had to be cut. For a complicated situation was encountered at this point. In the first place, the Channel fleet, still cruising, was apparently failing to find the French, and rumours were again gathering of preparations at Brest for an attack on Jersey, or even Ireland or England.[5] There was rising anxiety for news from Howe, and meanwhile it seemed unlikely that a further transfer of troops could be made from home. Ireland was already due to send a modest reinforcement to Toulon, and there were difficulties in finding transports to collect it.[6] And home defence had

---

1. See p. 288, n1 above.

2. 'Memoir respecting the proposed Expedition to the Coast of France Novr 12th 1793', unsigned but by Moira (W.O. 1/174). Amherst a few days later called the force 'a large Corps' (Diary, vol. II, Amherst Mss). See also Pitt to Elgin, Private, 16 November 1793 (P.R.O. 30/8/102).

3. The final aim, and limit, of the operation were not made completely clear. The Government was thinking in terms of St Malo alone, with the British part of the force proceeding to Toulon after an undisclosed period (cf. p. 317 above) while the Hessians remained in the port. But in these confused weeks it is doubtful if the implications were closely considered.

4. Moira's Memoir (W.O. 1/174).

5. See pp. 293, 322n6 above.

6. P. 319 above.

nothing to spare – though it had earlier been considered adequate[1] – after the needs of Flanders and the West Indies had been met. For the complications were not confined to Europe. Ever since the summer there had been preparations to strengthen the offensive in the Caribbean which had been given priority at the start of the war. The reasoning behind the strategy will be examined more fully later.[2] Here we need note only that the opening phase had produced a success followed by a reverse. The French Windward Islands were a prime target, and Tobago had been taken in April. But an assault on Martinique, in the centre of the chain, was beaten off in June, and at about the same time the Government learned that a French expedition had sailed for the West Indies. The Cabinet accordingly decided to send reinforcements,[3] and these were later settled at sixteen infantry regiments with a small naval squadron. The collection of shipping and equipment, however, held up their departure for another two months, and then events in Flanders raised some fresh problems. The force for the Caribbean was raided to defend Ostend, while other troops destined for England were held by the French advance.[4] The effects were felt by both expeditions, for the West Indies and the Vendée. The former was delayed further; the latter lost about half its strength, which was designed to consist of the Hessian contingent first planned for Toulon.[5] For the Hessians, retained earlier in Flanders by growing operational demands, had still not embarked in mid-November, when transport arrangements in any case were strained. The Cabinet, now faced by the need to decide on Toulon, the West Indies and the new undertaking, accordingly weakened the second to provide for a weakened third. They did not wish to starve a region to which they looked for their post-war rewards[6] – all the more in fact if the war should end soon; but that ending seemed likely at that moment to be hastened best inside France. The Caribbean force should not be further delayed, but neither should Moira.[7] In the Hessians' absence, therefore, eight of the regiments for the West Indies were taken for the Vendée. That venture was thus preserved, and it was deemed significant. But its planned strength was potentially reduced.

So indeed it proved in the end, for the Hessians did not arrive until the

1. See Amherst's diary for 25 June 1793 (vol. I, Amherst Mss).
2. See Ch. X, section III below; and pp. 262–3 above for the early thoughts.
3. Pitt to Grenville, [–June–July 1793] (*H.M.C., Dropmore*, II, 402–3). This refers to a Cabinet meeting to be called at once on the subject.
4. P. 297 above.
5. P. 308 above.
6. P. 269 above.
7. These arguments are noted by Amherst in his account of a Cabinet meeting on 18 November (Diary, vol. II; Amherst Mss), and reflected in Grenville to Auckland, 11 November 1793 (B.L. Add. Ms 34452) and letters between Pitt, Dundas and the King, 15–19 November (*L.C.G. III*, II, 121–6).

turn of the year. But the reduction of the force was not the only worry. The commanders of the West Indies expedition, Sir Charles Grey and Sir John Jervis, were not prepared to see it milked further or kept any longer at home. Jervis in particular, now down at Portsmouth, took charge of the final preparations; and when Jervis was in charge the effect was quickly felt. Moira suffered from the competition, since both enterprises were using the base. He hoped to embark on 25 November – soon changed to the 26th. But by then he was 'worn to death . . . endeavouring to work out my salvation amidst the perplexity and confusion'. Jervis had 'seized' all the harbour boats and lighters, the commisariat staff was in despair, and he himself so tired he could 'hardly hold the Pen'.[1] Emigré volunteers, hastily embodied, were proving an added burden. But his escorting naval squadron was ready, and on the 26th Grey and Jervis cleared Portsmouth with part of their convoy and headed down Channel. Moira sailed on 1 December, and was cruising off Cherbourg the next day. But his signals were unanswered, and on the 3rd the expedition anchored in the Channel Isles.

The empty coast in fact told its story. For the royalists had been beaten. Successful at first in their northward march, they hesitated and turned south again, to be defeated and dispersed later in the month. There was nothing for the expedition to find, and though it was not withdrawn for almost a month while possible coastal raids were debated, the whole affair fizzled out. In mid-January 1794 the exasperated Moira was off Cowes, seeking accommodation for a force now swept by disease.

The debacle was, as Moira himself remarked from Guernsey, 'embarrassing'.[2] Ministers had built extravagant hopes on highly uncertain evidence,[3] and the arrangements had proved chaotic. The Ordnance – or rather Richmond – came in for further criticism, and the nugatory venture attracted public attack. It was an awkward close to an awkward few months: Dunkirk not taken, Toulon evacuated, Howe empty-handed, Grey and Jervis delayed, and now the Vendée unsupported and apparently collapsed. The plan had also, predictably, left a diplomatic question mark: how to handle relations with a movement looking to an exiled Prince at its head. For d'Artois[4] naturally had been stirring, as he received invitations based on the prospect of an émigré

1. To Evan Nepean, 25 November 1793 (W.O. 1/174).
2. To Dundas, 3 December 1793 (loc. cit.).
3. The instructions for local offensives in the winter in Flanders, for instance (p. 297 above), were issued partly in order to stop the enemy concentrating against the royalists in north-west France – and this after Moira had failed to make contact (Dundas to Murray, no. 63, 9 December 1793; W.O. 6/8). See also same to same, no. 58, 20 November 1793, and same to York, 21 December 1793 (loc. cit.). The correspondence between Pitt and Dundas and the King from 5 to 8 December also reflects confusion (*L.C.G. III*, II, no. 983; Holland Rose, *Pitt and Napoleon*, 226).
4. See pp. 301–3 above.

force. His representative in London, the Duc d'Harcourt – an exception to the Princes' usual standard[1] – met with the familiar, and now uneasily, cautious response. The October statement on Toulon was cited as a necessary preliminary to conversations, and d'Artois was discouraged from making any move meanwhile.[2] The failure of the expedition spared Government further immediate problems. But it was symptomatic of this hurried bid to sustain counter-revolution that Pitt and Grenville could avoid defining, in the context of earlier statements, the role of the personal embodiment of the cause it was meant to support.

1. Grenville by this time doubted if any of their advisers on the continent was 'fit to be talked with on any point of business' (to Malmesbury, 9 December 1793; *H.M.C.*, *Dropmore*, II, 476).
2. Grenville – d'Harcourt correspondence from 11 November 1793 (F.O. 27/42 *passim*). As Windham, now becoming attracted to the Princes' cause, observed to Pitt, 'the Cabinet' seemed 'not in earnest in wishing to see them, for the present, at the head of the Royalist party' (16th, endorsed December 1793; P.R.O. 30/8/190).

CHAPTER X

Offensives Reversed

I

Parliament reassembled on 21 January 1794, after an interval of exactly seven months. At about that time, Pitt put on paper his defence of the conduct of the war. The last campaign had been successful, for Holland had been saved and Flanders recovered, and despite setbacks including Dunkirk there were gains elsewhere along the front. Sardinia and Spain had co-operated; French seaborne trade was interrupted while our convoys were not, and the enemy had taken care not to meet our fleet; Tobago was taken, and we had exerted pressure in both the West and the East Indies; and at Toulon we had created a 'Diversion – Intermediate Distress of Operations & Loss of Navy – Gen! Impression on the Mediterranean Powers'.[1] These results had been achieved in pursuit of objects given a definite order of priority:

1st Repelling the Enemy   2nd Acquisition of Places for Indemnity-Security, – And means of making further Impressions on Enemy.

× 4. Intermediate Means of annoying them, and providing for unforeseen Events.

× 3. Rendering the Effects of War as little grievous to Ourselves as possible.

5th. Destroying the present System of France as desirable in itself, and most likely to terminate the War[2]

---

1. B.L. Add. Ms 59065. The four pages in Pitt's hand form part of a series of notes in Grenville's papers for a Parliamentary speech – probably for the massive contribution by their friend Mornington in defence of Government on the opening day – and are attributed to a date after 6 January 1794. I have paraphrased in places. There are similar notes in P.R.O. 30/8/335.

Cf. pp. 292n4, 319n2 above for Pitt's debating defence of naval operations and of Toulon. Auckland, while acknowledging its 'lame & impotent Conclusion', had earlier made a similar judgment on the campaign in the Low Countries (to Lord Sheffield, 17 November 1793; B.L. Add. Ms 45728).

2. B.L. Add. Ms 59065. The marks 'x' and numbers against the initial order show the process of thought, perhaps revised with Grenville.

This was material for a debate. It may also have reflected a typical optimism,[1] and it certainly showed a readiness to face the coming year. The prime responsibility, to repel invasion, was in fact about to be reviewed, following recent, and current, tales of French intentions.[2] The Channel fleet's apparent inability to detect the enemy's movements, and the demands of equipment for operations overseas, sparked off an inquiry begun probably, once more, by Richmond at the Ordnance.[3] In January he started to assemble information on artillery and the Thames defences, and in February and March he, Dundas and Pitt reconsidered the whole question. The diagnosis was much as before, but the requirements were spelt out more precisely. There was particular need for defensive vessels along the Kent and Sussex coasts, and two floating batteries and over fifty gun boats were in fact provided by the end of the year. Plans were considered for requisitioning muskets, improving the system of ordnance supplies, continuing experiments on mortars, and strengthening certain key points.[4] Above all, the estimates of troops needed for the south-east underlined the importance of measures – some already under way, and for purposes other than defence against invasion – to enlarge both the regular army and its supplementary forces. The former had visible results. Starting in the late summer of 1793 and rising sharply from the following January, there was a 'deluge' of new regiments, many of them raised privately, and a renewed drive to bring older formations up to strength. A Corps of Waggoners saw the start of a specific transport service in the spring, even though that particular experiment was to prove abortive.[5] And the efforts were equally marked across the range of part-time forces. The foot militia – the ancient means of defence – was being augmented by county subscriptions, and Fencible cavalry, known in Scotland from the fifties and in England from the crisis year of '79, was added for horsed support. Almost a hundred

---

1. Not confined to himself; cf. Grenville in November, p. 317, n1 above. Pitt's own characteristic hopefulness emerges from a letter to George Rose of 25 December 1793 (B.L. Add. Ms 42772) in which he wrote of the 'still . . . very good Chance, of all proving right' at Toulon.

2. P. 323, n5 above. See also Amherst to Pitt, nd but probably early in 1794, in P.R.O. 30/8/243. The rumours persisted through the first half of the year.

3. Cf. p. 261 above.

4. For Richmond and Dundas see paper of 21 January 1794 (P.R.O., W.O, 1/60), and Richmond to Dundas, 24, 25 January and accompanying paper, 27 March 1794 (H.O. 50/371); for Pitt, lists of guns and gunners and militia, and plans for Volunteers, in P.R.O. 30/8/241, 244, his notes on artillery, nd and 27 March 1794, and on invasion, 16 February 1794, in P.R.O. 30/8/197. The earlier comparable study is mentioned on p. 261 above.

5. Fortescue, loc. cit., 209–11. The administration of the forces is discussed in Ch. XIII, section I below.

The change of attitude became marked from August 1793. In June Amherst had seen no need to raise more troops (Diary, vol. II, 25 June, Amherst Mss); but late in August Pitt was calculating deficiencies and the means to make them good ('Memd. respecting Force Aug. 27th 1793', in Pitt's hand; P.R.O. 30/8/196).

'troops' of the latter appeared by the summer of 1794; at the same time Volunteer companies, on the familiar basis but more fully supported by public funds, received statutory authority – an unprecedented step – and were formed into artillery and yeomanry as well as infantry. The army Estimates early in the session provided for 175,000 regulars, 52,000 militia (16,000 in Ireland), 40,000 Fencibles, and 34,000 hired foreign troops.[1]

The use of the regular forces – the strategy for the year – had been under consideration before the close of the preceding campaign. As early indeed as the previous July, Murray had suggested to Pitt from Flanders that the plan for 1794 should concentrate on striking for Paris in two complementary movements. One Allied army should advance from the north-east, another up the Seine after landing near Le Havre. The capital was the key to speedy victory – 'Such indeed seems to be your own opinion' – and the design should not be impracticable given proper strength.[2] Others later agreed on the object, though not on the method. The Austrians, increasingly anxious to wind up their commitments in the west, were convinced that Paris must be the target of the campaign. So York was told in December, [3] as were Ministers in February, when the Austrian General Mack arrived from Coburg's headquarters for a conference on plans. This was not the kind of 'congress', embracing all problems, for which the Government had earlier hoped: no one now, except perhaps the Dutch who had least to lose, wished to face the diplomatic issues round a common table.[4] But a certain feeling at least was apparent in the Austrian camp – though there were reservations – that 'in contradistinction to the Case of other Wars' efforts should be directed 'towards one common Point'.[5] York, himself about to leave for England, appealed to this sentiment, and Mack was allowed, despite some misgivings, to follow him to London. Strengths were soon agreed.

1. Fortescue, loc. cit., 216–18; J.R. Western, *The English Militia in the Eighteenth Century* (1965), 219, and *passim* for precedents. The Irish militia was placed on a new footing by an Act of the Irish Parliament in 1793 (33 Geo. III, c. 22); The Scottish was confined in practice to Fencibles (see the British Act 33 Geo. III, c. 36) – a term deriving from 'defensible': 'fit and liable for defensive military service' (*O.E.D.*). The main Act 'for augmenting the Militia' was 34 Geo. III, c. 16; it was debated from mid-March to early April (*P.R.*, XXXVII–XXXVIII (1794)).

2. Private & Confidential, 23 July 1793 (P.R.O. 30/8/162). This 'opinion' of Pitt's was specifically balanced against expectations from southern France – before, of course, the invitation from Toulon. That the Minister took the plan seriously is shown by his note on forces of 27 August 1793 (p. 304, n3 above).

3. Copy of York to Dundas, 22 December 1793 (P.R.O. 30/8/338). Slightly earlier information of the development of Austrian thinking was received from Elgin [see p. 286, n7 above] (copy of Elgin to Grenville, Confidential, 10 December 1793; P.R.O. 30/8/336).

4. Grenville had certainly become wary of a conference in which too many differing interests would be exposed (cf. Auckland to Pitt, 16 December 1793; P.R.O. 30/8/110). For the earlier view see p. 272, n2 above.

5. Elgin to Grenville (n4 above); and see, for slightly earlier and later Austrian sentiments, *L.C.G. III*, II, nos, 982, 992; *H.M.C., Dropmore*, II, 497–8.

The Austrians contemplated a force overall of 315,000 'effective fighting men'. Forty thousand of these should be British and Germans in British pay, the bulk forming part of the army – of some 170,000 – to subdue the barrier fortresses and march on Paris while the rest of the front remained on the strategic defensive. The telling blow would thus come from Flanders, preceded by the taking of strongpoints so that it could be safely launched as soon as the season allowed.[1]

The design had perforce to predicate answers to certain problems, administrative, diplomatic, and some affecting the command itself. These last indeed were already raising complications. For Pitt and Dundas were by now uneasy about the Duke of York: his position was due in a sense to chance,[2] and he had not filled it to the general satisfaction. There were points in his favour: he was loyal and zealous, open-minded and sensible, and he had a ready-made status at Allied headquarters. But royalty could also have its drawbacks when placed at the head of a British command, and York's personal qualities had failed to gain his army's confidence. He could not claim more than average ability – the Hanoverian manner made it look less – and he was widely supposed to be run by Murray, the intelligent but indecisive chief of staff.[3] Nor, at the age of twenty-nine, was he able to control his officers. As Wellington was to observe in the Peninsula, 'the whole business of an army upon service is foreign to our habits', and the Guards in particular brought the habits of the London clubs to the Flanders campaigns.[4] Influential and independent, their conduct and reports alike were harmful to a commander suffering in addition from the setback at Dunkirk. The King's intense interest in his son's fortunes was also far from welcome. At the turn of the year, therefore, the two Ministers wanted a change. A candidate was now to hand, and one of considerable weight; for Cornwallis had just returned from his Indian victories.[5] Pitt had long wanted his counsel – he had hoped at one time to make him Home Secretary[6] – and the General's experience and seniority placed

---

1. York to Dundas, 2 February 1794; paper from Coburg, 4 February 1794, via York (W.O. 1/168). For Cornwallis's comments see his letter to Pitt of 25 February 1794 in Stanhope Ms S5 02/4. The figure of 325,000 effectives allowed for a total strength of 340,000, as against one of 289,000 in December (York to Dundas, 23 December 1793; P.R.O. 30/8/338). Coburg had meanwhile modified his first intention to ignore some strongpoints in his rear; and Mack himself indeed, while subscribing to the aim, could not guarantee that there would be time for a final advance in the summer. Cf. pp. 286–7 above.

2. See p. 264 above.

3. In point of fact he had by then asked for Murray's recall (see *L.C.G. III*, II, nos. 982–4).

4. Wellington's comment was made in 1809. He took part in the Flanders campaign himself from the summer of 1794 – learning in the process, as he said later, what not to do.

5. See I, 453. He landed on 3 February, a week before Mack arrived.

6. See I, 130, 453, 458 n1, 622 n1.

him in quite another class from York. The Austrians however demurred – Cornwallis would have clearly proved a tougher proposition – and York remained, though the idea of introducing Cornwallis in some capacity was not dropped.

The Duke's retention had one immediate effect. It altered the disposition of the British troops, who had originally been intended to act as before on the seaward flank.[1] But that was now changed: the great part was placed under York at the service of the main attack, leaving a smaller contingent with some Austrians and Germans in west Flanders. Pitt was said to have thought this necessary to satisfy the King and the country:[2] George III wanted glory for his son, and the public might be happier if its army shared in the big push. There may have been further reasons: a stronger bargaining position at the peace table, and perhaps a feeling that York had best be under the eye of the central command.[3] The decision had administrative drawbacks, for it confused the lines of supply. It certainly – and literally – showed the distance covered since the start of the war, when British troops were confined to a day's march from their ports.[4]

The size of the force proposed suggests the same conclusion. For 40,000 effectives was a high figure to accept. Given the removal of part of the Hessians, it in fact meant finding some 20,000 men;[5] a number much greater than that granted to any other operation. The willingness to match the demand is in a sense the more telling because the Ministry was not prepared to devote everything it had. The West Indies posed no immediate problem, for Grey's expedition had recently sailed, and though it was below strength the operations were adjusted and two battalions earmarked to follow. No more were envisaged yet, and in fact none were allocated until August.[6] But there was another possible commitment which was not abandoned. Moira's force was largely kept in being, for home defence or a possible call from the Vendée.[7] Most of the drafts for the campaign had therefore to be raised in addition, and Pitt and Dundas settled to the familiar task. At first it seemed that 6,000 British should be sent by early April – an earnest of larger numbers

1. Elgin to Grenville, 10 December 1793 (P.R.O. 30/8/336).
2. See Duffy, 'War Policy', 82 n2.
3. This last is given great weight by Fortescue, loc. cit., 227.
4. P. 264 above
5. See Pitt's 'Mem^r for Campaign' in P.R.O. 30/8/242. This is endorsed in his hand, so far as I can see, 'Feb. 1793'. The last figure is obscure, though probably correct; but Pitt may have been careless, writing early in the new year, for the contents seem to point strongly to 1794. I have accordingly attributed them to that campaign. For the Hessians, see pp. 324–5 above.
6. Dundas to Major General Adam Williamson [in Jamaica], 25 August 1794 (P.R.O., W.O. 1/60); and see also Pitt's 'Proposed Distribution' of forces dated 27 August 1794 (P.R.O. 30/8/240). For the two battalions earmarked in January see Fortescue, loc. cit., 353.
7. P. 325 above.

which should 'enable us to begin acting' then. But this was soon changed to 4,800, all the rest to come from the Germans, while efforts were made to assemble a larger British artillery train.[1] The figures once more were to prove fallacious: neither men nor guns were so easy to find; administrative facts had yet to be faced and some hard lessons learned. In mid-June the British command was much the same size as in February, and while it then rose – in fact to a strength not far short of the target – this was in response to a crisis like that of the previous autumn, which again robbed Ministers of their freedom of manoeuvre. 1794 on the continent, for them, was to be 1793 writ large. But the emphasis was rather different; for while they had expected to raise resources which would avoid the need for strategic choice, the planned proportions of strength had shifted, and Pitt himself moved to a position not unlike his father's final balance in Europe between coastal assaults and a land campaign.

This however was to be effected by an increased reliance on hired troops; and the initial shortfall in the British contribution was not in · British resources alone. The drafts of Germans also failed to meet expectations. Much more seriously, so did the efforts of the Prussians and Austrians themselves. For the Government's difficulties were far from being confined to those of supply, whether of men or materials or transport. Its deeper problems stemmed from the nature of the Coalition, as the members' different preoccupations produced ever growing strains.

For exactly a month, from 22 November to 22 December 1793, Lord Malmesbury voyaged from London to Berlin.[2] His journey encapsulated the state of the Alliance. Talking to commanders, diplomats and Ministers as he moved across north-west Europe, he began to sort with his experienced eye the pieces of an obdurate jigsaw. A few indeed had been fitted together, and a few more perhaps were taking shape; for the most part, however, a coherent pattern had still to be found. Powerful figures in Holland were prepared to help support the Prussian war effort, and seemed genuinely anxious for 'one strong and common political chain'.[3] But they had reservations about the form of a Dutch contribution, and insisted on indemnities which the Austrians disliked.[4] The

---

1. 'Mem^{r}. for Campaign' (p. 331, n5 above); Richmond to Dundas, 13 March 1794, Dundas to York, 15 March 1794 (W.O. 6/11). The total of reinforcements by then was reckoned at 22,600, of whom 17,800 would be Hanoverians, Hessians (from Cassel and from Darmstadt), Brunswickers, and a corps from Salm on the upper Rhine. 2,500 of the Hessians would be returned from Moira's force.

2. See p. 299 above.

3. Malmesbury to Grenville, no. 4, Secret & Confidential, 3 December 1793 (P.R.O., F.O. 64/31). Cf. *Diaries and Correspondence of Malmesbury, III* (1844), 10–12.

4. Pp. 273–4, 286, 293–4, 296 above.

Austrians for their part were by now aware that the British sought their rewards outside Europe.[1] They accepted the fact, and had secured in return a promise of support – in men or in money – if either Power continued the war when the other had gained the conquests it sought. They had conceded improvements in principle for British trade with some of their territories – notably the Netherlands – and moved some way towards defining military commitments in a full treaty of alliance. But they remained opposed to the Dutch indemnities, they resented being pressed on their policy for the Netherlands, and they were extremely wary of involvement in any financial aid for Prussia.[2] Prussia herself was the most immediate cause for anxiety: a partner whose forces must at least be kept in being if the campaign was to succeed. For what would happen if the strategic defensive along the Rhine was seriously weakened; if active operations there had to be so reduced that large French forces were not pinned down? In such case, the advance in Flanders might be prejudiced. It seemed essential to the British that this measure of Prussian co-operation be secured.

Malmesbury's first reactions on reaching Berlin were not unhopeful. He was inclined to believe, as he was told, that the problem was 'Poverty' rather than 'Good will'.[3] In 1793 the Prussians had fielded some 50,000 men for the war in the west: they might provide 100,000 for 1794 – a figure which the Austrian command had now broadly in mind as a total for that front. But this would obviously be only in return for financial assistance; and there was a snag, for the balance to be met was not between the force found earlier and that now envisaged, but between the latter and the Prussian engagement of 1792 with the Emperor, which was for 28,000 men.[4] Such language did not allay the earlier suspicions in London. For by referring strictly to their Imperial commitment the Prussians were still ignoring their obligation to England under the treaty of 1788.[5] This 'striking difficulty' seemed 'to render the possibility of securing . . . future co-operation . . . in the War very doubtful'. Nevertheless the provision of a large Prussian force was worth 'very considerable sacrifice'. How considerable it was hard to

1. Cf. p. 315 above. This has been conveyed to them by Grenville on 7 September (to Morton Eden, no. 1; F.O. 7/34), and made public by the statement of 29 October to the Toulonese (p. 310 above).

2. See Duffy, 'War Policy', 62–74, and cf. pp. 296–7 above. Malmesbury was not in a position to gain an informed view of Austrian ideas on aid to Prussia. The Government had a foretaste in a despatch from Eden of 16 December 1793 (no. 78; F.O. 7/35).

3. To Grenville, Private, 27 December 1793, following his nos. 9 & 10 of 26 December (F.O. 64/31). See also his observation to Pitt on 9 January 1794 (*H.M.C., Dropmore*, II, 494–5).

4. Malmesbury to Grenville, no. 1, 5 January 1794 (F.O. 64/31). The Austrians' figure rose from something over 60,000 towards the end of 1793 (York to Dundas, 22 December 1793; P.R.O. 30/8/338) to about 100,000 by February 1794 (same to same, 2 February 1794; W.O. 1/168).

5. Cf. p. 295 above.

calculate, given scanty information; but it might well cost £2 million to meet the 'extraordinary' expenses of the Prussians under the Imperial agreement and the full expenses of the numbers required in addition for the coming campaign.

How could such a sum be supplied? 'Great as the resources of this Country are in point of finance the whole burthen . . . is far beyond what is possible to suppose that His Majesty should take upon Himself'. An Allied effort would be proposed – two fifths to come from Britain, one fifth each from Austria, the German Empire and the Dutch. The Prussians themselves should 'advance' a further sum, equal to one of those fifths, to meet the 'ordinary' expenses of their Imperial commitment. But that could be reimbursed later by the French as one of the peace conditions under a guarantee by Britain, Austria and Holland. As a further inducement, Prussia might secretly be offered some French fortresses on the Rhine, if first captured. In return, she must accept supervision of relevant expenditure, and adhere to a settled operational plan. This last might prove slow to negotiate. If so, or there were other difficulties, Malmesbury could conclude a provisional agreement which would keep a Prussian force, as at present, on the Rhine.[1]

These positive, indeed urgent, proposals derived from a specifically British view of both the value of the Prussian contribution and the need for a concerted Allied effort. The supply of aid in combination was not only financially desirable, but also the means to ensure a comprehensive plan of campaign. The sentiments were echoed in Holland – or at least in the anglophile parts of the Government. But there were doubts over the extent and the manner of support. Opinions had already been aired as to how the Dutch might raise a quota: they themselves had suggested an advance in cash from the British Treasury, to be repaid by loan subscriptions, while the British preferred a loan outright to be floated on the London market. Behind such reservations at The Hague – reflecting the responses from Dutch moneyed institutions – there lay the resentment over indemnities and a gloomy estimate of Prussia's aims. On the first, the British were prepared to repeat an earlier offer to restore the port of Negapatam in India, taken from the Dutch in the American War. But that prospect, once welcome in Holland, seemed now to have sunk in the scale: London was to be judged above all by its power to exert pressure on Austria.[2] Failure to do so was strengthening the substantial, perhaps growing, peace party; and even the most convinced adherents of the war, while prepared to contribute, had little confidence in Malmesbury's prospects at Berlin. Repeated urgings from London

---

1. Grenville to Malmesbury, no. 4, 28 January 1794 (F.O. 64/31). The despatch ran to 45 pages.

2. The Dutch also set less store by Negapatam now because the town was said to have been systematically 'dismantled' (William Eliot to Grenville, no. 22, 24 February 1794 (F.O. 37/52). For British offers in the eighties see I, 424–31.

sought to balance a continuing fear that 'the chain which bound Prussia to the common Cause was so rotten' that it was likely soon to break.[1]

Far worse was the reaction in Vienna. For if the junior partner was uncertain, the senior proved hostile. As against the British desire to use Prussians to free Austrian troops for the main advance, the Austrian Ministers so mistrusted their ally that, while underwriting the advance, they were opposed to increasing his force on the Rhine. They feared a large Prussian army poised between their own army and its homeland, and in a position from which it could influence smaller German states; and indeed the command in Flanders, and particularly Mack, were under a cloud for proposing dispositions that might yield such a result.[2] The Government in Vienna was divided, on almost every question affecting the west. The claims of Poland and eastern Europe were continually before its eyes. But Chancellor Thugut could rely for once on his colleagues' sympathy when he rejected any notion that they should help Prussia in this way.

The response therefore was unambiguous. Its tone was not improved by the fact that Grenville, hurrying to send Malmesbury's instructions, had failed to consult Vienna.[3] The negotiations centred on London over the next few important weeks had therefore to recognise that an alternative might have to be found. The British pressed their view, to the point of threatening to withdraw from Flanders if Austria in the end refused to pay her share.[4] But the bluff was called. Thugut observed that they themselves must then do the same; meanwhile he held his ground on the Allied subsidy and the Dutch indemnity.[5] By the middle of March it was clear that a different arrangement must be made; for as Grenville had already remarked, this would be 'infinitely preferable' to a break with Austria.[6] When it came to the pinch, there was no doubting where our principal interest lay; nor had the Prussians endeared themselves further by their own response. So annoying was it indeed that the Foreign Secretary would have been glad to end the talks were it not that 'in a Contest, in the Issue of which the happiness of all Civilized Society is so deeply engaged, much ought to be sacrificed to the Hope of acquiring present strength'.[7] The central problem remained the same: Prussia refused to admit that her war effort lay within the compass of her

1. Eg Eliot to Grenville sd, as above, and nos. 25, 38 of 26 October, 14 December 1793 (F.O. 37/50), no. 47 (Confidential), 7 January 1794 (F.O. 37/51).
2. See p. 330 above.
3. He first told the Austrian Government of the proposal on 4 February (to Eden, no. 5; F.O. 64/31), a week after the despatch to Malmesbury (p. 334, n1 above). The Austrian Minister in London, Starhemberg, seems to have been told nothing in advance when he saw Grenville on 21 January (*Quellen*, IV, 46–50).
4. This was on 18 February (Grenville to Eden, no. 8; F.O. 7/36).
5. See Duffy, 'War Policy', 84–6.
6. To Malmesbury, no. 9, 7 March 1794 (F.O. 64/32).
7. Ibid.

treaty with England. She could therefore bargain for aid entirely in the form of subsidy, rather than by way of a balance above a level of obligation. Long despatches went to and fro, to no particular purpose;[1] and the atmosphere was soured by the activities of the Prussian envoy in London, Baron Jacobi, who had been predicting Ministerial changes in the face of prospective Parliamentary criticism, in reports which were said to be 'dangerous and mischievous'.[2] The intense intrigues, and what Malmesbury called 'eternal Festivities' of the Court in Berlin also affected the pace of an inherently awkward negotiation.[3] But at least the opening stage had shown the British what to expect when the Austrian refusal forced them to pursue the matter on an altered footing.

In more than one respect, indeed, they could reflect that this might offer some immediate advantage. It removed the need to talk simultaneously to two mutually suspicious principals; and it gave the British the most direct say in defining Prussia's effort. The other side of the coin – the onus of enforcement – was something to be accepted in the light of events. Malmesbury was sent fresh instructions on 14 March – the day after the Austrian decision was known.[4] With the opening of the campaign in prospect, the Government felt bound to move fast. Persisting in its claim under the treaty of 1788, it reiterated its willingness to pay subsistence to the troops which Prussia was thereby required to furnish – some 30,000 men. If they were now raised to 50,000, the Maritime Powers – Britain and Holland – would provide an annual subsidy of £1 million, in quarterly instalments. In return, this Prussian force was to be at Britain's disposal – as laid down in the same treaty – and we would wish it to operate in Flanders, under its own commander but in concert with our army. These 'stipulations' were 'final': they were not to be varied; and if there was hesitation in accepting them we would regard the treaty of 1788 as 'broken'.

Tough talk. But in fact the message had already been overtaken, for the Prussians themselves, under Malmesbury's prompting, had proposed new terms the day before. They would place 60,000 men at the disposal of the Maritime Powers, for an annual subsidy of £800,000 plus the forces' expenses.[5] The gap was narrowing, though it was still in evidence, for the cost would be well over £1 million for Britain; and the

---

1. One from Malmesbury (no. 12, 16 February 1794; loc. cit.) occupied 49½ pages; one from Grenville (no. 9, 7 March, as above) 40 pages.

2. Malmesbury to Grenville, no. 5, 21 January 1794 (F.O. 64/31). Cf. p. 295, n2 above.

3. Same to same, Private, 6 January 1794 (B.L. Add. Ms 59019; omitted from the extract given in *H.M.C., Dropmore*, II, 491); 9 January 1794 (loc. cit., 492–4). For the impact of the proclivities of European Courts on negotiations cf. I, 513.

4. In Grenville's despatch no. 12 (F.O. 64/32).

5. Malmesbury to Grenville, no. 22, 13 March 1794 (loc. cit.). For the background, see his letter of sd in *Diaries and Correspondence of Malmesbury*, III, 77–82. A further 20,000 Prussians would be left to act as required by the treaty of 1792 with the Emperor (see p. 333 above).

talks were removed to The Hague, where the Dutch could effectively take part.[1] The stipulation that the Prussians should 'actually . . . join' the British in Flanders was finally dropped; 'concert' was acceptable – in fact an improvement, for flexibility might prove desirable – and on this basis progress was made. On 19 April a tripartite treaty was signed, as was an Anglo-Dutch financial Convention. Prussia would furnish 62,400 men under a Prussian commander by 24 May, to act as was judged most suitable to the interests of the Maritime Powers. Those two Powers would have at their disposal all resulting territorial gains. In return they would furnish a monthly subsidy of £50,000 from 1 April, and just under £100,000 a month for the upkeep of a full Prussian force. They would also pay a capital sum of £300,000 as 'preparation money' – an alternative to a demand for subsidies retroactively to 1 January – and later one of £100,000 on the Prussians' return home. Of these sums, the Dutch agreed to provide a quarter of the capital moneys, and £400,000 a year towards the subsidies and upkeep. To facilitate their contribution, Malmesbury tried to cut a knot by committing his Government to a loan from the Bank of England – which took Pitt by surprise.[2]

Meanwhile the search for a treaty with Vienna had made little progress. The clause in the Anglo-Dutch treaty with Prussia concerning conquests in Flanders offered a possible way out of the deadlock over the Dutch indemnity. Grenville shifted his ground in hope.[3] Otherwise the prospects were fortified only in the sense that the British had reaffirmed among themselves the priority of the Austrian connexion.[4]

By the time the Prussian treaty was signed, the campaign had opened. Pitt had hoped it would begin in April, and while the British drafts had failed to appear, the Austrians themselves were now ready to move. Both these facts, it could be held, justified an arrangement open to criticism – heard soon enough when Parliament debated the treaty at the end of the month. Pitt and Grenville defended the object, against attacks on the terms and on the danger of introducing the thin end of a financial wedge.[5] This last objection was not fully valid: Sardinia had been

1. And, as Malmesbury pointed out (see *H.M.C., Dropmore*, II, 533, 535), where the discussions would not be subject to the constant pressure of important opponents.

2. F.O. 64/33 for 28 March to 19 April: *L.C.G. III*, II, nos. 1035, 1043; *H.M.C., Dropmore*, II, 533–6, 541, 545–6, 552; *Diaries and Correspondence of Malmesbury*, III, 90–3. The disposal of conquests in Flanders by the Maritime Powers had first been suggested by Auckland in August 1793.

For the texts of the treaty and the Convention see *Consolidated Treaty Series*, 52, 199–207; *P.H.*, XXXI (1818), cols. 433–7. The treaty was for the term of 1794, but provision was made for renewal.

3. Duffy, 'War Policy', 87–8.

4. P. 296 above.

5. Debates in both Houses 30 April 1794; *P.R.*, XXXVIII, 212–24, XXXIX (1794), 256–9, 271, 273–4.

subsidised the year before.[1] But if Opposition could have known the extent to which Government had departed from its first terms – in the virtual abandonment of the earlier treaty rights, the negotiable formula for Prussian dispositions, the substantial increase in the sum itself – the result in the lobbies might have been less unequal.[2] At the same time, the Ministry could have claimed a consequential bonus from the main agreement. For one outcome of the talks was that the King of Prussia decided to command his troops in the west himself. Personally sympathetic to the cause, and always beguiled by military glory, he had proved responsive to an inducement which Malmesbury had been at pains to stress. His appearance would complete an impressive commitment by both the original Allies. For the Austrians too were to be commanded by their sovereign in person. The Emperor's presence in his Netherlands had been on the cards for several months. Accompanied by his brothers (one of whom, the Archduke Charles, was to prove his powers in the next few years), he arrived in Brussels on 9 April, and at army headquarters on the 14th.[3] Two days later he held a grand inspection, with the Guards and some Dragoons representing the British, and on the 17th the Allies opened their operations. The Prussians would thus play their part in an effort which, buttressed by its separate arrangements, would hopefully be that of a true Coalition. They would thereby be associated with an increased British role, or alternatively make up a shortfall in British reinforcements.

And then, on this not unpromising scene there fell the impact of central Europe. In fact this had made itself felt in the past few weeks. As the Emperor set out from Vienna, and Frederick William waited to leave Berlin, they were looking over their shoulders at an explosion in Poland. On 25 March the great rising began under Kosciuszko. His first battle was won on 4 April; the insurgents took possession of Warsaw on the 20th – a defeat of a foreign garrison which remained an inspiration for 150 years; by the end of the month they controlled almost all of the surviving independent territories. The partitioning Powers, deeply alarmed, reacted each in its own way. The Austrians watched closely, but allowed some reinforcements to leave for the west. The Russians from their greater distance sought their associates' aid. But this was

---

1. Pp. 278–9 above.

2. The votes were 134 to 33 for Government in the Commons, and 99 to 6 in the Lords. Cf. George III's comment two days earlier: 'perhaps a little more firmness in Ld Malmesbury's manner of treating might have in some particulars rendered the terms more advantageous' (to Pitt, 28 April 1794; Holland Rose, *Pitt and Napoleon*, 226). The King of course rather disliked Malmesbury: he had not been entirely happy with him in Holland in 1787, and the Ambassador's behaviour in the Regency crisis further depressed his standing at Court (see I, 525–32, 537; p. 296 above).

3. The decision was precipitated largely by the impossibility of otherwise naming a commander. Coburg was no longer looked on with favour, and the Archduke Charles, promoted as a candidate, was too young even for an Archduke. The result left Mack in effective charge under the Emperor.

already being offered, by an envoy posting north; for the Prussians wished to act against a rising, potentially dangerous to their own gains, which might moreover yield a more extensive reward.

These disturbing events could not affect the immediate move in the west. For the first ten days all seemed to go well. The opening target of Landrecies was taken, farthering the breach in the barrier fortresses – a series of operations which included 'the greatest day in the annals of the British horse'.[1] Soon, however, the impetus was lost. The Allies' thrust was pinched on its flanks, the French taking Menin to the north, and Mack decided to isolate and destroy the danger in the resulting salient. It was an ambitious plan – too ambitious, as it turned out. The enemy numbered some 60–75,000, in the area of Lille and Courtrai; the Austrians and British opposed to them, about 40,000. Reinforcement must come from Landrecies, and it demanded a swift march and co-ordinated manoeuvres if the design was to work. Neither was achieved. The troops could not move fast enough, orders were not sent expedi-tiously, and at the critical period the Austrian generals were strangely inactive. When battle was joined, at Turcoing on 18 May, the brunt fell on the British, barely assisted until too late by their stronger ally. They were forced to give way, York himself being chased about the countryside, and then retreat. The French might now threaten the Low Countries once more, and on the 23rd Mack resigned. The ensuing week was to prove a turning-point for the campaign, and in its longer consequences for the war in the west.

For depressed by the defeat, the Austrians were the more ready to measure their position against developments in the east. The reverse at Turcoing was not in fact necessarily disastrous: a French attack near Tournai was repulsed on the 22nd, the Austrian right wing gained a victory on the Sambre on the 24th, and that same day the Prussians won an engagement in the Palatinate. From Paris, the Jacobin Terror was having a growing effect on the armies. Given the will, the Allies might yet renew the offensive. But the Austrians did not see it like that, for many of them did not wish to do so. A lost battle in Flanders fields and the prospect of losing out in Poland weighed heavily on the Ministers now gathered in the Emperor's camp.

It was hardly surprising. In Vienna as in Berlin there had long been powerful voices raised against the Flanders campaign. It was proving expensive, the rewards were in doubt, and all the time there was the shadow of a closer Russo-Prussian alignment in central Europe. And now, in mid-May, the Prussians made an ominous move. Possibly the sequel to the recent tripartite agreement was lost by default: the transfer of Malmesbury's talks to Holland, while it freed them from immediate opposition, had given the opponents undisturbed access to the King in Berlin; and his own subsequent recall to England, for consultations

1. Fortescue, loc. cit., 243.

when the treaty was signed, may have removed a stiffening influence needed at a delicate point.[1] In any case, Poland beckoned. On 4 May the King left his capital: but to join his troops in the east instead of those for the west.[2] The provisions of the treaty itself held good; but this was a serious change of direction, and it reinforced the arguments of the Austrian 'eastern' party. Followed by Turcoing, and advice – from Mack himself – that west Flanders was lost, it led to a drastic reappraisal of policy. Although Thugut and Mercy staved off proposals for peace talks with France, they joined the rest in now favouring a defensive campaign. The Austrian forces must be conserved. The Netherlands should not be abandoned – treaty obligations and bargaining potential alike pointed that way. But the province must no longer consume too many resources in men or money: the Maritime Powers must help more, and the Prussian contribution should be enforced. These decisions were reached by 29 May; and they too were given dramatic expression. On that day the Emperor gave notice that he would be leaving for home.

So both sovereigns disappeared. The British had now to salvage the remains of a strategy undermined almost before it was set on foot. The Prussian force became even more significant. It had yet to be delivered. There was still the need – perhaps a greater need – to play a skilful hand.

On the contrary, however, one card was thrown away at once. The fault lay with Pitt, both departmentally and in a wider sense. As Chancellor of the Exchequer, he was responsible for arranging the treaty payments: initially, the 'preparation' money and the first monthly subvention. Malmesbury had promised that these would come quickly, to help the Prussians appear in time. But in fact a month went by before Pitt gave instructions.[3] The reason, according to Malmesbury himself, was Ministers' concentration on domestic unrest: a danger which certainly absorbed them just then, and confined him to 'very short and very few conversations'.[4] The result was unfortunate: the remittance, in bullion, did not reach Hamburg until 19 June, and it had then to be sent on to Berlin. This late arrival was to play its part in the disposition of forces, and in the atmosphere in which that had now to be discussed.

1. Malmesbury was summoned to England on 21 April, and left Holland on the 25th. Frederick William's departure for Poland was expected in Berlin a few days before. For the Austrian debate see Duffy, 'War Policy', 95–100.
2. Cf. p. 338 above.
3. To the Governor of the Bank of England, 20 May 1794 (cited in J.M. Sherwig, *Guineas and Gunpowder . . . 1793–1815* (1969), 46). The Prussians, it will be recalled, were due to be available by 24 May (p. 337 above). Malmesbury gave Pitt an explicit reminder about the need for prompt payment on 2 June (Stanhope Ms S5 03/3).
4. *Diaries and Correspondence*, 96. Pitt had meant to 'apply to the Bank' in the last week in April (*H.M.C., Dropmore*, II, 552). The current preoccupation with unrest is followed on pp. 394–5, 398–9 below.

For without the money the Prussians refused at first to move; and since they had always so warned, they can hardly be blamed.[1] Malmesbury on return failed to shift them; it was therefore against a depressing background that he at once encountered a greater and equally unforeseen problem. By the recent treaty, the force was to operate under its own commander as was 'judged most suitable' to its paymasters, the Maritime Powers. It was in fact to discuss this judgment that Malmesbury was recalled; for views had been shifting since the earlier thoughts in London of 'joining' the Prussians to the British. The Dutch now rather favoured the original idea of placing them on the Rhine; the Austrians – not responsible here, but obviously involved – vacillated between the same concept (formerly rejected, but now revived) and a concentration in the area between Luxembourg and the Meuse.[2] The British for their part were still anxious to keep the force in touch with themselves: they wanted it under their eye, and after Turcoing they were suspicious of Austrian motives in preferring to see it anywhere else.[3] To this end, Ministers contemplated a new British command, which would link a Prussian army lying north of the Meuse in the area Namur-Liège with York and the Allied forces on the Flanders front. It would have to be subordinate to York himself: apart from other considerations, the King was unlikely to stand for anything else.[4] But, particularly if the right man would serve, it could in fact be a step forward in reducing Government's sole dependence on the Duke. For the plan served a dual purpose. It would secure and anchor the Prussians: it might also introduce Cornwallis to the continental campaign.[5]

Cornwallis agreed to lend his authority. He was sent at once to combine with Malmesbury, now returned, to persuade the Dutch, inform the Prussians, incite them to move, and work out plans. The Dutch soon agreed. But the rest of the mission soon began to go wrong; for the approach to the Prussians produced an unexpected shock. In mid-June the two men arrived at headquarters near Mainz, to talk to Marshal Möllendorff, the force's commander designate.[6] They were

1. They were indeed offered aid in kind, in provisions and forage from the British army's stores. But this did not meet their greatest need, as they claimed, which was money rather than food; and it also of course prejudged their area of operation (see below) if the transfer was to be effective.
2. Cf. pp. 333–7 above.
3. This last feeling was brought out strongly in Dundas to Cornwallis (see below), 29 May 1794, enclosed in same to York, sd (P.R.O., W.O. 6/11), and Grenville to Malmesbury, 5 June 1794 (*H.M.C., Dropmore*, II, 566).
4. This became clear from Ministers' caution later on; and in any case George III was trying hard at this time to bring the German forces in British pay more exclusively under British (as against any Austrian) direction (see *L.C.G. III*, II, no. 1077). He would have been the less disposed to contemplate a division in the British command.
5. See pp. 330–1 above.
6. An earlier instance of whose relations with the British may be seen on p. 18 above.

given a frosty reception. Möllendorff could promise only 40,000 men – two-thirds of those agreed – and when he was told their destination he refused to comply. The trouble lay in the wording of the treaty: designed for flexibility of choice, the formula – a force under its own commander, acting 'in concert' with others where 'judged most suitable' to Dutch and British interests – converted an imposed commitment into a potential debate. Möllendorff protested against a foregone conclusion, and one of which he had been told nothing either by the Allies or by his own Government. He would not march without orders from his King – who was now in Poland; and though he later became personally more friendly, and British Ministers, under pressure of events in Flanders, began to have some second thoughts, deadlock supervened over the next few weeks.[1]

This was bad enough. The situation was made no better by further trouble over the subsidy remittances. The second instalment was again a month late; worse, it was not forwarded on reaching Hamburg, for the agents had been told by the bankers in London – Harman and Hoare, for the Bank of England – to make no further payments without express instructions. The embargo would seem to have stemmed from rumours that support was going to be suspended. When they were echoed in Prussia there was a short but intense row. Malmesbury's co-signatory of the treaty, the Foreign Minister Haugwitz, hitherto its bulwark, put in a bitter protest. The affair was cleared up, and the specie forwarded. But it showed the extent of mutual distrust. For the rumours indeed had some substance: Pitt and Grenville were furious at Möllendorff's delay, and while Pitt at least was not prepared yet to withhold the monthly remittances the idea was argued seriously, probably in Cabinet, during July.[2] By the end of that month relations were really badly strained. The architects of the treaty themselves, in England and in Prussia, were the angrier because early scepticism had yielded briefly to wary hopes.

The lack of Prussian troops was felt the more harshly from the turn of events in Flanders. For throughout June and July the front there was giving way. The abandonment of the offensive, underlined by the Emperor's departure, took the heart out of the Austrians and left them with no clear plans. Their movements were sluggish, and the French, recrossing the Sambre, soon had them in trouble. The cockpit was traversed once more, as famous names of the past and the future – Mons, Oudenarde, Ramillies, Waterloo – marked stages in a general retreat. After failing to exploit a chance at Fleurus the Austrians in fact virtually gave up, and York's forces, half-expecting to be isolated – possibly by an Austrian cease-fire – were pushed back along the flank. Brussels was

1. F.O. 64/34 *passim*.
2. Pitt to Grenville, 29 June 1794 (*H.M.C., Dropmore*, II, 592); Portland to Malmesbury, 23 July 1794 (*Diaries and Correspondence*, III, 124). Sherwig (op. cit., 48–50) gives an account of the fracas.

abandoned on 11 July, Antwerp on the 24th. It now became a question of defending Holland.

And, for the British, of securing the remaining communications with home. In mid-June the Government, alarmed by the danger in west Flanders, had moved to protect Ostend. There were troops available, for part of Moira's force was still in the Isle of Wight.[1] On the 17th it was ordered to sail, replenished notionally by drafts of recruits, and with reinforcements to follow from the Channel Islands and Ireland. The first elements arrived on the 21st and others on the 26th. But York's retreat forced evacuation by a timely march to Ghent, whence Moira withdrew early in July to join York himself. Meanwhile Nieuport to the west had surrendered, with a slaughter of French émigrés among the garrison. The coastal ports of Flanders, and Antwerp itself, were lost.

These misfortunes bred bad blood between the Allied commanders, and bad feeling in the British troops. The Austrians, admired a year before, sank in the scales. York and Cornwallis reported separately on incapacity and low morale. But the dangers of division – even a unilateral peace – roused the Government in London·to fresh efforts. With little prospect of aid from Prussia, Austria must be kept up to scratch. There was indeed really no choice if the campaign was to be rescued, and Ministers' preference, already marked,[2] gained further support at this point. For early in July the Portland Whigs, increasingly alarmed by the domestic unrest, joined Pitt to form a broad Coalition. As Portland himself was to put it, they had a 'partiality for the old Austrian system',[3] and their advent hastened a decision perhaps envisaged in any case. It certainly affected the execution. For Government now resolved to send a special mission to Vienna to rescue the talks on a full alliance;[4] and the choice fell on two of Portland's associates, Lord Spencer, himself now a Minister, and Thomas Grenville, the Foreign Secretary's brother. The process was swift; the decision was taken on 15 July, the two men were appointed on the 17th, and on the 19th their instructions were ready.[5]

The first object, naturally, was to restore the military situation. There must be changes in the Austrian command – the Government suggested names – and proper consultation on how to retake the lost barrier fortresses. Reinforcements must be raised: if possible 30,000 Austrians, 10,000 British and mercenaries, and 8,000 Dutch. The Prussians should bring their existing quota of aid to full strength,[6] and the British would

1. See p. 325 above.

2. P. 335 above.

3. To Earl Spencer, 2 September 1794 (quoted in Duffy, loc. cit., 107–8). For the junction see Ch. XI, section II below.

4. Pp. 337, 339–40 above. This was thought the more necessary because the resident Minister, Morton Eden, though viewed as rather ineffective, had left on home leave in May.

5. Duffy, loc. cit., 105–10.

6. See p. 336 above.

persist in their efforts to secure the extra men involved. Given the means and the will, the position could be retrieved. The better to achieve them, inducements were repeated and help proposed. The British, in 'defensive Alliance and . . . union', would guarantee an 'adequate' barrier of fortresses including some, unspecified, on the French side of the frontier. And by way of financial assistance the Government would give its backing to an Austrian loan, already floated but hanging fire, on the London market.[1] These proposals, as it happened, crossed others from the Austrians themselves, which were likewise to be presented by a special envoy: for a subsidy, or an immediate advance on it, or – as the British were suggesting – support for a loan.[2] When Spencer and Thomas Grenville set off, there was thus a renewed impulse for a closer connexion. It remained to be seen if the points of departure could be reconciled.

II

When Toulon was lost, there disappeared all immediate hopes of a southern strategy in which the British would play a leading part. As was recognised at once in London as well as the areas concerned, it was 'an Event which . . . completely changes the Face of Affairs in this part of the World'.[3] On the key Alpine front, the Sardinians looked to the defensive while talks dragged on with the Austrians over support and co-operation. In Genoa, keener fears of France left matters much where they were, with very limited scope for Allied influence. In Switzerland, that pool of trained men, the British Minister was similarly hamstrung, and the Foreign Office acknowledged that 'private endeavours' alone could be tried.[4] This depressed inaction gave way to a flurry when the enemy attacked in the mountains in April, invading northern Genoese territory in the process. The British envoys converged on Milan, where the talks with the Austrians were under way; but nothing was settled in the next two months, and it was lucky that late snowfalls held up an advance which seriously threatened the Val d'Aosta and the plains beyond. The front settled down, the French indeed retreated slightly, Sardinia and Austria reached a measure of agreement, and a late summer offensive was even envisaged. But in September the alarm

1. The instructions, together with their background explanation, were voluminous (Grenville to Spencer and Thomas Grenville, nos. 1–4, 19 July 1794; F.O. 7/38). Pitt's Minute on their military aspect is published in *H.M.C., Dropmore*, II, 599–600.
2. See Duffy, loc. cit., 103–4.
3. Trevor [in Turin] to Grenville, no. 3, 8 January 1794 (P.R.O., F.O. 67/14). Cf. Grenville to Trevor, no. 1, 3 January 1794 (loc. cit); correspondence from Genoa January 1794 *passim* (F.O. 28/7); Fitzgerald [in Berne] to Grenville, no. 1, 8 January 1794 (F.O. 74/4).
4. Grenville to Fitzgerald, no. 3, 18 March 1794 (F.O. 74/4).

returned: the enemy was massing once more on the coast, and the expense of withstanding fresh pressure was frightening the Sardinians. So far from a stroke in the south leading to the end of the war, the region was proving a suspect link in a generally shaky chain.

The British interest perforce returned to the exercise of naval influence. Hood's ships continued to cover the western Mediterranean, screening the trade with the Levant and Italy, maintaining pressure on the seaboard states, watching the French ports, interrupting their shipping, and settling the refugees from Toulon. An opportunity soon offered to underwrite this presence. Corsica had figured as a possible target in the imprecise plans before Toulon arose.[1] The potential advantages were obvious, particularly since the prospects looked not unhopeful. The island would provide a base east of Gibraltar not dependent on mainland goodwill, well placed to mask French movements and support the Sardinians along the coast.[2] An abundance of timber and naval stores would ease problems of supply from England, and deny the enemy a highly important source. And the operation might be relatively painless, since the Corsicans, notoriously troublesome to France, were again in partial revolt, and with some success. Nor in this case was the resistance movement wary of friendly foreign control. When closer contact was made in the summer the veteran leader Paoli asked for the island to be placed under British protection.[3] This was not necessarily an unmixed blessing: the rising had recently suffered some setbacks, Paoli himself was not fully trusted,[4] and the invitation might lead to difficulties with Spain. The British indeed had earlier taken care not to fan their ally's suspicions of a restored naval presence within the Straits which might be made permanent at the peace; nor in fact were they sure that Corsica should not go to Spain herself, as a possible European reward in return for agreement over the West Indies.[5] Such doubts were reflected in the view, before Paoli's message reached London, that 'a connexion' with the island might be 'more desirable than . . . possession'.[6] Toulon in any case then absorbed all efforts. But by January Corsica again looked attractive. Paoli was supposed to have improved his position, British troops were available with a British General, and a success would be welcome coming on top of failure. Hood

1. For which see pp. 278–82, 304–5 above.

2. For the desirability of a naval base inside the Straits see St Helens to Grenville, Private, 29 May 1793 (F.O. 72/27) on the former possession of Minorca, and Grenville to Mulgrave, Secret, no. 1, 8 July 1793 (H.O. 50/455) on Corsica and possibly Malta.

3. Paoli to George III, 1 September 1793, sent through the British Minister to Tuscany (F.O. 79/9).

4. Hood to Dundas, 7 October 1793 (H.O. 28/14).

5. On these two points see Grenville to St Helens, 13 April, 21 June 1793 (*H.M.C., Dropmore*, II, 392, 399); and for developing ideas on Spanish indemnification in Europe, p. 315 above.

6. Grenville to Mulgrave, no. 2, 10 September 1793 (H.O. 50/455).

would be glad of a base. The problem of Spain was brushed aside,[1] and on 12 January he sent Gilbert Elliot with two army officers (one being Colonel Moore, the future Sir John Moore) to talk to Paoli. While still rather sceptical of the latter's claims, they thought the odds looked promising. On 7 February the British force appeared before St Fiorenzo in the north, and ten days later the bay and the town were in its hands. Resistance had been stiffer than expected, and the French managed to withdraw a large part of the garrison to Bastia in the east. There might therefore be heavier fighting to capture that fortified port.

When Hood sent his emissaries to Paoli he had received a further assurance that the island would be placed 'under the Government and protection' of Britain 'without reserve'.[2] The British Government however was not prepared to commit itself too far at once. Ministers saw no point in hastening until Hood could report some success, and news of this came only in March. But Elliot was anxious to know where he stood, and at the end of that month, on the assumption that the 'main ports and stations' had been taken, the offer was accepted. Four 'general principles' were laid down. The Corsicans would become British subjects. A British governor would assume *'supreme Executive Power* with the *command* of the Military and with a Right of Negative in all legislative Acts'. His assent would not be required on the other hand for changes in 'domestic' laws. But foreign trade and 'all external Concerns' would be subject to Acts of the British Parliament.[3] Such arrangements broadly followed the lines – and as Hood described it, deliberately – adopted for the government of Ireland in the early eighties.[4] Within them Elliot was given a wide measure of discretion. It was left to his judgment how and with whom to implement the agreement, and how far it was to be binding on Britain – should there be an 'absolute' pledge or not. Allowing for the necessary latitude to the man on the spot, there was indeed a distinct air of reserve – almost of inattention – in taking what might appear to have been an important step. Perhaps Corsica was still viewed as a possible bargaining counter with Spain; as conceivably a temporary prize for the duration of the war. Certainly one senses a casual approach: Elliot was sent off to Italy in April, to step up the pressure for greater efforts there;[5] he was told to refer any further points on Corsica itself 'if practicable'; and recognition of the island's

1. This is implicit as early as November in Grenville to St Helens, 30 November 1793 (F.O. 72/28).
2. Paoli to Hood, 4 January, enclosed in Hood to Dundas, 7 January 1794 (H.O. 28/15), by which time the Admiral had decided to send two officers – though not as yet, apparently, Elliot – to Corsica.
3. Dundas to Elliot, 31 March 1794 (W.O. 6/54), in response to Elliot's despatches of 4, 21, 22 February. This would seem to have overtaken a message to Paoli himself, asking for his ideas on terms (copy of Dundas to Paoli, 7 March 1794; B.L. Add. Ms 22688).
4. See Holland Rose, *Pitt and Napoleon*, 64n2. Cf. I, 196.
5. See p. 344 above.

advantages was linked with the assumption that 'the future Preservation of it does not appear likely to be attended by any [equal] expense or Inconvenience'.[1] Pitt's reaction might be inferred here; as also from the lack of positive evidence. When the shape of the main campaign and the Prussian alliance was being hammered out,[2] Corsica doubtless did not seem very important.

This impression is strengthened by the way in which it was assumed at the end of March that the island by then would be effectively in British hands.[3] In point of fact the only development since the capture of St Fiorenzo had been a bitter quarrel between Hood and General Dundas. Their mutual 'disinclination'[4] underlay contrasting views on the chances of forcing Bastia, which was the next essential step. Dundas, as at Toulon, was pessimistic; Hood contemptuously the reverse. While the Ministry was counting its chickens, the General resigned and sailed for home.

It was not indeed until late in May that Bastia was taken, and mid-June before the island's Corte – the General Assembly – could meet. The change of sovereignty was endorsed, and Elliot was named Viceroy.[5] By then Calvi, the enemy's last fortified harbour, was under attack. The operations lasted until August – it was there that Nelson lost his right eye. But with its fall the conquest was completed of this new accession to the British Crown.

III

In the midst of these proceedings, early in June, a refitted French squadron emerged from Toulon, drawing Hood into a chase frustrated by bad weather. Possession of Corsica was linked above all with maritime undertakings in which British troops served a naval purpose and the Mediterranean fleet might support and encourage the movements of an Allied army. It promoted, and was made possible by, the exercise of seapower, that 'application of the limited method to the unlimited form'[6] which later thought regarded as 'the British way in warfare'.[7]

There is no indication that Pitt himself was subscribing effectively to such a school; or indeed that he had yet developed very definite strategic views. At the start he had favoured a series of seaborne limited blows;

1. Dundas to Elliot, 31 March 1794 (W.O. 6/54).
2. Pp. 329–37 above.
3. See above.
4. Gilbert Elliot to Lady Elliot, 13 March 1794 (*Life and Letters of Elliot*, II, 232).
5. On 19 June. The documents may be found in *The Annual Register* for 1794, Appendix to the Chronicle, 95–111.
6. Julian S. Corbett, *Some Principles of Maritime Strategy* (1911), 63.
7. As Liddell Hart entitled it in his book of 1932.

but the design was not developed enough to make him reject other demands, particularly those from the main continental campaign. He was ready to provide the latter with more men as well as money, and certainly not to remove British troops at seemingly critical moments for competing operations.[1] He was also ready to contribute a sizeable force to a northern thrust from Toulon,[2] which could have meant an indefinite commitment added to that in Flanders. He became increasingly involved in Europe. At the same time he remained hopeful that the growth of national resources would sustain a whole range of operations, there and overseas. '. . . Mere naval exertions are not sufficient against a country not possessing the command of the sea'. But that in itself was no justification for 'abandoning our prospects' of colonial success.[3] In essence this approach doubtless followed the two-headed strategy which had achieved success in earlier French and Spanish wars: the support of allies, including troops, to contain the enemy in Europe, while depriving him of overseas resources and increasing British trade and wealth which in turn would aid support of the continental allies. Such a policy in the end, however, required a balance of priorities as events and the state of the alliance itself might suggest. Pitt was content in these early days to act as opportunity offered, in a situation which was held not to posit the need for clear-cut choice.

The strategic developments of the next few years and the discussions they engendered, often taken as characterising the conduct of the war as a whole, have in fact been read back largely into a period to which they did not apply. Events were soon to remove for the British the prospect of a continental campaign, and later to revive it in a form posing the 'alternative' which Dundas had feared.[4] Some classic statements of policy resulted, not least from Dundas himself, which did much to shape subsequent thinking on British methods in war. They take their place in a pattern of argument emerging from the seventeenth century and stretching largely unchanged into almost our own day. One must be the more precise in tracing their application through the phases of the long conflict in which they reached so high a point.

This does not mean that seapower was viewed, in this phase, as anything but fundamental. The very range of the current possibilities ensured that. The navy was the essential instrument of any British strategy: the conveyor and cover of troop movements and supplies, the close or distant guardian of trade, a means of denying supplies to the enemy, the first line of defence. At the centre of such functions was the

1. Eg pp. 264–5, 289, 297, 330–1, 343 above.
2. Pp. 304–5, 318–20 above.
3. Pitt in the debate on the Army Estimates, 3 February 1794 (*P.R.*, XXXVII, 265, 269). For different wording in the first quotation see *The Senator*, VIII (nd), 185, and *P.H.*, XXX, col. 336. Cf. Walpole in 1739, on war with Spain: 'It is true our navy is much superior to theirs, but by a navy alone we cannot propose to force them to a peace'.
4. See p. 269 above.

presence of the Channel fleet; for, as always, their reach and flexibility turned on command of the home approaches. In 1793 its operations had been disappointing.[1] 1794 produced an encounter which demonstrated both the strength and the weaknesses of its direction. 'The Glorious First of June', the series of engagements in which Howe defeated the French fleet from Brest, marked a significant tactical victory within a strategic failure. When news of the battle was received, joy was unconfined. The performance of the Opera was broken off while Rule Britannia and the Anthem were sung; London was illuminated, bells rang, commemorative medals were struck. The King and Queen paid a four day visit to the returning ships at Portsmouth; peerages, baronetages and promotions followed, medals (the first for an action in British naval history) were awarded, a subscription was raised for widows and orphans. It was a genuine occasion of public acclaim, and a useful tonic for Government. Care was taken not to mar the achievement with less convenient considerations. Pitt, Dundas and Chatham, all on view at Portsmouth – Pitt briefly – were concerned in the background with resentments arising from the conduct of individuals and their claims·to distinction.[2] Pitt himself was in something of a scrape over the reward due to Howe, whose promised Garter he was determined should go to the Duke of Portland at this point.[3] Such problems were the stuff – far from trivial in effect – of naval and Ministerial life. More serious for the shape of events was the context of the battle itself. For the fleets had met in the course of operations around the passage of a large convoy laden with grain from America needed to make good a dearth in France. Distant blockade, based on Torbay, had already let the enemy slip out of Brest. In the engagement and its aftermath he managed to screen the precious cargo, which a fortnight later reached its destination intact. The deliverance was timely, at a moment of political and economic crisis for the Revolution. Against the defeat in battle could be set the attainment of the object.

The time indeed had not come when Britain could wield naval power 'as an absolute mistress'.[4] The history of the Channel fleet itself for the rest of the year bore witness to the fact. Ocean convoys were covered with minor loss, and the main French force stayed in harbour. But Howe's main body was at sea for less than a month in all after June, and in December the Brest fleet emerged and sailed south to join the Toulon

1. Pp. 292–3, 295, 323 above. Cf. Pitt's defence on p. 327.

2. Partly through Chatham's own fault in requiring that names should be included in Howe's despatch: a demand with which Howe complied reluctantly (see P.R.O. 30/8/367) and which affected the award of medals as well.

3. *L.G.C. III*, II, nos. 1093, 1095. The Admiral refused the Marquessate offered instead, and was given his Garter only three years later. On Portland's claim see p. 414 below.

4. Captain A.T. Mahan, *The Influence of Sea Power upon the French Revolution and Empire 1793–1812*, II (1893), 372.

fleet. It was turned back by a gale. Two smaller squadrons earlier in the year had likewise sailed into the Atlantic, one for West Africa, the other for the West Indies.[1] None the less, the public instinct was right: the Glorious First of June was an important success. The superiority in seamanship and gunnery, flawed though it may have been by the standards of a few years later, was sufficiently marked to confirm confidence in the future. It helped reinforce British morale, and depress the French. Whatever the strategic and even tactical shortcomings, it opened the great series of victories at sea.

It was fitting in a sense that the origin of the action should have lain in American waters. For the value of seapower, and the claims put forward on its behalf, rested prominently on its sustenance of world-wide trade and colonies, and in that framework the Atlantic took first place. The centre of interest for both French and British rested in the Caribbean. While Dundas thought success 'of infinite Moment' in the East and West Indies alike, the East had in fact to look after itself for over a year.[2] The forces in India – aided by the fact that news of the war reached them before the French[3] – took over the enemy's ports except Pondicherry, which fell later in the summer. A naval presence was maintained for some months by a single man-of-war – the rest of a small squadron having been sent home earlier – and from the autumn by three armed East Indiamen. This, rather fortunately, sufficed for coastal waters and some limited convoy. But the problem was the protection of shipping throughout the Indian Ocean, from the Indies and the Straits of Malacca to the Cape of Good Hope. The Dutch and British were too weak to contain French frigates and privateers based on Mauritius, or to blockade the island itself. Allied commerce suffered, and in May 1794, when the margin of strength in European waters had been increased by the damage to the French at Toulon, a small reinforcing squadron sailed from England, reaching Madras in October. Meanwhile the West Indies received attention on a quite different scale: a reinforcement from France in the summer of 1793, Jervis's and Grey's expedition in November, protection of Atlantic convoys by the fleets from Torbay and Brest.[4]

The reasons were not far to seek. They stemmed from a calculation which no British Government was likely to challenge seriously in 1793. For the West Indies were still held to provide resources of wealth and strength significant, and perhaps critical, to both competing Powers. The experience of almost a century had turned the argument into a

1. For the latter see p. 324 above.
2. P. 269 above. For application of the term East Indies to the East as a whole, see I, 423.
3. I, 439.
4. Pp. 292–3, 324–5 above.

truism – and built up strong, if sometimes competing, interests to defend it:[1] the current figures of trade appeared to confirm the fact. In 1789 two-fifths of France's commerce – taking imports, exports and re-exports – derived from her colonies, the vast bulk being with the West Indies. The British islands furnished over a fifth of the home country's imports in value – the largest single source – and if they took less by way of exports their raw materials, particularly cotton, did much to swell the sales to other parts of the world.[2] The depressing effects of the American War appeared to have been largely overcome; the relevant statistics were resuming their upward march, and the way seemed open once more to a growing share of the western Atlantic trade.[3] For the direct figures themselves were only part of the story; they underwrote wider advantages for France and Britain alike. The Caribbean was the hub of the triangular traffic between Europe, Africa and the American continent: a system involving manufactured goods and slaves, primary materials and produce, in a network of ocean passages and of re-exports nearer home. It nourished a supply of ships and seamen, and the life of some major ports: of Bristol, Nantes and Bordeaux, of Liverpool, Le Havre and Marseilles, of London itself. It assisted the growth of manufacturing industry, and, possibly still, of capital formation.[4] Its effects were imbedded in the national structures – according to some contemporaries, perhaps more than a fifth of the French population depended on the West Indies in some degree. Such considerations had largely overcome doubts about the islands' value raised in England in the great debate on American affairs.[5] With the advent of a new French war the traditional view held sway.

The strategic consequence was direct conquest, as in earlier wars: to strike at French resources in trade and shipping and increase the British, to strengthen bases and stop or reduce commerce-raiding in the western Atlantic, and to exploit the gains at the peace table for bargaining or retention. These familiar and important objects appeared particularly attractive in the particular context of this Revolutionary War. There was much to be said for holding control over the French colony of St Domingue, shaken by the negro and mulatto risings which might spread to Jamaica. Its seizure moreover, together with that of Martinique and Guadeloupe, might be quite easy given the pre-war approaches from the planters themselves.[6] And bearing more directly on metropolitan

1. For an important example in the eighties see I, 333–4.
2. One computation (by Dr Duffy, in an unpublished paper to which I am indebted for much that follows) puts the result at a quarter of total British exports and re-exports. For direct figures see Mitchell & Deane, *Abstract of British Historical Statistics*, 312, and Frances Armytage, *The Free Port System in the British West Indies* (1953), Appendix III.
3. See I, 332–9.
4. Cf. for Britain loc. cit., 158n3, 382n4.
5. Loc. cit., 158–9, 332–3.
6. See pp. 262–3 above.

France, the supply of colonial products might be even more important than usual in her state of increasing economic dislocation. It was against this background that the Government favoured reinforcements, and Pitt himself gave initial priority to 'offensive operations' in the Caribbean.[1]

The strategy proved expensive, and few of its aims were directly achieved. When peace was made in 1801, after operations against the French islands of Tobago, St Domingue, Martinique, Guadeloupe, St Lucia, the Saints, Marie Galante and Deseada, only Tobago, Martinique and St Lucia were in British hands, and all three were returned. The sole West Indian conquest retained was in fact Trinidad, captured from Spain after she had changed sides.[2] Of perhaps 120,000 soldiers and seamen involved in the various actions, probably more than 50,000 were killed, the majority by disease, while thousands again had to be discharged. Such effects of the climate were all too familiar from earlier wars; and although it had in fact been making fewer inroads in the past two decades, constant reinforcements were likely to be needed in a further conflict, which themselves were most vulnerable in their first year of operations. Offensive campaigns in such conditions were peculiarly wasteful of men. The efforts accounted for a sizeable proportion – it would be rash to specify exactly – of the costs of the war. They failed to cripple the French economy, which despite the problems was not so dependent on colonial supplies as those of Spain and Holland, and proved the better able to withstand the losses this time thanks to the conquests in Europe. They absorbed and destroyed formations whose presence was urgently needed for continental operations at a later, critical stage. Small wonder that a line of historians from Macaulay to Fortescue and beyond has anathematised this strategy of the 1790s.

> For this England's soldiers had been sacrificed, her treasures squandered, her influence in Europe weakened, her arm for six fateful years fettered, numbed and paralysed.[3]

Such a statement, if extreme, derived from sombre facts. Certain considerations have to be set against them. Whatever the longer consequences, and the fortunes of different products at the time, and despite the scale of local privateering which was high for much of the war, the overall figures of British trade with the West Indies – direct and by way of entrepôt – increased significantly during these same years.[4] It thereby helped sustain, as was claimed, the maritime strength on which naval power relied; and in ways that could not be replaced by other lines

1. Ibid; pp. 266, 324 above.
2. For which event see p. 631 below.
3. Fortescue, op. cit., IV–Part I, 565. And cf. loc. cit., 384–5, 496.
4. Mitchell and Deane, op. cit., 312. For an assessment of the factors see *The Trade Winds*, ed. C. Northcote Parkinson (1948), ch. VIII by Lucy Frances Horsfall.

of commerce. For such a change would have affected not only the structure of ports but of shipping itself, since much of this was of a special type – the smallish, beamy, fast West Indiaman – and the vessels, like the trade, would not have been filled elsewhere. These results, it can be argued, would not have been possible without an offensive strategy, particularly against islands masking the interspersed British possessions. The outcome moreover, if it failed to achieve their transfer in 1801, left a position that enabled the British to sweep the region after war was renewed, retaining a choice of conquests at the peace in 1815. The efforts of the Revolutionary War in other words paved the way, however expensively, for the easier gains of its Napoleonic successor. With all their shortcomings, they contributed to that accumulation of seapower which, by direct containment and pressure and by the sustenance of financial influence, formed a prime element in a policy that brought victory in the end.

This was broadly the case for the defence, developed by one school of naval historians of whom the classic exemplar was Mahan.

To control the whole Caribbean region was amongst those objects that lay within the scope of the British Government, the one most essential to the success of the general war.

He was not deterred by the orthodox tenet that command of distant regions was best secured by a concentration commanding the focal European waters. His argument was rather that in certain conditions the second, once gained, demanded the first.

In a contest between equal navies for the control of the sea, to waste military effort upon the capture of small islands . . . is a preposterous misdirection of effort; but when one navy is overwhelmingly preponderant, as the British was after 1794, when the enemy confines himself to commerce-destroying by crowds of small privateers, then the true military policy is to stamp out the nests where they swarm.

And this applied 'even' to 1793 and 1794, although operations in the second year had been stretched too far.[1]

Seen in the longer-term context, much of the debate might be represented as misconceived. For the liberal economists had been right to cast doubts on the value of the Western colonial commerce, even though they were concerned more with the mainland than the islands, and with the colonial system than the ingredients of the trade.[2] Not only was too high a value set by Pitt and his colleagues on its place within the French economy – though not, it could be argued later, within the

1. *The Influence of Sea Power upon the French Revolution and Empire*, II, 393, 252.
2. Cf. I, 161–2.

Spanish: the foundations of prosperity throughout the Caribbean – coffee, cotton, above all sugar – can be shown in retrospect to have been starting to shift. The island plantations were already faced by problems before the war began. Stimulated partly by the ensuing damage, in the British as well as the French islands, they were now progressively if unevenly overtaken by large-scale production elsewhere. The very rise in prices under wartime conditions, which boosted the value of the trade in the nineties,[1] hastened a process which, though gradual, was probable in any case. And beyond this absolute there was also a relative loss of importance, as industrialisation began to change the proportions of the British economy. The larger consequences of the West Indian campaigns were very different from those envisaged: an acceleration of the removal of slavery, and of the decline of the region itself. But such a fact, grateful as it is to historical irony, need not invalidate decisions which were necessarily short-term. In that sense, any study of war 'is not deeply concerned with the consequences. Its theme is the effort'.[2] And that type of effort has to be assessed against the day. The economic yields were buoyant, and despite military setbacks remained so – indeed improved – in the next few years. It is therefore perhaps more pertinent to return to the military sphere, and direct the questions to the plans and the operations themselves. What preferable course might Government have chosen, in the conditions of 1793–4? Its local resources had been determined by earlier strategic doctrine which – to a greater extent than the French – kept the garrisons low and rested on wartime reinforcements from home. Given this legacy (which it fully accepted), should – could – the Ministry have put greater forces into its early 'offensive operations'? Alternatively should it have stayed on the strategic defensive, releasing more strength for operations in Europe – themselves requiring assessment in the light of the administrative and diplomatic pressures? And within a central strategy bearing on the resources for local plans, were the latter themselves in this first stage such as to give the former a reasonable prospect? This indeed, it might be hazarded, was the nub of the matter. For whatever role the West Indian operations were designed to fill, success turned as always on a reconciliation of ends with measurable means.

The ends in this case in at least one instance were political as well as military – control of an area threatening to export insurrection; the means in most instances at the start, internal efforts with external support.[3] The combination favoured the adoption of an ambitious

---

1. P. 352 above. And for the continued buoyancy in the next decade see Seymour Drescher, *Econocide, British Slavery in the Era of Abolition* (1977).
2. W.K. Hancock and M.M. Gowing, *The British War Economy* (1949), 555.
3. See pp. 262–3 above.

design. A month before war began, Government had agreed to consider means of taking the French territory of St Domingue under British protection. Jamaica was alerted to prepare; meanwhile in February orders were sent to Barbados to attack Tobago and, with the planters' assistance, the Windward Islands of St Lucia ('the West Indian Gibraltar'), Martinique (a well-found naval base), Guadeloupe and Marie Galante.[1] In June the Governor of Jamaica was authorised to accept a capitulation from St Domingue,[2] and when this came in September some seven hundred troops and a small frigate squadron sailed to take possession of the fortified harbour of Mole St Nicholas.

These moves met with mixed success. Tobago was taken easily in April.[3] But an attack on Martinique in June was called off after a landing, when the French royalists' effective support was in doubt, and the plans for the other Windward Islands were not followed up. In St Domingue, a more uncertain position developed. The planters' message to Jamaica had been sent after a further massacre by negroes in the north: news which, together with a forecast of rising trouble in other islands, made the British the more anxious to recover the situation. The assurances of a friendly greeting were borne out at first, and Mole St Nicholas surrendered readily. Pressure from the negroes was lifted, the Republicans failed to mount a relief, and over the next four months focal points were taken around the western coast. The Windward Passage to Jamaica was now covered; trade was picking up; and the commanders decided to ensure the conquest by blockading the capital, Port-au-Prince. But at this point the thinness of the occupation was revealed. Reinforcements from Jamaica were stretched to the limit, for the garrison there was itself reduced, and at no time were there more than nine hundred British troops effectively available in St Domingue. The Government had earlier authorised the raising of militia, white and mulatto; but though this was done it was on a small scale, and the results did not ease relations between the two elements or bind the mulattoes to the British. A further possible source of aid lay in troops from the Spanish part of the island, and a small contingent was arranged on the spot. Anything more however, given the doubts about indemnities, was likely to need some thought in London and Madrid.[4] In these circumstances it

1. Ibid. The quotation on St Lucia dates from the War of American Independence; Alan G. Jamieson, 'War in the Leeward Islands: 1775–1783' (Oxford D.Phil. thesis, 1981).

2. For exchanges between the Ministry and the French planters to this end, and the instructions to Jamaica, see P.R.O., W.O. 1/158, which contains a copy in Pitt's hand of the 'proprietors'' final paper.

3. As, a month later, were the islands of St Pierre and Miquelon off Newfoundland, by a small expedition from Halifax in Nova Scotia. They too were returned to France in 1801.

4. See p. 315 above. After the operations had begun, Grenville indeed hinted at a possible accommodation to be reached locally; but he avoided proposing a 'precise plan' (to St Helens, no. 31, 30 November 1793; F.O. 72/28).

proved impossible to control the country beyond the strongpoints; and the lack of a solid British force was undermining the confidence of those expected to supply an alternative. The position began to deteriorate in the face of fresh negro and mulatto massacres; the Spaniards proved of little use, and the sickly season approached. By April 1794 the commanders were distinctly uneasy. But in May the long-awaited reinforcements arrived.

They came moreover crowned with the reputation of victory. Grey and Jervis had reached Barbados in January with some 7,000 troops.[1] They attacked Martinique in February, completing its capture in March, and St Lucia at the beginning of April, forcing surrender in a few days. Moving on to Guadeloupe, taking the Saints on the way, they won a series of engagements in an impressive example of naval and military co-operation. By the end of the month the island was reduced, setting troops free for St Domingue. They were used at once against Port-au-Prince, which fell early in June. As the rainy season set in, the position in the Caribbean thus looked dramatically better than it had done a few months before.

It seemed a triumph for the Ministry's judgment. In April, before news of the events was received, Pitt forecast 'valuable and important acquisitions . . . which . . . we had every prospect of making' in the West Indies.[2] At the end of May – when the success of St Domingue was still unknown – he was able to say, in a debate on the conduct of the war, that while gains in that area might not themselves bring peace at once,

> Is it . . . of little consequence in the first year of the war to cut up their [the French] resources, and destroy the sinews of their commerce? Is the injury to their revenue less fatal, though . . . it may not, in the first instance, be perceived? Is it of little consequence to us in the prosecution of a war for which we do not ourselves possess sufficient military force, and in aid of which we must have recourse to our pecuniary resources, thus to procure the means of increasing these resources, by extending our commerce, and opening new sources of industry?[3]

The colonial strategy in a nutshell; and apparently yielding results at a time when Allied operations in Europe were showing signs of going wrong.[4] But the satisfaction was short-lived. The distant blockade of the Atlantic ports, which had allowed the main French fleet to leave Brest in May, had failed to stop a squadron from Rochefort in April bound with

1. See p. 325 above.
2. In the Commons, 10 April 1794 (*P.R.*, XXXVIII, 128).
3. 30 May 1794 (loc. cit., 375). By 'the first year of the war' he presumably meant the year ending in the first campaigning season open in that part of the world to wartime reinforcements.
4. Pp. 338–9 above.

transports for the Caribbean.[1] Early in June they landed over 1,500 troops in Guadeloupe, and fierce fighting with varying fortunes followed for a month. In July the British were forced to evacuate the eastern part of the island, and consolidate on the isthmus with the western half. The operations had severely lowered their numbers, and disease was mounting. In September the French attacked again, and no relief was in sight. In mid-December the last troops had to be embarked for Martinique. Meanwhile some of the British positions in western St Domingue came under fire. The garrisons found themselves hard pressed, casualties and sickness took a rising toll, and in December a key strongpoint guarding the Windward Passage was lost. By then the British forces everywhere were being reduced by disease, and in the captured Windward Islands as well as St Domingue the mulattoes and negroes posed a growing threat. This last was something new, on such a scale, to be added to the experience of Caribbean warfare. In all the circumstances, could the recent gains be held?

The answer must depend on the degree of willpower in London. Some sense of moral support, and indeed the goodwill of two able commanders, had already been lost by Ministerial action. Grey had been told in May that he could return to England, as he himself had proposed, to discuss plans for the campaign of 1794–5. But in July he and Jervis were severely censured by Dundas for their method of exacting prize money, in a despatch which led them to demand replacements and prepare to leave at once. In the event the turn of operations held them until November, by which time indeed both men were tired and ill. But their feelings had been made very clear, successors had been appointed, and any threat to prize money – a prime inducement to service in the West Indies – was likely to have an effect on the officer corps as a whole. The accusations in point of fact had partial substance, they came from British as well as French interests, and Pitt's reaction – for as Grey appreciated, it must have been Pitt whose 'ear' had been 'gained'[2] – was in keeping with his wish to respect the 'protection' offered to the French colonies,[3] and his usual inclination to frown on reported misconduct. Admirable, no doubt. But it could also be noted that both commanders had some involvement with Opposition – Grey in local politics and as the father of the Friend of the People,[4] Jervis, though loosely to be counted as an Administration MP, in terms of personal friendship; and that being so, the Ministers should have been the more careful of their ground. As it was, Dundas was open to the comment that he had approved special rules for allocation of captures in advance,[5] even if he

1. See p. 324 above.
2. To Nepean, 29 July 1794 (P.R.O., W.O. 1/82).
3. For which see his remarks in the Commons on 30 December 1794 (*P.R.*, XLI (1795), 52).
4. See p. 109 above.
5. Contained in Grey and Jervis to Dundas, 16 January 1794, in P.R.O., C.O. 318/13.

could not be aware how the rights of seizure would be framed; and it was distinctly hasty to condemn men who had not been heard. In view of the time required to gather evidence, and the range of the charges, such a judgment on a distant expedition was scarcely likely to help morale.[1]

Of more critical importance, however, was the extent of material aid. There was no lack of good intentions on the Ministry's part. In July Dundas was hoping to ship recruits to the regiments in St Domingue, and a further contingent of 600 troops. As grave reports of sickness were received in August, more extensive plans were formed: for at least 1,700 men at once, followed by two 'Catholic Corps' from Ireland and 4–500 light cavalry, and for a medical staff and supplies. Gibraltar was ordered to send three regiments to Martinique, and this was done in October. But by then a familiar combination was taking effect at home. Despite all Dundas's efforts – and he made his urgency plain[2] – westerly winds in the Channel, too distant a blockade of the Atlantic ports, reverses on the continent and administrative inadequacies affected the main design. One regiment in England was unfit for service, and no other could be spared; the Irish formations could not be completed as quickly as had been hoped. Replacements however were earmarked from Europe, and meanwhile, in mid-December, some 1,500 of the original reinforcements at last sailed down Channel on a favourable wind. Encouraged by these signs, Dundas was still counting on 'a very respectable force' of over 6,000. But even while he gave the figures things were going wrong again. The Allies were pulling back in the Low Countries, and British troops could not be returned; and at the turn of the year the French fleet was thought to be at sea. The first troop convoy was therefore held until the Channel fleet could provide cover, and only the Gibraltar contingent, and one vessel blown separately out of Plymouth, reached Martinique and Jamaica by the close of 1794. Conversely, in January 1795 a convoy of French troops reached Guadeloupe, having evaded the watch on Brest.[3]

One means of helping to make good the deficiencies caused by 'the

1. The Ministry censured the two men for setting up prize courts, which they had no powers to do; and the scope of the provisions for seizure, as laid down by the same authority, formed a questionable extension of normal practice. The objections from British interests, echoing the French proprietors, stemmed from fears of possible Republican retaliation. Grey and Jervis took their case to law, and eventually won on every count but one – which however was a substantial one. Long before that, in 1795, Ministers had been made to look awkward by having to reject some badly framed charges raised in the Commons, and indeed to move counter-resolutions (*P.R.*, XLI, 490–502).

2. See in particular his Private letters to Chatham at the Admiralty of 13 and 14 September 1794 (P.R.O. 30/8/368).

3. In addition to the official correspondences, there is a précis of operational correspondence with Grey, endorsed 30 December 1794, among Pitt's papers in P.R.O. 30/8/350.

For events on the continent see section IV below.

unprecedented Sickness',[1] which was proving so hard from England, was to raise local levies seasoned against disease. Grey, and the command in St Domingue, had in fact taken this initiative earlier, and the latter was now anxious to enlarge the scale. The proposals soon ran into trouble, for they raised a triangular problem, of the relations of negroes and mulattoes with the French, their relations with the British, and the role and position of the French proprietors themselves. No aspect could be disentangled from the others. The French planters and merchants were owed support in return for assistance, offered in a formal agreement[2] containing assurances on their rights. They were an obvious source of supply for officers. But they could not meet all the requirements if substantial forces were needed quickly: the coloured populations alone were the likely answer to such a demand. This last indeed had been accepted by Ministers as applying to the British islands for the past few years, a fact reflected in Pitt's thinking before the war began.[3] It was one thing however to admit the principle; quite another to apply it. Could terms be granted to the negroes and mulattoes which would not offend the French planters? And would they indeed be approved, in the example they set, in the British islands? Difficulties soon arose. Grey's actions in the south were unknown;[4] but the news from St Domingue gave rise to objections. For in its efforts to enlist the mulattoes the command had gone as far as it dared, by conveying support for their claims to appointments under an ancient, but lapsed, French royal decree. Unfortunately, this ran counter to the planters' recent capitulation, which specifically confined mulattoes' rights to those applying in the British colonies. As a result, no one was happy. The mulattoes' confidence was not secured, and the French proprietors sent an envoy to London to propose a white legion for St Domingue, composed of exiles and deserters and to be financed by Britain in return for the promise of a tax on the island's produce. The idea was accepted – giving rise to trouble later. At the same time the command's approach to the negro problem caused a stir. For here it was anxious to gain support by some programme of emancipation: of a remission of slave status for those recruited outside the ranks of free negroes, perhaps after five years' service. In such case, it was claimed, important areas of the island could be secured at once. The initial reaction, however, was predictable, particularly since the Secretary of State was Dundas, a leading opponent of sudden change to the system over the past few years. Labour corps were desirable, and some levies militarily welcome; but

1. Dundas to Sir Adam Williamson, 10 February 1795 (W.O. 1/60).
2. P. 355 above.
3. See ibid; and Fortescue, loc. cit., 410 for thoughts in 1790 in the Nootka Sound crisis. For earlier attitudes, see Richard Pares, *War and Trade in the West Indies 1739–1763* (1936), 252–7.
4. See the paper prepared for Pitt (p. 358, n3 above) at the end of 1794.

at the same time I am clearly of opinion that if the Services of the Negroes could be obtained by pecuniary gratifications, it would be far preferable to the measures of promising freedom to them, which if carried to too great an extent would inevitably create the most serious evils.[1]

Recruitment was not stopped, in the particular circumstances of St Domingue: the French planters themselves indeed wanted it expanded. But a few months later, the raising of fresh negro levies for the Windward Islands was expressly forbidden without further instructions.[2]

This injunction was sent, at a critical moment for colonial strategy, following a long and important Cabinet meeting.[3] It therefore expressed the Ministry's collective view. Pitt himself, who had recently spoken again of the 'horror' of the slave trade, had gone on to condemn French anarchy as 'even more dreadful' than the slave system.[4] This was a comparison which in the circumstances looked suspiciously like a contrast; and there is no evidence that he was prepared at this point, against prevalent opinions, to press for a reduction of slavery as a weapon of war. Government's refusal to take such a step, at the time the decision was taken, was perhaps of immediate and certainly of potential significance. For the actions of the mulattoes and negroes proved to be one of the three factors, together with losses from sickness and the quality of the Atlantic blockade, governing the course of the West Indies' campaigns; and this pattern was first discernible, in its potential proportions, during the second half of 1794. It had not been so earlier, in 1793 when nothing much happened, or in the successful months following the arrival of Grey's expedition. In 1795 it was established, much to Britain's detriment; and one must therefore ask if a great opportunity had not been missed. For was not this factor of the coloured populations indeed a determinant of the others, in the extent to which it shaped the efforts of the contestants themselves? Given greater negro and mulatto sympathies, might the British have secured the French islands without the long succession of expensive reinforcements from home? Might such sympathies have deterred the enemy from sending his own reinforcements? Might they have spared the British islands the need for substantial forces to guard against unrest? For the impact was

1. Dundas to Williamson, 7 October 1794 (P.R.O., W.O. 1/60); and see same to Vaughan, sd (Roger Norman Buckley, *Slaves in Red Coats* . . . (1979), 10). For his part in the debates on the abolition of the slave trade from 1788 to 1792 see I, 399–402.

2. Same to Major General Sir John Vaughan [successor to Grey], no. 9, 19 February 1795 (W.O. 1/83).

3. Same to same, nos. 5–9, sd; and see also no. 4, 18 February 1795 (loc. cit.), showing that the King had seen Vaughan's opinions before the Cabinet met.

4. In the Commons, 30 December 1794 (*P.R.*, XL, (1795), 52). For the distinction commonly drawn between the possibilities of abolishing the trade and abolishing the system see I, 390.

twofold: not only in the numbers sent out from Britain – with wastage from desertion before loss from disease – but also on the nature of the operations: whether these were to be strategically relevant or strategically negative. In St Domingue, for instance, the hinterland might have been left alone and a less costly effort confined to covering the Windward Passage. Perhaps such questions are put too simply. The populations' loyalties were quite often held; recruits were enlisted to fight both the French and also other negroes and mulattoes. Nor, even if the sympathies had been spread more widely, would they necessarily have been complete, in the French islands attracted by a guarantee from Paris of wholesale emancipation – could the counter-attraction have satisfied Toussaint l'Ouverture and Rigaud in St Domingue? – and, in the British, from populations suffering threats to subsistence, induced probably by a shortage of American foodstuffs which was the remaining legacy of the recent war.[1] Nor, again, might the military results have met all the expectations: the local commanders may have been pitching their claims too high. They may have proposed a reward out of scale with potential returns. It would seem still to have been worth-while, on a military view, to accept that risk.

But the problem of course was not only military. It was political as well. To bite into slavery was a hazardous proceeding. The system was imbedded in the economies for which the campaigns were being fought, and only if both seemed in real danger was such a step likely to be approved. Ministers perhaps not surprisingly were cautious in 1794, for a spate of recent gains was only then being followed by checks and reverses. Despite the warnings, they were not ready for a serious change of course. But the problem in fact would remain, and it was of great importance. For it embodied heavy restraints on the strategy itself.

IV

Whatever happened in the West Indies, and whatever weight was attached to it, could not compare in immediacy with events in western Europe. From July a period of intense uncertainty – of opportunity or of failure – opened. On the one hand, news from France revived some hopes of a crisis which might yield decisive advantage if only support could be applied. 'Thermidor' – the fall of Robespierre following the last frenzied stage of the Terror – was bound to turn British thoughts again to subversion and invasion. It was all the more frustrating, on the other hand, that at this very moment the Allies were falling back in Flanders

1. For the slaves' food supply in the British colonies, in relation to the islands' commercial achievements, see R.B. Sheridan, 'The Crisis of Slave Subsistence in the British West Indies during and after the American Revolution', in *William and Mary Quarterly*, XXXIII, no. 4.

and their relations were badly strained. Seen from England, Prussia was going wrong within months of receiving a subsidy; and a closer understanding with Austria had to be sought against military reverses which themselves stemmed from, as they threatened to seal, the failure to establish a common will.[1]

The efforts were two-way. For the decision to send a mission to Vienna was taken almost simultaneously with an Austrian decision to send a special envoy to London.[2] Unfortunately in the latter instance much of the effect was lost; for the man chosen was Count Mercy in Brussels,[3] and after delay from bad weather and a horrible three and a half days in the Channel, the elderly diplomat, already in poor health, died towards the end of August. The talks were taken up by the resident Minister, Starhemberg. But he was not of the same calibre, and Mercy's loss was a definite blow.

It was the more severe because experienced sympathy was badly needed. The starting points of the two Governments remained uncomfortably far apart. The British, interested in defending Holland and retaining Austrian sovereignty in the Belgic provinces, geared their proposals very obviously to those ends. The Austrians, lukewarm or hostile to their Netherlands, increasingly worried about central Europe, suspicious of Prussia, and financially embarrassed, required inducements for their efforts in the west. Mercy's instructions were to extract, in return for the promise of fulfilling engagements, as many British troops as possible, renewed British influence for Dutch and Prussian troops, and financial aid in the form of official support for a loan already on the London market, or of a subsidy from the Maritime Powers, or a mortgage on assets in the Netherlands.[4] These were specific demands to set against a general assurance. Spencer's and Grenville's instructions likewise were firmer on demands than rewards. In return for the removal of Coburg and Austrian reinforcements in Flanders, they could offer an intention to supply reinforcements from England and Holland, the hope (perforce subject to Parliamentary approval, and the terms of the Government's own fund-raising) of official support for the Austrian loan, and the guarantee of 'a respectable and adequate barrier' in Flanders, to be included in a system of alliance and of mutual support at the peace. Less agreeably in this last connexion, and to be kept in the wings, was the need to press for the Dutch indemnity once the Convention was signed.[5]

It was perhaps hardly surprising that terms of this kind were at once rebuffed. The imprecise offer of a barrier for territory which its sovereign

1. See pp. 341–4 above.
2. On 15 and 12 July respectively. Cf. p. 343 above.
3. For whom see p. 272, n2 above.
4. Duffy, 'War Policy', 103–4.
5. Loc. cit., 110–12. For the Dutch territorial indemnity at Austrian expense see pp. 273, 296 above. When going to the money market for its own recent needs, the Government had stated that it would not take formal responsibility for any foreign loan.

no longer cared for, the prospect rather than the assurance of more British and Dutch troops, the carrot of alliance when none was held out specifically on treatment in relation to other allies,[1] failed to meet demands that were now insistent on tangible help. Above all, the financial proposals came as a disappointment; for unlike the year before,[2] finance was now displacing other issues as the prime point for negotiations. The Austrians had not fared well so far in an attempt to raise money in London – the only real source available since Amsterdam was hard hit by the war. A loan for £3 million, floated in May, had raised only £300,000 by July, when the evacuation of the Belgic provinces threatened its collapse. Official cover therefore seemed vital, and the British Government was not unwilling: Pitt gave some verbal encouragement, and an 'advance' of £150,000, was made in August to be followed by two more, in return for a stand in defence of Maastricht.[3] But this could not provide what the Austrians wanted: the advances did not necessarily presage a loan, and a guarantee, however phrased, must await Parliamentary approval.[4] Some assurance of substance was needed for a serious response to a mission which after all had been sent because of a crisis. For if that crisis was acknowledged in Vienna, it was not necessary in the same light; the balance of forces there was delicate – more so perhaps than Pitt and Grenville knew. Thugut, now formally in sole charge of foreign affairs, was none the less in an exposed position: looked on as an upstart by the great nobility, and dependent on an Emperor whose priorities were shifting.[5] He could not afford to give much away without proof of the necessary aid; nor indeed was he himself committed to a campaign in the west on a scale which could risk damage to Austrian interests elsewhere. Beneath all the turns of attitude, stemming from circumstance and also from character, he was genuinely anxious to sustain a major effort against France. He saw grave dangers otherwise. But he was certainly not prepared to do all that the British asked unless he could show a worth-while return.

Spencer and Grenville were able to bring London up to date on this situation. They had also to transmit Thugut's demands, one of which came as a surprise. For these included not only the promise of some fortresses beyond the mission's private instructions, and a definite undertaking to provide security for the loan, but also the transfer of the Prussian subsidy to Austria when its period expired. A neat reversal of the earlier British plan for Austria to help provide that sum![6] In any case, it was obviously a proposition that had to be referred home. Thugut's

1. Spencer was in fact informed that the Government was concerned to protect 'the close bonds of Anglo-Dutch friendship' (Grenville to Spencer, no. 1, 19 July 1794; F.O. 7/38).
2. See pp. 293–4 above.
3. See Karl F. Helleiner, *The Imperial Loans* (1965), 3–14, 19–20.
4. See pp. 344, 362 above.
5. Pp. 338–40 above.
6. See pp. 334–5 above.

tone, and the prevailing atmosphere, moreover discouraged the two envoys: they found 'weakness and inefficiency' and 'a total want of vigour', and in Thugut himself, the only capable figure, 'a cold, narrow and contracted view'. Nothing, they were sure, would happen 'till they can hear the money jingle in Count Mercy's courier's portmanteau'. It might well be better to give up and seek auxiliary troops elsewhere.[1]

This was depressing. The only point indeed that had been met was the demand for the removal of Coburg and one of his subordinates. But here too disagreement followed. The Austrians had not been pleased to receive British advice on a replacement,[2] though their temporary appointment, General Clerfayt, was at first agreeable to both parties. But they were soon confronted by something much more obnoxious: nothing less in fact than the prospect a British commander-in-chief. This proposal formed part of Pitt's and Dundas's continuing efforts to dispose of York: still anxious to see Cornwallis in charge, with the Duke as a subordinate, they now suggested that he be sent to command Clerfayt as well. It was an attempt to kill two birds: it might also be said to have marked the climax of involvement in a campaign which initially had seemed a temporary, limited commitment. The idea, however, did not fare well. George III was resentful, though he did not immediately refuse – Dundas sensed his strong suspicion, and Cornwallis, himself reluctant and embarrassed, presumed that he had been 'completely ruined . . . at St. James's.' York, informed orally on a special visit by the new Secretary at War William Windham, agreed to be superseded but insisted on then returning home. These difficulties, which Pitt did not underrate, could doubtless be overcome. But the scheme in any case was killed, as an Allied arrangement, in Vienna. Though British Ministers complained, perhaps with reason, that Starhemberg had been in favour, Thugut at once threw it out of court.[3] It was indeed an unpromising idea to put to a partner with larger forces. And it had one particularly unfortunate, and lasting, effect.

For the proposal was linked as a condition with others that could in themselves have been welcome: with an assurance to seek a Parliamentary guarantee for the loan,[4] and – equally interesting – an acceptance of Thugut's request on the Prussian subsidy. In return for the latter, the Austrians must supply the troops associated with it, and use their weight to secure money for Prussia from the Empire. These

1. Duffy, loc. cit., 114–19. The quotations are from Thomas Grenville to Lord Grenville, 15 August, 1 September 1794 (*H.M.C., Dropmore*, II, 618–19, 628).
2. Pp. 343, 362 above.
3. The affair may be followed in *Correspondence of Cornwallis*, II, 261–73; *L.C.G. III*, II, 233–42; *Stanhope*, II, Appendix, xxi; Holland Rose, *Pitt and Napoleon*, 227–9; Buckingham, II, 274–5, 295; Pitt's and Windham's letters in B.L. Add. Ms 37844, and Dundas's and Windham's in Add. Ms 37874 (and see also Dundas to Pitt, nd but endorsed 'later 1794', in P.R.O. 30/8/157); *Quellen*, IV, 412–14, 425; Duffy, loc. cit., 124–5. For the earlier attempt to reduce York's role, see pp. 330–1 above.
4. Which would be over and above the Ministry's.

terms, a distinct advance, were meant to stiffen resolution at a time of serious but not, it was hoped, uncheckable retreat.[1] But the naming of Cornwallis would not be forgotten; nor for that matter would the earlier condition – to stand in defence of Maastricht – for the cash advances.[2] Thugut had received an impression of what financial dependence could mean. He dropped all idea of a future subsidy (granted directly by Government) and – a decision of consequence – opted for market loans. Declaring himself satisfied with the proposed guarantee for 1794, he demanded its repetition for the sum of £3 million in 1795. At the same time he rejected London's immediate operational plans as wholly impracticable in the light of current events.[3]

In this last he was right, given a growing reluctance among the Austrians to fight hard for Flanders. When the latest British message was sent, two fortresses, Valenciennes and Condé, were still unsubdued. Within a few days both had tamely surrendered, while the retreat continued apace. To British Ministers, fed continuously with complaints from their commanders, this was intolerable, and by mid-September the wave of disillusionment had gathered strength. On the 9th Pitt told the King that circumstances were changing fast; on the 14th, while the earlier proposals were still under debate in Vienna, the disconsolate Spencer and his colleague were informed of another change of direction.[4] If the Austrians had already accepted Cornwallis and the terms of support, the arrangements must stand. But if not we withdrew his name and the offer of a subsidy, and in return for covering the loan of 1794 would require only a force of 80–100,000 Austrians in the Low Countries, without stipulating strategic plans. A new Convention might still be signed – now with less latitude over the barrier; but only on the basis that Austria would honour her obligations to press the war against France. Grenville greatly doubted if such an approach would succeed; but one way or another he wanted no further delay.

His forecast proved correct. Thugut exploded, the more angrily because Grenville also called for an account of the recent surrenders.[5] Couched in the loftiest Grenvillian language – which was adding its

---

1. Grenville to Spencer and T. Grenville, no. 5, 29 August 1794 (F.O. 7/38). The package also contained a more extended but still qualified and imprecise guarantee of a barrier. For the Prussian troops see pp. 337, 342 above.

2. P. 363 above. Pitt indeed told York that Government had 'positively require[d]' the Austrians to defend Maastricht (? to York, Downing Street, 25 September 1794; P.R.O., W.O. 6/11).

3. Spencer to Grenville, no. 8, 22 September 1794 (F.O. 7/38). And see same to same, 15 September (loc. cit.), and Thomas Grenville's letters in *H.M.C., Dropmore*, II, 630–2, 635.

4. Pitt to George III (*L.C.G. III*, II, no. 1120); Grenville to Spencer and T. Grenville, no. 7 (F.O. 7/38). See also *H.M.C., Dropmore*, II, 629 and, for some Cabinet consultation, Grenville to Fitzwilliam, 13 September 1794 (Wentworth Woodhouse Muniments F31/23, Sheffield). Portland seems to have agreed (to Grenville, Private, 14 September 1794; B.L. Add. Ms 58934).

5. In his no. 8 of 14 September (F.O. 7/38).

personal flavour to what had long been looked on as a condescending national style[1] – the messages evoked 'much soreness', though not a decisive break. 'Les procédés de l'Angleterre sont révoltants', Thugut commented privately. But he was not quite prepared to burn his boats; there was next year's loan to think of, and the wider advantages of the disagreeable connexion. The demand for the second £3 million stood; an inquiry on the fortresses was already under way; and on this indeterminate note the British envoys took their leave. They set out from Vienna on 7 October. The prospect of an alliance appeared to be no closer than before they arrived.[2]

Indeed if anything it was more distant. On 26 September the British cancelled payment of the last instalment of their cash advance. Since no stand was being made on the Meuse, the conditions had not been met.[3] But the action clearly reflected wider doubts of the Austrian role.

It was not the only one of its kind. For only four days later Pitt summoned the Prussian Minister in London to tell him that the October instalment of the subsidy would 'probably be suspended'.[4] The manner of the telling – like so much of the business throughout – appears to have been clumsily handled. Pitt may have held the interview without Grenville; he may indeed have acted on his own; at any rate he allowed a statement, meant presumably as a threat, to be taken as an accomplished fact by an envoy who had long been ill-disposed. Jacobi reported in that sense to Berlin, and the last flicker of hope disappeared of any Prussian movement to the north in defence of Holland. The Foreign Secretary, whatever his own view of Prussia, tried to soften the blow, and Malmesbury also did what he could. But the remittance was stopped – care being taken this time to bring past payments up to date.[5]

Pitt's heavy-handedness, if excessive, can scarcely have made a difference to the immediate issue. Although Malmesbury saw some belated signs of tractability, he too was sure that nothing effective would

1. This last was an old complaint in Europe, dating back to the fifties at least.
2. See Duffy, loc. cit., 132–4.
3. Pp. 363, 365n2 above.
4. Grenville to Malmesbury, 30 September 1794 (F.O. 64/35). The date of the meeting is also established in *H.M.C., Dropmore*, III, 536.
5. See *L.C.G. III*, II, no. 1131, and cf. pp. 340, 342 above. Grenville wrote an undated angry letter to Pitt which Holland Rose, who gives an extract in *Pitt and Napoleon*, 260, ascribes to 12 October, and which could be taken to imply that the Foreign Secretary had been excluded from, or overuled by, the interview and that Pitt had been supported by Dundas, who might himself have been present. The full contents however, which can be read in P.R.O. 38/8/140, could apply equally well to a quite different occasion. Malmesbury uses words – very briefly (*Diaries and Correspondence*, III, 141) – which again might or might not mean that Pitt saw the Prussian Minister on his own. Whatever happened, Grenville did seem concerned to soften the blow in his no. 3, of 12 October 1794, to Arthur Paget [in Berlin], (F.O. 64/30).

be done.[1] He had assumed indeed for some weeks that his mission would shortly be ended;[2] and his deepening depression had been fully shared in London. Whatever their differences over tactics, all the Ministers were fed up; over £1 million had been sent, and nothing gained. For some two months they had been debating how far they dared go, and with a real crisis approaching in Holland shock treatment perhaps had its attractions.[3] Whether, given a less abrupt approach, the Prussians' response might have been less drastic, it is hard to say. As it was, Jacobi soon had the pleasure of announcing that their army was withdrawing entirely from the Rhine. The news was followed by rumours of talks with the French for a peace treaty. The British subsidy was cancelled and Malmesbury told to leave. Nevertheless, the lines were kept open: if Grenville gave Jacobi a bad half-hour, he studiously refrained from threats to Berlin.[4] The dangerous weeks ahead must be faced, as expected, without Prussian aid; the larger strategic picture would have to be reviewed. But that did not necessarily mean accepting a loss to the Coalition. So long as Prussia remained at war with France, relations should be maintained.

It was much the same with Austria. In the anger of September, Pitt saw an end to joint operations, and Grenville even to any 'idea of . . . concert between the two Courts'.[5] No serious talks with Vienna in fact took place in the next two months, although they were provided for when the Spencer mission left. There was indeed no resident British Minister until mid-December, though this was due more to personal problems than to those of policy.[6] But again links were maintained. Advances of cash were resumed in October when the Austrians seemed willing to help defend Holland, and discussions continued, if rather gloomily, on the question of a second loan. While the British knew that they could not look to a major effort in the short term, and were indeed wondering if and how they should seek hired forces elsewhere, the Austrians at least were in the field and might still represent the best hope of eventually recovering the Low Countries and of maintaining pressure on France. For the Prussians were now an unknown quantity; and as for the Dutch, their familiar deep-seated divisions were producing a general paralysis and a rising fear of involvement as the Allies fell back. York was

1. To Grenville, nos. 61, 62, 26 September, 6 October 1794 (F.O. 64/35).

2. Same to same, 27 August 1794 (*H.M.C., Dropmore*, II, 625–6).

3. See Sherwig, op. cit., 49, for the recent past; Grenville to St Helens [in The Hague], no. 71, 30 September 1794 (F.O. 37/55) for the argument now. Cf. 339 above.

4. Grenville's Minute of meeting with Jacobi, 23 October 1794 (F.O. 97/324); Grenville to Paget, no. 4, 24 October 1794 (F.O. 64/30); same to Malmesbury, no. 31, sd (F.O. 64/35).

5. Pitt to Chatham, 24 September 1794 (P.R.O. 30/8/101); Grenville to Spencer and T. Grenville, no. 10, 25 September 1794 (F.O. 7/38).

6. In the end Morton Eden returned to the post, which he had left in May (see p. 343, n4 above), after unsuccessful searches for a replacement.

finding it impossible to draw them properly into his plans, and 'Under this System the Republic cannot be saved'.[1] As they looked about for ways to shore up the defences, and beyond that to preserve a strategy, Ministers in London could not build on, but neither could they dismiss, the Austrian connexion.

Meanwhile, however, could not something be done elsewhere? As news came out of France itself, it revived some hopes. The fall of Robespierre was hard to interpret, and assessments varied at first. But by October the prospects were engaging serious attention. Two possibilities emerged, neither of them unfamiliar: support for the north-west, and for the émigré army on the Rhine.

Both, naturally enough, were raised by the royalist movement itself, in communications readily received at this time of general disarray. The more pressing came out of Brittany; for late in September there appeared in London, smuggled from the northern coast, one of the most attractive figures of the resistance. Joseph Comte de Puisaye was of higher calibre than his quarrelling fellow Breton chiefs; 'L'esprit le plus éclairé, la meilleure et la plus forte tête'. Personally impressive, in physique and argument, he was also known to be a Constitutionalist, and thus on the royalist wing that most appealed to the British Government.[2] By the same token he was far from popular with the exiled Princes. But his reception in London placed him in a favoured position. For the circumstances were unusually propitious. Windham, the new Secretary at War, had been moving for some months from sympathy towards commitment. His recent visit to Flanders[3] had made an adverse impression, he shared the Portland Whigs' interest in the exiles and resisters – though not, in any marked degree, Burke's attachment to the 'ultras' – and his knowledge now of the state of the Coalition combined with his own predilections to swing him (as it proved, enduringly) to active support. Other, less personal factors helped. Contact with northern France had been improving through the Channel Islands Correspondence, stimulated in part by a naval officer from Jersey, Philippe d'Auvergne, who was now known by the French title of Prince de Bouillon as adopted heir of the late Duke.[4] He was in fact about to be

1. Grenville to St Helens, no. 39, 25 September 1794 (F.O. 37/55). The usual exhortations to Holland had been continuing through recent weeks.
2. See p. 313 above. The assessment of Puisaye, from the Chancellor Pasquier's memoirs, is quoted in Emile Gabory, *L'Angleterre et la Vendée*, I (1930), 126.
3. P. 364 above.
4. For the Correspondence see p. 299 above. Bouillon, 'whose life would seem to belong to fiction rather than history were it not so well documented' (Cobban, in *E.H.R.*, LXXXVII, no. 302, 407), was styled by the lesser title of Prince although the Duke had died in 1792, because he could not yet enter into his inheritance.

placed in charge of a growing organisation undoubtedly more effective than the sketchy arrangements of the year before. The French exiles in England, too, were in a better military posture, following arrangements in the summer for the formation of émigré regiments under statutory terms.[1] And there were some British troops and a commander again available, to serve as a basis for any plan that might be devised. For Moira and his men, who in June had been shipped to Ostend after lying unused for some months, were still destined in theory for 'a particular service' in north-west France; and while the men themselves were held on the continent in the confusion of the retreat, the General had returned, and other regiments, rushed to defend the port of Sluys in August, were recalled in September to take the force's place in part.[2] A camp was found near Southampton Water. There was thus, at least in theory – for most of the troops were raw and Moira himself was largely absent on his private affairs – a nucleus in existence if its use was approved.

This seemed hardly likely when Puisaye reached London. Despite a modest revival of interest, and Pitt's own intermittent hopes,[3] Ministers were uncertain how much there was to exploit. A few supplies and some money had been sent in the past few months, but more ambitious projects were rejected or ignored. British thoughts were concentrated on success in Flanders; and when that gave way to failure there was no strength at first to spare. In the first half of September Pitt could not see how 'any Attempt on the Coast' was possible, for Moira's force was tied up and the season was growing late. Such an operation 'ought to be deferred till next Spring'.[4] But a fortnight later he was changing his mind. The latest accounts of reviving resistance in the north-west left him sceptical – he was warier by now and knew some of the sources too well. But Puisaye made an impression, largely by not claiming too much. He wanted enough support to enable the Royalists in Brittany to survive the winter, after which the British might act on a larger scale. He was not concerned with any other area – which might require a separate effort – and this limitation at once served him well. 'Considerable Facility', Pitt wrote with relief, 'will certainly arise from these Operations being so near home; and I think the Prospect seems at first View a

1. The Act was 24 Geo. III, c. 43.

2. P.R.O., W.O. 1/175, 6/11 *passim*; and see p. 343 above.

3. Eg *H.M.C., Dropmore*, II, 599, 604. And see his remarks to Portland in mid-June, made admittedly to ease the Whigs' path into Government (E.A. Smith, *Whig principles and party politics* . . . (1975), 167).

4. To Windham, 10 September 1794 (B.L. Add. Ms 37844), and see also same to same, 23 September 1794 (loc. cit.), and Dundas to same, 10 and 15 September 1794 (B.L. Add. Ms 37874). A somewhat different impression, however, is given in Dundas to Portland, 16 September 1794 (Portland Ms PwF 3845, University of Nottingham). For earlier months see the theses of Richards and King (Note on Sources to Chs. II, IX above).

tempting One, if We can find the Force'.[1] His ready optimism was excited; he read Puisaye's memorandum attentively, and called for an immediate examination of the plans.

The response was discouraging. Dundas was taken aback. He may have felt some political disgruntlement, following the new arrangements of the summer, and some fear that Pitt's 'yielding nature'[2] was under pressure from the Whigs. But he was a fair man, and accustomed to handling connexions as they came, and his answer was essentially to the merits of the case. Puisaye was asking for 5 or 6,000 British troops (a number that later rose to 10,000) for 'an adventure' which 'should be very distinctly explained and understood'. The military implications would be hard to weigh, given 'the desultory information' that, apart from Puisaye himself, was all we had received so far.[3] Cornwallis was likewise sceptical.[4] Pitt persisted nevertheless; the camp at Southampton was sent supplies, and papers passed to and fro in London. Puisaye remained through October and, impatiently, November. But early in December, Moira finally extinguished the plan. His British troops, he stressed, were mostly inexperienced; the Bretons were not properly embodied; he was required to make a landing in winter and then strike rapidly into the province without the artillery needed to take a major town. And if he succeeded, what then? Would ports become available for supplies and, no doubt, demands for reinforcements? For 'Retreat is impracticable', and the enemy would himself reinforce against a resistance movement hitherto held to be inferior to that of the Vendée. Puisaye seemed a 'clear and sensible' man; but not one used to large-scale operations, and of course he had an interest to farther amidst the guerrillas' intrigues.[5] It was a decisive rejoinder. The project was

1. To Chatham, 24 September 1794 (P.R.O. 30/8/101). Two days before, when he had not met Puisaye, he was still dubious about the kind of plans which others were presenting for the west coast as well (same to same, 22 September 1794, loc. cit.; notes in Pitt's hand, nd but summarising proposals from May to July and a subsequent 'Verbal Project', P.R.O., W.O. 1/389). But he was beginning to busy himself with detail at about the same time (see P.H. Crew, at the Ordnance Office, to Pitt, 23 September 1794; P.R.O. 30/8/127). By the 27th he had ordered arms 'for a Secret Service' (list of issues (loc. cit.).

2. See I, 322; an expression used by Dundas, if in a wider context, at about this time. His role in the arrangements is discussed on pp. 412–14 below.

3. To Pitt, 24 September 1794 (P.R.O. 30/8/157).

4. To Windham, 30 ? October 1794 (B.L. Add. Ms 37874). And see also his letter to Pitt of 30 October in P.R.O. 30/8/242.

5. Moira to Dundas, 5 December 1794; forwarded to Pitt (P.R.O. 30/8/160). For the General's earlier reaction to operations embracing the Vendée see ibid, and Cornwallis to Dundas, 14 September 1794 (*Correspondence of Cornwallis*, II, 267); for the camp at Southampton, P.R.O. 1/176; for Dundas's continued caution and Pitt's persistence, Dundas to Pitt, 13 October 1794 (Cambridge University Library Ms 6958(8)), Pitt to George III, 23 November 1794 (*L.C.G. III*, II, no. 1161); for Puisaye, vols. III–IV of his *Mémoires* (1804, 1806), B.L. Add. Mss 7976, 7979–80, 7982, *H.M.C., Dropmore*, III, 536–41, and P.R.O., F.O. 95/604–5.

dropped, and operational plans were put back in storage for the time being.

In his own initial reply, Dundas had touched on questions other than the military. For Puisaye wanted three things: first, men, supplies and money from England; secondly, recognition of the movement and a declaration from the Princes: and thirdly, a supply of *assignats* – paper money on the Republican model – printed in England to help finance the resistance. These last were forthcoming: issued, as the Breton Council of War had decreed, on the security of a restored monarchy, as well possibly as forgeries of Republican paper.[1] The latter practice – if it occurred here – was not new: such notes had been supplied to York for use in French Flanders – a device more typical of our own days than of warfare in the eighteenth century. The issue on a future régime had some diplomatic significance, for it recognised the allegiance of the Breton resistance to the exiled monarchy whose blessing of the movement was in turn being sought. The production of the notes under British auspices was thus one expression of a development towards a more explicit connexion of Government with the Princes themselves.

This took place in two other distinct ways. In August d'Artois was told, in answer to a request, that he could come to England for consultations on the émigré force.[2] As the pace quickened in September he went for a start to York's headquarters, after which however he remained on the continent until well into 1795. Ministers in point of fact were not displeased by his absence once the immediate plans were shelved, and the Prince for his part was not anxious to depend too much on the 'moderate' Puisaye. Nevertheless, given a real possibility of reviving Royalist pressure, 'the re-establishment of some Monarchical Government' in France was again a weapon;[3] and in that case, whatever the problems and the need for caution, d'Artois could not be left entirely in the cold. At the same time he was not the only Royalist card that might be played. Puisaye had scarcely landed when a message arrived from another quarter. The main émigré army, which had long been commanded by the Prince de Condé in Germany, was languishing on the Rhine, dependent on and virtually unemployed by the Austrians. The Prince had apparently tried in the spring to get in touch with Pitt. He certainly did so in September, with a plea for money. It was well received. Pitt toyed with the prospect of tempting the force into British service, where it might be directed 'much more usefully' than by the Austrian command. George III agreed: Condé was 'certainly the best man we could employ at the head of the royalists' – much better, it was

1. See Holland Rose, II, 261.
2. Cf. p. 29 above.
3. Pitt in the Commons, 26 January 1795 (*The Senator*, XI (nd), 337), which seems preferable to the wording in *P.R.*, XL, 324. And, Pitt maintained as before, in private as in public, no more than a weapon, the best available at this time 'to maintain *Security*' in Europe for the future (Canning's journal, 28 January 1795; Canning Ms 29 dii, Leeds).

inferred, than d'Artois himself.[1] These thoughts applied to the north-west. But encouragement in any event seemed worth-while, and an advance of £15,000 was agreed. A reliable émigré was also sent, to report on the state of the army. He found it neglected and despondent, and thus well disposed to British support. The idea indeed was becoming attractive. For over the following months there was quickening interest in a fresh scenario, for possible action in eastern France.

This itself was stimulated, if abortively, at the same interesting point, when Puisaye was seeing Pitt and Condé's appeal had just been received. Early in October a remarkable message reached London which increased the renewed attention being paid to French affairs. It came out of Switzerland. The Constitutionalists there, now reinforced by Mounier,[2] had been busy since Thermidor; their contacts were becoming more hopeful, and speculation was rife. They now sent a set of proposals purporting to come from moderates in Paris, including no less a figure than Tallien, who was emerging as a leader in the new Administration. It was a call for direct negotiation with the British Government on the Allies' behalf, to be based on a return to the Constitution of '1789'[3] with a restored monarchy, the repeal of seizures and proscriptions on the one side and an amnesty on the other, and no cession of pre-war French territory. A wide range of subjects was covered, from arrangements for a general armistice, including the Sardinian and Spanish fronts, to the treatment of public worship and property and the *assignats*. Such scope suggested authority, Mounier and his circle were respected, the moment was propitious for a ready hearing, and Ministers were at once aroused.

Their interest indeed was such that an agent was despatched in the course of the month, for talks to be reported direct and kept out of the Foreign Office files.[4] The choice proved to be a good one, both from personality and from background, and a man had in fact been found who, despite its final failure, was probably the best available to conduct liaison with resistance in France. William Wickham was to become the principal director of what would now be called subversive policy over the period – the next three years – of its most active life. Some two years younger than Grenville and Pitt, he was a friend of the former's since Oxford days, and like the latter a member of Lincoln's Inn. He had already been employed on contacts with the Vendée in 1793, and was

1. Pitt to George III, 18 September 1794 (*L.C.G. III*, II, no. 1123); George III to Pitt, 19 September 1794 (Holland Rose, *Pitt and Napoleon*, 229).

2. See p. 313 above. Exactly how the message first reached London it is hard to say: probably the earliest intimation came from the British Minister in Berne, but private sources too seem to have had wind of the plan, and to have contacted Pitt (eg Malouet in his *Mémoires*, I, and Sir John Macpherson in P.R.O. 30/8/154).

3. See p. 309, n2 above.

4. Communication with Grenville was to be through the Lord Chancellor, Loughborough.

now Superintendent of the Alien Office attached to the Home Office. Moreover he knew Switzerland – or at least Geneva – quite well, having had the not uncommon experience of studying civil law there,[1] and the less common one of marrying the daughter of a Swiss professor. Finally, he was thought to be bright, and as George III commented, a 'very wary' man was needed, which the resident Minister in Berne was not.[2] His instructions were framed accordingly: he was taken fully into Government's confidence, while the Minister himself – told of Wickham's purpose – was allowed to take local leave.[3]

The proposals proved delusive. Wickham concluded in November that the contacts with Paris had been tenuous and no proper talks had taken place. He discounted the immediate prospect. But he did not discount the future, and, appointed chargé d'affaires, was told to gather information and promised funds to that end. Emphasis was laid on 'the inland and southern Provinces',[4] for the last of which Switzerland was well placed. And it was increasingly in that direction that thoughts turned in the following months, when the fortunes of war brought the upper Rhine into greater prominence and Wickham's network, well supplied with money, had increasing hopes of south-east France. As the threads were drawn together Condé seemed to merit serious attention; and he was soon to receive it, in a period when efforts were also applied to the north-west. For indeed by then both were facets of a developing British strategy in which French action, by resisters and émigrés, held an important place.

This sudden interest, arising in the last quarter of 1794, thus gains significance from events in 1795. At the time, however, it was intensified by hopes of an antidote to potential disaster in the Low Countries.

For over those same three months operations there went from bad to worse. Early in September the French had entered Holland, taking Sluys in the north-west and Eindhoven in the south. In the course of the next three weeks York was driven beyond the Maas, where he tried to form a line from west of Grave through Gennep to Venloo as a point of junction with the Austrians, themselves fallen back beyond the Roer. Only Maastricht survived to the west, and that was left to its fate as Clerfayt late in September continued towards the Rhine. On 6 October the French were in Cologne, while the Austrians took up positions on the east bank of the river from Duisburg to Bonn. Meanwhile York and the Dutch were in trouble. Bois-le-Duc fell on 10 October, and the enemy

1. Cf. I, 69.

2. 'Lord Robert Fitzgerald is certainly not an able nor quick-sighted man' (to Grenville, 6 October 1794; *H.M.C., Dropmore*, II, 638).

3. P.R.O., F.O. 74/4, October 1794 *passim*.

4. Grenville to Wickham, 9 December 1794 (*The Correspondence of . . . William Wickham from the Year 1794*, ed. by His Grandson . . ., I (1870), 17).

was soon pushing to the north-east. He was also advancing north from Venloo, threatening the flank; and the Duke accordingly decided to pull back beyond the Waal. This in itself might be tricky, for the Dutch had failed to strengthen Nijmegen, a pivotal point to cover the river crossings. It was abandoned early in November. Something of a pause then ensued, for the French were apparently tiring, and there seemed some prospect of forming a defensive river line with the Dutch on the right beyond the Waal, the British and Germans in the centre, and an Austrian force on the left from Emmerich to Wesel on the Rhine. But two things were necessary if this was to hold: some purposeful effort on the part of the Dutch, so far conspicuously lacking, and either pressure to draw some French troops away from the front or signs of their taking up winter quarters, giving the Allies time to breathe.

As the British force was bundled back, Pitt and his colleagues tried to take stock. Robbed of the victory which they badly needed, strategically and politically, they were keenly conscious of the 'Embarrassment of a Situation, . . . sufficiently discouraging'. At the same time it was 'one of the Peculiarities of that Situation, that there is no Sense of difficulty which it does not oblige us to encounter'.[1] This was an early reaction. As the threat of 'Calamity'[2] came ever closer, they did what they could with a sense of growing despair. Of one thing they were certain: there should be a change of command. York perhaps could not be displaced in the midst of active operations; but when a lull came in November he was recalled, ostensibly for talks. Pitt and Dundas had in fact decided that their long-running efforts must be brought to a point. At the same time the Duke must clearly not be disgraced. George III would not have allowed it; nor was such an outcome necessary, for an opening offered, if not at once, which had been in their minds for some time. York could become Commander-in-Chief, replacing Amherst who was something of a passenger.[3] Indeed there were also thoughts of making a clean sweep in the military departments, bringing Cornwallis to the Ordnance in place of Richmond, who had not attended Cabinet meetings for some time. But whatever might transpire, York should not return to Holland, and on 23 November Pitt wrote a 'long and dutiful' but 'very honest and firm' letter to the King.[4] It was 'felt as a severe blow': George III did not

1. Pitt to Windham, 21 September 1794 (B.L. Add. Ms 37844). For the 'badly needed' victory, see Dundas to same, 10 September 1794 (B.L. Add. Ms 37874).
2. Pitt to same, 19 September 1794 (B.L. Add. Ms 37844).
3. As indeed had been foretold (Richmond to Pitt, 12 January 1793; Stanhope Ms S5 03/14). Pitt was not in fact much in favour of any replacement, relying on the War Office to do the work. But he was content to accept York if the King wanted it (Dundas to Windham, 30 November 1794; B.L. Add. Ms 37874).
4. Dundas to Cornwallis, 27 November 1794 (*Correspondence of Cornwallis*, II, 274). Pitt's letter is in *L.C.G. III*, II, no. 1161; his much corrected draft of it, in Stanhope Ms S5 010/15.

hide his displeasure; but he acquiesced, to the Cabinet's relief.[1] No single successor could be found for the British and Hanoverians together, or indeed, as was briefly hoped, for the Allies in the Low Countries as a whole. For attempts to induce the Duke of Brunswick to act in this latter capacity, which had been under way for some weeks, were showing little sign of success. He finally refused at the end of November.[2] The British troops were therefore placed under Lieutenant General Harcourt, the senior officer left, and the Hanoverians under their own senior General. It was a pyrrhic victory for Ministers, extracted at a point when they themselves were highly doubtful if there was any real future for the command.

This indeed was shown in the most practical of ways, for Harcourt was soon told that it had been found 'expedient to withdraw a considerable part of the British Infantry from the Continent'. Seven regiments were to come home, the first three at once: the force remaining should suffice to defend the line of the Waal.[3] The intended movement followed an absence of reinforcements in the past three months – a period, one might think, in which they could have been considered. But there had been reasons enough to give pause: the wish to keep a force in being for Brittany, fears of a possible French descent on England, uncertain conditions in the Dutch harbours.[4] These however were now overtaken by a disincentive of a different order: the suspicion, fast becoming a belief, that the Dutch were going to give in.

If that in fact were to happen, the British position was untenable. We had gone to war to save a country which would then have made peace. Nor was it likely to do so reluctantly, or cushion the blow for its ally: the lack of co-operation, the animosity, were too open for that. For Dutch passivity had now turned to resentment and active obstruction of the British movements. The Patriots once more sprang forward, and their opponents hung back. Holland had long been a house divided, and it

1. George III to Pitt, 24 November 1794 and correspondence of 26–27th (Stanhope II, Appendix, xxi–xxii; Holland Rose, *Pitt and Napoleon*, 234); Amherst's diary, vol. IV, 24 November; Dundas to Cornwallis, 27 November (as above).

2. Apart from the unenviable nature of the task, Brunswick was closely connected with Prussia, and the Duke was not prepared to accept without the King of Prussia's approval. The Cabinet had agreed to the suggestion (initially Dundas's) on 10 October, and the Dutch followed suit on the 21st. Hugh Elliot, the British Minister at Dresden, was sent to Brunswick on an errand of persuasion, supported late in November by Malmesbury, who was despatched primarily to arrange the marriage of the Duke's daughter Caroline to the Prince of Wales. But the unfortunate success of the second object was matched by the failure of the first.

For York's command of the Hanoverians, see p. 264 above.

3. Dundas to Harcourt, 13 December 1794 (P.R.O., W.O. 6/11). According to one tale, the decision had been taken at least a fortnight before (Burges to Anne Burges, 2 December 1794; Bland Burges Ms 10, Bodleian Library).

4. For the second see pp. 367–8 above.

was not going to stand; the unfortunate Ministers – the Pensionary and the Greffier – who still stood for the British connexion could find no effective support in a supine Stadholter and a dispirited people.[1] Nor indeed could they extract much help from the British Government. Pleas for more money met with the answer that their own resources were far from exhausted, and when the Greffier Fagel went to London in November on a last attempt, he was received with personal sympathy but very little else. By then it was known that the French had made approaches, and the Dutch were prepared to negotiate: Fagel's visit indeed was largely to warn that they must probably close with terms of some kind. Late in the month it even looked as if they might seek an immediate armistice – a unilateral step which was denounced as 'inexcusable'.[2] Meanwhile the British commanders were angrily complaining that their troops were 'hated and more dreaded than the enemy, even by the well-disposed inhabitants'.[3] The situation could not but grow worse when the brief lull broke. For the French were not going to rest in their quarters: as the ice began to form in December they attacked across the estuaries, driving the Dutch until the British and Germans counter-attacked north of the Waal. The attempt was checked for the moment. But it was clear that it would be renewed, and that hard times were coming in a bleak winter and a hostile land.

When Fagel disclosed his position, he was striving to act within his Alliances, and more loosely the Coalition, with the object of 'a general and honourable peace'. The British replied that they proposed to go on with the war. But the Prussians, the other ally in question, might be in different case; and sure enough, the gloom in London was compounded in December by the news – known already unofficially – that they were talking to the French. The detail remained unknown, for the meetings, in Basle, were shrouded in secrecy. But their attitude when tackled was so unfriendly that the worst was feared. In any case they could not be expected to take the field in the coming year without prior receipt of a subsidy which was withheld until they showed results. The British Government was not disposed to bargain, after the events of the past few months. The fact had therefore to be faced that the Triple Alliance might cease to exist.

It was thus almost predictable that Austria began to be wooed again. In November, Ministers were still annoyed at the outcome of the Spencer mission, though prepared to keep the ball in play to the extent

---

1. Cf. p. 273 above.

2. Grenville to St Helens, nos. 53–58, 11–25 November (P.R.O., F.O. 37/56); and *H.M.C., Dropmore*, II, 646–7 for a Cabinet Minute of the 18th. See also *L.C.G. III*, II, no. 1152.

3. This remark, typical of many, was in a letter to Cornwallis which he showed to others (Cornwallis to Dundas, 20 November 1794, in S.R.O., Melville Castle Ms GD 51/1/608/1; same to Colonel Alexander Ross, 23 November 1794, in *Correspondence of Cornwallis*, II, 273–4).

of supporting a 'limited' loan.[1] But by mid-December they moved significantly, under the pressure of what George III called 'the strange state of public affairs'.[2] They now offered a Parliamentary guarantee for the whole £6 million demanded, in return for 200,000 Austrians in the field next year from Basle to the sea, with 80,000 of them committed to defend Holland if the Dutch were still at war. A force, it was hoped, might also be available to act with the British against north-west France, while operations were mounted with the Sardinians in Piedmont supported by the Mediterranean fleet. Given agreement, a treaty of alliance could follow quickly.[3] This approach was made against the background of Pitt's sustained exertions. He was already active in the capital market, for a second domestic loan within the year; but he now resolved to 'encounter' this further 'difficulty', which raised the amounts to be found £18 to £24 million.[4] He was prepared furthermore to consider linking the two operations, by making the more attractive terms designed for subscribers to an Austrian loan conditional on the same subscribers taking a proportion of the British stock. This proposition stemmed from a financier, Walter Boyd, to whom Pitt was turning increasingly as a thrusting and so far successful operator in the money market. They had been in touch since the early summer, and were constantly so at this time, and the Minister decided to adopt the scheme. Despite the misgivings of the Bank of England he was determined to go ahead, for the Austrian loan in his opinion was 'a public measure of necessity'. Boyd, he knew, was ready to manage it. The rumour was public on 15 December. On the 18th the approach to Vienna was formally made.[5]

Without greater Austrian efforts, the prospects indeed looked unpromising. In the south, as the British stressed, more effective support was essential: the Sardinians were pessimistic, and thought to have made discreet soundings for peace, Tuscany might have done likewise

---

1. Grenville to Morton Eden, no. 1, 26 November 1794 (F.O. 7/39): '. . . a loan, to some limited amount, . . . that . . . should not be a drain upon the capital of this country . . . it being always understood that the exertion of Austria must be proportional to any such assistance, and . . . unquestionable security . . . given on that head'.

2. To Grenville, 1 December 1794 (*H.M.C., Dropmore*, II, 648).

3. Grenville to Eden, no. 5, 18 December 1794 (F.O. 7/39).

4. Cf. pp. 364–5 above. Helleiner, op. cit., 26. Funding operations are discussed in Ch. XIII, section III below.

5. Helleiner, op. cit., 26–32; Sir John Clapham, *The Bank of England . . .*, I (1944), 193; Boyd's letters to Pitt, 1794 *passim*, in P.R.O. 30/8/115 (and see also P.R.O. 30/8/169). Boyd's bank – Boyd, Benfield & Co. – was a newcomer to the City, Boyd himself having been a successful banker in Paris until March 1793, while Paul Benfield had returned to England finally in 1790 after a highly profitable and notorious Indian career. Some of the latter's gains went, as at an earlier stage, into Parliamentary elections, including his own. As an old-fashioned corrupt nabob, a boroughmonger and venal MP, he might indeed be said to have stood for everything of which Pitt was supposed to disapprove.

and was certainly unco-operative, and even Naples was preparing for a possible collapse.[1] Stronger action in Piedmont might also pay a dividend in Spain; for in November the Spaniards urged the Ministry to use its influence with Austria so that they could plan an advance on the Catalonian front with greater prospect of success, following a transfer of French forces, as it was hoped, to the Alps and Savoy. In Germany, the effort was needed to offset Prussia's attitude: the Duke of Brunswick would not take command, Baden withdrew its troops from British service, the British Minister in Bonn was told to move away from the Rhine.[2] In the Imperial Diet there was a proposal for peace. And beyond these fringes the neutrals were showing how the wind blew. In the south, Venice and Turkey were increasingly friendly to France. In the Baltic, the Swedes and the Danes still threatened an Armed Neutrality, continued to trade with France as they could, and maintained a joint naval squadron. The British envoys were finding life difficult, in Copenhagen as well as in Stockholm; nor was Russian influence as prominent as it had been,[3] for the Polish troubles were not over and without some inducements from England the Baltic would take second place.[4] There was little cheer to be had throughout Europe. The one relief lay farther afield, in an adjustment of the old problems with the United States which had been reaching new heights in wartime conditions. Against a background of American resentment that even threatened a rupture, skilled diplomacy here produced a treaty – Jay's Treaty – which, if it could not avert trouble for the future, went far towards marking the end of the aftermath to an earlier war. Nevertheless it could be attacked in both countries as conceding too much, and Pitt and Grenville knew that they had to tread a narrow path.[5] They were glad to emerge as they did, avoiding an added conflict without undue loss to the maritime system as the Coalition showed signs of collapse.

A gloomy scene, then, within the Alliances. And there were causes for disquiet within the British effort itself. The state of the army in Holland was fast becoming chaotic. The supply of transport and medical arrangements and clothing – though not of food – had broken down; the regiments were filled with untrained recruits, the officers were undisciplined. Complaints had been flooding in since the summer, and there was now widespread alarm. 'The evil ... to discipline ... increases every day', one General complained in August; another warned in November that 'order, discipline and confidence' must be

1. Francis Jackson to Grenville, no. 56, 5 November 1794 (F.O. 72/35).
2. For Brunswick and Baden see pp. 375, 281 above.
3. Pp. 276–7 above.
4. F.O. 65/28 *passim*; 'Conduct of Russia affecting Neutrals since 1793', anon, nd, in Pitt's papers (P.R.O. 30/8/196).
5. Fuller discussion of this important aspect of wartime trade follows in Ch. XIII, section II below. For the problems inherited from the eighties see I, Chs. XII, XIII.

restored if there was to be a further campaign. 'Despised by our enemies, without discipline, confidence, or exertions among ourselves, . . . every disgrace and misfortune is to be expected': so Cornwallis was told.[1] When Wellington remarked later that he had 'long been of opinion that a British army could bear neither success nor failure',[2] he was drawing in part on his vivid memory of the winter of 1794–5.

The discontent and unease were reflected in the effort to reshuffle the higher administration.[3] But this was not confined to the army: it embraced the navy as well. For all was not well at the Admiralty. The reforming Middleton, recalled to service in May, may have been a stern witness; but the scene he depicted was real enough.[4] There was a slackness within the Department, and a lack of cohesion in its dealings with others. The blow fell – on the whole justifiably – on the First Lord himself. For while he was not untalented, Chatham had long lost the public's confidence, and, it would seem, weight in the Cabinet.[5] He was expendable, and his brother did not try to argue the fact. Barely a fortnight after moving York, Pitt obtained an exchange between Chatham and Spencer, the former taking the latter's post of Lord Privy Seal. 'Some new arrangement', he told the King, 'is become *indispensably necessary*', as 'the present situation of affairs . . . made him look with additional anxiety to all the Departments'.[6] The Ministry indeed was not functioning smoothly, and the fact was causing speculation. There was an urgent need to show that something was being done.

Not the least of the reasons lay in the approaching Session. For to add to Pitt's problems, Parliament must meet on 30 December. The prorogation had been extended at short notice from the original date in November, possibly at the King's urging,[7] and the course of the war had

---

1. Major General Craig to Nepean, 5 August 1794 (Fortescue, op. cit. 298); Major General Abercromby to Dundas, 27 November 1794 (N.L.S. Ms 3835); *Correspondence of Cornwallis*, II, 274.

2. This characteristic observation was made in the Peninsula in 1809. And see p. 330 above.

3. P. 374 above.

4. This is followed on pp. 497–9 below. He had resigned from the Navy Board in 1790 (I, 317).

5. See pp. 293, 318 above; and I think the impression is conveyed in Pitt's letter to him of 12 July [1794], copy in P.R.O. 30/8/10, and in Dundas's letters of 13 and 14 September in P.R.O. 30/8/368.

Newspaper comment had been unfavourable to Chatham since the summer of 1793 at least, and it reflected some informed opinion at that time. According to Gilbert Elliot, the First Lord was indolent, 'said to get drunk every evening', and to command little confidence within the navy (journal, 11 September 1793; N.L.S., Minto Ms 11159). See also *The Diary of Joseph Farington*, ed. Kenneth Garlick and Angus Macintyre, I (1978), 201 (though also 218), 278.

6. 8 December 1794 (*L.C.G. III*, II, no. 1170).

7. See George III to Grenville, 10 November 1794 (*H.M.C., Dropmore*, II, 647). A change of date in the summons was not in itself uncommon, but the lateness of the notice on this occasion attracted comment.

not improved since. Obviously there might be trouble, for the public was in an unsettled mood:

> a mixture of rage at the triumph of the Jacobins, of mortification at our own disgraces, of extreme indignation and horror at the . . . turpitude of some of the allied powers, of grief and alarm at the ruin which is coming upon Holland and upon the whole European continent; and all this with a score of difficulties inextricable, and a suspension between two doubts – . . . whether we can prosecute the war, and . . . whether it is possible to make any step towards peace.[1]

This was a diplomat's perspective; but it was reflected elsewhere, in newspapers, in private correspondence, in the armed forces themselves.[2] Would it now be shown at Westminster? The Foxites would obviously do their worst. But shortly before the meeting a more disturbing threat arose. Wilberforce had been moving, in personal misery, towards the painful conviction that he must call for exploratory talks for an honourable peace. He would not side fully with Opposition by denouncing the causes of the war itself; but he would move his own amendment to the Address. It was hard to tell what the effect might be. On the one hand Wilberforce was noted, with others of Pitt's early circle, for his '*absurd refinement*': this would not be the first time that he had failed to follow a Ministerial line.[3] But it would be far the most striking instance, and coming from such a source his action could provide a focus for wavering opinion. It might prove politically dangerous: it was certainly a private wound. Pitt was as miserable as Wilberforce himself when the latter rose to speak. He 'seemed pretty seriously hurt', and tradition indeed has it that this was one of the very few nights on which he lost his sleep expressly over public business.[4] It was Wilberforce's amendment that mainly shaped his own remarks in the debate, and that may have prompted some uncharacteristic language – perhaps a private appeal.

> It has pleased inscrutable Providence that this power of France should triumph over every thing that has been opposed to it! but let us not therefore fall without making any efforts to resist it; – let us not sink without measuring its strength.

---

1. Auckland to Lord Henry Spencer, 20 November 1794 (*A.C.*, III, 261). And see his long letter to Pitt of the 28th, and a further one to Spencer on 22 December (loc. cit., 265–76).

2. For an expression of feeling as far distant as the Mediterranean fleet see *Life and Letters of Gilbert Elliot*, II, 278–80.

3. Cf. I, 230.

4. Portland to Fitzwilliam, 7 January 1795 (quoted in John Pollock, *Wilberforce* (1977), 129); R.I. and S. Wilberforce, *Life of William Wilberforce*, II, 71. Cf. I, 131.

This was interjected, as Pitt himself said, with 'emotion' in a fighting speech.[1] But as he looked back on two years of war – on hopes almost always frustrated, offensives that turned to retreats, a last case potentially worse than the first – it was scarcely surprising if he felt momentarily driven to speak as he did.

1. I find the wording here the more striking – going beyond the 'looking difficulties in the face' which had been his habit and pride from the first (cf. I, 279) – precisely because of the characteristically firm and hopeful nature of the rest, and the cheerful face which Pitt wore in company (eg the impressions of Lord Hood to Sir Gilbert Elliot, 8 December 1794, National Maritime Museum, Minto Ms ELL/140; and of Canning, journal, 25–30 December 1794, Canning Ms 29 dii). But one has to consider discrepancies in the Parliamentary reports in trying to decide what was actually said. Unlike my usual practice, I have followed *P.H.* (XXXI, cols. 1036–7, for 30 December 1794) in preference to the less dramatic phraseology of the contemporary *P.R.*, (XL, 46–7) and *The Senator* (XI, 79) because the more vivid tone, in a passage of 'emotion', seems to me to ring true. It was the version adopted in the earliest collection of Pitt's speeches, published the year after his death (ed. W.S. Hathaway, IV (1806), 239), and has been repeated since, from John Gifford's *History of the Political Life of . . . William Pitt* (1809) to Coupland's edition of *The War Speeches* (1915). But I am not sure from what source it came.

The passage certainly seems to have made an impression. The young Duke of Rutland for instance, the son of Pitt's friend, wrote of the first sentence (in whichever version he saw) that it was 'the strongest ever read' (to W.H. Fremantle, 11 January 1795; Fremantle Mss, Buckinghamshire C.R.O.).

Part Four

CHAPTER XI

The Defence of an Order

I

At this same juncture, at the end of 1794, the state of the country gave less immediate cause for Ministerial concern than that of operations. But this was not because all had been calm. On the contrary, the summer had witnessed a profound scare; and if recovery had been swift, and the scare itself added to Pitt's Parliamentary strength, the memory was recent and vigilance was required.

The swings of feeling, and the pressures on Government, largely repeated in 1794 the experience of 1792–3. When England went to war, public attitudes seemed more reassuring than a short time before. Pitt himself may not have fully shared the vivid fears of recent months; but in any case there was now an impression that things had improved. The last quarter of 1792 had been alarming. But it quickly produced a reaction which forced the radical Societies onto the defensive. If the Loyalist Associations in their turn were by no means always representative, they spearheaded pressures already proving effective in the last weeks of peace.[1] This applied at any rate south of the border; and in Scotland too, while the movement for reform mounted a second Convention in April, there was a widespread reaction against the recent spate of violence.[2] But Scotland in any case was far off, to most Ministers other than Dundas. And as Pitt surveyed the other main element in the foundations of a war effort, he rested his view of the economy on the satisfaction of the previous year. It was encouraging, he concluded his first wartime budget, to look back on 'that flourishing state'. For it was that 'prosperous situation' which 'at . . . present . . . supplies us with the exertions, and furnishes us with the means, which our exigencies demand'.[3]

This confidence was soon to face a challenge. For, in a sense surprisingly, the first domestic upset of the war was financial, reaching a climax in the next few weeks. Pitt may in fact have been conscious of a threat even as he spoke,[4] and certainly the signs were gathering by then.

1. See pp. 229–33 above.
2. Pp. 217–19 above.
3. 11 March 1793 (*P.R.*, XXXV, 57). See I, 273–5 for February 1792.
4. There is a hint of this in Bishop Tomline's (Pretyman's) unpublished part of his *Life* of Pitt (see I, xi); B.L. Add. Ms 45107(A), ch. 16, 23.

Towards the end of October 1792 three per cent Consols had stood at an average of $90\frac{1}{2}$. A month later the figure was $84\frac{1}{2}$, towards the end of December $75\frac{1}{2}$, by the end of February $71\frac{1}{2}$. Such a fall was unprecedented in the past decade.[1] Equally disconcerting, the number of bankruptcies doubled from 1792 to 1793, to a figure not reached again for another seventeen years.[2] These were 'dreadful failures'. They lay as an 'alarming evil' at the centre of a 'general distress' contrasting sharply with the recent prosperity.[3]

In point of fact, however, the former sprang from the latter. For conditions of boom in the past few years had led to a '*hazardous Expansion of . . . Capital*' in overseas trade which then came under pressure from continental developments combined with a bad harvest at home.[4] There had undoubtedly been widespread 'Speculation' in European markets by British manufacturers selling direct to customers who commanded insufficient credit. This trend, described by one well-informed observer as significant in scale,[5] was now exposed by the tide of events. As the Allied armies retreated in the autumn, trade fell off and cash was husbanded in Europe, not least by sales of British funds which led to a fall in sterling further induced by large British purchases of foreign grain. It was thus on a downturn in exports, a declining exchange rate and agricultural constriction that there began to loom in November the possibility of an Anglo-French war. The consequences followed. Domestic credits were threatened, coin began to be hoarded, many manufacturers and merchants drew in their horns. The outbreak of hostilities was a final depressant. In March 1793 there was a run on the country banks and a drain of specie from the Bank of England. Some of the former failed, as did not a few of their customers. A period of escalating growth came to an abrupt halt.

The rising momentum of the process demanded Pitt's intervention. In mid-April he was being flooded with 'Deputations from every Class of the mercantile World' and 'forced to attend to their melancholy cases'.[6]

1. See, for these and comparable movements in the funds, *The Gentleman's Magazine*, LXII *Part the Second* (1792), LXIII *Parts the First and Second* (1793). The depression in the textile industry in 1788 (p. 000 above) had had no significant repercussions on the stock market, and a brief fall during the war scare of 1790 was minor by comparison; cf. Ashton, *Economic Fluctuations in England 1700–1800*, 130–3.

2. Sheila Marriner, 'English Bankruptcy Records and Statistics before 1850' (*Ec. H.R., 2nd ser.*, XXXIII, no. 3), 353. Taking a broad view of differing lists none of which may be accurate, the figures were rather more than 600 and just over 1,300 respectively.

3. See *The Annual Register for . . . 1793* (1794), British and Foreign History, ch. III, 73 *et seq.*

4. For the quotation from a former Secretary of the Treasury, Sir Grey Cooper, which was shown to Pitt, see p. 94, n2 above.

5. By Thomas Irving of the Customs (for whom see I, 163, 179, 324); report among Pitt's papers, endorsed 'From Mr. Irving', 10 April 1794 (P.R.O. 30/8/286).

6. William Huskisson [Superintendent of the Alien Office] to William Haley, 15 April 1793 (B.L. Add. Ms 38734).

By the end of the month he had 'devised a Plan'.[1] The Bank of England could advance no more bullion. The Royal and Chartered Banks in Scotland had exhausted their facilities. There was in fact, in marked contrast to the position a year before, a lack of cash and negotiable paper for which there were urgent calls. The money supply should therefore be increased and Government's own credit facilities extended. Pitt met the need by sanctioning an issue of £5 notes from the Bank of England, and advancing a maximum of £5 million in Exchequer bills to merchants depositing goods worth double the sum taken up and returnable on repayment of a loan which was in the usual negotiable form. These expedients required Parliamentary sanction. Pitt accordingly put them to a Commons' committee set up on 25 April and reporting two days later. The issues of notes and bills were approved, six Customs' warehouses named to cover the country, Commissioners appointed to manage the deposits, and the scheme went into effect in May.[2]

It contained a bold and, as Pitt himself acknowledged, unprecedented set of measures. The Bank of England had always been forbidden to issue notes of less than £10 denomination, and a loan to the public of such a nature had never been 'resorted to in this or any other country'.[3] It proved a great success. Some £2,200,000 worth of bills were taken up, and since they bore interest at $3\frac{1}{2}$ per cent but were issued to the borrowers at five, the Commission paid for itself and indeed produced a surplus. Not a single merchant, it was claimed, defaulted.[4] The rate of bankruptcies eased after May. By the end of the summer the crisis was a memory and the Bank beginning to restore its reserves. The collapse had not been due to the war: both the causes and the process were of earlier origin. But the war had given a final dramatic impulse, and the sequel was seen at the time in the same partly irrelevant terms. For as Pitt's measures took effect, two conclusions were widely drawn. The result was taken, rightly, as something of a personal triumph. It also suggested that the peacetime financial saviour could adapt to the problems of war.

The spring and summer months indeed, until near the latter's close, were months of widespread confidence. Military operations were going well with the relief of Holland and the advance in Flanders, the crisis of credit was weathered, radicalism, it seemed, being broadly contained. The tone of Ministers and their supporters was assured, at times buoyant. It was also determined: no concessions were to be made. In May Charles Grey introduced the motion for Parliamentary reform to which he had pledged himself a year before. He did so without marked

1. Pretyman's account, B.L. Add. Ms 45107(A), ch. 16, 23v.
2. *P.R.*, XXXV, 282–372. *H.C.J.*, 48 (1803), 702–7 contains the committee's report.
3. Ashton, op. cit., 133n; B.L. Add. Ms 45107(A), ch. 16, 25.
4. B.L. Add. Ms 45107(A), ch. 16, 26.

enthusiasm.[1] There was indeed a clear anxiety to keep his distance from the popular Societies: a precaution, always a shifting plank in the Friends of the People's platform, which was the more advisable against a background of quite numerous but unimpressive petitions from 'out of doors'. Thirty-six in all had been sent in, the London Corresponding Society's with over five thousand signatures. But two-thirds of them came from Scotland, none from the English counties – that touchstone of strength – and the impression was indeed of a 'ragged fusilade'.[2] The prayers were dismissed, and the motion itself was lost by 282 to 41. Pitt spoke as expected. The proposal was 'capable of producing much mischief, and likely to be attended with no good'.[3] That expressed the feeling behind the vote. Experienced reformers such as Wyvill and Stanhope had known that any move would fail.[4]

Parliamentary reform, as a matter of Parliamentary business, was thus dead for the foreseeable future. This did not mean that the Ministry was given its head against all dangers entirely unopposed. A few weeks before Grey's motion Government brought in a bill on traitorous correspondence with the enemy, making it treasonable for a British subject to supply military stores, provisions or money without licence, to buy property in France (an asset, often seized, whose price would fuel the enemy's efforts), or be admitted from that country without a permit. The object was to clarify in current circumstances the long line of statutes on high treason.[5] The measure would also confirm the stop on certain exports imposed in the last days of peace, and reinforce the recent Aliens Act.[6] It did not pass without much debate and some real misgivings. Introduced on 15 March it was discussed also on the 21st and 22nd, on 4 and 8 and 9 April before it left the Commons and went through the Lords on the 15th and 22nd. The hard core of Foxites was not alone on this occasion. While their procedural objections were steadily defeated amendments of substance were accepted from others, Pitt's wish for speed was disappointed, and he had to accept prolonged consideration.[7] Much eloquence was expended on the powers that must accrue to a Secretary of State for licences and permits; the sanctity of the

1. Speech of 6 May 1793; *P.R.*, XXXV, 376–86. Cf. for his remarks on 30 April 1792, op. cit., XXXII, 449–51, 490–2.

2. John Cannon, *Parliamentary Reform 1640–1832* (1973), 125. See also Goodwin, *The Friends of Liberty*, 279–80, and for the English counties in the eighties, I, 67, 69.

3. Speech of 7 May, *P.R.*, XXXV, 470; op. cit., 507 for the vote.

4. See Cannon, op. cit., 125; O'Gorman, *The Whig Party and the French Revolution*, Appendix 4, for the limited response from the Foxites themselves; I, 68–9 for Wyvill and Stanhope.

5. Pitt stressed the object of clarification, in the light of earlier enactments the sense of which might be disputable for current purposes (speech of 21 March 1793; *P.R.*, XXXV, 111–12).

6. Pp. 225, 238, above.

7. For the debates see *P.R.*, XXXV, 71–210, XXXVI (1793), 163–96. The Act was 33 Geo. III, c. 27.

principles of 1688 could be at stake. Pitt indeed justified the measures by weighing their 'mildness' against the precautions taken by the 'great men' of William's and Anne's French wars,[1] which themselves would not be called oppressive given their context. It was true that

> There often had been mentioned two classes of men, who were supposed to have opposite principles – Whigs and Tories. There often had been those who called themselves Whigs, but who in principles were Tories, and afterwards proved to be such. He knew how often it had happened that Tories had availed themselves of the popularity of the character of Whig, and had therefore assumed the title and language without the principles.

But – when Sheridan at once picked up the point – he for his part 'held not the principles of some persons who had lately called themselves Whigs, but the principles of liberty settled at the Revolution.'[2]

Outside Parliament, the balance of sentiment was expressed in the pressures brought to bear on 'sedition'. Government itself acted most directly by bringing prosecutions, as it had started to do following the Proclamation of May 1792. Most were successful; but some features are of interest. If one takes the eleven English cases contained in the later *Collection of State Trials* for 1793, six resulted in a verdict of guilty without qualification, two of not guilty, one of guilty with a recommendation to mercy, and two of guilty on counts more restricted than those brought by the Crown. This list is by no means complete, either for London or the provinces, in both of which discharges seem to have been rare.[3] The sentences however were not extreme by the standards of the time: imprisonment ranging from six months to two years for each offence plus fines of up to £200 and often securities for subsequent behaviour over a period, or in one case plus securities, the pillory and dismissal from his profession; and in one instance, where imprisonment by a court of law was not in question, dismissal from a University.[4]

There are other circumstances and questions to be taken into this account.[5] With one glaring set of exceptions the punishments themselves

1. In 13 & 14 Will. III, c. 3, and 2 & 3 Anne, c. 20.
2. Debate of 21 March 1793 (*P.R.*, XXXV, 111, 118).
3. Though two more at least, both affecting the idealistic tractseller Thomas Spence, can be added for London. The relevant volume of *A Complete Collection of State Trials . . .*, compiled by T.B. Howell, is XXII (1817). For juries' defiance over the counts see the cases of Daniel Isaac Eaton, op. cit.
4. Op. cit. In two cases the prison sentence meant four years consecutively in total. Dismissal from his profession was possible in the instance of the attorney John Frost as 'an attorney of the Court'. In that of William Frend the case was brought and heard by the University of Cambridge.
In one other instance a convicted defendant was moved to a different prison, on his own plea, to save him from having to live with felons.
5. See pp. 391–3 below.

could be argued not to have exceeded the most recent precedent, imposed on Lord George Gordon for two libels in 1787.[1] After the panic he had caused in 1780 Lord George was perhaps a special case, and sentences of four years (the harshest in England in 1793) were not light. But compared with those meted out for some other crimes,[2] and given the fears of past months, even they could be regarded as not outrageously severe. The exceptions however were exceptions indeed. They came, under a different system of law, in Scotland. The early prosecutions there produced terms of imprisonment broadly analogous to the English.[3] But the trials of Muir and Palmer in August and September roused feelings not confined to radicals. Lord Justice Clerk Braxfield's behaviour on the Bench – an appalling echo of Jeffreys –, his handling of juries selected under Scots law finally by the Court, the sentences of fourteen and seven years' transportation, shocked many on both sides of the border. The Foxites raised the matter no less than five times in Parliament. But they had to rely on technicalities, on which a defence could be mustered sufficient for the Ministry to crush the attacks.[4] The Scottish judges were exceptional, in tone and at this time in punishment.[5] But they left an early sense of savage repression which has been cited ever since.

Elsewhere in 1793 reactions were more complex, and restraints visible. Judges' predilections in England were sometimes clear, and juries sometimes picked. Widespread evidence of this last, however, seems hard to establish; juries could go against the prosecution – and judges' wishes – and they could not be taken for granted.[6] The Courts themselves could occasionally direct cases to be dropped if an indict-

---

1. Imprisonment for three and two years respectively, making a consecutive total of five, with a fine of £500 in the second case and securities for subsequent behaviour. According to Fox, this was the longest sentence for such offences ever given (speech of 25 March 1794; *The Senator*, IX (nd), 734). The first libel was on the administration of the law, the second on the Queen of France.

2. Cf. pp. 127–8 above.

3. See *Collection of State Trials*, XXIII (1817); Henry W. Meikle, *Scotland and the French Revolution* (1922), 112–14.

4. *P.R.*, XXXVII, XXXIX for debates on 4 and 24 February, 10 and 25 March 1794 in the Commons, and 15 April in the Lords. Fox himself seems to have been rather reluctant at first to contemplate Parliamentary discussion, so long as hope remained of influencing Ministers privately (Grenville in particular); but he had clearly come round following that failure (to William Adam, 13 and 17 December 1793, 3 January 1794; B.L. Add. Ms 47569).

Cf. pp. 218, 385 above for reactions to unrest in Scotland.

5. Braxfield himself indeed was unique in his coarse and sustained ferocity. But his colleagues Lords Swinton and earlier Henderland, for example, voiced similar opinions or sentiments (see *State Trials*, XXIII, *passim*).

6. Landsdowne for instance, who opposed the war and its works from the start, remarked after a few months that 'The Tide is evidently turning ... The Crown Lawyers do not find it so easy to influence Jurys' (to Lord Holland, 25 July 1793; B.L. Add. Ms 51682).

ment was wrongly drawn.[1] And certain features of the law indeed tended to make the Crown lawyers cautious. Prosecutions would be for libel or sedition or high treason, and the last carried a capital sentence – and in a form so barbarous if strictly followed that it could sway the verdict the other way. It was a well-known feature of the British system – remarked on by foreigners – that juries were often reluctant to convict for capital crimes.[2] Treason would not necessarily be an exception; and in cases of libel juries had a more extensive voice since Fox's Act of 1792. They were now the judges of matter as well as of fact; a restriction which Pitt, a supporter at the time, may have come to regret.[3] Ministers themselves tended to concentrate on challenges – as they saw it – which would have a popular effect: the story is well known of Pitt's alleged decision not to prosecute William Godwin for his *Inquiry Concerning Political Justice*, published in February 1793, because it cost three guineas.[4] Such factors bore on the occasions on which the Law Officers or the Home Office held their hand; and indeed only a small proportion of the prosecutions came before a higher Court. Most were tried in the Quarter Sessions before magistrates; and here much turned on the state of local feelings and on personalities. For the justices on their Benches reflected, in their degrees of support or disagreement, their impressions of the surrounding sentiment as well as their own views and temperaments. Mostly, it would seem, they were prepared to enforce, and often ready to stimulate, the law. There were also places where they were not, sometimes actively, sometimes passively: Derby, Nottingham, Sheffield (at first), Trowbridge and Bridport at times, are examples. Indifference or cowardice could produce the same effect as deliberate choice. But zealous or idle, in support or (more rarely) recalcitrance, the justices were easier to direct than control.

The Courts' reactions in fact bring one to the wider, and in the end the critical, question. What was the climate which decided the extent and the strength of indirect as well as legal pressures? The latter carried their own penalties other than the sentences: costs (which could be a serious matter), and damage to or loss of occupation. But there was also a whole range of the former that could be brought to bear: from a refusal to give one's custom to a supplier or allow one's premises to be used for meetings, from withholding favours in tenancies or jobs, to the more continuous threat of subjection to informants and the more extreme danger of a mob. It would often be hard to differentiate between an official and a purely spontaneous origin; Government's strictly limited

1. Cf. p. 389, n3 above. Eight cases of the latter kind have been spotted by one authority (Clive Emsley, 'Public Order in England 1790–1801', 325, and see also 154).
2. See Radzinowicz, *A History of English Criminal Law*, I, 719–24; and cf. p. 127 above.
3. See p. 81 above.
4. C. Kegan Paul, *William Godwin, His Friends and Contemporaries*, I (1876), 80; and see p. 167 above. The source was Godwin's daughter Mary Shelley; Pitt was said to have made the remark at a meeting of the Privy Council (see p. 396 below).

resources could shade into influence or approval. The reports from the small number of Home Office agents – a handful employed more or less continuously, others intermittently – were only one element in the flow of information, solicited and unsolicited, credible or dubious. It is hard to tell, too, how far hostile crowds were set on foot, encouraged, or tacitly ignored.[1] To generalise is almost inevitably to distort the kaleidoscope. Perhaps one might say that the advent of war strengthened the impression of Governmental approval of pressures which in fact turned very largely on local conditions, and often could not, and sometimes would not, have been applied by Government direct.

The effects were correspondingly uneven. 1793 saw a rising flow of reformers and radicals to America. It saw a decline for several months in recruitment for the popular Societies, and the disappearance of some of the debating clubs. It was marked by a drop in circulation, and some closures, among radical newspapers. The greater part of the year reversed the radicals' hopes of 1792. The panic of the previous winter did not wholly die away, as was shown by the notorious Bristol bridge riot in September, when ten people were killed and more than thirty wounded by troops sent in by the magistrates to disperse a demonstration which had probably more to do with local rights and resentments than, as was feared, a potential upsurge based on the Rights of Man.[2] There were growing signs of authorities linking familiar kinds of disturbance with political aims; not surprisingly perhaps given the former's customary incidence.[3] There were also cases to the contrary. Government's own record was variable. Its language and some of its actions were stiff; but Ministers moved within the parameters of locality and uncertain information, an area in which they were often less clear than they were apt to sound. Nor were all attempts at amelioration and improvement suddenly lost. The first half of the year witnessed the first statutory recognition of Friendly Societies, in an Act, introduced by the Treasury, for their 'encouragement and relief' which 'at once protected and emancipated' bodies, long known but hitherto unsheltered, that would soon be associated with trade combinations. Pitt himself followed the returns with interest over the first few years.[4] All in all, he and his colleagues had regard to familiar constraints and attitudes as they began to operate powers taken to respond to an unfamiliar threat. They were 'not . . . men committed to a new kind of total war, but they recognised that France was fighting in a different fashion'.[5] For if hostilities had

---

1. Cf. pp. 135–8, 103–4, 132–4 above.

2. Philip D. Jones, 'The Bristol Bridge Riot and Its Antecedents . . .' (*The Journal of British Studies*, XIX, no. 2), 74–92.

3. Cf. Ch. IV, sections I, II above.

4. Brought in by George Rose in April, the bill became law in June; see p. ooo, no above. The quotation is from Halévy's *History of the English People in the Nineteenth Century* (1949 edn.), I, 330. Pitt's papers are in P.R.O. 30/8/309.

5. Clive Emsley, *British Society and the French Wars 1793–1815* (1979), 21.

come about because of a traditional challenge to a strategic interest,[1] the enemy was proclaiming principles 'not levelled against particular nations, but against every country where there was any form of Government established; . . . calculated every where to sow the seeds of rebellion and civil contention.[2] The defences were raised against that prospect in the framework available. And while the initial phase was not of long duration its features should be noted if the later developments are to be properly assessed.

For a change was becoming visible from the autumn and winter. Although many of the Societies continued to suffer from falls in numbers and funds, others picked up, activities revived and some new ones indeed began to develop. In October 1793 the London Corresponding Society held an outdoor meeting in Hackney, and in November the formidable John Thelwall gave his first public lectures, the forerunners of a celebrated series. These events were in aid of a project which had been in the air for some months, was now coming to the fore, and would cast its shadow on the year ahead. As early as April there had been thoughts in London of a national Convention, following the Scottish example and soon reinforced by the failure of Grey's motion for Parliamentary reform. They persisted through the summer, in discussion with the provinces, and in October the LCS and SCI received invitations to a third assembly in Edinburgh.[3] Delegates were chosen and subscriptions raised, though not without some doubts. The provincial Societies were thinly represented. There was a distinct air of caution. But, in part unsure, in part enthusiastic, the English movements were caught up in the Scottish incentive. 'The British Convention' in November and December was a heady affair, and the London delegates – Margarot, Gerrald, Charles Sinclair – in the event played a dominant part. The proceedings were dated from 'the First Year of the . . . Convention', 'divisions' and 'sections' formed on French lines, resolutions passed for annual Parliaments and proclaiming defiance to 'unconstitutional' acts. Speeches became more fiery, phrases more exalted, as the days went by. The result was a crop of arrests and trials, once more under Braxfield, which temporarily broke the Scottish movements, made martyrs for the English, excited fresh recruits for them; and raised the temperature afresh.[4]

This last was not surprising. To active radicals and reformers the repeated repression was an outrage. To others broadly in sympathy with

1. See pp. 257, 269 above.
2. Pitt's speech of 12 February 1793 (*P.R.*, XXXIV, 445–6). He was referring specifically to the decree of 19 November 1792 (p. 206 above).
3. See pp. 217, 385 above.
4. For the trials themselves see *State Trials*, XXIII. Margarot and, a little later, Gerrald were sentenced to transportation for fourteen years.

them, it was worrying and deeply distasteful. To their opponents, to a mass of opinion varying in degree, and specifically to most politicians, the Convention was a shock. The defiance of Parliament – the claim that the assembly more truly represented the people – the mounting extremism, the preparations for the future, above all the use of French terms, frightened and infuriated those who took them at face value and disgusted many who perhaps did not. The next few months underlined the contrast – not yet complete, but deepening after the comparative lull of the previous year. In particular they heightened the Government's suspicions, leading it to act, as it hoped decisively, in May 1794.

For the Societies were now once more on the move. They themselves were conscious of a new spirit, to counter a rising threat. Correspondence again grew closer, numbers again increased, meetings and resolutions, some in public, showed a much firmer tone. The SCI (reviving from sleep) and LCS held general meetings in January, the latter with over 1,000 people present, approving a system of Conventions and the rights of free men to stand together against tyranny. The language, if imprecise, was strong[1] – a growing feature of these occasions – and within the movement itself organisation was tightened. By the end of the month a secret committee of the LCS was set up to plan for an emergency Convention: a decision sparked by the recent landing of Hessians in the Solent area – part of the complicated and increasingly confused programme of troop movements, which was taken, almost inevitably, as a domestic threat.[2] The public and semi-public demonstrations continued. A large meeting in Sheffield at the end of February called for a reform of Parliament even if the efforts ended in Botany Bay. Another, attended by perhaps 6–7,000 in the open air on 7 April, resolved that further petitions to Parliament were useless – an invitation, as the Ministry saw it, to a Convention. A week later the LCS met publicly at Chalk Farm by the foot of Primrose Hill, to voice its feelings on the Scottish trials and the threats to liberty in England and Ireland. An 'immense multitude' turned up, many of them serious and attentive spectators, and the proceedings ended, calmly but defiantly, with the resolution that any further attempts to 'violate those yet remaining laws' should be 'considered as dissolving entirely the social compact between the English Nation and their Governors'. Within another three weeks, on 2 May, the SCI held its annual anniversary dinner, where an enlarged company, first regaled by the *Ça Ira* and *Marseillaise*, heard some highly provocative, and doubtless bibulous, speeches and toasts. None of these occasions lost in the telling from the Ministry's informants – 'Bow Street runners, . . . Government spies and reporters', as Francis

1. And of course subject later to conflicting interpretations. For a balanced assessment see Goodwin, op. cit., 306–10. Cf. pp. 109, 113, 115 above for the SCI in 1793.

2. See p. 324 above. The landings were challenged by the Foxites over the next two months, as having been effected without the necessary Parliamentary consent for the admittance of foreign troops.

Place recalled of the Chalk Farm meeting. They became the more disturbing as they drew larger audiences and, so it seemed, came thick and fast.[1]

There were other disquieting signs, not all of them so public. In printed letters circulated widely to the provinces in April, the SCI virtually dropped the old nostrum of Parliamentary reform for the alternative – or opposite – of an urgent Convention. The direction of much – not all – of the talk inside the LCS seemed dangerous, as relayed by the spies who had penetrated its ranks. The volume of reports from all over the country was swelling once more, much as it had done towards the end of 1792.[2] And the Foreign and Home Offices were following the activities of an agent from Paris, the Irishman William Jackson, sent to assess the amount of support and sympathy an invasion might command. He arrived late in February, going on to Dublin at the end of March after receiving – discouraging – answers supplied to his English contact, William Stone, from a range of opinion that included two MPs. The visit took place in a period of rumours of French preparations for a descent and when Pitt, Richmond and Dundas were reviewing the defences.[3] Jackson was arrested in Ireland late in April, and Stone in England early in May. It was against this background, in an atmosphere charged further by reports of the Societies' own links with Ireland, that on 12 May the Government struck.

Early that morning the Secretary of the LCS, Thomas Hardy, was arrested at his shoemaker's shop in Piccadilly. On the same day a Royal Message was delivered to Parliament stating that the books and papers of the London Societies had been seized. On the 13th Pitt moved for the appointment of a Secret Committee of the Commons to examine them, and two more arrests, one being of Thelwall, were made. The Committee's first report was received on the 16th – the day after it met – alleging a conspiracy, and calling for suspension of the Habeas Corpus Act for eight months. The bill passed on the 18th, by 146 to 28, after fourteen 'delaying' divisions called by the Foxites.[4] Meanwhile, on the 16th, four more activists in London, including Horne Tooke, were taken up. Over the next few weeks others were sought in the provinces, some going into hiding successfully and one escaping abroad. In Scotland the search was intensified when some pikeheads and axes were discovered in Edinburgh; material evidence, it seemed, of a wider plot. The same was

---

1. Place's account of Chalk Farm is quoted in Goodwin, op. cit., 328; the resolution – on Thelwall's motion – in Thompson, *The Making of the English Working Class*, 131.

2. Cf. p. 216 above. In the series P.R.O., H.O. 42 there are two volumes for 1791 and four (the last two being the bulkier) for 1792; similarly, four volumes for 1793 are followed by six (three covering January to May inclusive) for 1794. This was the highest number reached in the decade.

3. P. 328 above.

4. *P.R.*, XXXVIII, 237–328. Pitt used the word quoted, when writing to the King (17 May 1794; *L.C.G. III*, II, no. 1070).

suggested by information that pikes had been made in Sheffield. Such facts were disclosed in the second report from the Commons' Committee on 6 June, which also drew on simultaneous examinations in the Privy Council. These, unlike its own, were of witnesses as well as of papers. They yield a vivid glimpse of Pitt from a hostile hand, for Thelwall wrote of one scene not long after the event.[1]

> I was called in and beheld the whole Dramatis Personae intrenched chin deep in Lectures and manuscripts . . . all scattered about in the utmost confusion . . .
>
> *Attorney-General (piano)*. Mr. Thelwall, what is your Christian name?
> *T. (somewhat sullenly)*. John.
> *Att. Gen. (piano still)*. . . . With two l's at the end or with one?
> *T.* With two – but it does not signify. (*Carelessly, but rather sullen, or so*). You need not give yourself any trouble. I do not intend to answer any questions.
> *Pitt.* What does he say? (*Darting round, very fiercely, from the other side of the room, and seating himself by the side of the Chancellor.*)
> *Lord Chancellor (with silver softness, almost melting to a whisper)*.
> He does not mean to answer any questions.
> *Pitt.* What is it? – What is it? – What? (*fiercely*) . . .

In August and September two further trials, this time for high treason, took place in Edinburgh; conducted more decently than before, and resulting in one of the accused being hanged and the other found guilty but pardoned. In September a grand jury of Middlesex was directed to find that a charge of high treason could be brought against twelve men including Hardy, Tooke, Thelwall, and the novelist and playwright Thomas Holcroft.[2] It complied in October, and on the 25th the first prosecution, that of Hardy, opened at the Old Bailey.

The trial went badly for the Ministry. As things turned out the Attorney General erred by going for too high a charge. The alternative would have been sedition, and this indeed had been the preference of his advisers in more hypothetical conditions before arrests were made. But several factors now disposed the other way. The judges in the Privy Council who had attended the examinations were convinced that treason had been committed; Parliament had referred to 'a seditious and traitorous conspiracy' after debating the Commons' Committee's reports; and the jury in September had been instructed by the presiding judge (in the celebrated, or notorious, charge of Justice Eyre) that a true bill for high treason should be found. There was also a legal dilemma: if

---

1. *Tribune*, 4 April 1795; quoted in E.P. Thompson, op. cit., 18–19. For the lectures see p. 393 above. The Attorney General was Sir John Scott, the Lord Chancellor Loughborough (see p. 403 below).
2. For whom see p. 118 above.

sedition was preferred and evidence of treason then emerged in Court, the accused could be acquitted of the lesser crime while it would be awkward to act on the greater. And – an important consideration – given that the evidence pointed as was thought, 'it would have been impossible that the Country could ever have been made fully acquainted with the dangers, to which it was exposed' without the whole being presented. It was for this reason above all that a lengthy process was adopted, even at the risk of tiring and confusing a jury; for it appeared 'essential to securing the public safety' that the Societies' transactions should be exposed.[1]

But the calculation proved disastrously wrong – and a lesson against proceeding on any but strictly legal grounds. For the Crown would have to prove 'constructive treason'; to show that 'any act intended to put the King in circumstances in which his life would be in danger' was 'an overt act of compassing his death' as required by statute.[2] This was uncertain ground, in the very nature – the length and conflicting constructions – of evidence which encompassed the Societies' aims and proceedings over several years. The language of the treason Acts as they stood was not precisely adapted to the circumstances; and a superb defence by Thomas Erskine – one of the great forensic performances of the century – threw the jury into growing doubt. Hardy was acquitted, and escorted triumphantly through the streets. The trial attracted intense excitement. Crowds milled around the Court every day, hooting and besieging the judges and the Attorney General, cheering Erskine and finally drawing his coach down the Strand. A fortnight later Tooke's case followed; and this time with an obviously packed jury. But it did no good. Erskine displayed his talents once more, Tooke was a witty and skilful defendant, and the jury, despite its origins, took only eight minutes to acquit him. Thelwall was tried next, at the beginning of December – in point of fact Government's most likely chance, for his language had been much more consistently subversive than Hardy's or Tooke's, and he himself was a less attractive personality.[3] The jury this time was out for two hours. But the earlier cases had left their mark. Thelwall too was found not guilty, and in mid-December the remaining prosecutions were dropped.

Government had thus failed at least directly: the strategy of 'acquainting the Country with the dangers'[4] had not ended with the desired result inside the Courts. The proceedings had also been

1. Sir John Scott's reminiscences in the 1820s of his reasoning (*Lord Eldon's Anecdote Book*, 56).

2. See W.S. Holdsworth, *A History of English Law*, VIII (1925), 318.

3. Not the least of Erskine's skills indeed was to prevent him from playing too prominent a role: exactly the opposite to Tooke's case. It was said that when Thelwall scribbled a note to his Counsel, 'I'll be hanged if I don't plead my own cause!' he received the reply, 'You'll be hanged if you do!' (Stanhope, II, 273).

4. See above.

personally embarrassing for two Cabinet Ministers; for Richmond and Pitt had been called as witnesses by the defence. It was ironical that they should have been thus linked, at a time when their relations were growing steadily worse.[1] But of course they were subpoenaed as former Parliamentary reformers, who had professed doctrines and uttered sentiments similar to those of the men in the dock.

> Yet in the mouths of PITT and RICHMOND'S LORD,
> *Once* what a sweet and inoffensive word![2]

There had been a hint of such a possibility in Frost's trial some eighteen months before: Erskine had then alluded to Pitt's and Richmond's activities in 1782.[3] The Duke was now called twice, in Hardy's and Tooke's trials, and Pitt himself once.[4] This last was by Tooke, who made good use of the occasion. He obliged his witness finally to agree that he had taken part in a meeting at Richmond's which included 'delegates' from counties and cities – a fact which he had been at pains to deny as a feature of the subsequent celebrated meeting at the Thatched House Tavern,[5] but which Tooke argued had made of its predecessor something analogous to a Convention. Pitt's residual legal training in fact did not enable him to escape from the well-placed questions. Erskine must have watched with considerable pleasure, after his own early treatment by the Minister in Parliament.[6]

Had the Government misjudged the real situation as well as the legal tactics? Were the Societies' more respectable aims, as Pitt stated, a mere 'pretext of reform', a 'mask of attachment to the state and country' behind which lay, combined with a Convention, a conspiracy for a rising, above all in the manufacturing towns? For those were 'the places where those people dwelled . . . who were naturally supposed to be the most . . . likely to raise into an enormous torrent of insurrection, which would sweep away all the barriers of Government, law and religion, and leave the country a naked waste for their usurped authority to range in'.[7] The language was high-flown, in the style of the day; there can be little doubt that it meant what it said. All the evidence suggests that Pitt was

1. Pp. 293, 316n5, 374 above.
2. 'Ode to Certain Foreign Soldiers'; *The Works of Peter Pindar*, III (1794), 391.
3. *State Trials*, XXII, cols 492–4. See I, Ch. III *passim*, and particularly 70–1.
4. *State Trials*, XXIV, cols. 1047–65, XXV, cols. 344, 375–81 for Richmond; XXV, cols. 381–6, 394 for Pitt.
5. Cf. I, 70–1.
6. See I, 611.
7. Speech of 16 May 1794 (*P.R.*, XXXVIII, 245–53, particularly 248). It is worth noting that this passage, often quoted as a generalisation, bore a specific reference. And cf. p. 164 above.

convinced of a potential immediate danger serious enough to demand urgent precautions. If he was perhaps sceptical in some degree in 1792, and not unduly worried in 1793, his fear of widescale trouble was real in 1794. There were too many indications within a short period for him to ignore them; above all it was the increasing boldness of the calls for a British Convention that impelled him and Dundas to act. The rigid defence of the Scottish judges[1] was conducted against a background of rising Governmental disquiet; in May itself Ministers were 'so fully employed in their discoveries' that, as Malmesbury found on his return from the continent, they could not attend to the problem of Prussia.[2] They were intent on scotching a threat which, as Pitt implied, they might earlier have underrated even if it might still be thought unlikely to succeed. He resorted to the means 'usual . . . in time of danger', the temporary suspension of the Habeas Corpus Act. In doing so he claimed the agreement of the Commons' Committee; and the ensuing votes showed how fully the fears were shared.[3]

Unnecessary panic? Probably so in the sense that a general rising would probably have misfired. It would have taken much organisation, which the Government's spies would almost certainly have rumbled. A wave of local disturbances, some of them fierce, might not have been so unlikely – with a suppression, all the messier because of the limited resources, that would have exacted its toll of sentences and possibly lives. The Gordon and Priestly riots[4] had underlined the danger, and increased the sensitivity to violence. It was not unreasonable to apprehend troubles whose familiar problems of control might be intensified by less familiar, and less measurable, aims. But would such troubles in fact have occurred without real provocation? Were the more extreme symptoms truly representative? Was it reasonable to dismiss the element of restraint which still informed much of the movement for reform? Many in the Societies, Tooke and Hardy themselves, were not men of violence. The strands were too varied, the tradition was too deep, for the case to be simplified in that way, and indeed some at least of the Societies' language and activities were signs of their own excessive fears. Each side in point of fact was compounding the other's sense of crisis; a process hastened by the rejection of Grey's motion and springing immediately from the Scottish trials.[5] To radicals, and reformers, these last were an open declaration of war – and radicals are seldom guilty of minimising the pressures. Many genuinely believed that repression

1. P. 390 above.
2. P. 340 above.
3. *P.R.*, XXXVIII, 252; and see p. 395–6 above.
4. Pp. 123, 131–2 above.
5. 'It was by these proceedings [the trials] more than by any other wrong, that the spirit of discontent justified itself throughout the rest of that age'. Lord Cockburn (in *Memorials of His Time*, 102) was speaking of Scotland itself. But the conclusion applies to the immediate sequel in England as well.

would now mount swiftly, and saw their own moves as essentially defensive. It was the Crown, they claimed, that had struck first, and showed signs of striking harder. They were entitled to draw on their resources in their turn.

This was not a line likely to appeal to Pitt. He had shown in his earlier treatment of the Dissenters a readiness to associate sheep with goats.[1] When he made up his mind to move he could hit hard, ignoring valid distinctions; he was not going to respect them now, and he struck at what he thought the most vulnerable points. Nor were other Ministers prepared to accept the reformers' claim: the Scottish trials themselves had been caused after all by the excesses of a Convention, and the rising defiance since then could be interpreted in quite another way. It could be held to show that extremists had taken over, and at a time when the French Revolution, so often in their mouths, was reaching ever more terrible heights. The moderates were not in the saddle; nor in fact were they still so moderate. Sedition was being encouraged, real trouble was brewing whatever its dimensions, and even if these might not be substantial there was the example of Paris in '89, despite its much greater resources for maintaining order.[2] This was the first group of men in office in England for more than a century to experience a conflict driven by ideas of such force. If they were not sure exactly how powerful the impulse was, they were sure that they would be remiss to sit passively by.

Taken at the two extremes this represented a new confrontation. It certainly marked a step along a steepening path. But the extremes were still extremes, they did not occupy all the ground, and there were constraints indeed on the main actors themselves. It has been well remarked that in 1794 'the antagonists appear to be strangely amateurish and uncertain of their role . . . Civility and violence are mixed together', to produce sometimes haphazard effects.[3] The conditions of imprisonment that summer were strict, the search of Hardy's house was brutal. Troops had to be used to cover the judges' comings and goings at the Courts. The Attorney General was surrounded by a mob. He was able to argue them out of assault, and to reflect many years later that if sensibly handled 'Englishmen are generally either reasonable, or good natured'.[4] Dundas and Horne Tooke, neighbours in Wimbledon, greeted each other affably after the trials. And in the public at large the differences were often those of degree. There were many who had no truck with sedition but disapproved of some of the Ministry's methods; who, like the highly respectable painter Farington, could be thought 'a Democrat' by a man like Windham and 'a violent aristocrat' by a fellow

1. See pp. 66–71 above.
2. Cf. p. 125 above.
3. Thompson, op. cit., 19.
4. *Lord Eldon's Anecdote Book*, 101.

Academician.[1] The authorities themselves were acting largely on accustomed lines and within traditional limitations. This was by no means the first time, as Pitt observed, that Parliament had suspended Habeas Corpus, and the trials showed flaws in the prosecution's case which could not survive in the Courts. The Ministry learned indeed from the experience that if it decided to bring charges of treason the best hope of securing convictions would be by way of new statutes rather than judicial interpretation. In 1794 it was attacking with the weapons available. The lessons were evident in the following years.

Nevertheless Government had its successes. For if the defendants escaped, the Societies once more lost impetus, as quickly it seemed as they had recently revived. The SCI – whose secretary turned King's evidence – ceased to meet, the LCS again lost members and its finances sank, the burgeoning contacts with provincial Societies were temporarily cut. Some of the leaders themselves disappeared, if again temporarily, from the scene: Hardy, Tooke and Thelwall themselves withdrew from active effort. The feared conspiracy melted into air; and indeed by the time the trials took place the most promising conditions for a rising had been removed. The Glorious First of June owed much of its reception to the damper it put on a French descent:[2] not the least of its significance was, it seemed, to seal the arrests of May. And in the spring Pitt brought in a bill for the statutory raising of Volunteer corps, which soon came to bear on an internal as well as an external threat. Plans against the latter had been under way from early in the year, stimulated by the reports of possible invasion.[3] They were soon linked, in Parliamentary debates and meetings in the country, with efforts to mobilise opinion against 'Jacobinism' within as well as without. For the Volunteer bill did not stand alone. It followed one to augment the militia, and included a plan to raise voluntary subscriptions for local defence.[4] This last (despite a precedent in 1782) was attacked by the Foxites as illegal, and as reflecting adversely on those who might not choose to take part. But Ministers were not averse to a fight, 'out of doors' as well as in the House; they had the best of it; and the Volunteers in due course tapped sources in local society which would form an effective line against popular disturbance. The cavalry in particular – long regarded as normally the most effective arm in a riot[5] – was allowed

1. *Diary of Joseph Farington*, I, 193–4.
2. P. 349 above.
3. See p. 328 above.
4. Ibid. The specifically military aspects of the measures are discussed on pp. 486–8 below. The rest of this paragraph relies much on J.R. Western, 'The Volunteer Movement as an Anti-Revolutionary Force, 1793–1801' (*E.H.R.*, LXXI, no. 281) and 'The County Fencibles and Militia Augmentation of 1794' (*Journal of the Society for Army Historical Research*, Volume Thirty-Four, 3–11). For the debates see *P.R.*, XXXVII–XXXIX and *The Senator*, IX *passim* for 17 March–11 April. The Acts were 34 Geo. III, cs. 16, 31.
5. See p. 126 above. And, as a volunteer force, socially the most reliable.

to operate, unlike the infantry or artillery, outside its own county. The success of the scheme – the rapid growth of its Corps[1] – might be seen in part as some insurance against a danger to which Government was naturally always alert: any appearance of disaffection in the regular army. In point of fact there had been little of this, though some incidents had occurred: a few active reformers among the officers were removed early on, and there had been isolated troubles in the ranks. The programme of barracks in place of quarters was seen as one prophylactic:[2] a healthy establishment of part-time soldiers could perhaps be another. But of greater significance was the proof that some at least of the well-disposed were prepared to act on their disposition, and that the disposition was widespread. A flow of recruits, and perhaps at least equally the weight of sentiment in the meetings on the bill, gave the Ministry the impression that its Parliamentary strength was not unduly misleading. The measures of the spring formed the first real chance of testing sections at least of propertied opinion.[3] The reception suggested its 'real sense'[4] within a wider context of varying degrees of support.

II

And in Parliament itself the summer witnessed a major event. The Ministry was joined in July by the Portland Whigs. It was a step that broke immediately the pattern of a decade. Equally, by thrusting on the Foxites a role that proved crucial to the more distant future, it marked, paradoxically, a milestone in the winding development of party.

Paradox indeed had not been absent from Opposition's courses in the past eighteen months. Fox's speeches in November and December 1792, more uncompromising than ever before, had caused rising trouble.[5] Portland and his associates, though thoroughly uneasy, were not prepared for a break, or to do more than refrain from opposing the Government's attitude to France. But after a brief respite in the Christmas recess they were faced by fresh difficulties, for on 1 February, within a fortnight of the news of Louis XVI's execution, Fox made a comprehensive defence of the Revolution from which he excepted only that event.[6] The Whig Club split on approval of the speech; Portland found an ameliorating formula; but early in March forty-five members resigned. By then moreover moves were under way for a further step, towards forming a distinctive, quasi-independent Parliamentary force.

1. Pp. 328–9 above.
2. There might however be limits in practice to this, cited on p. 451 below.
3. Cf. Pitt's remarks in the debate of 7 April (*P.R.*, XXXVIII, 489).
4. George III to Pitt, writing of 'the landed property of the Kingdom', on 29 March 1794 (*L.C.G. III*, II, no. 1039).
5. See pp. 225–7 above.
6. *P.R.*, XXXIV, 409–21.

This was made easier because one source of suspicion had recently been removed, for Loughborough, the go-between in the early negotiation for an extended Ministry, had finally decided to join Pitt on his own, and in January became Lord Chancellor.[1] His disappearance spared his former friends the embarrassment of association with a compromising influence. But in any case the deepening rift was becoming harder to conceal. In February a group centred on Windham, Burke, Gilbert Elliot and some others considered the prospect of a new connexion, to separate from Fox and 'give a cordial support to the Executive against French Principles at home and abroad'.[2] Early in March the self-styled 'Third Party' could be said to have come into existence. As far as could be seen it might count on some thirty-eight MPs.

There had been more hopeful estimates. Windham himself, the 'sort of head' of the group,[3] thought at first of a possible eighty-six names, and another forecaster, Lord Sheffield, went rather higher. But their details differed to some extent, a few proved disastrously wrong – fourteen men on Windham's list actually joined Fox in opposing the war – and the composition of the eventual 'party' pointed likewise to a more diminished return. For of the thirty-eight identifiable members only twenty-six could be called regular Whigs: the other twelve were of that familiar species, the independent Member. The new formation had not gathered in all of the secessionists from the Whig Club, let alone a substantially wider element of support. After all the signs from the beginning of the year, it mustered just more than a fifth of Opposition's earlier normal voting strength.[4]

The uncertainties were not surprising. In the first place the 'Third Party' was not a fully independent body. It was rather a pressure group on Portland to break with Fox on the issue of the war: on other questions, of a more familiar nature, it remained at least implicitly in the main stream. Windham himself had been willing until recently to agree that a difference of principle could be accepted over France;[5] and support for the Ministry was confined – subject to some reservations[6] – to the admittedly broad areas of order at home and the prosecution of hostilities abroad. Such an intermediate stance was imposed on difficulties likely to be experienced in any case. New political groupings,

1. Pp. 228–9, 176–9 above.
2. See O'Gorman, *The Whig Party and the French Revolution*, 126.
3. His own phrase; quoted in Butterfield, 'Charles James Fox and the Whig Opposition in 1792' (*Cambridge Historical Journal*, IX, no. 3), 329–30.
4. I.e., 26 out of a broad figure of 126; see O'Gorman, op. cit., 127 and Appendices 1, 2. The forthcoming *History of Parliament* gives slightly different figures. Broadly speaking, Portland could count on some 51–54 MPs (op. cit., 128 and Appendix 3). For a brief attempt to form a distinctive party in peacetime based intrinsically on independents see I, 615.
5. See his denial of 'a difference [with Fox] that amounted to principle in the Commons on 15 December 1792 (*P.R.*, XXXIV, 120–1).
6. Cf. pp. 388–9 above.

however placed, are seldom sure of their numbers; the past months had been testing, and shifts in alignment were bound to prove painful; and Parliamentary groupings, in the forms long known, were moreover not cut and dried. The adhesion of independents in their varying degrees was in fact a sign of life; but that of course was not a consolation for Windham and the rest. For a traditional connexion was not what was required. The Third Party leaders indeed were in a curiously ambivalent position: that of challenging in its own name something in which they believed. The basis of the grouping was not the old one of territorial or electoral influence: none of them possessed those attributes in marked degree. On the contrary it rested on a premise and a policy, responding in fact to a conception of party as defined earlier by Burke himself.[1] The Third Party, minor as its impact may have been, thus represented a step along that road. Its emergence however seemed to the main body of Whigs a deplorable threat to party cohesion.

And this, to Portland and his loyalists, threatened principle itself. If the new formation was calling on the need for clarity over a major issue, to many it was raising a single issue to a point endangering the greater good. Windham and his friends seemed as bad as Fox himself and those who followed his line on France. Both sections were striking at the unity essential to preserve a larger cause. This was a threat to which the old Rockingham wing of Opposition was perhaps particularly sensitive; for the earlier moves towards the Ministry, followed now by partial secession, while involving itself, undoubtedly contained a Northite element from the original Coalition.[2] If Windham and Burke hailed from an unsullied background, Loughborough and Elliot came from another, subsumed for a decade, whose reviving influence could possibly be discerned. It behoved those of the pure succession all the more to hold the line. The Whigs looked on themselves as the Parliamentary guardians of principles venerable and fundamental. To damage their own effectiveness was to commit a political crime. Portland and his peers in short found both dissident wings attached disproportionately to one object. It was to take a major scare to make the centre admit that the object must take precedence over all else.

Again this was perhaps not surprising. The Whig grandees could not bring themselves to part from Fox in a way that would benefit Pitt: to leave the great if wayward champion of liberties, the admired companion, the friend of their youth,[3] and bring comfort to the prime enemy, the successful deceiver of '83–4. The talks in the summer of 1792 had not lessened their suspicions: as late as January 1794 Portland could remind Windham that 'the present Ministry was formed' 'to annihilate,

---

1. See 1, 35.

2. Cf. op. cit., 98–101, 618–19.

3. In the spring of 1793 Fox's debts had come to the point where a subscription was raised by his friends. Portland contributed and urged others to do so.

if possible, the Whig Party'.[1] The main body of Opposition solidly supported prosecution of the war: their reservations indeed arose where they thought that more might be done, or the direction improved. If they criticised in private or in society they scarcely did so in Parliament, where they consistently contested Fox's views. They resolutely opposed Parliamentary reform – in this instance with some of the Foxites.[2] But the Portland Whigs could not agree to give up all hopes of their falling angel; and when at last they did, they remained reluctant to throw in their lot with Pitt.

Nor for that matter were Windham and his associates prepared yet to take a further step. They had after all set up largely as a pressure group; and for much of 1793 they concerted, at first awkwardly, with the Portland Whigs in responses to the Ministry.[3] For the Ministry began to test the prospects after the war began; with Pitt on this occasion – unlike the last – making the running from the start.[4] The soundings seem to have begun in May, after some conversations between Gilbert Elliot and Loughborough, ostensibly at least to see if Malmesbury might be employed.[5] Pitt however, though prepared to favour that prospect, had not entirely overcome his resentment at the veteran diplomat's behaviour in the Regency crisis,[6] and it was to Elliot himself that the first overture was made. He was offered the Governorship of Madras; and while he declined on domestic grounds, he stayed in touch, half disposed to office and continuing to suggest particular friends.[7] Meanwhile Pitt was making other moves. He gave an Earldom to Lord Porchester and a Garter to Lord Carlisle, both supporters of Portland's and the latter sympathetic to the new developments; and on the same day, 14 June, three days before Fox was due to introduce a motion for peace with France, he wrote to Windham suggesting a meeting. It took place on the 17th itself; Windham was offered the Secretaryship at War, and Lord Spencer – a Whig of the old connexion, the brother of Georgiana

1. 11 January 1794 (B.L. Add. Ms 37845). Cf. Ch. VI, section I, above for the summer of 1792.

2. P. 388, n4 above. When Parliament reassembled at the beginning of 1794 Pitt and others were afraid that 'the Middle [i.e. Third] Party' itself might support the war but criticise its conduct in the past year – which could have been 'embarrassing'. But this last did not happen (Canning's Journal, 25 January 1794; Canning Ms 29 d ii, Leeds Archives Department).

3. They also continued to sit on the same side of the House (see O'Gorman, op. cit., 137). Cf. I, 39.

4. See p. 185 above.

5. Elliot to Malmesbury, 6, 8 April 1793 (N.L.S., Minto Ms IE 68).

6. See p. 296 above. Pitt's fading resentment can be followed in Elliot's letter of 8 April (n5 above) and William Elliot to Gilbert Elliot, 17 June 1793 (N.L.S., Minto Ms 11138).

7. Henry Dundas to Gilbert Elliot, 26 May 1793: 'It is known to Mr. Pitt alone that I write this letter' (Minto Ms 11139); Elliot to Malmesbury, 14 June 1793 (Minto Ms 11111). His efforts in the summer concentrated on Malmesbury and Sylvester Douglas (for whom see pp. 406–7 below).

Devonshire, but sympathetic to the Third Party – the Lord Lieutenancy of Ireland.[1]

The approach was rebuffed. Spencer turned it down the next day, and Windham, who had seen Portland on the 16th, at once followed suit with 'a great load off my mind'. He found his own arguments 'much inferior' to Pitt's in telling him of the decision;[2] but he was glad to escape what he still regarded as a snare. No member of Opposition was in fact ready to take a Ministerial post: the farthest anyone could go was to seek or consider an official position. And so it remained throughout the rest of the year. Elliot accepted the abortive Commissionership of Dunkirk in September, and a Commissionership at Toulon in October (taking Douglas with him as Secretary); Malmesbury was sent on his mission to Prussia in November.[3] But while the former, always the most inclined towards co-operation, was talking in the autumn of an enlarged Ministry, Windham and others remained unconvinced and Ministers themselves were now more cautious of making a further approach.[4] Throughout these months and into the winter contacts were maintained and indeed strengthened. Those members of Opposition who saw Pitt at this period found him more agreeable than in the past. He had been 'very courteous' to Malmesbury in the summer; he was cordial to Portland in September; Spencer found him affable if inconclusive in November; and when Thomas Pelham, of the Newcastle clan, a follower of Portland and a friend of Fox, renewed acquaintance at Loughborough's in December, the Minister appeared 'improved in his manners' and despite 'a sort of awkwardness' 'there was no reserve'.[5] Conversations however left matters as they were. The suspicions were strong; all the stronger as Elliot and Malmesbury took official posts and missions. Portland, uncomfortable and miserable, wavered over his duty, half convinced when he had seen Pitt that there were grounds for 'a ministerial arrangement',[6] but equally fearful when he talked to his friends of betraying the cause. Some of his associates however were

1. For Carlisle's Garter and Porchester's elevation to Carnarvon see *G.E.C.*, III, 36, 46; for Pitt's meeting with Windham, Pitt to Windham, 14 June 1793 (*The Windham Papers . . .*, I (1913), 137: 'the first note from Pitt', *The Diary of . . . William Windham*, 277, and see 278). For Duchess Georgiana, I, 218.

2. *Diary* for 19 June, 278; see also 277 and O'Gorman, op. cit., 144 for the meeting with Portland.

3. Pp. 286n3, 310, 296–7 above. Elliot refused the Secretaryship for Ireland (an openly political post) in June.

4. Elliot's journal, 8–9 September 1793, recording conversations with Dundas (Minto Ms 11159). See also O'Gorman, op. cit., 153.

5. William Elliot to Gilbert Elliot, 17 June 1793 (Minto Ms 11138); Portland to Fitzwilliam, 22 September 1793 (Wentworth Woodhouse Muniments, F 31a, Sheffield City Libraries); Spencer to Windham, 11 November 1793 (*The Windham Papers*, I, 176–82), and Thomas Grenville's memorandum of 18–19 November 1793 (B.L. Add. Ms 42058); Thomas Pelham to Lady Webster, 7 December 1793 (B.L. Add. Ms 51705). Pelham however still found 'the same unpleasant continued laugh at almost everything he says in the way of observation'.

6. Portland to Fitzwilliam, 22 September 1793 (n5 above).

growing impatient of his indecisiveness, and by the end of the year Spencer and Pelham, with Tom Grenville (the third Grenville brother) among others, were moving more clearly in Windham's direction. But this was still with the aim of achieving a strength sufficient 'to have weight with Ministers and Parliament', not of any reinforcement of the Ministry itself.[1]

Such was the position on the eve of a new year, and a month before a new session. Just before the latter opened, however, Portland took a further step. Under growing pressure and a deepened if painful personal conviction, he decided that he must effectively and finally part from Fox. At a meeting at Burlington House on 20 January 1794 he announced that he would no longer regard himself as in 'systematic opposition'.[2] This was not meant to suggest a junction with Government. But in itself it was a decisive resolution. It removed the need for a Third Party. It allowed the whole corps other than the Foxites to speak and act with one voice. It was in fact necessary for the health of the conservative Opposition and thus also for its relations with the Ministry, reducing the dangers of internal division and of individual losses by inducements from outside.

These last continued. Pitt had given both Portland and Spencer the impression that he was open to 'a ministerial arrangement': 'upon those principles and that basis', according to the former, 'upon which alone I could ever take a part'; 'only on the supposition', according to the latter, 'of our [the main Opposition and Third Party] doing it jointly'.[3] How far the Minister was in earnest it is hard to tell. Spencer at least had heard of a recent conversation implying that Pitt would like to pursue individual accessions; and one indeed followed when Douglas in December was offered and accepted the Irish Secretaryship. Ireland was always a sensitive subject to the Whigs, and to Portland himself; moreover Douglas acted after consulting Lord Mansfield, formerly Stormont, a senior member of the Whigs' inner circle who had originally been a Northite.[4] The defection was a personal blow to Portland, the more threatening since it could be seen as a renewed inducement to Spencer.[5] Nor could the Whigs be convinced that, whatever Pitt's own views, his colleagues would welcome an extended accession. Dundas

1. Spencer to Thomas Grenville, 10 December 1793 (B.L. Add. Ms 42058). Windham himself was taking the same line over the immediate future, while leaving more distant prospects obscure; see his letter of 26 December 1793 to Mrs Crewe (*The Windham Papers*, I, 192). Spencer however thought that he was now not so averse to accepting office (Thomas Grenville's memorandum, 19 November 1793; B.L. Add. Ms 42058).

2. O'Gorman, op. cit., 178–9; and see Portland to Fitzwilliam, 25 December 1793 (Wentworth Woodhouse Muniments, F 31a).

3. Portland to Fitzwilliam, 22 September 1793 (Wentworth Woodhouse Muniments, F 31a); Spencer to Windham, 11 November 1793 (*The Windham Papers*, I, 180).

4. See I, 123, and for Ireland and the Rockinghams op. cit., 196. The background is discussed more fully in section III of this Chapter.

5. Portland to Windham, 11 January 1794 (B.L. Add. Ms 37873). He alluded to it more than once in the next few months. See pp. 105–6 above.

certainly had not seemed so keen in the autumn; there appeared to be 'a great indisposition towards a connexion with the Duke of Portland', said to arise from the King's dislike of the Duke's conduct in '92.[1] A major rearrangement of the Ministry would indeed raise some hard problems of the distribution of power and patronage throughout the ranks. Pitt may well have been more open to the prospect than any one around him: he had entire confidence in his own capacity, and patronage always left him bored. If he had to take the Whigs on a joint basis he was probably prepared to do so; if some of them acceded individually, or from the Third Party alone, that doubtless would suit him at least as well. He knew that certain competent individuals could strengthen the Administration: if they were accompanied by some of public substance that could be an added boon.[2] He looked at the Whig notables themselves with his usual calm and sardonic eye.

> I recollect [wrote Pretyman much later] that in private Conversation ... in 1793, I expressed some surprise at the support his measures were receiving from certain Peers & Members of the House of Commons of large Property, who had hitherto opposed his Administration, & at the disposition they manifested to connect themselves with him, upon which he observed, "they see that their titles & possessions are in danger, & they think their best chance for preserving them is by supporting Government & joining me."[3]

He would welcome the isolation of the Foxites. He was happy to gain some selected strength. If the accession was to be comprehensive he would accommodate that as it came. Meanwhile he kept personally in touch with Windham, learning in return something of Opposition's intentions and views.[4]

This may have been his attitude at the start of the year. The developments of the next few months drove the two sides towards each other. The Ministry fuelled the process with some local and military patronage – and the offer of a Lord Lieutenancy for Portland himself.[5] Pitt kept the Whig leaders informed, directly or indirectly, of some Ministerial plans: of the Prussian subsidy, and the formation of an émigré corps in England. Portland in his turn sent his views in March on

---

1. Conversation with Gilbert Elliot, 8–9 September 1793 (see p. 286, n3 above). Presumably this referred to the Duke's continued countenance of Fox late in that year; and see p. 414 below.

2. Cf. pp. 188–9 above.

3. Unpublished chapter 18 for his *Life* of Pitt, 16na (B.L. Add. Ms 45107(c)).

4. See the correspondence in B.L. Add. Ms 37844. On 16 January 1794 Pitt showed a draft of the King's Speech for the coming session, with a request for a talk 'on the general Situation of affairs'. This would have been not unconnected with his hope of disarming criticism of the conduct of the war (p. 405, n2 above). Cf. too p. 189 above.

5. Of Middlesex, in February or March 1794 (O'Gorman, op. cit., 186). It was not accepted at the time; cf. *L.C.G. III*, II, no. 1097.

military dispositions.[1] A selective working arrangement, where it suited the Ministry, particularly for Parliamentary purposes, was emerging by the spring of 1794. Neither of the parties was urgently impelled to anything more. Both recognised the hazards and inconveniencies of a junction which in other ways made good sense. The Government was doing quite well: its majorities held with broad consistency, and operations on the continent were still in a not unpromising stage.[2] But matters began to change for both sides in May, in face of the supposed conspiracy. Dundas and Pitt kept Windham informed, they promoted the inclusion of some of the former Third Party in the Commons' Committee of Secrecy,[3] and on the 23rd – after Windham had made it clear that there was now no moving 'separately' – Pitt requested an interview with Portland.[4] The two men met the next day, and discussed 'the probability of our forming a ministerial arrangement' such, as Pitt hoped, 'might make us act together as one Great Family' against the Jacobin danger.[5] The Duke summoned his friends for the 30th, by which time all could be in town; but his Duchess then fell ill, and indeed died, the meeting was postponed to 3 and then 13 June, and it was the 18th of that month before Portland saw Pitt again. He was now empowered to explore terms, and negotiations could begin. Whatever else might come from the Ministry's measures against sedition, they had brought to a point the prospect of an important political change.[6]

There were bargains however to be struck before this could be achieved. Pitt and Portland each had much to defend, and both had to sell the results to their colleagues. All connexions placed a premium on posts and patronage; but the Rockinghams had been outstanding, imposing a justification of principle on a universal practice. Their heirs maintained the tradition. One of the deterrents to a coalition with Pitt in 1792 had

1. See O'Gorman, op. cit., 186–7; pp. 337, 369 above.
2. Cf. pp. 338–9 above. Charles Greville, formerly an Opposition member, even thought Government 'stronger than I ever knew it' in March (to Sir William Hamilton, 7 March 1794; B.L. Add. Ms 40715).
3. See p. 395 above. Five of the 21 members could be so described, with at least one more (Thomas Grenville) in active sympathy.
4. Pitt to Portland, 23 May 1794 (Portland Ms PWF 7702; Nottingham University). Windham's statement, which was made to Dundas on 1 May, is mentioned in his *Diary*, 308. But for Spencer's view as recently as 12 May that 'union' with the Ministry was still 'distant', and his continuing reservations on the eve of Pitt's move, see the memorandum of his conversation with John Pratt (Camden) in Camden Ms O 256/1 (Kent C.A.O.), and also Spencer to Thomas Grenville, 27 May 1794 (B.L. Add. Ms 42058).
5. Portland to Fitzwilliam, 25 May 1794 (Wentworth Woodhouse Muniments, F 31b).
6. I have put it like this because, while there had been an almost simultaneous reverse on the continent when the Allies were checked in the battle of Turcoing on 18 May, turning their advance into a retreat (p. 339 above) it was the domestic danger in my view that first impelled the talks.

been the inadequacy of the offers: too few Cabinet offices, and an 'insignificant' share of the lesser loaves and fishes.[1] Portland must now exact a greater 'equality' if the Whig cause was to survive; and there were in any case many mouths to be fed after so long in the wilderness. Public principle and private satisfaction alike demanded the fruits. And Pitt for his part had to take note of feelings among his colleagues and supporters. However boring he found questions of patronage – particularly minor patronage – he had to deal with them in such a case when it came to the point. For there were lively apprehensions. The last few years had heightened the sense of party over and above the earlier divide, sharpening the natural suspicion of newcomers' designs on power and profit.[2] While some accession was accepted and in places welcomed, there were reservations about the effects of a general rearrangement on existing cohesion and loyalties.

The talks continued for four weeks. Portland gained some limited assurances on war policy. Pitt told him that a restored French monarchy was, in the Duke's version, 'the first and determined aim of the present Ministry', and that while recognition of a Regent did not seem currently feasible it was favoured when conditions were right. This in fact was not immediately so promising as the conservative Whigs imagined. Nor indeed was Pitt's assertion that he still agreed with the desirability of aiding the French royalists – which of course might involve the exiled Princes more closely than hitherto. Such statements were those of intent, according to circumstances and competing priorities. But the last did represent a 'dream' of the Minister's to which he was becoming personally attached within the context of a strategy determined very largely by responses to events.[3] Greater difficulties centred on the attitudes of individual Whigs to office. Fitzwilliam, always a potent influence on Portland, at first preferred to remain outside, and Spencer was still undecided (as indeed, less seriously, was Mansfield) about the wisdom of full-scale coalition. But the news from Flanders now increased the pressures: as the Allied retreat continued, Fitzwilliam agreed to come in provided a proper balance was recognised by 'such marks of real substantial favour and confidence on the part of the Crown . . . as will mark beyond dispute the return of weight, power and consideration to the Old Whigs', and he himself could be Lord Lieutenant of Ireland, the one post to which, if pressed, he felt a duty. Since Spencer persisted in refusing that Office the way there might be clear, and Spencer himself, if also reluctantly, consented in the end to join.[4] At the beginning of July

1. See p. 178 above.
2. Pp. 54–5 above.
3. Portland to Fitzwilliam, 19–20 June 1794 (Wentworth Woodhouse Muniments, F 31b); Dundas to Pitt, 13 October 1794 (Cambridge University Library Ms 6958(8)). Cf. pp. 368–73 above.
4. Fitzwilliam to Portland, 23 June 1794 (Portland Ms PWF 3765). For Spencer at the outset see p. 409, n4 above; for developments in general in June E.A. Smith, *Whig principles and party politics*, 166–9, and O'Gorman, op. cit., 196–204.

therefore Fitzwilliam received the promise of Ireland once arrangements had been made to satisfy the incumbent, Westmorland, and meanwhile the offer of the Lord Presidency of the Council. Within the next few days, after Pitt had tentatively proposed Hawkesbury for the succession to the latter Office, it was established that Spencer or Mansfield would have it, the other taking some unspecified Cabinet post.[1] Windham had already been sounded on the possibility of becoming Secretary at War; Portland himself would become Home Secretary. On 3 July the King was told the details, to which he gave his consent.[2] At that point therefore the two negotiators expected a junction within forty-eight hours.

But one problem had not in fact been solved. What was to happen to the existing Ministers? There was some room for manoeuvre. Camden, the Lord President of the Council, who would gladly have retired in any case, had recently died;[3] and Stafford, the elderly Lord Privy Seal, would not object to going. Westmorland (outside the Cabinet) must be consulted and met as far as possible, but he could be brought back from Dublin. This allowed a reshuffle affecting three Cabinet posts. But Pitt had agreed to four, and one involved Portland as a Secretary of State. It was important to retain William Grenville and Dundas in the central direction of the war. How could that be done to every one's satisfaction?

The proposed answer in point of fact almost wrecked the prospects. It centred on Dundas. Grenville, it seems, was not intimately involved in the negotiation: he had not been so on the previous occasion, in 1792, and he may moreover have been feeling somewhat sensitive, as a true member of his family, over a suggestion from Pitt some months before aimed at reducing the fees of his Office. He stayed at Dropmore throughout the critical week.[4] But his post in any case had not been in debate: it was the Home Office that was under offer, and Dundas's wartime functions that must be preserved. Pitt's preferred solution was to separate them from the Department in a Secretaryship for War and the Colonies (with Dundas retaining his authority for 'the East Indies') while Portland remained responsible for Britain and for order in Ireland.[5] He gained the impression that Portland was content. But two snags quickly became apparent. The Whigs were not sure if Dundas was meant to hold on to the Indian and the Scottish patronage. And

1. Pitt to Portland, 2 July 1794 (Portland Ms PWF 7703: there is a copy in Pitt's papers, in P.R.O. 30/8/102); Portland to Pitt, sd (copy in Cambridge University Library Ms 62958/8).

2. Pitt to Portland, 3 July 1794 (Portland Ms PWF 7704).

3. In April.

4. See p. 188 above for 1792. His correspondence with Pitt, in February 1794, over a reduction in his fees in return for taking an Auditorship of the Exchequer may be followed in *H.M.C., Dropmore*, II, 511–13, 515; and see I, 311. His absence at Dropmore was noted by his Under Secretary Burges (to Anne Burges, 10 July 1794; Burges Ms 10, Bodleian Library).

5. Cf. I, 329, and Nelson, *The Home Office*, 6–7; for the term 'East Indies', I, 423.

Windham, who was confidently expected to accept the Secretaryship at War, if necessary with an added seat in the Cabinet, rejected the offer on learning that there would be a new Secretaryship of State for War in Dundas's hands.[1] For that would leave war policy as it was. Portland should take the Home Office with unaltered powers. On 5 July deadlock therefore supervened.

Pitt's first thought was to turn to Grenville. He asked him to take the Home Office on the terms held out to Portland, allowing the Duke to succeed to the Foreign Office while Dundas occupied the new Department. Grenville to his credit assented. But Portland did not: he did not want foreign affairs, and though he would sanction the Secretaryship for War he now refused to part with the Colonies. Dundas at first accepted this division. But on reflection he changed his mind; and on the morning of 9 July he wrote to Pitt that he would resign if the change was made.[2]

It is not hard to see why. Dundas may have been moved to some extent by a residual feeling of insecurity. For while his influence may now have seemed well founded it had been built up as Home Secretary from an uncertain start, and precisely because of this success he must have feared a prospective check. It was noticeable indeed that, in contrast to his role two years before, he was not disposed this time to take a leading part in the negotiation.[3] And his anxiety grew as he watched the Minister making the running, yielding possibly five Cabinet posts and truncating the initial arrangements for his own.[4] At the same time his fears were by no means exclusively for himself. For Dundas was genuinely opposed to the creation of an Office which in his opinion would prove to be a 'Puppet' in the arrangements for directing a war.

> The Idea of a War Minister as a Separate Department ... cannot exist in this Country. . . . All modern Wars are a Contention of Purse, and unless some very peculiar Circumstance occurs . . . the Minister for Finance must be the Minister for War.

This particular Minister of Finance moreover was known to be a dominant figure. A Secretary of State purely for war was therefore likely to fall between all the stools, promoting 'Wrangling' and complicating

---

1. For the minor Office of Secretary at War, with its limitations, see I, 170.

2. The developments of the brief period leading up to Dundas's decision may be followed in Windham's published *Diary* and *Papers* and his unpublished papers in B.L. Add. Ms 37845, in *H.M.C., Dropmore*, II, in Portland's and Fitzwilliam's papers, in Stanhope Mss S5 03/13, 06/23), and Holland Rose, *Pitt and Napoleon*, 227, 250–1. Summaries exist in O'Gorman and in Smith, op. cit.

3. See I, 458, and pp. 176, 185 above. Dundas may also have reflected that he had taken care to stress in February 1793 the benefits of his staying where he was 'while the war continues' (see Holland Rose, II, 124–5); a judgment that had been accepted.

4. Cf. his comment to Pitt a few months later, in another context, on the latter's 'yielding nature'; 13 October 1794 (I, 322).

'the Channel of Correspondence' with other interested parties which were themselves in Cabinet. And if this would be his status in general war business when divorced from the weight of his former Department, a division of colonial responsibilities would add 'inexplicable confusion'. It was for these reasons that Dundas told Pitt not to 'mention, or more think of' the idea of his being 'a Secretary of State with a War Department'.[1]

Pitt was horrified. He had already informed Portland that he could not agree to place such a 'Department' in new hands,[2] and he now told Dundas that the latter's resignation would leave him 'really completely heart broken'. He would have to 'carry on the business' of completing a Ministry, but without the hope of any 'comfort'; and he therefore made 'a personal request in the strongest manner' that his colleague would accept the revised post.[3] Dundas, 'with the most poignant concern', did not give way. But neither did Pitt. He went at once to the King, and asked him to write direct. George III did so. He agreed that the retention of 'the West Indies' by the Home Office was not particularly satisfactory; but he called on Dundas 'in the strongest manner' to continue as Secretary for the war.[4] Faced with this, Dundas consented.[5] He was soon to prove that his main fear was groundless, and to preside over a Department which, after acquiring all colonial business seven years later, was to endure unaltered until the Crimean War began.

With the last obstacle removed the arrangements went ahead.[6] On 11

1. Dundas to Pitt, 9 July 1794 (P.R.O. 30/8/157); printed in part in Holland Rose, II, 271. The constitutional and administrative questions are discussed more fully in Ch. XIII, section IV below. Dundas might perhaps also have had in mind the failures of the American War, with its three Secretaries of State (see I, 307). But these in point of fact had occurred with a weak First Lord of the Treasury, whereas he was now thinking in terms of the opposite.

2. Pitt to Portland, 5 July 1794 (Portland Ms 7705; the date – disputed by O'Gorman, op. cit., 206n1 – seems to be confirmed by Pitt's draft of sd in Stanhope Ms S5 06/23). Cf. same to Grenville, sd (*H.M.C., Dropmore*, II, 595). The importance of avoiding 'a chasm' in business and retaining Dundas in charge in particular was further stressed by Grenville to his brother Thomas on the 6th (B.L. Add. Ms 42058).

3. 9 July, '¾ past 11' [a.m.] (Stanhope, II, 253). The original is in S.R.O., Melville Castle Ms GD 51/1/24/2.

4. Stanhope, II, 254–5. The King wrote, 'to continue Secretary of State for the War, namely, to keep up the correspondence wherever the war is carried on'. Contrary to his own earlier correct definition (I, 329), he now in point of fact described 'the West Indies' as being 'added to the Home Department'. The original is in S.R.O., Melville Castle Ms GD 51/1/204.

5. To George III, sd, 11 p.m. (*L.C.G. III*, II, 222; and see op. cit., no. 1091). The next day he sent the King his correspondence with Pitt (op. cit., no. 1092).

6. Not without a characteristic reminder from Hawkesbury, on being apprised, to look at 'the Act of 1782' (the Act for Economical Reform, 22 Geo. III, c. 82), which would seem to forbid three Secretaries of State, and one of them in the Commons. He was not quite clear however if he was right about this (to Pitt, 7 July 1794; Stanhope Ms S5 02/15). Chatham too had earlier had doubts about the constitutional propriety of the proposed new Secretaryship (see Pitt to Chatham, 1 July [1794]; P.R.O. 30/8/101).

July Portland became Home Secretary, Dundas Secretary of State for War, Fitzwilliam Lord President, Spencer Lord Privy Seal, Mansfield a Cabinet Minister without a portfolio, and Windham (as Portland had thought likely) Secretary at War with a seat in Cabinet. That body accordingly now numbered thirteen in place of ten – Mansfield and Windham being added as well as Dundas's new Office – of whom five had joined from the main ranks of Opposition.[1]

III

The coalition was accompanied by the desired marks of 'favour and confidence'.[2] Portland took the Garter he had declined in 1792, and his son and heir the Lord Lieutenancy of Middlesex.[3] Windham became a Privy Councillor on joining the Cabinet, four Whig supporters received English baronies, one a promotion in the peerage, one Irish Earl a British barony; and Burke, appropriately, a pension. Two others were given posts in the King's household. Such largesse was thought excessive outside the beneficiaries' circles. The King, who had wanted the Garter for Lord Howe, could not 'see why on the Duke of Portland's head favours are to be heaped without measure'; and Pitt's supporters felt much the same. Portland, grumbled Rose from the Treasury, was 'an atrocious jobber'.[4] Others fastened more on the apparent distribution of power. Wilberforce thought that too many Cabinet places had been given away; Pratt (now Camden) and Mornington felt aggrieved; many friends, reported Canning, 'either grumble pretty audibly at the distribution of so great a part of the powers among new comers, or at best, shake their head, and wish that it may answer in the end'.[5] The Minister's closer colleagues were neither pleased nor confident. Hawkesbury can hardly have relished being passed over for a senior if less 'efficient' post; Dundas watched for new influences with a suspicious eye; all were aware that Pitt had conceded more than had been forecast.[6]

1. And as George Rose noted, Loughborough made a sixth, if uneasily, from the same source (*Diaries and Correspondence*, I, 193). Hawkesbury on the other hand was able to single out Mansfield as an 'old Friend' – like Loughborough himself – from the days of North (to Pitt, p. 413, n6 above).
2. P. 410 above.
3. See pp. 183, 408 above.
4. George III to Pitt, 13 July 1794 (Stanhope, II, Appendix, xx) and see p. 349 above; Rose to Pretyman, 14 July 1794 (*Diaries and Correspondence of George Rose*, I, 194).
5. Wilberforce to Lord Muncaster, 9 July 1794 (*Correspondence of Wilberforce*, I, 103–4); Pellew, *Life of Sidmouth*, I, 122–3; Dorothy Marshall, *The Rise of Canning* (1938), 75.
6. For Dundas see eg p. 412 above; for the unexpected scale of the concessions, Buckingham to Grenville, 8 July 1794 (*H.M.C., Dropmore*, II, 597): 'I cannot but recollect how widely such an arrangement differs from the ideas which both Mr. Pitt and you had upon it some months since'. The extent of Hawkesbury's dissatisfaction would have depended on whether or not he knew of Pitt's initial proposal for the Lord

Many wondered how he would now fare. Auckland, affecting disengagement as an elder statesman from his unsummoned Kentish retreat, thought the 'experiment to be hazardous, and likely to end in disgusts and disappointments'. Burges was 'far from thinking this so advantageous a manoeuvre for my friend Pitt as he seems to suppose'. Rose prayed 'From the very bottom of my heart' that he might be 'mistaken as to the consequences'. It was 'absolutely necessary' that the Minister should continue in effective direction; but he could not raise his hopes much, even though he had 'great confidence in Mr. Pitt'.[1]

Pitt himself as always fully shared the last sentiment. When the Speaker mentioned 'the measure worthy of [a] great and daring mind' of bringing into Cabinet a group that might 'almost . . . have outvoted him', he replied that 'he was under no anxiety on that account, since he placed much dependence on his new colleagues, and still more on himself'.[2] Of course he had to say something; but the response, in both its parts, rang true. Once he had taken a decision he usually acted wholeheartedly: Eden in the eighties had found him almost alone in treating a convert without reserve.[3] He was prepared to believe that others would respond; and in any event he was not worried about maintaining his ascendancy. Some observers thought that the new arrangement would cause uncertainty in the conduct of the war; some that it might play into the hands of the King. George III indeed, according to one view, might be 'the greatest gainer' from the new balance, operating in Cabinet through a member such as Hawkesbury. So Hawkesbury's son indeed was said to have hinted.[4] But to Pitt such a verdict would have seemed problematical at most. He did not necessarily trust the King[5] – less indeed perhaps than he did many politicians. But if he was to encounter such a problem he could reflect

Presidency (p. 411 above). But the way in which he singled out Mansfield alone for approval among the concessions (p. 414, n1 above) suggests – as one would expect – considerable reserve, and many years later his son the Prime Minister recalled his ill-treatment on this occasion (Keith Grahame Feiling, *The Second Tory Party 1714–1832* (1938), 196). See however below.

Within the next few weeks Hawkesbury had a further cause for serious disquiet, over possible terms on trade with the United States (see pp. 513–14 below; foreshadowed by his son Robert in a letter to his father of 27 July, B.L. Loan Ms 72, vol. 53).

1. Auckland to Lord Henry Spencer, 10 July 1794 (*A.C.*, III, 220) – he was in point of fact, as might have been expected from his nature, aggrieved that he had not been called (to Pitt, 14 July 1794; copy in B.L. Add. Ms 34452); Burges to Anne Burges, 9 July 1794 (Burges Ms 10); *Diaries and Correspondence of Rose*, I, 195. Rose, it should be added, was talking about the state of the war as well as the Cabinet changes.

2. Pellew, *Life of Sidmouth*, 121.

3. Ehrman, *The British Government and Commercial Negotiations with Europe*, 38.

4. Burges to Anne Burges, 9 July 1794 (Burges Ms 10). He was not necessarily a good judge. According to this letter Pitt had 'hitherto been absolute' in Cabinet. But in 1791 Burges had likewise forecast a new 'restraint' after Ministerial changes (I, 633, 635), which he now seemed to be denying.

5. Cf. I, 65, 136, 187, 641–3; pp. 31–3, 174 above.

that the balance contained a Whig establishment not normally in sympathy with or favourably viewed by the monarch. Some of the feelings he may have held two years before in favour of a wider combination would doubtless have persisted; if so, they were blended with a much keener search for unity. For Fox, the great conundrum then, stood now for a cause far more deeply discredited in a war which moreover was not going too well. That particular 'coach' no longer 'stopped the way':[1] its occupants were isolated in Opposition, and this in itself was surely worth a risk of future 'embarrassments in . . . Cabinet'.[2] In the last resort the Minister's attitude was simple. There were threats demanding a united front, and the coalition represented a great weight of authority in and out of Parliament. He had his close colleagues Grenville and Dundas still at his side in directing strategy. But strategy needed domestic support, and there was an equal need for domestic order.

πὒγον ὀλέγειν εὔχεδθε πολέμον δόρυ
οὐκδυν ταδ ἔδται πρόξ θεῦν αλλ οὖν θεοὺξ
τοὺξ τηξ αλούδηξ ἐκλείπειν λόγοξ [3]

And in that defence the arrangement could form 'the most powerful Government this country ever knew'.[4]

Pitt could rely on himself the more safely because of the calibre of his new colleagues. For the advantages of the Whig accession lay chiefly in the political and the subordinate executive spheres. So far as the Cabinet itself was concerned, Windham seems to have been considered the ablest of the recruits: probably indeed the future leader of 'that set'.[5] Despite his secondary Office[6] he was expected to influence the direction of policy: a prediction that in point of fact was only partly and temporarily fulfilled. For Windham did not prove as effective or formidable as was forecast. A man of high attainments and attractive personality, he was a comparative failure in Government. Starting with almost every advantage – an ample property in Norfolk, riches, good looks, a fine taste and intelligence, an equal facility for sport and letters – he seemed destined for great things. He had indeed refused a first step, as Secretary to the Lord Lieutenant of Ireland, while an undergraduate at Oxford.

1. See p. 181 above.
2. *Diaries and Correspondence of Rose*, I, 194.
3. Pray rather that our wall unshaken stand –
   That helps the gods as well; for while the wall
   Holds, the gods hold, and when it falls they fall
       Aeschylus, *The Seven Against Thebes* (Gilbert Murray's transln.).
4. Burges's description of Pitt's own attitude, and that of his patronage Secretary and confidant Charles Long 'and others', who were 'immoderate in their joy' (9 July 1794; Burges Ms 10).
5. See loc. cit.; *Diaries and Correspondence of Rose*, I, 194.
6. Cf. p. 412, n1 above.

But he did not enter public life at once. The devoted friend of Burke – as of Johnson – but equally happy in his fields and his library, it took the American War to lead him into politics; and his pleasures remained. He did not have to be one of those who endured the dust for the palm. But in any case that was not his real nature. Ambitious as he became, he was also indecisive. He did not genuinely want to lead: he could argue and urge, but he lacked the steel. His best work indeed was as an administrator helping to improve conditions in the army:[1] in the higher issues, through a long career, he more often protested than carried the day. In 1794 his views on the war were undergoing a gradual change, from reliance on the campaign in Flanders to reliance on action through the French royalists. In changing circumstances, in fact, he was a proponent of a continental policy. A growing number of Ministerialists, including Dundas, watched with an increasingly wary eye.

There were two other new Ministers who, like Windham, had not held office before. Unlike Windham, neither aroused high expectations from their former opponents. In one case this proved a mistake; for Spencer emerged as a great First Lord of the Admiralty over six gruelling years. But that lay, if not far, in the future. For the present he was Lord Privy Seal, having steadily declined the frequent offers of Ireland. There was nothing to indicate how he would shape. He seemed a typical Whig peer, landed, cultivated – he formed the collection at Althorp on which the John Rylands Library was built – descended from the great Duke of Marlborough and, more important, connected with the Cavendishes, 'trusty and confidential',[2] apparently unambitious, rather dry. At this time he was thirty-five, almost a year older than Pitt. Windham was forty-four; the third untried newcomer, Fitzwilliam, forty-six.

In this last case the question of experience or abilities did not really arise. Fitzwilliam quite simply was Rockingham's nephew and heir. He owned the rent rolls and the patronage that had underpinned his uncle's leadership: he represented, as much as any one, the tradition of the past thirty years. His influence with Portland, at least since Fox's receded, was greater than that of any other intimate. The high and steady message from Wentworth Woodhouse was received as the milk of Whiggery itself. And so indeed it was, in the Burkeian formulation which Burke himself however had now reinterpreted. Fitzwilliam was one of the sternest critics of Fox's aberrant views, and perhaps the most reluctant of all the Old Whigs to join forces with Pitt. He condemned the former unreservedly and was deeply suspicious of acting with the latter. This devotion to principles long imbibed, in a situation calling for painful thinking, this dislike and distrust of adaptation, were soon to be shown in an important sphere. They were the products of a proud and

---

1. In two spells of office, the second, after the turn of the century, as Secretary of State.
2. Lord Sheffield to Auckland, 30 July 1794 [misprinted 1793] (*A.C.*, III, 223).

honourable nature – an unswerving sense of responsibility – and a pedestrian and simplifying mind. A description by a younger contemporary summed up a type, still evolving, which reached its final flowering in the next century: the independent peer of great property doing his, sometimes reluctant, public duty.

> With little talent and less acquirements, he was, throughout life, one of the most considerable men in the country and a striking instance of that most agreeable truth – that courage and honesty in great situations more than supply the place of policy or talent.[1]

Such a man was quick to suspect too much cleverness by half. Beloved by his friends – it was the loss of Fitzwilliam, 'the person in the world of whom . . . I have the best opinion', that Fox lamented most keenly when the break came –,[2] respected and admired throughout his own countryside, he was ill suited to the one political post he was genuinely prepared to take.

The oldest of the new Ministers, at sixty-six, was Mansfield, a nephew of the great judge, who as Lord Stormont had been an Ambassador, a Secretary of State under North, and Lord President in the Coalition. Sensible, shrewd, a good scholar – Winckelmann thought well of him – rather stiff, rather mean, he was a useful member of the outer Cabinet circle in the two years before he died. Portland himself was now fifty-six. The troubles of the past few years were not those he was best equipped to meet, and he had not cut a very impressive or happy figure. His strength had lain rather in persistent attention to the detail of system and patronage in a position, as First Lord of the Treasury in 1783 and *primus inter pares* with his colleagues since, which was raised as usual on the sure foundation of influence and wealth.[3] In the recent lengthy and troubled sessions at his town mansion of Burlington House he sat embarrassed and indecisive – he 'fell', wrote Malmesbury once, 'into one of those paroxysms of dead Silence so peculiar to him & in which we have so often seen him' – nor was he always able to keep his balance in Parliamentary tactics.[4] Once freed, however, from such constraints he could show some solid virtues. While there was no temptation to exaggerate his talents it was possible to underrate them.

1. Henry Richard Vassall, Lord Holland, *Further Memoirs of the Whig Party (1807–1821)*, ed. Lord Stavordale (1905), 255.

2. To Lord Holland, 18 August 1794 (*Memorials and Correspondence of Charles James Fox*, ed. Lord John Russell, III (1854), 79).

3. Cf. I, 38, 616, 620–1.

4. As on the confused occasion in December 1792 when he passively allowed two flatly contradictory statements of the Whigs' position in relation to support for Government – the adverse one by his own son – to be delivered in the Commons (see p. 229 above). The quotation is in Malmesbury to Gilbert Elliot, 4 December 1793 (N.L.S., Minto Ms IE 65), and see also a similar description a year earlier in Malmesbury's *Diaries and Correspondence*, II, 477–8.

Without any apparent brilliancy [it had been written of his brief period as Lord Lieutenant of Ireland], his understanding is sound and direct, his principles most honourable and his intentions excellent.[1]

This was a fair summing up, which was to be confirmed in his years at the Home Office. Highly conservative and placed in the Department responsible for law and order, he administered his responsibilities with a regard for the first as well as the second. Less vigorous and sharp than his predecessor, his congenital steadiness was valuable: in a period of increasing trouble and repression there might well have been a worse Secretary of State.[2] Within the Cabinet he was loyal and soon worked easily with his former opponents. His standing was shortly to be tested in a peculiarly painful way.

The Ministry could also draw strength in various respects at less exalted levels: at those indeed where it had felt a need for some time.[3] To the very useful Malmesbury and Elliot could now be added other likely men of ability, and one, Thomas Grenville, the great book collector and the only one of three brothers never to have been employed, was given a task and emolument at once. He was sent with Spencer to Vienna – and surely no British mission has ever boasted two more splendid bibliophiles.[4] As a Portland Whig intimate with all parties in the talks, a Grenville, and a clever man,[5] he was an obvious immediate choice. But similar prospects could now be spread more widely through the political world, and over the next few years Government tapped a fuller range.

Meanwhile there was a Cabinet that had to be made to operate. As one Under Secretary put it, the extent of inexperience should be good for men like himself. Some of the new members, 'entirely ignorant of every thing . . . must have recourse to some one for information'.[6] Their education would have to be fostered at once. Certainly Ministers seem to have been called together formally more often than in recent months; undoubtedly in part at least because of the worsening state of the campaign. According to one source there were twenty-two Cabinet meetings in 1793, six from January to the dividing line in 1794 and

---

1. Earl of Buckinghamshire to Rev. Mr Elliot, – 1783 (*H.M.C., Lothian Mss*, 419). Portland had been in Ireland in 1782 (see I, 79).

Cf. for a view of Portland in 1789 as 'an honest man', I, 662 n1.

2. It is not unremarkable, for instance, that when the incessant conspirator John Binns was imprisoned before trial on one of several occasions in the later nineties, Portland, accompanied by his wife and two daughters, paid him a social visit (see E.P. Thompson, op. cit., 19 n2).

3. See p. 408 above.

4. P. 343 above. The Grenville Library may be seen in its glory in its room within the British Library.

5. Eg Sheffield to Auckland, 30 July 1794 (*A.C.*, III, 223).

6. Burges to Anne Burges, 10 July 1794 (Burges Ms 10).

twenty-seven from then to the end of December. The Cabinet dinners on the other hand may have slightly fallen off: by the same account there were twenty-five in 1793, eighteen from January to the change in July and eleven thereafter to the end of the year.[1] There was opportunity for the recruits to learn what was going on, whatever the extent of their contributions to the main business, that of the war.[2] But the 'experiment'[3] was a tender shoot: it could all too easily be chilled. And the new Ministry was only two months old when it had to weather a domestic storm.

Of course there were important differences in outlook between Pitt himself and his new allies. It has been said that they 'did not join a reactionary Government; they rather made it reactionary by joining it':[4] and when one considers the record of the peacetime decade there is a good deal in that view. Pitt's attitudes to administration, to the slave trade, to reform in essence, were not those of the Old Whigs. But there was nothing now on the near horizon to divide them on English or Scottish questions. The main preoccupation there was the same, they agreed on the measures against discontent, and the sharing of posts there had also been decided. Such common ground however, it was soon apparent, did not apply to Ireland; and it was that persistent source of problems which suddenly caused trouble.

This was not, as it happened, because Ireland itself was in an immediately critical state. On the contrary, both the Parliament and the country were comparatively calm. The Catholic Relief Act of 1793 was an expedient rather than an answer, and long-term Anglo-Irish relations had still to be designed.[5] But the measure served for the time being; and some recent signs of conspiracy, linked apparently with England,[6] had been dealt with in the same way. Arrests were made, books and papers seized, in May 1794, and in the summer and autumn things seemed to be under control. The Cabinet crisis stemmed directly from London, not Dublin; as much a legacy of the Whigs' own past and a sign of belief in their current 'equality' as the result of a response to an undoubted but scarcely an instant need.

For Ireland lay close to Whig hearts, particularly to Portland's and Fitzwilliam's. The former's brief spell as Lord Lieutenant had been at a formative time; the latter had been offered the post in 1783, possessed

---

1. Amherst's Diary, vols. I–IV (Amherst Mss, Kent C.A.O.). His record, apparently kept regularly for his own attendances, would not of course necessarily cover every occasion. He seems – but one cannot be entirely sure – to have distinguished carefully between Cabinet meetings and others among Ministers, and likewise in the matter of dinners.

2. This last is discussed in Ch. XIII, section IV below.

3. P. 415 above.

4. Richard Pares, *King George III and the Politicians* (1953), 194. And cf. p. 181 above.

5. See pp. 86n2, 222 above; 424–5 below.

6. P. 395 above.

large Irish estates and (like Portland) Irish family connexions, and above all was the friend and disciple of Burke. This almost proprietary approach was strengthed by the fact that the connexions in both cases were the Ponsonbys, a great clan which had lost out in the political upheaval of '84;[1] and the habitual addiction to 'the old and sleepy game of patronage'[2] may have been further heightened in reaction to the constraints of coalition in England. The disposal of places across the Irish Sea was to fall, it seemed, in the Whigs' Other Island. Its public motive was to service a policy deemed to be essential and to need new men.

Matters came to a head in October 1794. Portland and Fitzwilliam had wasted no time in preparing for the future. In mid-August they invited Thomas Grenville to take the Irish Secretaryship, and later that month they asked Grattan and George Ponsonby, the Irish Whig leaders, to come to London.[3] Appointments and policies were drawn up enthusiastically over the following month. Fitzwilliam's rapid translation to Dublin, armed with measures and men, was eagerly awaited; for the group had agreed that not only Westmorland but also the Lord Chancellor Fitzgibbon would disappear. So too in fact would John Beresford, the other great champion of the Protestant ascendancy and a close adviser of the British Ministry over the past ten years.[4] Fitzwilliam himself was now impatient. It was generally known that he was destined for the post. The understanding indeed had been confirmed in August.[5] When was Westmorland going to come home?

This was not how Pitt interpreted the earlier exchanges. He had thought at first of a Cabinet place for Westmorland – the Duchy of Lancaster if Hawkesbury was promoted – and when that was abandoned he meant to find something that would not smack of dismissal and would satisfy his friend.[6] But he seems to have assumed there was no particular hurry, he did nothing in the next two months, and apparently failed to appreciate that Fitzwilliam insisted on action soon.[7] His awakening was rude. Early in October Portland warned him that

---

1. They included cousins of Portland, while Lady Charlotte Ponsonby was Fitzwilliam's wife.

2. Auckland to John Beresford, 23 October 1794 (*A.C.*, III, 253).

3. Fitzwilliam was later accused of having been responsible for a premature invitation to Dublin, and it was certainly he who sent it, as also that to Thomas Grenville. But as E.A. Smith has shown in *Whig principles and party politics*, 178–80, he did not move at this time without Portland's knowledge and indeed direction. For the invitations themselves see Portland Ms PWF 3769, 3771, and Buckingham, II, 277, 282–3; *Memoirs of . . . Henry Grattan, by . . . his son Henry Grattan*, IV, 173–4.

4. Eg I, 201, 211–12.

5. Smith, op. cit., 179, 213 n7.

6. For the idea of the Cabinet post see Pitt to Portland, 2 July 1794 (Portland Ms PWF 7703), and see p. 411 above; for the friendship, p. 221 above.

7. Pitt to Chatham, 24 September 1794 (P.R.O. 30/8/101) strongly suggests this.

Fitzwilliam's wish was 'no longer to be resisted', and by the 8th the importunate Lord President was threatening to resign.[1] He told his associates in both London and Dublin, and by the 12th the Cabinet was 'upon the brink of Rupture'.[2] Ministers sprang into action, in a state of muddled and often angry alarm.

Portland hoped that the business could be brought to 'a speedy issue': he confided it indeed to Windham for that purpose, as one less intimately involved. But it was not to be so easy. There were already ruffled feelings over Fitzwilliam's broadcast consultations: Westmorland complained, justifiably, that his position was being undermined since his successor's plans were known in Dublin; and when Portland asked Pitt to a dinner to meet Grattan, 'the Ponsonbys and the Grenvilles . . . looked as if they would cut each other's throats'.[3] The Grenvilles indeed could hardly be pleased at the revival of an influence which the head of their family, Buckingham, had opposed while Lord Lieutenant. His objurgations may have had an impact, if a limited one, on his brother William; they were certainly enough to make Thomas in the end decline the offer of the Irish Secretaryship.[4] Dundas for his part was thoroughly roused. 'I have seldom in my lifetime been more astonished'; 'It is abominable swindling'; 'barring the awkwardness of the moment, I know not if you are not better off without them'.[5] The new Ministers for their part, except for Spencer who was in Vienna and would clearly have agreed, were prepared to leave *en bloc* if Fitzwilliam went. Nevertheless, there were some grounds for hope that a way out could be found; 'the awkwardness of the moment' was real, and induced some caution in both parts of the Cabinet. Windham and perhaps Mansfield felt that Fitzwilliam was behaving rashly, Grenville was embarrassed, Loughborough as always ready to mediate. Forces were at work on both sides. But a great deal of explanation was needed if the episode was not to produce a fatal split.

A flurry of activity ensued. Talks were held, letters passed: Grenville even offered to hand over the Foreign Office to Mansfield if the latter did

---

1. Portland to Pitt, 4 October 1794 (P.R.O. 30/8/229); same to Windham, 8 October 1794 (*The Windham Papers*, 256).

2. Portland to Windham, 11 October 1794; Fitzwilliam to same, sd; Mansfield to same, 12 October 1794 (op. cit., 256–9).

3. Westmorland's complaints to Pitt, which became a stream, are in P.R.O. 30/8/331; his retrospective statement of 16 November (printed in *L.G. III*, II, no. 1158, as 'Edward Cooke's Memorandum') is in P.R.O. 30/8/324. The dinner at Portland's is described in *Memoirs of Grattan*, IV, 174–5; it took place 'shortly after' Grattan's arrival. The wording may be partly his son's.

Cf. also, for September, Pepper Arden to Pitt in Holland Rose, II, 341.

4. Cf. I, 43; and for William Grenville see p. 55, n1 below.

5. To Pitt, 13 October 1794 (The Rt Hon. Edward Gibson, Lord Ashbourne, *Pitt, some Chapters of his Life and Times* (1898), 183–4).

not become Lord President.[1] Pitt himself stood firm on the immediate issue. On 15 October he asked Grattan to call, and 'very plain and very civil in his manner' made it clear that Westmorland must be properly provided for. The conversation led him to believe 'the Business more desperate than ever'; but he told Windham the next day that he could not consent to Fitzgibbon being removed or to 'leaving either Him or any of the Supporters of the Government exposed to the Risk of a new System'. He repeated his assurances to Westmorland.[2] At the same time however he wished to be conciliatory about the fuss itself and was prepared to examine the prospects at large. For of course the concentration on the appointments was very largely a symptom. A deeper cause of the dispute lay in questions of policy itself.

This emerged from the talks. Pitt soon concluded that the crisis had arisen from 'Indiscretion' rather than 'any settled Plan', and he was anxious not to 'force' his new colleagues 'to a Breach if it can be avoided, with Honor'. He was lucky to be aided in this by Fitzwilliam's wish to await Spencer's return so that the whole group could have been consulted and resign together.[3] This in fact gave a further three weeks, during which Ministers were co-operating on other pressing matters; and although Grenville thought that 'This Irish subject seems to grow worse instead of better', Fitzwilliam himself, after seeing Pitt probably on 12 November, believed that it was 'now brought . . . nearly to a point'.[4] Westmorland, after some juggling, had been found a dignified billet as Master of the Horse. The way to Dublin in that respect was thus open, and Mansfield's future also clear. Pitt and Grenville – the latter brought firmly to the centre of a business which Dundas disliked – met Fitzwilliam and Spencer on the 14th and advanced far enough for a

1. To Pitt, 11 October 1794 (Stanhope, II, 284–5). His financial prospects would have been secured in that event by the earlier provision for an Auditorship of the Exchequer (see p. 411, n4 above).
  The offer possibly showed a desire to be clear of the issue under competing pressures.
2. Grattan's account printed, with glosses, by his son (*Memoirs of Grattan*, IV, 178–9); Pitt to Grenville, 'Wednesday ½ p 6' (*H.M.C., Dropmore*, III, 17, where it is attributed to February 1795: on the original, in B.L. Add. Ms 58907, the ascription is more reasonably to October 1794); same to Windham, Private, 16 October 1794 (B.L. Add. Ms 37844, and see Stanhope, II, 289); same to Westmorland, endorsed in Pitt's hand 19 October 1794 (P.R.O. 30/8/325, and see *Miscellanies, collected and edited by Earl Stanhope* (1863), 8–12).
3. Pitt to Westmorland as in n2 above; Fitzwilliam to Countess Fitzwilliam, nd, cited in Smith, op. cit., 183; same to Burke, 21 October 1794 (*Correspondence of Burke*, VIII, 59).
4. W.W. to Thomas Grenville, '11 p.m.', endorsed 12 November 1794; Fitzwilliam to same, endorsed 14 November 1794 (B.L. Add. Ms 42058). Fitzwilliam saw Pitt two days before he wrote, and on the 13th the King told the Queen that 'all differences . . . were now made up' and Fitzwilliam would be going to Ireland (*L.C.G. III*, II, no. 1156n5). Spencer and Thomas Grenville reached England on the 8th.
  For Ministers' simultaneous preoccupation with affairs on the continent see pp. 366–74 above.

further meeting the next day. It was held accordingly on the 15th, with Portland and Windham added. By then the understanding seemed to warrant a discussion of 'all the other points . . . respecting Ireland'.[1]

But what exactly the understanding was, it is hard to say. Pitt had made it clear that his Irish supporters were not to be sacrificed to a 'new System' at Fitzwilliam's dictation. He had further laid down, equally clearly, that 'the very Idea of a *new System* (as far as I understand what is meant by that Term) and especially one formed without previous Communication or Concert with the rest of the King's Servants here, or with the Friends of Government in Ireland, is in itself what I feel it utterly impossible to accede to'. This was of the first importance, and he was anxious 'to leave no Part of it liable to be misunderstood'.[2] At the same time he was prepared to consider individual changes that might be agreed.[3] Nor was he so far removed, in principle, from the Whigs' central panacea. They were convinced that nothing short of representation in the Irish Parliament would reconcile the Roman Catholics and remove the persistent fear of subversion. Pitt had never gone as far as that; but he had favoured admittance to the borough (though not the county) franchise before Westmorland and his Secretary Hobart had temporarily closed the door. The Relief Act of 1792 had been an unconvincing attempt to keep things quiet 'for a time'. It did not work, and in February 1793 the Irish Government introduced a much wider measure.[4] Catholics were now granted the Parliamentary franchise on the same qualifications as Protestants, and allowed to hold civil and military posts apart from the higher Offices of state, judgeships and those of king's counsel, high sheriff, and general on the staff. They could

1. Pitt to Portland, 14 November 1794 (Holland Rose, *Pitt and Napoleon*, 28). This, and an account by Fitzwilliam of the meeting of the 15th (Wentworth Woodhouse Muniments, F 29b), establish the dates. Together with a retrospective account of the second meeting by Grenville (*H.M.C., Dropmore*, III, 35–8), it also establishes attendance. Some authorities have ascribed the second conference to a date in December (Holland Rose, *Pitt and Napoleon*, 28; Barnes, *George III and William Pitt*, 340), but the evidence cited in this n. seems to me to favour November.

Dundas's feelings may be inferred from Burke's letter to him of 5 November 1794 (*Correspondence of Burke*, VIII, 72). He had earlier told Loughborough that 'The idea of Lord Fitzwilliam going to Ireland was at all times a bad one' (19 October [1794; misdated 1792]; S.R.O., Melville Castle Ms GD 51/1/17/14), and it seems to me possible that a memorandum starting on much the same lines, and endorsed '1794' in Pitt's papers (P.R.O. 30/8/325), which was attributed to Pitt by Pretyman (B.L. Add. Ms 45107) and by Stanhope (II, 290–1), reflects his colleague's views.

2. To Windham, 16 October 1794, '3.30 p.m.' (B.L. Add. Ms 37844; and see Stanhope, II, 289–90), following up his letter of the same day on p. 423, n2 above.

3. I think this is strongly implied in the papers which survive among Pitt's records, in P.R.O. 30/8/328: Loughborough to Pitt, two letters nd but one endorsed, after the Chancellor had seen Grattan and Burke, 'November 1794' (and see Holland Rose, *Pitt and Napoleon*, 24–7); and Pitt to Westmorland, corrected draft, 19 November 1794. See also Burke to Fitzwilliam, 7 November 1794 (*Correspondence of Burke*, VIII, 74–5).

4. P. 222 above. The new Act was 33 Geo. III, c. 21 in the Irish series.

keep arms on a property qualification, at the lower levels after subscribing to an oath of allegiance; and take degrees in the university in Dublin. Not much, it might therefore seem, remained in practice: only a few Parliamentary seats might be held to be at stake;[1] and Grattan at any rate gained the impression that this further relief would not be contested. Pitt, he is said to have noted, remarked on the question, '*Not to bring it forward as a Government measure, but if Government were pressed*, TO YIELD IT'.[2] Within the context of this alleged observation – the proscription of a sweeping 'new system', prior consultation with London and Ministerial passivity meanwhile – it would not have run counter to feelings he had held, if loosely, for some time. And Fitzwilliam for his part had now apparently been brought to acknowledge that Ireland was not 'a thing separate from the general mass of the King's Government; but . . . to be governed by the same concert, and the same communication of Councils, with which all Business in England had been and would . . . be carried on'.[3] Such statements, if properly understood, promised a reasonable basis for the further meeting that was now to take place.

In the event that meeting was to prove highly important. The more the pity that no proper record was agreed at the time. Two accounts survive: one by Fitzwilliam, based on his notes and stated to have been shown to Pitt 'after' the discussion; the other by William Grenville, written, it would seem, four months later to be approved by all the rest except, by inference, Fitzwilliam himself.[4] Five questions were brought up, four of them affecting appointments. The influential Office of

1. Burke in (probably) September had put them as low as three (to Fitzwilliam, nd; *Correspondence of Burke*, VIII, 21–2).
2. *Memoirs*, IV, 177. One has to qualify Grattan's evidence with the comment that his son, who published it later, was not scrupulous in selection and gloss.
3. Burke's account to Fitzwilliam of his and Grattan's assurances given on Fitzwilliam's behalf to Loughborough (see p. 424, n3 above), 7 November 1794 (*Correspondence of Burke*, VIII, 74).
4. For these two sources see p. 424, n1 above. Fitzwilliam's version was headed 'Heads of a Conversation at Pitts, Novr. 15.1794 – Shewn to him after the conversation – Shewn afterwards to Grattan & the Ponsonbys'. Grenville's, of March 1795, was later stated by himself to be a 'first draft', for in 1799 he made an endorsement on it, 'The corrected copy is interlined with an addition in Mr. Pitt's hand, and a note added by myself, stating its having been communicated to the different persons there mentioned'. This is in P.R.O., H.O. 110/46, ff. 312–19v. It is endorsed as having been shown to Portland, Spencer, Pitt and Windham and 'settled' at a meeting in Grenville's office. One of the *marginalia* suggests that the original conversation 'must have been towards the end of Nov. or the beginning of December', but I have preferred Fitzwilliam's evidence here. Clean copies of the corrected record are to be found in the papers of Lord Camden (Camden Ms 0142A/4; Kent C.A.O.) and Thomas Pelham (B.L. Add. Ms 31118; see p. 439 below). Extracts are printed in Lecky's *A History of Ireland in the Eighteenth Century*, III (1892 edn.), 309–10, and Ashbourne, op. cit., 187–90.
The first draft and the final version in point of fact do not vary greatly. I draw attention on pp. 426–7, 436 below to what I consider to be one important difference.

Provost of Trinity College Dublin, soon likely to be vacant, was to be filled on Fitzwilliam's nomination. His proposal for an Office close to himself for one of the Ponsonbys (William) was vetoed, and another agreed instead. Pitt and Grenville objected likewise to William's brother George Ponsonby's becoming Attorney General, with a view to his being the chief spokesman in the Irish Commons. This would suggest 'a change of system', and he was to be given the secondary post of Solicitor General instead, other rearrangements having been agreed. Fourthly, the abolition of some revenue posts, established in Buckingham's day, was postponed for further study by Fitzwilliam on the spot and, it was 'desired', consultation with London. Finally, after 'mention' of some less important subjects, 'the question of further concession to the Catholics was discussed, though not at much length'. According to Grenville's 'draft',

> The subject was considered as one of much delicacy, and no decided sentiment as to the line which it might ultimately be right to adopt upon it was expressed by any person present. The result of the discussion was an unanimous opinion that Lord Fitz-William should inform himself in Ireland as to the state and disposition of the country in this respect, and should transmit that information with his opinion, to the King's servants here; that he should, as much as possible, endeavour to prevent the agitation of the question during the present session; and that, in all events, he should do nothing in it which might commit the King's Government here or in Ireland without fresh instructions from hence.[1]

A variation should be noted in the final agreed text.[2] After the 'subjects of less importance'

> the conversation turned to the course to be pursued respecting Public Measures, in which it was understood that on all important subjects Lord Fitzwilliam should transmit all the information he could collect with his opinion to the King's servants here, and that He should do nothing to commit The King's Government in such cases without Instructions from hence. It is also distinctly recollected by some of the Persons present that The Catholic Question was particularly mentioned, tho' not discussed at much length, that no decided sentiment was expressed by any one as to the Line which it might be right ultimately to adopt, but that the same general principles beforestated were considered as applying to this as well as to other Questions of importance; and that a strong opinion was stated that Lord

1. *H.M.C., Dropmore*, III, 38.
2. P.R.O., H.O. 100/46, ff. 318v–19.

Fitzwilliam should if possible prevent the agitation of the Question at all during the present Session.

A significant difference of emphasis. It was consultation that was stressed, rather than any specific issue, including the Catholic issue. Fitzwilliam's own notes stated simply, for their part, 'Roman Catholick [question] not to be brought forward by Government, that the discussion of the propriety may be left open'.[1]

The meeting then ended. Fitzwilliam was still not entirely happy. 'I go to Ireland', he wrote three days later, ' – though not exactly upon the terms I had originally thought of', particularly as far as Fitzgibbon was concerned.[2] But he went. The appointment was announced in the second half of December, and on 5 January 1795 the new Lord Lieutenant reached Dublin.

This autumnal episode did not aid the Ministry's consolidation. In other areas – in the main work of government – the new partners were co-operating well. Pitt himself remarked that 'On every other Point, the Conduct of our new Friends has been perfectly cordial and Satisfactory';[3] and in both the preservation of order at home and the conduct of the war there is no evidence of regular division on sectional lines.[4] But the intensity of the crisis over Fitzwilliam, which none of the Cabinet underrated, showed how vulnerable the accord could be. The suspicions lay close to the surface: there had scarcely been time for them to submerge. Shaken and still in parts inexperienced, the Government in the autumn and winter was certainly not emerging as 'the most powerful . . . this country ever knew'.[5]

The consolidation in any case had to evolve over an intrinsically difficult period. The disappointments of the war, above all in the Low Countries, were raising public criticism. The early facile confidence was giving way to as facile grumbling and rumour, and Pitt's own reputation was under something of a cloud. His opponents naturally saw signs of hope: of accessions to their ranks, a turn in public sentiment, even the Minister's supersession.[6] Such reactions may not have meant much; but

---

1. Wentworth Woodhouse Muniments, F 29b. It should be remarked that the brevity of these notes could have rendered them susceptible of the later differing interpretations of the conversation, despite their apparently having been shown to Pitt (p. 425, n4 above).

2. To Burke, 18 November [1794] (*Correspondence of Burke*, VIII, 78).

3. To Westmorland, 19 October 1794 (P.R.O. 30/8/325).

4. For the war cf. Ch. X, sections III, IV above. By December it was even being rumoured – fallaciously – that Dundas was 'inclining' in Cabinet 'to the Portland side' (*Diary of Farington*, I, 276).

5. P. 416 above.

6. Eg Fox to Holland, 25 December 1794 (*Memorials and Correspondence of Fox*, III, 98); same to [Duke of Norfolk], 2 January [1795] (B.L. Add. Ms 47569); Landsdowne's alleged opinion in December (*Diary of Farington*, I, 274).

Pitt's own supporters were not immune. Many were uneasy, and there was a growing feeling that Ministers were out of touch.[1] It was at least partly to counter such signs as Parliament reassembled at the turn of the year that he exchanged Chatham and Spencer.[2] And a few weeks later he moved again, in the military Departments. A comprehensive arrangement emerged, involving two posts and four men, all of whose prospects were in fact already in question. The first was Amherst, the Commander-in-Chief, who was ripe to go. He should retire, and this would have the added benefit of finding something appropriate for York, at last brought home, to the King's displeasure, from his continental command.[3] As a royal Prince – and in Pitt's eyes nothing else – he would not be a member of Cabinet; but as the sovereign's direct military representative he would have an honourable place. The proposed appointment sealed another decision which itself was overdue: to remove Richmond from the Ordnance and the Ministry. For able as he was, the Duke's doubts on strategy and his consequential absence from meetings made him, as he acknowledged (or claimed), 'merely . . . a nominal member of the Cabinet'.[4] He had further disadvantages: marked unpopularity with the public, and now an unwelcome prominence – more prolonged than Pitt's – in the sedition trials.[5] York's new post would be the last straw: the young Commander-in-Chief would have to work with an acerbic colleague and senior General who 'greatly disliked' him, in a Ministry already attacked for defects in communication. There would be a marked 'want of concert'.[6] Everything thus pointed to Richmond's going. It was indeed already under discussion, and at the end of January he was dismissed. He went in a sequence of angry letters, to be replaced by Cornwallis – always favoured by Pitt, and constantly in his thoughts over the past year.[7] By the spring the Cabinet thus looked rather different from that of the previous July; and it endured with only small alterations for the next six years. The changes by and large were in fact to prove successful; some notably so. But the process necessarily imposed some further political – and as it turned out, personal – disturbance at the time.

1. Eg for perhaps extreme examples Baron Hotham to Auckland, 15 November 1794; Auckland to Lord Henry Spencer, 20 November 1794 (*A.C.*, III, 256–8, 261). Cf. Auckland to Pitt, 5 January [endorsed 1795] (P.R.O. 30/8/110).

2. P. 379 above.

3. See pp. 374–5 above.

4. To Pitt, 14 July 1794 (Stanhope Ms S5 03/14). Cf. pp. 293, 374 above.

5. Richmond, unlike Pitt, was called in Hardy's trial as well as Tooke's (p. 398 above); and his evidence in the latter case was subjected to much longer examination.

6. As George III put it to Richmond himself (to Pitt, 29 January 1795; *L.C.G. III*, II, no. 1198). Fox remarked on 'my uncle's great dislike to the Duke of York' in September 1793 (*Correspondence*, III, 50); cf. pp. 287–8 above.

7. See pp. 330–1, 364 above. Richmond's letters in December 1794–January 1795 are printed in *H.M.C., Bathurst*, 706–12; originals, covering February 1795 as well, may be found in Stanhope Ms S5 03/14, P.R.O. 30/8/171. He knew of the possibility as early as mid-December.

Nor did they allay the doubts that had partly occasioned them. Many of these continued to fasten on the fact of the coalition itself. Towards the end of January 1795, shortly before the new appointments were announced, Pitt received one of the bluntest letters in his whole career. It came from the Solicitor General, John Mitford: never, as he remarked of himself, a 'forbearing' man.[1]

> . . . I know not whether truth reaches your ears. If it does, probably this will be only troublesome to you. My situation, & my character, induces men often to speak freely to me, & I therefore frequently hear the most disagreeable assertions with respect to the conduct of H.M. ministers & particularly of yourself. The present state of affairs sours the minds of the best friends of government; & they are particularly affected by observing, as they conceive, a languor in every department . . . They say they . . . did look upon you as a man of spirit & activity . . . They now doubt whether they have justly conceived your character. They say they have seen you, looking about for support, & resting on broken reeds. That you have called to your assistance those who only bring you weakness, who want every moment your protection, & daily consume your good fame; whilst some of them are ruining you by their indiscretion, & others are not unwilling to negotiate with your opponents . . . & [the letter ended after long passages on the conduct of the war] they profess themselves angry to see *you*, as they assert, employed by your colleagues in the pursuit of party, in defending what is indefensible, in negotiating jobs, bargaining for places, hunting for boroughs, & lavishing dignities & honours, instead of preserving the integrity which once distinguished your administration . . .

This missive did not receive an answer. Nothing daunted, Mitford sent another, which showed no reassurance from the fresh appointments.[2]

> . . . the evident difficulty of your present situation, the solitude in which you seem to be placed amongst a throng of cabinet ministers, the ignorance in which I believe most of your friends are with respect both to your real situation & your intentions, & their apparent uncertainty whether you are not acting upon the impulse of the moment because you are unwilling to look at the evil in its full extent, gives me the greatest uneasiness. This . . . is increased by knowing that your conduct of late has turned, some warm friends, into cold friends, or perhaps bitter enemies. . . . Many of them apprehend what they long ago foretold has at length happened; that you are completely surrounded; . . . that you are no longer your own master; & that if you can extricate yourself . . ., you have not a moment to lose . . .

1. 25 January 1795 (P.R.O. 30/8/170).
2. 14 February 1795 (loc. cit.; partly printed in Stanhope, II, 305–6).

Some of this, and the accompanying detail, was, and was later shown to be, wide of the mark. Again it seems not to have drawn a written answer,[1] and Pitt went his own way. If his spirits faltered at times – as they did – he appeared as resilient as ever: 'in very good spirits', 'very hearty', 'very merry', 'undismayed'.[2] Few of his supporters for their part were prepared to follow Wilberforce in opposing his war policy.[3] Nevertheless, Mitford's warnings showed how the land lay. Coming in a period of failure, they revealed a widespread impression, which the Minister himself must try to do something to remove.

IV

One of Mitford's most anguished sentences in his second letter referred to Ireland. 'What has happened to Ireland seems to be generally considered as a death-blow'.[4] He was alluding to the early stages of the major eruption which followed, in London as well as Dublin, within weeks of Fitzwilliam's arrival.

For Fitzwilliam moved fast. Three days after reaching the Castle he dismissed John Beresford, on whom so much had rested, from his post as First Commissioner of the Revenue.[5] A series of other arrangements, some highly controversial, was in train. George Ponsonby was moved towards the Attorney Generalship which had been opposed in London, the incumbent being persuaded to retire voluntarily on offers of the Chief Justiceship for himself and a peerage for his wife. Brother William was to be placed temporarily in the post which Fitzwilliam had earlier proposed as a permanency.[6] And a group of appointments, removals and retirements, the last usually on advantageous terms, surprised and impressed – delighted or angered – beneficiaries, victims and public alike. Dublin buzzed with comment and rumour. Fears and expectancies grew. By the second half of January the Irish Administration was assuming a new look.

Pitt was engaged at this point with 'so many *pressing* things' that he was reluctant to 'interrupt' them 'by renewing the unlucky Subject of

---

1. It does not appear at any rate to have survived in the collections I have read; and Dr R.F. Mullen informs that there is none in Mitford's papers in the Gloucestershire Record Office. Lord Redesdale, as he became, could later find only three letters to himself from Pitt over the years (to Bishop Pretyman-Tomline, 7 May 1820; Pretyman Ms 562: 1820, West Suffolk R.O.).

2. Robert Jenkinson to Hawkesbury, 7 September 1794 (B.L. Loan Ms 72, vol. 53); Canning's diary, November 1794–February 1795 (Canning Ms 29 d ii). Cf. pp. 380–1 above; I, 587, 589.

3. P. 380 above.

4. 14 February 1795 (P.R.O. 30/8/170).

5. Cf. p. 421 above. Beresford was to retain his salary as *douceur*. For the use of the term the Castle for the Irish Government see p. 221, n2. above

6. See p. 426 above.

Ireland'.[1] But he could not entirely ignore it. Portland had not objected to the first arrangements of which he learned, affecting George Ponsonby. But as the list grew in the next fortnight so did the protests. Beresford came over to London. Other dispossessed persons lobbied. Former Lord Lieutenants wrote in; and Ministers themselves were becoming alarmed. On 2 February Portland changed his mind about Ponsonby, and on the 9th Pitt wrote direct.[2] These decisions, he stated bluntly, were 'in contradiction to the ideas which I thought were fully understood among us'. He had not had time to get in touch before on the matter, owing to the weight of business, and he greatly regretted having to do so now when there were 'so many others of a different nature to which all our minds ought to be directed'. By this of course he meant Irish defence, law and order and thus, at one remove, policy. But he knew all too well when he wrote that these had not in fact been ignored.

For Fitzwilliam had by then indeed directed his mind to policy. He had become convinced within ten days of his arrival that discontent was such that 'No time is to be lost'. Administration must be tightened up – which was partly, he answered Pitt, why new hands are needed.[3] But above all the Catholic gentry and monied men must be brought into active co-operation. He wanted to form a Yeomanry, as had been done in England,[4] which they would officer. But such a step, and real support in general, meant removing their most glaring civil disability. Catholics must be eligible to sit in Parliament; that was the key to reduce the tension, and so the number of British garrison troops. He had therefore reached the conclusion, as early as mid-January, that '*not to grant cheerfully* on the part of government all the Catholics wish, will not only be exceedingly impolitick, but *perhaps dangerous*'.[5]

Fitzwilliam went on to say that if he received 'no very peremptory directions to the contrary' he would 'acquiesce with a good grace in the demands'.[6] The occasion for his doing so might come very soon. A new Irish session opened on 22 January, and while the Lord Lieutenant's speech contained no reference to a Relief bill he was making his sentiments clear enough in conversation.[7] His despatch, written on 15 January but held up by bad weather, reached London on the 27th. It was then held up further, at this period of '*pressing* things',[8] for another

---

1. To Windham, 'Friday' [endorsed 16 January 1795], 17 January [endorsed 1795] (B.L. Add. Ms 37844). Some of the pressing things are discussed on pp. 547–8, 560–2 below.
2. Portland to Fitzwilliam, 2 February 1795, with which cf. same to same, 13 January 1795; Pitt to same, 9 February 1795. William Grenville had already expressed worry on 28 January (to same; all in Wentworth Woodhouse Muniments, F31).
3. 14 February 1795 (copy loc. cit., F5).
4. Pp. 401–2 above.
5. To Portland, 15 January 1795; and see also same to same, 10 January 1795 (Wentworth Woodhouse Muniments, F5).
6. 15 January 1795: 'even *the appearance of hesitation* may be mischievous to a degree beyond calculation'.
7. See Smith, op. cit., 196.
8. P. 430 above.

eleven days. This was peculiarly unfortunate. It proved to be unwise. But when the reaction came, delay or no delay, it was predictable. A lead came from the King. For George III erupted, on a subject on which his opinion must carry weight. Such a step, he told Pitt, would be a 'total change of the principles of government', 'overturning the fabric' of the Glorious Revolution. It would not even bring personal benefit to most of the Irish Catholics, who were too poor to qualify for a vote; and the wider consequence must be 'sooner or later to separate the two kingdoms' or lead to fatal change in Great Britain itself. More immediately, it would be highly unpopular here, for while 'persons of rank' might dismiss their religious 'indifference' under the name of 'toleration', 'the bulk of the nation' would not feel like that. The Cabinet, he knew, was going to discuss the question, and he wished it to know his views; but this was one which in any case lay outside its sole determination. 'I cannot conclude without expressing that the subject is beyond the decision of any Cabinet of Ministers.'[1]

Prophetic words; even if the King meant, as seemed possible, that if Ministers wished to send an answer encouraging to Fitzwilliam this should not be done 'without previous concert with the leading men of every order in the State'.[2] He wrote, as he observed, hastily, and the constitutional implications of the phrase were far from clear. But any such concert would of course have to take account of the royal prerogative, and the Cabinet now knew how the monarch felt. The warning would have underwritten, but it can hardly have shaped, its own response. For, particularly after the discussion in November, Ministers could not simply have given Fitzwilliam a free hand. They did in fact what might have been expected: they asked for further information on the likely effects upon 'the present ecclesiastical establishment and the present constitution of the House of Commons'. Meanwhile he was to do all he could to defer the introduction of a bill, and to give no appearance of encouraging those who would bring it in.[3]

The instructions were couched politely: they came after all from Portland as Home Secretary. Fitzwilliam was told that if he could put off a bill he might 'afford the means of doing a greater service to the British Empire' than any since 1688 or 1707. He would give time, by his general administration, for Government's good intentions to be revealed; a better course than urging a bill the long-term effects of which could not be foretold. But in any event the despatch was sent too late. Fitzwilliam had asked Grattan, as the potential mover, to wait until the Cabinet and the King approved the measure; and he wrote to London for advice on

---

1. 6 February 1795 (Stanhope, II, Appendix, xxiii–xxv. The original is in P.R.O. 30/8/103).

2. Ibid.

3. Portland to Fitzwilliam, 8 February 1795 (Wentworth Woodhouse Muniments, F31). Ministers met on the 7th.

10 February. He repeated his own opinion that the question must be 'finally and conclusively settled' by giving the relief. But two days later Grattan asked leave in the Commons to introduce a bill, reserving the details at the Lord Lieutenant's request until the latter gained London's approval. Of this Fitzwilliam seems to have had little doubt.

> I think myself fully authorised to decide for myself upon the subject, but still, considering the extent proposed, I am desirous to have the mode considered in England . . . whilst I hope it is still within my reach to have it limited or modified.

At the same time he requested confirmation of his proposals for George Ponsonby and another appointment.[1]

The impasse, and confusion, were now complete. It was clear that Fitzwilliam knew the contents of the proposed bill, and was doing nothing to delay it. He for his part was unaware, when he wrote, that contrary instructions were on their way. For the pace and hazards of communication again made their impact.[2] Portland's despatch and Pitt's letter[3] reached Dublin only on the 14th. The Lord Lieutenant now knew that the Ministry was not going to support him. He had committed his sympathy to a measure which he was ordered to deprecate and postpone. He replied angrily, and rashly, on the same day. 'I will not be the person so to put it off on the part of Government'. 'If they [his policies] are not such as to entitle me to a cordial & unequivocal support of the Cabinet, recall me: these are not the times for the fate of the Empire to be trifled with'.[4]

The Cabinet agreed. Portland was by now thoroughly worried: indeed he was in an agony as the full sense of the confusion dawned. Two letters, one official, one private, on 16 and 18 February repeated his instructions, relayed his grief, and finally advised Fitzwilliam to give up his post.[5] The Cabinet, 'in the plainest and most direct terms', called on the Lord Lieutenant to 'take the most effectual means in your power to prevent any further proceeding on that Bill' until he was told otherwise. This was the result of a meeting on the 20th.[6] There was another the next day, at which the unhappy but now resolute Home Secretary suggested that Fitzwilliam be brought home. It was bold advice, and doubtless a relief coming from such a quarter, and it may well have been decisive. Portland himself recorded that he 'chose to be the first to give it, and I was, I believe, the only member of the Cabinet who gave it decidedly'.

1. To Portland, 12 February 1795 (loc. cit., F5; quoted in Smith, op. cit., 197).
2. Cf. pp. 241, 317 above.
3. P. 431, n2 above.
4. Wentworth Woodhouse Muniments, F5; first quotation to Portland, second to Pitt.
5. Loc. cit., F31.
6. Ibid, for that date.

The rest concurred, and on 23 February Fitzwilliam was sent notice of recall.[1]

The rights and wrongs of the affair have been argued over the years. Fitzwilliam certainly had causes for complaint. His important despatch of 15 January, containing his intentions, which was received on the 27th, was not considered for another eleven days. Given his strong – his overmastering – feeling of the vital need for speed, he was justified in thinking that he was not being given proper attention. The Irish Parliament was meeting. There was a strong movement for a Catholic Relief bill and a likelihood, he was sure, of its being introduced. When this seemed certain he had asked for postponement while he waited to hear from the Ministry, and thereafter for the omission of detail. Yet he was left in the dark throughout an eventful month, only to learn too late, and as he thought quite unrealistically, that he was to halt a process by then under way. His plans for appointments were likewise not dealt with conclusively for several weeks. Ministers complained, and increasingly, in February; but not until then, and meanwhile he had received no official rebuke.[2]

On these reasonable grounds for grievance, Fitzwilliam was driven to build much more. The Ministry's behaviour in these vital weeks must amount to betrayal. He pointed to two central instances within the context of his brief as he saw it: to the removal of Beresford, and 'the Catholic question' itself. The first, quite simply, had not been specifically mentioned in the conversations before he left London; and this indeed was confirmed by his colleagues in due course. Why then should he not have acted as he wished, particularly since Beresford had appeared to be satisfied with the terms on which he was to go?[3] The Catholic question for its part had been 'mentioned' only briefly, at the end of a long discussion covering other matters. Every one agreed that it was 'not to be brought forward by Government'. It was also appreciated that 'no decided sentiment was expressed . . . as to the Line which it might be right ultimately to adopt'.[4] Fitzwilliam knew that he had therefore to inform the Government of his views, and try to prevent precipitate action in Ireland until its response was known. He had done this: the former on 15 January followed by a request for guidance on 10

1. Ibid, for that date.
2. Grenville's letter towards the end of January (p. 431, n2 above) could not weigh seriously against Portland's initially mild, even favourable, despatch followed by his and Pitt's silence on the subject.
3. He retained the salary of the post (p. 430, n5 above). Grenville's later statement, in both its forms, was clear that his position was not discussed (*H.M.C., Dropmore*, III, 36, 38; P.R.O., H.O. 100/46, ff. 318–v, where the wording differs slightly from *Dropmore*, 36).
4. P. 426 above; note both versions.

Earl Fitzwilliam, *by Henry Edridge*

Earl Spencer, *by Henry Edridge*

February, the latter by an appeal to Grattan and, when that failed, a successful request to omit an immediate announcement of detail. In return he had heard nothing from the Cabinet until late in the month, and then its instructions were followed at once by notice of his dismissal.

Fitzwilliam also felt aggrieved on the vexed subject of his appointments in general. Much had been made of his plan for George Ponsonby; but if this had been vetoed in London it was because it would mean the dismissal of a predecessor, whereas a voluntary retirement (and promotion) had proved possible.[1] William Ponsonby was to be placed temporarily, not permanently, in his post; and other apparently controversial rearrangements had either not been covered by the talks in November or were achieved through inducement and agreement. And all these points, the Lord Lieutenant stressed, must be seen against the background of his mission. For this was not an ordinary, conventional event, in anything like ordinary times. Why, after all, had he accepted? Because he had understood he would be given support and wide discretion in a necessary task. And what was that task? Nothing less than to bring immediate peace to Ireland, through a policy on which, as he put it later,

> by the cheerful and unanimous acquiescence of the Protestants in the earnest desire of the Catholicks, both descriptions should forget all their former differences: . . . should have no quarrel but with republicanism; no enemy, but the common enemy to order . . .

And to effect this an essential preliminary was to ensure 'arrangements of office formed to obtain unanimity, confidence, and co-operation'. If this approach was to be called 'precipitation' he could only answer that the right terms were rather 'expedition and promptitude'.[2]

Pitt and the other Ministers saw the matter in a very different light. Those who had taken part in the talks of mid-November were astonished at what ensued. Maybe Beresford's name had not been raised: in retrospect this reflected on Fitzwilliam, for given his 'assurances . . . that he had not in view the establishment of any new system'[3] he should certainly have warned his colleagues of what he intended in so central a case. Nor was it true to say that Beresford had been satisfied with his compensation. Rather he had acquiesced, and was not slow to make his resentment plain.[4] The arguments for the Ponsonbys were disingenuous: they had been placed precisely where he had been urged not to place them. And while there was a consensus that the Catholic question had

1. P. 431 above.
2. To George III, 22 April 1795 (*L.C.G. III*, II, no. 1243).
3. *H.M.C., Dropmore*, III, 36.
4. Pitt to Fitzwilliam, 9, 21 February 1795 (Wentworth Woodhouse Muniments, F31). The Minister also pointed out that the removal was in fact illegal, since it required 'a direct authority' from the Treasury, under whom the post fell.

435

not been fully discussed there was equally a consensus that – all the more necessarily – no step should be taken without full consultation. To Pitt and the rest Fitzwilliam's requests to Grattan by no means covered the case. He was known to have made his feelings clear: the promoters of a bill were assured of his unofficial sympathy. The points he was raising could not disguise the fact that he had broken the spirit of an understanding; and in this vital instance the letter as well. For the crux of the complaint was stated clearly in the passage of the subsequent record in which Grenville's draft was significantly amplified by others. The essence of it was that 'on all important subjects' Fitzwilliam 'should do nothing to commit The King's Government . . . without Instructions from hence'.[1] And what had happened? He had pursued a headlong course, remodelling his administration as soon as he arrived, and conspicuously failing to make it plain that a Catholic Relief bill must wait.

How had such confusion arisen? Why the contrasting interpretations? They were based on an inherently tricky political situation in London. The talks in mid-November, summing up the terms on which Fitzwilliam went to Ireland, were aimed at saving the Cabinet while preserving conditions thought to be essential. The latter, it was reckoned, were the minimum necessary while the former object was achieved. Room for misunderstanding therefore persisted when there was inducement to suspend awkward points. And this, one may hazard, was increased by the fact that Pitt was giving the problem only intermittent attention. He had been culpably slow to appreciate the strength of Fitzwilliam's sentiments in the late summer. He was absorbed thereafter, in a worsening campaign, with diplomatic and military business. And he does not give the impression of devoting sustained thought to what in any case he may have looked on as an annoying distraction. Grattan is said once to have been told that Pitt 'was a good minister for England, but a bad minister for Ireland'.[2] There was truth in this in the sense that he no longer applied himself to Dublin's affairs more than he had to. There seems to have been a drop in interest, almost a disgust, after the failure of his Irish Propositions; when he now talked of 'the unlucky subject of Ireland' he may have had more than the immediate complication in mind.[3] If one balances his remarks against such a background, he probably did suggest sympathy with the principle of a Relief bill and acknowledge that Government might concede under pressure. Fitzwilliam himself, as well as Grattan, appears certainly to have thought so: 'Your M's Ministers', he told the King later, in a sentence which must have caused disturbance, 'had agreed on the principle of the Bill for quieting the minds of the Catholicks'.[4] Such an

1. See p. 426 above. Again note both versions.
2. By 'a friend'; *Life and Times of Grattan*, IV, 176.
3. Cf. I, 215–16, 663; pp. 430–1 above.
4. *L.C.G. III*, II, no. 1243; and cf. p. 425 above.

attitude was not new: Pitt had long been disposed in that direction. But it was at least equally important to grasp that his Irish tactics varied easily according to advice. In this instance, moreover, his other preoccupations may have led him to underrate the strength of George III's feelings. In all these ways he was probably guilty of misleading men who needed little incentive as to what he would accept as constituting pressure in Dublin. But if this was so – and one may judge that it was – it was mainly because he, with others, in turn let himself be misled as to Fitzwilliam's state of mind.

For if Pitt was careless he was not alone here in misreading the signs. The whole basis of an understanding rested on Fitzwilliam's acceptance of the need to proceed with some precision, with balance if with firmness, and in controversial matters only after reference. It posited a calm if alert approach, and a certain readiness to look and learn. But this was far from the mood in which Fitzwilliam himself faced his task. He had been certain from the previous summer of the only solution: it had been taught him by Burke, and had become his gospel. Seized of its truth, deeply wary of Pitt and of any constraints from that suspect quarter, he was in an excitable and defiant temper when he left.[1] His devotion to principle made him resolved not to be deflected. It also increased his inability, perhaps congenital, to appreciate the subtleties of a delicate discussion. Not for Fitzwilliam a sensitive response to distasteful implications or things left unsaid. He had reluctantly granted that there must be some compromise through limits to his freedom, but he was not well equipped, and did not really wish, to see where the compromises fell. Convinced before he reached Dublin that he must start to act at once, he was ready to hear on arrival that there was no room for delay. Portland was soon sure that he had been completely influenced. 'Do you feel that the Government of Ireland is really in your hands?' There was 'such a concurrence in', 'such a deference to' the views and wishes of Grattan and the Ponsonbys.[2] So there was; but it was not imposed suddenly on an uncertain newcomer. It was part and parcel of the equipment with which Fitzwilliam came.

Given such a frame of mind it is hard to see how an understanding could survive. No precision, no subtlety, no compromise were possible in pursuit of an aim demanding them all. Portland was right when he told Fitzwilliam that he could do great service by a graduated approach.[3] As it was, the collapse of his mission was an unnecessarily dramatic setback. The consequences, like the event, have been argued continually. Was it, as has often been said, a turning-point in Irish history: the abrupt and

1. The excitability may have been heightened, as Dr Mullen has suggested to me, by the fact that his young only son Lord Milton, whom he took with him as his secretary, was ill when they left – and seriously ill by the time they returned.
2. 20 February 1795 (Wentworth Woodhouse Muniments, F31).
3. P. 432 above.

shameful ruin of a policy which could have prevented a long tragic sequel – the insurrection of only three years later and the bitter troubles beyond? Some contingent facts should be borne in mind. The Relief Act of '95 would not have been as extensive as that of '93: it might, as Burke maintained, have proved of symbolic value rather than an immediate measure of substance. Antagonism to British rule in its existing form, or to British rule itself, was not moreover confined to Roman Catholics: the United Irishmen had been founded by a Protestant, and they included members of both denominations. Not all Catholics themselves, by the same token, would necessarily have been reconciled by an Act linked with appeals on law and order to their upper ranks. The radicals were now feeling their strength: becoming more articulate and organised; and they were far from wedded to the Grattan Whigs.[1] Finally, the impact of British commercial policy had still to be taken into account; but Pitt had turned away from that problem after 1785, and he paid little heed when it was raised in the talks in London in 1794.[2] Such considerations may make one cautious about claiming too much for a single measure; as has been said of the affair, 'History does not permit controlled experiments'.[3] But however that may be, two things at any rate can be said. The collapse of Fitzwilliam's mission became a part of the history to which the men of '98 pointed, and was imbedded thereafter in the attitudes of the nineteenth century. In whatever degree, it figured as a cause of the rising intensity of the troubles, and in that sense could claim a high importance. And this was the sadder because the failure came at a point when, for the first time in recent years, there was the prospect of real co-operation in the British Parliament on an Irish issue. The new combination of Ministerial interests could have reduced the area of division, and in this instance the Foxites too would presumably have given support. What might have happened if the King had then dug his heels in, it is hard to say. A sizeable force of peers and MPs would doubtless have rebelled against the Ministry. But if Fitzwilliam had followed the lines of his instructions, as his colleagues had understood them, and the Cabinet had time for a considered review, it is not impossible that a balanced conciliatory policy would have emerged. As it was, the collapse was dramatic, with sombre implications for the middle term. One need not endorse its overriding significance to view the event as anything but a tragedy.

The immediate sequel was bound to be painful. Pitt was, and remained,

---

1. Cf. pp. 424–5, 220–1 above.

2. He was not prepared for a major readjustment while the war was under way; memorandum of conversation between Pitt, Fitzwilliam and Sir John Parnell, 27 November 1794 (P.R.O. 30/8/331).

3. R.B. McDowell, *Ireland in the Age of Imperialism and Revolution 1760–1801* (1979), 458.

furious. Looking back some years later he 'said, that the conduct of Lord Fitzwilliam in Ireland, was the strongest instance of the breach of political Faith, which had ever occurred to him'. The affair made 'a lasting breach' between the two men – not that there had been any real confidence before.[1] For Fitzwilliam himself felt exactly the same about Pitt. He wanted to leave Dublin at once, but had to wait until a successor was found in March; and when he returned, from a city draped in mourning, it was in righteous and outspoken anger. Convinced by then that the Minister had duped his new colleagues to discredit and split the Old Whigs, he cut his former friends[2] and set about stating his case. Two long explanations had already been sent to his old associate Carlisle, which soon escaped into print. Now Burke helped him draft a submission to the King.[3] He made a formal Protest in the Lords, which occasioned debates in both Houses in May; and a final postscript was added in June by a duel with Beresford, whom he had accused of malversation, which fortunately had an amicable ending. This, as Fitzwilliam himself said, marked the end of his Irish administration. Unreconciled but dignified, he resumed his English life.

Meanwhile the Government was looking for a replacement. Pitt soon decided on his close friend John Pratt, now Lord Camden, who was a Junior Lord of the Treasury. He had to use all his powers of persuasion, for Camden did not want to go. But old ties and public need prevailed, and he set out in the course of the month.[4] He took with him as Chief Secretary Thomas Pelham, a 'man of confidence' among the Portland Whigs. They were armed for the 'peculiar circumstances' with a full account of background, and copies of the agreed record of the talks with Fitzwilliam.[5] One of the immediate measures must be to cancel the latter's principal changes of posts; another, to block or defeat the Relief bill now introduced. This last was in fact achieved, not surprisingly, in May. A more difficult task, as the instructions stressed, might be to deal with the 'misrepresentations' and 'unjust inferences' from recent events.

---

1. Pretyman's unpublished chapters of his *Life* of Pitt (B.L. Add. Ms 45107, ch. 18, 52v, 53na). And see his letter to his wife in similar terms, nd but presumably 1795, in Pretyman Ms 435/45.

2. There was a partial exception in Windham, who he felt had tried to bridge the gap. But he was prepared only to acknowledge his greeting 'with a decent openness', in contrast to his treatment of Spencer, *'whose shame was upon his Countenance, and I did nothing to wipe it off'* (see Smith, op. cit., 217n60). More reluctantly, but firmly, he rejected Portland's plea for a reconciliation.

3. See *H.M.C., Carlisle*, 704–11, 713–21; *L.C.G. III*, II, no. 1243. Burke's role appears in his *Correspondence*, VIII, 226–30.

4. His account of Pitt's persuasion, from 5 to 8 March 1795, is in Camden Ms 0102, with a complement in 0103 which suggests that he had been in mind for the post for some time. An initial letter of refusal, nd but endorsed by Pitt 'March 1795', is in P.R.O. 30/8/119.

5. The draft of the former, with corrections in Pitt's hand, is in P.R.O., H.O. 100/46, ff. 301–8v. For the latter see p. 425, n4 above.

The near prospect looked uncertain. But it proved calmer than had been feared. Camden's reports were soon conveying relatively soothing assurances. Troops could be spared, as was badly needed, for duties elsewhere in the summer, and to English eyes at any rate the position seemed broadly under control. Even in May the 'clouds' were thought to be 'dispersing' after the violent 'storm'. In June it was apparently forgotten in both Dublin and London. By August Camden was high in the King's favour – a significant sign.[1] Ministers once more assumed with relief that Ireland was not an urgent issue.

The affair also did a good deal to unite the hitherto uneasy Ministry. With Ireland conveniently out of the way, much embarrassment disappeared. The Portland Whigs could now feel more free to work closely and steadily with Pitt, and their suspicions gradually sank as they entered more deeply into affairs. The storm had perhaps cleared the air more sharply than a milder introduction would have done. It certainly forced the two wings of the Cabinet into greater mutual dependence. And this was just as well. For sterner times lay ahead. The Fitzwilliam episode was scarcely over before a wider threat emerged.

---

1. J[ames] Grenville to Camden, 17 May 1795 (Camden Ms C113); Camden to Dundas, 9 June 1795 (P.R.O., W.O. 1/612); Wilberforce to Camden, 18 June 1795 (Camden Ms C 269/1); Pepper Arden to same, 14 August 1795 (loc. cit., C93). There are letters and reports from Camden to Pitt in P.R.O. 30/8/119, 326. The relief in London was the greater after the hostility shown on his arrival, when he had to be hustled into the Castle by a side door.

CHAPTER XII

Dearth and Discontent

I

In the spring and early summer of 1795 Ministers and their friends were feeling relieved about one important fact. Contrary to their forebodings,[1] the Parliamentary session was broadly under control. Wilberforce's call for peace talks, so distressing to Pitt, had been rejected at the outset – as, not surprisingly, was one by the Foxites – and a renewed effort in May met with little response.[2] The Alliance was in deepening trouble; but there was no slackening of resolve to give it funds.[3] The Act for suspending Habeas Corpus was extended with no difficulty.[4] And Government found ample majorities on a range of other questions, from the financial problems of the Prince of Wales (eventually) to Fitzwilliam's recall itself.[5] Speeches from Opposition were sometimes briefer than expected, the 'spirit of debating' seemed exhausted towards the end,[6] and the Ministry emerged in June less bruised than it had feared.

This did not mean that there was not dissatisfaction in the Commons. Mitford's observations had been made from knowledge, and in the following months he was not alone. 'Our Session,' wrote Pitt's friend Mornington, '. . . was the most unpleasant I ever remember, more ill

1. Pp. 427–8 above.
2. P. 380 above. Wilberforce's amendment to the debate on the Address in December 1794 was defeated by 246 to 73; motions in both Houses to much the same effect by Grey and the Duke of Bedford in January 1795, by 269 to 86 and 88 to 15 respectively; Wilberforce's motion in May by 201 to 86. According to Dundas, the last 'was certainly received with much greater coldness than any of the former discussions' (to Camden, 1 June 1795; Camden Ms C 106/1). Canning on the other hand noted (incorrectly) that, all the same, it was 'the strongest Minority I believe that has yet appeared against the War' (Journal, 26 May 1795; Canning Ms 29 d ii).
   In March Pitt himself found 'Business . . . getting thro' very smoothly' (to Pretyman, 9 March 1795; Pretyman Ms 435/42).
3. These developments are followed in Chs. XIII section III, XIV section I below.
4. See p. 395 above. But with some labour, in a series of debates in January and February.
5. *P.R.*, XL–XLII (1795) *passim*. In one case, that of the treatment of Sir Charles Grey and Sir John Jervis, the commanders in the West Indies (see pp. 357–8 above), the attack was beaten off with Opposition's help.
   The Prince's affairs were awkward, and the Ministry had to modify its first intentions in order to ward off trouble from its own supporters.
6. The phrase comes from Canning's Journal for 28 May (Canning Ms 29 d ii).

temper of all sorts floating in the House', with a desire for 'an honorable peace'.[1] His impression was not always shared by others looking at the division figures.[2] But, as so often, those were not the full answer. They were the products of the junction with the Portland Whigs, in circumstances which by their uncertainty favoured a resolute show of support. It was the very fact that the war was thought to be in a state of fine balance, and that there were causes for growing anxiety at home, that entered into the normal patterns of voting and, on the basis of the coalition, steadied the ranks. The enlarged Ministry must be upheld. No alternative was in sight. Pitt himself remained the obvious, the necessary, leader. These were compelling incentives to display a 'common principle of action' among old supporters who were growing 'less cordial'[3] and allies recruited solely by events.

The need for firmess and unity was clear after the session ended. For the most familiar cause of social unrest was by then present once more. The effects of war on an economy are seldom easy to measure – quite as much for the short as for the longer term – and it would be rash to try to do so at all exactly in this case. Some features however can be discerned at the end of the first two years, if sometimes only dimly through the indices and figures. Both the volume and the balance of overseas trade had recovered from its sudden depression – which, as Pitt repeatedly claimed, had itself not been due in essence to the war.[4] In 1794 exports regained the level of 1791, re-exports almost doubled that rate, and the balance was almost as favourable as in the boom year of '92. Associated undertakings likewise responded, both to opportunity and to damage. Ports, dockyards and shipyards were busy, for naval and military and commercial needs; the shipyards in part to replace losses from a *guerre de course*.[5] Production was sustained or increased in a range of important sectors: in textiles – particularly cottons –, paper, tanning, glass, pig iron, to take some known figures. Transport continued to attract investment: more indeed was put into canals and river 'navigation' than ever before. The number of patents again rose, slightly, and bankruptcies fell sharply. Judged by the criteria of specie reserves, interest rates and rates of foreign exchange, the period from mid–1793 to mid–1795 was one of vigorous if uneven activity.[6]

1. Cf. pp. 429–30 above; Mornington to Camden, 22 July 1795 (Camden Ms C 121/1).

2. Eg Auckland to Gilbert Elliot, 2 April 1795: 'We are stout and victorious in Parliament' (N.L.S., Minto Ms 11105).

3. Mornington to Camden (n1 above).

4. Speeches of 30 April, 17 June 1793, 5 February, 6 March 1794 (*P.R.*, XXXV, 339–40; op. cit., 678, 680; XXXVII, 312; op. cit., 496). Cf. his remark, according to one report, on 11 March 1793: 'Experience had taught, that commerce could flourish during war' (*The Senator*, VI, 473). And see pp. 385–7 above.

5. For which see pp. 500–1 below.

6. Figures are given in Gayer, Rostow, Schwartz, *The Growth and Fluctuation of the British Economy, 1790–1850* . . ., II, Mitchell and Deane, *Abstract of British Historical Statistics*, Ralph Davis, *The Industrial Revolution and British Overseas Trade* (1979), and Sheila Marriner as in p. 386, n2 above. They differ to some extent, but the patterns are much the same. Cf. Ashton, *Economic Fluctuations in England 1700–1800*, 169.

The unevenness should not be ignored. Not all areas of the economy were doing well; and those that were contained plenty of exceptions under wartime conditions. Seaborne trade itself was subject to loss, delay and inconvenience – the latter partly from the convoy system which was shipping's best protection, all three from the privateers raiding coastal, and West Indian, waters.[1] Not every one would recognise his situation from a national or regional graph. And there were sectors in temporary decline. Perhaps the most significant of these lay in the brick industry, where there was a marked fall in production from 1793 to '94 and again to '95.[2] As the main constituent of housebuilding this was important, though the explanation may lie largely in the exceptional activity of the past few years followed by caution after the ensuing credit crisis – and perhaps, a little later, by rising interest rates. It was one of the elements that limited but was far from halting a process which economic historians have seen as the 'recovery' or 'upswing' of 1794–6.

One of the sharpest indications of the decline in brick production – and a fall in demand for glass and cotton goods as well – occurred however in one well-marked period, the spring and summer of 1795. And this points to the influence of a basic element of the economy which was then far from sharing the fortunes of so much other industry and trade. For the largest industry in the country was agriculture. The results of the harvests were always pervasive; and while of course there were different harvests, whose crops could differ widely – with varying impacts on animal husbandry – the yardstick, economically and socially, was corn. The early war years were unlucky here, for a poor corn harvest in 1792, which had led to a great rise in the import of wheat, was followed by a disappointing aggregate yield in 1794 and then by one of the severest winters on record. There was already a shortage of wheaten flour early in 1795. It stood no chance of recovery in what was to prove a disastrous year.

Such fluctuations were naturally familiar. The eighties themselves had witnessed deficits, followed by surpluses, followed in '89–'90 by deficits again.[3] It was the country's misfortune that the first decade of these long wars saw a series of harvests which, interrupted but far too frequent, stamped it as one of dearth. With exceptions in 1796–8 they varied in fact from moderate to appalling, causing crises in supplies of cereals, sometimes of livestock and, in a period of continued rising population, above all in the subsistence diet of bread. The effects on prices were all too visible, and wheat in particular, now the staple ingredient in the most basic of foods, entered on a new range. Seldom costing more than 50 shillings a quarter from 1784 to '94, it then never fell below that figure until 1849. The first dramatic rise came in 1795–6, from some 52 shillings in 1794 to some 75 and then to over 78. There had

---

1. This is discussed on pp. 501–2 below.
2. Mitchell and Deane, op. cit., Ch. IX, table 1.
3. See p. 92 above.

never been an increase of this magnitude, in the tables of the past two hundred years. But the combination of factors was itself unprecedented: one of the hardest winters of the century, which unlike the other two notorious occasions in 1709 and 1740 followed on an existing deficiency, for a population which had increased in the interval and moreover become largely accustomed to the wheaten, rather than the rye or barley, loaf.[1] To those in the lower ranges of society, and inescapably to the poor, this overmastering fact was far more important than – to many made nonsense of – the graphs of 'upswing'. To those in authority, local and national, the historical consequences were not encouraging. If the past was anything to go by, such a phenomenon was bound to cause trouble.

It certainly undermined the aims of policy as embodied in the latest Corn Laws. The Act of 1791 had been intended, in a changing balance of import and export, to secure the support of domestic production in face of rising overseas supplies which by various devices were evading the stipulations of a run of recent statutes.[2] Against a growing demand for cheap food by freer trade, mounted by the midland and northern towns, it endeavoured to reinforce the old framework combining agricultural protection with reasonable prices. In a repeal of a long series of statutes, from 1663 to 1789, the level of the price at which corn could be exported was raised from 44 to 46 shillings a quarter, the former bounty of five shillings a quarter being continued at the lower price, and duties on imports were charged at a rate of 24s 3d on entry prices below 50 shillings, 2s 6d on those between 50 and 54, and 6d on those above the last figure. A preference was introduced on supplies from Ireland and British North America, setting the same duties 2s lower at the intermediate price levels in each case. The machinery of administration, amended by Acts of 1781 and 1789, was further modified on the basis of the latter.[3] These regulations were not unreasonable for conditions at the time. But they were very soon overtaken by events. The onset of war and of so many poor harvests placed them under excessive pressure; particularly of a war in which seaborne trade was controlled strictly from the start. For the Government was doubly reluctant to allow export of corn when much of it might go, one way or another, to France; restricting food supplies to the enemy was now indeed deemed to be a

---

1. See eg Donald Grove Barnes, *A History of the English Corn Laws from 1660–1846* (1930), Appendix B, and 72. Of course the price could vary locally, and also sharply within the year: in 1795 it rose indeed in places at one time to over 100 shillings.

These considerations apply particularly to England – and particularly southern and midland England – and Wales. In much of the north and of course in Scotland oats continued substantially to meet Dr Johnson's definition.

2. See pp. 43–4 above; Barnes, op. cit., Ch. IV.

3. Op cit., 59, 66–7. The Act was 31 Geo. III, c. 30. It included regulations similar in principle for trade in rye, barley, beer and oats. For the term British North America see I, 354 n4.

weapon of war.[1] This policy however, it might almost be said, 'came nearer to starving England than France.'[2] Merchants, upset by the uncertainties, drew in their horns all round, and this, combined with the scale of the enemy's own purchases in other countries, ensured that British domestic shortages were not filled adequately by imports. All these circumstances bore hard on the new attempt to keep supplies and prices in harness. The old measure of temporary prohibition of exports was applied in the winter of 1792, a result of the poor harvest as well as a precaution against the French.[3] Fresh amendments to the methods of determining import prices – long a thorny problem – were made in 1793. And in 1794 imports were allowed in duty free; another old expedient in time of shortage which pointed the limitations of the latest remedies.[4]

The crisis of 1795 thus fell on a system which embodied an uncertain approach. There were inner contradictions, which could scarcely be resolved quickly under stress. For the combination of measures accepted in practice reflected an uneasy mixture of attitudes deriving from a range of theories and traditions. After the easier decades in the first half of the century – a period broadly of better harvests and rising real wages – the problem was recognised as one of great importance. Adam Smith himself had summed it up, in a long 'Digression on the Corn Trade' embedded in *The Wealth of Nations*.

> The laws concerning corn may every where be compared to the laws concerning religion. The people feel themselves so much interested in what relates either to their subsistence in this life, or to their happiness in a life to come, that government must yield to their prejudices, and, in order to preserve the public tranquillity, establish that system which they approve of

– and which was therefore unlikely to be a 'reasonable system'.[5] In many ways he was right. Pragmatic caution, religious principle, ancient assumptions of a 'moral economy', more recent aspirations of 'benevolence', combined to weigh on the authors and agents of policy with sufficient force to make them in some degree 'prisoners of the people'.[6]

1. A policy treated at greater length in Ch. XIII, section II below.
2. Barnes, op. cit., 76.
3. See pp. 154, 238 above.
4. Effected respectively by Order in Council (and reinforced a few months later by 33 Geo. III, c. 3); 33 Geo. III, c. 65; Order in Council.
5. Bk IV, Ch. V,b (ed. R.H. Campbell and A.S. Skinner, I (1976), 539). I owe this reference to Professor Daniel A. Baugh, in an unpublished paper, 'Whose "Moral Economy"? Friends and Foes of the Free Market in the Speenhamland Era' (1978), to which I am much indebted.
6. The phrase is E.P. Thompson's, used of supporters among the upper ranks of the concept or assumption of a 'moral economy' (*Past and Present*, No. 50, see p. 102, n2 above).

The people themselves however in this instance should probably be broadly defined. There were identities as well as contrasts of feeling through the range of ranks and denominations; a good deal of common ground among men who in practice recognised similar limits. Equally there were very great differences in theories of treatment, some of which bore on practice in an opposite direction. The current orthodoxy in the eighties and nineties was that of Smith himself; or rather of those elements in an eclectic philosophy which were generally taken as forming its core.[1] One of the most forthright exponents of the doctrine was Burke, in a pamphlet addressed to this very crisis: 'Of all things, an indiscreet tampering with the trade of provisions is the most dangerous, and it is always worst in the time when men are most disposed to it: that is, in the time of scarcity'.[2] It was no kindness to interfere with the operations of a free market. High food prices, however serious – and precisely because of – their temporary effects, were in point of fact the latter's best remedy. Rationing by cost promoted conservation of current supplies; a good level of return was the surest inducement to future increase. This was a lesson it might be hard to swallow in the midst of shortage. But, as the master had shown, historical experience pointed to its truth.

The logic was not accepted universally. Older modes of feeling and thought were not dead; and there were also reservations among some political economists who were not convinced that a principle acknowledged as applying to normal fluctuations was necessarily suited to a wartime emergency. But these last were scattered, they were individually uninfluential, and had little apparent effect on the proclaimed arguments of leading politicians.[3] For there was a remarkable consensus among the latter, on both sides of the current divide, from men who prided themselves on being abreast of the latest thought. The central thrust of *The Wealth of Nations* was all the more welcome perhaps in such quarters for providing theoretical support to administrative limits well recognised by those concerned.[4] Acclaimed from the start, it had been swiftly embedded in classical whig doctrine, and its basic tenets, so interpreted, would not be lightly overturned. Among the party Whigs themselves, Fox could not agree to 'coercion' in the grain market – or others – and Portland similarly, and unwaveringly, was wedded to a self-regulating trade.[5] The strength of his

1. For Smith as '*the* great eclectic' cf. I, 512.

2. Opening sentence of *Thoughts and Details on Scarcity, Originally Presented to the Right Hon. William Pitt, in the Month of November, 1795* (1795).

3. The names for instance of David Davies, John Howlett and John Vancouver, all of whom published on such lines in 1795–7, were not prominent at the time and have not figured prominently since.

4. Cf. p. 155 above.

5. Fox's speech in the Commons of 2 November 1795 (*P.R.*, XLIII, 73). On Portland see Thompson, loc. cit., 129–31; Baugh, loc. cit., agrees in stressing the Duke's 'implicit' and enduring faith in the doctrine.

commitment indeed was perhaps exceptional within the Government; but held as it was by the Home Secretary, the Minister most concerned, it carried weight and represented the official response. Pitt himself had shown – or so it seemed to a close colleague – a similar approach in an earlier shortage, and his most explicit statement in the current crisis repeated principles distilled from 'the most celebrated writers upon political oeconomy, and the experience of those states where arts had flourished the most'. Their agreement made it

> unnecessary to argue the general expediency of any Legislative interference . . . [but] only to inquire, therefore, whether the present case was strong enough for the exception. . . . It was indeed the most absurd bigotry in asserting the general principle, to exclude the exception; but trade, industry and barter would always find their own level, and be impeded by regulations which violated their natural operation, and deranged their proper effect.[1]

This pronouncement had a significant context. It was made at a point when Pitt was abandoning, in answer to Parliamentary objections, a responsibility for handling the import of wheat which Government had assumed earlier;[2] and, of equal and complementary importance, his words were addressed not to the question of prices themselves but to that of agricultural wages.[3] As such they fitted neatly into current teaching. For if ceilings on prices were not to be set directly by central decree – if policy was confined to influencing a free market by restrictions and guarantees through the ports – the remedies, or palliatives, must be sought elsewhere; and it was here in fact that a wider admixture of attitudes and policies was brought to bear. This was certainly so with Pitt himself, accustomed to taking elements of Smithian doctrine in the extensive, irregular area of Governmental choice.[4] As the crisis deepened, so did his awareness of the problems. And it ended by focusing not on detailed price regulation but on relief: of supplies by schemes of limitation and substitution, and of consumption by an added plan of Poor Relief.

There had been developments, in thought and legislation, affecting this last problem in turn. It was natural enough that this should have

1. Speech of 12 February 1796 (*P.R.*, XLIV, 23; and see pp. 154–5 above). Cf. his suggestive remarks three months before in *P.R.*, XLIII, 76. And in June 1795, referring specifically to the price of bread, he remarked that if local levels were set by magistrates 'too low, tho they will give temporary Relief & Satisfaction, they will ultimately encrease the Mischief' by preventing reduced consumption in a shortage (to Pretyman, 29 June 1795; Pretyman Ms 435/42).

For Dundas's suspicions of his attitude in 1792 see p. 154 above.

2. This is discussed on pp. 464–6 below.

3. The occasion of the debate was 'Mr. Whitbread's Bill to regulate the Wages of Labourers in Husbandry'.

4. Cf. I, Ch. XVI, sections II–VI and particularly 511–12.

been so. The Poor Laws, held in the frame of Elizabethan and Carolean tenets, amounted to a system of social welfare which was coming increasingly under strain. Rising population and mobility of labour, dawning signs of wider movements in prices – the indications of a changing economy – were bound to bring their pressures. Since broadly the middle of the century questions had been raised of the two main elements, the laws of settlement of paupers and the organisation for indoor workhouse relief. The foundations had not been shifted – as they were not to be shifted for another forty years – and much of the discussion itself was not new. The Acts of Settlement in particular, enabling a parish to remove indigent entrants to their places of origin, had long been criticised. But the debate was taking some altered forms, and these had coalesced recently to produce one significant legislative expression. 'Gilbert's Act' of 1782, introduced largely to improve the management of workhouses, also marked a reversal of the trend favouring maintenance and employment in those institutions. Its chief thrust allowed, in fact encouraged, parishes to give outdoor relief, and not only in time of accident or sickness but indefinitely to the 'orderly and industrious poor'. The measure – and its easy acceptance – reflected a range of influences on an attitude which here in any case would rather permit than dictate: dissatisfaction with workhouse costs and efficiency, which a run of poor harvests had now underlined, increasingly articulate economic reasons for aiding the deserving poor, combined with the wider tide of benevolence now lapping into Parliament itself.[1] When further bad harvests came in the nineties both attitudes and methods were thus rather mixed. There were the old provisions for local resettlement. There was a network of workhouse relief. There was also sanction for an alternative which distinguished the deserving from the undeserving and transferred the burden again more directly and visibly to the parish itself.

All this was on the statute book. But even where the directions were clearly pointed that did not mean that practice had been uniform. On the contrary, the very principle of the statutes, that responsibility lay with the parish, meant that 'System' was never more than 'a portmanteau word'.[2] The intense diversity of local life within the national identity was nowhere more clearly visible in fact than in the matter of poor relief. One must not dismiss the common denominators. The doctrines informing a long series of Acts moulded, as they drew on, local habits: if there was a patchwork of responses, autonomy had its limits. It is probably excessive to see 'only a casual connection' between the laws and what happened on the ground. But it is certainly true that 'to

---

1. The influences behind Gilbert's proposals, maturing over several decades, are discussed in A.W. Coats, 'Economic Thought and Poor Law Policy in the Eighteenth Century'; *Ec.H.R.*, 2nd ser., XIII, no. 1. The Act was 22 Geo. III, c. 83.
2. J.D. Marshall, *The Old Poor Law, 1795–1834* (1968), 10.

understand the old Poor Law it is necessary to concentrate on administration rather than on legislation'.[1] Parish officers had always adapted the Act of Settlement and Removal to their circumstances: they were often reluctant to incur the expense, or impose the hardship, of rapid ejection. Some kept a close eye on their workhouses and preferred to manage them themselves; many opted for the institutions, proliferating under private Acts, which tended to cover more than one parish under contract. There was harshness, there was kindliness, and, one may guess, there was much indifference within a legislative approach that limited mobility, tried to discourage 'pauper' marriages, penalised the resulting immorality, and for better for worse made the ratepayer, and where relevant the magistrate, the arbiter. For the legislation was not only subject to a wide spectrum of response: of enforcement or avoidance, supplementation or restriction. It was itself, as its complexity suggested, the product, in large measure the codification, of practices already being followed within the country at large. Parishes were building workhouses increasingly before the encouragement of the Workhouse Test Act of 1723. Some were developing forms of outdoor relief, themselves deriving from the past, before Gilbert's Act of 1782. The very volume of the statutes comprising the old Poor Law pointed to the impact of local examples on a body of central doctrine which, conservative in essence and by now haphazard in detail, embraced a choice of their experiences in a policy designed to contain and to guide.

The correlation was shown once more in 1795. For as the shortage of flour began to bite, local authorities began to act, and to produce an expedient which not only spread selectively through parts of the country but, perhaps more notably, influenced theory until the old Poor Laws were at length repealed. It was in May of that year that the magistrates of Berkshire, meeting at Speenhamland by Newbury, made the regulations for poor relief which became known nationally by that name. While not in point of fact quite the first of a crop of similar provisions, they soon passed into the language as a means of combating pressing need.[2] The aim was to provide a scale of allowances in aid of wages, proportioned by the price of bread and the amounts determined by the number of a man's dependants. With a gallon loaf costing one shilling, and relief rising with each extra penny to a cost of two shillings, a single man would be guaranteed a minimum weekly income of three shillings with a further 1s 6d for each dependant; at the upper level of cost the respective sums would be five shillings and 2s 6d. These calculations were founded on the premise that one-third of a labourer's

1. The second quotation is from Dorothy Marshall, 'The Old Poor Law, 1662–1795' (*Ec.H.R.*, VIII, no. 1, 38); the first from the Webbs (*English Poor Law History*, Part I (1927), 149).

2. The Speenhamland meeting followed the county Quarter Sessions of April. Almost identical rules had been drawn up in their January Sessions by the magistrates of Berkshire and of Oxfordshire.

income was spent on bread; and in practice the allowance was
sometimes made – as customarily by charities – in kind: in flour itself. An
alternative would have been to raise the agricultural wage. But the
justices, while 'recommending' farmers to do this 'in proportion' to the
price of food, resolved that it was 'inexpedient to grant . . . assistance by
regulating Wages'; a conclusion shared by Pitt.[1] Speenhamland thus
married a system of parish relief to prevalent economic doctrine in the
face of an unprecedented threat to subsistence.

The occasion was not without precedent. Apart from the almost
simultaneous plans in neighbouring counties, there had been something
of the kind in Dorset in 1792, and the origin of Speenhamland itself
probably lay in a scheme worked out by a Berkshire magistrate in –
curiously enough – the bumper year 1791.[2] Since Elizabethan times
many parishes had given support as they deemed proper in times of
emergency; and the more highly articulated system of 1795 was
intended to deal with a temporary crisis. It had its roots in tradition. But
its fame, and the pace of its selective adoption, showed not only the
impact of the latest shortage but the scale of the rising discontent.

II

For the summer witnessed a spate of protests at the price of bread, from
appeals for help from Government to full-blown riots. Taking the
numbers of these last, through reports to the Privy Council and
mentions in some London newspapers, there was one in March, one in
April, nine in July and perhaps six in August (when prices rose most
steeply), and another four over the next three months.[3] But these were
occasions identified strictly with the one object – they did not include for
instance a serious outbreak in Sheffield in August in which two men were
killed[4] – and riots in any case, involving the magistrates and even troops,
were the tips of an iceberg. Other lesser but deeply felt action was not
necessarily dignified by the term. There were smaller demonstrations,
attacks on individual targets – in Birmingham a large flour mill was
burned – and forcible detentions of grain in transit to other areas. On the
same basis of computation, eight of these stoppages occurred in July and
three over the next three months; and, if concentrated more in the

1. The Speenhamland Minutes are printed in, *inter alia*, *English Historical Documents*,
XI, ed. Aspinall and Smith, 414–15. Cf. p. 447 above for Pitt's statement of the general
argument.
2. See Mark D. Neuman, 'A suggestion regarding the origin of the Speenhamland
plan' (*E.H.R.*, LXXXIV, No. CCCXXI), 317–21; and cf. p. 92, n5 above.
3. Walter M. Stern, 'The Bread Crisis in Britain, 1795–6' (*Economica, New Series*,
XXXI, No. 122), 169, 172. There were three more in March and one in April 1796.
4. And which may possibly have originated in a plan to seize stocks of corn, flour and
bread; see Goodwin, *The Friends of Liberty*, 382.

producing regions, like the riots they were widely spread.[1] The appeals themselves flooded in to Government: nine in June, 55 in July, 34 in August, three in November–December.[2] In intensity and range it all added up to an exceptionally fierce wave of unrest.

Such a phenomenon was worrying to magistrates and Ministers alike. The latter had to take it in a wider context. They were particularly alert to one potential danger of which a few instances emerged: discontent, or even rioting, among the troops themselves. There was in fact little trouble from the regulars; now contained more fully in barracks. But there were some disturbing incidents in the militia, of which the worst were a two-day 'rampage' in Oxfordshire and seizures of corn and flour in two Sussex coastal towns.[3] No great threat in point of fact developed. But Government was watchful of military forces for which greater numbers were now required, in which service broadly speaking was unpopular, and whose sympathies might be affected by the spreading hardship that was aiding enlistment on the one hand and surrounding part-time soldiers on the other. The detestation of anything smacking of compulsion for the army itself had indeed been amply demonstrated over the past months. A series of riots, some particularly ferocious, had been taking place since the previous summer against the activities of the crimps – the civilian agents hired by the military to deliver 'voluntary' recruits. An incident in which a young man died while trying to escape their attentions led to several days of violence in London in August 1794, and similar trouble lasted intermittently into the middle of 1795. Service in the militia was also widely avoided where possible.[4] While Volunteers were now available, there was thus reason in an anxious year to keep an eye on any hint of disaffection from the customary means of defence.

For the Ministry had to take the food riots along with other causes for discontent. A shortage of bread might always be *sui generis* in rousing violent fears and passions; but it stood out now against a background of general inflation and a frustrating war. Figures of prices are hard to determine, even as an average; but by the end of 1795 the cost of living may have risen broadly by some 30 per cent since 1790, the rate of increase perhaps doubling from 1793. Many foodstuffs were rising fast: cattle sold at Smithfield for over 20 per cent more than in 1794, and sugar increased by some eight per cent. Other articles were also more expensive; cottons in particular by some ten per cent. And while not all of course were necessities – though meat was eaten widely down the social scale – the burdens were felt by others than the very poor. Wages

1. Ibid. The areas most affected in this way were Oxford-Wales and Northamptonshire-East Anglia. The riots covered places throughout the country, villages as well as towns.
2. And one in January 1796; Stern, loc. cit., 171.
3. Loc. cit., 172; Emsley, 'Public Order in England 1790–1801', 295–6. For the barracks see p. 195 above.
4. See Emsley, loc. cit., 194–202; p. 158 above.

too had been broadly on the increase: in agriculture itself by an aggregate (with some marked regional exceptions) of perhaps 11 per cent in the past five years. But this could not compensate at the bottom for the price, and sheer scarcity, of the loaf, and in a society where the structure of labour was characterised largely by underemployment the gains were also being threatened, increasingly sharply, across a wider range.[1]

These were serious facts to be weighed with a buoyant industry and overseas trade. And they had to be seen at a time of rising taxation and military disappointment. The former in point of fact was modest – the main financing of the war was effected mainly through loans, not current revenue – but it took a wide variety of forms, falling on the 'luxuries' of the middle and upper orders, and any increase in tax, however slight, was always vociferously remarked. The latter was felt particularly strongly from the summer onwards, and Government, having been fortunate in the earlier Parliamentary session, had to endure the effects at the point of sharpest economic distress.[2] The combination tended to affect most strongly those elements not affected by distress itself: those with higher standards of living, and interested most keenly in the course of the war. It spread the scepticism and irritation already voiced at the start of the year among articulate critics and supporters alike, and the Ministry was increasingly conscious in the long recess that if its continuation was broadly accepted its reputation was on the ebb.

It was thus in an atmosphere, as far as the dearth and the war itself were concerned, compounded at different levels of fear, confusion and widening doubt, that Government faced its culminating threat, a fresh wave of radical defiance. For the check to 'subversion' after the trials of 1794[3] could not survive the onset of hardship and popular anger. The graph of radicalism did not always coincide with that of popular unrest. The two phenomena had distinctive conditions and aims and could follow separate courses.[4] But the second half of 1795 saw the biggest explosion so far of political and economic protest combined: one with a greater economic content than in '92 or '94 – and, more markedly,

---

1. Cf. pp. 98–9 above for structural underemployment. The whole subject of prices and real and money wages remains of course a thorny one – not surprisingly, given the unreliability of so much of the data apart from anything else. It has attracted and will doubtless continue to attract a literature of its own. For some figures – a judicious selection from earlier work – see Mitchell and Deane, op. cit., Ch. XII, tables 2, 3, 5, 6.

2. The two subjects are followed in Chs. XIII section III, and XIV *passim* below. See p. 450 above for the particular steepness of the rise in bread prices in July and August.

Petitions in favour of peace began to come in from northern towns early in the year (Austin Mitchell, 'Radicalism and Repression in the North of England, 1791–1797', 357). But they were not very numerous or weighty at that time.

3. See pp. 401–2 above.

4. Cf. Chs. III–V above.

covering areas of the countryside as well as the towns[1] – and a political challenge, formulated then, unknown to earlier decades. It was a tense, a traumatic, period. It shook Ministers and tested their nerve. It looked to Pitt at one point like revolution. It drew a strong response.

This experience could not necessarily have been predicted earlier in the year. The radicals' discouragement following the treason trials persisted into the spring. The SCI effectively disappeared, the LCS remained weakened by resignations and dissension, the provincial Societies, likewise disheartened, ceased to correspond closely with London. The retrogression proved in due course to have fostered fresh development, for as old leaders disappeared new emerged – John Gale Jones, John Binns, Francis Place.[2] But that was of prospective rather than immediate interest. In June the Ministry felt confident enough to lift the suspension of the Habeas Corpus Act.[3]

Once more however its relief was temporary.[4] As distress grew and spread in the summer, so did the revival of political dissent. Two new features moreover appeared, one at least of which was highly significant. Thelwall was developing his lectures into a regular system of popular instruction; and the LCS, building likewise on a precedent of 1794, turned to the mass outdoor meeting as the most telling form of protest.[5] Both these developments, it could be argued, in fact provided an alternative to riot; they were peaceful means of voicing grievances; they could be – and were – used to condemn violence. But however justifiable such a claim – and it was stressed throughout the major demonstrations – it did not impress Ministers studying the aims and the language in a period of violence itself.

The first of the large meetings was held late in June, at St George's Fields south of the river. Attended by many thousands – estimates varied from 10,000 to 100,000 – it heard a highly charged attack on the Ministry, and ended by approving Addresses to the King and the Nation, demands for manhood suffrage, annual Parliaments, recognition of 'the brave French republic', and condemnations of the war and the price of food. The proceedings were orderly, the crowd was quiet, and recruitment to the LCS received a fillip. Where 400 new members

---

1. Cf. p. 166 above.
2. See p. 401 above.
3. Cf. p. 441, above.
   The general easement, as it seemed, of course had its limits. Pitt himself received a rather refreshingly abusive letter from the town of Leeds – beginning 'You are one of Damn'd scoundrel rascals that ever trod upon English ground' – promising a rising of 10,000 armed men in the next few months (J. Lloyd to Pitt, 19 March 1795; P.R.O. 30/8/153). No doubt he took it in his stride.
4. Cf. pp. 387, 393 above.
5. Cf. pp. 393–4 above. Reeves (see p. 229 above) had been perceptive in appreciating, when Thelwall's lectures started, that their 'mischief . . . is of a new kind' (in a report of 29 April 1794; Goodwin, op. cit., 320).

joined in June, 800 were added the next month, and the Society's divisions, 17 in March and 29 at the start of July, numbered 41 early in August and over 70 by October.[1] Provincial activity was likewise burgeoning, above all in the old centres. Norwich and Sheffield, to take two prominent instances, leapt to life again; Leicester and the West Riding towns revived; and the LCS was now spreading its own tentacles directly into different parts of the country. In October it held two further public meetings in the capital: outside Copenhagen House in Islington on the 20th and in Copenhagen Fields on the 26th. The latter was said to have attracted a concourse of over 100,000. It endorsed an Address to the Nation and a string of familiar resolutions, dispersing quietly once more, well pleased, according to one account, with 'A DAY WELL SPENT'.[2]

As they studied the reports of these occasions, however, Ministers were not reassured by the peaceable behaviour. They were concerned at least as much with the oratory and the resolutions themselves. Warnings that neglect of the voice of the people could incur the reward of high treason, that their 'aggravated feelings' could not for ever be restrained, above all that the towns of the kingdom should associate to procure a Parliamentary reform – an ominous renewed hint of a Convention[3] – were as seditious as before. Such language moreover coincided with a crop of inflammatory pamphlets and handbills, widely dispersed. Nor was London itself in these months a particularly peaceful place. As generally in the eighteenth century, the capital was spared much in the way of bread riots: supplies, easily accessible by both land and sea, were always carefully watched by authorities alert to the dangers of shortage and excessive fluctuations in price. Even in 1795 measures were taken in the summer to cushion the worst of the blows.[4] But trouble lay not far below the surface, and it was breaking out in other forms. The crimping riots may well have been intensified by the growing unpopularity of a war now associated with the cost of food; and one of the last such demonstrations, in July, was marked by a crowd breaking some of Pitt's windows in Downing Street. He played down the occasion.

> A mob [he commented to his mother] is magnified by report; but that which visited my window with a single pebble was really so young and so little versed in its business, that it hardly merited the notice of a newspaper.

There was no repetition, and he was unperturbed when the Speaker saw him a week or so later.[5] The incident indeed was minor. But a more

1. Op. cit., 371, 373. For the LCS's organisation see pp. 108 above.
2. Op. cit., 384–5; and 375–84.
3. Op. cit., 385–6.
4. See George Rudé, *Hanoverian London 1714–1808* (1971), 203–4; p. 467 below.
5. Pitt to Hester Countess of Chatham, 18 July 1795 (Stanhope, II, 324); Henry Addington to Camden, 29 July 1795 (Camden Ms C 224/1). And see p. 451 above.

serious one followed in October. The price of bread, and of life in general, had by then suffered its steepest rise so far,[1] and the temper, if often smouldering, was volatile. When the new session of Parliament opened on the 29th, a few days after the LCS's latest meeting, Pitt was 'surrounded' on his way by a cursing mob;[2] and the King himself fared worse. An 'immense' crowd, shouting 'No Pitt, No War, Bread, Bread, Peace, Peace', booed and hissed as he passed through St James's Park, and a missile – whether stone or bullet was never discovered – broke against a window of the state coach as it neared the House of Lords.[3] George III, who was convinced he had been shot at, appeared his usual resolute self – the unfortunate Westmorland, accompanying him as Master of the Horse,[4] was less calm – but further trouble ensued on his return, and the Guards had to earn their name. The episode, coming when it did, alarmed the politicians and produced a swift reaction. Habeas Corpus was suspended once more, and within a fortnight the Ministry introduced a Treasonable Practices and then a Seditious Meetings and Assemblies bill.[5]

The constitutional means at Government's disposal in combating sedition had remained unaltered since the Proclamation of May 1792. Their limits – or uncertainties under construction – had been exposed only the year before.[6] If Ministers believed that disaffection was being organised by men 'whose purposes and practices through life' this was,[7] some more effective weapons would have to be devised to control assemblies on the one hand and prosecute successfully on the other. The bills were designed as a pair for those purposes: the first to encompass the definition of treason, the second 'to prevent', as Pitt put it, 'the mischief which such meetings might otherwise produce'. He recognised that this last was 'a matter of considerable . . . delicacy'. It demanded 'a nice hand, so as to preserve' the subject's 'legal right'. But while the House could debate the detail later, he was sure of agreement that some measure was required.[8]

---

1. Wheat, which had risen from 7 shillings a bushel to 7s 9d between January and June, leapt to 13s 6d in August and was still at 9s 6d in October (Stern, loc. cit., 169). The wholesale price index has been reckoned at 101.9 in January, 114.2 in June, 130.9 in August, and 118.3 in October (Gayer, Rostow, Schwartz, op. cit., I, 468).

2. Canning's description (see *L.C.G. III*, II, 416 n2). He was in Pitt's carriage.

3. The account is by Francis Place (see his *Autobiography*, 145–7). He made the point, or claim, that hissing and groaning on such occasions was not uncommon in itself: 'it had long been the custom' of those who wished 'to show their dislike of the proceedings of the court', and continued into the next century.

4. See p. 423 above.

5. By Grenville in the Lords and Pitt in the Commons, on 6 and 10 November respectively. For Habeas Corpus in the summer see p. 453 above.

6. Pp. 91, 396–7 above.

7. Pitt on 10 November 1795 (*The Senator*, XIII, 151). I have preferred this source in this instance to *P.R.*, which is rather less full and whose report is wrongly dated the 9th.

8. Op. cit., 149–53.

The problem was clear enough. The constitutional right of petition-ing should be protected. How should this be done, and lawful and honest meetings remain unhampered, while bearing down on others, including those called allegedly for that purpose, which from experience pro-ceeded to dangerous agitation? Pitt's opening explanation was con-cerned with the balance: the terms of the Seditious Meetings bill itself were open-endedly severe. In a context giving them a summary power, the result would depend on the magistrates. No public meeting, with some corporate exceptions, of more than fifty persons was to be held without due notice being given by seven resident householders. The justices were given the authority to attend, to make arrests at discretion, treat obstruction as a felony, and disperse the assembly if necessary under the Riot Act. This applied to the larger meetings. There were also the more restricted gatherings to listen to 'lectures on political subjects, . . . where', as Pitt put it, 'sedition was the source of livelihood of certain persons' – he had Thelwall obviously in mind.[1] These must be licensed by two magistrates (or university authorities where relevant); otherwise they would become 'disorderly houses' – a treatment based on an Act ('Mansfield's Act') whereby the 'house' was closed down and a fine imposed.

The measure was to be 'temporary': for a period of three years. The Treasonable Practices bill applied in part to the same period and in part to the life of George III and one session following his death. This latter period related to the bill's first object: to clear up old ambiguities and 'adapt' existing statutes in such ways as were necessary to 'the situation of the times'. The words were Grenville's by way of introduction,[2] and as Pitt had done in the complementary measure he was careful to give a balanced, restrained look to the terms that followed. The 'variations' would be few, to a body of law 'notoriously inefficient' as it stood; and indeed some of his comments in the course of the debates may have perturbed die-hard peers, including some of his colleagues. Our danger, he announced, stemmed from radical Societies which could be com-pared to the Clubs in France, which in turn had destroyed a revolution initially excusable, even welcome; one springing from 'a government in itself bad' and wasteful.[3] These remarks in point of fact were aimed at the current situation in the war: at possible developments in France and in the Ministry's own policy. They were for note in that context.[4] But they supported the impression of a measured response, which the bill itself certainly did not convey. The scope of treason was now widened to include pressure on the King to change his measures or his counsels,

1. Op. cit., 153.
2. 6 November 1795 (op. cit., 122). See p. 455, n5 above. For the element of clarification cf. p. 388, n5 above; it was also stressed later by two Lord Chief Justices, Ellenborough and Abbott (Radzinowicz, op. cit., I, 613 n12).
3. Speech of 13 November 1795 (*The Senator*, XIII, 228–9).
4. For which see pp. 599–602 below; and also p. 588.

and intimidation of either or both Houses of Parliament; its expression, which hitherto had to be proved an 'overt' act, could now be revealed in writing or speech on the evidence of two witnesses. Such crimes would be punishable, like all cases of treason, by death. The second part of the bill dealt with persons who, in the terms of the Act as it passed, 'shall maliciously and advisedly, by writing, printing, preaching, or other speaking, express, publish, utter, or declare, any words or sentences to excite or stir up the people to hatred or contempt of the person of his Majesty, his heirs or successors, or the Government and Constitution of this realm, as by law established'. They could be subject on a first conviction to the penalties of a high misdemeanour, and on a second to transportation for seven years.[1]

This was comprehensive enough. It could embrace a squib on the Prince of Wales. Almost any hostile criticism in fact could be liable to prosecution – though conviction could still be another matter.[2] There is no explicit evidence on Pitt's approach to the bills, though there are some clues. He was relaxed enough in June to readmit Habeas Corpus, just before the scarcity of bread began to make itself really felt. He was much absorbed by the war throughout the summer, at what he thought a critical time, and was ready to include a body of the Guards – the troops responsible for London – in an expedition to the West Indies, against the King's wish.[3] He felt free to leave his desk in September, and after reporting to George III at Weymouth carry on to Burton Pynsent for one of his increasingly rare visits. It was the mass meetings followed by the insult and possible danger to the King in October that made him fear a recrudescence of the danger of 1794. Thereafter he moved fast, bringing in the legislation and summoning reinforcements to the area of London: regular cavalry, Fencibles and militia from as far away as Lancashire, Pembrokeshire and Cornwall.[4] Early in November he told Wilberforce and Mornington, 'My head would be off in six months, were I to resign'. 'I see', Wilberforce commented, 'that he expects a civil broil'.[5]

Perhaps not everyone was convinced of Pitt's 'firmness'.[6] To many, stronger measures were long overdue, and there was some flavour in his introduction of the bill of a continuing desire to preserve a balance.

1. 36 Geo. III, c.7. The Seditious Meetings and Assemblies Act was 36 Geo. III, c.8.

2. And the Scottish penalty of transportation in some of the cases was now introduced to England and Wales (cf. p. 390 above).

3. See pp. 535, 597n2 below. The proposal was made in a Cabinet minute of 14 August (*L.C.G. III*, II, no. 1285), and Pitt would have known of Dundas's subsequent efforts to stick to it despite the King's disapproval precisely on the ground of internal security (loc. cit.).

4. Holland Rose, II, 285.

5. *Life of Wilberforce*, I, 114.

6. This might have been Buckingham's meaning when he wrote to his brother William, 'you will have a serious struggle, and I do not doubt *your* firmness' (19 November 1795; *H.M.C., Dropmore*, III, 147).

Much of his speech was devoted to the need to preserve legitimate rights, and the hope was to deter, and thereby prevent trouble. Such remarks could be dismissed by his opponents on the other hand as camouflage – as they claimed the attack on the King to be merely a pretext for measures already planned or desired. The sentiment indeed could be seen as meaningless, since deterrence involved the same repression, the same loss of freedom, as prosecution itself. Alternatively it could be taken as the best that could be hoped in highly dangerous circumstances. At least Pitt applied pressure even-handedly at this point. The bills had scarcely passed when the Foxites brought a motion condemning a libel on the Constitution in a recent publication by John Reeves, the anti-Jacobin organiser of the Loyal Associations of 1792. In his *Thoughts on the English Government* he had argued that 'the Kingly government' could operate in all its functions without Lords or Commons, and that the protection of law and government derived 'unceasingly' from the King alone.[1] Windham sprang to the defence. But Pitt disagreed with him. After some initial delaying action, he found the 'real meaning incompatible with the existence of the Constitution', and supported a proposal to prosecute.[2] He naturally laid himself open to expostulation from the victim: the more so as Reeves had just been offering aid in his 'prior way' and giving advice including, as it happened, a proposal to license pamphlets.[3] The decision however drew some approbation from a member now voting normally with Opposition, who told Ministers, following Pitt's speech, that 'some of their lost confidence they would regain'.[4]

But any such tendency on Pitt's part was of course confined within compelling limits. His prime task was to bring a fast-growing challenge once more under control. The bills are not remembered for explanatory phrases of restraint but as marking the crucial stage in – the legislative opening of – his celebrated 'Reign of Terror'. The degree and effects of that terror fall to be considered later. When the bills appeared they were at once bitterly fought. All elements of protest joined forces, focused for the first time in the war by Fox himself, abandoning the Parliamentary Opposition's reluctance to come too close to the movements outside.[5] Recalling as so often the days of the American Revolution, he appealed

1. Speech of Charles Sturt in the Commons, 23 November 1795 (*P.R.*, XLIII, 287–8). For Reeves's activities and relations with the Ministry in 1792 see pp. 229–33 above.

2. Speech of 26 November 1795; *P.R.*, XLIII, 416–18.

3. Letters to Pitt, 7–25 November 1795 (P.R.O. 30/8/170). Reeves was brought to Court in May 1796, and acquitted by a jury which found the publication 'very improper' but not guided by the motives stated by the Attorney General.

4. Thomas Stanley, 26 November 1795 (*P.R.*, XLIII, 425). He noted the 'affection for whig principles' occasioned by the debates. Similarly an independent, Robert Buxton, who preceded him, called for 'exemplary punishment' of 'a libel on the glorious Revolution' (op. cit., 424–5). For Stanley's political affinities see L.G. Mitchell, op. cit., 288, and O'Gorman, op. cit., 137, 251.

5. Pp. 76, 173, 387–8 above.

for a national wave of petitions and held a meeting in New Palace Yard. The petitions rolled in: perhaps 94 in all with a total of over 130,000 signatures. They came mostly from public meetings up and down the country, convened by the provincial Societies as urged by the LCS. The latter itself held two meetings, on 4 November near Copenhagen House and on 7 December in Marylebone Fields (now Regent's Park). The orators were almost a roll-call of the radical leaders – Thelwall, John Ashley, Richard Hodgson, John Richter, John Gale Jones, Matthew Brown from Sheffield, William Frend of Cambridge fame.[1] After the recent tumult, the tone with some exceptions – Gale Jones threatened Pitt with execution[2] – was sober if defiant, and one of the resolutions in November deplored the attack on the King's coach. Both assemblies dispersed quietly, and no violence was shown to those spectators who failed to raise their hands for the resolutions – among them, as in New Palace Yard, several of Pitt's friends.[3] The demonstrations 'out of doors' were combined with an assault by the Foxites in Parliament which sought to enlist sympathy from independents. It was naturally defeated: Government's majorities were overwhelming – on the Treasonable Practices bill 66 to 7 in the Lords, 226 to 45 in the Commons; on the Seditious Meetings bill 266 to 51 in the Commons, 107 to 18 in the Lords – and both measures became law on 18 December.[4] By then the Societies were organising themselves for life under the new pressures.

As always, it is hard to tell how representative these efforts were. The volume of petitions was exceptional, the anger real and widespread. It was not confined to the Societies and their audiences: some minorities on local bodies, in London and the northern towns, were quick to register their own protests. One must note qualifications, made at the time. Estimates of the sizes of meetings varied widely: Fox was said to have attracted a crowd of 30,000, the LCS in Islington one of 200,000 if not more. But some observers found the Westminster meeting 'not large', filling only two-thirds of New Palace Yard, and if the Islington assembly was huge its successor in Marylebone struck one onlooker as smaller than expected.[5] The petitions included only four from English counties by the beginning of December,[6] and there were plenty of others in favour of the Ministry. These did not equal the protests in number: perhaps 65

---

1. For the last of whom see p. 389, n4 above.

2. Cf. p. 457 above.

3. Goodwin, op. cit., 390–5; *Diary of Joseph Farington*, II, 403–6, 427–30.

4. *P.H.*, XXXII (1818), cols. 270, 527, 470, 554; *H.L.J.*, XL (nd), 571–2. In the course of the heated debates, Fox let slip an expression which implied a popular right to resist the bills if they became law. Pitt was quick to accuse him of 'advising an appeal to the sword' (23 November 1795; *P.R.*, XLIII, 322). Fox was equally quick to qualify his remark, and in a note of the same date, apparently for his own keeping, Pitt seems to have accepted the explanation (P.R.O. 30/8/197).

5. Goodwin, op. cit., 390–1; Thompson, *Making of the English Working Class*, 145; Loren Reid, *Charles James Fox . . .* (1969), 318; *Diary of Farington*, II, 405, 430.

6. Charles Abbot in the Commons, 3 December 1795 (*P.R.*, XLIII, 556).

as against 94, with some 30,000 signatures;[1] and the last figure reflected the fact that some of the documents came from corporate bodies, which mustered fewer hands than could be mobilised at public meetings. It may also have suggested the relative efficiency of organisation on either side; and the relative scarcity in populous towns of the minor loyalist gentry and clergy who were active as they had been in 1792.[2] The statistics were disturbing for Government. They could not be lightly dismissed. Taken at face value they discounted the claim which could be made in 1794 that nine out of ten people in the country were sound and 'loyal',[3] and that the agitation was limited to small numbers of disaffected men.

But this very fact raises questions wider than the detail of the figures. How symptomatic were the activities, on either side, of feelings at large? And what elements indeed, as part of that question, surrounded and informed the protests themselves? There were probably many beyond the activists and petitioners, at different social levels, who greatly disliked the bills and had growing reservations about events. There were probably more whose fears outweighed any such sentiments, and who accepted that the time had come to stamp on a threat. There were many whose feelings may have been mixed but who clung to Pitt's leadership; who thought, as Francis Place acknowledged many years later, that 'a year of extraordinary difficulty . . . needed such men as Pitt, Dundas and Grenville to carry on the Government'.[4] And how extensive or how precise, how persistent or how temporary, were the grievances of many who subscribed to the petitions or the resolutions? A web of circumstance, a nexus of factors, comes into play here. 1795 saw perhaps the most vivid example of the conflict and combination of elements which together determined the dimensions of unrest.[5] It encapsulated complex pressures, experiences, doctrines, relationships which in a moment of crisis, as always, were projected in simplified forms. Judgment on the outcome could be made, if instinctively, only on that basis. Only so, in the last but now urgent resort, could meaning be given to the term 'loyal'.

The year obviously made great demands on Pitt himself: on his control of the Ministry and, a prerequisite, on his health and spirits. The former was not seriously in doubt. Whatever his concessions to the Whigs' demands for places, and his own supporters' strictures thereafter, he remained in much the same charge of the Cabinet and the machinery of government. As always, constitutional balances defined the scope of his

1. Goodwin, op. cit., 391 and n180.
2. Cf. p. 232 above.
3. Auckland on 30 May 1794 (*A.C.*, III, 213).
4. *Autobiography*, 144. He continued, 'and yet sustain the bad proceedings which had been in progress since 1792'.
5. Chs. IV–V above.

power;[1] as hitherto, he fully occupied his sphere. The Fitzwilliam affair, and the substitution of Portland for Dundas at the Home Office, may even have bolstered his authority in the domestic arena; and, it will be argued, it remained potent in the conduct of the war.[2] War administration was creaking, policy failing to grip. But it was over events rather than his colleagues that the degree of his control was reduced.

His spirits seem to have held up well through most of 1794. Pretyman, visiting him on one occasion, was 'cheered up' as usual; the young MP Robert Jenkinson, seeing him 'very often' in September at Walmer, thought him 'on the whole . . . in very good spirits' with a party that included the Dundases, Charles Long and an old Cambridge friend William Meeke.[3] He took Parliamentary business with seasoned aplomb: Canning, making excuses for the Minister's late arrival at an important debate on the suspension of Habeas Corpus, found later that he had simply been eating a good dinner.[4] Those dinners included plenty of wine. Canning, again, was struck by his consumption of 'I know not how much madeira' before going down to the House; though the results were still not often publicly visible.[5] Sometimes however they were. On one occasion not long before the war itself began, he and Addington did themselves well when dining with the Corporation of Canterbury before emerging to a crowd which, in those months of rising unrest, showed some signs of 'disapprobation'. '"A pretty story," said Mr. Pitt, "this will make in the papers. The Minister and the Speaker dined with the corporation . . ., got very drunk, and were hissed out of the town."' *The Morning Chronicle*, Addington recalled, reported that 'the Chancellor of the Exchequer was observed, in walking to his carriage, to oscillate like his own bills'.[6]

These habits began to bear on his health. So did the strain of the war. Jenkinson thought that the first indication of its impact came after the failure at Dunkirk.[7] Several of his friends in fact noticed an alteration in the course of 1793; but it was not serious enough for him to pay attention for at least another two years.[8] In 1795 or 1796, however, possibly at

---

1. Cf. I, Chs. VII section III, XI.
2. Ch. XIII, section IV below.
3. Pretyman to Mrs Pretyman, nd but ascribed to 1794 (Pretyman Ms 503:1); Robert Jenkinson to Hawkesbury, 7 September 1794 (B.L. Loan Ms 72, vol. 53). Jenkinson was in camp nearby. For Meeke see I, 17.
4. Wendy Hinde, *George Canning* (1973), 38. The debate was that of 17 May.
5. Op. cit., 35. Cf. I, 585.
6. Pellew, *Life and Correspondence of Sidmouth*, I, 91.
7. Loc. cit., 152–3. See pp. 290–3 above.
8. Pretyman's retrospective assessment of Pitt's health, nd; Tomline Mss, Box 29, 1, 35.2, Pembroke College, Cambridge. This was written for the part of his biography which Rosebery published as 'Bishop Tomline's Estimate of Pitt together with Chapter XXVII from the Unpublished Fourth Volume of the Life' (*The Monthly Review*, August 1903).

Pretyman found Pitt looking thin, after having been unwell, in October 1794 (to his wife, 15 October 1794; Stanhope Ms S5 C 67/6).

Dundas's urging, he consulted the physician Walter Farquhar, then fast building up the practice which made him a baronet and an enduringly fashionable doctor. Farquhar was not unduly worried; but his recollection is of interest.

> I found him in a state of general debility – the functions of the stomach greatly impaired & the Bowels very irregular – much of which I attributed to the excess of public business & the unremitting attention upon subjects of anxiety and interest.

He accordingly urged the need for 'some relaxation from the arduous Duties of Office' – a prescription which Pitt naturally 'stated to be impossible'.

> There appeared at this time [Farquhar concluded later] to be little or no constitutional mischief done, but the symptoms of debility with a gouty tendency, which Dr. Addington (as Mr. Pitt mentioned to me) had always remarked from his infancy, were likely to become formidable if neglected.[1]

This gout indeed was becoming more frequent and acute. Pitt had 'a very moderate and regular' attack in April, and one other at least in August;[2] and Farquhar's advice (if he gave it then) was proved true enough in time. But the course had a long way to run. Pitt certainly had his moments of depression – sometimes deep depression – over the state of the war, and of anxiety over developments at home.[3] His temperament was mercurial: it was also predominantly resilient. The optimism may have served when required in self-defence: it was also real – which was why it could be called on.[4] The good spirits in bad times were not assumed purely for the sake of appearances, though no doubt they sometimes were in part. If Pitt was cast down he could show it; and this was so in 1795 itself. But while it would be easy to presume that public affairs then gave cause enough, the principal reason, interacting with them, seems in fact to have been of a personal nature.

As often with Pitt, the private experience had a public context. In this

1. 'Letters Relating to the Love Episode of William Pitt together with an Account of his Health by his Physician Sir Walter Farquhar', ed. the Earl of Rosebery (*The Monthly Review*, December 1900), 31–2. Cf. I, 9, 105–6, 594–5.

Farquhar's recollection, much later, placed the occasion in 1795; but it may have been at fault. He received his baronetcy in March 1796, and in writing to Pitt in January to thank him for his 'approbation' he observed that 'As I have not the honor of being personally known to you' he was sending the letter through Rose (18 January 1796; P.R.O. 30/58/1).

2. Pitt to Hester Countess of Chatham, 20 April 1795 (Stanhope, II, 317); Pepper Arden to Camden, 14 August 1795 (Camden Ms C 93).

3. Pp. 380–1, 457 above for December 1794 and November 1795 respectively.

4. See I, 109–10, 322.

case it arose from the need to make a change of Offices. Events in the winter of 1794 had already brought some personal sadness, when Wilberforce's views on the war removed him from '*the old firm*'.[1] Both men felt the break keenly, as their joy was to show when agreement returned. But a more painful embarrassment followed with the decision to take Chatham away from the Admiralty.[2] For although he was given another Cabinet post he felt he had been made a scapegoat, and was not slow to make his sense of injustice known. Pitt was enough of a Grenville to respect the attention due to the head of the family:[3] his own temperament, with its need for old and simple affections, was deeply engaged. His brother's resentment left him disturbed and unhappy for several months. He confessed to his friend Pepper Arden in August that he had had more sleepless nights in the past year 'than during the rest of his administration put together'. But this, Arden understood, stemmed not so much from public pressures as 'principally from domestic occurrences in which as a public man he was obliged to sacrifice private feelings'. Chatham's anger was such that the personal 'breach' looked 'irreparable'. Pitt was 'very miserable', and his circle worried about what could be done.[4] This cannot have improved his uncertain health, and the difficulty lasted, in the midst of all the others, well into the next year. Only promotion for Chatham at the end of that summer relieved it; and Pitt's 'natural' spirits responded noticeably at once.[5] He had learned to live with the situation by then, and was often his resolute and cheerful self. But the episode showed the strength of his dependence on

1. Wilberforce's Journal, 12 February 1795 (*Life*, II, 71).

2. P. 379 above.

3. Cf. I, 43.

4. Arden to Camden, 14 August 1795 (see p. 462, n2 above); Addington to same, 29 July 1795 (Camden Ms C 224/1) – though he then reported Pitt as being cheerful.

5. Edward Wilson (see I, 6) to Hester Countess of Chatham, 5 June 1795, 24 September 1796 (P.R.O. 30/8/67); Lord Bathurst (see I, 592) to Camden, 27 February, 3 September [endorsed 1796], 27 November [1796] (Camden Ms C 195/2, 226/1–2); J.C. Villiers (see I, 17) to same, 15 September 1796 (loc. cit., C 131/2); Mornington to same, 24 November 1796 (loc. cit., C 121/3); Lord Carrington to same, nd but 1796 (loc. cit., C 97). Chatham's own feelings are made clear in his letters to Camden – the recipient, particularly while in Ireland (p. 439 above), of correspondence from others in Pitt's inner circle – between 13 December 1794 and 15 September 1796 (loc. cit., 254/1–5). He was made Lord President of the Council in the latter month.

Pitt suffered one other, minor, embarrassment of the kind in the summer of 1795. Hood, returning from the Mediterranean with part of the fleet needing relief, and long anxious not to return, wrote a letter to the Admiralty, on receiving orders to sail again with what he conceived to be inadequate strength, which was deemed to be insubordinate, and was ordered to haul down his flag. The Hoods were old family friends of the Pitts and Grenvilles, and had earlier benefited in their careers thereby. The *contretemps* could therefore have been awkward; but in the event both men took it well and Pitt showed the Admiral 'unabated' regard (Addington to Camden, 29 July 1795; loc. cit., C 224/1). Hood's letters at the time to Pitt, and a copy of one to Addington himself, are in P.R.O. 30/8/146.

personal affections and conceptions of honour, and it came, with an impact that his intimates took seriously, on top of growing problems confronting a system which needed his control.

III

Dearth and discontent in 1795 impelled a two-handed response. 'The State acted to relieve the cause of unrest and to repress its manifestations.'[1] The two Acts themselves came in the midst of efforts to cope with the effects of shortage; conditioned of course by permissible doctrines and practice, as the Acts too relied on public countenance.

The stoppages of exports and the adjustments of bounties and duties on wheat since 1792 had embodied a familiar approach to the problem of balancing supplies and prices.[2] Early in 1795, however, it appeared that Government had embarked on a more novel course. This may indeed even have started late in 1794; certainly it was well under way by the following spring.[3] The policy rested on the fact that merchants by now were cautious about buying wheat from overseas; a result largely of Government's own interference with commercial practice in its successive port regulations and its treatment of supplies to the enemy.[4] This last had already led to official absorption of individual neutral cargoes which could otherwise end up in France. It now further encouraged a decision, made in the face of growing domestic need, to take over directly the purchase of overseas wheat. There was undoubtedly a serious threat to such supplies. The harvest in northern Europe had been good; but the bitter winter delayed cargoes from the Baltic, and the Prussians furthermore had imposed an embargo which affected the large Polish shipments. Higher wartime freight rates were limiting purchases from the Mediterranean. The harvest had been bad in the United States. And Canadian wheat, though always of poor quality, was being bought up fast by the Spaniards, the Portuguese and the French themselves.[5] In these circumstances there was a strong case for Government to step in. By March it was doing so through the Committee of Trade.

The action was comprehensive. The official contractor, the wheat merchant Claude Scott, bought as heavily as he could through agents on both sides of the Atlantic; and the Ministry indeed sent a total of 56 vessels to Canada to collect supplies which it hoped to secure by outbidding the Spaniards and the Portuguese. The efforts in aggregate

1. Gayer, Rostow, Schwartz, op. cit., 9.
2. P. 444 above.
3. See Stern, 'The Bread Crisis in Britain', 178.
4. Pp. 444–5 above.
5. Stern, loc. cit., 177–8.

were on a major scale. They were only partially successful – and the competition in Canada led to an embargo by the Governor General in the late summer. By then, too, patchy harvests across the world and administrative delays in shipments meant that imports of wheat for the year again fell sadly short. They amounted in fact only to some 300,000 quarters – a total bettered regularly over the next ten years. But when an improvement came in 1796 it owed much to the fulfilment of earlier orders; and the authorities could claim moreover that not only were they active in a difficult situation, but were also ensuring that supplies bought by Britain reached and stayed in Britain itself.[1]

There appears to have been general agreement on the policy among the Ministers most closely concerned. One might perhaps see Hawkesbury's hand in the early stages: such action would suit his approach, and he was firmly in control of the Committee of Trade.[2] But there seems to have been no demur from the Treasury, to which Scott was financially responsible, or from Portland, that convinced free-trader, who as Home Secretary was a regular attendant.[3] Pitt himself in any case must have approved.[4] For someone with his views and sympathies there would have been conflicting arguments. The method of purchase was probably not cheap: costs fell directly on Government, and the knowledge overseas of the virtual monopoly may have tended to keep prices high. On the other hand world markets could be scoured, the French correspondingly denied, and the effects of monopoly possibly offset by the removal of wartime combination among merchants. Taking shortage and war policy together, the exercise may have seemed well worth-while. But it was vulnerable to objections based on received doctrine.

This was seen clearly enough in the last months of 1795. Almost as soon as Parliament met the Commons debated the high price of corn. The subject in fact was introduced by Pitt himself, to gain support for various domestic expedients.[5] But the Committee of the House which he

1. This was an argument of Claude Scott's (loc. cit., 179).

2. Eg Auckland to Pitt, 'In confidence', 18 November 1795, on Hawkesbury's choosing 'whom he pleases' to attend from outside, and on his self-confidence (P.R.O. 30/8/110). For Hawkesbury's position and general approach see I, 330–2. He may not however have been responsible for the policy: Lord Sheffield suspected 'a sure little junto' of Pitt, Dudley Ryder (see I, 108, 310) and 'young Jenky' (Hawkesbury's son, who unlike Ryder was not on the Committee); to Auckland, 26 June 1796 (*A.C.*, III, 349).

The extent of activity over the scarcity of wheat in all its aspects is shown by the frequency of the meetings devoted to the subject: thirteen from 31 January to 6 August 1795, of which Hawkesbury attended twelve (four on his own). He also attended 40 of the 43 meetings of the parent Privy Council at which wheat was discussed between 23 April and 25 November (Stern, loc. cit., 181).

3. Minutes, P.R.O., B.T. 5/9–10; and see pp. 446–7 above for Portland's views.

4. Might this in fact have been an early instance of the process which Grenville later described as 'Lord Liverpool [as Hawkesbury became] lur[ing] you from our arms into all the mazes of the old system' (I, 359n2)?

5. On 3 November (*P.R.*, XLIII, 66–9; misdated 2 November).

wished to set up to examine and report for that purpose immediately condemned the Government's buying overseas. The 'preponderant Opinion' of experts favoured a freer trade. Official intervention should accordingly be dropped, and a bounty granted 'for the encouragement of private speculation'. The pressure was strong, and immediately successful. Ministers at once gave public assurances, the purchases ceased, and within three days of the Commmittee's first report a bill was introduced for bounties on certain imported grains, which became law in December.[1]

The concession may have been the easier because the policy's impact had in fact been marginal. It had not proved significant within the total supply, the bulk of which had still to come from domestic production; and the effect on prices and distribution was confined directly to cargoes at the ports. Government exercised no such authority over inland produce. Such reasons led the agriculturist Arthur Young to believe – though he may have exaggerated – that the system was of value only to morale. If it represented, as has been suggested, 'the first example of state trading in essential supplies during war time', the full exercise was brief and touched the problems only at the fringe.[2]

Even so, it could still have a certain bearing on events; and this indeed was shown after the policy changed. The early months of 1796 seem to have witnessed some confusion: official purchases ceased, but the merchants had not had time fully to take over. Substantial quantities of wheat however were starting to arrive in the spring from earlier orders,[3] and Government of course continued to manage its reserve. It was here in fact that it had been able to exercise some modest influence on prices, by judicious releases and by holding back when possible from domestic purchases at excessive levels. The increasing shortage throughout the winter, forcing up demand, now coincided with a partial loss of control over the future of the official stocks. The Ministry husbanded them until the late spring, when merchants' cargoes, like its own delayed purchases, began to reach the ports. It then released substantial supplies on the market, and the combination pulled down prices at once. From a peak of 12s $6\frac{1}{4}$d a bushel in March they fell to 10s $5\frac{3}{4}$d in April and to 9s $5\frac{1}{4}$d in May; and although they rose again to just over 10s in the next two months they declined in August and, aided at last by a good harvest, fell to 8s in September and to 7s 4d by the end of the year.[4] The easement was not experienced without a row between Pitt and the importers, who

---

1. First Report of the Select Committee, 16 November 1795 (*Reports from Committees of the House of Commons*, IX (1803), 45); *P.R.*, XLIII, 248–55; *H.C.J.*, 51 (1803), 91–2. The Act was 36 Geo. III, c. 21. Import duties had by then been freshly removed, by statute (36 Geo. III, c. 3); cf. p. 445 above.

2. Stern, loc. cit., 178–80. The quotation refers specifically to British experience, in 'modern' times.

3. See p. 465 above.

4. Stern, loc. cit., 169. Cf. p. 455, n1 above.

John Horne Tooke, *by Thomas Hardy*   Thomas Hardy. *Unknown*

John Thelwall. *Attributed to William Hazlitt*

'The Republican-Attack', by Gillray, November 1795

later accused him of holding out hopes of compensation for losses incurred on purchases at higher levels and then reneging, after Government itself had brought about the fall. They may well have had a case at least up to a point. For they had been obliged to buy in ignorance of the state and prospects of official stocks; information which, however hard to specify in the latter instance, given the hazards of wartime shipping and events at the vendors' end, had been promised when the Ministry abandoned its own operations. To the merchants its market manoeuvres in the spring and early summer therefore looked unscrupulous: a not unreasonable conclusion which, however, may well have exaggerated its capacity. The handling of the situation in fact probably arose more from uncertainty at an anxious time than from wholly premeditated choice. On the other hand Pitt's reaction, when finally brought to defend himself in Parliament – an event delayed for over two years – did nothing to allay his accusers' resentment. Indeed he comes badly out of the whole affair: initial signs of sympathy, even if qualified, then procrastination, then refusal, and finally angry condemnation of the claimants for misrepresenting the case.[1] The tone may have stemmed to some extent from an uneasy conscience. It also showed a readiness, when it suited him, to give expression to the popular suspicions – always easily roused, and consonant here with both tradition and Smithian theory – of a 'combination', open or tacit, to keep prices high.[2]

Such feelings of course were rife at a time of crisis, and one of this magnitude was no exception. In 1795–6 they were reflected in newspapers and a spate of pamphlets. Forestalling, regrating, engrossing – the medieval crimes rife in Tudor and Stuart England, and still punishable at common law – figured prominently in the accusations. Some parishes, scattered throughout the country, applied an equally traditional remedy. There were instances of magistrates setting permissible prices: not a step of which enlightened opinion could properly approve,[3] but – as in London itself, where the Common Council acted – designed to show humanity and avoid unrest. Pitt himself would have liked to take powers to secure returns of supplies by area, but he was brought to agree that this would be thought high-handed, and might increase the alarm.[4] Instead, Government confined itself to introducing a bill to end the local stoppages of grain in transit, making hindrance a

1. Speech of 10 May 1798. After this onslaught, the importers' cause was defeated by 63 to 24. An account of the episode from their point of view is given in Barnes, op. cit., 75–6, 96; a perhaps more balanced assessment of Government's position in the first half of 1796, in Stern, loc. cit., 180–1.
2. Cf. Adam Smith on manufacturers, in I, 208.
3. Cf. p. 447, n1 above.
4. Holland Rose, II, 289.

criminal offence. This was a first-line defence. So were statutory measures to prohibit exports and, in accordance with the Commons' Committee, to give bounties on imports.[1] They were naturally of some help. But they could not be enough in themselves.

Two other, more extensive contributions could be envisaged, one for immediate effect, one for the longer term. The latter was fundamental: to increase production towards renewed self-sufficiency, an exercise which must rest on further improvements in methods and the use of land. Given past and current developments, it seemed there could be grounds for hope. The agricultural revolution continued, on the results of earlier successes, and poor harvests and wartime disturbances gave a fresh impetus to effort and thought. Government had become directly if cautiously involved in 1793, when Pitt agreed to set up and help fund a Board of Agriculture. He may not have attached much importance to it. The institution was a brainchild of the prolific Sir John Sinclair, allowed its life possibly as a reward for his aid in securing the success – he himself claimed the introduction – of the scheme for meeting the recent crisis of credit.[2] It was given a constitution, modelled probably in part on some Scottish societies in which he was active, which carried almost to absurdity the ideal of a balance of interests and of powers. The Board was a closed corporation, with a blend of Parliamentary and external members, some appointed – certain of them *ex officio* – some elected by their colleagues, relying largely on part-time private labours co-ordinated through a paid (but not salaried) Secretary, accommodated in the President's house, and funded partly by individual subscriptions and partly by Government grant. Its accounts were not submitted to the Treasury; its minutes were those of a private society. At the same time it spent public moneys, and enjoyed a semi-official charter. In its extreme version of a broadly cherished concept it was odd even by current standards: the Lord Chancellor, required to approve its charter, declined to do so for several months. Sinclair, as President, accordingly lent the Board £1,000 of his own to get started.[3] The arrangement hardly indicates Pitt's whole-hearted concern.

Once constituted, the new body set to work at once; or rather its President and Secretary did so, for they were very much the driving force. Sinclair wanted Arthur Young, the well-known writer on agriculture, for the latter post; a fairly obvious choice in itself, which was ratified by Government the more swiftly perhaps because Young had recently published a pamphlet, after some years of hostility, that amounted to strong support. High on the list of the Board's objects was a

1. See pp. 444–5, 466 above. The bill on inland transit became law as 36 Geo. III, c. 9.
2. For which see p. 387 above. Sinclair's role, or influence, is discussed and rather discounted in Sir John Clapham, *The Bank of England* . . ., I (1944), 264. For an earlier contact between the two men on a financial plan see I, 262, 266.
3. Rosalind Mitchison, *Agricultural Sir John* . . . (1962), 137–43, 146–8.

series of reports based on county surveys; and it was here in fact that it soon began to make its existence felt. By 1795 the first was ready for public consumption, to be followed by others over the next two decades. The dearth in the same year also brought it to the fore. Detailed recommendations were published, for a programme of potato planting, economies in the use of finer grains and in the feeding of livestock. It was also preparing an extensive General Enclosure bill. For after the great surge in mid-century the numbers of enclosures had been falling steadily – from a peak of 660 in the seventies to under 300 in the past ten years[1] – and the Board, in active correspondence with landowners and farmers, was far from believing that this was because most of what was needed had already been done. On the contrary, the key to increased production was fresh expansion; and the best incentive was to reduce the expense and trouble of the process. A comprehensive Act would replace the need for a host of costly and time-consuming individual applications: it should also remove the discrepancies in treatment which individual cases produced. Much hard work was put into the project, and by the end of the year it was ready. The Commons themselves seemed aware of the problem, and in February 1796 Sinclair asked leave to introduce the bill. But the measure at once ran into trouble. Parts of it had to be amended, as practical objections and legal complications were brought to bear; and faced by the keen sense of property rights and competing demands for Parliamentary time, the sponsors found themselves steadily losing ground. The session in any case was a short one, for Pitt was looking to a general election in the early summer.[2] Hints and an appeal from Sinclair to him in April and May accordingly fell on stony ground.[3] The Minister did not intervene, and the bill faded away. Government was too much occupied in other directions to involve itself here.[4]

Pitt thus did nothing to encourage legislation for increased production.[5] He relied rather on hopes of reduced consumption, to provide an immediate effect.[6] Some months before the measures affecting movements of wheat, inland and at the ports,[7] he brought in bills prohibiting the use of grain and other foodstuffs in distilling – which among other things meant a ban on whiskey –, and of grain and flour in starching and

---

1. Synopsis in Phyllis Deane and W.A. Cole, *British Economic Growth 1688–1959* . . . (1962), 94n3. They had however recently been rising again: 40 bills apiece in 1791 and 1792, 60 in 1793, and 74 in 1794 (see Gayer, Rostow, Schwartz, op. cit., I, 14, 35).
2. See p. 622 below.
3. See P.R.O. 30/8/178.
4. The Parliamentary debates do not give an adequate sense of what happened. Mitchison, op. cit., 154–8, is useful.
5. In some notes of November 1795 he did include among other ideas '? Genl Enclosure Bill (Substitute for Tithes)' (P.R.O. 30/8/197). But unlike the rest this carried a query, and it was not developed further.
6. See the same notes in his hand, endorsed in another's 'Nov: 1795 – Mda. respecting Corn'.
7. Pp. 467–8 above.

hair powder – thus abetting a major change in fashion. Passed in the spring, the duration of the Acts was extended when Parliament met again in the winter.[1] By then Pitt was also prepared to amend the assize of bread. This ancient system, governing quantity, quality and price, remained unsatisfactory despite revisions, and the regulations were widely disregarded; but they could still hinder changes in the composition of the loaf. An attempt to abolish them in London had recently been lost only by the Lord Mayor's casting vote. But Parliament went at least part of the way, repealing prohibitions on quality,[2] and while the assize itself was not abolished in London until 1822, and in the rest of the country until 1836, much of its surviving power was henceforth removed. Pitt's emphasis here was linked with a further expedient; designed in this instance to persuade rather than forbid. For in addition to the statutory measures he called for economy in consumption by outright reduction within families, and changes in the baking of bread.

Such possibilities indeed were being widely, if often imprecisely, canvassed: in pamphlet literature and private advice, in correspondence and papers from the Board of Agriculture. That body in fact had reached the point in November 1795 of sending out specimen loaves for comment; an advance on more straightforward substitutes tried or advised by other institutions – potato flour by the naval victuallers, sailors' biscuits by the City of London. Pitt was attracted by the idea, and when Parliament assembled he recommended it to the Select Committee on the Price of Corn.[3] The Committee took it up, proposing both parts of the package in December. Compliance should be voluntary – 'they are far from proposing any legislative measure to enforce . . . this suggestion'[4] – and the two Houses swiftly agreed on an engagement, a 'pledge', to reduce the normal consumption of wheat in their families by at least a third, whether by cutting down outright on the quantity of wheaten bread or using bread containing substitutes, for which various choices had been proposed by now. In order to facilitate such production an Act was passed allowing the baking and sale of certain types of 'mixed' bread, which would be marked with the letter M.[5]

This last part of the plan, however, was a failure. Parliament's lead,

---

1. They were 35 Geo. III, c.s 11, 49, 119, 36 Geo. III, c.s 6, 20. But in order to relieve the revenue, whiskey was to be distilled again after February 1796.

2. By 36 Geo. III c. 22.

3. On 3 November (*P.R.*, XLIII, 67). See pp. 465–6 above. Whether or not this procedure originated with him, Auckland, who was bombarding Pitt on the subject of scarcity (see P.R.O. 30/8/110), suggested its advantage in a paper (nd, but 1795; P.R.O. 30/8/291).

4. Third Report, 9 and 23 December 1795 (*Reports from Committees of the House of Commons*, IX, 54).

5. The Commons took the pledge on 11 December (*P.R.*, XLIII, 735–6), the Lords on the 16th (op. cit., XLV (1796), 209–13). The Act was 36 Geo. III, c.32.

supported conspicuously by the King (as the law on hair powder had been), doubtless had effect in some direct savings and in use of substitutes. But the latter foundered, partly on opposition from the bakers and mainly on the refusal of the poorer orders themselves to eat the marked loaves. The earlier change of diet from barley to wheat was now too well entrenched, and the new loaf possibly too inferior, for the former to be lightly abandoned by those to whom bread after all was a staple, and who were sensitive to a threat to nutrition. One authority has gone so far as to say of London that 'The poorer the district, the finer the bread sold.'[1] Certainly experience was to show that it was easier to induce some voluntary denial in those least affected than in those closer to the margin and jealous of their preferences and needs.

There was thus no lack of efforts, whatever their shortcomings, to attack the shortage. But could anything be done by Government to farther the aid to those in want? Parish assistance or employment, 'Speenhamland' schemes, all fell in the last resort within the ambit of the Poor Laws. In a crisis of this magnitude, was there room for fresh legislation?

In two respects it was agreed that there was. In the summer of 1795 the Acts of Settlement were amended once more, to forbid the removal of indigent persons until they became an actual charge on the parish. And early in the next session the principle of 'Speenhamland' was recognised by an Act sanctioning outdoor relief through removing the workhouse test of destitution.[2] By that time Pitt had decided that something more comprehensive might be tried. He may have been drawn or pushed in that direction by the proposal of an alternative. In December 1795 the Foxite Samuel Whitbread moved for a bill to regulate agricultural wages, which received its second reading on 12 February 1796. Opposing the scheme in principle, in a speech whose sympathetic tone and reasoning power were admired by the mover, Pitt 'threw out' some ideas of his own, which he hoped might attract enough approval for him to work on them further. He was certainly prepared to 'do every thing in his power to bring forward or promote . . . measures' on this 'subject of the utmost importance'.[3]

The Minister claimed that these preliminaries were based on careful examination. 'He was not bold enough to imagine that [they] were the result of his own investigations, but . . . they . . . arose from . . . an extensive survey of the opinions of others.'[4] This indeed was clear when the measures were presented in due course. Almost a year elapsed before that happened: a delay castigated by some later historians, and due

---

1. Stern, loc. cit., 183. For the earlier shift to wheaten bread see p. 444 above.
2. 35 Geo. III, c. 101, 36 Geo. III, c. 23.
3. Speech of 12 February 1796 (*P.R.*, XLIV, 27). Cf. p. 447, n3 above.
4. Loc. cit.

almost certainly in large measure to the other calls on Pitt's attention, coupled perhaps with a further easing of wheat prices encouraged by a good harvest, and by a reduction in open unrest.[1] On 22 December 1796 he asked leave to introduce a bill 'for the better support and maintenance of the poor'. After swift scrutiny and some amendments in committee it was printed for public comment, and on 28 February 1797 was brought before the House.[2]

I have used this last phrase because the measure, apparently after little debate, was then at once withdrawn, or put aside for further and it would seem distant consideration. In the event it was not reintroduced. What, one may ask, was the cause of this fiasco, when the bill emanated from a powerful Minister on questions which had long attracted critical discussion?

In the first place, the degree of Ministerial pressure was doubtful. The contents of the bill were associated very much with Pitt himself, almost as a personal initiative; it was not – the Poor Laws never were – a matter of confidence in Government, and in any case the Ministry as an entity does not seem to have been closely concerned. Moreover, in taking personal responsibility Pitt did not pretend to personal expertise. He acknowledged as much: he was anxious at the start for his proposals to be widely circulated so as to gain 'the most serious and mature investigation', and later confirmed that 'Inexperienced himself in country affairs, and in the condition of the poor, he was diffident of his own opinion'.[3] He was not indeed at all well acquainted with the problems. A story survived that, staying in Essex in 1795, probably with his private secretary Joseph Smith, he commented on the relative well-being of the lower orders. He was horrified when his host took him to the town of Halstead the next day, and showed him what conditions could really be like.[4] As one of his Cambridge constituents observed, he was also 'a stranger to the police of a village'.[5] With this confessed lack of certainty and, it would appear, little direct Governmental involvement, the plans perforce stoody uneasily on their merits.

And as such, not surprisingly, they were vulnerable. It was indeed the immediate widespread reaction that killed their chances by the time they came up for Parliamentary debate. Not all the responses in point of fact were unfavourable: Pitt received some plaudits, and as one

---

1. The price which stood at an average of 11s 6d in January and 12s 6¼d in April, was less than 10s throughout most of the second half of 1796, and 7s 4d by its close (Stern, loc. cit., 168). Cf. pp. 455n1, 466 above.

2. *P.R.*, XLIV, 517–19; *H.C.J.*, 52 (1803), 229, index under *Poor*.

3. Speech of March 1800, quoted in J.R. Poynter, *Society and Pauperism . . . 1795–1834* (1969), 75–6.

4. Rosebery, Pitt, 169. For Smith see I, 578. But cf. also Pitt's conjectures on the poor in February 1796, in *P.R.*, XLIV, 22.

5. James Nasmith, in his *The Duties of Overseers . . .* of 1799, quoted Poynter, op. cit., 63n28.

supporter pointed out, the poor themselves were not voicing the complaints.[1] But it was not hard to fault a series of proposals which was so largely a hotchpotch, and the weight of informed opinion was crushing. Pitt, who had relied on published studies, found himself assailed by a tribe of authors; and the helpers he had gathered for the bill could not redress the balance. One cannot tell precisely who they all were: possibly a selection drawn more strongly than usual from outside the Departments – perhaps Wilberforce and Pretyman, the lawyer and MP Charles Abbot, Sylvester Douglas, returned from office in Ireland, the writer Thomas Ruggles, in addition to Rose at the Treasury who had the further advantage of knowing about Friendly Societies.[2] They could not supply what was needed in an intrinsically difficult situation: a command of detail sufficient to meet criticism on specific issues while providing a coherent framework for partial revision of a diffuse and exceptionally complex whole. For a major reshaping was scarcely possible: the climate was not ripe for such an exercise; there was not an agreed social or political approach. And the way in which the matter was handled compounded the problems of inserting extensive but intermediate improvements.[3] As Charles Abbot admitted, where 'the principles were good in substance' their presentation was 'bad in the mode'.[4] 'Administrative incoherence, and extremely poor drafting' overlaid a more excusable 'confusion in aim'.[5]

The main points in the bill can be summarised in a note by Pitt of its 'Heads'.

Removals. Relief in Proportion to Children. Advances. Property not to prevent Relief. Parochial Funds for Superannuation. Work to be found. Schools of Industry. Work at home.[6]

A good deal of attention was given to the appointment and qualifications of 'Visitors' – the men who would be responsible for superintending the Schools of Industry, on which Pitt laid much stress. As usual, they would be drawn predominantly from the gentry – and they would

---

1. See Poynter, op. cit., 66 – a study to which, being like Pitt diffident in this matter, I am much indebted. There are letters of support as well as criticism in P.R.O. 30/8/308.

2. Op. cit., 63, for most of these names. Pretyman sent or returned to Pitt a copy of the bill as amended in committee (p. 472 above), which suggests involvement (P.R.O. 30/8/307). Douglas's [see p. 407 above] part appears in his letters to Pitt of 4 and 10 January 1797, in P.R.O. 30/8/138. Abbot and Ruggles seem to have been recruited at the drafting stage. For Rose and the Friendly Societies see p. 392 above; for Pitt's use of aid, I, 324–5, 510, and for Pretyman op. cit., 4.

3. Cf. Pitt in February, looking to 'an extension of those reformations . . . which had been begun' (*P.R.*, XLIV, 24).

4. *Diary and Correspondence of . . . Lord Colchester*, ed. by his son, Charles, Lord Colchester, I (1861), 82.

5. Poynter, op. cit., 76.

6. P.R.O. 30/8/307; notes in Pitt's hand.

work with the JPs to choose and supervise the Guardians.[1] He was highly critical of the Acts of Settlement, and wished to strengthen the *right* to reside by introducing permission for five years' stay or payment to a Parochial Fund which would provide age and sickness benefits. More drastically, parishes were to be obliged to relieve non-settled poor, reclaiming the cost from their parishes of origin. He insisted that large families should receive relief, and provided for aid in a wider variety of forms: by a compulsory Friendly Society scheme, to encourage frugality and reduce the rates; by loans in certain cases, and a plan for help to owners of small properties. At the same time he emphasised the need to find employment: by the establishment above all of the Schools of Industry, intended at first to be compulsorily standardised, for which he produced a new and elaborate administration. Neither they nor the workhouses, which he hoped to bring into line, should mean however that outdoor relief yielding employment or sustenance, and conceived as a matter of right, was to be abolished. He went into some detail here, of allowances or payments in kind as well as money, proportioned to circumstances and the number of dependants.[2]

The range of proposals showed good intentions. But their shortcomings and inconsistencies were real. Some were attacked as too harsh, either to the ratepayers or to the poor themselves, others – such as the provisions for outdoor relief – as too generous. Contradictions could be argued between the Friendly Society scheme and the Parochial Fund, and strong objections raised to compulsion. There was widespread doubt about the terms and administration of the Schools of Industry and their relations with workhouses. The harnessing of relief to the size of the family was soon to attract the attention of Malthus. Such a range as well as weight of criticism discouraged Pitt. He did not return to the charge, and the next attempt at a bill – also unsuccessful – was made a decade later, after he had died.[3]

It was a sad, an unfortunate, and, it has often been held, a discreditable episode. Pitt, it has been claimed,[4] should at the very least have tried again. This of course would have meant his giving personal detailed attention to a wide-ranging, well-conducted exercise brought within the aegis of Government. He should then have attacked the problems with the intensity he had shown in earlier complicated matters – in the series of measures that had made his reputation in the eighties. It

1. Loc. cit.; Pitt's notes on another copy. There are further notes by him of headings, probably for a speech to the Commons, on another sheet; and copies of the bill as amended in committee. Earlier extensive notes, indicating his intentions, are in P.R.O. 30/58/8.

2. See Poynter, op. cit., 62–76. The *Heads of a Bill* as presented to Parliament were printed in Arthur Young's journal *Annals* (XXVI) and by Sir Frederick Morton Eden (Auckland's nephew) in his influential (and critical) *The State of the Poor . . .* (1797).

3. By Whitbread, in 1807.

4. Particularly by the Hammonds, in *The Village Labourer*; see op. cit., I (1927), 148.

was not beyond his powers to learn fast: he had not lost his dazzlingly swift grasp; his capacity for thorough assimilation remained exceptional. Sinclair was referring to financial concerns when he remarked at this time that 'You take up any hint so quickly, and understand those subjects so thoroughly, that it is sufficient to suggest any idea, and You soon see it in all its bearings'.[1] But if the Poor Laws were much less familiar they could have yielded to treatment, at the hands of a Minister with his experience and gifts. It was a question of will; which meant of priorities; which at this point above all meant of time. For neither in 1796 nor 1797 did circumstances easily favour such an effort.

The weight of accusation indeed might perhaps lie more heavily on Pitt's failure to confide the case to someone else: to another Minister – though who but Hawkesbury could have been considered competent? –, or to a private person – Auckland? – enjoying Ministerial support. He himself was too much engaged in unremitting business – in the conduct of war and attendant diplomacy, and increasingly urgent financial issues – to devote proper care to a large question on which he did not feel at home. If he could already have claimed some knowledge, perhaps he would have found some opportunity. But uninstructed sympathy was not enough in itself. The failure left its accustomed mark. As on some other occasions – the Irish Propositions spring to mind in particular – he did not try again.[2]

One may allow that the sympathy was genuine. Pitt honoured his expressed intentions, and did so indeed at a time when the political incentive might be said in some ways to have declined.[3] The incursion into the Poor Law was postponed; nevertheless it took place, in circumstances rather different from those of the earlier measures directed at shortage. But the background in fact was the same: the need to try to meet a crisis, felt from the start of 1795.[4] That the sum of attempts was limited in effect was due to long-standing constraints, which may have suffered a shock but were not undermined. That attempts were made, including the daunting task of grappling with the Poor Laws, showed the fear as well as concern induced by events. And those events comprehended developments outside as well as inside the country; for while relief schemes might have been expected in any case from the scale of dearth and discontent, the discontent was now directly linked with the state of the war. It was no longer possible to separate the two: by the autumn of 1795 the petitions for aid were also containing urgent pleas for a return to peace.[5] That hope had not diminished a year later: very far from it. The war was going ever more badly and had

1. To Pitt, 11 April [endorsed 1796] (P.R.O. 30/8/178).
2. Cf. I, 110, 215–16.
3. See p. 472 above.
4. See p. 464 above.
5. Cf. p. 452, n2 above for the spring.

become a target for abuse. If its demands therefore hindered a sustained effort to tackle the effects of poverty, it also raised the need for moves, in this respect as in others, to try to calm and reassure.

CHAPTER XIII

The Management of War

I

W hen Pitt aired his views on strategy soon after the war began, they derived, undigested and naturally coloured by immediate events, from concepts brought to their height in the middle decades of the century.[1] Set against a history of public debate, inheritance doubtless played its part. His obvious predilection for coastal assaults and overseas expeditions echoed Chatham's doctrine, particularly in its early phase. But the retention of troops in Flanders after Holland had been saved followed – without much forethought but with growing conviction[2] – the policy which Chatham had come increasingly to accept, contributing a presence to an Allied pressure by land which was accompanied by and underwrote pressure from Britain by sea. It was never easy to maintain 'that fine balance between maritime and continental interests' which, often controverted or seen as paradoxical, was in fact 'the pre-requisite of her rise to naval mastery'.[3] The truism was illustrated directly in the opening years of the First Coalition; as also when conditions altered and the tension was apparently removed. The geographical opportunities produced their corresponding difficulties for an island Power with a smallish population – and representative institutions. Supply of men and materials, logistics, bases, the need to keep Parliament willing to pay, the nature of the current alliances, had all to be managed against the enemy's own performance. The problems were thrown into sharp relief in the years of the First Coalition, as disappointments followed from Allied divergencies which misjudgments in London at times underlined but did not cause. But they were enhanced throughout the period by a strictly British factor which Pitt himself was far from appreciating fully at once. For if the strategic concepts were often hard to apply it was also because they operated, in a struggle of growing complexity, on administrative assumptions that were equally traditional, and in their basic tenets hostile to change.

The influences were reciprocal. Administrative practice helped shape

1. See pp. 266–8 above.
2. Cf. pp. 264–5, 271–2, 294 above.
3. Paul M. Kennedy, *The Rise and Fall of British Naval Mastery* (1976), 88.

as it responded to the lines of policy; underlying national habits of mind owed much to the policies' limited demands. The management of war reflected attitudes developed on the premise that operations were conducted at a distance, through resources which on aggregate the operations themselves could enlarge. This of course, with its accompanying distrust of continental involvements, was the hallmark of 'maritime' thought, and a central reason for the importance assigned to the West Indies throughout the French wars. But however the balance was struck it contained distinctive elements not shared by the other main Allied Powers,[1] which set the mould of administrative form.

Certain features could be noted at the beginning of 1793. The country had a pool of 'prime seamen' in naval and merchant ships and the fisheries, whose voluntary recruitment could be accompanied by the press.[2] There was in fact a reserve of trained manpower, though never large enough for wartime – when the trades that filled the pool also restricted its size – and equally the resolve, however unpopular the effects, to conscript. Neither was the case for overseas military service.[3] If the fighting fleets had to admit competition from the seaborne activities which supplied them, the regular army at first was scarcely a competitor in the manpower market at all. As Pitt was told at the start, Britain was not like those continental states which could count on large numbers of men 'having little Else to do than to come forth for War when wanted'. Our human resources were severely limited (perhaps an undue discounting of the population growth), and predominantly engaged in agriculture and trade. We had 'no Redundancy', and 'ought very much' therefore 'to economise our Men for we had no second army to produce if we waste the first'.[4] It was a cry that would be echoed in later 'Great Wars'. But its strength was the greater at this time from the political connotation. The traditional distrust of a standing army – permitted by the shape of past wars – confined that force in size and quality, and had lately ruled out any form of conscription.[5] There was no impressment even of criminals in 1793; only the county militia, sanctified by an

1. This wording is designed to exclude Spain, whose strategic conditions – like those indeed of France – could be said to resemble Britain's in some respects within a different combination.

2. The legal validity was disputable; but the custom was accepted. Government was able also, and here with indisputable legality, to take vessels for privateering.

3. Until 1780 such military impressment could apply, by a series of statues, to insolvent debtors, convicted criminals, and certain types of pauper – all of them classes of men who in some degree had forfeited their liberty. But the current provisions, expiring then, were not renewed or replaced.

4. Richmond's 'Minutes of Conversation with Mr. Pitt 10 April 1793' (P.R.O., W.O. 30/81. See p. 266, n3 above). And even the horses must be carefully watched, for 'our Cavalry is not like foreign Hussars' who used up indifferent beasts in wasteful succession. It was 'too good & too expensive' to fritter away, and we could not afford to treat lightly 'what by maturity might be a most respectable force'.

5. See n3 above.

Anglo-Saxon origin, could call out the subjects to defend the realm.[1] In operations of war – which meant out of the country – emphasis was placed as before on hiring or subsidising Europeans to augment or avoid the need for British troops. The use of manpower, basic to the conduct of policy and administration, was a prime index of attitudes by now well entrenched.

A complementary manifestation lay in the role assigned to finance. For the attention paid to the needs of trade with its constraints on naval manpower, the reluctance to divert men to the army from the creation of wealth, the practice of hiring foreign troops and when necessary of subsidising allies, were all aspects of its central importance. No one was more convinced of this than Pitt, the instrument of a post-war recovery, the more so as he faced an enemy already in financial trouble. He drew the comparison from the start – undeterred, and rightly, by the early crisis of credit[2] – and it was cardinal to his hopes for more than another two years. 'All modern wars had been remarked to depend on a comparison of the means by which they were to be carried on', and 'the balance of pecuniary resources' was 'on the side of Great Britain'. The French might have 'found a substitute for money', but their success 'could not be permanent'; and 'if he was asked, where was the money to combat their resources?' he could answer in 'the proud situation of this happy island'.[3] The proportions of the thesis began to change as the campaigns progressed. More was heard of the French troubles, rather less of British strength. The concentration on finance could indeed threaten the confidence it had sustained. But this was not in sight when the country settled to providing for another war.

The cultivation of 'pecuniary resources' in turn accorded with established principle. They should in fact be cultivated rather than excessively pressed. The goose must be nourished to lay the eggs, by means which at first were virtually unquestioned. Finance should come, as in earlier wars, from public lending rather than taxes: the latter being used, as in peacetime though naturally on a larger scale, to service the former and the reduction of past (mainly wartime) debt. The levies on land, manufactures and commerce were accordingly kept within strict bounds. And despite the frequent impressions to the contrary among those concerned, as Government took their men and sometimes vessels[4]

1. Cf. pp. 112, 122 above. The Fencibles, as descendants of an earlier idea for 'select militia' (see p. 328 above), may be included in this statement.

2. See pp. 385–7 above.

3. Speeches of 31 December 1794 – when he showed briefly something like despair about the military operations – (*P.R.*, XL, 53, *et seq.* on France's financial plight), 5 February 1795 (op. cit., 395–6). Other examples could be cited from the first three years of war, eg on pp. 523, 580 below.

Notes on French finances may be found among his papers in P.R.O. 30/8/197.

4. See p. 478, n2 above.

and frequently ignored the complaints, the overseas trades, the most sensitive barometer of a wartime economy, were apt to receive particular consideration. Ministers, often wearily, were conditioned to study their interests – Parliamentary pressures were enough to see to that. The great Chartered Companies, with the partial exception of the East India Company, may now have declined; but contact with the last remained regular and close, as it was with some of the burgeoning trading Associations. Whatever the shortcomings, their members were supported in ways which produced results: in a century since 1689, for half the years of which the country was at war, tonnage and port facilities increased despite the incidence of losses and setbacks, and were able to exploit the compensating gains. And based on these facts, an extensive network of activities matured. The measures to protect ocean shipping, some of them enshrined in legislation, formed the apex of a triangle that was broadly based.

Seaborne trade indeed, to a maritime nation, served attack as well as defence. There was the question not only of war trade but also of trade war.[1] The direct denial of supplies to the enemy, by embargoes from this country (laid selectively on this occasion before the war began),[2] by the interruption of his colonial imports and the capture of posts and colonies themselves, was a tried weapon – whose short-term effects might sometimes be overrated, but even then could aid longer-term expansion. Equally tried, but far more controversial and delicate in operation, was indirect denial by preventing the carriage of contraband goods in neutral ships. Posing hard questions of definition – of 'effective blockade' and contraband itself –, and of principle – rights of passage, the freedom of the seas – this was a thorn for diplomats to grasp as well as a stick for the navy to wield. For the belief in the efficacy of such pressure had always to be balanced against the danger of driving neutrals too far. The League of Armed Neutrality was a recent warning, and a diplomatic target in 1793.[3] But while the problems were perceived there was no disposition to moderate the claim: Ambassadors and Ministries pursued their efforts in the context, it was held, of legitimate need. Blockade and neutral rights were prominent questions for Britain from the start, as in earlier wars. They were handled, like others, in a firm framework of inherited doctrine.

Financial strength, fed partly by and in turn feeding maritime power, was a distinct and prominent ingredient of military strategy as well. It allowed – and perhaps encouraged – the policy on a substantial scale of hiring mercenaries and, one way or another, subsidising continental states. Developed mainly in the Seven Years' War, this was applied at

1. Cf. G.N. Clark's article on the later seventeeth century, 'War Trade and Trade War', in *Ec.H.R.*, I.
2. P. 238 above.
3. See pp. 275–7 above.

once, if at first reluctantly, in 1793. The amounts were considerable, and they rose very soon: taking sums authorised or guaranteed by Government,[1] from almost £800,000 for the first year to over £2½ million for 1794 and some £5½ million for 1795. The last figure indeed was to prove the highest for another eighteen years, though only because it included a large loan as well as a subsidy and mercenary payments.[2] It probably accounted for something like one fifth of naval and military expenditure, as that for 1794 probably did for about one seventh.[3] Such proportions were significant. They would have been impossible without the strong belief in an active economy as a weapon of war.

They also showed the importance attached to the existence of an Allied Coalition. The American War in particular had taught a lesson in that respect. 'France', it had been prophesied earlier in the century, 'will outdo us at sea when they have nothing to fear on land', and the Admiralty could confirm the danger in due course when there was 'no other . . . object' to distract the enemy and England for a change had 'no one friend or ally'.[4] The direct challenge was perhaps less now that the French navy had been hit by revolution; but it was not removed,[5] and in the wider context of grand strategy the arguments prevailed. 'Mere naval exertions are not sufficient against a country not possessing the command of the sea';[6] military pressures too must be sought, and sustained where they occurred. The proportions of the British commitments in men might vary with events. 'British gold' was the more necessary to the concerted effort.

A strategy so dependent on a concept of complementary functions posed distinctive problems for administrative control. There is always a narrow line, in allotting resources, between mutual support and competition, and it was particularly likely to be blurred in this instance. An unusually wide combination of Powers, whose natural interests were largely opposed, placed a heavy strain on British options and their implementation. Given the traditional limits of the executive machinery, scarcely altered by the most recent war and three naval 'armaments' since,[7] it was not surprising that the response was

1. As distinct from funds raised on the London money market without such backing.
2. For which see pp. 519–20 below. Figures are broad and some of the calculations disputable (see Sherwig, *Guineas and Gunpowder*, 362–8); and the former, it should be stressed, apply to allocations and not necessarily to payments.
3. Mitchell and Deane, *Abstract of British Historical Statistics*, 391. But again one must recall the contemporary warning quoted in I, 276 on the unreliability of exact calculations.
4. Duke of Newcastle in 1742, Earl of Sandwich in 1779 (see Admiral Sir Herbert Richmond, *Statesmen and Sea Power* (1946), 107, 151).
5. Cf. p. 349 above.
6. Pitt in 1794 (p. 348 above).
7. For the Dutch crisis, Nootka Sound, and Ochakov.

inadequate at first and development patchy and slow.

Running through the system was the acceptance of diffused authority. In war as in peace the executive should not be given too much unitary power. The Crown should be restrained by a supporting Parliament, and its Departments of State weighed in a balance of constitutional responsibilities. This last fact could be seen at one point of final impact, the battle front itself. For the soldier, whose recruitment and service already fell under three autonomous military authorities, was largely kept in being on campaign by an organisation under the Treasury. Pitt's official contact with the army in the Low Countries was as First Lord of that Department, communicating with the Commissary General, who performed those tasks. The arrangement was not, and was known not to be, particularly satisfactory. Commissaries, like certain other account-ants to the Treasury, were personally responsible for their public funds – an obligation that could last for decades until the books were cleared.[1] They were the more liable to grasp personal opportunities, and the fact was widely accepted: as Cornwallis put it to Pitt, there were so many 'inviting examples'.[2] But if the officials were in a lucrative, they were also in an exposed position: civilians in a military setting, not on the peacetime establishment and generally looked on as not quite gentle-men.[3] They always needed the 'Countenance & protection' of their Minister as well as the goodwill of the commander on the spot.[4] In this instance York proved co-operative, and Pitt seems to have done his best, particularly perhaps in the first campaign. He picked a good man, with professional experience and also some political substance: Brook Watson, the leading (Pittite) MP for the City of London until his appointment, who was subsequently Lord Mayor in a critical year. Such a choice gave Pitt the added advantage – which he sought deliberately – of placing a personal source of information at head-quarters:[5] an example of his turning a given arrangement to profitable use. But that was to make the best of a poorish job. This particular separation of functions was more in tune with theory than helpful in practice, and even with more intimate contact the old difficulties remained.

The fact was of more than marginal importance. Subsistence in the field could always raise stern problems. 'Famine,' it had recently been

1. Cf. I, 301. This particular Commissary General's accounts were wound up in 1812, by which time he was dead.

2. See *Correspondence of Cornwallis*, III, 103.

3. Cf. Wellington, quoted in Richard Glover, *Peninsular Preparation* . . . (1963), 256.

4. Brook Watson to Pitt, Private, 6 June 1793 (P.R.O. 30/8/187).

5. See Watson's letters, 1793–5, loc. cit. and P.R.O. 30/58/1. He had been a Commissary in the Seven Years' War and a Commissary General in the War of American Independence. His name may be more familiar as the subject of the remarkable painting by Copley, depicting him losing his leg as a boy to a shark in the Caribbean. He became Lord Mayor in 1796.

said, 'makes greater havoc of an army than the enemy',[1] and there was to be an ample reminder in the winter of 1794–5. It would be absurd to lay the blame on that occasion entirely on these administrative shortcomings: there are times when no system can be expected to save the day, and the causes of the British retreat themselves lay elsewhere.[2] Nor must it be forgotten that the enemy suffered almost equal muddle and hardship in success. War is a hard master, and the circumstances of the late eighteenth century often made nonsense of radical as of traditional measures. But this was not the point. Revolutionary France was in essence challenging the limits: in tactics, methods of conscription, movement and supply. She did so by exploiting quite recent developments as elements of transformation: 'The secret of the success of the new French armies was to lie in the combination of the professionalism of the *ancien régime* with the enthusiasm of a Nation in Arms'.[3] And both halves of the equation were necessary. Professional improvements were not confined to France: they had counterparts, if less searching, among the Allied states. But no Allied army, or national organisation, was designed to rest on a popular will. However far short the French might fall in their aim, or the people tire of the effects, there was as yet no counterpart to that principle elsewhere. It would be many years in fact before some other nations were driven to discover an equivalent. Meanwhile the Coalition approached conditions which often baffled both sides without the stimulus which set those conditions in a changing light.

It might be thought curious that in England the approach should find perhaps its most extreme expression in the management of 'what for simplicity may be called the Army'.[4] After all, here was an area of business calling for integrated decisions. The reasons of course stemmed from historical fears. For it was not that the British tradition necessarily precluded effective management: the national system throughout the century served a marked expansion of power. Nor was the calibre of the officials always to be despised: if – in a sense because – there were sinecurists and idlers, there were also capable men at work.[5] It was rather that the courses of politics and strategy had produced a climate of thought in which the military organisation could be kept in compartments without excessive risk to the country's physical defence. Very occasionally, in invasion scares, its effectiveness was publicly discussed. More often it could be ignored, and projects for improvement indeed held in suspicion. Even after years of a great war, the army was not

1. Thomas Simes, *Treatise of Military Science* (1780); quoted in Glover, op. cit., 255–6.
2. Pp. 337–44, 373–5 above. And, as Pitt was informed, the arrangements in the field were improved in some respects during its course (see the manual on the Commissariat by Havilland Le Mesurier among Pitt's papers, in P.R.O. 30/8/242, which is reproduced in Glover, op. cit., Appendix B).
3. Michael Howard, *War in European History* (1976), 80.
4. Mackesy, *The War for America*, 14.
5. Cf. I, 179.

looked on as 'the characteristic and constitutional force of Britain'.[1] The feeling ran deep at the outset, in face of a range of sudden demands.

The 'principle of multiple diffusion' therefore survived.[2] The King in person was head of the army, and like his predecessors actively so: involved in appointments, regimental affairs, the conduct – and employment – of his troops. His authority could be exercised, outside the financial and Parliamentary spheres, through a Commander-in-Chief; and one was appointed in 1793 shortly before the outbreak of war. But while the occasion, as it proved, reintroduced an Office that then endured continuously for over a century, with a staff soon ensconced in what were to become familiar quarters in the Horse Guards, such a project might well have seemed surprising at the time. Commanders-in-Chief had been temporary figures; the sovereign could always resume his functions directly; and Pitt was in fact prepared to see the appointment lapse only two years after it had been revived.[3] He did so on the ground that the War Office could carry out the executive duties. But the Secretary at War, if advancing in political status at that point,[4] was still a constitutionally minor figure. He prepared the Estimates, and answered financial and administrative questions in the Commons; but, as one of the incumbents had remarked in the American War, he 'was no minister, and could not be supposed to have a competent knowledge of . . . how the war was to be carried on'.[5] Nor did the War Office draw and distribute the moneys for which it estimated: that was the province of the Paymaster General of the Forces. Its responsibilities moreover covered only the regular infantry and cavalry in Great Britain: artillery and engineers and their supplies fell to the Master General of the Ordnance, the 'unembodied' militia and Volunteers to a Secretary of State, and much of the system was duplicated in Ireland.[6] When one adds to this pattern the semi-autonomous functions of the regimental colonels with their agents, it was not surprising that the army could look as if it belonged to several 'different sovereign states'.[7]

Such autonomy made for cumbersome and often inefficient processes. Again one must not exaggerate – which is easy enough to do. As one studies the administrative chart and then experiences suffered, it is tempting to draw conclusions about cause and effect. Not all of them would be justified: sensible men often managed to sidestep and

---

1. Quotation of 1808; op cit., 313.

2. See op. cit., 312.

3. For Amherst's appointment see p. 261, n1 above and, together with the administrative arrangements, Charles M. Clode, *The Military Forces of the Crown*, II (1869), 263–4, 335. Pitt's attitude early in 1795 appears on p. 491 below.

4. See pp. 368, 412n1, 414 above.

5. Mackesy, op. cit., 15.

6. And the forces in India fell partly under the East India Company; cf. I, 170–1, 454–5.

7. Quoted op. cit., 171.

sometimes to leap the hurdles; there were institutions outside the Departments which could supplement the latter's efforts, and were regularly used; and when one particular set of shortcomings is removed another in any case is apt to develop. Every war can show its characteristic failures in management. But when that has been said, one has to underline what was characteristic of the late eighteenth century. For the current arrangements were singularly suited to foster two major defects. They harboured, indeed they promoted, a legalistic approach; at the same time, and in a sense paradoxically, they did nothing to discourage the amateurism which permeated the British system at large. The latter fact, widely approved in this instance as a protection, was continually visible both in the offices and in the field. It accounted for instance for the quality of much of the planning and intelligence – the inadequate checking and assessment, the lack of briefing, even of maps.[1] The former was endemic in the organisations it served; an easy shelter in times of trouble, a barrier often of first resort. Separate in their natures, the two characteristics combined to set a premium on personal efforts in conditions strongly resistant to change.

The efforts were often forthcoming. The Government was far from inactive; and its measures were not unskilfully adapted to the case. For given the pattern of the military system, in the Departments and the forces themselves, there could be no real likelihood early in the war of substantial innovations. Those would come, if at all, only from urgent need, and that was acknowledged only towards the end of the First Coalition. Meanwhile Ministers and officials, often grouped around Pitt in person, took such steps as they thought the constraints would allow.

The sequence was perhaps most marked in the essential business of raising men. Tentative and makeshift as the methods were, the results numerically were impressive. In fact by the spring of 1795 – assisted by rising rural distress – recruiting had reached a peak which was not surpassed, and seldom sustained, for the rest of the decade. The regular forces on the British establishment, some 35,000 at the start of the war, rose to almost 125,000 two years later. Even so, in mid-1795 there was a deficit of some 50,000 on the authorised strength. These facts were cause both for congratulation and for serious thought. They contained the highest returns from recruitment in the wars of the past half-century. They also suggested the scale of the demands and of the achievable current response.[2]

---

1. Eg pp. 288–90, 299, 318–19 above.
2. See Fortescue, op. cit., IV – Part II, 887, 938–40; J.R. Western, 'The Recruitment of the Land Forces in Great Britain, 1793–99' (Ph.D thesis, University of Edinburgh, 1953), 8, 10. These authorities show some discrepancies in their figures, but both exclude for this purpose the Irish and East India Company's establishments and foreign mercenaries. Cf. also Sir George Yonge's claim for 1793, in the Commons on 3 February 1794 (*P.R.*, XXXVII, 254), which included some enlistment beyond the regulars themselves.

The Government made use of the traditional arrangements – the recruiting lieutenant and sergeant with the bounty, and the contractor or 'crimp' whose methods could sometimes be closer to impressment than inducement. Its first recourse in 1793 was to augment the existing regiments: to bring them up to strength – according to Dundas later, only one was fully effective, and that was in India[1] – and if possible expand by direct recruitment and absorbing 'independent companies' privately raised. But as the campaign made ever greater demands, a plan was adopted in the autumn to raise new regiments on a sizeable scale. These soon brought in very useful numbers – some 30,000 by the following March – in contrast to the process of augmentation, which was a failure. Nevertheless, the dual policy suffered as losses rose in the next two years, and by the end of 1795 the emphasis in recruiting had shifted again to the existing regiments. Pitt followed the efforts closely.[2] He had his own lists of services and requirements, of dispositions, targets and results. From the late summer of 1794 at least he kept the detailed weekly states of infantry and cavalry. And in July of that year he launched a scheme to raise regiments under the auspices of individual towns. Put quickly into effect, this had some immediate success: sixteen were formed by their respective towns in 1794–5, all but two for the Line.[3] Of equal significance, the experiment had an implication for the future, in shifting recruitment for the regular army in part from the central to the local authorities. But that would await a later period, in sterner circumstances. The first phase of the war saw Ministers working through somewhat haphazard expedients to limits which they thought it wise to accept.

Experiments were tried more widely, with varying rates of success, on the non-regular forces confined, initially, to home defence. Not surprisingly, this happened mainly when fears of invasion rose, and the first of such occasions was early in 1794. Following the review of precautions by Richmond with Pitt and Dundas, a major development of the auxiliaries began in the spring.[4] It branched out in some new directions, adding to recruitment for the foot militia the formation of Fencible cavalry and the extension and statutory recognition of Volunteer corps. Subscriptions were also sought towards local defence. Some of these proposals, with their political as well as military connotations, brought the pressures on the latter at once to the fore. The battle in Parliament and in the country indeed underlined the classic connexion, central to national attitudes for the past century and a half.

1. To Grenville, 21 July 1798 (*H.M.C., Dropmore*, IV, 264).
2. See particularly P.R.O. 30/8/196–8, 239–45.
3. Western, loc. cit., 7, 52. Pitt's role appears clearly in Nepean to Matthew Lewis [at the War Office], 14 July [1794] (B.L. Add. Ms 37874).
4. See pp. 328–9 above.

It was not surprising that the Foxites should have headed attacks on subscriptions to local defence, or felt nervous about the nature of the Volunteers.[1] And while the Ministry had its way, at Westminster and beyond, the episode confirmed the constant need for caution where military forces were concerned.[2]

The results were useful. It can be argued that the policy robbed the regular army of men. How far this may be true it would seem impossible to tell. One may doubt, however, if the men in question were likely to have so enlisted: they, much more than the regulars, were a cross-section of the population. The augmentation of the militia yielded only some 2,700 by the end of the year. But, aided by high bounties, there was a spate of Fencible regiments and Volunteer corps,[3] and it was here that developments indeed were most marked, in type as well as in numbers. Although some artillery had been formed on the coasts in the invasion scare of 1779, it had been on an uncertain footing, and when there was small-scale recruiting in 1793 it was by the Commander-in-Chief, which caused confusion later.[4] The Act now set up three types of corps: coastal artillery, infantry, and cavalry – the first Yeomanry. Government made a contribution to the costs, and the officers held their commissions from the King. But they were entered and administered by the Lords Lieutenant, whose authority the Crown was careful to accept, and in training and terms of service the formations were essentially local.[5] The same applied of course to the Fencibles, privately raised, and the militia itself, the latter embodied by stages in 1793 and extended – for the first time in many years and without much success – to the City of London in 1794.[6] The organisation was also amended to allow regiments to recruit directly, which eased some of the complications of the militia ballots. These were interesting steps in the evolution of a system. In the counties themselves the effect was to add further ingredients to the perennial brew of local alliances and conflicts.

1. See pp. 401–2 above, and for Pitt's papers on the measures P.R.O. 30/8/244.

2. Not least by a Foxite argument that there was 'a wide distinction' in such matters between the military and the navy (*The Senator*, IX, 872).

3. Fortescue lists 88 of the former, 33 being cavalry (loc. cit., 941–4). For the latter see n5 below

4. Western, 'Recruitment of the Land Forces', 236–7.

5. See 34 Geo. III, c. 31. The Yeomanry, of which 81 troops may have been raised in 1794 – more, probably, than artillery and infantry (Fortescue, loc. cit., 892; Western, loc. cit., 237) – could serve in neighbouring counties if required at any time, and anywhere in the kingdom in an invasion (see pp. 401–2 above); infantry only within five miles of the recruiting centre. Artillery was designed to be stationary in coastal defence.

The sense of the relations between the Crown and the Lords Lieutenant is forcibly conveyed in Clode, *The Military Forces of the Crown*, I (1869), 281 – an admirable work by a War Office veteran, which among its sources of interest encapsulates an older constitutional approach then coming under strain.

6. By 34 Geo. III, c. 81, and recapitulatory Acts of 1795 and 1796. The Tower Hamlets (likewise a Lieutenancy) were also considered in 1794, but left alone until 1796.

Such a pattern reflected Government's position very clearly: its tentative efforts to enter more fully into arrangements on which it must depend.[1] The new Acts, in forwarding the first, had to recognise the second. The part-time forces were self-contained, and could not be moved as Government might wish, though some Fencible regiments did agree to serve in Ireland or the Channel Islands if required.[2] Nor was tighter control favoured by the compromise reached between the Secretaries of State themselves when their duties were redefined in 1794.[3] The retention of the militia by the Home Secretary gave him the Volunteers under the new Act, a function which he retained for another four years; and while Portland and Dundas worked together quite amicably the former had no love of innovation, and was in any case on the fringe of the group that conducted the war. When fear of invasion rose next, in 1796, the structure of the forces remained the same, as did the attachment to the voluntary principle, maintained under an equally resolute division of responsibilities.

One of the main reasons indeed for the emphasis on Fencibles and Volunteers, who retained such independence, was that they would come forward willingly. Given the unpopularity of military service and the resistance to undue pressure – shown in the past in militia riots, and at this point in the crimping riots as recruitement for the regular army was stepped up[4] – quality was at a premium and never easy to find. The part-time soldiers varied widely according to the source: the Yeomanry perhaps at the top, the urban infantry formations at the bottom. But while there was plenty of desertion from the militia, and the bounty could play as great a part in all quarters as patriotism, those two inducements could secure a reasonable proportion of reliable men. The authorities' reports indicate a not unrepresentative cross-section of the country. This was certainly not so with the regular troops. Wellington was far from being the first General to regard his recruits as 'the scum of the earth', and while the verdict can be softened slightly it was basically true. Drawn so largely from the unemployed, the young man in trouble, the petty criminal, the hard case, the army was a legion foreign to the stream of ordinary life. One can exaggerate the extent to which it took the sweepings of society: the recruiting officers, particularly as the regiments themselves took over increasingly from the professionals,

---

1. A process pointed by Pitt's acceptance of the need, in face of Parliamentary pressure, to introduce the Militia and Volunteer bills ministerially himself. His speech on the latter was said by one hearer, politically opposed, to have been outstandingly effective (see *Diary of Joseph Farington*, I, 179). Eight years before, when a bill for militia reform had been proposed, he thought it more appropriate for a private Member (see J.R. Western, *The English Militia in the Eighteenth Century* (1965), 200–2).

2. Western, 'Recruitment of the Land Forces', 52.

3. See pp. 412–13 above.

4. Pp. 103, 451 above; and cf. p. 485.

tried, if often without much hope, to reject the worst.[1] Some regiments indeed had their loyalties, and their own savage code of behaviour. The difficulty was discipline, at least off the field. It was typical of the Guards, for instance, to step forward to a man when called on to volunteer for Holland at the start of the war, and to arrive drunk almost to a man at the end of their march to the ports. Once beyond the picked flank company of a battalion, quality could be quite uncertain. And so it could be among the officers, above all perhaps in the cavalry and the Guards. York may have suffered exceptionally from insubordination;[2] but Wellington himself in due course was to have a perpetual struggle. Throughout the corps moreover there were scattered gentlemen with commissions given for raising their companies:[3] an intensification of the independent flavour which permeated the regiments as a whole. It would have been surprising to be told that the British army would end the wars as the finest Allied fighting force. In the earlier phases the Austrians and Prussians were not highly impressed.

Pitt himself at first had little idea of the level of performance; and, as he was told, counting heads was of limited use.[4] In the early nineties he had been involved in a review of pay and conditions, to try to improve peacetime enlistment and reduce desertion.[5] But his concern was centred on economy, as it then was in all military affairs,[6] about which in point of fact he knew very little. He confessed as much when the war was under way – 'I distrust extremely any Ideas of my own on Military Subjects'[7] – and his study of them seems to have been confined, at least judging by his library, to manuals of drill and fortification; matters moreover touching mainly his last years.[8] His one pre-war intervention, made to provide against the threat of domestic unrest, was to set up a new department to build and maintain barracks.[9] An administrative departure, this was not a financial success. Barracks hitherto had fallen

---

1. There was always a division of opinion about how best to recruit. Some of the highest authorities, including Dundas and the King himself, disliked the professional corps and agents. The War Office however tended to prefer them. In the event there was a shift to the regiments from 1795.

Pitt seems personally to have approved the use of 'the Crimps in London', which was suggested by Amherst in August 1794 (Stanhope Ms S5 01/1; Kent CAO).

2. P. 330 above.

3. See p. 486 above.

4. See p. 267 above.

5. See papers from Sir William Fawcett [Adjutant General] and Richmond, August–November 1791, in P.R.O. 30/8/243. Problems of enlistment for Britain and for Ireland as seen in 1787 are surveyed in a memorandum from 'D.D' (presumably David Dundas; see pp. 316–17 above, and 490 below) in P.R.O. 30/8/323.

6. Eg p. 262 above for the West Indies at this time.

7. To Windham, 21 September 1794 (*The Windham Papers*, I (1913), 246).

8. Pretyman Ms 562:21 (Suffolk R.O., Ipswich); cf. I, 14 n2.

9. See p. 195 above.

under the Ordnance Office, and it was perhaps with an eye to the fiasco of 1786, when the Commons rejected Richmond's plan for fortifications,[1] that Pitt thought of a separate instrument to circumvent delay. In June 1792 a Barrackmaster General's Department was formed, its accounts being placed under the Army Extraordinaries, which meant that they were not immediately submitted to Parliament. The scheme, not unnaturally, soon aroused attacks in the Commons, and these grew when it was examined by a series of committees and commissions from 1797. A disquieting picture was revealed. The Barrackmaster General appeared to be largely independent, even of the Secretary for War whose subordinate he was presumed to be; and the financial supervision which Pitt claimed for the system[2] was proved to be illusory – on the contrary, over £9 million was spent without proper record in just over a decade. The arrangements were revoked in the end, though not until the year after his death. They were a sad commentary on the judgment of a Minister who, with whatever restrictions, had created the Commission for Auditing the Public Accounts.[3]

A temporary pressure, considered urgent, had thus dictated an uncharacteristic move. The barracks' programme, however, did serve its purpose in making for a greater mobility of troops[4] and helping to reduce the ancient problem of quartering them on the populace. Other aids to efficiency came more directly from within the army itself. Both training and conditions of service were in fact attracting professional attention. Richmond (a General as well as a Minister), and David Dundas – a better staff officer than commander[5] – had recently published studies of tactics, and the latter was responsible in 1792 for new regulations for exercises and drill. If there was scarcely the flowering of thought that distinguished the last decades of the old French army – with Bourcet and Guibert, du Teil and Gribeauval – if indeed doctrine looked rather to Prussia, some thought was at least being applied; and Guibert was translated. Wartime experience now began to lead to further changes in training and equipment. Cavalry exercises were reorganised in 1795, weapons and saddlery improved, veterinary surgeons regularly appointed, and the breeding of the horses themselves was reviewed. In 1795, too, infantry drill was taken seriously in hand, and the first two companies of riflemen were formed in Britain.[6] Less was done in this early period for other aspects of service; but the men's pay was raised, at least temporarily, in 1795 to compensate

1. I, 517–19.
2. Speech in the Commons, 8 April 1796 (*P.R.*, XLIV (1796), 389–90).
3. See I, 301–3.
4. Cf. p. 126 above.
5. Pp. 267n2, 489n5 above.
6. Riflemen in point of fact dated back to the 1750s; but only on an *ad hoc* basis in colonial warfare. Grey (see p. 356 above) trained and used them in the West Indies in 1794.

partially for the rise in the price of bread.[1] The provision of clothing remained a matter of chance, depending mostly on the colonels, and the campaigns of 1793-4 were in fact supplied largely by public subscriptions, the War Office even proving unable to find enough boots. In 1795 the cavalry benefited from a transfer of some of these items to public funds. But it was another three years before there was a wider survey, and then the recommendations were not carried out. A more serious attempt was made to take the medical arrangements in hand, as the opening campaigns revealed their futility. A Medical Board was set up in 1794 to direct a unified service, with supplies and hospitals financed by Government and the surgeons placed on a more regular footing. This sensible reorganisation was unfortunately altered a few years later, when the regiments and the Ordnance Board reasserted traditional claims. But at any rate some attention was being paid to the subject; and in 1795 an advance was made with the setting up of a special Board to advise on supplies, conditions and practice for a new expedition to the West Indies. Commanders themselves, here and there, were also doing what they could for the soldier's lot: Grey and later Abercromby in the Caribbean[2] gained the confidence of their men and showed that consideration was no enemy of discipline. They set standards which others – Charles Stuart and Sir John Moore perhaps most prominently – would equal, and which meanwhile were recognised increasingly in Whitehall itself.

For it was not by chance that so many of the improvements were set on foot in 1795. They came for the most part from a new Commander-in-Chief.[3] Pitt's role in this development was not deliberate. York was proposed for the Office purely to remove him from Holland while assuaging the King,[4] and no one foresaw his success – as notable for the army as were Middleton's proposals for the navy. The Minister indeed would have been content to leave the post vacant, relying on the War. Office; and it had an implication perhaps likewise unforeseen. For the revival of the Office, now effectively filled, had been followed by the establishment, itself essentially for political reasons, of the new Secretaryship of State for War.[5] Whatever the causes, and despite the addition indeed of one more – and reluctant – authority, there were thus in embryo revised possibilities with which to face the problems of an inchoate system. As it turned out, the latter were too deep-rooted to be properly subdued. But the machinery now afforded a prospect at least of

1. Cf. pp. 443-4 above.
2. For the latter see pp. 566-7 below.
3. Building not infrequently on the experience gained recently in Flanders. The improvements to the cavalry for instance were based on lessons learned, and already being applied, by David Dundas and Major Le Marchant (a few years later to be the founder of the Royal Military College).
4. P. 374 above.
5. P. 411 above.

greater uniformity in effecting improvements to the material on which policy must rest.

Such a prospect might have seemed more promising at first in the Ordnance. For that Department was designed for an ampler control of its affairs. These were varied: the Ordnance supplied its material to both the military and the naval forces, managed its own sea transport, built most forts and fieldworks,[1] and controlled the artillery and the engineers. But unlike the other military Offices it was master of its own house, administratively and financially, through the Master General and the Board. The former moreover was a functionary of high and ancient standing: normally – when there was no Commander-in-Chief – regarded as Government's principal military adviser. While not necessarily a member of the Cabinet he was often politically important,[2] and if his duties were complicated by a division between military and civil, and by a balance of power in the latter between himself and the Board, he carried an authority which offered real scope to an active incumbent. No one could deny that quality to Richmond – even Shelburne had acknowledged it – and the Department bore witness to his efforts in the decade before the war.[3] The foundation of the Trigonometrical (better known as the Ordnance) Survey and of the Royal Military Artificers (later to be absorbed into the Royal Engineers), the first public examination of entrants to the old Royal Military Academy at Woolwich, a notable improvement in gunpowder: all showed his zeal in reform. Further steps were taken in the early years of war. On the eve, in January 1793, a Horse Artillery was formed on the Prussian model, and in 1794 – six years before Buonaparte, the great gunner, followed suit – a corps of Royal Artillery Drivers within the Field Artillery. These novelties were set in a context of steady application across much of the spectrum of the Ordnance's work. Over twenty years after he had gone, Richmond was remembered as a head 'whom no man went before in knowledge of the details of his Department'.[4]

But such a personal contribution in fact attested the need. The Duke's successors, first Cornwallis then Chatham, himself interrupted briefly by Moira, made little mark – unless Chatham's lethargy is counted as a negative impression – and their lack of impact threw into relief the constraints on Richmond's own performance. These lay in the public as well as the Government's own domain. The Ordnance's prime task was

1. And before 1792, barracks (cf. p. 195 above).
2. Cf. p. 261, n1 above. The mixture of the professional and political aspects was exemplified by Richmond, who as Master General in Shelburne's Ministry resigned from the Cabinet but retained his Office, which he regarded as a military responsibility.
3. See I, 91, 312.
4. The verdict of R.H. Crew, Secretary of the Ordnance, in 1817; quoted Glover, op. cit., 109.

that of supply. But its system of procurement intensified the problems. The Department produced some of its goods itself: cannon (apart from mortars) and their carriages, ammunition of all kinds, and more recently some of the gunpowder. It relied however on private sources for the weapons most widely needed – for small arms, with their parts[1] – and this added greatly to the complications of programmes which in any case were hard to meet. There was not a vast immediate gap between peacetime and wartime Ordnance orders for the navy. But it was large enough – and of course it grew steadily – to cause problems in the main loading areas, at Woolwich and Portsmouth, where the dockyard authorities were jealous of space. The position was far more serious initially for the army, in an industry scarcely capable of rapid expansion. Peacetime military demands had been low, stocks must now be quickly increased, and there was bound to be a shortage of skilled men. The difficulties were compounded by competition, which the Department failed to overcome for some years. Some of this came from Europe; and while one large buyer, France, was removed – leaving stocks however that would not take British ammunition – others began to emerge from Allied Powers now taking British patterns. A greater part was domestic: from the East India Company for its forces, and also from within the Government itself. The Treasury and the War Office were never reluctant to raid the industry for short-term needs in the successive emergencies of 1794–5. The problems facing the Ordnance in fact led to practices that increased them, as different Departments vied with each other as well as with the outside world. Richmond and his officials did their best. They scoured the workshops, tried to hasten payments, took steps with the East India Company. But, as they recognised, their efforts were inadequate. Orders had to be placed abroad – in Liège, later in Germany and Denmark – against a background of rising prices and sometimes falling standards at home. It was not until the second half of the decade that the Ordnance began to get a grip of the position, in ways that eventually were to make Britain the armourer of the final Alliance.

The inter-departmental rivalry for arms was symptomatic of a wider problem. For the Ordnance was placed in a sensitive relationship with the other armed services. This of course was endemic, as it usually is, in an arrangement which, whatever its merits, provides for a separate authority in an area of supply. The files of the Defence Departments and the Ministry of Supply in the Second World War will bear that out. But the hazards were heightened in the eighteenth century by the Ordnance's control of troops as well as material, by the greater physical obstacles to effective co-ordination, and not least by the extreme ease with which normal bureaucratic jealousies could be translated into constitutional terms. Such factors bore hard on practices and habits as

1. A tentative proposal in 1794 to manufacture these in Ordnance workshops was rejected within the Department.

rife within the Department as outside: procrastination, local independence, the blurring of public and private benefit. The effects indeed had bedevilled its reputation for a least a century: from the days of Pepys to those of Wellington the Ordnance was accused of corruption and delay. There was no exception in the 1790s, as the failure of Dunkirk first proved;[1] and the fact that the Master General was Richmond was certainly no help. For unfair as this may seem – and was – when his achievements are remembered, his unpopularity with the public and his awkwardness as a colleague[2] strengthened the temptation to lay the blame at his door. The Department's shortcomings were moreover underlined in these years by comparison in the field. The British could not match the French in artillery, the arm in which the latter excelled. But the main cause of the Ordnance's persistent bad press lay, as hitherto, elsewhere: in the combination of its autonomy in important, sometimes difficult, processes with a necessarily continuous, intimate involvement in its customers' affairs.

The most powerful of the customers, viewed as an entity, was the navy. The Admiralty with its subordinate Boards was in a position of strength. It stood second only to the Treasury at the head of an administrative pyramid,[3] based on a network of establishments – dockyards, victualling and rope yards, hospitals – and a range of operational business rivalled by no other single Department. The system was exceptionally self-contained. If the Ordnance supplied the guns, it did not – as with the military – supply the gunners: no men indeed in the sea service came under an extraneous authority, and the navy had its own 'sea soldiers' – though seldom enough – in the form of Marines. To a much greater extent than the Ordnance the Navy Board possessed its own means of production. The Victualling Board was unique in the scale of its arrangements for food and drink. The Commissioners for Sick and Wounded, likewise under the Admiralty, ran two permanent hospitals among their other duties.[4] And the whole system was reproduced with variations in the bases overseas. Such an organisation – producing its own measure of Parliamentary patronage – naturally carried weight in its relations with others. Even more than the Paymaster General for the army, the Treasurer of the Navy was free in practice of detailed Treasury supervision;[5] and in a degree unknown to any of the military authorities, the Admiralty had a structure capable of accommodating the exercise of policy and administrative control.

1. Pp. 290, 293 above.
2. See pp. 287–8, 293 above.
3. Cf. I, 282.
4. At Haslar and Plymouth. Greenwich Hospital was the equivalent of the army's Chelsea: a home for pensioners, under its own Board.
5. See I, 302–3, 312.

The structure; but not necessarily the skill to exploit the assets. The navy started the war in good shape in many ways. Its ships indeed were in perhaps 'an unprecedented state of preparation',[1] a state of affairs for which Pitt himself could take much of the credit. A substantial programme of rebuilding and repair had been carried out in the past decade; and, aided by experience in the mobilisations from 1787 to 1791,[2] the 93 sail of the line had a healthy stock of equipment and stores. In contrast to the army as shown by the level of supplies for the Low Countries, the fleet by and large was ready for the necessary intake of men and not unduly hampered in its main operations. The capacities of the yards were stretched when unforeseen needs arose in competition – when Jervis for instance stripped Portsmouth in 1793 at Moira's expense.[3] But in strictly naval terms maintenance and repairs were sustained without excessive interference to construction, particularly of smaller ships which had been somewhat neglected in the peacetime programme. Victualling arrangements on the whole likewise took the strain. And the health of the fleets in European waters, above all in the main Channel fleet, improved conspicuously over previous wars. It continued indeed to do so, thanks to some unusually intelligent physicians and to standards of hygiene maintained by Howe and later improved by St Vincent. Matters of course were much worse in the West Indies, where the squadrons were hard struck despite the example of improvements in the American War; but even there the early years were the worst, before medical supplies were reorganised and a naval hospital was set up in Martinique. Taking the navy a whole, the figures in the hospital records are significant: some 31,600 sick and 2,200 dead out of an establishment of 100,000 (probably rather fewer actually serving) in 1782, some 21,400 and 990 respectively out of some 81,700 serving in 1794 – and some 12,000 and 1,600 out of just under 100,000 serving ten years later.[4] The naval medical service, horrifying as its methods would appear to us, showed a not unimpressive application of official effort.

There were other signs in these opening years of a willingness to improve. In 1794 the sea transport organisation was tidied up. Hitherto, or at least in living memory, the various administrative Boards – Navy, Victualling, Sick and Wounded as well as Ordnance – were responsible for their own vessels. The arrangements had come under fire in the eighties on the experience of the American War, particularly in the Enquiry of the Commissioners for Fees influenced largely by

---

1. P.L.C. Webb, 'The Rebuilding and Repair of the Fleet, 1783–93', in *Bulletin of the Institute of Historical Research*, L, no. 122, 194.

2. I, 313, 520, 534–5, 557, 562, 566; pp. 17, 50 above.

3. P. 325 above.

4. Christopher Lloyd and Jack L.S. Coulter, *Medicine and the Navy*, III (1961), 183, where some of the figures' limitations are stated. There was some reorganisation of the hospitals themselves in 1795.

Middleton's proposals.[1] This had recommended centralisation in the Navy Board. But nothing was done, and in the second year of war Middleton tried again. As often, he seems to have gone direct to Pitt, and this time a response was forthcoming,[2] though not in the form earlier proposed. The Government instead turned to an older answer, from the wars of William III and Anne, in the shape of a Transport Board which on this occasion absorbed all responsibilities under the Admiralty apart from those of the Sick and Wounded Board. Established in July 1794, and expanded in September 1795 to take over transport of prisoners of war, it was wound up – as its predecessor had been – in the post-war period.[3] With its introduction the Admiralty acquired its final wartime quiver of subordinate institutions.

Another early administrative adjustment was to prove useful, and this time for an unforeseen purpose. Of all the challenges to naval expansion the most apparent was that of manpower. The numbers now voted by Parliament soon approached the highest of the American War: 45,000 – an increase of 20,000 from the previous year – for 1793, 85,000 for 1794, 100,000 for 1795. There were various ways to raise the men: by the usual royal bounty; by contracting with independent agencies – merchant companies, waterway and fishing interests, individual ports – in return for honouring exemptions from the press or refraining from embargoes on sailings; by encouraging extra bounties and inducements from corporations such as Lloyds and Trinity House; and of course by the press itself. Direct impressment in point of fact played a smaller part than is often assumed, and a progressively smaller part than in recent wars. Between January 1793 and January 1795 it produced perhaps 14,900 men out of some 76,900 raised, and ten years later possibly only 2,000 out of 30,000.[4] The results indeed were apt to receive a disproportionate amount of attention, for the activities, understandably, were always vigorously resented. But this is not least because they often strayed into forbidden territory, seizing men and boys theoretically protected by the Admiralty's own rules. The traditional method, whereby captains fended for themselves, was bound to underline the chances – already high – of offences. On the eve of war in 1793 it was largely superseded by the establishment of an Impress Service with its own gangs and facilities. Building on a piecemeal organisation set up in places in the American War, this soon grew into a comprehensive

1. For which see I, 313–17.
2. The evidence is given in M.E. Condon, 'The Establishment of the Transport Board – a Subdivision of the Admiralty – 4 July 1794', in *The Mariner's Mirror*, 58, no. 1, 79.
3. In 1816. The Sick and Wounded Board, which until 1795 had handled the carriage of prisoners of war, surrendered the rest of its transport duties in 1806.
4. Christopher Oprey, 'Schemes for the Reform of Naval Recruitment, 1793–1815' (M.A. thesis. University of Liverpool, 1961), 31; and see also 32. Numbers in the first case to the nearest hundred. Cf. Stephen F. Gradish, *The Manning of the British Navy during The Seven Years' War* (1980), ch. 3 and Appendix A; Mackesy, op. cit., 176–7.

agency employing some thousands of men. The calibre was often low, in the hands of captains and lieutenants on the beach; but not always, particularly after reforms in 1794, and the Service actively sought its share of volunteers as well as pressed men. It brought a more professional character to a basic task. It also provided a ready-made instrument for a later extension of the task itself.

For two years after the Impress Service was formed measures were taken to raise men for the navy on an enlarged and more deliberate system. Like those for the military in the previous summer they were given statutory protection and force.[1] As in that case, too, the bills were introduced by Pitt. The Minister was clearly not happy about the press as it stood – it was possibly unconstitutional and certainly too random in practice – and he could draw on ideas stemming once more from Middleton in the eighties.[2] In February 1795 he moved in the Commons for a combination of schemes: for a quota of men – seamen or landmen – from merchant ships, by tonnage and employment; a quota from parishes, proportionately graded; a quota from inland navigation; and, as on earlier occasions, most recently in 1778-9, a supply of 'idle, disorderly and vagrants' from the local authorities. Debate refined the plans into two bills, for counties and ports respectively, which passed in March.[3] In the event some 31,000 men were recruited by such means in 1795, roughly the number expected. In theory, and largely in practice, they were volunteers, paid a bounty for joining – higher than the original bounty of '93. The vexed question of their quality, brought to the fore by the naval mutinies two years later, can be left to that event: in large degree, it may be said here, they were thought broadly satisfactory at the time. There were risks attached to the scheme. But as an administrative innovation the Quota Acts, implemented through the Impress Service, may be judged in contemporary terms – and largely were judged – a distinct success.

These various measures marked real achievements. They did not mean that all was well with the Admiralty's system. On the contrary, reformers on the one hand and many officers and men on the other would have echoed one great Admiral's verdict that 'the Civil Branch

---

1. Pp. 329, 487 above.

2. For Pitt's misgivings about the legality of the press see his speech in the Commons of 2 February 1795 (*P.R.*, XL, 379). Oprey, loc. cit., 128-9 disucsses the origins of the measures. Like the Admiralty, the Minister was the recipient of many proposals for improving naval recruitment. Very few made an impact; but in January 1795 one did reach the Department – Patrick Holland's plan 'for Manning the Navy without Impressment' – which eventually received serious attention from the First Lord (by then Middleton himself) and Pitt. This however was only in 1805, the year after the author published the scheme, and there is no sign of its influence earlier.

3. 35 Geo. III, cs. 5, 9. The former was extended to Scotland – the latter included that country – by 35 Geo. III, c. 29, and the package was repeated in the following year by 37 Geo. III, cs. 4, 5. The debates in 1795 may be followed in *P.R.*, XL-XLI.

. . . is rotten to the core'.[1] Mutiny, whatever the circumstances, is not a good testimonial, and 1797 brought to a head misgivings voiced over many years. Much of the period indeed which saw British superiority reach unprecedented heights at sea was filled with vociferous criticism of the organisation ashore. From the mid-1780s to the first decade of the nineteenth century there was a series of official and Parliamentary reports against a background of complaints from the fleets. Some of the attacks were ignorant and others were overstated. The Admiralty rejected proposals on occasions which it bettered, if belatedly, itself; the navy was perforce hard pressed, and failures could not always be avoided; and many of the comments came from normal Service grousing, or from political exploitation – not least by officers with Parliamentary interests. But the criticisms could scarcely have continued in such force if there had not been cause; and they were no harsher than were coming at times from within the organisation itself. Middleton's comprehensive strictures may sometimes be faulted in detail. His recommendations were apt to change according to the source of resistance. He himself may have been, as a later Secretary of the Admiralty put it, 'a prig and a bore'.[2] So are many reformers; it is their achievements that count. Middleton could point to some structural improvements in the first four years of war: besides the Impress Service and the Transport Board, a reconstituted Navy Board in 1796 on lines which he had recommended in the previous decade, and the almost simultaneous creation – which he had come to favour for want of something better – of an Inspector General of Naval Works with a roving commission into the dockyards.[3] In the person of Samuel Bentham, the formidable brother of the formidable Jeremy, this last appointment was to yield some notable results. In the context of Middleton's own daily efforts – scrutinising, checking, prodding, proposing – such institutional changes were a significant feat.

But they remained marginal to what he and others knew was needed. And it was ironical that the last moves took place after he himself had gone. For Middleton, who had resigned once, from the Navy Board in 1790, was brought back as a Lord of Admiralty in May 1794 only to resign again in October 1795, over a change of command in the Caribbean affecting relations with the army.[4] The dispute came as the climax to an unhappy experience; he was already finding his position 'disagreeable',[5] and the departure would now have seemed final: no one

---

1. St Vincent (Jervis) in 1797.

2. Sir Oswyn Murray, 'The Admiralty', VI (*The Mariner's Mirror*, XXIV, no. 3, 335). This remark occurs in a passage of praise for Middleton's merits. It must be borne in mind that the Admiral was an Evangelical.

3. Introduced respectively in June and March.

4. See I, 317; pp. 567, 613 below. He remained nominally a member of the Board until late November.

5. Middleton to Dundas (and for Pitt), 9 November 1795 (*Letters and Papers of Lord Barham*, II, 429).

could have guessed at his return as Lord Barham to direct the Admiralty in the Trafalgar campaign. The cause of his going illuminated not only processes he deplored but also some of the consequences for the Department's relations with the rest of Government. For his objection was to signing an order which, being 'officially proposed to the Board by the first Lord', was held by that personage to place the responsibility 'unquestionably' on himself, 'the other members . . . [being] always understood to concur in his Measures'.[1] This Middleton considered inadmissible.

> I did not, till then, understand, that I was to dwindle into the wretched insignificance of sitting as a numerical Member of a naval Board, to receive a Salary for signing my Name to whatever might be put before me . . .[2]

The measure was not merely unjust, from which, as a good Evangelical, he appealed to 'a much higher tribunal than any on earth'.[3] It pointed limits to effectiveness which lay at the centre of his attacks. For while Middleton vacillated over the years in his definitions of the ideal Board – the answers usually not unrelated to his own prospects of a powerful voice – he had always held the vision of well distributed, regulated business, with its consequences of informed control over the subordinate bodies and a professionally coherent stance within the executive as a whole. And as his own searches for the answer showed, the two aspects were interrelated: the Admiralty's place in the direction of policy turned on an administrative management which itself would respond to the character of the Admiralty Board. Recent history had shown the Department standing at an intermediate point: too powerful to be seriously shifted by pressures from inquiries or associates, not powerful enough to fill a consistently assured positive role. Howe had proved the difficulties of 'connecting' it 'with the rest of the Administration' when the First Lord in peacetime decided to remain aloof.[4] Chatham, his replacement, carried too few guns in war. Spencer was to achieve a more considerable success. But these variations pointed the extent of the system's dependence on the First Lord in person: the problem which defeated all Middleton's approaches in the absence of central managerial reform. The workings of the Admiralty Board, to his frustration, remained fitful and unco-ordinated:[5] it failed to consolidate its authority fully with either lower or higher levels. The possibilities, inherited from the earlier wars, were to be more largely realised in the course of this prolonged struggle. By its close the Admiralty was handling its world-

1. Spencer to Middleton, 25 October 1795 (op. cit., 421).
2. To Dundas, as in p.498, n5 above.
3. To Spencer, 26 October 1795 (*Private Papers of . . . Spencer*, I, 183).
4. See I, 315.
5. Eg to Dundas, Private, 26 July 1794: 'There is no Method in the Office – no Arrangement, nor due Attendance' (B.L. Add. Ms 41079).

wide commitments with a sophistication born of a generation's experience. Still constitutionally conservative, its skills in practice had grown. But in the early phase maritime fortunes were still in the making. The navy's place among the elements and then in the exercise of strategy were thus, in that period, not necessarily on a par. The former was fundamental; nothing else was possible without it. The latter was less predictable, as a largely self-contained sector of government proved largely impervious to outside pressure while not always providing effective support.

II

'The aim of maritime strategy is . . . not so much to establish complete control of all sea communications' – which usually can be only an ideal – 'as to develop the ability to establish zones of maritime control.' And this if achieved has a dual effect, positive to the one side and negative to the other, enabling 'commercial and military seaborne traffic . . . to pass in reasonable safety' while 'it will automatically bring about the denial to the enemy of the same sea communications'.[1] Such doctrine, given prominence by a concept of economic warfare, made demands in this instance, as it normally does, beyond those on the navy itself. Resting firmly on seapower, its application also embraced diplomacy, financial expertise, domestic and international law.

The safety of British shipping – the positive effect – relied of course ultimately on the fleets, holding their opponents in port or deterring or beating them at sea. Immediate protection however centred from the start on convoy, which might or might not involve direct cover from a fleet or squadron. This could apply only in part to the mass of coastal trade, where a *guerre de course* must be discouraged by cruisers patrolling singly or in company; and, at the other end of the spectrum, to the outer areas – Indian Ocean, South Atlantic, Caribbean – where naval strength at the start was low in relation to the hazards.[2] In all such instances, unescorted ships took the brunt of the attacks, from privateers and, particularly in the farther oceans, small cruising squadrons. The ensuing complaints were incessant, as was not surprising from the scale of loss. Privateers in European waters may in point of fact have been fewer than in some previous wars, and less successful than their victims readily supposed;[3] but they, and their counterparts and the naval squadrons in distant seas, accounted for probably 1,350 to 1,400 British

---

1. Captain S.W. Roskill, *The War at Sea 1939–1945*, I (1954), 3–4.

2. Cf. pp. 349–50 above. And see p. 292, n4 for Pitt's notes in defence of the measures for protection of shipping in the first year of war.

3. See Patrick Crowhurst, *The Defence of British Trade 1689–1815* (1977), particularly 21–80.

500

ships in the years 1793–5.[1] This gives an annual average of 450 at least, probably rather less at the start and more later; and it was small comfort to owners and masters to be told that trade in general continued to grow. For in point of fact the sinkings and captures, serious as they were, could be accepted in proportion to the volume and value of traffic. Given a total of some 16,300 vessels registered in the British dominions in September 1793 and some 17,000 three years later, the numerical loss throughout would have been under 3 per cent.[2] This was not much higher than that caused by storm and accident, it was reduced by prizes taken from the enemy, and more than offset – numerically again – by construction. Eight hundred new vessels were registered in the British dominions in 1793, 714 in 1794, 719 in 1795.[3] And if tonnage as well as numbers is considered, and also the value of goods, the proportions of loss may well have been less.

For however depressing and sometimes humiliating the failure to stifle the *guerre de course*, much of it fell on relatively modest cargoes in the inshore fisheries and trades. It is hard to be exact in a complicated subject. In the trade with Europe for instance – the largest of all sectors[4] – where the aggregate value was rising and the volume of unescorted British sailings was large, a not insignificant proportion was nevertheless carried in neutral bottoms. Even there however British convoys were assembled when possible for both north and south – for the Baltic and the Mediterranean; and with some exceptions – East Indiamen, Hudson's Bay ships, some of the West Indian 'runners' – the ocean trades were conducted likewise and the convoys themselves for the most part were safe. The danger in fact was likely to arise after ships detached or dispersed to their ports. And most of these sailings had a seasonal character, for both the outward and inward voyages,[5] which lent itself to a convoy system. This was introduced at once, following experience in the American War, and supported in June 1793 by an Act containing some regulations.[6] The whole thrust of policy indeed was towards such

1. Mahan's calculations in *The Influence of Sea Power upon the French Revolution and Empire*, II, 221–3 have remained a basis for subsequent treatment. Cf. however those in Charles Wright & C. Ernest Fayle, *A History of Lloyds* . . . (1928), 183–5.

2. David Macpherson, *Annals of Commerce* . . ., IV (1805), 287, 331, 368. These figures are for England, Scotland, Ireland, the Colonies, the Channel Islands and the Isle of Man. I give the totals to the nearest hundred tons. A similar proportion has been calculated, less satisfactorily, from (incomplete) figures of British clearances in home ports.

3. Macpherson, ibid.

4. See Mitchell & Deane, *Abstract of British Historical Statistics*, ch. XI, table 10.

5. Cf. Pitt's 'Accounts of the Seasons outwards & Inwards of Ships in different Trades', compiled by Thomas Irving of the Customs [see I, 179, 324] in October 1790 (P.R.O. 30/8/257).

6. 33 Geo. III, c.66: an Act for the encouragement of seamen, in which certain obligations relating to convoy were included. For recent experience see David Syrett, 'The Organization of British Trade Convoys during the American War, 1775–1783', in *The Mariner's Mirror*, 62, no. 2.

an organisation; and the emphasis grew as that improved while the *guerre de course* persisted. In 1798 a Convoy Act, with detailed compulsory powers, was passed.[1] The machinery was established which would control the argosies of the renewed Napoleonic War.

Such an achievement – and it was one of the Admiralty's successes – would not have been possible without co-operation from the interests concerned. There was plenty of grumbling about delays and failures, in the ports and the markets, the City and Parliament. Prices could be depressed when large quantities of similar goods were thrust on the public at one time. There was always controversy about the merits of convoy. But the weight of opinion was increasingly in favour; and particularly in a most important quarter, among the insurance men at Lloyd's. For Lloyd's was now accepted as the focus and spokesman of an interest which by its nature could not only represent but also bring pressure on the trades it served. Freed from earlier internecine struggles – the former 'New Lloyd's' had emerged victorious – and concentrated mainly in the capital, the marine underwriters were in a position to influence their clients and Government alike. The extent and variety of shipping business called for, in fact required, solid insurance; and Lloyd's pinned its faith on convoy from the start of the war. Its lobbying indeed was partly responsible for the speed with which that was brought in, and the powerful Committee threw its weight in the scales when shipowners argued against the discipline. The arrangements benefited from – were buttressed by – a series of legal judgments, dating largely from the days of Lord Mansfield but extending through the nineties themselves, which defined risks and liabilities, the nature of convoy and of escort: many in fact of the conditions for reliable wartime insurance. While far from covering all possibilities, these test cases were significant for finance. The underwriters were severely strained in the Revolutionary and still more the Napoleonic Wars: in the years of the First Coalition, depending on the season, the voyage and the state of operations – let alone the rumours – premiums could vary from perhaps 6–7 to over 10 per cent.[2] But the market held, unlike those of France and Holland which ended in collapse; and the Admiralty found in Lloyd's a close and increasingly effective partner in the management, and championship, of the system for shipping defence.

On aggregate, Government could take heart from the results in the first three to four years. Against a background of military stalemate with

1. 38 Geo. III, c. 76.
2. One would be rash to be too precise; and the suddenness of the fluctuations has also to be borne in mind. They could be very sharp, the worst in its general effect perhaps being that at the turn of 1794–5, when fears of Holland leaving the war drove the Committee of Lloyd's to ask Pitt – unsuccessfully – for legislative relief (Wright & Fayle, op. cit., 192).

more than its share of disappointments, and an economy which was coming under serious if selective strain, Ministers could point to the growth in the volume of overseas trade.[1] This of course did not mean that there were not shortages or inadequacies in imports needed for war: the navy itself faced increasing problems over hemp, sailcloth and masts. But despite dislocations and setbacks the graphs continued to rise, more sharply in some useful respects than before the war.[2] The achievement, due primarily to maritime and financial organisation, also owed something in one area to timely diplomacy. The package of treaties and Conventions in 1793 did not wholly overlook commercial advantage: where apposite they ensured port facilities, and a promising climate for British goods by providing naval cover for the ally's trade. And while conditions scarcely allowed a resumption of the more comprehensive talks which in certain cases – Portugal, Spain, The Two Sicilies – had shown fluctuating promise in the previous decade,[3] the war served in one instance to clinch a prolonged stubborn effort. A commercial Convention with Russia, on British terms, accompanied the Convention of mutual support.[4] The earlier negotiation in this quarter had looked like ending with the Ochakov affair.[5] But it surfaced again in the changing circumstances, and by March 1793 the Empress was anxious enough for a *rapprochement* to drop the arguments for a better deal. She now consented without further ado to renew the commercial treaty of 1766, which, expiring in 1786, had given Britain marked advantages.[6] Although the new agreement was restricted to six years, and many harassments continued in practice, the upshot was thus a restatement of an unreciprocal *status quo*. Whatever the recent context – for the issues had been fought hard from London in peacetime – it was a perhaps not inappropriate greeting to a sterner period.

Defence and expansion of British trade was one side of the coin. The other, equally important, was denial of overseas trade to France. Colonial conquests were seen as one means of strangling her economy.[7] Capture or destruction of her shipping was a second, and this had quite considerable results. Perhaps eight hundred French vessels were taken in the first three years of war, and the incentives, first laid down in the Convoy and Cruizers Act of Queen Anne's time, were repeated in the provisions for prize money in the manning Act of 1793, often itself called the Convoy Act.[8] The effects, heightened by the dearth of new building

1. See p. 442 above.
2. Cf. for re-exports p. 351, n2 above.
3. Pp. 279–80 above; I, Ch. XVI, sections II, IV, and, for The Two Sicilies, Ehrman, *Commercial Negotiations with Europe*, 155–67.
4. See pp. 275–6 above.
5. I, Ch. XVI, section V; Ch. 1 *passim* above.
6. Ehrman, op. cit., 134–6.
7. See pp. 351–2 above.
8. Cf. 33 Geo. III, c. 66 (p. 501, n6 above) with 6 Anne, c. 65.

in France though diminished at least temporarily by her accession of Dutch tonnage in 1795,[1] became progressively greater in the middle and later nineties. But this achievement further pointed the importance of other measures that were less direct. For it was little use to drive the enemy from the seas if his objects could be met by other means. The reduction of his shipping forced more of his commerce into neutral bottoms. It thus stressed the need, always readily grasped, for Britain to state terms for neutral trade.

This was a complex and delicate matter, as it long had been and would long remain. The maintenance of blockade and embargo against the claims of 'free ships, free goods' was accepted as a basic doctrine of British wartime policy.[2] All the Allied agreements contained clauses denying supplies to France; and so far as London was concerned the chief value of the Conventions with Russia was that they undermined the system of Armed Neutrality.[3] At the same time, there were limits. The neutrals should not be driven too far. Some, if treated with consideration, might be converted into allies; and the American War had shown the danger of excessively harsh restriction. These caveats were strengthened by the anxiety to attract seamen from abroad as British seamen were taken into the naval fleets: one of the earliest wartime measures was to modify the Navigation Act to permit three-quarters of a merchant crew to be foreign subjects.[4] The response from neutrals would not be improved if their Governments had been excessively offended. In framing and enforcing trade regulations such thoughts had to be borne in mind.

The British case, looking directly to precedent and treaty,[5] rested on a definition of contraband and a claim to a capacity for effective blockade. It did not extend to the stoppage of all neutral trade with the enemy; and when the Russians proclaimed such an intention in respect of the Danes and Swedes the Ministry in London was quick to dissociate itself.[6] Its own Order in Council of June 1793, clarifying its measures, repeated the

1. P. 548 below.
2. There was one recent exception – on which at least one neutral seized. In the Anglo-French commercial treaty of 1786, its author Eden had conceded that France could protect enemy property in her own ships if she was neutral in a conflict in which Britain was engaged. Eden himself claimed, however, that this was purely a tactical move designed to facilitate a treaty, because it was virtually inconceivable that France would not be a belligerent in any general war (to Morton Eden, 1 February 1787; B.L. Add. Ms 34434).
3. See pp. 274–80 above.
4. 33 Geo. III, c. 26. There was also the anxiety, of course, to recover British seamen from foreign ships.
According to an anecdote of Sir William Scott [see p. 506 below], Pitt at first favoured a 'mild' treatment of neutrals, partly on the ground that 'the war could not last more than a year' (*Diary of William Windham*, 386).
5. Cf. Hawkesbury's earlier emphasis here, on pp. 276–7 above.
6. P. 277 above.

decision, communicated to the main neutral Powers in the spring, to forbid the carriage of enemy goods in neutral vessels and of 'warlike stores' and provisions into enemy ports.[1] But this in itself raised quite enough questions, of principle and of practice, to bedevil relations within a matter of months. The inclusion of foodstuffs was particularly resented, for it enlarged the prohibitions of earlier, or at least recent, wars.[2] It was defended on the ground that this was unlike 'ordinary cases of hostility': a conflict to which the familiar limitations could not fully apply.[3] And the same argument was used in another issue which soon became prominent: the sale in neutral Courts of British vessels captured and brought in by French privateers, the proceeds of which, as prizes of war, went to France. This was said to be inadmissible, for the French authorities were not recognised internationally *de jure*.[4] But the objections were contested; and even when a Government admitted a contention – as the Danes did sometimes over merchants' behaviour, and eventually over the British claims to have established a blockade of certain French coasts – it imposed, so it seemed to London, a remarkably feeble control over a much wider range of practices which ignored such rules as were officially agreed.

The British attitudes towards the two main neutrals, Denmark and Sweden,[5] differed somewhat in the period of the First Coalition. Despite a minor upset in the Russo-Swedish war of 1788, when the Ministry had ruffled feelings in Copenhagen as well as Stockholm, and a disappointment in the Ochakov affair,[6] relations seemed inherently likely to be better with the former than with the latter. The Danish Minister Bernstorff was thought to be still something of an anglophile, and a closer connexion had once been considered.[7] A feeler indeed was put out in the spring of 1793, when the British were constructing their web of alliances;[8] and while they scarcely expected a response, they were not unhopeful of reasonable co-operation in restraining trade. Russia's voice might also count, in a country sharing an habitual hostility to Sweden. Such hopes were disappointed. The Danish Government, it was true, issued regulations for its merchants; but it joined with Sweden in a joint squadron to protect their shipping against a threat from Russia, and

1. Ibid; Grenville to Hailes [in Copenhagen], no. 5, 29 March 1793 (P.R.O., F.O. 22/16); same to Henry Wesley [in Stockholm], no. 4, 4 April 1793 (F.O. 73/14).

2. Grain and flour had in fact been declared contraband in Queen Anne's war, in 1709 – as Hawkesbury well knew (see his copies of the Orders, in B.L. Add. Ms 38353). But that was a long time ago.

3. Grenville to Hailes, no. 9, 3 July 1793 (F.O. 22/17).

4. Ibid; and cf. Grenville to Lord Henry Spencer [in Stockholm], no. 1, 9 August 1793 (F.O. 73/16), where a clause in a treaty of 1661 was also invoked.

5. The two were so much the most significant of the European neutrals that they were often called 'the Neutral Powers' *tout court*.

6. I, 543–4; pp. 13–14, 17, 23–4, 27 above.

7. See I, 467–8, 471.

8. Grenville to Hailes, no. 5, 29 March 1793 (F.O. 22/16).

Britain's own standing, uncertain in any case against French purchases and influence, suffered from the personality of the envoy, the intelligent but agressive Daniel Hailes.[1] As French buying – direct and indirect – increased, as the privateers began to bite, and British counter-measures were refined, the mutual protests grew. In the spring of 1794 there were even rumours that Denmark and Sweden would revive an Armed Neutrality, and by the late summer there was something of a crisis, brought to a point by yet another dispute over rights of search and procedural delays. British Ministers by now were quite as angry as the Danes themselves; but it was none the less noticeable that they took the occasion to try to lower the temperature. Although Grenville was sure that 'every Dane hates England'[2] he negotiated seriously, and the Government agreed to suspend the invariable carriage of Baltic ships into British ports, there to await judgment from an Admiralty Court, when foodstuffs for France were found aboard. Certain exceptions were now allowed for destinations where blockade was doubtful, so long as these were validated by the search at sea. The concession helped; and in 1795 the atmosphere further improved. There was more than one reason. Russia was again working more closely with Britain, after an interval in which policies on both neutral trade and support for the Bourbons diverged.[3] Joint representations and a revived Russian squadron had their effect; and in a year of fluctuating fortunes for the belligerents, with even some prospect of a peace, the Danes moreover were reflecting on the implications of a French victory which would probably favour Sweden rather than themselves. Meanwhile the British, as indeed they told the Russians, wished to be 'as considerate as possible'[4] and in particular to reduce delays in contraband judgments. Sir William Scott – later the great luminary of the Admiralty Court – was consulted, and improvements were made which proved acceptable to the Danes.[5] The earlier instructions on the search of 'corn ships' were confirmed as a result in September; and the Government's readiness to pay for the wheat and flour where the exceptions did not operate may also have helped soothe feelings at the other end.[6] At a time when the future of the war was uncertain, the British could reflect that, partial as their success had been in damming the flow of contraband, they had

---

1. Cf. Ehrman, *Commercial Negotiations with Europe*, 36 n2, 38 n1, 133 n4, for his earlier career. He arrived in Denmark, from Poland, in November 1792. Within a year his 'warm' representations of his country's case had made him personally unpopular, and after threatening to become involved in a libel action he was allowed to come home in the autumn of 1794.

For the joint squadron see p. 378 above.

2. To St Helens [in The Hague], 13 August 1794 (*H.M.C. Dropmore*, III, 615).

3. Cf. pp. 301–2, 378 above. The new moves can be followed in F.O. 65/30.

4. Grenville to Whitworth, no. 11, 12 June 1795 (loc. cit.).

5. See F.O. 22/23–4 *passim*.

6. P. 464 above.

achieved a *modus vivendi* with Denmark which left their policy substantially intact; and in fact would allow them, at a critical juncture in the following year, to make use of Danish good offices as a point of contact with France.

Matters were rather different with Sweden. There was little hope of co-operation there, with a particularly weak Government and a population largely partial to the French. Although the British argued the leniency of their measures compared with the Anglo-Swedish treaty of 1661 – still in certain respects the charter of commercial relations· – they could hardly have looked for agreement, and they did not try very hard. Instructions on policy from London were conspicuous by their rarity.[2] The Swedes benefited from the Danes' success in relaxing the procedures of search for food ships.[3] But the British knew there was little they could do to affect policy in Stockholm, and relied on the Russians to keep it in check. The tergiversations of the domestic politics were regularly reported to London. But they had no real bearing on the response in the North Sea.

The other maritime European neutrals lay in the south. Diplomats and sailors did their best to contain 'the perfidious and mischievous . . . Italian States',[4] and the perennial game of search and complaint went on indeed throughout the Mediterranean. But the value of the traffic there was small compared with that of the north, and it was to their Baltic policies that the British had mainly to look. The Government could reflect after three years of war that – thanks to Russia – the Neutral League was defunct, while neither Denmark nor Sweden had become allied to France. If much contraband was getting through, much certainly was not, while Baltic imports to Britain were not drastically withheld. We could still count on the use of neutral shipping to supplement or replace our own – a growing use in fact as France gained fresh coastlines and the *guerre de course* did not decline. If her seaborne trade in Europe was not suppressed it was undoubtedly diminished: our naval and diplomatic deterrents, if not complete, were bringing their rewards. It was a not insignificant achievement. But again it was not the whole story, for neither sea routes nor neutrals were confined to Europe. One source of trade lay at the start in a new relationship to the belligerents. For the first time in a European war there was a legally independent United States.

Ten years after the American War British relations with the former

---

1. See p. 505, n4 above.
2. Lord Henry Spencer to Auckland, 16 May 1794 (B.L. Add. Ms 34452). Grenville's despatches to Sweden are numbered in single figures in each of the first three years of war.
3. P. 506 above.
4. Lord Henry Spencer to Grenville, no. 17, 6 December 1793 (F.O. 73/16).

colonies still turned on questions bequeathed by the peace. Three main issues remained causes of resentment, and the first two of active dispute: payment of American debts, agreed in principle, to British merchants and to loyalists, and an American claim for compensation from Britain for slaves removed in the war; the final settlement of 'the Old Northwest' and the treatment of the Indians in the backlands with Canada; and restrictions on American shipping in the British West Indies, a matter central to any prospect of a fresh comprehensive commercial agreement.[1] The despatch of a British Minister to Philadelphia for the first time in 1791 could be seen as a step towards serious talks. But while it was taken, after some delay, following a threat of greater American protectionism – to which London was sensitive from its post-war trading success – the Government was not going lightly to abandon positions tenaciously held to a new federation thought to be weak and even open to disruption.[2] The envoy, George Hammond, made modest headway on the frontier problem. But not on the others, and his exchanges with Jefferson, the Secretary of State, were nugatory from the start and sometimes acrimonious. This was in fact not necessarily as unhopeful as it seemed, for Jefferson's ready suspicions – and Jefferson was much to blame – were all the keener because he was fighting a running battle within his own Government. Throughout the community of the States indeed there was a highly vocal difference between interests making for conciliatory tactics at least in certain matters of trade, and those seeking a hard line throughout. Given some fresh turn of events, which might affect this balance and simultaneously induce greater urgency in London, some response could conceivably emerge from either capital. But both sides were obstinate, one was divided and the other complacent, and in 1792 no compelling event arose.

War, it might be thought, would have been a catalyst; and so it proved. But not immediately: not in fact for about a year. The Order in Council of June 1793 was bound to raise complaints.[3] But while the British were determined that American grain must be stopped from reaching France whenever possible, they were also anxious to avoid undue friction and see that procedures were impartially observed. By and large their efforts paid off; an initial 'lukewarm' acquiescence survived;[4] and a major indiscretion by the French envoy Genêt, in commissioning American ships as privateers, evoked a fury in Philadelphia that for a time eclipsed any other irritation. Anglo-American relations in the autumn appeared calmer than before. But the next few months showed how misleading the appearance could be.

1. I, Ch. XII *passim*; Ch. XIII, 355–8 and section II.
2. For British ideas on supporting separatism in Vermont and Kentucky in 1789–90 see op. cit., 372–5.
3. P. 277 above.
4. Hammond to Grenville, 7 July 1793 (P.R.O., F.O. 5/1), describing Jefferson's early reaction.

For in the winter and spring there was a whole crop of untoward events, produced mostly by the war but viewed in America in the light of older issues. Perhaps the worst – certainly the stupidest in its handling from London – arose from developments in the West Indies which had led to a concentration of American shipping. The process began early in 1793, following a French decision to open the ports to the United States. It soon reached extraordinary heights, as the planters in St Domingue fled the negro risings with their possessions or exported produce as soon as they could.[1] The local British authorities added their contribution, keeping the French ports open where they took over and exploiting the American access to stock up with imports for their own islands, particularly of food.[2] But when the situation was appreciated in London the Government decided to act; moved, it claimed later, by the state of affairs arising from St Domingue which could allow large amounts of foodstuffs to be shipped for France under a neutral flag. It was best to strike at the source; orders were accordingly sent in November to seize American vessels in the Caribbean and adjudicate on contraband in the usual way. The bag was high: some 250, of which 150 were 'condemned'. So was the anger in the United States.

The business may well have been muddled, as the sequel indeed suggests. It was possibly a product of the natural sternness of Hawkesbury at the Committee of Trade which escaped the full attention of Grenville at the Foreign Office.[3] If so, the episode foreshadowed attitudes in the following year. But however that may be, the effect was certainly not foreseen. Ministers would naturally expect a complaint, and one was forthcoming from the American envoy. But they were used to that: they had been advised in the summer not to take such representations too seriously, and they gave no sign of being particularly worried now.[4] It was only when British merchants warned that the measure could cause real trouble that the Committee of Trade decided to think again. A fresh Order, of 8 January 1794, restored the former limits of search; and a copy was sent at once, with a belated copy of the Order of November, in an attempt to assuage American opinion. But it was too late. News of the seizures reached Philadelphia in mid-March; the despatch from London only at the end of the month. The fat was already in the fire when Hammond tried to explain.[5]

1. Cf. p. 355 above.
2. By calling on emergency powers under the Act of 1788 (28 Geo. III, c. 6) regulating shipping and trade in the West Indies (see I, 337), which allowed imports from friendly foreign islands in case of need – though this should still be in British ships.
   See pp. 355–6 above for British operations in the region in 1793.
3. Hawkesbury's role as defender of the Navigation system in the West Indies is discussed in I, 332–41.
4. Burges's 'Foreign Office Journal', 28 December 1793 (*H.M.C. Dropmore*, II, 488–9); Hammond to Grenville, 7 July 1793 (F.O. 5/1).
5. A good account of the affair is given in Charles R. Ritcheson, *Aftermath of Revolution . . . 1783–1795* (1969), 299–306.

It was indeed boiling the more fiercely because of another incident. Ever since the peace of 1783 the Americans had been plagued by the Algerine pirates, no longer needing to consider even the possibility of a British reaction. Ships were seized, crews held for years, regardless of diplomatic efforts. A negotiation however was at last due to start in the autumn of 1793. At that moment the Americans learned that Portugal – which always took the brunt of naval measures to confine the corsairs to the Mediterranean – had signed a year's truce with Algiers. They also learned that the British Government had lent its good offices to that end. It was useless for Grenville to point out that this was done to help an ally. The aggrieved shipowners and merchants saw it as another deliberate blow at their trade.

As if all this was not enough, the frontier problem reared its head again. It had never indeed disappeared, and the threat of trouble could seldom be discounted. Since 1792 the authorities in Canada had been half-expecting American incursions – reasonably so as they watched the restless armed movements on the other side. In 1793 they sounded London to see if they might take some preventive measures. And while they were told sternly to forget such thoughts their fears did not decline. At the turn of the year they heard that an American expedition was on its way. In February 1794 the Governor-General, Dorchester,[1] made a bellicose speech to the Indians, and a week later he ordered the reoccupation of a key frontier post. The move was defensive. But coupled as it was with Dorchester's language, its confirmation in May fell on a Congress and public by now thoroughly incensed.

Such events seemed the more provocative because they could be set in a perspective provided by the American Government itself while some of them were taking place. Washington had acted in December by making available to the Congress papers relating to the dealings with both Britain and France. The emphasis was plain: troubles with the former were more deep-rooted than with the latter; and the message was underlined almost simultaneously by a report, long awaited from Jefferson, on foreign trade. The mass of information thus suddenly disclosed gave a sombre background to current developments, and it was followed by a renewed attempt in Congress to impose higher protectionist measures.[2] The angry debates marked a further step in the deepening rift between Jeffersonians and Federalists – the conflict from which the first great American parties were to be formed. But although a temporary embargo was laid on the West Indian islands, the motions failed; and the Government likewise was unwilling to bring matters to a head while there was still a chance of improvement. Washington, looking to a neutrality 'friendly and impartial to the belligerent

---

1. For whose connexions with the secessionists in Vermont and the anglophiles in Philadelphia see I, 373, 375–6, 562.
2. Cf. p. 508 above.

Powers',[1] represented and held a balance between the political groups. The growing prospect of a war with Britain sobered those whom it did not excite. And when the danger at last dawned on London the feeling there was much the same. The turn of events had come which, perhaps alone, could evoke a mutual response. The way was opening, if uninvitingly, to serious negotiation.

The initiative came from the United States. In April 1794, as tempers rose further and Hammond – who was losing his grasp – failed to calm them, the American Government decided to send a special envoy to review all the issues and attempt a settlement. The choice fell on John Jay. He sailed that month and arrived in June. With his coming affairs moved into a more helpful stage.

For both Jay and Grenville, and the British Ministry in general, were now anxious to defuse the crisis. The reports from America were muddling – only two days before Jay landed the envoy was still expected to be Jefferson – but the embargo was ominous, even if it was lifted in the event after two months, and in the current state of the war a fresh enemy at sea would not be welcome. Jay for his part was prepared to try conciliation if he could. A long record of moderation, laced with resolution, and of respect for Britain even in conflict, disposed him, despite a French and Dutch ancestry, towards a balanced agreement. A roll-call of high achievements, as one of the fathers of the Republic, a President of the Continental Congress, Ambassador to Spain and Secretary for Foreign Affairs, and now Chief Justice of the United States, gave him the stature to conclude. His personality as well as experience was suited to the task. For while he was prey to a certain self-righteousness, which was well known in London – 'almost every man has a weak . . . quarter, and Mr. Jay's weak side is *Mr. Jay*'[2] – and had a liking for good English society on which his critics were quick to seize, such particularities could not seriously disturb an intense patriotism bearing on innate good sense and a capacity for measured judgment. His qualities struck a chord in Grenville, himself disposed to settle. The two men soon became, and remained, firm friends.

This of course did not mean that the outcome was predictable. On the contrary, the mutual regard grew out of concentrated talks. There was too wide an assortment of questions for one side to have its way throughout; and if the pressures had not been real, and Jay remote from his sources, the bargaining would doubtless have dragged on as it usually did on such occasions.[3] The process began seriously in late July, after delays while the Americans in London sought greater detail on the seizures of their vessels and the British were absorbed in other more

---

1. 'The Declaration of Neutrality', 22 April 1793.
2. Auckland to Grenville, 22 June 1794 (*H.M.C., Dropmore*, II, 578).
3. Cf. the periods of pre-war British commercial negotiations with European states listed in I, 513.

urgent business. For June and July were busy months. The new Ministry was being formed; Grenville, absenting himself at one point, was not immediately sure of his post; and then he was occupied with the important approach to Vienna, while much of Pitt's time was taken up with events in Flanders.[1] Jay submitted 'Outline' proposals on 6 August; Grenville replied with a 'Project' on the 30th; a 'Counter-*Projet*' was returned on 30 September; on 19 November a treaty was signed. This was fast work, made possible by accepting the points at which the other party might stick, and aided by a conciliatory move from the British at the start. For on 6 August – the day on which Jay presented his Outline – two Orders in Council were issued, one extending the period of appeal for the vessels seized in the West Indies and the other superseding the Order of June 1793 in so far as that applied to the shipment of American grain.[2] The Glorious First of June, it might seem, had been fought just in time. But the concession was to prove a tactical step in paving the way for agreement rather than a retreat embodied in the agreement itself.

The Jay treaty, as it came to be known, applied to almost all the issues in dispute: the American debts, the frontier question, belligerent rights, commercial relations. Jay himself dropped the question of 'abducted' slaves as a counter in the first of these problems,[3] where he agreed that claims could go to Anglo-American arbitration instead of the American courts. On the frontier, the British consented to leave the objected posts by 1 June 1796, while both parties would allow free passage by their citizens and Indians, and trade on terms specified largely in 1783. Such provisions left one problem unsolved: the unmapped hinterland of the Mississippi valley, a region likely to cover many thousand square miles. British claims rested on a conjectural definition at the peace and the right to navigate freely up the river, itself now reconfirmed. Jay naturally refused to connect this freedom with a cession of territory; and the matter was assigned to joint survey and – significantly again – arbitration.[4] On the third, and great, question of belligerent rights, careful wording was needed. The Americans recognised that certain goods could legitimately be captured in neutral ships, the British the obligation to proceed to speedy judgment. Contraband should cover arms and implements for war, which could be confiscated; but since there was 'difficulty' in deciding when foodstuffs fell under the heading, such seizures, where they occurred, should lead not to confiscation but to purchase in full. For commercial relations the central issue lay of course in the West Indies, and this was indeed to prove the hardest test

---

1. Pp. 409–14, 342–4 above; John Jay to Edmund Randolph, 30 July 1794 (*American State Papers, Class I, Foreign Relations*, I (1832), 480).

2. See pp. 509, 277 above.

3. P. 508 above. But he claimed later that it was largely solved in effect by the results reached in other parts of the treaty.

4. 'The period of modern arbitration begins with the Jay Treaty of . . . 1794' (Oppenheim's *International Law*, ed. H. Lauterpacht, II (1952), 34).

for both sides. The answer contained in the treaty gave American vessels of seventy tons and under the same trading rights as British, provided that the produce of the islands in molasses, sugar, coffee, cocoa and cotton – rum being omitted – were taken only to the United States and not re-exported thence in American ships. Other subjects proved less contentious and evoked little debate. They were treated broadly on the basis of reciprocity, as a favoured nation where relevant, in duties, quantities of tonnage, and individual rights.[1]

The merits of the treaty have been argued from that day to this. Did it fudge too many issues which then continued to cause trouble? Did Jay concede too much? Should the British have been firmer over the frontier regions and the West Indian trade? There was an illuminating contrast in the immediate sequel in either country, which also sheds light on decisions within the British Ministry while the talks were under way. In sum, the agreement raised little controversy in England. No Parliamentary debate was called; the public remained quiescent; and the one attempt to mount a campaign against a part of the treaty failed conspicuously to gather real weight. This effort centred, scarcely surprisingly, on the terms for the West Indies. Its author, again not surprisingly, was Hawkesbury at the Committee of Trade. For to Hawkesbury, the great proponent of a neo-mercantilist trading empire, the supporter of the shipping interest in a closely similar peacetime debate, the framer of the most recent Navigation Act,[2] the offending article was offensive indeed. As seen from his office, the question was 'whether this Country shall give up the principal advantages which it derives from her Sugar Islands' and allow a competition from which 'the United States will in a short time become Masters in effect'.[3] Although he had some doubts on certain other matters, particularly the consequences of the boundary settlement for British influence with the Indians, he was prepared to approve them having made his points.[4] He had been consulted from the start, though probably not included in the negotiation itself, which seems to have been confined strictly to the Foreign Office. But as soon as Grenville showed signs of compromising over the Caribbean trade he did all he could to forestall and discredit the process. The result was negligible: within the Ministry, perhaps partly because Hawkesbury had to miss a decisive Cabinet meeting through illness; with the public, because by temperament and training as a loyal King's servant and office holder he was not the man to press a campaign

---

1. For the text of the treaty see, *inter alia*, *Consolidated Treaty Series*, 52, 245–67; *P.H.*, XXXII, cols. 216–35.

2. I, 330–41.

3. George Chalmers [Chief Clerk to the Committee of Trade] to Hawkesbury, 21 June 1794 (B.L. Add. Ms 38229); Hawkesbury's paper of 29 August 1794 (B.L. Add. Ms 38310).

4. See Hawkesbury to Grenville, 29 August 1794 (B.L. Add. Ms 58935); Ritcheson, op. cit., 328–31 and, for subsequent British efforts with the Indians, 338–40.

too far 'out of doors',[1] and the public itself was not in a mood to respond. Even the West Indian interest, in a time of growing general anxiety, was not inclined to act on his inducements. Nothing much happened; and long before the terms were published he retired from the field. When a final British draft for a treaty was circulated to the Cabinet in October, he declined to comment on the relevant article or attend a meeting on the subject.[2]

The fact was that Hawkesbury's guns were too slight when ranged against Grenville supported by Pitt over a matter essentially of foreign policy. Such sympathy as he may have commanded – from Dundas, for instance[3] – was not enough. Pitt's own role in the negotiation cannot be followed in detail, for little seems to have survived on paper either of the Foreign Office talks or of Ministerial discussions. He met Jay, initially at least, and there were occasional Cabinets on the questions.[4] One catches glimpses in the summer of his being consulted and informed.[5] But however much he may have left the conduct to Grenville his attitude was not in doubt when a decision was due on this controversial topic. It was taken in response to the state of the war at a point of some 'urgency' and 'crisis',[6] against his own earlier balance, or mix, of commercial policies for the Caribbean. But one must remember what that mix had been – how on balance it still favoured flexible protection[7] – and what precisely the Cabinet now laid down. This was far from being a complete surrender, as its reception showed. For if Hawkesbury saw the admittance of American shipping as a heavy blow, the Americans were outraged by the restriction placed on its benefits for themselves.

In the event indeed they went so far as to reject the terms – an ironical fate for a solution that could be attacked in Britain as seriously damaging. When Jay's treaty came up for ratification in the summer of 1795, Congress 'suspended' the article on the West Indies, which did not come into effect. The reason lay in the fury roused by the constraint on re-export of the islands' produce: the agreement that American shipping could be used to take it only to American ports.[8] If it was sold overseas thereafter, transport was reserved to foreigners – doubtless largely to the

---

1. Cf. I, 41, 330–2. The Cabinet meeting was on 29 August, and the Project was sent to Jay on the 30th (p. 512 above).

2. Hawkesbury to Grenville, 17 October 1794 (B.L. Add. Ms 38230); a copy for Pitt is in P.R.O. 30/8/152. For the attempts at a public campaign see Ritcheson, op. cit., 345–6, and Jerald A. Combs, *The Jay Treaty* . . . (1970), 154.

3. Dundas to Grenville, nd but of this period (B.L. Add. Ms 58915).

4. Eg Jay to Alexander Hamilton, 11 July 1794 (*The Correspondence and Public Papers of John Jay* . . . ed. Henry P. Johnston, IV (1893), 30; Grenville to Hawkesbury, 20 June 1794 (B.L. Add. Ms 38229); Hawkesbury to Grenville, 29 August 1794 (B.L. Add. Ms 58935).

5. See P.R.O. 30/8/344.

6. Pitt's description of the current circumstances in general; to George III, 26 August 1794 (*L.C.G. III*, II, no. 1110).

7. See I, 335–9.

8. P. 513 above.

British themselves. Taken with other parts of a suspect instrument – for which Jay found himself ferociously abused – it proved too much. For the first time in its short history Congress refused to confirm, in part, a treaty undertaking signed on behalf of the United States.[1]

To many Americans the proof of the result lay in the fact that the British approved it. Pitt and Grenville professed themselves satisfied with the treaty's 'fairness and mutual accommodation', and Pitt further proclaimed that there had been no 'dishonourable submissions'.[2] Such statements were made for Parliamentary consumption. But they were none the less within the ambit of truth. The Ministry was looking forward to a period of greater amity on a balance of advantage in which the concessions were not in fact all on one side. The British denied to the United States the full benefits of admission to West Indian markets; but that admission was on new and potentially favourable terms. The frontier settlement secured the continuation of the valuable fur trade for Britain; it kept open the dream, dating back to Shelburne, of commercial penetration of the western hinterland; but not through acceptance of a British claim to controversial territory or of influence with the Indians through a disputed or neutral zone.[3] Commercial privileges and treatment in general were based on reciprocity; and the Americans were admitted specifically into Eastern markets on better terms. The belligerent's right of search at sea was confirmed: the existence of contraband in fact admitted; but obligations and limits were enjoined in the vexed question of foodstuffs. And beyond – or provided by – the detail there lay a mutual deeper benefit, proportioned to their circumstances, which the cooler heads on either side perceived. At a point in the war of growing disappointment and sudden widespread pessimism, the British Government forestalled fresh difficulties without 'dishonourable submissions'.[4] At the same time the Americans gained what they most needed, a prospect of peace and development substantially freed from continued British pressures.[5] When one considers that in 1794 the British looked on the Americans as largely 'Jacobinical',[6]

1. And, largely because it set a precedent, the occasion remained perhaps the most celebrated and controversial until in 1920 the Senate refused to ratify the Versailles treaty. In that instance of course the whole instrument was rejected, whereas in 1795 one article only was 'suspended'.

2. Speeches of 24 (Pitt) and 30 (Grenville) March; *P.R.*, XLI, 125, XLII, 328. The second quotation comes from the version in *The Senator*, XII (nd), 773; *P.R.* has 'humiliation'.

The debates in either House were on 'the State of the Nation', not on the treaty itself, which was laid before Parliament only in November 1795 and caused no discussion (cf. p. 513 above).

3. Cf. I, 93–5, 355–8.

4. N2 above.

5. Cf. Washington to Charles Carroll, 1 May 1796; quoted in Combs, op. cit., 187.

6. This very widely held view was said to have been shared by Pitt in June, in a report of a conversation with the Committee of [British] American Merchants (*The Morning Chronicle*, 20 June 1794).

and that 'hatred of Britain was the . . . most primitive force of American nationalism',[1] it was a not unremarkable feat to have concluded an agreement which, if it left some old claims to be settled, and failed to check old feelings of resentment, aimed at and largely succeeded in turning the page of the recent past.

III

The assertion of belligerent rights was distinguished in one respect among the elements of strategy. It applied equally in principle to a short or a long war. Wartime finance on the other hand, as enshrined by Pitt at the heart of the efforts, depended for its form on their duration and scale.

In ledger terms, the former did not matter too much if the latter was not too large. Expenditure on the war in the first two years – on army, navy and ordnance – was less than it had been on aggregate in the last three full years of the American War. At £8,137 million for 1793 and £16,837 for 1794 it compared – probably on a slightly depreciated purchasing power – with £14,869, £17,063 and £20,126 million for 1780–2. In 1783, when peace was signed, £13,667 million had still been spent on the forces.[2] The new burdens were unwelcome, and in a sense worrying given the earlier fears of bankruptcy from similar figures.[3] But they fell within the range of experience, and also, as it seemed, of a still buoyant economy. If prices were rising, so were sectors of industrial production and overseas trade; and confidence, if shallow in some quarters, survived broadly from the past decade.[4] But in point of fact the picture was changing, for in 1795 war expenditure rose steeply to an unprecedented height. The figure for that year turned out to be £26,273 million – almost £10 million more than for 1794 – and it was followed by £28,254 million for 1796.[5] At this stage therefore the factors of scale and duration began to merge in a relationship unsettling to earlier assumptions. The costs exerted a new pressure to seek ways of ending the war.[6] And if these last should fail they argued the need to review financial methods themselves.

1. F. Thistlethwaite in *The New Cambridge Modern History*, IX (1965), 611.

2. Mitchell & Deane, *Abstract of Historical Statistics*, ch. XIV, table 2. The figure for 1794 includes £1,907 million of funded naval debt contracted earlier. Differing amounts are given in P.K. O'Brien, 'Government Revenue, 1793–1815 . . .' (D. Phil thesis, Oxford, 1967), 497, table 17.

3. See I, 157–8.

4. Cf. pp. 442–4, 451–2, 387 above.

5. Mitchell & Deane, ibid.; including £1,491 and £4,227 million respectively of funded naval debt contracted earlier.

6. This statement may stand even though the costs as finally accounted, producing the figures cited above, were almost always rather higher than the Estimates on which the public could judge (see below). The fact indeed, amply appreciated in 1795–6, increased a pressure which was joined to that of rising economic distress.

Such a prospect could indeed be foreseen in part in the spring of 1796. For by then the forecasts of expenditure at least were clearly breaking down. Pitt had to introduce a supplementary budget in April to follow his statement for the year in December 1795; and the fact reflected not merely the uncertainties now inherent in the course of events but also a lack of control inherent in administrative forms. The Minister was well aware of the growing gap between the Estimates and reality: some $£2\frac{1}{2}$ million for the navy in 1793 and some $£6\frac{1}{2}$ million in 1795, while the army in the same year overspent its supply by some $£3\frac{1}{2}$ million.[1] The proportions of the totals were significant; but it proved impossible to apply proper checks either to forestall or seriously to scrutinise the process. The army and navy retained their old immunity from detailed Treasury supervision: they presented their Estimates to Parliament without the Department's prior vetting, and their financial officers escaped the immediate attention of a central audit.[2] Nor were the Estimates themselves reliable guides even to intentions: the navy's in particular rested largely on a figure expressed as upkeep per man per month which dated back to the seventeenth century.[3] On this archaic formula, which continued to account for the 'ordinary' cost, a further sum was then imposed: an addition which itself could be deployed departmentally between several accounts. The Barrackmaster General's procedures showed the lengths to which military accounts could be taken – and accepted.[4] All in all, the degree of financial independence in the different forces was one of the strongest indications of the limits to effective centralised power.

Pitt indeed failed for the next few years to bring his annual forecasts within a single statement. A 'circumstance' which in 1796 was 'before unknown in the history of this country' became the rule from then until 1799.[5] The state of the war and constraints in Whitehall combined to produce persistent deficiencies; and his remedies concentrated not so much on the Estimates themselves as on the best ways to provide for the ensuing debts. Such an approach could do nothing to discourage immediate borrowing by the spending Departments, in the shape of their own debentures, warrants and bills. The navy by tradition was

1. Cf. figures of expenditure in Mitchell & Deane, ibid., with budget calculations and notes in Richard A. Cooper, 'British Government Finance 1793–1807 . . .' (Ph.D thesis, University of California, 1976), 375 *et seq*. Accounts from the Navy Office showing discrepancies for 1793 (dated 22 January 1794) and the last quarter of 1795 may be seen in Pitt's papers, P.R.O. 30/8/247.

2. Cf. pp. 482, 494 above, and I, 312 for rather stricter treatment of the Ordnance. Cf. also Pitt's remarks in May 1796 on the practical limits to Parliament's 'command of a retrospective authority' over the application of expenditure (*The Senator.*, XV (nd), 1665).

3. I, 312.

4. See p. 490 above.

5. J.J. Grellier, *The History of the National Debt* . . . (1810), 391–2. The same applied in 1803. Cf. however I, 253n6 for an inexact and doubtful precedent.

responsible for more of these than the other Services, and even after much of its debt had been dealt with it was thought to account for £4.6 million in early 1797 compared with £4.4 million for the army and the ordnance together.[1] Pitt had never liked these 'floating' Departmental deficits – the navy bills in particular – or the size of the unfunded debt of which they formed a part. Some of his earliest financial measures had been devoted to its reduction, by converting such instruments and certain types of Exchequer bills into funded stock. He did the same now as far as he could, to lessen the proportion of higher interest rates and opportunities for speculation which short-term borrowing involved – attractions which also absorbed loan money that could otherwise go into the Funds.[2] At first he was unsuccessful – or did not try hard enough: the nominal total of unfunded debt rose by almost half between 1793 and 1795. But action was then taken in two large operations, in May and November 1796, which mopped up outstanding obligations on an unprecedented scale. The terms of conversion were expensive – discounts of 1 to 5 per cent, depending on the interest rates, on market prices already historically low. Nevertheless the results brought the nominal amount of the remaining unfunded debt below its immediate pre-war level, and the cost of servicing it to 0.4 per cent of total expenditure compared with 1.1 in 1793.[3] The problem would resurface. But it had proved, expensively and perhaps belatedly, containable; and its impact in any case was greater on confidence than on the amount of debt as a whole.

For the vast proportion of the National Debt remained funded, as it long had been: £231.5 in nominal value out of £241.6 million in 1793, £301.9 out of £310.4 in 1796.[4] Costing almost £9 and £11⅓ million respectively to service, it claimed over a quarter of net annual expenditure in the fourth, swollen year of war.[5] The rate of increase was approaching a point at which policy would be questioned. Meanwhile it underlined the need to seek expedients for restraint. Pitt employed one device from the start, at the expense of the Bank of England: he secured an annual advance of £1 million on the sale of Exchequer bills, which

1. According to a contemporary calculation; see Cooper, loc. cit., 37. O'Brien (loc. cit., 495, table 16) gives a figure for the Navy bills of £4.2 million.

2. See I, 258–60, and Pitt's budget speeches of 11 March 1793 and 6 December 1796 (*P.R.*, XXXV, 48; XLVI (1797), 262). Thomas Coutts – his own banker – stressed the effect of the 'ruinous floating securities' on funded loan operations in a private letter (19 March 1797; P.R.O. 30/8/126).

3. Mitchell & Deane, op. cit., ch. XIV, tables 5,2; Cooper, loc. cit., 40–1. O'Brien, loc. cit., 507, table 21, gives premiums or discounts on Exchequer and Navy bills, 1793–6.

The conversions of 1796, absorbing some £26½ million of Exchequer and Navy bills, covered some pre-war as well as wartime issues (cf. I, 268n6).

4. Mitchell & Deane, op. cit., ch. XIV, table 5.

5. Op. cit., ch. XIV, tables 5, 2. In 1792 the charge was over half of a much lower expenditure.

was then retained for the period in which a larger amount was theoretically paid off.[1] The same cause affected his approach to one element of expenditure which was directed beyond the strictly British effort. For the desire to avoid a further burden from falling wholly on the Exchequer was one of the factors that influenced his handling of financial support for the Allies.

It was no coincidence that the greatest rise in British payments to continental Powers during the period of the First Coalition was to be met by way of public loan. Of the £5,546,480 allocated to partners, auxiliaries and mercenaries in 1795, £4,600,000 was for Austria in the form of guaranteed subscription. All such payments in the two previous years, on a smaller though growing scale, had been entirely by Governmental subsidies and remittances for hired troops: to Sardinia, Hanover, Hesse Cassel, Hesse Darmstadt, and Baden in 1793, and to Prussia and Brunswick as well in 1794.[2] But now Austria would have to borrow, and moreover borrow from the public, for the money would be sought on the market with the Treasury as guarantor. Government had never before devised or been involved in such an operation.

There were several reasons for its being tried. When the idea was first being considered – and increasingly thereafter – Ministers were unhappy about the subsidy to Prussia. The payments, it was said, were producing no results, and Parliament might become restive; given Austria's own uncertain intentions, would a further drain on capital be wise?[3] While they were prepared at one point to switch the same remittances to Vienna, it was on stiff military terms which were refused in the event.[4] The loan scheme had its complications, viewed in the light of domestic finance: its very size, which argued in favour of avoiding a fresh burden on the Debt, could affect the latter's own funding for the year.[5] Nevertheless it might seem, financially, to offer fewer immediate hostages. A loan carried terms for interest and repayments, and even if the borrower defaulted on them Government was committed only to those sums, which would be cheaper in the short term than a subsidy. Moreover the arrangement, novel as it was, could be seen against a

1. Cooper, loc. cit., 38. Cf. I, 251 for his not dissimilar method with the Bank on the threat of war in 1790.
2. Pp. 480–1 above; Sherwig, op. cit., 365. And cf. pp. 278–9, 281, 332n1, 337 above.
3. See pp. 340–2, 362–8, 376–7 above. The condemnation of Prussia of course ignored Pitt's failure to ensure regular remittances.
It was the fear of drain on capital (eg Grenville's remark on p. 377, n1 above) that could arguably be weighed against the relative loss of control over Austria's military efforts under a market loan, compared with the allegedly greater discipline of successive subsidy payments.
4. Pp. 364–5 above, and cf. the preceding n.
5. P. 377 above, developed further on p. 525 below.

background already in place; for Austria was already in the market for a loan, which had been undersubscribed,[1] and if Government now acted as guarantor a further approach could be made. Yet again, it was an arrangement that the Austrians themselves favoured;[2] and in the end there was really no alternative. For the final determinant was strategic need, becoming increasingly urgent even as the financial terms were being hammered out.[3] The loan as it emerged had serious drawbacks, and was never popular in either country. Pitt, who worked hard to secure its acceptance at home, had to argue on the ground of 'necessity'.[4] The precedent was followed with another country only once, much later,[5] though it was repeated with Austria herself. It stemmed from a particular set of circumstances, which occasioned some relief to Government's accounts.

The occasion was important as an element in the use of 'Pitt's gold' for Europe. For the Austrian loan of 1795 was the largest single allocation to the continent throughout the Revolutionary and Napoleonic Wars: almost double the size in fact of the next largest, to Russia in 1814. When it was out of the way, the total in 1796 (entirely for hired troops) was some £120,000; and in the final year of the First Coalition a further loan to Austria accounted for £1,620,000 out of allocations of some £1,665,000.[6] Hardly surprisingly, given the amount and the poor state of Imperial credit, Pitt had some trouble in 1795 in finding suitable terms. Largely at the prompting of his principal loan agent Walter Boyd, he linked the operation with the funding system itself to avoid excessive competition. Subscribers to the Imperial loan were obliged to have subscribed to the Government's own loan for the year.[7] The inducements had to be quite substantial. In taking up the British stock, the investor would receive an extra annuity payment proportioned to any shortfall on the other loan; and that loan itself would yield an annual interest starting at just under 7 per cent, diminishing to just under 3 per cent by the terminal date of 25 years.[8] This was a favourable rate at the start compared with a British fund: the lender was receiving an attractive return under Treasury guarantee. The scheme showed the importance attached to the Austrian connexion. It also threw instructive light on the normal terms for financing the war.

For, as in the past, the cost of the struggle was to be paid in borrowed

1. P. 363 above.
2. Though not without some changes of mind on the way; see pp. 363, 365 above.
3. This will be followed in Ch. XIV, section I below.
4. P. 377 above.
5. Sherwig, op. cit., 365–8. In 1809, with a loan of £600,000 to Portugal.
6. Op. cit., 365. For a calculation of payments, as distinct from allocations, to Austria in 1796–7, see Duffy, 'British War Policy', Appendix C, dissenting from Sherwig, 91n.
7. See p. 377 above.
8. See Duffy, 'British War Policy', 148–9, for the complicated calculations.

money. Government counted on loans to meet the great bulk of 'extraordinary' expense.[1] Doctrine rested on the experience of a century in which debt could be treated as a 'branch of . . . property' from which the creditor could draw an income while his taxes were kept within bounds. The threat to this wisdom from the American War had been contained, as it seemed, by Pitt's Sinking Fund;[2] and if the new war was not too prolonged, the economy could sustain some further debt. Pitt himself did not hesitate to follow in the steps of Walpole, Pelham and North, and to persevere in them for as long as he could.

The correspondence was particularly close in matters of taxation. Indeed in one respect Pitt was if anything more cautious. The Land Tax – the basic tax – had generally risen in previous wars; but he had already increased it in peacetime, and preferred not to do so again.[3] He continued his pre-war policy of spreading the load as widely, and thinly, as possible, placing the emphasis, as doctrine decreed once more, on 'optional' or luxury consumption. As he put it in his final budget of the Revolutionary War, opinion had 'always adhered to a principle . . . of laying on taxes which should fall as much as possible on articles . . . which should bear upon the higher orders, and from which the lower classes might be exempt'.[4] And within that range he opted for articles under the so-called permanent taxes – excise, customs, stamps, posts, hereditary Crown revenues, now gathered into the Consolidated Fund – rather than for imposts under the assessed taxes which he had increased to meet an earlier war scare,[5] and made perpetual in 1794. This was in fact much more effective, since the former were by far the greater source of revenue. It also helped avoid the kind of outcry he had encountered when first in office over the introduction of something unfamiliar or new.[6]

For five years of war, in fact, Pitt imposed no fresh type of tax. His measures fell on the traditional sources of customs, excise and stamps: on bricks and glass, wines and spirits, tea and coffee, cocoa and tobacco, some imported fruits, marine insurance, the wearing of hair powder,

1. Cf. pp. 479, 518 above. A smaller source also lying outside taxation was the lottery, which Pitt always liked (I, 255); see Mitchell & Deane, op. cit., ch. XIV, note 3.

2. I, 157–8, 248–9, 260–7.

3. Op. cit., 255. And cf. his remarks on its permissible level in a paper on redemption of the tax, nd but probably 1798, in P.R.O. 30/58/1. Cf. also, however, p. 522 below.

4. Speech of 18 February 1801 (*The Senator, 2nd ser.*, I (nd), 223). Cf. I, 244–56. If the report was accurate, this is a nice example of the use of 'classes' and 'orders' as discussed on pp. 142–4 above.

5. In 1790 (I, 251). The assessed taxes had to be voted on each occasion, whereas the existence of the permanent taxes did not, though changes in their scope or rate required approval after introduction in the budget. For Pitt's achievement of the Consolidated Fund see I, 271–3.

6. Figures are in Mitchell & Deane, op. cit., ch. XIV, table 1; the assessed taxes never reached one-sixth of the total revenue in the first four years of the war. Pitt's early experiences with them are discussed in I, 251–5.

hats, horses and dogs.[1] The constraints on novelty were shown by his one move in that direction; to convert a levy, introduced by North, on receipts for objects by personal inheritance into a direct tax on collateral succession to such objects and also to landed property. The former was allowed, in 1796. But the latter, though passed after controversy by the Speaker's casting vote, was then withdrawn.[2] Pitt thus had to be careful, and it was by familiar means that he increased his net revenue from 1793 to 1796. Not surprisingly, the increase was modest. A rise of £1¼ million, when net expenditure rose by more than £20½ million, was no more heroic than that produced in the last four years of the American War.[3] But by contemporary theory it met its designed purpose: to pay for the annual 'ordinary' expenses of Government and the servicing of past and current debt. The former rose only gently thanks to budgetary methods, in which the 'ordinary' expenditure on the armed forces formed a small part of their wartime needs.[4] It was thus more largely to meet the latter, which in peacetime had swallowed over half the total, that more budget revenue was needed in face of a growing charge. 'Pitt', it has been truly said, 'did not intend his taxation policy to pay for the war but to support the funding system which would pay for the war'.[5]

The funded loans themselves were at first assigned on the system which Pitt had developed in peacetime. Government, through the Bank of England, invited competition by sealed tender from contractors (usually in syndicate) for subscriptions on terms announced by the Treasury in advance.[6] The practice varied in the course of the long wars: of the 26 loans raised from 1793 to 1815, fifteen were by this method and the rest were not.[7] The latter fell mostly within the period of the Napoleonic War; but there was a precedent during the years of the First Coalition, when the bank of Boyd Benfield obtained the contracts for 1795 to 1797 without other tenders being considered in the event.[8] The reward to the initial subscribers lay in the premium on the scrip, particularly at the launching – a profit dependent of course on a buoyant market. As in peacetime, Pitt had to rely mainly on 3 per cent stocks: an attempt to float a loan at 5 per cent in 1793 met the same fate

1. And he suffered a defeat on printed calicoes and linens, in 1796, as he had done once before, in 1785 (I, 250, 253).

2. And, furthermore, defeated on every occasion that it was reintroduced over the next half century. It passed eventually in 1853.

3. See Mitchell & Deane, op. cit., ch. XIV, tables 1, 2. Cf. p. 523, n3 below for some annual figures before civil expenditure was deducted. The figure of total expenditure contains the provision for past naval debt mentioned in p. 518, n3 above: it would otherwise be some £16½ million.

4. Cf. p. 517 above; and see Pitt's remarks on the incidence of 'ordinary' and 'extraordinary' costs, on 6 May 1796 (*P.R.*, XLIV, 619).

5. Cooper, loc. cit., 89. For figures see Mitchell & Deane, op. cit., ch. XIV, table 2.

6. Cf. I, 257–8.

7. O'Brien, loc. cit., 225.

8. This is discussed on pp. 525–6, 619 below.

as an earlier effort at the start of his Administration – for, as North was said to have put it, 'in order to establish a 5 per cent stock "certain poor ignorant men on the other side of Temple bar must concur"'.[1] The Minister sometimes contrived in these years to include a higher denomination: the issues for 1794 and '95 contained some 4 per cent stock.[2] But for the most part he operated within the market's familiar preference, necessarily accepting some disadvantages of which he was well aware.

The results of borrowing were substantial, taking funded loans and conversions. Perhaps the most satisfactory figures show annual receipts for 1793–6 of £6.7, 12.4, 22.8, and 32.5 million.[3] They were the bulwark of the war effort: the animators of its springs. And their role in turn was sustained by belief in the reformed Sinking Fund. The reformer himself fully shared the sentiment. Pitt had increased the sum paid to the Fund out of revenue in 1792, and also provided for a second Fund to redeem new debt.[4] The arrangements breathed the confidence of a triumphant year.[5] They were not altered as conditions perforce began to change. In the period following 1792 payments continued to be made from revenue over and above the sum originally laid down, and the redemption of debt was steadily pursued. Costing £1.6 million in 1793, it absorbed £2.5 million in 1796,[6] and Pitt had no intention of compromising on his plans. In May 1790, when the prospect of war began to dawn over Nootka Sound, he noted that in such an event 'the Act . . . for the Reduction of the Debt should continue to be regularly put into Execution'. Seven years later he told the Commons that the operations would be 'continued in full vigour'.[7] And so they were. They were in fact maintained continuously until the 1820s.

For the first two years of the war these financial policies commanded wide assent; and for a further year at least they could be defended with conviction. Pitt himself naturally did so, at regular intervals, and in December 1795 he reiterated his 'pride and satisfaction' with the results.[8] He could claim support from some notable facts. Taxes,

1. I, 259. Pitt's undated notes for the 'Loan 1793' are in P.R.O. 30/8/195.

2. See S.R. Cope 'The History of Boyd, Benfield & Co . . .' (Ph. D thesis, University of London, 1947), Appendix B.

3. O'Brien, loc. cit., 9, table 4. Cf. Mitchell & Deane, op. cit., ch. XIV, table 6. O'Brien's comparable figures for new 'war' taxes collected (i.e., gross receipts from taxes levied in addition to the continuing peacetime imposts, from which revenue remained broadly steady) are £1.2, 0.9, 2.1, and 3 million.

4. I, 268.

5. See op. cit., 273–5.

6. Mitchell & Deane, op. cit., ch. XIV, table 6.

7. Memorandum of 14 May 1790 (P.R.O. 30/8/197); speech of 5 December 1797 (*P.R.*, XLIX (1798), 375). And cf. his speech of 24 November 1797 (op. cit., 282–3).

8. Debate of 7 December 1795 (*The Senator*, XIV (nd), 600). Cf. p. 479 above.

imposed on familiar lines, were meeting the objects for which they were intended. Loan money was available in increasing quantities. The Sinking Fund – the final bastion – was being sustained as planned. Given Pitt's premises, these were achievements he had designed. His measures were endorsed retrospectively for 1793–5 by the Commons' Select Committee on Finance of 1797.[1] They fell within a framework broadly accepted in the years concerned.

The Select Committee's verdict was the more interesting because the case by then had somewhat changed. An intervening year of rising troubles had thrown rising doubt on some at least of the policies and on their management. No clear alternative had been offered, and the bulk of the criticisms were of specifics; but the apprehensions were real, and some had been voiced more privately even in 1795. This in fact was not surprising, for that year saw a sudden rise not merely in the total of expenditure but in that of remittances overseas. A sum for the latter of some $£1\frac{1}{2}$ million in bills and bullion in 1793 had increased to perhaps some $£5\frac{1}{2}$ million in 1794 and was now reaching perhaps $£9\frac{1}{2}$ million. This last indeed was a figure which would not be surpassed for another sixteen years, and the annual sums in the interval were mostly less than a quarter as large.[2] But given the initial development, it was only natural that fears were felt particularly by the guardian of the reserves, the Bank of England itself; and it was highly significant that this should have been so. For the co-operation of the Directors and the Treasury was fundamental to wartime finance. The Bank had been founded in a war, with war needs immediately in mind. It managed the National Debt, and was Government's consultant on loans. It advanced money on the Departmental bills and debentures, and discounted them for the market. It was vital to the control of a money supply consisting increasingly of bankers' liabilities, and thus to the tone of the banking system throughout the country. Government had come in the course of the century to count on its support; and signs of serious recalcitrance had been remarkably rare.

It was therefore perhaps not surprising that Pitt tended to dismiss such indications now. He had shown himself inclined earlier to take a fairly high hand with the Directors, and he was not going to curtail wartime needs at an increasingly interesting stage. For the Bank's forebodings stemmed initially from the Minister's proposal for an Austrian loan added and linked to the domestic funding for 1795.[3] This,

1. First Report, 31 March 1797 (*Reports from Committees of the House of Commons ...*, XII (1803), 2–4, 6).
2. Figures taken broadly from those of Norman J. Silberling, 'Financial and Monetary Policy of Great Britain during the Napoleonic Wars' (*The Quarterly Journal of Economics*, XXXVIII), table V, 227. Sherwig, op. cit., 365 has different figures for payments to allies – he is not concerned there, as Silberling is, with remittances for British forces in addition.
Cf. p. 520 above.
3. See p. 377 above.

it was feared, might raise liabilities dangerously far above reserves of specie; always a banker's dread, and already a matter of intermittent concern.[1] As Pitt pursued and effected his intention and the large volume of stock was issued, as unfunded debt continued to be floated, and bullion to be sent overseas, the uneasiness in Threadneedle Street turned to alarm. In June the Bank threatened to withhold further advances on Treasury bills. In July it increased its warnings, with no apparent effect. In August it declined to consider a request for an advance on Exchequer paper.[2] The dissatisfaction persisted for the rest of the year, and beyond.

The Bank's ill humour was fanned by the Minister's alternative expedients in facing his difficulties. For while Pitt was justified in claiming that money was forthcoming in 1795,[3] his methods of obtaining it throw light on problems that were now beginning to show. His resolve to meet ever wider demands, in what proved to be a period of mounting gravity, drove him to courses which perforce involved him in risks. They came to centre on an agent of conspicuous and increasingly convenient nerve and resource: Walter Boyd, who came to notice through the business of the Austrian loan.[4] Its connexion with the main loan for 1795 led the Minister to place the latter in the hands of Boyd's syndicate without opening it to competition. When the Bank of England became reluctant to make cash advances on Departmental bills, he then turned to Boyd to anticipate payments on the loan contract. And when this was done, without publicity, it was by a device – anticipating bills on Hamburg – itself facilitated by Boyd's operations in managing credits for Government abroad.[5] Such interlocking arrangements brought Pitt into a contact implying reliance and support, and the fact was evident at the end of the year. Boyd's syndicate at that time still held unsold stock on the loan for 1795. Pitt decided that this entitled them to preferential 'consideration' for its successor.[6] After first inviting tenders for the new loan he awarded it – after a dramatic meeting with the bidders in Downing Street – as he had done before, without competition. The terms had in fact already been discussed in person with Boyd. This was the peak of a relationship of recent and rapid growth, the benefits of which thereafter became less assured.

Pitt's conduct was attacked. The aspirant contractors were naturally

1. For pre-war, as well as early wartime warnings, cf. pp. 386–7 above. The proportions were in fact not unduly adverse at the turn of 1794–5; but they became progressively worse from the early summer.
2. O'Brien, loc. cit., 113–16. Serious warnings in July from the Directors to Pitt may be found in P.R.O. 30/8/276.
3. P. 523 above.
4. And for whom see p. 377, n5 above.
5. The best account of 'the Hamburg Bill Transaction' is in Cope, 'The History of Boyd, Benfield & Co', 51–134.
6. The word is his (loc. cit., 150). The contract was awarded in November.

angry, and one of them – William Morgan, already disgruntled[1] – took the matter farther. He secured a petition to Parliament, which produced a debate. And while the Minister was exonerated after a 'long and desultory conversation',[2] he was soon caught up in a disturbing epilogue to the affair. For on the very next day he announced to the House that the Government would be open to receive French proposals for peace – the first public statement of its kind in the course of the war[3] – and the stock market rose sharply on the news. The premium on the loan advanced from 7 to 13 per cent in a matter of hours: a very handy profit, where taken, for Boyd and his partners. The coincidence stirred the Commons to life. There was a move for an inquiry, and a Committee was appointed which reported in February 1796. The tenor of its findings was critical; but Pitt was again supported by a heavy majority in the House itself. This however was not quite the end: there was a last challenge, for Boyd's Hamburg bill transaction, which had leaked out earlier, was now subjected to hostile resolutions. They in turn were heavily defeated, and nothing more ensued. But the episode left a taste, and not least with the Bank of England.[4]

Pitt would seem to have acted from mixed motives. He undoubtedly felt a sense of gratitude – perhaps, too, of embarrassment – which affected his judgment. He was also influenced by a less subjective consideration. For the decision on the loan for 1796 established that if a previous issue remained under payment the new issue would be offered to the contractors in the earlier case. This was a not unreasonable way of trying to reassure bidders who might otherwise feel exposed. It would have been less open to question in this instance if the terms, which were favourable to Boyd, had not been settled so largely with him in advance.[5]

The Minister in fact was in a corner from which he could not escape entirely unscathed. Jealousy of Boyd in the City was now mixed with keener suspicion; the Commons' majorities – a closing of the ranks –

---

1. See I, 263–4 for his hostile pamphlet of 1792 on Pitt's obligation to Dr Price in forming the plan for the Sinking Fund in 1786 – a work that roused high resentment in the Minister's circle (I, 263–4). He had approached Pitt unsuccessfully over the loan for 1795 (paper, endorsed by Pitt, of 7 November 1794; P.R.O. 30/8/272).

2. *The Times*, 8 December 1795. The petition was presented on the 4th (*H.C.J.*, 51, 189–90).

3. This is discussed in Ch. XIV, section V below.

4. *P.R.*, XLIII, 621–2, 640–5; XLIV, 117–96, 194–212. The final occasion may have been the more unpleasant for Pitt because the resolutions were moved by an acquaintance from his early days at the Bar, Joseph Jekyll, who had not only been an early supporter but, despite a connexion with Lansdowne, had remained on friendly terms (see I, 24). Jekyll had indeed already put down a question on the matter in October 1795 (*P.R.*, XLIII, 56–7).

5. Cope, loc. cit., 159–61 underlines this last point as reflecting on a judgment swayed unduly by gratitude. O'Brien, loc. cit., 118 stresses the need to reassure contractors in an uncertain time.

could not conceal the doubts in its committee. The affair is of interest not only for the shifts to which Pitt was being put, but also for the light it cast on a changing situation. For 1795 was a significant year in the financial history of the war. It saw the emergence, if implicitly, of a threat to accepted assumptions which would become an open challenge as the conditions hardened. One must not exaggerate the dangers when the constraints were still quite mild: there was no immediate cause to suppose, in that autumn and winter, that the policies could not yield fresh fruits. But they did contain a latent paradox which adversity might always reveal – which indeed had been exposed in the recent American War. For if taxes were to follow familiar lines, as was considered so important, this must depend on restraint in the borrowing which was incurred to restrain their own growth. If the debt became too great they must be overhauled to meet its charges; and while no such prospect was in sight, or considered, as Government's credit came under strain, that was in fact inherent in a development caused – unlike that in 1793 – mainly by external pressures arising from the war. These moreover bore on a year of sharp if uneven depression at home, unsettling to one of Pitt's assumptions, that the economy was elastic and strong. It was one thing to restore a confidence damaged by excessive domestic expansion; another to increase the calls for loan money, at a time of economic disturbance, in support of commitments abroad which were depleting the reserves.[1]

The risks were not lessened – they were held justifiable – by the emphasis placed on the Sinking Fund: a trust indeed cardinal to Pitt's reliance on the policy of borrowing. The absorption of debt into 'annuities, subsisting for a given number of years' meant that, despite wartime increase, it would be terminable eventually; the uninterrupted allocations themselves would reduce the rate of that increase – Pitt even once said that they would 'leave us where we were'.[2] But for the immediate future in a state of war, there was a flaw in the argument; for the operations' success must depend on a surplus of revenue over expenditure. Reverse that process, and you were in ever-tightening coils: raising borrowed money to pay for your borrowing, and moreover, if credit deteriorated, redeeming earlier, cheaper loans from funds raised at higher interest. Such a process, as Gladstone said later, was a 'form of mischief'.[3] The system was maintained because it was seen as the sole means, under solemn pledge, of removing an otherwise indefinite burden of debt from the future. If the current generation was not being

1. Cf. pp. 385–7 above for the credit crisis of 1793, and 443–5 for the possible extent of wartime pressures as causes of the depression in 1795.

2. This was said in November 1797 (*P.R.*, XLIX, 283) – a year in which the rise in the nominal amount of the public debt again greatly exceeded the sum devoted to redemption (Mitchell & Deane, op. cit., ch. XIV, tables, 5, 6). The observation on terminable annuities was of later date – June 1799 (*The Senator*, XXIII (nd), 1657).

3. Speech of 8 May 1854; cited in Cooper, loc. cit., 92. And cf. I, 268–9.

asked to shoulder more in the way of taxes, it was finding money to help liquidate the deficit by a constraint not imposed in any previous war.[1] And the commitment had its short-term as well as more distant rewards. It helped keep up the price of stocks as the authorities made their purchases for redemption, assisting Government to borrow more cheaply than might otherwise have been the case. It supported confidence in Government's solvency, at home and abroad, and was thus a source of comfort to ourselves and our allies, and discomfort to the enemy.[2] If it was abandoned, there was no recourse elsewhere: in this sense Pitt was the willing victim of his earlier success. For it was the widespread fears felt by the end of the American War that sustained the much greater liabilities under its successor.

The question therefore would be not whether to drop the obligation but rather how best to meet its annual charge; and it would be here that changes in fact were made in the next few years. For by then the country was committed to a task, seen as unavoidable, which none the less had been accepted the more readily from an expectation which was not fulfilled. No doubt Pitt would have clung to his Sinking Fund from 1793 under any circumstances; given his reasoning, it is hard to see how he would not. But the precise shape of his policies for taxes and loans in the years of the First Coalition reflected his early belief that the war would be short. In that case the size of the National Debt could of course be contained, borrowing take the brunt of 'extraordinary' costs, and the budget look to a single campaign. Only as the expectation faded, and the policies showed undue signs of wear, was he driven, by stages, to review and innovation. That point was far from being reached by the end of 1795, and twelve months later Pitt was clearly still hoping for an end to the war within the budgetary span.[3] But by then any such expectation rested on an altered basis. For if the finances had hitherto been seen as a weapon to achieve outright victory, those twelve months did much to turn them into a pressure making for a negotiated peace.

IV

Whatever its context, financial management remained a key element in Pitt's handling of a wartime Administration. As in the previous decade, he ruled supreme over Treasury business. After four years of unremitting attention to domestic and foreign pressures, the content and detail of

1. Pitt's speech, 7 June 1799 (as in p. 527, n2 above).
2. Pitt's speech, 24 November 1797 (ibid).
3. For a typical impression of the tone of his budget speech of 7 December 1796 see *The Diaries of Sylvester Douglas (Lord Glenbervie)*, ed. Francis Bickley, I (1928), 103. The background is discussed in Ch. XV, section III below.
    There was of course liable to be more than one budget in the course of the year (p. 517 above).

financial policy remained in his personal charge. 'You will find the office quite a sinecure', a new junior Lord of the Treasury was told.

There are seldom Boards. Mr. Pitt does all the material business at his own house, signs the papers, and then two other Lords sign them of course. Other business the Secretaries judge of without carrying it to him, and lay the papers on the table and circulate them for signature to any of the Lords.

In his own experience, the informant added, 'he had not seen Pitt at a Board he did not know when'.[1]

The Secretaries' scope in turn was recognised for what it was. Rose, the financial expert of the pair,[2] was the constant informant and adviser: a valuable aide, sometimes a corrective, but not more than that. His material was supplemented by others' from the limited circles which Pitt liked to consult:[3] by Departmental officials, and a few colleagues present or past – Hawkesbury among the latter, used cautiously, and Auckland perhaps above all.[4] But such calls, as likewise unsolicited advice from acquaintances, supporters or critics – from Auckland himself given half a chance, from self-appointed helpers such as Sinclair given none[5] – and the flow from interests and institutions, official and unofficial, all related to a Minister known to be master of his house. However Pitt manoeuvred outside with individuals or corporate bodies, however he exploited, circumvented or retreated there, his control was unchallenged in the Treasury itself. And the processes reacted on each other. A powerful First Lord had the greater impact on the financial community; the community's support or acquiescence bolstered a First Lord's power.

At the same time one must remember what the Treasury could and could not do in its relations with the principal wartime Departments. If Pitt laid the lines of central policy and dominated the revenue boards, he had little effective control over much of the expenditure. The army and navy and ordnance could go largely their own ways, subject in such areas in practice only to distant retrospective review.[6] This duality was

1. John Smyth's information to Sylvester Douglas (*Diaries of . . . Douglas*, I, 128). Smyth had been on the Board since May 1794. His description is confirmed by the Minutes, in P.R.O., T.29/65–70.

2. The other, Charles Long since 1791 (see p. 211 above), was mainly concerned with patronage and Parliamentary support; and sometimes involved accordingly in what might be called the politics of finance – he made the principal speech in Pitt's defence over the Hamburg bill transaction in 1796 (p. 525 above).

3. Cf. I, 324, 590.

4. The reader may possibly recall their personalities and relations with Pitt from I, Chs. VI section II, XII section I, XIV section III, XVI section III; and pp. 15, 411, 414n6, 415, 465, 513–14 above.

5. For the two of them see P.R.O. 30/8/110, 178; and cf. I, 239 for the second.

6. P. 517 above.

crucial to the system from which it sprang. It had given to First Lords of the Treasury the potential on which to build; it also, and equally, defined their institutional limits.

Such facts must be borne in mind in considering Pitt's own conception of his role. When Dundas told him that 'All modern Wars are a Contention of Purse, and unless some very peculiar Circumstance occurs . . . the Minister for Finance must be the Minister for War', he was voicing an impression which had been growing for some time, for which an argument could be made, but which the recipient certainly wished to hear.[1] For Pitt himself had no doubt either of the decisive function of finance or, as his experience lengthened, of the consequence for Government. He made his view crystal clear in the one interval of peace which he was to know again.

> He stated . . . his sentiments with regard to the absolute necessity there is in the conduct of the affairs of this country, that there should be an avowed and real Minister, possessing the chief weight in the Council, and the principal place in the confidence of the King. In that respect there can be no rivalry or division of power. That power must rest in the person generally called the First Minister, and that Minister ought, he thinks, to be the person at the head of the finances. He knows, to his own comfortable experience, that notwithstanding the abstract truth of that general proposition, it is noways incompatible with the most cordial concert and mutual exchange of advice and intercourse amongst the different branches of Executive Departments; but still . . . the sentiments of the Minister must be allowed and understood to prevail . . .[2]

This high claim, 'often taken as the first real definition of the office of Prime Minister',[3] was made in particular circumstances, when Pitt was out of office and receiving an offer of an inadequate share of power. It had an immediate connotation. Nevertheless it was a statement of principle, and while not limited to war or 'critical times'[4] it responded to the recent struggle, which had confirmed and strengthened his opinion in its opening phase.

Dundas's earlier statement, however, was rather more ambiguous than the conclusion suggested. The emphasis lay on the personal as well as the institutional position. If the 'Contention of Purse' suggested the

1. P. 412 above. Cf. Mackesy, *The War for America*, 20–1.

2. This well known statement came again from Dundas, staying with Pitt at the time; Lord Melville to Henry Addington, 22 March 1803 (Pellew, *Life . . . of . . . Addington*, II, 116).

3. *English Historical Documents, XI, 1783–1832*, ed. A. Aspinall and E. Anthony Smith (1959), note to no. 64.

4. As by North, in 1778; see I, 281.

senior financial Minister as 'the Minister for War', it was still not impossible to conceive of that place being filled from another post. There could be a 'peculiar Circumstance'; there had been in the past: Chatham himself had been a notable 'Exception'.

> I do not mean to say that there is not at all times in His Majesty's Councils some particular Person who has and ought to have a leading and even an overruling Ascendancy in the conduct of Publick affairs, and that Ascendancy extends to War as it does to any other Subject. Such you are at present as the Minister of the King; Such your Father was as Secretary of State[;] Such you would be if you was Secretary of State, and Such Mr. Fox would be if He was Secretary of State and the Duke of Bedford First Lord of the Treasury. In short it depends and ever must depend on other Circumstances than the Particular name by which a Person is called . . .[1]

even if the name of First Lord of the Treasury had a presumptive advantage.

Pitt certainly had the 'leading Ascendancy' when war broke out. Even those who, tracing a decline in success in the last years of peace, connected it with Cabinet changes,[2] could hardly deny his continued if no longer unqualified pre-eminence. The influences cited then – Dundas and Grenville – were unlikely to be weaker now, when the latter's functions as Foreign Secretary were crucial and the responsibility of the Home Department for the affairs of overseas settlements[3] gave the former a specific place in the shaping of strategy. Over and above these Departmental cares, however, was the Secretaries of State's recognised role as the linchpins of an Administration. And this was true of war perhaps even more than of peace. 'All warlike preparations, every military operation, and every naval equipment must be directed by a Secretary of State before they can be undertaken'. So one of their Under Secretaries had written in the American War, and, in remodelled Offices, the same had held good in more recent scares.[4]

The Secretaries of State were in fact the connecting links essential to a system of dispersed powers. Without them the administrative structure for war could hardly have been articulated. It was this indeed that made Dundas doubt if a new Secretary with less ample authority could fill the role for which he was designed.[5] For not only might his administrative powers be weakened but, as a result, his intimate contact might be reduced with the Minister at the head of affairs. And it was highly

1. To Pitt, 9 July 1794 (P.R.O. 30/8/157).
2. See I, 633–5. This was a Foreign Office view.
3. I, 329. And cf. p. 413, n4 above.
4. The quotation is cited by Mackesy, op. cit., 17. And cf. I, 309, 570 n4.
5. See pp. 412–13 above.

important that this should not happen: that the Secretaries and a powerful First Lord of the Treasury should work closely and if possible harmoniously together. Given a strong combination at the centre the other relevant Ministers could both be restrained from encroaching on policy (whether or not that was desirable) and, in some degree, spurred in execution. The former at any rate was true in the first two years of this war – and so far as Dundas himself was concerned, despite his forecast, thereafter. Richmond at the Ordnance was excluded, for better or worse, from discussions on strategy. Amherst, Sir George Yonge and Chatham were held, and held themselves by nature, in their places. And if a certain change took place when Windham became Secretary at War, it was still not one of extended scope.[1] The Cabinet, in which most of them sat, retained its position as the ultimate forum – an authority indeed which was to gain in continuity over a generation of war. 'The operations', as Dundas himself stated with constitutional rectitude, '. . . are canvassed and adjusted in Cabinet and become the joint act of His Majesty's Confidential Servants'. This last was valid. It was proper but less convincing in practice, at the time he wrote, to add that 'the Secretary of State who holds the Pen does no more than transmit their Sentiments'.[2]

For while the trio of Pitt, himself and Grenville reported and referred to their colleagues – perhaps not least at the Cabinet dinners at which business could sometimes be done[3] – they had found little need by that point to seek judgment on any doubts of their own. One cannot specify how far operations, or their diplomatic context, were 'canvassed and adjusted in Cabinet' in 1793–4. Few Minutes seem to have survived, and while there are not infrequent mentions of meetings the exact gist and tone are seldom known.[4] Some subjects, largely predictable, emerge from the obscurity: the formation of Conventions or treaties with Russia and with Mediterranean Powers; military movements and instructions, perhaps most thickly in the early days and again towards the end of 1794; naval movements against sorties from Brest; the eventual scale and timing of expeditions to the West Indies; the decision to hold Toulon, and efforts to muster Allied aid; reinforcements for the Channel Islands against a possible threat; Gilbert Elliot's appointment in Corsica, and Malmesbury's mission to the continent; the treaty with the United States; the British command in the Low Countries in 1794; support for Prussia, and Austria, and French émigrés, mostly in that year; possible

1. See pp. 293, 374, 484, 379 above. Windham's influence is also discussed on p. 535 below.

2. To Pitt, 9 July 1794 (P.R.O. 30/8/157).

3. Cf. I, 581, 632.

4. One of the best sources is Amherst's Diary (Kent C.A.O.), which contains 22 references to Cabinet meetings, and 25 to Cabinet dinners, from March to December 1793, and 33 and 29 respectively in 1794. But all too often the topics are not given.

withdrawal from Holland at its close.[1] There will have been other occasions and topics of the kind, how significant one cannot tell. But there are few indications for that period of what George III called 'anything unpleasant'[2] – of serious differences of view in or brought to the notice of Cabinet. This might appear a surprising statement, when the First Lord of the Admiralty had to be removed for a failure in relations between his and 'the other Departments'. But the bad feeling related more to administrative practice than to the moulding of policy, in which Chatham's opinion – as over Toulon – carried little weight.[3] Undesirable though this last may have been – and the position was soon to alter, as his successor Spencer began to make himself felt – it saved his colleagues from having to adjudicate on disputes, and he himself was able to stay with them in a less 'efficient' post. Where more substantial figures brought objections these seem to have related mainly to foreign affairs: to Hawkesbury's dislike of part of the Jay treaty, and – more directly relevant to operations – possibly to Grenville's uneasiness over an incident in the treatment of Prussia.[4] The latter however is not certain, and neither episode in any case caused significant trouble. The only member to cast serious doubt on strategic thought began to absent himself from meetings within a year.[5] The impression in fact is of a powerful small group settling their own minds and differences in advance, and by and large, with shades of emphasis, then presenting a solid front. When they did not – and the first clear instance was to occur in 1795 – the Cabinet perforce moved, temporarily, to the centre of the stage.[6]

1. Grenville to George III, 18 March 1793 (*L.C.G. III*, II, no. 858), Minute of 17 April 1793 (B.L. Add. Ms 59306); Amherst's Diary *passim*, vols. I–IV; Dundas to George III, 17 March 1793 (*L.C.G. III*, II, no. 857, and see loc. cit., nos. 852, 855), Pitt to Grenville [June–July 1793] (*H.M.C., Dropmore*, II, 402), Amherst's Diary, vol. IV, 24 October, 18 November 1794; Dundas to George III, 26 October, 16 November (*bis*) 1793 (loc. cit., nos. 963, 969, 972), 10, 25 October 1794 (loc. cit., nos. 1138, 1145); same to same, 14 September 1793 (loc. cit., no. 938); draft of Pitt to George III, 5 December 1793 (P.R.O. 30/8/301); Dundas to same, 24 September 1793 (*L.C.G. III*, II, no. 949), Grenville to same, 9 April 1794 (loc. cit., no. 1043); p. 514 above; pp. 374–5 above, Pitt to George III, ?24 August (Holland Rose, *Pitt and Napoleon*, 227–8), 30 August 1794 (*L.C.G. III*, II, no. 1113), Amherst's Diary, vol. IV, 18 November 1794; same to Grenville, 10 October [1793] (*H.M.C., Dropmore*, II, 441–2), Grenville to George III, 24 July 1794 (*L.C.G. III*, II, no. 1096), same to Pitt, ?12 October 1794 (Holland Rose, op. cit., 260), same to George III, 14 November, 6 December 1794 (*L.C.G. III*, II, nos. 1157, 1167), Pitt to Hawkesbury, 7 February 1795 (B.L. Loan Ms 72, vol. 38); Minute of 14 November 1794 (*H.M.C., Dropmore*, II, 644); Minute of 18 November (loc. cit., 646), Dundas to Windham, Private, 21 November 1794 (B.L. Add. Ms 37874).
2. To Dundas, 18 March 1793 (*L.C.G. III*, II, no. 857).
3. See pp. 379, 318 above; Pitt to George III, 8 December 1794 (loc. cit., no. 1170).
4. Pp. 513, 366n5 above.
5. See pp. 267–9, 293, 428 above.
6. The incident is followed on pp. 549–56 below.

The degree of consensus in the inner circle makes it harder to measure Pitt's own contribution. There may indeed seem to be a paradox in claiming an ascendancy for someone who distrusted 'extremely' his feel for military affairs.[1] He certainly looked for advice and as always listened carefully; and he could yield in the face of real resistance, as when Dundas and the Generals opposed him over Puisaye in 1794.[2] But if his interest was roused he would return to the charge, and, if determined enough, he could well carry others with him. The degree of effort put into Toulon, and still more into north-west France, as was to happen in the latter instance within months of his initial rebuff, were examples of personal impact on a process he largely shaped.[3] These were choices which, wise or not, fell clearly enough within his scope. He sometimes followed such decisions in detail, as his peacetime experience had accustomed him to do. The intermittent raids, understandable and likely as they were, could be more confusing than helpful; as could the legacy, when they ceased as suddenly and the Minister withdrew with partial knowledge. That is the price of a powerful head of Government. More often however the policy emerged with less trace of individual stimulus. The commitment to the Low Countries once Holland was saved, the early refusal to concentrate on Brittany, the Dunkirk operation, the scales of resources and orders of priority for the West Indies, the treatment of Austria and Prussia and of neutrals, of the Bourbons and their possible restoration, all appear to reflect a natural concert of views. And this in its turn does not necessarily imply that Pitt's were largely moulded by others; that the military choices in particular emanated always from Dundas. If the Secretary influenced the Minister the reverse was also true. As Pitt himself once put it, without trying for effect, 'every act of his being as much *mine* as *his*'.[4] Dundas's role was established at the start by a combination of causes: the powers of his Office, Amherst's nullity, Chatham's laxity, Richmond's awkwardness. Although, as he pointed out, all those three Ministers were in the Cabinet,[5] none was personally in a position, and only Richmond wished, to be a force. Dundas by contrast had long been at Pitt's elbow, increasingly so since 1789. But this was the point, as he himself knew. When he told Pitt that, whatever his own post, 'not a Person living would ever look upon . . . any other Person but yourself as the War Minister',[6] he was not being merely plausible and polite. Richmond's views were discounted largely because he had lost Pitt's confidence; and if Dundas's were influential, and accepted or shared in the first two

1. P. 489 above.
2. Pp. 370–1 above.
3. See pp. 303–6 above, 568–79 below.
4. To Grenville, 5 July 1794 (*H.M.C., Dropmore*, II, 595). This was written on the eve of the agonised moment when Dundas was trying to resign (pp. 412–13 above).
5. To Pitt, 9 July 1794 (P.R.O. 30/8/157).
6. Ibid.

years, it was largely because he already held it. The appointment to which he referred, of Secretary of State for War, in the event codified a status he had enjoyed for some eighteen months. But when, as was to happen in 1795, he doubted the wisdom of a military undertaking, he refrained from opposing a plan on which he knew Pitt was intent.[1]

The Minister's initial ascendancy in fact derived not from an expertise in war but from the position he had carved for himself in peace. It rested on a tenure of the Treasury which he exploited to the full, and a personal involvement, by now familiar, in any area of business he chose. Working as closely with Grenville in foreign affairs as with Dundas in the military, he was at a focal point for strategic decisions. It was indeed when an operation had or was affected by wider implications that he was apt to make his own wishes felt.[2] And when he did so the effect was apt to be conclusive, as Grenville was to find, more sharply than Dundas, also in 1795.[3] The same, it may be said, in the last resort applied to George III, watching alertly and sometimes suspiciously in the wings. His influence was always to be reckoned with in the treatment of the army – above all the Guards – and the Hanoverian troops. It always bore on the functions and career of the Duke of York. It added to the disfavour in which Richmond was held.[4] And on wider issues it had naturally to be weighed. It was one factor in making up the strategic account. But it was not more than that: when it came to the point Pitt remained the arbiter. His authority was still too firmly based for any of his associates, or a minority of them, directly to challenge his final resolve.

That this remained true – that in fact it was shown most clearly – in 1795 suggests that in matters of strategy little had changed with an altered Cabinet. In the first few months of the broadened Administration this was certainly so, for while Portland and Windham among the accessions were then in relevant posts, the former was concerned in the military sphere mainly with home defence and though the latter's interest was keen his views hardened only in the winter.[5] They had an effect thereafter, to Dundas's annoyance. But that was due largely to a turn of circumstances which led Pitt himself in the same direction— and when they changed again the effect declined. A similar favourable process, combined with his own qualities, was by then bringing another Portland Whig to the fore, as Spencer introduced a clearer naval voice to an increasingly maritime strategy. In the closing stages of the First

1. This is discussed in Ch. XIV, section III below.
2. Eg his personal involvement in the early stages of Dunkirk in 1793, and, as will be shown, in the plans for north-west France and indeed for France in general two years later.
3. Ch. XIV, section I below.
4. See pp. 331, 374, 428 above.
5. Cf. pp. 368, 417 above.

Coalition the old trio acquired an adjunct. But the trio was still at the hub of direction, debating intimately among themselves and laying the lines of policy where the main areas converged.

The impression of such continuity, however, was far from complete; nor did Pitt's own authority always appear convincing. The fear of divided counsels and the consequences for himself, which agitated Government supporters when the new element joined, and had grown by the end of 1794,[1] included the management of the war. This last was not the only source of discontents which covered the Government as a whole. But it increased them, and brought them to a point. When Mitford wrote his long, bold first letter of complaint, he dwelt largely on the war Departments. Stressing the 'neglect to provide for that moment of danger which the country very generally expects soon to arrive', he insisted on the 'inertness . . . prevalent in all parts' of the Administration. But according to those with whom he talked

> particularly throughout the naval & military establishments neglect pervades every office . . . in all, a most thorough reform is necessary, to give real activity to the springs of government. According to them, there is an absolute want of many of the most important necessaries in the Naval department [where indolence, corruption and extravagance were said to be rife among both clerks and naval officers] . . . The army is in some degree the object of similar animadversion, & particularly the board of ordnance. But that which seems most to occupy the minds of well meaning men is the apparent want of means for the internal defence of the country . . . They all look to *you* . . . If *you* have not spirit & exertion sufficient for the exigency, they think they have good reason to despond . . .

And the worst of it was that Pitt, so addressed, appeared to have lost his 'spirit' and become captive to the new political arrangements he had made. 'Resting on broken reeds', involved with men who were 'consuming his good fame', he no longer seemed in active and unfettered command. Such was the talk among old friends and supporters; but, Mitford ended, not among them alone. Some of it came even from men connected with Opposition, who 'still think they must look to *you* for the safety of the country.[2]

Strong stuff. And in its way a strong tribute to Pitt. The dissatisfaction, reported also by others as well placed to know as Mitford, was hardly surprising at this particular time. The political ructions and indiscretions of the autumn focused attention on the state of the Ministry;[3] and the sudden retreat through Flanders sparked a wave of

1. See pp. 414–15, 427–9 above.
2. 25 January 1795; p. 429 above.
3. Pp. 420–4 above.

anger and alarm. Parliament, the country, Pitt himself, were baffled at the turn of the year.[1] Chances had miscarried, there was little to show for them, and now another season of war lay ahead. Some of the criticisms were in point of fact not strictly on target. Pitt had just changed one of the Ministers and was about to change others in the main war Departments;[2] and various administrative efforts, some sponsored by himself, were ignored. Mitford for instance reported a widespread feeling that 'a vast body could be instantly raised' by voluntary enlistment if the Ministry would recognise the extent of popular support. But only some months before it had acted precisely to this end, and if the augmentation of the militia – which apparently he favoured – was not proving particularly successful, the new provisions for Volunteer corps were meeting with a real response. Recruitment for the regular army, while still short, was the highest in memory. And in the navy, the transport and (more modestly) impress services had been recently remodelled, and the health of the fleet was being significantly improved.[3] Not all was inactive, and larger reforms would soon be introduced – not the less soon, no doubt, because of the criticisms.[4] Nor was the assumption that wells of support existed, untapped and easily exploitable, an accurate reflection of the true state of affairs. Undoubtedly there was a feeling, expressed most keenly among men of property, that more should and could be done to organise loyal means of defence. They '*profess*', as Mitford himself put it, 'their readiness to meet the emergency' – the immediacy of which, one might say, was itself exaggerated. But the underlining was not so wide of the mark. When Government sought greater effectiveness or a wider central capacity, particularly in the traditionally sensitive military sphere, it soon encountered the familiar obstacles and constraints.[5] Pitt, so Macaulay pronounced for a generation raised in the memory of Waterloo,

> was at the head of a nation engaged in a struggle for life and death, of a nation eminently distinguished by all the physical and all the moral qualities which make excellent soldiers. The resources at his command were unlimited. The Parliament was even more ready to grant him men and money than he was to ask for them. In such an emergency, and with such means, such a statesman as Richelieu, as Louvois, as Chatham, as Wellesley, would have created in a few months one of the finest armies in the world . . .[6]

1. See pp. 379–81 above.
2. Pp. 379, 428 above.
3. Section I above.
4. The improvement of medical supplies for the West Indies, for instance, was doubtless impelled in part by a growing dread of service in that quarter among the troops.
5. Cf. pp. 481–500 above.
6. 'William Pitt', in the *Encyclopaedia Britannica* (1859).

Such a description of 1793–4 would have seemed strange to the Ministers concerned.

But when all this has been said, the contemporary critics were right in fastening on administration. For the failures or successes of strategy cannot be assessed in an administrative void. The decisions in the years of the First Coalition were framed in a context which was not always simple or susceptible of obvious choice. The period was one of sudden crises and equally sudden opportunities, and responses, perforce often immediate, were often piecemeal. Many arose, as usual in war, from the enemy's initiative. Such were the early involvement on the continent in defence of Holland, and some of the incessant diversions affecting Moira's force in the first two campaigns.[1] But in the framework of an alliance, it was also the case that judgments contained considerations wider than the military alone. If we take the first three years (or more precisely, slightly less), certain features develop which come increasingly to underlie actions that can otherwise appear incoherent. One may start with the first significant choice, made when Holland had been saved, to remain in the Low Countries and enlarge the original British force. For this was taken to preserve the Belgic provinces in their pre-war relationship with Austria; and that object, considered vital, had diplomatic and military implications which helped shape the British contribution to the following year's campaign. The preservation of the Low Countries, and Austria's place there, remained of prime importance, and it was not easy or safe to remove or greatly reduce York's army. But its presence should also promote a more direct influence on the plans – and the movements – of partners now receiving or actively seeking British money; and it was further desirable if there was a decisive Allied drive into France.[2] The prospect of victory in 1794 seemed tantalisingly close; and if it materialised the British would do well to be on the spot. It did not, and hopes for the main front receded thereafter. But as seen from London against a changing and increasingly uncertain background, the outcome remained in balance for a further year. The more violent the swings then, indeed, the greater the inducement to seize other openings in Europe, supported by continued pressure on eastern France. Like the first venture, at Toulon, these must lie in France itself; and again the weighing of factors ranged beyond the strictly military. It embraced in fact the whole spectrum of the enemy's internal state, including the diplomatic implications of acting in concert with domestic resistance – a form of warfare, novel in degree, which governed the treatment of the various French interests, internal and émigré, whose shifting fortunes contributed to its formation.[3] A British presence on the continent, in whichever form, was therefore accepted, at first in

1. Pp. 263–4, 297, 322–5, 343, 369 above.

2. See Ch. VIII section 1, Ch. X ooo section 1 (including p. 331 for a discrepant effect from this combination of reasons) above.

3. This is followed in Ch. XIV, sections III, IV below.

the confident and then the urgent hope of rapid victory. And this naturally had consequences for the maritime strategy which, instinctively adopted at the start, remained fundamental. The navy was sustained, reinforcements were sent to the West Indies and offensives planned. Blockade and colonial conquest were seen once more as basic pressures on France. But as the Coalition developed, naval warfare was viewed as not enough in itself; and when a close and a distant interest competed for immediate resources the former was usually favoured in fact during the first two and a half years.[1] This was doubtless to be expected: the need would appear more pressing, and there was a temptation to think that men could be extracted or replaced to meet the latter's programme. No stark 'alternative' was admitted.[2] But one must note that in practice the Government had moved from a starting point which held no firm place for action in Europe to an acceptance of that theatre as the decisive prospect within a current year. The fact that such an attitude would soon change again with a further change of circumstance does not remove the reality, however limited its term. And while there was no real dispute as the events of this period unfolded, Pitt's own approach, quite uncertain at first and ambiguous for some time, became more explicit, ironically, in what proved to be a final phase.

A strategy that relied heavily on exploiting opportunities was not necessarily indefensible in principle. Pitt himself confronted his critics with a reasoned case at successive stages – increasingly as he had to explain hopes deferred. Their own proposals indeed – when offered – often shrink under examination; and later critics in their turn have often, less excusably, ignored relevant factors. They have been inclined furthermore to foreshorten the time scale, attributing to one period the conditions of another. History of course is written with hindsight. But historians should not be dominated by hindsight, and Pitt and Dundas – and Grenville – were not as simple as some of their detractors.[3] They were not blind to the interactions of the demands and chances to which they worked, within what they knew to be a diplomatic and military and economic frame. There was an alliance to be considered. There were overseas interests to guard and to build on. There was a state of affairs in France to which experience was proving a shaky guide.

All these ingredients of a combination offered prospects within a reasonable term: a basis for a strategy of diversified effort and bargaining points at the peace. But success must rest on three assumptions none of which in fact was certain. And in the event none was to be fulfilled.

1. Cf. p. 348 above for Pitt's statement on the naval contribution, and ibid, n5 and p. 369, for competing interests in 1793–4. 1795 is followed in Ch. XIV below.

2. P. 269 above.

3. Fortescue being the extreme example, in his *History of the British Army* and *British Statesman of the Great War*.

In the first place, the Alliance must be made to work to some effect. The story of the first two years on the contrary – as again of the next – was one of missed opportunities arising from diverging or contrasting interests. Of course a united, determined Coalition might still not have beaten France in that time. Its Generals were cautious, its staffs deliberate, and on the Flanders front itself, from which the main thrust was expected in 1794, they had first to clear the barrier fortresses unless the French obliged by concentrating in the open.[1] The pace was unlikely to be swift, and the enemy had shown a gift for recovery and a spirit and tactical power which had already made their mark. Few commanders in the century had achieved a clear-cut victory – which was what might be needed – in a single campaign; and when different nationalities had to act together the technical constraints were usually underlined. Nevertheless, on both sides of the Alps with monotonous regularity, the Coalition Powers failed to press their advantages thanks to concerns beyond the battlefields themselves. The territorial quarrel between the Dutch and the Austrians, the Germanic rivalries of Austria and Prussia, the mutual suspicions of Austria and Sardinia, of Spain and Britain, undermined co-operation. Above all, the Polish Partition, focusing Austrian and Prussian ambitions, hampered and finally ruined the plans for the west.

> It was in the north and east of Europe that the crisis occurred which, from 1789 to 1795, stirred up the great Powers of Europe against each other, revealed the antagonism of their pretensions, called forth their rivalries, . . . for long delayed their coalition, paralysed it when formed, and finally broke it up.

And in that great question, following Ochakov, England had no voice.[2]

The British were justified in their irritation, rising to digust and fury, as they watched much of this melancholy spectacle of disarray. Pitt and Grenville fought and fought and fought again throughout the long struggle to build and sustain the Alliances that rose and fell and rose once more. They tried hard in the opening phase, employing special envoys when necessary – Malmesbury to Prussia, Spencer and Thomas Grenville to Austria, later Macartney to the émigré Court.[3] They worked indeed incessantly. But they did so under certain disadvantages endemic to their role and some of their own making. The lack of say in the Polish question was one. Their function as paymaster was another; for while this was central to British influence, and probably essential to the Coalition itself, it did not make them better liked by the bene-

---

1. Cf. pp. 286–7 above. The consequences for supply were also significant, since armies normally living off the country had to assemble depots when static for too long.
2. P. 28 above; and for this quotation from Sorel, I, 553.
3. See pp. 332, 343 above, and 582 below.

ficiaries. Nations, like people, usually resent those who help them financially, more openly when, as most often, there are terms attached. The necessary bargaining with Prussia and with Austria soured relations; and any subsequent pressure or apparent pressure or default by the paymaster could quickly cause disproportionate tension. England was not particularly popular on the continent when she joined the war; success and growing self-satisfaction had not greatly endeared her to others. Grenville's lofty language now, Pitt's carelessness with remittances to Prussia, had their places in a failure the main causes of which lay elsewhere.[1]

The shakiness of the Alliance was the more serious because the enemy seemed even more shaky. Continued pressure was the surest catalyst of a quick French collapse. For the intensity of their weakness was the second assumption in this period, and it was one which Pitt held particularly strongly. Imbued from the first with a vivid impression of France's economic strains, and a financier's emphasis on the evils of excessive paper money, he could not believe in her prolonged survival if wartime costs had to be maintained.[2] Effective operations on the continent were a vital element in the process: with them, internal unrest would soar and the French armies themselves would be starved; without them, the Revolution would have a breathing space at the least, and at the worst could resume its conquests. The first part of the argument cannot be proved, for the pressure was not sustained: the French were let off the hook, as Pitt saw it, time and time again. But his reading may well have been optimistic in any case: their overseas possessions, while important to their system, were less so than the British supposed, and the domestic economy, pressed near the margin, was exasperatingly resilient, until a military genius arrived to place it on a different footing.

Two linked assumptions, then, which proved inadequate. Their success would have relieved the burden on a third which related to the British capacity itself. For a strategy embracing a diversified effort posited sufficient and flexible resources, which meant an organisation able to provide both. The greatest weakness, in the last resort, of the British management in this period was the assumption that these would be forthcoming when the odds were that they would not. Again one should be careful not to overstate the case. The charge of frittering away men and material between too many targets, valid as it sometimes was against the administrative estimates, must allow for urgent defensive needs in face of the enemy's successes, and for disappointments and delays from auxiliaries and allies. It must recognise that those other

1. See pp. 365–6, 340–2 above.
2. Cf. p. 479 above. Wilberforce held that Pitt first came to believe in the prospect of a short war from 'Dundas's influence' on the eve (*Life of Wilberforce*, II, 391). It seems to me more likely that this was only one of the factors, and his own financial reasonings, strong at the start, strengthened as time went by.

Powers, and the French émigrés, were sometimes designed to furnish much of the strength for operations planned to include a British element. It should also not overlook the extent to which some resources were in fact increased, or the progress, restricted though it was, in improving some aspects of organisation. Such facts should be borne in mind. But really they prove the point: the conditions which promoted the strategy placed it constantly at risk. If the enemy was capable of sudden rapid advances, the more important to retain an adequate reserve. If auxiliaries and allies were unreliable in delivery, the greater the need for one's own troops. If recruitment was raised to an unprecedented level, which however was still strained by operational demands and a higher pressure on supplies, that meant that the demands must be carefully watched. If there was some visible but still obstinate progress in improving organisation, that reflected not only the need to heighten the effort but also the existence of constraints which could not be ignored. If, in short, the prospect of victory seemed to lie around the corner for almost three years, the more important to master hard problems of priority and choice.

The need was the greater because it was not merely a question of the size of the resources. It was also, as Pitt was slow to grasp fully, a question of quality. Not only were numbers and quantities limited, and some incapable of rapid expansion. All too often the calibre of men and material and organisation was painfully low. Once again we should not ignore the efforts to improve: the growing concentration on volunteers to take over part of the home defence, the emphasis where possible on professionalism in the naval Quota Acts, the gradual impact of an advance in military training.[1] But the obstacles were formidable. And so it proved in the higher reaches; in the vital areas of intelligence and planning. Departmental arrangements and staffwork were mediocre, co-operation between different arms virtually non-existent – Grey and Jervis in the West Indies were the exception to something very like a rule. And good intelligence, in both London and the theatres, was conspicuous by its absence, as a series of reverses from Dunkirk onwards amply proved. These were not the foundations for a strategy whose very range and flexibility demanded precision. As in the West Indies, so in general, success required 'a reconciliation of ends with measurable means'.[2]

We end therefore where we began.[3] The system for war was not geared to providing what was needed at an ever-growing pace. Compared with previous conflicts the demands of this occasion rose and spread with unusual speed, while the traditional framework of response remained much the same. Men might become unhappy with the results;

1. Section I above.
2. P. 354 above. For Grey and Jervis see p. 356; for Dunkirk pp. 287–90.
3. Pp. 477–8 above.

but they were not ready for the appropriate changes, and neither was the Government prepared for a task which implied a lengthy struggle. Even as it was, an extension of powers, a disturbance of equipoise, was suspect and apt to be resisted as inimical to the traditions it was meant to defend. The conduct of strategy thus contained a serious flaw in what proved to be this early stage. It was seeking to respond to demands and chances which soon outran the handling of resources themselves dependent on a complex of attitudes which restricted their quality and supply.

This was a conditioning fact. Pitt himself in the same period did something to compound a process of which he was a, partly unconscious, victim. His profound belief in a short war, raising his resolve to keep the Allies together and to pursue a diversified strategy, also made it easier to work to a given system in the broad expectation of meeting short-term needs. Such aims and assumptions suited a temperament for which, arguably, they were becoming rationalisations. For by 1795 there were signs that Pitt was avoiding inconvenient thoughts. He had always prided himself on 'looking our situation in the face',[1] and could claim that on the whole he had enjoyed marked success. But he was used now to success, and he did not like it to escape his control. For there was equally that side to his nature: '*I cannot allow myself to doubt*',[2] and if will and argument could be given their chance he would not easily contemplate failure. If he had seriously to do so he would adjust to altered facts. But meanwhile he intensely disliked – he shrank from – losing hope. Such a disposition in a dominant figure produced its public as well as private strengths: it injected a personal spirit into the national mood. Conversely, the disappointment, public and personal, could be serious if beliefs and reality began to drift apart. That process in his own case, as already suggested, was not likely to be swift, since public conditions in their turn bore here on private inclination. Pitt could not have operated as he did outside a context that offered the hopes he craved; one that provided a reasonable prospect for the lines on which he worked. The British position, flawed as it was, had great attributes of strength. It was this that enabled him to stand at the centre of the formulation of policies the instruments of which were not under firm control.

1. See I, 279.
2. Written, on Ireland, in 1785; I, 215.

Part Five

CHAPTER XIV

Strategy Adapted

I

Never the best of correspondents, Pitt sat down in April 1795 to write to his mother after a lapse of, probably, half a year. So much had happened in the past four to five months, he observed, that he would not know where to start; he would have liked to come down to Burton Pynsent and talk over 'the long History of this short Period'. He must have been referring in part to the Fitzwilliam affair; but also to the war, which had had its share of 'Interesting Occurrences', with plans in train moreover for others soon to come.[1]

Their course revealed a shift of pattern since 1794. At the same time it marked a, largely involuntary, return to Pitt's own earlier hopes – and after his momentary confession at the end of that year he continued, with his usual resilience, to hope.[2] Colonial conquests, a descent on the French coast, closer links with Russia: such developments and prospects in 1795 looked back to his first, unformed notions.[3] Now they were given an impetus and a sharper focus. For, together with plans to support a counter-revolution inside France, the emphasis was shaped by the collapse of the Triple Alliance.

Holland was, effectively, the first partner to go. This of course was not unexpected: by December 1794 the British were prepared for the Dutch to give up.[4] Co-operation no longer existed, the Patriots were taking over, Amsterdam fell in January and the Stadtholder fled to England. From that point the Government assumed that Dutch sovereignty had disappeared, and the safety of the British force became the 'primary object'.[5] This indeed was pressing, for the troops were facing disaster as they continued, after a brief respite, to pull back beyond the rivers. In

---

1. 20 April 1795 (P.R.O. 30/8/12). The preceding letter, in a series which Lady Chatham seems to have preserved carefully, is dated 17 September 1794.

For Pitt's letter-writing see I, 323–4; for his visits to Burton Pynsent, op. cit., 589; for Fitzwilliam, Ch. XI, section IV above.

2. See pp. 380–1 above.

3. Cf. pp. 266–7 above.

4. Pp. 375–6 above.

5. Dundas's expression (to York, 16 January 1795; P.R.O., W.O. 6/12). By then, according to Burges at the Foreign Office, there were 'Councils sitting every day' (to Anne Burges, 21 January 1795; Bodleian Library, Bland Burges Ms 10/151).

bitter weather and a hostile country, frozen and starved and harried by marauders, their transport in chaos and the sick unattended, discipline finally broke down.[1] The events of January and February were some of the most tragic in British military history, and only a slackening of the French pressure, as talks began with the Patriots, saved the remains of the army from disintegration. Order indeed was partly restored as the retreat continued through eastern Holland and into Prussia to a line on the Ems. Headquarters were set up at Osnabrück – the see of which York had been bishop since he was six months old. But this was a temporary halt, allowing the Prussians to take over their frontier, for on 8 February the Cabinet had confirmed the intention to withdraw the infantry and guns from the continent.[2] Communications, disrupted for some weeks, were re-established through Emden, and in mid-March the force moved east once more, to meet the transports ordered to the Weser. A month later the infantry and part of the artillery embarked at Bremen, leaving the cavalry and the rest of the gunners, with the Hanoverians and other auxiliaries, to co-operate with the Austrian command in Germany itself.

In the event, the Dutch were not allowed by their conquerors to change their status until May. When they did so, it was not to withdraw from the war but to change sides. As well as providing for a French army almost as starved of supplies as the British, they had then to meet the terms of a full defensive and offensive alliance. France obtained a strong naval squadron, some troops, a heavy financial indemnity, the territory of Maastricht, part of southern Holland, and the defences of Flushing. So far as the British were concerned, something like a state of war already existed, for shipping had been held in Dutch ports since February and in British ports since March. Dutch warships could be taken. But the treaty of 16 May was proof not only that the Coalition had lost a member but that the enemy had added to his strength.

Meanwhile the second partner went. Prussia signed a treaty with France in Basle on 5 April. Perhaps this could not have been averted, at least to useful purpose given the frustrating experience of the past year.[3] Prussia's prime fear and prime hope – fear of Austria, hope of eastern gains – were always liable to outweigh the merits of a western crusade; and never more so than now, when throughout the winter she was deep in talks for a further partition of Poland. With a tactful French negotiator and Britain's unpopularity, inducements from London might well have failed or, worse, been wasted. None the less they were mooted, and indeed pressed so strongly as to threaten a crisis in the inner circle of the Ministry itself.

The adversaries were Pitt and Grenville. Their positions, curiously it

---

1. Cf. pp. 378–9 above.
2. Minute in *L.C.G. III*, II, no. 1199. And see p. 375 above.
3. See pp. 339–42, 366–7 above.

might seem, were in each case opposite to those they had taken, briefly, a few months before. Then Pitt had held up the Prussian subsidy to Grenville's irritation:[1] now he was anxious to make a fresh approach, against Grenville's advice. But in point of fact the earlier difference of emphasis had centred on tactics not on policy; and the Foreign Secretary's response now was hardened by surprise and anger that the Minister was departing from what had appeared to be common ground.

Pitt's proposals were made probably towards the end of February[2] – by which time the main British army had left Holland. He returned to the old stipulation for 60,000 fresh Prussians, whose services were now to be rewarded by stages for reconquering the country. £400,000 would be paid when they crossed the river Yssel, £400,000 when the French were driven back beyond the Waal, and a further £1,200,000 when the Stadtholder was restored. These sums would be in addition to the terms of the original subsidy, set now to produce £1,600,000 a year while a Prussian force remained on the Ems. The objects were thus to regain Holland and (through the force on the Ems) defend north-west Germany.[3] And if these could be secured, the Prussian (and in due course the Triple) Alliance was saved.

Pitt could therefore argue that his proposition was related to a well defined need. We would not be subsidising Prussia in a vacuum, but for specific returns. Grenville however was far from impressed, and he set his rejoinder in a wider context.[4] As to the military benefits themselves, he doubted if they would be gained at the stipulated price, or perhaps at any price whatever. Even if the Prussians agreed to the offer, they might find it did not cover the costs, and we would have embarked on an indeterminate process which Parliament would certainly dislike. Nor was our experience reassuring: we knew the gap between promise and performance. But in any case the offer would probably be refused. The hostile pressures in Berlin were strong, their authors were in the ascendant, and while the King might be personally disposed to stay in

---

1. P. 366 above.
2. To Grenville; *H.M.C., Dropmore*, III, 25–6. The letter is ascribed there to the 20th–28th. The ms, in B.L. Add. Ms 58907, is headed 'Thursday night' and carries the endorsement of the 26th. By Grenville's Minute on the proposals (see n3 below), which is headed '1795, January–March', Pitt may have been forming his ideas for some weeks.
3. Grenville's Minute 'on the Project of a New Convention'; *H.M.C., Dropmore*, III, 26–30. Pitt's copy is in P.R.O. 30/8/338. According to this Minute, the maintenance of the Prussian force was linked with the defence of Westphalia.
   By the beginning of March Pitt had added what would seem to have been a further proposition, to furnish at least 25,000 men for co-operation with these Prussian forces (draft Cabinet Minute, 1 March 1795, for which see p. 553, n5 below). They may of course have been intended to be largely Hanoverians and German mercenaries – doubtless with some British cavalry (see p. 548 above). Even so, their presence would represent a continued British interest in the reconquered Holland.
4. *H.M.C., Dropmore*, III, 26–30.

the war his actions had scarcely been conclusive and his interests were conflicting. Every Prussian General and Minister on whom we counted had proved unreliable. On balance, he saw little reason to throw good money after bad.

And if his assessment was right, Grenville saw great dangers in a further approach. For this would not only be useless; it could do real harm. It would expose the Ministry to Parliamentary attack. It would not necessarily revive the Triple Alliance, since Prussia on the contrary might prefer to guard her influence in Holland by bargaining with France. And any Prussian bargain for peace might in fact be forwarded rather than prevented by a financial inducement from Britain which could be used to bid up French concessions. Pitt's proposal would fail in its objects. Furthermore, in the process it would also threaten hopeful prospects with other Powers.

This last indeed was Grenville's greatest fear. For early in 1795 he was looking forward to agreements with Russia and with Austria. An earnest of the former in fact came, in limited but promising form, at the very time that Pitt advanced his plan. It was hastened by the fate of Holland. Only two months before, the long talks for an alliance had been in the doldrums. But early in February Whitworth was told that the recent French successes made a 'favourable termination . . . of the highest importance'.[1] One stumbling-block was removed, for in the changed circumstances the British were ready to accept the former offer of naval aid in immediate preference to troops. They now wanted a 'Fleet' in the North Sea, to tighten the measures against neutral contraband and also to strengthen the watch which would be necessary on the Texel. The Russians, themselves shocked by the loss of Holland and relieved of a call for offensive land forces, were equally happy to sign a treaty of defensive alliance. They would provide 12,000 troops on demand if Britain or her overseas possessions were attacked; the British likewise a naval squadron if Russia was attacked, even as a result of defensive operations beyond her borders. These definitions embodied concessions on either side. The treaty, signed provisionally on 18 February, gained immediate point from a secret article providing for limited naval co-operation outside the Baltic.[2]

The British however had larger possibilities in mind. Before news of the agreement reached London they were floating more ambitious ideas. If Prussia made peace, as seemed highly possible, Austria must be kept in the war at all costs. To this end, we would waive our old hopes of

1. Grenville to Whitworth, no. 2, 6 February 1795 (P.R.O., F.O. 65/29). Cf. p. 378 above.

2. For the French text see *Consolidated Treaties*, 52(1969), 317–26, and for the English, *inter alia P.H.*, XXXII, cols. 207–11; for the background, Whitworth to Grenville, nos. 9, 10, 19 February 1795 (F.O. 65/29), and cf. pp. 275–6, 300–2 above.

the 12,000 Russians for offensive operations[1] if that number was allotted to the Austrians instead. But we were prepared to subsidise a separate force of up to 55,000 men who could be used, at the Russians' discretion, in one of three ways. They could further reinforce the Austrians on the Rhine, or act with us in a descent on France, or be applied to both purposes in proportion. By an earlier treaty in 1755, we had paid £500,000 a year for a force of this size. We would now pay £1 million, or proportionately to a minimum of 12,000 men. The proposal of course looked once more to a full offensive alliance. Meanwhile we wanted the squadron to co-operate in the North Sea.[2]

Such moves indicated the need. The immediate treaty was primarily concerned with the uncertain prospects at sea; with the tasks imposed by Dutch merchant shipping and an unknown future for the Dutch fleet, and the effects of French successes on the Baltic neutrals. Whatever the doubts about her competence, Russia might help ease the naval strain: a closer link with Britain could also raise the pressure on the uneasy partnership of Sweden and Denmark. For while the watch on their trade with France was demanding a growing effort, exacerbated by the quarrels of the previous year, the recent turn of events did not suit both countries equally: the Danes were perturbed by an Allied reverse which delighted the Swedes.[3] Reports from Copenhagen indeed suggested a revival of the old jealousies, and a certain disposition to try to iron out the problem with London. An alliance with Russia, however restricted, which impinged on our maritime policies could thus bring a dual form of relief at an anxious time.

The latest version of the larger plan, for an offensive alliance, turned substantially on the prospects of the Anglo-Austrian connexion. The two indeed were deliberately linked, in a somewhat delicate state of affairs. Ministers were aware that the two Imperial Powers had themselves been moving closer together, and had in fact signed a treaty in January, though its contents were unknown. They were told that the Empress was urging the Emperor to sustain the war in the west; and also that she was tired of Prussia, following the latter's failure to crush resistance in Poland.[4] It thus seemed a favourable moment to offer her inducements on the lines proposed; and all the more so from the course of the negotiation between London and Vienna. Throughout January and most of February Pitt and Grenville were waiting for a reply to the proposals of 18 December,[5] offering a guarantee of £6 million for a specified military return. The message indeed had been adjusted while

---

1. As distinct from those now specified for possible aid in the defensive treaty.
2. Grenville to Whitworth, nos. 4, 5, 9 March 1795 (F.O. 65/29). News of agreement on the defensive treaty was received on the 20th.
3. See pp. 13, 277, and cf. p. 378 above.
4. See pp. 338–9 above.
5. See p. 377 above. It was held up by bad weather and the disruption of communications from the chaos in Holland.

still in transit towards a possible Austrian preference, £4½ million with certain benefits being offered for 200,000 men or £6 million, less existing advances, for 240,000.[1] A favourable answer was confidently expected: Pitt asked the Commons on 5 February to approve the loan even though he could not specify the sum. He had put his full weight behind it, and at that point he was deeply committed: 'it was necessary ... we should look to some great Power on the Continent. And to whom could we look but to the Emperor?'[2] A fortnight later, however, there was an unforeseen setback; for to the Government's dismay Thugut turned down the proposals. His most effective objections centred on the technical terms; by his interpretation of a complicated formula the rate of interest was too high, and the link with domestic funding which Pitt had arranged meant in effect that Austria would be helping to pay for a British loan.[3] Both contentions were arguable, and both were to be stubbornly argued, though the full force of the dispute was not gauged in London at first. But the sequence of hope and disappointment, the balance of opportunity and danger, reinforced the case for pressing the approaches to both Imperial Powers.

Grenville's feeling about Pitt's plan was intensified by the conviction that these approaches could not be reconciled with fresh support for Prussia. In fact he was sure that they were mutually exclusive. He stressed

> The danger that by negotiating at all with Prussia under the present circumstances we alienate the Austrian and Russian Governments, with whom it should be our policy to endeavour to form the closest union –

For

> The hope of uniting those three Courts in one common system is one

1. Grenville to Eden, no. 6, 13 January 1795 (F.O. 7/40), sent in response to Eden's no. 1, 18 December 1794 (F.O. 74/39) reporting a conversation with Thugut before, of course, the new British offer was received.

2. *P.R.*, XL, 396; and cf. pp. 376–7 above. The motion was carried by 173 to 58. The figure of £6 million was widely known by this time, in the City and beyond, and according to Canning the business 'passed as easily as you would borrow half-a-crown to pay a hackney coachman' (journal, 5 February 1795; Canning Ms 29 dii). Nor did it encounter much difficulty from thin Houses in its successive stages.

3. Other objections were less effective. Thugut maintained that he had not authorised Boyd (p. 377 above) to negotiate for the new loan – a rather weak point seeing that Ministers had been constantly in touch with the Austrian representatives in London; and that no more than 170,000 of the 200,000 men could be deployed north of the Alps, the rest being needed in Italy – which the British were soon disposed to accept (p. 559 below).

which neither our past experience nor any view of their . . . present disposition towards each other seem to justify. If this cannot be done, the option must be made, and being made, must be adhered to.[1]

Since Prussia in his view could not be trusted, he was clear what the option should be. Austria should be supported, partly through the medium, and with the addition, of Russia.

Pitt by contrast rested his argument on a more open – or optimistic – assessment of Prussia. He was impressed by – he seized on – reports that the mood in Berlin was changing again. A new British envoy was struck on arrival by the air of indecision, and the hints that all would yet be well if financial aid was assured. The veteran Malmesbury, though cautious and no longer on the spot, was himself now inclined to think that the Franco-Prussian talks at Basle would fail.[2] It could therefore be held a duty to make a last attempt. An ally should not be lost by default; and Pitt could point to his graduated payments as an insurance that the money would produce results. The pattern indeed suggested once more – this time for quite obvious reasons – the way in which his mind always liked to work. '. . . The *advantage* and the *obligation* should be reciprocal; one cannot be so without the other'.[3] Safeguards would be provided, and the benefits could be real.

The resulting dispute lasted for some six weeks. Pitt took his proposal quickly to Cabinet, and since he had failed to budge Grenville beforehand, their colleagues, already involved with Fitzwilliam,[4] faced another serious issue. They supported the Minister's opinion by a bare majority of six to five; but 'one is enough', and Grenville told Pitt that he would resign.[5] The latter's response naturally was to play for time. A further Cabinet meeting was apparently in prospect for the next day, at which, he acknowledged, the decision might well be reversed. And if it was not, the instructions could be sent by Dundas or Portland (shades of

1. *H.M.C., Dropmore*, III, 29.

2. Lord Henry Spencer to Grenville, January–February 1795 *passim* (F.O. 64/37); Malmesbury to same, Private, 3 February 1795 (F.O. 64/36). Spencer was a promising young diplomat who had served under Auckland in Holland and then been sent – his ability doubtless reinforced by the fact that he was a son of the Duke of Marlborough – as Minister to Sweden. He arrived in Berlin, succeeding Paget, in January, and was to die there in July.

3. His remark on the first version of his Irish Propositions in 1785 (I, 202).

4. See pp. 433–4 above.

5. Pitt's initial attempt to convert Grenville is suggested in *H.M.C., Dropmore*, III, 25–6. The Cabinet met on 1 March, and Loughborough, Portland, Dundas, Cornwallis and Windham supported Pitt, while Mansfield, Chatham, Spencer and Hawkesbury agreed with Grenville (draft of proposed Minute of 1 March 1795; Pitt Mss, Cambridge University Library Add. Ms 6958 (9). Pitt's original draft is in Stanhope Ms S5 09/28). Confirming his intention to resign, Grenville wrote to Pitt on 2 March that he had 'as yet said nothing to any of our colleagues' (*H.M.C., Dropmore*, III, 30–1, with ascription of date only. The letter, and one of 1 March, are in P.R.O. 30/8/140).

Leeds and Grenville himself in 1791) and he hoped there would be no resignation until the arrangements were formally concluded – 'which must also be near the conclusion of the Session'.[1] This, it might be thought, was asking a good deal, even bearing in mind the need to present a united front if Fitzwilliam broke ranks. But as it turned out, the decision itself was to be postponed. If the planned Cabinet meeting took place, nothing conclusive emerged,[2] and Pitt may indeed have been coming under pressure. He certainly failed to gain immediate support, as he may have hoped, from George III, on behalf of a scheme that might be held to offer better prospects of defending Hanover. For when that question arose as a result of separate Hanoverian inquiries, the King showed a wariness of Prussia in his Electoral capacity, as well as a practical scepticism in declining to let his Hanoverian interests favour a subsidy which he doubted if Parliament would pass.[3] This may have helped Grenville. His hand was also strengthened by a report received early in March that Prussia had signed her treaty with France. The news was not confirmed; but it was credited, and the sequel followed in the British approach to Russia for an offensive alliance.[4] Pitt could hardly have objected to this, for it was his wish to keep options open. But if Grenville gained ground, it was not for long. For Prussia, it soon emerged, had not signed a peace treaty after all; more hopeful reports were resumed from Berlin, while those from Vienna were worse. On 12 March Ministers learned that the Austrians could not engage to help Hanover, at a time when they were pulling back from their northern sector on the Rhine; on the 28th, that the terms of the loan were still considered unacceptable, and that an official was coming to London to examine them.[5] This settled the matter. The King, 'a little staggered', lined up with Pitt, the more strongly after hearing Malmesbury's views

1. Pitt to Grenville, 'Monday evening' [2 March 1795] (B.L. Add. Ms 58907; see also *H.M.C., Dropmore*, III, 30). Cf. p. 21 above for 1791.

So far as I can interpret his rather obscure wording in the same letter, Pitt intended to accept the Cabinet's final verdict whichever way it went.

2. Portland also mentioned a meeting on the subject arranged for the 6th (to Pitt, 5 March 1795; P.R.O. 30/8/168). Nothing seems to have survived to show if it took place.

3. Correspondence of George III and Pitt, 2–3 March 1795 (*L.C.G. III*, II, no. 1210), where it seems to me that the King's caution had a distinctively Electoral flavour.

The occasion might be borne in mind in assessing Richard Pares's remark that 'George III thought and acted as a German prince very much more in the 1790's than in the 1760's' (*King George III and the Politicians*, 5 n3). Arguments here might be adduced either way; but perhaps in point of fact no real conflict was raised, at least in this instance, between his two interests.

4. Spencer to Grenville, no. 7, 21 February (F.O. 64/37); Malmesbury to Grenville, 26 February 1795 (*Malmesbury*, III, 250); pp. 550–1 above, and see also Starhemberg to Thugut, 10 March 1795 (*Quellen*, V, 126–7). The connexion was made clear by Grenville in his no. 8 of 10 March to Spencer in Berlin (F.O. 64/37).

5. Spencer to Grenville, nos. 9, 12, 28 February, 17 March 1795 (F.O. 64/37); Eden to same, nos. 25, 27, 11, 27 February, Private 12 March 1795 (F.O. 7/40), dates of receipt endorsed.

when the latter reached England early in April. On the 8th the Cabinet decided that the approach should be made to Prussia, Pitt drafted the instructions, and since Grenville refused to sign them Dundas did so in his place. On the night of the 20th they arrived in Berlin.[1]

But the decision was irrelevant. Before it had even been taken, the Prussians had at last signed their treaty at Basle. Spencer in Berlin was disconsolate; had the despatches come 'a few Days sooner, I may venture to assert that England would have had at her disposal the best appointed Army in Europe'.[2] His natural disappointment may have been misplaced. The treaty was then a fortnight old, and whether the subsidy would ever have prevented it, or the result proved effective, may be open to doubt. But the question was now closed. Grenville could feel himself vindicated; the Austrian, with the Russian, connexion was the only one to pursue.

One significant point may be noted at the close of the affair. While the Foreign Secretary would not sign the despatches to Berlin, and his dissent was recorded in the Cabinet's Minute – perhaps the first occasion on which this was done[3] – he no longer talked of resignation. Informing the King of his refusal, he added that he was 'very far from presuming to press [his] opinion upon Your Majesty in opposition to the sentiments of those whose opinion ought on every account to have more weight than his'. George III assured him that 'his dissent on the present occasion will not in the least diminish my opinion of him', and went on to explain his own change of mind.[4] This was not the language of separation. Grenville had chosen to stay. Exactly when, one cannot tell; nor how far Pitt had reckoned on the fact.

For if Grenville were really to go, Pitt certainly faced what he called an '*éclat*',[5] on an issue of such importance and at a politically troubled time. The two men of course had had their disagreements over the past two years. But the sharpest had turned on status, in a triangle including Dundas; on policy the differences had been those of emphasis.[6] This was their first fundamental clash, and one may ask why Pitt accepted the risk. Hardly, one may think, because of a strong inherent preference for

---

1. Correspondence of George III and Pitt, 28–29 March, 5 April, 8–9 April 1795 – the last including the Cabinet Minute of the 8th (*L.C.G. III*, II, nos. 1223, 1228, 1233); Dundas to Lieutenant Colonel Calvert [carrying the instructions], 10 April 1795 (P.R.O., W.O. 1/408); drafts of despatches to Spencer (with Dundas's *marginalia* and for his signature) sd, in Pitt's hand (loc. cit.); Spencer to Grenville, no. 20, 21 April 1795 (F.O. 64/37). There seems to have been an idea of a Cabinet in the last days of March, but I do not know if the meeting took place.

2. Spencer to Grenville, ibid. He thought the treaty imminent on the 14th, and learned of it on the 18th from the Berlin *Gazette* (nos. 18, 19, loc. cit.). The news was known in London on the 16th.

3. A. Aspinall, *The Cabinet Council, 1783–1835* (1952), 217.

4. Correspondence of 8–9 April 1795 (*H.M.C., Dropmore*, III, 50). Cf. p. 554 above.

5. To Grenville, 2 March 1795 (B.L. Add. Ms 58907).

6. Cf. pp. 310n3, 366 above.

Prussia. Whatever his earlier feelings, and the attractions of the Triple
Alliance, he had become as disgusted with her conduct as Grenville; and
if he was less committed than Grenville – and the Portland Whigs[1] – to
Austria, he recognised the need for that connexion when it came to the
point. As he had recently declared in Parliament, what other Power was
so well placed to sustain the Coalition in its fullest range and effect?[2] It
was vital geographically, on both sides of the Alps. And despite its failure
in the Low Countries – partly at least from non-military causes – the
Emperor's army was still respected, for its quality as well as its size. Pitt,
it may be hazarded, did not prefer Prussia if he had to choose; it was
rather that, unlike Grenville, he would not admit that a choice was
necessary. His great aim was to preserve the Coalition wherever that was
possible: to continue to 'bring down every power on earth to assist' us
against France.[3] And so long as that could be done, while the partners to
that extent remained partners, he was sanguine enough to strive for an
adjustment of their disagreements. The alliances might be disappointing; but the loss of an ally could be worse. His heart quite as much as his
head led him in that direction. The answer did not meet Grenville's
reasoning. It was a hope more than a programme, a typical combination
indeed of some of Pitt's weaknesses and strengths. But one cannot tell if
he would have pressed it so firmly under any circumstances: if he would
have faced the certainty of Grenville's going, even with a balance of
Cabinet support.[4] Perhaps he knew this would not arise after the latest
reports from Austria; perhaps he could judge, then or earlier, that it was
unlikely. At any rate events favoured him, until the decision was
overtaken, and his reading of the odds on his cousin proved, if
pointlessly, correct.

It was ironical not only that Prussia had made peace by the time the
Cabinet moved, but also that the news from Austria on which it acted
was out of date. The latest reports had taken up to a month to arrive,[5]
and in fact the position had changed for the better on 2 April. The
sequence of events, indeed, illustrated yet again the habitual effects of
slow communications. For Thugut then suddenly announced that he
would accept the financial conditions for a loan of £4½ million, almost
certainly on learning of the approach to Russia.[6] Grenville's case was

1. See p. 343 above.
2. 5 February 1795 (*P.R.*, XL, 396; see p. 552 above).
3. P. 272 above.
4. And that balance itself might have been in doubt if the rest of the Cabinet had been
aware of Grenville's threat (see p. 553 above).
5. P. 551, n5 above.
6. News of which reached Vienna on 29 March. For Thugut's announcement see
Eden to Grenville, no. 38, 2 April 1795, enclosing copy of same to Whitworth [in St.
Petersburg], Secret, sd (F.O. 7/40). Cf. p. 550 above.
There had been a hint of an easier attitude on the question of the interest rate over a
week before (Eden to Grenville, no. 35, 23 March 1795; loc. cit.), but that in itself was
still far from acceptance of the terms as a whole.

holding good, for the Austrian Minister was under pressure at home in his advocacy – however slight that seemed in London – of the British connexion. As Austria's interests in central and eastern Europe received a fresh fillip from the Russian treaty – which, though requiring that she remain at war with France, was concerned mainly with Poland and Turkey – the forces hostile to western commitments were rapidly gaining ground. The Emperor himself had recently questioned the value of a strategy which seemed mainly to benefit Prussian ambition and British maritime power. But the new turn of events gave Thugut a breathing space and a prospect. He could now argue for a Triple Alliance on the lines he had long sought.[1] It must have been this stimulus, at such a juncture, that allowed him to counter the financial interests which, in Vienna as in London, disapproved of the loan.[2]

This did not mean that all was now plain sailing. The expert from Vienna was on his way, and the Austrian Department of Finance – the *Hofkammer* – was not going to be easily defeated. It was always a slow-moving body; there was little goodwill in this instance; and the Ministers themselves on either side were not disposed to yield too much. Neither party indeed looked on the terms as financially attractive. If the British saved themselves subsidy payments they had to raise a large sum for two associated loans, with the danger of depressing Government funds and the likelihood – since remittances to Austria were required partly in specie – of repeated losses to the bullion reserves. Austrian credit was bad, and there was the risk of default on interest. As the Bank of England pointed out, it was a doubtful business proposition. Nor could the Austrians be happy for their part with a rate of interest which, even if agreed to be lower than first thought, was significantly higher than that for the domestic loan which they had thus to subsidise. If their credit was said to be poor, they thought it all the more necessary that it should not be placed under such extortionate pressure.[3] Another month followed while the two sides were finally brought together. But on 4 May the loan Convention, with its military provisions, was signed.[4]

The financial forebodings were well founded, for both the short and the long term. The loan was to prove a source of trouble to the connexion it underwrote. The very delay in reaching agreement had at least a partial repercussion on one of the military objects the British hoped to

1. See p. 271 above.
2. Duffy, 'War Policy', 150–1, 153–4, 157–61 (differing here from Helleiner, *The Imperial Loans*, 46, 48), and cf. pp. 377, 520 above for Pitt's not dissimilar position in relation to the City.
3. Cf. p. 552, n3 above. Duffy, loc. cit., 149 n1, gives a succinct explanation of the differences, arising from misunderstanding and lack of clear explanation, in calculating the true effective rate of interest. Pitt's version of the initial 'misconception' is recounted in Auckland to Gilbert Elliot, 6 April 1795 (N.L.S. Add. Ms 11105).
4. The French text, including the secret article for the provision of troops (see pp. 377, 551 above), is given in *Consolidated Treaties*, 52, 371–81; the English, without the secret article, in (*inter alia*) *P.H.*, XXXI, cols. 1558–64. Some papers for Pitt on the transaction are in P.R.O. 30/8/339.

gain. But the settlement had been made for a range of reasons, diplomatic and military as well as financial, and its signature opened the way to the conclusion of a formal Alliance. The British indeed, as the talks dragged on, had made the latter conditional on the former; they now forced the pace on disputed points, and a treaty was signed on 20 May.

The real bait lay in an engagement to approach Russia for a Triple Alliance. Otherwise the treaty, like the Anglo-Russian in February,[1] was for a defensive partnership. If either party was attacked in any of its possessions (a definition the Austrians had not much liked) the other would provide on demand 20,000 infantry and 6,000 cavalry, or a sum of money – a commutation which again the Austrians accepted with reluctance. Neither party would harbour vessels belonging to the other's enemy; and arrangements were made for captured property and goods.[2] It was a limited measure, pending an offensive Alliance with Russia. Meanwhile the British looked forward to building on the military promise of the loan Convention.

Pitt had earlier defined this prospect in its varied aspects, including its bearing on the premise which now increasingly governed his thoughts.[3]

> . . . To whom could we look but the Emperor? Both from the extensive means which he possessed, from his local situation, from the military character of his subjects, and from his interest in the prosecution of the present contest. If the road of conquest was found to be shorter than that of negociation; if we looked for a Power who was interested in the preservation of the Italian States, . . . whose interest it was to defend Savoy, and preserve Piedmont, the emperor was that Power. If we wanted a Power who would defend Spain, or be a barrier to the French in the Low Countries; for all these objects the House of Austria was concerned . . .
>
> But he did not merely rest upon this argument . . . It was an object of policy to increase our force when considered as acting upon our enemy in another mode. . . . the internal pressure of France was such, that it could not long be supported, unless the immense mass of paper currency was reduced. There existed no way of diminishing this mass, but by a diminuation of their expences, and those expences could not be lessened, unless their forces were reduced. . . . It was necessary, therefore, that we should keep them up to the same scale of exertions which must ultimately be fatal to their resources, and that by bringing into the field a force equal to any which they could possibly supply . . .

This was a comprehensive case embracing an indefinite term, and the last argument was underlined when Prussia left the war. At that same

1. Pp. 550–1 above.
2. For the French text see *Consolidated Treaties*, 52, 401–6, and for the English *P.H.*, XXXII, cols. 212–16; for the preliminary Austrian objections, Duffy, loc. cit., 172–4.
3. 5 February 1795 (*P.R.*, XL, 396–7). Cf., or contrast with, p. 541 above.

time, however, a more urgent possibility was added which for a spell was taken seriously in London. For the spring of 1795 was a baffling period, in which the enemy's military success was balanced by waves of fierce internal unrest. The hopes of a crisis in France, fluctuating since the previous summer,[1] were rising sharply once more in the weeks after Pitt spoke. By mid-April they were at a peak, and the British Government was calling for action from the only source of external pressure, the Austrian army on the Rhine. The expectations were high, and the language corresponded.

> The whole of what is at stake in this contest depends on the means of profiting from this favourable moment. We can never hope that the circumstances as far as they regard the state of France can be more favourable than they now are. . . . What must be obvious . . . is the infinite advantage of acting soon, and (at all hazards) acting offensively.[2]

But whether this judgment was right or not, there was unlikely to be an immediate response. Any action, as the Austrians had stressed, must depend on a promise of money, and the talks on the loan were still dragging on.[3] The peace party, and the *Hofkammer*, had yet to be overcome. And after the Convention was signed, this particular prospect looked less clear.

The others however remained, some with their own immediacy. Pitt had stressed Austria's role in the south, particularly in northern Italy – so important for our Mediterranean interests and as a base for an offensive.[4] The case needed no elaboration as the troubles in France grew on the one hand, while on the other the Allies lost pressure in the north and the Italian states themselves wavered. For the news from there was disquieting. Tuscany, that reluctant partner, withdrew from the war in February, and Naples was said to be in danger of losing heart. More important, Sardinia – the hinge of the position – would need support and encouragement; for if there was less talk of peace in Turin than a few months before, the issue was going to turn on Austria's attitude and Austrian reinforcements. The same factor would influence Venice, whose neutrality was inclining now towards France. It was not surprising therefore that the Government was happy for the loan to cover forces in the Milanese, while it kept up its efforts to bring Austria and Sardinia closer together.[5]

1. See pp. 372–3 above.
2. Grenville to Eden, Private, 17 April 1795 (F.O. 7/40).
3. See Eden's reply of 4 May (*H.M.C., Dropmore*, III, 67–8). 'Advances' moreover were held up in the process, lest the Austrians exploit the ready cash to procrastinate on the terms of the loan.
   The questionable validity of the British judgment is discussed in section III below.
4. See pp. 278–9, 347, 377–8 above.
5. Cf. pp. 305, 307 above.

The other Power which Pitt mentioned was Spain; and there too the position was uncertain. Over the past few months the French had advanced on the Catalonian front, and the Spaniards were calling for Allied operations to relieve the pressure. Austrian action would therefore be welcome, in Piedmont or Savoy; indeed it might be crucial, for there were signs in Madrid of a growing wish for peace. These were soon in fact proved correct; but there was little to be done when hopes of an Austrian offensive could not be fulfilled. The French, predictably, began to make offers, and while these met with no ready response – speed was not a Spanish characteristic – they stood a fair chance of success. There was indeed no real counter-attraction after a period of Allied reverses with which to tempt an historically suspicious and weak ally. It was therefore recognised in London that Spain might withdraw, either by treaty or, it was suggested, by 'some kind of *composition* with France'.[1] This could not be taken for granted; events might yet prevent it. But if it were to happen, there could be several results. As in the case of Prussia, French forces would be freed for other operations. British strength in the Mediterranean and the eastern Atlantic would be further stretched. By the same token, Corsica might be more open to attack. And finally, in the case of Spain – unlike that of Prussia or an Italian state – enforced neutrality might affect strategic developments beyond Europe which were already being augmented by the Dutch defeat.

II

At the end of 1794, commitments and plans for campaigns overseas were concentrated, as hitherto, on the French West Indies. It was for this purpose that the largest reinforcements had sailed or were sailing, and even in the routine movements for 'foreign stations' in the next few months the Windward Islands, Jamaica and St Domingue accounted for over half the numbers.[2] There should now be no threat in North America, and the East had been left virtually to itself.[3] But in January 1795 this last assumption suddenly changed. The Dutch collapse raised menacing problems across the oceans as well as in Europe, and the reaction in London was unequivocal and swift.

It was facilitated, or at least given cover, by the presence of the Stadtholder. As George III forecast at the time, his arrival proved 'of

1. Earl of Bute [Ambassador in Madrid] quoting the Spanish Minister Alcudia (Godoy), to Grenville, no. 1, 23 June 1795 (F.O. 72/37). For past Spanish attitudes see pp. 280, 314–15, 345 above.
2. See p. 358 above for recent months, and for troops earmarked to 'complete' and relieve those on foreign stations, anon. calculations, 29 December 1794, in Pitt's papers (P.R.O. 30/8/240).
3. Cf. p. 350 above.

utility'.[1] For with his consent some legitimacy could be given to measures which the authorities in Holland were no longer free to sanction. There were some difficulties at first, for William V wavered as always – not unnaturally perhaps in this particular case. Had it been necessary indeed the British Government would have acted without him, for while it was an 'extremely nice . . . point' to say how Holland should now be regarded, 'the whole Cabinet' was determined to forestall any overseas risk from the French. Members therefore resolved, if he proved indecisive, 'to take possession of everything we could lay our hands upon' including 'the Dutch East Indies and the Cape and American possessions'.[2] But in the event agreement was reached: the Stadtholder gave the use of his name, and armed with that 'approbation' the Cabinet prepared to move.[3]

The speed and unanimity of the decision were not surprising. Over the past decade and a half the British had been seeking to own or operate Dutch bases. Strategic concern in the American War was combined with commercial thrust to foster plans for seizure at one time, negotiations for access at another. A force was mounted in 1780–1 to capture the Cape of Good Hope. Trincomalee was taken in 1782, but had to be returned at the peace. Both might have been attacked in 1787 – in the Stadtholder's name – if the Dutch crisis had then led to a war with France. The transfer of Trincomalee and of Rhio on the Malacca Straits were on the list of British demands in the trade talks of 1787–91. So was a request for exclusive rights to garrison Cape Town if necessary, together with Dutch possessions in India and beyond.[4] These objects were associated above all with Dundas at the Indian Board of Control, and the case for urgency certainly did not suffer now that he was Secretary of State for War. But it did not depend on that.[5] The dangers and opportunities were clear. The latest turn of events can have left no one in doubt.

The immediate target was the Cape of Good Hope. Its safety was

1. To Grenville, 24 January 1795 (*L.C.G. III*, II, no. 1196). For that event see p. 547 above.

2. Portland to Fitzwilliam, Secret and Confidential, 26 January 1795 (copy in Portland Ms PwV 109, University of Nottingham).

3. Minute of 8 February 1795 (*L.C.G. III*, II, no. 1199). All members were present, on a Sunday: according to Amherst (Diary, vol. VI; Amherst Mss) 'at Grenville's'. Grenville's draft for the Stadtholder's signature and the final, altered version are discussed in Nicholas Tarling, *Anglo-Dutch Rivalry in the Malay World 1780–1824* (1962).

4. I, 50, 94–5, 162, 423–40. The Cape, it should be noted, unlike the other focal points, was valued almost entirely for strategic purposes; its direct commercial advantages were few (cf. op. cit., 388).

5. For instance, preparations to attack the Cape and Trincomalee if necessary in 1787 were authorised by Pitt (op. cit., 425 n3).

Dundas had again shown his concern for the Cape in November 1794, as the position deteriorated in Holland (to Grenville, 16 November 1794; *H.M.C., Dropmore*, II, 645–6.)

important for the passage to India; and once secured, it could support the same expedition for further operations. It was a highly desirable foundation for defence and conquest alike: above all, 'a feather in the hands of the Dutch' which 'would be a sword in the hands of France'.[1] Preparations went ahead at once for a small advance force and a larger naval squadron. They sailed early in March and in April, followed in May by the main expedition, which was shipped in East Indiamen via the Brazilian coast.[2] Cape Town was expected to compound or surrender before this last force arrived, so that after helping provide a garrison it could carry on to the east. But if the French reached the Cape first in such strength that an attack proved impossible, it should sail to India nevertheless to join local forces against the Dutch. In either case, Trincomalee should then be the prime target, others being the settlements at Cochin and on the Malabar coast.[3] If this series – as it was hoped – of operations was fully successful, it would complete a significant stage in an expansion of power along the Eastern sea routes.

Success was in fact achieved, though not in the sequence expected. The burghers of the Cape did not comply with the Stadtholder's wishes; attacks had to be mounted, the main expedition was delayed on passage, and the colony surrendered only in September. Even then a strong garrison was needed, and no troops could be spared for India. It was November before a naval force set sail. But in the event these disappointments did not block the eastern operations. Orders for the King's and the Company's troops,[4] sent in February, arrived by July. At the end of that month a force from Calcutta and Madras embarked for Ceylon, the main part to attack Trincomalee while the rest sailed on to Malacca. Both places fell in the second half of August, and the force in Ceylon then proceeded to mop up the island. Colombo surrendered in the following February – Cochin on the mainland had done so earlier – and by March the Malaccan force had reduced the keypoints in the southern Moluccas. Under these pincer attacks the Dutch position in the East largely crumbled. Although useful bases remained unassaulted, from which trade routes could still be threatened, the decision to 'take everything we could lay our hands upon' had produced major gains.[5]

1. The aphorism came from Captain John Blankett, an authority on communications with the East whose views were well known to Ministers, and who was now about to be sent in command of an advance naval force for the Cape (quoted in Vincent T. Harlow, *The Founding of the Second British Empire 1763–1793*, I (1952), 389).
2. On the customary passage taking advantage of favourable winds (see I, 388 n2).
3. P.R.O., W.O. 1/323, January–May 1795 *passim*.
4. See I, 451–6.
5. P. 561 above. The determination to bring everything possible to bear was further shown by the despatch (on his initiative) of an agent – Hugh Cleghorn, the Scottish professor who became a spymaster (see p. 138 above) – to induce a regiment of Swiss mercenaries in Cochin and Ceylon to desert from the Dutch. He succeeded in the latter instance, after an odyssey which can be followed in W.O. 1/361.

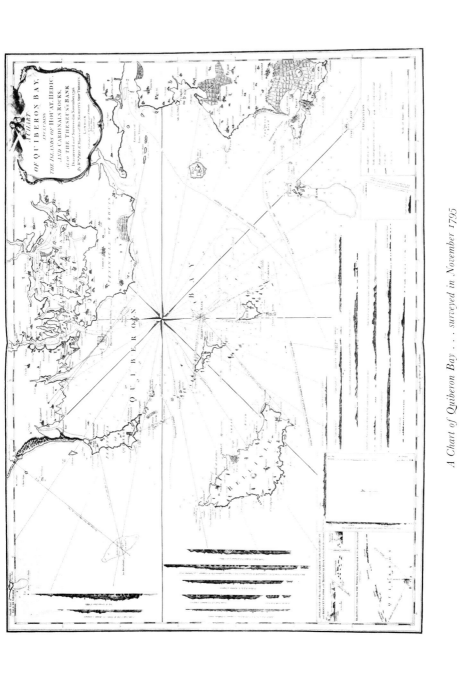

A Chart of Quiberon Bay . . . surveyed in November 1795

The Duke of York with troops in Flanders, *by William Anderson*

Whatever its significance, however, this effort had only a marginal impact on resources for overseas at the time it was set on foot. The Western hemisphere – the transatlantic theatre – remained the prime concern, and its demands revealed the effective limits to a global strategy.

This was underlined by the question of the Dutch 'American possessions' themselves, included in the undertaking to forestall the French.[1] An order was sent to the Windward Islands to occupy settlements as far as possible, particularly Surinam, Curacoa and St Eustatius. But it was no sooner written than cancelled, and the cancellation was at once followed by a proposal to take Demerara with troops to be sent from the Channel Islands.[2] Such instantaneous changes of mind reflected a confused situation not only in respect of Holland but in the main West Indies' campaign. For the Dutch problem had to be added to a general review which was now being forced on Ministers by news arriving from the Caribbean.[3]

The position was certainly not reassuring. Guadeloupe had been abandoned, and while Martinique and St Lucia were held as conquests the occupying forces were weak, and the British Windward Islands had no garrisons left. In St Domingue too the force was reduced by fighting and, above all, disease, and confined to separated points round the western bay. Command of the sea – inherently difficult within the Caribbean – was less than complete. Privateering was rife, and bound to benefit from the enemy's recapture of Guadeloupe; and recent weeks had shown once more how hard it was to stop reinforcements from France. Early in January, some 1,500 troops and a small squadron reached Guadeloupe from Brest. Meanwhile larger British reinforcements had been delayed. Part of a force for Jamaica and St Domingue, meant to leave in September, did so in December, while the rest, now released from the continent, suffered a final brief postponement from the need for stronger cover since the Brest fleet was thought to be at sea.[4] The replenishment for the Windward Islands had likewise met with administrative setbacks which at length cut its strength from disease aboard the ships before the convoy sailed.[5] It was this last consideration that led to second thoughts about the Dutch possessions. Given the new French strength, and 'the unprecedented sickness' among the British troops throughout the islands, even the most eager Ministers were forced to admit there might be little to spare.[6]

1. P. 561 above.
2. Dundas to Major General Vaughan, nos. 5, 6, 7, 11 – the last mentioning pressure from mercantile interests – all 19 February 1795 (W.O. 1/83).
3. Dundas to Vaughan, no. 4, 18 February, no. 7, 19 February 1795 (W.O. 1/83).
4. See p. 375 above.
5. Cf. p. 358 above; Dundas to Sir Adam Williamson, no. 1, 9 January 1795 (W.O 1/62).
6. Same to same, 10 February 1795 (W.O. 1/60); same to Vaughan, no. 7, 19 February 1795 (W.O. 1/83).

However, troops were now on their way, whatever their quality. Even if offensives were temporarily abandoned, we should be able to strengthen what we held. 'Internal defence' was in fact the immediate watchword.[1] It very shortly proved to be the need.

The blows fell first in the Windward Islands. For the French reinforcement of Guadeloupe had a dual effect: on their own strength, and on the native populations. The link was once more the hope of improvement of status or, for slaves, of liberation, rekindled as fresh resources were provided in a key strategic point.[2] The British authorities awaited trouble they could not accurately predict. It came suddenly in March in Grenada, St Vincent and St Lucia. Risings of caribs and, except in St Vincent, negroes swept the three islands. The garrisons were forced into pockets, and St Lucia was abandoned in June. To the north Toussaint l'Ouverture kept up the pressure in St Do ningue, the seas were alive with privateers, and in July the negro maroons rose in the northern mountains of Jamaica. Fighting there continued until December, when the outburst was finally put down. But the operations, and the islands' terror – for the mountain maroons were dreaded – affected the campaign in St Domingue, which received virtually none of the replenishment from England. These widespread dangers had to be faced, from May, in the 'sickly season', as disease struck once more at strengths and morale. The effects were felt progressively. Some ground at first was recovered in Grenada and St Vincent. But the strain began to tell, particularly among the young depleted drafts; many of the gains were lost, by apathy and demoralisation; and in its later stages the year's campaign in the Windward Islands has indeed been ranked as 'perhaps the most discreditable . . . in the records of the British Army'.[3] Together with that in the Leeward Islands, it was certainly expensive. Several thousand more men – some 2,000 in St Domingue – had to be written off.

None of this was encouraging. The fact did not weaken Ministers' resolve, and only partially affected their attitude to one material demand. They were not going to alter their policy or, as they saw it, sap a main foundation. The very dangers led them rather to redouble their efforts, and define their ground.

This last was shown in respect of one 'important and serious' problem.[4] In February 1795 the Cabinet stopped the raising of further negro levies in the Windward Islands. Alarmed by ideas, from there and from Jamaica, of offering remission of slavery in return for service, it wished to review the whole matter afresh.[5] This was done over the next two months, and in the course of the spring and summer both commands

1. And, for St Domingue, concentration of forces, which might mean abandoning outlying gains (Dundas to Williamson, no. 2, 19 February 1795; W.O. 1/62.)
2. Cf. p. 361 above.
3. Fortescue, op. cit., 454.
4. As Dundas put it to Vaughan, no. 14, 17 April 1795 (W.O. 1/83).
5. See pp. 359–60 above.

were allowed to form three 'Black Corps' of 1,000 infantry each, and small bodies of cavalry. But one condition was reaffirmed. It was 'absolutely necessary' not to raise expectations of freedom among enlisted slaves.[1] The terms of the ensuing Proclamation in Jamaica therefore came as a shock; for not only were the 'pecuniary gratifications' larger than had been recommended, but – far worse – emancipation was promised for slaves after five years' service. The Government was angry and affronted. Its 'most positive' orders had been disobeyed. Nothing doubtless could be done about the Corps in question. But expense in future must be kept down if possible, and no such promise must be made again.[2]

There was thus no yielding on this point. Other conciliations might be offered, at least in French islands under attack. In St Domingue a further concession was made for negro and mulatto support: the 'gens de couleur' could be promised greater civil rights if practicable, and possibly even political privileges.[3] Nothing so specific, however, was said about their counterparts in British territories. The whole question of the coloured populations in fact was treated warily, step by step.[4] For the case of the local commands was not fully accepted in London: it was scouted in 1794, and again in the reverses of 1795. Even then, the Government could claim, the picture was not wholly gloomy. The risings were not uniformly supported; coloured populations did not always unite. In St Vincent, broadly speaking, negroes fought caribs; in Dominica, by Martinique, they repelled the French, in Jamaica the mountain maroons were isolated from the rest. French promises of freedom could win adherents, and provoke insurrection; but comparable offers might not be essential to stimulate resistance. The local argument, that only the coloured inhabitants could bring success to the West Indian strategy without a great drain on resources from home, was in essence correct.[5] But Ministers, even in this adverse year, could point to the limits of the enemy's successes; and they were prepared to supply those home resources, with all the implications for transport and health, rather than

1. Dundas to Vaughan as in p. 564, n4 above, and no. 16, 4 June 1795 (loc. cit.); same to Williamson, no. 7, 4 June 1795 (W.O. 1/62).

2. Dundas to Major General Gordon Forbes, no. 1, 29 September 1795 (W.O. 1/62). Cf. p. 360 above.

This was not in fact the only occasion on which the local commands acted on their own. The Windward Islands raised some 'Black Rangers' before permission was given.

3. Ibid. Cf. p. 359 above for the awkward situation here in regard to the French planters.

4. Thus the command in the Windward Islands was allowed to employ a 'Black Carolina Corps' – foreign mercenaries – while negro levies from the islands themselves were forbidden (Dundas to Vaughan, no. 2, 23 January 1795; W.O. 1/83). And the subsequent permission to raise such local 'Corps' was itself regarded in London as 'temporary' (see draft for instructions to the command in St Domingue, September 1795, in W.O. 1/61).

5. See p. 359 above.

endanger the social and economic structure of valuable possessions.

The readiness to meet the commitment, and indeed extend it, became ever more plain as the year went by. One reinforcement of the familiar kind was ordered at the end of June – 4,000 men for the Windward Islands, half of whom seem to have sailed in the end. But a greater expedition was soon being put in hand. Preparations began probably at the end of May,[1] and some two months later these were suddenly enlarged for both resources and plans. The addition was caused by Spain. For on 22 July, after their months of indecision, the Spaniards finally withdrew from the war; and while the event of course was half expected the terms certainly were not. The British had counted on a strict neutrality; they were shaken to learn that the treaty – signed, like Prussia's, at Basle – included the cession of San Domingo, against the return of French conquests in Spain. The transaction was a double blow. As the neighbouring territory to St Domingue, San Domingo was operationally important; and both strategically and economically, it was significant in the longer term. The British indeed had not disguised their hope of themselves acquiring it at the peace table, in return for supporting Spanish gains on the mainland of Europe. The island's affairs had been a source of friction throughout the brief alliance, as London complained of inadequate military support and harassment of shipping and merchants, and Madrid of commercial incursions and attempts to dictate. San Domingo in fact had become, with Corsica, a prime cause of worsening relations, and when the Spaniards had promised to reinforce it – which they did not do – this could have served to deter excessive British interest as well as to defeat the French.[2] The news of its transfer therefore left Ministers in no doubt. Troops must be made available to prevent the colony falling into enemy hands. They were reserved accordingly, to form part of the expedition; and while due caution was necessary – for we were not at war with Spain – the command should feel free to occupy places evacuated by our late allies.[3]

This committment was inserted into a general offensive: to clear Grenada and St Vincent if that had not already been done, and retake Guadeloupe or St Lucia; to consider attacks on Surinam, Demerara and other Dutch settlements when resources allowed; to conquer St Domingue, and ensure the safety of San Domingo. An experienced General was appointed, with the new title of Commander-in-Chief, West Indies – Sir Ralph Abercromby, recently knighted for his handling

---

1. It is hard to specify exactly. But in November Dundas referred to 'an Expedition determined upon Six Months ago' (to General Abercromby, Private, 3 November 1795; W.O. 1/84), and Fortescue relates a series of orders for strengthening battalions returned from the continent, which were initiated on 30 May, to that design (loc. cit., 477).

2. Pp. 345, 355 above; F.O. 72/27–8, 33–7 *passim*.

3. Cabinet Minute, 14 August 1795, in Dundas to George III, 15 August 1795 (*L.C.G. III*, II, no. 1285); draft Secret Instructions, 9 October 1795 (W.O. 1/84); Dundas to Forbes, Most Secret, 4 November 1795 (W.O. 1/62).

of the unnerving retreat in Holland and, in Cornwallis's view at least, the best available from a 'melancholy list'.[1] Over fifteen thousand troops were earmarked, with a naval squadron, and unusual provision was made for medical advice and supplies.[2] With such resources Government was confident of success. 'You will be reinforced', the commander in St Domingue was told, 'by an armament which . . . cannot fail to carry everything before it'.[3]

The effort indeed was of a different order from anything hitherto: double the size of Grey's expedition, which had been followed by piecemeal drafts. Here was a substantial force, to serve an integrated command. It expressed the resolve to recover positions and then master the theatre, in pursuit of 'Means of making further Impression on Enemy' (now including the Dutch) and ensuring 'Acquisition of Places for Indemnity' at the peace.[4] It underwrote the rising emphasis on overseas gains as events were changing. And it did so in reference not only to the plans themselves but to a competing effort. For when Spain pulled out of the war, at a point when the armament was being prepared, the design was given precedence over another that was closer to hand. 'I incline to think', Pitt observed immediately, 'that our Plan must now be changed, and that the only great Part must be in the West Indies' to 'counterbalance' the enemy in Europe. In particular the cession of San Domingo – against developments throughout the region – 'makes it a new Question, whether any British Force can . . . be hazarded on the Continent of France'.[5]

III

This was written at a dramatic moment: just as such a force was about to be launched, to recoup a venture whose early success had ended in defeat and slaughter. On the very day indeed that the Spanish treaty

1. Dundas to Abercromby, 28 September, 9 October 1795 (W.O. 1/84); same to Forbes, no. 1, 29 September 1795 (W.O. 1/62). For the intended sequence of operations see same to Spencer, 28 [September]; *Private Papers of . . . Spencer*, I, 154.

Abercromby was chosen by the middle of August (see *L.C.G. III*, II, no. 1285), and may have known of such a prospect (on a smaller scale) a month before – at any rate he was then suggesting plans for the West Indies (to ? Pitt, 14 July 1795; P.R.O. 30/8/107.) His name seems to have been suggested, by Cornwallis, at the beginning of the month (to Pitt, 2 July 1795; Stanhope Ms S5 02/4).

For the dispute which his terms of appointment raised over the naval command see pp. 498 above, 613 below.

2. Cf. p. 495 above.

3. Dundas to Forbes, no. 2, Most Secret, 30 September 1795 (W.O. 1/62).

4. Pitt's notes on strategic principles, almost certainly written in January 1794 (p. 327, n1 above).

5. To Chatham, 3 August 1795 (P.R.O. 30/8/101). By 'Continent' he of course meant mainland.

was signed at Basle, the remnants of a French royalist expedition were being rescued from the Breton coast.

For the assault on Brittany, so often conjectured, had now been tried and lost. This might not have seemed probable – again as so often – six months before. At the turn of the year the Channel Isles Correspondence suffered the capture of its best agent, 'le fameux Prigent', who was suspected by some of then betraying its methods. A further blow came in February, when the Breton guerrilla leader Charette – a prominent figure in the peasant *chouan* resistance – signed a truce in the Vendée. Other groups, always loosely linked, differed in their attitudes to the arrangement: a reflection of the habitual feuds which made judgment of the prospects so difficult. But some, including Charette himself, were stirring once more in the spring, Prigent reappeared in April to reanimate the Correspondence, and the favoured royalist commander Puisaye, who had stayed on in London, was able – perhaps encouraged – to revive his case. He certainly had a ready audience, for his failure in the autumn and winter did not preclude the earlier idea of some kind of landing in 1795.[1] Pitt in particular had shown keen interest – Dundas went so far as to call it his 'Dream'[2] – and he was unlikely to have been less enthusiastic now. For circumstances were propitious. The prospect of a crumbling Coalition – Holland gone, Prussia and Spain perhaps going –, reports from Wickham and others of rising discontent in France, the need to restore the Ministry's standing by some military success, all provided good reasons for looking at the problems again.[3] Plans were studied in April and May, a design was approved early in June, and from the 6th to the 10th the orders were drafted for the commanders.[4]

The plan was for an émigré force to land on the Quiberon peninsula in southern Brittany, to establish a base for supplies and join the *chouans* in a general rising. As such it accorded with the original desire of the resistance, expressed in the summer of 1793.[5] Help from outside, at least in the first instance, would come from Frenchmen themselves. The decision however was not taken solely to meet that early demand: after all, Puisaye had called more recently for a substantial British force. It contained a diplomatic element; but on purely military grounds it may have reflected a continuing caution bequeathed from the autumn,[6] and must have been largely affected by the fact that spare British forces were inadequate. This was not due to demands for the West Indies, for news of the reverses had not yet arrived. But the infantry from the Low Countries was embarked only in April, its replenishment began only at

1. Cf. pp. 369–71 above. The reference to 1795, by Pitt, is on p. 369.
2. To Pitt, 13 October 1794; see p. 410, n3 above.
3. For Wickham cf. pp. 372–3 above.
4. Puisaye to Pitt, January–April 1793 *passim* (P.R.O. 30/8/169); P.R.O., W.O. 1/390, 1/687; P.R.O., Adm. 1/4164, 2/1349; B.L. Add. Ms 7975: all for early June.
5. P. 300 above.
6. For which see p. 370 above. The diplomatic element is discussed on pp. 575–6 below.

the end of May, and the British troops in reserve under Moira were not impressive in numbers or quality.[1] Meanwhile however there were obvious arguments for the assault to be launched soon. It had a bearing on the efforts, now mounting, to stimulate operations on other fronts, to encourage unrest elsewhere in France, and to keep Spain in the war.[2] Even, therefore, if thoughts may have been harboured of an immediate British back-up for émigré landings, or – as Pitt himself may have wished – of a more ambitious scheme,[3] the means were not readily available in the available time.

Since the force was to be wholly French, two consequences arose. Its strength must be recruited; and the command must be related to British responsibilities. The handling of both these matters has been attacked ever since: in the first case justifiably, in the second almost certainly not. Recruitment on the necessary scale was obviously going to be difficult. Puisaye had sent out calls through Europe, and more exiles were flocking in; but this was not enough in itself, and, probably at his suggestion, Ministers decided to enrol willing prisoners-of-war.[4] They may have assumed that experienced volunteers would be good for quality as well as numbers; but the move was to prove a costly mistake. So too, it was later claimed, was the pattern of command which the Government laid down. For while the expedition was composed of Frenchmen, its instructions perforce were British. The troops would be landed from British ships, they were paid and supplied by Britain, and indeed formed under British regulations by an Act of Parliament.[5] Their

---

1. Pp. 357, 369, 548 above. One point might be made here. The lack of British troops has been attributed (Holland Rose, II, 261, 273–4) to George III's refusal to spare those still on the continent from the defence of Hanover – now a pressing problem – until overruled, too late, by his British Ministers. But this in fact referred to the *cavalry*, not all of which had been earmarked, as had the much more numerous infantry, for return to England (see eg George III to Dundas, 8 February 1795; W.B. Hamilton, 'Some Letters of George III', in *The South Atlantic Quarterly*, LXVIII, no. 3, 419–20). The other troops remaining in British pay on the continent were precisely that: hired Hessians, and Hanoverians.

2. The first two themes are discussed later in this Chapter. News of the imminent royalist landings was sent to Spain as one of the arguments to dissuade her from making peace (Grenville to Bute, no. 6, Most Secret, 12 June 1795; F.O. 72/37).

3. There is a memorandum by Pitt, in P.R.O. 30/8/196, for a force of 4,000 men to secure Calais, which apparently was expected to be 'delivered'; to be followed by landings by 30,000 British troops, possibly on Belleisle and then into western France, or if this was not feasible in 'diversions . . . on different Points of the North Western Coasts of France, and the Coast of Flanders and Holland'; while an émigré force under d'Artois joined the resistance in the most suitable place. The hope of establishing a British 'Position in France', by landing from Belleisle, was linked with a prospective rising in Paris. The force for Calais was to act as soon as possible after 15 May, and the larger body to be ready on 15 June, The paper is not dated; but taken in conjunction with the hopes of a rising in the capital and plans for eastern France (for which see pp. 579–87 below) it may well refer to 1795.

4. I do not know how many Ministers were involved.

5. See p. 369, n1 above.

commander, the veteran Comte d'Hervilly, held his commission from George III. His status and that of Puisaye must therefore be clearly defined. In the aftermath of Quiberon, when accusations were being flung about, the outcome was said to have turned, on the contrary, on misunderstanding or worse. And since the charges, which included treachery, were levelled at Pitt himself among others, one must consider if or how far those particular instructions were to blame.

The issue has been debated from that day to this. Sometimes the charge is of deliberate intention, to destroy émigré influence and leave the field free for British interests; sometimes of confused thought, or muddled or careless drafting. The first accusation seems hard to sustain. It makes little sense against the background of British policy hitherto – or indeed as currently shaped for possibilities elsewhere in France;[1] and if Pitt had wished to ruin the enterprise and condemn its members to capture or death, he could quite easily have arranged a leak to the Committee of Public Safety.[2] This, one might think, would have been much less risky than to count on the effects of divided command, or for that matter on treachery – belated and uncertain – on the spot. The second charge, however, merits closer attention; there had been plenty of cloudy thinking and administrative muddle before, and some evidence has been adduced to support one or other aspects of the claim.

The problem turns on the wording of some of the instructions to the various persons and bodies affected, above all those to the Admiralty and to the naval commander.[3] Puisaye's own orders were quite clear: he was told that the force came under his command once it was ashore. There was no equivocation about this; both the Secretary of State and the Secretary at War were explicit, and d'Hervilly equally was informed.[4] At the same time it was laid down that while the expedition was on passage it remained responsible to d'Hervilly, the commander of the émigré regiments at the time of embarkation; and he was moreover responsible for deciding whether the troops should land or not. The command, in short, would change when the passage was completed and there were orders to be given on land.

Such an allocation of authority was sensible enough. Puisaye's

1. Pp. 579–87 below.

2. Cf. Holland Rose, 'Was Pitt Responsible for the Quiberon Disaster?', in *Pitt and Napoleon*, 58. The charge of betrayal, soon rife among émigrés on the continent, was given an airing in England when Fox chose to mention it in apparent disbelief in the Commons (29 October 1795; *P.R.*, XLIII, 37) and Sheridan followed with an attack on 'British honour'. An alternative accusation of treachery has fastened on a rival royalist organisation in Paris – itself in touch with British agents (Gabory, *L'Angleterre et la Vendée*, I, 203).

3. The following account draws on Maurice Hutt, 'The British Government's Responsibility for the 'divided command' of the Expedition to Quiberon, 1795', in *E.H.R.*, LXXVI, no. 300, which surveys the literature as well as the primary material of the debate.

4. Loc. cit., 481, 488 for the evidence.

knowledge centred on the position in Brittany; the safety of the regiments formed under d'Hervilly was a British concern. The latter was the proper man to consult with the commander of the naval squadron, responsible with himself for the safety of the troops until they were ashore. Nor does there seem reason seriously to doubt that d'Hervilly knew the scope of his authority. He had been informed by Dundas of Puisaye's position when the instructions were framed. So far therefore, one might say, so good. The responsibilities were delineated, and those responsible acquainted with them.

But the doubts have arisen, and the controversy has continued, from a different set of orders: those given by the Admiralty to the naval commander, Captain Sir John Warren. The Department itself was fully apprised. It knew that Puisaye would 'take command of the troops from the time of their disembarkation'. It was also notified that until that time he should be consulted on all questions relating to the landing, 'every possible attention' being paid to his views subject to d'Hervilly's overriding authority.[1] In its own instructions to Warren, however, the clause was omitted which specified Puisaye's command on shore: he was described as 'employed in a confidential situation', 'accompanying' d'Hervilly and to be consulted, but so far as can be seen his role thereafter was not mentioned.[2] Why, it has been asked, was this? Was the omission deliberate, designed to confuse? Or the result of incompetence? Or of a copyist's error? The conjectures have been amply debated. But a simpler, and traditional, explanation may be preferred. It is that the Admiralty was officially informing its commander of the position so far as it concerned himself. For it was d'Hervilly with whom Warren would deal, taking Puisaye's opinion into account; the naval orders covered the passage and landing, and did not extend to the time beyond. In point of fact it is clear that Warren was aware of the pattern of command for the later period, for in a letter to the First Lord he referred to Puisaye as the commander-in-chief ashore.[3] It would have been better if the Admiralty had informed its subordinate formally at the start that this was so. Historians would certainly have been saved some trouble. But given all the circumstances it would seem unreasonable to argue that the naval orders could have caused confusion in the mind of either of the French commanders.

For this exegesis on texts draws its importance from the relationship which developed; one that precipitated the final disaster, and thereafter

---

1. Loc. cit., 481–2.

2. This is in the Department's copy of the orders, dated 6 June 1795 (Warren's original not having been found). It is obviously to be preferred to the 'Extract' of them sent to Puisaye, to be opened on sailing, which has been the document studied and analysed in the past; see Hutt, loc. cit., 482–3.

3. Warren to Spencer, 3 July 1795 (*Private Papers of . . . Spencer*, I, 80). The commander in the Channel fleet also knew this, from the Secretary of the Admiralty (Hutt, loc. cit., 485).

was laid at the British door. In view of what happened, a different charge might perhaps be preferred: it might be argued that Puisaye and d'Hervilly should never have been sent out together. For both were known to be forcible and prickly, d'Hervilly particularly so; and when it was notoriously hard in any case to combine the two wings of the royalist cause why, one might ask, underline the difficulties in the persons of these particular men? As George III remarked, 'I hope the two Counts will not from private vanity forget the main object'.[1] But the comment, valid as it was, only underlined the problem. For the very difficulties of the situation in fact left no other choice. Puisaye had a clear claim to lead an expedition that must rely on the resistance, while the émigrés would have taken umbrage if their General was replaced at the last moment by someone else. Beggars in the form of sponsoring Powers often cannot be choosers. If the venture was to go ahead at all in the form determined, the best – the only – answer was to clarify the structure of command.

And at first indeed all seemed to go well. The vanguard sailed on 17 June, and the Channel fleet ensured its safe passage. Anchoring off Quiberon ten days later, it had an immediate effect; the *chouans* mustered, and on 3 July a combined force gained the fort guarding the approaches. On the 10th the royalist numbers were said to have risen to 4,000. By then Pitt's 'dream' was clearly thriving under the promise of the early reports.[2]

Beneath this surface, however, there were ominous signs. The émigrés and the *chouans* were very soon on the worst of terms, so much so in fact that they had to be formed into distinct units. Puisaye and d'Hervilly, who had already had some differences over the landings, now disagreed on tactics at a time when there was little to check an advance. And farther afield the divided counsels and jealousies of the royalist movements were shown in the fate of a diversion to the east which Puisaye had ordered, and in a mission despatched from England to Charette in the interior.[3] For the first was soon sent instructions, purporting to come from d'Artois himself but probably emanating from the secret Royalist Agency in Paris, to march to northern Brittany – a singularly irrelevant movement – while the latter completely failed to rouse a guerrilla leader who had often been at odds with Puisaye and now resented the direction of British support.[4] Nothing could have revealed more sharply the 'purists'' animosity towards the 'constitutionalists', and the suspicions and rivalries among the Vendéan

---

1. To Dundas, 14 June 1795 (*L.C.G. III*, II, no. 1258).

2. Pitt to Grenville, 6 July (*H.M.C., Dropmore*, III, 89). Cf. p. 410 above. And see also his letter to Camden of 28 June (Pratt Ms C 123/4; Kent C.A.O., Maidstone).

3. For whom see p. 568 above. The diversion to the east was commanded by Tinteniac, for whom see p. 299, n6 above.

4. The report, from the Baron de Nantiat, to Grenville is in *H.M.C., Dropmore*, III, 105–24. It shows that the mission's brief came from the Foreign Secretary through Windham, on 3–4 July.

groups. The combination would have brought trouble if the expedition had thrust inland. But it never did. As Puisaye and d'Hervilly continued to bicker, it stayed where it was. The Republican forces gathered, and a belated advance was defeated on 16 July. Hope revived when a second wave of émigrés reached the coast in the next few days, and a further move was planned for the 20th. But in the night of the 19th some of the prisoners-of-war from England deserted, and told the enemy of a weak spot in the defences. Disaster followed. The fort fell, the royalists were routed, and those not rescued by the navy surrendered. A few days later, believing themselves safe, they were slaughtered to a man. The act disgusted even the executioners. It stirred the resistance, too late, to fury. And it was seen as a fresh and shocking indictment of Pitt's conduct of the war, raising the bitter accusations which were to last for years.

By this time preparations were almost complete for the despatch of British forces. There had been plans from early in July for something to be sent. The Government had been ready from the start to exploit purely naval co-operation: to provide transport and cover for a diversionary landing of émigrés from the Channel Islands, and to help secure the port of Lorient if Puisaye could take it by land.[1] But as the early reports were received Ministers resolved to build more boldly on success. Troops, now coming to hand, could be committed in support. The choice of commander was easily settled, for Moira was still available, and on 15 July he was given his orders. It had already been decided that the initial attack would be 'exclusively . . . of an Island'. The objects thereafter were first to ensure the safety of the Quiberon peninsula, then to take Lorient and Port Louis, and thereafter act as circumstances allowed. Seven thousand infantry and 2,400 cavalry would be provided, 4,000 of the infantry in two to three weeks and the rest about a month later, the cavalry as it could be raised in England and Ireland. Moira would be in 'general command' of all the forces in France, but his expedition would be 'auxiliary' to the French themselves, who would remain under Puisaye acting as Moira's subordinate while d'Artois, it was hoped, would arrive soon to head the royalist cause. The French regiments in British pay would not be enlarged beyond 10,000 infantry and 5,000 cavalry. Expectations clearly rested on a rapid spread of resistance in the Vendée itself.[2]

---

1. Draft of Dundas to Count Williamson, 10 June 1795; drafts of same to Puisaye, Most Secret, and Separate & Most Secret, 30 June 1795 (P.R.O., W.O. 1/390). Neither of these ideas came to fruition. The Channel fleet had driven a French squadron into Lorient when clearing the passage of Puisaye's expedition.

2. W.O. 1/176. For the development of Ministers' thoughts see Moira to William Aushisson, 2 July 1795 – when cavalry were not envisaged (loc. cit.); notes by Pitt, nd, of reports from 5–11 July (W.O. 1/390); notes by Pitt, 12 July (P.R.O. 30/8/196); Pitt to Grenville, 13 July 1795 (*H.M.C., Dropmore*, III, 90); York to George III, sd (*L.C.G.* III, II, no. 1265); Pitt to Moira, 19 July (loc. cit., no. 1270).

So all was set for a fresh attempt at the old elusive target, the establishment of a British force on the mainland of France. It was doomed once more, and this time the shadows fell almost at once; for on 20 July, five days after these orders were issued, the royalists were routed, and two days later Spain left the war.[1] The combination was bound to cast doubts on the future and at any rate the scale of the enterprise. Was there anything to be salvaged? And if so, could resources be spared? Government was already searching for the drafts needed for the next Caribbean campaign – an enterprise which Dundas, still not inclined to place too much weight on the Quiberon venture, considered 'to be of all others the most essential'.[2] By 3 August, as a consequence of the Spanish news, received a day or two before, Pitt was doubtful if 'any' British troops should be risked on the mainland of France.[3] At the same time a decision must be reached on the implications of Puisaye's defeat; for if he was to be sustained the support must be mounted at once. In short, rather as in November 1793 when Toulon was in question, Ministers were faced by the pressing emergence of events whose timing was unforeseen.[4] Pitt as usual took a hopeful view. He was encouraged by Moira's reaction to Puisaye's 'check' of 16 July, and, perhaps wishfully, by his response to the calamity that followed. At a meeting on the 31st at Hartford Bridge, on the Portsmouth road by Hartley Wintney, the two men, with Dundas, agreed to carry on. But the objects were reduced, and over the next ten days a review of the 'setback' at Quiberon combined with the need to reinforce the West Indies to produce a new set of orders.[5] The Cabinet by then was about to approve a major allocation of force to the Caribbean.[6] Moira's force was cut to 4,000 infantry with some cavalry. He was not to operate on the mainland, but only to attack an island – Noirmoutiers, south of St Nazaire, which had figured in past plans.[7] If even that target proved too difficult the troops should return home, and they should not be exposed to material risk. But possession was desirable if it could be made secure, to furnish a base for supplying the royalists if they were still 'determined to persevere'. These instructions were shortly amended to cover an attack on a smaller island, Isle Dieu (or d'Yeu) if Noirmoutiers appeared formidable. Their phrasing – their whole tone – bore Dundas's

---

1. P. 566 above.

2. To George III, 27 July 1795 (*L.C.G. III*, II, no. 1273).

3. P. 567 above.

4. Cf. pp. 322–4 above.

5. Moira to Pitt, 20 July 1795 (P.R.O. 30/8/160); same to same, 24 July 1795 (W.O. 1/176), 30 July 1795 (see *L.C.G. III*, II, no. 1277); Pitt to Camden, 25 July 1795 (Camden Ms C 123/5); Pitt to Grenville, 31 July (*H.M.C., Dropmore*, III, 93); Dundas to Moira, Most Secret, 11 August 1795 (*L.C.G. III*, II, no. 1282). I am indebted to Mr S.G.P. Ward's knowledge in locating Hartford Bridge.

6. By a Minute of 14 August (*L.C.G. III*, II, no. 1285). Cf. pp. 566–7 above.

7. P. 323 above. Noirmoutiers, though termed an island, was virtually a peninsula, for it was separated from the mainland only by two or three feet of water at most times.

mark.[1] He was now clearly anxious to be rid of a commitment which might have proved costly and indefinite. At the same time however he had to issue other orders which, if arguably complementary, stemmed from a different quarter and a more positive approach.

For while the British role was thus restricted, measures had to be included to cover the arrival of the nominal leader of the enterprise, d'Artois himself. In June Ministers had finally decided that the Prince must be associated with it, not least because the second wave of the landings at Quiberon would come from émigrés recruited in Germany, where he had taken up quarters several months before. He was asked if he would wish to join Puisaye if the venture went well, and accepted at the beginning of July. On the 6th, in the flush of enthusiasm from the first reports of success, Pitt asked Spencer and Windham, at the Admiralty and the War Office, to see if he could be brought over at once.[2] Neither of those Ministers was likely to object: the Portland Whigs had espoused the émigrés, and Windham was the chief spokesman for the Princes' cause. D'Artois reached England on 7 August and remained in Spithead. When the force sailed, just over three weeks later, he was on board.

Events had thus fortified the hopes, and influence, of that wing of the Ministry which for a year had been vainly urging a strong commitment to the Prince. At the same moment, moreover, there was a complementary pressure to reassess British policy towards French monarchical demands. For in June the young King Louis XVII was reported to have died in prison, and his uncle Provence claimed recognition as successor. The problems raised by his former claims as Regent thus reappeared. The Government indeed was about to send an envoy to Italy to assess his views and the prospects for influence. But meanwhile its position remained as it had been since the Declaration at Toulon in 1793. Moira's first instructions included a Declaration to the royalist forces on those same terms; and the Princes' representative in London, d'Harcourt, was given a similar reply. The tone was more sympathetic than before, not surprisingly in the circumstances; but if the monarchy was to be restored it could be only by the wishes of the people, and that in turn would demand moderation, a recognition of change, and some measure of forgiveness.[3] D'Artois sailed with the hope but not the

---

1. See particularly p. 371 in *L.C.G. III*, II, no. 1282. The amended instructions are in Dundas to Moira, 13 August 1795, loc. cit. pp. 373–4; and see Moira to Windham, 12 August 1795 (forwarded to Pitt; P.R.O. 30/8/160).

2. Grenville to d'Artois, 19 June 1795 (P.R.O., F.O. 27/44); d'Artois to Grenville, 1 July 1795 (loc. cit.); Pitt to Grenville, 6 July *(H.M.C., Dropmore*, III, 89). For the Prince's earlier movements see pp. 301–3 above; for the continuing coolness towards him personally, George III to Grenville, 12 June 1795 *(H.M.C., Dropmore*, III, 77–8).

3. Dundas to d'Harcourt, 22 June 1795 (F.O. 27/44); same to Moira, 15 July 1795 (W.O. 1/176). There is a draft of Moira's Declaration, marked 'For Mr. Pitt', in P.R.O. 30/8/335. Policy in regard to Louis XVIII is treated within its broader context in section IV below. For the Toulon Declaration see pp. 310–11 above.

certainty of British recognition of a King of France. He was also uncertain what he might be called on, and allowed, to do.

For of course the military prospects were by no means the same as when the Prince had been invited. He had been told then that concern for his safety precluded his being sent with the first assault, and this concern was now underlined.[1] Since Puisaye's force was out of the reckoning, the Government was thinking of Charette once more, to arrange to supply him and, if this proved feasible and the *chouans* were regaining the initiative, to see if d'Artois could then land and place himself at their head. But meanwhile the Prince must consult the British naval and military commanders – Warren, and Major General Doyle, in charge of what should have been the vanguard of the larger expedition.[2] Nothing therefore was firm as preparations drew to a point. There were alternative targets, in Noirmoutier or Isle d'Yeu. Contact and agreement with Charette were uncertain. And so accordingly was the future of a potentially focal figure whose status was still undecided but whose person if possible must be preserved.

It was not the best of foundations for a venture which was already in trouble. For the preparations were going badly wrong. At a time when Government was scraping the barrel to find men for a range of duties – for the West Indies above all, but also to replenish the Cape of Good Hope and Corsica[3] – it soon became clear that, as so often, numbers on paper meant little in themselves. Moira, long unhappy with his seemingly endless series of diversions and disappointments, was soon complaining bitterly of both the quality and the strength of his force. The first was as bad as anything he was used to, the second seriously short; and in fact Doyle had to leave with nearer 3,000 than 4,000 infantry.[4] There was an added misfortune. Although Ministers stressed the need for secrecy, the prospect was known at once and Noirmoutiers itself soon named in the newspapers. As a result two fresh possible targets were hastily introduced, the small islands of Houat and Hedic in Quiberon bay. Moira by then was fed up. He was not in operational command of the reduced force, and the rest of the troops in his charge were destined for the West Indies 'under other Generals'. He asked to resign as early as 14 August, and by the 23rd his request was granted. As the expedition sailed he quitted the scene.[5]

1. Grenville to d'Artois, 19 June 1795 (cf. p. 575 above); same to d'Harcourt, 7 August 1795; copy of Pitt to d'Artois, 15 August 1795 (F.O. 27/44).

2. Dundas to Moira, 13 August 1795 (*L.C.G. III*, II, no. 1282); Grenville to d'Artois, 15 August 1795 (F.O. 27/44); Moira to Doyle, ?17 August 1795 (*L.C.G. III*, II, no. 1286).

3. Dundas was calling attention to the needs of the Cape (see Dundas to George III, 18 August, *L.C.G. III*, II, no. 1285; cf. p. 562 above), and the Cabinet was soon to add those of Corsica to other demands (Minute of 7 September 1795, loc. cit., no. 1300).

4. Cf. pp. 573–4 above.

5. W.O. 1/176, *L.C.G. III*, II, *passim* for mid and late August. Moira had not himself been discreet about the expedition (see Pitt to Moira, 31 July 1795, Stanhope Ms S5 07; Buckingham to Grenville, 2 August 1795, *H.M.C., Dropmore, III*, 93).

The operation was a fiasco. Noirmoutiers proved on inspection to be hopelessly vulnerable from the mainland,[1] and at the end of September Isle d'Yeu was taken instead. The news that d'Artois had arrived excited Charette's hopes. But the Prince, having ordered the partisans to strike for the coast, was reluctant to venture farther; he declined to land even as they approached, and Charette began to despair. A last deputation in November was met with a flat ungraceful refusal: '*Je ne veux pas aller Chouanner*'. And by then the British Government had also given up. Isle d'Yeu was impossible in the winter. Small, exposed, and soon hit by storms, it was virtually isolated; and if d'Artois was going to place the need for his safety unreservedly above anything else there was little point in trying to face the odds.[2] In the second half of October Doyle was sent orders to pull out. He received them in mid-November, but could do nothing for the next few weeks. At last in December, in foul weather, the troops were taken off by skilful seamanship. They reached England at the end of the month, with d'Artois still in tow.[3]

The return of the expedition was a melancholy climax to a sorry tale. The Vendée had been left, as it proved finally, to 'Fire, Famine, and Slaughter'; and there was one obvious figure to accuse.

Slaughter	He came by stealth, and unlocked my den,
	And I have drunk the blood since then
	Of thrice three hundred thousand men.

| *Both* [*Fire* and *Famine*] | Who bade you do't? |

| *Slaughter* | The same! the same! |
| | Letters four do form his name.[4] |

And as an exercise in planning and power, the lessons were rubbed in afresh. Once again, a hopeful view of resources and a hopeless lack of

---

Pitt, who was clearly feeling guilty about the General's frustration – he recommended him for an advance in the peerage – seems to have thought briefly of sending him to command in 'St. Domingo' (to Portland, 6 August 1795; Portland Ms PwF T114). But the idea was given up.

1. See p. 574, n7 above.

2. I put it like this because while his conduct was despicable, the emphasis laid by British Ministers on the importance of his person (p. 576 above) gave him some pretext for behaving as he did.

3. He was sent off to live in Holyrood, in which, as a royal palace, he could shelter from the creditors whose potential importunities dogged his every approach to British soil (cf. p. 302 above). The problem had arisen most recently when he was due to arrive in August.

4. Coleridge, 'Fire, Famine, and Slaughter' (1798) – '*The Scene a desolated Tract in La Vendée*'. He had already made the charge, giving the numbers as 'more than *Three Hundred Thousand*' for 'La Vendée and other places', in *Conciones ad Populum* in 1795 itself.

information had betrayed a plan which this time moreover was itself entirely imprecise. Islands were suggested in rapid succession with no detailed intelligence; no reliable – or indeed regular – liaison existed with Charette or anyone else. It was a lamentable performance, thoroughly depressing after a run of failures. Not surprisingly, it brought finally into question the policy of which it had been a part.

The issues were raised most clearly by Dundas himself. His scepticism and fears had been hardening throughout the affair. Although he acquiesced in the decision, he was not happy about Moira's instructions in July;[1] and later developments left him in no doubt of what should have been done. If we had confined ourselves, he wrote a few months later,[2] to sending regular and substantial supplies, 'which was at all times in the Reach and within the Means of this Country . . ., We would . . . [have] acted [a] wise and efficient Part'. Instead, 'We have constantly amused ourselves and triffled away the time in forming fancies about Splendid Expeditions' to work with forces best left to themselves. For even if Moira and his army 'had ever got among them, it would not have kept together for a Month'. This was partisan warfare, and if it was to grow into anything more it could not be with foreign troops under foreign command. He acknowledged that his 'Reveries' did not seem to have been shared by others. Nor were they meant to discredit the policy of aiding unrest in France in face of the 'Necessity' of safeguarding 'all our Distant Possessions'. It was a question of the best means. The arguments were not entirely the result of hindsight: Dundas had long been worried by the prospect of 'starving every other service' in a militarily doubtful cause.[3] But the tone was now much firmer, for the recent experience had brought him closer to the strategic 'Alternative' which he had once been able to discount.[4]

The strength of Dundas's expressions, addressed as they were to Windham, showed his feelings about Pitt's involvement and support of the opposite view.[5] They had implications not only for military but also for diplomatic policy, and indeed they may have been fuelled partly by concurrent experience in that respect. For Quiberon did not stand on its own, though it would have been undertaken in any case. It had a place in a pattern embracing action in south-east France and Paris itself. The

1. Dundas to York, 25, 28 July 1795 (B.L. Add. Ms 40102). He had been absent – in Scotland – from the meeting at which the main decision was taken, but (as his concurrence on the 31st proved; see pp. 574–5 above) then saw it as his duty to give the plan 'the most effectual assistance in my power'. His apprehensions centred on committing British troops to the possibility of operations 'in the interior'.
2. To Windham, 31 March 1796 (B.L. Add. Ms 37876).
3. Cf. p. 322 above. In July 1795 however he had agreed, if uneasily, with Pitt that British troops were necessary on the coast for a time (cf. n1 above) to give a French royalist army a proper chance to develop (to York, 25 July 1795; B.L. Adds Ms 40102).
4. P. 269 above.
5. Cf. pp. 370, 412 above.

hopes there had in fact been rising even as the first expedition was preparing. And these rested quite as much, if not more, on the prospect of a unifying British influence as on the provision of any limited military aid.

IV

'The whole of what is at stake in this contest depends on the means of profiting from this favourable moment. We can never hope that the circumstances as far as they regard to the state of France can be more favourable than they now are'. When Grenville wrote these words in April 1795 about the internal situation in France he was genuinely excited, even if he was trying to excite an ally.[1] Too many openings for victory had been lost in the past two years; and here was one which must not be let slip in the critical state of the Coalition. It offered an escape from the proposition which Pitt himself had advanced, that the war might be won only by raising French financial pressures to the point of collapse, which in turn could mean an unremitting military pressure that was not itself decisive.[2] If this last prospect was to be forestalled there should be 'offensive action' now, in a quarter where it could ride on a great tide of domestic unrest.

The argument was not chimerical if the reports were to be believed. And many of the reports were accurate enough. The Vendée was not the only region on the boil. The south and south-east, if less well organised, were indeed in a more violent state. Insurrection there had as long though perhaps a more uneven history: the risings centred on the Rhone valley in 1793[3] were peaks in a process that was never entirely subdued. Throughout the Revolution there had been fierce discontent, more often localised than not; but now the criss-cross of antagonisms, largely inherited from the *ançien régime* – of classes and interests (agrricultural and urban, and urban themselves), between the provinces and the capital, Catholics and a prosperous Protestant minority – were increasingly if not wholly overlaid by general shock and distress. The purges of Year II had brought some old foes together in common fear of the Terror. The winter of Year III fell on communities already suffering from hardship and inflation. The earlier federalist movement, by no means monarchical,[4] was able to revive after Thermidor. Many of its adherents were now drawing closer to the Bourbon cause. And while royalism drew from this background more shades of difference than in the Vendée, the solid core remained likewise rural – though here

1. To Morton Eden [in Vienna], Private, 17 April 1795; see p. 559 above.
2. Speech of 5 February 1795 – in which the depressing word 'ultimately' was reported as being used (p. 558 above).
3. See p. 284 above.
4. Cf. p. 311, n2 above.

without feudal overtones – and fiercely Catholic, which was the real binding force. It faced a discredited Jacobin organisation, though one that was not completely crushed. The opportunity had come for revenge, as savage as the earlier repression. 'The White Terror' mounted in the spring of 1795: a wave of prison murders, arson and assassinations. Jacobins were in hiding, revolutionaries turning monarchist, churches filling, food and money running short. In April the reports to London suggested that 'not a single person . . . supposes . . . the Republican government can exist'.[1]

This was an overall picture; as was soon to be clear, Allied action would need to be selective if it was to reap a reward. But while the ferment was strongest in the south there was encouragement also elsewhere, in the spreading anger at shortages and soaring prices. In May the *assignat* had lost 68 per cent of its face value, and a month later 97 per cent; not surprisingly, every region was suffering financial and material crisis. It may have been in this period that Pitt talked of 'a gulf of bankruptcy' in France such that 'he could almost calculate the time by which their resources would be consumed!'[2] If so, the chance for immediate action would fulfil his strategy for financial pressure. And the situation in Paris itself was raising royalist hopes. In April and May there were popular risings, and *sansculottes* once more invaded the Convention. But they were put down, while the Constitution of '93 was revoked and the 'moderates' in the Assembly took the lead in drafting a successor. Some of these men were said now to be secretly in sympathy with some form of monarchy, enough at least to warrant a more serious approach. There might be elections under a new Constitution, and who could tell what might not follow? The 'Constitutionalist' royalists in particular sniffed a heady air.

The reports were coming in from a range of sources: from agents, from émigrés, above all from British envoys. Of the last, the most prolific were Drake in Genoa, Trevor in Turin, and Wickham in Berne;[3] and Wickham, now well installed and organised, was in charge of arrangements for support. Increasing his contacts in the south and east through the tangle of conspiracies underlying the White Terror, he built up a network centred on the veteran resistance in Lyons. As so often in such cases it is hard to be sure how significant this was; the evidence is patchy and confusing, and Wickham's sources were not the only ones involved. The south had lines to Vienna and St Petersburg, to northern Italy and western Germany. But the Swiss connexion was the most productive, and may have exercised the greatest effect. The pattern of violence was probably influenced, at times may even have been dictated, by the men

---

1. William Wickham on 19 April; see *H.M.C., Dropmore*, III, 84, and 80–6 *passim*.
2. This at least is the impression given in *Life of Wilberforce*, II, 92, quoting Pitt's conversation at dinner.
3. See pp. 281n1, 205n1, 372 above.

– the Comte de Précy and Dominique Allier – on whom Wickham mainly relied. The plans for the future, which he largely financed, were very much under their guidance, and could thus take account of his advice and demands. The main source of intelligence for Paris was still Mallet du Pan and his circle,[1] though Wickham also sent in an agent to assess and report. His impact there however was limited, for the capital's central Royalist Agency had many links with the outside world and was focused on the exiled Princes. It contained men of differing backgrounds and aims. But the Legation at Berne held prospective funds, and now that it was showing an interest it began, if at first rather clumsily, to draw into closer touch. The prospects remained to be proved if elections were held. But meanwhile they could be fuelled with money and advice and, as Pitt suggested later, inducements of protection;[2] and they seemed not unhopeful if the Vendée and the south were brought into play.

The response in London to these developments, positive as it was, could not be comprehensive or in many respects precise. Wickham found his instructions 'so far as they relate to France . . . extremely general'; in fact he had none 'regularly drawn up'.[3] The handling of agents and movements was left very much to his discretion, as was not unreasonable in the circumstances. But beyond this need for latitude there lay larger uncertainties which might well govern the outcome, and affect the role of the Allies. If the favourable situation was to be exploited there were two imponderables in particular neither of which was easily amenable to British control.

One was external to France: the guarantee of Austrian military support, without which domestic action might be crushed yet again. Ministers were clear what they wanted on this basic question. They were equally clear that the southern rising should not be premature. The other problem was internal: the need, familiar but now more urgent, to foster an understanding that would really unite a counter-revolution. This was not only intensely desirable for the immediate purpose – for there could no longer be any doubt about the mutual hatreds of the different royalists, which could wreck all the hopes:[4] it might also let the British themselves off a hook, already uncomfortable, on which they could well be impaled at the peace. For the possibility of victory accompanying or following a French counter-revolution revived, more acutely, the problem arising at the time of Toulon. The Ministry

1. Cf. p. 313 above.
2. To Grenville, 29 August 1795 (*H.M.C., Dropmore*, III, 29).
3. To Trevor, 25 June 1795 (*Correspondence of William Wickham*, I, 108).
4. Cf. the suspicions of the Paris Agency's role in the orders for Puisaye's diversionary operation at Quiberon (p. 572 above).

maintained its stance, that it would not seek to dictate a form of government – the more so indeed since the swing of opinion within French governing circles themselves might give it room to negotiate if necessary with a Republican authority.[1] But each time that plans were drawn up for active support of movements in arms, it was carried a pace farther towards endorsing a restored monarchy. Hitherto it had avoided commitment to any one group or any one person. But events now combined to force a fresh step, and a greater attempt at control.

For the coincidental pressures, coming at this point, were hard to avoid: the decision to be associated with d'Artois – and possibly Condé – as a commander in France; and the problem of the Comte de Provence, with his claim for recognition as King.[2] The Allied Powers, apart from Russia, remained cautious on the latter question.[3] But strategy was viewed at this point in London rather differently from the other capitals. The 'Lawful King' was no longer a child in prison, but an adult who could head a rising:[4] his attitudes could prove important, and they should at least be tested.

The Government therefore resolved to send a special envoy without delay. It chose Lord Macartney, not long returned from his famous mission to China.[5] The new King (as he was styled) was to be told that acceptance of his claim must await agreement from our allies. But they were being approached, in the hope – now 'considerable' – that the royalists 'in Brittany or elsewhere' would soon gain strength for 'some formal step' to be taken 'with Propriety and Advantage'. If recognition came, he would thus owe it to British initiative. Indeed he and d'Artois must understand – as according to d'Harcourt[6] they now did – that it was only to England they could look in general for success. They should therefore 'put themselves entirely in His Majesty's [i.e. British] Hands, leaving to Him the Direction of their Conduct'. The first requirement would be to publish a manifesto designed to broaden the base of the cause. The King would be most unwise to 'disgust' the Constitutional royalists of whatever type, though equally he should avoid pledges which would commit him to any 'one small Subdivision'. It would be best to postpone questions on the exact shape of government, while making it clear that this too did not preclude consideration of change in due course. Unity must be the aim within the monarchical movement. And there must be a serious attempt to reassure the country at large. It

1. Cf. pp. 312 – and 204 – above.
2. See pp. 575–6, 371–2 above.
3. Cf. pp. 301, 312n4 above.
4. As George III observed to Grenville, 15 June 1795 (*H.M.C., Dropmore*, III, 78).
5. For which see I, 421–3. He had arrived home in September 1794.
Provence's notification of his 'accession' was received on 26 June. By 6 July at the latest the Ministry had decided to send an envoy, and the instructions were ready on the 10th (P.R.O., F.O. 27/45; *Correspondence of Wickham*, I, 114).
6. See p. 326 above.

was important above all to remove the fear of retribution: of widespread punishment, and also of 'Insolence' when the émigrés returned. There should be an amnesty for all but regicides, and even they should be narrowly defined. Nor should all arrangements of property under the Republic be overturned: that would endanger peace for the future and revive memories of former 'Oppression'. Like the shape of government, it was a question whose detail had better be postponed. The immediate need was for the King to show that he did not insist on a complete return to the past.

Given 'a proper Declaration' on such lines, two other matters should be raised. The King should be encouraged to join one of his armies, conceivably Condé's but preferably d'Artois' where, all being well, he could be at once on French soil. If neither however proved possible there were other choices, including Gibraltar if that did not raise problems with Spain. And Macartney should also introduce the question of indemnities at the peace, making clear that for Britain these 'of course' would lie outside Europe. No commitments were pressed at this point; but 'explanations' were desirable. Finally, the King could be given up to £10,000 to meet his immediate wants.[1]

This approach – so different in tone and content from earlier messages to Provence – reflected the state of current expectations. The style, unofficially given, of King, the sympathetic if conditional response to recognition, the staking of claims to protect and to guide and for indemnities at the peace, all suggested the desirability of insuring on a restored monarchy. Macartney set off for Verona, where Provence (or Louis XVIII) had his Court. But by the time he arrived, early in August, his chances had been greatly reduced. For a royal manifesto had indeed been issued, the text of which was known by then, but with a phrasing and a spirit far removed from those of his instructions.[2] The Pretender could claim to be conciliatory according to his lights: a good deal more so than in any previous declaration from the Princes. He recognised a Constitution which limited the royal prerogatives, the role of the Estates General in taxation and that of Parliaments in guarding the laws. He proclaimed an amnesty to all who accepted his functions, apart from regicides and terrorists. But both the statements and omissions did little to reassure. The Constitution to be acknowledged was the 'ancient and venerable' one of the kingdom: there was nothing to attract Constitutionalists of more recent date. The Estates General, the Parliaments, were those of the *ançien régime*; the amnesty depended on acceptance of a thinly limited monarchy. The silences too were eloquent. Nothing was said in detail about reforms, or the highly

1. Grenville to Macartney, no. 1, 10 July 1795 (F.O. 27/45). The document is headed 'Draft', but appears to have been issued on the same date.
2. The manifesto was in fact dated 24 June, before Macartney had even been appointed. Its contents percolated through Europe in July.

important subject of property rights. The Declaration of Verona might almost have been drafted by Louis XVI in the late eighties. It did nothing to advance the pretensions of Louis XVIII.

The effect, not surprisingly, was dismal. It discouraged politicians in Paris, and failed to remove the widespread fears of revenge by the returning émigrés. Macartney did his best with an uphill task. But he had little effect on men who, as Grenville observed, were 'pertinaciously attached to their own Ideas and Systems'.[1] Nor indeed were they necessarily prepared to place themselves too much in pawn; for while Macartney received some overtures for a bilateral alliance – an idea heard once before, at the time of Toulon – these were made at least in part to play off one member of the Coalition against another. There was still a strong disposition, he found, to rely on Austria.[2] Sceptical but persistent, he lingered on through the rest of the year, while the plans for action inside France eddied to and fro. But in February 1796 he left Verona for some other Italian centres, and in May he set off home. The mission had been a failure, of greater interest as a reflection of strategic developments than for any achievements or influence it could claim.

For the chances of a British success at Verona, as of instilling unity elsewhere, were further reduced by the course of events on the ground. The failure in the Vendée was a sharp deterrent, and the problems were not eased when risings in the south and south-east hung fire throughout the summer. The prospects in those quarters, resting as they did so largely on Austrian intentions,[3] were to suffer from the fluctuations of policy on a wider stage. But British hopes remained high for some time, as the Government tried to play a double hand, pressing Vienna for action while it concerted plans with Condé. In the heady days of May, Ministers decided to give these last a high priority, building on the exchanges of the previous autumn.[4] An experienced staff officer, Colonel Charles Craufurd, was sent to Condé's headquarters, empowered to draw on much ampler funds than had been granted earlier and to propose operations in the light of Wickham's intelligence and the Austrians' strategy. If the Comte de Provence agreed, we would take the army entirely into British pay, enlarging it if possible from other émigrés in northern Germany; meanwhile a sum of £140,000 would be held at Frankfurt for its needs, out of which Wickham could draw a total of up to £30,000 for his own affairs. Action should follow quickly; if the Allied commander Clerfayt approved, Condé should join in an attack across the border on Franche-Comté, which would open the way for risings

1. To Macartney, no. 2, 8 September 1795 (F.O. 27/45).
2. To Grenville, no. 4, 23 August 1795 (loc. cit.). Richards, 'British Policy and the Problem of Monarchy in France', 272–5, gives an account of the overtures and their reception.
3. P. 581 above.
4. See pp. 371–2 above.

there and at Lyons.[1] The urgency rose over the next few weeks. By early in June Wickham's reports were so suggestive of 'a sudden emergency' that Craufurd was authorised to finance him beyond the recent limit; and the enlargement of Condé's force was correspondingly of 'such immense importance' that the Government would 'regret no expense' to that end.[2]

The costs certainly mounted. Four months later they had reached an effective total of £278,000, and a further £80,000 was envisaged for the coming quarter.[3] The return soon proved disappointing. Condé was 'elated' by his new funds; but his politics were the Pretender's, and his movements still depended on the Austrian command. The first fact was worrying from the start – 'You see', wrote Craufurd to Wickham, '. . . how difficult it is to make use of these Arch Royalists'.[4] The second was crucial; for, as the British accepted, the Austrians held the military key. Condé's force, however financed, remained under Austrian direction. It was the Austrian armies – whether or not with the benefit of the Vendée – that must hold down the French. And the plans of insurrection themselves suggested the need for action in one quarter which required Austrian consent to an offensive on more than one front.

For the heart of the internal risings would be Lyons, and, particularly with memories of '93, it was essential to protect that area against a doubtless savage counter-attack. In the British view this meant an Allied advance from the Alpine front into Savoy as well as from the Rhine into Franche-Comté, which was farther from the nerve centre. Throughout the past year the Government had been trying to bring Austria and Sardinia into greater harmony, and persuade the latter to accept an Austrian commander of the combined forces. This in fact had come about; and the atmosphere in Turin was also somewhat healthier,[5] as reports were received of the growing disaffection in France. In May and June the British envoy was urged, like his colleague in Vienna, to stress the need for a move into Savoy, taking risks if required. But the response was lukewarm. An Austro-Sardinian advance was initiated along the

---

1. Grenville to Craufurd, no. 1, Most Secret, 22 May 1795 (F.O. 29/5). The remittance to Frankfurt was handled by Boyd Benfield (see pp. 377, n5 above) with the aid in Germany of Colonel Craufurd's uncle Quintin, for whose correspondence see F.O. 29/7. They were members of a remarkable family – which also included Robert Craufurd, the future commander of the Light Division in the Peninsula – some of whose lives can be followed in *D.N.B.* For Clerfayt see p. 364 above.

2. Grenville to Craufurd, Secret, 8 June 1795 (F.O. 29/5). Cf. Fox's impression of Pitt's optimism at this time (to Lord Holland, 14 June 1795; B.L. Add. Ms 47572).

3. Craufurd to Grenville, no. 35, 30 October (loc. cit.). Some £30,000 in addition had been consumed at that date, in credit facilities and charges. Cf. a note of 27 August 1795, with a rather different estimate, in Pitt's papers, P.R.O. 30/8/338.

4. 26 June 1795 (*Correspondence of Wickham*, I, 106). Wickham himself had been rather sympathetic to the Princes. But cf. his reaction now to Grenville, 10 July 1795 (loc. cit., 115–17).

5. Cf. p. 559 above.

Riviera coast. But not far west of Genoa it turned into a campaign of attrition, designed to starve out the French with the help of a blockading British squadron. At the end of July the hopes of a descent on Savoy disappeared. And by then there was little comfort to be had from the prospects farther north.

The British had been pressing for action on the Rhine continuously since their request in April;[1] and at first indeed it seemed that the Austrians might agree. Clerfayt was ordered to open an offensive, and drew up a plan for operations from Düsseldorf to Basle, with a thrust, as asked, into Franche-Comté. Nothing, however, happened. No Austrian troops moved. And as the weeks and then months went by there were ominous signs that they might never do so. For Clerfayt was stalling on his instructions, starved – as he justifiably complained – of supplies, and apprehensive of a threat to his communications if the Prussians made themselves unpleasant; and in June and July, as reports reached London of Austria's problems elsewhere, the reality of the assurances from Vienna began to fade. In July the Foreign Ministers exchanged acrimonious reproaches. Some revised planning for Franche-Comté followed. But early in August the British were told that Condé's army would not be 'immediately' employed.

Behind these developments, or lack of them, there lay a combination of reasons, deriving from and affecting the state of the Alliance as a whole. For indeed the signing of the treaty in May,[2] so long in the making, was followed by a period of mutual suspicion worse perhaps than any so far. The situation in Poland and its bearing on Austro-Prusso-Russian relations, the divisions of power in Vienna, the Germanic Empire's desire for peace, the first failure at Quiberon, the British needs in the West Indies, all impinged on a connexion always beset by inherent differences and now increasingly, and dangerously, exposed. The problems were wider and deeper than those of operational planning. But they were brought to a point in its frustration, which precluded a test of the British hopes. Wickham himself remained optimistic. If the resistance in Lyons had to wait, it was ready against the day. If he lacked controlling influence in Paris, he gathered that the Agency was preparing. He had made contact with Charette in the Vendée.[3] And in the later summer a new development was reported from the upper Rhine, where Condé was negotiating with the republican general Pichegru to bring over his army. The secret talks raised high hopes in the émigrés and Wickham himself. But early in October they had to be balanced against a serious blow. For the royalists in Paris then indeed acted, taking to the streets in the Vendémiaire rising, only to

---

1. Ibid; and for the rest of this paragraph see P.R.O., F.O. 7/41–2 and 29/5, and *Correspondence of Wickham*, I, *passim*. Cf. p. 335 above for Austrian fears for their lines of communication.

2. P. 558 above.

3. Cf. p. 577 above.

be met by Buonaparte's whiff of grape-shot. Whatever the Austrians might still do, there was now little left of the British design. The Vendée was being abandoned. Condé was denied his role in the east. An armed take-over in the capital was out of the immediate reckoning. And though funds continued to be sent to Lyons, the resistance there was splitting up.[1] There were different elements to be considered which might yet offer promise for the coming year. France remained in a parlous state, the Allies had cards to play. Revised possibilities might be assembled from the failure of the earlier hopes. But those hopes themselves, as pursued in London, had been effectively blocked.

Perhaps they had always been extravagant. For there were some real dilemmas. Allied forces were assumed to be necessary, and indeed their absence could be held to have been decisive. But foreign invasions would arouse a hostility which might react on the domestic risings. British or Austrian troops would not make counter-revolution more popular – a fact which the British accepted in the role they gave to émigré forces. But here again there was a problem, for the royalists might not work properly together – which threw the burden back in part on the Allies. London was not ignorant of these conflicting dangers. Wickham stressed the hatred for the Allies; William Huskisson at the War Office argued the case against sending émigré regiments;[2] and while little was known in detail of the resistance in the south or in Paris, intelligence on the north-west had improved over the past two years. At the same time, the range of factors could never be assessed within a firm plan. The very nature of the design meant that much was unknown. For the hope was to exploit what was thought to be a developing situation, in which confusion was likely and chances must be seized. The odds in point of fact may well have been misjudged: France may not have been so ripe for insurrection, or the resistance as powerful, as the British trusted. Nor, outside France, was the state of the Alliance conducive to any easy acceptance of action which in the British view was needed to keep the Alliance alive. The contradictions and uncertainties were serious. The efforts to overcome them showed the degree of importance ascribed to the aim.

The result affected the evolution of strategic thought. For 1795 saw a change of emphasis which, further modified and gaining momentum, was to govern the approach over the next few years. The ejection of the British from the continent[3] set a new scenario, whose features were progressively underlined by the loss of Holland, Prussia and Spain. There was indeed a certain analogy with a more recent situation: the

---

1. Harvey Mitchell, *The Underground War against Revolutionary France* . . . (1965), 63.
2. Richards, loc. cit., 200. Huskisson had recently become Under Secretary.
3. See p. 548 above for the evacuation of the bulk of the force in March. The rest – cavalry and some artillery – followed in the autumn.

search for a strategy in 1940–1, after the evacuation from Dunkirk. This of course must not be pressed too far. There were significant differences. In 1795 Britain retained, and acquired, allies on the continent to an extent unknown between June 1940 and June 1941; as compared with Greece in the latter instance, there were Austria, Sardinia, The Two Sicilies, and Portugal and Russia with greater limitations. On the other hand the Government was not engaged in a Mediterranean land campaign: its efforts were devoted, apart from north-west France, entirely to distant theatres. The strategic formulations themselves moreover were tentative in both cases: in neither can one talk of firm conclusions formally accepted. Historical parallels, never exact, relate here to tendencies rather than facts. Nevertheless a certain broad comparison suggests itself. In 1940–1, both before and after Soviet Russia was forced into war – thus restoring, if only potentially, the concept of continental pressure which Austria and Sardinia represented in 1795 – the British Chiefs of Staff developed, unevenly and with unresolved contradictions, an 'indirect strategy' based on bombing, blockade and subversion.[1] Substitute distant operations for bombing, and the cap fits for 1795. And while the third element disappeared later, after 1797, the main structure was well adapted to conditions that endured for some time. For whereas in 1941 the acquisition first of Russia and then of the United States held out the prospect, however delayed, of a British return to the continent, in 1796–7 the First Coalition was finally tottering, and the prospect was one of virtual isolation unless peace could be secured. The strategy responded accordingly, taking a form indeed which in due course was to complicate attitudes under a fresh European Alliance. Much of the interest of events and their impact in the second half of 1795 thus lies in the signs of a phase emerging in what was to prove an important process.

Interest attaches likewise to an evolution within the phase itself. For the failure of the plans for the summer campaign, in the south and Paris as well as the Vendée, altered Ministers' views on their future course in French affairs. In the first place, they abandoned the idea of expeditions to the north-west. But they were also led, by the Austrians' reluctance to make prominent use of Condé and still more by the collapse of the Vendémiaire rising, to place greater reliance on strictly political internal change. This was the easier because of developments which Vendémiaire interrupted but did not destroy. For in August 1795 the Thermidorean Convention passed its new Constitution,[2] and the first stage of the consequent elections produced a crop of conservative deputies, some of them suspected royalists and others sympathetic to a 'moderate' restoration. With a similar second stage in prospect, the way thus seemed to be opening for discreet but intimate British support

1. See J.M.A. Gwyer, *Grand Strategy (U.K. Official Military Histories of the Second World War)*, III, Part I (1964), Ch. II.
2. See p. 580 above.

within the Convention itself. There was accordingly a shift of direction in 1796, towards financing and influencing a political organisation and bringing the Pretender into sympathy with it, against a background of Austrian operations aided, it was hoped, by Pichegru's change of allegiance.[1] Money and supplies were still sent to the Vendée; but the 'great design' was of a different kind. And this reinforced the probability, introduced by Spain's withdrawal and dismally advanced by the aftermath of Quiberon, that British operations in the foreseeable future would be purely naval and colonial. Subversion would continue, and its role would complement the financing of continental armies. But it was taking a form that would also complement, rather than conflict with, a maritime strategy through which trade would be covered, blockade enforced, and military enterprises sustained which related to both those purposes and employed resources freed from Europe. Strategic and diplomatic interests argued alike: the very fact that we might take a lesser share in deciding the outcome inside France made it the more important to pursue conquests overseas. As early as July 1795 Dundas expressed the view that – whatever happened in Brittany – 'by success in the West Indies alone you can be enabled to dictate the terms of peace'.[2] With that region now claiming an immediate priority, his closest colleagues were soon echoing his approach.

V

For such a strategy now seemed central both to continued war and to terms for peace. It could be said to meet Pitt's statement of strategic aims after the first year's fighting.[3] Its relevance to the next campaign, in the altered circumstances, was stated unequivocally in the last quarter of 1795. Whatever hopes Wickham may still have cherished, the Government accepted in October that 'All the ideas which had been in question for affording Assistance to the Royalists on the Eastern Frontier of France are now become impracticable', while the resistance in the north-west could not maintain itself. Given Austria's passivity, a different scene was opening. And it was one in which the British role, if questioned, should be self-evident. '. . . It is merely necessary to remark that . . . [British] Efforts by Sea will prevent the Operations of the Enemy on that Element, and prolong the present distresses and

1. For which last see p. 586 above.
2. To York, 28 July 1795 (B.L. Add. Ms 40102). Cf. a similar if less strenuous expression of views before the French force sailed for Quiberon, in Dundas to Camden, 1 June 1795 (Camden Ms C106/1). A more restricted indication came in a letter to Pitt a month before, professing, in favour of sending reinforcements to the Leeward Islands, that 'British subjects there have a right to expect priority over all other claims on our armed services' (29 June [1795]; copy in Manchester University Library, Rylands English Ms 907).
3. See p. 327 above.

difficulties of France, while the powerful Armament sent against the West Indies affords a justifiable expectation that much of the remaining possessions of France in that quarter, will be wrested from Her at an early period'.[1] In fact we could do with some Allied help to achieve these objects: our new partner Russia, which had recently sent a squadron to co-operate in the North Sea, should be asked for a further force, to be maintained at British expense, either to act in concert across the oceans or, no doubt more likely, release further British strength for that purpose.[2]

This lofty approach met, not surprisingly, with a cool response. So did a suggestion in August, made rather half-heartedly, that 10–12,000 Russian troops might be sent to Quiberon to help restore the position.[3] There was little real chance in point of fact of the Empress doing much in the summer or autumn: her priority was to gather the fruits of the latest Polish Partition, and when that was settled she continued to proffer advice and demands for support of the Bourbons rather than any firm indications of aid. Russian influence reinforced British efforts to exploit the differences of Denmark and Sweden, with some helpful effects on the management of the blockade. The treaty of February[4] – ratified in May – was a compensation for the loss of Holland, and could be seen later as a possible means, through Russia's links with Prussia, of limiting the consequences of the latter's withdrawal. But British requests to St Petersburg, which gathered pace towards the end of the year, stemmed in the main from a greater preoccupation. The real significance of Russia in the latter half of 1795 lay in her potential impact on the Austrian Alliance.

This might take one of two forms. Ever since the spring there had been hopes in London of a Triple Alliance with Austria as the third member.[5] Progress was slow: the two Imperial Powers had first to reach final agreement in Poland, and then there were difficulties of etiquette and protocol. But declarations were subscribed in September, though ratifications had still to follow; and the British viewed the object as important. It would commit Russia to certain engagements: more significantly in their eyes, to a degree of persuasion and involvement which could stiffen Austria's resolve. The Coalition would find a replacement for Prussia, and one moreover that the Austrians preferred. This was the prospect to be hoped for. But there was an alternative, assuming that there would be a further campaign the next year. It was

1. Grenville to Whitworth, draft unnumbered, – October 1795; same to same, Most Secret, 22 December 1795 (P.R.O., F.O. 65/32).

2. Same to same, Most Secret, 19 September 1795 (F.O. 65/31). The Russian squadron arrived in August; cf. p. 551 above.

3. Same to same, no. 16, Most Secret, 5 August 1795 (F.O. 65/30). For a subsequent, equally unrealistic idea of using Russians to reconquer Holland, see Dundas to Grenville, 28 August 1795 (*H.M.C., Dropmore*, III, 128).

4. P. 550 above.

5. See pp. 550–1, 558 above.

possible to cast Russia in another role: as a partial substitute for Austria herself.

Such a possibility might seem absurd. But the British were brought at least to consider it as their hopes of action in France faded and their suspicions of Vienna increased. By the later summer misunderstanding between the two Allied capitals was almost complete. In London it was 'mortifying' to reflect that the best chance of victory in the current year had been lost (so it was claimed) 'wholly' from Austrian 'Inactivity' and 'Weakness'.[1] The Government had met the financial demands; but where were its rewards? The armies on the Rhine had done nothing, and Condé was forbidden to move. To the Austrians such complaints seemed largely hypocritical. The British refusal to provide a financial advance while the loan was being discussed[2] had led at a critical time to embarrassments which prevented an offensive. The Ministry had done nothing to deter Prussia from posing a threat to Austrian communications,[3] although Russia was said to have suggested a subsidy, to be handled through St Petersburg, for that purpose. More ominously, what was to be made of recent Hanoverian behaviour – always held on the continent to indicate British policy? For the Hanoverian delegate to the Imperial Diet was among those pressing hardest for peace,[4] even proposing that if Austria hung back Prussian mediation should be sought. The resentment rose as the Electorate showed signs of withdrawing from the war in August; and, following the departure of the last British troops from Germany, it did so in September. In point of fact the British Cabinet was embarrassed by the event, of whose precise origins it was ignorant and which caused awkward exchanges with the King.[5] The confusion was not unfamiliar. Its significance on this occasion lay in the doubts it raised in Vienna of what England really had in mind.

The lack of trust was reciprocated, indeed exceeded, in London. This may have been partly because the complexities at the Emperor's Court were not fully understood. The Chancellor Thugut was in fact as usual in favour on balance of a war against France whose success would isolate Prussia, confirm Austria's leadership in the Germanic Empire, and lay the necessary claim to British diplomatic support. He could see the connexion, which others denied, between Austria's western and eastern interests, and his reasoning was strengthened by a successful stand

1. Grenville to Whitworth, – October 1795 (F.O. 65/32). And cf. same to Eden, nos. 47, 49, 24 July 1795 (F.O. 7/42); George III to Grenville, 27 July 1795 (*H.M.C., Dropmore*, III, 92).

2. See pp. 559, n3 above.

3. P. 586 above.

4. See p. 378 above.

5. For the troops' withdrawal see pp. 568–9 above. It was occasioned finally by the imminence of Hanoverian neutrality, which in turn it sealed. Ministers and the King were annoyed with each other; the correspondence, revolving around the reports of the Hanoverian Baron Steinberg, may be followed in P.R.O., W.O. 1/409 (where Pitt's concern may be glimpsed); *H.M.C., Dropmore*, III, 92, 94, 128, 133–4, 148–9; *L.C.G. III*, II, nos. 1290, 1295, 1300, 1301, 1303–4; *Pitt and Napoleon*, 237–8.

against Prussia's pretensions in Poland. But his opponents remained powerful and the Emperor indecisive, and his own unpopularity and failure to communicate did his case no good. The British as always tended to decry his motives when faced by his complaints. But this time there were altogether more suggestive causes for disquiet.[1] The persistent lack of movement on the fronts began to give rise to suspicion, heightened by the commanders' grievances to Craufurd as he toured their headquarters.[2] Even more disturbing, however, were reports from Russia and Switzerland that the inactivity was a prelude to negotiations for peace. Intercepted letters from the French envoy in Berne were particularly interesting, for while they disclosed no hard information there was a significant change of tone. The indications, rising in August, seemed all the stronger when the Austrians failed to collect the latest instalment of the British loan from the German agents. By the end of that month Ministers were seriously worried. And then, early in September, there came a sudden blow. On the 6th the French crossed the Rhine by Düsseldorf virtually unopposed. The German states were in a panic, and Clerfayt was said to hold out little hope. There seemed to be a real danger that the front might disintegrate. Was the moment at hand when Austria might try to leave the war?

The possibility of collapse on the continent brought matters to a head in London. It was essential that Vienna should not act on its own. Such of the Cabinet as were in town met on 19–20 September, in the light of Hanover's threatened neutrality and the latest news.

> Most of us [Pitt wrote] are strongly inclined to think that with a view to prevent the Emperor being alarmed into a separate peace, or at least being deserted by most of the princes of the Empire, as well as in order to satisfy the public mind here at the meeting of Parliament, it would be very useful to come immediately to such an explanation with Austria, as may put it in our power, if things soon assume a settled shape in France, to make use of any opening for ascertaining on what terms the new government may be disposed to treat, and may on the other hand establish in time a full consent for the prosecution of the war, if necessary, next year.[3]

1. The rest of this paragraph draws on Duffy, 'War Policy', 195–7.
2. See p. 584 above.
3. To Portland, Private, 20 September 1795 (Holland Rose, *Pitt and Napoleon*, 254–5). Those present on the two days besides himself were Loughborough, Spencer, Grenville, Dundas and Windham, with Mansfield on the 19th. Windham was said to have opposed 'any idea of even the possibility of negotiation'. This would have been because it meant treating with the Republic, and Portland too was disturbed by the possible threat to support for the Bourbons. But he approved the decision to approach Vienna, as did Chatham a few days later (23, 28 September respectively; P.R.O. 30/8/168, 122).

Pitt had told the King of the idea in the course of a visit to Weymouth on the 15th (see *H.M.C., Dropmore*, III, 134–5; *L.C.G. III*, II, no. 1301).

This long sentence contained all the ingredients and implications of the British position.

The move was decided by pressure of events on an ally. Nevertheless, it brought to a point the acceptance of an object – to prepare for an opening that might lead to peace talks – which had been looming in England itself for some time. We have seen how unpopular the war had become in that year of distress and dearth, giving rise to a feeling in Parliament not expressed by the divisions. Motions for such talks had earlier been easily defeated.[1] But if the figures represented the refusal, or reluctance, to be seen to take an initiative which could only weaken the Ministry's position at home and abroad, this did not mean that Members were content. On the contrary, they were wondering when and how the war was to be won, and becoming restive under the rising financial demands. Pitt was well aware from the early summer that some movement was desirable; it was a feeling indeed which he shared himself. As he said later, he of all people had a personal interest in promoting peace, 'by which alone I could be enabled to effect the favourite objects I had in view'.[2] He was essentially a peacetime Minister: he longed to return to those tasks, the more so as he considered the current economic and financial pressures. But the movement must still be seen to come from the French. The position was stated, and acknowledged, in the King's Speech at the end of the Session.

> It is impossible to contemplate the internal situation of the enemy . . ., without indulging an hope, that the present circumstances of France may, in their effects, hasten the return of such a state of order and regular government as may be capable of maintaining the accustomed relations of amity and peace with other powers.[3]

Exactly when, however, was 'out of the reach of human foresight', and meanwhile of course the war would go on.

This stance in fact was in accord with the Minister's own convictions. His belief that France faced a bankruptcy which must bring her to terms was now intense; and these words were spoken moreover in the hope of Allied invasions and counter-revolution. As that subsided, the more distant pressure of success in the West Indies took their place; and Pitt's optimism, now concentrated there, lent a distinctive note to Dundas's belief that the Caribbean's role was 'essential' to 'Peace or War'.[4]

> It may perhaps be well doubted whether the moment will be ripe for obtaining . . . secure, honourable, and advantageous . . . terms till we have had the benefits of success in the West Indies.[5]

1. By 246 to 75, and 201 to 86 respectively. See p. 441, n2 above.
2. Debate of 10 May 1796 (*The Senator*, XV, 1753). This passage does not appear in the version of the speech in *P.R.*, XLIV, which indeed differs throughout.
3. 27 June 1795 (*P.R.*, XLI, 620).
4. Dundas to York, 20 July 1795 (B.L. Add. Ms 40102).
5. Pitt to Portland, 20 September 1795 (p. 592, n3 above).

The two were being drawn, perhaps rapidly, together. But the Austrian crisis could upset the prospect, for the latter could scarcely be awaited without movement in other directions while our main partner was lost and 'our relative situation . . . thus upon the whole' became 'less favourable instead of more so'.[1] The alternative of Europe and overseas theatres, as seats for British operations, was growing. But the immediate conjunction of events demanded an Allied balance which must not be so tilted that failure in the first forestalled the results expected from the second.

The need for military persistence as the basis for negotiation underlay the approach to Vienna that followed the Cabinet meetings. At their outset, Pitt drew attention to the two most likely dangers. If the Germanic Empire, or significant parts of it, withdrew, the Emperor could act only from Italy, 'where however his Efforts may be very considerable'. But if Sardinia too made peace – as she would do if the Austrians reduced their strength on that front – then it would be a case of 'The War on the Continent ended'. We must assume that Spain, Sweden and even Denmark were potential enemies, that Holland would equip a hostile fleet, and Prussia act in Poland or Hanover against Russo-Austrian or Allied interests. We had therefore to keep all those unfriendly Powers 'quiet', ensure that the Austrians were committed in Italy, 'secure Russia', and prevent the states of the Empire from suing for terms piecemeal.[2]

Such was the background to the despatches over the next few weeks. The Austrians were urged to consider plans for 'a great and formidable army' in 1796. Britain would supply financial assistance provided there was evidence of activity now, enough at least to convince Parliament that further aid was worth while. Diplomatic action was also needed if the German states were to be kept at war – an exercise in which the Austrians were said to have proved conspicuously weak. Allied cohesion was vital if the partners were not to be picked off separately. The two Governments should therefore consult on possible terms of peace while the Coalition maintained its pressures by land and sea. No diplomatic detail was advanced: the ball was left in Austria's court, though the British stated their abiding preference for the retention (and recovery) of the Austrian Netherlands.[3] But if the approach was exploratory, there must be no doubt it was in earnest. Pitt and Grenville had hoped to send out a special envoy at the end of September, and in fact had picked on the Irish Secretary Thomas Pelham.[4] But he refused, and a Foreign

1. Ibid.
2. Memoranda, 'Supposing Peace not to be made by this Country before the next Spring', 'Sept 19th', in Pitt's hand; endorsed (not in his hand) '19 Sept: 1775' (P.R.O. 30/8/197). For a more sanguine view of Denmark see p. 551 above.
3. Grenville to Eden, no. 64, Most Secret, 23 September 1795 (P.R.O., F.O. 7/43).
4. *H.M.C., Dropmore*, III, 135; Thomas Pelham to Lord Pelham, nd but September 1795 (B.L. Ad. Ms 38129). For Pelham see p. 439 above. He was over in London from

George Canning, *by Hoppner*

George Rose, *by Beechey*

Lord Malmesbury. *Unknown*

Office man, Francis Jackson, left in mid-October, carrying with him an outline of the terms to be suggested if opportunity arose.[1] At the same time, the Russians were asked to warn the Emperor not to make a separate peace,[2] a prospect which was being rumoured increasingly throughout Europe. By this time indeed the reports were such that Ministers were seriously alarmed.[3] When Parliament reassembled on the 29th, the King's Message combined a call for 'maintaining and improving our naval superiority, and for carrying on active and vigorous operations in the West-Indies' with an assertion that 'a disposition' on the part of France 'to negotiate for general peace on just and suitable terms will not fail to be met . . . with an earnest desire to give it the fullest and speediest effect'.[4]

Events, however, were once more producing their familiar see-saw effect. Nothing could illustrate more sharply the unstable nature of Allied expectations than the sudden if temporary swing from gloom to confidence that now took place. When Jackson arrived in Vienna he found the Austrians cock-a-hoop. For to London's surprise their armies had launched a counter-offensive in the middle of October, and on the day that Parliament met defeated the French in front of Mainz. Moreover, they kept it up. In the next few weeks they cleared much of the Palatinate and raised the sieges of Mannheim, Mainz itself, and Frankfurt; while the problems in Poland were finally removed with the belated signing of the treaty of partition.[5] There therefore seemed to be a real prospect of exploiting success in the west. Thugut's tone at once altered. His procrastination disappeared.

The result was seen in the response to the British approach. Caution and vagueness, with one significant exception, were replaced by definite views and demands.[6] The war must certainly go on, and Austria would field some 200,000 men next year. England for her part should guarantee a further loan of £3 million – on better terms; extract a firm promise of troops from Russia – if necessary by means of subsidy; and – a

---

Dublin at the time, and known to want to leave his post in the not too distant future. It is possible that Thomas Grenville was then considered (letters to him from Lord Grenville, 23 September 1795, 1 October, 3 October; B.L. Add. Ms 41852). Morton Eden, the resident Minister, was thought not to carry enough weight on his own.

1. Paper in Grenville's hand, 5 October 1795 (B.L. Add. Ms 59306); almost certainly for, or approved by, the Cabinet.
See p. 10, n1 above for Jackson's German experience. Aged 25 at this time, he happened to be in London on leave from Madrid (see p. 209, n5 above).
2. Grenville to Whitworth, 10 October 1795 (F.O. 65/32).
3. See Duffy, 'War Policy', 203.
4. P.R., XLIII, 2–3.
5. On 24 October, the Austrian copy arriving on 13 November.
6. Jackson to Grenville, no. 1, 10 November 1795 (F.O. 7/43); and see also Eden to Auckland, 8 November 1795 (*Auckland*, III, 320–3). The contents were probably relayed to the Cabinet on 2 December (Minute in Grenville's hand, 2 December 1795; B.L. Add. Ms 59306).

riposte to the expostulations from London – enable the German states to pull their weight. Otherwise there would be a defensive campaign confined strictly to Italy, while the Empire procured an armistice and the Austrian Government, like the British, awaited the climax of exhaustion in France. There was one area of discussion, however, where a clear answer was not forthcoming. Nothing specific could be said about the Netherlands until Russia had been consulted, and Jackson himself was convinced that Vienna still wanted the Bavarian Exchange.

The news of the Austrian successes was greeted with delight and relief. The first reports came just in time for a passage to be inserted in the King's Speech,[1] and Pitt, who a few weeks before had been contemplating peace 'before Easter',[2] could now return to his anticipations from the West Indies. There might no longer be the need to hope, rather desperately, that the mere sailing of the large expedition would incline the enemy, 'from the extreme pressure upon them', 'to give us all the sacrifices we should require'.[3] We could now afford to await results, probably in the spring, which would play a major part in bringing France to terms.[4] This turn of events – or assumptions – was indeed just as well, for the expedition itself was inordinately delayed. The date for completion of the preparations had already been postponed from the first half of September to the first week of October; but this in turn passed before the commander, Abercromby, was given his instructions on the 9th.[5] Autumnal westerlies then set in. But when they relented early in November the expedition was still not ready to sail. It was hard to tell why – though one can now see that the reason lay largely in the late arrival of East and West Indiamen indispensable to make up the tonnage needed for so large a force and its supplies.[6] Dundas, who had been in 'Agony' while the adverse winds lasted, clearly thought that the Generals were waiting on perfection.

> I do not see any reason to hope that you will be more ready to go a Month hence than you are now. I really feel it a Disgrace to the Executive Government of the Country, and every Branch acting under it, that an Expedition determined upon Six months ago, should

1. *P.R.*, XLIII, 2. They reached the Foreign Office on 27 October (*L.C.G. III*, II, no. 1318; *H.M.C., Dropmore*, III, 143).

2. To Henry Addington, 4 October 1795 (Pellew, *Life and Correspondence of Sidmouth*, I, 156–7).

3. Pitt to Portland, 20 September 1795 (Holland Rose, *Pitt and Napoleon*, 254). This follows the passage quoted on p. 593 above.

4. Cf. Grenville to Eden and to Whitworth, Most Secret, 22 December 1795 (F.O. 7/43, 65/32).

5. Dundas to Abercromby, Secret Instructions, 9 October 1795 (P.R.O., W.O. 1/84); see p. 566, n3 above. For the earlier expectations see same to same, 28 September, 3 November 1795 (loc. cit.).

6. M.W.B. Sanderson, 'English Naval Strategy and Maritime Trade in the Caribbean, 1793–1802' (Ph.D thesis, University of London, 1968), 336–7.

not be in a State to sail Seven Weeks later than its appointed time.[1]

He must have been the more infuriated after all the efforts he had made to find the troops, from the French expedition, from the garrisons and Ireland, from Germany, from the Guards brigade.[2] However, the convoy weighed anchor at last on the 16th and sailed down Channel in a light breeze, watched by crowds along the coast. Two nights later a gale set in, catching it off Portland, sinking some of the transports and forcing the rest back to Portsmouth. It sailed again on 3 December. Again it was caught by a gale which held Abercromby himself, on board the escorting flagship, in the mouth of the Channel for seven weeks, until he was driven into port once more. Some thirty transports had returned by then; the other hundred disappeared into the ocean, whether to the West Indies or the bottom was unknown. Most of them in fact reached their destination by driblets. But it was the end of February before the rest sailed finally, Abercromby preceding them and arriving in March 1796.

While all this was going on, the plans themselves had to be changed. The initial delay had been caused partly by the absence of foreign troops expected from Germany, and since these were intended for St Domingue offensive operations there were postponed. This however should enable St Lucia to be attacked at the same time as Guadeloupe, and the revisions affected dispositions throughout the Leeward Islands.[3] But the further setback in December caused further discussion at the turn of the year, for there was now a real conflict of interests between the different areas of the Caribbean. Considerable risks would have to be taken whatever was decided, and there were strong divisions in Cabinet which were resolved only as Abercromby left.[4] This was on the plane of local strategy. But it raised a more far-reaching question. For whatever was done the season would now be 'advanced . . . before operations can commence', so much so indeed that they could not be 'prosecuted with full effect' until the *end* of 1796.[5] The implications were grave, and they led to a grave dispute. But even as the old year closed the brief euphoria was fading, and the promise of the autumn was being drastically reduced.

1. Dundas to Abercromby, 3 November (W.O. 1/84), quoted in Fortescue, op. cit., 479. Cf. p. 566, n1 above.
2. In the last of which he failed, after a brush with the King over the numbers to be taken from a force desirable 'for the interior quiet of the Kingdom' (16 August 1795; p. 457, n3 above). 3,000 of the infantry, and smaller drafts of cavalry and artillery, were to be mercenaries.
3. Dundas to Abercromby, Most Secret, 23 November 1795 (W.O. 1/84). Cf. p. 566 above.
4. These are followed in Ch. XV, section I below.
5. Pitt to Grenville, 3 January 1796 (*H.M.C., Dropmore*, III, 166); same to George III, 30 January 1796 (Stanhope, II, Appendix, xxx). Cf. pp. 266, 564 above for the limits to the campaigning season in the Carribean.

The curve of expectation in Europe flattened as well. The victories in Germany were somewhat offset late in November by an Austro-Sardinian defeat at Loano which led to the evacuation of the coast west of Genoa. The gains of the summer in the south, meagre as they had been, were lost.[1] Nor was there much prospect of further immediate success on the Rhine: the Austrian armies w.re exhausted, and Clerfayt signed a local armistice at the end of the year. Nor again was the news from St Petersburg encouraging. The hopes of a Russian force for 1796 were shaken when the Empress declined to act in Germany without Prussian co-operation. This last of course was desirable to protect the lines of route. But such a prospect was by no means to the Austrian taste. The Imperial Powers indeed were beginning to eye each other once more. The Russians were said to be concentrating troops on the Turkish frontier, and they seemed to be taking a cautious line on the Bavarian Exchange.[2] The facts of power east of the Rhine were overtaking a transient military advantage. It was in these circumstances that the British decided to spell out formally their own ideas for peace.

They did so late in December, to Vienna and St Petersburg.[3] Russia's influence was sought to oppose the Bavarian Exchange. For the principal British object in Europe was to restore the *status quo* in the Netherlands: 'as [these] constitute the great link of connection between this Country and Austria', their retention by the Emperor 'will, it is hoped, be considered as the first object in any plan of pacification'. An adequate barrier should be secured, perhaps by adding Liège and some former Dutch territory.[4] As for the other Allies, Sardinia should regain her possessions in Savoy.[5] The Two Sicilies and Portugal, which had lost no territory, should merely be included in the general terms; the arrangements for the German states in the Empire were primarily Austria's affair. Britain's own indemnities would lie outside Europe (Corsica being kept as a possibility in the background).[6] Her proposals for the continent were thus simpler than those of 1793–4. The collapse of the first Triple Alliance had in fact removed some of the complications. But a fundamental divergence still lay at the root of the second. For as Pitt and Grenville lobbied Russia to keep Austria in the Netherlands, Thugut remained determined to enlist her influence in favour of Bavaria, linked perhaps with Alsace.[7] As the Coalition faced the

1. See pp. 585–6 above.
2. Pp. 551, 557, 595–6 above.
3. Grenville to Eden, no. 72, Most Secret, 22 December 1795 (F.O. 7/43); same to Whitworth, Most Secret, sd (F.O. 65/32); printed in J.H. Rose, 'France and the First Coalition before the Campaign of 1796' in *E.H.R.*, XVIII, no. LXX.
4. Cf. p. 273 above.
5. See p. 278 above.
6. The island had at any rate been mentioned in the outline of possible terms in October (B.L. Add. Ms 59306; see p. 595, n1 above).
7. Duffy, 'War Policy', 210–12, 218.

uncertainties of peace negotiations or a further campaign, it had no concerted plans for either at the end of the third year of war.

In their despatches to the two capitals, the British also offered some ideas on France. They would not insist on a restored monarchy; but there must be an amnesty for royalists, with the right for those inside the country to remain there undisturbed, perhaps with their effects wholly or partly returned, or to sell their possessions and emigrate if they wished. This statement, keeping options wide open, embodied a further shift in applying the formula to which the Government clung as its aim, and defence.

No one clung harder than Pitt. For the formula had always had the virtue, to a Minister concerned strictly for future security, that it need not tie him closely as to means. Having expressed the aim, it left any policy of political choice or intervention adjustable, within the military limits, to situations as they arose. The commitment to monarchy, hardening by stages since the autumn of 1793, reached a point in the summer of 1795 which might have seemed binding. The support for d'Artois, the aid to Condé, the mission to Verona, raised the involvement with royalism to a new level, with a new tone. If purists like Burke could still fear the attractions of the Constitutionalists, it was broadly, almost universally, assumed that Britain was now at any rate pledged to see a King returned. But this was not what the formula, or any Cabinet Minister, had said. The preference for monarchy, increasingly explicit, rested on the two foundations of operational advantage and the superiority of the system for future security – despite the suspicions of a long past – to the republicanism of recent years. The first, however, was now brought into question, and the second might be irrelevant as the political climate seemed to be on the turn. The tone and then the direction of policy began accordingly to change. The process was shown clearly in a series of remarks by Pitt himself. At the end of August he suggested that temporary asylum might be offered to members of the Convention who, though republicans, engaged to work for the restoration of a monarchy; our future co-operation with Louis XVIII might even be made conditional on his guaranteeing their safety and rewards. In September he listed as an object of any campaign for the next year, 'To encourage as much as possible the Exertions of the Royalists without committing ourselves to the Continuance of the War'.[1] This was hardly a clarion call, and in October he faced the implication. The order had then just been drafted to pull out the British troops from the Vendée coast.

. . . This will so change Monsieur's [d'Artois'] situation and

1. Pitt to Grenville, 29 August 1795 (*H.M.C., Dropmore*, III, 129); memoranda of 19 September 1795 (P.R.O. 30/8/197).

expectations that . . . we are, I think, bound to explain to him that the present crisis in Paris, though on the one hand it may lead to a continued state of distraction, or to a new order of things more favourable to his prospects, yet, on the other hand, may possibly produce some established form of Government with which the country may think it necessary to treat, provided it should find them inclined to negotiation on a footing consistent with our honour and interest, and that of our allies. That we should still see the restoration of monarchy with infinitely more satisfaction than any other result, and that . . . while the war continues (which may be necessarily prolonged . . .) every effort will be used on our part to continue supplies . . . for the use of the Royalists on different parts of the coast; but that, feeling it possible that there may be such an issue of the present crisis as may lead sooner or later to negotiation with some form of government different from monarchy, we have thought it right to apprise him of what may eventually be our line of conduct . . .[1]

From there it was a short step to the despatches of December.

Obvious problems could be envisaged, in the Alliance, within England, and in the substance of the question itself. The effect on the Austrians was likely to be less unfavourable than on the Russians. The former had not recognised the Comte de Provence as King, and had taken shelter behind the British by announcing that they would do so if the two Powers acted together. To the Russians, on the other hand, recognition was still a central plank of policy,[2] so that this pronouncement from London would not be well received. At home, there was much uneasiness among the Portland Whigs. The Duke himself, while admitting the 'probability' of having to negotiate with the present French Government, was averse to any declaration in advance that would weaken the monarchy's claims; Windham went farther, and opposed any hint of talks with republicans;[3] and outside the Ministry, the father figure of Burke was voicing his extreme alarm.[4] As Pitt said later, 'many things which fell from that great man' showed 'a difference' from official policy.[5] But clearly trouble might arise from one section of the Cabinet. There were also Parliament and the King to be considered

---

1. Pitt to Grenville, 16 October 1795 (*H.M.C., Dropmore*, III, 140). See p. 577 above for the order to pull out.

2. Grenville to Whitworth, 10 November 1795 (F.O. 65/32); and see p. 582 above. For the Austrians in the same month see Duffy, loc. cit., 214.

3. P. 592, n3 above.

4. Burke to Pitt, 28 October; to Auckland, 30 October; to Dundas, c. 4 November 1795 (*Correspondence of Burke*, VIII, 330–1, 334–5, 337). It was the second of these letters, passed on to Pitt, that provoked the response quoted on p. 80 above; and which was indeed the first sign of the composition of Burke's *Letters on a Regicide Peace*, published after his death.

5. Debate of 10 May 1796 (*The Senator*, XV, 1756).

very carefully. The reaction in the Commons in point of fact was favourable enough at first. The opening debate of the session went much better than expected; and if Pitt's disciple Canning is to be believed, his 'declaration respecting the *possibility of treating* with the new Government seemed to take a weight off people's minds'. Indeed it 'set them a-shouting with approbation', and there was equal approval when he followed up by 'stipulating *vigorously* for *good* terms'.[1] Wilberforce and his friends returned to the Government lobby in the division,[2] and the majority was much larger than the Foxites had anticipated. So far so good.[3] But the relief was bound to be mixed with doubts. Would the present French leaders survive? And had they, and the country, really changed their spots? Pitt himself was becoming increasingly anxious to find out the answer to this last question. He was guarding his position, balancing his movements, taking things step by step. It was an exploratory exercise. But he was pushing it along, in concert with Grenville[4] but with a personal initiative. As the Commons remained broadly quiescent, and the West Indies' expedition was still held up, he decided to repeat and elaborate on the statement of six weeks before. On 8 December he presented a royal Message to the Commons.[5]

> . . . The crisis which was depending at the commencement of the present session has led to such an order of things in France as will induce His Majesty (conformably to the sentiments which He has already declared) to meet any disposition to negociation on the part of the enemy, with an earnest desire to give it the fullest and speediest effect, and to conclude a treaty of general peace, whenever it can be effected on just and suitable terms for Himself and His allies.

This, as George III was careful to remark, was 'guardedly drawn'; and the Minister, equally carefully, had given as his reason the need to forestall a confused debate on a prospective Opposition motion for peace.[6] True enough; but perhaps not the whole truth. For while Pitt intended to wait for an overture, there was soon a hint that if it failed to appear something more might be done. It was important to discover the true weight of the reports coming out of France in the past few months; above all, to test the private signals against an opportunity for popular expression. For this if for no other reason, therefore, much advantage

---

1. Quoted in *L.C.G. III*, II, no. 1320n5.
2. Cf. p. 463 above.
3. Canning to the Marchioness of Stafford, 5 November 1795 (P.R.O. 30/29/4(10)).
4. Eg, for this and the questions, Lord Mornington to Grenville, nd but ascribed November–December 1795 (*H.M.C., Dropmore*, III, 149–50).
5. *P.R.*, XLIII, 624.
6. Correspondence of 5 December 1795 (*L.C.G. III*, II, no. 1340). Opposition's motion had already been tabled.

might eventually be derived (probably after 'the Winter') 'even from a more direct declaration conveyed to that Country of a willingness to enter into the discussion of terms of Peace'.[1]

1. Grenville to Eden and to Whitworth, 22 December 1795 (p. 58, n3 above).

CHAPTER XV

Policy Undone

I

T he tenor of the King's Speech at the end of 1795 pointed the fact
that Pitt's impressions and emphases were different from those of
a year before. Then he had been despondent, if momentarily,
about the course of the war,[1] but was confident enough about the
situation at home. He had had to make some Cabinet changes within the
still recent coalition. But the coalition was achieved, at some sacrifice of
political goodwill; the threat of subversion seemed to have been met;
neither the finances nor the economy gave cause for immediate worry;
and the depression over operations was itself due largely to a sense of
chances missed, rather than to real fear of stalemate or defeat. The view
was not so reassuring twelve months on, and now the domestic factors
counted for more. The shortage of wheat was still acute; discontent was
vocal and recently alarming; the finances, so central to Pitt's being, were
leading him to shifts he would earlier have scorned;[2] and the public's
sense of chances missed – of an enemy, groggier than ever, again let off
the ropes – was much keener, and the sense of foreboding more real.
Parliament and the people were all too obviously restive, after three
years of expense with no apparent return. Fear of the Revolution
remained vivid, and patriotism had deep roots; the propertied orders
were very far from the end of their tether. But they were growing tired of
disappointments and resentful of failures; they could see little prospect of
success in the coming year; by and large, while they were probably not
prepared to yield too much in the terms, they were also probably not
averse, particularly from what they had read of events in France, to
some exploration of the possibilities for a negotiated peace.

So at any rate it seemed to Pitt and others at the opening of the
session.[3] The handling of the business would clearly be delicate: there
were allies to be considered, and if anything was to be attempted it must

1. See pp. 380–1 above.
2. And cf. Rose's view from the Treasury of the cost of the war compared with the
absence of 'the smallest possible Advantage' (to Pretyman; quoted in Robin Reilly, *Pitt
the Younger, 1759–1806* (1978), 242).
3. Pp. 600–2 above.

be on the basis that it rested on elements of strength.[1] There must first of all be broad agreement in the inner circle of Government. It was the more annoying to find that 'His Majesty', publicly prepared in the light of French developments to show 'an earnest desire' for 'a treaty of general peace',[2] was in private entirely opposed to his Ministers taking any step. The initiative should come from the enemy, whose situation gave them plenty of cause; he saw no purpose, and much possible damage, in Britain making a move. The King acknowledged the possible usefulness of having said something in Parliament to forestall a worse proposal from the Foxites.[3] But he felt 'compelled by the magnitude of the subject' to state his thoughts at some length – a rare and significant occurence – without more loss of time. As usual they were forthright, and they were introduced with some tactical skill.

> This I do with the greater ease at the present moment, when I am persuaded none of my Ministers can seriously look on this as the proper time for entering on the consideration of that subject [a negotiation], and consequently that my ideas may [be] of more use . . . The great force which has been collected and sent to the West Indies . . . [together with future additions] ought to have sufficient time allowed for it to be seen what success may be obtained in that part of the globe. I perhaps am too sanguine, but I really believe it may secure the possession of St. Domingo, without which acquisition I cannot think our possessions in the islands secure, and that peace can be but of short duration.
>
> The further successes in the E. Indies, which cannot but be expected, are additional reasons not to hamper ourselves with a negotiation. We are trying to persuade both the Courts of Vienna and Petersburg to come forward and commence an early campaign . . . we cannot honourably move without first giving them notice, which will be a solid cause for their waiting the issue of the measure prior to making preparations which cannot be effected without expense.

And then there was the state of France, financially overburdened and filled increasingly with discontent. Her mounting 'disasters' could be averted only by our proposing peace, which 'would give a momentary

1. Eg notes by Grenville of 27 January 'as to declaration of readiness to make Peace' (almost certainly referring to a forthcoming Opposition motion, made on 15 February 1796), 'Not fit . . . unaccompanied by that of a vigorous prosecution of the War as affording at present the only reasonable prospect of Peace' (B.L. Add. Ms 59067A).

In Stanhope Ms S5 09/27 (Kent C.A.O.) there is a memorandum in Pitt's hand, 'Notes respecting France Jan. 1795'. Since these notes consist of possible peace terms, and refer to the restoration of Holland (cf. p. 548 above), they would seem to be misdated for 1796. They are of interest as showing the compass of his thoughts at that point; but the options are so wide that little can be gained by setting them out.

2. P. 601 above.

3. Ibid.

weight' to her Government and 'put a stop to the various engines' threatening the destruction of the Revolutionary system.[1]

Such a paper demanded an answer rather more explicit than Pitt might have wished. Relying on the tenor of the approach to our main ally, Austria, for that of an opening to France,[2] he was obliged to disclose as background his apprehensions of the feeling at home. His respect for the sense of the Commons, as he claimed to detect it, was plain. The King unfortunately would be wrong to depend on an early contribution from events in the West Indies.[3]

> The return of [the main naval force] with a large part of the convoy to Spithead (of which accounts were received this morning),[4] and the advanced season, make it now impossible that operations on a large scale can be prosecuted with full effect (though they may still be successfully begun) till the close of the year; and it cannot be expected that Parliament or the country will wait to so distant a period for *some* pacific explanation. It seems equally clear that if Government takes in time steps to remove the possibility of cavil on its real desire to make peace in conjunction with your Majesty's Allies, on suitable terms whenever they can be obtained, that this will ensure the continuance of a zealous support in and out of Parliament.
>
> On the other hand if Government delay taking steps so late as to be obliged to take them in consequence of any declaration of the sense of Parliament, all hope of good terms would be at an end. In the first case, the issue of the war (though far from equal to all that might at some periods have been hoped) would still be honourable and probably advantageous; in the other case, it can hardly be expected to be otherwise than the reverse.

And if the French were led, as a result of the need for a response, to repeat their 'inadmissible' pretentions, that would strengthen support for the war, remove 'any Parliamentary difficulties', and give Government a strong hand if the negotiation survived.

Not surprisingly, these arguments evoked a fairly dusty response. George III was not unduly impressed by a politician's sensitivities, or by such reservations on the extent of military success.

> . . . it is not the return of the force sent to the West Indies that can in the least alter my opinions . . .; but I do not in the least mean by this to make any obstinate resistance to the measure proposed, though I own

1. Paper enclosed in George III to Pitt, 27 January 1796 (Holland Rose, *Pitt and Napoleon*, 238–9). For the new expedition to the West Indies see pp. 566–7, 596–7 above; for the Far East in the past year, pp. 561–2 above. 'St Domingo' = St Domingue.

2. Cf. pp. 594–5, 598 above.

3. To George III, 30 January 1796 (Stanhope, II, Appendix, xxx–xxxi).

4. See p. 597 above.

I cannot feel the utility of it. My mind is not of a nature to be guided by the obtaining a little applause or staving off some abuse; rectitude of conduct is my sole aim. I trust the rulers of France will reject any proposition from hence short of a total giving up of any advantage we may have gained, and therefore that the measure proposed will meet with a refusal.[1]

Despite his apparent readiness not to press his views, the King in point of fact was most unlikely to lapse into silence if it came to the point. For he knew well enough that there was division within the Cabinet. He sent his paper to Loughborough, Portland and Dundas, as well as to Pitt; and he was particularly hopeful of Dundas, as the closest to the Minister and one whose 'sentiments' on the question he believed to be 'as steady' as his own.[2] Such messages could overshoot the mark: politicians could be wary of royal manoeuvres, even though Dundas had reason to wish for some favour from the closet after the recall of the Duke of York.[3] But in any case George III was counting, as he wrote, on a rejection from France. Meanwhile he stayed watchful in the wings, not letting his opinion be forgotten and showing a marked suspicion of Pitt's firmness.[4]

Events proved his scepticism. The French were not interested. Neither for that matter were the principal Allies. The Russians were as averse as might have been expected to any negotiation that did not rest on the return of the Bourbons. The Sardinians, discouraged by failure in 1795 and as always at odds with the Austrians, were too depressed and uncertain to have any specific views. And the Austrians themselves, the key to the success – the continuation – of the diminished Coalition, did not respond well to proposals which once more ignored the Bavarian Exchange. While not committed as was the Empress to support of the exiled French monarchy, the Emperor remained wedded to the concept of relinquishing the Netherlands. The differences of policy were moreover exacerbated in the last two cases by a British failure to promise, or indeed implement, further immediate financial support. Sardinia was calling for a higher subsidy, Austria needed a regular supply. But the embarrassments in London, rising in the latter half of 1795, increased sharply in the winter to a point where the former was refused and the latter interrupted.[5] These developments, becoming

---

1. To Pitt, 31 January 1796 (Stanhope, II, Appendix, xxxi–xxxii).
2. To Dundas, 6 February 1796 (*L.C.G. III*, II, no. 1367 n1). For the King's distribution of the original paper see op. cit., no. 1361 n1; and for Portland's earlier misgivings, p. 600 above.
3. See pp. 364, 374–5, above.
4. See George III to Dundas, 16 February 1796 (*L.C.G. III*, II, no. 1371).
5. Whitworth to Grenville, nos. 1, 4–5, 2, 12, 19 January 1796 (P.R.O., F.O. 65/33); Trevor to Grenville, no. 83, 28 November 1795, nos. 1, 5 and 7, 6, 23, 30 January, Grenville's 'Minutes of Conference' [with Count Front], 9 February 1796 (F.O. 67/19–20); Duffy, 'British War Policy', 220–3. For finance in 1795 see pp. 523–8 above.

clear in February, did not bode well for Allied agreement if a negotiation had got seriously under way. But it did not. The soundings were entrusted to Wickham in Berne: he was told to approach the French envoy Barthélemy, which he did on 8 March. On the 26th Barthélemy returned an answer which put paid to any hopes. All British colonial conquests should be restored, and France, it was implied, should hold her 'natural frontiers' of the Rhine, the Alps, the Pyrenees and the ocean.[1] This 'insolent paper' at once ended the matter. It showed, remarked Pitt, that we still had to wait 'for the return of reason in our deluded enemy'.[2]

The Government published the main exchanges, to demonstrate its good faith to our partners and our resolve to leave 'the first advances' – by which was meant the first proposals for terms – to the French. Now we had 'no option between war and peace'. In saying this, Pitt did not disguise the depth of the previous year's disappointments (a not unreasonable aid, one might have said, to the enemy's delusion):

> when we experienced the sad reverse of fortune; when the spirit of our allies was broken, our troops discomfited, our territories wrested from us, and all our hopes disconcerted . . .[3]

A shaky basis on which to build. But Ministers of course did not stop searching for a strategy while the approach in Berne was made, and they went doggedly on in the spring and summer. In most respects it was a cheerless task. Indeed on one front it was pursued against disaster. In April 1796 Buonaparte opened his Italian campaign. Taking over an army starved of supplies and food itself, he was through the passes in a matter of weeks and storming through the hills to the Lombard plain. Stunned by 'the Torrent of this victorious Enemy',[4] Sardinia made peace on the 28th. By mid-May Lodi had been fought, the French were in Milan and the Austrians retreating fast. The fears spread through the peninsula, and at the end of the month The Two Sicilies, the remaining ally, signed an armistice which was followed by a peace treaty in October. In June the Austrians were holed up in Mantua, the last stronghold in their Italian territories, and Buonaparte was turning south to attend to the neutral states.

The repercussions were soon felt. The Directory in Paris had approved the plan for the attack on Italy in order to relieve pressure on

---

1. And in the list of acquisitions the Austrian Netherlands (Belgic Provinces) were not even mentioned, since the French had 'incorporated' them by decree in October 1795.
   See *Correspondence of William Wickham*, I, 269–74, 312–14, 320–1; *The Cambridge History of British Foreign Policy*, I, 263–5.
2. Grenville to George III, 9 April 1796 (*L.C.G. III*, II, no. 1387); Pitt's speech of 10 May 1796 (*The Senator*, XV, 1763).
3. Speech of 10 May.
4. Trevor [from Turin] to Grenville, no. 34, 25 April 1796 (F.O. 67/21).

the central front, and the calculation was correct. In the last days of May the Austrians moved their army on the upper Rhine through the Alps. The gains along the western bank of the river, made before the winter armistice, had accordingly to be given up, together with plans for operations beyond.[1] In the first half of June a new commander, the Archduke Charles, withdrew from Mainz. There appeared to be no prospect for the time being of an offensive in any quarter.

Something very like the threat of the previous September had thus arisen. Sardinia had made peace, and if the German Empire as such was still in the war the Austrians were confined effectively to acting in Italy, and under much more adverse circumstances. Was 'The War on the Continent' about to be 'ended'?[2] Pitt and Grenville were hard at work to shore up the tottering frame. There were four candidates to be considered, in combination or distinctly. The first, unpromising as it might seem, was Prussia. Grenville was alert throughout the winter to the possibility of yet another change of direction in Berlin, and early in February the Government thought conditions favourable enough for an approach. The Prussians appeared uneasy about French pretensions. They had now concentrated their force for the protection of a neutral northern Germany. The British proposed that it should be used for an attack on Holland – where from their reports discontent was rife – which would restore the Stadtholder in advance of proposing a general peace the Allied terms for which might be entrusted as a first step to Prusso-Russian talks with Austria. While the Emperor's retention of his Netherlands was as usual strongly favoured, there was even a hint of British consent to an arrangement which would leave them 'in such a situation as to be neither directly nor indirectly dependant on France'. England would defray, retrospectively, the costs of the reconquest of Holland – which we might recoup, at least in part, from retaining the Dutch colonies we had taken over. This approach may well have been made in part at least to forestall a similar French use of Prussia, as a channel for a peace treaty but on very different terms. It held out the bait of a restored influence in Holland. But over the next few months the prospect faded away, and by June there were renewed fears of Prussia actively joining with France.[3]

Russia figured in the scheme. And obviously she was another party to be pursued. The Empress seemed disposed to come once more into rather closer relations with Prussia, and if that Power could be brought

1. See pp. 595, 598, 586 above.
2. P. 594 above.
3. P.R.O., F.O. 64/38–40 *passim*; *H.M.C., Dropmore*, III, 170–215. The peak of the effort was in February and March. The quotation is from Grenville to Eden, no. 3, Most Secret, 9 February 1796; for the Prussian defensive force see pp. 548–9 above.

into play perhaps she would send a force into Germany.[1] The British envoy was instructed to disclose the idea of reconquering Holland. But no clear answer was received; by April Whitworth was complaining of 'scandalously evasive Conduct'; and in June, 'While other Countries are in a State of Convulsion, this scarcely furnishes . . . Matter sufficient for a Despatch'.[2] In point of fact the Russians were proving useful in the Baltic, where their threats to the Swedes restrained and later diminished the latter's ties with France and bolstered the more sympathetic neutrality of Denmark. But while that was important for our trade and naval power, it was marginal to the immediate concern, and some quarters at least in London were still anxious to induce the Empress to act. Dundas above all was prepared to persuade her 'to come forward at any price'.

> For my part I would give her St Domingo, or even overturn the Turkish Empire in Europe rather than not combine Europe in the present moment.

Only supreme 'pecuniary Embarrassments at home' should be allowed to prevent a major effort.[3] But there was little likelihood of a speedy decision at the other end.

There remained Austria. All that could be done directly was to see that she did not collapse for want of funds. Since a fresh loan was presenting difficulties at a time of rapidly deepening financial problems, an advance of £100,000 was made at the end of April for the army under the Archduke Charles. Great secrecy was observed in case of objections at home. Three weeks later a further advance of £150,000 was authorised in case of need. The defeats of May not surprisingly gave rise to rumours of a separate peace, and the Austrian envoy in London reported that he had never seen Ministers so gloomy. But early in June he was able to say that his Government would continue to fight, and in the next few weeks £300,000 was promised to cover July and August. Monthly sums of £150,000 would be provided, it was hoped, for the rest of the year, the whole to be repaid from a subsequent loan, still impossible to make at that time. These advances would amount in all to £1,150,000. They remained substantially short of the Austrians' earlier demand.[4]

Not much therefore was to be expected from present or past allies. The only other possibility lay within enemy territory. The great disappoint-

1. Grenville's Most Secret Minute, circulated to some of the Cabinet, 2 February 1796 (B.L. Add. Ms 59306).
2. Whitworth to Grenville, nos. 20, 26, 19 April, 7 June 1796; and see F.O. 65/33 *passim*.
3. Dundas to William Huskisson (see p. 587 above), 14 June [1796] (B.L. Add. Ms 38734). 'St Domingo' again = St Domingue.
4. Duffy, loc. cit., 227–8. Cf. p. 595 above.

ments of the previous year had swung British thoughts towards a purely political rather than an armed counter-revolution in France. Wickham had not lost hope of the latter, and flickers of rebellion could still rouse momentary enthusiasm in London.[1] But it did not compare with the feelings in 1795, and the last blow to expectations of military action came with the removal of Pichegru, for some time in contact with the Allies, from his command on the Rhine.[2] The General was still at large, and still in a plotting mood. But he himself now recognised that a different way must be found, and as Buonaparte's army swept through northern Italy Wickham concentrated his efforts, with his Government's support, on encouraging a broad political front.

The story is a tortuous one. It is always hard to co-ordinate active resisters, disaffected politicians and soldiers, and unrealistic exiles, and none in this case moreover produced an obvious leader. Wickham struggled through the spring and summer to build bridges between the 'pure' royalists and the Constitutionalists whom England preferred and who were now well represented in the Convention. He had some success. But the Directory was in a stronger position as the news from Italy continued to roll in. Jacobinism was increasingly discredited, and direct measures were being taken against it; many who might earlier have been expected to rally to a moderate royalism were now more inclined to leave things as they were. There was undoubtedly a widespread wish for peace in France. But it needed careful and skilful nourishment, and by midsummer Wickham had not managed to wean the exiled Court from its unyielding pretensions. There was thus little basis for agreement on the future at a time when the Revolution was in a new phase, which would include a second round of elections. That last prospect had been one of the planks on which London was now building its hopes. But the poll was not due until 1797, and the possibility of bringing matters to a point earlier, although not submerged, was beginning to seem rather faint.[3]

The prospects on the continent thus continued to look sombre. And the fruits of maritime war were not for immediate picking. Despite its growing ascendancy, the navy indeed was under growing strain. It was becoming clear that the French would try to avoid a major action in European waters; there had been no such encounter since the previous July, when the Channel fleet had opened the way for the landings at Quiberon, and the Mediterranean fleet forced the enemy back into

1. Eg Grenville to Wickham, 15 April 1796 (*Correspondence of Wickham*, I, 342–3); and see for Wickham op. cit., II, *passim* and P.R.O., F.O. 74/17.

2. See p. 586 above. The Directory decided on this in March, but he was not recalled at once and forestalled dismissal by requesting prolonged leave.

3. Cf. pp. 580, 588–9 above. This paragraph is based largely on Harvey Mitchell, *The Underground War against Revolutionary France*, ch. 7. Much of Wickham's correspondence with Grenville is printed in *Correspondence of Wickham*, I, and *H.M.C., Dropmore*, III.

Toulon though failing to exploit its advantage. The moral superiority in that sea moreover had since risen significantly, for Jervis had arrived on the station, replacing Hood,[1] and was bending the command to his will. The famous band of brothers – Troubridge, Foley, Berry, Hardy, Collingwood, Nelson – was taking shape in 1796 under that eagle eye. Blockade of Toulon became close and continuous, discipline was tightened, supplies and health were improved. But the pressures on the fleet increased greatly when Buonaparte turned south; in June the French were in Leghorn, the main source of supplies and the base for coastal operations. The neutrality of Naples was another blow. And potentially more serious, the entrance to the Mediterranean itself was coming under threat.

For Spain's attitude was increasingly in doubt. There had been rumours from the previous autumn that she would sign an alliance with France; and while this might be restricted to the defensive the terms could still be awkward, and an offensive partnership would raise serious problems. The British tried to reach a settlement of differences on the basis of neutrality; but Ministers were half prepared for the result which came in the end.[2] On 19 August 1796, after much uncertainty, the Spaniards plunged for an offensive alliance; and while they were still not at war with England, naval dispositions had to be made. The fleet, and Corsica, were now sandwiched between a Spain that in effect was hostile and a neutral Italy to which the enemy dictated the terms of access. Jervis was not dismayed. But the danger was clear; and even if it could be accepted, maintenance of strength in the Mediterranean could now seriously affect commitments elsewhere.

For the Channel too might be threatened. There were the Dutch to watch as well as the French – a demand not much lessened for the British by the acquisition of a Russian squadron.[3] More to the point were rumoured developments farther west. There had been intermittent fears of an invasion before, particularly in 1794.[4] They were revived in the summer of 1796, with some reason and with growing force. By August reports were suggesting preparations at Brest aimed possibly at Ireland but possibly at England itself. The climate was not eased by Spain's new move, and even those most confident of naval protection – 'Home', Dundas had pronounced in March, 'will take care of itself'[5] – were now obliged to consider military plans. The army was better placed to do so

1. See p. 463, n5 above.

2. P.R.O., F.O. 72/39–43 *passim*.

3. See p. 590, n2 above. It was later described by a British observer as 'a curious squad'.

4. See pp. 323, 328 above.

5. To Spencer, 24 March 1796 (*Private Papers of . . . Spencer*, I, 240). He stated that he had 'always differed in opinion from those who have thought that everything was to be sacrificed to a strong Channel fleet' and that this applied particularly to the present, as distinct from an 'ordinary', war. France on this occasion could only do 'real injury . . . to this country' through our 'distant possessions'.

than it had been, for it had re-examined the English and southern Irish coastal defences over the past eighteen months.[1] The Channel fleet itself meanwhile followed the familiar policy of the distant blockade, with cruisers watching Brest and other ports while the main line of battle cruised intermittently in the Western Approaches, leaving smaller squadrons to do so in the winter from the anchorage at Spithead. With the growing possibility, should Spain take a final step, of combined hostile forces in the eastern Atlantic, the advantages of greater British strength there loomed large.

If the maritime position in Europe was strategically defensive, could more distant operations raise Allied hopes? Dundas, always attentive to the dangers and possibilities in the East, took care to reinforce the Cape and India against suspected attacks. The policy paid off. A Dutch attempt to reconquer the Cape with a naval squadron was frustrated in August, and at the end of the year a troublesome strongpoint was taken in Madagascar. Recent conquests in the region were consolidated. But further immediate operations were discouraged: when the commander at the Cape suggested that Mauritius and Batavia might be captured, he was told in the autumn not to 'indulge . . . in speculations' from a position in which he could not judge 'the state of the whole Empire'.[2] It was true that a Spanish war might bring fresh gains in the Pacific. But they would take time; meanwhile those already made throughout the Eastern theatre offered useful bargaining points for peace rather than short-term strategic relief.

The emphasis as usual in fact lay in the West. And there the hopes were no longer so high. Ministers, dejected by the repeated delays to Abercromby's expedition, did not expect major results from the West Indies until late in the year. The postponement had a bearing on the prospect for peace negotiations. It also caused a further dispute over the shape of operations themselves. The earlier misfortunes had severely reduced the original plans.[3] In November 1795 Pitt was brought to agree that simultaneous assaults in the Windward Islands and St Domingue were impossible; the first reinforcements, of some 5,000 men, should therefore concentrate on St Lucia and Guadeloupe while the rest would follow to swell the garrisons in St Domingue until the campaigning season allowed of an offensive.[4] But as further mishaps followed opinions continued to fluctuate; and discussions, difficult in any case,

1. See P.R.O., W.O. 30/61–3 *passim*.
2. Dundas to Major General Craig, 20 November 1796 (P.R.O., W.O. 1/325). See also in general W.O. 1/320, 323, 344, 356, 358–9, 6/67. Dundas's fears of enemy efforts in the East are clearly expressed in his letter to Spencer of 24 March 1796 (n1 above). See pp. 562–3 above for the gains.
3. Cf. pp. 566–7, 596–7 above.
4. Pitt to Dundas, 21 November 1795 (S.R.O., Melville Castle Muniments, GD 51/1/675); Dundas to Abercromby, Most Secret, 23 November 1795 (W.O. 1/84).

took place in an uncomfortable atmosphere provoked by earlier clashes between the army and the navy. For in the more spacious circumstances of the summer and autumn the sailors had favoured a principal attack on Guadeloupe, placed centraly to threaten sea operations in both the Leeward and the Windward Islands. The soldiers however always preferred St Domingue as the first target, and Dundas ensured that they had their way in the priorities of an extensive programme. The arguments became the sharper from an accompanying disagreement over command, in which Abercromby and Dundas clashed with Spencer, who in turn ended by clashing with Middleton. The First Lord was again defeated, Middleton then resigned, the naval command itself was disrupted, and the Admiralty Board, already disturbed by Spencer's assertion of a brisker authority than Chatham's, was left resentful and aggrieved.[1] These disgruntlements underlay a debate which however closed in uneasy consensus. For in January 1796 the strategic decision was referred to Cabinet, an event which precipitated a final exchange. Pitt and Dundas now seemed disposed to abandon thoughts of St Lucia and Guadeloupe; measures should be taken to secure 'what we still retain' in the Leeward Islands, and then '(with a view either to war or peace)' to concentrate on an offensive in St Domingue when conditions allowed.[2] Spencer gloomily agreed. He pointed out what he saw as illusions: any lingering idea, based on fallible estimates of the strength of reinforcements, of mounting any other operations, particularly against Guadeloupe; and the expectation of holding most, perhaps any, of our possessions in the 'Islands to the Windward' of St Domingue, which – Windward and Leeward alike – were excessively vulnerable while Guadeloupe remained in enemy hands. Operations in St Domingue moreover might provoke a rupture with Spain, from her possession of the adjoining San Domingo. And while it was true that we had faced the combined navies of France, Spain and Holland before, this was in different circumstances, when we had no large fleet or commitments in the Mediterranean. Such dangers were formidable, and should not be optimistically disguised. Nevertheless St Domingue was incontestably valuable, important in itself and for the security of Jamaica. He was therefore prepared, '(not without great reluctance), to give Preference' to an offensive there.[3]

1. Sanderson, 'English Naval Strategy . . . in the Caribbean', 306–33, gives a good account of these disputes, in which Pitt declined to refer the question of command to the Cabinet (loc. cit., 327). Spencer had started by dismissing two members of the Board within five months, and making Hood haul down his flag (p. 463, n5 above). The *Spencer* and *Barham Papers* (I and II respectively) do much to cover the rows over the naval command. See p. 498 above for Middleton.

2. Pitt to Grenville, 3 January 1796 (*H.M.C., Dropmore*, III, 166).

3. Spencer to ?Dundas, 4 January 1795 [but clearly 1796] (W.O. 1/63). He referred to a Cabinet meeting on the coming Wednesday, which would make the date the 6th. He too (pp. 605n1, 609n3 above) used 'St Domingo' for St Domingue.

This broad agreement settled the matter at least in outline. It still seems however to have left room, at least to Dundas, for flexibility over the months before the main operations began. For despite intermittent doubts Dundas was not wholly reconciled to the need for standing on the defensive meanwhile – or indeed to the figures designed to show that St Lucia and Guadeloupe must be dropped. He therefore left Abercromby to decide. Those two importance targets should not be attempted if they seemed on the spot to demand too much strength. St Domingue of course must be the prime object. But it might be possible at any rate to regain St Vincent and Grenada beforehand as well as making our Leeward Islands more secure. No time, Dundas thought, need be lost in such restricted attacks.[1] And so it proved. Abercromby in fact elected on a compromise. He moved against St Lucia in April, took it towards the end of May, and occupied St Vincent and Grenada in June. The Dutch possession of Demerara and the small adjoining islands had already been occupied 'quietly' in April. And in these months modest reinforcements were put into St Domingue, where minor combined operations were started, though with no effect.

Some successes could therefore be claimed. But the two greatest hopes of the original enterprise, St Domingue and Guadeloupe, remained unfulfilled. The former perhaps would be realised later – though the odds were rising against it, when French reinforcements once more reached the island from Brest[2] – the latter almost certainly not; and in any case neither could affect the state of the war as seen in midsummer. The first half of 1796 was indeed a curious period: so much business abroad to be followed, so little to show from British arms. Of course the time lag of communications has always to be borne in mind. News from the West or East Indies or the Cape could take months – from the last two, many months – to arrive. Even so, compared with the past three years there was something of a vacuum: no British involvement on the continent and little of note farther afield. The navy was active, cruising, convoying, transporting and supporting troops across the oceans, blockading in the North Sea and Mediterranean, engaged in small, often individual, encounters. Its movements and those of merchant ships were reported regularly in the newspapers. But there was no great fleet action, and the work as usual persisted very largely unseen. The public's main interest perforce was fixed on events in Europe, in which we no longer took part directly and which were going from bad to worse. The inner ring of Ministers was fully occupied, trying to preserve the remains of the Alliance, considering a balanced peace package, pursuing a Caribbean strategy, reviewing the home islands' defence. The country

---

1. Dundas to Abercromby, Secret, Most Secret & Separate, and Separate & Confidential, all of 10 January 1796 (W.O. 1/85). And see also same to same, Secret, 3 February 1796 (loc. cit.).

2. And see in general pp. 292–3, 356–7, 563 above.

at large could only watch a deteriorating situation, and one where British efforts and influence were apparently of no avail.

II

Nor was the domestic position reassuring, particularly perhaps to Pitt. The recent fierce unrest had largely died down, under the joint impact of falling wheat prices and the Two Acts.[1] Bread riots were notably fewer, the great outdoor meetings were not repeated, there were no more calls for a Convention, and while the King – this time with the Queen – was assaulted again on 1 February the London crowd was quieter in general than had been feared a few months before.[2] The radical Societies by and large were once more in disarray. If there were a few additions to their numbers – notably in the north-west – the general pattern was one of decline. In the capital, the Friends of the People disappeared finally early in 1796, and the LCS was struggling against severe odds. Adapting its organisation and activities to meet the fact of the new laws, it did its best to whip up attendance in the reshaped divisions and sections, embarked on a monthly journal to be financed by members' subscriptions, and sent delegates into the provinces to rally the faithful and attract fresh support. The efforts largely failed. The journal proved an almost crippling liability, membership sank dramatically, and the two missionaries, whose preparations were known to the Government, were arrested after an interval and legally defended at further heavy cost.[3] Thelwall likewise fared badly in his lecturing campaign. Addressing his discourses now ostensibly to the history of Greece and Rome, he was driven out of London into the more sympathetic atmosphere of East Anglia. But after a successful stay in Norwich he encountered organised disruption – set on foot, it would seem, by naval press gangs – in Yarmouth, and was forced to give up by 'the petty tyranny of provincial persecution'[4] That 'tyranny' indeed proved an effective deterrent in many parts of the country. It reinforced the Societies' own inclinations not to challenge the Acts outright but rather to try to manoeuvre within their limits.

In what appeared to be an endless see-saw between the authorities

---

1. Pp. 455–60, 466, 472 above.

2. And at the close of the session in May the royal coach was actually cheered on its way through St James's Park (*Diary of . . . Joseph Farington*, II, 551–2). Cf. p. 455 above.

3. Their fate was instructive. Arrested without specific charges in Birmingham in March 1796, and bailed by Francis Place a few days later, the costs of their defence were raised by the Society, with difficulty, against trials which took place only in 1799. One of the delegates, John Gale Jones, was then found guilty under the Seditious Meetings Act, but not sentenced; the other, John Binns, who a few months later was defended by Romilly, was acquitted.

4. His own phrase; see Goodwin, op. cit., 405.

and the radical movements, the balance thus seemed to be tilted once more to the former. Nevertheless this was far from meaning that the country was content. Ministers could take comfort from the likelihood that reforming zeal had lost much of its impetus, and that the prospect of immediate revolutionary action was fading again. But they could be under few illusions that they were thought to be doing well. On the contrary, the signs were mounting of a widespread wish for peace. The spirit of discontent in fact may now often have stemmed less from positive radicalism than from an increasingly sullen pessimism about the war; equally there was a growing impatience diffused, no doubt unevenly, among different ranks of the better-affected. Burke estimated that a fifth of the 'political citizens' of Britain were 'pure Jacobins' at this time.[1] He was an unreliable guide; but the question was also how the rest were feeling. The 'Commercial people' were said in May to be 'entirely for peace'; by August 'all' the former 'good friends of government' in the West Riding were 'sadly dissatisfied'; many who would not normally have echoed his comments might now have agreed with Lord Sheffield that they were 'never . . . thoroughly alarmed before'.[2]

Such an atmosphere was serious for Ministers. It affected Pitt particularly, not only because he could be the main target, the incontestable head of the Ministry whose own authority might be at stake, but also because he shared the frustration and impatience of economic uncertainties and growing financial strain. It was this last indeed that disturbed and influenced him most directly; and it underlay the shift in economic fortunes themselves. For the first wartime boom, uneven though it had been, was showing signs of flagging from the summer. If the figures of output by and large held up well for the year in aggregate, overseas trade was coming under pressure, and the reasons stemmed largely from movements of specie and of the exchanges. Support for the Allies lowered British reserves in 1795,[3] even while it boosted exports to Austria into 1796. The French, despite the hardships and confusion which so encouraged Pitt, were gradually resuming cash payments abroad and thus increasing competition. And the course of operations, removing the Low Countries as the European entrepôt of trade and centre of finance, helped produce considerable if temporary dislocation in England. This was the context for the 'Commercial people's' rising disenchantment with the war. Pitt and the authorities

1. The estimate appeared in his *Letters on a Regicide Peace*, written mostly in the summer of 1796.
2. *Diary of Farington*, II, 556; *Life of Wilberforce*, II, 169; Sheffield to Auckland, 26 June 1796 (*A.C.*, III, 349). For Sheffield see I, 148, 207–9.
  The feelings were reflected in the price of 3 per cent Consols, which dropped some $5\frac{1}{2}$ points on monthly average ($69\frac{1}{2}$ to 64) from January to June (see *The Annual Register* for 1796, which indeed in its Preface described 'the spirit of innovation' as 'strong, rampant, and daring').
3. See p. 524 above.

were worried more immediately about the impact of its costs on finance as a whole.

As he emerged from the bruising experience of arranging his loan for the new year,[1] the Minister faced an expenditure assigned to the armed forces which he put at some £1½ million less than for 1795. The reason lay, after allowing for an increase on the navy, in a reduction on the army and ordnance arising from the enforced curtailment of land operations.[2] Other expenses, by way of loan interest, past deficits and current conversions, with the stable costs of civil government, raised the total slightly above that of the preceding budget. But as usual Pitt was under-estimating, and this time he had to present a further bill, in which the army and ordnance accounted for a sum in fact about £1½ million higher than the savings forecast only four months before.[3] The war was continuing to run away with money. Given the policy of restraining taxes, it was therefore necessary to raise a further loan.[4]

In doing so, Pitt could reflect that the market rate of borrowing on Government funding had fallen slightly in recent months.[5] But this was a temporary – almost a momentary – fluctuation in a depressing trend, and the cost of such operations was becoming inescapably higher. The price of the 3 per cent Consols in which the new loan was floated fell steadily through the spring and summer; and its undertakers, the house of Boyd Benfield, which had been allotted the contracts on the past two occasions, still had substantial amounts of the main loan for the year on their hands.[6] The prospect on the markets was uncertain. And the reasons were not far to seek. They lay in the growing difficulties of finding satisfactory credit on a day to day basis, a problem then accentuated by the delays in receipts from subscriptions to the latest loans themselves.

The difficulties had been first experienced in 1795, when the Bank of England became seriously worried by the ratio of liabilities to reserves. Its recalcitrance to Pitt's demands for advances forced him into less desirable expedients which in turn increased the Directors' displeasure. In the last quarter of the year they demanded repayment of £1 million of

---

1. Pp. 524–6 above.

2. Cf. notes in Pitt's hand, 'Possible Reduction in Expenses in 1796 below 1795', in Stanhope Ms S5 09/29.

3. For the budget calculations, presented by Pitt on 7 December 1795 and 18 April 1796, see Cooper, 'British Government Finance 1793–1807', 380–2. See also p. 517 above.

4. Cf. pp. 521–2 above.

5. From 5 per cent in November 1795 to 4.49 per cent on 15 April 1796 (O'Brien, 'Government Revenue, 1793–1815', Table 18, 499).

6. For the price of the Consols see p. 616, n2 above; by August they stood at a mean of 57¾. For Boyd Benfield, p. 525 above, and Cope, 'The History of Boyd, Benfield & Co', 168 for the difficulties in selling the main loan.

advances on Treasury bills, suspended some payments on Navy bills, and continually remonstrated with the Minister. At the end of December they decided to limit the volume of their discounts, by determining the amounts on a weekly basis.[1]

The policy was not strictly new – though the precedents, of 1745 and 1782, were scarcely encouraging –, it was meant to be short-lived, and was applied as flexibly as possible. In practice indeed the rationing proved less in total than unofficial restrictions in 1795.[2] But it was formulated and operated now in circumstances which had graver effects. It introduced greater uncertainty into the rates at which Goverment could borrow on its paper, particularly on its bills, debentures and warrants, now competing more openly with commercial bills. The last too were now subject more openly to restriction as the Bank might decide. The Bank's own issue of notes was reduced – from an average quarterly $£11\frac{1}{2}$ million in 1795 to some $£10\frac{1}{4}$ million and finally just over $£9\frac{1}{2}$ million in 1796.[3] And all this caused a fall in the money supply which encouraged demands for cash, at a time when, thanks to the bankers' past successes in meeting the bulk of commercial liabilities, less bullion was being minted than for the past twenty years.[4] The whole process increased the Bank's unwillingness to meet the Treasury's full demands. In May 1796 the Directors refused to follow their custom of accepting the scrip of the new loan 'at the second payment', as security for advances made on subsequent instalments.[5] And while in July they agreed to advance £1 million on Pitt's urgent request for double that sum, they stressed that 'in so doing they apprehend that they render themselves totally incapable of granting any further assistance to Government during the remainder of this Year & unable even to make the usual advances on Land & Malt for the ensuing Year should these Bills be passed before Xmas'.[6] This was sombre news, when such accommodation was needed for immediate expenditure. Not only was all Government borrowing becoming ever-

1. Clapham, *The Bank of England*, I, 267, 269. See also O'Brien, loc. cit., 116. Some of the Bank's correspondence with Pitt (for which see also P.R.O. 30/8/195, 276), as well as its summaries of meetings with Pitt and his and its oral evidence, was printed in the Report of the Commons' Committee of Secrecy on the Outstanding Demands of the Bank of 1797 (*Reports from Committees of the House of Commons*, XI (1803), 119–92). See also p. 525 above.

2. Clapham, op. cit., 269.

3. Op. cit., 270, and cf. his Appendix A. Pitt was warned in the summer that this could accelerate (Samuel Hoare to Pitt, 11 June 1796; P.R.O. 30/8/145).

4. In 1793 the Mint coined £2,747,400 in gold, and in 1794 £2,558,900; in 1795, £493,400 (and £300 in silver); in 1796, £464,700 (Mitchell and Deane, op. cit., ch. XV, table 1).

5. Loans were payable by the subscribers in instalments as an alternative to full payment which attracted a Treasury discount.

6. To Pitt, 28 July 1796 (P.R.O. 30/8/276). They were later driven to make a further advance of £800,000 from 'a sense of public service'.

For the land and malt taxes see I, 240, 273, and p. 521 above; for their anticipation, Binney, *British Public Finance and Administration 1774–1792*, 127.

more expensive: the great traditional channel of business seemed in danger of drying up.

Pitt had already tried to ease the situation by funding a quantity of 'floating' paper, a process he repeated in November. He did so with the Bank's approval, and with some success.[1] But this was only one factor, and not a preponderant one, in a massive problem; and the loan contractor himself, Walter Boyd, was in deepening trouble. The fall in the prices of Government stock left him holding a substantial loss. In an effort to stem the process he bought more, which he could not afford. His firm was over-extended, and it was not helped by the resentment it had already aroused, not least from the Bank of England.[2] Nor did this diminish as Boyd, true to form, sought to gamble his way through, counting largely on Pitt's continued need and support. He agreed, though with some reluctance in this case, to manage the second loan; and to organise the further monthly advances to Austria.[3] But it was no use: the position was basically untenable unless confidence returned and the price of stock rose. As it was, a discount on the main loan of $4\frac{3}{4}$ per cent in June rose to $8\frac{1}{2}$ per cent in October and 13 per cent in November.[4] By 1797 the firm's liabilities were too great, and it slid slowly into bankruptcy, declared in 1799. In one respect at least Boyd had been partly right in his expectations: Pitt did make an effort, dictated by a sense of obligation and a desire to avoid added instability, to rescue an agent who had served him in a difficult relationship. The effort indeed was a bold one: in fact thoroughly 'improper'.[5] The Minister found some £40,000 in cash from naval funds, an expedient suggested by Dundas as Treasurer of the Navy. In return Charles Long, as Secretary of the Treasury, accepted an equivalent from Boyd in East India Company and Government bills. No one else was told of this dangerous transaction. It remained unknown, and the diversion of funds, to still undisclosed purposes, was revealed only in a Parliamentary report in the year before Pitt died.[6]

But Boyd was not content merely to practise; he was concerned also to preach. If his own greatest danger lay in contraction, so, he maintained,

1. P. 518 above.
2. See pp. 525–6 above.
3. For which see p. 609 above. Nor was he averse to other commitments; he listened not unsympathetically to a Portuguese request for a loan, subject to Pitt's approval, to be made on the security of diamonds lodged in the Bank of England (Boyd to Pitt, 2 January 1796; P.R.O. 30/8/115).

Boyd also chose this summer to go into Parliament at a general election, for his partner Benfield's pocket borough (and seat) of Shaftesbury.

4. Cooper, loc. cit., 109.
5. The word is Clapham's, *Bank of England*, II, 17.
6. The report in fact which led to Dundas's impeachment, to be discussed in vol. III. For the transaction see Cope, loc. cit., 235–7; for the Commons' debate on it of 14 June 1805, *Cobbett's Parliamentary Debates . . .*, V (1805), cols. 385–423. Boyd's letters to Pitt in the last phase are in P.R.O. 30/8/115.

did the country's. The doctrine suited the temperament of 'a man of vast views, who could sketch out a project in a few minutes which should produce' large sums 'without any possible loss'.[1] It was also a serious proposal to counter a set of circumstances which the Bank of England met in quite a different way. The argument indeed, which Boyd put to Pitt in the spring of 1796, is of interest as the first shot in what was later a famous war: the long debate on currency and bullion that Boyd himself opened publicly in 1801[2] and that continued, graced meanwhile by Ricardo and the Commons' bullion committee, into the age of Lord Liverpool and Peel. Restriction of the Bank's notes was bound to cause commercial embarrassments and failures. Adequate means of exchange were essential to an adequate provision of credit, without which trade and industry would swiftly decline. In the crisis of 1793 the Treasury had made a special issue of Exchequer bills and authorised the introduction of a lower denomination of Bank notes.[3] The experiment did the trick then, and while Exchequer bills were not so popular now something comparable was needed to prevent the economy from slowing down. The Bank itself, the cause of the trouble and 'oppressive' to himself, was not available. He therefore proposed a new institution, a Parliamentary board of credit, which would issue notes in the same way, secured on a Government fund of £4–5 million. Arguing on these lines, Boyd succeeded in forming a committee which included some influential men: John Julius Angerstein, who had helped Pitt's arrangements in 1793, and Stephen Lushington, the East India director and MP, in the chair. The proposals were published, attracting much interest, notably in Ministerial newspapers; and early in April the committee discussed the plan with Pitt.[4]

It met with a cool response. Pitt wished to secure any such scheme, if adopted, on Exchequer bills, and he must have been influenced in the days that followed by widespread scepticism in the City. In 1793 he had found much support there; but now, while Angerstein (obviously) and Sinclair approved and there was some enthusiasm, 'monied men' on the whole were doubtful and the Bank of England itself of course was hostile.[5] The Minister's attitude is revealed in a letter from Boyd. 'It is not surprising that you should regard with a suspicious eye every thing that looks like Innovation in the principles and practice of finance,

1. Boyd's description of himself, in a letter to Benfield of autumn 1796 quoted by Samuel Whitbread in the debate on naval finances in 1805 (Clapham, op. cit., II, 17).
2. With his *Letter to the Right Honourable William Pitt on the Influence of the Stoppage of Specie at the Bank of England on the Prices of Provisions and other Commodities*; written in 1800 and published the next year.
3. P. 387 above.
4. On the 5th, according to *The True Briton* of the 7th. Since that newspaper was founded and funded with Government's support the information was probably accurate. This paragraph in general has followed Cope, loc. cit., 173–9.
5. Loc. cit., 180–1. Sinclair (for whose connexion with 1793 see p. 468 above) came up with a supporting scheme of his own; see *The Morning Chronicle* of 11 April 1796.

which have raised this Country to its present eminence, and therefore it is natural that you should be averse to the Measure proposed for the establishment of a Board of Credit'. The financier still held out the double bait of a fund that 'would infallibly, in time, prove the most fertile of all the Sources of Revenue' and also 'form a Barrier against the Oppression of the Bank of England'.[1] But it was in vain. The Bank made it crystal clear that it would fight the scheme. It urged the Minister to adopt the alternative easement he already had in mind, of funding floating debt.[2] And while Pitt, against renewed complaints, gave the new loan to Boyd at this very time, he would have nothing to do with the contractor's idea.[3]

At first sight one might perhaps wonder that he should have turned it down so firmly, after his own action three years before. But in fact Boyd's analysis of the situation was wrong. There was a fundamental difference between the two crises, one stemming from an over-extension of credit leading to a loss of confidence which could be restored by the knowledge that Treasury aid was readily available, the other from a drain of the specie reserves caused by an adverse balance of payments and reflected in a fall in sterling. Boyd's answer in such a circumstance could even have made the position worse. His argument was ingenious, and was to prove attractive as adapted to other conditions; but in this instance he was accusing an accessory of the crime.

The firm's problems compounded those facing the Treasury in the summer and autumn. Commercial interests, though holding up better than expected, were convening meetings and passing resolutions; and by September Ministers themselves were becoming really alarmed. A new note was evident as they viewed a situation they did not understand, and which Pitt for once seemed unable to bring under control.

> . . . I cannot help being persuaded [wrote Dundas], that there is a serious Danger to be apprehended from the Present Scarcity of Money be the cause . . . what it may. It seems the most extraordinary Phenomenon that has ever happened in the monied or commercial concerns of this Country. We have frequently seen casual or temporary interruption to the Progress and Operations of commercial Credit, but it has always been easy to trace it to some pretty obvious Cause *either* of particular Branches of trade too rapidly extended . . ., *or* of an Artificial Circulation prevalent in the Country founded on no solid Basis, . . . but I have never heard it insinuated that these or any similar causes at present exist . . . it is absolutely necessary that you find some Remedy . . .
>
> I shall call upon you tomorrow at one . . . .[4]

1. 14 April 1796 (P.R.O. 30/8/115).
2. Ibid; Cope, loc. cit., 183–5. Its stance was echoed in Opposition newspapers, rallying to one of the great Whig institutions.
3. Cope, loc. cit., 191–4; cf. p. 525 above.
4. To Pitt, 3 September 1796 (P.R.O. 30/8/157).

He cannot have been reassured by what he heard. Pitt had some perception of the causes, but he could not hope to find an immediate remedy. Still unwilling to change the role or basis of taxation, he must have recourse yet again to borrowing; and, as was soon to be shown, he was turning his mind to this. 'Our great apparent Difficulty is Finance, which can only be removed by bringing People to a Temper for very unusual Exertions'.[1] But the temper at the time seemed far from determined for the purpose, and the channel for the exertions had to be worked out.

In the midst of these pressures, abroad and at home, the Ministry decided on a general election. One was not necessary under the Septennial Act until the summer of 1797 at the latest; but as in 1790 Pitt and the Treasury managers opted for an earlier date. As on that occasion too the event was preceded by intermittent rumours: in October 1794 after the coalition, and in September 1795.[2] The timing would seem to have rested finally on some fairly obvious grounds: steady majorities in Parliament, the numbers unaffected by the underlying doubts and criticisms; public acceptance of the Government's declared intention to consider an overture for peace, the rejection of which however meant that the war went on; and an impression of broad support for measures to hold down domestic threats – certainly of a reaction to the threats themselves.[3] Pitt may also have wanted the result behind him in facing an uncertain prospect; one where he might need to probe farther for peace or adjust to fresh strategic problems.[4] Whatever the calculations, they were justified by the event. The Ministry emerged from the election even better than it had hoped.

The Treasury had of course made a series of forecasts, from November 1795 at least. In what may have been the final estimate it reckoned on 346 pro, 67 con, 56 hopeful and 44 doubtful, with the Scottish seats incomplete; and a final survey of the last added a total of 43 to the first and third categories and of 2 to the second and fourth. By taking half the hopefuls as pros, with the other half and all doubtfuls as cons, Rose reached an estimate of 417 to 141. In the event – after the polls closed, and before the petitions against returns were heard – it can be calculated

1. To Chatham, 4 September 1796 (P.R.O. 30/8/101); see Stanhope, II, 381–2.
2. See the Introductory Survey to the forthcoming volumes in *The History of Parliament*.
   The precise date seems to have been decided at the end of April (Portland to Thomas Pelham, 2 May 1796; B.L. Add. Ms 33102). Parliament was dissolved on 20 May.
3. Cf. pp. 441–2, 593, 601, 615 above. The first two factors were shown once more in the months running up to the dissolution, when motions for peace talks by Grey in February and Fox in May were defeated by 189 to 50 and 216 to 42 respectively.
4. This is perhaps suggested by a remark quoted on p. 624 below; and by the course of events that followed shortly.

that 424 Ministerialists faced 95 in Opposition, with 29 independents and 10 doubtful.[1]

Such figures were markedly better than in 1790. This was not surprising. The Portland Whigs were now part of the Ministry, and the rest of Opposition, including some gains of fairly regular support from among the less committed, had settled at a maximum of about 100 over the past two years.[2] As even important divisions showed, this was not a predictable voting strength: as always, that varied with the subject and with habits of attendance.[3] Large Ministerial majorities were thus normally assured; and the election itself was unusually quiet. There were only 66 contests – over a third less than in 1790 – and rioting and licence seem to have been relatively subdued.[4] Altogether Pitt and his colleagues could take comfort from an easy reinstalment. This did not mean that the quietness or the figures signalled enthusiastic support.

Of course election returns were at best an indirect guide to opinion. The system filtered rather than mirrored the public's feelings and views.[5] In so far as it did so here it was probably often by way of negative expression. Those who could vote made no efforts by and large to challenge the subdual of Fox. Such activity would have to be exceptional to make a dent on solid forces. There was little sign that it was going to be seriously tried. The Foxites were at a low ebb. So was active radicalism in the country.[6] The relative lack of violence at the polls may itself have stemmed from a discouraging atmosphere – and a wary respect, as the other side of the coin, of the Two Acts as locally interpreted.[7] The general mood was sombre compared with that of six years before. While the war more often than not touched only lightly on daily life, its shadow was coming closer, and dearth and unrest had been – still were – felt as vivid dangers. Any threat to the Ministry was less likely to come directly from the enfranchised public than from a falling off of support in the Commons. But this last, if it should come, would itself now acknowledge a further loss of confidence, not confined to the House, which did not include a turn to Opposition. The conduct of Government was being anxiously watched. It elicited support in some degree by default. And Pitt's own position, commanding in Cabinet and in the public's linkage of events with himself, was bound to suffer from that recognition and identification. He remained to all appearance

1. See *The History of Parliament* as in p. 622, n2 above; and p. 56 above for a calculation for 1790.
2. Op. cit. for detailed calculations on various divisions.
3. Cf. p. 57 above; and eg p. 622, n3 above.
4. *History of Parliament*, op. cit. Cf. p. 56 above.
5. Cf. I, Ch. VI, section III.
6. Though Burke could presumably have claimed, in his estimate of 'pure Jacobinism', that the political public itself could return a broadly Foxite Opposition amounting to more than a sixth of the House of Commons (see p. 616 above).
7. P. 615 above.

secure. There was no obvious challenger, or replacement. But he was becoming associated increasingly with a stalemate which promised no clear escape.[1] There was a certain air of expectation – not diminished by the recent French intransigence[2] – to see how he would respond. A successful election did nothing to change his awareness of the fact.

III

But in any case the Minister was now anxious to make a further move. For by the end of June he, with most of the Cabinet, was close to despair about the war in Europe. Early in that month the Under Secretary for War reported 'We [in the Ministry] are in a crisis', with 'every gloomy impression . . . greedily received, immediately rebounded with increased force by the nation'.[3] The atmosphere lightened slightly when it was learned that the Emperor meant to go on fighting; and financial advances were accordingly agreed.[4] But no sooner was this done than there were fresh rumours that Vienna had in fact made peace, and while Pitt did not credit them he no longer had any real hope of an effective partnership. The first remittances should be honoured, the rest depending on what we heard of the Austrians' intentions. But the future as he put it to Grenville looked bleak.[5]

> I am . . . clear that (unless there happens some unexpected turn in the state of things) any idea of our enabling Austria to act with any effect beyond the present year is out of the question. In this situation it would be inexcusable not to try any chance that can be tried, honourably and safely, to set on some foot some decent plan of pacification; and I can conceive no objection in the mind of any of our colleagues to see whether the arrangement to which you have pointed can be made acceptable both to Austria and Prussia. But though I think it should be tried, I do not flatter myself with much chance of success. On the whole my notion is that most likely, either now or a few months hence, we shall be left to sustain alone the conflict with France and Holland, probably joined by Spain, and perhaps favored more or less openly by the Northern powers. But with proper exertion we can make our party good against them all. If however there should be any appearance of this situation taking place soon, I believe it will be right to meet Parliament as early as possible. [An] Austrian loan

1. Cf. p. 603 above.
2. Pp. 606–7 above.
3. Huskisson to Dundas, 9 June 1796 (B.L. Add. Ms 38734).
4. Cf. p. 609 above.
5. 23 June 1796 (*H.M.C., Dropmore*, III, 214–15). Two days later Rose echoed the view that the Emperor would make peace; to Pretyman, 25 June 1796 (Pretyman Ms T 108/44).

will, on such a supposition, be out of the question, and strong measures must be immediately taken to procure a large addition of seamen, and of fencible troops for home defence. Such steps cannot be taken too soon, in the event I am supposing, in order to prevent the impression of danger gaining too much ground, before preparation is made to meet it.

There were thus two things to do: to prepare for a war on our own, and simultaneously, with the parties most concerned, for 'some decent plan of pacification'.

One of the parties mentioned was Prussia. For the British had not dropped the idea of luring her back into active operations. The inducement of a powerful influence in Holland had apparently failed.[1] It was replaced by a more extensive, indeed a bold proposal, in the desperate hope of salvaging the war on the continent. 'The arrangement' to which Grenville 'had pointed'[2] was defined in the course of July. Prussia should be offered possession of the Austrian Netherlands, in return for proposing on behalf of the Allies 'reasonable terms of peace' which would include Austria's long-coveted hope of the Bavarian Exchange. If terms were refused, Prussia – on this territorial prospect – should act once more with her former partners. In order to press the plan and ascertain reactions, an Under Secretary at the Foreign Office, George Hammond – formerly Minister in the United States – should be sent at once to Berlin and Vienna.[3]

Why France should accept Prussia instead of Austria on her northeast frontier was far from clear; if indeed she would be prepared to relinquish the Belgic provinces at all.[4] But such a question could be left for the moment. The immediate need was to shore up a campaign, and the Bavarian Exchange might be the surest – perhaps the only – key to an Austro–Prussian *rapprochement*. It might tempt the Prussians themselves, never averse to a piece of territory. And from England's point of view it would at least block independence for a vital area which otherwise would probably become a *de facto* dependency of France.[5] Above all, Ministers could not think of an alternative. They accepted that the state of the finances made a fresh loan impossible: the Bank of England would not stand for it, and neither – unlike the previous year – might the Commons.[6] But without some real, timely inducement the

1. See p. 608 above.
2. Above.
3. Cabinet Minute, 28 July 1796 (*L.C.G. III*, II, no. 1429). For Hammond see pp. 508, 511 above.
4. Cf. p. 607, n1 above.
5. See pp. 596, 598 above.
6. Pp. 617–22 above. George Rose at the Treasury had recently made it very clear that no fresh loan was possible; to Pretyman, 25 June 1796 (p. 624, n5 above).

Emperor was expected to make a unilateral peace. The plan they proposed seemed therefore 'indispensably necessary'.[1]

How much faith Pitt and Grenville placed in the design it is hard to say. Both disclaimed great hopes of success, and they may have meant what they said.[2] They fought for it hard, however, when it was opposed by the King. For George III, unreconciled in principle to what could be precipitate moves for peace, particularly disliked 'language' which could easily 'raise the demands of both Austria and Prussia'. He spoke for the smaller German Powers, whose right and interests England was thus disposing – ignorantly, he made clear by sketching a few of the further implications;[3] but also against assuming a settlement which must bear on British conquests, silent though his Ministers were on this point. His views were not shaken by strenuous letters from Grenville and from Pitt, and it took a meeting with them at Windsor to make him consent to 'the experiment'.[4] Certainly both Ministers put its importance very high: 'almost the only chance of terminating the contest on the Continent without an accession of power to France which must be considered as essentially injurious to this country'; 'measures' which 'the exigency of the present crisis appears to them to press in the most urgent manner'.[5]

So Hammond was despatched. He did not have much success. His instructions were to take the temperature, if possible inform the Prussians of the plan, and ask if they would prefer territory in the Low Countries, as we hoped, rather than in Germany. As soon as they concurred he was to proceed to Vienna with a draft agreement.[6] The Austrians would thus be presented with something approaching a *fait accompli*. But it did not work out like that. Hammond reached Germany on 7 August and three days later had an apparently satisfactory talk with the Duke of Brunswick, at which he was given hopes of the King of Prussia's support. But while the royal reaction indeed seemed not unfriendly that of the Minister, Haugwitz, had 'an Air of carelessness and indifference', so marked in fact that Hammond decided not to make his proposition. The conversations thus remained 'vague and desultory', and he left for home at the beginning of September; the more readily since Eden, the British envoy in Vienna, had written by then that the

1. Minute of 28 July 1796 (p. 625, n3 above).
2. For Pitt a little earlier see p. 624 above; for Grenville slightly later, Grenville to Buckingham, 14 August 1796 (Buckingham, II, 348).
3. To Grenville, 30 July 1796 (*H.M.C., Dropmore*, III, 227–8). Cf. p. 624 above.
4. As Pitt put it to him on 30 July (*L.C.G. III*, II, no. 1430). For the exchange see ibid. and *H.M.C., Dropmore*, III, 228–30. The meeting would seem to have taken place on the 31st.
5. Pitt to George III, 30 July; Grenville to George III, 31 July 1796, as in n4 above.
6. Three documents of Instructions: 'August', and two 'Separate and Most Secret, August' (P.R.O., F.O. 64/41).

Austrians attached no importance to his remaining in Berlin.[1]

At first sight it might have seemed that Hammond had not done all he could. But it would almost certainly have made no difference if he had presented the offer. For two days before he landed the Prussians had in fact signed a secret treaty of neutrality with France, whereby they were to be given the lands of the bishopric of Münster at the peace. The first part of the British plan was thus abortive. And the designed second part merely led to trouble. For the Austrians, informed that Hammond would be coming via Berlin, though not of his instructions, were far from pleased, even without such knowledge, that he was seeing the Prussians before themselves.[2] The news was the more depressing coming as it did at a time of fresh defeat in Italy; for while their reinforcements had lifted the siege of Mantua in July, Buonaparte had struck back at Castiglione and forced them once more into the Alps. The cry for peace was being heard in Vienna more strongly than ever; and it was swollen by a further diminution of British financial support. The Austrians already felt a sense of grievance; they had expected a new loan, and could claim some encouraging hints on the eve of disappointment. The monthly advancements that emerged fell far short of their hopes; and, now, on top of that, one was held up – a consequence of Boyd's growing problems.[3] To Thugut's credit – and it was a tribute to his power at an adverse point – he prevented any overture to France; on the contrary he asked London to co-operate in a fresh appeal which was going to Russia.[4] Meanwhile the Austrians would await the results of their own further operations. They had certainly gained no encouragement from the British initiative.

Nor were they heartened by what followed. For while Hammond was preparing to come home Pitt and Grenville decided to take a further sounding from France. They did not then know of the appeal to Russia; but experience raised few hopes. On 2 September the Foreign Secretary minuted the proposal.[5] The channel, it was hoped, would be the Danes.[6] Their Minister in London would be asked to request his colleague in Paris to seek a passport 'for a person to be sent from hence to open

1. Correspondence of Hammond, Grenville and Elgin [Minister in Berlin], *H.M.C., Dropmore*, III, 230–9; Hammond to Grenville, nos. 1–8, 8 August–6 September 1796; Elgin to Grenville, nos. 72, 76, 1, 3 September 1796 (loc. cit.).

2. Thugut learned of the programme on 13 August. The Russians were similarly informed, but soon after Hammond had arrived in Berlin.

3. See pp. 595, 609, 619, 624 above. One junior Minister at least was explicit that the Austrians had been given grounds in May for thinking that the difficulties in London would soon ease or vanish, and a new Parliament, meeting in July, would be approached for renewed aid on a proper scale (Huskisson to Dundas, draft of 20 June 1796; B.L. Add. Ms 38734). Parliament met in October, and inadequate sums were meanwhile provided with embarrassed circumspection.

4. Duffy, loc. cit., 243.

5. *H.M.C., Dropmore*, III, 239–42.

6. Cf. p. 507 above.

discussions on the subject of peace'. If that was granted, the person would be Francis Jackson, the emissary to Vienna almost a year before and just named as Ambassador to Turkey.[1] His instructions would of course relate largely to procedure – talks about talks, where to be held and with which associated Powers. But some of our opening terms would be disclosed. France should return all her conquests from the Austrians; though, in the only reference to a prime British preoccupation, it might be found that she would 'perhaps absolutely refuse to restore the Netherlands to Austria, and the latter will be more ready to relinquish them than any other of it's possessions before the war, especially if any prospect is offered of indemnification or compensation elsewhere'. She could keep Savoy and Nice, taken from Sardinia, and 'all the conquered countries on the Rhine not belonging to Austria'. Outside Europe, she could have her pre-war possessions, and also her gains from Spain in San Domingo – and 'It would not be too much . . . in the course of the negotiation' to let her take the whole of that Spanish colony. The Dutch for their part might also perhaps be handed back their losses in the Caribbean, and possibly, though not necessarily, those in the East apart from Ceylon, Cochin in India, and the Cape of Good Hope. But whatever happened these last three, as 'the most valuable of her conquests', should be held by Britain – Dundas's views, it would seem, were momentarily visible here.[2] Something should be done for the Stadtholder, whose loss of position was accepted, and this could form part of the bargain to be struck with Holland. Other former allies would have to recognise the principle of *uti possidetis* – what the French had they would hold.

This document had several important features. It differed greatly from the terms outlined in December 1795, and from the plan for Prussia as recently as July.[3] Most significant of all was the vagueness over the settlement of the Austrian Netherlands. Opposition to the Bavarian Exchange seemed to be tacitly dropped; no alternative safeguard was mentioned: only the aim of 'placing the Netherlands in a situation of as little dependence as possible on France'. Doubtless this was something which it was hoped would emerge from the talks. Since Prussia moreover had shown no interest in possession of Holland, and the Stadtholder's

1. See p. 595 above.

2. According to one account, Pitt told him as they rode to the meeting on 1 September which decided on the approach, 'We must keep Ceylon or the Cape'. Dundas replied that they should do both (*Diaries of Sylvester Douglas, Lord Glenbervie*, I, 111).

Cf. Pitt's emphasis at the end of 1795 on Martinique, the Mole in St Domingue, and the Cape of Good Hope as 'most important conquests' – among the 'means which entitle us to enter on any negociation with effect' (speech of 9 December; *P.R.*, XLIII, 668). Only one of these was mentioned now.

3. Pp. 598, 625 above. In his notes probably of January 1796 (p. 604, n1 above) Pitt had ranged more widely; but these had not reached the point of precise consideration, let alone formal communication, and they contained some demands which were dropped or put in question here.

return was no longer sought, the prospects for the Low Countries, that vital British interest and a principal *casus belli*, appeared at this stage to be left in the air. This was something new, whatever intention there may have been to redress it. So, formally, was the abandonment of Savoy, though that and Nice had been ceded in the Franco-Sardinian peace treaty; and of the territories on the Rhine, which earlier were recognised to be primarily Austria's affair. So for that matter was the generous bestowal of a Spanish colony, in part or whole, on a former enemy who, at the time of drafting, seemed quite likely to become Spain's ally. And there was a noticeable change in the form proposed for the negotiation. The British ideas were not sent in advance to Austria, and there was no suggestion of proposing a joint initiative. The talks should open between French and British Ministers on neutral soil if possible or otherwise in Paris, 'where they may also be met by a Minister from the Emperor, if his Imperial Majesty shall think fit'. The document added at once that if France objected to a joint negotiation thereafter 'the interests of Great Britain cannot be so separated from those of the Continent. That no peace can be concluded between Great Britain and France, nor even any progress made . . ., without constant reference to the manner in which it may be proposed to arrange the affairs of the Continent, and particularly the interests of Austria', to which we were 'bound'. The British would argue that the terms – 'Austria would recover all she has lost by the war' – together with this formula protected their ally. But the former (even if the Netherlands were kept) gave her no gains in what was supposed to be a negotiation from reasonable strength, and the latter's wording did not carry precision. A not entirely happy precedent indeed was cited – that of the end of the Seven Years' War, when Britain and France began talks with each other which continued in combination with the Franco-Prussian negotiation.[1] All in all, it could be held, this was not the spirit of past exchanges with Vienna.

The whole tenor of the paper in point of fact reflected something very like panic – a word used by the Austrian Minister in London to convey the atmosphere.[2] Pitt himself was the driving force. He was in touch in August with apparently clandestine approaches from moderates across the Channel, particularly with a certain Nettement, a member of the Convention whom he saw and who claimed that an envoy might succeed.[3] This was what he wanted to hear. Always liable to sudden fluctuations of mood between 'a garrett or a cellar',[4] he had been subject

---

1. *H.M.C., Dropmore*, III, 239–41.

2. Starhemberg to Thugut, 6 September 1796; quoted by Duffy, loc. cit., 245. For less alarmist but confused reactions, from someone closely in touch, see Canning to Lord Granville Leveson-Gower, ? 19 and 27 July, 16 August 1796 (P.R.O. 30/29/8(1)), same to Marchioness of Stafford, 8 September 1796 (P.R.O. 30/8/4(10)).

3. Auckland to Pitt, 30 July 1796 (B.L. Add. Ms 34454); *Cambridge History of British Foreign Policy*, I, 267–8.

4. Dundas's description (I, 110).

to brief intense spells of depression before. He was so again now, 'dispirited', 'very uneven' and 'not in his usual spirits', where some weeks before he had appeared to 'support himself wonderfully amid ... increasing Difficulties'.[1] By the close of July indeed it was evident that Pitt was becoming desperately anxious for talks.[2] And in such a case he could be careless of past policy. Dundas indeed related his own phrase of a garrett or a cellar precisely to this point: 'when aiming at peace, there is no sacrifice which at times he has not been ready to make for the attainment of it'.[3] Until quite recently such temptation had been held in check. Dundas himself, seeing Pitt before going to Scotland in May for the election, did not suspect any weakening of resolve.[4] Nor would Pitt himself have admitted to more than a move designed 'to bring the question of peace or war to a point', as a necessary preliminary, if matters fell thus, to 'very unusual exertions'.[5] This was true as far as it went. But how far would he go for the point to be tested? The eagerness to talk, the slant of the proposals, suggested quite a long way.

Nevertheless he did not stand alone. Grenville composed the Minute and was said to be eager now for peace,[6] and Dundas, earlier critical, did not object. At least two other Ministers, Portland and Loughborough, agreed; and after seeing Pitt the King gave his consent on 4 September.[7] Two days later the Danish envoy was asked to send his message to Paris.[8]

In their discussions over this period, Ministers had also to take account of the prospect of war with Spain; something they had faced for at least several months. By now indeed they were prepared for the worst: the reports from Madrid left them little choice. Early in August the Spaniards had escorted a French squadron into the Atlantic from Cadiz.

---

1. Hawkesbury to Liverpool, 28 August 1796 (B.L. Loan Ms 72, vol. 54); Bathurst to Camden, 3 September [1796] (Camden Ms C 226/1); Rose to Pretyman, 11 July 1796 (Pretyman Ms T108/44, Addington to Camden, 30 July 1796 (Camden Ms C 224/2), and cf. 29 July (C 224/1), Mornington to Camden, 16 August 1796 (Camden Ms C 121/2). For Pitt's health see pp. 461–2 above.

2. Eg Rose to Auckland, 29 July 1796 (B.L. Add. Ms 34454).

3. To Spencer, 17 November 1801; in the sentence preceding the phrase (Feiling, *The Second Tory Party*, 165–6).

4. To Huskisson, 14 June [1796] (B.L. Add. Ms 38734).

5. To Chatham, 4 September 1796 (see p. 622, n1 above).

6. Bathurst to Camden, 3 September [endorsed 1796] (Camden Ms 226/1). He contrasted Grenville's attitude at this point with that of the previous year. But see p. 601 above.

7. George III to Grenville, 4 September 1796 (*H.M.C., Dropmore*, III, 242). In this letter the King referred only to Portland, Loughborough and Pitt of the rest of the Cabinet. This was probably because all three were with him at Weymouth – Pitt having arrived recently – and the first two may have completed or made up the numbers required for a decision. I do not know how many Ministers attended the meeting on the 1st; certainly Dundas was present (see p. 628, n2 above; and p. 609 for his attitude in June).

8. Grenville to Count de Wedel, 6 September 1796 (copy in P.R.O., F.O. 27/48).

A flurry of despatches from London, still conciliatory, had no effect. At the end of the month an embargo was placed on British ships at Corunna. In mid-September Spanish ships were ordered to be held in British ports. By then indeed there was little hope, and after a last spell of procrastination Spain declared war on 5 October.[1]

The event did not depress most of the Cabinet unduly. No one had a high opinion of the Spaniards, and there could be plums overseas for the picking, particularly across the Atlantic if forces could be spared in the Caribbean. Extensive plans were set on foot at once, for both West and East, and for action on the Spanish coast itself. But there was a remaining area which entered into the balance and, of immediate and central concern, aroused fierce if brief debate.

This was the Mediterranean. What should be done about the fleet, and Corsica, when the Strait of Gibralter could be the door of a trap instead of a passage? A decision, soon to be altered, had in fact been taken in advance of war. At the end of August orders were sent to evacuate Corsica, and withdraw the fleet to Gibraltar.[2] The prospect of hostilities with Spain was of course one reason for this; so too in the latter case was the likelihood, as it then seemed, of the French sweeping down to Naples, one of the two close bases for naval maintenance and supplies.[3] Corsica itself, the other, had in any cast lost most of its attraction, as Buonaparte's victories removed much of its strategic significance and increased the island's unrest. It had proved an unruly accession to the British Crown. The veteran Paoli, the great bulwark at first, had had to be removed in the previous autumn, and sent into retirement in England – with eventually a monument in Westminster Abbey. The threat of attack from the mainland, discouraged by a swift naval seizure of Elba, roused some sympathy and sporadic unrest. The Viceroy and the garrison were unperturbed, and the work of government went on. But, as Nelson recognised, in a case of war with Spain, 'we must give up Corsica, that is all'. He addded, with equal truth, 'Our fleets will cover every sea but the Mediterranean'.[4] The Admiralty wished to concentrate its forces where they would not run the risk of confinement in support of an ally who could no longer be reached and might soon give up.

Evacuation would not be simple. The order was received on 25 September, and Jervis would have to assemble transports for a lengthy passage, which could come only from Gibraltar, to which he had himself

---

1. P.R.O., F.O. 72/43–4 *passim*; Pitt to Grenville, 15 September 1796 (*H.M.C., Dropmore*, III, 251). Cf. pp. 560, 566–7, 569n2 above.

2. Cf. p. 611 above. The decisions were taken by 28 August, according to a letter from Dundas to the Board of Admiralty of that date (P.R.O., W.O. 6/147). The orders to Elliot in Corsica (see pp. 346–7 above) and to Jervis in the fleet were sent on the 31st.

3. At least according to Dundas; to Spencer, 31 October 1796 (*Private Papers of . . . Spencer*, I, 333).

4. Quoted in Holland Rose, 'British Rule in Corsica' (*Pitt and Napoleon*), 75.

been ordered to retire.[1] The problems were recognised in the Admiralty, and he was told to stay inside the Mediterranean as long as possible; he accordingly decided – if he had not already done so – to base the ships and troops on Elba pending the withdrawal. This information was sent off in mid-October.[2] At almost the same moment, the Cabinet resolved that the evacuation of Corsica should be 'suspended' and the fleet 'continued' in the inland sea.[3]

The background to this resolution was unexpected. The resolution itself showed the volatility and uncertainty in which Pitt and his closest colleagues were moving. Its immediate origin was a message from Russia. When the Austrians had made their appeal to the Empress,[4] any prospect of success was discounted in London. On experience, there would be fair words and no suggestion of troops. This time, however, there was in fact one difference: Poland had suffered its Third Partition in 1795, the spoils had been finally adjusted since, and the former priority was thus reduced. Ministers' scepticism was proved wrong; at least there were grounds for thinking that it might be, though as recently as August there had been an unhelpful move when the Russian squadron was recalled from the North Sea.[5] But early in October news also arrived, of a different nature, which in point of fact stemmed from much the same time. The Empress – and it was emphasised that it was very much her personal decision – was prepared to send 60,000 men to the Austrians if Britain would subsidise them to the tune of £120,000 a month plus an 'extraordinary' payment of £300,000. The British envoy's immediate reaction was to say that this was far too much. At the same time he was surprised by the offer, and urged its serious consideration. Ministers in London were not backward. A reply was quickly sent. If the Russians would sign a treaty with ourselves and Austria, and Parliament ratified the cost, we would supply the £300,000 plus £100,000 a month for twelve months, conditional on the troops being really 'in motion' and 'actually quit[ting] the Russian Dominions'. Payments could be stopped with two months' notice. The total would thus be £1½ million; but a further £600,000 could be guaranteed by way of a credit to be repaid after the war, since our current remittances to Austria, in our financial difficulties, prevented

---

1. Jervis to Secretary of Admiralty, no. 49, 27 September 1796 (P.R.O., Adm. 1/395). For his command of the fleet see p. 611 above. For the receipt of the order see *Private Papers of Spencer*, 319 n1.

2. Jervis to Secretary of Admiralty, no. 53, 16–18 October 1796 (Adm. 1/395).

3. Minute of Cabinet, 19 October 1796 (*H.M.C., Dropmore*, III, 261).

4. P. 627 above.

5. Whitworth to Grenville, 12/23 August 1796 (P.R.O., F.O. 65/34); Woronzow [Vorontsov] to Grenville, 4/15 August 1796 (B.L. Add. Ms 59044). The move was unwelcome more as a possible reflection of Russian ambivalence than for its impact on British effectiveness. The navy had a very low opinion of the squadron; see p. 611, n3 above.

anything more immediately to Russia. In an accompanying 'most secret' despatch, Whitworth was told that if absolutely necessary the £300,000 would be paid when the treaty was signed without awaiting ratification; that the sum by way of credit could be £800,000 'or even £1,000,000' – an earnest to the Russians to spend more freely meanwhile; and that *in extremis* we would accept 50,000 or even 40,000 men. This was a measure of 'the utmost limit' to which we were ready to go to secure real Russian co-operation.[1]

The inducements however did not end there. Over the next fortnight Ministers thought they could find an extra bait. By the time the Cabinet met on 19 October they had decided to offer Corsica to the Empress. She was known to be interested in the island, as the only base in the Mediterranean available in the sense that it had been French. If British trade was placed on a preferential footing, and we were guaranteed naval supplies and facilities, we would 'obtain the consent of the people' to the transfer.[2] Possibly the idea stemmed from Dundas. At all events it seems to have been easily agreed.[3] In order to carry it into effect, the earlier orders were countermanded.

But the prospects from Russia were not the only good news at this point. The Austrians' fortunes themselves seemed suddenly to change for the better. Late in August the Archduke Charles had defeated the French in eastern Bavaria, and on 3 September, as they fell back down the Main, he repeated his success at Würzburg. The advance continued into October, until the enemy was forced across the Rhine. Meanwhile in Italy Mantua still held out, and the Austrians were preparing for a renewed effort. These events lifted spirits in London, and Pitt's own mood changed. 'Everyone here', came a report from Holwood in mid-September, 'in high spirits', and early in October Canning found 'tricks, frolics and fooleries', quite in the old style.[4] The main cause may have been the end of the rift with his brother;[5] but it was certainly aided by this less private relief. On 6 September Pitt was taking comfort from the report, received that day, of the first Austrian victory. A fortnight later he found the news from Germany 'every Thing that can be wished', and he and the King, while cautious about Italy, were alike looking forward

---

1. Whitworth to Grenville, nos. 35–37, 12/23 August–3 September 1796; Grenville to Whitworth, nos. 18, 20, 7 October 1796 (F.O. 65/34). There are undated notes by Pitt in P.R.O. 30/8/196 which may relate to this occasion.

2. Minute of Cabinet, 19 October 1796 (p. 632, n3 above). See also Grenville to Whitworth, no. 25, Most Secret, 21 October 1796 (F.O. 65/35).

3. George III in fact 'never received a minute of Cabinet that more heartily met with my approbation' (to Grenville, 20 October 1796; *H.M.C., Dropmore*, III, 261–2). Cf. p. 635 below for Dundas on the subject; also *Private Papers of Spencer*, I, 332–3.

4. J.C. Villiers to Camden, 15 September 1796 (Camden Ms C 131/2); Canning to Rev. William Leigh, 4 October 1796 (Canning Mss, Leeds, 52–3, packet 14). See I, 18, 107–8, 589; and cf. pp. 430, 461–2, 629–30 above.

5. See pp. 462–4 above.

to an 'annihilation' of the enemy along the Rhine. In mid-October Dundas found that 'the Circumstances of the moment brighten wonderfully upon us'.[1] It was in this context that the Russian message was received, and plans for the war with Spain were set on foot.

Those plans were extensive. Much, it was thought, might be done in the West Indies. Abercromby had taken advantage of the close campaigning season to sail home, and was being consulted. He was ordered to take Trinidad if possible, and, on the eve of his departure in November, to consider the subsequent capture of Porto Rico. A design was also being worked out for an attack on Buenos Aires, if a naval squadron could be sent quickly. Troop reinforcements could not be large, but small numbers might be spared from Ireland, and perhaps some Hessians, currently stationed in various areas. At the same time there was thought of preparing for operations in the Pacific, against Manila, though these could not take place in the near future.[2] And in Europe, some reinforcements could be sent to Gibraltar, and some form of attack – it was debatable whether purely naval or with shipborne troops – might be mounted quickly against Cadiz.[3] At the same time Ministers looked hard at the feasibility of sending a British force to Portugal, which was asking for aid in case of invasion. They thought at first, reluctantly, that nothing could be done; but after further 'minute Investigation', that perhaps 5,000 'disciplined' men might be spared. So too might some 2,500 hired Germans. The preparations went ahead accordingly, and a commander was chosen in November. He sailed the next month; but by then other problems had made themselves felt, and he was reduced from 'a great auxiliary Force' to 'a few discontented and disunited Frenchmen' drawn from the exiled royalists.[4]

These world-wide movements thrust to the fore the future in the Mediterranean. The Admiralty and Dundas held contrasting views. The former was facing a position not unlike that of the later years of the American War. In place of the Allied fleets of Britain, Spain and Holland, with Russian co-operation, they now confronted an alliance of

1. Pitt to Hester Countess of Chatham, 6 September 1796 (Stanhope, II, 383); same to Auckland, 22 September [1796] (B.L. Add. Ms 46519), and same to George III, 20 September 1796 (*L.C.G. III*, II, no. 1441); George III to Grenville, 22 September 1796 (*H.M.C., Dropmore*, III, 255); Dundas [to Pitt], 19 September [1796] (P.R.O. 30/58/1).

2. Draft of Dundas to Abercromby, nos. 1, 2, Secret, September–October 1796 (P.R.O., W.O. 1/65); same to Spencer, 28 October 1796, Spencer to same, 31 October 1796 (*Private Papers of Spencer*, I, 323, 326); [Huskisson] to Dundas, Private, 30 October, 1 November [1796], Dundas to Huskisson, 3 November [1796] (B.L. Add. Ms 38734); Dundas to Abercromby, 13 November 1796 (W.O. 1/85).

3. Dundas to General O'Hara [in Gibraltar], 8 November 1796 (W.O. 1/288); Grenville to Dundas, 15 November 1796 (*Private Papers of Spencer*, I, 335–7).

4. Lt. General Charles Stuart to Dundas, 20 December 1796 (P.R.O., W.O. 1/217; and see loc. cit. and F.O. 63/23 *passim* for November–December, and also Dundas to Grenville, 8 November 1796 (*H.M.C., Dropmore*, III, 266–7). Cf. p. 369 above for the royalist regiments.

the French, Dutch and Spanish fleets – and the Russian squadron was withdrawn. This was at a point when we wished to launch attacks on Spanish colonies, sustain our operations against the French in the West Indies, watch and if possible harass Cadiz;[1] and guard against invasion at home. For the reports of the summer, centring on Brest, were followed by a stream in the autumn which intensified the attention given to plans of defense. The coastal surveys begun in 1795 formed the basis of a paper from General Dundas, now Quartermaster General; and Cornwallis had already, in August, supplied 'Additional Hints' on invasion.[2] But by then the fears were for Ireland rather than England. In the middle of that month the Admiralty warned the watching squadron off Brest; and it was highly anxious in the early autumn to reinforce its strength in the Channel and Western Approaches. As things stood, it could reckon in October on 36 sail of the line for the Channel fleet, while 21 were in the Mediterranean. Six of the former were supposed to be found immediately for the attacks on the Spanish colonies in the West. And there were thought to be at least 25 French sail of the line in the Atlantic ports – 17 'ready' at Brest – with about 12 Spaniards almost ready in Cadiz and the north-western port of Ferrol. Given all these tasks and responsibilities, including the 'enormous drains' of the distant theatres, 'a decided superiority' over the hostile navies could not be achieved if the Mediterranean fleet was 'cooped up . . . in that sea'.[3]

Under such circumstances, therefore, the Admiralty stressed that the orders of August to that station were only 'suspended'.[4] It assumed that its ships would not remain indefinitely. Dundas disagreed. Like everyone else he was not impressed by the Spaniards' strength on paper.[5] It was pusillanimous to 'begin the war by running out of the Mediterranean', one of the four great naval theatres – with the Channel and the East and West Indies – and the one in and from which we were best placed to harry and divide the new enemy. His arguments were in part rather confused; he saw Corsica, as before, as not 'good for anything', but placed a greater reliance on continued use of Naples than

1. There was also a short-lived design in September–October, known as the Texel Project, for a combined assault on the Helder to damage the Dutch fleet and marine and, by luring troops to the area, give more chance to any possible insurrection in a period when the French, thanks to the Austrian operations, were in no position to reinforce. See P.R.O., W.O. 1/178, and *Private Papers of Spencer*, I, 299–310.
2. W.O. 30/64 (for General Dundas – see p. 490 above), 30/58 (for Cornwallis – see p. 428 above). W.O. 30/63 contains a report on the south of Ireland. For the regional reports begun in 1795 see p. 612 above; for the summer reports, ibid.
3. Board of Admiralty Minute, 11 August 1796 (P.R.O., Adm. 3/117); Spencer to Dundas, 31 October 1796 (*Private Papers of Spencer*, I, 323–9), and see also op. cit., 363–5.
4. P. 631 above.
5. To Spencer, 28 October 1796 (*Private Papers of Spencer*, I, 321–2). And cf. Canning to Granville Leveson-Gower, 28 August 1796 (P.R.O., 30/29/8(1)); Jervis to Spencer, 2 October 1796 (*Private Papers of Spencer*, II, 58); George III to Spencer, 25 October 1796 (op. cit., I, 320).

its peace treaty might bear.[1] While he had some justification for thinking the Admiralty's figures weighted towards the worst of the case, he hardly did justice to the need for a conservative assessment as the basis for a responsible strategy. By the time of the dispute, moreover, the Mediterranean fleet had just been seriously weakened, leaving it in a state of real numerical inferiority. For the commander of a squadron, Admiral Man, detached to Gibraltar for stores, had decided on 9 October to cruise outside the Straits for about a fortnight and then carry on home. Unduly impressed by the strength of an enemy between him and the main fleet – the Toulon force, now assisted by a Spanish squadron – he saw no point in trying to rejoin. Jervis was thus left with two-thirds of his former strength. When the news reached the Admiralty on the 25th, the situation was judged to be grave.[2]

Both parties to the dispute claimed Pitt's agreement.[3] Dundas's uneasiness – indeed his excitement – may well have been due largely to a feeling that, as earlier, he did not quite know where the Minister stood. Although consenting to the opening for peace, he clearly found it unpalatable; his instinct intensified his arguments for standing fast and giving no sign. Obviously subject to his colleagues' reasoning, and not prepared to break ranks, he nevertheless still shared the King's reluctance – as the King took care to suggest.[4] Like others, he may have regretted the move in the light of the Austrian victories.[5] He might also have agreed silently that what followed was 'an humiliating step'.[6] For while operational plans were actively in train, so was an increasingly open pursuit of talks with France.

The Danish envoy in Paris duly passed on his message. The reply was received in London on 23 September. The French would not grant a passport through an intermediary. The British must apply for one direct. This was accordingly done, and the document received early in October. But Jackson – hardly surprisingly – was no longer considered of sufficient weight. Pitt, apparently with some reluctance, was brought to agree, and from the other end of the spectrum Malmesbury was summoned yet again. On 18 October he landed in France.[7]

1. Dundas to Spencer, 28 and 31 October 1796 (op. cit., I, 321–3, 329–33). By the treaty (p. 607 above), The Two Sicilies were not compelled to exclude British ships from Naples, but it would have been rash to count on the former scale of repair, maintenance and supply.

2. Man's movements had been muddled on earlier detachment, and he seems in fact to have been in a depressed state of mind for some time. He was not employed again.

3. Dundas on 28 October, Spencer on the 30th (*Private Papers of Spencer*, I, 321, 327).

4. See the similar tone used by George III to Dundas on 3 July and on 17 November (*L.C.G. III*, II, nos. 1422, 1467).

5. Eg Sheffield to Auckland, 23 September 1796 (*A.C.*, III, 358).

6. George III to Grenville, 23 September 1796 (*H.M.C., Dropmore*, III, 256). See also his letter of the 24th, ibid.

7. Grenville to George III, 23 September, 5 October 1796 (*H.M.C., Dropmore*, III, 255–6); same to same, 5 October 1796 (*L.C.G. III*, II, no. 1449); George III to Grenville, sd (*H.M.C., Dropmore*, III, 258–9); Grenville to George III, 12 October 1796 (*L.C.G. III*, II, no. 1451); *Life of Wilberforce*, II, 170; *Diaries and Correspondence of Malmesbury*, III, 267.

These proceedings, it seemed to the sceptics, showed indecent haste, and argued an excessive importance for the mission. Their misgivings may have had some effect in stiffening the spirit of Malmesbury's instructions. For in two vital respects this was more definite than that of the initial Minute. The negotiation, once under way, was to be conducted 'conjointly' with Austria, and her consent – and this was underlined privately – was 'a *sine qua non*' of any result. Moreover, it was stressed privately again, we were 'bound' by treaty not to make peace 'except' by 'procuring for that Power the restitution of *all* it may have *lost* in the war'.[1] The shift in emphasis stemmed probably from a combination of events. In the first place, the Austrians had reacted angrily to the disclosure of the British intention. In fact they refused to be associated with the approach. It would hearten the enemy at a time when he was being beaten on the German front, would discourage the Italian neutrals, might discourage the Russians, and in any case was a disgraceful step to take without prior consultation. This unwelcome news reached London on 15 October, after a passage of three weeks.[2] It was responsible for the urgent order which Grenville sent to Malmesbury, by then on his way to Dover, to 'take still more care' to safeguard the Austrians' position.[3] But his instructions in any case showed some firmness in their statement of the need for 'conjunction', and they had been composed before the despatch from Vienna was received. It has been held that this was due to Grenville's influence: that he stiffened Pitt. And while there may be hindsight in such a claim, not least from his views on peace the next year, there may be something to it, the more so as Dundas would have been in support.[4] There may also have been an incentive for Pitt himself to shift to some extent. By mid-October his wish could have been father to the thought that 'the tide of success' was 'turned', and that, though the news remained often confusing, we held new negotiating cards.[5] Reports moreover continued to come in of the war-weariness in France itself. It was thus in a context of failure and hope, of diverse opinions and sentiments, and the need, made brutally plain, to take proper account of an angry ally, that Pitt, driven by public feeling and his financial preoccupations, had to hold a mercurial temperament to the balance required.

1. Grenville to Malmesbury, no. 1, 14 October 1796 (P.R.O., F.O. 27/46); same to same, 16 October 1796 (*Diaries and Correspondence of Malmesbury*, III, 265–6).

2. Eden to Grenville, no. 106, 23 September 1796 (F.O. 7/46); Duffy, loc. cit., 249–50.

3. 16 October 1796 (n1 above).

4. Adams, *The Influence of Grenville on Pitt's Foreign Policy*, 47–8. But cf. p. 630, n6 above. A paper had also been received on peace terms from Hawkesbury, now Lord Liverpool, which struck a firmer balance (B.L. Add. Ms 58907; in Grenville's files, but endorsed in Pitt's hand 'Octr 9th 1796').

5. *Life of Wilberforce*, II, 170, for conversation at dinner with Pitt and Rose on 20 September; before further Austrian successes had been gained. Cf. pp. 633–4 above. Canning however, at the Foreign Office and seeing much of Pitt at this time, stressed the 'state of ignorance' of fast-moving events (eg to Granville Leveson–Gower, 7 November 1796; P.R.O. 30/29/8(1)).

When arrangements had been made for the mission to Paris, and plans put in hand for the Spanish war, Pitt turned to the means for 'very unusual' financial 'Exertions'.[1] The loan for the year would soon have to be raised to sustain continuing commitments; particularly if they were to include larger remittances of specie abroad – a prominent cause of the domestic problems.[2] And this seemed not impossible. Austria was still demanding a loan, on a scale comparable with that of 1795, and might anyway extract increased monthly advances; Russia would have to be paid for sending troops into Germany. Such aid would almost certainly be the only hope for the Alliance. But if the Alliance survived it could be, paradoxically, at a cost to Britain which, if not disproportionately high, and lower than two years before, was nevertheless the tip of an iceberg which could bring the ship to a stop.[3] The familiar channels of loan money were in danger of drying up; in any case the market rates of interest were making them dangerously expensive. With a growing tightness of credit and consequential shortage of coin, the system was no longer working properly. It might even break down.

Some alternative must therefore be sought to the normal method of raising a loan. Pitt's answer, returning to a method not tried since the reign of William III, was to go to the public direct.[4] He did so in order to borrow more cheaply than was currently possible through contractors;

1. P. 622 above.

2. See pp. 524, 621 above.

3. Remittances, current and proposed, to Austria and Russia (the latter not including deferred payments – pp. 632–3 above) could amount to some £2¾ million (pp. 609, 632 above) – as against demands for £6–7 million – which would then represent some 11 per cent of expenditure attributed directly to the war in the past year (see p. 516 above). Pitt allowed in his budget, on 7 December 1796, for support amounting to £3 million (*P.R., 3rd ser.*; I (1797), 271–2). Cf. p. 519 above for 1795.

By no means all of these transactions of course were made in bullion; but the total had to be accounted for against bullion reserves (cf. p. 617 above). There had been other particular drains on specie from the Bank of England in 1796; for higher imports from the Baltic, largely naval, than in recent years; for continuing compensation to owners of confiscated neutral vessels; for imports of grain to Britain and also to Ireland, to which coin was sent as it had been in 1795 – all over and above the general needs of trade in a year during most of which there was an adverse balance of payments (see O'Brien, 'Government Revenue', 111–12).

4. He seems to have been thinking on these lines by mid-September (J.C. Villiers – from Holwood – to Camden, 15 September 1796; Camden Ms C 131/2). Shortly afterwards, on the 20th and 27th, he received suggestions from Sinclair, who by his own account had first mentioned the prospect in conversation at the start of the year (P.R.O. 30/8/178; Mitchison, *Agricultural Sir John*, 164). Whether this advice was the origin of the subsequent scheme it seems impossible to say. If it was, Pitt certainly showed no immediate gratitude. Sinclair complained, at the very time it was put into effect, that the Minister was doing nothing to fulfil an earlier 'promise' to find him a seat in Parliament (to Pitt, 3 December 1796; P.R.O. 30/8/178). There was clearly consultation with others when the matter came to the point; eg *Life of Wilberforce*, III, 183–4, A.C., III, 363.

to avoid 'incurring so heavy an annual Charge, and so great an Encrease of Capital as would attend a Loan made in the accustomed Mode at the present Price of the Funds'.[1] There was some debate whether to opt for a forced or a voluntary contribution. The Minister began by favouring the former, perhaps on the argument that market discounts were such that a voluntary loan would probably fail, and that since a call of this kind was 'partly in the nature of a Tax . . . some Compulsion or fear of future Compulsion' could be held 'to be necessary'.[2] Towards the end of November he therefore aired his idea: a forced loan to be levied on incomes above a level to be decided – privately, he thought at a rate of 25 per cent – carrying 5 per cent interest and with the capital repaid within four years.[3] But there would have been disadvantages, and his mind was not made up. Incomes would have to be assessed, and the rate of contribution; measures smacking of arbitrary power, and involving administrative expense. Within a few days, it seems, he decided after all on the voluntary method. On 1 December the details were announced.[4]

The Loyalty Loan, as it was called, was made, as Pitt envisaged, in 5 per cent stock, subscribers receiving £122 10s of stock for a contribution of £100. It was redeemable three years after the redemption or reduction of the existing 5 per cents, with an option of repayment at par not less than two years after the conclusion of a peace treaty, and an alternative of repayment in a 3 per cent stock valued at 75. The target was £18 million – the same sum as had been sought in the main budgets of the past two years.[5] The subscription books were opened on 1 December, and the sum was reached in four days. The Bank of England itself led the way with £1 million, the Directors and officers subscribing a further £½ million as individuals. The East India Company produced

1. Pitt to Governor and Deputy Governor of the Bank of England, 23 November 1796 (copy in P.R.O. 30/8/195).

2. Henry Thornton to Pitt, 18 November 1796 (P.R.O. 30/8/183). Writing, as a banker, at the urging of Wilberforce, who shared his house in Clapham, he was an acquaintance of some standing. Indeed Pitt had designed his library. Coutts too was sceptical of success from a voluntary loan (to Pitt, 28 November 1796; P.R.O. 30/8/126). Sinclair (to Dundas, 15 November 1796; N.L.S. Ms 641) had the impression that the Minister was thinking of compulsion.

3. Pitt to Bank of England, 23 November 1796. The copy in P.R.O. 30/8/195 contains a mention of the 25 per cent; the letter as sent did not (Cooper, loc. cit., 112n6). In a 'List of proposed Acts' in Pitt's hand dated 'Sept' 1796' (P.R.O. 30/8/196), the first is for 'raising a given Sum by a Loan, on all descriptions of Income'. This would account for the comment that it was in the nature of a tax, and in fact Pitt seems earlier to have been contemplating a direct tax on incomes if a loan failed (Lord Carrington [Robert Smith] to Camden, nd but 1796, probably October; Camden Ms C 97).

4. The decision was given in a letter from him to the Bank of England on 30 November. It is printed in *P.R.*, *3rd ser.*, I, 276.

5. Memorandum by Pitt, on a forced or voluntary loan, 30 November 1796 (P.R.O. 30/8/195); Pitt to Bank of England, sd (n4 above). And see Cope, loc. cit., 113–14, 378, 380. The target was mentioned by Rose on 3 December (to Pretyman; Pretyman Ms T.108/44). Cf. pp. 522–3 above for the more normal choice of a 3 per cent stock for loans.

£2 million, leading banks £100,000 each. Trinity House subscribed £100,000, as did the Dukes of Bedford (a noted Foxite) and Bridgwater (the reverse). Pitt's banker Coutts lent £50,000; Bob Smith, created Lord Carrington four months before, £40,000. Cabinet Ministers did what they could. Grenville, Dundas and Pitt each subscribed £10,000; the last two, Grenville expected, 'with still more difficulty in finding it than I shall'.[1] The lists held several thousand names by the day the sum was met.

This was a splendid boost to morale. 'I really do not think,' wrote Rose, 'so extraordinary an Instance of public Spirit, Zeal & Firmness has been given as in the Subscriptions'. 'We now', he added, 'avoid the coercive Plan or at least all offensive Parts of it' – an indication that Pitt would not have shrunk from such a course if required.[2] Pitt himself found the first reception of the appeal 'Comfortable News', the more so as the sums seemed likely to be found largely in the City 'without even giving Time for Subscriptions from the Country'.[3] He could reckon to have made a saving – the Treasury calculated one of almost £50,000 a year despite the higher interest rate – as well as avoiding fresh strain on his seriously embarrassed contractors.[4] Government's immediate purpose had been met, and with a heartening public demonstration. But the result was to prove less satisfactory in the longer term. For if money was to go on being raised in this way the lenders must make a profit; and in the event they made a pronounced loss. The loan scrip at the start sold on the market at a premium of 10s. But it soon sank to a discount of 5 per cent; in three months' time, to one of 9 per cent; and in six months' time to 11–14 per cent. Pitt by then was seriously worried – fortunate for him he had not tried compulsion. He proposed a scheme of compensation whereby the investors would be granted a long annuity worth about £5 for every £100 of their stock. Given the rate of discount on the latter, this would not make up all the deficit; but it would help, at a cost to Government of £60–70,000. The plan however ran into difficulties. It was passed in the Commons by only one vote. There were strong objections to favouring one class of investors over all the others, and as a result the Minister dropped the idea. He must have guessed what the

1. Grenville to Buckingham, 2 December 1796 (Buckingham, II, 351); Cooper, loc. cit., 114–15. Hawkesbury, created Earl of Liverpool six months before, subscribed the same sum. For Bob Smith see I, 107, 579–80.

2. Rose to Pretyman, 3 December 1796 (Pretyman Ms T.108/44); and cf. Grenville to Malmesbury, 10 December 1796 (*H.M.C., Dropmore*, III, 282).

3. To Auckland, 'Friday' [1 December 1796] (B.L. Add. Ms 46519; cf. *A.C.*, III, 364). There may have been some point to this. John Hatsell, the Clerk to the Commons, gathered, almost certainly in mid-November, that a loan would be 'totally impracticable' for some of the country gentlemen, even 'those of pretty large incomes', because they would not wish to lose money by transferring from existing securities, whose sale would have to be at a discount (to John Ley, 'Friday 18th' [attributed to November 1796] (Ley of Trehill Mss, Devon R.O.).

4. Figures based on Rose's (P.R.O. 30/8/302). And see Cooper, loc. cit., 116–17.

consequence would be. The 'example to future occasions' which he had sought was now dimmed; and in fact an open subscription was not tried again.[1] He had gained a breathing space. The loan for 1797, at least as foreseen, was secure. But hopeful though it seemed, the immediate success did nothing to meet problems which were more deep-seated and would have to receive a more radical response.

The 'Instance of public Spirit' owed much to the persisting and now open threat of a landing, whether on the Irish or the English coast.[2] Rumour ebbed and flowed through the autum with French dispositions at the Atlantic ports; the King's Speech to the new Parliament spoke of the enemy's 'intention of attempting a descent';[3] and despite delays and the time of year, an expedition was indeed preparing at Brest. It was destined for Ireland, where plans had been made to act in concert with the United Irishmen, whose leader Wolfe Tone would accompany the force.[4] Ministers however were not sure – the French cover suggested Portugal – and the uncertainty did nothing to stimulate or focus the movements of the Channel fleet. The watch on Brest was in stark contrast to Jervis's earlier watch on Toulon. Beyond the inshore frigates the main cruising squadron stood well out at sea, circumscribed in this instance by a long spell of easterly winds. The reserve lay for the winter at Spithead, some two hundred miles distant; and the Commander-in-Chief, Lord Bridport, was living ashore in Somerset. On 16 December the French fleet was observed leaving harbour, and a frigate sent to warn the watching squadron. But no squadron was found, and six days passed before it received the report. Meanwhile another frigate had brought the news to Falmouth. Bridport prepared to put to sea, which he did at his own pace on Christmas day. By then the French expedition, with 20,000 troops embarked, had entered Bantry Bay.

It did so, however, in a state of confusion. Things had gone badly wrong from the start, and the senior Admiral and the General – Hoche, the victor of Quiberon, who had Tone with him – became separated from the force and from each other. The weather now took a hand, more effectively than the Channel fleet. Gales rising to a hurricane kept the French from landing, and forced them back, scattered and demoralised, to the far shelter of Brest. The attempt which had promised an Irish rising ended in a Parliamentary debate. But it might well have succeeded, for despite the earlier survey there was no proper local

---

1. Pitt's speech of 31 May 1797 (*P.R., 3rd ser.*, II (1797), 667–8. By the end of 1797 the loan stock was selling at 70, compared with existing 5 per cent stock at 86 when the loan was floated.

2. P. 635 above.

3. On 6 October. And this passage was given a debate to itself on the 18th (*P.R., 3rd ser.*, I, 87–121).

4. See p. 220 above.

defence.[1] The Lord Lieutenant was sure that another attack would be made. As he set to work to rouse efforts and opinion, he looked in his turn 'with anxiety' to peace.[2]

The bungled landing was lampooned in London. But it was a shock. The enemy had evaded the cruising squadron; what might have happened if he had been heading for England? For, again despite the earlier surveys, it was clear in the autumn that we had 'no real security' other than the fleet. The comprehensive paper from General Dundas showed what needed doing. 'For God's sake', wrote Spencer to the General's kinsman, 'exert yourself to carry [its] ideas . . . into execution'.[3] Pitt himself meanwhile had been considering various measures: an Act, analogous to the Quota Act of 1795 for the navy, to bring the infantry up to strength, another 'for raising a Supplementary Militia', and one to give emergency powers, under Order in Council, in case of an attempt at invasion.[4] When the new Parliament met, in October, the first two were brought forward. After consulting some peers and MPs Pitt gave notice on the 18th, and four bills were introduced, one for levying quotas of men, 15,000 in all, to be divided between the army and the navy, one for raising a supplementary militia of 60,000 men, and two (one applying to Scotland) for a further 20,000 men to be used as a 'provisional force of cavalry'.[5] After initial objections to the need for compulsion against what could be a hypothetical danger, Opposition allowed the bill for militia augmentation but contested that for the cavalry, which, from the greater mobility allowed to that arm, might be sent to Ireland, a kingdom that should look after itself – and could have done so better under Fitzwilliam.[6] All the measures nevertheless passed quickly, and were put into effect.[7] But as on a

1. See p. 612 above for the survey.

2. Camden to Spencer, nd (*Private Papers of Spencer*, I, 378–9).

3. To Henry Dundas, 15 November (op. cit., 335). See p. 635 above for General Dundas's paper of that month, clearly that to which Spencer was referring.

4. 'List of proposed Acts Septr 1796', in Pitt's hand (P.R.O. 30/8/196). See p. 497 above for the naval Quota Act of 1795.

5. *P.R., 3rd ser.*, I, 89–92, 121; Western, *The English Militia in the Eighteenth Century*, 221. Grenville and Dundas were concerned in plans for the militia (the former from a scheme sent in by Buckingham) at or by the beginning of October (Dundas to Grenville, 2 October 1796; *H.M.C., Dropmore*, III, 257).

The Act for emergency powers was not introduced, doubtless because the others gave largely what was wanted, and such a measure might have roused opposition at a point when unity was required.

6. Fox in the debate of 2 November 1796 (*P.R., 3rd ser.*, I, 214–23); and see op. cit., 92–6, 98–106, 111–16, 118–19. Cf. pp. 401–2 above for the scope allowed to Volunteer cavalry.

Opposition however did succeed in forcing the withdrawal of a separate bill within the scheme for the milita, requiring landowners to furnish one gamekeeper each to produce a force of 7,000 marksmen – a measure described by Sheridan as 'a bill given to Pitt in the form of a bad translation of a German romance' (Western, op. cit., 222 n1).

7. 37 Geo. III, cs. 3–6, amended by cs. 22–4; all passed on 11 November, and the amendments on 30 December.

previous notorious occasion, in 1757, the augmentation of the militia provoked serious riots. Service of this kind was never popular, and hatred of conscription always rife. There were rumours – spread deliberately, Government thought – that men would be sent overseas, fears (justified in the event) that they would be kept under arms for some time, and familiar grievances over pay and the practice of hiring substitutes.[1] Trouble broke out across the country, mainly in November: in the southern Midlands, north Wales, Lancashire, Cumberland, above all in East Anglia. North Lincolnshire and Norfolk saw the worst of the violence, in the course of which Pitt was burned in effigy in Norwich. But it did not last long. Special constables were sworn, the Yeomanry called out, and troops sent to the Eastern Counties. Deputy Lieutenants and magistrates held meetings, the Treasury underwrote the costs of some prosecutions. By the turn of the year things were generally quiet again.[2] But the scale of the demonstrations, predictable perhaps though it should have been, could not but reinforce the feelings, spreading once more, that there was 'a very unpleasant spirit in the common people'.[3]

The growing prospect of an expedition from Brest, and the possible subtraction of Man's squadron – over which confusion reigned for some time – led to a further change of heart on the Mediterranean. The latest order, for the troops to stay in Corsica, had no effect in point of fact, for by the time it reached Jervis, late in October, the evacuation had been carried out.[4] The Viceroy and garrison were in Elba, with Nelson and his squadron; and Jervis himself left for Gibraltar in November to re-store. While he sailed west Ministers decided to return to something like their first intention, given greater exactness by intervening events. The fleet should operate west of the Straits, covering the Portuguese and Atlantic Spanish coasts, and the Tagus was recommended as a base for the time being. The Admiral learned this when he reached the Rock on 1 December. On the 16th he sailed for Lisbon to meet, as he trusted, a reinforcement from home. Meanwhile he sent orders to Nelson to rejoin with the former Corsican garrison after landing reinforcements at Gibraltar, and in January 1797 the latter set sail in his turn. His departure marked the last phase of the British evacuation of the Mediterranean, after a century of continuous naval presence.[5]

The same period saw growing pessimism about the outlook in the

1. Western, op. cit., 223, 299, 301; and cf. pp. 451, 478–9, 488 above.

Pitt had been warned of these objections and of the likely unpopularity of the augmentation, by John Mitford in another of his frank letters while the bills were being introduced (26 October 1796; Stanhope Ms S5 03/5; cf. pp. 429, 536 above), and by Pretyman (sd; loc. cit., C34).

2. Western, op. cit., 290–302.

3. Hatsell to John Ley, attributed 18 November 1796 (p. 640, n3 above).

4. Cf. p. 632 above.

5. See pp. 634, 641 above for the impact of Portugal on strategic thought. Jervis was sent his new instructions on 8 November (*Private Papers of Spencer*, II, 69–71).

Caribbean. For after the hard-won agreement to regard St Domingue as the principal target, operations there bogged down in the summer and were now recognised as having failed.[1] The entry of Spain into the war confirmed the fact; the reverse pressure indeed was such that the result would probably be the 'winding up of our affairs in that Island'.[2] Guadeloupe, the other major prize, had earlier been ruled out. Only the Spanish territories of Trinidad and possibly Porto Rico offered immediate prospects; for if Brazil too might perhaps be attacked, that would take time for an expedition from home.[3] No further reinforcements, naval or military, could be spared for the West Indies themselves. The great design of 1795 was blocked, and in 1797 the French might deploy an advantage based on the shift in the balance of power. While the past year had seen some gains in a theatre which had recently carried the main British hopes, those hopes were thus sadly diminished, whether for war or peace, at the close.

The evacuation of Corsica might have had diplomatic repercussions. The island after all was just being offered to Russia.[4] But an event of far greater import made that question irrelevant. On 16 November, quite unexpectedly, the Empress Catherine died.

It could hardly have happened at a worse moment. The gap between Russian words and deeds, when it suited, was no less wide than that of other Powers, and the Austrians and British were all too well aware of the reluctance to use troops in the West. But there did seem a chance in this crisis that a force would really be sent; the appeal from Vienna had at least evoked the first notable initiative to London since 1793.[5] Now suddenly all was uncertain. The new Emperor Paul was known to hate the Revolution as his mother had done. But there resemblances ended. Morose and capricious, obsessed with military discipline, and now emerging from physical exclusion, he was an unknown and umpromising factor. His predominant instincts were to banish Catherine's shadow and to preserve his army; and, devoted to the Prussian model, his sympathies did not lie with Austria. The result was seen very quickly. By the end of November Whitworth had little hope of aid by land; in mid-December he reported that there would be only naval co-operation; on Christmas day he wrote that the offer of Corsica had been refused, and

1. Pp. 612–14 above.
2. Dundas to Abercromby, Private, 14 November 1796 (P.R.O., W.O. 1/85); and see W.O. 1/65 *passim* for these months.
3. See p. 634 above.
4. P. 633 above.
5. See pp. 627, 632, and cf. pp. 301–2, 550–1, 590–1, 598, 606, 608–9 above.

that Russian policy seemed almost certain to veer from Vienna towards Berlin.[1]

This was indeed effectively the end of the matter. The only consolation for Britain could be said to lie in the relief on prospective remittances abroad. To the Austrians it was a further blow at a point when they were already feeling let down, removing the promise of strength on the Rhine so as to allow reinforcement in Italy. It also robbed them of an argument with which to discourage British efforts for peace. Thugut had placed great hopes on the Russian offer as a disincentive; and even though it failed to stop the talks from opening, its disappearance further weakened his capacity for pressure. His constraints were revealed progressively in the last two months of the year. For the British, if momentarily discomposed, were not going to be deterred by Austrian disapproval. When it became clear that Thugut's reaction was not a mere flash in the pan, Pitt and Grenville settled down to bring pressure in their turn.

Something indeed would have to be done, for Malmesbury was in an awkward position. He had reached Paris on 22 October, a week after leaving London – giving rise to Burke's remark that the journey was slow because 'he went the whole way on his knees'.[2] The next day he opened his talks with the Foreign Minister, Delacroix. It was soon plain that the Directory was going to play on the possibility of a bilateral peace, since the Emperor apparently intended to continue at war. This would obviously raise 'puzzle and embarrassments' which Malmesbury hoped he would not be left to 'unravel'.[3] His messages strengthened the need for an understanding with Vienna, and on 7 November two despatches were completed in London. The first repeated the request, but now as a demand, that an Austrian negotiator be sent to Paris or that Malmesbury be empowered to act on behalf of both Allies. If neither of these things was done, we would conduct the talks to conform with our views of the Emperor's interests; and if Austria still refused to co-operate, 'it might eventually become necessary . . . to go one step further, and conclude peace with France, securing only to [her] the offer at the same time of such terms as the faith of treaties and the King's regard to the general interests of Europe would in such case induce him to require

1. To Grenville, nos. 61, 64, 66, 68, of 1, 13, 25 December 1796 (P.R.O., F.O. 65/35). At the same time however, possibly influenced by his reaction against his mother, the Emperor was thought to be suspending some tariffs on British imports which she was supposed to have been introducing in 1797 (Grenville to Whitworth, no. 36, 30 December 1796; loc. cit.).

2. A '*mot*', Malmesbury himself commented a month later, which 'is too good; I fear it will not be forgotten' (to Canning, [at the Foreign Office; p. 637, n5 above], 27 November 1796; *Diaries and Correspondence of Malmesbury*, III, 323). Nor has it been.

3. Same to same, 27 October 1796 (op. cit., 292); and see same to Grenville, 23, 27 October 1796 (op. cit., 268-83).

from France'. Lack of co-operation moreover could mean no further financial support. The second despatch sought detailed information on Austria's terms, particularly of course on the Austrian Netherlands. If their future was the chief cause of Thugut's holding back, we would not insist on their being retained by Austria herself. But in that case they should pass to Prussia, as the only real guarantee against their passing effectively to France.[1]

This was stern, not to say harsh, language. But distasteful as it was, the British in fact were right in judging that they could bring it to bear. Before the despatches were sent, a messenger reached Vienna direct from Malmesbury asking that he be joined by an Austrian envoy. Thugut's reaction was instructive. He greeted the request, the British Minister commented, 'with more agitation than I ever saw'; but also with the confession that if all French conquests were returned he would have to consent, for England would then have fulfilled her treaty obligations.[2] His agitation rose even higher when the messages from London arrived. He 'expressed the utmost astonishment'; what had happened to the Bavarian Exchange? Apparently the Elector was no longer to be given the Netherlands if Bavaria passed to Austria; he 'asked what we would do with [him] – would we strangle him, or send him to Botany Bay?' In any case, Austria would certainly not agree to any gains for Prussia.[3] Nevertheless Thugut knew in the last resort that he could not dispense with British aid, inadequate as its immediate prospects remained.[4] He was in fact holding out until he saw what became of the current military operations; and as November wore on these were failing his hopes. Italy had been reinforced, and there were fresh plans to relieve Mantua and even drive on beyond the Milanese. On the Rhine front, too, a plan had been prepared to invade Alsace. But the Archduke Charles could not keep up the momentum of the past three months; and Buonaparte's victory at Arcole in mid-November halted the Austrians in their tracks. At the same time the Empress died, the news reaching Vienna on 10 December. By then the British had decided broadly how to proceed in Paris.

It was high time. Malmesbury had been stalling for over a month. His first instructions limited his freedom of manoeuvre while he gauged the atmosphere, which in turn did nothing to lower the caution on the other side. The Directory moreover resorted to the practice which it had earlier adopted with Wickham, of publishing the opening correspon-

1. Grenville to Eden, nos. 52, 53, 7 November 1796 (P.R.O., F.O. 7/47).

2. Eden to Auckland, 16 November [1796] (*A.C.*, III, 361); same to Grenville, no. 128, sd (F.O. 7/47).

3. Same to Auckland, 9 December 1796 (*A.C.*, III, 368). The official despatch, no. 135, 26 November 1796 (F.O. 7/47) is rather less vivid.

4. Duffy, 'War Policy', 263, quoting a letter of 26 November. The latest indications were only of an increase in monthly advances for 1797 from £120,000 to £125,000 (cf. pp. 609, 632–3 above).

dence with a harsh response of its own.[1] A second set of instructions, equally limiting, accordingly centred on matters of form.[2] But in the course of November Malmesbury concluded, though not without strong doubts at times, that Delacroix and his colleagues did not quite dare break off the talks. If nothing else, the negotiation was developing into a public relations exercise, and the French public, as tired of war as any other, would not forgive a frivolous stoppage. His impression encouraged Ministers to allow him greater latitude; and this was made rather more easy since they now had some notion of Austrian ideas. For while Thugut was rejecting participation he felt driven to sketch broad lines of preference: he remained wedded to the Bavarian Exchange, though with a guarantee to protect the Netherlands, and wished to see the Empire restored to its former bounds, and a barrier created against French designs on Italy.[3] That seemed at least something to go on, and on 10 December, after much discussion, Malmesbury was sent his fresh instructions. He was now allowed to negotiate on five main points. The Austrian Netherlands should either be returned to Austria (by preference) or rendered independent of France while Austria received an adequate equivalent. In the latter case they might be joined to Liège and some Dutch territory (Maastricht and part of Flanders) ceded in 1795, forming a barrier which could compensate for French acquisitions in Germany. Secondly, the Empire should if possible regain its former bounds, or at least be restored to its communication with the Netherlands. Thirdly (depending on the extent of Austrian success) the Milanese should be given some former Sardinian territory to the west, or its bounds should be restored and the French evacuate Lombardy. Outside Europe, several options were suggested to avoid French acquisition of San Domingo, a gain which would seriously upset the balance in the Caribbean. Lastly, we intended to keep Ceylon, Cochin and the Cape of Good Hope, with possibly some settlements in the East Indies. Other conquests from the Dutch would be restored if it was agreed that they would not be ceded later to France and France was not given any privileges denied to Britain.[4]

The proposals were stiffer than those of 2 September.[5] The enemy was not to have San Domingo, or retain all his German conquests. It has

---

1. Cf. p. 607 above. The unhelpful tone of the answer was greeted with satisfaction by the King (*H.M.C., Dropmore*, III, 265); but although Pitt thought that the publication of the correspondence might have met with 'some short and spirited notice' from Malmesbury, it was not allowed to disrupt the negotiation (Canning to Malmesbury, 7 [?8] November 1796, *Malmesbury*, III, 298; and see, more strongly, same to Granville Leveson-Gower, sd, P.R.O. 30/29/8(1)).

2. Grenville to Malmesbury, no. 7, 7 November 1796 (P.R.O., F.O. 27/46), partly printed in *Malmesbury*, III, 298–303.

3. Eden to Grenville, no. 128, 16 November 1796 (F.O. 7/47).

4. Grenville to Malmesbury, nos. 11, 12, 11 December 1796 (F.O. 27/46).

5. Cf. pp. 627–9 above.

been held that the terms represented Grenville's influence, and were designed to force an ending of the talks for which the blame could be put on France.[1] Both parts of the claim seem too crude. Grenville was not regularly in London, and missed Cabinet business, in the first half of November, when he had to attend to family affairs arising from the death of a sister. Pitt, already very much involved, took over then even more directly; and he was aided by his protégé Canning at the Foreign Office. The negotiation indeed was not insignificant in intensifying a contact which had been growing closer since the summer. For Canning had then learned to ride, and so could visit his elders near London: Auckland at Beckenham among others, and above all Pitt himself at Holwood. He did so as much as he could, and an intimacy crept – or rushed – into his accounts; by November he was referring (as few dared do) to 'Pitt' *tout court*.[2] Under that shade in fact he prided himself on influencing the spirit, and even marginally the detail, of directions to Malmesbury – who for his part had taken care before leaving to put himself on cordial private terms.[3] Pitt, as was his habit in important cases, wrote to the envoy and sought his views direct.[4] It could therefore be argued that Grenville's return, marking a reassumption of authority, also indicated a significant change of course. Some remarks of Malmesbury's, if truly reported, asserting Pitt's wish for peace and complaining of 'la mauvaise tournure que le lord Grenville a donnée à la négotiation', could give colour to that view. But one cannot tell from the brief quotation whether this was a criticism of the Foreign Secretary's influence or of his competence, and in any case it was spoken (if it really was spoken) in Paris.[5] Other remarks, made on the spot in London, one by a Cabinet Minister, refer by contrast to Pitt's 'great superiority' over Grenville at this time.[6] The Minister agreed to terms less abject than those at the low point early in September. Intervening events, and reflection on others' opinions, would have seen to that. He and the Foreign Office late in November expected little of the negotiation. But this was after some gloomy despatches from Malmesbury, which were followed by his forecast that the Directory would not break off. That estimate appeared to be greeted with pleasure; and a disapproving

1. This is the view of E.D. Adams, in *The Influence of Grenville on Pitt's Foreign Policy*, 49–50, and of Holland Rose, in *The Cambridge History of British Foreign Policy*, I, 272.

2. Eg to Granville Leveson-Gower, 8 November 1796 (P.R.O. 30/29/8(1)). Cf. I, 132.

3. Eg same to same, 7, 8 November 1796 (loc. cit.); Malmesbury to Canning, 27 October 1796 (*Malmesbury*, III, 291–3). And see Canning Mss, Leeds, packet 63.

4. *Malmesbury* III, 295–6; and see return letters, op. cit., 305–7, *H.M.C., Dropmore*, III, 278–9. Cf. I, 324–5.

5. The remarks occur in a despatch from the Prussian Minister in Paris to his Government of 20 December, reporting a conversation on that day with Malmesbury (quoted Adams, op. cit., 49–50). But see *H.M.C., Dropmore*, III, 282 for earlier strong doubts of his reliability.

6. *The Diary of . . . Windham*, 347, for 29 November; and cf. Vorontsov [Russian Minister in London] to Count Razumovski, 9 December 1796 (cited Duffy, loc. cit., 510).

colleague certainly thought that the new instructions were meant to forward, not to end, the talks. Windham, who had not dropped his long-standing disapproval of overtures, stayed away from the meeting on that account.[1] Nor were Ministers in a good position to go too far; they had to bear in mind a popular wish for peace which should not be flouted too easily.[2] The terms, in the circumstances, could be taken as reasonable. They could appear as such if they were summarily rejected; but there is no real ground for thinking that rejection was the aim.

The circumstances themselves, however, were about to change; were changing indeed even as the despatches were sent. The position in Italy was only now becoming clear, and the news of the Empress's death reached Paris on 14 December. On the 17th Malmesbury presented his new message. It was civilly received, and the Directory may still have felt some hesitation. That same day an order was sent to delay the expedition at Brest. But by the time it reached the port the ships had sailed for Ireland, and by then the Russian development moreover had been assessed.[3] On the 18th the British proposals were rejected as an 'ultimatum', and the next day Malmesbury was told to leave Paris within forty-eight hours. On the 20th he set out, hoping that 'we have died well; certain I am that I quit *this* world without regret'.[4]

The Government could proclaim that, in the event, it was the enemy who had stopped the talks. England, it could be asserted to Europe, had done her duty by Austria; the refusal, it could be hoped, would lead to 'discontent and demur' in France; the attempt, unsuccessful as it was, by proving our desire for a reasonable peace should 'contribute . . . to a cheerful and vigorous support of the war'. 'If the treaty was to fail', Pitt concluded, 'I think it could not do so on better grounds for us'.[5]

1. *Diary*, 348 for 10 December; this seems to be the clear meaning. Cf. pp. 600 above for his feelings in 1795. Grenville to Malmesbury, sd (*H.M.C., Dropmore*, III, 282–3), while firm and ultimately sceptical, does not appear to me suggestive of an intention to force a break.

2. One of the law officers indeed went so far as to say after Malmesbury was sent to Paris that '*all* people wish for peace' apart from 'Mr. Burke & a few others', though few expected it (Edward Law – the future Lord Ellenborough, then Attorney General of the County Palatine of Lancaster – to Bishop of Elphin, 29 October 1796 (P.R.O. 30/12/17(2)).

3. See p. 641 above for the sailing of the expedition: the order of posponement may have been actuated by exaggerated reports of British strength in the Western Approaches. Malmesbury was convinced, from what he could learn, that the death of the Empress had 'very much influenced' the French (to Grenville, 20 December 1796; *H.M.C., Dropmore*, III, 287).

4. Ibid. A minor reason for the Directory to be glad to see the back of him would have been the (correct) suspicion that he was in touch with British agents in Paris (see Grenville's no. 9 of 7 November 1796; F.O. 27/46) and of course also sending back impressions of what he saw.

5. Pitt to Auckland, 24 December 1796 (*A.C.*, III, 370). The other quotations are from the earlier predictions of Grenville to George III, 30 January 1796 (*H.M.C., Dropmore*, III, 169) and Pitt to same, sd (Stanhope, II, Appendix, xxxi: cf. p. 605 above).

The Government published a Manifesto on 27 December (see, *inter alia*, John Gifford's *Life of . . . Pitt*, III (1809), Appendix A).

Nevertheless it was a very bad moment. If the Loyalty Loan was a marked success the loan system itself was in deep trouble, the drain on the reserves continued, and there was a marked shortage of coin. Austria seemed prepared to fight on, after the uncertainty of the summer; but the resolve turned on operations which were faltering yet again. Little if anything could be expected from Russia. We had quitted the Mediterranean. The plans for the Caribbean, now our main theatre, had proved too ambitious, and the balance was changing with Spain's entry into the war. There was undoubtedly war wearines in France; but her finances had improved, discontent lacked effective focus, and the Directory was strengthened by Buonaparte's victories. And if the threat of invasion and the failure of the talks rallied feeling at home, this overlaid a dissatisfaction the causes of which were not removed. Another year of war was now in prospect, and there could be no clear idea how to win. The view was discouraging in whichever direction one looked.

It was the more deeply so to Pitt because it seemed to confirm a fact borne in on him increasingly over the past year. The struggle, to all appearances, could continue indefinitely. From 1793 until well into 1795 he had looked to a foreseeable end: confidently for some eighteen months and then with rising anxiety. But when success eluded him, by force of arms and from risings in France, he suffered a season in which the British effort was marginal to the main campaign. And at its close the Alliance seemed hardly more likely to endure than it had in the summer; we would probably have to fight on alone, relying on maritime pressures which, substantial as they might prove, were unlikely to bring swift results.[1] To look back was a melancholy task. In 1793 it had been France that stood alone, against a Coalition which swelled to eight nations. By the end of 1796 Holland and Spain had changed sides, Prussia, Sardinia and The Two Sicilies had withdrawn,[2] and of the three survivors of the original Alliance one, Russia, scarcely counted. Nor was the tale for Britain itself reassuring. Trouble had still been avoided in Ireland, Scotland was subdued again, and unrest in England (and Wales) less strident than in 1795. But discontent remained, and the spirit in the higher orders was defensive. The changes were depressing; and they challenged the basis of Pitt's own career. He had been forced out of the image of reform, albeit earlier reduced,[3] into one of repression. He was being forced into questioning the adequacy of his financial methods. He was now forced to recognise that he could see no timely issue to the war. It was a climax to a long transition, marked brutally by Malmesbury's return. And in the next few months there would be worse to come.

1. Cf. his remarks on pp. 624–5 above. The improvement in the French finances, moreover, and the military disappointments in the West Indies had now removed much of his earlier confidence of effective economic pressure from that quarter (see pp. 351, 356 above).

2. As had Hanover (see p. 591 above), bound to Britain by ties other than those of alliance.

3. See Ch. III above.

Notes on Sources

CHAPTER I

The published accounts of the Ochakov affair in its European setting can be followed by countries in J.S. Bromley and A. Goodwin's *Select List of Works on Europe and Europe Overseas, 1715–1815* (1956). The best is Dietrich Gerhard's *England und der Aufstieg Russlands* . . . (1933) which may be supplemented by Robert Howard Lord, *The Second Partition of Poland: A study in Diplomatic History* (1916), Felix Salomon, *William Pitt der Jüngere*, I, (1906), and David Bayne Horn, *Great Britain and Europe in the Eighteenth Century* (1967). An interesting article by Jerzy Łojek in the journal *East Central Europe*, II, no. 1 (Pittsburgh, 1975), looks at the crisis from the Polish point of view. Paul L.C. Webb, 'Sea Power in the Ochakov Affair' (*The International History Review*, II, no. 1), concentrates on that aspect. Of the three principal biographies of Pitt (Tomline, Stanhope, Holland Rose), the last, in chs. XXVI, XXVII, of *William Pitt and National Revival* (1911), contains the most ample and thoughtful discussion. It should be read with M.S. Anderson's *Britain's Discovery of Russia, 1553–1815* (1958), ch. VI. John Ehrman, 'Pitt the Younger and the Ochakov Affair' (*History Today*, IX, no. 7) rehearses some of the ground covered in this Chapter. The lists of *British Diplomatic Representatives, 1689–1789*, ed. David Bayne Horn (1932) and *1789–1852*, ed. S.T. Bindoff, Elizabeth F. Malcolm Smith and C.K. Webster (1934), are useful.

The most valuable published collections of contemporary material on British policy are *The Political Memoranda of Francis Fifth Duke of Leeds* . . ., ed. Oscar Browning (1884), *H.M.C., Dropmore*, II, and *A.C.*, II (see Abbreviations). Alison Gilbert Olson, *The Radical Duke* (1961) includes some of Richmond's protests, and *Memoirs and Correspondence of Sir Murray Robert Keith* . . ., ed. Mrs Gillespie Smyth, II (1849) is of marginal interest. *The Annual Register* for 1791 and 1792, the files of *The Times* and other London newspapers in the Burney Collection in the British Library, and M.D. George, *Catalogue of Prints and Drawings in the British Museum: Division I, Political and Personal Satires*, VI (1938), should be consulted for public reactions and their manipulation. *P.R.*, XXIX–XXXI, XXXIII (1791–2), *The Senator: or Clarendon's Chronicle*, II–IV (nd) – a sometimes fuller record – and *P.H.*, XXIX (1817) need to be compared for the debates. Burke's accusation of Robert Adair is contained in *Observations on the Conduct of the Minority, Particularly in The Last Session of Parliament, Addressed to the Duke of Portland and Lord Fitzwilliam, 1793* (1797), which may be found in *The Works and Correspondence of the Right Honourable Edmund Burke* . . ., ed. Earl Fitzwilliam and Sir Richard Bourke, V (1852). *Two letters from Mr. Adair to the Bishop of Winchester, In Answer to the Charge of a High Treasonable Misdemeanour* . . . (1821), and *Memorials and Correspondence of Charles James Fox*, ed. Lord John Russell, II (1853), cover the exchanges between Adair and Tomline in 1821.

Much, however, is left untouched by the printed sources, and the full story can be followed only from ms material. The relevant Foreign Office files are P.R.O., F.O. 7/23–5 for Austria, 22/13, 97/116 for Denmark, 37/33 for Holland, 62/3–4 for Poland, 64/19–21, 97/323–4 for Prussia, 65/19–20, 95/8 for Russia, 72/21 for Spain, 73/11–12, 97/399 for Sweden. F.O. 78/12B contains a small selection of printed documents concerning Ochakov. It is not worth consulting F.O. 78/12A (Turkey), or F.O. 95/1,6,8 (for several of the states above). F.O. 353/64, 66, 68, 88, in the collection of F.J. Jackson's papers, include interesting private correspondence between some of the British envoys involved; so do B.L. Add. Ms 46822 (Francis Drake's papers), and NLS (see Abbreviations) Ms 556 (Robert Liston's papers).

A good deal of material is scattered among Pitt's files, the most important of which are P.R.O. 30/8/102 (copies of out-letters, for Ewart), 110 (from Auckland), 132 (from Elgin), 133 (from Ewart, very important), 248, 258 (a few naval papers), 337 (containing part of the material on Adair's mission), 338 (Prussia). There are 11 pages of Pitt's notes defending his final decision, undated but endorsed 1791, in P.R.O. 30/8/195. A few copies of his letters to Ewart in the later part of 1791 are in P.R.O. 30/58/1 (the Dacres Adams Mss). Ewart's own papers, in the Ewart Mss belonging to Sir Hector Monro at Kirtlebridge, Dumfriesshire, are of great value.

So too are the Burges Mss in the Bodleian Library, which include private letters from and to British envoys. Mss 9, 34–7, 45, 47, 49, 51, 58, 61–2, 74, 84, 95 are of interest, with 47, 51, 62, 95 bearing particularly closely on Adair's mission. Of the other principal actors, Leeds's papers in B.L. Add. Ms 28066 are useful, and there is some background material in B.L. Add. Ms 28065 and Egerton Mss 3502, 3504. Sir Robert Keith's papers in B.L. Add. Mss 35543–4 include some letters from Foreign Office personalities as well as, more fully, from Auckland. Auckland's own files, as one might expect, are voluminous and highly interesting; B.L. Add. Mss 34432–9 hold the plentiful material which is not to be found in *A.C.*, II. Grenville's papers in the British Library contain little here that is not in *H.M.C., Dropmore*. There is one interesting letter from Pitt to Stafford, on 28 March 1791, in the latter's papers, P.R.O. 30/29/384.

The naval preparations may be followed in P.R.O. Adm. 3/107–8, 106/3037. Chatham's papers as First Lord include one letter on the subject from George III (P.R.O. 30/8/364).

CHAPTER II

British foreign policy in relation to France from 1789 to early in 1792 is well summed up in *The Cambridge History of British Foreign Policy 1783–1919*, I, ed. Sir A.W. Ward and G.P. Gooch (1922). See also Horn, *Great Britain and Europe in the Eighteenth Century* (Note on Sources to Ch. I), Holland Rose, *William Pitt and National Revival* (Ch. I), and J.H. Clapham, *The Causes of the War of 1792* (1899). Pitt's attitude is discussed in J.T. Stoker, *William Pitt et la Révolution Française* (1935), and in E.D. Adams, *The Influence of William Grenville on Pitt's Foreign Policy, 1787–98* (1904); and Alfred Cobban's 'British Secret Service in France, 1784–1792' (*E.H.R.*, LXIX, no. 271) – reprinted as ch. 10 in his *Aspects of the French Revolution* (1968) – throws light on the Government's activities and French impressions of them. Primary material in published sources includes

H.M.C., Dropmore, I, II; *The Correspondence of Edmund Burke*, VI, ed. Alfred Cobban and Robert A. Smith (1967); *A.C.*, II (Abbreviations); the two collections of *Despatches from Paris 1784–1790*, II, ed. Oscar Browning (1910), and *The Despatches of Earl Gower . . .*, ed. Oscar Browning (1885); and *The Correspondence of William Augustus Miles on the French Revolution 1789–1817*, ed. the Rev. Charles Popham Miles, I (1890). Mile's role, and that of Hugh Elliot, in 1790, is examined by H.V. Evans in 'William Pitt, William Miles and the French Revolution' (*Bulletin of the Institute of Historical Research*, XLIII, no. 108). Pitt's correspondence with them and with the King is in P.R.O. 30/8/159 (for Miles), P.R.O. 30/8/102, 132 (for Elliot) – and see also Tomline (Abbreviations), III, 131–5, and *L.C.G. III*, I (see Abbreviations) and *H.M.C., Twelfth Report, Appendix, Pt IX* (for the King). Talleyrand's reports during his first mission to London in 1792 are in G. Pallain's edition (1889) of the volume of that title in *Correspondence de Talleyrand*. One of the émigré Princes' early communications is printed by Holland Rose in 'The Comte d'Artois and Pitt in December 1789' (*E.H.R.*, XXX, no. 118).

There are collections of Pitt's papers on French affairs in P.R.O. 30/8/333–4. The copies of his out-letters in P.R.O. 30/8/102, the letters to his mother in P.R.O. 30/8/12, and his correspondence with Auckland, Gower, and Grenville – the last for one letter in 1788 – in P.R.O. 30/8/110, 139, 140 respectively, contain items of interest. For his attitude to the export of flour to France in 1789 see P.R.O. 30/8/163 (for Luzerne) and P.R.O., B.T. 5/5, 6/130. P.R.O. 30/8/196 contains his notes on the reductions in the armed forces early in 1792.

P.R.O., F.O. 27/32–8, 95/99 and 100, include the despatches from the Foreign Secretary to Paris omitted in Browning's full collection of the reverse side of the correspondence (see above). They also contain some material on de la Bintinnaye's mission to England in 1791, more of which may be found in F.O. 95/3 and Burke's *Correspondence* (see above). F.O. 95/2 has an interesting intercept of a French view on Pitt's attitude in May 1789.

Leeds's papers in B.L. Add. Mss 28064–6 include some relevant correspondence with British diplomats, particularly Dorset and Fitzherbert; but there is little in Grenville's unpublished papers at the B.L. to supplement *H.M.C., Dropmore* here. Calonne's dealings with Pitt may be followed in P.R.O. 30/8/119 and 134, P.R.O., P.C. 1/125–7, 130, and – more doubtfully as to period – F.O. 95/620, 632.

A large amount of paper exists on the affairs of the Austrian Netherlands in 1790 – not least perhaps because Auckland was involved –, in his own papers in B.L. Add. Mss 34434–6, 34519, and in P.R.O. 37/32–8. There is nothing, however, in Pitt's collections in P.R.O. 30/8/336, 339.

CHAPTER III

The state of parties and the general election of 1790 are examined in the Introductory Survey to the forthcoming volumes in *The History of Parliament* for 1790 to 1818, ed. Roland Thorne. Other studies, bearing on the subject from Opposition's point of view, are Donald E. Ginter's *Whig Organization in the General Election of 1790, Selections from the Blair Adam Papers* (1967), F. O'Gorman's *The Whig Party and the French Revolution* (1967), L.G. Mitchell's *Charles James Fox and the Disintegration of the Whig Party 1782–1794* (1971).

William Combe's anonymous *Considerations on the Approaching Dissolution of Parliament*... (1790) and Joseph Towers, *Thoughts on the Commencement of a New Parliament* (1790) are interesting examples of pamphleteering opinion; Henry Mackenzie's *A Reveiw of the Principal Proceedings of the Parlimanet of 1784* (nd), his (anonymous) *The Letters of Brutus to Certain Celebrated Political Characters* (1791) and *Additional Letters of Brutus* (nd, but 1793), gain in significance from the author's connexion with Pitt. Pitt's own correspondence contains scattered references to the election, of no great importance; the files on election matters in P.R.O. 30/8/234 and 314 are disappointing.

Much has been written on the state of the Anglican Church and of Nonconformity in this period. Charles J. Abbey and John H. Overton, *The English Church in the Eighteenth Century*, 2 vols. (1878) and Abbey's *The English Church and Its Bishops 1700–1800*, I (1887) are major accounts in the older tradition. Greater depth, however, is provided by the Rev. Norman Sykes's seminal *Church and State in England in the XVIIIth Century* (1934), G.F.A. Best's *Temporal Pillars, Queen Anne's Bounty, the Ecclesiastical Commissioners, and the Church of England* (1964), and Charles Smyth's *Simeon & Church Order, A Study of the Origins of the Evangelical Revival in Cambridge in the Eighteenth Century* (1940). R.A. Soloway has discussed *Prelates and People, Ecclesiastical Social Thought in England 1783–1852* (1969) and E.R. Norman, *Church and Society 1770–1970* (1976) is interesting. Ursula Henriques, *Religious Toleration in England 1787–1833* (1961) is a valuable survey from within and outside the Establishment. For Dissent, Herbert S. Skeats, *A History of the Free Churches of England, from A.D. 1688–A.D. 1851* (1868) is an equivalent to Abbey; Michael R. Watts, *The Dissenters*, I (1970) gives the background to the 1790s. Among other studies of which the sects form a central or major element may be mentioned B.L. Manning, *The Protestant Dissenting Deputies* (1952), Anthony Lincoln, *Some Political and Social Ideas of English Dissent 1763–1800* (1938), E.D. Bebb, *Nonconformity and Social Life 1660–1800* (1935), Alan D. Gilbert, *Religion and Society in Industrial England . . . 1740–1914* (1976), R.B. Barlow, *Citizenship and Conscience* (1962), Gerald R. Cragg, *Reason and Authority in the Eighteenth Century* (1964), Caroline Robbins, *The Eighteenth-Century Commonwealthman* (1959). Richard W. Davis, *Dissent in Politics 1780–1830* (1971) illustrates its theme by reference to the career of the MP William Smith; James E. Bradley, 'Whigs and Nonconformists: "Slumbering Radicalism" in English Politics, 1739–1789' (*Eighteenth-Century Studies*, 9, No. 1), provides criticism of some these views of the political content. *A History of the Methodist Church in Great Britain*, I, ed. Rupert Davies and Gordon Rupp (1965), particularly chs. I, VI and IX, treats of the Anglican body which became a Dissenting sect.

A large contemporary literature exists on the efforts to repeal the Corporation and Test Acts, to which there are good guides in some of the works cited above and in William Thomas Laprade, 'England and the French Revolution 1789–1797', in *Johns Hopkins University Studies in Historical and Political Science, Series XXVII*, nos. 8–12 (1909). Price and Priestly were, as usual, to the fore. William Belsham, *Memoirs of the Reign of George III. To the Session of Parliament Ending A.D. 1793*, IV (1795), and his *Essays Philosophical and Moral, Historical and Literary*, II (1799), contain interesting comments from a good historian of the moderate Dissenting school. William Paley's *The Principles of Moral and Political Philosophy* (1785) is important not only in its own right, but also for Pitt's admiration of the author. Pitt's own attitude emerges more clearly from the

Parliamentary debates – covered in *P.R.*, XXI (1787), XXVI (1789), XXVII (1790), Stockdale (see Abbreviations), II–IV and unnumbered, *P.H.*, XXVI, XXVIII (1816) – than from his correspondence in the P.R.O. 30/8 series. Robert Isaac Wilberforce and Samuel Wilberforce, *The Life of William Wilberforce*, I (1839), and the same authors' edition of *The Correspondence of William Wilberforce*, I (1840), show the doubts and hesitations of a close friend. A volume of 'Minutes of the Meetings of the Committee Appointed to Conduct the Application to Parliament for the Repeal of the Corporation and Test Acts, 1787–90', in the Guildhall Library, City of London, Ms 3804/1, records the Minister's reception of a deputation in 1787. Archbishop Moore's Mss in Lambeth Palace Library, No. 17, contains copies of the Minutes of the Bishops' meeting in February 1787, and Moore's subsequent letter to Pitt. An analysis of the Parliamentary campaign itself, and the effects on the general election in 1790, is to be found in G.M. Ditchfield, 'The parliamentary struggle over the repeal of the Test and Corporation Acts, 1787–1790' (*E.H.R.*, LXXXIX, no. 352).

The classic accounts of the stirrings of reforming interest after 1788 are Philip Anthony Brown, *The French Revolution in English History* (1918), Henry Meikle, *The French Revolution and Scotland* (1912), and above all George Stead Veitch, *The Genesis of Parliamentary Reform* (2nd edn., 1965). Laprade (see above) is also helpful, and there is much material on rather the same lines in S. Maccoby, *English Radicalism 1786–1832, From Paine to Cobbett* (1955). John Cannon, *Parliamentary Reform 1640–1832* (1973) places the issues in a wider context. *The Debate on the French Revolution 1789–1800*, ed. Alfred Cobban (1950) contains extracts from contemporary publications. Further sources for the whole question, in the light of the spread of activity, are given in Chs. IV–V below; but *An Abstract of the History and Proceedings of the Revolution Society in London ...* (1789) and *The Correspondence of the Revolution Society in London, with the National Assembly, and with Various Societies of the Friends of Liberty in France and England* (1792) record the proceedings of the main centre in these early years, while Thomas Walker, *A Review of the Political Events which have Occurred in Manchester, during the Last Five Years ...* (1794) briefly describes the foundation of the first new major provincial Society. The literature on Burke and Paine is of course immense, and continuing. Burke's contacts with the Ministry from the summer of 1791 may be followed in his *Correspondence*, VI (see Ch. II above). *P.R.*, XXV (1789) – XXX (1791), Stockdale (as above), *The Senator; or Clarendon's Parliamentary Chronicle*, I–III (nd), *P.H.*, XXVIII (1816), XXIX (1817) cover the debates (over and above those on the Corporation and Test Acts, above) to the end of 1791. There is a clear summary of Fox's Libel Act in Sir William Holdsworth's *A History of English Law*, X (1938). Pitt's role in the passing of the Catholic Relief Act is examined best in Bernard Ward, *The Dawn of the Catholic Revival in England 1781–1803*, I (1909), which may be supplemented by *Reminiscences of Charles Butler, Esq., of Lincoln's-Inn* (1822 and 1827); and, here as elsewhere, Lecky's great *History of England in the Eighteenth Century* should not be forgotten. P.R.O. 30/8/310 includes the Minister's papers on the Roman Catholics, as also the abortive plan for the partial commutation of tithes. P.R.O. 30/8/102 contains a copy of his letter on this last subject to Archbishop Moore, P.R.O. 30/8/161 the reply, and the Moore Mss, Lambeth Palace Library, No. 9 some further relevant correspondence of the Archbishop's.

CHAPTERS IV & V

In treating of such large themes, on which so much study has fallen or impinged, I can note only a few of the many sources available, which I have found particularly helpful. Malcolm I. Thomis and Peter Holt, *Threats of Revolution in Britain 1789–1848* (1977), chs. 1, 6 is concerned with much the same ground; and a stimulating comprehensive survey is provided by Harold Perkin, *The Origins of Modern English Society 1780–1880* (1969). When one starts to examine the different interests in that society one is led at once to the growing body of work on particular regions, places and groups in books, articles and theses, and to the older local histories and published records. This is not the place for a selective list; bibliographical guides to current studies may be found regularly in *E.H.R.*, *Ec.H.R.*, and the Royal Historical Society's *Annual Bibliography of English and Irish History*. There is, however, a good general introduction to the circumstances and attitudes of the landowning interest in G.E. Mingay's *English Landed Society in the Eighteenth Century* (1963); similarly, Dorothy Marshall's *The English Poor in the Eighteenth Century . . .* (1926) – like some of her wider social surveys – provides a useful background. Links between social discontent and economic forces on a national scale are suggested in W.W. Rostow, 'Business Cycles, Harvests, and Politics' (*The Journal of Economic History*, I, no. 21) and more generally in Arthur Gayer, W.W. Rostow, and Anna Jacobson Schwartz, *The Growth and Fluctuation of the British Economy 1790–1850* (2 vols., 1953). These have attracted critical debate, to which there are guides again in *Ec.H.R.* A particularly useful article on a central problem is M.W. Flinn's 'Trends in Real Wages, 1750–1850', in *Ec.H.R., Second Series*, XXVII, no. 3.

The reforming and revolutionary Societies of the 1790s in England have naturally attracted much attention. The older standard works are those of Laprade, Veitch, and Brown (see Note on Sources to Ch. III above) and Robert Birley, *The English Jacobins from 1789 to 1802* (1924). To these may be added Eugene Charlton Black, *The Association . . .* (1963), Cannon, Maccoby (for both of which see Ch. III above), W.P. Hall, *British Radicalism, 1791–7* (1912), Carl B. Crone, *The English Jacobins: Reformers in the Late Eighteenth Century* (1968), T.M. Parssinen, 'Association, convention and anti-Parliament in British radical politics, 1771–1848' (*E.H.R.*, LXXXVIII, no. 348), and – a magisterial survey – Albert Goodwin, *The Friends of Liberty, The English Democratic Movement in the Age of the French Revolution* (1979). Two lives of Thomas Paine, by Moncure Daniel Conway (2 vols., 1823) and by Audrey Williamson (1973), are useful. P.J. Brunsdon, 'The Association of the Friends of the People' (M.A. thesis, University of Manchester, 1961) examines that largely aristocratic Society; Henry Collins, 'The London Corresponding Society', in *Democracy and the Labour Movement . . .*, ed. John Saville (1954), and Allan W.L. Seaman, 'Reform Politics at Sheffield, 1791–7' (*Transactions of the Hunterian Archaeological Society*, VII, Part 5), inquire into two of the most important of the new popular bodies. Collins's chapter adds much to the near contemporary accounts in Thomas Hardy's *Memoir* (1832) and Francis Place's *Autobiography*, ed. Mary Thrale (1972).

There have been other valuable contributions, not all accessible in print; some regional and some from less institutional points of view. They include Norman McCord and David E. Brewster, 'Some Labour Troubles of the 1790's in North East England' (*International Review of Social History*, XIII, Part 3), Austin Vernon Mitchell, 'Radicalism and Repression in the North of England 1791–1797' (M.A. thesis, University of Manchester, 1958), J. Money, 'Birmingham and the West Midlands, 1760–1793 . . .' (*Midland History*, I, no. 1), D.J.V. Jones, *Before Rebecca, Popular Protests in Wales 1793–1835* (1973), a debate on the West Riding between J.R. Dinwiddy and J.L. Baxter & F.K. Donnelly in *Past and Present*, no. 64; W.A.L. Seaman, 'British Democratic Societies in the Period of the French Revolution' (Ph.D thesis, University of London, 1954), James Walvin, 'English Democratic Societies and Popular Radicalism, 1791–1800' (Ph.D thesis, University of York, 1969); J. Stevenson, 'Food Riots in England, 1792–1818', in *Popular Protest and Public Order*, ed. R. Quinault and J. Stevenson, (1974), R.B. Rose 'Eighteenth Century Price Riots and Public Policy in England' (*International Review of Social History*, VI, Part 2), and E.P. Thompson, 'The Moral Economy of the English Crowd in the Eighteenth Century' (*Past and Present*, no. 50; with discussion by others in later issues). R.B. Rose, 'The Priestly Riots of 1791' (*Past and Present*, no. 18) provides a thoughtful investigation of the subject.

Much of this more recent work has been stimulated by the inquiries into the structure and attitudes of the lower classes, earlier ignored, which are associated with the names of Rudé, Hobsbawm, and E.P. Thompson. G.F. Rudé's 'The Gordon Riots . . .' (*Trans. R. Hist. S.*, *5th series*, 6), 'The London "Mob" in the Eighteenth Century' (*The Historical Journal*, 2, no. 1), and *Hanoverian London 1714–1808* (1971) – the last drawing in part on Dorothy George's *London Life in the Eighteenth Century* (1951) – and E.P. Thompson's seminal if uneven study of *The Making of the English Working Class* (1963, 2nd edn. 1968), concern England above all. So does John Stevenson's *Popular Disturbances in England 1700–1870* (1979). Rudé's *The Crowd in History . . . 1780–1848* (1964) – which he has followed with other similar studies –, E.J. Hobsbawm's *Primitive Rebels* (1959) and *Labouring Men* (1964), and Gwyn A. Williams, *Artisans and Sansculottes* (1968), suggest comparisons with movements elsewhere. Other contributions have traced popular attitudes through the use of terms: among them Asa Briggs in 'The Language of "Class" in Early Nineteenth Century England' (in *Essays in Labour History . . .*, ed. Asa Briggs and John Saville (1960)), Christopher Hill in 'The Norman Yoke' (in *Democracy and the Labour Movement*), J.G.A. Pocock, *Politics, Language and Time* (1972); and see also Quentin Skinner, 'History and Ideology in the English Revolution' (*The Historical Journal*, 8, no. 2). Assessments and bibliographies of recent lines of thought, covering this as well as later periods, are provided by Gertrude Himmelfarb in *The Journal of British Studies*, XI, no. 1, Norbert J. Gossman in *The British Studies Monitor*, IV, no. 1, and John W. Osborne, loc. cit., IV, no. 3.

The sources and weapons of order have been described from various starting points. Clive Emsley, 'Public Order in England 1790–1801' (M. Litt thesis, University of Cambridge, 1970), examines the effects of the system on the ground. For the regular land forces themselves C.M. Clode, *The Armed Forces of the Crown* (2 vols., 1869) and vol. III of the Hon. J.W. Fortescue's standard *A History of the British Army* (1902) provide a background to other studies, among which Clive Emsley, 'Political Disaffection and the British Army in 1792' (*Bulletin of the Institute of Historical Research*, XLVIII, no. 118) is immediately relevant here. J.R. Western, *The English Militia in the Eighteenth Century . . .* (1965) deals admirably with its subject. There are useful chs. in R.R. Nelson,

The Home Office, 1782–1801 (1969), and Kenneth Ellis, *The Post Office in the Eighteenth Century* (1958), on the Government's handling of agents and information. The classic treatment of local government and its resources remains that of Sidney and Beatrice Webb in *English Local Government from the Revolution to the Municipal Reform Act* (9 vols., 1906–1929). There is a comprehensive account of crime and the law in Leon Radcinowicz, *A History of English Criminal Law and Its Administration from 1750* (4 vols., 1948–68), which may be supplemented, for some of the environs of London, by J.M. Beattie's 'The Pattern of Crime in England 1660–1800' (*Past & Present*, no. 62). Chapters by Douglas Hay and E.P. Thompson in *Albion's Fatal Tree* (1975) offer suggestive comment.

For the important and complex influence of religion, in its various denominational aspects, see the Note on Sources to Ch. III above, to which may be added Elie Halévy's survey in vol. I of his great *A History of the English People in the Nineteenth Century* (English transln., 2nd edn., 1949), Robert K. Wearmouth, *Methodism and the Common People of the Eighteenth Century* (1945), and W.R. Ward, *Religion and Society 1790–1850* (1972). Popular education and readership are discussed in R.K. Webb, *The British Working Class Reader 1790–1848* (1955), Richard D. Altick, *The English Common Reader . . . 1800–1900* (1957), John William Adamson, *English Education, 1789–1902* (1930), and Michalina E.F. Vaughan and Margaret Scotford Archer, *Social and Educational Change in England and France, 1789–1848* (1971). The work of R.S. Schofield, Lawrence Stone, and David Cress (see the last's list of sources in *The Historical Journal*, vol. 20, no. 1) throws interesting light on antecedent periods; and the whole subject is attracting much study at present. Two useful books on the press are A. Aspinall's *Politics and the Press c. 1780–1850* (1949), and Donald Read, *Press and People 1790–1850, Opinion in Three English Cities* (1961). They are supplemented by Ian R. Christie, *Myth and Reality* (1970), chs. 15 and 16, by the theses of Seaman, Walvin and Mitchell (above), and I.S. Asquith, 'James Perry and the *Morning Chronicle* 1790–1821' (Ph.D thesis, University of London, 1973). J.M.S. Tompkins, *The Popular Novel in England 1770–1800* (1932) is a pioneering work that, among a growing list of successors, shows the enduring value of perception.

All these are secondary authorities. *The Debate on the French Revolution*, ed. Cobban (see Ch. III above), *British Working Class Movements 1789–1875: select documents*, ed. G.D.H. Cole and A.W. Filson (1951), and *The Early English Trade Unions . . .*, ed. A. Aspinall (1949), contain selected primary material. The publications of the Societies, and the voluminous pamphlet literature, are signposted in the bibliographies of Laprade, Veitch and Black in particular, as well as those of the theses mentioned above. Newspapers of course are mines of information, and misinformation. *A Complete Collection of State Trials*, ed. Thomas B. Howell, XXII (1817) throws valuable light on the early structures of the popular Societies and the attitudes of some leading members, as well as on the nature of Government's information. Governmental sources themselves will be mentioned in the Notes on Sources for Chs. XI, XII below. It is sufficient here to specify the Home Office papers most relevant to England and Wales in 1789–92, in P.R.O., H.O. 14/207–8, 14/216, 33/1, 42/14–23, 48/1–2, 50/18, 50/380–3, 98/1–2, 119/1.

CHAPTER VI

There have been four interesting analyses of the party talks in the summer of 1792: in Donald Grove Barnes, *George III and William Pitt, 1783–1806* (1939), H. Butterfield, 'Charles James Fox and the Whig Opposition in 1792' (*The Cambridge Historical Journal*, IX, no. 3), F. O'Gorman, and L.G. Mitchell (for both of which see Note on Sources to Ch. III above). Butterfield has returned tangentially to the theme in 'Sincerity and Insincerity in Charles James Fox' (*Proceedings of the British Academy*, LVII).

Published accounts of participants exist in *Memorials and Correspondence of Charles James Fox*, ed. Lord John Russell, II, III, IV (1853–7), *Diaries and Correspondence of James Harris, First Earl of Malmesbury . . .*, ed. by his Grandson, the Third Earl, II (1844), *Life and Letters of Sir Gilbert Elliot, First Earl of Minto, from 1751 to 1806*, ed. by the Countess of Minto, II (1874), and *Political Memoranda of . . . Duke of Leeds* (see Ch. I above). Material is also to be found in *A.C.*, II (Abbreviations), and – marginally – *H.M.C., Dropmore* II, Buckingham, II, and *Correspondence of Burke*, VII, together with Stanhope, II and *L.C.G. III*, I (Abbreviations) for Thurlow's dismissal. Tomline, III and Stanhope, II (Abbreviations) contain some of the correspondence on Pitt's appointment as Lord Warden of the Cinque Ports. *Miscellanies Collected and Edited by Earl Stanhope, Second Series* (1872) contains George Canning's account of his first meeting with Pitt; his earlier letter is in the Stanhope Mss at the Kent C.A.O. (Abbreviations), Maidstone, 'Pitt Papers: Autograph Letters from Colleagues, &c. II', and Pitt's answer in the Canning Mss, Harewood Deposit, Leeds Archives Department, bundle 30.

Unpublished sources for the party talks include P.R.O. 30/8/102, 110, 153, 157, 168 (Pitt's correspondence); B.L. Add. Mss 34441–2, 45728, 46519 (Auckland), 27916 (Leeds), 38192 (Hawkesbury), 47560–1, 47580 (Fox), 51705 (Thomas Pelham); Portland Mss, University of Nottingham, PwF 9220–4 (Portland's correspondence with Loughborough); Wentworth Woodhouse Muniments, Sheffield City Libraries, F31a (Fitzwilliam's correspondence with Portland); S.R.O. (see Abbreviations), Melville Castle Mss GD 51/1/17/2–13, 51/1/20/1,7,8, and Melville Correspondence, 1780–1830, nos. 85–9, 94–6 in the W.L. Clements Library, University of Michigan (Dundas). The Minto Mss in the N.L.S. do not add anything in this instance to the published letters; neither do Burke's papers in the Fitzwilliam Mss in the Northamptonshire Record Office to his published correspondence or to Butterfield (above).

The building of barracks in the summer is discussed in Radcinowicz (see Chs. IV–V above), IV (1968), ch. 4, section 2; the significance of the Westminster Justices' Act, op. cit., III (1956), ch. 5, sections 3 & 4. The Home Office papers, P.R.O. H.O. 1/1, 42/20–1, 42/208, 48/2, 48/216, 98/2, 102/60, 119/1, Pitt's file P.R.O. 30/8/240, and *Correspondence of Burke*, VII, throw light on domestic affairs, apart from those in Scotland and Ireland; Lucyle Werkmeister, *The London Daily Press 1772–1792* (1963) has information on its subject which is useful but not always well digested.

The Polish question is admirably treated by Gerhard and by Lord (see Ch. I above). Two unpublished theses, by Norman Frank Richards, 'British Policy and the Problem of the Monarchy in France, 1789–1802' (Ph.D, University of London, 1954), and J.T. Murley, 'The Origin and Outbreak of the Anglo-

French War of 1793' (D.Phil, Oxford, 1959) follow British policy towards France in these months. *H.M.C., Dropmore*, II, Buckingham, II, *A.C.*, II (Ch. I above), and *Letters and Correspondence of Sir James Bland Burges . . .*, ed. James Hutton (1885), contain valuable material on European affairs, which is amplified in P.R.O. 30/8/333 (for Pitt) and B.L. Add. Mss 59064 (for Grenville), 34441–4 (for Auckland). P.R.O., F.O. 7/29–30, 26/18–19, 27/38–40, 37/37–40, 62/5, 64/24–6, 65/23, 67/9–10, 72/23–4, 97/247 cover the countries of greatest interest in the summer and early autumn.

CHAPTER VII

Unrest in England at the winter of 1792–3 is covered in the sources given for Chs. IV–V above, to which may be added P.R.O., H.O. 42/24, Pitt's papers in P.R.O. 30/8/198, 284, 313, and letters from him to Dundas in December 1792 in the Clements Library, University of Michigan, the published papers and correspondence and biographies of individuals from other Chs., and, for a particular episode, Clive Emsley, 'The London 'Insurrection' of December 1792: Fact, Fiction, or Fantasy', in *The Journal of British Studies*, XVII, no. 2. Scotland is the subject of two good older studies, William Law's *The Awakening of Scotland . . . 1747 to 1797* (1910) and Henry W. Meikle's *Scotland and the French Revolution* (1912). Kenneth J. Logue, *Popular Disturbances in Scotland 1780–1815* (1979) incorporates more recent lines of interest. For the Episcopalians' disabilities see F.C. Mather in *E.H.R.*, XCII, no. 364, and for the failure to secure repeal of the Test Act, G.M. Ditchfield, 'The Scottish Campaign against the Test Act' in *The Historical Journal*, 23, no. 1. For Ireland there is still Lecky's great *History of Ireland in the Eighteenth Century* (III, 1892 edn.), to which may be added Edith M. Johnston, *Great Britain and Ireland 1760–1800 . . .* (1963), J.C. Beckett, *The Making of Modern Ireland 1603–1923* (1966), and R.B. McDowell, *Ireland in the Age of Imperialism and Revolution* (1979). P.R.O., H.O. 102/4–7, 102/60–1, and P.R.O. 30/8/157 (Dundas's correspondence with Pitt) for Scotland, P.R.O., H.O. 100/31–9, and P.R.O. 30/8/331, 369 (Westmorland's correspondence with Pitt and with Chatham) for Ireland, give body to the published accounts. Reeves's Loyal Association published proceedings and pamphlets in 1793 under the title of *Association Papers*. His own collection of documents for the period is in B.L. Add. Mss 16919–28; some correspondence with Nepean in 1792 in P.R.O., H.O. 42/21, 23, and with Pitt at different times in P.R.O. 30/8/170 and John Johnson Ms 3 (Bodleian Library). A careful, hostile study of the movement appears in Black (Note on Sources to Chs. IV–V above), ch. VII. Some of its conclusions, and those of Austin Mitchell, 'The Association Movement of 1792–3', in *The Historical Journal*, 4, no. 1, have attracted critical comment from Donald E. Ginter, 'The Loyalist Association Movement of 1792–93 and British Public Opinion', loc. cit., 9, no. 2. For the developments within Opposition see the sources cited in Ch. VI above, to which may be added B.L. Add Mss 47565, 47568, 47570 (for Fox), B.L. Add. Ms 37873 (for William Windham), P.R.O. 30/8/153 (for Loughborough).

There are many studies, British and French, of the events leading up to the war; publication of the documents themselves has not been so well served. J. Holland Rose edited some 'Documents relating to the Rupture with France in 1793' in two Parts in *E.H.R.*, XXVI, nos. CV, CVI, and published others in

Appendix A of *The Cambridge History of British Foreign Policy 1783–1919*, I. The Foreign Office papers for the period November 1792 to February 1793 are P.R.O., F.O. 7/31–2, 97/59 (Austria), 26/19–20 (Flanders), 27/40–1, 95/3/1 (France), 37/40–4, 97/247 (Holland), 64/26–7, 97/324 (Prussia), 65/23–4 (Russia), 67/10–11 (Sardinia), 72/25–6 (Spain). Auckland's papers in P.R.O. 30/8/110 and B.L. Add. Mss 34445–7, of which a small selection is published in *AC*, II, are valuable. So are Grenville's, published extensively in *H.M.C., Dropmore*, II with some of interest in Buckingham, II (Abbreviations). See also Bland Burges's *Letters and Correspondence* (Ch. VI above), and, for the French West Indies, Hawkesbury's papers in B.L. Add. Mss 38192, 38228, 38351–2. Lord Amherst's Diary (vol. I) in the Kent C.A.O. supplies dates of meetings in the final weeks. *The Correspondence of William Augustus Miles on the French Revolution* (Ch. II) is essential; but it needs to be read in the light of Howard V. Evans's articles cited for the same Ch. Some of Miles's unpublished correspondence with Pitt is in P.R.O. 30/8/159, and there is a copy of a letter from Pitt to him in P.R.O. 30/8/102. Other relevant files of Pitt's for foreign affairs – tantalisingly incomplete – are P.R.O. 30/8/195, 197, 333, and Stanhope Ms S5 09/14 (Kent C.A.O.). Murley (see Ch. VI above) remains an admirable guide for these last months of Anglo-French peace on either side of the Channel, and his bibliography should be read for the French sources. John G. Alger, *Englishmen in the French Revolution* (1889) and 'The British Colony in Paris, 1792–93' in *E.H.R.*, XIII, no. LII, and David Williams, 'The Missions of David Williams and James Tilly Matthews to England (1793)', loc. cit., LIII, no. CCXII, are useful for that aspect of an increasingly confused scene. The Parliamentary debates are in *P.R.*, XXXIV (1793) *The Senator . . .*, VI (nd), and *P.H.*, XXX (1817).

CHAPTER VIII

It is appropriate to open a list of sources for what was to prove a long war with the Hon. J.W. Fortescue, *A History of the British Army* (IV – Parts I, II, and Maps and Plans, 1906). For with all its shortcomings as an account of strategy, its circumscribed opinions of individuals, and its inaccuracies in detail, it remains indispensable for operations and dispositions of troops. Alfred H. Burne, *The Noble Duke of York . . .* (1949) provides a spirited defence of that commander. There is a useful article on the main Allied partner in G.A. Craig's 'Command and staff problems in the Austrian Army, 1740–1866' (G.A. Craig, *War, Politics and Diplomacy*, 1966), and William O. Shanchan discusses *Prussian Military Reforms, 1786–1813* (1965). For the enemy's forces, Colonel Ramsay Weston Phipps, *Armies of The First French Republic*, I–IV (1926–35) is a counterpart in its coverage to Fortescue.

Naval operations are described in the composite *The Royal Navy A History . . .* by Wm. Laird Clowes (and others) (IV, 1899), which itself draws on William James, *The Naval History of Great Britain from . . . 1793, to . . . 1820 . . .* (5 vols, 1822–24) and Edward Pelham Brenton, *The Naval History of Great Britain, from the Year MDCCLXXXIII to MDCCCXXII* (5 vols, 1823–5). G.J. Marcus, *A Naval History of England*, 2 (1971) is the most recent general account.

These are operational studies for the most part; sources for British military and naval administration are discussed in Ch. XIII below. When one comes to

British strategy, no comprehensive account exists for the years of the First Coalition. Mahan's *The Influence of Sea Power upon the French Revolution and Empire* (2 vols., 1892) remains a classic, and Admiral Sir Hubert Richmond's *Statesmen and Sea Power* (1946) a minor one; but both of course are concerned with one basic element, and subsume the first phase in a general analysis. Piers Mackesy's useful paper, 'Problems of an Amphibious Power: Britain against France, 1793–1815' (*Naval War College Review*, Newport, Rhode Island, Spring 1798), is necessarily brief in covering the wars as a whole. Fortescue's *British Statesmen of the Great War, 1793–1814* (1911) is not impressive. Holland Rose's article 'The Duke of Richmond on the conduct of the War in 1793' (*E.H.R.*, XXV, no. XCIX) is by its nature a limited study. But there is an enlightening discussion of the initial attitude to the Caribbean in David Geggus, 'The British Government and the Saint Domingue slave revolt, 1791–1793' (*E.H.R.*, XCVI, no. 379); and two valuable sources for the first campaign – one on a central theme of a longer period, the other on a facet of the campaign itself – are to be found in Michael Duffy's 'British War Policy: the Austrian Alliance, 1793–1801' (D.Phil thesis, University of Oxford, 1971), and the same author's ' "A particular service": The British government and the Dunkirk expedition of 1793' (*E.H.R.*, XCI, no. 360). Both are concerned with the interaction of military and diplomatic affairs. Published material for the latter is comparatively scarce in the case of Britain: treaty agreements are covered in *The Consolidated Treaty Series*, ed. Clive Parry, 51–2 (1961), and some of the English texts are given in the relevant volumes of *HCJ*, *HLJ*, and later *PH* (see Abbreviations). H.W.V. Temperley and Lillian Penson provide a broader selection of papers in *Foundations of British Foreign Policy from Pitt to Salisbury . . .* (1938), and material made available at the time in successive volumes of *The Annual Register* (some previously printed in the official *London Gazette*) was reproduced in *A Collection of State Papers, relative to the War in France . . .*, the first volume of which appeared in 1794. Correspondence is to be found in *AC, III, Diaries and Correspondence of Malmesbury* (Ch. VI above), Olson's *The Radical Duke* (Ch. I), *Life and Letters of Sir Gilbert Elliot* (Ch. VI), *Letters and Correspondence of Bland Burges* (Ch. VI), *LCG III*, II, Buckingham, II, and above all *H.M.C., Dropmore*, II and (marginally) III. *Arkhiv Kniazia Vorontsova*, ed. P.I. Bartenev (1870–95) is useful for British relations with Russia; and there is a fine series for Austria in *Quellen sur Geschichte der Deutschen Kaiserspolitick Österreichs während der französischen Revolutionskriege 1790–1801*, ed. A. von Vivenot & H.R. von Zeissberg (1873–90).

Published studies of British diplomacy in 1793 are also rare. Relations with Russia are examined by Dietrich Gerhard, and with Russia, Prussia and Austria in a particular context by Robert Howard Lord (Ch. I). One may also cite *The Cambridge History of British Foreign Policy*, I, and – less satisfactory – E.D. Adams (Ch. II); and there is always the great Sorel. John M. Sherwig, *Guineas and Gunpowder: British Foreign Aid in the Wars with France 1793–1815* (1969) and Karl F. Helleiner, *The Imperial Loans, A Study in Financial and Diplomatic History* (1965) examine a vital ingredient, though one barely visible as yet. Philip C. Jessup and Francis Deák, *Neutrality, Its History, Economics and Law* (I & II, 1935–6) is a useful introductory study.

P.R., XXXIV–XXXVI (1793), *The Senator*, VII (nd), *P.H.* XXX (1817) cover the debates.

Unpublished sources yield more. The relevant series in the P.R.O., F.O.

papers for 1793 (apart from France, for which see Ch. IX below) are 93 (for treaties, by countries), 7/32–5, 97/60 (Austria), 9/9 (Bavaria), 22/16–17, 97/117 (Denmark), 26/20–2 (Flanders), 28/6 (Genoa), 29/1–3 (Army in Germany), 31/5 (Cologne & Hesse Cassel), 33/8, 97/240 (Hamburg), 37/44–50 (Holland, 63/16–17 (Portugal), 64/27–8 (Prussia), 65/24–5, 97/342 (Russia), 67/11–13 (Sardinia), 68/8 (Saxony), 70/6 (Sicily), 72/26–8, 97/375 (Spain), 73/14–16, 97/399 (Sweden), 74/3 (Switzerland), 78/14 (Turkey), 79/8–9, 528/5 (Tuscany), 81/9 (Venice). The most useful P.R.O. files for military operations (not including the hinterland of France) are W.O. 1/15, 1/58, 1/166–7, 1/177, 1/287, 6/7–10, 6/23, 30/81 (for one important document only – Richmond's account of his conversation with Pitt in April 1793); and H.O. 32/3, 50/2, 50/368–70. For the navy (excluding plans for a descent on the French coasts, and Mediterranean operations), see P.R.O., Adm. 1/98–9, 2/123–5, 2/374, 2/1345–6, 3/110–11, and H.O. 28/9–13.

Private papers of similar coverage include B.L. Add. Ms 34446–52, 46519 (Auckland), 38192, 38288–9, 38351–2, 45278 (Hawkesbury), 47569, 47571 (Fox), 58877, 58968, 59006, 59065, 59080, 59279, 59306 (Grenville), Loan Ms 57, vol. 107 (Bathurst Mss, for correspondence between Pitt, Dundas and Richmond, published in part in *E.H.R.*, XXV, no. XCIX). In the N.L.S., Mss 11048–9, 11138, 11159–66 (Minto) are of interest, as is Ms 5569 (Liston, when in Sweden); but Dundas's extensive papers, there and in the S.R.O. and the B.L., are not significant in this case. Lord Amherst's Diary, vols. I & II (see Ch. VII above) are useful. There is material of varying importance in Pitt's papers in the P.R.O., in 30/8/195–7, 245, 336–42, 348–9, and among his correspondence in 12, 101, 102, 110 (for Auckland), 140 (Grenville), 162 (Sir James Murray; partly published, with letters from 102, by J. Holland Rose in *E.H.R.*, XXIV, no. XCVI), 187 (Brook Watson), for whom see also 30/58/1.

CHAPTER IX

Fortescue (see Ch. VIII above) and Holland Rose, II (Abbreviations) are the principal published accounts on the British side, together with J. Holland Rose, *Lord Hood and the Defence of Toulon* (1922). A. Cobban, *Aspects of the French Revolution* (see Ch. II above) ch. 11, and Maurice Hutt, 'Spies in France 1793–1808' (*History Today*, XII, no. 3) are good on the beginnings of the Channel Islands' contacts with resistance in France. To these may be added the unpublished Duffy, 'British War Policy' (Ch. VIII) for the Austrian role, Richards (Ch. VI), and Agnes King, 'The Relations of the British Government with the Emigrés and Royalists of Western France, 1793–5' (Ph.D thesis, University of London, 1931). Of a mass of French publications, one may cite Paul Cottin, *Toulon et les Anglais en 1793 . . .* (1898), Emile Gabory, *L'Angleterre et la Vendée . . .* (2 vols., 1930–1), and more generally Jacques Godechot, *La Contre-Révolution . . .* (1961).

Published sources are included in the list for Ch. VIII above; to which one should add here vol. VII of *The Correspondence of Edmund Burke* and J. Holland Rose, *Pitt and Napoleon, Essays and Letters* (1912), as well as the appendices in J. Holland Rose's study of Toulon (above) which include a wide selection of letters from Hood and from Mulgrave. Among unpublished private sources, Pitt's papers contain some significant material in P.R.O. 30/8/102, 140, 196,

331–4, and Stanhope Ms S5 07 (Kent C.A.O.). There are useful précis of correspondence with Toulon among Grenville's papers in B.L. Add. Ms 59064, and his relations with Mulgrave are suggested by a few letters in Add. Ms 58940. Dundas's papers (see Ch. VIII above) are again disappointing, apart from one letter on the first news of Toulon in the Buccleugh Mss, GD 224/30/9/12 in the S.R.O. Amherst's Diary vols. I and II (Ch. VII) is again useful, as is Gilbert Elliot's for September 1793 (loc. cit.). Thomas Grenville's papers contain an interesting letter from Fitzwilliam reflecting the Portland Whigs' views on the statements for Toulon (B.L. Add. Ms 42058); and Thomas Pelham's in B.L. Add. Ms 51706 throw further light on their attitude – and Burke's – to the royalists. Windham's papers become more important after 1793, but B.L. Add. Mss 37844, 37846 are relevant, and J. Holland Rose published some of the contents in *E.H.R.*, XXVII, no. CVIII; Auckland's (see Ch. VIII) are of interest as usual, although in this instance he was on the fringe of information. Among the diplomats, Francis Drake at Genoa provides some material from B.L. Add. Ms 46822.

The departmental files in the P.R.O. are of central significance for this Chapter. The F.O. series for France comprise 27/41–2, 95/3/1–3, 95/4/6. Other relevant F.O. series are those for Austria, France, Genoa, Russia, Sardinia, Sicily, Spain, Switzerland, and Tuscany (all in Ch. VIII above, with additions for Tuscany in 528/13–17). In the W.O. papers, 1/174 (correspondence with Moira), 1/177, 1/388–92, 1/396, 6/8 are relevant, and in the H.O. series 28/12–13, 28/14 (Dundas's correspondence with Hood), 50/370, 50/454–5 (Toulon material). P.R.O. Adm. 1/391 contains Hood's despatches and letters to the Admiralty, and Adm. 3/111 (Board Minutes) includes relevant information. P.R.O., P.C. 1/125 has the French texts of some of the declarations for Toulon of which the English versions were published at the time.

CHAPTER X

Most of the published material and unpublished theses repeat those for Chs. VIII and IX above. *The Correspondence of Charles, First Marquis Cornwallis*, ed. Charles Ross, II (1859) is of interest for the continental campaign. Paul M. Kennedy, *The Rise and Fall of British Naval Mastery* (1976) may be added to Mahan and Richmond (Ch. VIII above) for its survey of the use of seapower, a theme touched on here; naval administration is discussed in Ch. XIII below. M.W.B. Sanderson examines 'English Naval Strategy and Maritime Trade in the Caribbean, 1793–1802' (Ph.D thesis, University of London, 1968) – and there is a useful predecessor for comparison in Alan G. Jamieson's 'War in the Leeward Islands,. 1775–1783' (D.Phil thesis, Oxford, 1981) – and Michael Duffy has provided a stimulating unpublished paper, 'Motivation and Performance in the British Expeditions to the West Indies during the War against Revolutionary France'. See also the article by David Geggus cited in the Note on Sources to Ch. VIII above. Roger Norman Buckley studies *Slaves in Red Coats, the British West India Regiments 1795–1815* (1979); and there are valuable articles on losses in that area by Buckley in *The Journal of Army Historical Research*, LVI, by Geggus in the same journal and by Geggus in *Medical History*, 23, no. 1. Helleiner, *The Imperial Loans* (Ch. VIII) treats of a subject emerging as one of central importance to an Austrian alliance. *The Paget Papers, Diplomatic and Other Correspondence of the Hon. Sir Arthur Paget, GCB 1794–1807*, ed. . . Sir Augustus B. Paget . . ., I (1896) describes the situation in Berlin at a difficult time. Selected diplomatic correspondence is published in Appendix B of *The Cambridge History of British Foreign Policy*, I (Ch. II). The *Mémoires* of the Comte de Puisaye (III–IV, 1804, 1806) are useful for his visit to London, an episode discussed in the secondary material listed for Ch. IX. Maurice Hutt's bibliographical article on Puisaye in *Annales Historiques de la Révolution Française*, no. 175, is also of value. *Mémoires de Malouet*, I (1874) and *Memoirs and Correspondence of Mallet du Pan*, ed. A Sayons, I, II (1852) convey the views of two favoured 'Constitutionalists', and Harvey Mitchell's *The Underground War against Revolutionary France, The Missions of William Wickham 1794–1800* (1965) explores an area of strategy for which *The Correspondence of the Right Honourable William Wickham from the Year 1794*, ed. . . by His Grandson, William Wickham . . ., I (1870) provides some sketchy material at this early stage. *P.R.*, XXXVII–XL (1794–5), *The Senator*, VIII–XI (nd), *P.H.*, XXX–XXXI (1817–18) cover the Parliamentary debates.

Much of the ms material likewise repeats or follows on that given for Chs. VIII and IX. Relevant series in the P.R.O., F.O. papers (excluding the U.S.A., treated in Ch. XIII below) are 7/36–9, 97/59 (Austria), 9/10 (Bavaria), 22/18–21, 97/117 (Denmark), 26/23–5 (Flanders), 28/7–10 (Genoa), 29/4 (Army in Germany), 31/6 (Cologne & Hesse Cassel), 33/9, 97/240 (Hamburg), 37/51–6, 97/248 (Holland), 63/18–19 (Portugal), 64/29–35, 64/37, 97/324 (Prussia), 65/26–8, 97/342 (Russia), 67/14–15 (Sardinia), 68/8 (Saxony), 70/7 (Sicily), 72/33–5 (Spain), 73/17–18, 97/399 (Sweden), 74/4 (Switzerland), 78/15 (Turkey), 79/10–11, 528/5 (Tuscany), 81/10 (Venice). P.R.O., P.C. 1/130 contains correspondence between Pitt and Calonne. Useful files for operations on the continent are P.R.O., W.O. 1/168–70, 1/175–7, 1/388–92, 1/396, 1/602, 1/606–7, 6/1, 6/11, H.O. 50/371; for Corsica and the Mediterranean, W.O. 1/288, 1/302, 6/54, H.O. 28/14–18, 50/46, Adm. 1/392; for the West Indies, W.O. 1/31, 1/59–60, 1/82, 6/5, Adm. 1/245, 1/316, 1/492; for the East, W.O. 1/320, 1/356, 6/67, Adm. 1/167. Naval operations are further covered in P.R.O., Adm. 1/100–1, 1/221, 1/521, 2/374, 2/1347–8, 3/112–14.

Private papers (again excluding the United States of America) are voluminous. Some idea – patchy, as so often – of Pitt's range of interests can be gained from his papers in P.R.O. 30/8/196 and (marginally) 197, 240–2, 244, 258, 334, 338, 350, and, among his correspondence, 101 (for Chatham), 111 (Middleton), 115 (Walter Boyd, and see also Sir William Pulteney's letters in 169), 119 (Calonne), 122 (Charmilly), 125 (Cornwallis), 127, 135, 140 (William Grenville), 142, 145, 146 (Howe), 149, 154, 155 (Malmesbury), 157 (Dundas), 160 (Moira), 169 (Puisaye), 180 (Spencer, and Starhemberg), 187 (Brook Watson), 190 (Windham). Stanhope Mss S5 02/4, 03/3, 010/15 are also of some interest. William Grenville's papers in B.L. Add. Mss 58877, 58880, 58915, 58921–2, 58929, 58934–5, 58937, 59006, 59010–11, 59019, 59022, 59031, 59044, 59046, 59051, 59055–6, 59065, 59067A, 59068, 59080, 59279 supplement *H.M.C., Dropmore*, II–III, Buckingham, II, and the F.O. files. So, for the mission to Vienna, do those of his brother Thomas in the Stowe Mss at the Huntington Library, San Marino, California. As I have stated in the Introduction, Spencer's papers have been denied me. Windham's correspondence in B.L. Add. Mss 37844 (for Pitt's letters), 37846 (for William Grenville),

37874 (including Dundas) is full of interest; more so in fact than Dundas's in N.L.S., S.R.O., and B.L., though a Cabinet Minute of 10 October 1794 in B.L. Add. Ms 40102, and letters from Middleton in B.L. Add. Ms 41079 and S.R.O., Melville Castle Mss, GD 51/2/31, from Cornwallis loc. cit., GD 51/1/608/1–2, and from General Abercromby in N.L.S. Ms 3835 should be noted. Cornwallis's papers in P.R.O. 30/11/216–17 supplement the published *Correspondence* (above). Amherst's Diary (see Ch. VII), III–IV, is useful. Auckland's papers and those of Hawkesbury in B.L. are less so in this instance, though the former in Add. Mss 34452–3 contain some marginal information, and the latter in Loan Ms 72, vol. 53 has some reports on Pitt and Dundas in the autumn of 1794. Further personal information, and comments on Ministers' reactions, can be found in Bland Burges Ms 10 (Bodleian Library) and, in greater volume, in Canning's journal (Canning Ms 29 dii, Leeds Archives Department). Chatham's papers in P.R.O. 30/8/364–8 are of interest. So are Gilbert Elliot's in the Minto Mss in N.L.S. Mss 11105, 11138, 13001, as well as Mss 1707, 3112; his papers in the National Maritime Museum, Grenwich hold material on Corsica, while Paoli's in B.L. Add. Ms 22688 include letters from Dundas and from Hood. Liston's correspondence from Turkey, in N.L.S. Ms 5572, adds a little to the F.O. file. B.L. Add. Mss 7976, 7979–80, 7982, 8072 are of note among Puisaye's papers.

CHAPTER XI

Much of the material for section I has been cited in the Notes on Sources to Chs. IV–V above. The relevant volumes of *A Complete Collection of State Trials*, ed. Thomas B. Howell, are XXIII–XXV (1817–18). The debates arising from the trials of Muir and Palmer, on seditious practices, the suspension of the Habeas Corpus Act, and the Volunteer Corps bill are in *P.R.*, XXXVII–XLII (1794–5), *The Senator*, VIII–XI (nd), *P.H.*, XXX–XXXI. Relevant volumes in the P.R.O., H.O. series are 30/1, 33/1, 42/24–33, 48/3–4, 50/19–22, 384–5, 98/3–5, 100/39–52, 102/5–11, 62, 119/1. A great deal of material, for 1794 itself and for the three preceding years, was collected by the Privy Council and the Treasury Solicitor mostly in relation to the sedition trials. Useful guides may be found in Goodwin, *The Friends of Liberty* (see Chs. IV–V above), 518–19, and Black, *The Association*, 300–1 (ibid). The Privy Council's examination in 1794 can be followed in P.R.O., P.C. 1/22/A and 1/22/1; the relevant class in the Treasury Solicitor's files is P.R.O., T.S. 11. Letters from Robert to Henry Dundas in N.L.S. Ms 6 are of interest for Scotland in 1793–4.

Pretyman's account in B.L. Add. Ms 45107(A), and Sheila Marriner, 'English Bankruptcy Records and Statistics before 1850' (*Ec.H.R., Second Series*, XXXIII, no. 3), complement contemporary published discussion of the credit crisis of 1793.

The formation and first months of the remodelled Ministry are discussed by O'Gorman (Ch. III), and E.A. Smith, *Whig principles and party politics, Earl Fitzwilliam and the Whig party 1748–1833* (1975). Printed primary sources include *The Windham Papers*, I, *Correspondence of Burke*, VIII, *Life and Letters of Sir Gilbert Elliot*, II, *Diaries and Correspondence of George Rose*, II, *H.M.C., Dropmore*, II (all cited for earlier Chs.), *H.M.C., Bathurst* (for Richmond's dismissal), and of course Stanhope, II and Holland Rose, II (see Abbreviations). Published diaries, and newspapers, are full of reference to developments. There is unpublished material in P.R.O. 30/8/102, 110, 140, 153, 157, 169, 190 (for Pitt), S.R.O., Melville Castle Mss Gd 51/1/24–5 (for Dundas), B.L. Add. Ms 38192 (Hawkesbury), Portland Mss particularly classes PwF and PwV 107, 108 (University of Nottingham), Wentworth Woodhouse Muniments particularly classes F5 and F31 (for Fitzwilliam; Sheffield City Libraries), B.L. Add. Mss 37844–5, 37874.(for Windham), 41855, 42058 (Thomas Grenville, containing also some earlier indications of Spencer's attitude), 33629–31 (Thomas Pelham), Stanhope Mss S5 02/15, 03/13, 06/23 (Kent C.A.O.). Bland Burges Ms 10 (Bodleian Library) shows the reaction of an official. Amherst's Diary, vols. III–IV (Ch. VII), is of interest for its record of Cabinet meetings and dinners. P.R.O. 30/8/171, Stanhope Ms S5 09/14 contain correspondence between Pitt and Richmond supplementing *H.M.C., Bathurst* (above). Canning Ms 29 ii d (Leeds Archives Department), B.L. Loan Ms 72, vol. 53 (for Robert Jenkinson) give glimpses of Pitt's mood at various times.

The Fitzwilliam affair has been debated voluminously, with Lecky's *History of Ireland in the Eighteenth Century*, III (1892 edn.) providing the archetypal defence of Fitzwilliam. R.B. McDowell, 'The Fitzwilliam Episode' (*Irish Historical Studies*, XV, no. 58) is summarised in the same author's *Ireland in the Age of Imperialism and Revolution 1760–1801* (see Ch. VII). O'Gorman, E.A. Smith (both above), Edith M. Johnston, *Great Britain and Ireland 1760–1800* (see Ch. VII above) are three other fairly recent studies. Stanhope, II, the Right Hon. Edward Gibson, Lord Ashbourne, *Pitt: some Chapters of his Life and Times* (1898), Holland Rose, II, and the same author's *Pitt and Napoleon* in the chapter 'Pitt and Earl Fitzwilliam', print some of the documents. *The Windham Papers*, I, *Correspondence of Burke*, VIII, Buckingham, II, *H.M.C., Dropmore*, II–III, *H.M.C., Carlisle*, *L.C.G. III*, II, *Miscellanies, Collected and Edited by Earl Stanhope* (1863) – 'Mr. Pitt on the Irish Appointments' –, *Memoirs of the Life and Times of the Rt. Hon. Henry Grattan*, by his son, Henry Grattan, Esq., MP, IV (1842), *The Correspondence of the Right Hon. John Beresford ...*, ed. William Beresford, II (1854) are valuable. So is the unpublished material in the Portland and Fitzwilliam papers (see above), in B.L. Add. Mss 37874–5 (Windham), P.R.O. 30/8/324–5, 328–9, 331 (among Pitt's papers on Ireland), B.L. Add. Ms 45101 (Pretyman's account of Pitt's retrospective verdict on Fitzwilliam, P.R.O., H.O. 100/46. The aftermath for Ireland itself may be followed in P.R.O. 30/8/119, 326 (Camden's letters to Pitt, supplementing his despatches), Camden Mss C 95/1, 106/1–2, 113, 123/2–7, 2691, 0102–3, 0142A/1–5 (Kent C.A.O.), B.L. Add. Mss 33101, 33129 (for Thomas Pelham).

CHAPTER XII

The economy in 1795–6 has been broadly treated by Gayer, Rostow and Schwartz in *The Growth and Fluctuation of the British Economy* (see Chs. IV–V above), and significant elements in T.S. Ashton's *Economic Fluctuations in England 1700–1800* (1959). Statistics, as always arguable, are best taken from B.R. Mitchell and Phyllis Deane's *Abstract of British Historical Statistics* (1962), which in the vexed question of prices selects in part from the work of McCulloch, Tooke and Newmarch, Beveridge, Gilboy, Silberling, and the Schumpeters. *Ec.H.R.* provides guides to the discussion on real wages, well summed up by

Flinn (see Chs. IV–V above). J.L. Anderson seeks an answer to a complex of problems in 'Aspects of the Effect on the British Economy of the Wars against France, 1793–1815' (*Australian Economic History Review*, XII, no. 1). Rostow links economic forces with discontent in his article 'Business Cycles, Harvests, and Politics' (Chs. IV–V above).

The dearth of corn is treated in Walter M. Stern, 'The Bread Crisis in Britain, 1795–6' (*Economica, New Series*, XXXI, no. 122). Sir William Ashley, *The Bread of our Forefathers* (1928) investigates that subject, and Donald Grove Barnes, *A History of the English Corn Laws from 1660–1846* (1930) provides a painstaking guide, subject in its judgment on some aspects of 1795–6 to Stern's later account. There is a wealth of material on the treatment and relief of the poor. To the seminal works of Dorothy Marshall, *The English Poor in the Eighteenth Century* (Chs. IV–V) and the Webbs, *English Poor Law History*, vols. VII–IX (1929) of their *English Local Government* (ibid), may be added the admirable summary by J.D. Marshall of *The Old Poor Law 1795–1834* (repr. 1979); Mark Blaug, 'The Myth of the Old Poor Law and the Making of the New' and 'The Poor Law Re-examined' (*The Journal of Economic History*, XXIII, no. 2, XXIV, Number 2); James Stephen Taylor, 'The Mythology of the Old Poor Law' (loc. cit., XXIX, Number 2), criticising Blaug; W.E. Tate, *The Parish Chest* (1969 edn.). E.M. Hampson provides a valuable study of one locality in *The Treatment of Poverty in Cambridgeshire* (1934), Alan Booth of another in 'Food Riots in the North-West of England' (*Past and Present*, no. 77), and Roger A.E. Wells of a third in *Dearth and Distress in Yorkshire, 1793–1802* (*Borthwick Institute Paper* No. 52; 1977). D.A. Baugh assesses 'The Cost of Poor Relief in South-East England, 1790–1834' (*Ec.H.R., Second Series*, XXVIII, no. 1). He has also examined the wider problem of attitudes in *Poverty, Protestantism, and Political Economy: English Attitudes Towards the Poor, 1660–1800* (1981), and the question, 'Whose "Moral Economy"? Friends and Foes of the Free Market in the Speenhamland Era' (1978, unpublished). The same subject is covered in J.R. Poynter's comprehensive *Society and Pauperism: English Ideas on Poor Relief, 1795–1834* (1969), as well as in A.W. Coats, 'Economic Thought and Poor Law Policy in the Eighteenth Century' (*Ec.H.R., Second Series*, XIII, no. 1). There are two useful contributions on Speenhamland itself by Mark D. Newman: 'Speenhamland in Berkshire', in *Comparative Development in Social Welfare*, ed. E.W. Martin (1972), and 'A Suggestion regarding the origin of the Speenhamland Plan' (*E.H.R.*, LXXXIV, no. CCCXXXI). Pitt's Poor Law bill of 1796 is discussed expertly by Poynter (above), and also by Holland Rose in 'Pitt and Relief of the Poor' (*Pitt and Napoleon*).

Developments in agriculture may be studied in Lord Ernle, *English Farming Past and Present* (1961 edn.) and J.D. Chambers and G.E. Mingay, *The Agricultural Revolution 1750–1800* (1966), and certain features in A.H. Johns, 'Farming in Wartime: 1793–1815' (*Land, Labour and Population in the Industrial Revolution . . .*, ed. E.L. Jones and G.E. Mingay, 1967). The foundation of the Board of Agriculture and the fate of its General Enclosure bill are discussed in Rosalind Mitchison, 'The Old Board of Agriculture 1793–1822' (*E.H.R.*, LXXIV, No. 290), and the same author's *Agricultural Sir John, The Life of Sir John Sinclair of Ulbster 1754–1835* (1962). *The Autobiography of Arthur Young . . .*, ed. M. Betham-Edwards (1898) and John G. Gazley, *The Life of Arthur Young 1741–1820* (1973) are also useful.

Pitt's own papers are not unhelpful on dearth and poverty. P.R.O. 30/8/197 has notes showing his ideas on the former in November 1795, and P.R.O. 30/8/307–8, 30/58/8 his ideas on the latter at the turn of 1796–7. There is an interesting memorandum on corn from Auckland in P.R.O. 30/8/293. P.R.O. 30/8/292 and 296, on various other foodstuffs and on spirits, contain nothing of substance for the period. On the subject of unrest, the great bulk of published and unpublished material consulted for this Ch. is given in the Notes on Sources to Chs. IV–V above. P.R.O., H.O. 42/32–9 contain the main official files for the period. Parliamentary debates are covered in *P.R.*, XL – XLII (1795–6), *The Senator*, XI–XIV (nd), *P.H.*, XXXI–XXXII (1818).

Glimpses of Pitt's personal condition at the time may be gained from Camden's correspondents among the inner group of friends while he himself was in Ireland, in Camden Mss, series C (Kent C.A.O.), as well as in other scattered sources in my textual notes. Rosebery's editions of 'Letters Relating to the Love Episode of William Pitt together with an Account of his Health by his Physician Sir Walter Farquhar' (*The Monthly Review*, December 1900), and 'Bishop Tomline's Estimate of Pitt together with Chapter XXVII from the Unpublished Fourth Volume of the Life' (*The Monthly Review*, August 1903), provide interesting material.

CHAPTER XIII

The material here is taken largely from sources contained in the Notes to earlier Chs., particularly (though not entirely) VIII–X. I therefore confine myself to additions, to be taken in conjunction with that already cited. Richard Glover, *Peninsular Preparation, the Reform of the British Army 1795–1809* (1963), J.R. Western, 'The County Fencibles and Militia Augmentation of 1794' (*Journal of the Society for Army Historical Research*, Volume 34), and the same author's 'The Recruitment of the Land Forces, 1793–99' (Ph.D thesis, University of Edinburgh, 1953), are admirable studies of military organisation. J.A. Houlding, *Fit for Service, The Training of the British Army 1715–1795* (1981) is similarly useful for its subject, as is Arthur Forbes for *A History of the Army Ordnance Services* (1929). The navy has also been well served. N.A.M. Rodger, *The Admiralty* (1979), Bernard Pool, *Navy Board Contracts, 1660–1832* . . . (1966), Christopher Lloyd and Jack L.S. Coulter, *Medicine and the Navy, 1200–1900*, III (1961), Michael Lewis, *A Social History of the Navy, 1793–1815* (1960), P.K. Crimmin, 'Admiralty Relations with the Treasury, 1783–1806 . . .' (*The Mariner's Mirror*, 53, no. 1), and 'The Financial and Clerical Establishment of the Admiralty Office, 1783–1806' (loc. cit., 55, no. 3), M.E. Condon, 'The Establishment of the Transport Board – a Subdivision of the Admiralty – 4 July 1794' (loc. cit., 58, no. 1) – with which may be taken David Syrett, 'The Organization of British Trade Convoys during the American War, 1775–1783' (loc. cit., 62, no. 2) –, P.L.C. Webb, 'The Rebuilding and Repair of the Fleet, 1783–1792' (*Bulletin of the Institute of Historical Research*, L, no. 122), Christopher Oprey, 'Schemes for the Reform of Naval Recruitment, 1793–1815' (M.A. thesis, University of Liverpool, 1961), Clive Emsley, 'The Recruitment of Petty Offenders during the French Wars 1793–1815' (*The Mariner's Mirror*, 66, no. 3), and *The Manning of the Royal Navy: Selected Public Pamphlets, 1693–1873*, ed. J.S. Bromley (1974), are all of value. Some primary material is to be found in *Letters and Papers of Charles, Lord Barham, 1758–1813*, II, ed. Sir John Knox Laughton

(1910) and *Private Papers of George, second Earl Spencer . . . 1794–1801*, I, ed. Julian S. Corbett (1913). I have been able to consult the former's papers, in the National Maritime Museum, Greenwich; for Chatham's and Spencer's – or rather, not Spencer's – see the Note to Ch. X above. Richard Middleton, 'The Administration of Newcastle and Pitt: the Departments of State and the conduct of the war, 1754–1760 . . .' (Ph.D thesis, University of Exeter, 1968) and E.J.S. Fraser, 'The Pitt-Newcastle Coalition and the Conduct of the Seven Years' War, 1757–1760' (D.Phil thesis, University of Oxford, 1976) are of interest for comparison with a renowned example which was of personal concern to the elder Pitt's son.

Patrick Crowhurst, *The Defence of British Trade 1689–1815* (1977), C. Northcote Parkinson, *Trade in Eastern Seas, 1793–1813* (1937), *The Trade Winds: A Study of British Overseas Trade during the French Wars, 1793–1815*, ed. C. Northcote Parkinson (1948), Charles Wright and C. Ernest Fayle, *A History of Lloyds . . .* (1928), Judith Blow Williams, *British Commercial Policy and Trade Expansion 1750–1850* (1973), François Crouzet, 'Wars, Blockade, and Economic Change in Europe, 1792–1815' (*The Journal of Economic History*, XXIV, no. 4), and Ralph Davis, *The Industrial Revolution and British Overseas Trade* (1979), can be studied in conjunction with the statistical compilations noted for earlier Chs. Edward Stanley Roscoe, *Lord Stowell; His Life and the Development of English Prize Law* (1916) complements (as do the contemporary works of Sir James Park and of Ward Plumer) the two great compilations of Oppenheim's *International Law*, II, ed. H. Lauterpacht (1952) and Jessup and Déak, *Neutrality* (Ch. VIII above). For the treaty of 1794 with the United States one may compare Samuel Flagg Bemis, *Jay's Treaty . . .* (1923) with Jerald A. Combs, *The Jay Treaty . . .* (1970) and Charles R. Ritcheson, *Aftermath of Revolution . . . 1783–1795* (1969). *The Correspondence and Public Papers of John Jay . . .*, ed. Henry P. Johnston, IV (1893), and *American State Papers, Class I, Foreign Relations*, I (1832) contribute some American material. Charles Ritcheson, 'Thomas Pinckney's London Mission, 1792–1796, and the Impressment Issue' (*The International History Review*, II, no. 4), is a useful account of some other questions as well.

Three doctoral theses are important for financial policy: S.R. Cope, 'The History of Boyd, Benfield & Co: A Study in Merchant Banking in the last Decade of the Eighteenth Century' (Ph.D, University of London, 1947), P.K. O'Brien, 'Government Revenue, 1793–1815 – A Study in Fiscal and Financial Policy in the Wars against France' (D.Phil, Oxford, 1967), and Richard A. Cooper, 'British Government Finance 1793–1807: the Development of a Policy Based on War Taxes' (Ph.D, University of North Carolina, 1976). Helleiner (see Ch. VIII above) is also important. Some economic studies are listed in the Notes to Ch. XII above; but one may add here Sir John Clapham, *The Bank of England: A History, 1694–1914*, I (1944), Stephen Dowell, *A History of Taxation and Taxes in England . . .*, II (1884), William Kennedy, *English Taxation, 1640–1799 . . .* (1913), E.L. Hargreaves, *The National Debt* (1930), W.R. Ward, *The English Land Tax in the Eighteenth Century* (1953), Norman J. Silberling, 'Financial and Monetary Policy of Great Britain during the Napoleonic Wars' (*The Quarterly Journal of Economics*, XXXVIII). Henry Roseveare's *The Treasury . . .* (1969) is the standard account of that Department. Among a mass of older printed sources may be mentioned J.J. Grellier, *The History of the National Debt, from the Revolution of 1688 to the Beginning of the Year 1800 . . .* (1810), the same author's *The Terms of All the Loans which have been Raised for the Public*

Service during the Last Fifty Years . . . (1799), William Newmarch, *On the Loans Raised by Mr. Pitt during the First French War, 1793–1801* . . . (1855), Sir John Sinclair, *The History of the Public Revenue of the British Empire*, II (1803), *Reports from Committees of the House of Commons*, XII (1803). Correspondence of financial interest is of course scattered throughout Pitt's own papers. Many letters to him on taxation are collected in P.R.O. 30/8/264–71. The most relevant files of reports and calculations for 1793–6 are loc. cit., 195–6, 272–8, 303–5, P.R.O. 30/58/1, 8, Stanhope Mss 09/20, 23, 29, 38 (Kent C.A.O.).

A. Aspinall, 'The Cabinet Council, 1783–1835' (*Proceedings of the British Academy*, XXXVIII, 1952), Richard E. Willis, 'Cabinet Politics and Executive Policy-Making Procedures, 1794–1801' (*Albion*, 7, no. 1), and Charles Ronald Middleton, *The Administration of British Foreign Policy 1782–1846* (1977) may be added usefully for section IV of this Ch. to works cited earlier.

CHAPTER XIV

The primary printed material and unpublished theses for this Ch. repeat, individually or in series, those given in Chs. VIII – X above. To the secondary material may be added Ch. 3 in Holland Rose's *Pitt and Napoleon*, 'Was Pitt Responsible for the Quiberon Disaster?', and Maurice Hutt's valuable article in *E.H.R.*, LXXVI, no. 300, 'The British Government's Responsibility for the 'divided command' of the Expedition to Quiberon, 1795'. Gwynne Lewis, *The Second Vendée: The continuity of Counter-Revolution in the Department of the Gard, 1789–1815* (1978), and James W. Hood, 'Revival and Mutation of old Rivalries in Revolutionary France' (*Past & Present*, no. 82), throw light on the conditions for British hopes from France, particularly the south and south-east, in 1795; so do the works of R.C. Cobb, most notably perhaps *The Police and the People: French Revolutionary Protest, 1789–1820* (1970), and for other recent publications bearing on the subject see references in *The Historical Journal*, 23, no. 4, 793–812, 967–83. Richards, 'British Policy and the Problem of the Monarchy in France' (Ch. VI above), and W.R. Fryer, 'The Mirage of Restoration: Louis XVIII and Lord Macartney, 1795–6' (*Bulletin of the John Rylands University Library of Manchester*, 62, nos. 1, 2), are of direct interest. Cyril Northcote Parkinson, *War in the Eastern Seas, 1793–1815* (1954) and Nicholas Tarling, *Anglo-Dutch Rivalry in the Malay World, 1780–1824* (1962) are useful for their subjects. Holland Rose's study of 'France and the First Coalition before the Campaign of 1796', in *E.H.R.*, XVIII, no. LXX, covers relations with Austria and Russia from the autumn of 1795. The volumes of the Parliamentary debates are given in Ch. XII above.

Turning to the more voluminous ms sources, the relevant volumes in the P.R.O., F.O. series are 7/40–3, 97/60 (Austria), 9/11–12 (Bavaria), 22/22–4 (Denmark), 27/44–5, 95/3/4, 95/605–7, with P.C. 1/125 (France), 28/11–13 (Genoa), 29/5–7 (Army in Germany), 31/7 (Cologne, Hesse Cassell), 33/10–11, 97/240 (Hamburg), 37/57, 97/248 (Holland), 63/20–1 (Portugal), 64/36–9, 97/324 (Prussia), 65/29–32 (Russia), 67/16–19 (Sardinia), 68/9 (Saxony), 70/8 (Sicily), 72/36–9 (Spain), 73/19–22 (Sweden), 74/5–13 (Switzerland), 78/16 (Turkey), 79/12 (Tuscany), 81/10 (Venice). P.R.O., W.O. 1/172–3 with 6/12 cover the withdrawal of the British forces from the continent; W.O. 1/176 (correspondence with Moira and Doyle), 1/390 (with Puisaye and d'Hervilly),

1/392, 1/396, 6/1, and H.O. 50/372, the expedition to France; W.O. 1/408–9, missions to northern Germany; W.O. 1/320, 1/323–4, the Cape of Good Hope; W.O. 1/356, 1/358–9, 1/361 (for Cleghorn) – 2, 6/67, the Far East; W.O. 1/31, 1/61–3, 1/83–4, 1/92, 6/5–6, the West Indies. The sources for naval operations fall into Ch. XV below.

Among private papers, see, for Pitt, P.R.O. 30/8/12, 101 (for Pitt to Chatham), 102 (to Moira), 107 (for Abercromby), 110 (Auckland), 111, 115 (Boyd), 119, 122 (including Chatham), 127, 137, 140 (Grenville), 149, 154, 160 (Moira), 168 (Portland), 169 (Puisaye), 170, 180, 182, 187 (Brook Watson), 195-7, 332, 334–6, 338–9, 345–6, 348–52, and Camden Mss C 123/4–5, Stanhope Ms S5 09/28 (Kent C.A.O.). B.L. Add. Mss 59056, 59306 – and one letter to Thomas Grenville of September–October in 41852 – add a little for Grenville to *H.M.C., Dropmore*, III. There is some interesting evidence for Dundas's thought in B.L. Add. Ms 37876 (to Windham retrospectively in March 1796) and 40102 (to the Duke of York in July 1795), and in letters to him from Spencer in N.L.S. Ms 7199. For Windham see B.L. Add. Ms 37844, containing letters from Pitt, and P.R.O. 30/11/222, in Cornwallis's papers, for letters on ordnance supplies to France; for Portland, Ms PwV 108–9 and the PWF series at Nottingham University, for George III and for Pitt during 1795; for Canning, one letter of November 1795 in P.R.O. 30/29/4(10), and his Diary in Canning Ms 29D in Leeds Archives Department. Some of Puisaye's correspondence is in B.L. Add. Mss 7976, 7979–80. More marginally, one may consult Burges Ms (Bodleian Library) 10,150,151; N.L.S. Mss 5572, 5576 for Liston; B.L. Add. Ms 33129 for Thomas Pelham; B.L. Add. Ms 34453 and N.L.S. Ms 11105 for the profusion of Auckland's thoughts and advice.

CHAPTER XV

Much of the material for this Ch. again lies in sources cited for others. Such are the secondary accounts in *The Cambridge History of British Foreign Policy*, I (Ch. I above), in Duffy, 'British War Policy' and Helleiner (both Ch. VIII) for Austria, Harvey Mitchell (Ch. X) for France, E.D. Adams for Grenville's influence on Pitt (Ch. II), and in biographies already listed. To these may be added J. Holland Rose's article in *E.H.R.*, XVIII, no. LXX (Ch. XIV above). Published primary material on foreign affairs is contained in *Quellen* (Ch. VIII), in the diaries and correspondence of Gilbert Elliot, Malmesbury (Ch. VI), William Wickham (Ch. X), and Auckland (*A.C.*), in *H.M.C., Dropmore*, III, and *L.C.G. III*, II. The papers of Barham and of Spencer – II (1914) as well as I – (see Ch. XIII) are valuable for naval affairs, M.W.B. Sanderson's thesis (Ch. X) for the West Indies, and Commander E.H. Stuart Jones, *An Invasion That Failed . . .* (1950) for the French expedition to Ireland.

Goodwin (Chs. IV–V above) provides the best account of the radical movements in 1796. The theses of Cooper, of Cope and of O'Brien (Ch. XIII) are indispensable for the financial problems, and Clapham, I (ibid) with ch. I of II (1944), is also helpful. Ian P.H. Duffy, 'The Discount Policy of the Bank of England . . ., 1797–1821' (*Ec.H.R., Second Series*, XXXV, no. 1) is of interest also for 1796. *The Annual Register* gives prices of stocks; Grellier, and Newmarch (Ch. XIII), details of loans. Some of Pitt's correspondence with the Bank of England, together with his and its evidence to the Commons' Committee of Secrecy on the Outstanding Demands of the Bank of 1797, is printed in *Reports from Committees of the House of Commons*, XI (1803). The Reports of the Commons' Select Committee on Finance of 1797–8, printed op. cit., XII (Ch. XIII), are also relevant. Walter Boyd's *A Letter to the Right Honourable William Pitt . . .* of 1801 reproduces his arguments of 1796. For Sinclair see Ch. XII above. The Introductory Survey to the forthcoming volumes of *The History of Parliament* for 1790–1818 (Ch. III) is authoritative on the general election. The debates are covered in *P.R.*, XLIV (1796) – *3rd series*, I (1797), *The Senator*, XIV–XVI (nd), *P.H.*, XXXII.

P.R.O., F.O. 7/44–7, 22/25–6, 27/46–8, 63/22–3, 64/39–42, 65/33–5, 67/20–3, 70/9 cover Austria, Denmark, France (27/46 for Malmesbury's mission), Portugal, Prussia, Russia, Sardinia, The Two Sicilies respectively. F.O. 95/3/4, P.R.O., W.O. 1/388, 396 contain material on intelligence from France, and P.R.O., H.O. 69/1 shows Windham's continuing efforts for the royalists. W.O. 30/58, 61–6, 101 relate to home defence, 1/178 to the Texel Project, 1/217 to a force for Portugal, 1/302, 6/54 and H.O. 50/5 to Corsica, W.O. 1/606–7 to the Channel Islands, 6/20 to expeditions beyond Europe. W.O. 1/63 includes Spencer's misdated letter of 4 January 1796 on the West Indies; 1/64–5, 85 (Dundas's instructions to Abercromby), 92 are the most important of the files on that theatre; 1/356, 358–9, 361–2 of those on the Far East; 1/320, 323, 325 relate also to the Cape of Good Hope. W.O. 6/147 contains the Secretary of State for War's correspondence with the Admiralty; P.R.O., Adm. 1/395 despatches from the Mediterranean; Adm. 3/117 the Board's Minutes. I have relied otherwise on published accounts of naval events.

Pitt's notes on peace terms, probably of January 1796, are in Stanhope Ms S5 09/27 (Kent C.A.O.). S5 09/38 in the same collection holds some of his papers on finance, and S5 C34 a few letters from Pretyman relating to the general election at Cambridge and to the alarm caused by the bill for augmenting the militia. Another letter on this last subject, from John Mitford, is in S5 03/5. The Camden Mss (Kent C.A.O.) are again valuable for Pitt's health and spirits: in C 95/2, 97, 121/2, 123/11, 131/1–2, 224/2, 226/1–2; as are a few letters in Pretyman Ms T 108/44 at the Suffolk R.O., Ipswich. Canning's correspondence in the Leeds Archives Department, packets 3, 14, 30, and particularly 62–3, is useful for news of Pitt and for Canning's own relations with Malmesbury; his Diary for 1796 is loc. cit., Ms 29 D; his correspondence in P.R.O. 30/29/4(10), 30/29/8(1) and in B.L. Add. Ms 48219 is of value particularly for the second half of the year. The Barham Mss at the National Maritime Museum, Greenwich (in process of cataloguing) supplement his published papers (Ch. XIII above), though not significantly here. N.L.S. Mss 11210–11 complete Gilbert Elliot's correspondence from Corsica. Neither Portland's nor Burges's papers (in Nottingham University and the Bodleian Library respectively) are important for my treatment in this Ch.; nor are Rose's in the B.L., or Liverpool's voluminous Mss there apart from B.L. Loan Ms 72, vol. 54. Windham's papers in B.L. Add. Mss 37844, 37846 relate mainly to the French royalists; 37876 shows his disagreement with current strategy. Auckland's papers in B.L. Add. Mss 34454, 46519 have letters from Rose and from Pitt; Huskisson's in B.L. Add. Ms 38734 contain interesting correspondence with Dundas. Dundas's Melville Castle Mss in the S.R.O. include at G.D. 51/1/520/1–2 some material on plans against Spanish colonies; his archive in the N.L.S. has yielded me little of importance here from a scattered mass –

Mss 641, 1041, 3835, 7199 have a few useful letters. Grenville's papers in B.L. supplement *H.M.C.*, *Dropmore*, III: in 58877 (for Buckingham), 58907 (Liverpool's ideas on peace terms), 59044 (for Vorontsov), 59065, 59067A (for talks with France), 59076 (Russia), 59306 (Cabinet Minutes).

Of the three collections of Pitt's papers in the P.R.O., the Hoare papers in the 30/70 series hold nothing significant here. In the Dacres Adams papers, 30/58/1 is of marginal interest, and 30/58/8 has a mass of undated notes bearing on peace terms, some at least of which may relate to 1796. In the main series of the Chatham papers the following have been the most useful: P.R.O. 30/8/12 (letters to Hester Countess of Chatham), 101 (to Chatham), 102, 115 (for Boyd), 110 (Auckland), 155 (Malmesbury), 157 (Dundas), 170 (John Mitford), 178 (Sinclair), 183 (Henry Thornton), 196, 276 (Bank of England), 196–7 (for a wide range of subjects), 272, 275, 302 (finance), 315 (Cambridge University election), 333, 335 (France).

Index

Names and ranks of persons are given as far as possible in the style by which their owners were generally known in the period of this volume.

681

Index

Redwood Library and Athenaeum

Newport, R. I.